UCSMP ScottForesman

The University of Chicago School Mathematics Project

Transition Mathematics

Second Edition

Teacher's Edition

Part 1, Chapters 1-6

About the Cover The art on the cover was generated by a computer. The three interlocking rings signify the major themes of this book—algebra, geometry, and applied arithmetic.

Authors

Zalman Usiskin Cathy Hynes Feldman

Suzanne Davis Sharon Mallo Gladys Sanders David Witonsky

James Flanders Lydia Polonsky Susan Porter Steven S. Viktora

ScottForesman

A Division of HarperCollins*Publishers*

Editorial Offices: Glenview, Illinois

Regional Offices: Sunnyvale, California • Tucker, Georgia

Glenview, Illinois • Oakland, New Jersey • Dallas, Texas

ACKNOWLEDGMENTS

Authors

Zalman Usiskin
Professor of Education, The University of Chicago

Cathy Hynes Feldman
Mathematics Teacher, The University of Chicago Laboratory Schools

Suzanne Davis
Mathematics Supervisor, Pinellas County Schools, Largo, FL (Second Edition only)

Sharon Mallo
Mathematics Teacher, Lake Park H.S., Roselle, IL (Second Edition only)

Gladys Sanders
K–12 Mathematics Coordinator, Lawrence Public Schools, Lawrence, KS (Second Edition only)

David Witonsky
UCSMP (Second Edition only)

James Flanders
UCSMP (First Edition only)

Lydia Polonsky
UCSMP (First Edition only)

Susan Porter
Evanston Township H.S., Evanston, IL (First Edition only)

Steven S. Viktora
Chairman, Mathematics Department, Kenwood Academy, Chicago Public Schools (First Edition only)

UCSMP Production and Evaluation

Series Editors: Zalman Usiskin, Sharon L. Senk

Directors of First Edition Studies: Kathryn Sloane, Sandra Mathison; Assistant to the Directors: Penelope Flores

Directors of Second Edition Studies: Geraldine Macsai, Gurcharn Kaeley

Technical Coordinator: Susan Chang

Second Edition Teacher's Edition Editor: Suzanne Levin

Second Edition Consultants: Amy Hackenberg, Mary Lappan

First Edition Managing Editor: Natalie Jakucyn

We wish to thank the many editors, production personnel, and design personnel at ScottForesman for their magnificent assistance.

We wish to acknowledge the generous support of the Amoco Foundation and the Carnegie Corporation of New York in helping to make it possible for the First Edition of these materials to be developed, tested, and distributed, and the continuing support of the Amoco Foundation for the Second Edition.

Multicultural Reviewers for ScottForesman

Marion Bolden
Newark Board of Education, Newark, NJ

Seree Weroha
Kansas State University, Manhattan, KS

Efraín Meléndez
Dacatoh St. School, Los Angeles, CA

Yvonne Wynde
Educator, Sisseton-Wahpeton Dakota Nation, Waubay, SD

ISBN: 0-673-45746-X

2 3 4 5 6 7 8 9—DR—0 0 9 9 9 8 9 7 9 6 9 5 9 4

Contents
of Teacher's Edition

The complete Table of Contents for the Student Edition begins on page *vi*.

Your UCSMP Professional Sourcebook is found at the back of this book, starting on page T20.

Transition Mathematics

SECOND EDITION

"Every day I discover more and more reasons why the UCSMP curriculum works. The problems look so simple at first, but they show me new ways to get students to think—even after 24 years of teaching!"

Joyce Camara, teacher
Esmond, Rhode Island

The University of Chicago School Mathematics Project

It works

Carefully developed by a prestigious team of authors in full accordance with the goals of the NCTM Standards, UCSMP has been refined through field testing and feedback from users. Millions of successful students and an ever-growing network of enthusiastic teachers have proven that UCSMP is a program that works.

Why it works as today's curriculum

UCSMP's flexible six-year curriculum emphasizes connections within mathematics and to other disciplines, develops concepts through real-world applications, implements the latest technology, and encourages independent learning.

How it works for today's students

Clear and inviting, *Transition Mathematics* offers continual opportunities for problem solving, practice and review, and end-of-chapter mastery. Attention to individual needs and a broad approach to assessment help you offer success to all students.

The following section provides an overview of *Transition Mathematics*. For more detailed information see the Professional Sourcebook at the back of this book (page T20).

WHAT'S NEW in the Second Edition

In the Student Edition:

- Appealing, student-friendly layout
- Reading Organizers to outline each lesson
- In-class and In-lesson Activities
- Student Projects in every chapter
- More probability and statistics

In the Teacher's Edition:

- Warm-up ideas for introducing each lesson
- Enhanced integration and connections
- Optional activities to reinforce and extend topics
- Frequent suggestions for adapting to individual needs
- Ideas for Setting Up the Next Lesson

PLUS—

In the support package:

- Two forms of Lesson Masters for extra practice
- An enhanced Assessment Sourcebook
- Study Skills Handbook
- *Transition Mathematics* Software Tools
- Videodisc with multimedia CD-ROM

UCSMP — It works

The U.S. Department of Education has granted UCSMP its "A+ Award" for helping the nation work toward the six National Education Goals.

Program development

The UCSMP Secondary Component Materials have been developed with extensive input from classroom teachers and a special advisory board. The project has been funded by several major corporations which recognize the need for exciting new materials for mathematics education.

An innovative approach

UCSMP is the first full mathematics curriculum to implement the NCTM Standards by teaching concepts *through* their applications, emphasizing the reading and writing of mathematics, providing a wide variety of meaningful problem-solving opportunities, and incorporating the latest technology.

"Of 145 students who completed a summer project in Transition Mathematics *and are currently taking* UCSMP Algebra *with the same teachers, 86% of them are passing Algebra I. In addition, 95% of these students attend class 95% of the time or more. Preliminary results from the citywide, standardized mid-term examination in Algebra I indicate that everyone has passed. Needless to say, we are delighted."*

Sue Stetzer, director, Algebra Transition Project
Philadelphia, Pennsylvania

Middle School Curriculum Review Series has cited UCSMP as a "middle-school exemplary curriculum ... sensitive to the needs of urban, educationally disadvantaged students," with "demonstrated success in urban environments."

Proven success

The UCSMP materials have been carefully refined through years of field testing and feedback from users of the First Edition. Teachers throughout the country have discovered that UCSMP is the way to offer success to the greatest number of students.

The **best** book to help students make the *transition* has gotten even better!

Results of the Second Edition Evaluation

Group	Number of classes	Pretest HSST	Posttest HSST	Posttest Algebra	Posttest Geometry
UCSMP 2nd Edition	12	19.32	24.95	11.51	11.14
UCSMP 1st Edition	12	18.89	23.31	11.28	10.74
UCSMP 2nd Edition	4	17.55	22.89	9.91	9.62
Other Texts	4	17.60	22.83	8.00	7.40

For more details, see the Professional Sourcebook at the back of part 1 of the Teacher's Edition.

With results similar to those of the First Edition, the students in the *Transition Mathematics* Second Edition classes held their own on paper-and-pencil computation, and significantly outscored students in other texts in algebra and geometry knowledge.

"I have taught my students for two years. When they entered Grade 6, their achievement was two years below grade level. Presently they are at or above grade level. I attribute their growth this year to the use of Transition Mathematics.*"*

Frances L. Ostrander, teacher
Brookline, Massachusetts

Why it works as today's curriculum

Grades	Top 10% of 5th graders	50th-90th percentile of 6th graders	30th-70th percentile of 7th graders	15th-50th percentile of 8th graders
6	Transition Mathematics			
7	Algebra	Transition Mathematics		
8	Geometry	Algebra	Transition Mathematics	
9	Advanced Algebra	Geometry	Algebra	Transition Mathematics
10	Functions, Statistics, and Trigonometry	Advanced Algebra	Geometry	Algebra
11	Precalculus and Discrete Mathematics	Functions, Statistics, and Trigonometry	Advanced Algebra	Geometry
12	Calculus (Not part of UCSMP)	Precalculus and Discrete Mathematics	Functions, Statistics, and Trigonometry	Advanced Algebra

A flexible curriculum

UCSMP provides a complete program for students in middle school and high school. It spreads the usual secondary mathematics content over six years, allowing students to both broaden and deepen their understanding of each topic.

"Students understand math now— they aren't just memorizing. They are accepting responsibility for their learning."

Gail Sutton, math coordinator
Grand Rapids, Michigan

Real-world applications

By constantly answering the question, "When are we ever going to have to use this?," *Transition Mathematics* develops lessons more meaningfully and motivates students to learn. *See pages 79, 237, and 541 for further examples.*

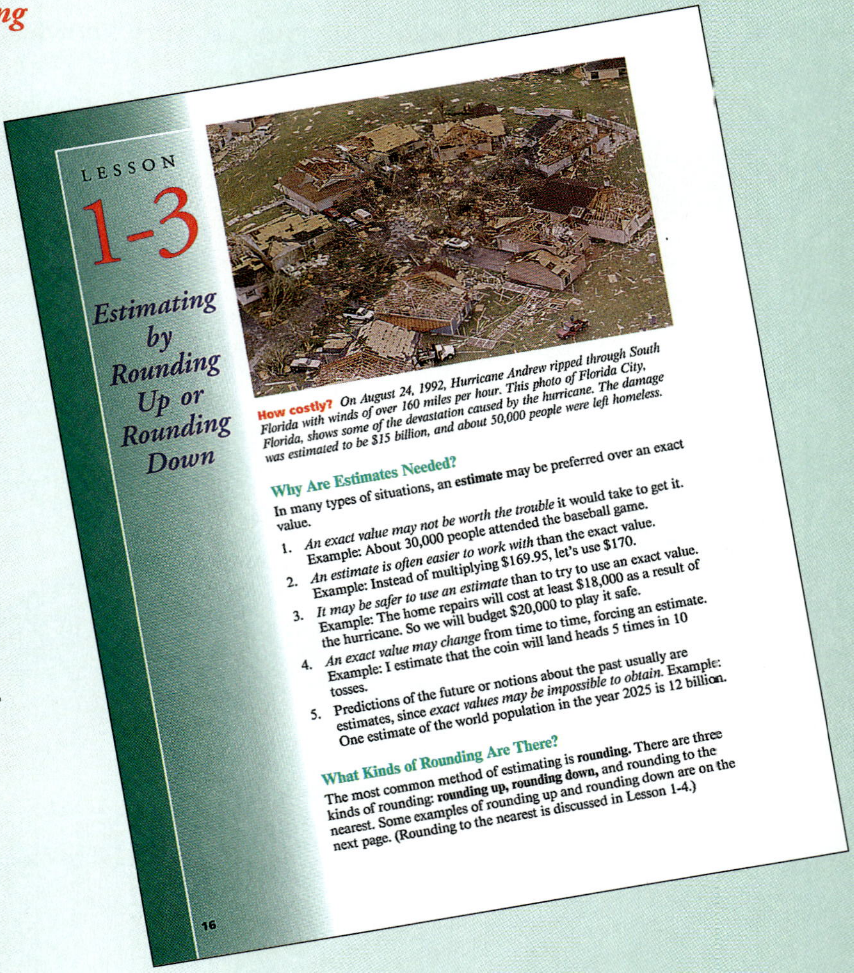
LESSON

1-3

Estimating by Rounding Up or Rounding Down

How costly? *On August 24, 1992, Hurricane Andrew ripped through South Florida with winds of over 160 miles per hour. This photo of Florida City, Florida, shows some of the devastation caused by the hurricane. The damage was estimated to be $15 billion, and about 50,000 people were left homeless.*

Why Are Estimates Needed?

In many types of situations, an **estimate** may be preferred over an exact value.

1. *An exact value may not be worth the trouble* it would take to get it. Example: About 30,000 people attended the baseball game.
2. *An estimate is often easier to work with* than the exact value. Example: Instead of multiplying $169.95, let's use $170.
3. *It may be safer to use an estimate* than to try to use an exact value. Example: The home repairs will cost at least $18,000 as a result of the hurricane. So we will budget $20,000 to play it safe.
4. *An exact value may change* from time to time, forcing an estimate. Example: I estimate that the coin will land heads 5 times in 10 tosses.
5. Predictions of the future or notions about the past usually are estimates, since *exact values may be impossible to obtain.* Example: One estimate of the world population in the year 2025 is 12 billion.

What Kinds of Rounding Are There?

The most common method of estimating is **rounding.** There are three kinds of rounding: **rounding up, rounding down,** and rounding to the nearest. Some examples of rounding up and rounding down are on the next page. (Rounding to the nearest is discussed in Lesson 1-4.)

16

Integration and connections

Transition Mathematics thoroughly integrates and makes connections to other areas of mathematics, to other disciplines, and to the real world. Students see how each mathematical idea fits into a larger context.
See pages 51, 308, 415-416, and 435-436 for further examples.

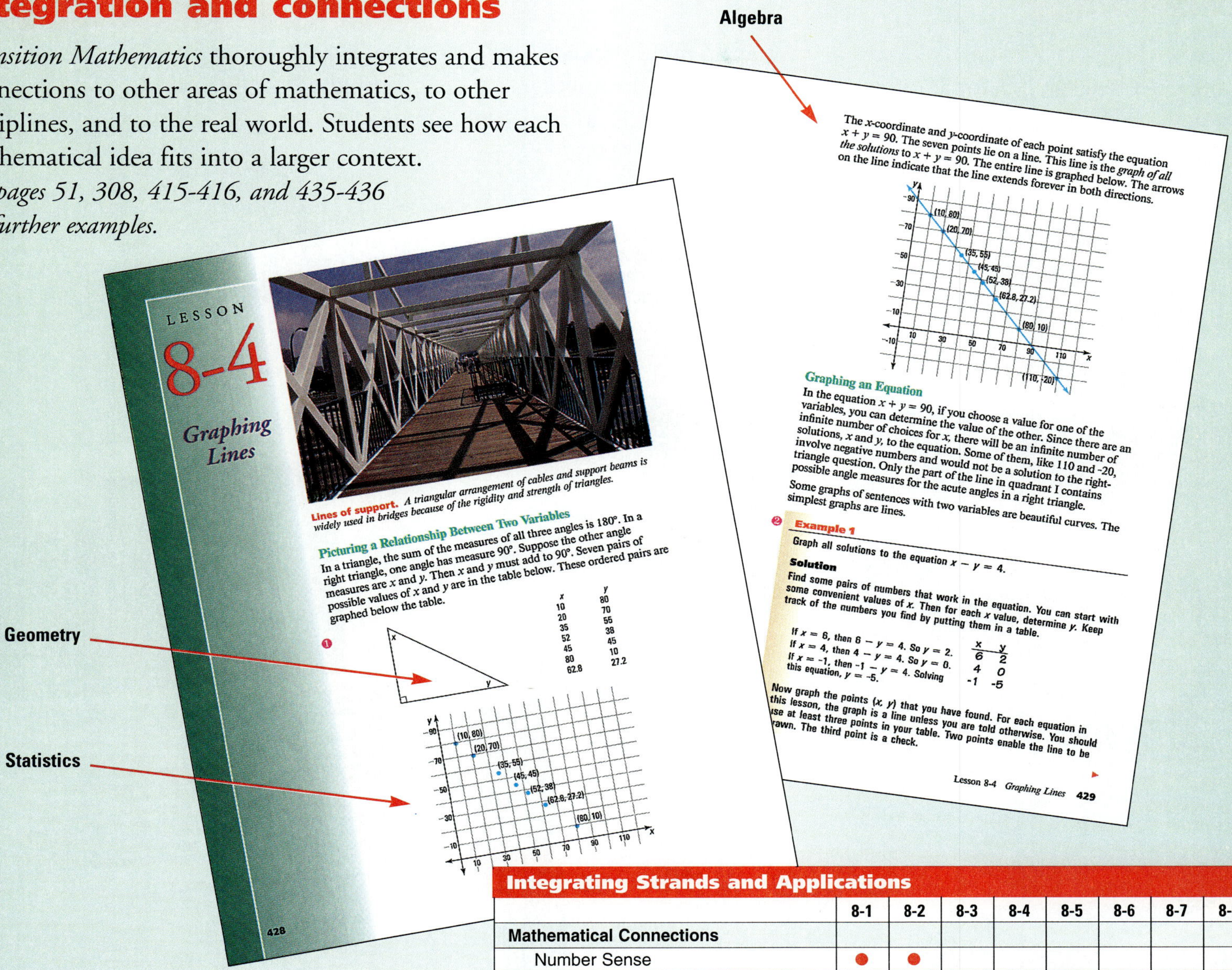

"Students never have to ask, 'Why are we studying this?'."

Mary Sanders, teacher
Homer, Alaska

On page B in each group of prechapter pages in the Teacher's Edition, integration and connections are summarized in a chart.

Integrating Strands and Applications

	8-1	8-2	8-3	8-4	8-5	8-6	8-7	8-8
Mathematical Connections								
Number Sense	●	●						
Algebra	●		●	●	●	●	●	●
Geometry	●	●	●	●	●	●	●	●
Measurement		●	●	●	●	●		
Statistics/Data Analysis	●	●	●	●	●	●	●	
Patterns and Functions				●	●	●		
Interdisciplinary and Other Connections								
Art					●	●	●	●
Literature	●							
Science	●	●	●	●	●	●	●	●
Social Studies	●	●	●	●	●	●	●	●
Multicultural		●					●	●
Technology		●	●	●		●	●	
Career					●			
Consumer			●	●				
Sports		●		●				

Why it works

Technology

State-of-the-art technology enhances mathematical understanding and strengthens problem-solving skills. Applications using calculators and computers are incorporated throughout the text. A new videodisc with multimedia CD-ROM makes learning more interactive and engaging. *See pages 75-76, 270, and 316-317 for further examples.*

Transition Mathematics integrates calculator and computer use throughout and offers an array of resources including interactive software, testing software, and videodisc with CD-ROM.

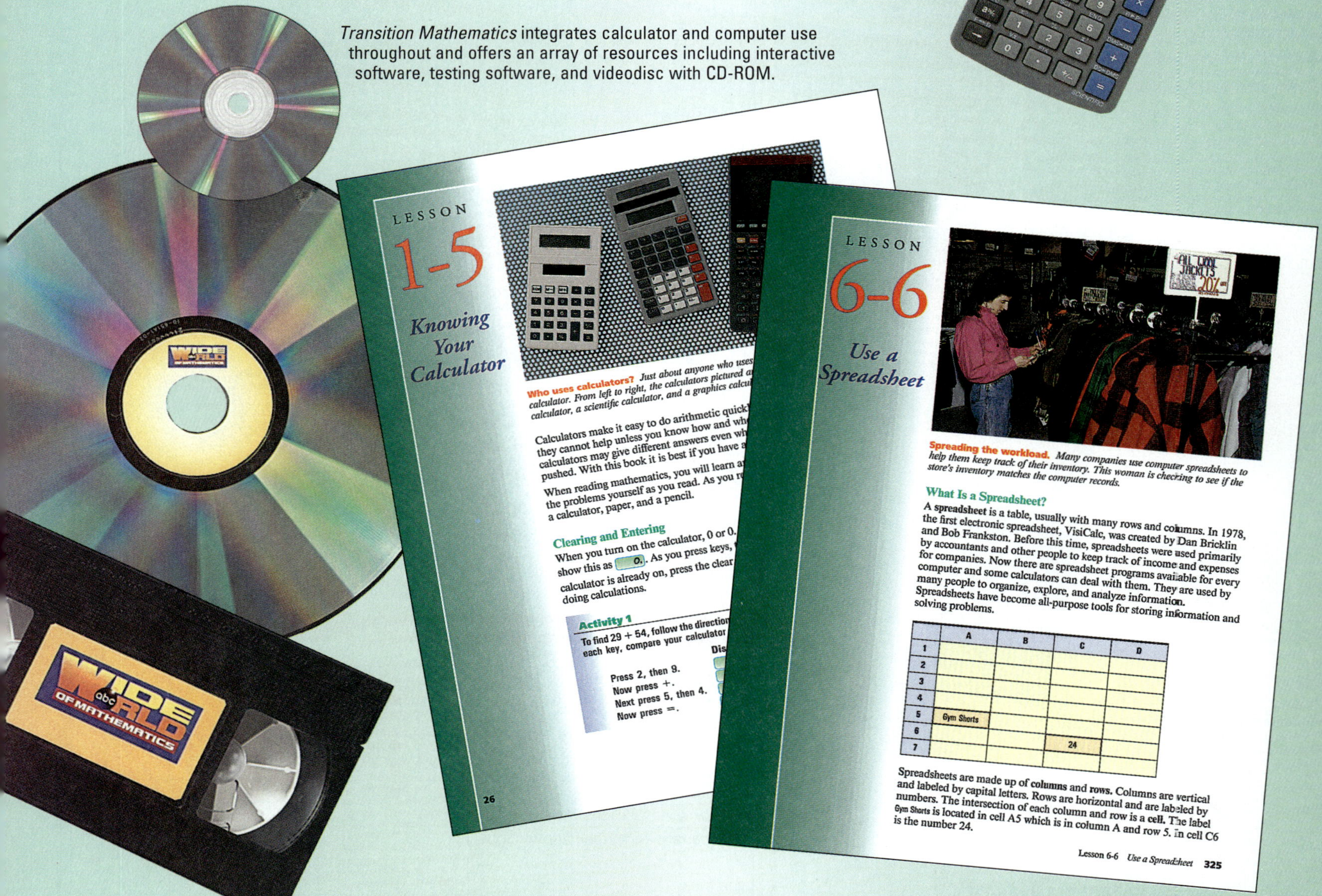

"In my opinion, this textbook style is one of the most significant advances in math education in recent years."

James T. Wise, teacher
Orlando, Florida

Activities and Projects

Activities and Projects in each chapter provide engaging ways for students to work individually or in groups to explore and extend their knowledge. Your Teacher's Edition also includes additional Optional Activities.

See pages 38, 209, and 213 for further examples of Activities.
See pages 5, 108, and 229-230 for further examples of Projects.

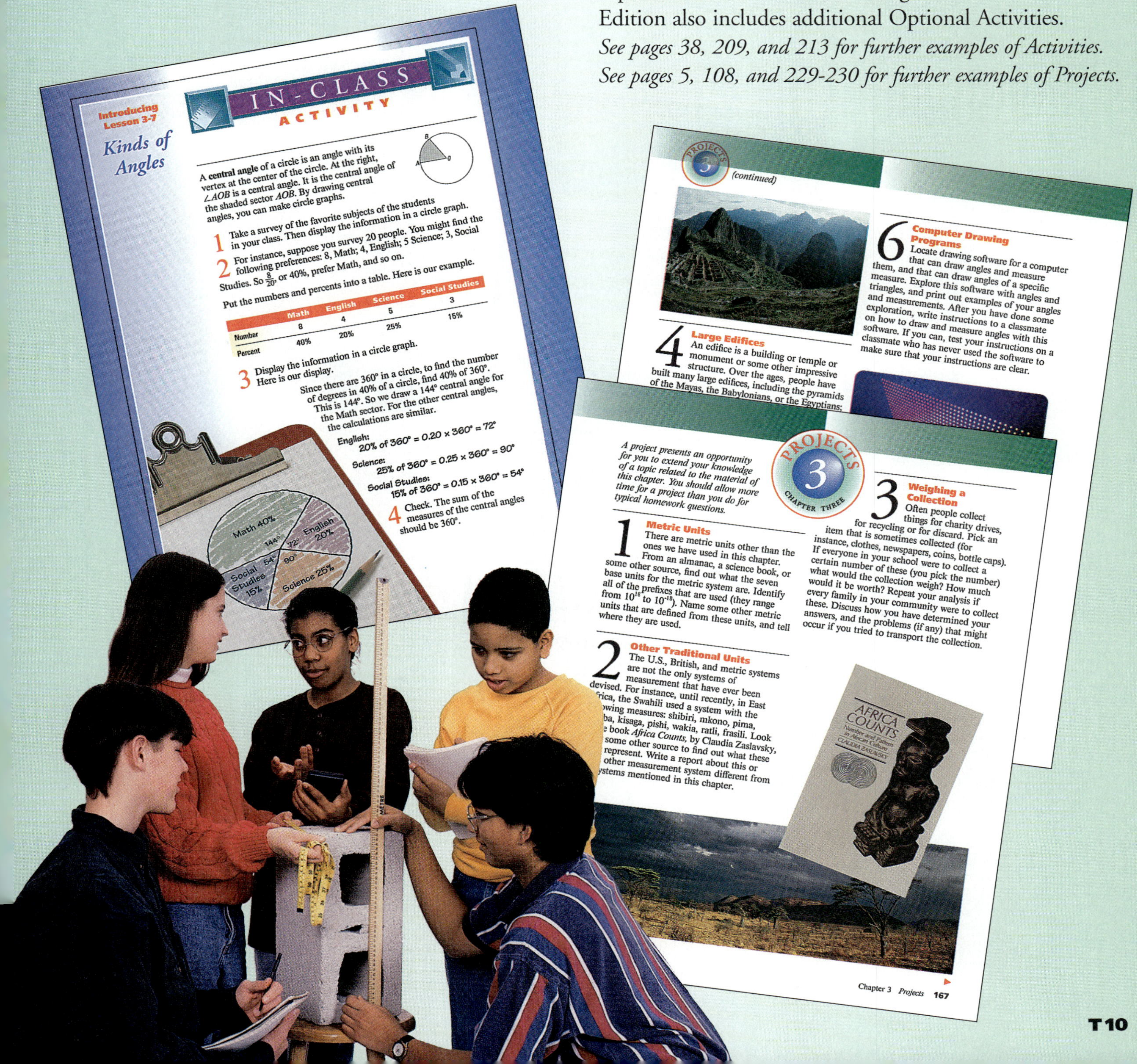

How it works for today's students

Inviting design

The text's appealing and functional format and unique lesson development make concepts easy to follow and comprehend. Colorful pages and a wealth of contemporary visuals — including greatly enhanced graphs — help stimulate students' interest throughout the course.

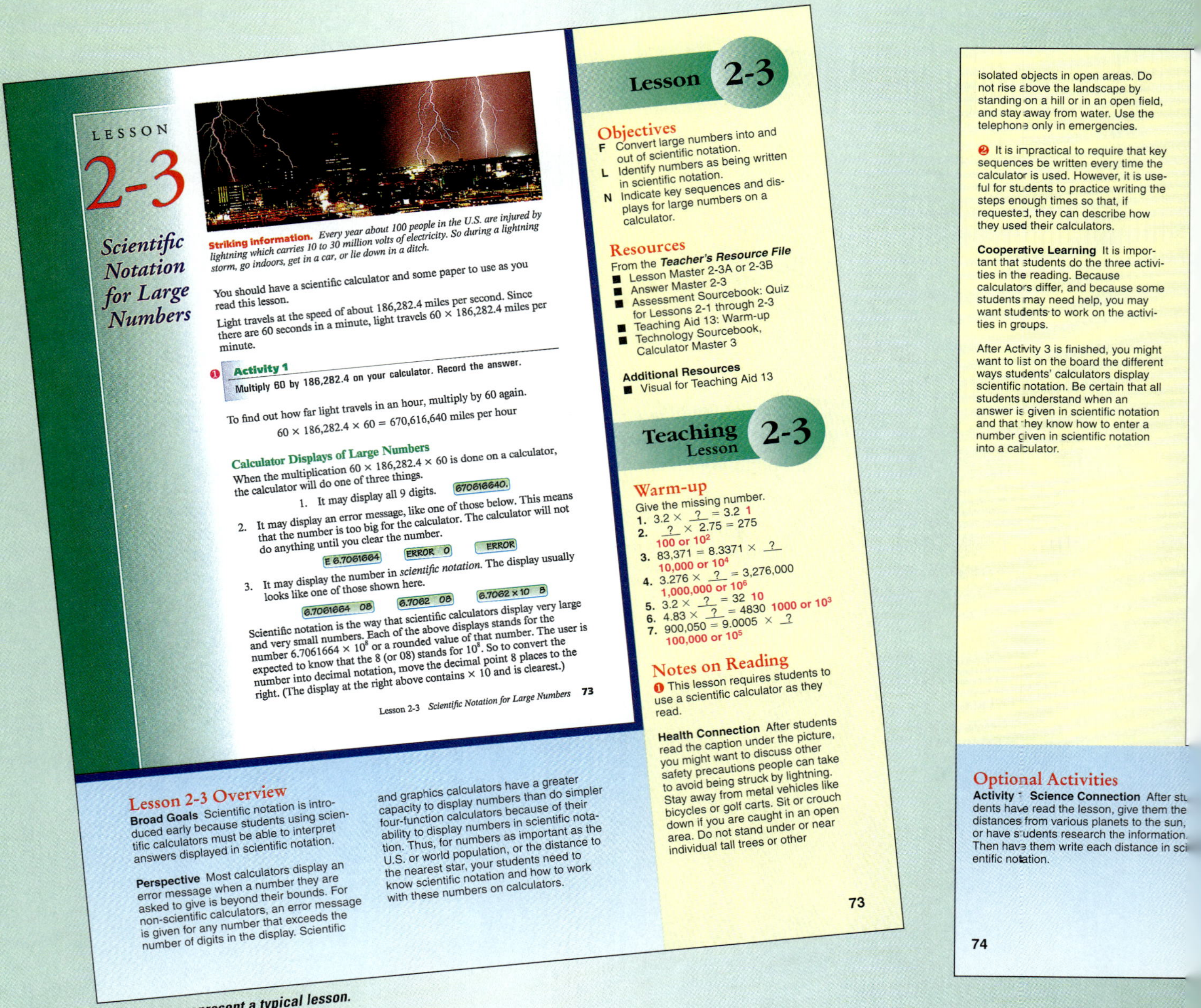

LESSON 2-3 *Scientific Notation for Large Numbers*

Striking information. *Every year about 100 people in the U.S. are injured by lightning which carries 10 to 30 million volts of electricity. So during a lightning storm, go indoors, get in a car, or lie down in a ditch.*

You should have a scientific calculator and some paper to use as you read this lesson.

Light travels at the speed of about 186,282.4 miles per second. Since there are 60 seconds in a minute, light travels 60 × 186,282.4 miles per minute.

❶ **Activity 1**
Multiply 60 by 186,282.4 on your calculator. Record the answer.

To find out how far light travels in an hour, multiply by 60 again.
60 × 186,282.4 × 60 = 670,616,640 miles per hour

Calculator Displays of Large Numbers
When the multiplication 60 × 186,282.4 × 60 is done on a calculator, the calculator will do one of three things.

1. It may display all 9 digits. 670616640.
2. It may display an error message, like one of those below. This means that the number is too big for the calculator. The calculator will not do anything until you clear the number.
E 6.7061664 ERROR 0 ERROR
3. It may display the number in *scientific notation.* The display usually looks like one of those shown here.
6.7061664 08 6.7062 08 6.7062 × 10 8

Scientific notation is the way that scientific calculators display very large and very small numbers. Each of the above displays stands for the number 6.7061664 × 10^8 or a rounded value of that number. The user is expected to know that the 8 (or 08) stands for 10^8. So to convert the number into decimal notation, move the decimal point 8 places to the right. (The display at the right above contains × 10 and is clearest.)

Lesson 2-3 *Scientific Notation for Large Numbers* 73

Lesson 2-3

Objectives
F Convert large numbers into and out of scientific notation.
L Identify numbers as being written in scientific notation.
N Indicate key sequences and displays for large numbers on a calculator.

Resources
From the *Teacher's Resource File*
- Lesson Master 2-3A or 2-3B
- Answer Master 2-3
- Assessment Sourcebook: Quiz for Lessons 2-1 through 2-3
- Teaching Aid 13: Warm-up
- Technology Sourcebook, Calculator Master 3

Additional Resources
- Visual for Teaching Aid 13

Teaching Lesson 2-3

Warm-up
Give the missing number.
1. 3.2 × _?_ = 3.2 1
2. _?_ × 2.75 = 275 100 or 10^2
3. 83,371 = 8.3371 × _?_ 10,000 or 10^4
4. 3.276 × _?_ = 3,276,000 1,000,000 or 10^6
5. 3.2 × _?_ = 32 10
6. 4.83 × _?_ = 4830 1000 or 10^3
7. 900,050 = 9.0005 × _?_ 100,000 or 10^5

Notes on Reading
❶ This lesson requires students to use a scientific calculator as they read.

Health Connection After students read the caption under the picture, you might want to discuss other safety precautions people can take to avoid being struck by lightning. Stay away from metal vehicles like bicycles or golf carts. Sit or crouch down if you are caught in an open area. Do not stand under or near individual tall trees or other

73

Lesson 2-3 Overview
Broad Goals Scientific notation is introduced early because students using scientific calculators must be able to interpret answers displayed in scientific notation.

Perspective Most calculators display an error message when a number they are asked to give is beyond their bounds. For non-scientific calculators, an error message is given for any number that exceeds the number of digits in the display. Scientific and graphics calculators have a greater capacity to display numbers than do simpler four-function calculators because of their ability to display numbers in scientific notation. Thus, for numbers as important as the U.S. or world population, or the distance to the nearest star, your students need to know scientific notation and how to work with these numbers on calculators.

isolated objects in open areas. Do not rise above the landscape by standing on a hill or in an open field, and stay away from water. Use the telephone only in emergencies.

❷ It is impractical to require that key sequences be written every time the calculator is used. However, it is useful for students to practice writing the steps enough times so that, if requested, they can describe how they used their calculators.

Cooperative Learning It is important that students do the three activities in the reading. Because calculators differ, and because some students may need help, you may want students to work on the activities in groups.

After Activity 3 is finished, you might want to list on the board the different ways students' calculators display scientific notation. Be certain that all students understand when an answer is given in scientific notation and that they know how to enter a number given in scientific notation into a calculator.

Optional Activities
Activity 1 Science Connection After students have read the lesson, give them the distances from various planets to the sun, or have students research the information. Then have them write each distance in scientific notation.

74

These pages represent a typical lesson.

"Students like the clarity, color, and presentation in the UCSMP books."

Edna Vasquez, teacher
Detroit, Michigan

Communication

Instead of spending valuable time explaining the textbook, you can devote more time each day to exploring additional examples and applications. Students learn to read and understand mathematics on their own, and to express this understanding both orally and in writing. Reading Organizers in each lesson help direct students' attention to key ideas in the reading.

Example 1

Calculate how far light travels in a day.

Solution

The key sequence below includes all the calculations done so far in this lesson and a multiplication by 24, the number of hours in a day.

❷ Key sequence: 60 [×] 186,282.4 [×] 60 [×] 24 [=]

The exact product is 16,094,799,360.

Many calculators must round the answer to 1.60948×10^{10} because they do not have enough room to display all digits.

Display: 1.60948 10

To write 1.60948×10^{10} as a decimal, perform this multiplication without a calculator. Move the decimal point 10 places to the right.

Answer: Light travels about 16,094,800,000 miles in a day.

Activity 2

Use your calculator to determine how far light travels in a 365-day year. This is the *distance* known as a **light-year**. Show your work as in Example 1.

What Is Scientific Notation?

The number 1.60948×10^{10} in Example 1 is in scientific notation.

In scientific notation, a number greater than or equal to 1 and less than 10 is multiplied by an integer power of 10.

decimal $\times$ $10^{exponent}$

Here are some more numbers written in scientific notation.

Decimal or word name	Scientific notation
670,620,000	6.7062×10^8
340.67	3.4067×10^2
2,380,000,000	2.38×10^9
60 trillion	6×10^{13}

Notice that there are three parts to scientific notation:
a number from 1 to 10, but less than 10
a multiplication sign
a power of 10.

Calculators often omit the multiplication sign and show the exponent instead of the power of 10.

Converting Decimals into Scientific Notation

Examples 2 and 3 show how to convert decimals into scientific notation.

India has two Delhis. The busy street pictured here is Chandi Chowk Street of Old Delhi. Just three miles south of Old Delhi is New Delhi, the capital of India and a modern, carefully planned city.

Example 2

The distance from Earth to the Sun is about 150,000,000 km. Write this number in scientific notation.

Solution

First, move the decimal point to get a number between 1 and 10. In this case, the number is 1.5 and this tells you the answer will look like this:

$$1.5 \times 10^{exponent}.$$

Second, find the power of 10. The exponent of 10 is the number of places you must move the decimal in 1.5 to the *right* in order to get 150,000,000. You must move it 8 places, so the number in scientific notation is:

$$1.5 \times 10^8.$$

Example 3

Write 45,678 in scientific notation.

Solution

Ask yourself: 45,678 equals 4.5678 times what power of 10? The answer to the question is 4. So

$$45{,}678 = 4.5678 \times 10^4.$$

Numbers with word names are easy to convert to scientific notation. Use the power of 10 equivalent to the word name.

Example 4

The population of India is expected to exceed 1.4 billion by the year 2025. This number is 1,400,000,000 and has too many digits for most calculators. Write it in scientific notation so that it can be entered into a calculator and used.

Solution

Since 1 billion = 10^9, 1.4 billion = 1.4×10^9. This is already in scientific notation.

You can enter a number in scientific notation directly into your calculator.

Activity 3

Enter 1.4 billion on your calculator, using one of the key sequences:

1.4 [EE] 9 or 1.4 [Exp] 9.

Either key sequence enters 1.4×10^9.

a. Identify the key sequence you need to use on your calculator.

b. Check by entering 1.4 [×] 10 [y^x] 9 [=]. Do you get the same answer?

Additional Examples

1. More than 300 million copies of Agatha Christie's mysteries have been sold. The mysteries have been translated into 103 languages. If each book contains about 75,000 words, write the approximate total number of printed words
   a. in scientific notation. 2.25×10^{13}
   b. as a decimal. 22,500,000,000,000
   c. using the place-value name. 22.5 trillion
2. Write each number in scientific notation.
   a. The *Mona Lisa*, which was painted by Leonardo da Vinci, has been valued for insurance purposes at $100 million . 1×10^8
   b. The distance from Earth to the star Proxima Centauri is 24,800,000,000,000 miles. 2.48×10^{13}
3. Hens at the largest chicken ranch in the United States—Croton Egg Farm in Croton, Ohio—produce over 1.35 billion eggs annually. Write this number
   a. as a decimal. 1,350,000,000
   b. in scientific notation. 1.35×10^9
4. Write a googol in scientific notation. 1×10^{100}

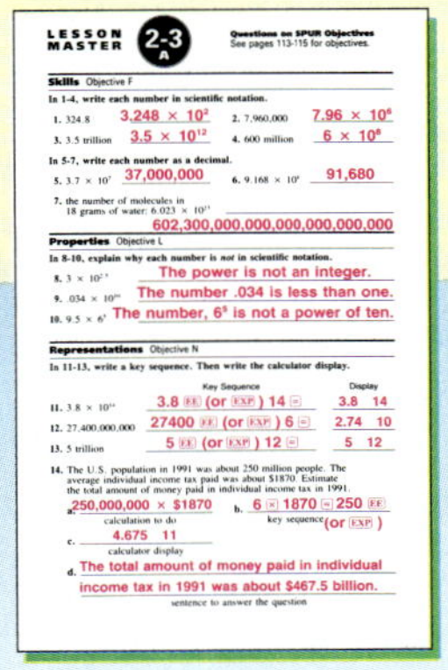

LESSON MASTER 2-3 A — Questions on SPUR Objectives. See pages 113-115 for objectives.

Skills Objective F

In 1-4, write each number in scientific notation.

1. 324.8 3.248×10^2 2. 7,960,000 7.96×10^6
3. 3.5 trillion 3.5×10^{12} 4. 600 million 6×10^8

In 5-7, write each number as a decimal.

5. 3.7×10^7 37,000,000 6. 9.168×10^4 91,680
7. the number of molecules in 18 grams of water: 6.023×10^{23} 602,300,000,000,000,000,000,000

Properties Objective L

In 8-10, explain why each number is *not* in scientific notation.

8. $3 \times 10^{2.5}$ The power is not an integer.
9. $.034 \times 10^{10}$ The number .034 is less than one.
10. 9.5×6^5 The number, 6^5 is not a power of ten.

Representations Objective N

In 11-13, write a key sequence. Then write the calculator display.

	Key Sequence	Display
11. 3.8×10^{14}	3.8 [EE] (or [EXP]) 14 [=]	3.8 14
12. 27,400,000,000	27400 [EE] (or [EXP]) 6 [=]	2.74 10
13. 5 trillion	5 [EE] (or [EXP]) 12 [=]	5 12

14. The U.S. population in 1991 was about 250 million people. The average individual income tax paid was about $1870. Estimate the total amount of money paid in individual income tax in 1991.
a. 250,000,000 × $1870 (calculation to do) b. 6 [×] 1870 [=] 250 [EE] (or [EXP]) (key sequence)
c. 4.675 11 (calculator display)
d. The total amount of money paid in individual income tax in 1991 was about $467.5 billion. (sentence to answer the question)

net	Approximate distance from sun	Scientific notation
cury	35.9 million miles	[3.59×10^7 miles]
us	67.2 million miles	[6.72×10^7 miles]
h	93.0 million miles	[9.3×10^7 miles]
s	141.6 million miles	[1.416×10^8 miles]
ter	483.6 million miles	[4.836×10^8 miles]
urn	886.7 million miles	[8.867×10^8 miles]
nus	1.8 trillion miles	[1.8×10^9 miles]
tune	2.8 trillion miles	[2.8×10^9 miles]
o	3.7 trillion miles	[3.7×10^9 miles]

Activity 2 Technology Connection
With *Technology Sourcebook, Calculator Master 3,* students determine when the positive-interger powers of 2, 3, and so on, become large enough to appear in scientific notation.

Reading Organizers

"With the UCSMP books, students are better thinkers and ask better questions. Students do not lose instructional time if the teacher is out of class."

Jim Wohlgehagen, math supervisor
Plano, Texas

How it works

Problem solving

Students learn to use mathematics effectively through problem-solving experiences that include use of higher-order thinking skills in daily assignments, a wide variety of problem types in the questions, and open-ended problems. *See pages 303, 312, and 334 for further examples.*

Notes on Questions

Question 17 Cooperative Learning Students enjoy comparing answers and figuring out which numbers are really the largest and smallest that can be displayed on their calculators. Have students write the answers that were shown on the calculators in their groups, and compare all the answers in a class discussion.

Follow-up for Lesson 2-3

Practice

For more questions on SPUR objectives, use **Lesson Master 2-3A** (shown on page 75) or **Lesson Master 2-3B** (shown on pages 76–77).

Assessment

Quiz A quiz covering Lessons 2-1 through 2-3 is provided in the *Assessment Sourcebook.*

Written Communication This is a good time for students to summarize what they have studied in Lessons 2-1 through 2-3. These three lessons have covered large numbers, whereas in the rest of the chapter, students will learn about small numbers and percents. [Summaries contain examples and explanations showing understanding of large numbers and how to write and read them.]

LESSON MASTER 2-3 B Questions on SPUR Objectives

Skills Objective F: Convert large numbers into and out of scientific notation.

In 1-8, write each number in scientific notation.

1. 578 5.78×10^2
2. 986,050 9.8605×10^5
3. 1,007 1.007×10^3
4. 95 9.5×10^1
5. 16.7 1.67×10^1
6. 750.23 7.5023×10^2
7. 2.8 million 2.8×10^6
8. 20 trillion 2×10^{13}

In 9-20, write each number as a decimal.

9. 8.2×10^6 8,200,000
10. 4.077×10^2 407.7
11. 6×10^8 600,000,000
12. 3.82×10^5 382,000
13. 2.6×10^{11} 260,000,000,000
14. 5.3×10 53
15. 7.4001×10^9 7,400,100,000
16. 1.145×10^3 1,145
17. diameter of Saturn: 1.151×10^5 kilometers 115,100
18. area of Pacific Ocean: 6.4×10^7 square miles 64,000,000
19. number of seconds in a day: 8.64×10^4 86,400
20. 1990 U.S. nuclear power generation: 5.8×10^{11} kilowatt hours 580,000,000,000

Properties Objective L: Identify numbers as being written in scientific notation.

In 21-24, explain why each number is *not* in scientific notation.

21. 17.6×10^4 The first number is greater than 10.
22. .0098 × 10[illegible] The first number is less than 1.
23. 3.6×8^2 There is no power of 10.
24. 5 × 10[illegible] The exponent of the ten is not an integer.

76

Using the EE key is more efficient than pressing the *three* keys × 10 y^x. The EE key is programmed to mean "times 10 to the power of."

On some calculators and computers, the number 1.4 billion may be written as 1.4 E 9 or even 1.4 E + 9. In this case the E means "exponent of 10" and does not indicate an error. The + sign indicates a positive number. In Lesson 2-9, you will learn about scientific notation with negative exponents.

QUESTIONS

Covering the Reading

1. a. How many miles does light travel in a 365-day year?
   b. What is this distance called? light-year
   a) about 5.87×10^{12} miles
2. How does your calculator display the number 9.01×10^{25}? 9.01 25
3. In scientific notation, a number greater than or equal to _?_ and less than _?_ is multiplied by an integer _?_ of 10. 1, 10, power

In 4–11, rewrite the number in scientific notation.

4. 800 8×10^2
5. 804 8.04×10^2
6. 63.21 6.321×10^1
7. 765.4 7.654×10^2
8. 3,500,000 square miles, the approximate land area of the U.S. 3.5×10^6
9. 6,588,000,000,000,000,000,000 tons, the approximate mass of Earth 6.588×10^{21}
10. 59.85 million people, the number of passengers handled by Chicago's O'Hare Field in 1991 5.985×10^7
11. 4 trillion dollars, the approximate U.S. national debt in 1993 4×10^{12}
12. Indicate how to enter 1.4×10^9 into your calculator
    a. using a key for scientific notation. 1.4 EE 9 or 1.4 Exp 9
    b. using a powering key. 1.4 × 10 y^x 9 =

In 13 and 14, what does your calculator display for the number?

13. 49×10^{14} Answers may vary. Sample: 4.9 15
14. 60 trillion Sample: 6. 13

Applying the Mathematics

15. The approximate weight of the largest blue whale ever measured is 1.9×10^5 kg. Multiply this number by 2.2 to estimate this weight in pounds. 4.18×10^5 or 418,000 lb
16. How many seconds are there in a 365-day year? 3.1536×10^7 or 31,536,000 seconds
17. a. Using scientific notation, what is the largest number you can display on your calculator?
    b. What is the smallest number you can display? (Hint: The smallest number is negative.)
    a) Sample: 9.9999 99 for 9.9999×10^{99}
    b) Sample: -9.9999 99 for -9.9999×10^{99}

76

Adapting to Individual Needs

Extra Help

Have students use the diagram below to write a number in scientific notation.

Example: Write 13,405,000 in scientific notation.

Move the decimal point to the left to form a decimal that is at least 1 but less than 10. Write the decimal. — 13405000 7 places; 1.3405

Write "× 10" after the decimal. — 1.3405 × 10

Count the number of places the decimal point was moved and write that count as the exponent for 10. — 1.3405×10^7

"The most important improvement I've seen while using the UCSMP materials is the enthusiasm that students have for learning. Students are talking about mathematics more and wanting to know why and how it works, rather than just trying to get an answer."

Carmen Grandy, teacher
St. Joseph, Michigan

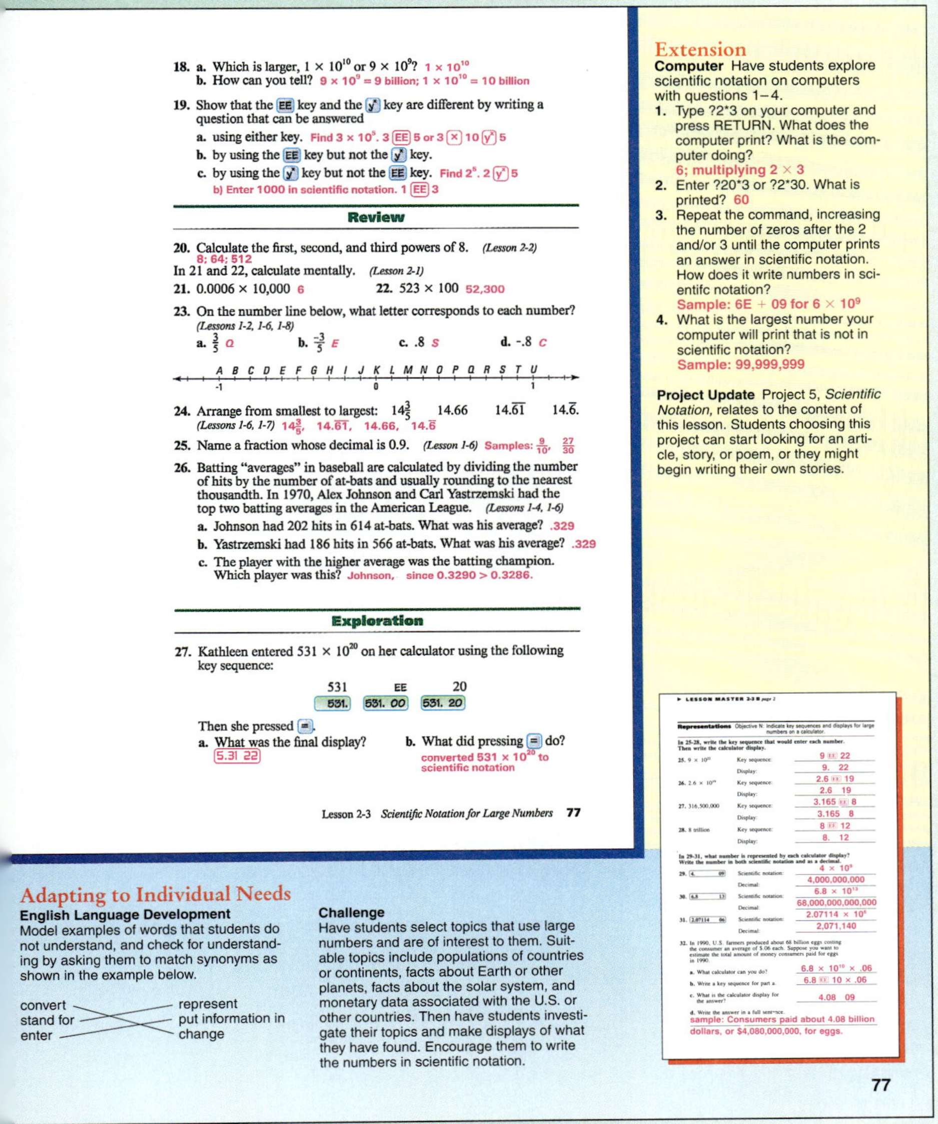

18. a. Which is larger, 1×10^{10} or 9×10^9? 1×10^{10}
b. How can you tell? 9×10^9 = 9 billion; 1×10^{10} = 10 billion

19. Show that the [EE] key and the [y^x] key are different by writing a question that can be answered
a. using either key. Find 3×10^5. 3 [EE] 5 or 3 [×] 10 [y^x] 5
b. by using the [EE] key but not the [y^x] key.
c. by using the [y^x] key but not the [EE] key. Find 2^5. 2 [y^x] 5
b) Enter 1000 in scientific notation. 1 [EE] 3

Review

20. Calculate the first, second, and third powers of 8. *(Lesson 2-2)* 8; 64; 512

In 21 and 22, calculate mentally. *(Lesson 2-1)*

21. $0.0006 \times 10{,}000$ 6
22. 523×100 52,300

23. On the number line below, what letter corresponds to each number? *(Lessons 1-2, 1-6, 1-8)*
a. $\frac{3}{5}$ Q
b. $\frac{-3}{5}$ E
c. .8 S
d. -.8 C

A B C D E F G H I J K L M N O P Q R S T U
-1 0 1

24. Arrange from smallest to largest: $14\frac{3}{5}$ 14.66 $14.\overline{61}$ $14.\overline{6}$.
(Lessons 1-6, 1-7) $14\frac{3}{5}$, $14.\overline{61}$, 14.66, $14.\overline{6}$

25. Name a fraction whose decimal is 0.9. *(Lesson 1-6)* Samples: $\frac{9}{10}$, $\frac{27}{30}$

26. Batting "averages" in baseball are calculated by dividing the number of hits by the number of at-bats and usually rounding to the nearest thousandth. In 1970, Alex Johnson and Carl Yastrzemski had the top two batting averages in the American League. *(Lessons 1-4, 1-6)*
a. Johnson had 202 hits in 614 at-bats. What was his average? .329
b. Yastrzemski had 186 hits in 566 at-bats. What was his average? .329
c. The player with the higher average was the batting champion. Which player was this? Johnson, since 0.3290 > 0.3286.

Exploration

27. Kathleen entered 531×10^{20} on her calculator using the following key sequence:

531 EE 20
531. 531. 00 531. 20

Then she pressed [=].
a. What was the final display? 5.31 22
b. What did pressing [=] do? converted 531×10^{20} to scientific notation

Lesson 2-3 *Scientific Notation for Large Numbers* 77

Extension

Computer Have students explore scientific notation on computers with questions 1–4.

1. Type ?2*3 on your computer and press RETURN. What does the computer print? What is the computer doing?
6; multiplying 2 × 3
2. Enter ?20*3 or ?2*30. What is printed? 60
3. Repeat the command, increasing the number of zeros after the 2 and/or 3 until the computer prints an answer in scientific notation. How does it write numbers in scientific notation?
Sample: 6E + 09 for 6×10^9
4. What is the largest number your computer will print that is not in scientific notation?
Sample: 99,999,999

Project Update Project 5, *Scientific Notation,* relates to the content of this lesson. Students choosing this project can start looking for an article, story, or poem, or they might begin writing their own stories.

▶ LESSON MASTER 2-3 B page 2

Representations Objective N: Indicate key sequences and displays for large numbers on a calculator.

In 25-28, write the key sequence that would enter each number. Then write the calculator display.

25. 9×10^{22} Key sequence: 9 [EE] 22 Display: 9. 22
26. 2.6×10^{19} Key sequence: 2.6 [EE] 19 Display: 2.6 19
27. 316,500,000 Key sequence: 3.165 [EE] 8 Display: 3.165 8
28. 8 trillion Key sequence: 8 [EE] 12 Display: 8. 12

In 29-31, what number is represented by each calculator display? Write the number in both scientific notation and as a decimal.

29. [4. 09] Scientific notation: 4×10^9 Decimal: 4,000,000,000
30. [6.8 13] Scientific notation: 6.8×10^{13} Decimal: 68,000,000,000,000
31. [2.07114 06] Scientific notation: 2.07114×10^6 Decimal: 2,071,140

32. In 1990, U.S. farmers produced about 68 billion eggs costing the consumer an average of $.06 each. Suppose you want to estimate the total amount of money consumers paid for eggs in 1990.
a. What calculator can you do? $6.8 \times 10^{10} \times .06$
b. Write a key sequence for part a. 6.8 [EE] 10 × .06
c. What is the calculator display for the answer? 4.08 09
d. Write the answer in a full sentence. sample: Consumers paid about 4.08 billion dollars, or $4,080,000,000, for eggs.

77

Adapting to Individual Needs

English Language Development
Model examples of words that students do not understand, and check for understanding by asking them to match synonyms as shown in the example below.

convert — represent
stand for — put information in
enter — change

Challenge
Have students select topics that use large numbers and are of interest to them. Suitable topics include populations of countries or continents, facts about Earth or other planets, facts about the solar system, and monetary data associated with the U.S. or other countries. Then have students investigate their topics and make displays of what they have found. Encourage them to write the numbers in scientific notation.

"As a teacher of Transition Mathematics, I can honestly say I have never, in twenty years of teaching, seen a better written math text. I enjoy teaching it and seeing the students succeed and learn to like math. The format and content is logical, challenging, and relevant."

Carol A. Connor, teacher
Olmstead Falls, Ohio

Practice and review

Continual opportunities for practice and review throughout *Transition Mathematics* help students strengthen conceptual understanding and ensure optimum performance. *See pages 15, 297-299, and 539 for further examples.*

Student diversity

UCSMP materials have been carefully designed to accommodate the full range of today's diverse student population. Your Teacher's Edition is full of ideas for addressing the needs of each student. *See pages 24, 132, and 313 for further examples.*

How it works

Progress checks for students

A Progress Self-Test at the end of each chapter helps students determine how well they've assimilated chapter concepts. Various types of problems, keyed to chapter objectives, provide ideal preparation for chapter tests and teach study skills.

CHAPTER TWO

PROGRESS SELF-TEST

Take this test as you would take a test in class. Then check your work with the solutions in the Selected Answers section in the back of the book.

In 1–10, write as a single decimal.

1. $100{,}000{,}000 \times 23.51864$
2. 34% of 600
3. 32 billionths
4. 824.59×0.00001
5. $\frac{1}{1000} \times 77$
6. 3456.8910×10^5
7. 2.816×10^{-3}
8. 10^{-7}
9. 8%
10. 6^3

In 11–13, consider 125^6.

11. 125 is called the _?_ and 6 the _?_.
12. a. What key sequence can you use to calculate this on your calculator?
    b. What is the resulting display?
13. Give a decimal estimate for 125^6.
14. What is the distance from a point on a circle to the center of the circle called?
15. What percent does a whole circle graph represent?

In 16 and 17, write in scientific notation.

16. 21,070,000,000
17. 0.00000 008

In 18 and 19, write a key sequence you can use to enter the number on your calculator.

18. 4.5×10^{13}
19. 0.00000 01234 56
20. Order from smallest to largest: 4^4 5^3 3^5.
21. Between what two integers is 40%?
22. Rewrite 4.73 as:
    a. a simple fraction b. a percent.
23. As a fraction, $33\frac{1}{3}\% =$ _?_.

24. Consider the circle graph below.

Type of Recording Media Sold 1991

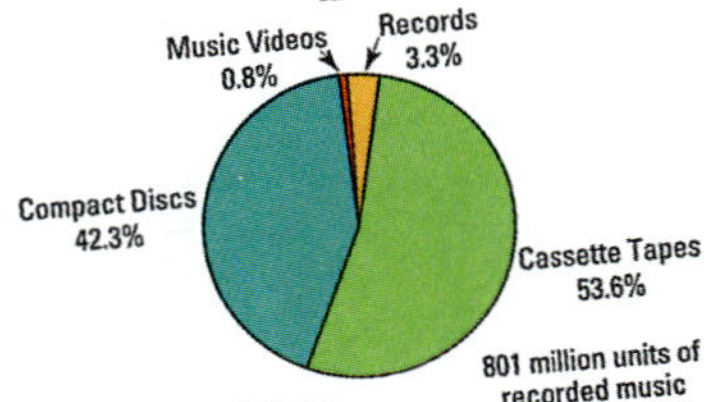

Source: *Recording Industry Association of America, Inc.*

a. Which type of recording med the most sales?
b. What percent of recorded m was not on compact disc?
c. About how many records w 1991?

25. A recent survey of 150 chefs r 30% of the chefs think brocco vegetable. How many chefs is
26. A computer system is on sale the regular price is \$1699, wh price to the nearest dollar?
27. Julio correctly answered 80% on a 20-item test. How many
28. Why is 22.4×10^3 not in scie
29. What power of 10 equals one million?
30. According to the Substitution Principle, $\frac{3}{5} - \frac{1}{10} =$ _?_ % − _?_ %.
31. It is estimated that a swarm of 250 billion locusts descended on the Red Sea in 1889. Write this number in scientific notation.

After taking and correcting the Self-Test, you may want to make a list of the problems you got wrong. Then write down what you need to study most. If you can, try to explain your most frequent or common mistakes. Use what you write to help you study and review the chapter.

The chart below keys the **Progress Self-Test** questions to the objectives in the **Chapter Review** on pages 113–115 or to the **Vocabulary** (Voc.) on page 111. This will enable you to locate those **Chapter Review** questions that correspond to questions you missed on the **Progress Self-Test.** The lesson where the material is covered is also indicated on the chart.

Question	**1**	**2**	**3**	**4**	**5**	**6**	**7**	**8**	**9**	**10**
Objective	A	G, K	B	E	E	A	E	D	G	C
Lesson	2-1	2-5	2-8	2-4	2-4	2-2	2-4	2-8	2-4	2-2
Question	**11**	**12**	**13**	**14**	**15**	**16**	**17**	**18**	**19**	**20**
Objective	Voc.	N	C	J	O	F	F	N	N	C
Lesson	2-2	2-3	2-2	2-7	2-7	2-3	2-9	2-3	2-9	2-2
Question	**21**	**22**	**23**	**24**	**25**	**26**	**27**	**28**	**29**	**30**
Objective	G, H	I	H	O	M	M	M	L	D	K
Lesson	2-4	2-6	2-4	2-7	2-5	2-5	2-5	2-3	2-2	2-5
Question	**31**									
Objective	F									
Lesson	2-3									

A chart for each Progress-Self Test (at the back of the Student Edition) keys test questions to chapter objectives.

"Students who received C's and D's last year are now scoring A's and B's on tests, quizzes, and homework assignments! They seem to have a more positive attitude toward math."

Melinda Henson-Parker, teacher
West Chicago, Illinois

End-of-chapter mastery

Comprehensive chapter reviews based on SPUR objectives — Skills, Properties, Uses, and Representations — ensure multidimensional understanding of key concepts.

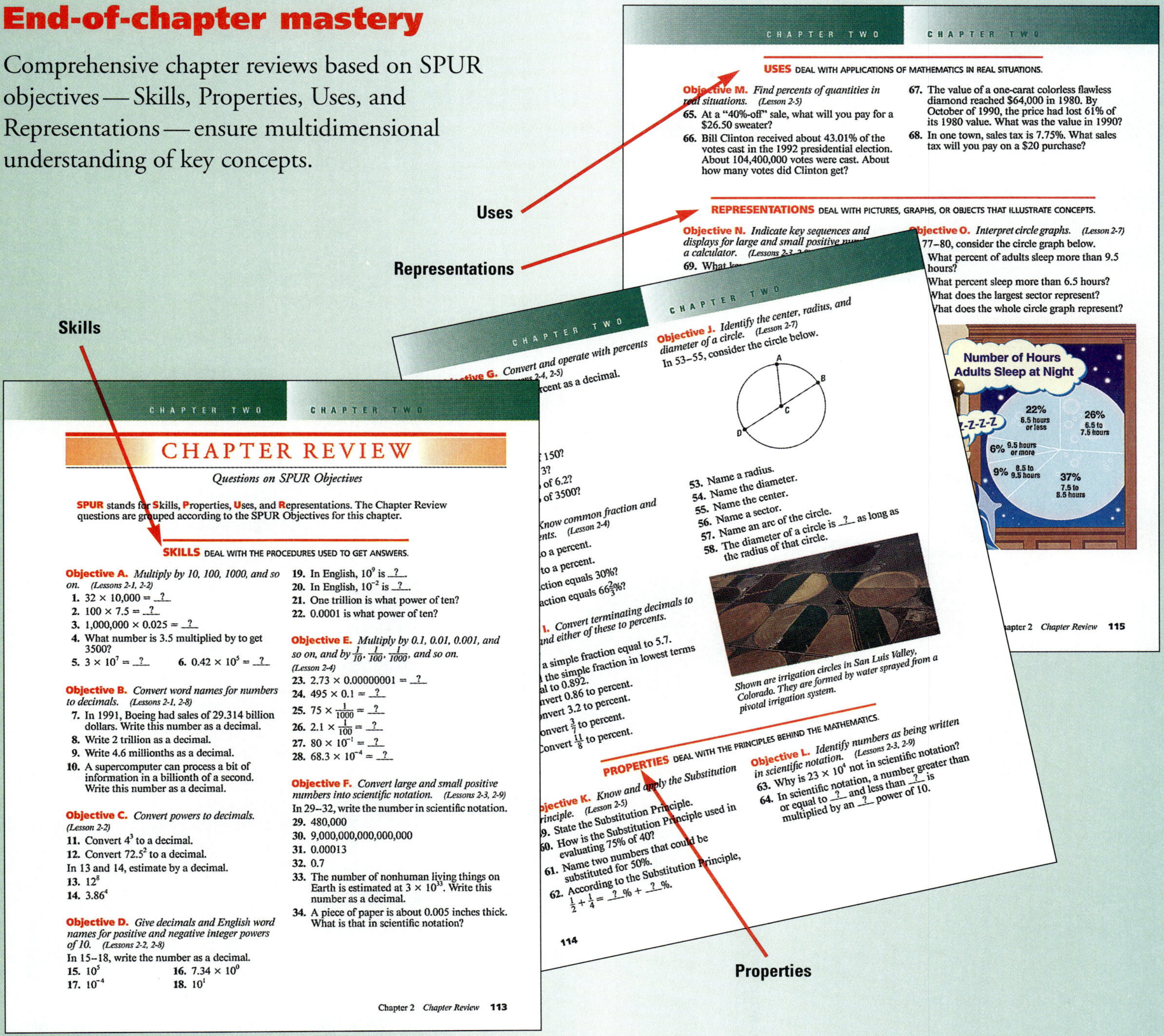

"Transition Mathematics is one of the best books I've seen to help students make the transition to algebra. It makes the students think. I appreciate the reading and writing in the book. It works toward the goals of the California Framework and the NCTM Standards."

Les Leibovitch, team leader
Van Nuys, California

How it works

Multiple forms of assessment

Your Assessment Sourcebook includes quizzes, test forms A and B, performance tests C and D, and a cumulative test for each chapter, and comprehensive tests after Chapters 3, 6, 9, and 13. Plus, Quiz and Test Writer software enables you to adapt existing tests or create your own in various forms. Your Assessment Sourcebook also includes abundant resources for portfolio, problem-solving, cooperative-group, and self assessment.

"UCSMP provides our students with good preparation for further studies in mathematics and other subjects."

Ibrahim Wazir, math chairperson
Vienna, Austria

Quiz and Test Writer Software for IBM and Macintosh lets you generate a variety of test and quiz forms quickly and easily.

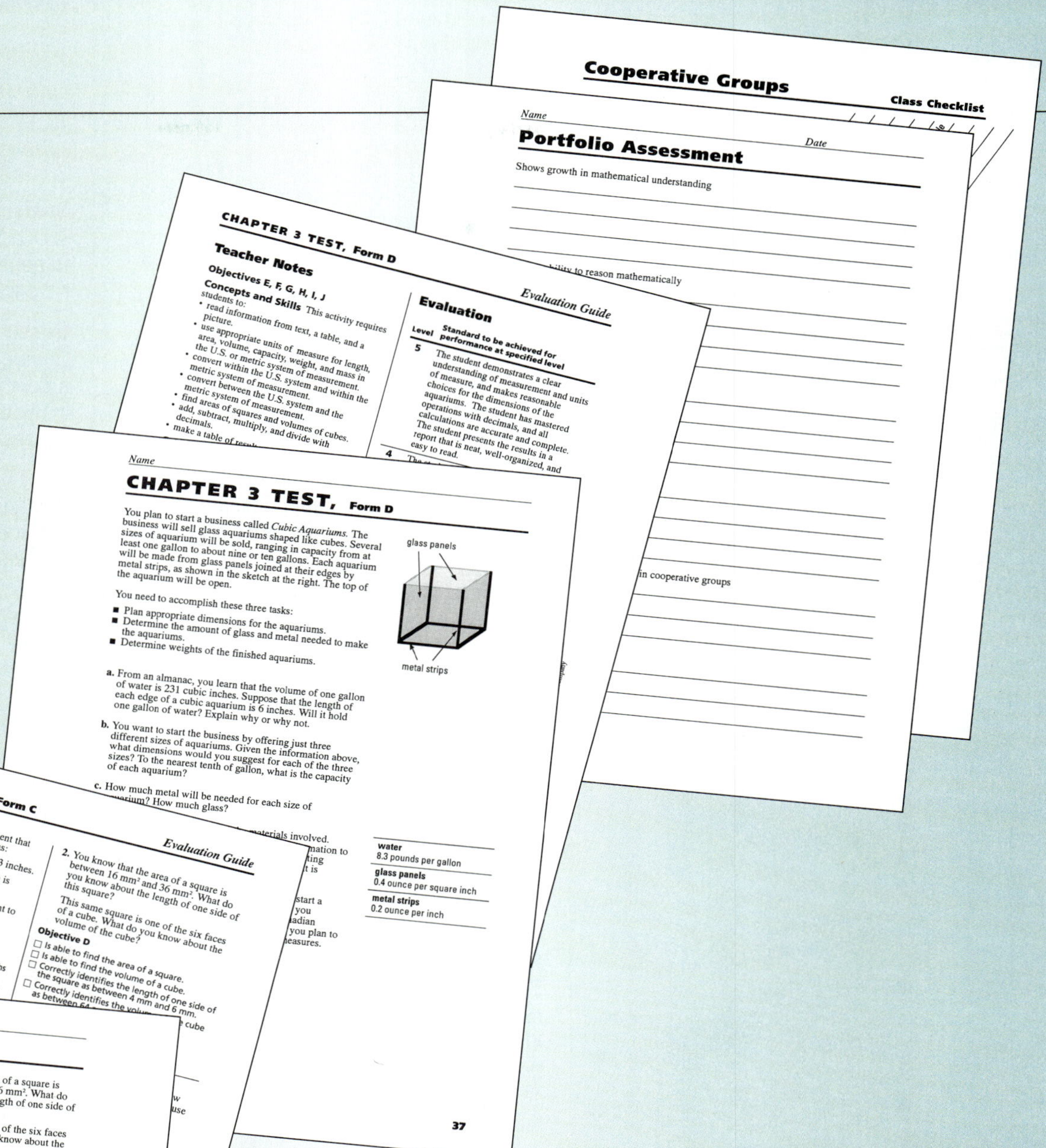

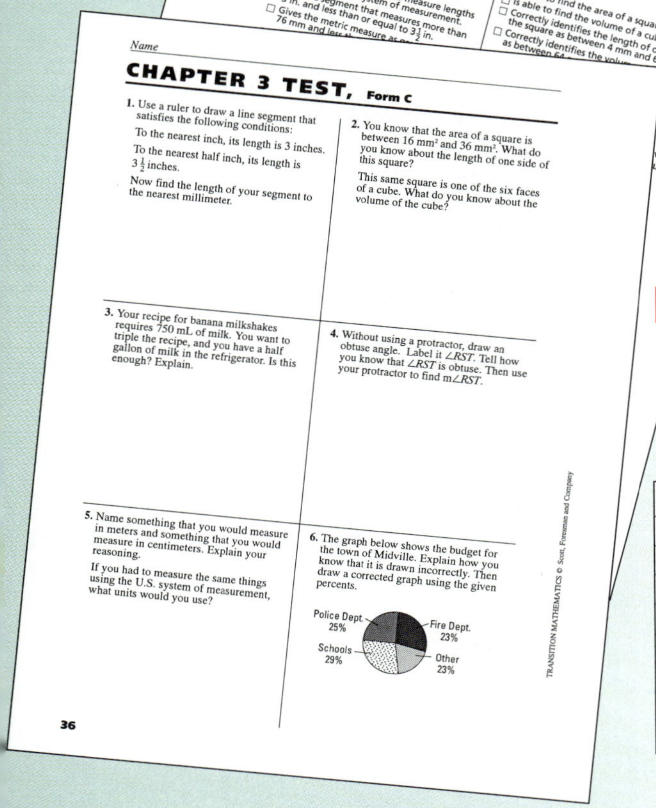

On page A in each group of prechapter pages, options for assessment alternatives are summarized in a chart.

In the Teacher's Edition...

Lesson	Optional Activities	Extra Help	Challenge	English Language Development	Error Alert	Extension	Cooperative Learning	Ongoing Assessment
3-1	●	●	●	●	●	●	●	Group
3-2	●	●	●	●	●	●	●	Written
3-3	●	●	●	●		●		Group
3-4	●	●		●		●	●	Oral
3-5	●		●	●	●	●		Written
3-6	●	●	●	●	●	●		Written
3-7	●		●	●	●	●	●	Written
3-8	●	●	●			●		Oral/Written
3-9	●	●	●	●		●		Oral

The works

Components of *Transition Mathematics, Second Edition*

Student Edition
0-673-45745-1. With calculator: 0-673-45759-1.

Teacher's Resource File
Contains a Teacher's Edition, hundreds of blackline masters and a Solution Manual correlated to the Student Edition. Booklets are also available separately. 0-673-45849-0.

- ☐ **Teacher's Edition** (in two parts). 0-673-45748-6.
- ☐ **Lesson Masters A.** Single-page blackline masters correlated to each lesson in the Student Edition—ideal for extra practice. 0-673-45750-8.
- ☐ **Lesson Masters B.** Two pages of practice for each lesson, for students who need extra help. 0-673-45749-4.
- ☐ **Teaching Aid Masters.** All Warm-ups and many Additional Examples from the Teacher's Edition margin notes, tables, graphs, drawings, visual organizers, and more. 0-673-45751-6.
- ☐ **Assessment Sourcebook.** Quizzes, standard tests, performance assessment, and cumulative tests for each chapter, plus comprehensive tests and guidelines for portfolio, problem-solving, cooperative-group, and self assessment. 0-673-45752-4.
- ☐ **Technology Sourcebook.** Ideas for teacher-directed computer demonstrations and blackline-master activities for use with both calculators and computers. Helps students explore and extend concepts through the latest technologies. 0-673-45754-0.
- ☐ **Answer Masters.** Answers for all questions in the Student Edition. 0-673-45753-2.
- ☐ **Solution Manual.** Complete step-by-step solutions to all questions in the Student Edition. 0-673-45755-9.

Visual Aids
Overhead transparencies of all Answer Masters and Teaching Aids, including Warm-ups and many Additional Examples from the Teacher's Edition margin notes to enhance your classroom presentations. 0-673-45758-3.

Activity Kit
Includes an Activity Sourcebook with blackline-master activities that enhance interest and understanding, encourage curiosity, and strengthen mathematical thinking. Also includes manipulatives for the overhead projector. 0-673-45764-8.

Study Skills Handbook
A UCSMP exclusive containing tips and models to help students develop study skills. 0-673-45823-7.

Geometry Template (package of 25)
Unique to UCSMP, this sturdy plastic tool is a combination compass and protractor and includes rulers, a grid, various geometric figures, and a center finder. 0-673-45825-3.

TI-30 Calculator
Designed by Texas Instruments with the assistance of the UCSMP team, this is the simplest scientific calculator on the market today. Available with the purchase of a Student Text. Also available in a caddy of ten and in an overhead version.
With Student Text: 0-673-45759-1.
Caddy of ten: 0-673-33990-4.
Overhead Version: 0-673-45406-1.

Transition Mathematics Software Tools (Apple II, IBM, Macintosh)
A geometry drawing tool, a spreadsheet tool, and a tool for graphing and exploring probabilities. Also includes a Reference Guide and blackline-master activities. Apple: 0-673-37449-1. IBM: 0-673-37450-5. Macintosh: 0-673-37451-3.

Quiz and Test Writer Software (IBM and Macintosh)
Create a wealth of custom quizzes and tests quickly and easily, with a minimum of computer expertise. Includes extra challenge problems.
IBM: 0-673-45827-X.
Macintosh: 0-673-45828-8.

Videotape/Videodisc with Multimedia CD-ROM (IBM and Macintosh)
Interactive activities for introducing lessons in the Student Edition. Can be used for teacher demonstrations or in a laboratory setting.
Videotape: 0-673-37473-4.
Videodisc: 0-673-37439-4.
CD-ROM Macintosh: 0-673-37443-2.
CD-ROM IBM: 0-673-37444-0.

UCSMP
SCOTT FORESMAN

The University of Chicago School Mathematics Project

Transition Mathematics

Second Edition

About the Cover The art on the cover was generated by a computer. The three interlocking rings signify the major themes of this book—algebra, geometry, and applied arithmetic.

Authors

Zalman Usiskin Cathy Hynes Feldman

Suzanne Davis Sharon Mallo Gladys Sanders David Witonsky

James Flanders Lydia Polonsky Susan Porter Steven S. Viktora

ScottForesman

A Division of HarperCollins*Publishers*

Editorial Offices: Glenview, Illinois
Regional Offices: Sunnyvale, California • Tucker, Georgia
Glenview, Illinois • Oakland, New Jersey • Dallas, Texas

ACKNOWLEDGMENTS

Authors

Zalman Usiskin
Professor of Education, The University of Chicago

Cathy Hynes Feldman
Mathematics Teacher, The University of Chicago Laboratory Schools

Suzanne Davis
Mathematics Supervisor, Pinellas County Schools, Largo, FL (Second Edition only)

Sharon Mallo
Mathematics Teacher, Lake Park H.S., Roselle, IL (Second Edition only)

Gladys Sanders
K–12 Mathematics Coordinator, Lawrence Public Schools, Lawrence, KS (Second Edition only)

David Witonsky
UCSMP (Second Edition only)

James Flanders
UCSMP (First Edition only)

Lydia Polonsky
UCSMP (First Edition only)

Susan Porter
Evanston Township H.S., Evanston, IL (First Edition only)

Steven S. Viktora
Chairman, Mathematics Department, Kenwood Academy, Chicago Public Schools (First Edition only)

Design Development

Curtis Design

UCSMP Production and Evaluation

Series Editors: Zalman Usiskin, Sharon L. Senk

Directors of First Edition Studies: Kathryn Sloane, Sandra Mathison; Assistant to the Directors: Penelope Flores

Directors of Second Edition Studies: Geraldine Macsai, Gurcharn Kaeley

Technical Coordinator: Susan Chang

Second Edition Teacher's Edition Editor: Suzanne Levin

Second Edition Consultants: Amy Hackenberg, Mary Lappan

First Edition Managing Editor: Natalie Jakucyn

We wish to thank the many editors, production personnel, and design personnel at ScottForesman for their magnificent assistance.

We wish to acknowledge the generous support of the Amoco Foundation and the Carnegie Corporation of New York in helping to make it possible for the First Edition of these materials to be developed, tested, and distributed, and the continuing support of the Amoco Foundation for the Second Edition.

Multicultural Reviewers for ScottForesman

Marion Bolden
Newark Board of Education, Newark, NJ

Seree Weroha
Kansas State University, Manhattan, KS

Efraín Meléndez
Dacatoh St. School, Los Angeles, CA

Yvonne Wynde
Educator, Sisseton-Wahpeton Dakota Nation, Waubay, SD

It is impossible for UCSMP to thank all the people who have helped create and test these books. We wish particularly to thank James Schultz and Glenda Lappan, who as members of the UCSMP Advisory Board, commented on early manuscripts; Carol Siegel, who coordinated the use of the test materials in schools; Liggy Chien and Kate Fahey of our editorial staff; Sara Benson, Anil Gurnarney, Jee Yoon Lee, Adil Moiduddin, Jeong Moon, Antoun Nabhan, Young Nam, and Sara Zimmerman of our technical staff; and Rochelle Gutiérrez, Nancy Miller, and Gerald Pillsbury of our evaluation staff.

A first draft of *Transition Mathematics* was written and piloted during the 1983–84 school year. After a major revision, a field trial edition was tested in 1984–85. These studies were done at the following schools:

Parkside Community Academy
Chicago Public Schools

Lively Junior High School
Elk Grove Village, Illinois

Kenwood Academy
Chicago Public Schools

McClure Junior High School
Western Springs, Illinois

Grove Junior High School
Elk Grove Village, Illinois

Wheaton-Warrenville Middle School
Wheaton, Illinois

Mead Junior High School
Elk Grove Village, Illinois

Glenbrook South High School
Glenview, Illinois

A second revision underwent a comprehensive nationwide test in 1985–86. The following schools participated in those studies:

Powell Middle School
Littleton, Colorado

16th St. Middle School
St. Petersburg, Florida

Walt Disney Magnet School
Gale Community Academy
Hubbard High School
Von Steuben Upper Grade Center
Chicago, Illinois

Hillcrest High School
Country Club Hills, Illinois

Friendship Junior High School
Des Plaines, Illinois

Bremen High School
Midlothian, Illinois

Holmes Junior High School
Mt. Prospect, Illinois

Sundling Junior High School
Winston Park Junior High School
Palatine, Illinois

Addams Junior High School
Schaumburg, Illinois

Edison Junior High School
Wheaton, Illinois

Golden Ring Middle School
Sparrows Point High School
Baltimore, Maryland

Walled Lake Central High School
Walled Lake, Michigan

Columbia High School
Columbia, Mississippi

Oak Grove High School
Hattiesburg, Mississippi

Roosevelt Middle School
Taylor Middle School
Albuquerque, New Mexico

Gamble Middle School
Schwab Middle School
Cincinnati, Ohio

Tuckahoe Middle School
Richmond, Virginia

Shumway Middle School
Vancouver, Washington

Since the ScottForesman publication of the First Edition of *Transition Mathematics* in 1990, thousands of teachers and schools have used the materials and have made additional suggestions for improvements. The materials were again revised, and the following teachers and schools participated in field studies in 1992–1993:

Charlotte Kulbacki
East Junior High School
Colorado Springs, Colorado

Patricia Gresko
Kerr Middle School
Blue Island, Illinois

Jane Sughrue
McCall Middle School
Winchester, Massachusetts

Audrey Reineck
Washington High School
Milwaukee, Wisconsin

Joseph Pierre-Lewis
Edison Middle School
Miami, Florida

Mary Fitzpatrick
Olson Middle School
Woodstock, Illinois

Cindy Urban
Forest Hills Central Middle School
Grand Rapids, Michigan

Barbara Pulliam
East Coweta Middle School
Senoia, Georgia

Kathy Hying
Northwood Middle School
Woodstock, Illinois

Garry J. Hopkins
Hillside Middle School
Kalamazoo, Michigan

Linda Ferreira
Osceola Middle School
Seminole, Florida

Karen Bloss
Northwest High School
Wichita, Kansas

Linda Kennley
C.A. Johnson High School
Columbia, South Carolina

THE UNIVERSITY OF CHICAGO SCHOOL MATHEMATICS PROJECT

The University of Chicago School Mathematics Project (UCSMP) is a long-term project designed to improve school mathematics in grades K-12. UCSMP began in 1983 with a 6-year grant from the Amoco Foundation. Additional funding has come from the National Science Foundation, the Ford Motor Company, the Carnegie Corporation of New York, the General Electric Foundation, GTE, Citicorp/Citibank, and the Exxon Education Foundation.

UCSMP is centered in the Departments of Education and Mathematics of the University of Chicago. The project has translated dozens of mathematics textbooks from other countries, held three international conferences, developed curricular materials for elementary and secondary schools, formulated models of teacher training and retraining, conducted a large number of large and small conferences, engaged in evaluations of many of its activities, and through its royalties has supported a wide variety of research projects in mathematics education at the University. UCSMP currently has the following components and directors:

Resources	Izaak Wirszup, Professor Emeritus of Mathematics
Elementary Materials	Max Bell, Professor of Education
Elementary Teacher Development	Sheila Sconiers, Research Associate in Education
Secondary	Sharon L. Senk, Associate Professor of Mathematics, Michigan State University Zalman Usiskin, Professor of Education
Evaluation	Larry Hedges, Professor of Education

From 1983 to 1987, the director of UCSMP was Paul Sally, Professor of Mathematics. Since 1987, the director has been Zalman Usiskin.

Transition Mathematics

The text *Transition Mathematics* has been developed by the Secondary Component of the project, and constitutes the core of the first year in a six-year mathematics curriculum devised by that component. The names of the six texts around which these years are built are:

Transition Mathematics
Algebra
Geometry
Advanced Algebra
Functions, Statistics, and Trigonometry
Precalculus and Discrete Mathematics

The content and questions of this book have been carefully sequenced to provide a smooth path from arithmetic to algebra, and from the visual world and arithmetic to geometry. It is for this reason that this book is entitled *Transition Mathematics*.

The first edition of *Transition Mathematics* introduced many features which have come now to be deemed essential in courses at this level. There is **wider scope,** including substantial amounts of geometry integrated with the arithmetic and algebra that is customary, to correct the present situation in which many students who finish algebra find themselves without enough prior knowledge to succeed in geometry. A **real-world orientation** has guided both the selection of content and the approaches allowed the student in working out exercises and problems, because being able to do mathematics is of little ultimate use to an individual unless he or she can apply that content. We require **reading mathematics,** because students must read to understand mathematics in later courses and must learn to read technical matter in the world at large. The use of **up-to-date technology** is integrated throughout, with *scientific calculators* assumed and *computer* exercises found in all content areas.

We continue to use two unique overall features designed to maximize performance. **Four dimensions of understanding** are emphasized: skill in carrying out various algorithms; developing and using mathematics properties and relationships; applying mathematics in realistic situations; and representing or picturing mathematical concepts. We call this the SPUR approach: **S**kills, **P**roperties, **U**ses, **R**epresentations. On occasion, a fifth dimension of understanding, the Culture dimension, is discussed.

The **book organization** is designed to maximize the acquisition of both skills and concepts. Ideas introduced in a lesson are reinforced through Review questions in the immediately succeeding lessons. This daily review feature allows students several nights to learn and practice important concepts and skills. At the end of each chapter, a carefully focused Progress Self-Test and a Chapter Review, each keyed to objectives in all the dimensions of understanding, are then used to solidify performance of skills and concepts from the chapter so that they may be applied later with confidence. Finally, to increase retention, important ideas are reviewed in later chapters.

Since the ScottForesman publication of the first edition of *Transition Mathematics* in 1990, the entire UCSMP secondary series has been completed and published. Thousands of teachers and schools have used the first edition and made additional suggestions for improvements. There have been advances in technology and in thinking about how students learn. We have attempted to utilize these ideas in the development of the second edition. We have found that many students are beginning this course with less experience with fractions than they should have, and so the sequence of some lessons has been changed, and there is more work with probability and fractions. At the same time, we assume a little more experience with measurement than we did in the first edition.

Those familiar with the first edition will note also a number of new features, including the following: **Activities** have been incorporated into many of the lessons to help students develop concepts before or as they read. There are **projects** at the end of each chapter because in the real world much of the mathematics done requires a longer period of time than is customarily available to students in daily assignments. There are many more questions requiring student **writing,** because writing helps students clarify their own thinking, and writing is an important aspect of communicating mathematical ideas to others. Each of these features is designed to involve students more actively in their learning. In the area of technology, **spreadsheets** are now being used as a tool to help solve problems.

Comments about these materials are welcomed. Please address comments to UCSMP, The University of Chicago, 5835 S. Kimbark, Chicago, IL 60637.

v

CONTENTS

CHAPTER 3 116

Measurement

CHAPTER 4 174

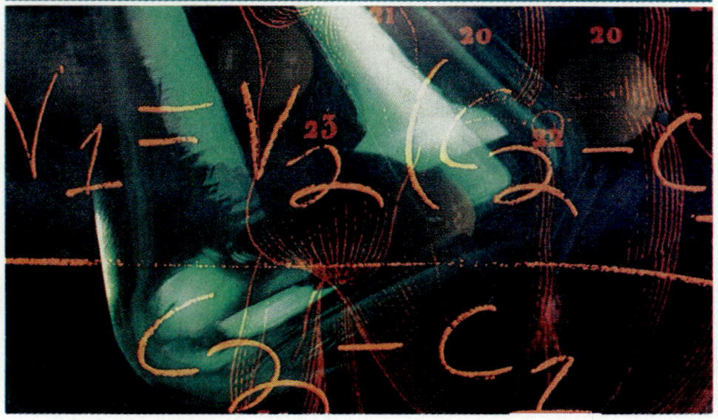

Uses of Variables

CHAPTER 5 236

Patterns Leading to Addition

CHAPTER 6 300

Problem-Solving Strategies

CHAPTER 7 344

Patterns Leading to Subtraction

To the Student

GETTING STARTED

Welcome to Transition Mathematics.
We hope you enjoy this book; it was written for you.

The Goals of *Transition Mathematics*

The goals of this book are to solidify the arithmetic you already know and to prepare you for algebra and geometry.

THERE IS ANOTHER important goal of this book: for you to be able to deal with the mathematics all around you—in newspapers, magazines, on television, in any job, and in school. To accomplish this goal you should try to learn from the reading in each lesson as well as from your teacher and your classmates. The authors, who are all experienced teachers, offer the following advice:

1 You can watch basketball hundreds of times on television. Still, to learn how to play basketball, you must have a ball in your hand and actually dribble, shoot, and pass it. Mathematics is no different. You cannot learn much mathematics just by watching other people do it. You must participate. Some teachers have a slogan: *Mathematics is not a spectator sport.*

Mathematics is not a spectator sport.

2 You are expected to read each lesson. Here are some ways to improve your reading comprehension:

Read slowly, paying attention to each word.

Look up the meaning of any word you do not understand.

Work examples yourself as you follow the steps in the text.

Reread sections that are unclear to you.

Discuss troublesome ideas with a fellow student or your teacher.

Notes on Reading

Reading Mathematics The reading abilities of students using Transition Mathematics differ. You might begin by calling on students in turn to read aloud a few sentences of this introduction. This will give you some idea of the reading levels of the students in your class. Alternatively, you could have students read this section on their own.

❶ Emphasize the cooperative nature of learning. Encourage students to discuss their mathematics assignments with each other in school or call one another at home if they have difficulty understanding a problem or concept. Be sure to distinguish *cooperation* from *copying.*

Overview

These pages contain three important bits of information:

1. a list of the materials that are needed for this book.
2. a description of the active approach taken to learning in this book, including participation, reading, writing, and problem solving.
3. a set of questions designed to familiarize students with the location of various features in the book.

❷ Encourage students to use the headline phrases that identify some of the key ideas taught in the lessons. Point out that these headlines can help students organize their thoughts, preview the reading, and find answers to questions about the lesson.

Also point out that as students read, they should stop to examine any graphs and charts and study all computations that might be in examples. Looking at pictures and photographs and reading captions is considered part of the lesson, too. Point out that throughout this book, important terms are printed in boldface type.

❸ Since some students may not know what a protractor looks like, have one in class to show them. Also show students the kind(s) of scientific calculator(s) you expect them to use with this book.

3 Writing can help you understand mathematics, too. So you will sometimes be asked to explain your solution to a problem or to justify an answer. Writing good explanations takes practice. Use the solutions to the examples in each lesson as a guide for your own writing.

4 If you cannot answer a question immediately, don't give up! Read the lesson, examples, or question again. If you can, go away from the problem and come back to it a little later. Do not be afraid to ask questions in class and to talk to others when you do not understand something.

What Tools Do You Need for This Book?

In addition to paper, pencils, and erasers, you will need the following equipment:

ruler with both centimeter and inch markings *(by Lesson 1-2)*

scientific calculator *(by Lesson 1-5)*

protractor to draw and measure angles *(by Lesson 3-6)*

The calculator should have the following keys:

EE or EXP to display very large or very small numbers in scientific notation

± or +/– (opposite)

^, x^y, or y^x (powering)

√x (square root)

x! (factorial)

π (pi)

1/x (reciprocal).

Your teacher may have more recommendations regarding what you need.

Getting Off to a Good Start

One way to get off to a good start is to spend some time getting acquainted with your textbook. The questions that follow are designed to help you become familiar with *Transition Mathematics.*

We hope you join the hundreds of thousands of students who have enjoyed this book. We wish you much success.

QUESTIONS

Covering the Reading

1. What are the goals of *Transition Mathematics*? See below.

2. Explain what is meant by the statement "Mathematics is not a spectator sport." See below.

3. Of the five things listed for improving reading comprehension, list the three you think are most helpful to you. Why do you think they are most helpful? See margin.

4. *Multiple choice.* Choose all correct answers. Which are good things to do if you cannot answer a homework question immediately?
(a) Give up.
(b) Look for a similar example in the reading.
(c) Relax, go on to the next question, and come back to this question later.
(d) Discuss the problem with a friend.
(e) Read the relevant part of the lesson again.
(f) Beg your teacher or parents to do it for you.
(g) Go watch *Wheel of Fortune.*
(b), (c), (d), (e)

1) To solidify arithmetic and prepare for algebra and geometry; to be able to deal with mathematics in different media, in any job, and in school

2) To be good at mathematics, you must do mathematics.

Knowing Your Textbook

In 5 and 6, refer to the Table of Contents beginning on page *vi.*

5. Algebra uses variables. In which chapter does work in algebra begin? Chapter 4

6. What lesson would you read to learn how to measure angles? Lesson 3-6

In 7–12, refer to other parts of the book.

7. Look at several lessons. What are the four categories of questions in each lesson? See below.

8. Suppose you have just finished the questions in Lesson 3-4. On what page can you find answers to check your work? What answers are given? See below.

9. When you finish a Progress Self-Test, what is recommended for you to do? See margin.

10. What kinds of questions are in the Chapter Review at the end of each chapter? Skills, Properties, Uses, and Representations

11. Where is the glossary and what does it contain? It begins on page 755; it has definitions of words and phrases introduced in the book.

12. Locate the index.
a. According to the index, where will you find information about David Robinson?
b. What is this information? See margin.

David Robinson

7) Covering the Reading, Applying the Mathematics, Review, Exploration

8) page 735; answers to odd-numbered questions in Applying the Mathematics and Review

Notes on Questions

Go through all the questions in class. Alternatively, you might have the class go through only the questions in *Covering the Reading* **(Questions 1–6),** and then let students work on **Questions 7–14** on their own or with a partner.

Cooperative Learning Another way to assign the questions is to divide the class into groups of 4. Have each group select a student to record answers. As each group goes through the questions, the recorder writes the answers on paper. You might want to walk around the room monitoring the groups to keep them on task.

Question 1 Note that there is more than one goal of this course. Point out that answers to *Covering the Reading* are often found literally in the lesson, but, when appropriate, students should try to write the answers in their own words.

Question 3 Writing Many questions in this book ask students to explain or justify an answer. Again encourage students to use their own words, but stress that their answers should be clear, both to themselves and to another person who might read them.

Additional Answers

3. Answers will vary. Choices may include: read slowly, look up meanings of words, work examples, reread sections, discuss ideas. (See the advice in step 2 on page 1.)

9. Check my work with the solutions given in the back of the book. Make a list of the problems I missed. Write down what I need to study most. Use what I write to help me study and review the chapter.

12. a) page 48; b) Robinson attended the U.S. Naval Academy in Annapolis earning a degree in mathematics. He is 7'1" tall and began his professional basketball career in 1989.

Setting Up Lesson 1-1

Homework If you have a short class period (15–30 minutes) tomorrow, you might assign the reading and the questions on *Covering the Reading* from Lesson 1-1. If you have a full-length period, assign the reading and all of the questions.

Error Alert Some students may feel that they can skip the *Chapter 1 Opener* on pages 4–5. Tell students that they should read all openers along with the first lessons of each chapter unless they are told otherwise.

Chapter 1 Planner

Adapting to Individual Needs

The student text is written for the vast majority of students. The chart at the right suggests two pacing plans to accommodate the needs of your students. Students in the Full Course should complete the entire text by the end of the year. Students in the Minimal Course will spend more time when there are quizzes and more time on the Chapter Review. Therefore, these students may not complete all of the chapters in the text.

Options are also presented to meet the needs of a variety of teaching and learning styles. For each lesson, the Teacher's Edition provides sections entitled: *Video* which describes video segments and related questions that can be used for motivation or extension; *Optional Activities* which suggests activities that employ materials, physical models, technology, and cooperative learning; and *Adapting to Individual Needs* which regularly includes **Challenge** problems, **English Language Development** suggestions, and suggestions for providing **Extra Help.** The Teacher's Edition also frequently includes an **Error Alert,** an **Extension,** and an **Assessment** alternative. The options available in Chapter 1 are summarized in the chart below.

Chapter 1 Pacing Chart

Day	Full Course	Minimal Course
1	1-1	1-1
2	1-2	1-2
3	1-3	1-3
4	1-4	1-4
5	Quiz*; 1-5	Quiz*; begin 1-5.
6	1-6	Finish 1-5.
7	1-7	1-6
8	1-8	1-7
9	Quiz*; 1-9	1-8
10	1-10	Quiz*; begin 1-9.
11	Self-Test	Finish 1-9.
12	Review	1-10
13	Test*	Self-Test
14		Review
15		Review
16		Test*

*in the Teacher's Resource File

In the Teacher's Edition...

Lesson	Optional Activities	Extra Help	Challenge	English Language Development	Error Alert	Extension	Cooperative Learning	Ongoing Assessment
1-1	●	●		●	●	●	●	Oral
1-2	●	●	●	●	●	●	●	Group
1-3	●	●		●	●	●		Written
1-4	●	●		●	●	●		Written
1-5	●	●	●	●	●	●	●	Group
1-6	●	●	●	●	●	●	●	Oral
1-7	●	●		●	●		●	Group
1-8	●	●	●	●	●	●	●	Group
1-9	●	●	●			●	●	Written
1-10	●	●	●	●		●		Written

In the Additional Resources...

	In the Teacher's Resource File								
Lesson	Lesson Masters, A and B	Teaching Aids*	Activity Kit*	Answer Masters	Technology Sourcebook	Assessment Sourcebook	Visual Aids**	Transition Mathematics Software	Video Segments
1-1	1-1	1, 4		1-1			1, 4, AM		
1-2	1-2	1, 5, 6, 7		1-2			1, 5, 6, 7, AM	Spreadsheet	1-2
1-3	1-3	1, 7		1-3			1, 7, AM		
1-4	1-4	1, 8		1-4		Quiz	1, 8, AM		
1-5	1-5	2		1-5			2, AM		
1-6	1-6	2, 9, 10, 11, 12	1	1-6	Demo 1, Calc 1		2, 9, 10, 11, 12, AM	Spreadsheet	
1-7	1-7	2, 8	2	1-7			2, 8, AM		
1-8	1-8	2, 8		1-8		Quiz	2, 8, AM		
1-9	1-9	3, 8, 11, 12	3	1-9	Comp 1, Calc 2		3, 8, 11, 12, AM	Spreadsheet	
1-10	1-10	3, 11		1-10			3, 11, AM		
End of chapter				Review		Tests			

*Teaching Aids, except Warm-ups, are pictured on pages 4C and 4D. The activities in the Activity Kit are pictured on page 4C.
**Visual Aids provide transparencies for all Teaching Aids and all Answer Masters.

Also available is the Study Skills Handbook which includes study-skill tips related to reading, note-taking, and comprehension.

Integrating Strands and Applications

	1-1	1-2	1-3	1-4	1-5	1-6	1-7	1-8	1-9	1-10
Mathematical Connections										
Number Sense	●		●	●	●			●	●	●
Algebra						●				
Geometry			●			●				●
Measurement		●	●			●	●		●	
Logic and Reasoning					●					●
Patterns and Functions	●	●				●	●	●	●	
Interdisciplinary and Other Connections										
Science				●					●	
Social Studies	●			●	●		●	●	●	
Multicultural	●	●		●	●				●	
Technology		●	●	●	●	●			●	
Career						●				●
Consumer		●	●	●	●	●	●	●		
Sports		●					●	●		

Teaching and Assessing the Chapter Objectives

Chapter 1 Objectives (Organized into the SPUR catetgories—Skills, Properties, Uses, and Representations)	**Lessons**	**Progress Self-Test Questions**	**Chapter Review Questions**	**In the Assessment Sourcebook: Chapter Test, Forms A and B**	**Chapter Test, Forms C**	**Chapter Test, Forms D**
Skills						
A: Translate back and forth from English into the decimal system.	1-1, 1-2	1, 2, 5, 6	1–10	2–5, 32		
B: Order decimals and fractions.	1-2, 1-6, 1-7, 1-9	7, 8, 31	11–18	6, 20, 26, 29	5	✓
C: Give a number that is between two decimals.	1-2, 1-8	14, 15	19–23	9, 12, 21	1	✓
D: Round any decimal place up or down or to the nearest value of a decimal place.	1-3, 1-4, 1-8	9, 10, 23	24–35	15–18	2	✓
E: Use a calculator to perform arithmetic operations.	1-5, 1-6, 1-8	24, 25	36–40	19	1	✓
F: Convert simple fractions and mixed numbers to decimals.	1-6, 1-7, 1-8	4	41–44	8, 22, 23	6	
G: Know by memory the common decimal and fraction equivalences between 0 and 1.	1-6	3, 20	45–52	24	6	
Properties						
H: Use the < and > symbols correctly between numbers.	1-9	16–19	53–56	13, 14	5	
I: Correctly use the raised bar symbol for repeating decimals.	1-6	26	57–60	25	5	
J: Use the Equal Fractions Property to rewrite fractions.	1-10	32–34	61–64	28, 30, 31	3	
Uses						
K: Deal with estimates in real situations.	1-3, 1-4	22, 29	65–69	7, 33, 34, 40	2	✓
L: Correctly interpret situations with two directions as positive, negative, or corresponding to zero.	1-8	11	70–72	14, 39		
Representations						
M: Graph and read numbers on a number line.	1-2, 1-7, 1-8	12, 13, 27, 28	73–78	10, 11, 27, 35	4	
N: Give people and rough dates for key ideas in the development of arithmetic.	1-1, 1-2, 1-6	35	79, 80	36		

Assessment Sourcebook
Quiz for Lessons 1-1 through 1-4
Quiz for Lessons 1-5 through 1-8
Chapter 1 Test, Forms A –D

Quiz and Test Writer
Multiple forms of chapter tests and quizzes; Challenges

Activity Kit

ACTIVITY 1

DECIMALS AND SIMPLE FRACTIONS
Use with **Lesson 1-6.**

Materials: Activity Aid A—Decimal Strips, scissors
Group Size: Partners

In this activity, you use a decimal strip from Activity Aid A to find decimals and fractions that are equal. Do all of the steps of the activity yourself. After each step, check to see if you and your partner agree. Try to resolve any differences.

1. Cut out a decimal strip. Fold it in half and make a crease. Then open the strip. Draw a tick mark at the crease, and write a fraction to label this point. Write the corresponding decimal for this fraction in the table at the right.
2. Refold your decimal strip in half and fold it in half again. Make a crease and open the strip. Draw a mark at each new crease and label each point with a fraction. Write the corresponding decimals for these fractions in the table.
3. With your partner, decide how to fold the decimal strip into eighths. Then fold it, mark each new crease, and label each point with a fraction. The corresponding decimals for these fractions are given in the table. Write the fractions in the table.
4. Fold the decimal strip into thirds and sixths and mark the new creases. Label the points with fractions, and write these fractions in the table.
5. Without folding, mark all fifths and tenths that have not yet been marked, and label the points with fractions. Then complete the table.

You will often use the fractions and the corresponding decimals shown in the table, so you should try to memorize them.

Fraction	Decimal
$\frac{1}{10}$	
	0.125
	0.166 . . .
$\frac{1}{5}$	
$\frac{1}{4}$	
$\frac{3}{10}$	
	0.333 . . .
	0.375
$\frac{2}{5}$	
$\frac{1}{2}$	
$\frac{3}{5}$	
	0.625
	0.666 . . .
$\frac{7}{10}$	
$\frac{3}{4}$	
$\frac{4}{5}$	
	0.833 . . .
	0.875
$\frac{9}{10}$	

ACTIVITY 2

DECIMALS AND MIXED NUMBERS
Use with **Lesson 1-7.**

Materials: Watch with second hand, ruler
Group Size: Small groups

1. Perform Activities A through C. Each group member should have another group member record the amount of time in minutes and seconds he or she needs to complete each task.
2. Write each time as a mixed number, and then change each mixed number to a decimal. Round decimals to the nearest hundredth of a minute.

   For example, 2 min 49 sec = $2\frac{49}{60}$ min. To change this mixed number to a decimal, recall from Lesson 1-6 that you can divide to find that the decimal for $\frac{49}{60}$ is about 0.82. When this decimal is added to 2, the sum is 2.82. Another method is to use a scientific calculator and key in 2 [+] 49 [÷] 60 [=].

Activity	Your Time		Your Time	
	Min	Sec	Mixed Number	Decimal
A. Count 120 of your heart beats.				
B. Multiply 589 by 23,489, without using a calculator.				
C. Find the distance around the edge of this worksheet.				

3. Graph your decimal times for Activities A through C on the number line. Label the points *A*, *B*, and *C*.

   0

4. For each activity, compare your time with times of another person in your group. Write a word sentence and a math sentence to describe the comparison. For example: "Joe took longer than I did to complete Activity C. 2.55 > 2.32."

ACTIVITY 3

COMPARING NUMBERS
Use with **Lesson 1-9.**

Materials: Activity Aid B—Square Decimal Models
Group Size: Partners

It is not always easy to compare numbers that are written as fractions. This activity shows you one method you can use.

1. Use the squares on Activity Aid B. One of you should shade $\frac{3}{4}$ of Square A and $\frac{4}{5}$ of Square B. The other should shade $\frac{3}{4}$ of Square C and $\frac{4}{5}$ of Square D. Together examine Squares A and B. Can you tell by looking which square has more shading?
2. Together examine Squares C and D. Explain how you can tell which square has more shading.
3. Based on Item 2, which sentence is true?

   (a) $\frac{3}{4} > \frac{4}{5}$ (b) $\frac{3}{4} < \frac{4}{5}$ (c) $\frac{3}{4} = \frac{4}{5}$
4. Which of the shaded squares show the *decimals* equal to $\frac{3}{4}$ and $\frac{4}{5}$? Explain why.
5. Give the decimals equal to $\frac{3}{4}$ and $\frac{4}{5}$. Write a sentence comparing the decimals. How does this sentence compare to the one in Item 4?
6. The dark lines divide Square E into tenths and Square F into twentieths. One of you should shade Square E to show $\frac{9}{10}$ and the other should shade Square F to show $\frac{17}{20}$. Write a sentence comparing these two fractions. Use >, <, or =.
7. Write the decimals equal to $\frac{9}{10}$ and $\frac{17}{20}$ and a sentence comparing the decimals. How does this sentence compare to the one in Item 6?
8. **Draw a Conclusion** With your partner decide how you can compare fractions without drawing a diagram.

Teaching Aids

TEACHING AID 1

Warm-up — Lesson 1-1

Write a number that satisfies the conditions. Then write the number in words.

1. A five-digit number that has two zeros
2. A six-digit number that has no zeros
3. An eight-digit number that has six zeros

Warm-up — Lesson 1-2

Work in groups. List situations in which you use decimals that are not whole numbers. Discuss some of the situations, emphasizing why a decimal is used.

Warm-up — Lesson 1-3

Use each number correctly in a sentence.

1. 18
2. 366
3. 3000
4. 100,000

Warm-up — Lesson 1-4

Locate each decimal on the same number line and give the nearest whole number.

1. 0.6
2. 1.1
3. 1.7
4. 2.3
5. 2.9
6. 3.2
7. 3.4
8. 3.8

TEACHING AID 2

Warm-up — Lesson 1-5

Work in pairs and add, subtract, multiply, and divide on a calculator. Keep a record of your problems and answers. Then write down things you notice about how the calculator works.

Warm-up — Lesson 1-6

Divide. Then check your answers. Do not use a calculator. Show your work.

1. 378 ÷ 9
2. 2438/23
3. 12)247.2
4. $\frac{1}{2}$
5. 39.9 ÷ 4.2

Warm-up — Lesson 1-7

Sketch rectangles or circles and shade them so that the shaded region represents the number. Then write a decimal for each fraction.

1. $\frac{3}{4}$
2. $\frac{2}{3}$
3. $\frac{5}{8}$

Warm-up — Lesson 1-8

Tell which number is larger.

1. .0078 or .011
2. $.4\overline{2}$ or $.\overline{3}$
3. 1.05 or 1.053
4. $\frac{2}{3}$ or $\frac{7}{8}$
5. $2\frac{3}{8}$ or $2\frac{3}{16}$
6. $\frac{18}{5}$ or $\frac{37}{10}$

For each problem, tell which number would be located to the left of the other on a number line (or below the other on a vertical number line).

TEACHING AID 3

Warm-up — Lesson 1-9

Find the number.

1. What number am I?
   Clue 1: I am greater than -4.
   Clue 2: I am less than -2.
   Clue 3: I am an integer.
2. What number am I?
   Clue 1: I am between 100 and 999.
   Clue 2: I am divisible by 8.
   Clue 3: The sum of my digits is 15.
   Clue 4: The product of my ones and tens digits is between 1 anc 10.
   Clue 5: No two of my digits are the same.

Warm-up — Lesson 1-10

Compare these sets of numbers using > or < signs.

1. 51.6 and 51
2. 0 and -8
3. 0 and .00329
4. -12 and -16
5. $5\frac{7}{8}$, 5, and $5\frac{4}{5}$
6. $-\frac{7}{15}$, $-\frac{14}{15}$, and $\frac{4}{15}$
7. $-\frac{5}{9}$, $-\frac{5}{6}$, and $-\frac{5}{12}$

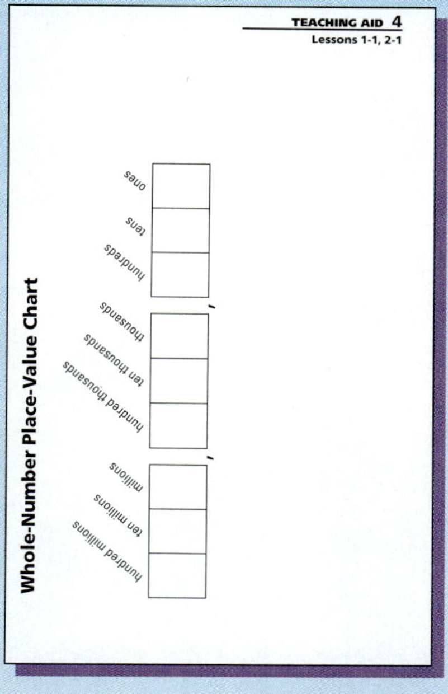

TEACHING AID 4
Lessons 1-1, 2-1

Whole-Number Place-Value Chart

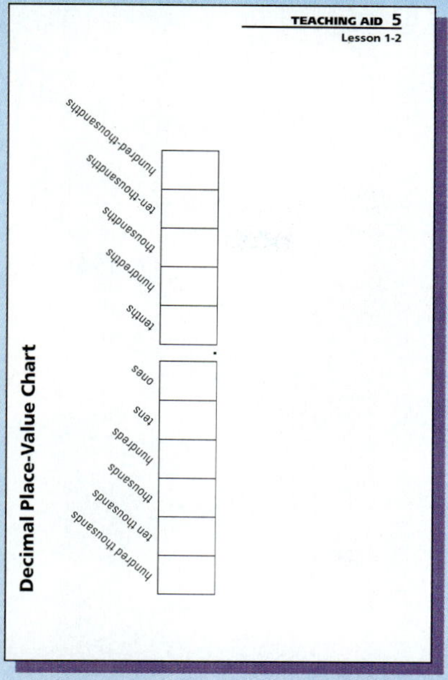

TEACHING AID 5
Lesson 1-2

Decimal Place-Value Chart

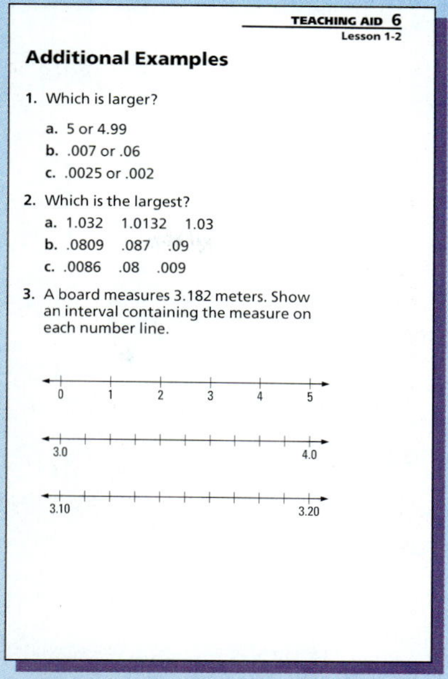

TEACHING AID 6
Lesson 1-2

Additional Examples

1. Which is larger?
   a. 5 or 4.99
   b. .007 or .06
   c. .0025 or .002
2. Which is the largest?
   a. 1.032 1.0132 1.03
   b. .0809 .087 .09
   c. .0086 .08 .009
3. A board measures 3.182 meters. Show an interval containing the measure on each number line.

TEACHING AID 7
Lessons 1-2, 1-3

Number Lines

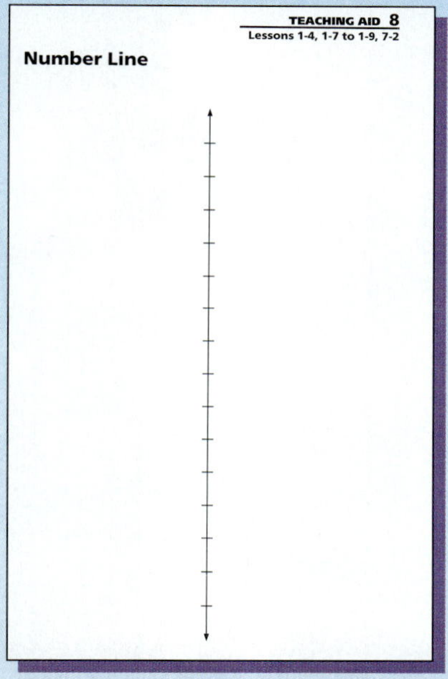

TEACHING AID 8
Lessons 1-4, 1-7 to 1-9, 7-2

Number Line

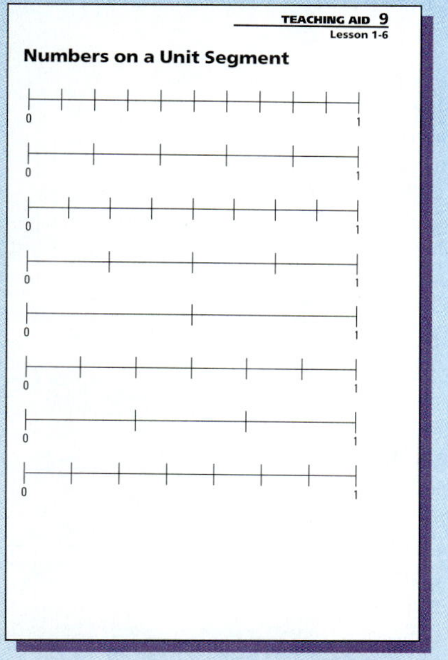

TEACHING AID 9
Lesson 1-6

Numbers on a Unit Segment

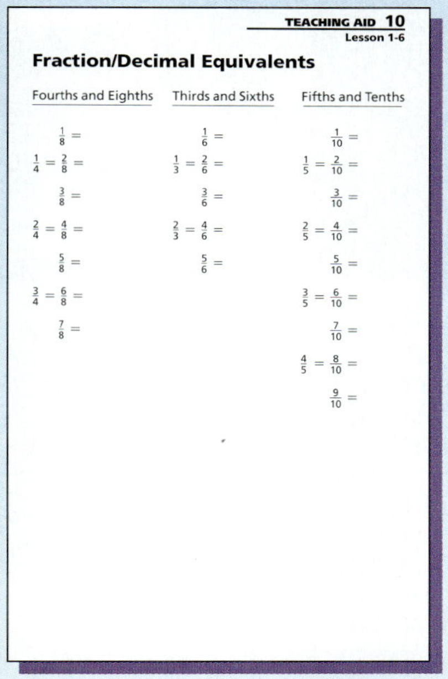

TEACHING AID 10
Lesson 1-6

Fraction/Decimal Equivalents

Fourths and Eighths

$\frac{1}{8} =$
$\frac{1}{4} = \frac{2}{8} =$
$\frac{3}{8} =$
$\frac{2}{4} = \frac{4}{8} =$
$\frac{5}{8} =$
$\frac{3}{4} = \frac{6}{8} =$
$\frac{7}{8} =$

Thirds and Sixths

$\frac{1}{6} =$
$\frac{1}{3} = \frac{2}{6} =$
$\frac{3}{6} =$
$\frac{2}{3} = \frac{4}{6} =$
$\frac{5}{6} =$

Fifths and Tenths

$\frac{1}{10} =$
$\frac{1}{5} = \frac{2}{10} =$
$\frac{3}{10} =$
$\frac{2}{5} = \frac{4}{10} =$
$\frac{5}{10} =$
$\frac{3}{5} = \frac{6}{10} =$
$\frac{7}{10} =$
$\frac{4}{5} = \frac{8}{10} =$
$\frac{9}{10} =$

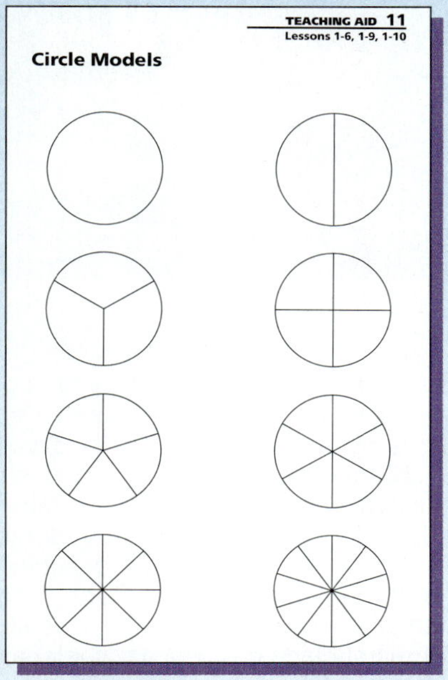

TEACHING AID 11
Lessons 1-6, 1-9, 1-10

Circle Models

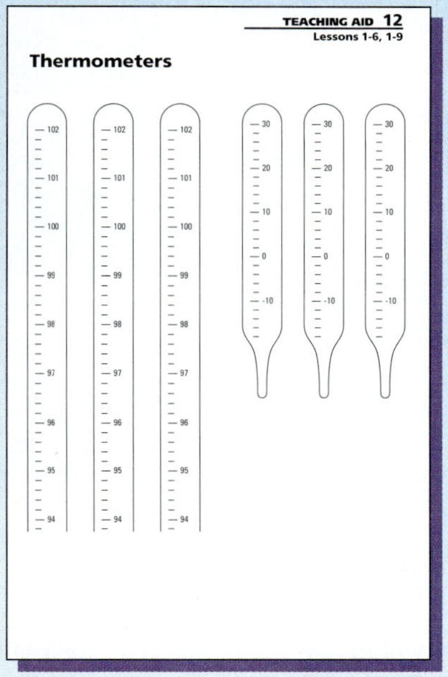

TEACHING AID 12
Lessons 1-6, 1-9

Thermometers

Chapter Opener 1

Pacing
We recommend 13 to 16 days for this chapter after an opening day introduction to the book. Some classes will be able to cover Lessons 1-3 and 1-4 in a single day, or Lessons 1-2 to 1-4 in two days. If you spend more than 16 class days on this chapter, you will be going too slowly to complete the book in a year. Remember that there is continual review to provide long-term mastery. The length of time it takes to cover this material will also depend on how many minutes and how often your class meets.

Using Pages 4–5
A history of the symbols we use for whole numbers is shown on page 5. Most people are surprised to learn that the symbols 0–9 developed relatively recently—about the time of Christopher Columbus.

Actually our symbols were developed even more recently than the table on page 5 suggests. In the 1500s and 1600s many people calculated with Roman numerals and the notation to the right of the decimal point was not developed until the late 1500s. The superiority of decimals over fractions and Roman numerals was recognized quickly by mathematicians. But their superiority was not generally recognized until the 1700s. The metric system was introduced in the late 1700s. Not until the 1800s did the present concept of "real number" develop.

You might point out that the ancient Greek symbol for 6 shown on page 5 is no longer used in the Greek alphabet.

CHAPTER 1

Chapter 1 Overview
Chapter 1 may strike you as a rather unusual first chapter for a book at this level. There is no paper-and-pencil computation with decimals, fractions, or whole numbers. There is an all-important reason for delaying computation—it makes very little sense for students to compute if they do not know what the numbers they are using represent.

Whereas this chapter deals with writing and ordering decimals, Chapter 2 deals with the relationships between decimals and the number 10. Do not worry if students do not have everything down pat by the time they complete this chapter because there is an entire second chapter in which these ideas get applied immediately.

Calculators are needed throughout this book, and it is assumed students have calculators for all tests. The first place calculators are required is in Lesson 1-5, giving you about a week to assemble a classroom set or for each student to obtain one. If a student buys a calculator, make certain that it is a scientific calculator. It is easier to explain how to use the calculator when all students have the same model, but many teachers think that students learn more if they see calculators that operate differently. Have students bring the instructions for their calculators to class.

DECIMAL NOTATION

Virtually every culture, from ancient times until now, has had spoken names for the numbers from one to nine. Many cultures have represented these numbers with written symbols. Most of these symbols are quite different from the ones we use today in the United States. The chart below gives some examples.

Culture	1	2	3	4	5	6	7	8	9
Greek	α	β	γ	δ	ϵ	ς	ζ	η	θ
Roman	I	II	III	IV	V	VI	VII	VIII	IX
Chinese (ancient)	—	=	≡	≣	X	∧	+	)(	ʃ
Chinese (modern)	一	二	三	四	五	六	七	八	九

❶

Among the earliest cultures to use the number 0 were the Mayas of Central America, and the peoples of India. The chart below shows how the ten **digits** we use, 0, 1, 2, 3, 4, 5, 6, 7, 8, and 9, have developed over the years.

The Development of Hindu-Arabic Numerals

By the year 900 A.D., some Hindus were using a *decimal system* to denote numbers. The Arabs wrote about this system. Europeans did not learn about it until 1202 A.D., when Leonardo of Pisa, an Italian mathematician also known as Fibonacci, translated an Arabic manuscript into Latin. This system is now used by mathematicians throughout the world, and we call the numerals **Arabic** or **Hindu-Arabic numerals.**

Photo Connections

The photo collage makes real-world connections to the content of the chapter: the early development of numbers and contemporary applications of numbers.

Mayan ruin in Palenque, Mexico: The Mayas were advanced in architecture as well as mathematics.

Jackie Joyner-Kersee: Decimals are commonly used to report the results of sporting events.

Numbers/Decimals: Contemporary applications of numbers and decimal notation includes uses in computers, engineering, construction, measurement, and business.

Waves: Early sea voyages and trading influenced the development of numbers and facilitated intellectual exchange.

Peaches: One early need for numbers was to account for produce and other traded goods.

Chapter 1 Projects

At the end of each chapter, you will find projects related to the chapter. At this time you might want to have students look over the projects on pages 55–56 and tentatively select one to work on. Then as students read and work further into the chapter, they can finalize their project choices.

Some students may elect to work independently on a project, while others might want to work in groups. At times a student might work alone and then collaborate with others for a class presentation and discussion. Allow for diversity—many, if not most, students have never done a mathematics project. Encourage students to use their imaginations when presenting their projects. As students work on projects throughout the year, they will see the many uses of mathematics in the real world.

For more information on projects, see *General Teaching Suggestions: Projects* in the *Professional Sourcebook* which begins on page T20 in Volume 1 of the Teacher's Edition.

Project Update Throughout each chapter of the Teacher's Edition, there are project updates which provide suggestions or reminders for you to give to your students about their projects.

We assume that students have whole-number computation well in hand before beginning this book. Computation with decimals, percents, fractions, integers, scientific notation, and powers is integrated throughout the book.

At all times, it is important to focus on reading for comprehension. Because many students are not accustomed to reading a mathematics text, we have provided specific suggestions in each lesson in Chapter 1 (and occasionally thereafter) for helping students adjust to this expectation. The first suggestions for students are found in the *To the Student* section that precedes this chapter. Although students are often uncomfortable reading and may find it difficult at first, they almost always improve after the first few chapters and become quite good readers of mathematics by the end of the year.

Lesson 1-1

Objectives

A Translate back and forth from English into the decimal system.

N Give people and rough dates for key ideas in the development of arithmetic.

Resources

From the ***Teacher's Resource File***

- Lesson Master 1-1A or 1-1B
- Answer Master 1-1
- Teaching Aids
  1 Warm-up
  4 Place-Value Chart

Additional Resources

- Visuals for Teaching Aids 1, 4

Teaching Lesson 1-1

Warm-up

You can use the *Warm-up,* or the *Additional Examples* on page 8, as questions for students to work on as you begin class.

As students arrive for class write the following questions on the board or use **Teaching Aid 1.**

Diagnostic Write a number that satisfies the conditions. Then write the number in words. **Sample answers are given.**

1. A five-digit number that has two zeros **59,800; fifty-nine thousand, eight hundred**
2. A six-digit number that has no zeros **142,561; one hundred forty-two thousand, five hundred sixty-one**

LESSON

1-1

Decimals for Whole Numbers

A taste of big numbers. *The Taste of Chicago draws big crowds who sample foods from Chicago's numerous ethnic restaurants. The 1993 attendance over ten days was 2,500,000, about the same as the population of Brooklyn, New York.*

What Is the Decimal System?

The **decimal system** is a system of writing numbers based on the number ten. A number written in the decimal system is said to be in **decimal notation.** In decimal notation, the smallest ten **whole numbers** need only one digit. Today we write them as 0, 1, 2, 3, 4, 5, 6, 7, 8, and 9. But look again at the chart on page 5. Notice that some of the symbols we use today did not appear until the 1400s.

Two digits are needed to write the next ninety whole numbers as decimals.

10 11 12 . . . 19 20 21 . . . 99

Notice that we call the whole numbers *decimals* even though there are no decimal points.

The next nine hundred whole numbers can be written with three digits.

100 101 102 . . . 200 201 . . . 999

By using more digits, very large numbers can be written. The 1990 census estimate of the U.S. population was 248709873 people. To make this easier to read, groups of digits are separated by commas.

In Decimal Notation:	In English:
2 4 8, 7 0 9, 8 7 3	Two hundred forty-eight million, seven hundred nine thousand, eight hundred seventy-three

Usually decimal notation is shorter than English words.

Lesson 1-1 Overview

Broad Goals There are two equally important goals in this lesson: reviewing how decimals serve to represent whole numbers and initiating the student in reading mathematics.

Perspective The discussion of decimals includes some history as well as place value. Some students are surprised that the word *decimal* is used with whole numbers, but decimal refers to a base-ten number system. You may wish to point out that *deci* is a Latin prefix meaning "ten." Stress the names of places up to hundred million. The names beyond hundred million are introduced in Lesson 2-1.

❶ Each digit in a decimal has a **place value.** Here are the place values for the nine digits of the number that represents the U.S. population in 1990.

2 4 8, 7 0 9, 8 7 3

2 — hundred millions; 4 — ten millions; 8 — millions; 7 — hundred thousands; 0 — ten thousands; 9 — thousands; 8 — hundreds; 7 — tens; 3 — ones

Counts and Counting Units

The U.S. population is an example of a **count.** The most basic use of numbers is as counts. For every count there is a **counting unit.** Counts are always whole numbers, never fractions between whole numbers. Here are some examples.

Phrase	Count	Counting Unit
0 eight-legged insects	0	eight-legged insects
28 letters in "antidisestablishmentarianism"	28	letters
U.S. population of 248,709,873	248,709,873	people

Why are dishes called China? *Porcelain dishes are often called china because porcelain was first made in China. The card shows the price of the dishes.*

QUESTIONS

Covering the Reading

Use these questions to check your understanding of the reading. If you cannot answer a question, you should go back to the reading for help in obtaining an answer.

1. What is the modern Chinese symbol for the number eight? 八
2. What letter did the Romans use to stand for the number of fingers on one normal hand? V
3. What people invented the decimal system? When was it invented? Hindus; 900 A.D.
4. Name two early cultures that used the number zero. the Mayas of Central America and the peoples of India
5. Name the smallest whole number. 0
6. a. Who was Fibonacci? an Italian mathematician also known as Leonardo of Pisa
   b. What did he do that relates to the decimal system?
   c. When did he do it? 1202 A.D.
   b) translated manuscripts containing the decimal system from Arabic into Latin
7. About when did all the symbols for the numbers zero through nine appear as we know them? the 1400s
8. Written in the decimal system, how many whole numbers have three digits? 900
9. Name the digit in the indicated place of the number 568,249.
   a. thousands 8 b. ones 9 c. hundreds 2 d. tens 4

3. An eight-digit number that has six zeros 34,000,000; thirty-four million

Notes on Reading

Reading Mathematics A very important aspect of this lesson is making a positive start on developing reading skills in mathematics. To help students get used to reading mathematics, you might have them take turns reading aloud.

❶ **Teaching Aid 4** is a whole-number place-value chart that can be used to illustrate this whole number and others through hundred millions.

Error Alert Some students may confuse the thousands period with the place value for thousands, or the millions period with the place value for millions. You might have these students play the game in *Extra Help* in *Adapting to Individual Needs* on page 8, or just have students read numbers from the chart in the game.

When the reading is finished, ask students to list the main ideas of the lesson. The list should include digits, decimal system, whole numbers, place-value names, count, and counting unit.

For more information on reading, see *General Teaching Suggestions: Reading* in the *Professional Sourcebook* which begins on page T20 in Volume 1 of the Teacher's Edition.

Optional Activities

Multicultural Connection After discussing the lesson, you might ask if any students know how to write and pronounce numbers in another language. For example, this is how to write and pronounce the numbers from one to ten in Japanese: ee-chee, nee, sahn, shee, go, ro-koo, shee-chee, hah-chee, koo, joo.

LESSON MASTER 1-1 A — **Questions on SPUR Objectives** See pages 59-61 for objectives.

Skills Objective A

1. Name the digit in each place of the number 602,543,210.
   a. thousands 3 b. millions 2
   c. hundred thousands 5 d. ones 0

In 2-6, write each as a decimal.

2. one thousand four hundred seven 1,407
3. eight billion, seven hundred million, two hundred forty-three thousand 8,700,243,000
4. three more than seven million 7,000,003
5. two hundred thirty thousand 230,000
6. three thousand fifty 3,050

In 7-9, write a word name for each.

7. 90,105,000 ninety million, one hundred five thousand
8. 180,000,035 one hundred eighty million, thirty-five
9. 7054 seven thousand, fifty-four

Culture Objective N

10. *Multiple choice.* About when was the decimal system first developed? b
    (a) 600-900 B.C. (b) 600-900 A.D.
    (c) 12th century (d) 15th century

Additional Examples

You might want to use these examples when discussing the lesson.

1. Give the count and the counting unit for each phrase.
   a. 28 students in class
   28; students
   b. 50-minute class
   50; minutes
   c. 3 classes per day
   3; classes
2. Name three things involving numbers that are not counts. **Sample answers: half a pizza, a .308 batting average, 10.3 gallons of gas, 35 miles per hour**

Notes on Questions

Question 14 Students often have an interesting variety of answers. Ask several students to give their responses during class discussion.

Question 18 Writing This question can provoke a nice discussion. First ask several students to read word for word what they wrote on their papers. Then ask them to explain all of what they were thinking. Use the discussion to show them that answers vary and that you care about what they write. Encourage students to write complete sentences.

Question 22 Error Alert If students write 1,111,111, remind them that 0 is a digit. If they write 0,000,000, by convention, we do not count leading zeros when counting the digits of a number.

LESSON MASTER 1-1 B Questions on SPUR Objectives

Skills Objective A: Translate back and forth from English into the decimal system.

In 1-2, name the digit in each place of the given number.

1. 315,976
   a. tens **7** b. thousands **5**
   c. hundred thousands **3** d. ones **6**
2. 8,677,008
   a. hundred thousands **6** b. millions **8**
   c. hundreds **0** d. tens **0**
3. 924,805,407
   a. ten thousands **0** b. millions **4**
   c. hundred millions **9** d. hundreds **4**

In 4-11, write each as a decimal.

4. seven thousand twenty-nine **7,029**
5. six hundred twelve thousand, nine hundred eighty-four **612,984**
6. eleven million sixty **11,000,060**
7. five more than three thousand **3,005**
8. twenty-two million, five hundred thirty-eight thousand, nine hundred seventy **22,538,970**
9. one less than ten million **9,999,999**
10. six hundred four million, seventeen thousand, nine hundred four **604,017,904**
11. twenty-five more than ten thousand **10,025**

10. A number is written as a decimal. Must there be a decimal point? Support your answer with an example. **No. 248,709,873**

11. Name one advantage of writing numbers as decimals rather than using English words. **A number written as a decimal is often shorter.**

12. A count is always what kind of number? **whole number**

13. Name something for which the count is between one million and one billion. **the population of the U.S.**

Applying the Mathematics

These questions extend the content of the lesson. You should study the examples and explanations if you cannot get an answer. For some questions, you can check your answers with the ones in the back of the book.

14. Describe a situation with a count that is larger than the 1990 U.S. population. **Samples: the number of grains of sand on a beach; the number of stars in the sky; the population of the earth**

15. Consider the number of stars on a U.S. flag.
   a. Name the count. **50** **b.** Name the counting unit. **stars**

16. One of the books of the Old Testament is called Numbers because it begins with a census of the adult males of the tribes of Israel. The ancients did not have our numerals. So they wrote out the population in words. ". . . of the tribe of Reuben, were forty and six thousand and five hundred." Write this number as a decimal. **46,500**

17. Federal aid is often given on the basis of population: the greater the population, the greater the aid. Use these 1990 Census data.

Corpus Christi, Texas	349,894
Pensacola, Florida	344,406
Portsmouth-Dover-Rochester, New Hampshire	350,078
Salinas-Seaside-Monterey, California	355,660

   a. Which of these four metropolitan areas would get the most aid?
   17a) Salinas-Seaside-Monterey, California
   b. Which of these four metropolitan areas would get the least aid? **Pensacola, Florida**

18. Tell why the counts in Question 17 are estimates, even on the day they were made. **Sample: The Census Bureau may have missed people in their count.**

A glimpse of Portsmouth. *Portsmouth, New Hampshire, is a community which prides itself on its historical homes, its art and cultural centers, and an international harbor.*

Adapting to Individual Needs

Extra Help Moving-Digits Game

Materials: sets of 9 cards, each card with 0 on one side and one of the digits 1–9 on the other side

Divide students into equal teams and distribute two identical sets of nine cards to each team. To begin a round, select a number with the same number of digits as the number of people on each team. Write this number in words on the board. The first team to arrange itself holding the cards in the order that represent the number is the winner of the round. Then write the number in a chart like the one shown below and ask a student to read the number aloud. Repeat the activity several times. (For larger numbers, or with unequal groups, some students in a group might have to hold more than one card.)

☐☐☐,☐☐☐,☐☐☐
millions thousands hundreds

In 19–21, write as a decimal.

19. 6 hundred million
600,000,000

20. ten thousand
10,000

21. five hundred six
506

22. In decimal notation, what is the smallest seven-digit whole number?
1,000,000

23. In decimal notation, write the number that is one less than ten thousand. 9,999

Review

Every lesson contains review questions to give you practice on ideas you have studied earlier.

24. Danielle saved $17 in May, $16 in June, and $18 in July. Elena saved three times as much as Danielle.

a. How much did Danielle save? $51
b. How much did Elena save? $153
c. How much did they save altogether? *(Previous course)* $204

25. a. How many years are in a decade? 10
b. How many years are in a century? *(Previous course)* 100

Exploration

These questions ask you to explore mathematics topics related to the chapter. Sometimes you will need to use dictionaries or other sources of information.

26. In Europe, the decimal numeral for seven is sometimes written as shown in the cartoon. Why do you think this is done?

Sample: so that the numeral for a 7 looks different from the numeral for a 1

Follow-up for Lesson 1-1

Practice

For more questions on SPUR objectives, use **Lesson Master 1-1A** (shown on page 7) or **Lesson Master 1-1B** (shown on pages 8–9).

Assessment

Oral Communication Write numbers in decimal notation on the board and call on students to say them aloud. Then, reverse the procedure. [Written and oral presentations of numbers will show an ability to state large numbers correctly, especially avoiding the use of the word *and* when stating whole numbers.]

Extension

Have students investigate how Roman numerals are written and then write these numbers using Roman numerals.

1. 344 [CCCXLIV]
2. 1994 [MCMXCIV]
3. 2505 [MMDV]
4. 1666 [MDCLXVI]
5. 3897 [MMMDCCCXCVII]

Project Update If you have not had students look over the projects on pages 55–56, you might want to do so now. Project 5, *Other Numeration Systems,* relates to the content of this lesson.

▶ **LESSON MASTER 1-1 B** *page 2*

In 12-18, write a word name for each.

12. 819 eight hundred nineteen
13. 12,862 twelve thousand, eight hundred sixty-two
14. 400,050 four hundred thousand, fifty
15. 3,002 three thousand two
16. 24,006,080 twenty-four million, six thousand eighty
17. 5,600,000 five million, six hundred thousand
18. 225,730,048 two hundred twenty-five million, seven hundred thirty thousand, forty-eight

Culture Objective N: Give people and rough dates for key ideas in the development of arithmetic.

19. *Multiple choice* When were all of today's symbols 0, 1, 2, 3, 4, 5, 6, 7, 8, and 9 first used? c
(a) 300 B.C. (b) Early 800s
(c) 1400s (d) 900-1200 A.D.

Review Ordering whole numbers (Previous course)

In 20-23, write the numbers in order from least to greatest.

20. 914 992 909 — 909 914 992
21. 12,677 12,767 10,977 — 10,977 12,677 12,767
22. 68,904 68,094 68,944 — 68,094 68,904 68,944
23. 124,762,098 124,767,098 124,761,098 — 124,761,098 124,762,098 124,767,098

In 24-26, write three whole numbers that are between the two given. Sample answers are given.

24. 80 and 90 — 82, 84, 86
25. 6,144 and 6,173 — 6,150; 6,160; 6,170
26. 120,940 and 120,950 — 120,941; 120,945; 120,949

Adapting to Individual Needs

English Language Development
Some students may wonder why the word *digit* is used to refer to both fingers and toes as well as the symbols 0–9. Explain that originally people counted numbers smaller than 10 on their fingers, and the word *digit* comes from the Latin word *digitus* meaning "finger."

Setting Up Lesson 1-2

Homework Have students read and answer all the questions in Lesson 1-2. Or they might answer only the questions on *Covering the Reading* and then answer the remainder of the questions in class or as part of their homework assignment for the next day. For more information on homework, see *General Teaching Suggestions: Homework* in the *Professional Sourcebook* which begins on page T20 in Volume 1 of the Teacher's Edition.

Lesson 1-2

Objectives

- **A** Translate back and forth from English into the decimal system.
- **B** Order decimals.
- **C** Give a number that is between two decimals.
- **M** Graph and read numbers on a number line.
- **N** Give people and rough dates for key ideas in the development of arithmetic.

Resources

From the ***Teacher's Resource File***

- Lesson Master 1-2A or 1-2B
- Answer Master 1-2
- Teaching Aids
  - 1 Warm-up
  - 5 Place-Value Chart
  - 6 Additional Example 3
  - 7 Number Lines (Questions 16–17)

Additional Resources

- Visuals for Teaching Aids 1, 5–7
- Spreadsheet Workshop

Teaching Lesson 1-2

Warm-up

You can use this *Warm-up,* or the *Additional Examples* on page 13, as questions for students to work on as you begin class.

Work in groups. List situations in which you use decimals that are not whole numbers. Discuss some of the situations, emphasizing why a decimal is used. **Samples: 8.7 gallons of gasoline; expressing 50 cm as .5 m; writing 456¢ as $4.56.**

LESSON

1-2 *Decimals for Numbers Between Whole Numbers*

What's next for Flo Jo? *Olympic track gold medalist Florence Griffith-Joyner holds the women's world record for the 200-meter sprint with a time of 21.34 seconds. In the summer of 1993, this popular athlete was named to co-chair the President's Council for Physical Fitness.*

Measuring is as common and important a use of numbers as counting. A **unit of measure** can always be split into smaller parts. This makes measures different from counts. For instance, you can split up measures of time.

❶ Intervals and Tick Marks

The women's world record for the 200-meter run is between 21 and 22 seconds. This time **interval** is pictured on the **number line** below. The marks on the number line are called **tick marks.** The interval on this number line is one second, the distance between two neighboring tick marks.

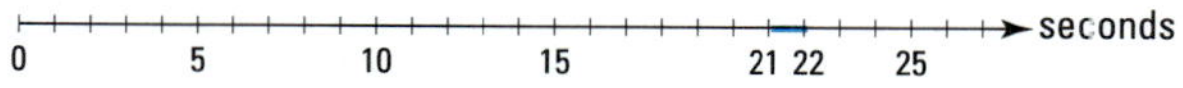

Notice the difference between intervals and tick marks. To divide a segment into three intervals requires two tick marks in the middle and two others at the ends.

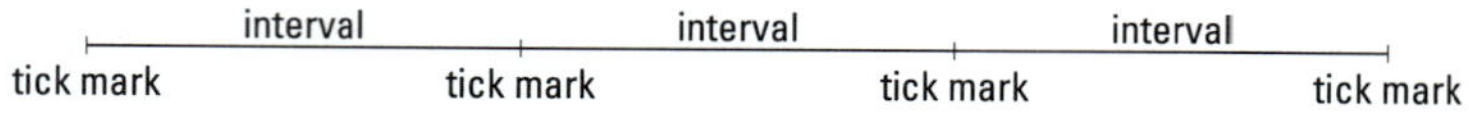

Measuring requires counting intervals, but some applications require counting tick marks.

Lesson 1-2 Overview

Broad Goals Students should see the creation of decimals as a natural outgrowth of attempting to measure something more and more accurately. Being able to order decimals is critical to the understanding of the meaning of decimals.

Perspective Since many students have learned to measure length by counting spaces, they think that measuring is just a special kind of counting. Actually, the reverse is true—counting is a special kind of measuring. The key difference is in the units. A measuring unit can be split whereas a counting unit cannot. Even money, which is a measure, can be split into units smaller than cents.

It is very important that students learn to order decimals. They will get more practice in the next two lessons, which are devoted to rounding.

To get more accuracy in the interval between 21 and 22 seconds, blow up the number line between 21 and 22. Then split that interval into ten equal parts. Nine new tick marks are needed. The interval on the new number line is **one tenth** of a second. The dot shown stands for the world record. Its location indicates that the time is between 21.3 and 21.4 seconds.

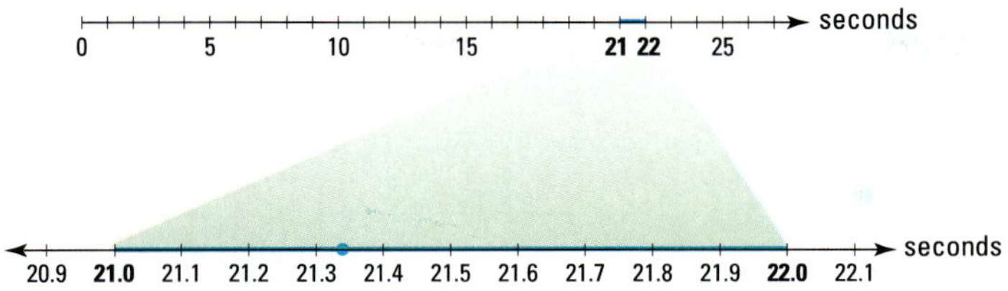

❷ Florence Griffith-Joyner set this world record in 1988. Her time of 21.34 seconds is what is being graphed. To graph 21.34, blow up the line again. Split the interval between 21.3 and 21.4 into ten parts. The interval on the new number line is one tenth of one tenth, or one **one-hundredth** of a second. In 21.34, the digit 3 is in the **tenths place.** The digit 4 is in the **hundredths place.**

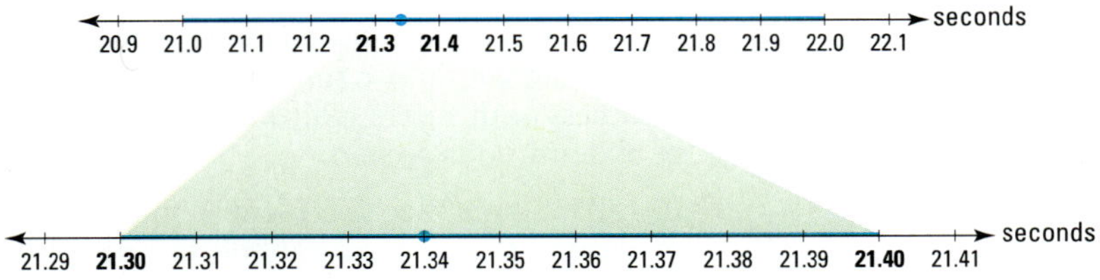

On the above number lines, we rewrote 21 seconds as 21.0 seconds, and 21.3 seconds as 21.30 seconds. A zero at the right of a decimal on the right side of the decimal point does not affect the value of the decimal. The same is true for money, for money is on the decimal system. $5 and $5.00 have the same value.

Who participates in the Special Olympics? *Everyone who is at least eight years old, has completed a medical application form showing cognitive delay or has at least 50% special education classes, and has trained with a coach for eight weeks is encouraged to participate.*

Notes on Reading

Reading Mathematics You might want to continue having students read aloud in class, especially if some students did not get a turn to do so with Lesson 1-1.

❶ Emphasize the difference between interval and tick mark. An interval is the set of numbers graphed between two tick marks, and sometimes including the tick marks. Students need to recognize that making n intervals requires $n + 1$ tick marks. For example, dividing an unmarked segment into 10 intervals requires 11 tick marks. Similarly, point out that dividing an interval into 10 sub-intervals requires 9 additional tick marks between the 2 tick marks at the ends for a total of 11 tick marks.

❷ Use Florence Griffith-Joyner's track record to discuss the idea that no measurement is exact. There is always the possibility that the measurement could be made more accurate by including more places to the right of the decimal point. The issue of what degree of accuracy is reasonable leads to the concept of estimating by rounding up or down, which is discussed in Lesson 1-3.

Video

Wide World of Mathematics The segment, *In 0.01 Second,* shows how advanced photographic techniques are used to examine events that happen in span of 0.01 second. The segment may be used to introduce or extend the topics of decimal place value and ordering decimals. Related questions and an investigation are provided in videodisc stills and in the Video Guide. A related CD-ROM activity is also available.

Videodisc Bar Codes

Search Chapter 4

Play

❸ Be sure students notice the similarities between the names of places to the right and left of the decimal point. You might want to use the decimal place-value chart in **Teaching Aid 5** to help students see the symmetry in place value.

❹ **Multicultural Connection** One of Simon Stevin's arguments for his new "decimal fractions" (digits to the right of the ones digit) was that many of the addition, subtraction, multiplication, and division algorithms used with whole numbers could be used with these numbers as well. It has been reported that decimal fractions first appeared in an Arab manuscript entitled *The Book of Chapters on Indian Arithmetic,* written in 952 or 953 by Abul Hassan al-Uqlidisi, and that it is possible that Stevin learned of decimal fractions from a Turkish translation of later Arab manuscripts.

It is interesting that Stevin did not use a decimal point; he put the symbols ①, ②, ③,..., above his new digits to indicate places to the right of the unit's place. For example, for 327.64 he wrote:

```
         ①  ②
3  2  7  6  4
```

The decimal point was first used in 1657 by William Oughtred, an English mathematician. The decimal point is still not commonly used in Europe. A comma is used after the units place and a space is used to separate periods in a number. For example, many Europeans write 328 417, 38 for 328,417.38.

❺ In this lesson, a distinct writing font is introduced in the Examples. The contrasting fonts are designed to show students what they are expected to write on their papers when they answer similar questions.

❸ Names for Decimal Places

Some situations require more places to the right of the decimal point. For instance, the famous number pi, written π, is the circumference of (distance around) a circle whose diameter is one unit. As a decimal, π never ends.

π = 3.14159265358979323846264338327950288419716939937510 . . .

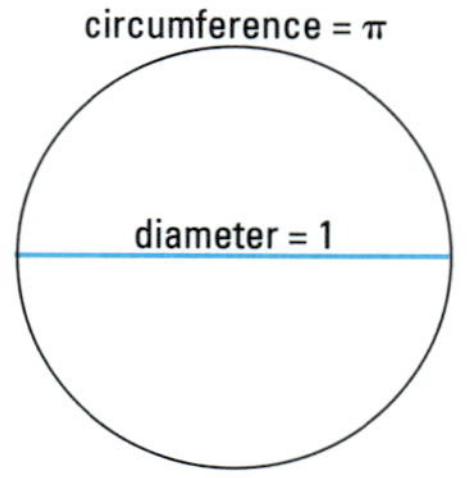

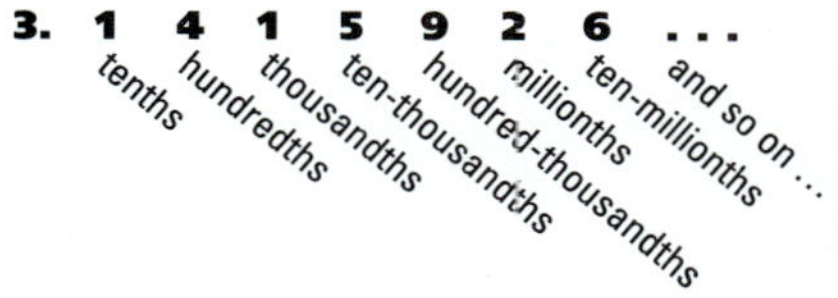

The names of the places to the right of the decimal point are similar to the names of the places to the left. Think of the ones place and the decimal point as the center. Then there is perfect balance of names to the right and to the left.

Today's uses often require many decimal places. Some grinding tools are accurate to within two millionths of an inch. (That's much less than the thickness of this page.) Supercomputers work at speeds often measured in billionths of a second.

❹ In 1585, Simon Stevin, a Flemish mathematician, first extended the use of decimal places to the right of the ones place. Before then, fractions were used. Decimals are now more common than fractions for measurements. An advantage of decimals is that they are easier to put in order and compare.

❺ Comparing Decimals

Most lessons in this book have examples. **What you might write in the solutions will look like this.** Whenever you can, try to answer the question in the example before reading the solution.

Example 1

Which is larger, 3.01 or 2.999?

Solution

Align the decimal points. "Align" means to put one above the other.

```
3.01
2.999
```

Start at the left of each number. 3 is larger than 2, so 3.01 is larger.

Optional Activities

Activity 1 After discussing the names for decimal places, you might have students complete this chart or make up a similar one to be completed by a classmate.

Number in words	Hundreds	Tens	Ones	.	Tenths	Hundredths	Thousandths
[Three tenths]			0	.	3		
Four and five hundred four thousandths			[4	.	5	0	4]
[Ten and fifty-one thousandths]		1	0	.	0	5	1
Three hundred fifty and eight hundredths	[3	5	0	.	0	8]	
Two hundred and two thousandths	[2	0	0	.	0	0	2]
[Fifty-five and fifty-five hundredths]		5	5	.	5	5	

Activity 2 Technology Connection You may wish to have students use Magic Squares Puzzle on the *Spreadsheet Workshop* to review addition and subtraction of decimals. The program displays a randomly-generated 3 × 3 or 4 × 4 puzzle with some open cells. Students enter numbers and try to create equal sums in the rows and columns. Students should select a difficulty level of 7 to work with decimals.

As you know, with whole numbers, the decimal with more digits always stands for a larger number. This is not true, however, for numbers which are not whole numbers.

Example 2

Which is the largest?

0.0073 0.007294 0.00078

Solution 1

Again, align the decimal points.

0.0073
0.007294
0.00078

The bottom number is smallest because it has 0 thousandths while the others have 7 thousandths. To find out which of the first two is larger, compare the ten-thousandths place. The 3 is larger than the 2, so *0.0073 is largest.*

Solution 2

Align the decimal points. Write all the numbers to show the same number of decimal places.

0.007300
0.007294
0.000780

Now it is easy to tell that *0.0073 is largest.*

⑥ In Example 2, a zero appears to the left of the decimal point of each number. This zero can make it easier to order numbers. It also draws attention to the decimal point and corresponds to the display on most calculators. Also notice that two different solutions are given to answer the question of Example 2. When there is more than one way of getting the answer to a question, you should try to learn all the ways. Then you can use the way that is easiest for you.

QUESTIONS

Covering the Reading

In 1–3, consider the number 21.34.

1. Between what two consecutive whole numbers is this number? 21 and 22
2. What digit is in the tenths place? 3
3. What digit is in the hundredths place? 4

⑥ In some books, the style is to place a 0 before every decimal between 0 and 1. For example, five tenths would be written as 0.5. However, decimals are not always represented in this way in the real world. Often, decimals are written without zeros; for instance, a team that wins 3 of 4 games is listed as having a winning percentage of .750, not 0.750. To help develop flexibility, this text uses both forms.

Additional Examples

1. Which is larger?
   a. 5 or 4.99 **5**
   b. .007 or .06 **.06**
   c. .0025 or .002 **.0025**
2. Which is the largest?
   a. 1.032 1.0132 1.03 **1.032**
   b. .0809 .087 .09 **.09**
   c. .0086 .08 .009 **.08**
3. A board measures 3.182 meters. Show an interval containing the measure on each number line.

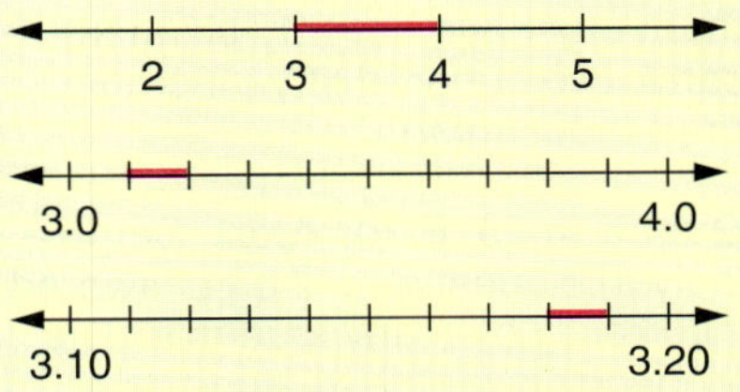

Notes on Questions

Emphasize that you expect students to attempt to answer all questions and to write down their attempts on their papers.

Adapting to Individual Needs

Extra Help

For students who are having difficulties comparing decimals, have them ask themselves the following questions: Did I

- align the decimal points?
- add zeros as place holders?
- compare the digits in each place moving from left to right until I found digits that were not equal?

LESSON MASTER 1-2 A Questions on SPUR Objectives
See pages 59-61 for objectives.

Skills Objective A

1. Write three and nine hundred one thousandths as a decimal. 3.901
2. Write thirty-three ten-thousandths as a decimal. .0033
3. Write 0.039 in words. thirty-nine thousandths
4. Write 2.46 in words. two and forty-six hundredths

Skills Objective B

5. Order from smallest to largest: 0.0689 0.069 0.068 — 0.068 0.0689 0.069
6. Which is largest: π, 3.142857, or 3.1415926? 3.142857

Skills Objective C

7. Write a number that is between 3.04 and 3.039. sample: 3.0395
8. Write a number that is between 2.53 and 2.54. sample: 2.531

Representations Objective M

In 9 and 10, use this number line.

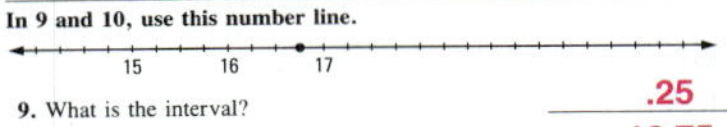

9. What is the interval? .25
10. What number is graphed? 16.75

In 11 and 12, use this line and a ruler.

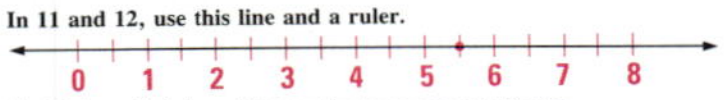

11. Mark and label an eight-centimeter segment indicating each half centimeter with a tick mark.
12. Graph a point at 5.5 centimeters.

Notes on Questions

Questions 16–17 One of the number lines on **Teaching Aid 7** is similar to the one shown here. You might want to have students graph the points as well as give the letters.

✎ **Question 18 Writing** Ask volunteers to read aloud exactly what is written on their papers. Be supportive of all attempts since many students may be unaccustomed to writing in mathematics. Remind them to write complete sentences when answering questions such as this one.

Questions 20–22 Do not give translation questions that are more complicated than those given here. While it is important that students know the decimal place for each digit, a long decimal such as 8.76259 is usually read "eight point seven six two five nine." This style is clearer and easier to understand than "eight and seventy-six thousand, two hundred fifty-nine hundred-thousandths."

Question 25 Error Alert Surprisingly this question will be answered incorrectly by many students. The tendency is for these students to think records are always larger numbers and therefore they add instead of subtract. If students answer the question incorrectly, ask them to reread the problem and consider the reasonableness of their answers.

In 4–7, consider the number 654,987.123456789. What digit is in each place?

4. thousands 4 **5.** tenths 1

6. thousandths 3 **7.** hundred-thousandths 5

8. What digit is in the millionths place of π? 2

9. Name a kind of measurement that can require accuracy to billionths. a supercomputer's speed

10. Who invented the idea of extending decimal places to the right of the decimal point, and when? Simon Stevin, in 1585

11. Name one advantage of decimals over fractions. Decimals are more easily compared.

In 12–14, put the numbers in order from smallest to largest.

12. 0.033 0.015 0.024 0.015, 0.024, 0.033

13. 6.783 .6783 67.83 .6783, 6.783, 67.83

14. 4.398 4.4 4.4001 4.398, 4.4, 4.4001

15. a. How many tick marks are needed to divide a number line into five intervals? 6

b. Draw a number line to represent any time from zero to five minutes. See left.

15b) 

In 16 and 17, use the number line drawn here. The tick marks are equally spaced.

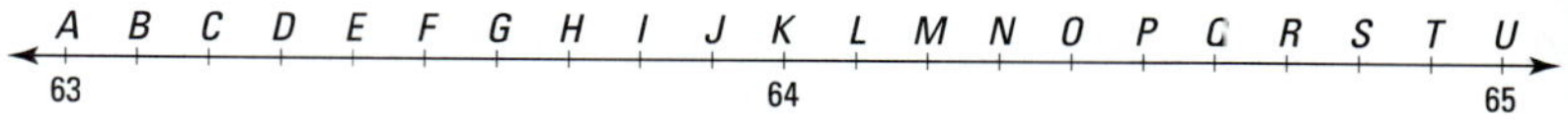

16. What is the length of each interval on this number line? .1

17. Which letter (if any) corresponds to the given number?
a. 63.4 *E* **b.** 64.8 *S* **c.** 64.80 *S* **d.** 64.08 none; between *K* and *L*

18. Explain the difference between a count and a measure. A count is always a whole number. A measure can be split into smaller parts.

19. a. What is the name of the number that is the circumference of a circle with diameter 1? π (pi)

b. Give the first five decimal places of this number. ("Decimal places" refers to places to the right of the decimal point.) 14159

Applying the Mathematics

Here are examples showing decimals translated into English.

3.5	three and five tenths
3.54	three and fifty-four hundredths
3.549	three and five hundred forty-nine thousandths

In 20–22, use the above examples to help translate the given number into English.

20. 5.9 **21.** 324.66 **22.** 0.024

20) five and nine tenths; 22) twenty-four thousandths
21) three hundred twenty-four and sixty-six hundredths

LESSON MASTER 1-2 B Questions on SPUR Objectives

Skills Objective A: Translate back and forth from English into the decimal system.

In 1-5, write as a decimal.

1. thirty-eight hundredths 0.38
2. fifty-six and nine tenths 56.9
3. two hundred one thousandths 0.201
4. ninety-five and four hundredths 95.04
5. four thousand seven and six hundred thirteen ten-thousandths 4007.0613

In 6-10, write in words.

6. 0.08 eight hundredths
7. 5.9 five and nine tenths
8. 3.003 three and three thousandths
9. 524.70 five hundred twenty-four and seventy hundredths
10. 16.202 sixteen and two hundred two thousandths

Skills Objective B: Order decimals and fractions.

In 11-15, write the numbers in order from smallest to largest.

11. 0.076 0.053 0.62 — 0.053 0.076 0.62
12. 0.24 0.212 0.2 — 0.2 0.212 0.24
13. 4.975 41.9 .4975 — .4975 4.975 41.9
14. π 3.56 3.1 — 3.1 π 3.56
15. 18.09 18.084 18.009 — 18.009 18.084 18.09

Adapting to Individual Needs

English Language Development
You might want to draw a place-value chart on the board or use **Teaching Aid 5**. Write numbers in the chart. Then read each number to help students see, hear, pronounce, and understand the difference between the following words: *ten, tens, and tenths*; *hundred, hundreds, and hundredths*; and *million, millions, and millionths.*

Challenge
Give students the following statement: *There are an infinite number of numbers between any two numbers.* Then have them **work in groups** to discuss the statement, decide whether it is true or false, and write a paragraph supporting their answer. Tell them they can use an example to illustrate their thinking. [Explanations will vary. Examples may show increasingly smaller intervals.]

23. To find a number between 8.2 and 8.3, write them as 8.20 and 8.30. Then any decimal beginning with 8.21, 8.22, and so on up to 8.29 is between them. Use this idea to find a number between 44.6 and 44.7. **Sample: 44.61**

24. A store sells 5 pairs of white tube socks for $16. Mel wants 1 pair and divides 16 by 5, using a calculator. The calculator shows 3.2. What should Mel pay? **$3.20**

25. In 1988, Florence Griffith-Joyner set a women's world record of 10.49 seconds in the 100-meter dash.
   a. Copy the number line below. Graph this number on your number line.

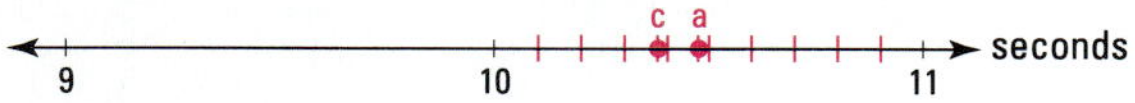

   b. If this record were lowered by a tenth of a second, what would the new record be? **10.39 seconds**
   c. Graph your answer to part **b** on your number line.

Trains will keep you on track. *This photo shows commuters at Shinjuku station in Tokyo, Japan.*

In 26 and 27, order the numbers from smallest to largest.

26. three thousandths
four thousandths
three millionths
3 millionths, 3 thousandths, 4 thousandths

27. sixty-five thousandths — **65 thousandths**
sixty-five thousand — **65**
sixty-five — **65 thousand**

28. Draw a number line six inches long. Indicate each inch with a tick mark. **Check students' drawings.**

29. A commuter train leaves Central Station every half hour from 6:30 A.M. to 9:00 A.M. How many morning trains could a commuter take? (Hint: Use a number line to represent this situation.) **6**

Review

In 30 and 31, write as a decimal. *(Lesson 1-1)*

30. four hundred million **400,000,000**

31. thirty-one thousand sixty-eight **31,068**

32. Written as a decimal, the number one million is a 1 followed by how many zeros? *(Lesson 1-1)* **6 zeros**

33. In "76 trombones," name the count and the counting unit. *(Lesson 1-1)* **count: 76; counting unit: trombones**

34. The metric system uses prefixes which are related to place values in the decimal system. What is the meaning of the three most common prefixes: kilo-, centi-, milli-? *(Previous course)* ***Kilo* means 1000, *centi* means one-hundredth, *milli* means one-thousandth.**

Exploration

35. Use an encyclopedia or a book on the history of mathematics to find out some additional information about the number π. Write a short report on what you find. **Answers will vary.**

Question 35 This is the first of many exploration questions asking students to look in other sources for information which clearly demonstrates that mathematics is not confined to math textbooks and math class.

Follow-up for Lesson 1-2

Practice

For more questions on SPUR objectives, use **Lesson Master 1-2A** (shown on page 13) or **Lesson Master 1-2B** (shown on pages 14–15).

Assessment

Group Assessment Divide the class into an even number of groups. Each group is to write five questions covering the lesson. Then have groups exchange papers, answer all the questions, and return the papers for checking. [Each student will participate in developing and answering the questions. Questions and answers should reflect an understanding of the content of the lesson.]

Extension

Project Update Students who select Project 1, on page 55, *Numbers in the Newspaper,* might start the project now by cutting out articles and advertisements that contain numbers.

Setting Up Lesson 1-3

Homework Have students read and answer all the questions for Lesson 1-3. If you are planning to cover Lessons 1-3 and 1-4 in a single day, then you might have students do all the reading and assign Questions 9–32 from Lesson 1-3 and Questions 1–9 from Lesson 1-4.

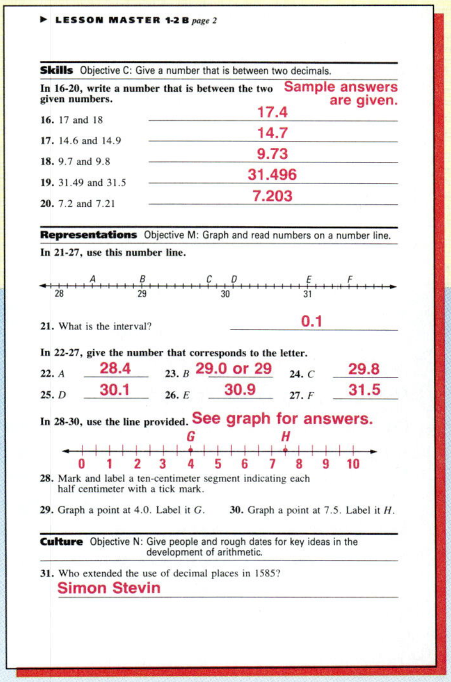

▸ **LESSON MASTER 1-2 B** *page 2*

Skills Objective C: Give a number that is between two decimals.

In 16-20, write a number that is between the two given numbers. Sample answers are given.

16. 17 and 18 — 17.4
17. 14.6 and 14.9 — 14.7
18. 9.7 and 9.8 — 9.73
19. 31.49 and 31.5 — 31.496
20. 7.2 and 7.21 — 7.203

Representations Objective M: Graph and read numbers on a number line.

In 21-27, use this number line.

A B C D E F
28 29 30 31

21. What is the interval? — 0.1

In 22-27, give the number that corresponds to the letter.

22. *A* 28.4 23. *B* 29.0 or 29 24. *C* 29.8
25. *D* 30.1 26. *E* 30.9 27. *F* 31.5

In 28-30, use the line provided. See graph for answers.

G H
0 1 2 3 4 5 6 7 8 9 10

28. Mark and label a ten-centimeter segment indicating each half centimeter with a tick mark.

29. Graph a point at 4.0. Label it *G*. 30. Graph a point at 7.5. Label it *H*.

Culture Objective N: Give people and rough dates for key ideas in the development of arithmetic.

31. Who extended the use of decimal places in 1585? Simon Stevin

Lesson 1-3

Objectives

D Round any decimal up or down.
K Deal with estimates in real situations.

Resources

From the ***Teacher's Resource File***
- Lesson Master 1-3A or 1-3B
- Answer Master 1-3
- Teaching Aids
  1 Warm-up
  7 Number Lines (Questions 26–27)

Additional Resources
- Visuals for Teaching Aids 1, 7

Teaching Lesson 1-3

Warm-up

You can use this *Warm-up,* or the *Additional Examples* on page 17, as questions for students to work on as you begin class.

Use each number correctly in a sentence. **Sample answers are given.**

1. 18 **There were 18 people invited to dinner.**
2. 366 **There are 366 days in a leap year.**
3. 3000 **It is about 3000 miles from the east coast of the U.S. to the west coast.**
4. 100,000 **About 100,000 newspapers were printed.**

LESSON

1-3 *Estimating by Rounding Up or Rounding Down*

How costly? *On August 24, 1992, Hurricane Andrew ripped through South Florida with winds of over 160 miles per hour. This photo of Florida City, Florida, shows some of the devastation caused by the hurricane. The damage was estimated to be $15 billion, and about 50,000 people were left homeless.*

Why Are Estimates Needed?

In many types of situations, an **estimate** may be preferred over an exact value.

1. *An exact value may not be worth the trouble* it would take to get it. Example: About 30,000 people attended the baseball game.
2. *An estimate is often easier to work with* than the exact value. Example: Instead of multiplying $169.95, let's use $170.
3. *It may be safer to use an estimate* than to try to use an exact value. Example: The home repairs will cost at least $18,000 as a result of the hurricane. So we will budget $20,000 to play it safe.
4. *An exact value may change* from time to time, forcing an estimate. Example: I estimate that the coin will land heads 5 times in 10 tosses.
5. Predictions of the future or notions about the past usually are estimates, since *exact values may be impossible to obtain.* Example: One estimate of the world population in the year 2025 is 12 billion.

What Kinds of Rounding Are There?

The most common method of estimating is **rounding.** There are three kinds of rounding: **rounding up, rounding down,** and rounding to the nearest. Some examples of rounding up and rounding down are on the next page. (Rounding to the nearest is discussed in Lesson 1-4.)

Lesson 1-3 Overview

Broad Goals Lesson 1-3, Estimating by Rounding Up or Rounding Down, and Lesson 1-4, Estimating by Rounding to the Nearest, are companion lessons. For students to understand rounding to the nearest, it is necessary to know what it means to round up and to round down. Since rounding to the nearest is not always preferred, the ideas in this lesson also need to be learned.

Perspective Students often learn to estimate by being asked to estimate the answer to a problem such as 39 × 51. However, because students know how to get the exact value in such problems, they think there is little reason to estimate. As a result, many students do not consider estimation as important as exact computation. The first paragraph of this lesson points out five types of situations in which estimates are preferred over exact values.

The most difficult idea for many students in rounding is semantic. Because we speak of doing something to a number, they want to do something even with numbers that are already rounded. And so, if asked to round 1200 down to the nearest hundred, they will say 1100 instead of keeping it at 1200. Emphasize that estimation is done to save time and energy, so students should be careful not to negate its effects by changing a number that doesn't need to be changed!

Rounding is almost always done with a particular decimal place in mind.

Example 1

A certain type of label is sold in packages of 100. If you need 1325 labels, how many labels must you buy? Give reasons for your answer.

Solution

You must buy more labels than you need. So you need to round up to the next 100. Since 1325 is between 1300 and 1400, you must buy 1400 labels.

The rounding of Example 1 can be pictured on a number line. Let the length of the intervals be 100. Rounding up 1325 to the next 100 means going to the higher endpoint of the interval. Rounding down would mean going to the lower endpoint, 1300.

Example 2

A store sells six bottles of fruit juice for \$4.69. You want one bottle. So you divide 4.69 by 6 to get the cost. Your calculator shows 0.7816667. What will you probably pay for the bottle?

Solution

The store will probably round up to the next penny. Pennies are hundredths of dollars, so look at the hundredths place in 0.7816667. The hundredths place is 8. That means that 0.7816667 is between 0.78 and 0.79. You will probably have to pay \$0.79, which is 79¢.

Some calculators round *down,* or **truncate,** all long positive decimals to the preceding millionth (the sixth decimal place).

Example 3

What will a calculator that truncates show for $\pi = 3.1415926535\ldots$?

Solution

The sixth decimal place is 2. The calculator will show 3.141592.

Notes on Reading

Reading Mathematics This is a good lesson for students to read on their own because the discussion is based on real situations and is not too technical. Also, most students have probably had some experience with rounding. You might ask students to make a list of the main ideas from the lesson. They should identify the following key points: reasons for estimating; rounding up; rounding down; and truncating.

Additional Examples

1. Eggs are packed in crates of 144 eggs. How many crates can be completely filled with 1500 eggs?
   10 crates
2. A store has bread on sale—three loaves for a dollar. What will you probably pay for one loaf of bread?
   \$0.34 or **34¢**
3. The product of 0.1349 and 0.00024 is 0.000032376. What will a calculator with an 8-digit display and that rounds show for the answer?
   0.0000324
4. Most banks will round down any fractions of a cent on interest paid on a savings account. How much interest would be paid if the calculated amount is \$75.625?
   \$75.62
5. A small airplane can carry 10,500 pounds of cargo. To be safe, what might the pilot show on the weight limit sign?
   Sample answer: 10,000 pounds

LESSON MASTER 1-3 A

Questions on SPUR Objectives
See pages 59-61 for objectives.

Skills Objective D

1. Round 7547.9 up to the next thousand. **8,000**
2. Round 182.16788932 down to the preceding millionth. **182.167889**
3. Round 71.345668 up to the next ten-thousandth. **71.3457**
4. Round 167,899,351.78 down to the preceding hundred. **167,899,300**
5. Round 88,088.888 down to the preceding thousand. **88,000**
6. Round 479.31 up to the next tenth. **479.4**
7. What will a calculator display for 0.454545454 . . . if it truncates and shows only 7 places? **0.4545454**
8. What will a calculator display for 3.11111177 . . . if it truncates at the millionths place? **3.111111**

Uses Objective K

9. A gourmet deli sells three packages of sandwich rolls for \$2.00. You want only one, so you divide 2.00 by 3 and get 0.66666667 on your calculator. How much will you pay for one? **\$0.67**
10. An office building elevator has been tested to hold 3,670 pounds. The inspector posting the safety warning in the elevator needs to round this figure to the nearest hundred pounds. Should she round up to the next or down to the preceding hundred? **down to preceding hundred**
11. Why are predictions of the future or notions about the past usually estimates?
    sample: Since the prediction is about the future, an exact answer is not known.
12. Give an example where you might be forced to use an estimate because the exact value changes from time to time.
    sample: a price on a share of stock; the number of people at a concert

Notes on Questions

This is a good lesson in which to cover the questions in class, ensuring that students understand how the answer to each question is found. Be sure students answer the *Review* questions and emphasize again how important it is for them to try to answer all the questions.

Question 10 Writing Ask for volunteers to read their answers aloud. If necessary, remind students to use complete sentences when writing their explanations.

LESSON MASTER 1-3 B **Questions on SPUR Objectives**

Skills Objective D: Round any decimal place up or down or to the nearest value of a decimal place.

1. Round 587 up to the next hundred. **600**
2. Round 23,209 down to the preceding thousand. **23,000**
3. Round 66.38 down to the preceding tenth. **66.3**
4. Round 0.4229 up to the next hundredth. **0.43**
5. Round 876.067304 up to the next thousandth. **876.068**
6. Round 19.009822 up to the next thousandth. **19.010**
7. Round 2.9116559 down to the preceding millionth. **2.911655**
8. Round 44,208.666666 down to the preceding ten-thousandth. **44,208.6666**
9. Round 114.6009 down to the preceding ten. **110**
10. Round 47.459 up to the next one. **48**
11. Round 56.97 up to the next tenth. **57.0**
12. Round 876.231 down to the preceding hundred. **800**

In 13 and 14, suppose a calculator truncates after 6 decimal places. What would the display show for each number?

13. 0.337337337337337 . . . **0.337337**
14. 9.4502697306520411 . . . **9.450269**

In 15 and 16, suppose a calculator truncates to the hundred-millionths place. What would the display show for each number?

15. 0.6848684868486848 . . . **0.68486848**
16. 2.1211211121111211112 . . . **2.12112111**

What is guacamole? *Peel and mash an avocado. Add a chopped tomato, a clove of garlic, one teaspoon of lemon juice, and a half-teaspoon of salt. The result is guacamole, a tasty dip for chips.*

QUESTIONS

Covering the Reading

1. Give an example of a situation where an estimate would be preferred over an exact value. Sample: You are deciding how much money to take on a trip.
2. Name five reasons why estimates are often preferred over exact values. See below.
3. The most common way of estimating is by __?__. rounding
4. Name three types of rounding. rounding up, rounding down, rounding to the nearest
5. Some drawing pencils are sold in packages of 10. A teacher needs one pencil for each student in a class of 32. How many pencils must be bought? 40
6. A store sells avocados at three for $1. You want one. So you divide $1.00 by 3 to get the cost. Your calculator shows 0.333333. How much will you probably have to pay for the avocado? 34¢, or $0.34
7. Refer to Example 2. If the store rounded down, what would you pay? 78¢
8. A store sells a dozen eggs for $1.09. You want a half dozen. To find out how much you will pay, you divide $1.09 by 2. You get 0.545. How much will you have to pay? 55¢, or $0.55
9. If a calculator rounds down to the preceding millionth, what will it show for 0.0123456? 0.012345

Applying the Mathematics

10. Explain what happens when a decimal is truncated. See below.
11. Suppose a calculator rounds down to the preceding hundred-millionth (the eighth decimal place). What will it show for 0.97531246809? 0.97531246
12. **a.** Round $1795 up to the next ten dollars. $1800
    b. Round $1795 down to the preceding ten dollars. $1790
    c. Graph $1795 and your answers to parts **a** and **b** on the same number line.

2) An exact value may not be worth the trouble. An estimate is often easier to work with. It may be safer to use an estimate. The exact value may change from time to time. Exact values may be impossible to obtain.

10) When a decimal is truncated to the preceding place, all decimal places after that place are dropped.

Optional Activities

Activity 1 Consumer Investigation As an ongoing activity, have students be alert as they visit various establishments (grocery stores, gas stations, and so on) and read advertisements for examples of misuse of the symbol for "cents." For example, .43¢ literally means less than a penny, but is often substituted for $.43. Compile a class file that includes both advertisements and a list of locations where this error occurs, and if possible, pictures of the misleading signs.

Activity 2 Reading Connection As an ongoing activity, have students read headlines and advertisements looking for examples in which numbers have been rounded to support a point of view. Students might rewrite the headlines and ads to convey opposite points of view. For example, if 4668 people attended a game, the headline MORE THAN 4000 ATTEND GAME! seems more positive than FEWER THAN 5000 ATTEND GAME.

13. a. Round 5280, the number of feet in one mile, up to the next 1000.
b. Round 5280 down to the preceding 1000.
c. Graph 5280 and your answers to parts **a** and **b** on the same number line. a) 6000; b) 5000; c) See below.

14. There are exactly 30.48 centimeters in one foot.
a. Round 30.48 up to the next tenth. 30.5
b. Round 30.48 down to the preceding tenth. 30.4

15. There are exactly 1.609344 kilometers in one mile.
a. Round 1.609344 up to the next thousandth. 1.610
b. Round 1.609344 down to the preceding thousandth. 1.609

Whose money is in the machine? *Banks place money in cash machines. When you withdraw money from a machine, your bank account is charged for the amount you take out.*

16. Suppose you have $97 in your bank account and you would like to withdraw as much as you can from a cash machine. Tell how much cash you can get from the machine if the only bill the machine dispenses is for the indicated amount.
a. $5 $95 b. $10 $90 c. $20 $80

In 17–20, tell whether a high or a low estimate would be preferred. Then explain why.

17. You are estimating how large a birthday cake to order for a party. High. You want everyone to have some cake.
18. You are estimating how much money you should take on a trip. High. You don't want to have too little money.
19. You are estimating how much weight an elevator can carry without being overloaded. Low. You don't want the cable to break.
20. You are estimating how many minutes it will take to do your math homework. High. You want to have enough time to do a good job.

Review

In 21 and 22, order the numbers from smallest to largest. *(Lesson 1-2)*

21. 5.1 5.01 5.001 5.001, 5.01, 5.1
22. .29 0.3 .07 .07, .29, 0.3
23. *Multiple choice.* Which number does not equal 0.86? *(Lesson 1-2)*
(a) 0.860 (b) .86 (c) .086 (c)

In 24 and 25, find a number that is between the two given numbers. *(Lesson 1-2)*

24. 5.8 and 5.9 Sample: 5.85
25. 5.9 and 6 Sample: 5.99

In 26 and 27, use this number line. *(Lesson 1-2)*

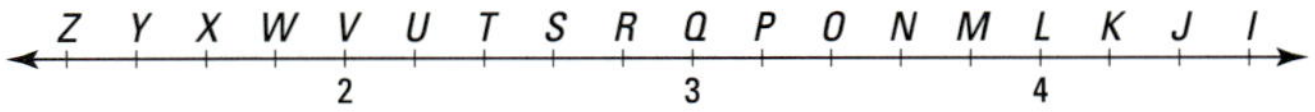

26. What is the interval on the number line? .2
27. Which letter on the number line corresponds to the given number?
a. 3.0 Q b. 2.8 R c. 1.4 Y

13c)
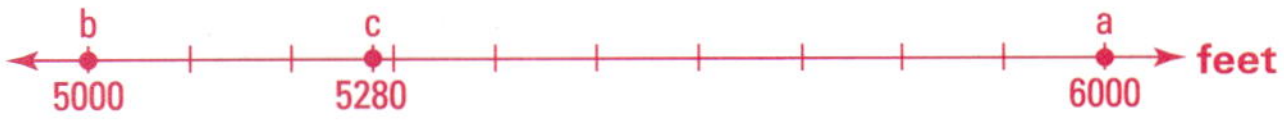

Question 15a Error Alert Some students might write 1.61. Explain that this answer does not indicate rounding to thousandths. The next thousandth after 1.609 is 1.610.

Questions 26–27 One of the number lines on **Teaching Aid 7** is similar to the one shown here. Be sure students are aware that this number line is not marked in unit intervals.

Adapting to Individual Needs

English Language Development
To help students picture a meaning of the word *truncate,* you might **use physical models** of truncated cones and pyramids. Demonstrate with models of the original cones and pyramids showing how each had a part cut off or *truncated.* Explain to students that when they truncate a decimal, they cut off part of it.

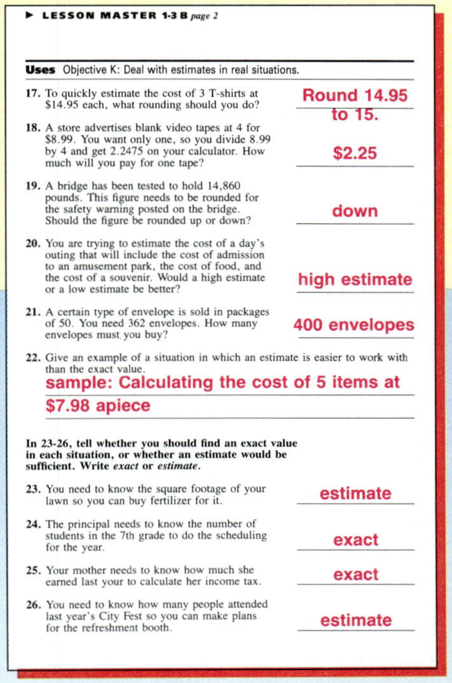
► LESSON MASTER 1-3 B *page 2*

Uses Objective K: Deal with estimates in real situations.

17. To quickly estimate the cost of 3 T-shirts at $14.95 each, what rounding should you do? Round 14.95 to 15.
18. A store advertises blank video tapes at 4 for $8.99. You want only one, so you divide 8.99 by 4 and get 2.2475 on your calculator. How much will you pay for one tape? $2.25
19. A bridge has been tested to hold 14,860 pounds. This figure needs to be rounded for the safety warning posted on the bridge. Should the figure be rounded up or down? down
20. You are trying to estimate the cost of a day's outing that will include the cost of admission to an amusement park, the cost of food, and the cost of a souvenir. Would a high estimate or a low estimate be better? high estimate
21. A certain type of envelope is sold in packages of 50. You need 362 envelopes. How many envelopes must you buy? 400 envelopes
22. Give an example of a situation in which an estimate is easier to work with than the exact value. sample: Calculating the cost of 5 items at $7.98 apiece

In 23-26, tell whether you should find an exact value in each situation, or whether an estimate would be sufficient. Write *exact* or *estimate*.

23. You need to know the square footage of your lawn so you can buy fertilizer for it. estimate
24. The principal needs to know the number of students in the 7th grade to do the scheduling for the year. exact
25. Your mother needs to know how much she earned last year to calculate her income tax. exact
26. You need to know how many people attended last year's City Fest so you can make plans for the refreshment booth. estimate

Notes on Questions

✎ **Question 30 Writing** Students should realize that dictionaries give more than one definition for many words, and that their definitions may differ because of the dictionaries used. Demonstrate this by having students read their answers aloud. Also ask them how the definition relates to rounding.

Question 32 This is the first time students encounter BASIC, the computer language used in this book. If students have access to a computer at home or at school, instruct them to put their computer in programming mode in order to access BASIC.

Follow-up for Lesson 1-3

Practice

For more questions on SPUR objectives, use **Lesson Master 1-3A** (shown on page 17) or **Lesson Master 1-3B** (shown on pages 18–19).

Assessment

Written Communication Have students write a sentence with an estimate and explain why they used an estimate instead of an exact value. [Sentences contain proper examples, citing one or more of the five reasons listed on page 16.]

Extension

Project Update Projects 2 and 4, *Comparing Estimates* and *The Advantages of Rounding,* on pages 55–56, relate to the content of this lesson. Students who have chosen Project 2 might decide on the subject of their survey and the age group they will interview. For Project 4, students might make a time schedule for collecting their data.

About the same? *The photo shows that the yardstick and meterstick are about the same length. A meter is a little more than three inches longer than a yard.*

28. For this question, you need a ruler that measures in centimeters. The metric system measures length in meters, centimeters, and millimeters.

- **a.** Draw a segment 10 cm long. Indicate each centimeter with a tick mark. **Check student drawings.**
- **b.** One millimeter equals one-tenth of a centimeter. Then how many millimeters equal one centimeter? **10**
- **c.** On your segment, mark off a point that is 38 millimeters from one end. *(Previous course, Lesson 1-2)* **Check student drawings.**

29. Write this number as a decimal: four million, thirty thousand. *(Lesson 1-1)* **4,030,000**

Exploration

30. What is the dictionary definition of the word *truncate?* How does this relate to the way truncate is used in this lesson? **See below.**

31. Look through a newspaper.

- **a.** Find a number which underestimates the value it is reporting.
- **b.** Find a number which overestimates the value it is reporting.

Write down enough about the examples to be able to report your findings to the class. **Answers will vary.**

32. On this and other computer questions in this book, it is possible that your computer will not act like other computers. If you get a strange message or no response, ask your teacher for help.

- **a.** Put your computer in programming mode, and type ?INT(4.57). The ? is short for PRINT. You could also type PRINT INT(4.57). Now press the RETURN key. What does the computer screen show? **4**
- **b.** Try part **a** with the following:

?INT(115.68)	**115**
?INT(789)	**789**
?INT(3000.12345)	**3000**
?INT(.995)	**0**

Based on what the computer shows, what does INT() do to the number inside the parentheses? **truncates all places to the right of the decimal point**

30) Sample: "to cut off a part of; cut short." *The World Book Dictionary* (1992). When a decimal is truncated, some of the decimal places are cut off.

Adapting to Individual Needs

Extra Help

You might help students round up and round down by having them show intervals in colors on a number line. Have them label a number line in tens from 190 to 310 and color only the interval from 200 to 300. Explain that when *rounding to hundreds,* for *any number* that is larger than 200 but smaller than 300, the next hundred is 300 and the preceding hundred is 200. So any number between 200 and 300 would *round up* to 300 or *round down* to 200. Ask students to round 287 to the next hundred [300] and then round it to the preceding hundred [200]. In another color, have students shade the interval from 280 to 290, and repeat the activity for rounding to the next 10 and to the preceding 10. Finally repeat the activity with a decimal, rounding it to the next whole number and to the preceding whole number.

Setting Up Lesson 1-4

Homework Because there is so little reading except for the examples, you might want to have students read Lesson 1-4 and answer all the questions on their own.

LESSON

1-4

Estimating by Rounding to the Nearest

What is a laser? Laser *is an acronym for Light Amplification by Stimulated Emission of Radiation. Because a laser beam can be focused more precisely than ordinary light, lasers are used in medical surgery, military range finders, bar code scanners, and compact disc players. Laser beams travel at the speed of light.*

If 38 is rounded *up* to the next ten, the result is 40. If 38 is rounded *down* to the preceding ten, the result is 30. Look at this number line.

The number 38 is nearer to 40 than to 30. So 40 is a better estimate of 38 than 30 is. When 38 is rounded to 40, we say that 38 has been **rounded to the nearest** 10.

Example 1

The speed of light is nearly 186,282.4 miles per second. Round this number to the nearest

a. whole number. **b.** ten. **c.** hundred.
d. thousand. **e.** ten thousand.

Solutions

a. 186,282.4 is between 186,282 and 186,283. Because .4 is less than .5, the number 186,282.4 is nearer to 186,282.

b. 186,282.4 is between 186,280 and 186,290. Because 82.4 is closer to 80 than to 90, round 186,282.4 down to 186,280.

c. 186,282.4 is between 186,200 and 186,300 and is closer to 186,300. So round up to 186,300.

d. The answer is 186,000.

e. The answer is 190,000.

Lesson 1-4

Objectives

D Round any decimal to the nearest value of a decimal place.
K Deal with estimates in real situations.

Resources

From the ***Teacher's Resource File***

- Lesson Master 1-4A or 1-4B
- Answer Master 1-4
- Assessment Sourcebook: Quiz for Lessons 1-1 through 1-4
- Teaching Aids
  1 Warm-up
  8 Number Line

Additional Resources

- Visuals for Teaching Aids 1, 8

Teaching Lesson 1-4

Warm-up

You can use this *Warm-up*, or the *Additional Examples* on page 23, as questions for students to work on as you begin class.

Diagnostic Locate each decimal on the same number line and give the nearest whole number. Students can use the number line on **Teaching Aid 8**.

1. 0.6 1 **2.** 1.1 1
3. 1.7 2 **4.** 2.3 2
5. 2.9 3 **6.** 3.2 3
7. 3.4 3 **8.** 3.8 4

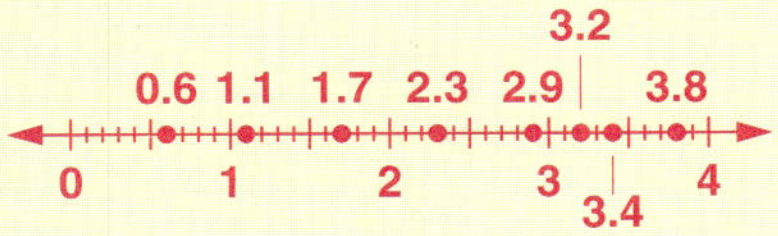

Lesson 1-4 Overview

Broad Goals This lesson covers the most common type of rounding, rounding to the nearest, and points out options when the number to be rounded is exactly halfway between two values.

Perspective The students' experiences with rounding up and rounding down should help them understand rounding to the nearest. This lesson also reinforces the importance of place value and order.

When mathematicians need to round up half the time and round down the other half, they use any one of a variety of strategies. One strategy is to round so that the digit preceding the rounding place is even. With this strategy, 7.45 is 7.4 and 7.55 is 7.6. Another strategy is to alternate rounding up and rounding down when the "critical digit" is 5.

Notes on Reading

Give students an opportunity to ask questions about the reading. You might ask them to explain what they think the purpose is for each example. [**Example 1** has examples of rounding a whole number while **Example 2** shows examples of rounding a decimal. Estimating with money is shown in **Example 3.**]

Stress the following key ideas about rounding.

1. It is typical to round to a particular decimal place.
2. If the digit to the right of the place to which you are rounding is larger than 5, round up. If the digit is smaller than 5, round down. If the digit equals 5, there is a choice.

The more accuracy that is needed, the closer one would want to be to the original value.

Tapes or CDs? *Although CDs are more expensive, they last longer and carry almost no background noise or reduction.*

Example 2

To calculate interest at 8.237%, you may use the number 0.08237 as a multiplier. Round this number to the nearest

a. tenth. **b.** hundredth.
c. thousandth. **d.** ten-thousandth.

Solutions

a. 0.08237 is between 0.0 and 0.1. It is nearer to 0.1, so *0.1* is the answer.
b. 0.08237 is between 0.08 and 0.09 and is nearer to *0.08*.
c. 0.08237 is between 0.082 and 0.083 and is closer to *0.082*.
d. 0.08237 is between 0.0823 and 0.0824 and is nearer to *0.0824*.

Rounding is often used to estimate costs.

Example 3

One tape costs $10.49, and Kiko wants to buy 7. Explain how she can use rounding to estimate the cost.

Solution

She can round $10.49 to the nearest ten cents, $10.50, to estimate.
Kiko's estimate:

$$\begin{array}{r} \$10.50 \\ \times \quad 7 \\ \hline \$73.50 \end{array}$$

In Example 3, the actual cost is $10.49 × 7, or $73.43. So, Kiko's estimate is only $0.07 more than the actual cost. Kiko could get a quicker but less accurate estimate by rounding $10.49 to the nearest dollar, $10. This would make it easy to estimate the cost in her head.

When Is There a Choice in Rounding?

There are situations in which there may be a choice in rounding. For instance, when rounding to the nearest dollar, you may round $10.50 up to $11 or down to $10, since $10.50 falls exactly halfway between the two. When there are many numbers that can be rounded either way, it makes sense to round up half the time and round down the other half of the time.

Optional Activities

History Connection After students finish the lesson, have them make time lines. Have them explain *century* and label the fifth, tenth, fifteenth, and twentieth centuries on their time lines. Explain that the first century started at the beginning of the year 1 A.D. and ended at the end of the year 100 A.D. The second century started at the beginning of the year 101 A.D. Ask students when the twentieth century began and when it will end [January 1, 1901 through December 31, 2000] and when the twenty-first century will begin [January 1, 2001].

You might have students locate the events listed at the right on their time lines and tell in which century the event occurred. [79: first; 1325: fourteenth; 1642: seventeenth; 1821: nineteenth; 1976: twentieth] Finally ask students to find the years for at least three other historical events and locate them on the same time line.

79 A.D.	Mount Vesuvius erupted, its lava burying the ancient city of Pompeii.
1325	Marco Polo visited China.
1642	Pascal invented the adding machine.
1821	Mexico gained its independence from Spain.
1976	The first commercial supersonic flight on the *Concorde* was from London to Washington, D.C.

QUESTIONS

Covering the Reading

1. Round 43
   a. up to the next ten. **50**
   b. down to the preceding ten. **40**
   c. to the nearest ten. **40**

2. Round 0.547
   a. up to the next hundredth. **0.55**
   b. down to the preceding hundredth. **0.54**
   c. to the nearest hundredth. **0.55**

3. Round 88.8888 to the nearest
   a. hundredth. **88.89** b. tenth. **88.9** c. one. **89** d. ten. **90** e. hundred. **100**

4. You wish to estimate the cost of 4 tapes at $8.69 each. What do you get for the rounded value, and what is your estimate of the cost in each situation?
   a. if you round $8.69 to the nearest ten cents **$8.70; $34.80**
   b. if you round $8.69 to the nearest dollar **$9.00; $36.00**

5. Pull-over shirts cost $19.95 each. Describe how to estimate the cost of 6 shirts. What is the estimated cost? **Round to the nearest dollar, then multiply by 6. The estimated cost is $120.00.**

6. Round the speed of light to the nearest hundred thousand miles per second. **200,000 miles per second**

7. When is there a choice in rounding to the nearest? Explain why there is a choice, using an example. **See below.**

8. The number 0.0325 is used in some calculations of the interest earned in a savings account. Round this number to the nearest thousandth. **0.033 or 0.032**

9. When there are many numbers that can be rounded either up or down, what is the sensible thing to do? **Round up half the time and round down half the time.**

Applying the Mathematics

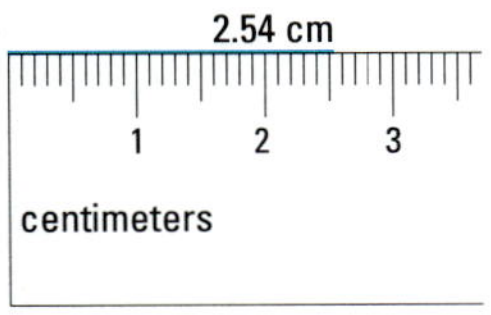

10. The U.S. Internal Revenue Service allows taxpayers to round all amounts to the nearest dollar. But half dollars must be rounded up. In figuring income tax, to what value can you round each amount?
    a. $89.46 **$89** b. $165.50 **$166** c. $100.91 **$101** d. $5324.28 **$5324**

11. Round 2.54, the number of centimeters in an inch, to the nearest tenth. **2.5**

7) There is a choice when the number being rounded falls exactly halfway between the two numbers. For example, $2.50 could be rounded up to $3.00 or down to $2.00 because 2.50 is exactly halfway between 2.00 and 3.00.

Additional Examples

1. On an overseas flight, a jet averaged 597.31 miles per hour. Round this quantity to the nearest
   a. tenth of a mile per hour. **597.3 mph**
   b. mile per hour. **597 mph**
   c. ten miles per hour. **600 mph**
   d. hundred miles per hour. **600 mph**

Point out that the answers to **parts c** and **d** are the same. You might want to discuss the idea of choosing the appropriate place to which to round. In this example, the average jet speed of 597.31 mph would almost always be rounded to 600 mph, or to the nearest ten miles per hour. But if one were interested in a world-record speed, then the average speed of 597.31 mph would be the appropriate expression.

2. The fraction $\frac{1}{7}$ is about equal to .142857. Round this decimal to the nearest
   a. hundred-thousandth. **.14286**
   b. hundredth. **.14**
   c. tenth. **.1**
   d. whole number. **0**

3. *Multiple choice.* A cassette tape costs $6.89. What will 35 such tapes cost? (No calculators or paper and pencil are allowed.)
   (a) $2.41
   (b) $24.12
   (c) $241.15
   (d) $2411.50
   (e) $24,115
   c

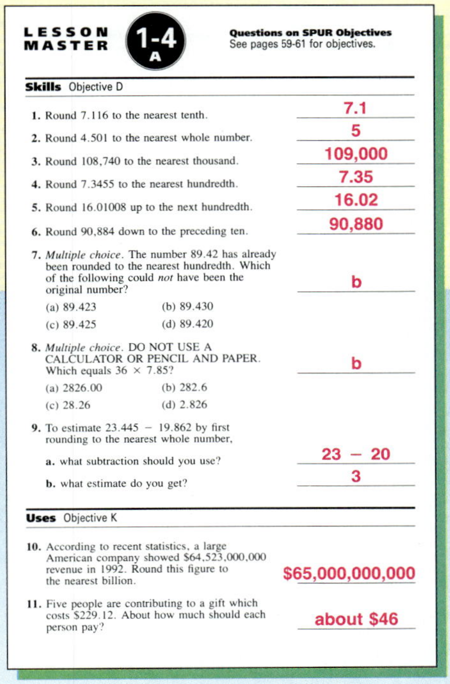

LESSON MASTER 1-4 A

Questions on SPUR Objectives
See pages 59-61 for objectives.

Skills Objective D

1. Round 7.116 to the nearest tenth. **7.1**
2. Round 4.501 to the nearest whole number. **5**
3. Round 108,740 to the nearest thousand. **109,000**
4. Round 7.3455 to the nearest hundredth. **7.35**
5. Round 16.01008 up to the next hundredth. **16.02**
6. Round 90,884 down to the preceding ten. **90,880**
7. *Multiple choice*. The number 89.42 has already been rounded to the nearest hundredth. Which of the following could *not* have been the original number? **b**
   (a) 89.423 (b) 89.430
   (c) 89.425 (d) 89.420
8. *Multiple choice*. DO NOT USE A CALCULATOR OR PENCIL AND PAPER. Which equals 36 × 7.85? **b**
   (a) 2826.00 (b) 282.6
   (c) 28.26 (d) 2.826
9. To estimate 23.445 − 19.862 by first rounding to the nearest whole number,
   a. what subtraction should you use? **23 − 20**
   b. what estimate do you get? **3**

Uses Objective K

10. According to recent statistics, a large American company showed $64,523,000,000 revenue in 1992. Round this figure to the nearest billion. **$65,000,000,000**
11. Five people are contributing to a gift which costs $229.12. About how much should each person pay? **about $46**

Notes on Questions

Question 25 Error Alert Some students may write 3.8 because they rounded 3.775 to the nearest tenth. Refer students to the definition of *truncate* in Lesson 1-3.

Question 31 *Dozen* is not a unit but a number name, just like *hundred*. Extending this idea, in "12 dozen eggs," *12 dozen* or 144 is the count and *eggs* is the counting unit.

History Connection You might point out that another number name is *score,* which means 20. Ask students how many years Abraham Lincoln was talking about in the Gettysburg Address when he said "Four score and seven years ago..." [87 years]

Question 33 This problem exemplifies the important skill of sorting out unnecessary information.

Follow-up for Lesson 1-4

Practice

For more questions on SPUR objectives, use **Lesson Master 1-4A** (shown on page 23) or **Lesson Master 1-4B** (shown on pages 24–25).

LESSON MASTER 1-4 B **Questions on SPUR Objectives**

Skills Objective D: Round any decimal place up or down or to the nearest value of a decimal place.

1. Round 84.248 to the nearest hundredth. 84.25
2. Round 0.833 to the nearest tenth. 0.8
3. Round 26.57 to the nearest whole number. 27
4. Round 518 to the nearest hundred. 500
5. Round 6.06755 to the nearest thousandth. 6.068
6. Round 19.09873 to the nearest hundredth. 19.10
7. Round 140,673 to the preceding ten. 140.670
8. Round 77.00513 up to the next thousandth. 77.006
9. Round 5,007 to the nearest ten. 5,010
10. Round 49.74381 to the nearest one. 50
11. *Multiple choice*. The number 44.83 has already been rounded to the nearest hundredth. Which of the following could *not* have been the original number?
(a) 44.830 (b) 44.825
(c) 44.837 (d) 44.833 c
12. *Multiple choice*. The number 18,400 has already been rounded to the nearest hundred. Which of the following could *not* have been the original number?
(a) 18,384 (b) 18,349
(c) 18,438 (d) 18,407 b
13. *Multiple choice*. DO NOT USE CALCULATOR OR PENCIL AND PAPER. Which equals 5.67 × 8?
(a) 453.6 (b) 4.536
(c) 45.36 (d) 4536.0 c
14. *Multiple choice*. DO NOT USE CALCULATOR OR PENCIL AND PAPER. Which equals 17.221 + 41.0789?
(a) 58.2999 (b) 582.999
(c) 42.8010 (d) 428.010 a

Where do American Indians live? *According to the 1990 census, about 739,000 of the American Indians in the U.S. live on reservations or in tribal designated areas, mainly in the states of Oklahoma, Arizona, and New Mexico. The accountants pictured above live in Texas.*

12. The total American Indian population in the United States in 1990, according to the census, was 1,878,285. Round this number to the nearest ten thousand. 1,880,000

13. Round 3.666666 to the nearest
a. tenth. 3.7 **b.** hundredth. 3.67 **c.** thousandth. 3.667 **d.** ten-thousandth. 3.6667

14. Round 12.3500 to the nearest hundredth. 12.35

15. You buy items costing $4.99, $6.99, and $8.99 in a store.
a. Add these quantities. $20.97
b. How close would you be to the actual cost if you rounded each given quantity to the nearest dollar and then added? $21, 3¢ off

16. Consider the addition problem 2.898765489 + 8.1898989898.
a. Estimate the answer by first rounding both numbers to the nearest whole number and then adding the estimates. 11
b. Explain how you could get a better estimate. Sample: Round each number to the nearest tenth or hundredth, for example.

In 17–20, what is the answer rounded to the nearest whole number? (Hint: You should be able to do these mentally.)

17. 6 × $3.99 $24

18. $11.95 divided by 2 $6

19. 920.9994 − 0.0003992 921

20. 2.0123456789 + 3.0123456789 5

21. A number is rounded to the nearest hundred. The resulting estimate is 9,600.
a. What is the smallest value the original number might have had?
b. What is the largest value the original number might have had?
a) 9550; b) 9650

Review

22. Sarah and George have $10 to spend at the grocery store. They want to buy 3 grapefruits at $0.96 each and 5 oranges at $0.83 each.
a. Use rounding to estimate the cost. Sample: $8.00
b. Do they have enough money? How do you know?
c. Calculate the exact cost. $7.03
d. How much change will they receive? *(Lesson 1-3)* $2.97
b) Yes, because the estimate is high, and they have $10.00.

23. If a calculator shows that you should pay $1.534 for something, what will a store probably charge you? *(Lesson 1-3)* $1.54

24. Round 1.008
a. up to the next hundredth. 1.01
b. down to the preceding hundredth. *(Lesson 1-3)* 1.00

25. Truncate 3.775 to one decimal place. *(Lesson 1-3)* 3.7

Adapting to Individual Needs

English Language Development
To help students grasp the meaning of *between,* you might **use a physical model** made up of students standing in a line or objects lined up on a table. For example, have two students, A and B, stand in the front of the room. Then direct students C and D to stand between A and B so that D is also between C and B yielding the arrangement A, C, D, B.

Extra Help
After students have rounded to a specific place, some do not know whether to drop the digits to the right of the rounded digit or to replace those digits with zeros. Suggest students ask this question—Is the number to be rounded a whole number? If the answer is yes, replace the digits to the right of the rounded digit with zeros. If no, drop all digits to the right of the rounded digit.

26. The Gardners are putting a picket fence along the sidewalk in front of their house. The fence has a post every 3 feet. If the front of the lot measures 45 feet, how many posts will they need? (Hint: Represent the fence with a number line.) *(Lesson 1-2)* **16 posts**

In 27–29, find a number that is between the two given numbers. *(Lesson 1-2)*

27. 3.2 and 3.4 **Sample: 3.3**
28. 6.3 and 6.29 **Sample: 6.295**
29. 14.23 and 14.230 **No number is between.**

30. Write one thousand, five hundred six and three tenths as a decimal. *(Lesson 1-2)* **1506.3**

31. John bought a dozen eggs. In "a dozen eggs," what is the count, and what is the counting unit? (Watch out!) *(Lesson 1-1)* **count: 12; counting unit: eggs**

32. The number ten million consists of a one followed by how many zeros? *(Lesson 1-1)* **7 zeros**

Exploration

33. a. Find the number that satisfies all of these conditions.

    Condition 1: When rounded up to the next hundred, the number becomes 600.

    Condition 2: When rounded down to the preceding ten, the number becomes 570.

    Condition 3: When rounded to the nearest ten, the number is increased by 4.

    Condition 4: The number is a whole number. **576**

    b. Are any of the conditions not needed? If so, which ones? **Yes, conditions 1 and 4 are not needed.**

34. How many decimal places does your computer show when it does a computation? Do this activity to find out.

    a. Type ?3/4 and press RETURN. What does the computer print, 0.75 or .75? **Answers will vary.**

    b. Type ?2/3 and press RETURN. How many decimal places does the computer print? Does the computer round to the nearest or does it truncate? **Answers will vary.**

Assessment

Quiz A quiz covering Lessons 1-1 through 1-4 is provided in the *Assessment Sourcebook.*

Written Communication Have students write a summary of Lessons 1-1 to 1-4. The summary should include the important concepts and also indicate the ideas that they found particularly easy or difficult. One way to organize the summary is by lesson. You might display the lesson titles or a list of objectives. Or you might allow students to write a summary using their books. [Summaries will contain the important concepts, an explanation of each, and a brief statement of how well the student has grasped the concepts.]

Extension

Multicultural Connection As an extension of Question 12, you might have students find the populations of other ethnic groups in the United States and round the numbers to the nearest ten thousand. They could combine their findings and display them on the bulletin board.

Project Update The two projects discussed for Lesson 1-3, Project 2, *Comparing Estimates,* on page 55, and Project 4, *The Advantages of Rounding,* on page 56, also relate to this lesson.

Setting Up Lesson 1-5

Beginning with Lesson 1-5, students will need to have calculators available.

Previewing the Reading Tell students that they are expected to have a calculator with them and to perform the activities in the lesson before doing the questions.

Homework If students are expected to have calculators at home for assignments (and we strongly recommend that they do), then Lesson 1-5 should be read and the activities performed at home. If students do not have calculators at home, you might assign the reading and Questions 1–8 and 11–22 of Lesson 1-6. Then do the reading and Questions 1–20 of Lesson 1-5 in class the next day and assign the rest of both Lessons 1-5 and 1-6 for homework.

▶ LESSON MASTER 1-4 B *page 2*

15. If you estimate 84.531 − 22.055 by first rounding to the nearest whole number,
    a. what subtraction should you use? **85 − 22**
    b. what estimate do you get? **63**

16. If you estimate 9.25 × 7 by first rounding to the nearest whole number,
    a. what multiplication should you use? **9 × 7**
    b. what estimate do you get? **63**

Uses Objective K: Deal with estimates in real situations.

17. In 1990, the public library in Wichita, Kansas, had 894,942 books. Round this number to the nearest thousand. **895,000**

18. In 1980, Buddy Baker won the Daytona 500 driving at an average speed of 177.602 miles per hour. Round this number to the nearest tenth **177.6**

19. Mrs. Thibideaux bought six house plants at $6.89 a piece. About how much did she spend? **about $42**

20. Eight calculators cost $55.86. About how much did each calculator cost? **about $7**

Review Estimation (Previous course)

Multiple choice **In 21-26, DO NOT USE A CALCULATOR OR PENCIL AND PAPER. Choose the *best* estimate.**

21. 5 × 731 **c**
    (a) 35,000 (b) 4,000 (c) 3,500 (d) 350

22. 714 − 388 **a**
    (a) 300 (b) 400 (c) 30 (d) 40

23. 32 × 69 **d**
    (a) between 180 and 210
    (b) between 1,800 and 2,100
    (c) between 180 and 280
    (d) between 1,800 and 2,800

24. $4.31 + $6.88 + $2.46 **a**
    (a) between $12 and $15
    (b) between $10 and $20
    (c) between $15 and $20
    (d) between $9 and $12

25. 293 ÷ 7 **d**
    (a) 4 (b) 30 (c) 50 (d) 40

26. 652 ÷ 81 **b**
    (a) 80 (b) 8 (c) 9 (d) 10

Lesson 1-5

Objectives

E Use a calculator to perform arithmetic operations.

Resources

From the ***Teacher's Resource File***
- Lesson Master 1-5A or 1-5B
- Answer Master 1-5
- Teaching Aid 2: Warm-up

Additional Resources
- Visual for Teaching Aid 2

Teaching Lesson 1-5

Warm-up

You can use this *Warm-up,* or the *Additional Examples* on page 28, as questions for students to work on as you begin class.

Calculator Work in pairs and add, subtract, multiply, and divide on a calculator. Keep a record of your problems and answers. Then write down things you notice about how the calculator works.

Notes on Reading

If you distribute calculators each day, develop a routine that takes no class time to pass them out or to collect them.

❶ If your students are not expected to have calculators at home, you may want to read this lesson aloud in class as students follow along with the classroom calculators. Or you might split the class into **pairs** or **small groups** and have the groups

LESSON

1-5 Knowing Your Calculator

Who uses calculators? *Just about anyone who uses numbers uses a calculator. From left to right, the calculators pictured are a four-function calculator, a scientific calculator, and a graphics calculator.*

❶ Calculators make it easy to do arithmetic quickly and accurately. But they cannot help unless you know how and when to use them. Different calculators may give different answers even when the same buttons are pushed. With this book it is best if you have a **scientific calculator.**

When reading mathematics, you will learn and remember more by doing the problems yourself as you read. As you read this lesson, you will need a calculator, paper, and a pencil.

Clearing and Entering

When you turn on the calculator, 0 or 0. will appear in the **display.** We show this as [0.]. As you press keys, the display changes. If your calculator is already on, press the clear key [C] or [CLEAR] twice before doing calculations.

Activity 1

To find 29 + 54, follow the directions in the left column below. After pressing each key, compare your calculator display to the one in the right column.

	Display shows
Press 2, then 9.	29.
Now press +.	29.
Next press 5, then 4.	54.
Now press =.	83.

Lesson 1-5 Overview

Broad Goals Both a content goal and a process goal appear in this lesson. The content goal is learning a language for discussing calculator use and for identifying keys that are needed for work in the rest of the book. The process goal regards the way in which students read mathematics. This lesson is written in activity format, and the student is expected to work through the activities with a calculator while reading the lesson.

Perspective Many students feel a calculator will do all their work for them and are surprised to find this is not the case. Stress writing key sequences, recording calculator results for steps leading to a solution, and knowing how to interpret the solution on the calculator. The goal is to help students make intelligent use of this tool.

The language developed in this lesson will be helpful in discussing calculator use for the rest of the year. For example, the phrase "key sequence" is particularly helpful in Chapter 4 when discussing order of operations. Some calculators may require second function keys for π, and those calculators will also use second function keys for many other purposes.

❷ Pressing a key on the calculator is called **entering** or **keying in.** The set of instructions in the left column of Activity 1 is called the **key sequence** for this problem. We will write the key sequence using boxes for everything pressed but the numbers.

29 [+] 54 [=]

Sometimes we show the display values underneath the last key pressed.

Key sequence:	29	[+]	54	[=]
Display:	29.	29.	54.	83.

Activity 2

Enter 85 + 9 × 2 on your calculator. After each key is pressed, compare your display with the display shown here.

Key sequence:	85	[+]	9	[×]	2	[=]
Display:	85.	85.	9.	9.	2.	103.

If your calculator first added 85 and 9, and then multiplied by 2, it gave you the incorrect answer 188. If you got 188, your calculator is not appropriate for this class.

Entering π

Most scientific calculators have a way of entering the number π. If you have a π key, simply press it. However, on some calculators, you must press two keys to display π. If there is a small π written above or below a key, two keys are probably needed. In this case, press [INV], [2nd], [SHIFT], or [F] before pressing the key with the π above or below it.

❸ ### Activity 3

Enter π. What number is displayed? How many places after the decimal point does your calculator show?

How Does Your Calculator Round Decimals That Are Too Long to Be Displayed?

Calculators differ in the way they round decimals to the right of a decimal point. This usually does not make much of a difference, but you should know what *your* calculator does. To check your calculator, try this activity.

Activity 4

This book's calculator symbol for division is [÷]. Key in 2 [÷] 3 [=].

The actual answer to 2 divided by 3 is 0.666666666666666 . . . , where the digit 6 repeats forever. No calculator can list all the digits. So the calculator must be programmed to round. (Calculators *are* computers; each key triggers a program.) If the last digit your calculator displays is a 7, your calculator rounds to the nearest. If the last digit your calculator

work on the activities. Then allow them to do as much of the assignment as they can together.

Students need to be reminded again and again that being active while reading mathematics is important. Encourage them *to do* the problems, examples, and activities *as they read* the lessons. Checking calculations on their own calculators is also important. Activities should not be viewed as optional (except where a computer is needed but not available).

❷ The ability to write a key sequence is important as a record of what was done in obtaining an answer using a calculator. Only the final display needs to be written as the answer; the intermediate displays are shown in the lesson as an instructional aid. Explain to students that writing key sequences is one way to communicate their thought processes to you and later to themselves as they review the lesson.

❸ If different models of calculators are used when doing **Activity 3** in class, a discussion should evolve as to what students feel the reason is for the different displays for π.

Optional Activities

Computing Methods

After students have read the lesson, they might **work in groups** and discuss kinds of computations for which they would want to *use a calculator* and kinds they could do faster *mentally* or with *paper and pencil.* Suggest that they write examples of each type of computation and give the answers. Then have the groups share their examples.

LESSON MASTER 1-5 A **Questions on SPUR Objectives**
See pages 59-61 for objectives.

Skills Objective E

In 1-5, use your calculator.

1. Round 8.3 ÷ 7 down to the nearest hundredth. **1.18**
2. 9.1 + 8.9 × 15.2 **144.38**
3. 2.57893 × 415 **1070.25595**
4. $\frac{8.25}{3}$ **2.75**
5. 343 + 48 ÷ 16 + 8 **354**
6. What does the [RCL] or [MR] key do? **It recalls information stored in memory.**
7. Write the key sequence for 2 times π. **2 [×] [π] [=]**
8. Write the key sequence for $\frac{23}{4}$. **23 [÷] 4 [=]**
9. Which is larger, 3 × π or $\frac{66}{7}$? $\frac{66}{7}$
10. **Step 1:** Key in your allowance of $6 a week. 6 [STO]
    Step 2: key in 150 [÷] [RCL] [=]
    How many weeks will it take you to save $150? **25 weeks**
    Step 3: Key in 450 [÷] [RCL] [=]
    How many weeks will it take you to save $450? **75 weeks**
    Step 4: Key in 200 [÷] [RCL] [=]
    How many weeks will it take you to save $200? **about 34 weeks**
11. Explain the difference between the [c] and [AC] keys. Include examples of when one key might be preferred over the other.
    sample: [c] means clear present entry. [AC] means clear all work done. If you input a 7 instead of a 5, you would use [c]. If you want to start over, you would use [AC].
12. Key in 9 [÷] 0. Explain the display.
    The display is E or error because division by 0 is undefined.

Additional Examples

1. A car ferry charges $15.00 for the car and driver and $3.75 for each additional passenger. How much would it cost for a car, driver, and three passengers? Write a key sequence, final display, and the answer to the question.
   3 [×] 3.75 [+] 15 [=]; 26.25; the cost for the car, driver, and three passengers is $26.25.
2. What key sequence could be used to calculate 87 + 43 - 10?
   87 [+] 43 [-] 10 [=]
3. What problem is represented by this key sequence?
   4.2 [-] .5 [×] 3 [=]
   4.2 - .5 × 3

displays is a 6, your calculator truncates. Does your calculator round to the nearest or truncate?

Memory Keys

Scientific calculators have keys that will store a value in "memory" for later use. Such a key might be labeled as [STO] or [M+]. In order to use a value that has been stored, you need to press [RCL] or [MR] for memory "recall." You should explore the use of that key. The memory on most scientific calculators is cleared when the [AC] key is pressed.

Writing Key Sequences

For many homework questions in this book, your teacher may wish you to "show your work." When you use a calculator, this means writing the key sequence and the final display.

Example

Vince bought four books at $12.95 each at a store that gives a discount of $5 if you spend more than $50. What was the cost of the four books (before tax)?

Solution

You must multiply $12.95 by 4 and then subtract 5. If you use a calculator and want to show your work, you can write:

Key Sequence: 4 [×] 12.95 [-] 5 [=]
Display: 46.8
The four books cost $46.80 before tax.

QUESTIONS

Covering the Reading

1. What is a *key sequence?* **a set of instructions for entering numbers and operations into a calculator**
2. *True or false.* If you follow the same key sequence on two different calculators, you will always get the same answer. **False**
3. What answer did you get for Activity 2? **103 on a scientific calculator; 188 on a non-scientific calculator**
4. Do the following key sequence on your calculator. Write down what is in the display after each key is pressed.

Key sequence:	8	[+]	7.2	[×]	10	[=]
Display:	**8**	**8**	**7.2**	**7.2**	**10**	**80**

5. a. Write a key sequence for the problem 15 ÷ 27. **15 [÷] 27 [=]**
   b. What is the final display?
   Sample: 0.5555556

LESSON MASTER 1-5 B Questions on SPUR Objectives

Skills Objective E: Use a calculator to perform arithmetic operations.

In 1-10, use your calculator.

1. Round 48 ÷ 11 to the nearest hundredth. **4.36**
2. Round 7.4 ÷ 9 down to the preceding tenth. **.8**
3. 4.2 × 18.9 − 6.5 **72.88**
4. 72.8625 × 892 **64993.35**
5. .846 + 2.9 × 17 **50.146**
6. 6.6 × .983 × 75 **486.585**
7. $\frac{25.28}{4}$ **6.32**
8. $\frac{1431.29}{16.1}$ **88.9**
9. 118 − 75 ÷ 3 + 762 **855**
10. 1,048 + 48,021 ÷ 3 **17,055**
11. What happens when you press the [AC] key?
    Everything including memory is cleared so a new calculation can be started.

In 12-15, write the key sequence for the given operation.

12. 8 times π **8 [×] [π] [=]**
13. 11.42 + 7.3 **11.42 [+] 7.3 [=]**
14. $\frac{118}{5}$ **118 [÷] 5 [=]**
15. 11 × 984.7 − 8.4 **11 [×] 984.7 [-] 8.4 [=]**
16. Which is larger, 10 × π or $\frac{100}{3}$? **$\frac{100}{3}$**
17. Which is smaller, $\frac{0.45}{36}$ or $\frac{0.36}{45}$? **$\frac{0.36}{45}$**
18. *Multiple choice.* What is calculated by the following key sequence? **c**
    136.8 [STO] 9 [×] [RCL] [-] 3 [×] [RCL] [=]
    (a) 136.8 × 9 − 3
    (b) 9 × 3 − 136.8
    (c) 9 × 136.8 − 3 × 136.8
    (d) 9 × 136.8 − 9 × 3

Adapting to Individual Needs

Extra Help
You might use an overhead calculator to explain what some of the keys do. Choose the keys that students should know at this time. Then give students sample problems to do on their calculators and have them explain each entry in finding the solutions.

Cooperative Learning Some of your students who know how to use a calculator might be paired with students needing extra help, thereby correcting any errors in thinking as they work through the sample problems.

6. **a.** What value does your calculator give for π?
b. Compare the value for π your calculator gives to the one on page 12. Does your calculator truncate or round to the nearest?
a) 3.1415927 (Answer may vary.) b) Answers may vary.

7. Explain the purpose of the [STO] key.
It is used to store a number in memory.

Applying the Mathematics

8. **a.** Follow the directions of Question 4, using this key sequence.
17.95 [STO] 6 [×] [RCL] [=] [+] 5 [×] [RCL] [=] See below.
b. What have you calculated in part **a**?
6 × 17.95 + 5 × 17.95 = 197.45

9. All calculators have a way of starting from scratch with a new calculation. How is this done on your calculator? [C] or [AC] or [CLEAR]

10. All calculators have a way of allowing you to correct a mistake in an entry. You press a key to replace one entry with another. On your calculator, what is this key called? [CE] clear entry, [CE/C], or [C]

11. How many decimal places does your calculator display? Enter the following key sequence to find out. Answers may vary.
13717421 [÷] 333 [÷] 333667 [=] [0.1234568]; 7 decimal places

How old is the calculator? *The calculator shown is the first scientific hand-held calculator, the TI SR-10, invented at Texas Instruments in 1967. It is about 6" by 4" by 2" and weighs about 3 pounds. By 1973, Texas Instruments had introduced a commercial version that sold for about $150.*

In 12–15, do the arithmetic problem on your calculator.

12. 3.5625 × 512 1824
13. 0.9 − 0.99 + 0.999 0.909
14. 6 × π 18.849556
15. 5 + 3 × 17 56

16. Perform the calculation and round the answer to the nearest tenth.
28.3 ÷ 5.1 − 3.71 1.8

17. What is the largest number in decimal notation that your calculator can display? 99999999. Answers may vary.

18. Which is larger, $\pi \times \pi$ or 10? 10

19. Explore the memory keys on your calculator. Write at least one key sequence using those keys and explain what the calculator has done.
Answers will vary.

20. Use this information and your calculator. Jeffrey is saving money each week to buy presents for his family. He wants to save $150. How much must he save each week if he saves for the given amount of time?
a. 3 weeks $50 **b.** 5 weeks $30 **c.** 8 weeks $18.75
d. 12 weeks $12.50 **e.** 20 weeks $7.50
(Hint: You may be able to save time by using a memory key.)

8a) 17.95 [STO] 6 [×] [RCL] [=]
[17.95] [M 17.95] [M 6.] [M 6.] [M 17.95] [M 107.7]
[+] 5 [×] [RCL] [=]
[M 107.7] [M 5.] [M 5.] [M 17.95] [M 197.45]

Notes on Questions

Question 15 Error Alert If a student has the answer 136, then either (a) the calculator is not scientific, or (b) the student pressed the equal-sign key to obtain the answer to 5 + 3 before multiplying. Remind students with scientific calculators to enter the problem as stated and then press the equal-sign key.

Adapting to Individual Needs

English Language Development
Some students who are just learning the English language will be familiar with the calculator and its uses but may not be familiar with common calculator terminology. Demonstrate what the following words represent: *key, enter, display,* and *clear.* Then write a key sequence on the board such as 45 [+] 27 [=]. Explain that this is a *key sequence* because it tells which keys to press and the order or sequence in which to press them.

▸ **LESSON MASTER 1-5 B** *page 2*

19. *Multiple choice.* Which key sequence can *not* be used for 124 ÷ 1.8 + 38 ÷ 1.8? c
(a) 124 [÷] 1.8 [=] [+] 38 [÷] 1.8 [=]
(b) 1.8 [STO] 124 [÷] [RCL] [+] 38 [÷] [RCL] [=]
(c) 1.8 [STO] 124 [÷] [STO] [=] [+] 38 [÷] [STO] [=]
(d) 1.8 [STO] 124 [÷] [RCL] [=] [+] 38 [÷] [RCL] [=]

20. Explain the difference between the [STO] and the [RCL] keys.
The [STO] key puts the number in the display in memory. The [RCL] key retrieves the number in memory and puts it in the display.

21. Key in 6 [÷] 0. Explain the display.
An error message, such as E, appears because dividing by 0 is undefined.

22. Pi has an infinite number of digits. The first 24 decimal places are shown here.
3.141592653589793238462643
Display π on your calculator with the touch of one or two keys. Can you tell by examining the display whether your calculator truncates or rounds? Explain your answer.
Answers will vary depending on calculator. For example, when 7 decimal places (8 digits total) are displayed for π, the calculator truncates if the last digit is 6, and it rounds if the last digit is 7. But when 8 decimal places are shown, you can't tell because the last digit will be 5 on both types of calculators.

Notes on Questions

Question 31 Make certain that each student knows how the error message is displayed on his or her calculator and what it means.

Follow-up for Lesson 1-5

Practice

For more questions on SPUR objectives, use **Lesson Master 1-5A** (shown on page 27) or **Lesson Master 1-5B** (shown on pages 28–29).

Assessment

Group Assessment Have groups of students work together to write a summary of what they have learned about calculators in this lesson. Tell them they can use examples to help with their explanations. [Each student will participate by stating key concepts and appropriate examples, which display an understanding of how the calculator can be used as a tool.]

Extension

History Connection Have students investigate the history of calculating devices from the abacus to the modern computer. They might include the first adding machine invented in 1642 by the French mathematician Blaise Pascal. In 1888, Hollerith's Tabulator was manufactured by a company that later became IBM. William Burroughs's adding machine was the first to print a tape of addends and their sum in 1892.

Review

21. Round to the nearest thousandth.
a. .44041 **.440** **b.** .44051 **.441** **c.** .40451 *(Lesson 1-4)* **.405**

22. a. Round 7.25 up to the next tenth. **7.3**
b. Round 7.25 down to the preceding tenth. *(Lesson 1-3)* **7.2**

23. You run a race in 53.7 seconds. Someone beats you by two tenths of a second. What was that person's time? *(Lesson 1-2)* **53.5 seconds**

24. Find a number between 2.36 and 2.37. *(Lesson 1-2)* **Sample: 2.365**

25. Mark began his math homework in school and needed to complete questions 10–30 at home. How many questions does he need to complete at home? *(Lesson 1-2)* **21**

26. Consider the number of buttons on your calculator.
a. Name the count. **40; answers may vary.**
b. Name the counting unit. *(Lesson 1-1)* **buttons**

27. Translate into English words: 3,412,670. *(Lesson 1-1)* **three million, four hundred twelve thousand, six hundred seventy**

28. Three hundred thousand is written as a three followed by how many zeros? *(Lesson 1-1)* **5 zeros**

29. What number is three less than three hundred thousand? *(Lesson 1-1)* **299,997**

30. Sandy made purchases of \$2.23, \$4.07, and \$2.49. She gave the clerk \$10.04. If Sandy received one bill and one coin from the clerk, what bill and coin were they? *(Previous course)* **a one-dollar bill and a quarter**

Exploration

31. Key in 5 [÷] 0 [=] on your calculator.
a. What is displayed? [E 0.] **Answers may vary.**
b. What does the display mean? **There is an error.**
c. Why did this happen? **A number cannot be divided by 0.**

Adapting to Individual Needs

Challenge
Some of your students might enjoy researching the abacus and telling classmates about its history and where it is used today. If possible have an abacus in class and ask these students to show how to operate it.

Setting Up Lesson 1-6

Previewing the Reading Emphasize again that students should have calculators in hand while reading.

Homework Have students read and answer all the questions in Lesson 1-6. Omit Question 25 if you plan to do the *Optional Activities* with number lines shown on page 32. You may wish to give students the option of answering any two of Questions 36, 37, and 38.

LESSON

1-6

Decimals for Simple Fractions

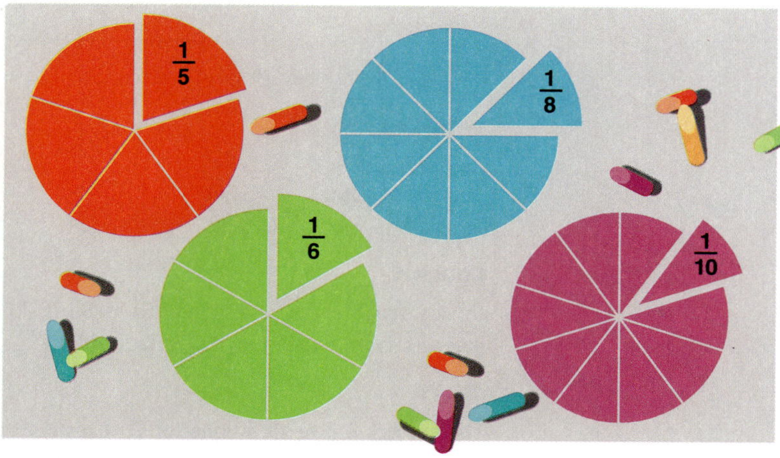

Fraction Vocabulary

The above picture shows *fractions* of four circles. A symbol of the form $\frac{a}{b}$ or a/b is a **fraction** with a **numerator** a and **denominator** b. The **fraction bar** — or **slash** / indicates division.

$$\frac{a}{b} = a/b = a \div b$$

In the language of division, the number a is the **dividend,** b is the **divisor,** and $\frac{a}{b}$ is the **quotient.** In $\frac{2}{3}$, 2 is the numerator or dividend, and 3 is the denominator or divisor. The fraction itself is the quotient, the result of dividing 2 by 3.

The fraction bar was first used by the Arabs and later by Fibonacci, but it was not widely used until the 1500s. A curved slash, *a∫b,* was first used by the Mexican Manuel Antonio Valdes in 1784. In the 1800s this developed into the slash in a/b.

A **simple fraction** is a fraction with a whole number in its numerator and a nonzero whole number in its denominator. (Because division by zero is not allowed, zero cannot be in the denominator of a fraction.) Here are some simple fractions.

$$3/4 \qquad \frac{72}{8} \qquad \frac{3}{11} \qquad \frac{0}{135} \qquad \frac{4}{180} \qquad \frac{34}{19}$$

Fractions and Division

Fractions are very useful because they are related to division. But fractions are harder to order, round, add, and subtract than decimals. So it often helps to find a decimal that equals a given fraction. This is easy to do, particularly with a calculator.

Lesson 1-6

Objectives

B Order decimals and fractions.
E Use a calculator to perform arithmetic operations.
F Convert simple fractions to decimals.
G Know by memory the common decimals and fractions between 0 and 1.
I Correctly use the raised bar symbol for repeating decimals.
N Give people and rough dates for key ideas in the development of arithmetic.

Resources

From the ***Teacher's Resource File***

- Lesson Master 1-6A or 1-6B
- Answer Master 1-6
- Teaching Aids
  - 2 Warm-up
  - 9 Numbers on a Unit Segment
  - 10 Fraction/Decimal Equivalents
  - 11 Circle Models
  - 12 Thermometers (Question 34)
- Activity Kit, Activity 1
- Technology Sourcebook
  - Computer Demonstration 1
  - Calculator Master 1

Additional Resources

- Visuals for Teaching Aids 2, 9–12
- Spreadsheet Workshop

Lesson 1-6 Overview

Broad Goals This lesson has two goals—to teach students how to convert fractions to decimals, and to reinforce the notion that a fraction represents a single number.

Perspective Work on operations with fractions is senseless if students do not know what the answers mean. So in this book we first deal with the meaning of fractions; operations with fractions are studied in later chapters.

Often a fraction is introduced via shading equal sectors of a circle, so that $\frac{a}{b}$ means that a of b sectors are shaded. If this is the *only* way that fractions are presented, students associate the numerator and the denominator of a fraction with counting and they have no meaning for the fraction bar. Thus, many students never think of the fraction as being a single number and it becomes more difficult for them to order fractions or rename a fraction as a decimal. Some students spend years of work with fractions before they are taught that $\frac{a}{b}$ means *dividing a* by *b*. The changing of fractions to decimals and the graphing of fractions on the number line help develop the concept of the fraction as representing a single number.

Teaching Lesson 1-6

Warm-up

Divide. Then check your answers. Do not use a calculator. Show your work.

1. $378 \div 9$ **42**
2. 2438/23 **106**
3. $12\overline{)247.2}$ **20.6**
4. $\frac{1}{2}$ **.5**
5. $39.9 \div 4.2$ **9.5**

Although we expect students to use a calculator throughout this book, long division is reviewed here because it is used in **Examples 2 and 3.**

Notes on Reading

Reading Mathematics One method of helping students grasp the many details in this lesson is to start by having them reread the text up to **Example 1,** listing the advantages of fractions and decimals as they read. Then discuss the examples with them, carefully pointing out the important concepts illustrated. **Example 1** is a straightforward easy example of converting a fraction to an ending, or terminating, decimal. **Example 2** is similar to **Example 1** but results in a number larger than 1. You might ask students why. [The numerator is larger than the denominator.] **Example 3** covers repeating decimals. **Example 4** illustrates a situation in which the calculator display does not indicate whether the decimal repeats or terminates. **Example 5** shows the case of a fraction representing an integer.

1 **Example 1**

Find a decimal equal to $\frac{3}{5}$.

Solution

Key sequence: 3 [÷] 5 [=]
Display: [0.6]
Answer: 0.6.

Check 1

(a very rough check) $\frac{3}{5}$ is less than 1. So is 0.6. (This checks that the numbers were entered in the correct order.)

Check 2

The answer 0.6 is six tenths, or $\frac{6}{10}$. Examine the circles at the beginning of this lesson. Do three of the $\frac{1}{5}$ pieces equal six of the $\frac{1}{10}$ pieces? Yes, they do. So it checks.

Activity

Draw fractions of the circles at the beginning of this lesson to show Check 2 to Example 1.

Example 2

Find the decimal equal to $\frac{7}{4}$.

Solution 1

Key in: 7 [÷] 4 [=]. The calculator displays the exact answer, 1.75.

Solution 2

Divide 4 into 7 using paper and pencil.

$$
\begin{array}{r}
1.75 \\
4\overline{)7.00} \\
\underline{4} \\
3\,0 \\
\underline{2\,8} \\
20 \\
\underline{20} \\
0
\end{array}
$$

Optional Activities

Activity 1 Using a Physical Model You might use *Activity 1* in *Activity Kit* to introduce Lesson 1-6, or you might want to use this activity after reading through **Example 4.** In this activity students fold a decimal number line to find equal decimals and fractions. After completing the activity, students can verify the common fraction-decimal equivalents given on page 34.

Cooperative Learning Students can then **work in pairs** and take turns pointing to a tick mark and naming it as a fraction and as a decimal.

Activity 2 Technology Connection You may wish to use *Technology Sourcebook, Computer Demonstration 1,* to introduce students to the treatment of decimals in the *Spreadsheet Workshop.* Fractions are converted to decimals, and values are rounded to fit within the cell. After the demonstration, have students experiment by entering various fractions and changing the column width

Activity 3 Technology Connection *Technology Sourcebook, Calculator Master 1,* has students explore patterns in the repetends for fractions with different denominators and make generalizations regarding the nature of the factors of the denominators.

Example 3

Find the decimal equal to $\frac{3}{11}$.

Solution

Key in: 3 ÷ 11 =. What the calculator shows depends on the way it rounds and the number of decimal places it displays. You might see 0.27272727 or 0.2727273 or 0.2727272, or something like this with fewer or more decimal places. This suggests that the 27 repeats again and again. That is the case.

$$\frac{3}{11} = 0.272727272727272727272727272727272727\ldots,$$

where the 27 repeats forever. For practical purposes an abbreviation is needed. It has become the custom to write

$$\frac{3}{11} = 0.\overline{27}.$$

The bar over the 27 indicates that the 27 repeats forever. The digits under the bar are the **repetend** of this **infinite repeating decimal.**

You can use long division to verify that a decimal repeats. Here we again determine the decimal for $\frac{3}{11}$, this time using long division.

$$\begin{array}{r} .2727\ldots \\ 11\overline{)3.0000} \\ \underline{2\,2} \\ 80 \\ \underline{77} \\ 30 \\ \underline{22} \\ 80 \\ \underline{77} \\ 3 \end{array}$$

Notice that the remainders, after subtraction, alternate between 8 and 3. This shows that the digits in the quotient repeat forever.

Example 4

Find the decimal equal to $\frac{87}{70}$.

Solution

Key in: 87 ÷ 70 =. Display: 1.242857142.

You cannot tell from this display whether or not the decimal repeats. Also, you cannot tell whether the last digit is rounded up or not. So write $\frac{87}{70} = 1.24285714\ldots$. That is all you are expected to do at this time.

In Example 4, the decimal actually does repeat.

$$\frac{87}{70} = 1.2\overline{428571}$$

In fact, *all* simple fractions are equal to ending or repeating decimals.

1 Students should learn to use a calculator to rewrite ("convert" or "change") any simple fraction as a decimal. But the conversion of simple fractions with denominators 2, 3, 4, 5, 6, and 10 should not require a calculator. (Some teachers also add eighths to this list.) Not only should the student know how to go from a fraction to a decimal, but for these cases, the student should be able to do the conversion mentally.

Calculator Some students may be able to convert a fraction to a decimal on their calculators by first entering the fraction (press the numerator, key in a fraction key, and press the denominator) and then pressing either = or F→D.

Note that we say that decimals are "equal" to fractions, not "equivalent." We also say "rewrite" or "convert" or "change" rather than "reduce." The word "reduce" carries with it the connotation that the value of the fraction is changed and it reinforces the notion that what matters most are the numerator and the denominator of a fraction and not the number it represents.

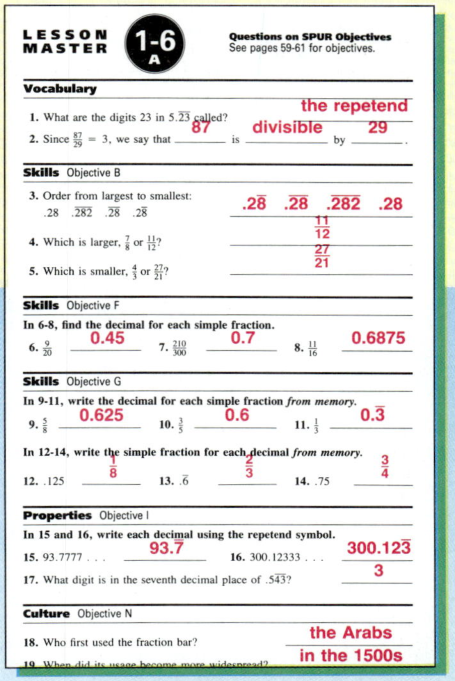

LESSON MASTER 1-6 A

Questions on SPUR Objectives
See pages 59-61 for objectives.

Vocabulary

1. What are the digits 23 in $5.\overline{23}$ called? the repetend
2. Since $\frac{87}{29} = 3$, we say that 87 is divisible by 29.

Skills Objective B

3. Order from largest to smallest: .28 $.\overline{282}$ $.\overline{28}$ $.2\overline{8}$ — $.2\overline{8}$ $.\overline{28}$ $.\overline{282}$ .28
4. Which is larger, $\frac{7}{8}$ or $\frac{11}{12}$? $\frac{11}{12}$
5. Which is smaller, $\frac{4}{3}$ or $\frac{27}{21}$? $\frac{27}{21}$

Skills Objective F

In 6-8, find the decimal for each simple fraction.

6. $\frac{9}{20}$ 0.45 7. $\frac{210}{300}$ 0.7 8. $\frac{11}{16}$ 0.6875

Skills Objective G

In 9-11, write the decimal for each simple fraction *from memory.*

9. $\frac{5}{8}$ 0.625 10. $\frac{3}{5}$ 0.6 11. $\frac{1}{3}$ $0.\overline{3}$

In 12-14, write the simple fraction for each decimal *from memory.*

12. .125 $\frac{1}{8}$ 13. $.\overline{6}$ $\frac{2}{3}$ 14. .75 $\frac{3}{4}$

Properties Objective I

In 15 and 16, write each decimal using the repetend symbol.

15. 93.7777 . . . $93.\overline{7}$ 16. 300.12333 . . . $300.12\overline{3}$

17. What digit is in the seventh decimal place of $.5\overline{43}$? 3

Culture Objective N

18. Who first used the fraction bar? the Arabs
19. When did its usage become more widespread? in the 1500s

Adapting to Individual Needs

English Language Development

To help students understand the words *repetend* and *infinite repeating decimal,* you might **use physical objects** to show students a repeating pattern, such as eraser, book, pencil, cup, book, pencil, cup, book, pencil, cup, and so on. Then replace the objects with numbers and write a pattern such as 9, 1, 2, 3, 1, 2, 3, 1, 2, 3, and so on. Then write .9123123123 ... on the board and explain that the three dots indicate that the digits 1, 2, and 3, continue to repeat forever and, therefore, the decimal is called an *infinite repeating decimal.* Write .9123123123 ... = $.9\overline{123}$ and explain that we call the repeating part of a decimal the repetend.

❷ To help students remember these commonly used fraction and decimal equivalents, you might use **Teaching Aids 9 and 10.** On **Teaching Aid 9,** students can write tenths, fifths, eighths, fourths, one half, sixths and thirds.

Additional Examples

Write a decimal equal to each fraction.

1. $\frac{9}{25}$ .36 2. $\frac{3}{2}$ 1.5 3. $\frac{5}{12}$ $.41\overline{6}$
4. $\frac{15}{13}$ 1.1538462 or calculator displays which might be 1.1538462 or 1.1538461.
5. $\frac{135}{15}$ 9

Notes on Questions

Question 6 You may want to use **Teaching Aid 10** when discussing this question.

Question 9 Some students will be able to write $\frac{4}{7}$ as a decimal using the repetend because they have used paper and pencil to divide or their calculators displayed enough digits. However, many calculators will only show 0.5714286 so that 0.571428 … is acceptable as an answer.

Question 13 Error Alert If students answer 9.8787878787, emphasize that the bar is placed only above the repetend 7.

(Notes on Questions are continued on page 36.)

LESSON MASTER 1-6 B **Questions on SPUR Objectives**

Vocabulary

1. In the number $6.3\overline{18}$ which digits make up the repetend? 18
2. In $\frac{91}{13}$, the dividend is 91 and the divisor is 13.
3. *Multiple choice.* Which of the following is *not* a simple fraction? a
(a) $\frac{4}{7.2}$ (b) $\frac{3}{10}$ (c) $\frac{22}{17}$ (d) $\frac{0}{14}$

Skills Objective B: Order decimals and fractions.

4. Order from smallest to largest: $.\overline{96}$ $.9\overline{6}$ $.96$ $.\overline{963}$ — $.96$ $.\overline{963}$ $.9\overline{6}$ $.\overline{96}$
5. Order from largest to smallest: $.3\overline{7}$ $.\overline{3}$ $.375$ $.\overline{37}$ — $.3\overline{7}$ $.375$ $.\overline{37}$ $.\overline{3}$
6. Which is smaller, $\frac{5}{8}$ or $\frac{2}{3}$? $\frac{5}{8}$ 7. Which is larger, $\frac{5}{9}$ or $\frac{8}{15}$? $\frac{5}{9}$

Skills Objective E: Use a calculator to perform arithmetic operations.

8. To simplify $\frac{62}{.31}$ on your calculator, which number should you enter first? 62

In 9 and 10, give the key sequence for converting each fraction to a decimal.

9. $\frac{13}{200}$ 13 ÷ 200 = 10. $\frac{5}{2.9}$ 5 ÷ 2.9 =

Skills Objective F: Convert simple fractions and mixed numbers to decimals.

In 11-16, find the decimal for each fraction.

11. $\frac{27}{40}$ .675 12. $\frac{7}{16}$ .4375 13. $\frac{135}{450}$ .3
14. $\frac{8}{15}$ $.5\overline{3}$ 15. $\frac{48}{64}$ .75 16. $\frac{6}{11}$ $.\overline{54}$

❷ What Decimals and Fractions Should You Know by Heart?

The common simple fractions in the chart below appear frequently in mathematics and in real-life situations. You need to know them.

Fourths and Eighths	Thirds and Sixths	Fifths and Tenths
$\frac{1}{8} = 0.125$	$\frac{1}{6} = 0.1\overline{6}$	$\frac{1}{10} = 0.1$
$\frac{1}{4} = \frac{2}{8} = 0.25$	$\frac{1}{3} = \frac{2}{6} = 0.\overline{3}$	$\frac{1}{5} = \frac{2}{10} = 0.2$
$\frac{3}{8} = 0.375$	$\frac{3}{6} = 0.5$	$\frac{3}{10} = 0.3$
$\frac{2}{4} = \frac{4}{8} = 0.5$	$\frac{2}{3} = \frac{4}{6} = 0.\overline{6}$	$\frac{2}{5} = \frac{4}{10} = 0.4$
$\frac{5}{8} = 0.625$	$\frac{5}{6} = 0.8\overline{3}$	$\frac{5}{10} = 0.5$
$\frac{3}{4} = \frac{6}{8} = 0.75$		$\frac{3}{5} = \frac{6}{10} = 0.6$
$\frac{7}{8} = 0.875$		$\frac{7}{10} = 0.7$
		$\frac{4}{5} = \frac{8}{10} = 0.8$
		$\frac{9}{10} = 0.9$

Some fractions are whole numbers in disguise.

Example 5

Find the decimal equal to $\frac{91}{13}$.

Solution

Key in: 91 ÷ 13 =.

Display: 7. . $\frac{91}{13} = 7.$

In Example 5, we say that 91 is **evenly divisible** by 13. Sometimes we merely say that 91 is **divisible** by 13.

QUESTIONS

Covering the Reading

1. Consider the fraction $\frac{15}{8}$.
 a. What is its numerator? 15
 b. What is its denominator? 8
 c. What is the symbol for division? c) — (bar)
 d. Does it equal 15/8 or 8/15? 15/8
 e. Does it equal 8 ÷ 15? No
 f. Does it equal 15 ÷ 8? Yes
 g. What is the divisor? 8
 h. What is the dividend? 15
 i. Find the decimal equal to it. 1.875
2. Before the 1500s, who used the fraction bar? the Arabs
3. Who first developed a slash symbol for fractions, and when? Manuel Antonio Valdes, 1784

Adapting to Individual Needs

Extra Help

To help students understand *ending decimal,* go through the long division computation for problems like 3 ÷ 4 and 17 ÷ 4. Students should notice the place at which the computation ends and realize why the decimal is an ending decimal. Use problems like 5 ÷ 11 and 16 ÷ 3 to show that sometimes the digits in the quotient repeat in a pattern. After dividing for a while, hopefully students will see that the pattern will continue forever because the same remainders are recurring. The quotient has a pattern of digits that occur over and over and that go on and on forever. Thus it is an *infinite repeating decimal.*

```
      .45454
 11)5.00000
    4 4
      60
      55
       50
       44
        60
        55
         50
         44
          6
```

4. Which of the following are simple fractions?
a. $\frac{15}{8}$ **b.** 2 **c.** $\frac{3.5}{2.3}$ **d.** $6\frac{2}{3}$ **e.** $\frac{0}{9}$ a and e

6)

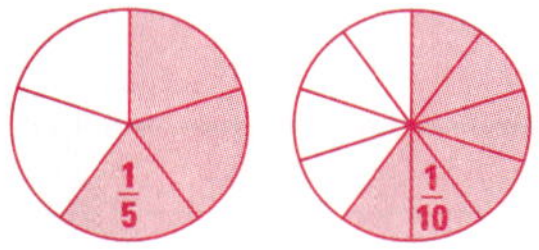

5. Why is it helpful to be able to find a decimal for a fraction?
Decimals are easier to order, round, add, and subtract.

6. Draw fractions of the circles on page 31 to confirm Check 2 to Example 1.

In 7–10, find a decimal for each fraction.

7. $\frac{3}{20}$ 0.15 8. $\frac{23}{20}$ 1.15 9. $\frac{4}{7}$ $0.\overline{571428}$ 10. $\frac{1}{27}$ $0.\overline{037}$

11. In $86.\overline{27}$, what is the repetend? 27

12. In $0.39\overline{8}$, what is the repetend? 8

In 13 and 14 write the first ten decimal places.

13. $9.8\overline{7}$ 9.8777777777 14. $0.\overline{142}$ 0.1421421421

15. If you do not know the decimals for these fractions, you should learn them now. Try to find each decimal without looking at page 34.

a. $\frac{1}{10}$ 0.1 **b.** $\frac{2}{10}$ 0.2 **c.** $\frac{3}{10}$ 0.3 **d.** $\frac{4}{10}$ 0.4 **e.** $\frac{5}{10}$ 0.5
f. $\frac{6}{10}$ 0.6 **g.** $\frac{7}{10}$ 0.7 **h.** $\frac{8}{10}$ 0.8 **i.** $\frac{9}{10}$ 0.9 **j.** $\frac{1}{5}$ 0.2
k. $\frac{2}{5}$ 0.4 **l.** $\frac{3}{5}$ 0.6 **m.** $\frac{4}{5}$ 0.8 **n.** $\frac{1}{2}$ 0.5 **o.** $\frac{1}{4}$ 0.25
p. $\frac{3}{4}$ 0.75 **q.** $\frac{1}{8}$ 0.125 **r.** $\frac{3}{8}$ 0.375 **s.** $\frac{5}{8}$ 0.625 **t.** $\frac{7}{8}$ 0.875
u. $\frac{1}{3}$ $0.\overline{3}$ **v.** $\frac{2}{3}$ $0.\overline{6}$ **w.** $\frac{4}{6}$ $0.\overline{6}$ **x.** $\frac{1}{6}$ $0.1\overline{6}$ **y.** $\frac{5}{6}$ $0.8\overline{3}$

In 16–21, give a simple fraction for each decimal. You should be able to find each fraction without looking at page 34.

16. 0.4 $\frac{4}{10}$ or $\frac{2}{5}$ 17. .25 $\frac{1}{4}$ 18. $.\overline{3}$ $\frac{1}{3}$
19. 0.60 $\frac{6}{10}$ or $\frac{3}{5}$ 20. 0.7 $\frac{7}{10}$ 21. $.\overline{6}$ $\frac{2}{3}$

22. $\frac{92}{23}$ = 4. So we say that 92 is _?_ by 23. evenly divisible (or divisible)

Who uses fractions? *Both salespersons and customers need to know decimal equivalents for common fractions. Someone requesting 1/4 pound of cheese should know that 0.25 pound is the same weight.*

Applying the Mathematics

23. Carpenters often measure in sixteenths of an inch.
a. Change $\frac{3}{16}''$ to a decimal. 0.1875″
b. Is $\frac{3}{16}''$ shorter or longer than $\frac{1}{5}''$? shorter

24. Rewrite $\frac{1}{14}$ as a decimal rounded to the nearest thousandth. 0.071

25.
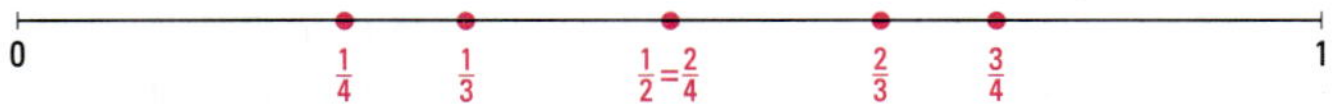

a. Trace this line segment onto your paper. Check 4-in. line segment.
b. Graph the fractions $\frac{1}{2}, \frac{1}{3}, \frac{2}{3}, \frac{1}{4}, \frac{2}{4}$, and $\frac{3}{4}$ on it. See graph above.

26. Order 3/10, 1/3, and 0.33 from smallest to largest. $\frac{3}{10}$, 0.33, $\frac{1}{3}$

Follow-up for Lesson 1-6

Practice

For more questions on SPUR objectives, use **Lesson Master 1-6A** (shown on page 33) or **Lesson Master 1-6B** (shown on pages 34–35).

Assessment

Oral Communication On the board write a list of all the terms used in this lesson and a list of fractions and decimals. Call on students to explain the terms and to write the fractions as decimals or vice versa. [Statements will show an understanding of how to read fractions, their relationship to decimals, and how to convert them.]

Extension

You might have students **work in groups** to discuss why the number of digits in a repetend cannot be greater than the value of the denominator (divisor). [The remainder must be less than the divisor, so the only possible remainders are numbers less than the divisor. At some point after zeros are annexed in the dividend, remainders will recur in sequence producing a repeating sequence of digits in the quotient.]

Project Update Project 3, *Which Fractions Equal Repeating Decimals?*, on page 56, relates to the content of this lesson.

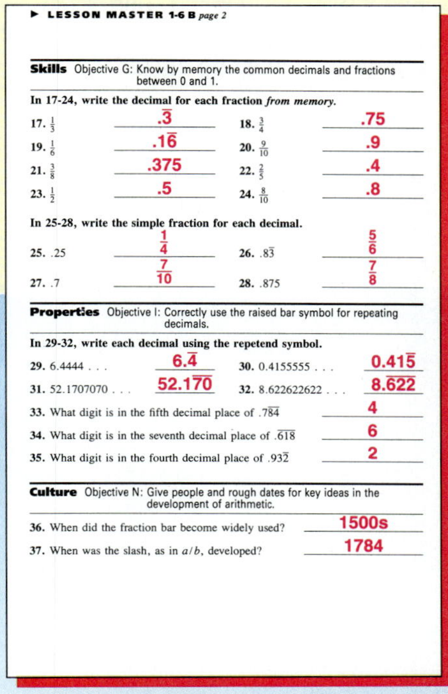
▶ **LESSON MASTER 1-6 B** *page 2*

Skills Objective G: Know by memory the common decimals and fractions between 0 and 1.

In 17-24, write the decimal for each fraction *from memory*.

17. $\frac{1}{3}$ $.\overline{3}$ 18. $\frac{3}{4}$ .75
19. $\frac{1}{6}$ $.1\overline{6}$ 20. $\frac{9}{10}$ .9
21. $\frac{3}{8}$ .375 22. $\frac{2}{5}$ .4
23. $\frac{1}{2}$ .5 24. $\frac{8}{10}$ .8

In 25-28, write the simple fraction for each decimal.

25. .25 $\frac{1}{4}$ 26. $.8\overline{3}$ $\frac{5}{6}$
27. .7 $\frac{7}{10}$ 28. .875 $\frac{7}{8}$

Properties Objective I: Correctly use the raised bar symbol for repeating decimals.

In 29-32, write each decimal using the repetend symbol.

29. 6.4444 . . . $6.\overline{4}$ 30. 0.4155555 . . . $0.41\overline{5}$
31. 52.1707070 . . . $52.1\overline{70}$ 32. 8.622622622 . . . $8.\overline{622}$

33. What digit is in the fifth decimal place of $.7\overline{84}$ 4
34. What digit is in the seventh decimal place of $.\overline{618}$ 6
35. What digit is in the fourth decimal place of $.93\overline{2}$ 2

Culture Objective N: Give people and rough dates for key ideas in the development of arithmetic.

36. When did the fraction bar become widely used? 1500s
37. When was the slash, as in *a*/*b*, developed? 1784

Adapting to Individual Needs

Challenge

You might want to show students how to add repeating decimals. For example, to add $0.\overline{39} + 2.\overline{7}$ first write the repetend of each decimal several times, showing the same number of digits for each decimal.

$$\begin{array}{rl} 0.\overline{39} & = 0.393939\ldots \\ +\ 2.\overline{7} & = 2.777777\ldots \\ \hline & \ 3.171716\ldots \quad = 3.\overline{17} \end{array}$$

Then give students these exercises. Tell them to write each sum as a repeating decimal with a bar over the repetend.

1. $4.\overline{5} + 3.\overline{1}$ [$7.\overline{6}$]
2. $2.\overline{53} + 6.\overline{2}$ [$8.\overline{75}$]
3. $0.\overline{64} + 0.\overline{7}$ [$1.\overline{42}$]
4. $1.\overline{724} + 0.\overline{6}$ [$2.\overline{391}$]
5. $0.\overline{521} + 0.\overline{3178}$ [$0.\overline{839353304699}$]

Notes on Questions

Question 28 Writing You might want to collect and read students' letters to gain insights about their understanding of fractions as decimals. Read aloud some of the exemplary letters.

Question 34 Few number-line contexts are as important as this one. Yet we have found that many students cannot read the thermometer often used for taking body temperatures. Point out that the interval between two consecutive tick marks on such thermometers usually represents 0.2°, and explain how body temperatures are read and interpreted. Make certain all students understand how the answer to this question is found. **Teaching Aid 12** has several thermometers which you might use when discussing this topic.

Question 36 Sometimes students will want to argue that the repeating decimal .9999... does not equal 1. The misconception is usually based on some notion that these infinite repeating decimals do end somewhere "way out there to the right." Of course they don't, and the cartoon on the page presents the appropriate challenge. To help students understand this, you might ask, "If .9999... is smaller than 1, what number is between them?" Since there is no number between them, .9999... must be equal to 1. Another explanation is to take the decimal for $\frac{1}{3}$ and multiply it by 3. Since $3 \times \frac{1}{3} = 1$, and $3 \times \frac{1}{3} = 3 \times .3333... = .9999...$, the two expressions must be equal.

Question 38 Students using scientific calculators might need to be reminded that the last digit in the display might be rounded up. They should consider this when looking for a pattern.

27. Order $\frac{2}{9}$, $\frac{2}{11}$, $\frac{2}{7}$ from smallest to largest. $\frac{2}{11}, \frac{2}{9}, \frac{2}{7}$

28. Write a letter to a younger student explaining how to change a fraction into a decimal. Include in your explanation how to do this with and without a calculator. **Answers will vary.**

Review

29. a. Do this arithmetic on your calculator: 8.868×6.668. What does your calculator display? **Sample: 59.131824**

b. Round your answer to part **a** to the nearest thousandth. *(Lessons 1-4, 1-5)* **59.132**

30. Round 3,522,037, the population of Puerto Rico in 1990 according to the U.S. census, to the nearest hundred thousand. *(Lesson 1-4)* **3,500,000**

31. Round 9.8978675645 to the nearest ten-thousandth. *(Lesson 1-4)* **9.8979**

32. Find a number between 0.036 and 0.0359. *(Lesson 1-2)* **Sample: 0.03595**

33. Which is larger, 34.000791 or 34.0079? *(Lesson 1-2)* **34.0079**

34. What temperature is shown by this thermometer? *(Lesson 1-2)* **99.6°**

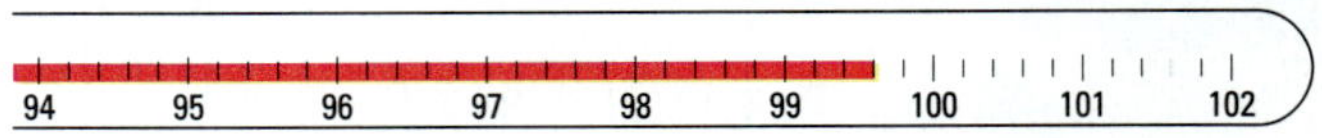

35. The Sanchez Dairy Farm sold 479 gallons of milk one day and 493 gallons the next. On the third day they sold twice as many gallons as on the previous two days. What was the total number of gallons sold on those three days? *(Previous course)* **2916 gallons**

36a) $0.\overline{1}$, $0.\overline{2}$, $0.\overline{3}$, $0.\overline{4}$, $0.\overline{5}$, $0.\overline{6}$, $0.\overline{7}$, $0.\overline{8}$

Exploration

36. a. Find the decimals for $\frac{1}{9}$, $\frac{2}{9}$, $\frac{3}{9}$, $\frac{4}{9}$, $\frac{5}{9}$, $\frac{6}{9}$, $\frac{7}{9}$, and $\frac{8}{9}$. **See above left.**

b. Based on the pattern you find, what fraction should equal $.\overline{9}$? $\frac{9}{9}$

c. Is the cartoon true? **Yes. These numbers are equal, so there are no numbers between them. $.\overline{9} = 1.0$**

37. a. Write down the decimals for $\frac{1}{2}$, $\frac{1}{3}$, $\frac{1}{4}$, $\frac{1}{5}$, and $\frac{1}{6}$. **0.5, $0.\overline{3}$, 0.25, 0.2, $0.1\overline{6}$**

b. Find the decimals for $\frac{1}{7}$, $\frac{1}{8}$, $\frac{1}{9}$, $\frac{1}{10}$, $\frac{1}{11}$, and $\frac{1}{12}$.

c. If you keep going, to what number are these decimals getting closer and closer? **0**

b) $0.\overline{142857}$, 0.125, $0.\overline{1}$, 0.1, $0.\overline{09}$, $0.08\overline{3}$

38. a. Explore the decimals for all simple fractions between 0 and 1 whose denominator is 7.

b. Use your results from part **a** to give the first twelve decimal places for each of these fractions.

a, b) $\frac{1}{7} = .\overline{142857} = .142857142857...$ $\quad \frac{4}{7} = .\overline{571428} = .571428571428...$

$\frac{2}{7} = .\overline{285714} = .285714285714...$ $\quad \frac{5}{7} = .\overline{714285} = .714285714285...$

$\frac{3}{7} = .\overline{428571} = .428571428571...$ $\quad \frac{6}{7} = .\overline{857142} = .857142857142...$

Setting Up Lesson 1-7

Previewing the Reading For a number of reasons, students should read Lesson 1-7 on their own as homework. First, Lesson 1-6 may require extended class time, so you may not have time for any introduction to Lesson 1-7. Second, the reading is short and closely related to the material in Lesson 1-6. Third, students have worked through six lessons learning how to read mathematics. They need to realize they are expected to be able to learn on their own when appropriate.

Homework Have students read and answer all the questions for Lesson 1-7. Note that a newspaper is needed for **Question 29.**

LESSON

1-7

Decimals for Mixed Numbers

What can you get for $2.75? *A hamburger, a tube of toothaste, a magazine, or 2 gallons of gas are examples of items that could each be purchased with $2.75 or less.*

The number $2\frac{3}{4}$ consists of a whole number and a fraction. It is called a **mixed number.** This mixed number is the sum of the whole number 2 and the fraction $\frac{3}{4}$. Only the plus sign is missing.

Graphing Mixed Numbers on a Number Line

Mixed numbers are common in measurement. The line segment below is three inches long and is divided into intervals each one inch long.

If each of these intervals is divided into two equal parts, the new intervals will be $\frac{1}{2}$ inch long.

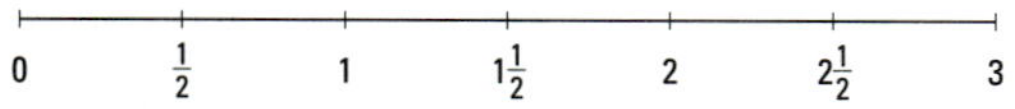

Dividing each half-inch interval into two equal parts creates intervals $\frac{1}{4}$ inch long.

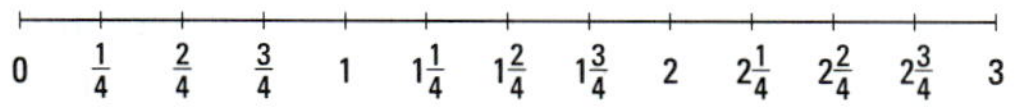

A line segment $2\frac{3}{4}$ inches long consists of 2 whole inches plus $\frac{3}{4}$ of an inch.

You can see that the segment is longer than 2 inches and shorter than 3 inches. This is because $2\frac{3}{4}$ is between 2 and 3.

Lesson 1-7

Objectives

B Order decimals and fractions.

F Convert mixed numbers to decimals.

M Graph and read numbers on a number line.

Resources

From the ***Teacher's Resource File***

- Lesson Master 1-7A or 1-7B
- Answer Master 1-7
- Teaching Aids
  - 2 Warm-up
  - 8 Number Line
- Activity Kit, Activity 2

Additional Resources

- Visuals for Teaching Aids 2, 8

Teaching Lesson 1-7

Warm-up

Sketch rectangles or circles and shade them so that the shaded region represents the number. Then write a decimal for each fraction.

1. $\frac{3}{4}$ 0.75 **2.** $\frac{2}{3}$ $0.\overline{6}$ **3.** $\frac{5}{8}$ 0.625

Ask for student volunteers to put their representations on the board. If students use only rectangles, ask for

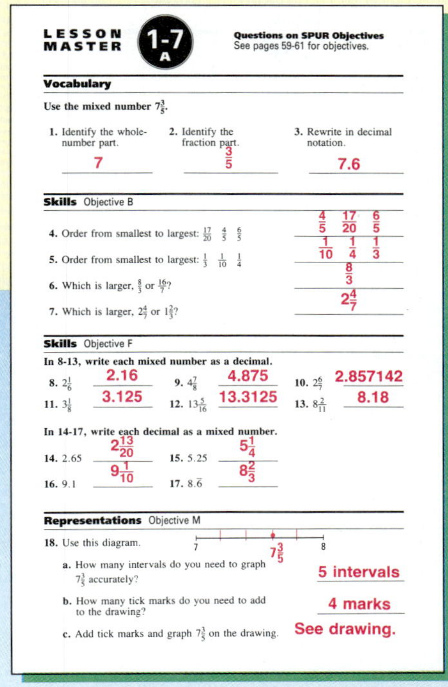

LESSON MASTER 1-7 A **Questions on SPUR Objectives** See pages 59-61 for objectives.

Vocabulary

Use the mixed number $7\frac{3}{5}$.

1. Identify the whole-number part. 7

2. Identify the fraction part. $\frac{3}{5}$

3. Rewrite in decimal notation. 7.6

Skills Objective B

4. Order from smallest to largest: $\frac{17}{20}$ $\frac{4}{5}$ $\frac{6}{5}$ — $\frac{4}{5}$ $\frac{17}{20}$ $\frac{6}{5}$

5. Order from smallest to largest: $\frac{1}{3}$ $\frac{1}{10}$ $\frac{1}{4}$ — $\frac{1}{10}$ $\frac{1}{4}$ $\frac{1}{3}$

6. Which is larger, $\frac{8}{3}$ or $\frac{16}{7}$? — $\frac{8}{3}$

7. Which is larger, $2\frac{4}{7}$ or $1\frac{2}{3}$? — $2\frac{4}{7}$

Skills Objective F

In 8-13, write each mixed number as a decimal.

8. $2\frac{1}{6}$ 2.16 **9.** $4\frac{7}{8}$ 4.875 **10.** $2\frac{6}{7}$ 2.857142

11. $3\frac{1}{8}$ 3.125 **12.** $13\frac{5}{16}$ 13.3125 **13.** $8\frac{2}{11}$ 8.18

In 14-17, write each decimal as a mixed number.

14. 2.65 $2\frac{13}{20}$ **15.** 5.25 $5\frac{1}{4}$

16. 9.1 $9\frac{1}{10}$ **17.** $8.\overline{6}$ $8\frac{2}{3}$

Representations Objective M

18. Use this diagram. (7, $7\frac{3}{5}$, 8)

a. How many intervals do you need to graph $7\frac{3}{5}$ accurately? 5 intervals

b. How many tick marks do you need to add to the drawing? 4 marks

c. Add tick marks and graph $7\frac{3}{5}$ on the drawing. See drawing.

Lesson 1-7 Overview

Broad Goals This is a rather easy lesson. The introduction of only one new idea—converting a mixed number to a decimal—allows time to review the many concepts from previous lessons.

Perspective The phrase "mixed number" is used inconsistently in our world. Both 3.5 and $3\frac{1}{2}$ have a whole-number part and a fraction part. We do not call the decimal 3.5 a mixed number, but we do call $3\frac{1}{2}$ a mixed number.

Changing Mixed Numbers to Decimals

On the previous page, we thought of $2\frac{3}{4}$ as $2 + \frac{3}{4}$. This suggests how the decimal for a mixed number can be found. First calculate the decimal for the simple fraction. Then add that decimal to the whole number.

Example

Express $2\frac{3}{4}$ in decimal notation.

Solution 1

Remember or calculate: $\frac{3}{4} = 0.75$.

Now add: $2\frac{3}{4} = 2 + \frac{3}{4} = 2 + 0.75 = 2.75$.

Solution 2

Use a scientific calculator. Key in 2 [+] 3 [÷] 4 [=]. On simpler calculators, the division must be done first, then the 2 must be added.

Display: [2.75]

Solution 3

Think money. You might write the following:

Fourths are quarters. Two and three-fourths is like two dollars and three quarters. Two dollars and three quarters is $2.75, which includes the correct decimal, 2.75.

QUESTIONS

Covering the Reading

1. Consider the mixed number $5\frac{3}{4}$.
   a. Between what two whole numbers is this number? **5 and 6**
   b. Identify the whole number part of this mixed number. **5**
   c. Rewrite this number in decimal notation. **5.75**
   d. Draw a line segment $5\frac{3}{4}$ inches long. **Check students' drawings.**

2. What is it about the mixed number of Question 1 that enables a person to think about it in terms of money? **Fourths are quarters, a term used in money.**

3. Consider the mixed number $4\frac{1}{3}$.
   a. What is the largest whole number less than $4\frac{1}{3}$? **4**
   b. Identify the fraction part of this number. $\frac{1}{3}$
   c. Write this number in decimal notation. $4.\overline{3}$
   d. Draw a number line 6 units long with intervals of 1 unit. Locate $4\frac{1}{3}$ on your number line.

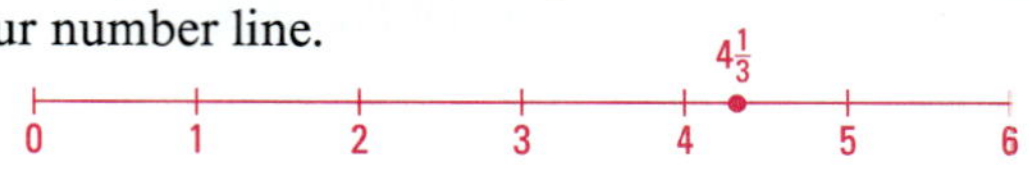

someone to represent at least one of the numbers using a circle and vice versa.

Notes on Reading

Begin class by drawing a number line on the board. Ask someone to locate $3\frac{1}{4}$ on the number line and explain how the point is found. Then go over the example in the lesson. It is important that students see many ways of writing mixed numbers as decimals.

If some students have nonscientific calculators, use the opportunity to discuss why these calculators display 1.25 for Solution 2 in the example. [It adds 2 and 3 first and then divides 5 by 4.] This discussion anticipates the work with order of operations in Chapter 4.

Additional Examples

1. Express $3\frac{7}{20}$ in decimal notation. **3.35**
2. Express $4\frac{5}{9}$ in decimal notation. $4.\overline{5}$

LESSON MASTER 1-7 B Questions on SPUR Objectives

Vocabulary

1. What do we call a number that consists of a whole number and a fraction? **mixed number**
2. Use the number $5\frac{7}{8}$.
   a. Identify the whole-number part of this number. **5**
   b. Identify the fraction part of this number. $\frac{7}{8}$
   c. Rewrite this number in decimal notation. **5.875**

Skills Objective B: Order decimals and fractions.

In 3 and 4, order from smallest to largest.

3. $2\frac{1}{5}$ $6\frac{1}{4}$ $3\frac{1}{6}$ — $2\frac{1}{5}$ $3\frac{1}{6}$ $6\frac{1}{4}$
4. $\frac{7}{20}$ $\frac{13}{10}$ $\frac{7}{10}$ — $\frac{7}{20}$ $\frac{7}{10}$ $\frac{13}{10}$

In 5 and 6, order from largest to smallest.

5. $8\frac{1}{3}$ $8\frac{2}{3}$ $4\frac{1}{3}$ — $8\frac{2}{3}$ $8\frac{1}{3}$ $4\frac{1}{3}$
6. $\frac{9}{8}$ $\frac{7}{8}$ $\frac{7}{10}$ — $\frac{9}{8}$ $\frac{7}{8}$ $\frac{7}{10}$
7. Which is larger, $2\frac{4}{5}$ or $2\frac{2}{3}$? $2\frac{4}{5}$
8. Which is larger, $7\frac{11}{12}$ or $7\frac{3}{4}$? $7\frac{11}{12}$
9. Which is smaller, $\frac{10}{7}$ or $\frac{13}{10}$? $\frac{13}{10}$
10. Which is smaller, $1\frac{3}{8}$ or $1\frac{1}{3}$? $1\frac{1}{3}$

Optional Activities

Activity 1 You can use *Activity Kit, Activity 2,* as an introduction to or as a follow-up for Lesson 1-7. In this activity, students time each other performing several tasks. Then they write their times as mixed numbers and decimals, and graph the decimals on a number line.

Activity 2 A Human Number Line At the beginning of the class, distribute cards with the digits 0 to 9 on them to 10 students. Have these students form a human number line at the front of the room. To the rest of the students, give cards with different non-whole numbers from 0 to 9 on them. The cards should contain assorted positive simple fractions, mixed numbers, and decimals. The task is for students to place themselves in the appropriate position of their number on the number line.

In 4–7, change the mixed number to a decimal. (The fraction parts are ones you should know, so try to do these without a calculator.)

4. $2\frac{1}{2}$ **2.5** **5.** $7\frac{2}{5}$ **7.4** **6.** $1\frac{3}{10}$ **1.3** **7.** $17\frac{5}{6}$ **$17.8\overline{3}$**

In 8–11, change the mixed number to a decimal.

8. $12\frac{5}{16}$ **12.3125** **9.** $4\frac{1}{11}$ **$4.\overline{09}$** **10.** $20\frac{8}{15}$ **$20.5\overline{3}$** **11.** $5\frac{7}{8}$ **5.875**

Applying the Mathematics

12. Most stock prices are measured in eighths. What is each value in dollars and cents?

a. A stock's price goes up $4\frac{1}{4}$ dollars a share. **\$4.25**

b. A stock's price goes up $1\frac{3}{8}$ dollars a share. **\$1.375**

13. Order from the smallest to the largest: $2\frac{3}{5}$ $5\frac{2}{3}$ $3\frac{2}{5}$. **$2\frac{3}{5}$, $3\frac{2}{5}$, $5\frac{2}{3}$**

14. Mouse A is $2\frac{3}{10}$ inches long. Mouse B is $2\frac{1}{4}$ inches long. Which mouse is longer? **Mouse A**

15. Round $12\frac{8}{15}$ to the nearest thousandth. **12.533**

16. The Preakness, a famous horse race, is $1\frac{3}{16}$ miles long. Convert this length to a length in decimals. **1.1875 miles**

17. A shelf is measured to be $35\frac{11}{32}$ inches long. Is this shorter or longer than $35\frac{1}{3}$ inches? **longer**

18. Trace this segment onto your paper. Graph each of the indicated numbers.

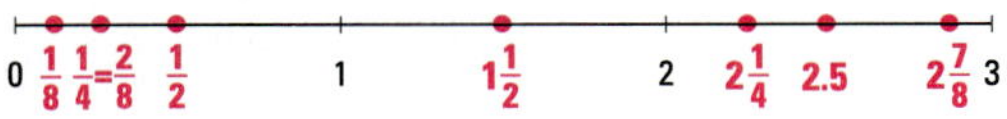

a. $\frac{1}{2}$ **b.** $\frac{1}{4}$ **c.** $\frac{1}{8}$ **d.** $\frac{2}{8}$

e. $1\frac{1}{2}$ **f.** $2\frac{1}{4}$ **g.** $2\frac{7}{8}$ **h.** 2.5

19. Draw a line segment 3.375 inches long. (Hint: What fraction equals 0.375?) **Check students' drawings for $3\frac{3}{8}''$ segment.**

Review

20. In parts **a–h**, give the decimal for each number. *(Lesson 1-6)*

a. $\frac{1}{8}$ **0.125** **b.** $\frac{2}{8}$ **0.25** **c.** $\frac{3}{8}$ **0.375** **d.** $\frac{4}{8}$ **0.5**

e. $\frac{5}{8}$ **0.625** **f.** $\frac{6}{8}$ **0.75** **g.** $\frac{7}{8}$ **0.875** **h.** $\frac{8}{8}$ **1**

i. Explain how the answer to part **a** enables a person to find the answers to all the other parts.

20i) The decimal for any of the other fractions can be arrived at by multiplying the numerator of that fraction by .125.

Notes on Questions

Question 5 Error Alert Some students may write 7.25 as the decimal equivalent for $7\frac{2}{5}$. Review the common fraction-decimal equivalents on page 34 and explain that $7\frac{2}{5} = 7 + \frac{2}{5} = 7 + \frac{4}{10} = 7 + .4 = 7.4$.

Question 9 The answer requires interpretation of a calculator display. Depending on the number of decimal places shown, a calculator may round the answer, as in 4.0909091, or truncate it, as in 4.0909090. Students should realize this is the best calculators with eight-digit displays can do for $4.\overline{09}$.

Question 12b The answer, \$1.375, would usually not be rounded because most people buy shares in multiples of 100. The value of a person's holding is the product of the number of shares and the value of each share. So a person who sold 1000 shares of this stock at this price would get (before subtracting broker's commissions) \$1375. Many people think that fractions of pennies are ignored, but this is often not the case in business. Even fractions of a penny can add to significant amounts. In this case, the difference is \$5.00.

▸ **LESSON MASTER 1-7 B** *page 2*

Skills Objective F: Convert simple fractions and mixed numbers to decimals.

In 11-18, write each mixed number as a decimal.

11. $6\frac{7}{10}$	**6.7**	12. $8\frac{1}{16}$	**8.0625**
13. $1\frac{4}{7}$	**1.571428**	14. $5\frac{8}{9}$	**$5.\overline{8}$**
15. $10\frac{3}{4}$	**10.75**	16. $4\frac{2}{3}$	**$4.\overline{6}$**
17. $12\frac{8}{15}$	**$12.5\overline{3}$**	18. $3\frac{7}{8}$	**3.875**

In 19-24, write each decimal as a mixed number.

19. 9.7	**$9\frac{7}{10}$**	20. 4.75	**$4\frac{3}{4}$**
21. 7.3	**$7\frac{3}{10}$**	22. 12.5	**$12\frac{1}{2}$**
23. 22.6	**$22\frac{3}{5}$**	24. 11.625	**$11\frac{5}{8}$**

Representations Objective M: Graph and read numbers on a number line.

In 25-27, give the mixed number that is graphed at each point.

25. A **$1\frac{1}{5}$** 26. B **$1\frac{3}{5}$** 27. C **$2\frac{4}{5}$**

28. Use this diagram.

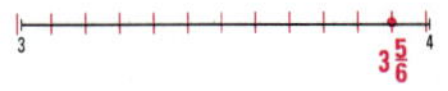

a. How many intervals do you need to graph $3\frac{5}{6}$ accurately? **6 intervals**

b. How many tick marks do you need to add to the drawing? **5 tick marks**

c. Add tick marks and graph $3\frac{5}{6}$ on the drawing. **See graph.**

Adapting to Individual Needs

English Language Development

Question 11 deals with the stock exchange. The word *stock* has several meanings and some students may not understand its use in this context. Explain that the ownership in a company is often divided into parts, or *shares of stock*. Shares of stock are bought and sold in stock exchanges. Stock prices are usually given as fractions or mixed numbers. For example, $2\frac{3}{8}$ means \$2.375. It might also be thought of as "2 dollars and $37\frac{1}{2}$ cents." You might ask students to tell the price of a stock selling at $52\frac{1}{8}$ [\$52.125 or 52 dollars and $12\frac{1}{2}$ cents] and of a stock selling at $16\frac{1}{2}$ [\$16.50].

Notes on Questions

Question 29 Cooperative Learning You might want to give a stock-market page from a newspaper to every group of 4 or 5 students. Have students discuss and try out estimation strategies. Then have a student from each group explain how the group arrived at its estimate.

Save the stock market pages for **Question 35** *in Lesson 1-8.*

✎ **Question 30 Writing** Ask some students to read their answers aloud. Then poll the class asking how many preferred each solution. Write the fraction of students making each choice.

Follow-up for Lesson 1-7

Practice

For more questions on SPUR objectives, use **Lesson Master 1-7A** (shown on page 37) or **Lesson Master 1-7B** (shown on pages 38–39).

Assessment

Group Assessment Give each group of three or four students the number line on **Teaching Aid 8** and a list of fractions, mixed numbers, and decimals to locate on the line. Tell students to write the fractions and mixed numbers below the line and the decimals above the line. [Statements made by individual students while completing the number line reveal their grasp of the concept.]

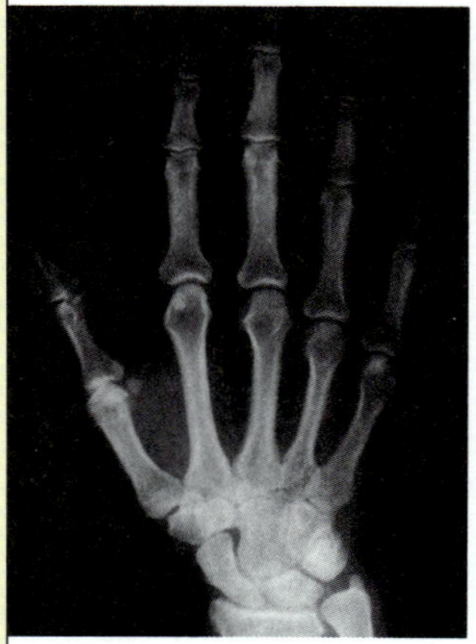

What's inside?
Discovered by Wilhelm Roentgen in 1895, X-rays play a vital role in determining the structure of matter and in treating diseases such as cancer.

21. a. Give an example of a simple fraction. Sample: $\frac{11}{12}$
b. Write a fraction that is not a simple fraction. *(Lesson 1-6)* Sample: $\frac{1.4}{7}$

22. What digit is in the eleventh decimal place of $7.\overline{8142}$? *(Lesson 1-6)* 4

23. Estimate 16.432893542050 + 83.5633344441 to the nearest whole number. *(Lesson 1-4)* 100

24. Find a number between 2 and 2.1. *(Lesson 1-2)* Sample: 2.07

25. *True or false.* 5 = 5.0 *(Lesson 1-2)* True

26. In decimal notation, write the whole number that is one less than one million. *(Lesson 1-1)* 999,999

27. Consider the following sentences. Each human hand has 27 small bones. Together the hands have over $\frac{1}{4}$ of the 206 bones in the whole body.
a. Name the counts. 27 and 206
b. Name the counting units. *(Lesson 1-1)* small bones and bones

28. Mark has four \$20 bills to buy school clothes. He bought a shirt for \$16.97, a pair of jeans for \$21.63, and a pair of sneakers for \$33.78. How much change should Mark receive when he pays for the clothes? *(Previous course)* \$7.62

Exploration

29. a. Examine a stock market page from a daily newspaper. Estimate how many mixed numbers there are on the page.
b. Explain how you found your estimate in part **a.**
29 a,b) Answers will vary.

30. Refer to the Example in this lesson. Write a brief explanation telling why you think three solutions are given instead of just one. Which solution do you prefer for solving the problem? Why is this your preference? Answers will vary.

Adapting to Individual Needs

Extra Help
Some students might benefit from **using physical models** to understand the meaning of mixed numbers and to help them write mixed numbers as decimals. For example:

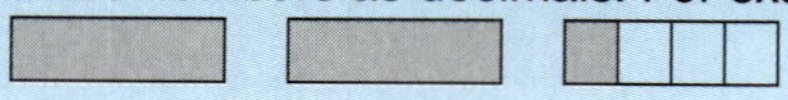

1 + 1 + $\frac{1}{4}$ = $2\frac{1}{4}$

1 + 1 + .25 = 2.25

Give students other mixed numbers and have them **work in pairs** to illustrate each number with fraction models.

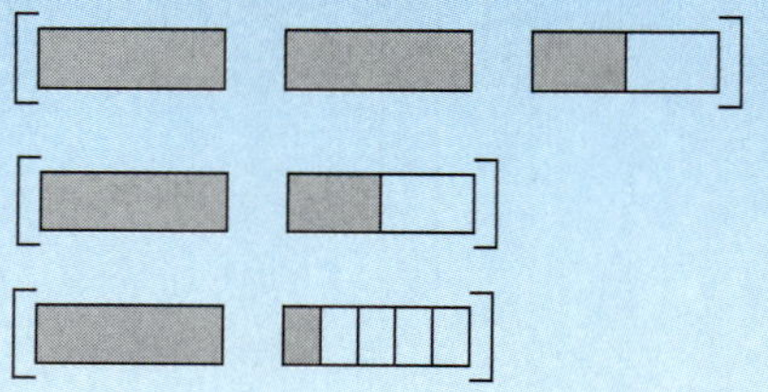

1. $2\frac{1}{2}$
2. 1.5
3. $1\frac{1}{5}$

Setting Up Lesson 1-8

Previewing the Reading Call attention to the structure of the chart on page 42 so that students realize they must read it across rather than down. Note that an almanac and newspaper stock quotations are required for **Questions 34 and 35** on page 45.

LESSON

1-8

Negative Numbers

Is the price right? *In this store, a shopper is considering unusual clothing and decorative items imported from all over the world. The amount the customer pays for these items must be greater than the store owner's cost in order for the store to avoid losses and remain in business.*

Situations with Negative Numbers

On every item a store sells, the store can make money, lose money, or break even. Here are some of the possibilities.

Using words and numbers	Using numbers only
make \$3	3
make \$2	2
make \$1	1
make \$0.50	.5
break even	0
lose \$1	-1
lose \$1.50	-1.5
lose \$2	-2
lose \$3	-3

The numbers along the number line describe the situation without using words. Higher numbers on the line are larger and mean more profits. The - (negative) sign stands for *opposite of.* The opposite of making \$1.50 is losing \$1.50. Similarly, the opposite of 1.50 is -1.50, and vice versa. The numbers with the - sign are called **negative numbers.**

Lesson 1-8

Objectives

C Give a number that is between two negative numbers.
D Round negative numbers up or down or to the nearest value of a decimal place.
E Enter negative numbers on a calculator.
F Convert negative mixed numbers to decimals.
L Correctly interpret situations with two directions as positive, negative, or corresponding to zero.
M Graph and read negative numbers on a number line.

Resources

From the ***Teacher's Resource File***
- Lesson Masters 1-8A or 1-8B
- Answer Master 1-8
- Assessment Sourcebook: Quiz for Lessons 1-5 through 1-8
- Teaching Aids
  2 Warm-up
  8 Number Line

Additional Resources
- Visuals for Teaching Aids 2, 8

Teaching Lesson 1-8

Warm-up

Tell which number is larger.

1. .0078 or .011 **.011**
2. $.\overline{42}$ or $.\overline{3}$ **$.\overline{42}$**
3. 1.05 or 1.053 **1.053**
4. $\frac{2}{3}$ or $\frac{7}{8}$ **$\frac{7}{8}$**
5. $2\frac{3}{8}$ or $2\frac{3}{16}$ **$2\frac{3}{8}$**
6. $\frac{18}{5}$ or $\frac{37}{10}$ **$\frac{37}{10}$**

For each problem, tell which number would be located to the left of the other on a number line (or below the other on a vertical number line). [the smaller number]

Lesson 1-8 Overview

Broad Goals The goal of this lesson is to give so many examples of negative numbers that students will realize they naturally arise from many situations. It is hoped that students will learn to take advantage of their intuition about such numbers.

Perspective The number line provides a wonderful representation for negative numbers and should help students visualize how to order them.

Notes on Reading

❶ Ask students to give additional real-world examples of using opposites. [Sample answers: a battery, a magnet, a compass, football gains and losses, above and below par in golf, and stock-market gains and losses]

❷ Emphasize the best ways of reading -3 ("negative three" or "the opposite of three"). Students often say "minus 3" because that is commonly used outside math class, even though it is misleading and can present trouble when they get to algebra.

❸ **Error Alert** When studying the number line, some students might think that, for example, -5 is larger than -4. Have these students think of colder temperatures, bigger losses of money, or lagging behind others in a timed race. You might ask students to draw and label a picture to represent each situation.

The graphs in this lesson show smaller numbers to the left or down. You might use **Teaching Aid 8** for graphing these numbers.

Most people know negative numbers from temperatures. But they are found in many other situations. On TV bowling programs, -12 means "behind by twelve pins." The symbol +12, called **positive** 12, means "ahead by twelve pins." The numbers 12 and +12 are identical. Since it is shorter and simpler to leave off the + (positive) sign, positive 12 is usually written as 12.

Negative numbers can be used when a situation has two opposite directions. Either direction may be picked as positive. The other is then negative. Zero stands for the starting point. The table below gives some situations that often use negative numbers.

❶

Situation	Negative	Zero	Positive
savings account	withdrawal	no change	deposit
time	before	now	after
games	behind	even	ahead
business	loss	break even	profit
elevation	below sea level	sea level	above sea level

Does anything live in the Dead Sea? *Brine shrimp and a few plant species are able to live in the Dead Sea, which is nine times as salty as the ocean. The salty nature of the Dead Sea increases the density of the water. Because of this density, people do not sink.*

For instance, the shore of the Dead Sea in Israel, the lowest land on Earth, is 396 meters below sea level. This can be represented by -396 meters.

There are three common ways in which the - sign for negatives is said out loud.

❷

write	say	
-3	negative 3	correct
-3	opposite of 3	correct
-3	minus 3	very commonly used, but can be confusing since there is no subtraction here

Example 1

A space shuttle is to be launched. Represent each of these times (in seconds) by positive or negative numbers.

a. 4.3 seconds before the launch
b. 1 minute after the launch
c. the time of the launch

Solution

a. Since the time is *before* the launch, it is negative.
The time is -4.3 seconds.
b. The time is *after* the launch, so it is positive. Since 1 minute = 60 seconds, The time is 60 seconds.
c. The time of the launch is represented by 0 seconds.

Optional Activities

Activity 1 Geography Connection After students complete Lesson 1-8, you might have them draw vertical number lines that show the highest point on Earth (Mt. Everest, which is about 29,000 feet above sea level), and the lowest point (Marianas Trench, which is about 36,200 feet below sea level), along with the elevations of some other locations. Some students might like to **work in groups** and make a poster showing what they found.

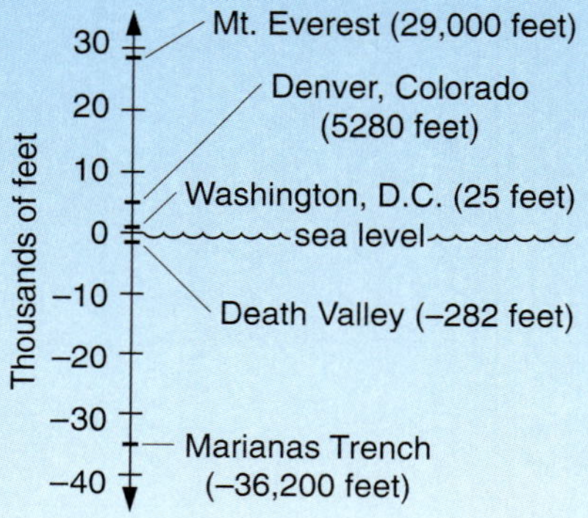

Activity 2 Extend the Human Number Line After students finish the lesson, you might modify the human number line from *Optional Activities* on page 38 to include integers from -4 to 4. Give students positive and negative simple fractions, mixed numbers, and decimals for the activity.

Example 2

The price of a share of stock went down $1\frac{7}{8}$ dollars.

a. How will this be written on the stock market pages of a newspaper?
b. Write the answer to part **a** as a decimal.
c. Round the answer to part **b** to the nearest penny.

Solution

a. Since the price went down, the change will be written as $-1\frac{7}{8}$. (Newspapers omit the dollar sign.)
b. $\frac{7}{8} = 0.875$, so $-1\frac{7}{8} = -1.875$.
c. -1.875 is halfway between -1.88 and -1.87. The answer is: either -\$1.88 or -\$1.87.

Graphing Negative Numbers on a Number Line

On a horizontal number line, negative numbers are almost always placed at the left. The numbers identified on the number line drawn below are the **integers.** The **positive integers** are the numbers 1, 2, 3, ... The **negative integers** are -1, -2, -3, ... Zero is an integer but is neither positive nor negative. All numbers to the right of 0 are **positive numbers.** All numbers to the left of 0 are **negative numbers.**

3
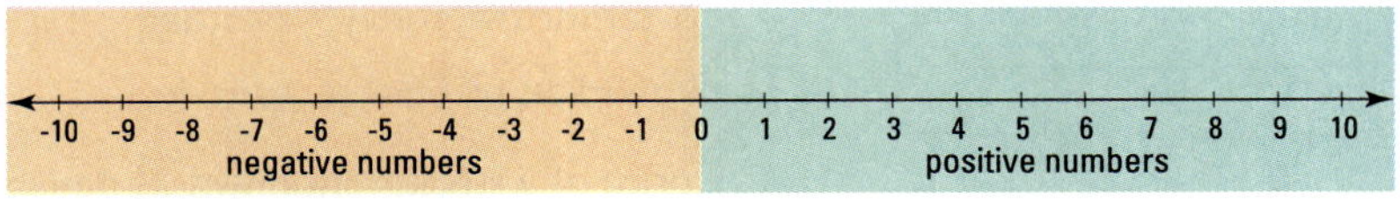

Example 3

Graph 1.3 and -1.3.

Solution

Use a number line from -2 to 2. To graph 1.3, split the interval from 1 to 2 into tenths. To graph -1.3, split the interval from -2 to -1 into tenths. Then graph each number by placing a dot on the appropriate tick mark.

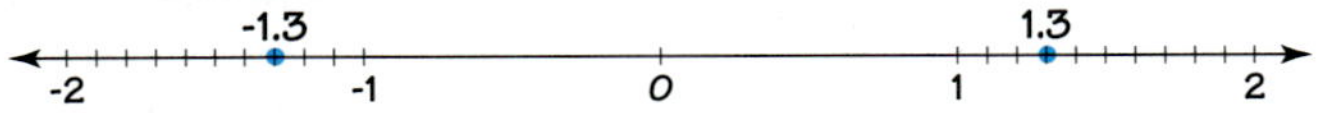

Entering Negative Numbers into a Calculator

All scientific calculators have a way to enter negative numbers. This is done by the opposite key [+/−] or [±] or [(−)]. For example, 7 [±] keys in -7 on some calculators.

Additional Examples

1. In golf, a score used as a standard is called *par.* Name an integer that represents each of the following golf scores.
   - **a.** 6 strokes below par -6
   - **b.** three over par 3
   - **c.** even with par 0
2. The elevation of some parts of New Orleans are $2\frac{3}{4}$ feet below sea level.
   - **a.** Write this number to show that the elevation is below sea level. $-2\frac{3}{4}$
   - **b.** Write this number as a decimal. -2.75
   - **c.** Round this number to the nearest foot. -3
3. Graph 0.7 and -0.7 on the same number line.

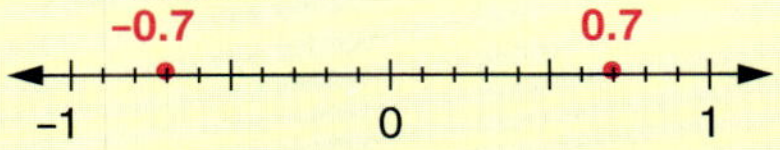

4. Write a number to represent the depth of the Marianas Trench, the deepest part of the Pacific Ocean. It is about 36,200 feet below sea level. -36,200

Adapting to Individual Needs

English Language Development
Review the meaning of the words below by encouraging students to give examples of each in context from their own experiences. Correct any misconceptions they may have and clarify the meanings of the words with additional examples as needed.

1. Above	2. Below
3. Loss	4. Gain
5. Decrease	6. Increase
7. Withdrawal	8. Deposit

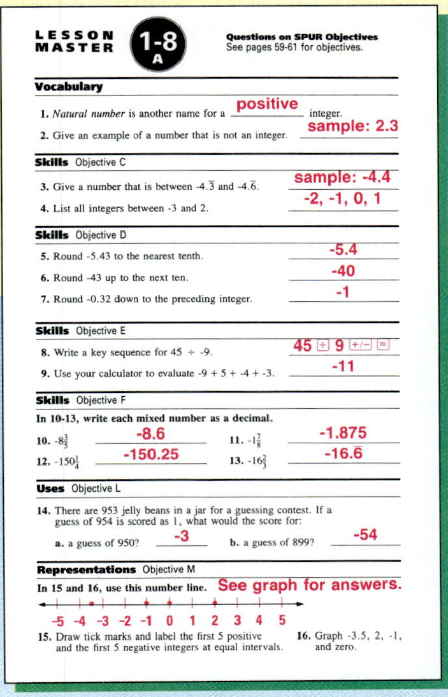
LESSON MASTER 1-8 A Questions on SPUR Objectives
See pages 59-61 for objectives.

Vocabulary

1. *Natural number* is another name for a positive integer.
2. Give an example of a number that is not an integer. sample: 2.3

Skills Objective C

3. Give a number that is between $-4.\overline{3}$ and $-4.\overline{6}$. sample: -4.4
4. List all integers between -3 and 2. -2, -1, 0, 1

Skills Objective D

5. Round -5.43 to the nearest tenth. -5.4
6. Round -43 up to the next ten. -40
7. Round -0.32 down to the preceding integer. -1

Skills Objective E

8. Write a key sequence for 45 ÷ -9. 45 [÷] 9 [+/−] [=]
9. Use your calculator to evaluate -9 + 5 + -4 + -3. -11

Skills Objective F

In 10-13, write each mixed number as a decimal.

10. $-8\frac{3}{5}$ -8.6
11. $-1\frac{7}{8}$ -1.875
12. $-150\frac{1}{4}$ -150.25
13. $-16\frac{2}{3}$ $-16.\overline{6}$

Uses Objective L

14. There are 953 jelly beans in a jar for a guessing contest. If a guess of 954 is scored as 1, what would the score for:
    a. a guess of 950? -3
    b. a guess of 899? -54

Representations Objective M

In 15 and 16, use this number line. See graph for answers.

-5 -4 -3 -2 -1 0 1 2 3 4 5

15. Draw tick marks and label the first 5 positive and the first 5 negative integers at equal intervals.
16. Graph -3.5, 2, -1, and zero.

Notes on Questions

Questions 5–6 Error Alert Some students think graphing a point means simply labeling the tick marks on a number line. Make sure these students understand that graphing a number on a number line means placing a dot on the line at the place corresponding to the number.

Questions 12–14 Emphasize that an integer is either a whole number or its opposite, and calling it an integer does not depend on how the number is written. For example, $\frac{6.2}{3.1}$ is an integer. Tell students that these definitions will be used throughout the text.

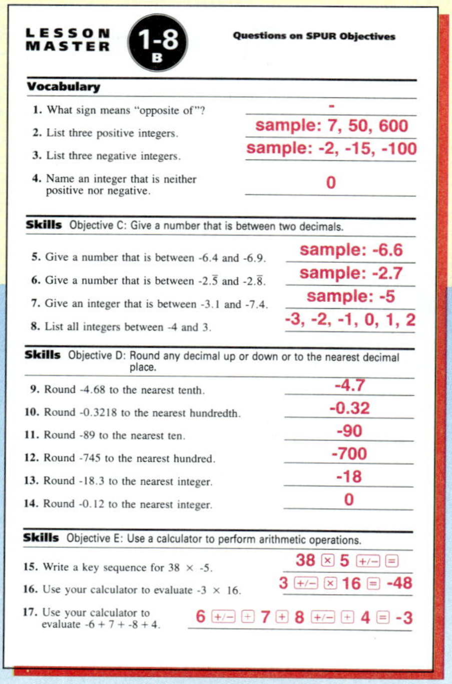

LESSON MASTER 1-8 B

Questions on SPUR Objectives

Vocabulary

1. What sign means "opposite of"? -
2. List three positive integers. sample: 7, 50, 600
3. List three negative integers. sample: -2, -15, -100
4. Name an integer that is neither positive nor negative. 0

Skills Objective C: Give a number that is between two decimals.

5. Give a number that is between -6.4 and -6.9. sample: -6.6
6. Give a number that is between -2.$\bar{5}$ and -2.$\bar{8}$. sample: -2.7
7. Give an integer that is between -3.1 and -7.4. sample: -5
8. List all integers between -4 and 3. -3, -2, -1, 0, 1, 2

Skills Objective D: Round any decimal up or down or to the nearest decimal place.

9. Round -4.68 to the nearest tenth. -4.7
10. Round -0.3218 to the nearest hundredth. -0.32
11. Round -89 to the nearest ten. -90
12. Round -745 to the nearest hundred. -700
13. Round -18.3 to the nearest integer. -18
14. Round -0.12 to the nearest integer. 0

Skills Objective E: Use a calculator to perform arithmetic operations.

15. Write a key sequence for 38 × -5. 38 [×] 5 [+/-] [=]
16. Use your calculator to evaluate -3 × 16. 3 [+/-] [×] 16 [=] -48
17. Use your calculator to evaluate -6 + 7 + -8 + 4. 6 [+/-] [+] 7 [+] 8 [+/-] [+] 4 [=] -3

Pins to spare. *For a spare, you get 10 pins plus the number of pins knocked down by the first ball of your next turn. For a strike, you get 10 pins plus the pins from your next 2 balls. In each case, the total number of pins is added in the frame where the spare or strike occurred.*

QUESTIONS

Covering the Reading

1. Translate -4 into English words in two different ways. **negative 4, opposite of 4**
2. Next to a bowler's name on TV is the number -8. Is the bowler ahead or behind? **behind**
3. On a horizontal number line, negative numbers are usually to the _?_ of positive numbers. **left**
4. On a vertical number line, negative numbers are usually _?_ positive numbers. **below**
5. Graph -7, $-3\frac{1}{2}$, $3\frac{1}{2}$, 0, and 7 on the same horizontal number line. **See below.**
6. Graph a profit of \$4, a loss of \$2.10, breaking even, and a profit of \$10 on a vertical number line. **See page 45.**
7. Write a key sequence for entering -3.5 on a calculator. **3.5 [±]**

In 8–10, three words or phrases relating to a situation are given. Which would usually be considered positive? which negative? which zero?

8. Football: losing yardage, gaining yardage, no gain **negative, positive, zero**
9. Time: tomorrow, today, yesterday **positive, zero, negative**
10. Stock market: no change, gain, loss **zero, positive, negative**
11. The price of a stock went down $2\frac{1}{8}$ dollars a share.
    a. How will this be written on the stock market pages of a newspaper?
    b. Write the answer to part **a** as a decimal. **-2.125**
    c. Round the answer to part **b** to the nearest penny. **either -\$2.12 or -\$2.13**
12. *Multiple choice.* Which of the following numbers is not an integer?
    (a) 5 (b) 0 (c) -5 (d) .5 **(d)**
13. Give an example of an integer that is neither positive nor negative. **0**
14. Give an example of a negative number that is not an integer. **Sample: -2.5**

Applying the Mathematics

15. Suppose time is measured in days and 0 stands for today.
    a. What number stands for yesterday? **-1**
    b. What number stands for tomorrow? **1**
    c. What number stands for the day before yesterday? **-2**
    d. What number stands for the day after tomorrow? **2**

5)
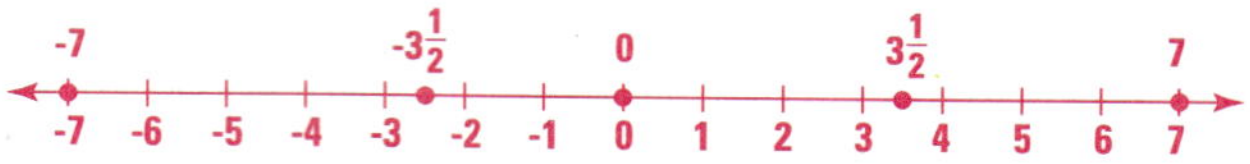

Adapting to Individual Needs

Extra Help

Draw a number line on the board or use **Teaching Aid 8.** Label the number line as shown at the right. Identify the positive and negative numbers and their opposites. Point out that 0 is an integer that is neither positive nor negative and that 0 has no opposite.

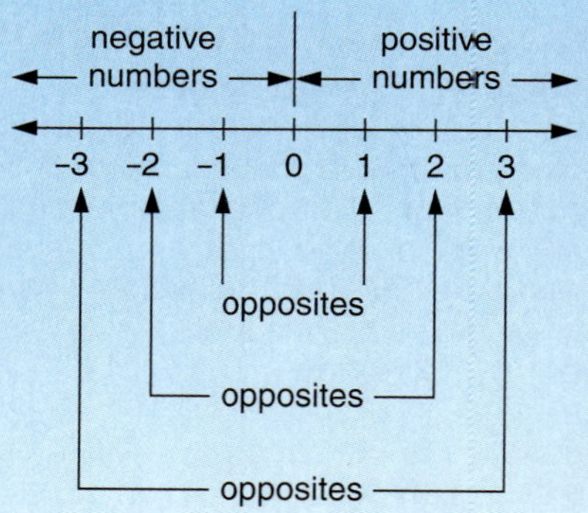

6)

In 16–19, use the number line drawn here. Which letter, if any, corresponds to the given number?

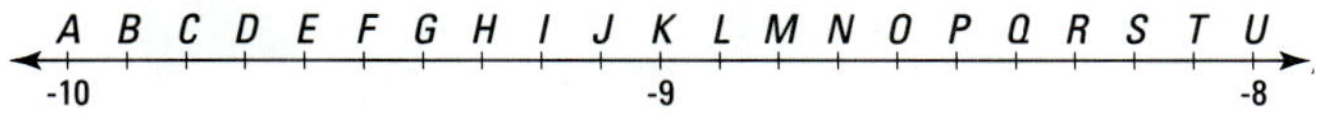

16. -9.1 J **17.** -8.4 Q **18.** -9.0 K **19.** -10.1 none

20. Pick the two numbers that are equal: (-43.3) -43.03 (-43.30) 43.3

21. Which of -1, 0, $\frac{1}{2}$, $\frac{2}{2}$, and $\frac{3}{2}$ are not positive integers? -1, 0, $\frac{1}{2}$, $\frac{3}{2}$

In 22–24, round to the nearest integer.

22. -1.75 -2 **23.** $-\frac{3}{5}$ -1 **24.** -0.4273 0

In 25–27, round to the nearest tenth.

25. -60.52 -60.5 **26.** -43.06 -43.1 **27.** $-9\frac{1}{3}$ -9.3

Review

28. Write each number as a decimal. *(Lessons 1-6, 1-7)*
a. $8\frac{3}{4}$ 8.75 **b.** $-\frac{2}{3}$ $-.\overline{6}$ **c.** $5\frac{3}{5}$ 5.6 **d.** $\frac{5}{16}$ .3125

29)

6	+	3
6.	6.	3.
×	4	÷
3.	4.	12.
2	=	
2.	12.	

29. Write the key sequence and the display after each calculator entry for 6 + 3 × 4 ÷ 2. *(Lesson 1-5)* See left.

30. Round $28.47
a. up to the next dollar. $29 **b.** down to the preceding dollar. $28
c. to the nearest dollar. *(Lessons 1-3, 1-4)* $28

31. Suppose the points are equally spaced on the number line drawn here. If *E* is 1 and *L* is 2, what number corresponds to *C*? *(Lesson 1-2)*
1.2 or $1\frac{1}{5}$

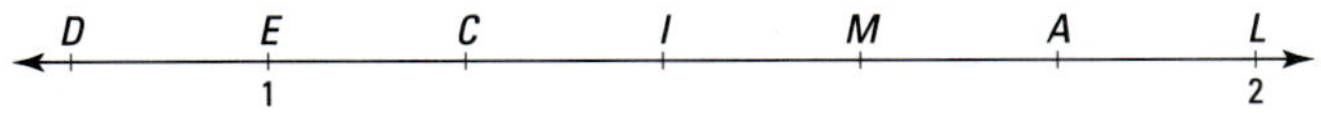

32. Order from smallest to largest: 5.67 5.067 5.607 5.60 *(Lesson 1-2)*
5.067, 5.60, 5.607, 5.67

33. Write as a decimal: four hundred sixty-two thousand and one hundredth. *(Lesson 1-2)* 462,000.01

Exploration

34. Use an almanac to find the place in the United States with the lowest elevation. What number represents this elevation? Death Valley, about -282 ft or about -86 m

35. Examine a page of a newspaper that has prices of stocks. Copy or cut out some rows with negative numbers. Answers will vary.

36. Find an example of negative numbers that is not given in this lesson.
Samples: east: positive, west: negative, clockwise: negative, counterclockwise: positive

Follow-up for Lesson 1-8

Practice

For more questions on SPUR objectives, use **Lesson Master 1-8A** (shown on page 43) or **Lesson Master 1-8B** (shown on pages 44–45).

Assessment

Quiz A quiz covering Lessons 1-5 through 1-8 is provided in the *Assessment Sourcebook.*

Group Assessment Write questions that correspond to the objectives of this lesson and prepare 4 to 6 copies to give to every group of 4 to 6 students. After the groups discuss the answers to the questions, have them write the answers. [Written work can verify your observation of the discussion group.]

Extension

Students might enjoy picking a stock listed in the newspaper and keeping track of it for a week. They should record the value of the stock at the close of each day along with the daily change. Some students might also want to graph the results.

Project Update Project 1, *Numbers in the Newspaper,* on page 55, relates to the content of this lesson.

▸ **LESSON MASTER 1-8 B** *page 2*

Skills Objective F: Convert simple fractions and mixed numbers to decimals.

In 18-25, write each mixed number as a decimal.

18. $-4\frac{1}{2}$ -4.5 **19.** $-37\frac{3}{4}$ -37.75
20. $-6\frac{7}{10}$ -6.7 **21.** $-1\frac{3}{8}$ -1.375
22. $-\frac{4}{5}$ -.8 **23.** $-19\frac{1}{3}$ $-19.\overline{3}$
24. $-522\frac{1}{4}$ -522.25 **25.** $-73\frac{5}{6}$ $-73.8\overline{3}$

Skills Objective L: Correctly interpret situations with two directions as positive, negative, or corresponding to zero.

26. If 10 represents climbing up ten feet, what number represents climbing down ten feet? -10

27. If 6 represents a gain of six pounds, what number represents a loss of four pounds? -4

28. If -17 represents a loss of seventeen dollars, what number represents a profit of eleven dollars? 11

29. If the flood stage of the Golden Berry River is 18 feet, and this height is called 0, what number represents
a. 16 feet? -2 **b.** 23 feet? 5
c. 19 feet? 1 **d.** 12 feet? -6

30. If zero represents today, and time is measured in days, what number stands
a. for yesterday? -1 **b.** for 6 days from today? 6

Representations Objective M: Graph and read numbers on a number line.

In 31 and 32, use this number line.

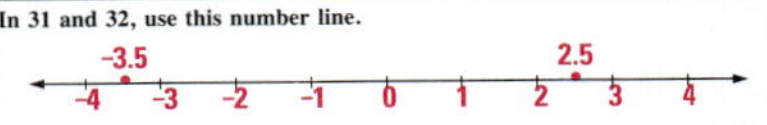

31. Draw tick marks and label the first four positive and the first four negative integers at equal intervals. See graph.

32. Graph 2.5, 0, -1, and -3.5. See graph.

Adapting to Individual Needs

Challenge
Many graphs in newspapers and magazines show values below a "zero" point. Suggest that students look for such graphs and **work in pairs** to analyze them. They might paste each graph on a sheet of paper and write a paragraph defining the zero point and explaining what the graph shows.

Lesson 1-9

Objectives

B Order positive and negative numbers.

H Use the < and > symbols correctly between numbers.

Resources

From the ***Teacher's Resource File***

- Lesson Masters 1-9A or 1-9B
- Answer Master 1-9
- Teaching Aids
  3 Warm-up
  8 Number Line
  11 Circle Models
  12 Thermometers
- Activity Kit, Activity 3
- Technology Sourcebook
  Computer Master 1
  Calculator Master 2

Additional Resources

- Visuals for Teaching Aids 3, 8, 11, 12
- Spreadsheet Workshop

Teaching Lesson 1-9

Warm-up

Find the number.

1. What number am I?
   Clue 1: I am greater than −4.
   Clue 2: I am less than −2.
   Clue 3: I am an integer. **−3**
2. What number am I?
   Clue 1: I am between 100 and 999.
   Clue 2: I am divisible by 8.
   Clue 3: The sum of my digits is 15.
   Clue 4: The product of my ones and tens digits is between 1 and 10.
   Clue 5: No two of my digits are the same. **816**

LESSON 1-9 Comparing Numbers

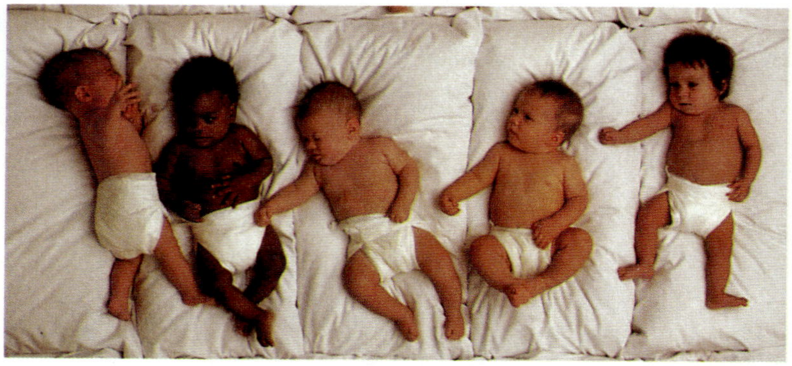

Comparing Counts

Counts are frequently compared. For instance, in 1990 there were about 4,179,000 births in the United States. In 1991 there were about 4,111,000 births. To indicate that there were fewer births in 1991 we write

$$4{,}111{,}000 < 4{,}179{,}000.$$

The symbol < means **is less than.** The symbol > means **is greater than,** so we could also write

$$4{,}179{,}000 > 4{,}111{,}000.$$

Comparison of populations is useful in knowing whether more schools or hospitals should be built, or how many people could buy a particular item or watch a television program.

The symbols < and > are **inequality symbols.** Thomas Harriot, an English mathematician, first used < and > in the early 1600s. You can remember which symbol is which because each symbol points to the smaller number: $3 < 5$ and $5 > 3$.

Comparing Measures

Measures can also be compared. You probably have compared your height and weight to those of other people.

Example 1

Mario is 5′6″ tall. Setsuko is 4′10″ tall.
a. Compare these numbers using the > sign.
b. Compare these numbers using the < sign.

Solution

a. Mario is taller than Setsuko.

5'6" > 4'10"

b. Setsuko is shorter than Mario.

4'10" < 5'6"

Lesson 1-9 Overview

Broad Goals Because of all the work on ordering numbers in the previous lessons, students should be prepared for the introduction of the inequality symbols given in this lesson.

Perspective It is not clear why some students find using inequality symbols so difficult. In a curriculum currently used in Hungary, the symbols < and > are introduced on the first day of *first* grade. The students are told that the symbol opens up to the larger number.

❶ Comparing Positive and Negative Numbers

Numbers can be compared whether they are positive, negative, or zero. You can always think of temperature. For instance, to compare 0 and 4, think: a temperature of 0°C is colder than one of 4°C. In symbols,

$$0 < 4.$$

A temperature of -7°C is colder than either of these temperatures.

$$-7 < 0$$

$$-7 < 4$$

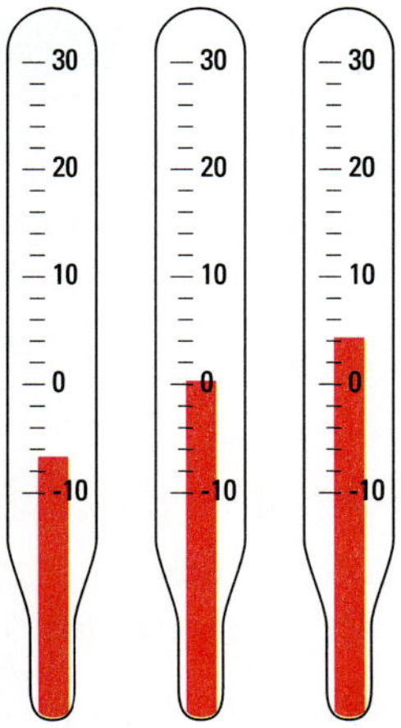

Numbers graphed on a number line are also easy to compare. Smaller numbers are usually to the *left* or *below* larger numbers. The numbers -7, 0, and 4 are shown on the vertical thermometers and the horizontal number line below.

When numbers are in order, inequalities can be combined. For the numbers pictured here, you could write either **-7 < 0 < 4** or **4 > 0 > -7**.

❷ *Caution:* Even though 10 is greater than 5, -10 is less than -5. In symbols, -10 < -5. For example, -10 could mean a lower temperature or bigger loss than -5.

Example 2

Rewrite the following sentence using inequality symbols: 12 is between 10 and 15.

Solution

Since 12 is between 10 and 15, it is larger than 10. So 12 > 10.
Since 12 is between 10 and 15, it is smaller than 15. So 15 > 12.
These inequalities can be combined into one sentence: **15 > 12 > 10**.
This is read "fifteen is greater than twelve which is greater than ten."
Another sentence uses the < sign: **10 < 12 < 15**.

Caution: Do not use > and < in the same sentence. For instance, do not write $5\frac{3}{4} > 3 < 4\frac{1}{3}$. A sentence comparing $5\frac{3}{4}$, 3, and $4\frac{1}{3}$ could be written as $\mathbf{5\frac{3}{4} > 4\frac{1}{3} > 3}$ or $\mathbf{3 < 4\frac{1}{3} < 5\frac{3}{4}}$.

Comparing Fractions

When numbers are written as fractions, it is not always easy to compare them. But if you convert them to decimals, they can be compared more easily.

Notes on Reading

Reading Mathematics Because Lesson 1-9 is a short, uncomplicated lesson with straightforward objectives, this is a good time to check on students' reading by asking them to write a list or summary of important points of the lesson at the beginning of class.

❶ You might want to give students **Teaching Aid 8** when comparing positive and negative numbers on a number line. Students might also find it useful to label and color in the thermometers in **Teaching Aid 12.**

❷ Ask students for the meaning of the word *caution.* The two cautions on this page warn students about common errors in working with inequalities. The first caution warns students not to just look at the number without the sign when comparing; 10 > 5, but −10 < −5 . For the second caution, using both < and > in the same sentence is a particularly common error. Note that 5 > 3 < 4 could be read "5 is greater than 3 is less than 4," which does not make much sense.

Optional Activities

Activity 1 You might want to use *Activity Kit, Activity 3,* to introduce this lesson. Students shade parts of 10-by-10 grids to compare fractions.

Activity 2 Technology Connection *Technology Sourcebook, Computer Master 1,* has students create a table of winter temperature data involving negative numbers. Students use the *Spreadsheet Workshop* to compare and order the data.

Activity 3 Technology Connection *Technology Sourcebook, Calculator Master 2,* shows how to compare both positive and negative fractions and mixed numbers by first expressing fractions and mixed numbers as decimals.

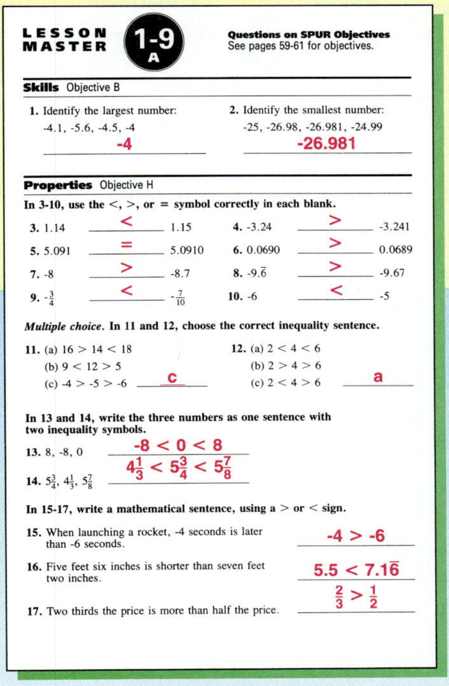

LESSON MASTER 1-9 A

Questions on SPUR Objectives
See pages 59-61 for objectives.

Skills Objective B

1. Identify the largest number: -4.1, -5.6, -4.5, -4 **-4**
2. Identify the smallest number: -25, -26.98, -26.981, -24.99 **-26.981**

Properties Objective H

In 3-10, use the <, >, or = symbol correctly in each blank.

3. 1.14 __<__ 1.15
4. -3.24 __>__ -3.241
5. 5.091 __=__ 5.0910
6. 0.0690 __>__ 0.0689
7. -8 __>__ -8.7
8. $-9.\overline{6}$ __>__ -9.67
9. $-\frac{3}{4}$ __<__ $-\frac{7}{10}$
10. -6 __<__ -5

***Multiple choice.* In 11 and 12, choose the correct inequality sentence.**

11. (a) 16 > 14 < 18 (b) 9 < 12 > 5 (c) -4 > -5 > -6 __c__
12. (a) 2 < 4 < 6 (b) 2 > 4 > 6 (c) 2 < 4 > 6 __a__

In 13 and 14, write the three numbers as one sentence with two inequality symbols.

13. 8, -8, 0 **-8 < 0 < 8**
14. $5\frac{3}{4}$, $4\frac{1}{3}$, $5\frac{7}{8}$ $4\frac{1}{3} < 5\frac{3}{4} < 5\frac{7}{8}$

In 15-17, write a mathematical sentence, using a > or < sign.

15. When launching a rocket, -4 seconds is later than -6 seconds. **-4 > -6**
16. Five feet six inches is shorter than seven feet two inches. $5.5 < 7.1\overline{6}$
17. Two thirds the price is more than half the price. $\frac{2}{3} > \frac{1}{2}$

❸ When discussing **Example 3**, you might want to use the circle models in **Teaching Aid 11**.

Additional Examples

1. The Amazon River in South America is about 4000 miles long. The length of the Nile River in Africa is about 4160 miles. Compare these lengths using
   a. the $>$ symbol. $4160 > 4000$
   b. the $<$ symbol. $4000 < 4160$
2. Rewrite the following sentence using inequality symbols: 0 is between -10 and 5.
   $-10 < 0 < 5$ or $5 > 0 > -10$
3. One circular spinner is divided into 6 equal parts with 4 parts labeled "You win!" On another spinner of the same size, 7 out of its 10 equal parts are winners. Is it easier to win with the first spinner or the second? Why?
   second; $\frac{7}{10} > \frac{4}{6}$

Notes on Questions

Question 17 Ask students if any negative number is less than any positive number. [Yes; every negative number is less than zero and zero is less than every positive number.]

Question 40 The answer will surprise some students. Use -4.3 as an example. When truncated it becomes -4, which is greater than -4.3.

LESSON MASTER 1-9 B **Questions on SPUR Objectives**

Skills Objective B: Order decimals and fractions.

1. Identify the smallest number: 21.44, -22.6, -22.9, -20.14 — -22.9
2. Identify the largest number: -8.99, -8.67, -8.673, -9 — -8.67
3. Order from smallest to largest: 7.32 -14 -6.2 — -14 -6.2 7.32
4. Order from largest to smallest: 0 -42 -41.5 — 0 -41.5 -42

Properties Objective H: Use the $<$ and $>$ symbols correctly between numbers.

In 5-16, use the $<$, $>$, or $=$ symbol correctly in each blank.

5. 1.36	$<$	1.39	6. -6.1	$>$	-7.3
7. 7.4	$=$	7.40	8. 0.0985	$<$	0.985
9. -5.4	$>$	-5.8	10. -12.42	$<$	11.9
11. 0	$<$	6.17	12. 0	$>$	-37
13. -0.288	$<$	-0.28	14. -78	$<$	-58
15. $\frac{9}{10}$	$>$	$\frac{7}{8}$	16. $-\frac{1}{6}$	$<$	$-\frac{3}{20}$

Multiple choice. **In 17-20, choose the correct inequality sentence.**

17. (a) $4 < 10 > 7$ (b) $19 > 17 > 6$ (c) $13 > 8 < 11$ — b
18. (a) $-8 < -7 < 6$ (b) $-8 > -7 < 6$ (c) $-8 > -7 > 6$ — a
19. (a) $0 < -7 < -10$ (b) $3 < 0 > -2$ (c) $-9 < -5 < 0$ — c
20. (a) $.009 > .09 > .9$ (b) $8.2 > -2.12 > -3$ (c) $-2.3 < -4.3 < -6.3$ — b

14) Negative three is less than three.
15) Seventeen is greater than negative one and five-tenths.
16) Negative four is less than negative three and a half which is less than negative three.

Example 3

Klaus ate 2 of the 3 pieces of a small pizza. Sonja ate 5 of the 8 pieces of a pizza of the same size. Compare $\frac{2}{3}$ and $\frac{5}{8}$ to find out who ate more.

Solution

Use the decimal equivalents. $\frac{2}{3} = .\overline{6}$ and $\frac{5}{8} = .625$.

Since $.625 < .\overline{6}$, $\frac{5}{8} < \frac{2}{3}$. So, Klaus ate more.

QUESTIONS

Covering the Reading

1. Give an example in which it would be useful to compare counts. Sample: comparing number of births
2. What is the meaning of the symbol $<$? is less than
3. What is the meaning of the symbol $>$? is greater than
4. *Multiple choice.* Which is true? (c)
   (a) $2 < -5$ (b) $2 = -5$ (c) $2 > -5$

In 5–8, rewrite the sentence using one of the symbols $<$, $>$, or $=$.

5. -5 is less than -3. $-5 < -3$
6. 6 is greater than -12. $6 > -12$
7. 4′11″ is shorter than 5′. 4′11″ < 5′
8. A height of 4.5 feet is the same as a height of $4\frac{1}{2}$ feet. 4.5 ft = $4\frac{1}{2}$ ft

In 9–11, write a sentence with the same meaning, using the other inequality symbol.

9. $2 < 2\frac{1}{10}$ $2\frac{1}{10} > 2$
10. $-18 < 0$ $0 > -18$
11. $0.43 < 0.432 < 0.44$ $0.44 > 0.432 > 0.43$
12. Write this inequality in two different ways: 0 is between -2 and 2. $-2 < 0 < 2$; $2 > 0 > -2$
13. Marissa ate 2 of the 6 pieces of a small pizza. Mal ate 3 of the 8 pieces of another pizza of the same size. Who ate more? Mal; $\frac{3}{8} > \frac{2}{6}$

In 14–16, translate into English words. See above left.

14. $-3 < 3$
15. $17 > -1.5$
16. $-4 < -3\frac{1}{2} < -3$

In 17 and 18, put the numbers in a mathematical sentence, using $<$, $>$, or $=$.

17. A temperature of -6°C is colder than a temperature of 15°C. -6°C < 15°C
18. Shawn Bradley, whose height is 7′6″, is taller than David Robinson, whose height is 7′1″. 7′6″ > 7′1″
19. On a horizontal number line, larger numbers are usually graphed to the __?__ of smaller numbers. right
20. On a vertical number line, larger numbers are usually graphed __?__ smaller numbers. above

Meet Mr. Robinson. *As a child, David was interested in music, electronics, and sports. He played basketball in eighth grade—but did not like it! With his father's encouragement, David attended the U.S. Naval Academy in Annapolis, MD, and earned a degree in mathematics. He began his professional basketball career in 1989.*

Adapting to Individual Needs

Extra Help
Materials: **Teaching Aid 11**

Have students cut out the circles on **Teaching Aid 11** and use them to compare fractions, such as the fractions $\frac{5}{8}$ and $\frac{2}{3}$ in **Example 3. Using physical models** can help students compare fractions without changing them to decimals. Point out that whenever students compare two fractions in this way, the size of the circles must be the same.

Applying the Mathematics

In 21 and 22, two numbers are given.
a. Graph the numbers on a number line.
b. Put the numbers in a mathematical sentence.

21. A profit of $1 is more than a loss of $2000. a) See below. b) $1 > -2000$

22. An elevation 300 ft below sea level is higher than an elevation 400 ft below sea level. a) See below. b) $-300 > -400$

In 23–30, choose the correct symbol: <, >, or =.

23. 0.305 __?__ 0.3046 >
24. $\frac{8}{8}$ __?__ $\frac{3}{3}$ =
25. $3.\overline{1515}$ __?__ $3.\overline{15}$ =

26. $10.\overline{8}$ __?__ 10.8 >
27. $\frac{10}{11}$ __?__ $\frac{67}{73}$ <
28. -14 __?__ $-14\frac{1}{2}$ >

29. -0.75 __?__ 0.75 <
30. 0.5 __?__ -0.6 >

In 31 and 32, put the three numbers into one sentence with two inequality symbols.

31. 62.1 6.21 0.621 $62.1 > 6.21 > 0.621$

32. $2\frac{1}{2}$ $2\frac{2}{3}$ $2\frac{2}{5}$ $2\frac{2}{3} > 2\frac{1}{2} > 2\frac{2}{5}$

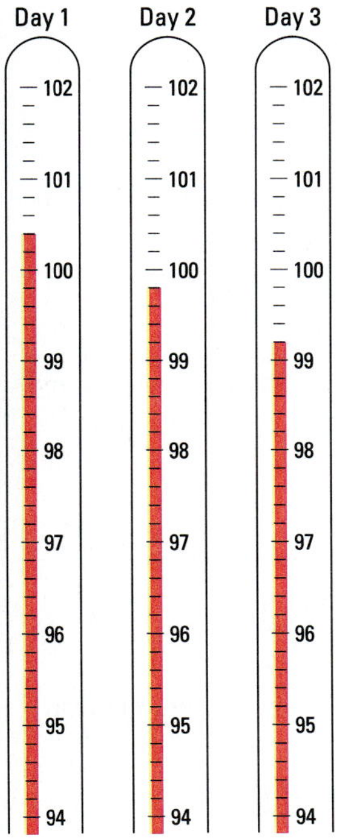

33. The thermometers pictured at the left show Joanne's body temperature on three consecutive days of a cold. Put the three numbers into one sentence connected by inequality symbols.
$99.2 < 99.8 < 100.4$

Review

34. Name all integers between -4 and 3. *(Lesson 1-8)*
-3, -2, -1, 0, 1, 2

35. Name all the positive integers less than 5. *(Lesson 1-8)* 1, 2, 3, 4

36. Suppose time is measured in years and 0 stands for this year. Tell what number each year stands for. *(Lesson 1-8)*
a. next year 1 **b.** last year -1 **c.** 2010 16 (in 1994) **d.** 1925 -69 (in 1994)

37. Round $2 \times \pi$ to the nearest thousandth. *(Lessons 1-4, 1-5)* 6.283

In 38 and 39, estimate each sum to the nearest whole number. Do not use a calculator. *(Lesson 1-4)*

38. 70.0392 + 6.98234 77

39. $14.95 + $2.99 + $7.89 $26

Exploration

40. Truncating decimal places in a positive number is the same as rounding down. When decimal places are truncated in a negative number, is the result a larger number, a smaller number, or equal to the original number? The result is a larger number.

21a)

22a)
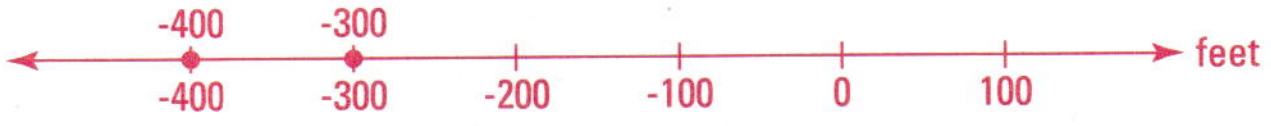

Follow-up for Lesson 1-9

Practice

For more questions on SPUR objectives, use **Lesson Master 1-9A** (shown on page 47), or **Lesson Master 1-9B** (shown on pages 48–49).

Assessment

Written Communication Give students the following questions.

1. Write two different ways to compare $\frac{5}{6}$ and $\frac{3}{4}$. $\frac{5}{6} > \frac{3}{4}$ and $\frac{3}{4} < \frac{5}{6}$
2. Order -4.5, -5.6, and -1.4 from least to greatest, using the inequality symbols. $-5.6 < -4.5 < -1.4$
3. Order the fractions, $-\frac{1}{3}$, $-\frac{1}{10}$, and $-\frac{1}{5}$ from largest to smallest using inequality symbols. $-\frac{1}{10} > -\frac{1}{5} > -\frac{1}{3}$

Extension

Multicultural Connection At Verchojansk in the northeast region of Russia, the average temperature in January is −58°F and the lowest recorded temperature is −90°F. At Eureka, in Canada's arctic region, winter temperatures average −35°F and summer temperatures average 43°F. Students might look up and report on customs related to climatic conditions.

Adapting to Individual Needs

Challenge Work with a partner.

1. Pick any two integers and compare them. Then find the opposites of the two integers and compare them.
2. Repeat Question 1 five more times with different pairs of integers.
3. If the first integer is greater than the second integer, what can you say about the opposites of the integers? [The opposite of the first integer is less than the opposite of the second integer.]

Setting Up Lesson 1-10

Previewing the Reading Because the reading for the next lesson needs to be done with care, you may wish to begin Lesson 1-10 in class and then give a homework assignment based on how much was covered.

▶ **LESSON MASTER 1-9 B** *page 2*

In 21-24, write the three numbers as one sentence with two inequality symbols.

21. -3, 0, 9 $-3 < 0 < 9$ or $9 > 0 > -3$

22. -11, -4, $-5\frac{1}{2}$ $-11 < -5\frac{1}{2} < -4$ or $-4 > -5\frac{1}{2} > -11$

23. $6.\overline{3}$, 6.3, 6.38 $6.3 < 6.\overline{3} < 6.38$ or $6.38 > 6.\overline{3} > 6.3$

24. $12\frac{3}{5}$, $13\frac{1}{4}$, $12\frac{1}{2}$ $12\frac{1}{2} < 12\frac{3}{5} < 13\frac{1}{4}$ or $13\frac{1}{4} > 12\frac{3}{5} > 12\frac{1}{2}$

In 25-29, write a mathematical sentence using a > or < sign.

25. Four feet eleven inches is taller than four feet six inches. 4′11″ > 4′6″

26. -7°F is colder than -4°F. -7°F < -4°F

27. A profit of $120 is more than a loss of $60. $120 > -$60

28. A quarter hour is shorter than a half hour. $\frac{1}{4}$ hr < $\frac{1}{2}$ hr

29. An elevation of 145 feet below sea level is higher than an elevation of 200 feet below sea level. -145′ > -200′

REVIEW Multiples (Previous course)

In 30-34, list the first five positive multiples of each number.

30. 4 4, 8, 12, 16, 20

31. 5 5, 10, 15, 20, 25

32. 9 9, 18, 27, 36, 45

33. 8 8, 16, 24, 32, 40

34. 12 12, 24, 36, 48, 60

In 35 and 36, which of the numbers given is *not* a multiple of the first number?

35. 6: 48, 12, 92, 84, 66 92
36. 7: 63, 700, 56, 72, 84 72

In 37-40, give a number that is a multiple of *both* numbers. Sample answers are given.

37. 2 and 5 10
38. 6 and 8 24
39. 4 and 10 20
40. 3 and 4 12

Lesson 1-10

Objectives

J Use the Equal Fractions Property to rewrite fractions.

Resources

From the ***Teacher's Resource File***

- Lesson Master 1-10A or 1-10B
- Answer Master 1-10
- Teaching Aids
  - 3 Warm-up
  - 11 Circle Models

Additional Resources

- Visuals for Teaching Aids 3, 11

Teaching Lesson 1-10

Warm-up

Compare these sets of numbers using > or < signs. **Sample answers are given using >.**

1. 51.6 and 51 **51.6 > 51**
2. 0 and -8 **0 > -8**
3. 0 and .00329 **.00329 > 0**
4. -12 and -16 **-12 > -16**
5. $5\frac{7}{8}$, 5, and $5\frac{4}{5}$ **$5\frac{7}{8} > 5\frac{4}{5} > 5$**
6. $-\frac{7}{15}$, $-\frac{14}{15}$, and $\frac{4}{15}$ **$\frac{4}{15} > -\frac{7}{15} > -\frac{14}{15}$**
7. $-\frac{5}{9}$, $-\frac{5}{6}$, and $-\frac{5}{12}$ **$-\frac{5}{12} > -\frac{5}{9} > -\frac{5}{6}$**

LESSON

1-10 *Equal Fractions*

❶ Eat 3 of 4 pieces, or 6 of 8 pieces, or 9 of 12 pieces of a pizza. You will have eaten the same amount.

The numbers $\frac{3}{4}$, $\frac{6}{8}$, and $\frac{9}{12}$ are graphed in the same place on a number line.

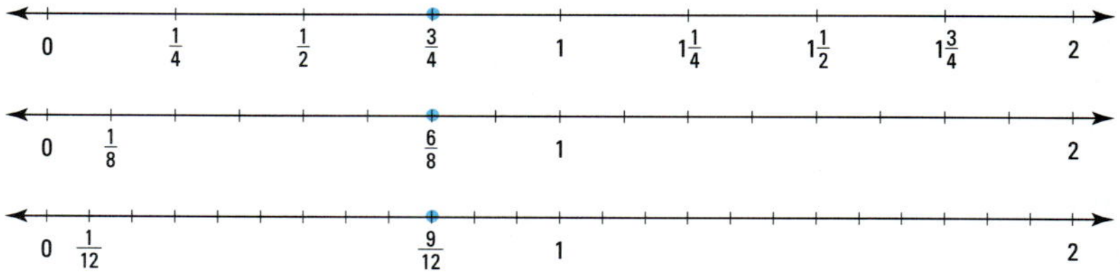

The above situations picture $\frac{3}{4} = \frac{6}{8} = \frac{9}{12}$.

You can verify this equality by changing each fraction to a decimal. You will get 0.75. The fractions $\frac{3}{4}$, $\frac{6}{8}$, and $\frac{9}{12}$ are **equal fractions.**

How Can You Create Equal Fractions?

Notice that $\frac{6}{8} = \frac{3 \times 2}{4 \times 2}$ and $\frac{9}{12} = \frac{3 \times 3}{4 \times 3}$. This suggests a way to create many fractions equal to a given fraction. Just multiply both numerator and denominator by the same nonzero number.

Example 1

Find three other fractions equal to $\frac{2}{3}$.

Solution

You can multiply the numerator and denominator by any nonzero number. We pick 6, 15, and 1000.

$\frac{2 \times 6}{3 \times 6} = \frac{12}{18}$ $\frac{2 \times 15}{3 \times 15} = \frac{30}{45}$ $\frac{2 \times 1000}{3 \times 1000} = \frac{2000}{3000}$

Check

You know that $\frac{2}{3} = 2 \div 3 = .\overline{6}$. Do the other fractions equal $.\overline{6}$? Divide to find out.

$12 \div 18 = 0.666...$ $30 \div 45 = 0.666...$ $2000 \div 3000 = 0.666...$

Yes they do.

Lesson 1-10 Overview

Broad Goals The purpose of this lesson is to show the applications of the Equal Fractions Property in creating fractions equal to a given fraction and in rewriting a fraction in lowest terms.

Perspective As mentioned in the notes to Lesson 1-6, we do not say "reduce fractions" because the fraction $\frac{2}{3}$ has the same value as $\frac{6}{9}$. We also do not use the phrase "reduce to lowest terms" because it gives the impression that the value of the fraction is getting smaller. However, the phrase "in lowest terms" is universal, and we recommend its use.

What happens if you divide the numerator and denominator of $\frac{2000}{3000}$ by the same number?

$$\frac{2000 \div 100}{3000 \div 100} = \frac{20}{30} \qquad \frac{2000 \div 500}{3000 \div 500} = \frac{4}{6} \qquad \frac{2000 \div 1000}{3000 \div 1000} = \frac{2}{3}$$

The results are fractions equal to $\frac{2}{3}$. They are equal because you are essentially multiplying or dividing by 1.

❷ **Equal Fractions Property**
If the numerator and denominator of a fraction are both multiplied (or divided) by the same nonzero number, then the resulting fraction is equal to the original one.

In the previous lesson, the fractions $\frac{2}{3}$ and $\frac{5}{8}$ were compared by changing each fraction to a decimal. You can also compare $\frac{2}{3}$ and $\frac{5}{8}$ by using equal fractions. First find a number that is divisible by both 3 and 8. We use 24. Then change the fractions to twenty-fourths.

$$\frac{2}{3} = \frac{2 \times 8}{3 \times 8} = \frac{16}{24} \qquad \frac{5}{8} = \frac{5 \times 3}{8 \times 3} = \frac{15}{24}$$

Since $\frac{16}{24}$ is greater than $\frac{15}{24}$, $\frac{2}{3} > \frac{5}{8}$.

❸ Using Factors to Write Fractions in Lowest Terms

A number that divides evenly into another number is called a **factor** of that number. For example, 3 and 8 are factors of 24. To find all the factors of 24, write all the whole number multiplication problems that equal 24. Be careful not to miss any.

$$1 \times 24 = 24 \qquad 2 \times 12 = 24 \qquad 3 \times 8 = 24 \qquad 4 \times 6 = 24$$

So the factors of 24 are 1, 2, 3, 4, 6, 8, 12, and 24.

Of the many fractions equal to $\frac{2000}{3000}$, the simple fraction with the smallest whole numbers is $\frac{2}{3}$. We say that $\frac{2000}{3000}$, written in **lowest terms,** equals $\frac{2}{3}$. To write a fraction in lowest terms, look for a factor of both the numerator and denominator.

Example 2

Write $\frac{20}{35}$ in lowest terms.

Solution

5 is a factor of both 20 and 35. It is the largest whole number that divides both 20 and 35. Divide both numerator and denominator by 5.

$$\frac{20}{35} = \frac{20/5}{35/5} = \frac{4}{7}$$

Check

You should verify that $\frac{4}{7}$ and $\frac{20}{35}$ equal the same decimal.

Notes on Reading

Reading Mathematics Students need to read the examples *carefully*. If students read this lesson at home, discuss each example in class before they answer the questions.

Being able to write equal fractions is an important skill. As the examples indicate, sometimes a person will need to multiply both the numerator and the denominator by the same nonzero number **(Example 1),** and sometimes the need is to divide **(Examples 2 and 3).** The purpose of finding factors of a number **(Examples 2 and 3)** is to enable students to divide more efficiently.

❶ **Teaching Aid 11** can be used when introducing this lesson.

❷ The Equal Fractions Property is based on the Multiplicative Identity Property, namely that the product of 1 and a number is the number. Because the Multiplicative Identity Property is not explained until a later chapter, it is not mentioned in this lesson. If you decide to discuss this property here, you may also want to show that you *cannot* add or subtract the same number in the numerator and denominator without changing the value of the fraction.

❸ You might want to use the geometrical approach given in *Optional Activities* below to introduce factors. Then discuss the section on Using Factors to write Fractions in Lowest Terms and **Examples 2 and 3.**

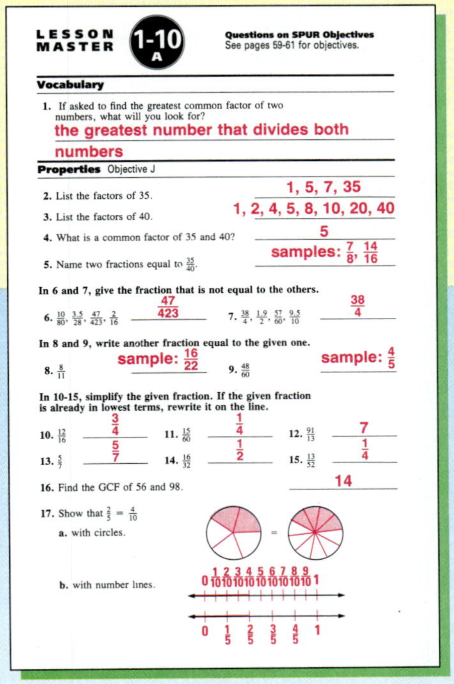
LESSON MASTER 1-10 A
Questions on SPUR Objectives
See pages 59-61 for objectives.

Vocabulary

1. If asked to find the greatest common factor of two numbers, what will you look for? the greatest number that divides both numbers

Properties Objective J

2. List the factors of 35. 1, 5, 7, 35
3. List the factors of 40. 1, 2, 4, 5, 8, 10, 20, 40
4. What is a common factor of 35 and 40? 5
5. Name two fractions equal to $\frac{35}{40}$. samples: $\frac{7}{8}$, $\frac{14}{16}$

In 6 and 7, give the fraction that is not equal to the others.

6. $\frac{10}{80}$, $\frac{3.5}{28}$, $\frac{47}{423}$, $\frac{2}{16}$ — $\frac{47}{423}$
7. $\frac{38}{4}$, $\frac{1.9}{2}$, $\frac{57}{60}$, $\frac{9.5}{10}$ — $\frac{38}{4}$

In 8 and 9, write another fraction equal to the given one.

8. $\frac{8}{11}$ sample: $\frac{16}{22}$
9. $\frac{48}{60}$ sample: $\frac{4}{5}$

In 10-15, simplify the given fraction. If the given fraction is already in lowest terms, rewrite it on the line.

10. $\frac{12}{16}$ $\frac{3}{4}$
11. $\frac{15}{60}$ $\frac{1}{4}$
12. $\frac{91}{13}$ 7
13. $\frac{5}{7}$ $\frac{5}{7}$
14. $\frac{16}{32}$ $\frac{1}{2}$
15. $\frac{13}{52}$ $\frac{1}{4}$

16. Find the GCF of 56 and 98. 14

17. Show that $\frac{2}{5} = \frac{4}{10}$
a. with circles.
b. with number lines.

Optional Activities

Geometry Connection
Materials: Grid paper

Before discussing **Examples 2 and 3,** you might want to present an alternative approach which represents the factors as dimensions of rectangles with area equal to the number. For example, to find the factors of 6, form all possible rectangles with whole-number dimensions and an area of 6 square units. The possibilities are 1×6 and 2×3. (Point out that 6×1 and 3×2 give the same factors.) Therefore, the factors of 6 are 1, 2, 3, and 6. Have students give the dimensions and describe all possible rectangles whose area is 48. [1×48, 2×24, 3×16, 4×12, 6×8; the factors of 48 are 1, 2, 3, 4, 6, 8, 12, 16, 24, and 48.]

❹ Although it is possible to find the prime factorization of the numerator and denominator to simplify a fraction, the drawbacks of this strategy are suggested by the fact that it often takes more time than successive division. Most people find just one number that is a factor of both the numerator and denominator, and divide both by it (as Heather did). Then they work with the simpler fraction, or simplify it further. After some practice, students learn to divide the numerator and denominator by the largest common factor they can readily identify (as Karen did).

Calculator Some calculators have keys that put fractions in lowest terms. Some allow the user to divide the numerator and denominator of a simple fraction by any common factor.

There are many ways to simplify a fraction. All correct ways lead to the same answer.

Example 3

Simplify $\frac{60}{24}$. (To simplify means to write in lowest terms.)

Solution 1

Vince saw that 4 is a factor of both 60 and 24. Here is his work.

$$\frac{60}{24} = \frac{60/4}{24/4} = \frac{15}{6}$$

Since 3 is a factor of both 15 and 6, $\frac{15}{6}$ is not in lowest terms. Vince needed a second step.

$$\frac{15}{6} = \frac{15/3}{6/3} = \frac{5}{2}$$

$\frac{5}{2}$ is in lowest terms. So $\frac{60}{24} = \frac{5}{2}$.

❹ **Solution 2**

Heather knew that 3 is a factor of both 60 and 24. Here is her work.

$$\frac{60}{24} = \frac{60/3}{24/3} = \frac{20}{8}$$

Then she saw that 2 is a factor of 20 and 8.

$$\frac{20}{8} = \frac{20/2}{8/2} = \frac{10}{4}$$

Dividing numerator and denominator again by 2, she got the same answer Vince got.

$$\frac{10}{4} = \frac{10/2}{4/2} = \frac{5}{2}$$

Solution 3

Karen got the same answer in just one step.

$$\frac{60}{24} = \frac{60/12}{24/12} = \frac{5}{2}$$

In Solution 3, Karen makes simplifying $\frac{60}{24}$ a one-step problem by dividing numerator and denominator by 12. We call 12 the **greatest common factor,** or GCF, of 60 and 24. To find the GCF of 60 and 24, write all the factors of 24:

1, 2, 3, 4, 6, 8, 12, 24.

Next write all the factors of 60:

1, 2, 3, 4, 5, 6, 10, 12, 15, 20, 30, 60.

The factors they have in common are 1, 2, 3, 4, 6, and 12. So the greatest common factor is 12.

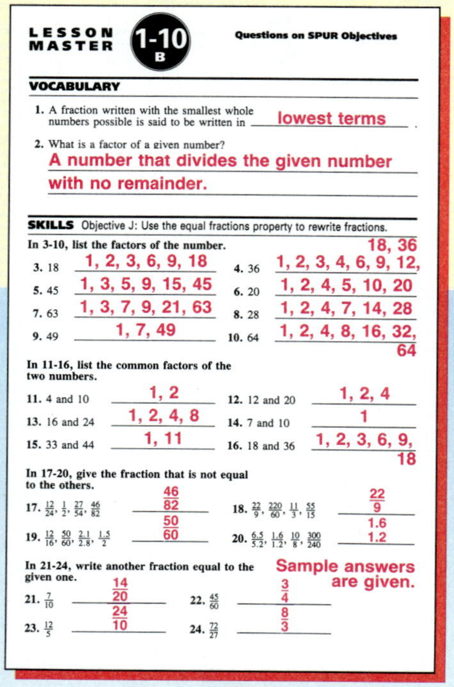
LESSON MASTER 1-10 B

Questions on SPUR Objectives

VOCABULARY

1. A fraction written with the smallest whole numbers possible is said to be written in **lowest terms**.

2. What is a factor of a given number? **A number that divides the given number with no remainder.**

SKILLS Objective J: Use the equal fractions property to rewrite fractions.

In 3-10, list the factors of the number.

3. 18 **1, 2, 3, 6, 9, 18**
4. 36 **1, 2, 3, 4, 6, 9, 12, 18, 36**
5. 45 **1, 3, 5, 9, 15, 45**
6. 20 **1, 2, 4, 5, 10, 20**
7. 63 **1, 3, 7, 9, 21, 63**
8. 28 **1, 2, 4, 7, 14, 28**
9. 49 **1, 7, 49**
10. 64 **1, 2, 4, 8, 16, 32, 64**

In 11-16, list the common factors of the two numbers.

11. 4 and 10 **1, 2**
12. 12 and 20 **1, 2, 4**
13. 16 and 24 **1, 2, 4, 8**
14. 7 and 10 **1**
15. 33 and 44 **1, 11**
16. 18 and 36 **1, 2, 3, 6, 9, 18**

In 17-20, give the fraction that is not equal to the others.

17. $\frac{12}{24}, \frac{1}{2}, \frac{27}{54}, \frac{46}{82}$ **$\frac{46}{82}$**
18. $\frac{22}{9}, \frac{220}{60}, \frac{11}{3}, \frac{55}{15}$ **$\frac{22}{9}$**
19. $\frac{12}{16}, \frac{50}{60}, \frac{2.1}{2.8}, \frac{1.5}{2}$ **$\frac{50}{60}$**
20. $\frac{6.5}{5.2}, \frac{1.6}{1.2}, \frac{10}{8}, \frac{300}{240}$ **$\frac{1.6}{1.2}$**

In 21-24, write another fraction equal to the given one. **Sample answers are given.**

21. $\frac{7}{10}$ **$\frac{14}{20}$**
22. $\frac{45}{60}$ **$\frac{3}{4}$**
23. $\frac{12}{5}$ **$\frac{24}{10}$**
24. $\frac{72}{27}$ **$\frac{8}{3}$**

Adapting to Individual Needs

Extra Help

As students work with you, demonstrate how to fold a sheet of paper into fourths. Have students shade three of the fourths. Next have them refold the paper into fourths and then into eighths. Ask how many parts are shaded now. [6] Ask if $\frac{3}{4}$ is still shaded. [yes] Write $\frac{3}{4} = \frac{6}{8}$ on the board. Repeat the activity to show other equal fractions.

QUESTIONS

Covering the Reading

3a)

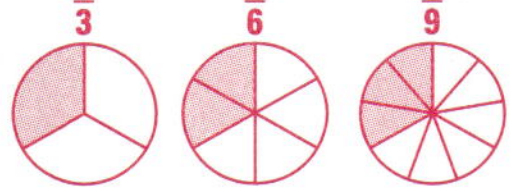

3b)

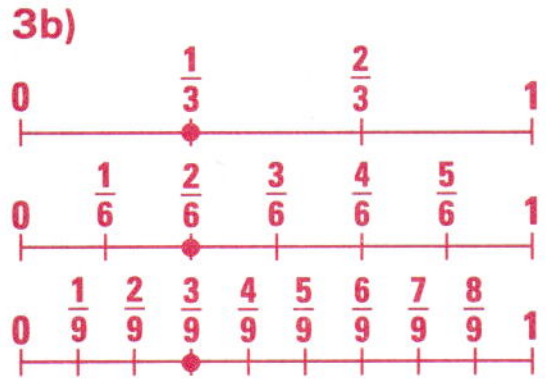

7a) 1, 2, 3, 4, 6, 8, 12, 16, 24, 48

7b) 1, 2, 3, 4, 5, 6, 10, 12, 15, 20, 30, 60

1. *Multiple choice.* Which of the following is not equal to $\frac{3}{4}$?
(a) $\frac{6}{8}$ (b) $\frac{8}{12}$ (c) 0.75 (d) $\frac{1.5}{2}$ **(b)**

2. *Multiple choice.* Which fraction, if any, is not equal to the others?
(a) $\frac{24}{36}$ (b) $\frac{48}{72}$ (c) $\frac{4.8}{7.2}$
(d) $\frac{24 \text{ million}}{36 \text{ million}}$ (e) All are equal. **(e)**

3. a. Picture $\frac{1}{3} = \frac{2}{6} = \frac{3}{9}$ with circles.
b. Picture this equality with number lines.

4. Find a fraction equal to $\frac{21}{12}$ that has a bigger numerator. **Sample: $\frac{42}{24}$**

5. *True or false.* Sixteen and twenty are both factors of 80. **True**

6. How can you tell when a fraction is in lowest terms? **There is no whole number other than 1 that is a factor of both the numerator and denominator.**

7. a. Write the factors of 48. **b.** Write the factors of 60.
c. Name all common factors of 48 and 60. **1, 2, 3, 4, 6, 12**
d. Name the greatest common factor of 48 and 60. **12**
e. Write $\frac{48}{60}$ in lowest terms. **$\frac{4}{5}$**

8. a. Find the GCF of 32 and 48. **16** **b.** Write $\frac{32}{48}$ in lowest terms. **$\frac{2}{3}$**
c. Write $\frac{48}{32}$ in lowest terms. **$\frac{3}{2}$**

In 9–14, a fraction is given.
a. Name a common factor of the numerator and denominator.
b. Rewrite the fraction in lowest terms.

9. $\frac{21}{12}$ **a) 3 or 1; b) $\frac{7}{4}$**
10. $\frac{15}{20}$ **a) 5 or 1; b) $\frac{3}{4}$**
11. $\frac{12}{32}$ **a) Sample: 2; b) $\frac{3}{8}$**
12. $\frac{52}{64}$ **a) Sample: 2; b) $\frac{13}{16}$**
13. $\frac{180}{16}$ **a) Sample: 4; b) $\frac{45}{4}$**
14. $\frac{240}{72}$ **a) Sample: 24; b) $\frac{10}{3}$**

Applying the Mathematics

15. a. Convert $\frac{3}{11}$ and $\frac{2}{7}$ to fractions with the same denominator to decide which is larger. **$\frac{3}{11} = \frac{21}{77}$, $\frac{2}{7} = \frac{22}{77}$; $\frac{22}{77} > \frac{21}{77}$, so $\frac{2}{7} > \frac{3}{11}$.**
b. Check by converting the fractions to decimals. **See below.**

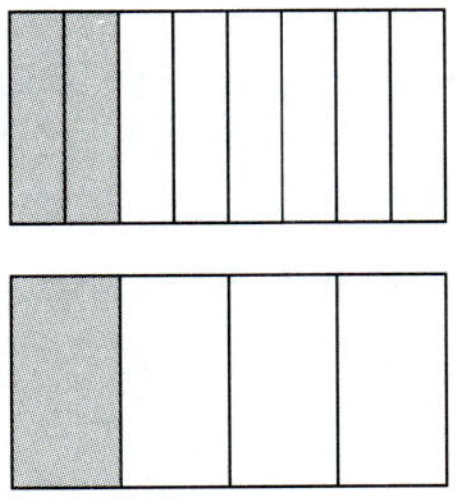

16. A carpenter finds that the height of a door is $75\frac{12}{16}''$. Reduce this mixed number to lowest terms. **$75\frac{3}{4}''$**

17. What equality of fractions is pictured at the left? **$\frac{2}{8} = \frac{1}{4}$**

18. As you know, $\frac{13}{1} = 13$. Find three other fractions equal to 13. **Samples: $\frac{26}{2}$, $\frac{39}{3}$, $\frac{52}{4}$**

19. Find three fractions equal to 1. **Samples: $\frac{2}{2}$, $\frac{3}{3}$, $\frac{5}{5}$**

15b) $\frac{3}{11} = .\overline{27}$ and $\frac{2}{7} = .\overline{285714}$; $.\overline{285714} > .\overline{27}$ so $\frac{2}{7} > \frac{3}{11}$

Additional Examples

1. Find three other fractions equal to $\frac{5}{6}$. Check by converting each to a decimal. **Sample answers: $\frac{5}{6} = \frac{10}{12} = \frac{20}{24} = \frac{15}{18} = .8\overline{3}$**

2. Rewrite in lowest terms.
a. $\frac{30}{45}$ **$\frac{2}{3}$** **b.** $\frac{42}{24}$ **$\frac{7}{4}$**

3. Consider $\frac{72}{48}$.
a. What are the factors of both the numerator and the denominator?
1, 2, 3, 4, 6, 8, 12, 24
b. Which factor will help you to simplify the fraction in the least number of steps? Why?
24; it is the GCF.
c. Simplify the fraction. **$\frac{3}{2}$**

▶ **LESSON MASTER 1-10 B** *page 2*

In 25-36, simplify the given fraction. If the given fraction is already in lowest terms, rewrite it on the line.

25. $\frac{12}{18}$ **$\frac{2}{3}$** 26. $\frac{42}{48}$ **$\frac{7}{8}$** 27. $\frac{24}{60}$ **$\frac{2}{5}$**
28. $\frac{55}{44}$ **$\frac{5}{4}$** 29. $\frac{16}{80}$ **$\frac{1}{5}$** 30. $\frac{14}{25}$ **$\frac{14}{25}$**
31. $\frac{20}{6}$ **$\frac{10}{3}$** 32. $\frac{18}{63}$ **$\frac{2}{7}$** 33. $\frac{6}{19}$ **$\frac{6}{19}$**
34. $\frac{10}{75}$ **$\frac{2}{15}$** 35. $\frac{20}{9}$ **$\frac{20}{9}$** 36. $\frac{25}{50}$ **$\frac{1}{2}$**

In 37 and 38, find the GCF of the two numbers.

37. 20 and 36 **4** 38. 72 and 18 **18**

39. Tell what equality of fractions is pictured.

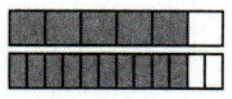

$\frac{5}{6} = \frac{10}{12}$

40. Show that $\frac{2}{3} = \frac{6}{9}$
a. with circles.

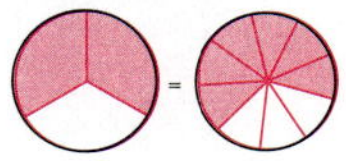

b. with number lines.

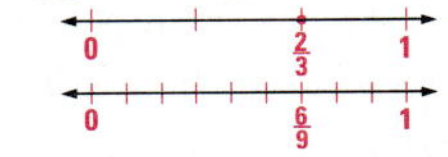

REVIEW Objective A, Lessons 1-1 and 1-2

In 41 and 42, write each as a decimal.

41. fifty-three million, two hundred eight thousand, fourteen **53,208,014**
42. forty-eight and seventeen thousandths **48.017**

In 43 and 44, write each in words.

43. .76 **seventy-six hundredths**
44. 602,007 **six hundred two thousand, seven**
45. What digit is in the tenths place of 514.903? **9**

Adapting to Individual Needs

English Language Development

To help students identify and understand the terms *factor(s), common factor,* and *greatest common factor,* write the following on the board:

45 = 5 × 9 Two factors of 45 are 5 and 9.
60 = 5 × 12 Two factors of 60 are 5 and 12.

Have students repeat as you point and say, "5 is a factor of 45; 9 is a factor of 45; 5 and 9 are factors of 45." Next repeat the procedure with 60. Then explain that since 5 is a factor of both 45 and 60, 5 is called a common factor of 45 and 60.

Ask students to find other common factors of 45 and 60 and then explain that the greatest common factor of 45 and 60 is 15.

Notes on Questions

Question 32 These four divisibility tests are of interest to many students, and should be learned. Divisibility in most situations can be easily checked by dividing on the calculator.

Question 33 This fraction has been chosen because neither the numerator nor the denominator has a factor between 1 and 10. (The only common factor of 323 and 493, other than 1, is 17.) Many students may think it is in lowest terms.

Follow-up for Lesson 1-10

Practice

For more questions on SPUR objectives, use **Lesson Master 1-10A** (shown on page 51) or **Lesson Master 1-10B** (shown on pages 52–53).

Assessment

Written Communication Have students write two paragraphs—one that explains how to find a fraction equal to $\frac{7}{8}$, and the other on how to simplify the fraction $\frac{75}{15}$. [Check that students use the Equal Fractions Property in their explanations.]

Extension

Different Ways to Write Fractions
Ask students to write two fractions equal to $\frac{3}{4}$ in which neither the numerator nor the denominator is an integer. [Four possible fractions are: $\frac{2.1}{2.8}$, $\frac{1.2}{1.6}$, $\frac{3/5}{4/5}$, and $\frac{6/3}{8/3}$]

20. Find a fraction equal to 8 that has 3 as its denominator. $\frac{24}{3}$

In 21 and 22, write the number as a fraction in lowest terms.

21. fourteen eighths $\frac{7}{4}$ **22.** seventy-five hundredths $\frac{3}{4}$

23. Sixty people are expected at a meeting and you are to arrange the chairs.

a. If you want the chairs in rows with equal numbers of chairs in each row, what choices do you have?

b. What idea in this lesson is applied in part **a**? These numbers are all the factors of 60.

23a)
1 row of 60 chairs
2 rows of 30 chairs
3 rows of 20 chairs
4 rows of 15 chairs
5 rows of 12 chairs
6 rows of 10 chairs
10 rows of 6 chairs
12 rows of 5 chairs
15 rows of 4 chairs
20 rows of 3 chairs
30 rows of 2 chairs
60 rows of 1 chair

Review

24. A 10th century Chinese mathematician, Liu Hui, used two approximations to π, $\frac{157}{50}$ and $\frac{3927}{1250}$. Fill in the blanks with $<$, $=$, or $>$. *(Lessons 1-2, 1-7, 1-9)*

a. π _?_ $\frac{157}{50}$ $>$ **b.** π _?_ $\frac{3927}{1250}$ $<$

25. Find three different numbers between 0 and -1. *(Lesson 1-8)*
Samples: $-\frac{1}{2}$, -0.2, -0.05

In 26–28, estimate to the nearest tenth. *(Lessons 1-4, 1-5)*

26. four thousand sixty-two times three thousandths 12.2

27. $\pi \times 567.34$ 1782.4 **28.** $18 + 1.8 - 0.18$ 19.6

In 29 and 30, round *up* to the next hundredth. *(Lessons 1-3, 1-7, 1-8)*

29. $4\frac{2}{17}$ 4.12 **30.** -0.00785 0

31. Try to find the decimal equal to each fraction without using a calculator or looking it up. *(Lesson 1-6)*

a. $\frac{4}{10}$ 0.4 **b.** $\frac{5}{8}$ 0.625 **c.** $\frac{3}{4}$ 0.75 **d.** $\frac{1}{3}$ $0.\overline{3}$ **e.** $\frac{5}{6}$ $0.8\overline{3}$

Exploration

32. There are easy ways to tell whether 2, 3, 5, and 9 are factors of numbers.

a. What about the digits of an integer tells you that 2 is a factor?

b. What about the digits of an integer tells you that 5 is a factor?

c. 3 is a factor of an integer when the sum of the digits of the integer is divisible by 3. Which of these numbers is not divisible by 3?

321 2856 198 4444 **4444**

d. 9 is a factor of an integer when the sum of the digits of the integer is divisible by 9. Which of these numbers is *not* divisible by 9?

198 44442 267 87561 **267**

e. Find a 5-digit number that is divisible by 5 and 9, but not by 2.
Samples: 49,995 and 83,115

32a) The ones digit will be even.

32b) The ones digit will be 0 or 5.

33. Some calculators display fractions and can rewrite fractions in lowest terms. If you have such a calculator, use it to write $\frac{323}{493}$ in lowest terms. $\frac{19}{29}$

Adapting to Individual Needs

Challenge 1 Geometry Connection
Materials: Grid paper

The greatest common factor of two whole numbers a and b is the length of the side of the largest square that can be used to completely fill a rectangle whose dimensions are a and b. For example, the largest square that can be used to fill a 10×15 rectangle is a 5×5 square, so the GCF of 10 and 15 is 5.

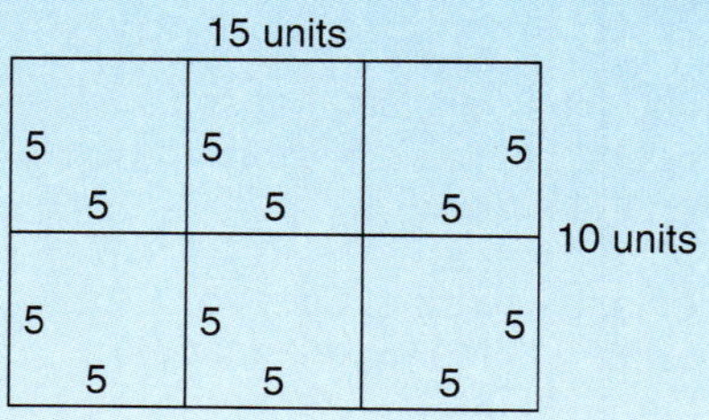

Have students use this idea to find the greatest common factor for other pairs of numbers.

Challenge 2 Mental Mathematics
Ask students to explain how they can tell if a fraction will end or repeat just by looking at the denominator of the fraction. [If the denominator can be written using only 2 and/or 5 as factors, the fraction can be written as an ending decimal. The decimals for all other fractions will repeat.]

A project presents an opportunity for you to extend your knowledge of a topic related to the material of this chapter. You should allow more time for a project than you do for typical homework questions.

PROJECTS 1 CHAPTER ONE

1 Numbers in the Newspaper

Pick one of the news pages of a daily or weekly newspaper. Make certain your page has at least five newspaper

articles on it. Find every number on this page, including those in advertisements. (Remember that some numbers may be written with their word names.) How many numbers are on this page? (If there are over a few hundred numbers, you may have to estimate.) Make a list of all of the counting units and all of the measure units used on the page. Write a paragraph describing what you have found and what you think is most interesting on this page.

2 Comparing Estimates

Take a survey of at least 25 people, asking them to estimate some quantity of your choosing. For instance, you might ask for an estimate of the population of a particular foreign country (such as India, where the population in 1990 was about 844,000,000). Or you might ask for an estimate of the year that the first Ph.D. in mathematics was awarded to a black woman (1949, to Marjorie Lee Browne at the University of Michigan and to Evelyn Boyd Granville at Yale University). Or you might ask for an estimate of the year we will run out of oil if we continue to use it at current rates and do not discover new sources (a 1989 estimate by British Petroleum is that we would run out in 2033). It is preferable if you pick some other thing to estimate. Then, once you have the estimates, write a paragraph about them. Are they usually too high or too low? Did anyone pick the exact amount? And so on.

Evelyn Boyd Granville

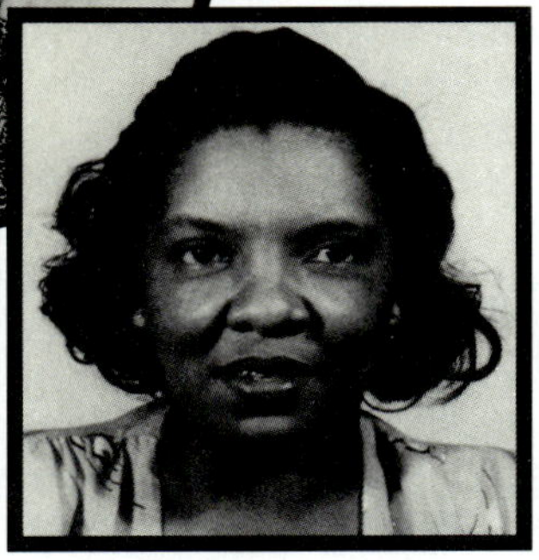

Marjorie L. Browne

Possible responses
1. **Responses will vary.**
2. **Responses will vary.**

Chapter 1 Projects

Discuss Chapter 1 projects and what you expect students to do with them. For more information about how projects can be incorporated into the mathematics program, see *General Teaching Suggestions: Projects* in the *Professional Sourcebook* which begins on page T20 of the Teacher's Edition.

Chapter 1 projects relate to the content of the lessons as shown below. They can, however, be used at any time after the lessons have been taught. Suggestions for using a project are given in the lesson notes under *Project Update.*

Project	Lesson(s)
1	1-2, 1-8
2	1-3, 1-4
3	1-6
4	1-3
5	1-1

1 Numbers in the Newspaper Students are expected to count every number on the newspaper page they select, including section and page numbers and numbers that appear in dates, photographs, charts and so on. If students choose pages that feature lists of data such as stock quotations, they should estimate the number of numbers used and explain their estimation process.

Anything counted gives rise to a counting unit. Students may recognize measuring units describing time, distance, area, volume, and rate. Numbers may also be used to label, to order, and to compare. These don't always have units. For instance, 50% is unitless.

2 Comparing Estimates Have students discuss what they want to survey, formulate their survey questions, and note the answers. Tell them that when conducting a survey, they should not alter the wording of the questions or add any comments, since this would bias the result.

When analyzing their survey, have students speculate on why responses might be unusually high or low and why estimates vary greatly or are all about the same.

3 Which Fractions Equal Repeating Decimals? Calculators can help students determine if fractions are terminating or repeating, even if the repetend has more decimal places than the calculator display. For fractions considered in this project, this happens with denominators of 17, 19, and 23; these fractions yield repetends of 16, 18, and 22 decimal places respectively.

4 The Advantages of Rounding Before students visit a local store, check with the store manager. Discuss with students how they might estimate the number of shoppers. [They could count the people entering the store for 10-minute periods during various times of the day or week, and then, based on the number of hours the store is open, make an estimate.] Also talk with students about how they might estimate the number of items for which prices are rounded up. [They could do this by walking through the store and tallying items or they could limit it to items advertised.] Students will have to estimate how many of these items are purchased by each shopper.

5 Other Numeration Systems Each student selecting this project might choose a different numeration system. Students can get information about numeration systems in encyclopedias, in books on the history of mathematics, or in books about the specific culture.

PROJECTS 1 *(continued)*

3 Which Fractions Equal Repeating Decimals?

From an Exploration in Lesson 1-6, you may have learned that the repetends of $\frac{1}{7}$, $\frac{2}{7}$, $\frac{3}{7}$, $\frac{4}{7}$, $\frac{5}{7}$, and $\frac{6}{7}$ have the same sequence of digits 142857 but they all start at different places in the sequence. This happens with other denominators and enables a person to determine the repetends of fractions even when the repetends have a large number of digits. Use your calculator to make a chart of the decimals for the fractions $\frac{1}{2}$, $\frac{1}{3}$, and so on, up to $\frac{1}{25}$. Which of these decimals terminate? Which of them repeat? For those that are repeating, determine the entire repetend by finding the decimal equivalents for other fractions with that denominator. (Sometimes the repetend has many places, but never more places than the value of the denominator.) Try to find a general pattern that will tell a person which fractions equal repeating decimals and which equal terminating decimals.

4 The Advantages of Rounding

Some people have suggested that pennies be taken out of circulation. Suppose all pennies were taken out of circulation and a food store changed its prices as follows: prices that end in 0 or 5 stay the same; prices that end in 1 or 6 are rounded down a penny to the nearest nickel; prices that end in 2, 3, 4, 7, 8, and 9 are rounded up to the next nickel. Does this make much of a difference? Go to a large store and try to estimate how many people shop there. Estimate how many items might be bought in which the store would round up, and then estimate how much the store might gain from rounding up. Report about what you have found.

5 Other Numeration Systems

Many cultures have written numbers differently from the way we write numbers now. Among these are the ancient Greeks of Europe, Aztecs of Mexico,

the Yoruba and Egyptians of Africa, the Hebrews, the Babylonians, and all the cultures of Southern and Eastern Asia. Read about the numeration systems of one of these cultures or some other culture with a different numeration system. Write a short report explaining how the numbers 1 through 10, 25, 100, and larger numbers were written by these peoples.

Responses

3. $\frac{1}{2} = 0.5$
$\frac{1}{3} = 0.\overline{3}$
$\frac{1}{4} = 0.25$
$\frac{1}{5} = 0.2$
$\frac{1}{6} = 0.1\overline{6}$
$\frac{1}{7} = 0.\overline{142857}$
$\frac{1}{8} = 0.125$
$\frac{1}{9} = 0.\overline{1}$
$\frac{1}{10} = 0.1$
$\frac{1}{11} = 0.\overline{09}$
$\frac{1}{12} = 0.08\overline{3}$
$\frac{1}{13} = 0.0\overline{76923}$
$\frac{1}{14} = 0.0\overline{714285}$
$\frac{1}{15} = 0.0\overline{6}$
$\frac{1}{16} = 0.0625$
$\frac{1}{17} = 0.\overline{0588235294117647}$
$\frac{1}{18} = 0.0\overline{5}$

SUMMARY

Today, by far the most common way of writing numbers is in the decimal system. In this chapter, decimals are used for whole numbers, for numbers between whole numbers, for negative numbers, for fractions, and for mixed numbers.

Decimals are easy to order. This makes it easy to estimate them. We estimated decimals by rounding up, rounding down, and rounding to the nearest decimal place. By dividing a number line into smaller intervals using tick marks, decimals can be represented on the number line.

Calculators represent numbers as decimals. So, if you can write numbers as decimals, then you can make a calculator work for you. By changing fractions to decimals, you can order them and tell whether two fractions are equal.

VOCABULARY

You should be able to give a general description and a specific example of each of the following ideas.

Lesson 1-1
digit
Arabic numerals, Hindu-Arabic numerals
decimal system, decimal notation
whole number
place value, ones place, tens place, hundreds place, thousands place, and so on
count, counting unit

Lesson 1-2
measure, unit of measure, interval
number line
tick marks
tenths place, hundredths place, thousandths place, and so on

Lesson 1-3
estimate
rounding up, rounding down
truncate

Lesson 1-4
rounding to the nearest

Lesson 1-5
scientific calculator
display [ ]
enter, key in, key sequence
RCL or STO
INV, 2nd, 0

Lesson 1-6
fraction, fraction bar, simple fraction
numerator, denominator
dividend, divisor, quotient
infinite repeating decimal, repetend
evenly divisible, divisible

Lesson 1-7
mixed number

Lesson 1-8
negative number, positive number
integer, positive integer, negative integer
+/– or ±

Lesson 1-9
inequality symbols
< (is less than), > (is greater than)

Lesson 1-10
equal fractions
Equal Fractions Property
factor
lowest terms
greatest common factor, GCF

Summary

The Summary gives an overview of the entire chapter and provides an opportunity for students to consider the material as a whole. Thus, the Summary can be used to help students relate and unify the concepts presented in the chapter.

Vocabulary

Terms, symbols, and properties are listed lesson by lesson to provide a checklist of concepts a student must know. Emphasize to students that they should read the vocabulary list carefully before starting the Progress Self-Test. If students do not understand the meaning of a term, they should refer back to the indicated lesson.

Some definitions of the terms in the vocabulary list may also be found in the Glossary at the back of the text. Have students locate the Glossary in their texts so they can use it as a reference.

$\frac{1}{19} = 0.\overline{052631578947368421}$
$\frac{1}{20} = 0.05$
$\frac{1}{21} = 0.\overline{047619}$
$\frac{1}{22} = 0.0\overline{45}$
$\frac{1}{23} = 0.\overline{0434782608695652173913}$
$\frac{1}{24} = 0.041\overline{6}$
$\frac{1}{25} = 0.04$

Sample response: Powers of 2 do not repeat. The same is true for powers of 5, 10, and 25. A broad generalization is: If a fraction has a denominator that is a factor of some power of 10, then it can be written as a terminating decimal. All other fractions result in the repeating decimals with various patterns. However, do not expect many students to come up with this.

4. Responses will vary.
5. For reference, here are some numbers represented in other numeration systems your students might locate.

(Responses continue on page 58.)

CHAPTER ONE

Progress Self-Test

For the development of mathematical competence, feedback and correction, along with the opportunity to practice, are necessary. The Progress Self-Test provides the opportunity for feedback and correction; the Chapter Review provides additional opportunities and practice. We cannot overemphasize the importance of these end-of-chapter materials. It is at this point that the material "gels" for many students, allowing them to solidify skills and understanding. In general, student performance should be markedly improved after they complete these pages.

Assign the Progress Self-Test as a one-night assignment. Worked-out *solutions* for all questions are in the Selected Answers section of the student book. Encourage students to take the Progress Self-Test honestly, grade themselves, and then be prepared to discuss the test in class.

Advise students to pay special attention to those Chapter Review questions (pages 59–61) which correspond to questions they missed on the Progress Self-Test.

Additional Answers

28.

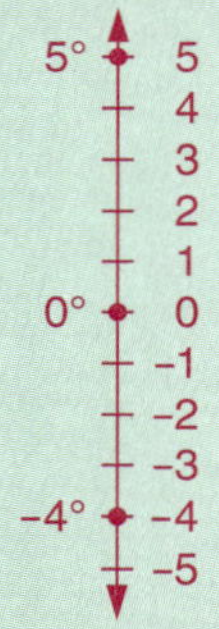

29. Sample: the number of people watching a parade

30. Sample: There are <u>4300</u> <u>people</u> watching the parade.

PROGRESS SELF-TEST

Take this test as you would take a test in class. You will need a calculator. Then check your work with the solutions in the Selected Answers section in the back of the book.

See margin for answers not shown below.

In 1–4, write as a decimal.

1. seven hundred thousand **700,000**
2. forty-five and six tenths **45.6**
3. $\frac{1}{4}$ **0.25**
4. $15\frac{13}{16}$ **15.8125**
5. What digit is in the hundredths place of 1234.5678? **6**
6. Write 0.003 in English. **three-thousandths**
7. Consider the four numbers .6, .66, $.\overline{6}$, and .606. Which is the largest? **$.\overline{6}$**
8. Consider the four numbers $\frac{1}{2}$, $\frac{2}{5}$, $\frac{1}{3}$, and $\frac{3}{10}$. Which is the smallest? **$\frac{3}{10}$**
9. Round 98.76 down to the preceding tenth. **98.7**
10. Round 98.76 to the nearest integer. **99**
11. Translate into mathematics: An elevation 80 ft below sea level is higher than an elevation 100 ft below sea level. **-80 ft > -100 ft**

In 12 and 13, use the number line pictured.

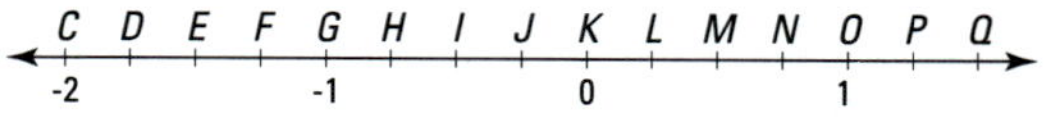

12. Which letter corresponds to the position of $\frac{1}{2}$? ***M***
13. Which letter corresponds to the position of -1.25? ***F***
14. Give a number between 16.5 and 16.6. **16.51**
15. Give a number between -2.39 and -2.391. **-2.3901**

In 16–18, which symbol, <, =, or >, goes between the numbers?

16. 0.45 __?__ 0.4500000001 **<**
17. -9.24 __?__ -9.240 **=**
18. $4\frac{4}{15}$ __?__ 4.93 **<**
19. -4 __?__ -5 **>**
20. What fraction is equal to 0.6? **Sample: $\frac{3}{5}$**
21. Give an example of a number that is not an integer. **Samples: 1/2, 0.43, $-5.\overline{3}$**
22. A store sells grapes on sale at 69¢ a pound. You need a quarter pound. So you divide by 4 on your calculator. The display shows 0.1725. What will you have to pay? **18¢**
23. Estimate 3.012012012 + 9.08888888888888 to the nearest integer. **12**
24. Indicate the key sequence for evaluating 3.456 × 2.345 on a calculator. **3.456 [×] 2.345 [**
25. Use your calculator to estimate 6 × π to the nearest integer. **18.849556 ≈ 19.**
26. What is the repetend in the repeating decimal 24.247474747 . . . ? **47**
27. Graph the numbers 7, 7.7, and 8 on the same number line. **See below.**
28. Graph these temperatures on the same vertical number line: 5°, -4°, 0°.
29. Give a situation where an estimate must be used because an exact value cannot be obtained.
30. Write a sentence containing a count and a counting unit. Underline the count once and the counting unit twice.
31. Which is largest: one tenth, one millionth, one billionth, or one thousandth? **0.1**
32. Find all the factors of 18. **1, 2, 3, 6, 9, and 18**
33. Find a fraction equal to 6 with 5 as its denominator. **$\frac{30}{5}$**
34. Rewrite $\frac{12}{21}$ in lowest terms. **$\frac{4}{7}$**
35. *Multiple choice.* When was the decimal system developed? **(c)**
    (a) between 2000 B.C. and 1000 B.C.
    (b) between 1000 B.C. and 1 B.C.
    (c) between 1 A.D. and 1000 A.D.
    (d) between 1000 A.D. and today

After taking and correcting the Self-Test, you may want to make a list of the problems you got wrong. Then write down what you need to study most. If you can, try to explain your most frequent or common mistakes. Use what you write to help you study and review the chapter.

27)

Response, page 56

5.

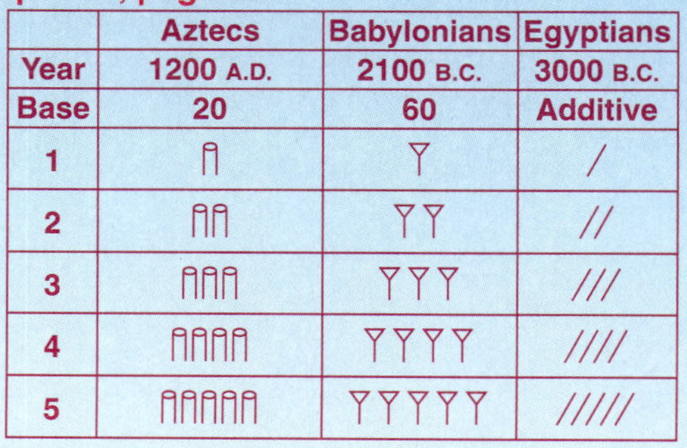

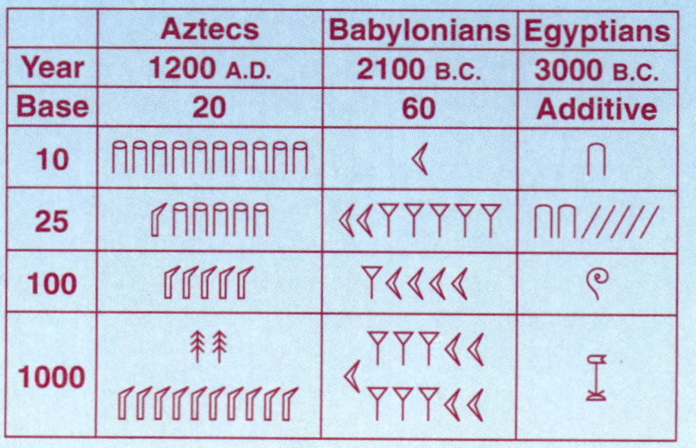

CHAPTER REVIEW

Questions on SPUR Objectives

SPUR stands for **S**kills, **P**roperties, **U**ses, and **R**epresentations. The Chapter Review questions are grouped according to the SPUR Objectives for this chapter. **See margin for answers not shown below.**

SKILLS DEAL WITH THE PROCEDURES USED TO GET ANSWERS.

Objective A: *Translate back and forth from English into the decimal system.* *(Lessons 1-1, 1-2)*

In 1–6, write the number as a decimal.

1. four thousand three **4003**
2. seventy-five hundredths **.75**
3. one hundred twenty million **120,000,000**
4. three and six thousandths **3.006**
5. seventy-five and six tenths **75.6**
6. nine hundred two thousand and nine hundred two thousandths **902,000.902**

In 7–10, translate into English words.

7. 500,400
8. 0.001 **one thousandth**
9. 3.041 **See below.**
10. 71,026,985 **See below.**

7) five hundred thousand, four hundred

Objective B: *Order decimals and fractions.* *(Lessons 1-2, 1-6, 1-7, 1-9)* **11) See below.**

In 11 and 12, which of the four given numbers is largest, which smallest?

11. 400,000 400,001 -.40000000001 0.4
12. .34 .3$\overline{4}$.$\overline{34}$.$\overline{343}$ **largest: .3$\overline{4}$; smallest: .34**

In 13–18, order from largest to smallest.

13. 0 -0.2 0.2 0.19 **0.2, 0.19, 0, -0.2**
14. -586.36 -586.363 -586.34 **See below.**
15. $\frac{1}{7}$ $\frac{1}{11}$ $\frac{1}{9}$ **$\frac{1}{7}$, $\frac{1}{9}$, $\frac{1}{11}$**
16. $\frac{2}{3}$ $\frac{6}{10}$ .66 **$\frac{2}{3}$, .66, $\frac{6}{10}$**
17. $3\frac{1}{3}$ $2\frac{2}{3}$ $4\frac{1}{6}$ **$4\frac{1}{6}$, $3\frac{1}{3}$, $2\frac{2}{3}$**
18. 5.3 5.$\overline{3}$ 4.33 **5.$\overline{3}$, 5.3, 4.33**

9) three and forty-one thousandths
10) seventy-one million, twenty-six thousand, nine hundred eighty-five
11) largest: 400,001; smallest: -.40000000001
14) -586.34, -586.36, -586.363

Objective C: *Give a number that is between two decimals.* *(Lessons 1-2, 1-8)*

In 19–23, give a number between the two numbers.

19. 73 and 73.1 **Sample: 73.05**
20. -1 and -2 **Sample: -1.3**
21. 6.99 and 7 **Sample: 6.995**
22. 3.40 and 3.$\overline{40}$ **Sample: 3.401**
23. -4 and 2 **Sample: 0**

Objective D: *Round any decimal place up or down or to the nearest value of a decimal place.* *(Lessons 1-3, 1-4, 1-8)*

24. Round 345.76 down to the preceding tenth. **345.7**
25. Round 5.8346 up to the next hundredth. **5.84**
26. Round 39 down to the preceding ten. **30**
27. After six decimal places, Joan's calculator truncates. What will the calculator display for 0.59595959595959 . . . ? **.595959**
28. Round 34,498 to the nearest thousand. **34,000**
29. Round 6.81 to the nearest tenth. **6.8**
30. Round 5.55 to the nearest integer. **6**
31. Round -2.47 to the nearest tenth. **-2.5**
32. Round -0.129 up to the next hundredth. **-0.12**
33. Round -14 down to the preceding ten. **-20**

In 34 and 35, estimate to the nearest integer without a calculator.

34. 58.9995320003 + 2.86574309 **62**
35. 6 × 7.99 **48**

Chapter 1 Review

Resources

From the ***Teacher's Resource File***

- Answer Master for Chapter 1 Review
- Assessment Sourcebook: Chapter 1 Test, Forms A–D

Additional Resources

- Quiz and Test Writer

The main objectives for the chapter are organized in the Chapter Review under the four types of understanding this book promotes—Skills, Properties, Uses, and Representations.

Skills include simple and complicated procedures for getting answers; at higher levels they include the study of algorithms.

Properties cover the mathematical justifications for procedures and other theories; at higher levels they include proofs.

Uses include real-world applications of the mathematics; at higher levels they include modeling.

Representations include graphs and diagrams; at higher levels they include the invention of new objects or metaphors to discuss the mathematics.

To the *lay person,* basic understanding of mathematics is usually found in Skills. The *mathematician* prefers to think of understanding in terms of Properties. The *engineer* often tests understanding by the ability to Use mathematics. The *psychologist* often views "true" understanding as being achieved through Representations or metaphors. The SPUR framework conveys the authors' views that all of these approaches have validity, and that together they contribute to the deep understanding of mathematics we want students to have.

Whereas end-of-chapter material may be considered optional in some texts, in *Transition Mathematics* we have selected these objectives and questions with the expectation that they will be covered. Students should be able to answer these questions with about 85% accuracy after studying the chapter.

You may assign these questions over a single night to help students prepare for a test the next day, or you may assign the questions over a two-day period. If you use two days, then we recommend you assign the *evens* for homework the first night so that students get feedback in class the next day, and then assign the *odds* the night before the test, because answers are provided to the odd-numbered questions.

It is effective to ask students the questions which they still do not understand and use the day or days as a total class discussion of the material which the class finds most difficult.

Assessment

Evaluation The *Assessment Sourcebook* provides four forms of the Chapter 1 Test. Forms A and B present parallel versions in a short-answer format. Forms C and D offer performance assessment.

For information on grading, see *General Teaching Suggestions: Grading* in the *Professional Sourcebook* which begins on page T20 in Volume 1 of the Teacher's Edition.

Objective E: *Use a calculator to perform arithmetic operations.* *(Lessons 1-5, 1-6, 1-8)*

36. Find 35.68 × 123.4. **4402.912**

37. Find 555 + 5.55 + .555 + 0.50. **561.605**

38. Find 73 − π to the nearest ten-thousandth.

39. What is the key sequence for entering -5 on a calculator you use? **Sample: 5 [+/−]**

40. Give the key sequence for converting $\frac{77}{8.2}$ to a decimal. **77 [÷] 8.2 [=]**

38) 69.8584

Objective F: *Convert simple fractions and mixed numbers to decimals.* *(Lessons 1-6, 1-7, 1-8)*

In 41–44, write the number as a decimal.

41. $\frac{11}{5}$ **2.2**

42. $\frac{-16}{3}$ **$-5.\overline{3}$**

43. $6\frac{4}{7}$ **$6.\overline{571428}$**

44. $5\frac{1}{4}$ **5.25**

Objective G: *Know by memory the common decimal and fraction equivalences between 0 and 1.* *(Lesson 1-6)*

In 45–48, give the decimal for the fraction.

45. $\frac{3}{4}$ **.75**

46. $\frac{2}{3}$ **$.\overline{6}$**

47. $\frac{1}{5}$ **.2**

48. $\frac{1}{6}$ **$.1\overline{6}$**

In 49–52, give a simple fraction for the decimal.

49. .8 **Sample: $\frac{4}{5}$**

50. $.\overline{3}$ **Sample: $\frac{1}{3}$**

51. 0.25 **Sample: $\frac{1}{4}$**

52. 0.625 **Sample: $\frac{5}{8}$**

PROPERTIES DEAL WITH THE PRINCIPLES BEHIND THE MATHEMATICS.

Objective H: *Use the < and > symbols correctly between numbers.* *(Lesson 1-9)*

In 53 and 54, choose the correct symbol <, =, or >.

53. 2.0 __?__ 0.2 **>**

54. 0.1 __?__ $0.\overline{1}$ **<**

55. Arrange the numbers $\frac{2}{3}$, .6, and .667 in one sentence with two > symbols between them.

56. Arrange the numbers -1, -2, and $-\frac{3}{2}$ in one sentence with two < symbols between them. **$-2 < -\frac{3}{2} < -1$**

Objective I: *Correctly use the raised bar symbol for repeating decimals.* *(Lesson 1-6)*

57. Give the 13th decimal place in $.\overline{1428}$. **1**

58. Give the 10th decimal place in $71.5\overline{36}$. **3**

55) $.667 > \frac{2}{3} > .6$

In 59 and 60, write the repeating decimal using the repetend symbol.

59. 6.8999 . . . (9 repeats) **$6.8\overline{9}$**

60. -0.002020202 . . . (02 repeats) **$-0.0\overline{02}$**

Objective J: *Use the Equal Fractions Property to rewrite fractions.* *(Lesson 1-10)*

61. Find two other fractions equal to $\frac{2}{7}$.

62. Find two other fractions equal to $\frac{280}{72}$.

63. Rewrite $\frac{80}{60}$ in lowest terms. **$\frac{4}{3}$**

64. Rewrite $-1\frac{12}{16}$ in lowest terms. **$-1\frac{3}{4}$**

61) Sample: $\frac{4}{14}$ and $\frac{6}{21}$

62) Sample: $\frac{35}{9}$ and $\frac{560}{144}$

USES DEAL WITH APPLICATIONS OF MATHEMATICS IN REAL SITUATIONS.

Objective K: *Deal with estimates in real situations.* *(Lessons 1-3, 1-4)*

65. According to U.S. census data, the population of Albany, Oregon was 29,462 in 1990. Round the population of Albany to the nearest thousand. **29,000**

66. To quickly estimate the cost of 5 records at $8.95 each, what rounding can you do?

66) Round to the nearest dollar, $9.00.

67. A store sells 6 granola bars for $2.99. You want 1 bar. Dividing on your calculator gives 0.4983333. What will the bar cost? **50¢**

68. Give a situation where an estimate would be used for a safety reason. **See below.**

69. Name a reason other than safety for needing an estimate. **Sample: An estimate might be easier to work with.**

68) Sample: maximum occupancy of a bus

CHAPTER ONE

Objective L: *Correctly interpret situations with two directions as positive, negative, or corresponding to zero.* *(Lesson 1-8)*

70. 350 meters below sea level corresponds to what number? **-350**

71. Translate into mathematics: A loss of $75,000 is worse than a gain of $10,000.
71) -75,000 < 10,000

72. An auto mechanic estimates the cost to fix your car. What number could stand for
a. an estimate $25 below the actual cost of repair? **-25**
b. an estimate $40 higher than the actual cost of repair? **40**
c. an estimate equal to the actual cost of repair? **0**

REPRESENTATIONS DEAL WITH PICTURES, GRAPHS, OR OBJECTS THAT ILLUSTRATE CONCEPTS.

Objective M: *Graph and read numbers on a number line.* *(Lessons 1-2, 1-7, 1-8)*

In 73–76, graph the numbers on the same number line.

73. $\frac{1}{3}$, $\frac{2}{3}$, and $1\frac{1}{3}$ **See below.**

74. 0, $\frac{1}{2}$, $\frac{1}{4}$, -1, and 1 **See below.**

75. 6, 6.4, and 7 **See below right.**

76. -3°, 1°, and -5° **See margin.**

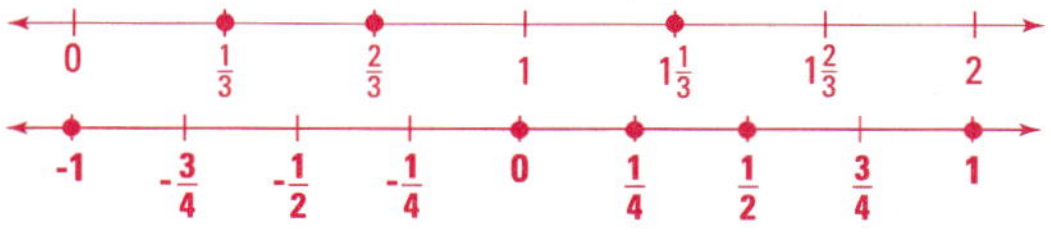

77. Use this number line.

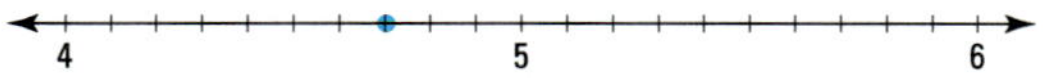

a. What is the distance between tick marks? **.1**
b. The dot is the graph of what number? **4.7**

78. Use this number line.

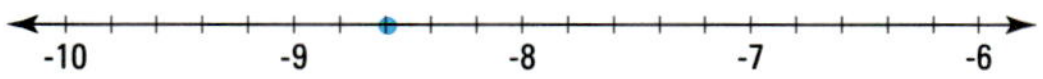

a. What is the distance between tick marks?
b. The dot corresponds to what number?
a) $\frac{1}{5}$ or .2 **b) $-8\frac{3}{5}$ or -8.6**

CULTURE DEALS WITH THE PEOPLES AND THE HISTORY RELATED TO THE DEVELOPMENT OF MATHEMATICAL IDEAS.

Objective N: *Give people and rough dates for key ideas in the development of arithmetic.* *(Lessons 1-1, 1-2, 1-6)*

79. *Multiple choice.* Our symbols for 0, 1, 2, 3, 4, 5, 6, 7, 8, and 9 did not all appear until about what date?
(a) 2000 B.C. (b) 1000 A.D.
(c) 1400 A.D. (d) 1900 A.D. **(c)**

80. Name a culture that used symbols quite different from the ones we use today in the United States. **Sample: Chinese**

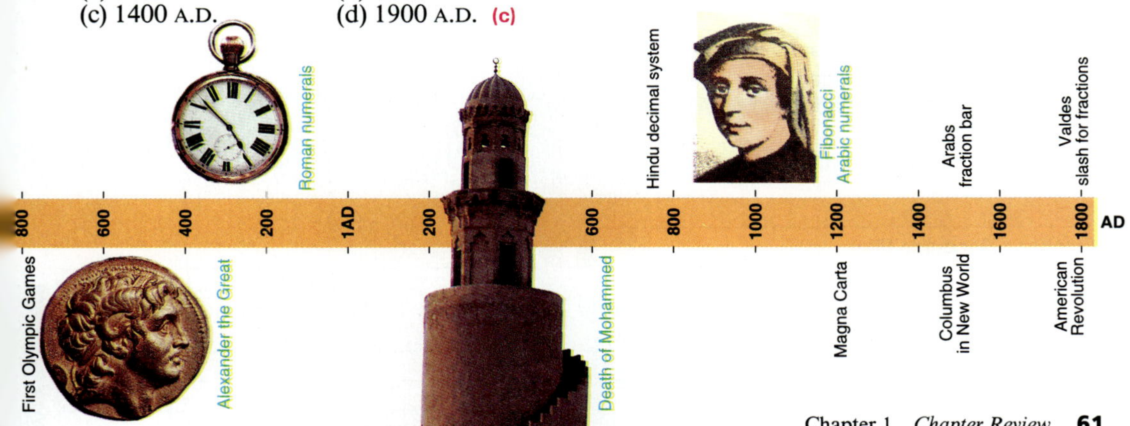

Additional Answers

76.

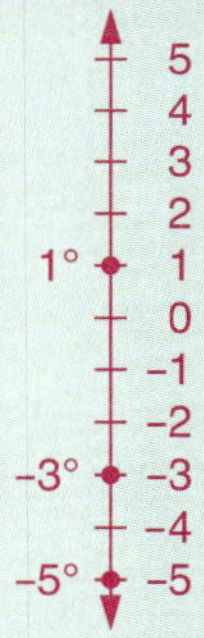

Setting Up Lesson 2-1

Homework We strongly recommend that you assign both the reading and some questions in Lesson 2-1 for homework the evening of the test. This assignment gives students work to do after they have completed the test and keeps the class moving. If you do not do this, you may cover one less chapter over the course of the year.

Remind students that this assignment includes reading the *Chapter 2 Opener.*

Chapter 2 Planner

Adapting to Individual Needs

The student text is written for the vast majority of students. The chart at the right suggests two pacing plans to accommodate the needs of your students. Students in the Full Course should complete the entire text by the end of the year. Students in the Minimal Course will spend more time when there are quizzes and more time on the Chapter Review. Therefore, these students may not complete all of the chapters in the text.

Options are also presented to meet the needs of a variety of teaching and learning styles. For each lesson, the Teacher's Edition provides sections entitled: *Video* which describes video segments and related questions that can be used for motivation or extension; *Optional Activities* which suggests activities that employ materials, physical models, technology, and cooperative learning; and *Adapting to Individual Needs* which regularly includes **Challenge** problems, **English Language Development** suggestions, and suggestions for providing **Extra Help.** The Teacher's Edition also frequently includes an **Error Alert,** an **Extension,** and an **Assessment** alternative. The options available in Chapter 2 are summarized in the chart below.

Chapter 2 Pacing Chart

Day	Full Course	Minimal Course
1	2-1	2-1
2	2-2	2-2
3	2-3	2-3
4	Quiz*; 2-4	Quiz*; begin 2-4.
5	2-5	Finish 2-4.
6	2-6	2-5
7	Quiz*; 2-7	2-6
8	2-8	Quiz*; begin 2-7.
9	2-9	Finish 2-7.
10	Self-Test	2-8
11	Review	2-9
12	Test*	Self-Test
13		Review
14		Review
15		Test*

*in the Teacher's Resource File

In the Teacher's Edition...

Lesson	Optional Activities	Extra Help	Challenge	English Language Development	Error Alert	Extension	Cooperative Learning	Ongoing Assessment
2-1	●	●	●	●		●	●	Diagnostic
2-2	●	●	●	●	●	●	●	Oral/Written
2-3	●	●	●	●		●	●	Written
2-4	●	●	●	●	●	●		Written
2-5	●	●	●	●		●	●	Group
2-6	●	●	●		●		●	Group
2-7	●	●	●	●		●	●	Written
2-8		●	●	●		●	●	Written
2-9	●	●	●		●	●		Written

In the Additional Resources...

	In the Teacher's Resource File								
Lesson	Lesson Masters, A and B	Teaching Aids*	Activity Kit*	Answer Masters	Technology Sourcebook	Assessment Sourcebook	Visual Aids**	Transition Mathematics Software	Video Segments
Chapter Opener									Opener
2-1	2-1	4,13		2-1			4, 13, AM		
2-2	2-2	13, 16, 17		2-2			13, 16, 17, AM		
2-3	2-3	13		2-3	Calc 3	Quiz	13, AM		2-3
2-4	2-4	14, 18, 19		2-4			14, 18, 19, AM	Spreadsheet	
2-5	2-5	14	4	2-5			14, AM		
2-6	2-6	14, 20		2-6	Calc 4	Quiz	14, 20, AM		
2-7	2-7	15, 21	5	2-7	Demo 2, Comp 2		15, 21, AM	Graphing/Probability	
2-8	2-8	15, 22		2-8			15, 22, AM		
In-class Activity		23		2-9			23, AM		
2-9	2-9	15, 22, 24		2-9	Calc 5		15, 22, 24, AM		
End of chapter				Review		Tests			

*Teaching Aids, except Warm-ups, are pictured on pages 62C and 62D. The activities in the Acitivity Kit are pictured on page 62C. Teaching Aid 23 which accompanies the In-class Activity is pictured with the lesson notes on page 104.

**Visual Aids provide transparencies for all Teaching Aids and all Answer Masters.

Also available is the Study Skills Handbook which includes study-skill tips related to reading, note-taking, and comprehension.

Integrating Strands and Applications

	2-1	2-2	2-3	2-4	2-5	2-6	2-7	2-8	2-9
Mathematical Connections									
Number Sense			●			●	●		●
Algebra	●	●		●	●			●	
Geometry							●		
Measurement								●	
Logic and Reasoning					●				
Statistics/Data Analysis							●		
Patterns and Functions	●	●	●	●	●	●		●	●
Interdisciplinary and Other Connections									
Art			●						
Literature			●						
Science	●	●	●	●	●			●	●
Social Studies	●	●	●	●	●	●	●	●	●
Multicultural	●	●			●	●	●	●	
Technology		●	●	●	●	●	●		●
Consumer		●		●	●	●	●	●	●
Sports	●	●	●		●				

Teaching and Assessing the Chapter Objectives

Chapter 2 Objectives (Organized into the SPUR catetgories—Skills, Properties, Uses, and Representations)	**Lessons**	**Progress Self-Test Questions**	**Chapter Review Questions**	**In the Assessment Sourcebook: Chapter Test, Forms A and B**	**Chapter Test, Forms C**	**D**
Skills						
A: Multiply by 10, 100, 1000, and so on.	2-1, 2-2	1, 6	1–6	1	1	
B: Convert word names for numbers to decimals.	2-1, 2-8	3	7–10	3, 6		
C: Convert powers to decimals.	2-2	10, 13, 20	11–14	4, 20, 21	1	
D: Give decimals and English word names for positive and negative integer powers of 10.	2-2, 2-8	8, 29	15–22	5, 7, 11–13, 18, 23	1	
E: Multiply by 0.1, 0.01, 0.001, and so on and by 1/10, 1/100, 1/1000, and so on.	2-4	4, 5, 7	23–28	2	6	
F: Convert large and small positive numbers into scientific notation.	2-3, 2-9	16, 17, 31	29–34	14–17, 25, 30	2, 3	
G: Convert and operate with percents as decimals.	2-4, 2-5	2, 9, 21	35–42	9	4, 6	✓
H: Know common fraction and percent equivalents.	2-4	21, 23	43–46	31–33, 35–38	6	✓
I: Convert terminating decimals to fractions, and either of these to percents.	2-6	22	47–52	23, 34, 39, 40		✓
J: Identify the center, radius, and diameter of a circle.	2-7	14	53–58	29		✓
Properties						
K: Know and apply the Substitution Principle.	2-5	2, 30	59–62	10	4	✓
L: Identify numbers as being written in scientific notation.	2-3, 2-9	28	63, 64	19	2, 3	
Uses						
M: Find percents of quantities in real situations.	2-5	25–27	65–68	28	4	✓
Representations						
N: Indicate key sequences and displays for large and small positive numbers on a calculator.	2-3, 2-9	12, 18, 19	69–76	24	2	
O: Interpret circle graphs.	2-7	15, 24	77–80	26, 27	5	✓

Assessment Sourcebook
Quiz for Lessons 2-1 through 2-3
Quiz for Lessons 2-4 through 2-6
Chapter 2 Test, Forms A–D
Chapter 2 Test, Cumulative Form

Quiz and Test Writer
Multiple forms of chapter tests and quizzes; Challenges

Activity Kit

ACTIVITY 4 — PERCENT OF A QUANTITY — Use with **Lesson 2-5.**

Materials: Grid paper
Group Size: Individuals

On your grid paper, outline a 10-by-10 square.

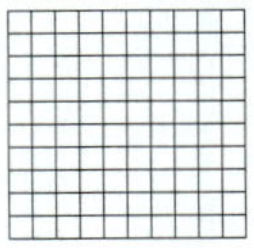

1. How many small grid squares are in the larger square you outlined? ________
2. Suppose each small square represents a package of 20 beads. How many beads are represented by all the small squares in the larger square? ________
3. Shade 30% of the larger square. How many small squares did you shade? ________
4. How many beads are shown by the shaded region? ________
5. **Draw a Conclusion** Suppose 30% of all the packages of the beads contain red beads. How many beads are red? Explain how your shaded grid shows this answer.

____

____

The sticker price of a car is $16,000. The car dealer is offering a 20% discount. What is the amount of the discount?

6. Use grid paper to illustrate this problem.
7. Refer to your work in Item 6 and complete the following.
   a. Each little square of the grid represents ______% of the whole grid and each little square also represents $______, so 1% of $16,000 = $______.
   b. 20 little squares of the grid represent ______% of the whole grid and 20 little squares also represent $______, so 20% of $16,000 = $______.
8. Which computation gives you 20% of $16,000? ________
   (a) 16,000 ÷ 20 (b) 20 × 16,000 (c) .20 × 16,000 (d) 16,000 ÷ .20
9. What is the amount of the discount? ________

ACTIVITY 5 — CIRCLE GRAPHS — Use with **Lesson 2-7.**

Materials: Ruler, compass, scissors, colored pencils
Group Size: Small groups

Everyone should draw and cut out a 4-inch circle and follow the directions in this activity. Then share your ideas within your group.

1. Fold the circle in half and make a sharp crease. Fold the circle in half again and make another sharp crease. Repeat this one more time. The folded circle should look like a wedge of pie.

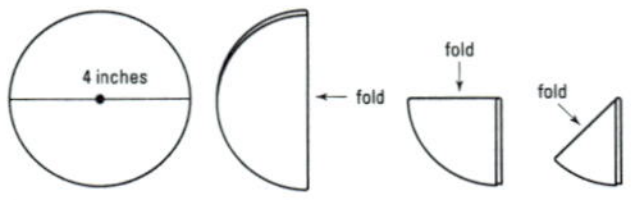

2. Open your circle. Using the creases as a guide, shade a region that shows half of the circle. Label this shaded region $\frac{1}{2}$.
3. Using a different color, shade a different region that shows one fourth of the circle. Label this shaded region $\frac{1}{4}$.
4. Using two more colors, shade two other regions that each show one eighth of the circle. Label each of these shaded regions $\frac{1}{8}$.

In your group, discuss the following situation: A class of 24 students was asked how they got to school. The results were:
6 walked, 3 rode in a car, 12 took a bus, and 3 rode bikes.

5. What fraction of the class is each group of students? Give the fraction in lowest terms.
   a. students who walked ____ b. students who rode in a car ____
   c. students who took a bus ____ d. students who rode bikes ____
6. Suppose the whole class is represented by your circle. Which region of the circle represents each group of students?
   a. students who walked ____ b. students who rode in a car ____
   c. students who took a bus ____ d. students who rode bikes ____
7. In your circle, label the regions *walk, car, bus,* and *bike.* Your labeled circle is a circle graph.

Teaching Aids

TEACHING AID 13

Warm-up — Lesson 2-1

Write each number in words as you would say it.

1. 22 2. 220
3. 22,000 4. 220,000
5. 2,200,000

Warm-up — Lesson 2-2

Compute.

1. 4 × 4 2. 8 × 8
3. 5 × 5 × 5 4. 10 × 10 × 10 × 10
5. 3 × 3 × 3 × 3 × 3 6. 1.2 × 1.2
7. .2 × .2 × .2

Warm-up — Lesson 2-3

Give the missing number.

1. 3.2 × ________ = 3.2
2. ________ × 2.75 = 275
3. 83,371 = 8.3371 × ________
4. 3.276 × ________ = 3,276,000
5. 3.2 × ________ = 32
6. 4.83 × ________ = 4830
7. 900,050 = 9.0005 × ________

TEACHING AID 14

Warm-up — Lesson 2-4

Write each fraction as a decimal.

1. $\frac{1}{4}$ 2. $\frac{7}{10}$
3. $\frac{2}{3}$ 4. $\frac{3}{8}$

Write each decimal as a fraction in lowest terms.

5. 0.5 6. 0.875
7. 0.6 8. $0.\overline{3}$

Warm-up — Lesson 2-5

Work in groups and discuss the following problem.

This week two stores have sales on the same brand of TV, originally priced at $329.95. Store A is selling the televisions for 50% off. Store B has marked the price down 30%, and if you buy a TV this weekend, you can take 20% off the marked down price. Which store has the better buy? Explain your answer.

Warm-up — Lesson 2-6

Write each decimal as a fraction in lowest terms and write each fraction as a decimal.

1. 0.5 2. 0.35 3. 1.3
4. $\frac{4}{5}$ 5. $\frac{3}{8}$ 6. $\frac{4}{9}$

TEACHING AID 15

Warm-up — Lesson 2-7

Use a compass or circle template and a ruler.

1. Draw a circle. Label the center *O*.
2. Draw a diameter and measure it.
3. Draw several more diameters and measure them. What can you say about the measures of the diameters of your circle?
4. Draw at least two different radii and measure them. What can you say about the measures of the radii of your circle?
5. What do you notice about the measures of the radii and diameters of your circle?

Warm-up — Lesson 2-8

Write each number in decimal form and give its word name.

1. 10^1 2. 10^2 3. 10^3
4. 10^4 5. 10^5 6. 10^6
7. 10^9 8. 10^{12}

Warm-up — Lesson 2-9

Write each number in scientific notation.

1. 1,230,000 2. 123,000
3. 12,300 4. 1230
5. 123 6. 12.3

TEACHING AID 16
Lesson 2-2

Powers of Two

2^1	2	2^{14}	16,384
2^2	4	2^{15}	32,768
2^3	8	2^{16}	65,536
2^4	16	2^{17}	131,072
2^5	32	2^{18}	262,144
2^6	64	2^{19}	524,288
2^7	128	2^{20}	1,048,576
2^8	256	2^{21}	2,097,152
2^9	512	2^{22}	4,194,304
2^{10}	1024	2^{23}	8,388,608
2^{11}	2048	2^{24}	16,777,216
2^{12}	4096	2^{25}	33,554,432
2^{13}	8192	2^{26}	67,108,864

TEACHING AID 17
Lesson 2-2

Powers of Ten

Power of 10	Word Name	Written as a Decimal
10^1	ten	10
10^2	hundred	100
10^3	thousand	1,000
10^6	million	1,000,000
10^9	billion	1,000,000,000
10^{12}	trillion	1,000,000,000,000
10^{15}	quadrillion	1,000,000,000,000,000
10^{18}	quintillion	1,000,000,000,000,000,000
10^{21}	sextillion	1,000,000,000,000,000,000,000
10^{24}	septillion	1,000,000,000,000,000,000,000,000
10^{27}	octillion	1,000,000,000,000,000,000,000,000,000
10^{30}	nonillion	1,000,000,000,000,000,000,000,000,000,000
10^{33}	decillion	1,000,000,000,000,000,000,000,000,000,000,000
10^{36}	undecillion	1,000,000,000,000,000,000,000,000,000,000,000,000
10^{39}	duodecillion	1,000,000,000,000,000,000,000,000,000,000,000,000,000
10^{42}	tredecillion	1,000,000,000,000,000,000,000,000,000,000,000,000,000,000

TEACHING AID 18
Lesson 2-4

Percents on a Number Line

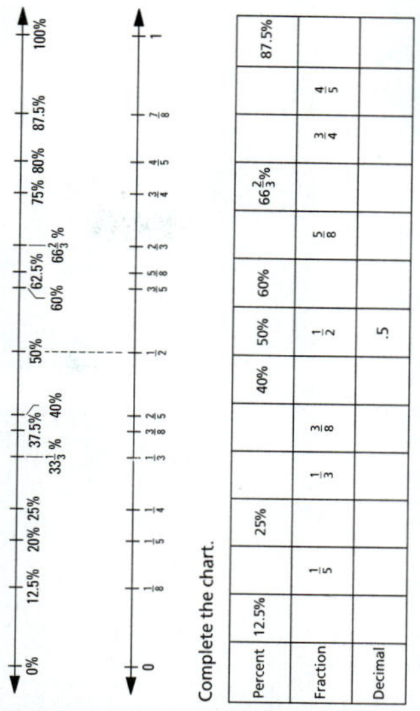

TEACHING AID 19
Lesson 2-4

Decimals and Percents

Changing a Percent to a Decimal

Write the percent. → Replace "%" with "× .01." → Write the product.

Changing a Decimal to a Percent

Write the decimal. → Multiply by 100. → Write "%" after the product.

TEACHING AID 20
Lesson 2-6

Fraction/Decimal/Percent Chart

Fraction	Decimal	Percent

TEACHING AID 21
Lesson 2-7

Circle-Graph Form

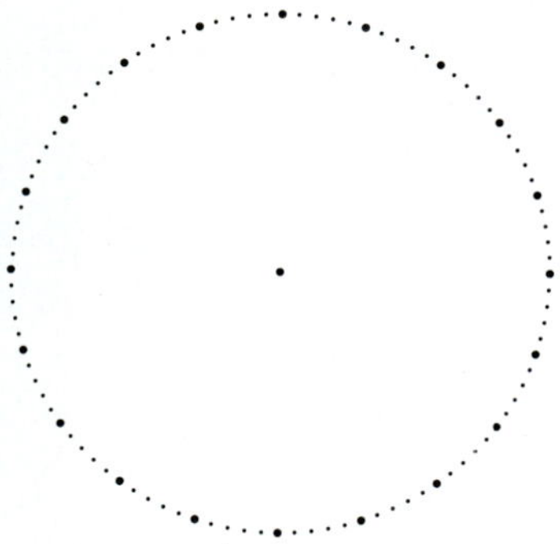

TEACHING AID 22
Lessons 2-8, 2-9

Integer Powers of Ten

10^1 = ten	10^{-1} = one tenth
10^2 = one hundred	10^{-2} = one hundredth
10^3 = one thousand	10^{-3} = one thousandth
10^6 = one million	10^{-6} = one millionth
10^9 = one billion	10^{-9} = one billionth
10^{12} = one trillion	10^{-12} = one trillionth
10^{15} = one quadrillion	10^{-15} = one quadrillionth
10^{18} = one quintillion	10^{-18} = one quintillionth
10^{21} = one sextillion	10^{-21} = one sextillionth
10^{24} = one septillion	10^{-24} = one septillionth
10^{27} = one octillion	10^{-27} = one octillionth
10^{30} = one nonillion	10^{-30} = one nonillionth
10^{33} = one decillion	10^{-33} = one decillionth

TEACHING AID 24
Lesson 2-9

Scientific Notation

Large Numbers

Scientific notation →	Power →	Move decimal point. →	Decimal
4.396×10^5	5	4 39600.	439,600

Decimal →	Write as number between 1 and 10. →	Count decimal places moved. →	Scientific notation
6,253,700	6.253700	6	6.2537×10^6

Small Numbers

Scientific notation →	Power →	Move decimal point. →	Decimal
4.55×10^{-4}	−4	.0004 55	.000455

Decimal →	Write as number between 1 and 10. →	Count decimal places moved. →	Scientific notation
.0057932	005.7932	3	5.7932×10^{-3}

Chapter Opener 2

Pacing

New notations are often hard for students to learn, since both a new concept and unfamiliar symbols must be mastered. Though many students will have seen powers and percents, they may be unsure of their abilities to deal with these topics. A student who has seen none of the notations will probably have an especially difficult time. With such students, you may want to move at a slightly slower pace to help them over the rough spots. We estimate 9 to 11 days on the lessons, 1 day to do the Progress Self-Test, 1 or 2 days for the Chapter Review, and 1 day for the chapter test. You may wish to spend a day on projects, and you may need a day for quizzes. We recommend 12–16 days for the chapter.

Using Pages 62–63

The cartoon presents a key idea in this chapter—extending the concepts that students have already seen to the positive numbers which are larger and smaller than those they may have encountered before. With a national debt of over 4 trillion dollars, one is tempted to ask: How much is that per person in the United States? How much is that per family? What is the interest (the amount that the government must pay the people from whom it borrowed the money) on that debt each year?

CHAPTER 2

Chapter 2 Overview

Four notations are introduced in Chapter 2: exponential notation; scientific notation with positive exponents; percent; and scientific notation with negative exponents. The first two notations are common ways of representing large numbers; the latter two represent small numbers. (For example, though 50% looks large, it is just another name for $\frac{1}{2}$.) The chapter title refers to the large and small numbers commonly represented by these notations.

The chapter could also be entitled "The Decimal System and Powers of Ten." All of the notations are based on the relationship between the decimal system and the number 10. Powers of 10 are used to write numbers in scientific notation, and the symbol % means to multiply by $\frac{1}{100}$, or 10^{-2}.

Although the content is standard, you may be surprised at the early introduction of percent and negative exponents. Percent is introduced here because the interpretation of the % symbol is very important, and we want to give students virtually the entire year to work with percents. Circle graphs are introduced here because they are the most common graphical representation of percents. Only some types of percent

LARGE AND SMALL NUMBERS

Decimal and fraction notations work well for most numbers in everyday use. But some uses require very large numbers. For instance, by 1992 the national debt of the United States, the amount the government has borrowed to finance its work, was over 4 trillion dollars. A trillion is a very large number. As a decimal it is 1,000,000,000,000. With so many digits, this decimal is difficult to work with. But, there are other notations that make things easier. One of these other notations is in the newspaper headline in the cartoon. This cartoon was drawn in 1982, near the time that the national debt first became more than a trillion dollars.

"BY THE WAY, WHAT COMES AFTER A TRILLION?"

In this chapter, you will study notations that are particularly useful for work with large and small numbers.

Photo Connections

The photo collage makes real-world connections to the content of the chapter: the use of large and small numbers.

Sky: The sky, which is the region of space visible from earth, contains countless tiny water droplets and ice crystals in the form of clouds and precipitation.

Horse Head Nebula: A nebula is a great cloud of gas and dust between stars. There are about 200 billion stars in the known universe, and most of them are between 1 million and 10 billion years old.

Subatomic Particle Tracks: As incredibly tiny as an atom is—more than a million times smaller than the thickness of a human hair—each one has subatomic particles which are even more minute.

Bacterium (Pseudomonas Aeruginosa): Electron microscopes project greatly enlarged images of bacteria—simple one cell organisms that measure from 0.3 to 2.0 microns in diameter. (1 micron = 0.000039 inch)

Penguins: Many species of penguins nest and raise their young in huge colonies called *rookeries.* A single rookery can contain as many as a million penguins.

Chapter 2 Projects

At this time you might want to have students look over the projects on pages 109–110.

problems are given in this chapter. Other types are introduced in later chapters.

Students' use of scientific calculators (which we encourage) persuaded us to introduce both positive and negative powers of 10 in this chapter. Students need to be able to interpret calculator displays in order to use them most effectively, and a few calculators display any positive number less than .01 in scientific notation.

Lesson 2-1

Objectives
A Multiply by 10, 100, 1000, and so on.
B Convert word names for numbers to decimals.

Resources
From the ***Teacher's Resource File***
- Lesson Master 2-1A or 2-1B
- Answer Master 2-1
- Teaching Aids
  4 Place-Value Chart
  13 Warm-up

Additional Resources
- Visuals for Teaching Aids 4, 13

Teaching Lesson 2-1

Warm-up
Write each number in words as you would say it.
1. 22 Twenty-two
2. 220 Two hundred twenty
3. 22,000 Twenty-two thousand
4. 220,000 Two hundred twenty thousand
5. 2,200,000 Two million, two hundred thousand

Notes on Reading
❶ **Reading Mathematics** After students have read this lesson independently, ask what clues on the printed page helped them locate the main ideas. [Sample answers: the boxed rule, the centered items, the use of italics, and boldface print]

Multicultural Connection Traditionally, baseball is considered to be

LESSON
2-1
Multiplying by 10, 100, . . .

This was not a rocky start. *A National League regular season record of 80,227 fans showed their support of the new expansion team, the Colorado Rockies, at Mile High Stadium during its 1993 home opener.*

❶ Multiplying by 10
On April 9, 1993, the baseball game between the Montreal Expos and the Colorado Rockies was attended by 80,227 (eighty thousand, two hundred twenty-seven) people. In this number, the 7 is in the ones place. There is a 2 in the tens place (so it stands for 20). There is also a 2 in the hundreds place (so it stands for 200). The 0 is in the thousands place. And the 8 is in the ten-thousands place (so it stands for 80,000). In this way, each place value is ten times the value of the place to its right. This makes it easy to multiply the number by 10. This is what you would do if the average price of a ticket were $10, and you wanted to know the total gate receipts for this game.

Attendance 8 0,2 2 7
80,227 × 10 = 8 0 2,2 7 0

The total gate receipts would be $802,270.

There is another way to think about this. Write 80,227 with a decimal point and a zero following it. (Remember that you can always insert a decimal point followed by zeros to the right of a whole number without changing its value. For example, $5 = $5.00.)

Attendance 8 0,2 2 7.0
80,227.0 × 10 = 8 0 2,2 7 0.

To multiply a number in decimal notation by 10, move the decimal point one place to the right.

For example, 62.58 × 10 = 625.8, and .0034 × 10 = .034.

Lesson 2-1 Overview
Broad Goals This lesson is the key lesson in Chapter 2. Two important ideas are introduced. The first is that from knowing how to multiply by 10, one can figure out how to multiply by 100, 1000, 10,000, and so on. The second important goal of this lesson is the interpretation of the use of words such as *thousand* or *million* as names for numbers to be multiplied, such as 3.7 million = 3.7 × 1,000,000 = 3,700,000.

Perspective The rule for multiplying by 10 is extended three times in the chapter. In Lesson 2-2, it is related to positive powers of 10. In Lesson 2-4, it is reversed and related to multiplication by $\frac{1}{10}$, $\frac{1}{100}$, and so on. In Lesson 2-8, the connection is made with negative powers. It is a wonderful example of the deduction of many properties from one single, simple property. Students should understand how later rules are related to the original rule given on page 64. Later in this chapter the use of word names is extended twice. The first extension is to tenths, thousandths, and so on in Lesson 2-4, and it is used only to describe the powers of 10. The second extension is to the word *percent,* which is interpreted as indicating to *multiply by .01.*

Multiplying by 100, 1000, 10,000, and so on

This simple idea is very powerful. Suppose you want to multiply a number by 100. Since 100 = 10 × 10, multiplying by 100 is like multiplying by 10 and then multiplying by 10 again. So move the decimal point *two* places to the right. For example, 59.072 × 100 = 5907.2.

The same idea can be extended to multiply by 1000, 10,000, and so on.

To multiply by 10, 100, 1000, and so on, move the decimal point as many places to the right as there are zeros.

$$\begin{aligned} 10 \times 47.3 &= 473. \\ 100 \times 47.3 &= 4730. \\ 1000 \times 47.3 &= 47{,}300. \\ 10{,}000 \times 47.3 &= 473{,}000. \end{aligned}$$

❷ Word Names for Some Large Numbers

In English, the numbers 10, 100, 1000, have the word names ten, hundred, thousand. Here are other numbers and their word names.

Decimal	Word name
1,000,000	million
1,000,000,000	billion
1,000,000,000,000	trillion
1,000,000,000,000,000	quadrillion
1,000,000,000,000,000,000	quintillion

❸ Now look again at the cartoon on page 63. The newsboy is holding up a newspaper mentioning a debt limit of 1.2 trillion dollars. The phrase 1.2 trillion means 1.2 *times* a trillion. Since a trillion has 12 zeros, move the decimal point 12 places to the right.

$$\begin{aligned} 1.2 \text{ trillion} &= 1.2 \times 1{,}000{,}000{,}000{,}000 \\ &= 1{,}200{,}000{,}000{,}000 \end{aligned}$$

Notice how much shorter and clearer 1.2 trillion is than 1,200,000,000,000. For these reasons, it is common to use word names for large numbers in sentences and charts.

❹ **Example**

A Bureau of Labor Statistics report in 1993 listed 118.451 million people in the United States as employed in February. Write this number in decimal notation (without words).

Solution

$$\begin{aligned} 118.451 \text{ million} &= 118.451 \times 1{,}000{,}000 \\ &= 118{,}451{,}000 \end{aligned}$$

Check

This is easy to check. Because 118.451 is between 118 and 119, you would expect 118.451 million to be between 118 million and 119 million.

the national pastime in the United States. However, organized baseball is also played in Cuba, Puerto Rico, Venezuela, the Dominican Republic, and in Panama during the winter months. Baseball was introduced to Japan in the 1870s and has become a national sport.

❷ Encourage students to memorize the word names for large numbers.

❸ In print, one sees a word name like *43 million* more often than one sees the pure decimal 43,000,000. Thus, for dealing with numbers in the real world, the ability to translate back and forth from word names to decimals is crucial.

❹ Writing a number like 118,451,000 as 118.451 million illustrates the combining of a decimal with a word, which is a form of representing numbers that is often ignored in mathematics classes but frequently required outside of them.

Additional Examples

Write each underlined number as a decimal.

1. In 1991, the United States exported 34.869 million tons of wheat to other countries.
   34,869,000
2. In 1992, the estimated population of China was 1.2 billion.
   1,200,000,000
3. There are approximately 5.88 trillion miles in a light year.
   5,880,000,000,000

LESSON MASTER 2-1 A

Questions on SPUR Objectives
See pages 113-115 for objectives.

Skills Objective A

1. Write a rule for multiplying a decimal by 10, 100, 1000, ...
   Move the decimal point 1, 2, 3, . . . places to the right.

In 2-5, write each product as a decimal.

2. 2.3 × 1,000 **2,300**
3. 100,000 × .0047 **470**
4. 36 × 10,000 **360,000**
5. 1000 × 1000 **1,000,000**

In 6-8, fill in the blank.

6. 3.9 × **1,000** = 3,900
7. **10,000** × 560 = 5,600,000
8. **100,000** × .026 = 2600
9. In earlier mathematics classes, you may have learned a rule for multiplying by powers of 10: add one zero for 10, add two zeros for 100, add three zeros, and so on. How does this rule compare to the one you learned in this lesson?
   Moving the decimal point to the right one place has the same effect as adding one zero and so on.

Skills Objective B

In 10-12, write a word name for each.

10. 6,000,000 **six million**
11. one followed by 9 zeros **one billion**
12. one followed by 15 zeros **one quadrillion**

In 13-16, write as a decimal.

13. 3.25 thousand **3,250**
14. 8 trillion **8,000,000,000,000**
15. China's estimated 1993 population: 1.183 billion **1,183,000,000**
16. Estimate of people watching Super Bowl XXVII (1993): 133.4 million **133,400,000**

Optional Activities

Multicultural Connection After students have read the lesson, you might want to point out that the prefixes *bi-*, *tri-*, *quad-*, and *quint-* are Latin prefixes for the numbers 2, 3, 4, and 5. If you have students who speak a Romance language, such as Spanish or French, you might compare these prefixes with the numbers in those languages as shown in the table.

Number	Latin prefix	Spanish	French
2	bi-	dos	deux
3	tri-	tres	trois
4	quad-	cuatro	quatre
5	quint-	cinco	cinq
6	sext-	seis	six
7	sept-	siete	sept
8	oct-	ocho	huit
9	non-	nueve	neuf
10	dec-	diez	dix

Notes on Questions

Questions 30–33 Have students explain the graph and provide a general interpretation of it. [The graph, entitled *World Population,* has dates in two-year intervals on the horizontal axis and population in half-billion intervals on the vertical axis; it shows that the world population is increasing.]

Question 43 Multicultural Connection In England and many other countries, the place-value names are the same as ours only up through hundred million. Then they continue as follows:

thousand million or *milliard* (U.S. billion)
ten thousand million
hundred thousand million
billion (U.S. trillion)
ten billion
hundred billion
thousand billion (U.S. quadrillion) and so on.

For example, in England, the world population of 5,200,000,000 might be written 5.2 thousand million.

Follow-up for Lesson 2-1

Practice

For more questions on SPUR objectives, use **Lesson Master 2-1A** (shown on page 65) or **Lesson Master 2-1B** (shown on pages 66–67).

LESSON MASTER 2-1 B Questions on SPUR Objectives

Skills Objective A: Multiply by 10, 100, 1000, and so on.

1. Give a general rule for multiplying a decimal by 1,000. Move the decimal point in the number 3 places to the right.

In 2-13, write each product as a decimal.

2. 48 × 100	4,800	3. 10 × 384	3,840
4. 7.1 × 10	71	5. 4.98 × 100	498
6. 75 × 1,000	75,000	7. 100 × 0.657	65.7
8. 100,000 × .0033	330	9. 4.09 × 10,000	40,900
10. 400 × 1,000	400,000	11. 100 × 100,000	10,000,000
12. .0056 × 100	.56	13. 10,000 × .093	930

In 14-19, fill in the blank.

14. 42 × 1,000 = 42,000
15. 100 × 6.4 = 640
16. 10,000 × 700 = 7,000,000
17. 0.083 × 1,000,000 = 83,000
18. 52 × 100 = 5,200
19. 10,000 × .00672 = 67.2

In 20-22, write the multiplication with decimals and then write the product as a decimal.

20. one tenth times ten .1 × 10 = 1
21. one hundredth times one hundred .01 × 100 = 1
22. one thousandth times one thousand .001 × 1000 = 1

In 23 and 24, DO NOT MULTIPLY. Extend the pattern from Questions 20-22 to write the product as a decimal.

23. one ten-thousandth times ten thousand 1
24. one millionth times one million 1

Leaner, meaner burgers. *Some fast-food corporations have begun offering leaner hamburgers as an alternative to the kind pictured here. The leaner burgers are lower in fat and cholesterol due to the use of fat substitutes, such as oat bran and a seaweed derivative, carrageenan.*

17) Sample: Move the decimal point as many places to the right as there are zeros following the 1.

QUESTIONS

Covering the Reading

1. In the number 81,345, the place value of the digit 1 is __?__ times the place value of the digit 3. 10

In 2–5, multiply the number by 10.

2. 634 6,340
3. 2.4 24
4. 0.08 0.8
5. 47.21 472.1
6. Give a general rule for multiplying a decimal by 10. Move the decimal point one place to the right.
7. Give a general rule for multiplying a decimal by 100. Move the decimal point two places to the right.

In 8–11, multiply the number by 100.

8. 113 11,300
9. .05 5
10. 7755.2 775,520
11. 6.301 630.1
12. Give a general rule for multiplying a decimal by 1000. Move the decimal point three places to the right.

In 13–16, calculate.

13. 32 × 1000 32,000
14. 1000 × 0.02 20
15. 1.43 × 10,000 14,300
16. 100,000 × 21.146 2,114,600
17. In your own words, write one rule for multiplying by 10, 100, 1000, etc. See left.

In 18–23, give the word name for the decimal 1 followed by:

18. 3 zeros one thousand
19. 6 zeros one million
20. 9 zeros one billion
21. 12 zeros one trillion
22. 15 zeros one quadrillion
23. 18 zeros one quintillion
24. According to "What America Eats" from *Parade Magazine,* November 24, 1991, "Sales in 1990 reached $15 billion, making pizza second only to hamburgers as America's most popular fast food." Write the underlined number in decimal notation. $15,000,000,000

In 25 and 26, the information is from the *Information Please Almanac,* 1993. Write the underlined numbers in decimal notation.

25. In the United States, there are 92.1 million homes with a TV. There are 90.8 million homes with a color TV. 92,100,000; 90,800,000
26. In 1988–1989, total funding for public elementary and secondary education in the United States was 191.21 billion dollars. $191,210,000,000

Applying the Mathematics

27. How can rounding help you check your answer to Question 15? See below.
28. 98.765 times what number equals 98,765? 1000
29. According to the U.S. Department of the Treasury, 9,324,386,076 pennies were minted in 1991. Round this number of pennies to:
    a. the nearest hundred million. 9,300,000,000
    b. the nearest ten million. 9,320,000,000

27) Sample: You can round 1.43 up to 2 or down to 1. Multiply 1 and 2 by 10,000. The answer should be between 10,000 and 20,000.

Adapting to Individual Needs

Extra Help

Use the place-value chart in **Teaching Aid 4** to show students patterns in the number names. Write digits in the chart and have students read the number. For example, 352,000,000 is read "three hundred fifty-two million" and not "3 hundred million 5 ten million 2 million."

English Language Development

Have students work in pairs and take turns saying aloud the different numbers which you write in the chart in **Teaching Aid 4.** Point out that numbers like 7 *million* and 14.2 *billion* are not read with a plural "s" as they are in some languages. After students have practiced, encourage them to try to read numbers aloud with the rest of the class.

In 30–33, use the graph to estimate world population for the given year to the nearest tenth of a billion. Write this number in decimal notation.

30. 1950 **31.** 1965 **32.** 1980 **33.** 1990

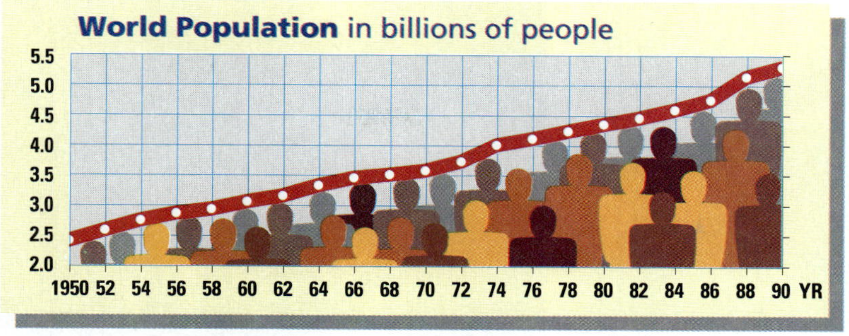

30) 2.4 billion; 2,400,000,000
31) 3.4 billion; 3,400,000,000
32) 4.3 billion or 4.4 billion; 4,300,000,000 or 4,400,000,000
33) 5.2 billion or 5.3 billion; 5,200,000,000 or 5,300,000,000

In 34–36, write the number as it might appear in a newspaper.

34. An estimated 15,000,000 people live in the Republic of Ghana. 15 million

35. Chile's gross domestic product was reported to be $27,800,000,000. 27.8 billion

36. The star *Proxima Centauri* is 24,800,000,000,000 miles from Earth. 24.8 trillion

37. Answer the question in the cartoon on page 63. the word name "quadrillion," or next whole number 1,000,000,000,001, or $1,000,000,000,000.01. See Assessment on page 67.

Review

38. Translate into mathematics: Negative ten is less than nine. *(Lesson 1-8)* $-10 < 9$

39. Change each number to a decimal. *(Lesson 1-8)*

a. $\frac{1}{8}$ .125 **b.** $\frac{1}{10}$ .1 **c.** $\frac{1}{50}$ .02 **d.** $\frac{1}{100}$ .01

40. The letters are equally spaced on the number line below.

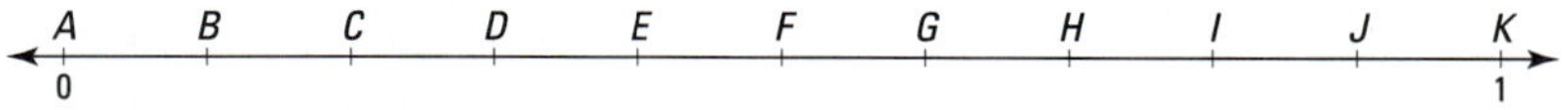

a. What number corresponds to *F*? .5

b. What number corresponds to *B*? .1

c. What letter corresponds to $\frac{3}{5}$? *G*

d. Between what neighboring letters is 0.0085? *(Lessons 1-2, 1-6)* *A* and *B*

41. Round 2.6494 *down* to thousandths. *(Lesson 1-3)* 2.649

Exploration

42. Locate, in a newspaper or magazine, at least two numbers written with a decimal followed by a word name (like those in the Example). Copy the complete sentences that contain the numbers. Answers will vary.

43. In England, the word *billion* does not always mean the number 1 followed by 9 zeros. What number does the word *billion* often represent in England? 1,000,000,000,000 (the American trillion)

Assessment

Diagnostic You might assess student understanding of Lesson 2-1 by having them write at least two answers to **Question 37.** [There are at least four possible correct answers.

(1) The word name after a trillion is quadrillion.
(2) The whole number after a trillion is a trillion one.
(3) Since the context is money, the number after a trillion is $1,000,000,000,000.01.
(4) There is no number that comes immediately after a trillion, for there is no next decimal.

With regard to answer (4), you might find how close students can come to naming numbers that come after a trillion, such as a trillion and a tenth, a trillion and a hundredth, and so on.]

Extension

Give students these problems and have them devise and describe a method for multiplying mentally.
Sample methods are given.

1. 6.24×50
   $6.24 \times 100 \div 2 = 312$
2. 25×3.6 $3.6 \times 100 \div 4 = 90$
3. 42×15 $42 \times 10 + 42 \times 10 \div 2 = 420 + 210 = 630$
4. 860×250
   $860 \times 1{,}000 \div 4 = 215{,}000$

Project Update Project 1, *One Million Pennies,* on page 109, relates to the content of this lesson. Students choosing this project might form discussion groups and decide how they will proceed.

▶ **LESSON MASTER 2-1 B** *page 2*

Skills Objective B: Convert word names for numbers to decimals.

In 25-31, write a word name for each.

25. 8,000,000 eight million
26. 12,000,000,000 twelve billion
27. 760,000,000 seven hundred sixty million
28. 32,000,000,000,000,000 thirty-two quadrillion
29. 156,000,000,000,000 one hundred fifty-six trillion
30. one followed by 12 zeros one trillion
31. one followed by 18 zeros one quintillion

In 32-36, write as a decimal.

32. 5.6 thousand 5,600
33. 3 billion 3,000,000,000
34. 5 trillion 5,000,000,000,000
35. 3.22 quintillion 3,220,000,000,000,000,000
36. 824 quadrillion 824,000,000,000,000,000

In 37-41, write the underlined numbers in decimal notation.

37. The temperature at the core of the sun is about *35 million* degrees Fahrenheit. 35,000,000
38. In four months, a pair of houseflies could produce *190 quintillion* descendants if all of them survived. 190,000,000,000,000,000,000
39. In 1990, *4.179 million* babies were born in the United States. 4,179,000
40. in 1870, the United States was *2.4 billion* dollars in debt. 2,400,000,000
41. In 1990, the U.S. Department of the Treasury collected nearly *4.7 trillion* dollars from individual (non-corporate) income taxes. 4,700,000,000,000

Adapting to Individual Needs

Challenge
You might have students find situations in which large numbers relate to populations of countries as a whole. Then have them interpret the situations on a per-person basis. For example, in 1993, it was reported that about $770 billion is spent each year on entitlement programs in the United States. (You may need to explain to students that entitlements are rights to guaranteed benefits under a government program such as Social Security or unemployment compensation.) Using 250 million as the population gives $3080 as the approximate amount spent per person on entitlements.

Lesson 2-2

Objectives

A Multiply by 10, 100, 1000, and so on.
C Convert powers to decimals.
D Give decimals and English word names for positive integer powers of 10.

Resources

From the ***Teacher's Resource File***
- Lesson Master 2-2A or 2-2B
- Answer Master 2-2
- Teaching Aids
  13 Warm-up
  16 Powers of Two
  17 Powers of Ten

Additional Resources
- Visuals for Teaching Aids 13, 16–17

Teaching Lesson 2-2

Warm-up

Compute.
1. 4×4 16
2. 8×8 64
3. $5 \times 5 \times 5$ 125
4. $10 \times 10 \times 10 \times 10$ 10,000
5. $3 \times 3 \times 3 \times 3 \times 3$ 243
6. 1.2×1.2 1.44
7. $.2 \times .2 \times .2$ .008

Notes on Reading

There is a lot for students to digest in this lesson. Students learn how to compute positive powers and should begin to appreciate the ease of finding powers of 10. Also, they should realize that powering is an operation that can give surprisingly large results.

LESSON

2-2 Powers

Where is it used? *Unlike our base 10 system which has ten digits (0, 1, 2, . . ., 9), the base 2 system has only two digits (0 and 1). Computers, laser discs, and CDs rely on the simple process of recognizing a 0 or 1 to generate sounds or pictures like the one above.*

What Are Powers?

In Lesson 2-1, you multiplied by 100. This was explained as multiplying by 10, followed by multiplying by 10. Repeated multiplication is so common that there is a shorthand for it. We write

$$10^2$$

(say "10 to the 2nd **power**" or "the second power of 10") to mean 10×10, or 100. In 10^2, the number 10 is called the **base,** and 2 is called the **exponent.** Similarly, 10^3 (say "10 to the 3rd power") means $10 \times 10 \times 10$, or 1000, and 10^4 (say "10 to the 4th power") means $10 \times 10 \times 10 \times 10$, or 10,000. In this book, only integers are used as exponents. With integer exponents, any number can be used as a base.

Words		Exponential form		Repeated multiplication		Decimal
3 to the 2nd power	=	3^2	=	3×3	=	9
8 to the 3rd power	=	8^3	=	$8\times8\times8$	=	512
1.3 to the 5th power	=	1.3^5	=	$1.3\times1.3\times1.3\times1.3\times1.3$	=	3.71293
1 to the 7th power	=	1^7	=	$1\times1\times1\times1\times1\times1\times1$	=	1

Some Important Powers to Know

We say that a number "to the first power" equals the number itself. So "3 to the first power" means 3^1, which equals 3. Also, $10^1 = 10$ and $\left(\frac{3}{4}\right)^1 = \frac{3}{4}$.

Lesson 2-2 Overview

Broad Goals In this lesson students learn about the positive integer powers of any number, but the positive integer powers of 10 are emphasized. Students should see that multiplication of a decimal by a power of 10 can be easily described in terms of the value of the exponent.

Perspective The operation that is implicit in 3^2 or 10^5 is called *powering or exponentiation* and more informally "taking the power." In powering, the first number is the base, the second number is the exponent, and the result is called the power. So we prefer the term "powering" because it conveys the idea of the result of the operation.

When the exponent is a positive integer, the relationship of powering to repeated multiplication can be used to change a number from exponential notation, say 4^5, to decimal notation, 1024. Without a calculator, the calculations are usually tedious, and only small integer exponents and bases can be considered. With a calculator, the y^x key can calculate powers directly, even when the exponent is not a positive integer.

Sometimes one does not have to resort to repeated multiplication to change from exponential notation to decimal notation. Such is the case when writing very large powers of 10.

❶ It is useful to know some powers of small numbers without having to calculate them every time. Here are the smallest positive integer powers of 2:

$2^1 = 2 \quad 2^2 = 4 \quad 2^3 = 8 \quad 2^4 = 16 \quad 2^5 = 32$
$2^6 = 64 \quad 2^7 = 128 \quad 2^8 = 256 \quad 2^9 = 512 \quad 2^{10} = 1024$

If you do not know the powers of 2, you have to calculate them.

Positive Integer Powers of Ten

The powers of 10 are very special in the decimal system. You can calculate them in your head. We have already noted that $10^1 = 10$, $10^2 = 100$, $10^3 = 1000$, and $10^4 = 10,000$. The next power, 10^5, is found by multiplying 10,000 by 10. So $10^5 = 100,000$. Notice the pattern: when written as decimals, 10^1 is a 1 followed by 1 zero, 10^2 is a 1 followed by 2 zeros, 10^3 is a 1 followed by 3 zeros, and so on. So 10^{12} is a 1 followed by 12 zeros; it is another way of writing one trillion.

You have now seen three different ways of representing the place values in the decimal system.

❷

Power of 10	Word name	Written as decimal
10^1	ten	10
10^2	hundred	100
10^3	thousand	1,000
10^6	million	1,000,000
10^9	billion	1,000,000,000
10^{12}	trillion	1,000,000,000,000
10^{15}	quadrillion	1,000,000,000,000,000
10^{18}	quintillion	1,000,000,000,000,000,000

Multiplying by Positive Integer Powers of Ten

You already know a quick way to multiply by 10, 100, 1000, and so on. It is just as quick to multiply by these numbers when they are written as powers.

$$53 \times 10^5 = 53 \times 100,000 = 5,300,000$$
$$2.38 \times 10^4 = 2.38 \times 10,000 = 23,800.$$

The decimal point moves to the right one place for each power of 10.

To multiply by a positive integer power of 10
Move the decimal point to the right the same number of places as the value of the exponent.

Error Alert When encountering powering for the first time, some students think that powering and multiplication are the same. For example, the student will think 3^4 is 12, not 81. Emphasize that powering means to use the base as a factor, computing $3 \times 3 \times 3 \times 3$. Also point out that the operation of powering would not be needed if the answer were always the same as the answer derived from multiplying. Alert students not to be fooled by the special case of the first power, $3^1 = 3$.

❶ At this time you might like to use the activity given below in *Optional Activities.* **Teaching Aid 16** shows students how rapidly the powers of 2 increase.

❷ Students can refer to **Teaching Aid 17** for names of some positive integer powers of 10.

It is fine for students to memorize that, when multiplying by a positive integer power of 10, one moves the decimal point by as many zeros as are in the number. But it is also important for students to know that if they forget the rule, there is an easy way of deriving it. We encourage you to emphasize how later rules are related to the original rule given in Lesson 2-1 on page 64.

Optional Activities

Materials: Paper, scissors

Use this activity after discussing the powers of 2. Have students cut a sheet of paper in half. Then have them put the halves one on top of the other, and cut the halves in half. Then cut those pieces in half, and so on. After each cut, record the number of pieces in a table. Point out how quickly the number increases to 512 pieces. Then show them **Teaching Aid 16.**

Cuts	Pieces	Power of 2
0	1	2^0
1	2	2^1
2	4	2^2
3	8	2^3
4	16	2^4
5	32	2^5
6	64	2^6
7	128	2^7
8	256	2^8
9	512	2^9

LESSON MASTER 2-2 A

Questions on SPUR Objectives
See pages 113-115 for objectives.

Skills Objective A

1. What is the general rule for multiplying by a positive integer power of ten? Move the decimal point to the right the same number of places as the value of the exponent.

In 2-5, write each product as a decimal.

2. 9×10^4 90,000
3. $10^6 \times 4.8$ 4,800,000
4. $.025 \times 10^5$ 2,500
5. $10^3 \times 10^4$ 10,000,000

Skills Objective C

In 6-9, write each power as a decimal.

6. 2^8 256
7. 23^2 529
8. 4^5 1,024
9. 0^{523} 0
10. Write a key sequence for evaluating 15^4. 15 [y^x] 4 [=]
11. Write 15^4 as a decimal. 50,625
12. Put in order from least to greatest: $2^5 \quad 5^2 \quad 3^5 \quad 5^3 \quad 3^2$ — $3^2 \quad 5^2 \quad 2^5 \quad 5^3 \quad 3^5$

Skills Objective D

13. How do you read 8^5? 8 to the 5th power
14. Write as a power: seven to the fourth power. 7^4
15. One hundred million is 10 to the eighth power.
16. What is the word name for 10^9? one billion

In 17-20, write as a decimal.

17. 10^1 10
18. 10^7 10,000,000
19. 10^4 10,000
20. 10^{12} 1,000,000,000,000

Additional Examples

You might want to use these examples when discussing the lesson.

1. Calculate each power.
   a. 4^3 **64** **b.** 10^7 **10,000,000**
2. Write as a decimal
   a. 8×10^5 **800,000**
   b. 2.03×10^4 **20,300**
3. Write the key sequence to calculate 9^4. **9 [y^x] 4 [=]**

Notes on Questions

Question 5 This question should help to dispel the common error of multiplying base and exponent. The question also demonstrates the power of the exponent; 20 gives a much larger result as an exponent than as a base.

Questions 24–25 Writing For each of these questions, you might have students write explanations about how they arrived at their answers. This kind of explanation of the method or process is sometimes referred to as *chatter.* Chatter helps the writer remember how an answer was found without having to redo the question.

Question 26 There is no universal convention for calculators regarding which comes first, powering or multiplication. Thus, this question helps to set up the issue of order of operations, formally addressed in Lesson 4-1.

(Notes on Questions are continued on page 72.)

LESSON MASTER 2-2 B Questions on SPUR Objectives

Vocabulary

1. In 9^4,
   a. which number is the base? **9**
   b. which number is the exponent? **4**

Skills Objective A: Multiply by 10, 100, 1000, and so on.

2. When you multiply by a positive integer power of ten,
   a. which way do you move the decimal point? **right**
   b. how many places do you move the decimal point? **same number of places as value of exponent**

In 3-10, write each product as a decimal.

3. 4×10^5 **400,000**
4. $10^4 \times 7.1$ **71,000**
5. $10^2 \times .048$ **4.8**
6. $10^6 \times 1.2297$ **1,229,700**
7. 123.4×10^3 **123,400**
8. $10^2 \times 10^6$ **100,000,000**
9. $.000096 \times 10^3$ **.096**
10. 249×10^4 **2,490,000**

Skills Objective C: Convert powers to decimals.

In 11-18, write each power as a decimal.

11. 2^7 **128**
12. 41^2 **1,681**
13. 3^5 **243**
14. 7^3 **343**
15. 1^{63} **1**
16. 1.6^2 **2.56**
17. 0^{142} **0**
18. $4{,}982^1$ **4,982**
19. Write a key sequence for evaluating 8^5. **8 [y^x] 5 [=]**
20. Write 8^5 as a decimal. **32,768**

Finding Other Powers

Besides powers of 10, only a few powers of small numbers are easy to calculate by hand. Powers of other small numbers can be quite large. For example, $9^8 = 43{,}046{,}721$. Usually it is quicker and more accurate to use a calculator. A scientific calculator has a special key labeled [x^y] or [y^x] or [^], the powering key. (If this label is in small print above or below a key, you will need to press [INV] or [2nd] or [F] before pressing the powering key.) For example, to evaluate 5^7, enter the following:

Key sequence:	5	[y^x]	7	[=]
Display:	5.	5.	7.	78125.

So $5^7 = 78{,}125$.

Note: Whether the key is labeled [x^y] or [y^x] or [^], the base is entered before the exponent.

Activity

Use your calculator to verify the value for 9^8 given above.

QUESTIONS

Covering the Reading

1. Consider 4^6.
   a. Name the base. **4**
   b. Name the exponent. **6**
   c. This number is __?__ to the __?__th __?__. **4 to the 6th power**
2. Calculate 3^1, 3^2, 3^3, 3^4, 3^5, and 3^6. **3; 9; 27; 81; 243; 729**
3. Give the values of 2^1, 2^2, 2^3, 2^4, 2^5, and 2^6. **2; 4; 8; 16; 32; 64**
4. Calculate 7^6. **117,649**
5. Calculate 2^{20} and 20^2. **1,048,576; 400**
6. Calculate 1^{994}. **1**
7. Calculate 1.08^3. (This kind of calculation is found in money matters.) **1.259712**
8. In decimal notation, 10^7 is a 1 followed by __?__ zeros. **seven**
9. Write 10^6 in the indicated form.
   a. decimal **1,000,000** **b.** word name **one million**
10. Write one thousand in the indicated form.
    a. decimal **1,000** **b.** as a power of 10 **10^3**
11. Write each number as a power of 10.
    a. million **10^6** **b.** billion **10^9** **c.** trillion **10^{12}**

Adapting to Individual Needs

Extra Help

Draw the table shown at the right on the board, or duplicate it on paper and distribute to students. After discussing 2^3, have students fill in the tables for various powers. Stress that the exponent tells how many times the base is multiplied by itself. Then call on different students to explain one of their powers.

Power	2^3	
Base	2	
Exponent	3	
Write the Base as Factors	$2 \times 2 \times 2 = 8$	

17) Move the decimal point to the right the same number of places as the value of the exponent.

26 b) If the calculator does the multiplication first, the answer will be 7776. If the answer is 96, the calculator took the power first.

28) forty-three quintillion, two hundred fifty-two quadrillion, three trillion, two hundred seventy-four billion, four hundred eighty-nine million, eight hundred fifty-six thousand

Are you a puzzlemeister? *The object of many puzzles is to mix them up and then return them to their original position. Rubik's Cube™, invented by Hungarian professor Erno Rubik, is shown at the bottom left.*

12. According to the table in this lesson, 10 to the first power is equal to what number? **10**

In 13–16, write the number as a decimal.

13. 5×10^2 **500**

14. 8×10^3 **8,000**

15. 3.7×10^4 **37,000**

16. 0.246×10^6 **246,000**

17. Write the general rule for multiplying by a positive integer power of 10. **See left.**

18. To multiply by 10 to the first power, you should move the decimal point how many places to the right? **one**

Applying the Mathematics

19. What number is 1 less than 10^3? **999**

20. Which is larger, 2^3 or 3^2? **3^2**

21. The table in this lesson skips from 10^3 to 10^6. Fill in the two rows that are missing. **10^4, ten thousand, 10,000; 10^5, hundred thousand, 100,000**

22. Ten million is the __?__ power of 10. **seventh**

23. **a.** Give the next number in this pattern of powers: 256, 64, 16, __?__. **4**

b. The smallest positive integer powers of what integer are in part **a**? **4**

24. *Multiple choice.* $3^{10} - 2^{10}$ is between

(a) 1 and 100. (b) 100 and 10,000.
(c) 10,000 and 1,000,000. **(c)**

25. Two ways 72 can be written as the sum or difference of powers are $72 = 9^2 - 3^2$ and $72 = 6^2 + 6^2$. Write 100 as a sum and a difference of powers. **Samples: $6^2 + 8^2 = 100$; $26^2 - 24^2 = 100$**

26. **a.** Enter the key sequence 3 [×] 2 [y^x] 5 [=] on your calculator. What number results? **96**

b. Some calculators do the multiplication first, then take the power. Other calculators take the power first, then multiply. What did your calculator do first? **See above left.**

27. *True or false.* $2^{10} > 10^3$. **True**

28. The object of a puzzle known as Rubik's Cube™ is to mix up the cube, then return it to its original position. There are 43,252,003,274,489,856,000 possible positions. Write this number in English. (This shows how much easier decimal notation is than English words.) **See above left.**

Follow-up for Lesson 2-2

Practice

For more questions on SPUR objectives, use **Lesson Master 2-2A** (shown on page 69) or **Lesson Master 2-2B** (shown on pages 70–71).

Assessment

Oral/Written Communication Divide the class into groups. Have them tell in writing what is wrong with each of the following sentences.

1. $9^2 = 18$
2. $10^7 = 1{,}000{,}000$
3. $12^3 = 12 + 12 + 12$

Sample answers are given.

1. **9^2 means 9×9, or 81.**
2. **When the base is 10, the exponent tells how many zeros there are after the one. There should be 7 zeros in this number.**
3. **Twelve to the third power means to use 12 as a factor, not as an addend.**

Extension

Multicultural Connection If you have not already done so, you might give students the place-value names used in Britain. (See the notes for Question 43 in Lesson 2-1.) Ask students if they can find a connection between the names and the number of zeros in the numbers. [In the British system, the prefixes bi-

▸ **LESSON MASTER 2-2 B** *page 2*

21. Which is larger, 3^6 or 6^3? **3^6**

22. Which is smaller, 0.2^5 or 1^3? **0.2^5**

23. Put in order from least to greatest: 4^2 2^5 3^4 4^3 2^3 **2^3 4^2 2^5 4^3 3^4**

24. Put in order from least to greatest: $.75^2$ $.75^4$ $.75^3$ $.75^1$ **$.75^4$ $.75^3$ $.75^2$ $.75^1$**

Skills Objective D: Give decimals and English word names for positive integer powers of 10.

In 25 and 26, tell how you read each power. Do not evaluate.

25. 4^7 **four to the seventh power**

26. 12^5 **twelve to the fifth power**

In 27 and 28, write as a power.

27. nine to the sixth power **9^6**

28. five to the second power **5^2**

29. One billion is 10 to the **9th** power.

In 30-35, give the word name for each number.

30. 10^6 **one million**

31. 10^{12} **one trillion**

32. 10^3 **one thousand**

33. 10^5 **one hundred thousand**

34. 10^{10} **ten billion**

35. 10^{15} **one quadrillion**

In 36-39, write as a decimal.

36. 10^2 **100**

37. 10^8 **100.000,000**

38. 10^{11} **100,000,000,000**

39. 10^{13} **10,000,000,000,000**

Adapting to Individual Needs

English Language Development
The words *base, factor,* and *power* have many definitions, some of which students know already. Have them write several meanings of the words including the mathematical definitions, and then draw a picture for each definition to help them remember the words.

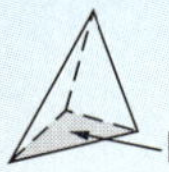

$5^2 \longleftarrow$ base

Challenge
Have students imagine they are going to work for 20 days. Which of the following payment schedules would they choose and why? (1) \$100 a day or (2) 2¢ the first day, 4¢ the second day, 8¢ the third day, 16¢ the fourth day, and so on. [For rate 1, \$100 a day earns \$2000 in 20 days. For rate 2, starting with 2¢ and doubling the amount each day gives \$20,971.50 in 20 days.]

(meaning 2), tri- (3), quad- (4), and quint- (5) stand for the number of groups of 6 zeros in the number. That is, a billion is 10^{12} (or 2 groups of 6 zeros); a trillion is 10^{18} (or 3 groups of 6 zeros); a quadrillion is 10^{24} (or 4 groups of 6 zeros); and so on.]

Project Update Project 4, *Powers of 10,* on page 110, relates to the content of this lesson. Students choosing this project might want to look for the book and/or film (or video) in the school library or in a public library. If neither the book nor the film is available locally, the librarian may be able to borrow them from another library.

Notes on Questions

Question 33 Barry Sanders, who plays for the Detroit Lions professional football team, is one of the premier running backs in football.

Question 34 Geography Connection Lake Baikal, one of the world's oldest lakes, lies in southeastern Siberia. While 336 rivers flow into Lake Baikal, only one, the Angara River, empties out of it. You might want to have students find Lake Baikal on a world map.

Question 40 The word *googol* is in some dictionaries and encyclopedias. Students will also find that googols are discussed in books that cover the history of mathematics. You might tell students that a *googolplex* is even larger than a googol. It is 10 to the googol power.

Question 41c You might use this question to promote interest in the next lesson. Most calculators and computers do not display enough digits to show the exact value 576,650,390,625. Instead they show the answer in scientific notation. The TI-30 displays

[5.7665 11].

The Casio fx-7700G displays

[5.766503906E+11]

and the TI-81 displays

[5.766503906E11].

Point out that students will learn to interpret these displays in Lesson 2-3.

How big is Lake Baikal? *Lake Baikal, 395 miles long, contains more water than all five of North America's Great Lakes put together. It holds $\frac{1}{5}$ of the world's fresh water supply and is home to 27 islands.*

Review

29. According to a 1993 estimate, the world population had grown by 2.5 billion people since 1960. Write 2.5 billion as a decimal. *(Lesson 2-1)* 2,500,000,000

In 30–32, multiply in your head. *(Lesson 2-1)*

30. $100 \times 10{,}000$ 1,000,000 **31.** $180 \times 10{,}000$ 1,800,000 **32.** 20×400 8000

In 33–35, write the positive or negative decimal suggested by the situation. *(Lesson 1-8)*

33. Barry Sanders ran for thirteen yards on the first play of the game. 13

34. The deepest lake in the world, Lake Baikal in Siberia, has a point that is eleven hundred eighty-one meters below sea level. -1,181

35. Absolute zero is four hundred fifty-nine and sixty-seven hundredths degrees Fahrenheit below zero. -459.67

36. Tell whether the number is or is not an integer. *(Lesson 1-8)*

a. -3 Yes **b.** 4.7 No **c.** 4.0 Yes **d.** $\frac{15}{3}$ Yes

e. $-17\frac{1}{3}$ No **f.** $\frac{89}{5}$ No **g.** 23 Yes

37. What digit is in the thousandths place when $\frac{15}{7}$ is rewritten as a decimal? *(Lessons 1-2, 1-6)* 2

38. What number results from this key sequence? *(Lesson 1-5)* $44.\overline{4}$

8 [÷] 9 [÷] 4 [×] 200 [=]

39. Suppose you buy 3 shirts at $8.95 each. What multiplication can you do to estimate the cost to the nearest dollar? *(Lesson 1-4)*
3 × 9 = 27

Exploration

40. A *googol* is one of the largest numbers that has a name. Look in a dictionary or other reference book to find out something about this number. 10^{100}, or 1 followed by 100 zeros

41. Calculate 3^5 using a computer. (You will need to type a symbol, usually either ^ or **, between the 3 and the 5.)

a. What did you type to get the computer to calculate 3^5?

b. Use this computer to compute 6^7. Compare this result with the result given on your calculator.

c. Repeat part **b** for the number 15^{10}.

a) Answers will vary. Samples: PRINT 3^5 or PRINT 3**5
b) 6^7 = 279936; they are the same.
c) Sample: 5.7665E11; the computer may use slightly different notation and give more decimal places in 5.7665 . . .

Setting Up Lesson 2-3

Materials Students will need a scientific calculator for Lesson 2-3.

Previewing the Reading Remind students that as they read, they should use their calculators when appropriate.

LESSON

2-3

Scientific Notation for Large Numbers

Striking information. *Every year about 100 people in the U.S. are injured by lightning which carries 10 to 30 million volts of electricity. So during a lightning storm, go indoors, get in a car, or lie down in a ditch.*

You should have a scientific calculator and some paper to use as you read this lesson.

Light travels at the speed of about 186,282.4 miles per second. Since there are 60 seconds in a minute, light travels 60 × 186,282.4 miles per minute.

❶ **Activity 1**

Multiply 60 by 186,282.4 on your calculator. Record the answer.

To find out how far light travels in an hour, multiply by 60 again.

$$60 \times 186{,}282.4 \times 60 = 670{,}616{,}640 \text{ miles per hour}$$

Calculator Displays of Large Numbers

When the multiplication 60 × 186,282.4 × 60 is done on a calculator, the calculator will do one of three things.

1. It may display all 9 digits. `670616640.`
2. It may display an error message, like one of those below. This means that the number is too big for the calculator. The calculator will not do anything until you clear the number.

   `E 6.7061664` `ERROR 0` `ERROR`

3. It may display the number in *scientific notation.* The display usually looks like one of those shown here.

   `6.7061664 08` `6.7062 08` `6.7062 x 10 8`

Scientific notation is the way that scientific calculators display very large and very small numbers. Each of the above displays stands for the number 6.7061664×10^8 or a rounded value of that number. The user is expected to know that the 8 (or 08) stands for 10^8. So to convert the number into decimal notation, move the decimal point 8 places to the right. (The display at the right above contains × 10 and is clearest.)

Lesson 2-3

Objectives

F Convert large numbers into and out of scientific notation.

L Identify numbers as being written in scientific notation.

N Indicate key sequences and displays for large numbers on a calculator.

Resources

From the ***Teacher's Resource File***

- Lesson Master 2-3A or 2-3B
- Answer Master 2-3
- Assessment Sourcebook: Quiz for Lessons 2-1 through 2-3
- Teaching Aid 13: Warm-up
- Technology Sourcebook, Calculator Master 3

Additional Resources

- Visual for Teaching Aid 13

Teaching Lesson 2-3

Warm-up

Give the missing number.

1. 3.2 × _?_ = 3.2 **1**
2. _?_ × 2.75 = 275 **100 or 10^2**
3. 83,371 = 8.3371 × _?_ **10,000 or 10^4**
4. 3.276 × _?_ = 3,276,000 **1,000,000 or 10^6**
5. 3.2 × _?_ = 32 **10**
6. 4.83 × _?_ = 4830 **1000 or 10^3**
7. 900,050 = 9.0005 × _?_ **100,000 or 10^5**

Notes on Reading

❶ This lesson requires students to use a scientific calculator as they read.

Health Connection After students read the caption under the picture, you might want to discuss other safety precautions people can take to avoid being struck by lightning. Stay away from metal vehicles like bicycles or golf carts. Sit or crouch down if you are caught in an open area. Do not stand under or near individual tall trees or other

Lesson 2-3 Overview

Broad Goals Scientific notation is introduced early because students using scientific calculators must be able to interpret answers displayed in scientific notation.

Perspective Most calculators display an error message when a number they are asked to give is beyond their bounds. For non-scientific calculators, an error message is given for any number that exceeds the number of digits in the display. Scientific and graphics calculators have a greater capacity to display numbers than do simpler four-function calculators because of their ability to display numbers in scientific notation. Thus, for numbers as important as the U.S. or world population, or the distance to the nearest star, your students need to know scientific notation and how to work with these numbers on calculators.

isolated objects in open areas. Do not rise above the landscape by standing on a hill or in an open field, and stay away from water. Use the telephone only in emergencies.

❷ It is impractical to require that key sequences be written every time the calculator is used. However, it is useful for students to practice writing the steps enough times so that, if requested, they can describe how they used their calculators.

Cooperative Learning It is important that students do the three activities in the reading. Because calculators differ, and because some students may need help, you may want students to work on the activities in groups.

After Activity 3 is finished, you might want to list on the board the different ways students' calculators display scientific notation. Be certain that all students understand when an answer is given in scientific notation and that they know how to enter a number given in scientific notation into a calculator.

Example 1

Calculate how far light travels in a day.

Solution

The key sequence below includes all the calculations done so far in this lesson and a multiplication by 24, the number of hours in a day.

❷ Key sequence: 60 [×] 186,282.4 [×] 60 [×] 24 [=]

The exact product is 16,094,799,360.

Many calculators must round the answer to 1.60948×10^{10} because they do not have enough room to display all digits.

Display: [1.60948   10]

To write 1.60948×10^{10} as a decimal, perform this multiplication without a calculator. Move the decimal point 10 places to the right.

Answer: Light travels about 16,094,800,000 miles in a day.

Activity 2

Use your calculator to determine how far light travels in a 365-day year. This is the *distance* known as a **light-year.** Show your work as in Example 1.

What Is Scientific Notation?

The number 1.60948×10^{10} in Example 1 is in scientific notation.

In scientific notation, a number greater than or equal to 1 and less than 10 is multiplied by an integer power of 10.

$$decimal \times 10^{exponent}$$

Here are some more numbers written in scientific notation.

Decimal or word name	Scientific notation
670,620,000	6.7062×10^8
340.67	3.4067×10^2
2,380,000,000	2.38×10^9
60 trillion	6×10^{13}

Notice that there are three parts to scientific notation:

a number from 1 to 10, but less than 10
a multiplication sign
a power of 10.

Calculators often omit the multiplication sign and show the exponent instead of the power of 10.

Converting Decimals into Scientific Notation

Examples 2 and 3 show how to convert decimals into scientific notation.

Optional Activities

Activity 1 Science Connection After students have read the lesson, give them the distances from various planets to the sun, or have students research the information. Then have them write each distance in scientific notation.

Planet	Approximate distance from sun	Scientific notation
Mercury	35.9 million miles	[3.59×10^7 miles]
Venus	67.2 million miles	[6.72×10^7 miles]
Earth	93.0 million miles	[9.3×10^7 miles]
Mars	141.6 million miles	[1.416×10^8 miles]
Jupiter	483.6 million miles	[4.836×10^8 miles]
Saturn	886.7 million miles	[8.867×10^8 miles]
Uranus	1.8 trillion miles	[1.8×10^9 miles]
Neptune	2.8 trillion miles	[2.8×10^9 miles]
Pluto	3.7 trillion miles	[3.7×10^9 miles]

Activity 2 Technology Connection With *Technology Sourcebook, Calculator Master 3,* students determine when the positive-interger powers of 2, 3, and so on, become large enough to appear in scientific notation.

Example 2

The distance from Earth to the Sun is about 150,000,000 km. Write this number in scientific notation.

Solution

First, move the decimal point to get a number between 1 and 10. In this case, the number is 1.5 and this tells you the answer will look like this:

$$1.5 \times 10^{exponent}.$$

Second, find the power of 10. The exponent of 10 is the number of places you must move the decimal in 1.5 to the *right* in order to get 150,000,000. You must move it 8 places, so the number in scientific notation is:

$$1.5 \times 10^8.$$

Example 3

Write 45,678 in scientific notation.

Solution

Ask yourself: 45,678 equals 4.5678 times what power of 10? The answer to the question is 4. So

$$45{,}678 = 4.5678 \times 10^4.$$

Numbers with word names are easy to convert to scientific notation. Use the power of 10 equivalent to the word name.

India has two Delhis. *The busy street pictured here is Chandi Chowk Street of Old Delhi. Just three miles south of Old Delhi is New Delhi, the capital of India and a modern, carefully planned city.*

Example 4

The population of India is expected to exceed 1.4 billion by the year 2025. This number is 1,400,000,000 and has too many digits for most calculators. Write it in scientific notation so that it can be entered into a calculator and used.

Solution

Since 1 billion $= 10^9$, 1.4 billion $= 1.4 \times 10^9$. This is already in scientific notation.

You can enter a number in scientific notation directly into your calculator.

Activity 3

Enter 1.4 billion on your calculator, using one of the key sequences:

1.4 [EE] 9 or 1.4 [Exp] 9.

Either key sequence enters 1.4×10^9.

a. Identify the key sequence you need to use on your calculator.

b. Check by entering 1.4 [×] 10 [y^x] 9 [=]. Do you get the same answer?

Additional Examples

1. More than 300 million copies of Agatha Christie's mysteries have been sold. The mysteries have been translated into 103 languages. If each book contains about 75,000 words, write the approximate total number of printed words
   - **a.** in scientific notation. 2.25×10^{13}
   - **b.** as a decimal. 22,500,000,000,000
   - **c.** using the place-value name. 22.5 trillion
2. Write each number in scientific notation.
   - **a.** The *Mona Lisa*, which was painted by Leonardo da Vinci, has been valued for insurance purposes at \$100 million . 1×10^8
   - **b.** The distance from Earth to the star Proxima Centauri is 24,800,000,000,000 miles. 2.48×10^{13}
3. Hens at the largest chicken ranch in the United States—Croton Egg Farm in Croton, Ohio—produce over 1.35 billion eggs annually. Write this number
   - **a.** as a decimal. 1,350,000,000
   - **b.** in scientific notation. 1.35×10^9
4. Write a googol in scientific notation. 1×10^{100}

LESSON MASTER 2-3 A

Questions on SPUR Objectives
See pages 113-115 for objectives.

Skills Objective F

In 1-4, write each number in scientific notation.

1. 324.8 3.248×10^2
2. 7,960,000 7.96×10^6
3. 3.5 trillion 3.5×10^{12}
4. 600 million 6×10^8

In 5-7, write each number as a decimal.

5. 3.7×10^7 37,000,000
6. 9.168×10^4 91,680
7. the number of molecules in 18 grams of water: 6.023×10^{23} 602,300,000,000,000,000,000,000

Properties Objective L

In 8-10, explain why each number is *not* in scientific notation.

8. $3 \times 10^{2.5}$ The power is not an integer.
9. $.034 \times 10^{10}$ The number .034 is less than one.
10. 9.5×6^5 The number, 6^5 is not a power of ten.

Representations Objective N

In 11-13, write a key sequence. Then write the calculator display.

	Key Sequence	Display
11. 3.8×10^{14}	3.8 [EE] (or [EXP]) 14 [=]	3.8 14
12. 27,400,000,000	27400 [EE] (or [EXP]) 6 [=]	2.74 10
13. 5 trillion	5 [EE] (or [EXP]) 12 [=]	5 12

14. The U.S. population in 1991 was about 250 million people. The average individual income tax paid was about \$1870. Estimate the total amount of money paid in individual income tax in 1991.
   - a. 250,000,000 × \$1870 (calculation to do)
   - b. 6 [×] 1870 [=] 250 [EE] (or [EXP]) (key sequence)
   - c. 4.675 11 (calculator display)
   - d. The total amount of money paid in individual income tax in 1991 was about \$467.5 billion. (sentence to answer the question)

Video

Wide World of Mathematics In the segment, *Hubble Telescope,* NASA scientists discuss the telescope's huge size and pinpoint accuracy. The telescope shows galaxies as they were billions of years ago. The data provide motivation for launching a lesson on scientific notation. Related questions and an investigation are provided in videodisc stills and in the Video Guide. A related CD-ROM activity is also available.

Videodisc Bar Codes

Search Chapter 9

Play

Notes on Questions

Question 17 Cooperative Learning Students enjoy comparing answers and figuring out which numbers are really the largest and smallest that can be displayed on their calculators. Have students write the answers that were shown on the calculators in their groups, and compare all the answers in a class discussion.

Follow-up for Lesson 2-3

Practice

For more questions on SPUR objectives, use **Lesson Master 2-3A** (shown on page 75) or **Lesson Master 2-3B** (shown on pages 76–77).

Assessment

Quiz A quiz covering Lessons 2-1 through 2-3 is provided in the *Assessment Sourcebook.*

Written Communication This is a good time for students to summarize what they have studied in Lessons 2-1 through 2-3. These three lessons have covered large numbers, whereas in the rest of the chapter, students will learn about small numbers and percents. [Summaries contain examples and explanations showing understanding of large numbers and how to write and read them.]

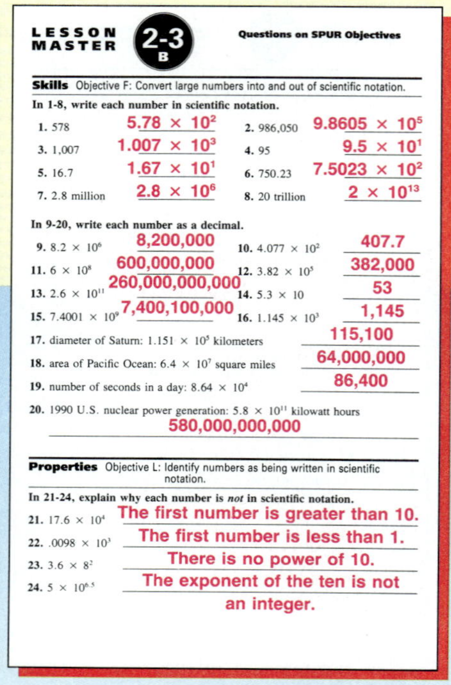

LESSON MASTER 2-3 B **Questions on SPUR Objectives**

Skills Objective F: Convert large numbers into and out of scientific notation.

In 1-8, write each number in scientific notation.

1. 578 5.78×10^2 **2.** 986,050 9.8605×10^5

3. 1,007 1.007×10^3 **4.** 95 9.5×10^1

5. 16.7 1.67×10^1 **6.** 750.23 7.5023×10^2

7. 2.8 million 2.8×10^6 **8.** 20 trillion 2×10^{13}

In 9-20, write each number as a decimal.

9. 8.2×10^6 8,200,000 **10.** 4.077×10^2 407.7

11. 6×10^8 600,000,000 **12.** 3.82×10^5 382,000

13. 2.6×10^{11} 260,000,000,000 **14.** 5.3×10 53

15. 7.4001×10^9 7,400,100,000 **16.** 1.145×10^3 1,145

17. diameter of Saturn: 1.151×10^5 kilometers 115,100

18. area of Pacific Ocean: 6.4×10^7 square miles 64,000,000

19. number of seconds in a day: 8.64×10^4 86,400

20. 1990 U.S. nuclear power generation: 5.8×10^{11} kilowatt hours 580,000,000,000

Properties Objective L: Identify numbers as being written in scientific notation.

In 21-24, explain why each number is *not* in scientific notation.

21. 17.6×10^4 The first number is greater than 10.

22. $.0098 \times 10^3$ The first number is less than 1.

23. 3.6×8^2 There is no power of 10.

24. $5 \times 10^{6.5}$ The exponent of the ten is not an integer.

Using the [EE] key is more efficient than pressing the *three* keys [×] 10 [y^x]. The [EE] key is programmed to mean "times 10 to the power of."

On some calculators and computers, the number 1.4 billion may be written as 1.4 E 9 or even 1.4 E + 9. In this case the E means "exponent of 10" and does not indicate an error. The + sign indicates a positive number. In Lesson 2-9, you will learn about scientific notation with negative exponents.

QUESTIONS

Covering the Reading

1. a. How many miles does light travel in a 365-day year?
b. What is this distance called? light-year
a) about 5.87×10^{12} miles

2. How does your calculator display the number 9.01×10^{25}? [9.01 25]

3. In scientific notation, a number greater than or equal to __?__ and less than __?__ is multiplied by an integer __?__ of 10. 1, 10, power

In 4–11, rewrite the number in scientific notation.

4. 800 8×10^2 **5.** 804 8.04×10^2 **6.** 63.21 6.321×10^1 **7.** 765.4 7.654×10^2

8. 3,500,000 square miles, the approximate land area of the U.S. 3.5×10^6

9. 6,588,000,000,000,000,000,000 tons, the approximate mass of Earth 6.588×10^{21}

10. 59.85 million people, the number of passengers handled by Chicago's O'Hare Field in 1991 5.985×10^7

11. 4 trillion dollars, the approximate U.S. national debt in 1993 4×10^{12}

12. Indicate how to enter 1.4×10^9 into your calculator
a. using a key for scientific notation. 1.4 [EE] 9 or 1.4 [Exp] 9
b. using a powering key. 1.4 [×] 10 [y^x] 9 [=]

In 13 and 14, what does your calculator display for the number?

13. 49×10^{14} Answers may vary. Sample: [4.9 15]

14. 60 trillion Sample: [6. 13]

Applying the Mathematics

15. The approximate weight of the largest blue whale ever measured is 1.9×10^5 kg. Multiply this number by 2.2 to estimate this weight in pounds. 4.18×10^5 or 418,000 lb

16. How many seconds are there in a 365-day year? 3.1536×10^7 or 31,536,000 seconds

17. a. Using scientific notation, what is the largest number you can display on your calculator?
b. What is the smallest number you can display? (Hint: The smallest number is negative.)
a) Sample: [9.9999 99] for 9.9999×10^{99}
b) Sample: [-9.9999 99] for -9.9999×10^{99}

Adapting to Individual Needs

Extra Help

Have students use the diagram below to write a number in scientific notation.

Move the decimal point to the left to form a decimal that is at least 1 but less than 10. Write the decimal.

↓

Write "× 10" after the decimal.

↓

Count the number of places the decimal point was moved and write that count as the exponent for 10.

Example: Write 13,405,000 in scientific notation.

13405000 **7 places**

1.3405

1.3405 × 10

1.3405×10^7

18. a. Which is larger, 1×10^{10} or 9×10^9? 1×10^{10}
b. How can you tell? 9×10^9 = 9 billion; 1×10^{10} = 10 billion

19. Show that the [EE] key and the [y^x] key are different by writing a question that can be answered
a. using either key. Find 3×10^5. 3 [EE] 5 or 3 [×] 10 [y^x] 5
b. by using the [EE] key but not the [y^x] key.
c. by using the [y^x] key but not the [EE] key. Find 2^5. 2 [y^x] 5
b) Enter 1000 in scientific notation. 1 [EE] 3

Review

20. Calculate the first, second, and third powers of 8. *(Lesson 2-2)* 8; 64; 512

In 21 and 22, calculate mentally. *(Lesson 2-1)*

21. $0.0006 \times 10{,}000$ 6

22. 523×100 52,300

23. On the number line below, what letter corresponds to each number? *(Lessons 1-2, 1-6, 1-8)*
a. $\frac{3}{5}$ Q
b. $\frac{-3}{5}$ E
c. .8 S
d. -.8 C

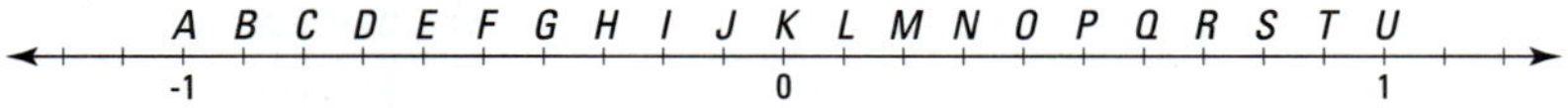

24. Arrange from smallest to largest: $14\frac{3}{5}$ 14.66 $14.\overline{61}$ $14.\overline{6}$. *(Lessons 1-6, 1-7)* $14\frac{3}{5}$, $14.\overline{61}$, 14.66, $14.\overline{6}$

25. Name a fraction whose decimal is 0.9. *(Lesson 1-6)* Samples: $\frac{9}{10}$, $\frac{27}{30}$

26. Batting "averages" in baseball are calculated by dividing the number of hits by the number of at-bats and usually rounding to the nearest thousandth. In 1970, Alex Johnson and Carl Yastrzemski had the top two batting averages in the American League. *(Lessons 1-4, 1-6)*
a. Johnson had 202 hits in 614 at-bats. What was his average? .329
b. Yastrzemski had 186 hits in 566 at-bats. What was his average? .329
c. The player with the higher average was the batting champion. Which player was this? Johnson, since 0.3290 > 0.3286.

Exploration

27. Kathleen entered 531×10^{20} on her calculator using the following key sequence:

531	EE	20
[531.]	[531. 00]	[531. 20]

Then she pressed [=].
a. What was the final display? [5.31 22]
b. What did pressing [=] do? converted 531×10^{20} to scientific notation

Extension

Computer Have students explore scientific notation on computers with questions 1–4.

1. Type ?2*3 on your computer and press RETURN. What does the computer print? What is the computer doing?
6; multiplying 2×3
2. Enter ?20*3 or ?2*30. What is printed? 60
3. Repeat the command, increasing the number of zeros after the 2 and/or 3 until the computer prints an answer in scientific notation. How does it write numbers in scientifc notation?
Sample: 6E + 09 for 6×10^9
4. What is the largest number your computer will print that is not in scientific notation?
Sample: 99,999,999

Project Update Project 5, *Scientific Notation,* on page 110, relates to the content of this lesson. Students choosing this project can start looking for an article, story, or poem, or they might begin writing their own stories.

Adapting to Individual Needs

English Language Development
Model examples of words that students do not understand, and check for understanding by asking them to match synonyms as shown in the example below.

convert	represent
stand for	put information in
enter	change

Challenge
Have students select topics that use large numbers and are of interest to them. Suitable topics include populations of countries or continents, facts about Earth or other planets, facts about the solar system, and monetary data associated with the U.S. or other countries. Then have students investigate their topics and make displays of what they have found. Encourage them to write the numbers in scientific notation.

▸ **LESSON MASTER 2-3 B** *page 2*

Representations Objective N: Indicate key sequences and displays for large numbers on a calculator.

In 25-28, write the key sequence that would enter each number. Then write the calculator display.

25. 9×10^{22} Key sequence: 9 [EE] 22
Display: 9. 22

26. 2.6×10^{19} Key sequence: 2.6 [EE] 19
Display: 2.6 19

27. 316,500,000 Key sequence: 3.165 [EE] 8
Display: 3.165 8

28. 8 trillion Key sequence: 8 [EE] 12
Display: 8. 12

In 29-31, what number is represented by each calculator display? Write the number in both scientific notation and as a decimal.

29. [4. 09] Scientific notation: 4×10^9
Decimal: 4,000,000,000

30. [6.8 13] Scientific notation: 6.8×10^{13}
Decimal: 68,000,000,000,000

31. [2.07114 06] Scientific notation: 2.07114×10^6
Decimal: 2,071,140

32. In 1990, U.S. farmers produced about 68 billion eggs costing the consumer an average of $.06 each. Suppose you want to estimate the total amount of money consumers paid for eggs in 1990.
a. What calculator can you do? $6.8 \times 10^{10} \times .06$
b. Write a key sequence for part a. 6.8 [EE] 10 × .06
c. What is the calculator display for the answer? 4.08 09
d. Write the answer in a full sentence.
sample: Consumers paid about 4.08 billion dollars, or $4,080,000,000, for eggs.

Lesson 2-4

Objectives

E Multiply by 0.1, 0.01, 0.001, and so on, and by $\frac{1}{10}$, $\frac{1}{100}$, $\frac{1}{1000}$, and so on.

G Convert and operate with percents as decimals.

H Know common fraction and percent equivalents.

Resources

From the ***Teacher's Resource File***

- Lesson Master 2-4A or 2-4B
- Answer Master 2-4
- Teaching Aids
  14 Warm-up
  18 Percents on a Number Line
  19 Decimals and Percents

Additional Resources

- Visuals for Teaching Aids 14, 18, 19
- Spreadsheet Workshop

Teaching Lesson 2-4

Warm-up

Write each fraction as a decimal.

1. $\frac{1}{4}$ .25 **2.** $\frac{7}{10}$ .7

3. $\frac{2}{3}$ $.\overline{6}$ **4.** $\frac{3}{8}$ .375

Write each decimal as a fraction in lowest terms.

5. 0.5 $\frac{1}{2}$ **6.** 0.875 $\frac{7}{8}$

7. 0.6 $\frac{3}{5}$ **8.** $0.\overline{3}$ $\frac{1}{3}$

LESSON

2-4 Multiplying by $\frac{1}{10}$, $\frac{1}{100}$, . . .

When was 43% enough? *Bill Clinton won the 1992 presidential election with 43.24% of the popular vote. He is shown here at inaugural festivities in Arlington, VA, getting a hug from daughter Chelsea as wife Hillary looks on.*

The numbers 10, 100, 1000, and so on, get larger and larger. By contrast, the numbers $\frac{1}{10}$, $\frac{1}{100}$, $\frac{1}{1000}$, and so on, get smaller and smaller. You can see that they get smaller by looking at the decimals for them.

$$\frac{1}{10} = .1 = \text{one tenth}$$
$$\frac{1}{100} = .01 = \text{one hundredth}$$
$$\frac{1}{1000} = .001 = \text{one thousandth}$$
$$\frac{1}{10{,}000} = .0001 = \text{one ten-thousandth}$$
and so on

Multiplying by $\frac{1}{10}$

To multiply a decimal by 10, remember that you move the decimal point one place to the *right*. Multiplication by $\frac{1}{10}$ undoes multiplication by 10. So, to multiply by $\frac{1}{10}$ or 0.1, you move the decimal point one place to the *left*.

$$\frac{1}{10} \times 15.283 = 1.5283$$

You can estimate to check. A tenth of \$15 is \$1.50.

Multiplying by $\frac{1}{100}$ and $\frac{1}{1000}$

Multiplying by $\frac{1}{100}$ is equivalent to multiplying by $\frac{1}{10}$ and then multiplying by $\frac{1}{10}$ again. So, to multiply by $\frac{1}{100}$ or .01, move the decimal point *two* places to the *left*.

$$\frac{1}{100} \times 15.283 = 0.15283$$

Lesson 2-4 Overview

Broad Goals In this lesson, students learn about negative integer powers of 10 and how to multiply by them. Percent is treated simply as meaning hundredths.

Perspective For many students, the relationship between positive and negative integer powers of 10 is clearer when demonstrated with fractions rather than decimals. That is, students more readily understand the connection between 1000 and $\frac{1}{1000}$ than the connection between 1000 and .001. And for some students, it is easier to see that $\frac{1}{10} \times \frac{1}{10} = \frac{1}{100}$ than to see that $.1 \times .1 = .01$. It may be harder for students to learn the fraction equivalents for .1, .01, .001, and so on.

Probably the simplest way for students to learn the fraction equivalents is for them to recall the place values to the right of the decimal point. Furthermore, just as the decimal point moves three places to the right when one multiplies by 1000, it moves three places to the left when one multiplies by $\frac{1}{1000}$ or .001.

The approach used for percent is simple. We treat the word *percent* as a word name, like *million* or *thousandth.* Percent is another name for *hundredths.* Thus, multiplying by .01 or $\frac{1}{100}$ for 1% is no different from multiplying by 1,000,000 for 1 million.

The pattern continues. Multiplication by $\frac{1}{1000}$ is equivalent to multiplying by $\frac{1}{10}$ three times. So move the decimal point three places to the left.

$$\frac{1}{1000} \times 15.283 = 0.015283$$

Activity

Check the above multiplications on your calculator by using decimals instead of fractions.

a. Multiply: $.1 \times 15.283$
b. Multiply: $.01 \times 15.283$
c. Multiply: $.001 \times 15.283$

❶ What Does % Mean?

If your calculator has a **percent key** %, enter 15.283 and press %. You should find the same display as when you multiplied by .01. This is because the **percent sign %** means to multiply by one hundredth. In general, to change a percent to a decimal, just multiply the number in front of the percent sign by $\frac{1}{100}$ or .01. Consider 50%.

As a fraction, $50\% = 50 \times \frac{1}{100} = \frac{50}{100} = \frac{1}{2}$.
As a decimal, $50\% = 50 \times .01 = .50 = .5$.

This confirms the idea that 50% of something is half of that thing.

The percent symbol is very common. Here are four examples of its use.

Example 1

Suppose a pair of designer jeans is on sale at 20% off. Rewrite 20% as a decimal.

Solution

We can use $\frac{1}{100}$ for the percent sign.

$$20\% = 20 \times \frac{1}{100} = .20 = .2$$

Recall that $.2 = \frac{1}{5}$. So $20\% = \frac{1}{5}$. Thus 20% off is the same as $\frac{1}{5}$ off.

Example 2

In the 1992 U.S. presidential election, an estimated 55% of the registered voters voted in the election. Rewrite 55% as a decimal.

Solution

Here we use .01 for the percent sign.

$$55\% = 55 \times .01 = .55$$

Here we multiplied by .01. Multiplying by $\frac{1}{100}$ would give the same answer. Use whichever is easier for you.

Notes on Reading

You may want to use a pattern to introduce multiplication by powers of 10. Write these two columns on the board:

23 million	230 million
430.5	4305
0.894	8.94

Ask students how the corresponding numbers in the columns are related to each other. [The numbers in the right column are 10 times the corresponding numbers in the left column; and the numbers in the left column are one tenth of the corresponding numbers in the right column.] Then, write another number in each column and ask for the corresponding number in the other column.

Change the pattern by making one number 100 times the other. Then repeat the procedure. The important concept for students to realize is that multiplication by $\frac{1}{x}$ undoes multiplication by x.

❶ Percent is such a pervasive concept that it is important for students to get off to a good start. Call attention to the idea that *percent* (%) is a word like *thousand* or *million*, which is used with numbers. Point out that just as 5 thousand can be written 5 × 1000, or 5000, and 9 million can be written 9 × 1,000,000, or 9,000,000, the symbol % means "$\times \frac{1}{100}$" or "× .01." Thus, an expression such as 25% can be written $25 \times \frac{1}{100} = \frac{25}{100} = \frac{1}{4}$ or $25 \times .01 = .25$.

Optional Activities

Activity 1 Percent Equivalent Game
After completing the lesson, you might want to have students play this game. Divide the class into teams of about five students each, and have each team choose one person to announce answers. Name a percent, and ask Team A for both its decimal and fraction. Team A scores one point for each correct response. If Team A fails to give the correct fraction and/or decimal, the first of the other teams to respond correctly scores the point or points. Proceed similarly by naming a percent for Team B, Team C, and so on. The winning team is the team with the most points when play stops.

Activity 2 Conduct a Survey
After completing the lesson, have students **work in groups** to design a survey on a topic that interests them. As part of their survey, students should consider whom they would like to survey. They also need to discuss the possible forms of questions they might write—multiple choice, yes or no, true or false, and free response—and how they will tally the answers. Then have students survey a given number of people and report their findings in a table that shows the percentage of people who answered questions the same way. You might have students save their data so they can represent the survey in a circle graph after studying Lesson 2-7.

Biology Connection After discussing **Example 4,** you might want to tell students that kangaroos are marsupials—mammals that give birth to extremely undeveloped offspring. The female generally gives birth to one offspring which is called a *joey.* A newborn joey measures only about 1 inch (2.5 centimeters) long. The joey will spend from six to eight months in a pouch on the belly of its mother. A full-grown adult male kangaroo stands about 6 feet (1.8 meters) tall. An adult female kangaroo stands about $4\frac{1}{2}$ feet (1.4 meters) tall. You might ask your better students to find the percent of increase in height from birth to adulthood for both male and female kangaroos [7100%; 5300%], or give the percents to the class and ask students to write them as decimals.

❷ It is essential that students learn decimal and fraction equivalents for the most common percents. Those shown on the number lines are a minimum. At this time you may wish to use **Teaching Aid 18.**

Additional Examples

Rewrite each percent as a decimal.

1. 40% .4
2. 12.5% .125
3. $5\frac{1}{3}$% $.05\overline{3}$
4. 1000% 10
5. 4369% 43.69
6. 2.076% .02076

Give a fraction (in lowest terms) or an integer for each percent.

7. $33\frac{1}{3}$% $\frac{1}{3}$
8. 80% $\frac{4}{5}$
9. 300% 3
10. 350% $\frac{7}{2}$

Notes on Questions

It might be helpful for students to use the *Visual Organizers* shown at the bottom of page 81. They are also given on **Teaching Aid 19.**

3 days old

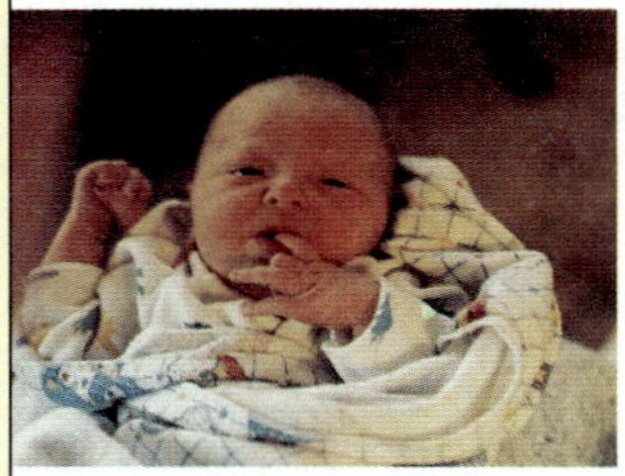

1 year old

What would happen if . . .? *If babies continued to grow at the rate of 200% per year, as they do during their first year, a baby with a birth weight of eight pounds would weigh 4,251,528 pounds by age 12.*

Example 3

A savings account gives a $3\frac{1}{4}$% interest rate. Rewrite $3\frac{1}{4}$% as a decimal.

Solution

First change the fraction to a decimal.

$$3\tfrac{1}{4}\% = 3.25\%$$

Now multiply by .01 instead of using the % sign.

$$= 3.25 \times .01$$
$$= 0.0325$$

The number 0.0325 is the number you can multiply by to determine the amount of interest paid in a savings account paying $3\frac{1}{4}$% interest.

Example 4

A baby weighs about 200% more at the age of one year than it does at birth. Rewrite 200% as a decimal.

Solution

$$200\% = 200 \times \frac{1}{100} = 2$$

A baby who weighs 200% *more* on its first birthday than it did at birth has increased its weight by a factor of two. If you want to determine the baby's weight, you need to add this increase to its original weight. So its final weight is 3 times its birth weight.

Graphing Percents on a Number Line

In Example 1, 20% was seen to equal the simple fraction $\frac{1}{5}$. Other percents equal commonly found simple fractions. Some of these are graphed on the number line below. You should learn these.

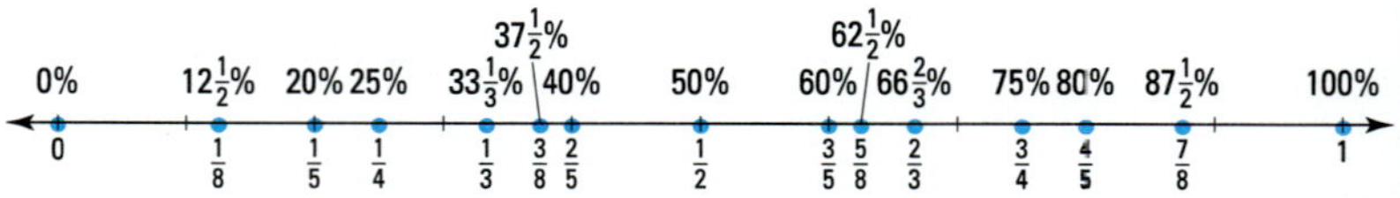

In Example 4, 200% was found to equal the integer 2. 100% = 1. Below is a different number line with some other percents indicated on it.

❷ 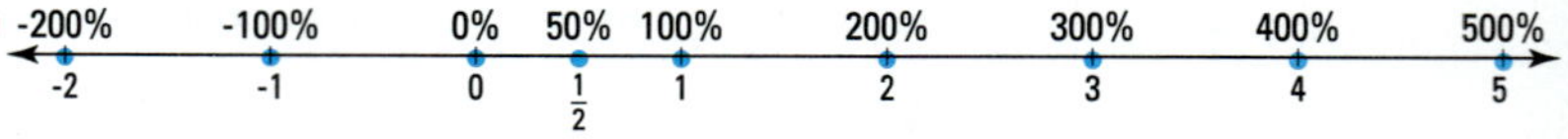

The idea of percent is old. The word *percent* comes from the Latin words *per centum,* meaning "through 100." (Sometimes it is useful to think of percent as "out of 100.") The symbol for percent is much newer. In 1650 the symbol $\frac{0}{0}$ was used. People have used the symbol % only in the last 100 years. Many writers still write "per cent" as two words. Either one word or two words are correct.

QUESTIONS

You should try to do all questions in this lesson without a calculator and without paper and pencil calculation.

Covering the Reading

In 1 and 2, write as a decimal.

1. one tenth .1

2. $\frac{1}{10{,}000}$ .0001

In 3 and 4, give a general rule for multiplying a decimal by the given number.

3. .01 Move the decimal point two places to the left.

4. $\frac{1}{10{,}000}$ Move the decimal point four places to the left.

In 5–8, write the answer as a decimal.

5. $46 \times \frac{1}{10}$ 4.6

6. $.01 \times 6$ .06

7. $\frac{1}{1000} \times 52$ .052

8. $250{,}000 \times .0001$ 25

9. Multiplying by $\frac{1}{100}$ is like multiplying by $\frac{1}{10}$ and then multiplying by __?__. $\frac{1}{10}$

10. To multiply by $\frac{1}{1000}$ using a calculator, what decimal can you use? .001

11. The symbol % is read __?__ and means __?__. percent, one-hundredth

12. About how old is the symbol %? about 100 years

13. To change a % to a decimal, __?__ the number in front of the % symbol by __?__. multiply, .01

In 14–22, rewrite the percent as a decimal.

14. 50% .5 **15.** 25% .25 **16.** 5% .05

17. 2% .02 **18.** 1.5% .015 **19.** 5.75% .0575

20. 300% 3 **21.** 150% 1.5 **22.** 82.3% .823

In 23–31, convert the percent to the indicated form.
a. decimal
b. simple fraction in lowest terms

23. 25% a) .25; b) $\frac{1}{4}$ **24.** 75% a) .75; b) $\frac{3}{4}$ **25.** 10% a) .1; b) $\frac{1}{10}$

26. 20% a) .2; b) $\frac{1}{5}$ **27.** 30% a) .3; b) $\frac{3}{10}$ **28.** $33\frac{1}{3}$% a) $.\overline{3}$; b) $\frac{1}{3}$

29. $66\frac{2}{3}$% a) $.\overline{6}$; b) $\frac{2}{3}$ **30.** $87\frac{1}{2}$% a) .875; b) $\frac{7}{8}$ **31.** 90% a) .9; b) $\frac{9}{10}$

In 32–37, change the fraction to a percent.

32. $\frac{1}{2}$ 50% **33.** $\frac{1}{4}$ 25% **34.** $\frac{1}{8}$ 12.5%

35. $\frac{3}{8}$ 37.5% **36.** $\frac{3}{5}$ 60% **37.** $\frac{1}{3}$ $33\frac{1}{3}$%

Questions 6 and 8 Error Alert When multiplying by .1, .01, .001, and so on, some students may mistakenly count the number of zeros in the multiplier and then move the decimal point that number of places. Students who make this error should check their work by replacing the decimal with its fraction equivalent and then repeat the multiplication.

Question 16 Error Alert If students get the answer .5 to this question, it might indicate that they have made an incorrect generalization from the examples. They might think that because 25% = .25, the % sign means to put a decimal point before the number. Their "trick" works only when there is a two-digit percent. Refer these students to Question 14. If 50% = .5, then 5% could not also equal .5. Again stress that % means to multiply by .01.

Questions 16–19 You might have students order their answers to these questions. Point out that the largest percent (5.75%) should also be the largest when written as a decimal; the smallest percent (1.5%) should be the smallest when written as a decimal.

Questions 25–27, 31 Discuss the pattern in the questions and answers. Ask students how they can easily compute 20%, 30%, 40%,... of a number. [First find 10% of the number. Then multiply that result by 2, 3, 4,....]

Visual Organizers

You might want to use **Teaching Aid 19** at this time.

Changing a Percent to a Decimal

Write the percent. → Replace "%" with "× .01." → Write the product.

Examples:

3.4%	3.4 × .01	.034
61%	61 × .01	.61

Changing a Decimal to a Percent

Write the decimal. → Multiply by 100. → Write "%" after the product.

Examples:

3.8	380	380%
.56	56	56%

LESSON MASTER 2-4 A

Questions on SPUR Objectives
See pages 113-115 for objectives.

Skills Objective E

1. Write a general rule for multiplying by $\frac{1}{10}, \frac{1}{100}, \frac{1}{1000}, \ldots$.
Move the decimal point to the left the same number of places as zeros in the denominator.

In 2-5, write each product as a decimal.

2. $3.5 \times .001$ 0.0035
3. $\frac{1}{10} \times 6$ 0.6
4. $43.8 \times \frac{1}{10^3}$ 0.000438
5. $500 \times .000001$ 0.0005

Skills Objective G

6. Explain the meaning of the % sign. Use an example in your explanation.
The % sign means to multiply by $\frac{1}{100}$.
$25\% = 25 \times \frac{1}{100} = \frac{25}{100} = \frac{1}{4}$

In 7-12, write each percent as a decimal.

7. 20% 0.2
8. 75% 0.75
9. 32% 0.32
10. 250% 2.5
11. 8.5% .085
12. 0.1% 0.001

Skills Objective H

13. Complete the charts. Fractions must be in lowest terms. Do as many as possible mentally.

Percent	Fraction
50%	$\frac{1}{2}$
25%	$\frac{1}{4}$
$33\frac{1}{3}$%	$\frac{1}{3}$
80%	$\frac{4}{5}$
12.5%	$\frac{1}{8}$

Percent	Fraction
20%	$\frac{1}{5}$
$66\frac{2}{3}$%	$\frac{2}{3}$
$62\frac{1}{2}$%	$\frac{5}{8}$
75%	$\frac{3}{4}$
100%	1

Notes on Questions

Question 39 Some students have trouble with the wording in this question. Discuss what is meant, and help them convert the question into the form: ____ × 46.381 = .46381

Question 57 You may want to provide a dictionary with the required terms for classroom reference.

Follow-up for Lesson 2-4

Practice

For more questions on SPUR objectives, use **Lesson Master 2-4A** (shown on page 81) or **Lesson Master 2-4B** (shown on pages 82–83).

Assessment

Written Communication Have students write about the relationships among percents, decimals, and fractions and how to convert from one to another. Suggest that they draw diagrams to help them organize their thoughts. Remind them that using examples can help them with their explanations. [Work shows understanding of the relationships among percents, decimals, and fractions through the use of diagrams and/or examples.]

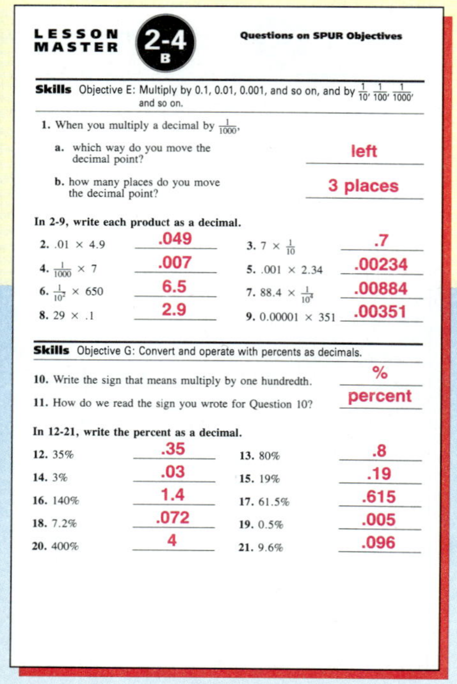

LESSON MASTER 2-4 B **Questions on SPUR Objectives**

Skills Objective E: Multiply by 0.1, 0.01, 0.001, and so on, and by $\frac{1}{10}$, $\frac{1}{100}$, $\frac{1}{1000}$, and so on.

1. When you multiply a decimal by $\frac{1}{1000}$,
   a. which way do you move the decimal point? **left**
   b. how many places do you move the decimal point? **3 places**

In 2-9, write each product as a decimal.

2. $.01 \times 4.9$	.049	3. $7 \times \frac{1}{10}$	.7
4. $\frac{1}{1000} \times 7$	.007	5. $.001 \times 2.34$	.00234
6. $\frac{1}{10^2} \times 650$	6.5	7. $88.4 \times \frac{1}{10^4}$	.00884
8. $29 \times .1$	2.9	9. 0.00001×351	.00351

Skills Objective G: Convert and operate with percents as decimals.

10. Write the sign that means multiply by one hundredth. **%**
11. How do we read the sign you wrote for Question 10? **percent**

In 12-21, write the percent as a decimal.

12. 35%	.35	13. 80%	.8
14. 3%	.03	15. 19%	.19
16. 140%	1.4	17. 61.5%	.615
18. 7.2%	.072	19. 0.5%	.005
20. 400%	4	21. 9.6%	.096

38. Trace this number line. Graph 10%, 20%, 30%, 40%, 50%, 60%, 70%, 80%, 90%, and 100% on it.

Applying the Mathematics

39. By what number can you multiply 46.381 to get 0.46381? $\frac{1}{100}$ or .01

40. Betty weighs 87.5 pounds. She weighed about a tenth of that at birth. To the nearest pound, what did she weigh at birth? 9 pounds

41. Multiply $\frac{1}{10^3}$ by 43.87. 0.04387

In 42 and 43, rewrite each underlined number as a fraction and as a decimal.

42. The teachers wanted a <u>7%</u> raise, and the school board offered <u>4%</u>.

42) $\frac{7}{100}$ or 0.07; $\frac{4}{100}$ or $\frac{1}{25}$ or 0.04

43. In 1983, the president of Brazil's central bank said, "We cannot live with <u>150%</u> inflation." Yet in 1990, inflation was <u>1,795%</u>.

43) $\frac{150}{100}$ or $1\frac{1}{2}$ or 1.5; $\frac{1795}{1000}$ or $\frac{359}{20}$ or 17.95

44. *Multiple choice.* Which is equal to 0.3?
(a) 300% (b) 30% (c) 3% (d) 0.3% (b)

45. *Multiple choice.* Which is closest to $0.\overline{3}$?
(a) 333% (b) 33% (c) 3% (d) .3% (b)

46. Between what two integers is 5.625%? Explain your thinking. 0 and 1. Since 5.625% = .05626, it is between 0 and 1.

47. Change 0.1% to a decimal and to a fraction. 0.001, $\frac{1}{1000}$

In 48–51, use the graph below:

Source: *Automotive News*, May 26, 1993

48. Which automaker had the largest percent increase in sales? Chrysler

49. Which automaker had the largest percent decrease in sales? Volkswagon/Audi

50. Which automaker had an increase, but the smallest percent increase in sales? Nissan/Infiniti

51. What percent would indicate no change in sales? 0%

Adapting to Individual Needs

Extra Help

Students can use the number lines on page 80 to help them make a table showing equivalent forms of fractions, decimals, and percents. Part of a table is shown below.

Fraction	$\frac{1}{8}$	$\frac{1}{5}$	$\frac{1}{4}$
Decimal	.125	.2	.25
Percent	$12\frac{1}{2}$%	20%	25%

English Language Development

You might help students understand the meaning of some of the words used in Examples 2 and 3, such as savings account, interest rate, and registered voters, by having other students act out scenes taking place in a bank or at a polling place. As students role play, you might ask them questions, such as *What are you doing now? What is that in your hand? How much money are you depositing?* and so on.

Review

52. Multiply 2.3 by each number. *(Lessons 2-1, 2-4)*

a. 1000 2,300 **b.** 10 23 **c.** 10^4 23,000 **d.** $\frac{1}{100}$ 0.023 **e.** 0.0001 0.00023

53. a. Write the three underlined numbers as decimals. *(Lesson 2-1)*

The number of students enrolled in grades 9–12 dropped from fourteen million, five hundred seventy thousand in 1980 to twelve million, four hundred seventy-two thousand in 1990. An estimate for the year 2000 is fifteen million, two hundred thousand.

b. Write the underlined numbers of part **a** in scientific notation. *(Lesson 2-3)* a) 14,570,000; 12,472,000; 15,200,000 b) 1.457×10^7; 1.2472×10^7; 1.52×10^7

54. Which number is smallest, 9×10^4, 8.2×10^5, or 3.01×10^9? *(Lesson 2-3)* 9×10^4

55. Which is greater, 8×3 or 8^3? *(Lesson 2-2)* 8^3

56. Consider the numbers -1.4, -14, and 0.14.

a. Order the numbers from smallest to largest. -14, -1.4, 0.14

b. Use the numbers in a sentence with two inequality symbols.

c. Graph the numbers on the same number line. *(Lessons 1-2, 1-9)*
b) $-14 < -1.4 < 0.14$ or $0.14 > -1.4 > -14$; c) See below.

Exploration

57. In the previous lessons, the largest power of 10 named was quintillion. But there are larger powers of 10 with names. Look up the given words in a dictionary. (You may need a large dictionary.) Write each number as a decimal and as a power of 10.

a. sextillion **b.** octillion **c.** nonillion **d.** decillion
See below.

58. Money rates are often given as percents. Find the following rates by looking in a daily newspaper or weekly magazine.

a. the prime interest rate charged by banks to companies with good credit ratings

b. a local mortgage rate on a new home purchase

c. the interest rate on an account at a local savings institution
Answers will vary.

56c)

57a) 1 followed by 21 zeros; 10^{21} b) 1 followed by 27 zeros; 10^{27}
c) 1 followed by 30 zeros; 10^{30} d) 1 followed by 33 zeros; 10^{33}

Extension

Multicultural Connection You might have each student select a different country and research "percent" facts about the country. (An almanac is a good source for such facts.) Students can make a bulletin board showing a world map and the facts they have found about various countries.

Technology Connection You may wish to have students use the *Spreadsheet Workshop* to explore multiplication by .1, .01, and .001. Have students enter these factors in the top row of the multiplication table from the Operation Forms menu. Students can enter other factors in the left column. Each number in the left column will be multiplied by each number in the top row. Encourage students to look for patterns as they study the products.

Project Update Students choosing Project 2, *Using the Symbols 1, 2, 3, and a Decimal Point*, on page 109, can begin writing their lists of decimal numbers. You might have these students pair off so they can check their lists.

Students selecting Project 3, *Percents in Print*, can begin their search for examples of percents in newspapers and magazines.

Adapting to Individual Needs

Challenge
Give students the following questions.

1. Can you multiply a number by 1000 and have fewer than three zeros in the product? Explain. [Yes, if the number is less than 1 but greater than or equal to .000001, or greater than -1 but less than or equal to -.000001.]

2. Write one tenth, one hundredth, one thousandth, and so on, using exponents, and then write them as decimals until you see a pattern. Describe the pattern.
[$\frac{1}{10} = \frac{1}{10^1} = .1$, $\frac{1}{100} = \frac{1}{10^2} = .01$, $\frac{1}{1000} = \frac{1}{10^3} = .001$; the number of zeros to the right of the decimal point is one less than the exponent.]

▸ **LESSON MASTER 2-4 B** *page 2*

Skills Objective H: Know common fraction and percent equivalents.

22. Complete the chart. Fractions must be in lowest terms. Do as many as possible mentally.

Percent	Fraction
50%	$\frac{1}{2}$
75%	$\frac{3}{4}$
$33\frac{1}{3}$%	$\frac{1}{3}$
25%	$\frac{1}{4}$
12.5%	$\frac{1}{8}$
37.5%	$\frac{3}{8}$
30%	$\frac{3}{10}$

Percent	Fraction
40%	$\frac{2}{5}$
87.5%	$\frac{7}{8}$
60%	$\frac{3}{5}$
70%	$\frac{7}{10}$
$66\frac{2}{3}$%	$\frac{2}{3}$
10%	$\frac{1}{10}$
62.5%	$\frac{5}{8}$

Review Multiplication of decimals (Previous course)

Multiple choice **In 23-26, DO NOT USE CALCULATORS OR PENCIL AND PAPER. Use estimation to choose the correct answer.**

23. .6 × .7 c
(a) .042 (b) .0042
(c) .42 (d) 4.2

24. 97 × .004 c
(a) .00388 (b) .0388
(c) .388 (d) 3.88

25. 216 × .8 a
(a) 172.8 (b) 17.28
(c) 1.728 (d) 1,728

26. 5.3 × 12.8 c
(a) 6,784 (b) 678.4
(c) 67.84 (d) 6.784

27. Write a problem that involves multiplication of decimals.
sample: An ounce of halibut contains about .34 grams of fat. How much fat is in 3.5 ounces of halibut?

Lesson 2-5

Objectives

G Convert and operate with percents as decimals.

K Know and apply the Substitution Principle.

M Find percents of quantities in real situations.

Resources

From the ***Teacher's Resource File***
- Lesson Master 2-5A or 2-5B
- Answer Master 2-5
- Teaching Aid 14: Warm-up
- Activity Kit, Activity 4

Additional Resources
- Visual for Teaching Aid 14

Teaching Lesson 2-5

Warm-up

Work in groups and discuss the following problem.

This week two stores have sales on the same brand of TV, originally priced at $329.95. Store A is selling the televisions for 50% off. Store B has marked the price down 30%, and if you buy a TV this weekend, you can take 20% off the marked down price. Which store has the better buy? Explain your answer.
Sample answer: Buy a TV at Store A any day this week for $164.98. Buying one at Store B on the weekend will cost $184.77.

LESSON 2-5

Percent of a Quantity

What percent graduate? *According to 1990 data, 71.2% of high school freshmen enrolled in U.S. public schools stayed in school and graduated. Vermont, Minnesota, and North Dakota had the highest rates.*

Why Are There So Many Ways to Write Numbers?

You have learned to convert percents to fractions and to decimals. You have learned to put some decimals in scientific notation. The purpose of all this rewriting is to give you *flexibility.* Sometimes it's easier to use fractions. Sometimes decimals are easier. Sometimes percent or scientific notation is needed.

But why does all of this work? Why can you use .01 in place of $\frac{1}{100}$, or 3×10^6 instead of 3 million, or 0.4 instead of $\frac{2}{5}$ or 40%? The reason is due to the general idea called the *Substitution Principle.*

> **Substitution Principle**
> If two numbers are equal, then one can be substituted for the other in any computation without changing the results of the computation.

Using the Substitution Principle with Percents

The Substitution Principle is used in many places. Here it is used to find percents of a quantity. The phrase "percent of" is a signal to multiply. Use a calculator as you work through the following examples.

Example 1

Suppose 30% of the 2000 students in a high school are freshmen. How many students is this?

Solution

	30% of 2000 students
Change "of" to "times."	= 30% × 2000 students
Now use the Substitution Principle, rewriting 30% as .3.	= .3 × 2000 students
	= 600 students

Lesson 2–5 Overview

Broad Goals Students should be able to find percents of quantities and encounter uses in real situations.

Perspective Finding percents of numbers, an important skill, will be reinforced many times in succeeding lessons, and by the end of the year this skill should be second nature to students. The mathematical procedure that is used relies on the Substitution Principle. To some students, the Substitution Principle seems so obvious that it should not need stating. But this principle makes *percent of* problems almost automatic. Using it encourages students to write out the steps of a problem, and for that reason it should be emphasized.

The Substitution Principle is the first property to be named. It is easy, and here it is in a place where all students understand its use. Later this principle is applied in the substitution of numbers for variables and in the solution of equations.

Example 2

Suppose 100% of the 2000 students live within the school district. How many students is this?

Solution

	100% of 2000 students
Change "of" to "times."	= 100% × 2000 students
Now use the Substitution Principle, rewriting 100% as 1.	= 1 × 2000 students
	= 2000 students

So, *all* of the students live within the school district.

Using Percents

From Example 2, you can see that "100% of" means "all of." Since 0% = 0, 0% of the students is 0 × 2000 students. So "0% of" means "none of." Since 50% is equal to $\frac{1}{2}$, "50% of" means "half of."

Percents are often used when items are put on sale.

Example 3

A sofa sells for $569.95. It is put on sale at 20% off.

a. How much will you save if you buy the sofa during the sale?

b. What will the sale price be?

Solution

a. You save 20% of $569.95.

20% of $569.95
= .2 × $569.95
= $113.99, the amount you save

b. Subtraction tells you what the sale price will be.

$569.95 original price
−113.99 amount saved
$455.96 sale price

Check

If you save 20%, you are paying 80% of the original cost.

80% of $569.95
= .8 × $569.95
= $455.96, the sale price

If you do not have a calculator, you might choose to estimate the answer to Example 3a. One estimate is found by rounding $569.95 up to $570. Because $570 is so close to the actual price, the estimate is very accurate.

20% × $570
= .2 × $570
= $114, only one penny off the actual amount saved!

Notes on Reading

The lesson has four examples. **Example 1** makes straightforward use of the Substitution Principle. **Example 2** demonstrates the meaning of 100%. **Example 3** is a two-step problem involving percent. Stress that finding "20% off" gives the dollar amount off, not the sale price. **Example 4** is a common application using a non-whole number percent.

LESSON MASTER 2-5 A

Questions on SPUR Objectives
See pages 113-115 for objectives.

Skills Objective G

In 1-4, rewrite each problem as a decimal multiplication and evaluate.

1. What is 75% of 40? 0.75 × 40 = 30
2. Find 30% of 54. 0.3 × 54 = 16.2
3. Evaluate 3.5% of 450. 0.035 × 450 = 15.75
4. Calculate 300% of 25. 3 × 25 = 75

Properties Objective K

5. How is the Substitution Principle used in calculating 80% of 400?
$\frac{4}{5}$ or 0.8 can be substituted for 80%.

6. According to the Substitution Principle, $\frac{3}{5} + \frac{1}{4}$ =
0. 6 + 0. 25 or 60 % + 25 %.

7. Name two numbers that could be substituted for 90%. 0.9 $\frac{9}{10}$

Uses Objective M

8. In a restaurant, the usual tip is 15% of the bill. How much should you and your friends tip on a bill of $15.43?

calculation to do	calculator answer	answer to question
0.15 × $15.43	2.3145	$2.31

9. On the average, college students pay 21% of their bills each year from earnings from a job. In 1992-93, the average cost for an in-state public college was $5929. How much did the typical student earn to contribute to this expense?

calculation to do	calculator answer	answer to question
0.21 × $5929	1245.09	$1245.09

10. You have $300 to spend on a new bike. Can you afford a $375 bike on sale for 25% off if sales tax is 5.5%? Justify your answer.
Yes. 0.25 × $375 = $93.75; $375 − $93.75 = $281.25; 0.055 × $281.25 = $15.46875; $281.25 + $15.47 = $296.72; $296.72 < $300

Multicultural Connection The 1991 inflation rate in the U.S is given in **Example 4.** You might have students find the inflation rates in other countries, and for each rate, have them work the example using this rate.

Additional Examples

1. During the 1986-87 basketball season, Larry Bird of the Boston Celtics attempted 455 free throws, missing only about 9% of them. About how many free throws did he miss? About how many did he make? **41 free throws; 414 free throws**
2. Suppose 100% of your class goes on a field trip. How many students is this? **the total number of students in the class**
3. Suppose a mountain bike that sells for $349 is on sale for $33\frac{1}{3}$% off.
   - **a.** What will the bike cost you before tax? **$232.67**
   - **b.** If there is a 5% tax, what will be the total cost? **$244.30**
4. Using the information given in Example 4, what would the cost of a computer be at the end of 1991 if it cost $2395 at the beginning of 1991? **$2469.25**
5. A large truck can be junked when wear and friction have taken a toll of more than .1% of its original weight. If a truck weighed 25,000 pounds when new, what weight loss would require it to be junked? **25 lb**

LESSON MASTER 2-5 B — **Questions on SPUR Objectives**

Skills Objective G: Convert and operate with percents as decimals.

In 1-8, rewrite each problem as a decimal multiplication and evaluate.

1. What is 50% of 88? .5 × 88 = 44
2. Evaluate 60% of 72. .6 × 72 = 43.2
3. Find 3% of 600. .03 × 600 = 18
4. Calculate 90% of 65. .9 × 65 = 58.5
5. Evaluate 200% of 46. 2 × 46 = 92
6. What is 4.8% of 750? .048 × 750 = 36
7. Calculate 12.5% of 30. .125 × 30 = 3.75
8. Find 375% of 25. 3.75 × 25 = 93.75

Properties Objective K: Know and apply the Substitution Principle.

9. State the Substitution Principle and give an example of how you might use it.
   If two numbers are equal, then one can be substituted for the other in computation without changing the results; sample: To find $12 \times \frac{1}{2}$, multiply 12 × .5.
10. According to the Substitution Principle,
    - a. as decimals, $\frac{1}{2} + \frac{7}{10} = 0.$ 5 $+ 0.$ 7 .
    - b. as percents, $\frac{1}{2} + \frac{7}{10} =$ 50 % + 70 %.

In 11 and 12, name two numbers that could be substituted for the given number. Sample answers are given.

11. 60% .6 $\frac{3}{5}$
12. $\frac{3}{4}$ 75% .75

How Percents Describe Inflation

Inflation is the general amount by which goods or services increase in price. Inflation is usually reported as a percent.

Example 4

In 1991, the U.S. inflation rate was 3.1%. Assume a house cost $60,000 at the beginning of 1991. If it increased in value at the rate of inflation, what was it worth at the end of 1991?

Solution

3.1% of $60,000
= 3.1% × 60,000
Change 3.1% to a decimal. = .031 × 60,000
= $1860, the amount of the increase

The value of the house at the end of 1991 was $60,000 + $1860 = $61,860.

QUESTIONS

Covering the Reading

1. Why is it useful to have many ways of writing numbers? **to give flexibility**
2. State the Substitution Principle. **See below.**
3. *True or false.* (Hint: Recall that 20% = $\frac{1}{5}$ and 30% = $\frac{3}{10}$.)
   - **a.** You can substitute $\frac{1}{5}$ for 20% in any computation and the answer will not be affected. **True**
   - **b.** 20% + 30% = $\frac{1}{5} + \frac{3}{10}$ **True**
   - **c.** 20% × $6000 = $\frac{1}{5}$ × $6000 **True**
4. **a.** In calculating 30% of 2000, when is the Substitution Principle used?
   b. Calculate 30% of 2000.
   a) when 30% is rewritten as .3 b) 600
5. Match each percent at the left with the correct phrase at the right.

all of 100% of		none of
half of 50% of		all of
none of 0% of		half of

In 6–9, determine the answer in your head.

6. 50% of 6000 **3000**
7. 100% of 12 **12**
8. 0% of 50 **0**
9. 150% of 30 **45**
10. A store normally sells futons at 2 for $899.
    - **a.** To estimate how much the beds would cost at 25% off, what value can be used in place of $899? **$900**
    - **b.** Estimate the price for the two beds at a "25% off" sale. **$675**

2) If two numbers are equal, then one may be substituted for the other in any computation without changing the results of the computation.

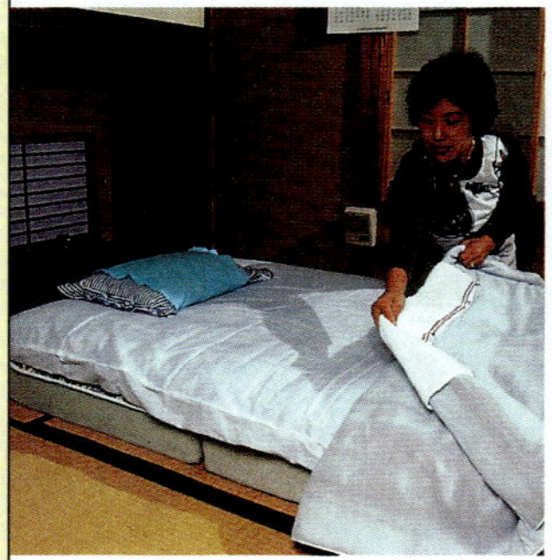

What's a futon?
A futon is a bed. It is a padded quilt generally placed on a mat or wooden frame. Originally used in Japan, futons are particularly functional in small homes as the futon can be rolled up and put away.

Optional Activities

Activity 1 You might want to use *Activity Kit, Activity 4,* to introduce Lesson 2-5. This activity gives students a visual representation of percent of a quantity.

Activity 2 Using Manipulatives to Find Percents
Materials: Red counters, yellow counters (or substitute with two other colors)

After completing the lesson, have students use the counters to solve problems like these.

1. Take 3 reds and 1 yellow. What percent are red? How many reds would you add so that 80% are red? [75%; 1 red]
2. Take 2 reds and 2 yellows. What percent are yellow? How many reds would you add so that 75% are red? [50%; 4 reds]

11. Use the information in Example 4. Suppose the cost of a vacation increased at the rate of inflation. If a vacation cost \$1200 at the beginning of 1991, what would you expect its cost to be at the end of 1991? **\$1237.20, or about \$1237**

12. Suppose the price of a CD increased 10% in the last year. What would you expect to pay for a CD that cost \$10.95 a year ago? **\$12.05**

Applying the Mathematics

14) Sample: "Let's split it equally, half for you, half for me."

In 13 and 14, what does the remark mean?

13. "We are with you 100%!" Sample: "We are with you totally."

14. "Let's split it 50-50."

In 15 and 16, assume the U.S. population to be about 250,000,000.

15. In your head, figure out what 10% of the U.S. population is. Use this to figure out **a.** 20%, **b.** 30%, **c.** 40%, and **d.** 50% of the population. a) 50 million; b) 75 million; c) 100 million; d) 125 million

16. The U.S. population is now increasing at the rate of about 1.06% a year. How many people is this? **2.65 million**

17. In Bakersfield, California, it rains on about 10% of the days in a year. About how many days is this? **36 or 37**

18. In store *A* you see a \$600 stereo at 25% off. In store *B* the same stereo normally costs \$575 and is on sale at 20% off. Which store has the lower sale price? **Store *A***

19. During the 1992–1993 season, the Detroit Pistons basketball team won 48.8% of its games. Did the Pistons win or lose more often? Justify your answer. **lose; 48.8% is less than 50% which is half.**

20. An interest penalty is charged on credit card purchases if you do not pay on time. Suppose you have \$1000 in overdue bills. If the penalty is 1.5% per month, how much interest will you have to pay the first month? **\$15**

21. The population of Los Angeles, California, was about 100,000 in 1900 and increased 1800% from 1900 to 1950. How many people is that increase? **1.8 million**

22. The caption below says that 46% of all revenues from sales of computers in 1991 were for personal computers. Did the writer round up or down to obtain this percent? **down**

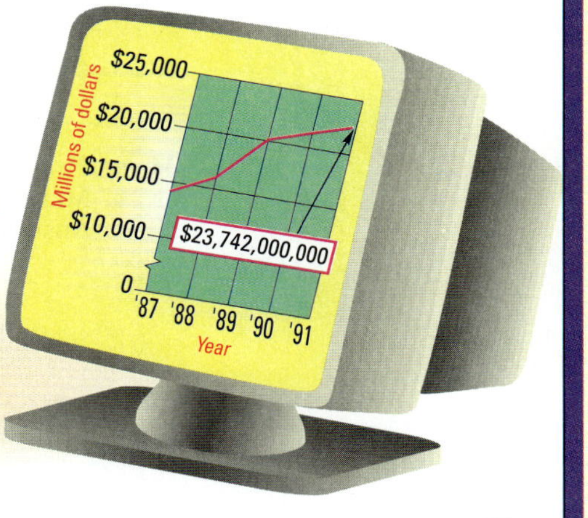

In 1991, total factory revenues from sales of computers were 50,885 million dollars. The percentage of the total for personal computers was 46%, up from just one-third of total revenues in 1987.

Source: Dataquest Inc., San Jose, CA, Consolidated Data Base

Notes on Questions

Question 10b Many students will do this problem in two steps, as was done in **Example 3.** They will find the amount of discount and then subtract that amount from the regular price. In a later discussion on the uses of multiplication, students will be encouraged to do this problem in one step by multiplying the regular price by 75%.

Question 17 This question provides another opportunity to discuss giving an answer in reasonable form. The exact answer is 36.5, but half a day makes no sense in response to the question asked. Students can round up or down to the nearest integer.

Question 21 An increase of 1800% means that the later population was 1900% of the original population.

Adapting to Individual Needs

Extra Help

Students who are having difficulties with percent problems might not understand how the Substitution Principle is used. Give these students several examples using colored chalk or markers (shown in bold on the right) to show what has been substituted.

Find 25% of 80.

$$
\begin{aligned}
& 25\,\mathbf{\%} \quad \mathbf{of} \quad 80 \\
= \ & 25 \times \mathbf{\tfrac{1}{100}} \quad \times \quad 80 \\
= \ & .25 \quad \times \quad 80 \\
= \ & 20
\end{aligned}
$$

▶ LESSON MASTER 2-5 B *page 2*

Uses Objective M: Find percents of quantities in real situations.

13. During a sale, a store is offering a 25% discount on a pair of speakers that normally sells for \$169. How much would you save on the speakers during the sale?

calculation	calculator answer	answer to question
.25 × 169	42.25	\$42.25

14. Employees at G. Hardcastle and Company receive a 10% discount on all purchases. What will an employee have to pay for a computer priced at \$1450?

calculation	calculator answer	answer to question
1450 − .10 × 1450	1305	\$1305

15. Houston, Texas, has clear skies about 20% of the days of the year. How many days each year is this?

calculation	calculator answer	answer to question
.2 × 365	73	73 days

16. For large groups, some restaurants automatically add a tip of 17% to the bill. On a bill of \$218.66, how much will the restaurant add for the tip?

calculation	calculator answer	answer to question
.17 × 218.66	37.1722	\$37.17

17. In 1989, the state of Washington spent about 15% more per person for their public libraries than did Hawaii. If Hawaii spent \$17.23 per person how much was spent per person in Washington?

calculation	calculator answer	answer to question
17.23 + .15 × 17.23	19.8145	\$19.81

18. Suppose your weekly allowance is \$5. How long will it take to save for a tape player that costs \$68, if you have a coupon for a 22% discount and sales tax is 6.5%? **12 weeks**

19. Simpson Sports normally prices the Land VII bike at \$310. Now on sale, the price is reduced 25%. At Cragin Bike Lot, the regular price of the Land VII bike is \$299, and the current sale price is 20% off. Which store currently has the better price? **Simpson Sports**

Follow-up for Lesson 2-5

Practice

For more questions on SPUR objectives, use **Lesson Master 2-5A** (shown on page 85) or **Lesson Master 2-5B** (shown on pages 86–87).

Assessment

Diagnostic You might use **Question 34** to diagnose if students understand the meaning of percent.

Group Assessment Have groups of students work together and write an essay on how and when they might need to find a percent of a number, including at least three worked-out problems. After collecting the papers, you might read some aloud for class discussion. [Statements made while composing the essays show comprehension and contain the examples. Class discussion reveals if there is a need for further development.]

Extension

Using Technology We do not teach **the percent key** on the calculator because it does not always follow the usual order of operations. But you may wish to discuss it after students read the lesson. On most calculators the percent key has two basic uses: (1) To convert a percent to a decimal by pressing the number and then the percent key and (2) To calculate an increase or decrease by following sequences similar to this one for **Example 3**: 569.95 [−] 20 [%] [=].

Project Update Students working on Project 3, *Percents in Print,* on page 109, might begin ordering the percents and describing how they are used.

Review

23. Multiply 990 by: **a.** 1 **b.** .1 **c.** .01 **d.** .001. *(Lesson 2-4)*
a) 990; b) 99; c) 9.9; d) 0.99

24. Change to a percent: **a.** $\frac{1}{4}$ **b.** $\frac{1}{3}$ **c.** $\frac{5}{4}$. *(Lesson 2-4)*
a) 25%; b) $33\frac{1}{3}$%; c) 125%

25. Write as a power of 10: **a.** quadrillion **b.** ten thousand. *(Lesson 2-2)*
a) 10^{15}; b) 10^4

In 26–30, write the number in decimal notation. *(Lessons 1-1, 1-7, 2-1, 2-2)*

26. 5^4 625 **27.** 8.3 million 8,300,000 **28.** 2.56×10^8 256,000,000 **29.** $4\frac{4}{5}$ 4.8

30. three billion, four hundred thousand
3,000,400,000

31. Write $\frac{48}{100}$ in lowest terms. *(Lesson 1-10)* $\frac{12}{25}$

32. The highest mountain in the world is Mt. Everest, in the Himalayas on the Tibet-Nepal border. Its peak is about 29,028 feet above sea level.

a. Should you call its height 29,028 feet, or -29,028 feet? 29,028 ft

b. Round the height to the nearest 100 feet. 29,000 ft

c. Round the height to the nearest 1000 feet. 29,000 ft

d. Round the height to the nearest 10,000 feet. *(Lessons 1-4, 1-8)* 30,000 ft

Would you climb it? *Mt. Everest is known in the Tibetan language as* Chomolungma, *"Goddess Mother of the World." It was first climbed in 1953 by Australian Edmund Hillary and Tenzing Norgay, a Sherpa of Nepal.*

33. Give the value of $\frac{\pi}{4}$ truncated to ten-thousandths. *(Lesson 1-3)*
0.7853

Exploration

34. a. Find a use of percent in a newspaper or magazine.
b. Make up a question about the information you have found.
c. Answer the question you made up.
Answers will vary.

Adapting to Individual Needs

English Language Development
Have students tell about some of their experiences with percents. Relate them to the lesson. You may need to explain the meanings of words such as sales tax and discount. Then have students act out situations involving percents. For example, one student might be a customer buying an item on sale, and another student might role-play a clerk who calculates the cost of the item.

Challenge
In **Question 15,** students devised a method to mentally find 10%, 20%, 30%, and so on, of a number. For the following questions, have students devise methods for finding the percents mentally. You might want to have students **work in pairs** so that they can try out their strategies with one another.

Sample answers are given.

1. 50% of 36 [Divide by 2; 18.]
2. 25% of 14 [Divide by 4; 3.5.]
3. 75% of 24 [Divide by 4 and then multiply by 3; 18.]
4. 5% of 48 [Find 10% and then divide by 2; 2.4.]
5. 15% of 80 [Add 10% and 5%; 12.]

LESSON

2-6

From Decimals to Fractions and Percents

Words without consonants. *In the words "ai," "oe," "aa," and "ae," 0% of the letters are consonants. All of these words are legal in some board games.*

In the word *power,* $\frac{3}{5}$ of the letters are consonants. Since $\frac{3}{5} = 60\%$, we could say 60% of the letters are consonants. Since 60% = .6, we could say .6 of the letters are consonants. Of these three choices, the decimal .6 is least used. It is usually converted to the fraction or the percent.

How to Convert a Terminating Decimal to a Fraction

If a terminating, or ending, decimal has only a few decimal places, just read the decimal in English and write the fraction.

Example 1

Convert 4.53 to a mixed number.

Solution

Read the decimal 4.53 as "four and fifty-three hundredths."

That tells you $4.53 = 4\frac{53}{100}$.

Another way to convert a decimal to a fraction is to write the decimal as a fraction over 1. Multiply the numerator and denominator by a power of 10 large enough to eliminate the decimal point in the numerator. This is an application of the Equal Fractions Property from Lesson 1-10.

Example 2

Write 0.036 as a fraction in lowest terms.

Solution

Write 0.036 as $\frac{0.036}{1}$.

Multiply both numerator and denominator by 1000. This moves the decimal point three places to the right in both the numerator and denominator to get $\frac{36}{1000}$. To write $\frac{36}{1000}$ in lowest terms, notice that 4 is a factor of both the numerator and the denominator. Divide each by 4.

$$0.036 = \frac{0.036}{1} = \frac{0.036 \times 1000}{1 \times 1000} = \frac{36}{1000} = \frac{36 \div 4}{1000 \div 4} = \frac{9}{250}$$

Check

Convert $\frac{9}{250}$ to a decimal using a calculator. You should get 0.036.

Lesson 2-6

Objectives

I Convert terminating decimals to fractions, and either of these to percents.

Resources

From the ***Teacher's Resource File***

- Lesson Master 2-6A or 2-6B
- Answer Master 2-6
- Assessment Sourcebook: Quiz for Lessons 2-4 through 2-6
- Teaching Aids
  14 Warm-up
  20 Fraction/Decimal/Percent Chart
- Technology Sourcebook, Calculator Master 4

Additional Resources

- Visuals for Teaching Aids 14, 20

Teaching Lesson 2-6

Warm-up

Write each decimal as a fraction in lowest terms, and write each fraction as a decimal.

1. 0.5 $\frac{1}{2}$ **2.** 0.35 $\frac{7}{20}$ **3.** 1.3 $1\frac{3}{10}$

4. $\frac{4}{5}$ .8 **5.** $\frac{3}{8}$ .375 **6.** $\frac{4}{9}$ $.\overline{4}$

Lesson 2-6 Overview

Broad Goals The broad goal of this lesson is to teach *flexibility.* A student should be able to write a number as a fraction, a decimal, or a percent, depending on the situation.

Perspective *Converting, changing,* and *simplifying* are different words for the same idea—rewriting. There are many reasons for rewriting, including the following:

(1) *Situational constraints* It may be necessary to perform a computation, and the algorithm or calculator requires that the number be in a certain form.

(2) *Clarity* A particular number may be easier to understand in a given notation.

(3) *Facility* It may be easier to work with a number in one notation than in another.

(4) *Consistency* When available data are given in different notations, it may be necessary to put all data into one form to compare or describe them.

LESSON MASTER 2-6 A **Questions on SPUR Objectives** See pages 113-115 for objectives.

Skills Objective I

In 1-8, complete the chart. You should be able to do this from memory.

	Fraction (lowest terms)	Decimal	Percent
1.	$\frac{1}{2}$	.5	50%
2.	$\frac{1}{3}$	$0.\overline{3}$	$33\frac{1}{3}\%$
3.	$\frac{3}{4}$	.75	75%
4.	$\frac{4}{5}$	.8	80%
5.	$\frac{9}{10}$	0.9	90%
6.	$\frac{2}{3}$	$0.\overline{6}$	$66\frac{2}{3}\%$
7.	$\frac{3}{8}$	0.375	37.5%
8.	1	1	100%

In 9-17, complete the chart. If necessary, you may use paper and pencil or your calculator.

	Fraction or Mixed Number (lowest terms)	Decimal	Percent
9.	$\frac{39}{100}$	0.39	39%
10.	$\frac{14}{25}$	.56	56%
11.	$\frac{3}{11}$	$0.\overline{27}$	$27.\overline{27}\%$
12.	$1\frac{3}{5}$	1.6	160%
13.	$3\frac{5}{6}$	$3.8\overline{3}$	$383.\overline{3}\%$
14.	$\frac{1}{80}$	.0125	1.25%
15.	$2\frac{1}{3}$	$2.\overline{3}$	$233.\overline{3}\%$
16.	$\frac{43}{1000}$	0.043	4.3%
17.	$\frac{1}{1000}$	0.001	$\frac{1}{10}\%$

How to Convert a Fraction with Decimals in It

Using the idea from Example 2, you can convert a fraction with decimals in it to a simple fraction.

Example 3

Find a simple fraction equal to $\frac{2.5}{35}$.

Solution

Remember that a simple fraction is a fraction with integers in its numerator and denominator. Multiply the numerator and the denominator by 10.

$$\frac{2.5 \times 10}{35 \times 10} = \frac{25}{350}$$

So $\frac{25}{350}$ is one answer. To put this fraction in lowest terms, notice that 25 is a factor of 25 and 350. Divide both numerator and denominator by 25.

$$\frac{2.5}{35} = \frac{25}{350} = \frac{25 \div 25}{350 \div 25} = \frac{1}{14}$$

Check

Use a calculator to verify that $\frac{2.5}{35} = .071428\ldots$ and $\frac{1}{14} = .071428\ldots$.

How to Convert a Decimal to a Percent

Now think about changing decimals to percents. Remember that to convert a percent to a decimal, move the decimal point two places to the *left*. For example, 53% = 0.53, 1800% = 18, and 6.25% = 0.0625.

To convert decimals to percents, reverse the procedure. Move the decimal point two places to the *right*. Here are a few examples.

0.036 = 3.6%
0.46 = 46%
3 = 300%
0.0007 = 0.07%

How to Convert a Fraction to a Percent

One way to convert fractions to percents is to convert them to decimals first. Then convert the decimals to percents.

Example 4

A worker receives time and a half for overtime. What percent of a person's pay is this?

Solution

time and a half = $1\frac{1}{2}$ = 1.5 = 150%

Notes on Reading

As with several previous lessons in Chapter 2, the concepts in Lesson 2-6 are represented in the examples. Since you have probably instructed students on the importance of examples, this might be a good time to have students look them over on their own, and then ask for volunteers to explain each example carefully.

Multicultural Connection Have students look at the opening photograph for the lesson, and ask how many of them have played Scrabble™. The class may be interested to know that the only wood used to manufacture the letter tiles in the Scrabble word game is the Bavarian maple which is from the Black Forest of Germany. The Bavarian maple wood has a tightly pressed grain that remains even when the letters are marked on the tiles. As a result, the playing tiles do not have defects that might give players an unfair advantage when picking tiles.

Example 1 is the easiest kind of conversion. You may wish to ask students to change the mixed number to a simple fraction, and to a percent. [$\frac{453}{100}$, 453%] **Example 2** is similar, except that the fraction needs to be written in lowest terms.

The fraction with a decimal in the numerator or denominator, the type in **Example 3,** fits in easily here and shows up often in applications. **Example 4 and 5** exemplify rewriting for the purpose of facility.

LESSON MASTER 2-6 B — **Questions on SPUR Objectives**

Skills Objective I: Convert terminating decimals to fractions, and either of these to percents.

In 1-16, complete the chart. You should be able to do this from memory.

	Fraction or Mixed Number (lowest terms)	Decimal	Percent
1.	$\frac{1}{2}$	.5	50%
2.	$\frac{3}{10}$	.3	30%
3.	$\frac{2}{5}$	.4	40%
4.	$\frac{1}{5}$	.2	20%
5.	$\frac{3}{5}$	.6	60%
6.	$\frac{1}{4}$	.25	25%
7.	$\frac{3}{8}$	.375	37.5%
8.	$\frac{3}{4}$	.75	75%
9.	$\frac{1}{8}$	.125	12.5%
10.	$1\frac{1}{2}$	1.5	150%
11.	$\frac{1}{3}$	$.\overline{3}$	$33\frac{1}{3}$%
12.	$\frac{1}{10}$	.1	10%
13.	$\frac{7}{10}$	.7	70%
14.	$\frac{2}{3}$	$.\overline{6}$	$66\frac{2}{3}$%
15.	$\frac{9}{10}$	.9	90%
16.	$\frac{7}{8}$	.875	87.5%

Optional Activities

Activity 1 After completing the lesson, students might enjoy playing **"I Have, Who Has?"** Obtain a set of large cards for as many students as there are in the class. On half the cards, write different numbers expressed as fractions, decimals, or percents. On the other half, write the same numbers in another way. Arrange the class in a circle, and distribute the cards, telling students not to show their cards to anyone. Call on a student. That student says: "I have ___ (naming the number), who has ___?" The student who has the equal number should say, "I do." The goal is to go around the circle, finding all the pairs as quickly as possible. Use a stopwatch. Add 15 seconds to the time for each incorrect answer.

When the pairs have all been found, collect and reshuffle the cards, distribute them again to students, and repeat the activity.

90

Example 5

A photographer reduces the dimensions of a photo to $\frac{5}{8}$ their original size. The final width is what percent of the original width?

Solution

First convert $\frac{5}{8}$ to a decimal. Then change the decimal to a percent.

$$\frac{5}{8} = 0.625 = 62.5\%$$

QUESTIONS

Covering the Reading

In 1–3, a decimal is given.
a. Write the decimal in English words.
b. Convert the decimal to a fraction or mixed number.

1. 8.27 See left. **2.** 630.5 See left. **3.** 0.001 a) one thousandth b) $\frac{1}{1000}$

4. The probability of a single birth being a boy is about .51. Convert this number to a percent. 51%

In 5 and 6, convert to a percent.

5. 0.724 72.4% **6.** 8 800%

7. A decimal approximation to π is 3.14. Convert 3.14 to a mixed number. $3\frac{7}{50}$

8. Explain how to change a fraction to a percent. Divide the numerator by the denominator, multiply by 100, and add a percent sign.

9. About $\frac{1}{4}$ of all families with two children are likely to have two girls. What percent of families is this? 25%

10. Write $\frac{4.2}{1.04}$ as a fraction in lowest terms. $\frac{105}{26}$

Applying the Mathematics

11. a. The cost of living in 1993 was about $3\frac{1}{2}$ times what it was in 1970. What percent is this? 350%
b. Suppose a slice of pizza cost 45¢ in 1970. Using the cost of living information in part **a**, estimate the cost of a slice in 1993. $1.58

In 12 and 13, use this information. Just as fractions can be represented by parts of circles, so can percents. Notice $\frac{1}{10}$ of a circle is 10%.

12. a. Draw a circle with a part representing 25%. See left.
b. What percent does the unshaded part of the circle represent? 75%

13. Draw a circle. Shade a part that represents $\frac{2}{5}$. What percent does this part represent? See drawing above left. 40%

How big are Bugs and Daffy? *Cartoons are enlarged and shrunk to fit on clothing, on comic pages, and so on. Thus, the same cartoon in one newspaper may appear larger or smaller in another newspaper.*

1a) eight and twenty-seven hundredths
1b) $8\frac{27}{100}$ or $\frac{827}{100}$
2a) six hundred thirty and five tenths
2b) $630\frac{1}{2}$ or $\frac{1261}{2}$

12a) 13)

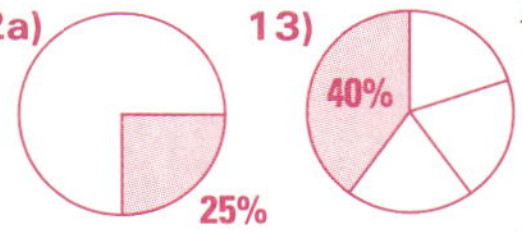

$\frac{1}{10}$ or 10%

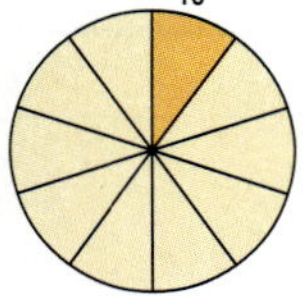

Pacing Practice on the skills taught in this lesson is interspersed in reviews throughout the book. You do not have to remain on this lesson more than a day.

Additional Examples

1. Convert 3.027 to a mixed number. $3\frac{27}{1000}$

2. Write .45 as a fraction in lowest terms. $\frac{9}{20}$

3. Find a simple fraction equal to $\frac{5.2}{9.36}$. $\frac{5}{9}$

4. A newborn baby typically triples his or her weight in the first year. What percent of the original weight is the weight after 1 year? 300%

5. A shirt is reduced by $\frac{1}{3}$. What percent is saved? $33\frac{1}{3}\%$

Notes on Questions

Before you begin discussing the questions for this lesson, you may wish to give students **Teaching Aid 20,** and have them place all relevant given information and the answers to the questions in the appropriate columns as they go through each of the questions. After all of the questions have been answered, have students go back and fill in the empty places. For example, for **Question 1** students would fill in the Decimal column (8.27) and Fraction column ($8\frac{27}{100}$) because they are the question and answer, respectively. Then 827% is written in the Percent column later.

▶ **LESSON MASTER 2-6 B** *page 2*

In 17-32, complete the chart. If necessary, you may use paper and pencil or your calculator.

	Fraction or Mixed Number (lowest terms)	Decimal	Percent
17.	$\frac{43}{100}$	.43	43%
18.	$\frac{3}{40}$	.075	7.5%
19.	$\frac{22}{25}$	.88	88%
20.	$\frac{1}{20}$	.05	5%
21.	$\frac{27}{400}$	.0675	6.75%
22.	$\frac{4}{9}$	.4	$44\frac{4}{9}\%$
23.	$2\frac{11}{20}$	2.55	255%
24.	$\frac{1}{200}$	.005	$\frac{1}{2}\%$
25.	$\frac{119}{160}$	.74375	74.375%
26.	$3\frac{7}{25}$	3.28	328%
27.	$\frac{719}{1000}$	.719	71.9%
28.	$\frac{3}{5000}$	.0006	.06%
29.	$4\frac{7}{8}$	4.875	487.5%
30.	$\frac{293}{2000}$	.1465	14.65%
31.	$1\frac{1}{3}$	$1.\overline{3}$	$133\frac{1}{3}\%$
32.	$\frac{1}{80}$	.0125	$1\frac{1}{4}\%$

Optional Activities

Activity 2 Technology Connection *Technology Sourcebook, Calculator Master 4,* provides work with equivalent forms of fractions, decimals, and percents and a variety of applications using them.

Notes on Questions

Questions 14–19 Error Alert Some students may have trouble with the uncommon percents. Review the process that is used with easy conversions, such as writing $\frac{1}{2}$ as a percent. Then have students apply the same process to the uncommon percents.

Follow-up for Lesson 2-6

Practice

For more questions on SPUR objectives, use **Lesson Master 2-6A** (shown on page 89) or **Lesson Master 2-6B** (shown on pages 90–91).

Assessment

Quiz A quiz covering Lessons 2-4 through 2-6 is provided in the *Assessment Sourcebook.*

Group Assessment Have groups of students explain to one another how to convert a terminating decimal to a fraction, how to convert a decimal to a percent, how to convert a fraction containing a decimal(s) to a simple fraction, and how to convert a fraction to a percent. [For each case, students participate by giving examples to show conversions and by helping others to understand.]

Additional Answers

35. The scientific calculator adds 7% of 500 to 500.

Key in: 500 [+] 7 [%] [=]

Display: [500.] [7.] [35.] [535.]

In 14–19, complete the table. Put fractions in lowest terms.

	Fraction	Decimal	Percent
	$\frac{1}{2}$	0.5	50%
14.	? $\frac{49}{500}$	? 0.098	9.8%
15.	? $\frac{16}{5}$	3.2	? 320%
16.	$\frac{5}{16}$	? 0.3125	? 31.25%
17.	? $\frac{27}{100}$	0.27	? 27%
18.	$\frac{3}{20}$	? 0.15	? 15%
19.	? $\frac{11}{25}$	? 0.44	44%

20. Ariel put 6.5 gallons of gasoline in a 12-gallon gas tank. So the tank is $\frac{6.5}{12}$ full. What simple fraction of a full tank is this? $\frac{13}{24}$

21. A money market account at a local bank pays 3.75% interest. What fraction is this? $\frac{3}{80}$

Who lives in the Sahara? *Over 2 million people live in the Sahara Desert. Most are nomads who herd sheep, goats, camels, and cattle near an oasis like the one pictured here.*

Review

22. a. Leslie used 30% of her $5.00 allowance to buy a magazine. How much did the magazine cost? $1.50

b. Explain how you could do part **a** in your head. *(Lesson 2-5)* 10% of $5 is 50¢, so 30% of $5 is 3 × .50 or $1.50.

23. Would you prefer to buy something at 30% off or $\frac{1}{3}$ off? *(Lesson 2-4)* $\frac{1}{3}$ off

In 24–26, calculate. *(Lessons 2-1, 2-2, 2-5)*

24. 1918.37 × 10,000 19,183,700 **25.** 14% of 231 32.34 **26.** 3^5 243

In 27 and 28, write the number as a decimal. *(Lessons 2-2, 2-4)*

27. 2.4×10^5 240,000 **28.** 3200% 32

In 29–31, rewrite the number in scientific notation. *(Lesson 2-3)*

29. 8,800,000 square kilometers, the approximate area of the Sahara Desert 8.8×10^6

30. 5280^3, the number of cubic feet in a cubic mile $1.47197952 \times 10^{11}$

31. 525,600 minutes, the number of minutes in a 365-day year 5.256×10^5

In 32 and 33, give the word name for the decimal. *(Lesson 2-1)*

32. One followed by nine zeros one billion **33.** One followed by fifteen zeros one quadrillion

34. Order from smallest to largest: .011 1/10 1/100. *(Lessons 1-2, 1-6)* $\frac{1}{100}$, .011, $\frac{1}{10}$

Exploration

35. If your calculator has a % key, try the following sequence: 500 [+] 7 [%] [=]. Explain what the calculator has done. See margin.

Adapting to Individual Needs

Extra Help

Before doing the examples in the text, you might want to review some simple problems. Be sure students understand the terms and the procedures.

1. Convert each decimal to a fraction or mixed number. (Hint: Reading the decimal will give you a clue.)
   a. .9 [$\frac{9}{10}$] **b.** 4.1 [$4\frac{1}{10}$]
   c. 2.17 [$2\frac{17}{100}$]
2. Convert each decimal to a fraction or mixed number in lowest terms.
   a. .6 [$\frac{3}{5}$] **b.** 15.6 [$15\frac{3}{5}$]
   c. 7.25 [$7\frac{1}{4}$]
3. Write each fraction with a denominator of 10, 100, or 1000. Then write the decimal.
   a. $\frac{2}{5}$ [$\frac{4}{10}$; 0.4]
   b. $5\frac{3}{4}$ [$5\frac{75}{100}$; 5.75]

Challenge

Have students write each decimal as a simple fraction in lowest terms.

1. -.00035 [$-\frac{7}{20{,}000}$]
2. 37.15625 [$\frac{1189}{32}$]
3. -1.001 [$-\frac{1001}{1000}$]
4. 15.0055 [$\frac{30{,}011}{2000}$]
5. 0.000048 [$\frac{3}{62{,}500}$]

LESSON

2-7

Circle Graphs

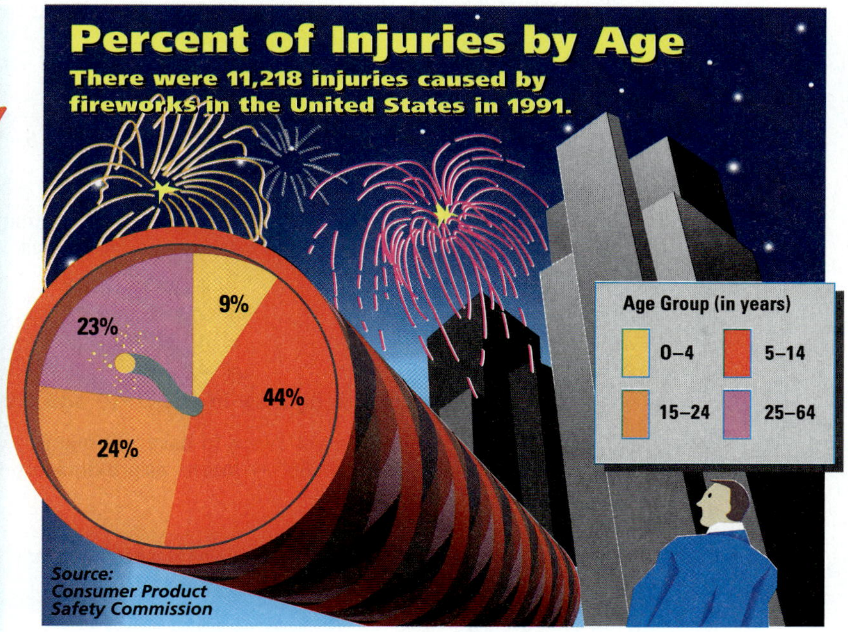

❶ Reading a Circle Graph

Percents of a whole are often pictured in a **circle graph** or **pie chart.** In a circle graph, you can quickly see the relationship of the parts. For example, the largest "pie piece" is the largest part of the whole.

Example 1

Use the information displayed in the circle graph above.

a. The entire circle represents what percent of the whole?
b. For the smallest piece of the circle, what does the 0–4 mean?
c. Which age group had the most injuries?
d. What percent of injuries are not in the 15–64 age groups?

Solution

a. Since the circle represents the whole quantity, it represents 100% of the injuries by fireworks.
Notice that 9% + 23% + 24% + 44% = 100%.
b. The 0–4 refers to children under the age of 5.
c. The 5–14 age group had the most injuries.
d. The percent in the 15–64 age groups is 24% + 23% = 47%.
Therefore,
100% − 47% = 53% are not in the 15–64 age group.

Lesson 2-7

Objectives

J Identify the center, radius, diameter, arc, and sector of a circle.
O Interpret circle graphs.

Resources

From the ***Teacher's Resource File***

- Lesson Master 2-7A or 2-7B
- Answer Master 2-7
- Teaching Aids
  15 Warm-up
  21 Circle-Graph Form
- Activity Kit, Activity 5
- Technology Sourcebook
  Computer Demonstration 2
  Computer Master 2

Additional Resources

- Visuals for Teaching Aids 15, 21
- Graphing/Probability Workshop
- Geometry Templates

Teaching Lesson 2-7

Warm-up

Diagnostic Use a compass or circle template and a ruler.

1. Draw a circle. Label the center *O.*
2. Draw a diameter and measure it.
3. Draw several more diameters and measure them. What can you say about the measures of the diameters of your circle? **They are =.**
4. Draw at least two different radii and measure them. What can you say about the measures of the radii of your circle? **They are =.**
5. What do you notice about the measures of the radii and diameters of your circle? **Sample: The diameter is twice the radius.**

Lesson 2-7 Overview

Broad Goals The most common display of percents is in circle graphs, also called *pie charts* or *pie graphs.* We also use these displays to represent fractions so that students have ways of visualizing equal percents and fractions. Circle graphs also provide a vehicle for introducing some terminology associated with circles.

Perspective Students are probably familiar with the use of pieces of pies (technically, *sectors*) to represent fractions between 0 and 1. The use of percents is similar in that the whole pie (technically, a circular region) stands for the number 1 (100%), and the sectors stand for parts of the circle (percents less than 100%).

At this point, we do not discuss the systematic drawing of circle graphs because that requires a knowledge of angle measure. However, simple circle graphs, such as those found in Example 3, or Questions 19 and 21, can be drawn by visually splitting up the circle as one would cut a pizza or other pie.

We have used *USA Today* as a source for two circle graphs in this lesson. Newspapers are a rich source for such graphs, and *USA Today* usually has one every day.

Notes on Reading

❶ Make sure students understand that the purpose of a circle graph is to show the relationships between a whole and its parts. In this graph, the whole is the total number of people injured by fireworks (11,218 or 100%). The parts are the numbers of people injured in each age group.

Multicultural Connection Fireworks probably originated in ancient China as a by-product of military explosives. During the Middle Ages, military technology, along with fireworks, was exported to Europe. Today, in many countries, fireworks are a part of celebrations which include national holidays such as the Fourth of July in the United States and Bastille Day in France and of festivals such as the coming of spring in Germany and the celebration of Holy Week in Mexico.

❷ Students are not required to make circle graphs by measuring angles in this lesson. Angle measures will be used in Chapter 3. Instead, students can approximate the sizes of the sectors by using the illustrations shown here.

After students finish reading the lesson, you might want to discuss the solution to Example 3 using the 100-Bead Circle which is discussed in *Optional Activities* below.

Additional Examples

Refer to the circle graph at the beginning of the lesson for Questions 1–2.

1. a. Redraw the circle graph as if the circle were not the top of a cylinder, but flat on a sheet of paper.

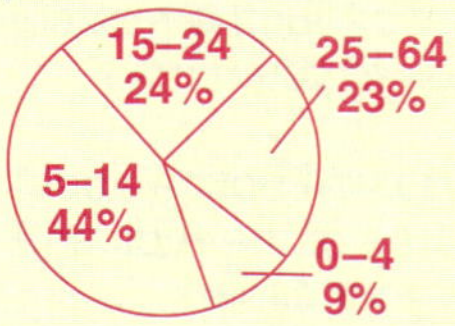

From information given in a circle graph, or next to the graph, you may be able to determine other information.

Example 2

Find the number of injuries by fireworks for the 5–14 age group.

Solution

To determine the number of injuries in any age group, multiply its percent of injuries by 11,218, the total number of injuries.

$$44\% \times 11{,}218$$
$$= .44 \times 11{,}218$$
$$= 4935.92$$
$$\approx 4936$$

There were 4936 injuries in the 5–14 age group.

Since it does not make sense to have .92 injuries, we rounded 4935.92 up to 4936. The symbol $\approx$ means **approximately equal to.**

Check

44% is less than 50%. The answer should be less than $\frac{1}{2}$ of 11,218, which is 5,609. It is.

Vocabulary for Circles

To discuss circle graphs, it is useful to know the names of parts of circles. A **circle** is the set of points which are all the same distance (its **radius**) from a certain point (its **center**). The plural of radius is **radii.** The distance across the circle is twice the length of its radius. That distance is the circle's **diameter.**

The words radius and diameter are used to name both distances and segments. The circle below at the left has center C and is named circle C. One radius of the circle is the line segment CD, written $\overline{CD}$. The radius of the circle is 5. One diameter of the circle is $\overline{DE}$. The diameter is 10.

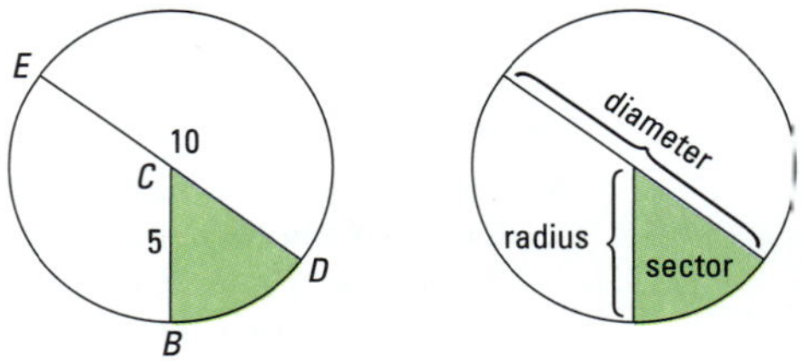

A part of a circle graph that looks like a slice of pie is called a **sector.** A sector is bounded by two radii and an *arc* of the circle. An **arc** is a part of a circle connecting two points (its endpoints) on the circle. The sector in the circle above bounded by $\overline{CB}$ and $\overline{CD}$ is named sector BCD or sector DCB. Sector BCD is also bounded by arc BD (written $\overset{\frown}{BD}$ or $\overset{\frown}{DB}$).

Optional Activities

Activity 1 You might want to use *Activity Kit, Activity 5,* to introduce the lesson or just after covering the reading of the lesson. In this activity, students make a simple circle graph by folding a paper circle into halves, fourths, and eighths.

Activity 2 The 100-Bead Circle
Materials: A string of 100 equal-sized beads and a large sheet of paper

After completing the lesson, have students **work in pairs.** The object of the activity is for students to put the string of beads on a circle, and use them to graph percents that result from a survey. Each sector is 1% of the circle. An alternative to using 100 actual beads is to use **Teaching Aid 21** which shows a circle with 100 "beads" on it. Begin by taking a survey of each student's favorite color, pet animal, or sport. Then have each pair translate the results into percents of the entire class. Students can use the 100-bead circle to draw a circle graph showing the results of the survey. The 100 beads enable students to draw circle graphs without using angle measures.

❷ Making a Circle Graph with Fractions or Percents

Fractions and percents are helpful in approximating the size of a sector on a circle graph.

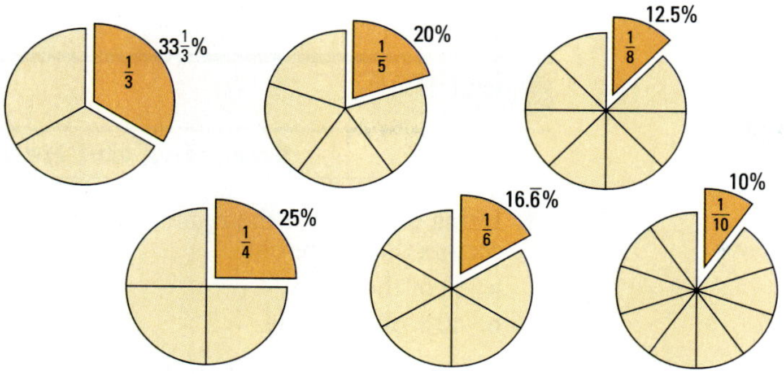

Example 3

Sixty students were asked to choose one dessert at a carnival. Draw a circle graph that displays the percent of students picking each dessert.

Dessert	Number of Students Choosing that Dessert
Ice Cream	30
Popcorn	15
Fruit	9
None	6

Solution

$\frac{30}{60}$ of the students chose ice cream. This is $\frac{1}{2}$, or 50%, of the students. So the sector for ice cream is half the circle.

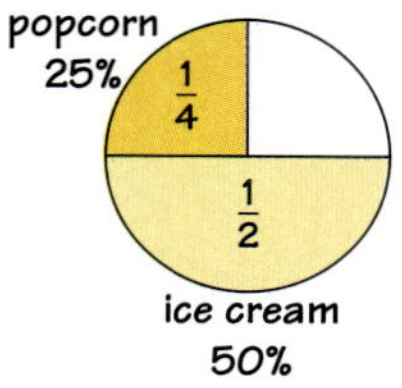

Popcorn was chosen by $\frac{15}{60}$, or $\frac{1}{4}$, or 25%, of the students. So the sector for popcorn is $\frac{1}{4}$ of the circle.

$\frac{6}{60}$ or $\frac{1}{10}$, or 10%, of the students chose none. The sector for none is $\frac{1}{10}$ of the circle. The circle piece for $\frac{1}{10}$ above can be used to approximate the sector for none.

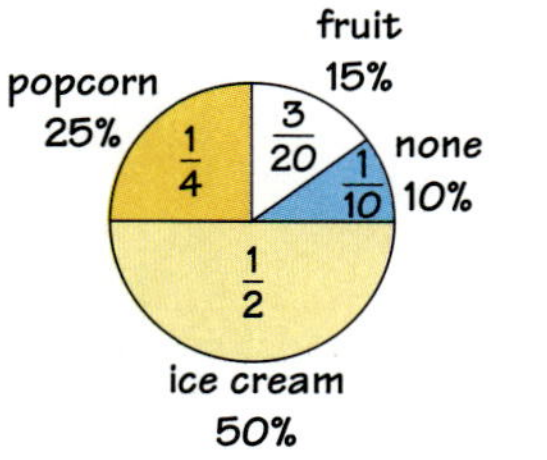

The remaining piece or unshaded part represents fruit. It is $\frac{9}{60}$, or $\frac{3}{20}$, or 15% of the circle.

A circle graph usually has the actual number or percent in each sector rather than the fraction.

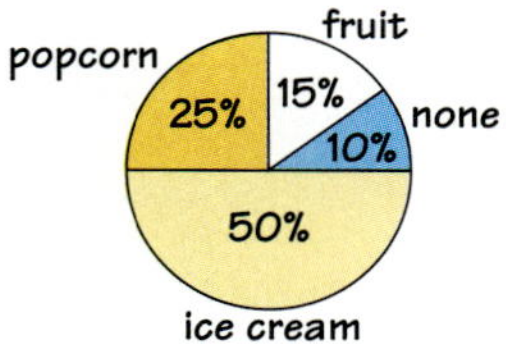

b. What percent of the injuries caused by fireworks in 1991 involved people under the age of 15? 53%

2. How many children under the age of 5 were injured by fireworks in the U.S. in 1991? about 1010 children

3. Suppose a family spends 17% of its income for taxes, 25% on housing, 20% on food, 10% on clothing and other necessities, 18% on entertainment and other non necessities, and 10% for savings. Put this information into a circle graph.

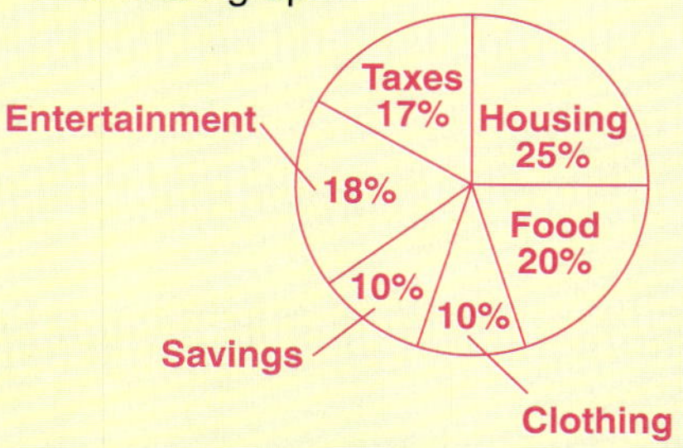

4. Draw a circle graph in which the sectors are the following fractions: $\frac{1}{3}$, $\frac{1}{6}$, $\frac{1}{4}$, $\frac{1}{5}$, and $\frac{1}{20}$. (Hint: change the fractions to percents.)

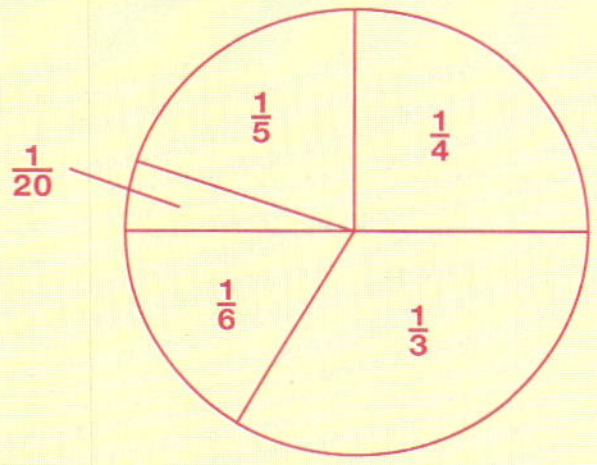

Optional Activities

Activity 3 Technology Connection You may wish to demonstrate how to make circle graphs using *Computer Demonstration 2* with the *Graphing and Probability Workshop*. Then, you could assign *Technology Sourcebook, Computer Master 2*. This activity involves collecting and displaying data about the ages of pennies.

LESSON MASTER 2-7 A

Questions on SPUR Objectives
See pages 113-115 for objectives.

Skills Objective J

In 1-5, give the name of the indicated part of the circle.

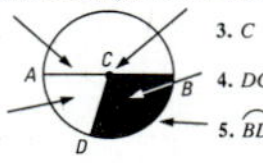

1. $\overline{AB}$ diameter
2. $\overline{CD}$ radius
3. C center
4. DCB sector
5. $\widehat{BD}$ arc
6. The diameter of a circle is 8 feet. Give the radius. 4 feet

Representations Objective O

7. Given the circle at the right,
   a. what percent is darkly shaded? 50%
   b. what percent is lightly shaded? 25%

In 8-11, use the circle graph picturing U.S. Household Income.

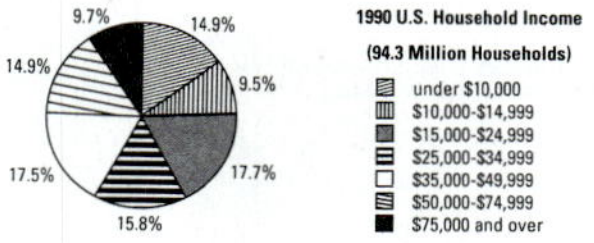

8. Which two income groups have the fewest households? $75,000 and over; $10,000-$14,999
9. Which two income groups have the most households? $35,000-$49,999; $15,000-$24,999
10. How many households have incomes under $10,000? 14,050,700 households
    0.149 × 94,300,000 (calculation) 14050700 (calculator answer) 14,050,700 households (answer to question)
11. How many households have incomes $75,000 or over? 9,147,100 households
    0.097 × 94,300,000 (calculation) 9147100 (calculator answer) 9,147,100 households (answer to question)

Notes on Questions

Questions 15–18 You might ask students how many people in the survey responded with each of the choices. [540, alarm or clock radio; 390, naturally; 50, need several alarms; 20, other] Then ask if they think the percents were rounded to the nearest integer percent. [It is very likely.]

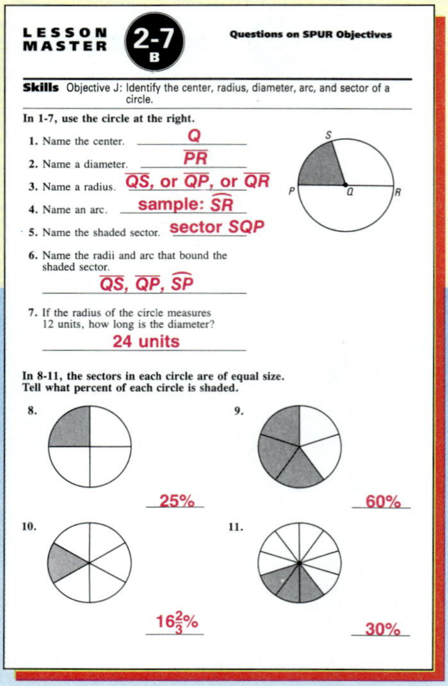
LESSON MASTER 2-7 B — Questions on SPUR Objectives

Skills Objective J: Identify the center, radius, diameter, arc, and sector of a circle.

In 1-7, use the circle at the right.

1. Name the center. Q
2. Name a diameter. PR
3. Name a radius. $\overline{QS}$, or $\overline{QP}$, or $\overline{QR}$
4. Name an arc. sample: $\overset{\frown}{SR}$
5. Name the shaded sector. sector SQP
6. Name the radii and arc that bound the shaded sector. $\overline{QS}$, $\overline{QP}$, $\overset{\frown}{SP}$
7. If the radius of the circle measures 12 units, how long is the diameter? 24 units

In 8-11, the sectors in each circle are of equal size. Tell what percent of each circle is shaded.

8. 25%
9. 60%
10. $16\frac{2}{3}$%
11. 30%

Circle graphs were first constructed by William Playfair in the late 1700s. Today circle graphs are found in many newspapers and magazines. There is software for most computers that will automatically construct circle graphs.

QUESTIONS

Covering the Reading

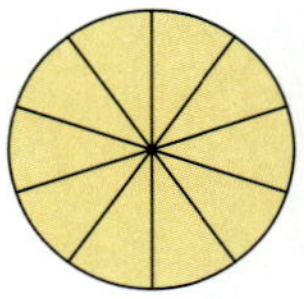

1. Using the circle at the right, state the number of sectors that represent
   a. $\frac{12}{40}$ of the circle. 3
   b. 40% of the circle. 4

In 2–4, use the circle graph on fireworks, page 93.

2. Which age group had the fewest injuries? 0–4
3. What percent of injuries are not in the 5–14 age group? 56%
4. Find the number of injuries for the 15–24 age group. 2692
5. What is the sum of the percents on a circle graph? 100%
6. Who first made a circle graph and when? William Playfair in the late 1700s
7. What is another name for circle graph? pie chart

In 8–10, use the circle graph on dessert choices, page 95.

8. The total number of people choosing to have desserts is _?_. 54
9. What fraction of people wanted fruit? $\frac{3}{20}$
10. Explain why the circle divided in 10 pieces helped in drawing the circle graph. The smallest sector is equal to the fraction $\frac{1}{10}$.
11. What is a circle? the set of points all the same distance from a certain point

In 12–14, use the circle at the right.

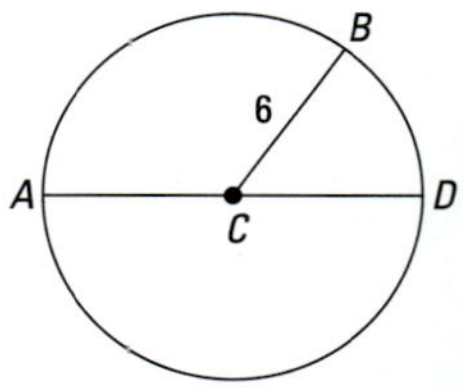

12. Name a radius. $\overline{BC}$ or $\overline{DC}$ or $\overline{AC}$
13. **a.** Name a sector. ACB or BCD
    b. Identify the radii and arc that bound the sector named in part **a.** See below.
14. The length of the diameter is _?_. 12

13b) for ACB, radii $\overline{CA}$ and $\overline{CB}$, and arc $\overset{\frown}{AB}$; for BCD, radii $\overline{CB}$ and $\overline{CD}$, and arc $\overset{\frown}{BD}$

Adapting to Individual Needs

Extra Help

Show students the circle graph at the right, and ask questions that help them understand that circle graphs are used to show all the parts that make up the whole. In this example, the whole is $160, and the amounts in each part add up to $160; the circle is 100%, and the sum of the percents is 100%. Discuss other circle graphs concentrating on the same concept.

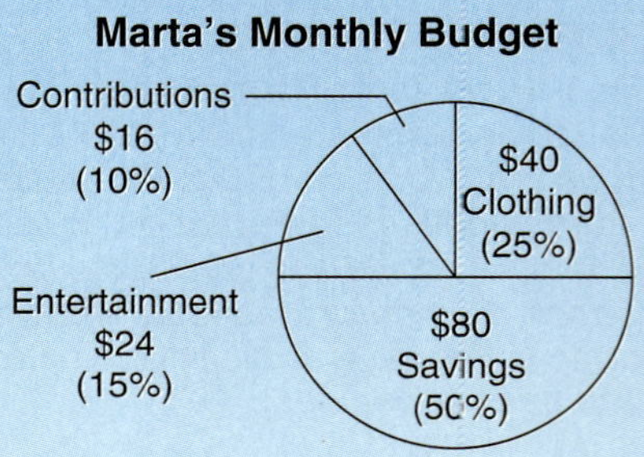

Applying the Mathematics

In 15–18, use the graph below.

How People Wake Up in the Morning

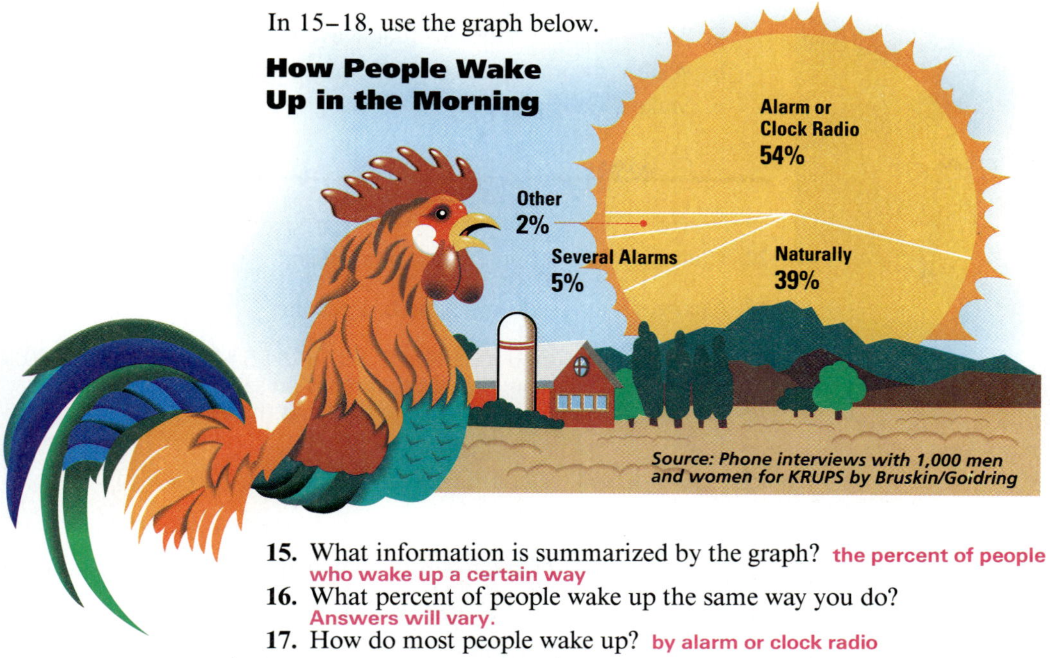

15. What information is summarized by the graph? the percent of people who wake up a certain way

16. What percent of people wake up the same way you do? Answers will vary.

17. How do most people wake up? by alarm or clock radio

18. How do you think the 2% of people included in "other" wake up in the morning? Samples: by a relative, by a rooster's crow, by a bugle (reveille)

19c)

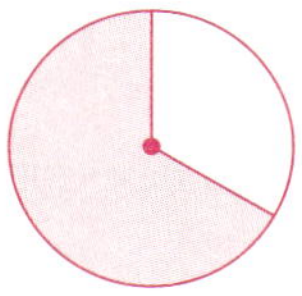

19. Refer to the table for dessert choices in this lesson. Suppose the number of students choosing ice cream was 40 and popcorn was 5.

a. The sector for ice cream should now be what fraction of the circle? $\frac{40}{60}$ or $\frac{2}{3}$

b. What percent of the circle is for ice cream? $66\frac{2}{3}\%$

c. Draw a circle on your paper. Shade the part that represents ice cream.

20. Use the circle graph below. It shows how many days the Williams family spent on their recent vacation in four states.

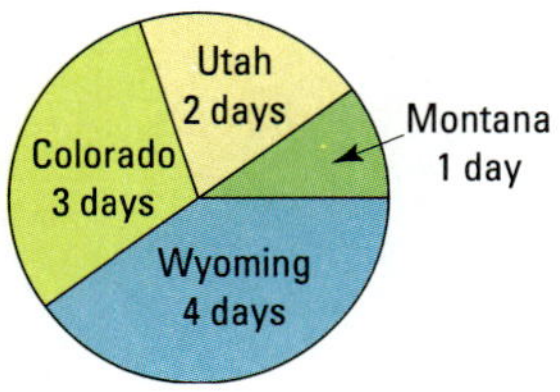

Give the percent of time they spent in each state.

a. Utah 20% **b.** Montana 10%

c. Wyoming 40% **d.** Colorado 30%

Adapting to Individual Needs

English Language Development

Some students may be familiar with the ideas conveyed by the following terms, but they may not know the words. Have students draw pictures to show what they know, and use illustrations to show them the meanings of terms they do not know.

1. circle **2.** center **3.** radius
4. diameter **5.** sector **6.** arc

Challenge

Students who saved their data from the survey they did in *Optional Activities* for Lesson 2-4 might show it now in a circle graph. Give them the circle graph form on **Teaching Aid 21**, or let them estimate the size of each sector in their graph based on those given on page 95.

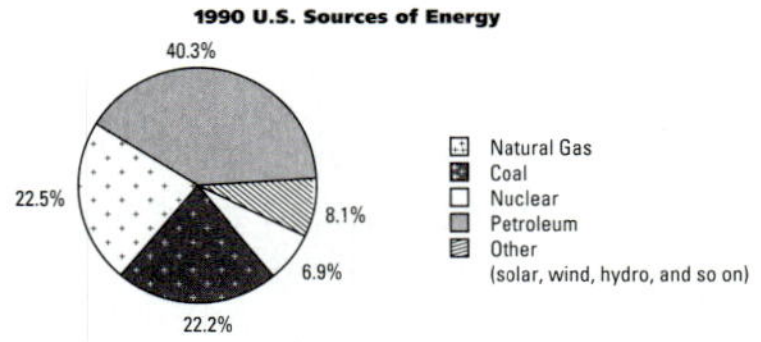

▶ **LESSON MASTER 2-7 B** *page 2*

Representations Objective O: Interpret circle graphs.

In 12-15, use the circle graph picturing U.S. sources of energy in 1990.

1990 U.S. Sources of Energy

12. In 1990, what percent of the energy in the United States came from nuclear power? 6.9%

13. What was the United States' largest source of energy? petroleum

14. Which two sources provided nearly equal amounts of energy? coal and natural gas

15. Did coal provide more than $\frac{1}{4}$ of the United States' energy or less than $\frac{1}{4}$? Explain your answer. Less; 22.2% < 25%, so 22.2% < $\frac{1}{4}$.

Review Objectives A and C, Lesson 2-2

In 16-23, write each as a decimal.

16. 3^4	81	**17.** 1.5^2	2.25
18. 1^{45}	1	**19.** 0^{17}	0
20. 55.911^4	9,772,125.6	**21.** 10^6	1,000,000
22. 6.8×10^3	6,800	**23.** $10^5 \times 0.0045$	450

Follow-up for Lesson 2-7

Practice
For more questions on SPUR objectives, use **Lesson Master 2-7A** (shown on page 95) or **Lesson Master 2-7B** (shown on pages 96–97).

Assessment
Written Communication Give students the following problem or a similar problem, and have them show the data in a circle graph. Kim budgets the $50 she earns each month as follows: clothes $20, food $10, entertainment $15, and savings $5.

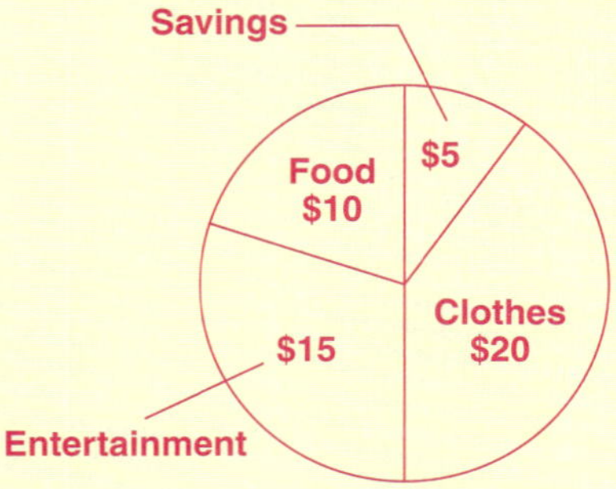

Extension
Tell students that some data cannot be represented by a circle graph and that some data can be represented better using a different kind of graph, such as a bar graph or a line graph. Then have students decide whether or not the following data can be represented by circle graphs. It might help students if they try to identify the *whole* and its *parts* for each case.

1. The budget for a class science project [yes]
2. Outside temperatures over a 24-hour period [no]
3. How time was spent over a 24-hour period [yes]
4. School days in December [yes]
5. The high and low temperatures for a month [no]
6. A city's comparison of the amounts of precipitation in 1993 with the normal amount [no]

Project Update Project 3, *Percents in Print,* on page 109, relates to the content of this lesson. Students can look for percents in circle graphs to include as parts of their projects and begin writing their paragraphs of explanation.

King's Dream. *Martin Luther King, Jr., shared his dream of people "not being judged by the color of their skin but by the content of their character," during his 1963 "I Have a Dream" speech. The speech, given after the March on Washington, was intended to urge Congress to pass the Civil Rights Bill.*

21. For their elective course, the students at Martin Luther King High School signed up as follows: 20 took Music, 10 took Woodshop, 5 took Drawing, and 15 took Keyboarding.

a. What percent of students took Keyboarding? 30%

b. What is the fraction of students who took either Music or Drawing?

c. Make a circle graph to display the given information. See below.

b) $\frac{25}{50}$ or $\frac{1}{2}$

Review

22. Change .7 to **a.** a fraction and **b.** a percent. *(Lesson 2-6)* $\frac{7}{10}$ 70%

23. Change $\frac{7}{20}$ to **a.** a decimal and **b.** a percent. *(Lessons 2-6, 1-6)* .35 35%

24. In one store a stereo usually sells for $179.95 but is on sale for 30% off. In a second store the same stereo is on sale for 25% off its normal price of $169.95. Which store has the better sale price? Explain how you arrived at your answer. *(Lesson 2-5)* See below.

25. Change 12.5% to a decimal and to a fraction. *(Lesson 2-4)* .125; $\frac{125}{1000}$ or $\frac{1}{8}$

26. Give a general rule for multiplying a decimal by 10. *(Lesson 2-1)* Move the decimal point one place to the right.

27. State the Equal Fractions Property in your own words. *(Lesson 1-10)* See below.

28. What numbers are the integers? *(Lesson 1-8)* the whole numbers and their opposites

29. Write the English words for 5.34. *(Lesson 1-1)* five and thirty-four hundredths

Exploration

30. a. Find an example of a pie or circle graph involving percent in your local newspaper. Answers will vary.

b. Make up a question about the information you have found and answer your question. Answers will vary.

31. Find a software package that enables a computer to display a circle graph on a monitor. If you have access to a computer, learn how to use it and the software to draw a circle graph. Draw the circle graph shown on the first page of this lesson. Appearance of graphs will differ depending on software used.

21c)

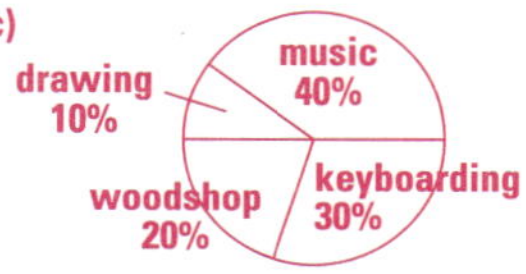

24) The first store has the slightly better price.
$179.95 – .3 × $179.95 ≈ $125.97;
$169.95 – .25 × $169.95 ≈ $127.47

27) If the numerator and denominator of a fraction are multiplied by the same nonzero number, the resulting fraction is equal to the original one.

LESSON

2-8

More Powers of Ten

The power of an abacus. *The picture shows an abacus used in a porcelain shop in Kweilin, China. Each column in an abacus represents a power of ten. Numbers are represented by properly positioning the beads in each column.*

What Is Exponential Form?

A number that is written with an exponent, such as 4^3 or 10^9, is said to be in **exponential form.** Exponential form is a short way of writing some large numbers. For example, $2^{20} = 1{,}048{,}576$. The decimal 1,048,576 is longer than the exponential form 2^{20} for the same number. Powers of 10 such as 100, 1000, and 10,000 are easily written in exponential form as 10^2, 10^3, and 10^4. Thus exponential form makes it possible to rewrite *large* numbers in the shorter scientific notation. Now we consider how to use exponential form to write *small* numbers.

What Is the Zero Power of a Number?

Examine this pattern closely. The numbers in each row going across are equal. Before turning the page, guess what should be the next entry in each column.

exponential form		decimal form		word name
10^6	=	1,000,000	=	million
10^5	=	100,000	=	hundred thousand
10^4	=	10,000	=	ten thousand
10^3	=	1,000	=	thousand
10^2	=	100	=	hundred
10^1	=	10	=	ten

Lesson 2-8

Objectives

B Change word names for place values to the right of the decimal point to decimals.

D Give decimals and English word names for positive and negative integer powers of 10.

Resources

From the ***Teacher's Resource File***

- Lesson Master 2-8A or 2-8B
- Answer Master 2-8
- Teaching Aids
  15 Warm-up
  22 Integer Powers of Ten

Additional Resources

- Visuals for Teaching Aids 15, 22

Teaching Lesson 2-8

Warm-up

Write each number in decimal form and give its word name.

1. 10^1 **10; ten**
2. 10^2 **100; hundred**
3. 10^3 **1,000; thousand**
4. 10^4 **10,000; ten thousand**
5. 10^5 **100,000; hundred thousand**
6. 10^6 **1,000,000; million**
7. 10^9 **1,000,000,000; billion**
8. 10^{12} **1,000,000,000,000; trillion**

Notes on Reading

Multicultural Connection An abacus is an ancient device used in China and other countries to make arithmetical calculations. The abacus can be used to add, subtract, multiply, and divide; it can also be used to find square roots and cube roots. The Chinese abacus is called *suan-pan,* which means counting, or reckoning, board.

Lesson 2-8 Overview

Broad Goals This lesson covers the zero power and the negative integer powers of 10.

Perspective Zero and negative integer powers of 10 are presented early in the course for several reasons. First, this material reinforces the work with powers of 10 and scientific notation introduced earlier. Second, scientific calculators display numbers very near zero in scientific notation with negative exponents, and it is important for students to be able to deal with these numbers. Third, by going so quickly to negative exponents, it becomes less likely that students will misinterpret powering as multiplication. Fourth, the use of negative powers to represent small numbers gives unexpected credibility for the existence of negative numbers.

The reading has three parts which correspond to three aspects of the lesson. The first part deals with the meaning of zero and negative exponents. The second part shows the nice correspondence between the names of the negative integer powers and the corresponding positive integer powers (just add "th"). The third part gives the rule for multiplying by negative integer powers of 10.

❶ You might show students a table of powers for a number other than 10 to point out that the zero power of any non zero number is equal to one. For example:

2^5	2^4	2^3	2^2	2^1	2^0
32	16	8	4	2	?

The pattern is that each number is one half the number before it. Following the pattern suggests that $2^0 = 1$.

❷ Emphasize that a negative exponent does not signify a negative result. Point out that all integer powers of 10 are positive. Only a negative number used as a base can give rise to integer powers that are negative.

❸ You might want to use **Teaching Aid 22** when discussing the names of the positive and negative integer powers of 10. Emphasize the patterns in the columns. You might want to display a poster showing the names of some of the positive and negative integer powers of 10. If you decide to make such a poster, leave space so that the metric prefixes found in Lesson 3-4 can be added. The connection of negative powers of 10 with metric prefixes is yet another reason for including negative powers here.

Pacing Mastery of the ideas in this lesson and the next lesson is not as important as mastery of earlier ideas in the chapter. There is ample time for review, and the ideas here are not as crucial. Do not spend more than a day on this lesson.

In the left column, the exponents decrease by 1, so the next entry should be 10^0. In the middle column, each number is $\frac{1}{10}$ the number above it. So the next entry should be $\frac{1}{10}$ of 10, or 1. In the right column are word names. Next to the tens place is the ones place. Here is the next row.

❶

exponential form		decimal form		word name
10^0	=	1	=	one

Activity 1

Verify with a calculator that 10 to the zero power is equal to 1.

Activity 2

Find the zero power of other numbers on your calculator.

❷ Negative Integer Powers of Ten

If the above pattern is continued, negative exponents will appear in the left column. This is exactly what is needed in order to represent small numbers.

10^{-1}	=	0.1	=	one tenth	=	$\frac{1}{10}$
10^{-2}	=	0.01	=	one hundredth	=	$\frac{1}{100}$
10^{-3}	=	0.001	=	one thousandth	=	$\frac{1}{1000}$
10^{-4}	=	0.0001	=	one ten-thousandth	=	$\frac{1}{10{,}000}$
10^{-5}	=	0.00001	=	one hundred-thousandth	=	$\frac{1}{100{,}000}$
				and so on		

Multiplying by Negative Integer Powers of Ten

To multiply a decimal by 10^{-1}, use the Substitution Principle. Since $10^{-1} = 0.1$, think of multiplying by 0.1, and move the decimal point one unit to the left.

$$829.43 \times 10^{-1} = 82.943$$

To multiply a decimal by 0.01 or $\frac{1}{100}$, you know you only have to move the decimal point two places to the left. Since $10^{-2} = 0.01$, the same goes for multiplying by 10^{-2}.

$$829.43 \times 10^{-2} = 8.2943$$

Do you see the simple pattern?

To multiply by a negative integer power of 10
Move the decimal point to the left as many places as indicated by the exponent.

Adapting to Individual Needs

Extra Help
Have students **work in groups** of two or three to make a chart of some of the powers of 10, giving the fraction form, the decimal form, and the word name for each power. A portion of a sample chart is shown below.

Power of 10	10^2	10^1	10^0	10^{-1}	10^{-2}
Fraction form	100	10	1	$\frac{1}{10}$	$\frac{1}{100}$
Decimal form	100	10	1	0.1	0.01
Word name	one hundred	ten	one	one tenth	one hundredth

Example 1

Write 72×10^{-5} as a decimal.

Solution

To multiply by 10^{-5}, move the decimal point five places to the left.

$72 \times 10^{-5} = 72.0 \times 10^{-5} = .00072$

❸ The names of the negative integer powers of 10 correspond to the names of the positive integer powers.

10^1 = ten	10^{-1} = one tenth
10^2 = one hundred	10^{-2} = one hundredth
10^3 = one thousand	10^{-3} = one thousandth
10^6 = one million	10^{-6} = one millionth
10^9 = one billion	10^{-9} = one billionth
10^{12} = one trillion	10^{-12} = one trillionth
10^{15} = one quadrillion	10^{-15} = one quadrillionth
10^{18} = one quintillion	10^{-18} = one quintillionth

Example 2

Write 6 trillionths as a decimal.

Solution

Think: one trillion $= 10^{12}$, so one trillionth is 10^{-12}.

6 trillionths $= 6 \times 10^{-12} = 0.00000\ 00000\ 06$

(When a decimal has many digits, we put a space after each five digits, starting at the decimal point, to make it easier to count the digits.)

QUESTIONS

Covering the Reading

1. *Multiple choice.* Which number is written in exponential form?
(a) $\frac{2}{3}$ (b) million (c) 2×10^6 (d) 7^3 (e) 1.45 **(d)**

2. Write $10 \times 10 \times 10 \times 10$ in exponential form. **10^4**

3. Give the place value name for each power.
a. 10^5 **b.** 10^4 **c.** 10^3 **d.** 10^2 **e.** 10^1
a) hundred thousands b) ten thousands c) thousands d) hundreds e) tens

4. Continue the pattern of Question 3 to give the place value name for each power:
a. 10^0 **b.** 10^{-1} **c.** 10^{-2} **d.** 10^{-3} **e.** 10^{-4}
a) ones b) tenths c) hundredths d) thousandths e) ten-thousandths

Additional Examples

Write each number as a decimal.

1. 9.8×10^{-4} **.00098**
2. 43 millionths **.000043**
3. 1200^0 **1**
4. half of a billionth
$.5 \times 10^{-9} = .00000\ 00005$

Adapting to Individual Needs

English Language Development

Materials: Map of the United States

For **Questions 30–33,** students from other countries may not understand what is meant by the regions of the United States. You might point out the general areas on a map when discussing the questions.

LESSON MASTER 2-8 A

Questions on SPUR Objectives
See pages 113-115 for objectives.

Skills Objectives B and D

In 1-8, fill in the chart.

	Exponential Form	Decimal Form	Word Name
1.	10^3	1000	thousand
2.	10^{-3}	0.001	thousandth
3.	10^{-6}	0.000001	millionth
4.	10^{-1}	.1	tenth
5.	10^{-9}	0.000000001	billionth
6.	10^0	1	one
7.	10^{-2}	0.01	hundredth
8.	10^{-4}	0.0001	ten-thousandth

9. Make up an example to explain how to multiply by a negative integer power of 10.
sample: To multiply by 10^{-3} move the decimal point three places to the left; $8.23 \cdot 10^{-3} = 0.00823$.

In 10-16, write each number as a decimal.

10. 4 ten-thousandths **0.0004**
11. 62 millionths **0.000062**
12. 7.2×10^{-4} **0.00072**
13. $.675 \times 10^{-5}$ **0.00000675**
14. $.9876 \times 10^{-8}$ **0.000000009876**
15. 5 microseconds (A microsecond is 10^{-6} seconds.) **0.000005 second**
16. approximate weight of a Jamaican hummingbird egg: 3.63×10^{-1} grams **0.363 gram**

Notes on Questions

Question 5 This question reinforces the fact that $10^0 = 1$. Although the reason "because the calculator says so" is not mathematically valid, seeing the display helps students who are still confusing powering with multiplication and think 10^0 equals zero.

Question 23 This pattern deserves special mention. Here, of course, the generalization $x^n \times x^{-n} = 1$ is valid, but at this point we do not expect students to use variables to describe the generalization. You might want to talk a little about the evidence one should have to make a generalization, and caution students against jumping to conclusions. To give students more intuition for the generalization, point out that multiplying a number by 10^4 moves the decimal point in the number 4 places to the right and that multiplying by 10^{-4} moves it 4 places to the left. This means that multiplying a number by both 10^4 and 10^{-4} brings the decimal point in the number back to its original position. This computation is the same as multiplying by 1.

Question 25 Diagnostic As you discuss this question, you might wish to diagnose student readiness for the metric-system discussion in Chapter 3 by asking if they know any of the other prefixes for these numbers. However, this is not the time to teach them.

LESSON MASTER 2-8 B **Questions on SPUR Objectives**

Skills Objective B: Change word names for place values to the right of the decimal point to decimals.
Objective D: Give decimals and English word names for positive and negative integer powers of 10.

In 1-15, fill in the chart.

	Exponential Form	Decimal Form	Word Name
1.	10^2	100	hundred
2.	10^3	1,000	thousand
3.	10^{-2}	.01	hundredth
4.	10^{-1}	.1	tenth
5.	10^{-3}	.001	thousandth
6.	10^{-5}	.00001	See below.
7.	10^0	1	one
8.	10^{-6}	.000001	millionth
9.	10^9	1,000,000,000	billion
10.	10^{-9}	.000000001	billionth
11.	10^{-12}	.000000000001	trillionth
12.	10^5	100,000	See below.
13.	10^{-15}	.000000000000001	quadrillionth
14.	10^{18}	See below.	quintillion
15.	10^{-4}	.0001	ten-thousandth

16. When you multiply a decimal by 10^{-5}
   a. How many places should you move the decimal point? 5
   b. In which direction should you move the decimal point? left

6. hundred-thousandth 12. hundred thousand
14. 1,000,000,000,000,000,000

5. What keys can you press on your calculator to verify that $10^0 = 1$? Sample: 10 y^x 0 =
6. Write each number as a decimal.
   a. 10^{-2} 0.01
   b. 10^{-3} 0.001
7. Tell whether each number is positive, negative, or equal to zero.
   a. 10^0 positive
   b. 10^{-1} positive
8. 10^7 = ten million. What is a word name for 10^{-7}? one ten-millionth

In 9–11, write the number as a power of 10.

9. one thousandth 10^{-3}
10. one millionth 10^{-6}
11. one trillionth 10^{-12}

In 12–17, write the number as a decimal.

12. 3×10^{-2} 0.03
13. 3.45×10^{-4} 0.000345
14. 41.3×10^0 41.3
15. four thousandths 0.004
16. sixty billionths 0.00000 0060
17. five millionths 0.00000 5
18. What is the general rule for multiplying by a negative integer power of 10? Move the decimal point to the left as many places as indicated by the exponent.

Applying the Mathematics

19. *Multiple choice.* Which of (a) to (e) does not equal the others?
   (a) 1%
   (b) .01
   (c) $\frac{1}{100}$
   (d) 10^{-2}
   (e) one hundredth
   (f) All of (a) through (e) are equal. (f)
20. Explain why 0^{10} does not equal 10^0. See below.
21. Describe the results you obtained for Activity 2 in this lesson. The zero power of any number other than 0 equals 1.
22. Write 10×10^{-7} as a decimal. 0.00000 1
23. a. Calculate $10^4 \times 10^{-4}$. 1
   b. What is a hundred times one one-hundredth? 1
   c. Make a general conclusion from parts **a** and **b**.

23c) When 10 to a power is multiplied by 10 to the opposite of the power, the product is 1.

24. Arrange from smallest to largest: 1 10^{-5} 0 10^2.
   0, 10^{-5}, 1, 10^2
25. In the metric system, all the prefixes have meaning. For example, kilo- means 1000, centi- means $\frac{1}{100}$ or .01, and milli- means $\frac{1}{1000}$ or .001. Using this information, explain the meaning of:
   a. kilometer
   b. centimeter
   c. millimeter. See below.
26. An electron microscope can magnify an object 10^5 times. The length of a poliomyelitis virus is 1.2×10^{-8} meter. Multiply this length by 10^5 to find how many meters long the virus would appear to be when viewed through this microscope. 0.0012 meter

In 27–29, write the number in exponential form. (For example, $64 = 4^3$.)

27. 81 9^2 or 3^4
28. 144 12^2
29. 32 2^5

20) 0^{10} is $0 \times 0 \times 0 \times 0 \times 0 \times 0 \times 0 \times 0 \times 0 \times 0 = 0$; 10^0 is defined to be 1, and $0 \neq 1$. So $0^{10} \neq 10^0$.
25) a) 1000 meters; b) .01 meter or one hundredth of a meter; c) .001 meter or one thousandth of a meter

Adapting to Individual Needs

Challenge

Have students investigate the electromagnetic spectrum, tell something about each wave in the spectrum, and give a typical wavelength in meters.

Wave	Sample Uses	Typical Wavelength
X rays	Rays that penetrate substances such as the body to "see" inside	10^{-11} meters
Ultraviolet rays	Rays that cause suntan or sunburn, as well as promote healing and give vitamins	10^{-8} meters
Light	Visible rays, ranging from violet to red	10^{-7} meters
Infrared rays	Rays that cause heat which can be felt (e.g. sunlight, lamps, and fire)	10^{-5} meters
Microwaves	Waves that can cook food	10^{-2} meters
Radio waves	Waves for radio and television	10 meters and on

It's a celebration. *This Bolivian folklore group at a New York street festival is celebrating* Día de la Raza, *a Columbus Day observance of "the Day of the Race." People from Bolivia are among the people classified by the Census Bureau as "Other Hispanics."*

Review

In 30–33, refer to the four circle graphs below. These graphs show how various Hispanic populations are distributed among the four regions of the United States: W = West, S = South, M = Midwest, and NE = Northeast. For instance, the left circle is about the 13.50 million people of Mexican heritage in the U.S. It shows that 58.0% of these people live in the West, 32.2% live in the South, 8.5% in the Midwest, and 1.3% in the Northeast. (Source: *Statistical Abstract of the United States: 1992*)

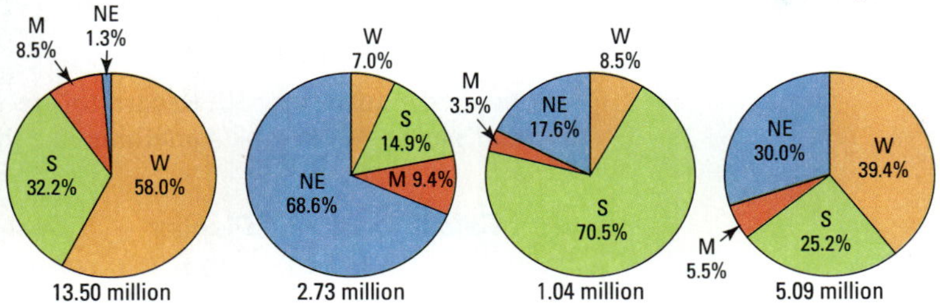

30. **a.** In which region do most people of Cuban heritage live? **South**

b. Why do you think more people of Cuban heritage live in this region than any other? *(Lesson 2-7)* **Answers will vary. Sample: The South region of the U.S. is closest to Cuba.**

31. How many people of Mexican heritage live in the West? *(Lessons 2-5, 2-7)* **7.83 million or 7,830,000**

32. **a.** Are there more people of Puerto Rican heritage or of Mexican heritage in the Midwest? **Mexican**

b. Explain your answer to part **a.** *(Lessons 2-5, 2-7)* **See below left.**

33. Fill in the blanks. Over $\frac{2}{3}$ of people of Other Hispanic heritage live in the __?__ or __?__ regions. *(Lessons 2-5, 2-6, 2-7)* **West, Northeast**

34. Change 1.03 to: **a.** fraction. $\frac{103}{100}$ **b.** a percent. *(Lesson 2-6)* **103%**

35. **a.** Change 0.1875 to a fraction in lowest terms. $\frac{3}{16}$

b. Change 0.1875 to a percent. *(Lessons 1-10, 2-6)* **18.75%**

36. Store *C* has a \$50 videotape marked 30% off. Store *D* has this tape for \$35. Which store offers the better buy? *(Lesson 2-5)* **Neither, the prices are the same.**

37. Write a rule for finding 10% of a number. *(Lessons 2-4, 2-5)* **Multiply the number by .1.**

38. 93,000,000 miles is the approximate distance from Earth to the Sun. Write this number in scientific notation. *(Lesson 2-3)* **9.3×10^7**

39. 512 is what power of 2? *(Lesson 2-2)* **ninth**

32b) **8.5% of 13.5 million ≈ 1.15 million which is larger than 9.4% of 2.73 million ≈ 0.26 million.**

Exploration

40. Large computers are able to do computations in nanoseconds. Look in a dictionary for the meaning of *nanosecond.* **one billionth of a second**

Question 26 We assume students will change 1.2×10^{-8} to .000000012, and then move the decimal point 5 places to the right to get .0012 meters. In Chapter 3, students will learn to convert from one unit to another; this virus is 1.2 millimeters long as seen through an electron microscope, and a millimeter is long enough to be seen.

Follow-up for Lesson 2-8

Practice

For more questions on SPUR objectives, use **Lesson Master 2-8A** (shown on page 101) or **Lesson Master 2-8B** (shown on pages 102–103).

Assessment

Written Communication Have students explain negative and zero exponents in letters to you or to another teacher in your school. Perhaps the language arts teachers would be interested in reading and commenting on them. [Letters include a coherent explanation and examples of negative and zero exponents.]

Extension

Project Update Project 4, *Powers of 10,* relates to the content of this lesson.

Setting Up Lesson 2-9

In-class Activity This is the first of a number of activities in this book that occur between lessons. As its location suggests, this activity should be undertaken before Lesson 2-9 is read. Its purpose is to set up that lesson by showing students how calculators display small powers of 10.

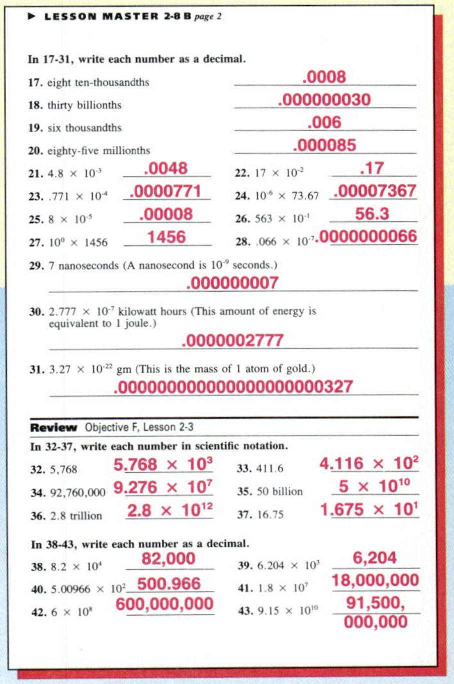

▶ **LESSON MASTER 2-8 B** *page 2*

In 17-31, write each number as a decimal.

17. eight ten-thousandths **.0008**
18. thirty billionths **.000000030**
19. six thousandths **.006**
20. eighty-five millionths **.000085**
21. 4.8×10^{-3} **.0048**
22. 17×10^{-2} **.17**
23. $.771 \times 10^{-4}$ **.0000771**
24. $10^{-6} \times 73.67$ **.00007367**
25. 8×10^{-5} **.00008**
26. 563×10^{-1} **56.3**
27. $10^{0} \times 1456$ **1456**
28. $.066 \times 10^{-7}$ **.0000000066**
29. 7 nanoseconds (A nanosecond is 10^{-9} seconds.) **.000000007**
30. 2.777×10^{-7} kilowatt hours (This amount of energy is equivalent to 1 joule.) **.0000002777**
31. 3.27×10^{-22} gm (This is the mass of 1 atom of gold.) **.000000000000000000000327**

Review Objective F, Lesson 2-3

In 32-37, write each number in scientific notation.

32. 5,768 **5.768×10^3**
33. 411.6 **4.116×10^2**
34. 92,760,000 **9.276×10^7**
35. 50 billion **5×10^{10}**
36. 2.8 trillion **2.8×10^{12}**
37. 16.75 **1.675×10^1**

In 38-43, write each number as a decimal.

38. 8.2×10^4 **82,000**
39. 6.204×10^3 **6,204**
40. 5.00966×10^2 **500.966**
41. 1.8×10^7 **18,000,000**
42. 6×10^8 **600,000,000**
43. 9.15×10^{10} **91,500,000,000**

In-class Activity

Resources

From the ***Teacher's Resource File***

- Teaching Aid 23: Small Numbers on a Calculator

Additional Resources

- Visual for Teaching Aid 23

In this activity, students use scientific calculators to successively divide, thereby determining the decimal place at which the calculator displays will change over from a quotient written as a decimal to a quotient expressed in scientific notation.

Teaching Aid 23 contains a table with four columns corresponding to the answers required for **Questions 2–4.** Students can use it for recording their successive divisions.

In **Question 4,** students are asked to write each calculator display as a decimal and in scientific notation. For students having difficulties writing the displays in scientific notation, you might suggest that they compare their displays with the displays using scientific notation for very large numbers which they learned in Lesson 2-3.

TEACHING AID 23
In-class Activity, Lesson 2-9

Small Numbers on a Calculator

Calculation	Display	Decimal	Scientific Notation
1 ÷ 10	0.1	0.1	
.1 ÷ 10			

Introducing Lesson 2-9

Scientific Notation for Small Numbers

IN-CLASS ACTIVITY

Work with a partner. One of you (person A) needs to have a scientific calculator. The other (person B) needs paper.

1 **Person A:** divide 1 by 10.
Person B: record the display.

2 Divide the answer by 10. Record this second display. Your paper should look something like this

Calculation	Display	Decimal
1 ÷ 10	0.1	.1
Ans ÷ 10		
Ans ÷ 10		
⋮		

3 Continue dividing the answers and recording the displays until you have 12 rows.

4 At some time, your display should shift into scientific notation. Together, determine what these answers are in scientific notation and what they are as decimals.
See margin.

4. In scientific notation and decimals, the answers for rows 1–12 are:

1.00×10^{-1}	.1
1.00×10^{-2}	.01
1.00×10^{-3}	.001
1.00×10^{-4}	.0001
1.00×10^{-5}	.00001
1.00×10^{-6}	.000001
1.00×10^{-7}	.0000001
1.00×10^{-8}	.00000001
1.00×10^{-9}	.000000001
1.00×10^{-10}	.0000000001
1.00×10^{-11}	.00000000001
1.00×10^{-12}	.000000000001

LESSON

2-9

Scientific Notation for Small Numbers

Crash! *At Sandia National Laboratories in Albuquerque, NM, subatomic particles with masses of 1.673 × 10^{-24} gram (at rest) are accelerated to nearly the speed of light. The particles collide to produce up to 900 billion electron volts. Operation of the particle accelerator creates the electrical discharges shown here.*

Converting Small Positive Numbers into Scientific Notation

The mass of one atom of hydrogen, the lightest element, is

.00000 00000 00000 00000 00016 75 gram.

(By comparison, a piece of notebook paper weighs more than a gram!) A number this small in decimal notation is difficult to read and use in computation. To help read this number, we have put a space after every fifth digit of the decimal. But there is a shorter way to write the number, namely, scientific notation.

> A small positive number written in scientific notation is a number greater than or equal to 1 and less than 10, multiplied by a negative integer power of 10.
>
> $$\textit{decimal} \times 10^{\textit{negative integer exponent}}$$

For instance, 1.91×10^{-5} is a small positive number written in scientific notation. The same ideas are involved in putting small numbers into scientific notation as are used with large numbers.

Example 1

Write the mass of one atom of hydrogen in scientific notation.

Solution

First place the decimal point between the 1 and the 6. This gives you 1.675, a number between 1 and 10. Now find the power of 10 by counting the number of places you must move the decimal to the *left* to change 1.675 into .00000 00000 00000 00000 00016 75. (The movement to the left is in the negative direction and signals the negative exponent.) The move is 24 places to the left. So the mass, in scientific notation, is:

$$1.675 \times 10^{-24} \text{ gram.}$$

Lesson 2-9

Objectives

F Convert small positive numbers into and out of scientific notation.

L Identify numbers as being written in scientific notation.

N Indicate key sequences and displays for small numbers on a calculator.

Resources

From the ***Teacher's Resource File***

- Lesson Master 2-9A or 2-9B
- Answer Master 2-9
- Teaching Aids
  15 Warm-up
  22 Integer Powers of Ten
  24 Scientific Notation
- Technology Sourcebook, Calculator Master 5

Additional Resources

- Visuals for Teaching Aids 15, 22, 24

Teaching Lesson 2-9

Warm-up

Write each number in scientific notation.

1. 1,230,000 1.23×10^6
2. 123,000 1.23×10^5
3. 12,300 1.23×10^4

LESSON MASTER 2-9 A **Questions on SPUR Objectives** See pages 113-115 for objectives.

Skills Objective F

In 1-4, write each in scientific notation.

1. .0042 4.2×10^{-3}
2. .000001 1×10^{-6}
3. $3.24 \times \frac{1}{100{,}000}$ 3.24×10^{-5}
4. 350×10^{-7} 3.5×10^{-5}

In 5-7, write each as a decimal.

5. 3.6×10^{-4} 0.00036
6. 8×10^{-6} 0.000008
7. 2.57×10^{-12} 0.00000000000257

Properties Objective L

8. Write a description of a number written in scientific notation. sample: In scientific notation an integer power of 10 is multiplied by a number greater than or equal to 1 and less than 10.

In 9 and 10, explain why each number is *not* in scientific notation.

9. 56×10^{-5} sample: The number must be less than or equal to 1 and less than 10 times an integer power of 10.
10. $3.7 \times 10^{-2.5}$ sample: The power of ten must be an integer.

Representations Objective N

11. For 7.29×10^{-5},
    a. what key sequence will enter this number on your calculator? 7.29 [EE] 5 [+/−]
    b. what is displayed on your calculator? 7.29 -05
12. What decimal number is represented by the calculator display [4.28 −06]? 4.28×10^{-6} or 0.00000428
13. Write the decimal for 1 ÷ 62,500,000. 0.000000016

Lesson 2-9 Overview

Broad Goals In this lesson, students use negative powers of 10 to write small numbers in scientific notation. This task is easier if students understand how to multiply by negative powers of 10 (Lesson 2-8). At the same time, the concepts in this lesson help students to master the material covered in Lesson 2-8. This lesson also extends the use of the calculator.

Perspective This brief lesson completes the chapter, giving students the power to represent very large and very small positive numbers. The examples are straightforward, and much of the lesson can be spent reviewing ideas from earlier lessons.

Notes on Reading

To show the pattern of scientific notation, write the following pattern on the board:

1230.	1.23×10^3
123.	1.23×10^2
12.3	1.23×10^1
1.23	?
.123	?
.0123	?
.00123	?

Ask students to continue the pattern. [1.23×10^0, 1.23×10^{-1}, 1.23×10^{-2}, 1.23×10^{-3}] Then have them use a calculator to confirm that the products are equal to the numbers at left.

Review the rules for writing a number in scientific notation. You might want to use the steps in *Adapting to Individual Needs* on page 107. Finally, carefully examine the examples with the students.

Visual Organizer At this time you may want to use **Teaching Aid 24** with students. It shows how to change both large and small numbers into and out of scientific notation.

LESSON MASTER 2-9 B Questions on SPUR Objectives

Skills Objective F: Convert small positive numbers into and out of scientific notation.

In 1-8, write each in scientific notation.

1. .03 3×10^{-2}
2. .8 8×10^{-1}
3. .000456 4.56×10^{-4}
4. 0.00000008 8×10^{-8}
5. .000090004 9.0004×10^{-5}
6. .76302 7.6302×10^{-1}
7. $5.45 \times \frac{1}{10{,}000}$ 5.45×10^{-4}
8. 480×10^{-9} 4.8×10^{-7}

In 9-16, write each as a decimal.

9. 2×10^{-8} .00000002
10. 3.1×10^{-3} .031
11. 1.0009×10^{-1} .10009
12. 9.99×10^{-11} .0000000000999
13. 5.72336×10^{-4} .000572336
14. 6.7×10^{-10} .00000000067
15. 8.0304×10^{-5} .000080304
16. 4.911×10^{-14} .00000000000004911

Properties Objective L: Identify numbers as being written in scientific notation.

17. A number written in scientific notation is the product of a decimal and a power of ten. Suppose a given number is a positive number less than 1. When that number is written in scientific notation,
   a. what is true about the decimal? It is greater than or equal to 1 and less than 10.
   b. what is true about the power of 10? The exponent is a negative integer.

Entering Small Positive Numbers into a Calculator

To enter 1.675×10^{-24} into a calculator, you may have two choices. One choice is to use the powering key.

Key sequence: 1.675 [×] 10 [y^x] 24 [±] [=]

A second choice is to use the scientific notation key.

Key sequence: 1.675 [EE] 24 [±]

The scientific notation key is usually easier to use. Using either sequence, you should see displayed the following or some equivalent.

[1.675 -24]

Activity 1

Enter 3.97×10^{-8} into a calculator.

Example 2

Change 3.97×10^{-8} to a decimal.

Solution

Recall that to multiply by 10^{-8}, move the decimal point 8 places to the left.

$$3.97 \times 10^{-8} = 0.00000\ 00397$$

To enter a small positive number written as a decimal into your calculator, first convert it into scientific notation.

Activity 2

Enter 0.00000 00000 6993 into a calculator.

From this activity, you should see [6.993 -11].

QUESTIONS

Covering the Reading

1. A small positive number in scientific notation is a number greater than or equal to _?_ and less than _?_ multiplied by a _?_ power of _?_. 1, 10, negative integer, 10
2. Why are small numbers often written in scientific notation? They are easier to use.
3. Give an example of a small quantity that is usually written in scientific notation. the mass of one atom of hydrogen
4. Write a key sequence that will display 3.97×10^{-8} on your calculator
   a. using the power key. See Sample below.
   b. using the key for scientific notation. Sample: 3.97 [EE] 8 [+/−]

   a) 3.97 [×] 10 [y^x] 8 [+/−] [=]

Optional Activities

Activity 1 Bring a set of science books to class. After students complete the lesson, give each of them or pairs of them one book. Have them search the book for examples of numbers given in scientific notation. As numbers are discovered, students should record them. This activity can be made competitive. Check that there are enough numbers in scientific notation to make the search interesting.

Activity 2 Technology Connection With *Technology Sourcebook, Calculator Master 5,* students determine when the negative-integer powers of 2, 3 and so on, become small enough to appear in scientific notation.

5. What number in scientific notation is given by this key sequence?

6.008 [EE] 5 [±] 6.008×10^{-5}

In 6–8, rewrite the number in scientific notation.

6. 0.00008052 second, the time needed for TV signals to travel 15 miles 8.052×10^{-5}
7. 0.28 second, the time needed for sound to travel the length of a football field 2.8×10^{-1}
8. 0.00000 00000 00000 00000 0396 gram, the mass of one atom of uranium 3.96×10^{-22}
9. Suppose a decimal is multiplied by a negative power of 10. Should its decimal point be moved to the right or to the left? to the left
10. What key sequence did you use for Activity 2? Sample: 6.993 [EE] 11 [+/−]

Applying the Mathematics

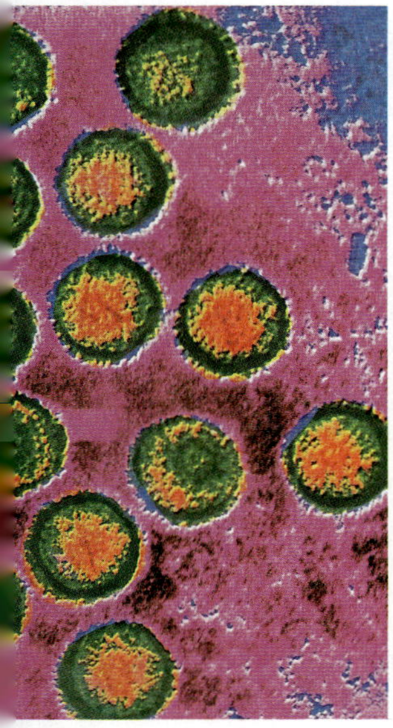

The photo shows Epstein-Barr virus particles, magnified 96,800 times.

11. Rewrite the number as a decimal part of a centimeter.
    a. 1×10^{-8} centimeter, the angstrom (a unit of length) 0.00000 001 cm
    b. 0.529 angstrom, the radius of a hydrogen atom 0.00000 000529 cm
12. Write the number in *decimal* notation given by the key sequence

    4.675 [EE] 7 [±]. 0.00000 04675
13. Calculate $\frac{3 \times 10^{-8}}{6 \times 10^{-7}}$. Give the answer in the indicated form.
    a. scientific notation 5×10^{-2}
    b. decimal .05

In 14 and 15, choose one of the symbols <, =, or >.

14. 5.37×10^{-5} _?_ 5.37×10^{-4} <
15. 49×10^{-9} _?_ 4.9×10^{-8} =
16. When an object is magnified at "100×" under a microscope, it appears 100 times as large as its actual size. Measurements of objects too small to be seen with the human eye are often written in scientific notation. Suppose the longest known virus, *citrus tristeza,* with length 2×10^{-5} meters, is viewed with a microscope at a magnification of 20,000×. How long does the virus appear to be? 0.4 meter or 4×10^{-1} meter

Review

17. Write as a power of 10.
    a. one million 10^6
    b. one millionth 10^{-6} *(Lessons 2-2, 2-8)*

In 18 and 19, order from smallest to largest.

18. -.6 -.66 -.666 -.656 -2/3 *(Lessons 1-6, 1-8)*
    -2/3, -.666, -.66, -.656, -.6
19. kilometer, millimeter, centimeter *(Lesson 2-8)*
    millimeter, centimeter, kilometer

Additional Examples

1. An electronic charge measures about .00000 00004 803 electrostatic units. Write this number in scientific notation. 4.803×10^{-10}
2. The volume of a water molecule is about 3×10^{-23} cubic meters. Write this number as a decimal. .00000 00000 00000 00000 003
3. Enter 0.00000 00000 0082 into a calculator. 8.2 [EE] 13 [±]

Notes on Questions

Questions 6–8 Error Alert A common mistake made in converting from a decimal to scientific notation with negative exponents is matching the number of zeros to the exponent. For example, some students might write the incorrect answer of 5.3×10^{-4} rather than the correct answer of 5.3×10^{-5} for the decimal .000053. Stress that the exponent describes movement of the decimal point which, in this case, does not translate into the number of zeros.

Question 13 You might ask students whether the answer should be more or less than 1 and why. [Less than one, because the denominator, 6×10^{-7}, is greater than the numerator, 3×10^{-8}]. Many students think that the 3 and the 6 determine the size of this fraction; the size actually depends more on the exponents.

▸ LESSON MASTER 2-9 B *page 2*

In 18-21, explain why each number is *not* in scientific notation.

18. $.17 \times 10^{-5}$ The first number is less than 1.
19. 67×10^{-2} The first number is greater than 10.
20. 5.8×5^{-10} There is no power of ten.
21. $8.4 \times 10^{-1.5}$ The exponent of ten is not an integer.

Representations Objective N: Indicate key sequences and displays for small numbers on a calculator.

22. For 6.84×10^{-9},
    a. what key sequence will enter this number on your calculator? 6.84 [EE] 9 [+/−]
    b. what is displayed on your calculator? 6.84 -09
23. For 0.00000 00000 07801,
    a. what key sequence will enter this number on your calculator? 7.801 [EE] 12 [+/−]
    b. what is displayed on your calculator? 7.801 -12

In 24 and 25, tell what decimal is represented by each calculator display.

24. [.8 -09] .000000008
25. [7.906 -15] .000000000000007906
26. A number is entered into a calculator by the following key sequence:
    7.2009 [EE] 12 [±]
    a. Write this number in scientific notation. 7.2009×10^{-12}
    b. Write this number as a decimal. .0000000000072009
27. Write the decimal for 1 ÷ 185,500,000. .0000000053908

Adapting to Individual Needs

Extra Help

Have students use four steps to write a number such as .000000239 in scientific notation.

Step 1 Put your pencil on the decimal point. Move your pencil to the right, counting the digits until you have a number that is at least 1 but less than 10. [For .000000239 this means moving 7 places to the right.]

Step 2 Write the number that is at least 1 but less than 10. [2.39].

Step 3 Write a power of 10. The exponent is the number of places you counted when moving your pencil to the right. [10^{-7}]

Step 4 Write the number in scientific notation. [2.39×10^{-7}]

Notes on Questions

Question 25 This question is fun for many students, and it is a good one to generate lively discussion. It also reviews the idea that percent is a fraction, and taking a fraction of a fraction results in a smaller quantity.

History Connection Some states levied individual income taxes before 1850. The federal government didn't pass individual income-tax laws until 1861 and 1862 when the Union government needed revenue to pay for the costs of the Civil War. Collection of those taxes ended in 1872. Congress passed another income-tax law in 1881. However, this tax was declared unconstitutional because the amount was based on the size of a state's population. Wisconsin passed a state individual income tax-law in 1911; its success led other states to enact similar laws. In 1913, the Constitution was amended and, consequently, the Underwood Tariff Act of 1913 included an income-tax section.

Question 33a Some computers will put small numbers into scientific notation before a calculator will do so. This is yet another reason for introducing negative exponents early.

Follow-up for Lesson 2-9

Practice

For more questions on SPUR objectives, use **Lesson Master 2-9A** (shown on page 105) or **Lesson Master 2-9B** (shown on pages 106–107).

Assessment

Written Communication Have students write short paragraphs explaining how to write 0.000345 in scientific notation and how to write 3.18×10^{-6} in decimal notation. [Students write clear, concise explanations of each process.]

Extension

Project Update Project 5, *Scientific Notation*, on page 110, relates to the content of this lesson. Students choosing this project can look for an article, story, or poem that contains very small numbers. If some students choosing this project want to write their own stories, they also can begin at this time.

20b)

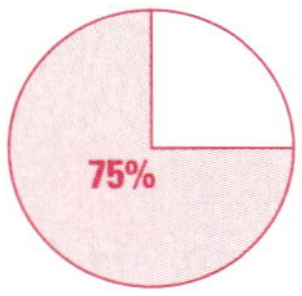

20. **a.** What percent is equal to $\frac{3}{4}$? 75%

b. Show this percent as part of a circle. *(Lessons 2-6, 2-7)*

21. The Skunks baseball team lost 60% of its games. Did the team win or lose more often? *(Lesson 2-5)* The team lost more often.

In 22–24, write the number as a decimal. *(Lessons 1-7, 2-5)*

22. 3% 0.03 **23.** $-19\frac{7}{10}$ -19.7 **24.** 150% 1.5

25. Newspaper columnist Georgie Anne Geyer once wrote about receiving a tax bill for \$0.01. The payment was due on June 30th.

a. If Ms. Geyer did not pay her bill by June 30th, she would have to pay a penalty of 10% of her bill. How much is this? \$0.001 or 0.1¢

b. Also, if she paid late, she would have to pay an additional interest penalty of 1% of her bill. How much is this? \$0.0001

c. What would be the exact total she owned if she paid the bill late?

d. Round your answer to part **c** to the nearest penny. *(Lessons 1-4, 2-5)*
c) \$0.0111; d) \$0.01

26. Between what two integers is 3.4%? (Watch out! Many students miss this one!) *(Lesson 2-4)* 0 and 1

27. Write 4,500,500,500 in scientific notation. *(Lesson 2-3)*
4.5005005×10^9

28. Calculate 5 to the 7th power. *(Lesson 2-2)* 78,125

What is "Squeeze-Belly Alley?" *That is the name given to the passageway pictured above and described in Question 29. It is Great Britain's narrowest street and is located in Port Isaac, Cornwall.*

29. There is a street in Great Britain that is only $19\frac{5}{16}$ inches wide.

a. Accurately place $19\frac{5}{16}$ on this number line.

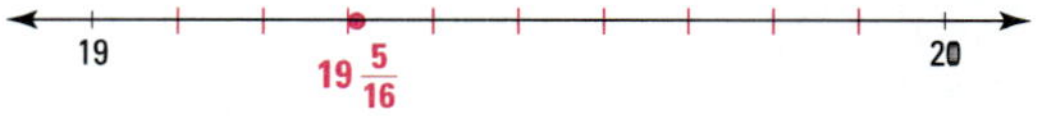

b. If you were 19.3 inches wide, could you walk down this street? *(Lessons 1-7, 1-9)* Yes

30. Change 76.23 to

a. a percent. 7623% **b.** a fraction. *(Lesson 2-6)* $\frac{7623}{100}$

In 31 and 32, tell whether a high or a low estimate would be preferred and why. *(Lesson 1-3)*

31. An airline estimates how much baggage an airplane can carry without being overloaded. Low; too much baggage would endanger the safety of the passengers.

32. A caterer estimates how much food to prepare for a graduation party. High; you want to have enough food for the guests.

Exploration

33. **a.** On your calculator, what is the smallest positive number that can be displayed? 1×10^{-99}; answers may vary.

b. What is the largest negative number that can be displayed?
-1×10^{-99} Answers may vary.

Adapting to Individual Needs

Challenge

Have students use a computer as they answer each of the following questions:

1. Type ?0.25*0.3 on your computer and press return. What does the computer display? What is the computer doing? [.075; multiplying]
2. Place a zero before either ?0.025*0.3 or ?0.25*0.03. What does the computer display? [Answers may vary. .0075 or 7.5E −03]
3. Continue increasing the number of zeros until an answer is shown in scientific notation. How does your computer write small numbers in scientific notation?
4. Write a comparison of how your calculator and computer handle scientific notation. [Answers may vary.]

PROJECTS 2 CHAPTER TWO

A project presents an opportunity for you to extend your knowledge of a topic related to the material of this chapter. You should allow more time for a project than you do for typical homework questions.

1 One Million Pennies

How tall might a stack of one million pennies be?

a. Guess at the height, and record your guess.

b. Now try to determine the height without guessing. Of course, you will not be able to actually use a million pennies, so you must use an indirect method. Measure the thickness of ten pennies. Based on this measurement, how tall is a stack of one million pennies?

c. Write a paragraph in which you tell how you made your determination, and compare the calculated height with your guess.

d. Think of some related questions. If the pennies were put down next to each other, how far would the million pennies stretch? Imagine a million of some other object. Indicate how high you think they would be if placed in a stack.

2 Using the Symbols 1, 2, 3, and a Decimal Point

How many different decimal numbers can you make with the digits 1, 2, and 3 and a decimal point, if you can use any or all of the digits? (One such number is 1.23, and obviously there are many others.) Make a list of your numbers from smallest to largest, and explain how you know that you have found all the possibilities. Then explore what would happen if you also included the digit 4.

3 Percents in Print

Look through a newspaper or magazine for twenty-five uses of the word *percent* or the symbol %. Make sure all the percents are different. Order the percents (now all different) from smallest to largest, and describe how each one was used. (For instance, you might write: "3.75%—rate on a savings account.") In a paragraph, summarize what you have found.

Chapter 2 Projects

Chapter 2 projects relate to the content of the lesson as follows:

Project	Lesson(s)
1	2-1
2	2-4
3	2-4, 2-5, 2-7
4	2-2, 2-8
5	2-3, 2-9

1 One Million Pennies Students predict how tall a stack of one million pennies would be by multiplying the height of 10 pennies by 100,000. However, the units used for measuring 10 pennies may not be appropriate for measuring 1,000,000 pennies. So students need to convert to larger units of measure such as meters, kilometers, yards, or miles.

2 Using Symbols 1, 2, 3, and a Decimal Point Make sure that students understand that it is their task to find the number of possible arrangements using the decimal point with all three digits, with any two of the digits, and with any one of the digits. You might suggest they find all the arrangements in each category and then order the numbers.

3 Percents in Print This project is straightforward, but it may take a considerable amount of time. News magazines or newspapers are recommended because they contain an abundance of percents, both in articles and in advertisements. You might suggest that students categorize how the percents were used or where they were found before they write their summaries.

Possible responses

1. a. Estimates will vary.
   b. Sample response: The measured height of 10 pennies is about 1.5 cm.
   c. Based on the measurement given in part b, the height of one penny would be 0.15 cm, and equivalent to 1.5 kilometers and just less than one mile.
   d. Some sample questions might be: Would walking one million paces take you from Miami to Juneau? How tall would 1,000,000 milk cartons stand?
2. Sample response: There are 48 possible arrangements; 24 using all 3 digits, 18 using 2 digits, and 6 using one digit. The possibilities from smallest to largest are: .1, .12, .123, .13, .132, .2, .21, .213, .23, .231, .3, .31, .312, .32, .321, 1, 1.2, 1.23, 1.3, 1.32, 2, 2.1, 2.13, 2.3, 2.31, 3, 3.1, 3.12, 3.2, 3.21, 12, 12.3, 13, 13.2, 21, 21.3, 23, 23.1, 31, 31.2, 32, 32.1, 123, 132, 213, 231, 312, and 321. There are no other possible arrangements because they have been systematically listed, and duplicates have been eliminated. If the number 4 were included, there would be 260 possible arrangements; 120 using all 4 digits, 96 using any 3 of the digits, 36 using any 2 of the digits, and 8 using any one digit.

4 Powers of 10 You might want to tell students that the reading level and subject matter of *Powers of Ten* is challenging. However, they should be able to understand the general concept of the book, which is viewing objects from different distances. The photographs shown in *Powers of Ten* provide plenty of examples of things they might include in their book reports.

5 Scientific Notation If students have trouble thinking of a story topic, you might suggest the following topics: recipes, money, speed, and time. Upon completing their stories, students should realize that scientific notation is not an effective means of communicating numbers that are neither excessively large nor excessively small.

PROJECTS 2 *(continued)*

4 Powers of 10

A book entitled *Powers of Ten* is published by Scientific American Books, Inc. Find a copy of this book in your school or public library, and write a book report on it. (The book is based on a short film also entitled *Powers of Ten.* You may be able to find that, also.)

Michael Jordan scored a total of 2.1541×10^4 points in 6.67×10^2 games—and led the NBA in scoring for 7 consecutive seasons.

5 Scientific Notation

Explore what would happen if we wrote all numbers in scientific notation. Write a story, or copy a published story that has many numbers (at least 10) in it. It is best if some of the numbers are big, some small. Change every number in the story to scientific notation. For instance, if you were writing about Shiing-Shen Chern, one of the greatest mathematicians of the 20th century, you would write that he was born in the year 1.911×10^3.

Groucho, Harpo, and Chico appeared as the Marx Brothers in 1.3×10^2 movies.

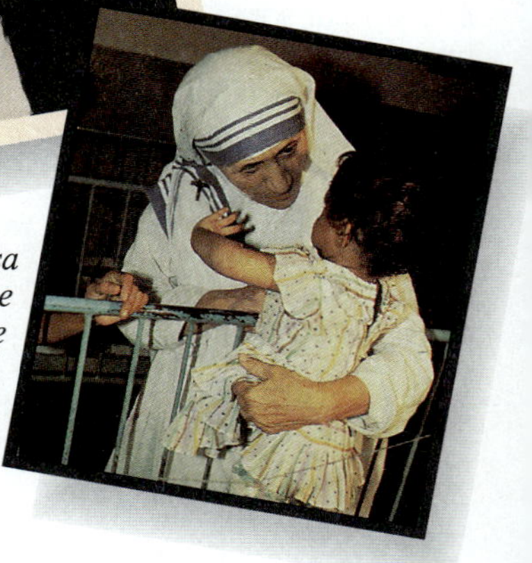

Mother Teresa received the Pope John XXIII Peace Prize in 1.971×10^3 for her work with the poor.

Lucille Ball appeared in 1.92×10^2 episodes for a total of 6.15×10^3 minutes of I Love Lucy.

Al Unser, Jr., set the world record for a 5.00×10^2–mile car race in 1990 with an average speed of 1.897×10^2 mph.

110

Possible responses

3. Responses will vary.
4. Sample response: Students might mention some of the following observations. At a distance of 10^{17} meters from earth, the sun is a speck in space. At a distance of 10^{10} meters, earth is visible and distinguishable. Focussing on a human hand, from a distance of 10^{-5} m, you can see white blood cells as well as the concave disks of the red blood cells. At a distance of 10^{-7} m and 10^{-8} m, the intricate double helices of DNA are visible. At a 10^{-14} m, the Carbon-12 atomic component of DNA is visible. The protons and neutrons of Carbon-12 are spherical.
5. Responses will vary.

SUMMARY

In Chapter 1, you learned three advantages of the decimal system. (1) All of the most common numbers can be written as decimals. (2) Decimals are easy to order. (3) Decimals are used by calculators to represent numbers. In this chapter, decimals are combined with other notations to write large and small numbers.

Positive integer powers of numbers arise from repeated multiplication. For instance, $7^3 = 7 \times 7 \times 7$. The numbers 10, 100, 1000, . . . (or 10^1, 10^2, 10^3, . . .) are positive integer powers of 10. The numbers $\frac{1}{10}$, $\frac{1}{100}$, $\frac{1}{1000}$ . . . or their decimal equivalents 0.1, 0.01, 0.001, . . . (or 10^{-1}, 10^{-2}, 10^{-3}, . . .) are negative integer powers of 10. The number one is the zero power of 10.

The decimal system is based on powers of the number 10. So it is easy to multiply decimals by powers of 10. To multiply a decimal by a positive (or negative) power of 10, move the decimal point to the right (or left) the same number of places as the value of the exponent.

Percent means multiply by $\frac{1}{100}$, so decimals can easily be converted to percents. To find a percent of a number, multiply the percent by that number. Percents, decimals, and fractions are all used often and sometimes interchangeably. So it is useful to be able to convert from one form to another.

Information involving percents and fractions is often represented visually using circle graphs. Sectors in the circle graph represent parts of a whole quantity.

Large and small numbers are also often written in exponential form. Scientific notation combines exponential form with decimal notation. Scientific notation is a standard way used all over the world to express very large or very small numbers.

VOCABULARY

You should be able to give a general description and a specific example of each of the following ideas.

Lesson 2-1
million, billion, trillion, and so on

Lesson 2-2
base, exponent, power
x^y, y^x

Lesson 2-3
scientific notation for large numbers, light-year
EE, exp

Lesson 2-4
percent, %

Lesson 2-5
Substitution Principle

Lesson 2-6
terminating decimal

Lesson 2-7
circle graph, pie chart
$\approx$
circle, center, radius, diameter
sector, arc

Lesson 2-8
exponential form
millionth, billionth, trillionth, and so on

Lesson 2-9
scientific notation for small numbers

Summary

The Summary gives an overview of the entire chapter and provides an opportunity for students to consider the material as a whole. Thus, the Summary can be used to help students relate and unify the concepts presented in the chapter.

Vocabulary

Terms, symbols, and properties are listed by lesson to provide a checklist of concepts that a student must know. Emphasize to students that they should read the vocabulary list carefully before starting the Progress Self-Test. If students do not understand the meaning of a term, they should refer back to the indicated lesson.

Progress Self-Test

For the development of mathematical competence, feedback and correction, along with the opportunity to practice, are necessary. The Progress Self-Test provides the opportunity for feedback and correction; the Chapter Review provides additional opportunities and practice. We cannot overemphasize the importance of these end-of-chapter materials. It is at this point that the material "gels" for many students, allowing them to solidify skills and understanding. In general, student performance should be markedly improved after these pages.

Assign the Progress Self-Test as a one-night assignment. Worked-out *solutions* for all questions are in the Selected Answers section of the student book. Encourage students to take the Progress Self-Test honestly, grade themselves, and then be prepared to discuss the test in class.

Additional Answers

12. a. 125 [y^x] 6 [=]

b. 3.8147 12

Answers may vary.

18. 4.5 [EE] 13 or 4.5 [×] 10 [y^x] 13 [=]

19. First write in scientific notation: 1.23456×10^{-7}. Then enter either 1.23456 [EE] 7 [±] or 1.23456 [×] 10 [y^x] 7 [±] [=].

PROGRESS SELF-TEST

Take this test as you would take a test in class. Then check your work with the solutions in the Selected Answers section in the back of the book. **See margin for answers not shown below.**

In 1–10, write as a single decimal.

1. $100{,}000{,}000 \times 23.51864$ **2,351,864,000**
2. 34% of 600 **204**
3. 32 billionths **0.00000 0032**
4. 824.59×0.00001 **0.0082459**
5. $\frac{1}{1000} \times 77$ **0.077**
6. 3456.8910×10^5 **345,689,100**
7. 2.816×10^{-3} **0.002816**
8. 10^{-7} **0.00000 01**
9. 8% **0.08**
10. 6^3 **216**

In 11–13, consider 125^6. **11) base; exponent**

11. 125 is called the __?__ and 6 the __?__.
12. a. What key sequence can you use to calculate this on your calculator?
    b. What is the resulting display?
13. Give a decimal estimate for 125^6. **See below.**
14. What is the distance from a point on a circle to the center of the circle called? **radius**
15. What percent does a whole circle graph represent? **100%**

13) 3,814,700,000,000

In 16 and 17, write in scientific notation.

16. 21,070,000,000 **2.107×10^{10}**
17. 0.00000 008 **8×10^{-8}**

In 18 and 19, write a key sequence you can use to enter the number on your calculator.

18. 4.5×10^{13}
19. 0.00000 01234 56
20. Order from smallest to largest: 4^4 5^3 3^5. **5^3, 3^5, 4^4**
21. Between what two integers is 40%? **0 and 1**
22. Rewrite 4.73 as:
    a. a simple fraction **$\frac{473}{100}$** b. a percent. **473%**
23. As a fraction, $33\frac{1}{3}\% =$ __?__. **$\frac{1}{3}$**

24. Consider the circle graph below.

Type of Recording Media Sold 1991

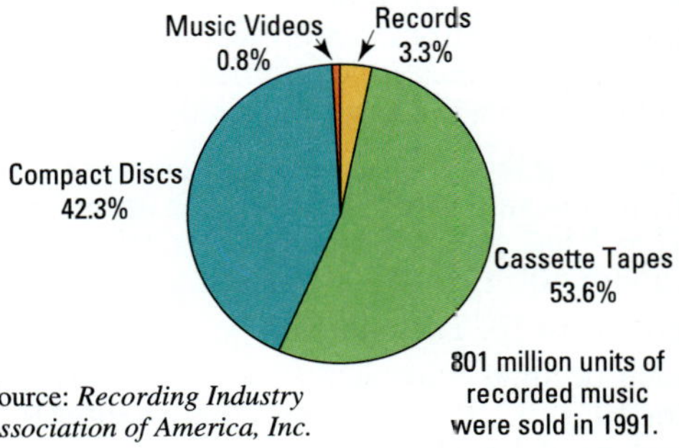

Source: *Recording Industry Association of America, Inc.*

a. Which type of recording medium had the most sales? **cassette tapes**
b. What percent of recorded media sold was not on compact disc? **57.7%**
c. About how many records were sold in 1991? **≈26.4 million**

25. A recent survey of 150 chefs reported that 30% of the chefs think broccoli is the top vegetable. How many chefs is this? **45**
26. A computer system is on sale at 25% off. If the regular price is \$1699, what is the sale price to the nearest dollar? **\$1274**
27. Julio correctly answered 80% of the items on a 20-item test. How many did he miss? **4**
28. Why is 22.4×10^3 not in scientific notation?
29. What power of 10 equals one million? **sixth**
30. According to the Substitution Principle, $\frac{3}{5} - \frac{1}{10} =$ __?__ % $-$ __?__ %. **60, 10**
31. It is estimated that a swarm of 250 billion locusts descended on the Red Sea in 1889. Write this number in scientific notation. **2.5×10^{11}** **28) 22.4 is not between 1 and 10.**

After taking and correcting the Self-Test, you may want to make a list of the problems you got wrong. Then write down what you need to study most. If you can, try to explain your most frequent or common mistakes. Use what you write to help you study and review the chapter.

CHAPTER REVIEW

Questions on SPUR Objectives

SPUR stands for **S**kills, **P**roperties, **U**ses, and **R**epresentations. The Chapter Review questions are grouped according to the SPUR Objectives for this chapter.

SKILLS DEAL WITH THE PROCEDURES USED TO GET ANSWERS.

Objective A. *Multiply by 10, 100, 1000, and so on.* *(Lessons 2-1, 2-2)*

1. $32 \times 10{,}000 =$? 320,000
2. $100 \times 7.5 =$? 750
3. $1{,}000{,}000 \times 0.025 =$? 25,000
4. What number is 3.5 multiplied by to get 3500? 1000
5. $3 \times 10^7 =$? 30,000,000
6. $0.42 \times 10^5 =$? 42,000

7) 29,314,000,000 8) 2,000,000,000,000

Objective B. *Convert word names for numbers to decimals.* *(Lessons 2-1, 2-8)*

7. In 1991, Boeing had sales of 29.314 billion dollars. Write this number as a decimal.
8. Write 2 trillion as a decimal.
9. Write 4.6 millionths as a decimal.
10. A supercomputer can process a bit of information in a billionth of a second. Write this number as a decimal.

9) 0.00000 46 10) 0.00000 0001

Objective C. *Convert powers to decimals.* *(Lesson 2-2)*

11. Convert 4^3 to a decimal. 64
12. Convert 72.5^2 to a decimal. 5256.25

In 13 and 14, estimate by a decimal.

13. 12^8 ≈ 429,980,000
14. 3.86^4 ≈ 221.99808

Objective D. *Give decimals and English word names for positive and negative integer powers of 10.* *(Lessons 2-2, 2-8)*

In 15–18, write the number as a decimal.

15. 10^5 100,000
16. 7.34×10^0 7.34
17. 10^{-4} 0.0001
18. 10^1 10
19. In English, 10^9 is ?. one billion
20. In English, 10^{-2} is ?. one hundredth
21. One trillion is what power of ten? twelfth
22. 0.0001 is what power of ten? negative fourth

Objective E. *Multiply by 0.1, 0.01, 0.001, and so on, and by* $\frac{1}{10}, \frac{1}{100}, \frac{1}{1000}$, *and so on.* *(Lesson 2-4)*

23. $2.73 \times 0.00000001 =$? 0.00000 00273
24. $495 \times 0.1 =$? 49.5
25. $75 \times \frac{1}{1000} =$? 0.075
26. $2.1 \times \frac{1}{100} =$? 0.021
27. $80 \times 10^{-1} =$? 8
28. $68.3 \times 10^{-4} =$? 0.00683

Objective F. *Convert large and small positive numbers into scientific notation.* *(Lessons 2-3, 2-9)*

In 29–32, write the number in scientific notation.

29. 480,000 4.8×10^5
30. 9,000,000,000,000,000 9×10^{15}
31. 0.00013 1.3×10^{-4}
32. 0.7 7×10^{-1}
33. The number of nonhuman living things on Earth is estimated at 3×10^{33}. Write this number as a decimal. See below.
34. A piece of paper is about 0.005 inches thick. What is that in scientific notation? 5×10^{-3} in.

33) 3,000,000,000,000,000,000,000,000,000,000,000

Chapter 2 Review

Resources

From the ***Teacher's Resource File***

- Answer Master for Chapter 2 Review
- Assessment Sourcebook: Chapter 2 Test, Forms A–D Chapter 2 Test, Cumulative Form

Additional Resources

- Quiz and Test Writer

The main objectives for the chapter are organized in the Chapter Review under the four types of understanding this book promotes—Skills, Properties, Uses, and Representations.

Whereas end-of-chapter material may be considered optional in some texts, in *Transition Mathematics* we have selected these objectives and questions with the expectation that they will be covered. Students should be able to answer these questions with about 85% accuracy after studying the chapter.

You might assign these questions over a single night to help students prepare for a test the next day, or you might assign the questions over a two-day period. If you work the questions over two days, then we recommend assigning the *evens* for homework the first night so that students get feedback in class the next day, then assigning the *odds* the night before the test, since answers are provided to the odd-numbered questions.

It is effective to ask students which questions they still do not understand, and use the day or days as a total class discussion of the material which the class finds most difficult.

Assessment

Evaluation The *Assessment Sourcebook* provides five forms of the Chapter 2 Test. Forms A and B present parallel versions in a short-answer format. Forms C and D offer performance assessment. The fifth test is Chapter 2 Test, Cumulative Form. About 75% of this test covers Chapter 2; 25% of it covers Chapter 1.

For information on grading see *General Teaching Suggestions: Grading* in the *Professional Sourcebook* which begins on page T20 in Volume 1 of the Teacher's Edition.

CHAPTER TWO

Objective G. *Convert and operate with percents as decimals.* *(Lessons 2-4, 2-5)*

In 35–38, write the percent as a decimal.

35. 15% **0.15**

36. 5.25% **0.0525**

37. 9% **0.09**

38. 200% **2**

39. What is 50% of 150? **75**

40. What is 3% of 3? **0.09**

41. What is 100% of 6.2? **6.2**

42. What is 7.8% of 3500? **273**

Objective H. *Know common fraction and percent equivalents.* *(Lesson 2-4)*

43. Change $\frac{1}{2}$ to a percent. **50%**

44. Change $\frac{4}{5}$ to a percent. **80%**

45. What fraction equals 30%? $\frac{3}{10}$

46. What fraction equals $66\frac{2}{3}\%$? $\frac{2}{3}$

Objective I. *Convert terminating decimals to fractions, and either of these to percents.* *(Lesson 2-6)*

47. Find a simple fraction equal to 5.7. $\frac{57}{10}$

48. Find the simple fraction in lowest terms equal to 0.892. $\frac{223}{250}$

49. Convert 0.86 to percent. **86%**

50. Convert 3.2 to percent. **320%**

51. Convert $\frac{3}{7}$ to percent. **≈ 42.9%**

52. Convert $\frac{11}{8}$ to percent. **137.5%**

Objective J. *Identify the center, radius, and diameter of a circle.* *(Lesson 2-7)*

In 53–55, consider the circle below.

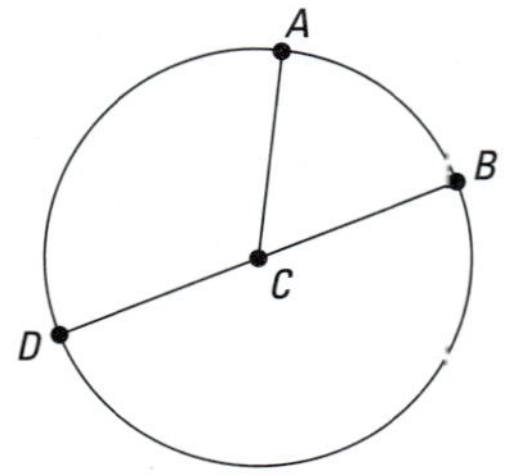

53. Name a radius. $\overline{AC}$, $\overline{BC}$, or $\overline{DC}$

54. Name the diameter. $\overline{BD}$

55. Name the center. *C*

56. Name a sector. *ACB* or *DCA* or *DCB*

57. Name an arc of the circle. $\overset{\frown}{AB}$ or $\overset{\frown}{AD}$ or $\overset{\frown}{BD}$

58. The diameter of a circle is __?__ as long as the radius of that circle. **twice**

Shown are irrigation circles in San Luis Valley, Colorado. They are formed by water sprayed from a pivotal irrigation system.

PROPERTIES DEAL WITH THE PRINCIPLES BEHIND THE MATHEMATICS.

Objective K. *Know and apply the Substitution Principle.* *(Lesson 2-5)*

59. State the Substitution Principle.

60. How is the Substitution Principle used in evaluating 75% of 40?

61. Name two numbers that could be substituted for 50%. $\frac{1}{2}$ **and .5**

62. According to the Substitution Principle, $\frac{1}{2} + \frac{1}{4} =$ __?__% + __?__%. **50, 25**

63) 23 is not between 1 and 10.

Objective L. *Identify numbers as being written in scientific notation.* *(Lessons 2-3, 2-9)*

63. Why is 23×10^4 not in scientific notation?

64. In scientific notation, a number greater than or equal to __?__ and less than __?__ is multiplied by an __?__ power of 10.
1, 10, integer

59) If two numbers are equal, one may be substituted for the other in any computation without changing the results of the computation.

60) .75 is substituted for 75%.

CHAPTER TWO

USES DEAL WITH APPLICATIONS OF MATHEMATICS IN REAL SITUATIONS.

Objective M. *Find percents of quantities in real situations.* *(Lesson 2-5)*

65. At a "40%-off" sale, what will you pay for a \$26.50 sweater? **\$15.90**

66. Bill Clinton received about 43.01% of the votes cast in the 1992 presidential election. About 104,400,000 votes were cast. About how many votes did Clinton get? **≈ 44,900,000**

67. The value of a one-carat colorless flawless diamond reached \$64,000 in 1980. By October of 1990, the price had lost 61% of its 1980 value. What was the value in 1990?

68. In one town, sales tax is 7.75%. What sales tax will you pay on a \$20 purchase? **\$1.55**

67) \$24,960 ≈ \$25,000

REPRESENTATIONS DEAL WITH PICTURES, GRAPHS, OR OBJECTS THAT ILLUSTRATE CONCEPTS.

Objective N. *Indicate key sequences and displays for large and small positive numbers on a calculator.* *(Lessons 2-3, 2-9)*

69. What key sequence will enter 32 billion on your calculator? **Sample: 3.2 [EE] 10**

70. What key sequence will enter one trillionth on your calculator? **Sample: 1 [EE] 12 [+/−]**

71. a. What key sequence will enter 2^{45} on your calculator? **Sample: 2 [y^x] 45 [=]**

b. Write an approximation to 2^{45} in scientific notation. **≈ 3.5184×10^{13}**

72. If a calculator displays [4.73 08], what decimal is being shown? **473,000,000**

In 73–76, use a calculator to find the answer.

73. Estimate $1{,}357{,}975 \times 24{,}681{,}086$.

74. Estimate $.0025 \times .00004567$. **1.14175×10^{-7}**

75. What key sequence will enter 1.93×10^{-15}?

76. What key sequence will enter 3×10^{21}?

73) ≈ 3.3516×10^{13}
75) Sample: 1.93 [EE] 15 [+/−]
76) Sample: 3 [EE] 21

Objective O. *Interpret circle graphs.* *(Lesson 2-7)*

In 77–80, consider the circle graph below.

77. What percent of adults sleep 9.5 hours or more? **6%**

78. What percent sleep more than 6.5 hours?

79. What does the largest sector represent?

80. What does the whole circle graph represent?

78) 78%
79) percent of adults who sleep more than 7.5 hours up to 8.5 hours
80) 100% of the adults surveyed for the data

Setting Up Lesson 3-1

Materials: Students will need the *Transition Mathematics* Geometry Templates or rulers for Lesson 3-1 and most of the other lessons in Chapter 3.

Homework There is more than the usual amount of reading in Lesson 3-1. For students who can handle the reading, we strongly recommend that you assign the reading and some questions for homework the evening of the test. It gives students work to do after they have completed the test and keeps the class moving.

For students having difficulty with reading, you might suggest they read only the Chapter 3 Opener for homework. Then these students might read the lesson aloud and work through the activities in class the next day.

Chapter 3 Planner

Adapting to Individual Needs

The student text is written for the vast majority of students. The chart at the right suggests two pacing plans to accommodate the needs of your students. Students in the Full Course should complete the entire text by the end of the year. Students in the Minimal Course will spend more time when there are quizzes and more time on the Chapter Review. Therefore, these students may not complete all of the chapters in the text.

Options are also presented to meet the needs of a variety of teaching and learning styles. For each lesson, the Teacher's Edition provides sections entitled: *Video* which describes video segments and related questions that can be used for motivation or extension; *Optional Activities* which suggests activities that employ materials, physical models, technology, and cooperative learning; and *Adapting to Individual Needs* which regularly includes **Challenge** problems, **English Language Development** suggestions, and suggestions for providing **Extra Help.** The Teacher's Edition also frequently includes an **Error Alert,** an **Extension,** and an **Assessment** alternative. The options available in Chapter 3 are summarized in the chart below.

Chapter 3 Pacing Chart

Day	Full Course	Minimal Course
1	3-1	3-1
2	3-2	3-2
3	3-3	3-3
4	Quiz*; 3-4	Quiz*; begin 3-4.
5	3-5	Finish 3-4.
6	3-6	3-5
7	3-7	3-6
8	Quiz*; 3-8	3-7
9	3-9	Quiz*; begin 3-8.
10	Self-Test	Finish 3-8.
11	Review	3-9
12	Test*	Self-Test
13	Comprehensive Test*	Review
14		Review
15		Test*
16		Comprehensive Test*

*in the Teacher's Resource File

In the Teacher's Edition...

Lesson	Optional Activities	Extra Help	Challenge	English Language Development	Error Alert	Extension	Cooperative Learning	Ongoing Assessment
3-1	●	●	●	●	●	●	●	Group
3-2	●	●	●	●	●	●	●	Written
3-3	●	●	●	●		●		Group
3-4	●	●		●		●	●	Oral
3-5	●		●	●	●	●		Written
3-6	●	●	●	●	●	●		Written
3-7	●	●	●	●	●	●	●	Written
3-8	●	●	●			●		Oral/Written
3-9	●	●	●	●		●		Oral

In the Additional Resources...

	In the Teacher's Resource File								
Lesson	Lesson Masters, A and B	Teaching Aids*	Activity Kit*	Answer Masters	Technology Sourcebook	Assessment Sourcebook	Visual Aids**	Transition Mathematics Software	Video Segments
3-1	3-1	25, 28		3-1			25, 28, AM		
3-2	3-2	25, 29		3-2			25, 29, AM	Spreadsheet	
3-3	3-3	25, 30		3-3		Quiz	25, 30, AM		
3-4	3-4	26, 31		3-4	Comp 3		26, 31, AM	Spreadsheet	
3-5	3-5	26, 32		3-5	Calc 6		26, 32, AM		
3-6	3-6	26, 33		3-6	Demo 3		26, 33, AM	Geometry	
In-class Activity		34					34, AM		
3-7	3-7	27, 35		3-7	Comp 4	Quiz	27, 35, AM	Geometry	
3-8	3-8	27, 36	6	3-8			27, 36, AM		3-8
3-9	3-9	27, 37, 38	7	3-9			27, 37, 38, AM		
End of chapter				Review		Tests			

*Teaching Aids, except Warm-ups, are pictured on pages 116C and 116D. The activities in the Activity Kit are pictured on page 116C. Teaching Aid 34 which accompanies the In-class Activity is pictured with the lesson notes on page 152.

**Visual Aids provide transparencies for all Teaching Aids and all Answer Masters.

Also available is the Study Skills Handbook which includes study-skill tips related to reading, note-taking, and comprehension.

Integrating Strands and Applications

	3-1	3-2	3-3	3-4	3-5	3-6	3-7	3-8	3-9
Mathematical Connections									
Number Sense	●	●	●	●	●	●	●	●	
Algebra	●	●	●	●	●				
Geometry						●	●	●	●
Measurement	●	●	●	●	●	●	●	●	●
Statistics/Data Analysis					●	●	●		●
Patterns and Functions	●	●	●	●					
Interdisciplinary and Other Connections									
Music			●						
Literature		●							
Science				●	●	●	●	●	●
Social Studies	●	●	●	●	●	●	●	●	●
Multicultural	●		●		●	●	●		●
Technology		●		●		●	●	●	
Consumer					●		●		
Sports		●			●			●	

Teaching and Assessing the Chapter Objectives

Chapter 3 Objectives (Organized into the SPUR categories—Skills, Properties, Uses, and Representations)	**Lessons**	**Progress Self-Test Questions**	**Chapter Review Questions**	**In the Assessment Sourcebook** Chapter Test, Forms A and B	Chapter Test, Forms C	Chapter Test, Forms D
Skills						
A: Measure lengths to the nearest inch, half inch, quarter inch, or eighth of an inch, or to the nearest centimeter, or tenth of a centimeter.	3-1	1	1–4	13, 14	1	
B: Measure angles to the nearest degree using a protractor.	3-6	15, 17	5–8	15	4	
C: Distinguish between acute, right, and obtuse angles by sight.	3-7	20	9–12	5, 16, 17	4	
D: Find areas of squares and volumes of cubes given the length of one side or edge.	3-8, 3-9	22, 25	13–17	4	2	
Properties						
E: State and apply the Multiplication Property of Equality.	3-2	6	18–21	2	3	✓
Uses						
F: Give appropriate units for measuring mass, length, and capacity in the U.S. or metric system of measurement.	3-2, 3-3, 3-4	4	22–25	6–8	5	✓
G: Convert within the U.S. system of measurement.	3-2, 3-3	5, 9, 10	26–31	11, 12, 28	3	✓
H: Convert within the metric system.	3-4	2, 7, 8, 24	32–38	3, 9, 10, 27	3	✓
I: Convert between different systems.	3-2, 3-5	3, 11–13	39–47	21–26	3	✓
J: Find areas of squares or volumes of cubes in real contexts.	3-8, 3-9	26	48, 49	18		✓
Representations						
K: Draw a line segment of a given length.	3-1	2	50–53	20	1	
L: Draw an angle with a given measure.	3-6	19	54–57	19	6	
M: Read, make, and interpret circle graphs.	3-7	21	58–60	29, 30	6	
Cultures						
N: Give countries and approximate dates of origin of current measuring ideas.	3-1, 3-4, 3-6	14	61–63	1		

Assessment Sourcebook
Quiz for Lessons 3-1 through 3-3
Quiz for Lessons 3-4 through 3-7
Chapter 3 Test, Forms A–D
Chapter 3 Test, Cumulative Form
Comprehensive Test, Chapters 1–3

Quiz and Test Writer
Multiple forms of chapter tests and quizzes; Challenges

Activity Kit

ACTIVITY 6 MEASURING AREA Use with **Lesson 3-8.**

Materials: Grid paper, ruler, scissors, tape
Group Size: Partners

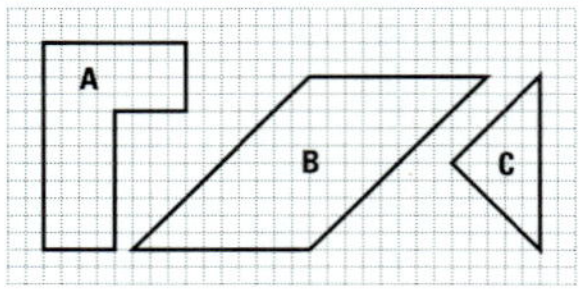

1. Carefully draw each figure shown above on grid paper. Work alone to find the area of each figure by finding the total number of squares inside the figure. Be sure to include the half squares, as well. Compare your answers with those of your partner. If you do not agree, recount together.

   Figure A: _______ squares Figure B: _______ squares

   Figure C: _______ squares

2. With your partner, cut each figure apart and tape the parts together to form a square. Find the area of each square.

   Square A: _______ square units Square B: _______ square units

   Square C: _______ square units

3. Compare the area of each figure in Item 1 to the area of each square in Item 2. What do you notice?

   ____

4. On grid paper, both partners should draw a square of the same size. What is the area of the square? _______ square units

5. Cut out the square you drew in Item 4. Cut the square into smaller pieces and rearrange the pieces to make another figure. What is the area of your new figure? the area of your partner's new figure?

   Your figure: _______ sq. units Partner's figure: _______ sq. units

6. **Draw a Conclusion** Does a figure have to be a square to have an area of 1 square unit? 16 square units? Explain.

   ____

ACTIVITY 7 MEASURING VOLUME Use with **Lesson 3-9.**

Materials: 150 centimeter cubes
Group Size: Partners

Work alone on Items 1–5 and with your partner on Item 6.

1. Grab a handful of centimeter cubes. Count them. How many are there?

   ____

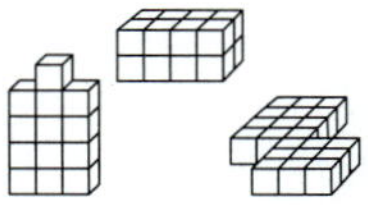

2. Arrange all the cubes to form any shape you like. Some possibilities are shown at the right.

3. Each cube is 1 cubic centimeter. The number of cubic centimeters (cm^3) in the shape you made is its *volume*. What is the volume of the shape you made? _______ cm^3

4. Using the same number of cubes as before, arrange them to form a different shape. What is its volume? _______ cm^3

Each shape drawn below is a cube. Notice that each side is a square.

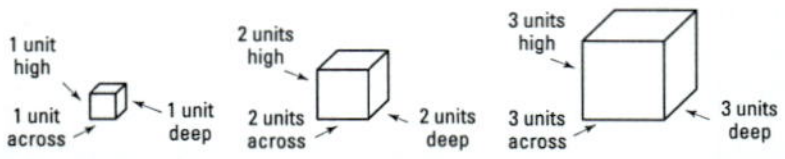

5. Use your centimeter cubes to build the cubes described in the table. Then complete the table.

Dimensions of Cube	Volume in Cubic Centimeters
1 cm by 1 cm by 1 cm	
2 cm by 2 cm by 2 cm	
3 cm by 3 cm by 3 cm	
4 cm by 4 cm by 4 cm	
5 cm by 5 cm by 5 cm	

6. **Draw a Conclusion** Discuss and describe two different ways to find the volumes you gave in the table.

   ____

Teaching Aids

TEACHING AID 25

Warm-up Lesson 3-1

Round each mixed number to the nearest half and to the nearest quarter.

1. $3\frac{3}{5}$ 2. $6\frac{3}{8}$ 3. $8\frac{15}{16}$ 4. $7\frac{1}{8}$

Round each number to the nearest whole number and to the nearest tenth.

5. 2.51 6. 6.22 7. 8.83 8. 1.37

Warm-up Lesson 3-2

Compute mentally.

1. 3×12 2. $60 \div 12$
3. $36 \div 3$ 4. 15×3
5. $72 \div 12$ 6. $72 \div 36$
7. 20×3 8. 20×12

Warm-up Lesson 3-3

You have 30 seconds to fill in the blanks.

1. 1 ft = _______ in.
2. 1 yd = _______ ft
3. 1 mi = _______ ft
4. 1 in. = _______ cm
5. 1 yd = _______ in.

TEACHING AID 26

Warm-up Lesson 3-4

Work with a partner. Choose the most sensible measure and explain your reasoning.

1. The length of a football field
   a. 1100 cm b. 11 km c. 90 m
2. The capacity of a picnic cooler
   a. 20 L b. 2400 cm c. 80 g
3. The area of an envelope
   a. 240 cm^2 b. 400 mm^2 c. 1 m^2
4. The mass of a shoe
   a. 4 kg b. 0.4 kg c. 40 g

Warm-up Lesson 3-5

You have one minute to fill in the blanks.

1. 1 gal = _______ qt 2. 1 km = _______ m
3. 1 mi = _______ ft 4. 1 in. = _______ cm
5. 1 mg = _______ g 6. 1 mL = _______ L

Warm-up Lesson 3-6

You need straws and a protractor. Estimate each of the following angle measures with your straws. Then place the "straw angle" on a sheet of paper and draw the angle by tracing the inside of the straw angle. Finally, measure each angle to see how close it is to the given measure.

1. 30° 2. 135° 3. 45°
4. 110° 5. 80° 6. 170°

TEACHING AID 27

Warm-up Lesson 3-7

Work in groups and find objects in the classroom that show acute angles and objects that show obtuse angles. List at least three examples of each kind of angle.

Warm-up Lesson 3-8

Place the decimal point correctly in each product. Do not use a calculator.

1. $3.2 \times 3.2 = 1024$
2. $6.01 \times 6.01 = 361201$
3. $7 \times 7 = 49$
4. $9.4 \times 9.4 = 8836$
5. $6.3^2 = 3969$
6. $7.25^2 = 525625$

Warm-up Lesson 3-9

Work in groups. Solve the following problem. Cheese wedges like the one at the left are packed in the wedge-shaped box at the right. How many wedges will fit in the box? Explain how you got your answer.

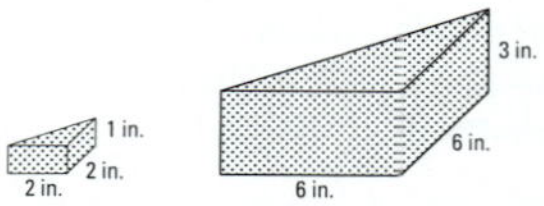

TEACHING AID 28
Lesson 3-1

Measuring Length

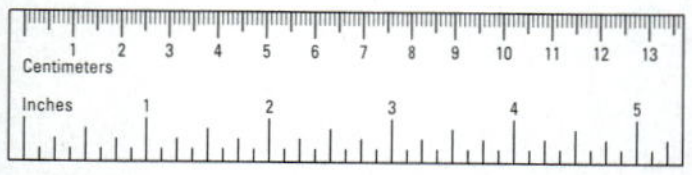

Measure each of the following segments using the specified units.

1. a. nearest centimeter ________
   b. nearest millimeter ________
   c. nearest inch ________
2. a. nearest in. ________
   b. nearest $\frac{1}{2}$ in. ________
   c. nearest $\frac{1}{8}$ in. ________
3. Draw a segment that is $2\frac{1}{4}$ in. long.

4. Draw a segment that is 8.5 cm long.

TEACHING AID 29
Lesson 3-2

Customary Units of Length

1 foot (ft) = 12 inches (in.)

1 yard (yd) = 3 ft

1 mile (mi) = 5280 ft

TEACHING AID 30
Lesson 3-3

Customary Units of Weight and Capacity

For weight:

1 pound (lb) = 16 ounces (oz)

1 short ton = 2000 lb

For capacity (liquid or dry volume):

1 quart (qt) = 2 pints (pt)

1 gallon (gal) = 4 qt

TEACHING AID 31
Lesson 3-4

Metric Units of Measure

place value	thousands	hundreds	tens	ones	tenths	hundredths	thousandths
power of 10	10^3			10^0			
unit of length	**kilometer**					**centimeter**	
unit of mass		hectogram			decigram		
unit of capacity			dekaliter				**milliliter**

place value	trillions	billions	millions	millionths	billionths	trillionths
power of 10	10^{12}		10^6		10^{-9}	10^{-12}
prefix	tera-	giga-	mega-	micro-	nano-	pico-

TEACHING AID 32
Lesson 3-5

Conversions to Know

1 inch = 2.54 centimeters (exactly)
1 kilogram ≈ 2.2 pounds
1 liter ≈ 1.06 quarts
1 kilometer ≈ 1.6 miles
1 meter ≈ 39.37 inches

For which conversion(s) can you use the Substitution Principle?

For which conversion(s) should you use estimation as well?

TEACHING AID 33
Lesson 3-6

Measuring Angles

Measure each angle.

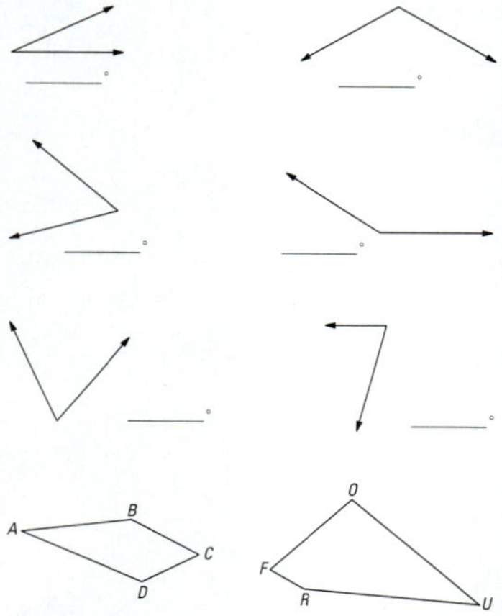

m∠D = ________ m∠F = ________

TEACHING AID 35
Lesson 3-7

United States Map

TEACHING AID 36
Lesson 3-8

Centimeter Grid

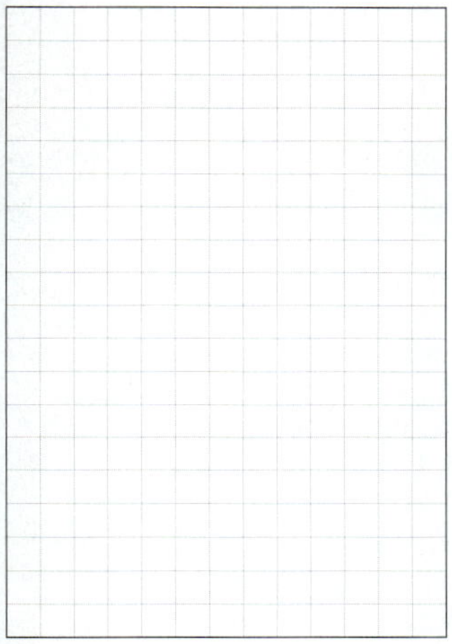

TEACHING AID 37
Lesson 3-9

Square Foot

1 square foot = ________ square inches

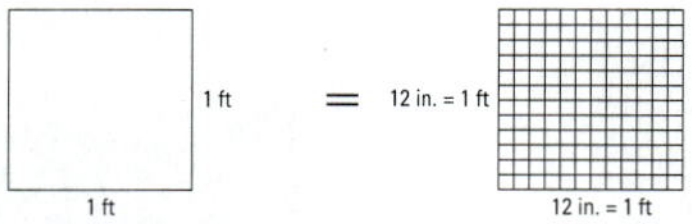

Cubic Foot

1 cubic foot = ________ cubic inches

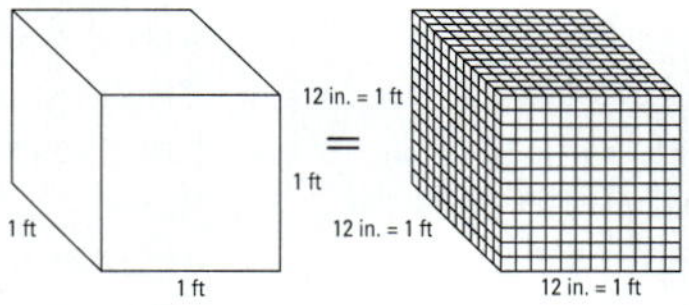

TEACHING AID 38
Lesson 3-9

Patterns for 1-Inch Cube

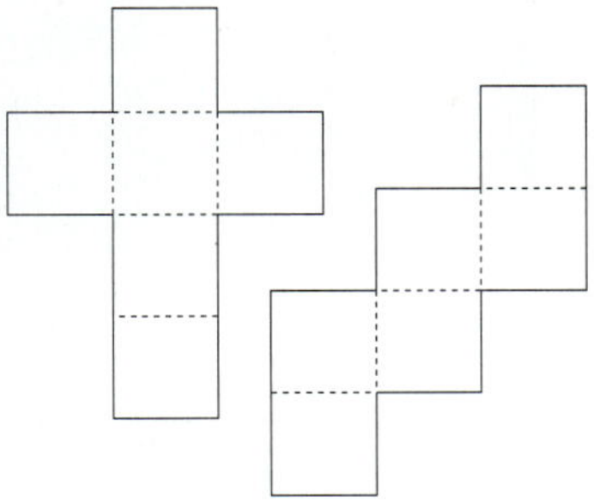

Chapter Opener 3

Pacing

We recommend spending 12 to 15 days on this chapter, including 1 day to review the Progress Self-Test, 1 to 2 days on the Chapter Review, and 1 day for testing. A test covering Chapters 1–3 is provided in the *Assessment Sourcebook.* This Comprehensive Test can be used as a quarter exam.

Using pages 116–117

Use the photograph of the ballet dancer to point out that many of the first measuring units were based on the lengths of body parts. You may want to mention other early measures of length. For example, the pace was the distance of a stride—which was measured from the spot where a heel lifted off the ground to the spot where the same heel touched the ground. Soldiers in the Roman Empire measured distances by counting paces. The pace was equal to 5 feet, which meant that 1000 paces was 5000 feet, a measure close to the length of the mile. In fact, the Romans used the word *mille* for 1000. This word is the origin of the unit we call the mile.

Photo Connections

The photo collage makes real-world connections to the content of the chapter: measurement.

Pyramids: The Pyramids of Giza stand as testaments to the early technical skill and engineering ability of the Egyptians. The linear measurement used in their construction, the cubit, gives us a glimpse of the builders themselves. Based on the human form, a cubit represented the length of the arm from the elbow to

CHAPTER 3

Chapter 3 Overview

We assume that students have seen most of the units of measure that are in this chapter. But we assume that they need more work on them. If your students have little or no experience with measuring, you may wish to spend a couple more days on actual physical measurement of lengths, angles, and areas. Do not spend extra time reviewing things students already know, and spend no more than 15 class days on the chapter; there is much more information on measurement in later chapters.

An entire chapter on measurement is included at this point for several reasons. First, quantities with units of length, weight or mass, area, volume or capacity, and angle measure are used throughout this book. (We use the word *quantity* to indicate the combination of a number and a count or measure unit; *25 books* and *7.62 kilograms* are quantities.) Second, measurement often involves computing with fractions and decimals, and most students need practice with these skills. Third, the metric system, one of the main topics in this chapter, is based upon powers of 10 and reinforces the work in Chapter 2. Fourth, the calculations of both area and volume are connected with the second and third powers, respectively. And fifth, after about a month on arithmetic, some geometry is a nice break.

MEASUREMENT

The first units of length were based on the human body. Some of these units are shown in the picture below. For instance, a "hand" was the width of a person's palm. So the size of a hand differed from person to person. Initially, these rough units were sufficient for most purposes. But as time went on, more accurate units were needed. So units began to be *standardized.*

According to tradition, the *yard* originally was the distance from the tip of the nose of King Henry I of England (who reigned from 1100 to 1135) to the tips of his fingers. The *foot* is supposedly based on the foot of Charlemagne (who ruled France and neighboring areas from 768 to 814).

the extended finger tips, 20.623 inches.

Hands: Early linear measurements derived their meanings from body measurements. Hands, arms, and fingers provided convenient bases for units of length. In some instances this practice continues today.

Market: At a marketplace in Bali, Indonesia, various forms of measurement are used to determine weight, volume, or length of the goods. Some of the earliest measurements of weight probably were based on estimates of what a man or pack animal could lift or haul.

Caliper: A micrometer caliper is an instrument used to provide an accurate measurement of the diameter or thickness of an object. Here a technician is using one to measure the dimensions of a gasket. The measurements will be used to determine if the gasket falls within prescribed tolerances.

Astrolabe: Early astronomers and navigators used an astrolabe to measure the angles of celestial bodies above the horizon. The astrolabe is the predecessor to the sextant and other more accurate instruments.

Chapter 3 Projects

At this time you might want to have students look over the Chapter 3 projects on pages 167–168.

Various units of measures are introduced in the lessons as follows:

Lesson 3-1: inch, meter, centimeter, millimeter
Lesson 3-2: foot, yard, mile
Lesson 3-3: ounce, pound, short ton, fluid ounce, cup, pint, quart, gallon
Lesson 3-4: gram, liter (metric prefixes)
Lesson 3-5: monetary units
Lesson 3-6: degree (for angle measure)
Lesson 3-8: square units
Lesson 3-9: cubic units

Students will need a ruler and a protractor for this chapter. If students need to buy them, you may want to make specific suggestions about what they should get so that all of the students have similar equipment. We recommend the clear plastic variety. A suitable ruler and protractor are on ScottForesman's Geometry Template.

You will find it helpful to have the following equipment available:

- yardsticks, meter sticks, and tape measures
- centimeter cubes and small boxes or containers
- 1-liter and 2-liter containers; quart, pint, and cup containers
- a balance
- empty food packages labeled with both customary and metric units of measure

Lesson 3-1

Objectives

A Measure lengths to the nearest inch, half inch, quarter inch, or eighth of an inch, or to the nearest centimeter or millimeter.

K Draw a line segment of a given length.

N Give countries and approximate dates of origin of current measuring ideas.

Resources

From the ***Teacher's Resource File***
- Lesson Master 3-1A or 3-1B
- Answer Master 3-1
- Teaching Aids
  25 Warm-up
  28 Measuring Length

Additional Resources
- Visuals for Teaching Aids 25, 28
- Ruler or Geometry Template

Teaching Lesson 3-1

Warm-Up

Diagnostic Round each mixed number to the nearest half and to the nearest quarter.

1. $3\frac{3}{5}$ $3\frac{1}{2}$; $3\frac{1}{2}$ **2.** $6\frac{3}{8}$ $6\frac{1}{2}$; $6\frac{1}{4}$ or $6\frac{1}{2}$

3. $8\frac{15}{16}$ 9; 9 **4.** $7\frac{1}{8}$ 7; 7 or $7\frac{1}{4}$

Round each number to the nearest whole number and to the nearest tenth.

5. 2.51 3; 2.5 **6.** 6.22 6; 6.2

7. 8.83 9; 8.8 **8.** 1.37 1; 1.4

LESSON

3-1

Measuring Length

Poetic license. *As far back as the 1780s, when the preamble to the U.S. Constitution was being written, the nation's leaders were concerned with standardizing units of measure. Today, license plates have standardized dimensions. The automobile plates for all states must be 12″ by 6″.*

How Did Standardized Measuring Units Come to Be?

Around the year 1600, scientific experimentation began and still more accurate measurement was necessary. Scientists from different countries needed to be able to communicate with each other about their work. With the manufacturing of lenses and clocks, accurate measurement was needed outside of science. Around 1760, the Industrial Revolution began. Hand tools were replaced by power-driven machines. Accurate, consistent measurement was needed everywhere.

The writers of the U.S. Constitution in 1787 recognized the need for standardized units. One paragraph in the Constitution reads:

> *The Congress shall have power . . . to fix the standard of weights and measures.*

1 In 1790, Thomas Jefferson proposed to Congress a measuring system based on the number 10. This would closely relate the measuring system to the decimal system. Five years later the *metric system,* based on the number 10, was established in France. We could have been the first country with a measuring system based on the decimal system. But we were emotionally tied to England, which was at that time an enemy of France. So we adopted the system of measurement used in England instead. Not until 1866 did the metric system become legal in the United States.

Lesson 3-1 Overview

Broad Goals One broad goal of this lesson is to make students realize that units of measure are inventions that have changed over time. This goal is important because, in your students' lifetimes, it is quite possible that the United States will officially change to the metric system. In order to bring this point across, we review measuring with two units of length with which we hope students are familiar: the centimeter and the inch.

Perspective Many students like the description of when, why, and how measures were standardized, so the introductory paragraphs in the chapter opener and in this lesson can make for lively class discussion. Once aware of the invention and development of measures, students can gain perspective and realize that mathematics is still growing and changing.

Conversions of length from the customary system to the metric system can be exact because 1 in. = 2.54 cm exactly. At the U.S. National Institute of Standards and Technology, the inch is defined in terms of the centimeter and thus in terms of the meter. The meter itself is officially defined (since 1960) as "1,650,763.73 wavelengths in a vacuum of the orange-red line of the spectrum of krypton-86."

At first the metric system was used mainly in science. But as years have gone by, it has been used in more and more fields and in more and more countries. The United States is the only large country in the world that has not officially converted to the metric system. The old "English system" or "British Imperial system" has evolved into the **U.S. system** or **customary system of measurement.** Today in the U.S., we measure in both the metric and U.S. systems.

All systems of measurement have units of length. For the metric system, the base unit of length is the **meter.** A **centimeter** is $\frac{1}{100}$, or .01, of a meter. For the U.S. system, the base unit of length is the **inch.** Here are the actual lengths of these units.

Figures appear smaller than actual size in Teacher's Edition.

Measuring Lengths in Centimeters and Millimeters

The ruler pictured below is scaled in centimeters on the top and inches on the bottom.

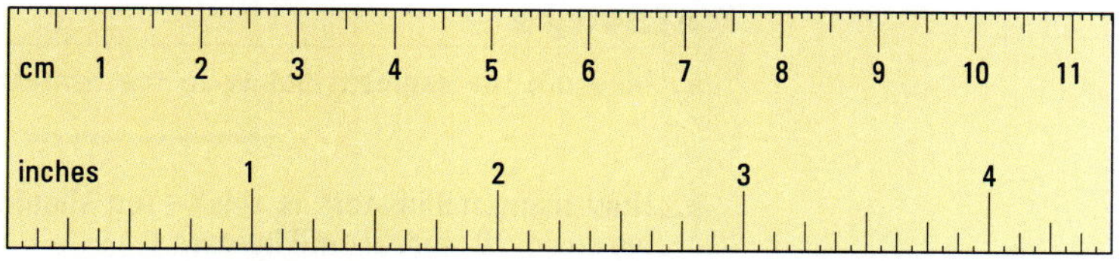

Since a centimeter is .01 of a meter, there are 100 centimeters in one meter. On the ruler, each centimeter is divided into 10 parts, each a **millimeter,** or .001 meter. Since a millimeter is .001 meter, 1000 millimeters equal 1 meter. Since 1000 millimeters and 100 centimeters both make up a meter, 10 millimeters equal 1 centimeter. Each small interval on the top scale of the above ruler is 1 millimeter.

The three segments drawn below have lengths of about 6, 6.3, and 7 centimeters.

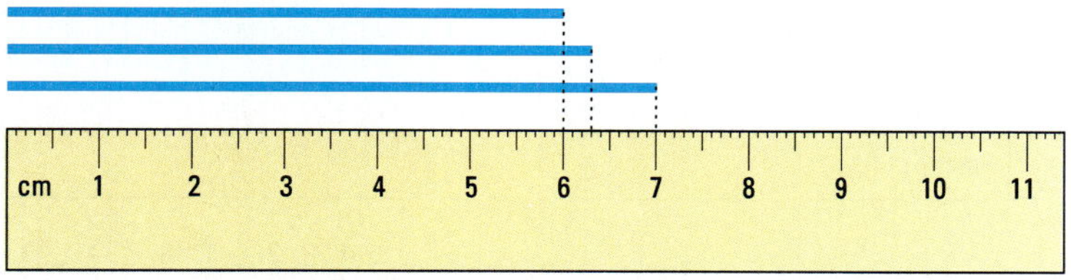

Notes on Reading

In previous chapters, students have been asked to have a calculator with them as they read. Here students need a ruler with both a centimeter and an inch scale. They should check the scale on any ruler they have with the scales we use in this book. Even in our days of standardized units, not all rulers match!

Throughout the lesson, stress that any measure of length is an approximation. Ask students how accurate they think they can really be and what factors could cause variations in their results. Students should be allowed leeway in the accuracy of their measurements. A variation of a tenth of a centimeter or an eighth of an inch is reasonable.

Reading Mathematics This lesson has more than the usual amount of reading, so you might wish to separate the class into groups and have students in each group take turns reading aloud. Note that the chapter opener and the first section of the lesson, *How Did Standardized Measuring Units Come to Be?* comprise six major paragraphs. After students complete the reading, you might ask each group to write a question they would put on a test for each paragraph.

If students do the reading on their own, you should plan to have a thorough class discussion.

1 Social Studies Connection
The references to Thomas Jefferson, the Constitution, and our attachment to England provide an opportunity to relate mathematics and social studies. The beliefs of Thomas Jefferson with respect to weights and measures directly affected the adoption of systems we still use today. Your students may not realize how brilliant Thomas Jefferson was. At a White House dinner honoring Nobel prize

Optional Activities

Activity 1 After reading about Thomas Jefferson's contributions at the beginning of the lesson, some students might be interested in finding out more about Jefferson. They could write about his many professions and how they may have influenced his beliefs.

Activity 2 Cooperative Learning After discussing **Example 2,** students might **work in groups,** and draw three segments with different lengths that satisfy each condition.

1. The segment is 3 inches long if measured to the nearest inch. [Any segment greater than or equal to $2\frac{1}{2}$ in. and less than $3\frac{1}{2}$ in.]
2. The segment is $5\frac{1}{2}$ inches long if measured to the nearest half inch. [Any segment greater than or equal to $5\frac{1}{4}$ in. and less than $5\frac{3}{4}$ in.]
3. The segment is 4 inches long if measured to the nearest half inch. [Any segment greater than or equal to $3\frac{3}{4}$ in. and less than $4\frac{1}{4}$ in.]
4. The segment is $2\frac{3}{4}$ inches long if measured to the nearest eighth inch. [Any segment greater than or equal to $2\frac{11}{16}$ in. and less than $2\frac{13}{16}$ in.]

winners in 1962, President Kennedy said, "I think this is the most extraordinary collection of talent, of human knowledge, that has ever been gathered together at the White House, with the possible exception of when Thomas Jefferson dined alone."

Among Jefferson's many professions were those of surveyor and architect, two vocations requiring accurate measurements. Jefferson saw the advantage of a measuring system based on 10 and tried unsuccessfully to get the new republic to adopt it. This was a revolutionary idea at the time—the metric system had not yet been developed. However, Jefferson was successful in two respects. First, partly as a result of his efforts, our monetary system is based on 10 and was the first system in the world to be so based. Second, Jefferson's thinking influenced the Constitutional requirement that gave Congress the power to establish a system of weights and measures.

Pacing This lesson may take longer than a day, particularly if you do a thorough review of the Chapter 2 test. However, Lesson 3-2 is brief.

Figures appear smaller than actual size in Teacher's Edition.

Example 1

Find the length of this small paper clip
a. to the nearest centimeter, and
b. to the nearest millimeter.

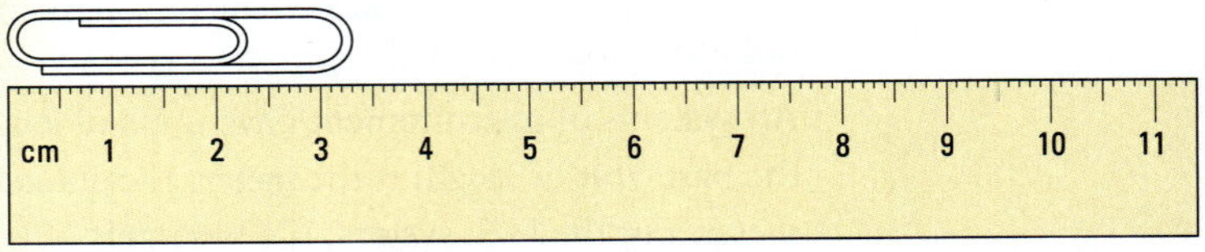

Solution

a. The numbered tick marks are 1 centimeter apart. So the length of the clip is *3 centimeters*, to the nearest centimeter.

b. The small tick marks are 0.1 centimeter apart. So the length of the clip is 3.3 centimeters, to the nearest tenth of a centimeter. To the nearest millimeter, the length is *33 millimeters*.

Activity 1

a. Measure the segment below to the nearest tenth of a centimeter.

2.6 cm

b. How many millimeters is this? (You should get a length somewhere between 20 and 30 millimeters.)

Measuring Lengths in Inches

On rulers, inches are usually divided into halves, fourths, eighths, and sixteenths. On most rulers, the tick marks have different lengths. The shortest interval is sixteenths.

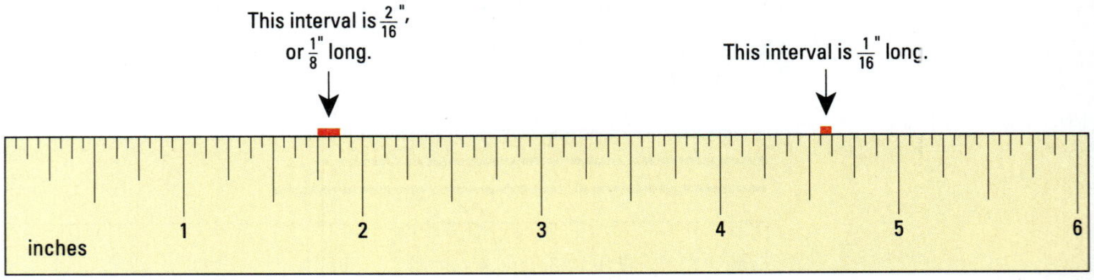

These equal fractions, $\frac{4}{16} = \frac{2}{8} = \frac{1}{4}$, $\frac{8}{16} = \frac{4}{8} = \frac{2}{4} = \frac{1}{2}$, $\frac{12}{16} = \frac{6}{8} = \frac{3}{4}$, and so on, are used in measuring inches. The segments drawn at the top of page 121 have lengths of about 1, $1\frac{1}{2}$, $1\frac{5}{8}$, and $1\frac{3}{4}$ inches.

Adapting to Individual Needs

Challenge

Explain that when a machine part is manufactured, the amount a measurement can vary from a specified size is called the tolerance. For example, a bolt might be designed to have a tolerance of ±0.01 inch. If the specified length is 5 inches, then the actual measurement can be in the range from (5 − 0.01) in. to (5 + 0.01) in. Any bolt that is out of that range should be discarded.

Point out that some parts have a tolerance in one direction only. For example, an engineer might designate a length of 9 − 0.02 inch. That means the measurement can be between 8.98 in. and 9.00 in.

Have students find the allowable range of measurement for each part.

Designed length	Tolerance
1. 0.34 in.	±0.01 in.
2. $7\frac{1}{2}$ in.	$\pm\frac{1}{4}$ in.
3. 8 cm	±1 mm
4. 2.5 cm	±0.001 cm
5. 7 m	−1 cm

[**1.** 0.33 in. to 0.35 in. **2.** $7\frac{1}{4}$ in. to $7\frac{3}{4}$ in. **3.** 7.9 cm to 8.1 cm **4.** 2.499 cm to 2.501 cm **5.** 6.99 m to 7.00 m]

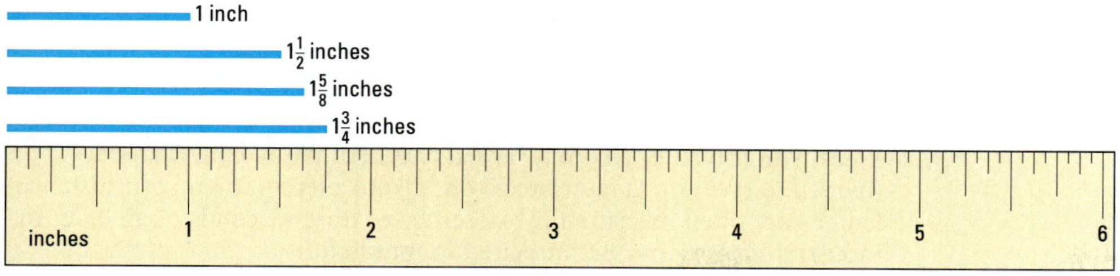

The above ruler is marked off in inches and fractions of inches.

Look at the segment that is $1\frac{3}{4}$ inches long. How do we know its length? The ruler's numbers show that its length is between 1 and 2 inches. The $\frac{3}{4}$ is not so easy to see. Notice that there are 16 intervals between 1 inch and 2 inches. So each interval is $\frac{1}{16}$ of an inch long. The segment reaches 12 intervals past 1 inch. So its length is $1\frac{12}{16}$ inches. Written in lowest terms, this is $1\frac{3}{4}$ inches.

Example 2

Find the height of this photograph:

a. to the nearest $\frac{1}{2}$ inch.

b. to the nearest $\frac{1}{4}$ inch.

c. to the nearest $\frac{1}{8}$ inch.

Modern Robin? *The photo is of some of the characters from 20th Century Fox's* Robin Hood: Men In Tights. *In this comedic version of the legend, Robin Hood is in the center, portrayed by Cary Elwes.*

Solution

The tick marks are $\frac{1}{16}$ in. apart, so the height is a little more than $2\frac{2}{16}$ in., or a little more than $2\frac{1}{8}$ in.

a. Rounded to the nearest $\frac{1}{2}$ in., $2\frac{1}{8}$ in. is 2 in.

b. Rounded to the nearest $\frac{1}{4}$ in., a little more than $2\frac{1}{8}$ in. is $2\frac{1}{4}$ in.

c. Rounded to the nearest $\frac{1}{8}$ in., a little more than $2\frac{1}{8}$ in. is $2\frac{1}{8}$ in.

Additional Examples

Have students **work with a partner.** Tell them to select classroom objects for which they can measure the length. Possible items to have in class for students to measure might include an unsharpened pencil, a paperback book (length and width), a new piece of chalk, a large paper clip, a straw, and a stamp. Things in the classroom might include a desk top, bulletin board, blackboard, door, floor tile, and a blackboard eraser. **Answers will vary.**

1. Select an object. Find its length
   a. to the nearest centimeter.
   b. to the nearest millimeter.
2. Select another object. Find its length
   a. to the nearest half inch.
   b. to the nearest fourth inch.
   c. to the nearest eighth inch.
3. Select another object. Give a customary and a metric unit that would be appropriate for measuring its length.

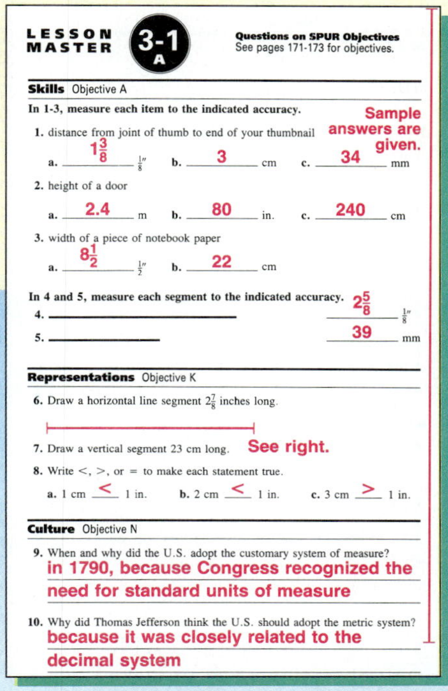
LESSON MASTER 3-1 A

Questions on SPUR Objectives
See pages 171-173 for objectives.

Skills Objective A

In 1-3, measure each item to the indicated accuracy. **Sample answers are given.**

1. distance from joint of thumb to end of your thumbnail
   a. $1\frac{3}{8}$ $\frac{1}{8}''$ b. 3 cm c. 34 mm
2. height of a door
   a. 2.4 m b. 80 in. c. 240 cm
3. width of a piece of notebook paper
   a. $8\frac{1}{2}$ $\frac{1}{2}''$ b. 22 cm

In 4 and 5, measure each segment to the indicated accuracy.

4. ______ $2\frac{5}{8}$ $\frac{1}{8}''$
5. ______ 39 mm

Representations Objective K

6. Draw a horizontal line segment $2\frac{7}{8}$ inches long.
7. Draw a vertical segment 23 cm long. **See right.**
8. Write $<$, $>$, or $=$ to make each statement true.
   a. 1 cm $<$ 1 in. b. 2 cm $<$ 1 in. c. 3 cm $>$ 1 in.

Culture Objective N

9. When and why did the U.S. adopt the customary system of measure?
   in 1790, because Congress recognized the need for standard units of measure
10. Why did Thomas Jefferson think the U.S. should adopt the metric system?
   because it was closely related to the decimal system

Activity 2

Measure the height of this page to the nearest eighth inch.

When you measure, you may have a choice of units. Units can be divided to give you greater precision in your measurement. For instance, lengths are often measured in sixteenths or thirty-seconds of an inch. In industry, lengths may be measured to hundredths or thousandths or even smaller parts of an inch. Whatever unit you work with, you are rounding to the nearest. The rounding unit (tenth of a centimeter, for example) indicates how precise your measurement is.

Example 3

Give a U.S. unit and a metric unit that would be appropriate for measuring the length of a pencil.

Solution

A pencil would probably be measured in inches or centimeters. A millimeter would be too tiny a unit; feet, yards, miles, meters, and kilometers would be too large.

A man for any era. *Thomas Jefferson (1743–1826) was an American revolutionary leader, a political philosopher, author of the Declaration of Independence, and third president of the U.S. He also pushed for public schools and libraries.*

QUESTIONS

Covering the Reading

1. The first units of length were based on _?_. lengths of the human body
2. The heights of horses are sometimes measured in hands. How was the length called a hand originally determined? width of a person's palm
3. The yard originally was the distance from the _?_ to the _?_ of what king of England? tip of the nose; tip of his fingers; King Henry I
4. Whose foot is said to have been the foot from which today's foot originated? Charlemagne
5. Why did units become standardized? More accurate measurements were needed for scientific experimentation.
6. About when did accurate lengths become needed everywhere? 1760

In 7–10, *true or false.*

7. Thomas Jefferson wanted the United States to adopt the English system of measurement. False
8. The metric system was established in France in 1795. True
9. The metric system became legal in the United States over 100 years ago. True
10. Congress has the power to set standards of measurement in the United States. True
11. The base unit of length in the metric system is the _?_. meter

Notes on Questions

You might want to review **Questions 1–11** in class to check that the basic ideas of the lesson and the history of measurement are clear to students.

LESSON MASTER 3-1 B — **Questions on SPUR Objectives**

Skills Objective A: Measure lengths to the nearest inch, half inch, quarter inch, or eighth of an inch, or to the nearest centimeter or millimeter.

In 1-5 measure each item to the indicated accuracy. 1-4 answers will vary.

1. thickness of a door
 a. ________ $\frac{1}{8}''$ b. ________ cm c. ________ mm
2. height of a window
 a. ________ in. b. ________ $\frac{1}{2}$ in. c. ________ cm
3. length of a pen
 a. ________ $\frac{1}{4}''$ b. ________ $\frac{1}{8}''$ c. ________ cm
4. height of a table or desk
 a. ________ in. b. ________ $\frac{1}{2}''$ c. ________ cm
5. diameter of a penny
 a. $\frac{3}{4}$ $\frac{1}{4}''$ b. $\frac{6}{8}$ $\frac{1}{8}''$ c. 19 mm

In 6-10, measure each segment to the indicated accuracy.

6. $\frac{1}{4}''$ ________ $2\frac{3}{4}''$
7. $\frac{1}{8}''$ ________ $3\frac{1}{8}''$
8. mm ________ 38 mm
9. $\frac{1}{2}''$ ________ $3\frac{1}{2}''$
10. cm ________ 9 cm

Adapting to Individual Needs

Extra Help
Some students may not have learned proper measurement techniques. You might let students who have mastered the skill review with them the centimeter and millimeter markings on the metric scale of a ruler and the inch and fraction-of-an-inch markings on the customary scale. Then, after illustrating proper placement of the ruler when measuring, watch students measure objects to ensure that they do it properly.

English Language Development You might use measuring with rulers (inch and centimeter) and a tape measure to assess students' understanding of the vocabulary. As students measure common objects, check that they understand the words *length* and *height* and how "long" an object is.

12. In Activity 1, give the length of the segment.
a. in centimeters **2.6 cm** **b.** in millimeters **26 mm**

In 13–15, measure the length of the segment to the nearest millimeter.

13. **56 mm**

14. **104 mm**

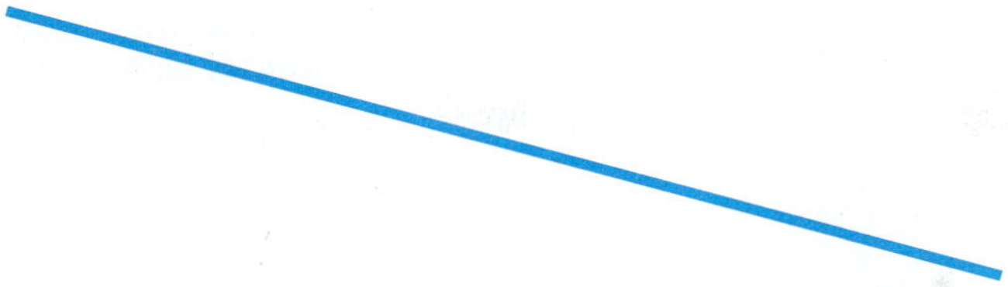

15. **35 mm**

16. What is the answer in Activity 2? **10 in.; answers may vary.**

In 17–19, use this ruler to find the length of the segment to the nearest eighth of an inch. Write the length in lowest terms.

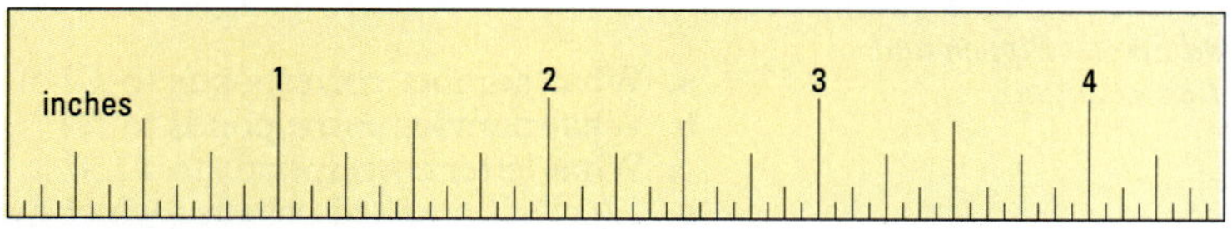

17. **$2\frac{1}{8}$ in.**

18. **$1\frac{3}{8}$ in.**

19. **$\frac{3}{4}$ in.**

Applying the Mathematics

In 20–24, *multiple choice.* Match the quantity with an appropriate metric unit of measure.

20. length of a swimming pool **(c)**
21. distance from London to Paris **(d)**
22. thickness of the cover of your math book **(a)**
23. height of your desk **(c)**
24. length of your thumb **(b)**

(a) millimeter
(b) centimeter
(c) meter
(d) kilometer

25. Draw a segment that is 6 cm long. Use your ruler to estimate its measure in inches. **6 cm ≈ $2\frac{3}{8}$ in. Check student's drawing.**

26. Draw a vertical segment with length 3.5 inches. **Check student's drawing.**

27. Draw a horizontal segment with length 12.4 centimeters. **Check student's drawing.**

Questions 13–19 and 25–27
These questions provide practice measuring segments and drawing segments of a specified length. You might wish to use **Teaching Aid 28** to give students more practice drawing and measuring segments.

For students having difficulty measuring, see *Extra Help* in *Adapting to Individual Needs* on page 122.

Questions 26–27 Error Alert
Some students may not understand the words vertical and horizontal. If so, review the meanings of the terms. You might relate horizontal to horizon.

▸ **LESSON MASTER 3-1 B** *page 2*

Representations Objective K: Draw a line segment of a given length.

11. In the space below, draw a horizontal line segment $3\frac{1}{4}$ inches long.

12. On the left side of this page, draw a vertical line segment $5\frac{7}{8}$ inches long.

13. In the space below, draw a horizontal line segment 51 mm long.

14. On the right side of this page, draw a vertical line segment 13 cm long.

In 15-18, write <, >, or = to make each statement true.

15. 1 mm __<__ 1 cm
16. 1 in. __>__ 1 cm
17. 1 cm __=__ 10 mm
18. 1 cm __<__ $\frac{1}{2}$ in.

Culture Objective N: Give countries and approximate dates of origin of current measuring ideas.

19. Which U.S. document gives Congress the power to set the standard for weights and measures? **U. S. Constitution**

20. From which country did the U.S. system of measurement evolve? **England**

21. When did the metric system become legal in the United States? **1866**

22. Name two historical figures associated with units of measure and describe the units.
Samples: King Henry I: The yard ran from the tip of his nose to the tips of his fingers; Charlemagne: The foot was based on his foot.

Notes on Questions

Question 33 History Connection In surveying, the term *chain* refers to both a unit of measure and a measuring instrument. As a unit, a chain is a length of 66 feet and as a measuring device, it is an actual chain comprised of 100 links. Today, however, the cumbersome chain has been replaced by a steel band or tape. It is interesting to note, however, that many country roads and town streets in the United States are 66 feet, or one chain, wide. Also, a chain is $\frac{1}{10}$ of a furlong, or $\frac{1}{80}$ of a mile.

Follow-up for Lesson 3-1

Practice

For more questions on the SPUR objectives, use **Lesson Master 3-1A** (shown on page 121) or **Lesson Master 3-1B** (shown on pages 122–123).

Assessment

Group Assessment Have students **work in pairs** and take turns drawing and measuring segments. The student drawing the segment should decide if his or her partner should measure in customary or metric units. The student measuring should decide on an appropriate unit. Both students should discuss the answer. [Observation indicates that students know how to measure with a ruler and have facility with the terminology.]

Extension

Multicultural Connection You might suggest that students investigate and write reports on how lengths were measured in ancient cultures, such as those in Central America, Egypt, and China. Students might also make a bulletin-board display to illustrate their findings. Encyclopedias and books about the history of mathematics are references they might use.

Project Update Project 2, *Other Traditional Units,* on page 167, relates to the content of this lesson. Students choosing this project might start researching other traditional units of length at this time.

From top to bottom, the athletes shown are Andre Agassi; Kristi Yamaguchi; and Scottie Pippen and Michael Jordan.

Review

28. Some people believe that if a sports team or individual appears on the cover of *Sports Illustrated,* then the team or individual becomes jinxed and will suffer a decline in performance. Researchers at the University of Southern California examined 271 covers. They found that 57.6% of the cover subjects improved in performance.

a. Did more cover subjects improve or decline in performance? improve

b. How many of the 271 cover subjects improved in performance? *(Lessons 2-4, 2-5)* 156

29. Since $\frac{1}{20}$ = 5%, what percent is equal to $\frac{9}{20}$? *(Lesson 2-4)* 45%

30. Which is larger, 5×10^6 or 6×10^5? *(Lesson 2-3)* 5×10^6

31. Which is larger, 5 to the 6th power, or 6 to the 5th power? *(Lesson 2-2)* 5^6

32. Use the number line drawn here. The letters refer to points that are equally spaced. *(Lesson 1-2)*

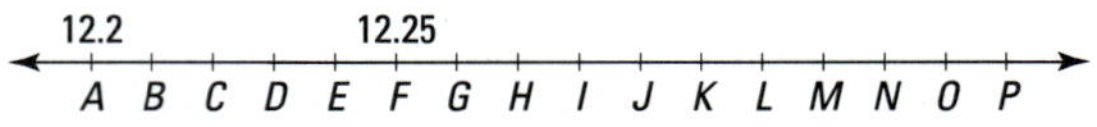

a. What number corresponds to *E*? 12.24

b. What number corresponds to *N*? 12.33

c. What letter corresponds to 12.3? *K*

d. 12.213 is graphed between which two points? *B* and *C*

Exploration

33. There are many units of length that have specialized uses. Find out something about each of these specialized units of length.

a. pica
b. ell
c. link
d. chain

See below.

34. Look at the picture that opens this chapter. Find out what these lengths are today.

a. fathom 6 ft
b. cubit approximately 18 in. or 45.72 cm

33. a) a size of type, $\frac{1}{6}$ inch high
b) length used to measure cloth, 45 in.
c) $\frac{1}{100}$ of a surveyor's chain, 7.92 in.
d) 66 ft, used in surveying

Setting Up Lesson 3-2

Materials If you plan to have students do the Extension on page 129, you will need to have a road map for each pair of students.

LESSON

3-2

Converting Lengths

A whale of a catch. *The coho salmon shown at the left is about 25 in., or 2 ft 1 in., or about $\frac{2}{3}$ yd long. It weighs about 22 lb. The largest coho salmon ever caught weighed 33 lb 4 oz.*

Converting Lengths Within the U.S. System

Carlos is 5 feet 3 inches tall. Theresa is 65 inches tall. Who is taller? To compare these measures, the units of measure need to be consistent.

First you need to know how these units of length are related. Three relationships are used so often you should memorize them if you do not know them already. We call them **conversion equations** because they have an equal sign and they are used for converting from one unit to another.

Conversion Equations for Customary Units of Length

1 foot (ft) = 12 inches (in.)
1 yard (yd) = 3 feet
1 mile (mi) = 5280 feet

Except for the inch, it is now recommended that periods not be used in abbreviations for units of measure. Periods may be confused with decimals.

The conversion equations make it possible to convert from one unit to another by multiplying. The property that follows is extraordinarily useful.

Multiplication Property of Equality
When equal quantities are multiplied by the same number, the resulting quantities are equal.

Lesson 3-2

Objectives

E State and apply the Multiplication Property of Equality.
F Give appropriate units for measuring length in the U.S. system of measurement.
G Convert within the U.S. system of measurement.
I Convert from inches to centimeters.

Resources

From the ***Teacher's Resource File***

- Lesson Master 3-2A or 3-2B
- Answer Master 3-2
- Teaching Aids
  25 Warm-up
  29 Customary Units of Length

Additional Resources

- Visuals for Teaching Aids 25, 29
- Road maps
- Spreadsheet Workshop

Teaching Lesson 3-2

Warm-up

Mental Mathematics Compute mentally.

1. 3×12 36 **2.** $60 \div 12$ 5
3. $36 \div 3$ 12 **4.** 15×3 45
5. $72 \div 12$ 6 **6.** $72 \div 36$ 2
7. 20×3 60 **8.** 20×12 240

Notes on Reading

You might begin by asking students to name things they measure in inches, feet, yards, and miles. Then ask why they think there are different units of length. [Possible answer: to

Lesson 3-2 Overview

Broad Goals The goal of this lesson is to give students a formal process for converting lengths from one unit to another. This process will be used in other situations in later lessons.

Perspective There are at least three ways to convert units. We use the Multiplication Property of Equality, as illustrated in **Example 1**. Note we begin with the *conversion equation* 1 mile = 5280 feet, which relates feet and miles. Then we multiply both sides by 1.7 to find the number of feet in 1.7 miles. This method has the advantage of preparing students for solving equations, and many teachers believe it is the simplest method to learn.

A method which uses the Substitution Principle is shown in *Optional Activities* on page 126. It is a viable alternative to the method in the text.

A method using proportions is presented in many texts. Using this method, the following proportion could be solved to find the number of feet in 1.7 miles.

$$\frac{1 \text{ mile}}{5280 \text{ feet}} = \frac{1.7 \text{ mile}}{x \text{ feet}}$$

We do not favor using proportions at this time because the method is too complicated for the simple problems being considered.

be able to use whole numbers for as many measurements as possible]

Example 1 The solution shows the strategy of the lesson—use the Multiplication Property of Equality. This strategy is very powerful and will be used throughout the year in many types of situations.

Example 2 This example involves a measurement that has two units, so working with it requires converting one of the units to the other. Note the use of the Addition Property of Equality—the quantity 3 inches has been added to each side.

Example 3 The common conversion from inches to yards can be derived from two of the conversions given on page 125. Thus, students do not need to memorize all relationships between units; they only need to know one relationship connecting that unit to another.

We introduce the conversion from inches to centimeters at this time because it is exact and because it involves the same principles presented in the lesson.

Activity To find the number of centimeters in 4 inches, students can use the conversion equation and the Multiplication Property of Equality as follows:

$$1 \text{ in.} = 2.54 \text{ cm}$$
$$4 \times 1 \text{ in.} = 4 \times 2.54 \text{ cm}$$
$$4 \text{ in.} = 10.16 \text{ cm}$$

Example 1

How many feet are in 1.7 miles?

Solution

Start with the conversion equation relating feet and miles.

$$1 \text{ mi} = 5280 \text{ ft}$$

Multiply both sides by 1.7. $\quad 1.7 \times 1 \text{ mile} = 1.7 \times 5280 \text{ ft}$

$$1.7 \text{ miles} = 8976 \text{ feet.}$$

There is also an Addition Property of Equality. When the same quantity is added to equal quantities, the resulting sums are equal.

Example 2

Of the two people mentioned on page 125, who is taller, Carlos or Theresa?

Solution

Carlos's height is 5 feet 3 inches, so we convert this into inches.

Start with the conversion equation relating feet and inches. $\quad 1 \text{ foot} = 12 \text{ inches}$

Multiply both sides by 5. $\quad 5 \times 1 \text{ foot} = 5 \times 12 \text{ inches}$

$$5 \text{ feet} = 60 \text{ inches}$$

Add 3 inches to both sides. $\quad 5 \text{ feet } 3 \text{ inches} = 63 \text{ inches}$

Since Theresa's height is 65 inches, she is taller than Carlos.

Sometimes more than one conversion is needed in a problem.

Example 3

How many inches are in a yard?

Solution

Start with the conversion equation relating yards to feet. $\quad 1 \text{ yard} = 3 \text{ feet}$

Now convert 3 feet into inches. Use the conversion equation relating feet and inches. $\quad 1 \text{ foot} = 12 \text{ inches}$

Multiply both sides by 3. $\quad 3 \times 1 \text{ foot} = 3 \times 12 \text{ inches}$

$$3 \text{ feet} = 36 \text{ inches}$$

This shows 1 yard = 3 feet = 36 inches. So there are 36 inches in a yard.

Optional Activities

Activity 1 As an alternate approach to **Example 1,** you might show students how to use the Substitution Principle to solve conversion problems. For example, to change 1.7 miles to feet, substitute "5,280 feet" for "mile" and multiply.

$$\begin{aligned} &1.7 \text{ miles} \\ &= 1.7 \cdot 1 \text{ mile} \\ &= 1.7 \cdot 5{,}280 \text{ feet} \\ &= 8{,}976 \text{ feet} \end{aligned}$$

Activity 2 A Running Stride
Materials: Yardstick or tape measure

As an introduction to the lesson, you might have students **work in pairs** to find their running strides. One student should run while his or her partner watches the strides and marks the backs of two consecutive footprints. Then students can measure the distance between the marks. Ask students to find how far they could run in 10 strides, 100 strides, and 1000 strides.

Activity 3 Literature Connection
After completing the lesson, some students might enjoy reading *Gulliver's Travels* and then converting various measures into Lilliputian size ($\frac{1}{12}$ normal size) and Brobdingnagian size (12 times normal size). Students might draw the sizes of an item in all three ways.

Converting from Inches to Centimeters

Because the metric system is now the worldwide system, the inch is officially defined (even in the U.S.) in terms of centimeters.

1 inch = 2.54 centimeters

Because 1 inch is about 2.5 centimeters, 2 inches are about 5 centimeters. In general, it is easy to convert any number of inches to centimeters.

Activity

Determine exactly how many centimeters are in 4 inches. (Your answer should be close to 10.)

QUESTIONS

Covering the Reading

1. Name four units of length in the customary system. inch, foot, yard, mile

In 2–6, complete the relationship.

2. 1 ft = _?_ in. 12
3. 1 yd = _?_ ft 3
4. 1 yd = _?_ in. 36
5. 1 mi = _?_ ft 5280
6. 1 in. = _?_ cm 2.54
7. What value did you get for the Activity? 10.16 cm

In 8–10, convert.

8. .62 mile to feet 3273.6 ft
9. 4 yards to feet 12 ft
10. 10 inches to centimeters 25.4 cm
11. Who is taller if Natalie says she is 4 feet 6 inches tall, and Nathan gives his height as 50 inches? Natalie
12. Why is it recommended to abbreviate feet *ft* rather than *ft.*? The period may be confused with a decimal point.
13. Why is the inch defined in terms of the centimeter? The metric system is now the worldwide system.

Applying the Mathematics

14. a. Measure the height of your eyes from the ground, in inches, by standing next to a wall and marking the height. Answers will vary.
    b. Measure this height in centimeters. Answers will vary.
    c. Convert the inches to centimeters to check whether your measurements are correct. (Use 1 in. = 2.54 cm.) Answers will vary.

Additional Examples

1. A basketball player is $6\frac{1}{2}$ feet tall. How tall is the player in inches? 78 in.
2. A hall is 4 yd 2 ft long. Is a piece of carpeting that is 13 ft long enough to run the entire length of the hall? No
3. How many yards are in one mile? 1760 yd
4. a. One yard is how many centimeters? 91.44 cm
   b. Is this conversion exact or approximate ? Exact

Notes on Questions

When students do their homework, you might want to have them use **Teaching Aid 29.** The conversion equations for customary units of length are given for reference on the Teaching Aid.

Questions 2–6 Have students memorize these relationships.

Question 8 Note that .62 mile is about one kilometer.

Question 13 You might point out that the U.S. loses opportunities to export goods because many items manufactured in the U.S. are not in measurements easily handled in other countries.

Question 14 Students need two different measurement scales—inches and centimeters.

LESSON MASTER 3-2 A

Questions on SPUR Objectives
See pages 171-173 for objectives.

Properties Objective E

1. In your own words, explain what the Multiplication Property of Equality allows you to do.
   Multiply equal quantities by same number, and results are equal.
2. *Multiple choice.* Which step uses the Multiplication Property of Equality to find the number of feet in $\frac{1}{4}$ mile? b
   (a) 1 mile = 5280 feet
   (b) $\frac{1}{4}$ mile × 1 mile = $\frac{1}{4}$ × 5280 feet
   (c) $\frac{1}{4}$ × 1 mile = .25 × 5280 feet
   (d) $\frac{1}{4}$ × 1 mile = 1320 feet

Uses Objective F

In 3-6, tell whether the quantity would probably be measured in inches, feet, yards, or miles.

3. the length of a municipal swimming pool feet or yards
4. the length of the Mississippi River miles
5. the altitude of Mt. Hood feet
6. the dimensions of your calculator inches

Uses Objectives G and I

In 7-9, fill in the blank.

7. 1 yd = ______ ft
8. 1 mi = 5280 ft
9. 2.54 cm = 1 in.

In 10-11 convert. Show your work. Student work is not shown.

10. $2\frac{1}{2}$ miles to feet
    $2\frac{1}{2}$ mi = 13,200 ft
11. 1 foot to centimeters
    1 ft = 30.48 cm

Adapting to Individual Needs

English Language Development
Non-English speaking students might be paired with English speaking classmates so that they can help one another to understand how to convert lengths between the U.S. and metric systems.

Notes on Questions

Question 17 Students will probably convert 100 yards to feet and then divide.

Question 23 When we read this in the news, we thought there must be an error because 1 million percent seems too high for any actual situation. However, the answer to **part b** is reasonable, and the data are correct.

Question 29 Error Alert Caution students regarding the care that must be taken in typing the BASIC program. In line 40, there is a space after "IS" so that there will be a space when the computer prints the information.

15. **a.** In the U.S. system, a *rod* is defined as $5\frac{1}{2}$ yards. How many feet are in one rod? **1 rod = 16.5 ft**
b. A furlong is equal in length to 40 rods. How many feet is this? **1 furlong = 660 ft**
c. The Kentucky Derby, held every May in Louisville, Kentucky, was originally thought of as a 10-furlong horse race. How many feet long is the Kentucky Derby? **6600 ft**

16. Some city blocks are $\frac{1}{8}$ mile long. Convert this to feet. **660 ft**

17. If your running stride is 2.5 feet long, how many strides will you take in running 100 yards? **120 strides**

18. Convert $7\frac{1}{2}$ yards to feet. **22.5 ft**

19. Convert 7 yards, 2 feet, 6 inches to inches. **282 in.**

20. **a.** How many inches are in a mile? **63,360 in.**
b. How many centimeters are in a mile? **160,934.4 cm**

The National Autonomous University in Mexico City, originally opened in 1551, is Mexico's foremost center of higher learning. The Central Library, shown here, was built in 1951 and is completely covered with brilliant mosaics that include symbolic devices from early Mexican civilizations.

Review

21. Measure this segment **Figures appear smaller than actual size in Teacher's Edition.**
a. to the nearest $\frac{1}{8}$ of an inch, and **$3\frac{3}{8}$ in.**
b. to the nearest centimeter. *(Lesson 3-1)* **9 cm**

22. Measure the length of a dollar bill as indicated.
a. to the nearest inch **6 in.**
b. to the nearest fourth of an inch **$6\frac{1}{4}$ in.**
c. to the nearest eighth of an inch *(Lesson 3-1)* **$6\frac{1}{8}$ in.**

23. The National Autonomous University of Mexico has about 250,000 students. Since tuition had not been raised since 1948 and was equal to about six U.S. cents, in 1992 administrators announced a tuition increase of about 1 million percent!
a. Write one million percent as a decimal. *(Lesson 2-4)* **10,000**
b. Estimate the new tuition. *(Lesson 2-5)* **≈ $600 per student**
c. After the tuition raise was finalized, about how much total tuition did the university collect? Give your answer in both scientific notation and as a decimal. *(Lesson 2-3)* **$\$1.5 \times 10^8$; $150,000,000**

24. Which is larger, $\frac{3}{10}$ or $\frac{29}{97}$? *(Lesson 1-8)* **$\frac{3}{10}$**

25. **a.** Order -1, -2, and -1.5 from smallest to largest. **-2, -1.5, -1**
b. Write the numbers in part **a** on one line with inequality signs between them. *(Lesson 1-6)* **$-2 < -1.5 < -1$ or $-1 > -1.5 > -2$**

26. What number does the key sequence 89 [+/-] yield? *(Lesson 1-5)* **-89**

27. Estimate 896.5555555555 + 7.96113 to the nearest hundred. *(Lesson 1-4)* **900**

LESSON MASTER 3-2 B — Questions on SPUR Objectives

Properties Objective E: State and apply the Multiplication Property of Equality.

1. In your own words, state the Multiplication Property of Equality. **sample: Equal quantities can be multiplied by the same number and the products will be equal.**

2. *Multiple choice.* Which step uses the Multiplication Property of Equality to find the number of inches in $2\frac{1}{2}$ feet? **a**
(a) $2\frac{1}{2} \times 1$ foot $= 2\frac{1}{2} \times 12$ inches
(b) 1 foot = 12 inches
(c) $2\frac{1}{2}$ feet = 30 inches
(d) $2\frac{1}{2} \times 1$ foot = 30 inches

3. *Multiple choice.* Which step uses the Multiplication Property of Equality to find the number of centimeters in 7 inches? **d**
(a) 1 inch = 2.54 cm
(b) 17.78 cm = 7 inches
(c) 2.54×1 cm $= 2.54 \times 1$ inch
(d) 7×1 in. $= 7 \times 2.54$ cm

Uses Objective F: Give appropriate units for measuring length in the U.S. system of measurement.

In 4-9, tell whether the length would probably be measured in inches, feet, yards, or miles.

4. the altitude of Pikes Peak **feet or miles**
5. the dimensions of a note pad **inches**
6. the length of the Ohio River **miles**
7. fabric for a dress **yards**
8. the dimensions of a kitchen **feet**
9. the length of a newborn baby **inches**

Adapting to Individual Needs

Extra Help

To be successful with any measurement conversion, students should ask themselves if the number of new units will be greater than, or less than, the number of original units. If they are converting to smaller units, the number will be greater. If they are converting to larger units, the number will be less. You might demonstrate this by using a yardstick—the length of the stick is both 1 yard and 36 inches. In any given length, there will be more inches than yards.

This same concept is important when converting between measurement systems. Some students might remember to use the conversion factor 2.54 when converting inches to centimeters, but they forget whether to multiply or divide. If they realize that there will be more centimeters than inches in a given length, they will understand that they multiply.

Exploration

28. Having a frame of reference for a given measure can help you picture the length of a quantity. For example, an adult finger is about half an inch wide. Find something with a length that is about the same as the given unit.

a. inch **b.** foot
c. yard **d.** mile
e. millimeter **f.** centimeter
g. meter
Answers will vary.

29. The computer program below instructs a computer to convert a length in miles to one in feet. The line numbers 10, 20, and so on, at left must be typed. The computer executes the program in the order of the line numbers, which can be any positive integers.

a. Type in the following.

```
NEW
10 PRINT "WHAT IS LENGTH IN MILES?"
20 INPUT NMILES
30 NFEET = 5280 * NMILES
40 PRINT "THE NUMBER OF FEET IS "NFEET
50 END
```

To see your program, type LIST and press RETURN. You can change any line by typing it over. You need not type the entire program again.

b. To run your program, type RUN and press RETURN. The computer will execute line 10 and ask you to input a number. Input 5 and press RETURN. The computer will then execute the rest of the program. What does the computer screen show? THE NUMBER OF FEET IS 26400

c. Run the program a few times, with values of your own choosing. Write down the values you input and the answers the computer gives. Answers will vary.

Follow-up for Lesson 3-2

Practice

For more questions on the SPUR objectives, use **Lesson Master 3-2A** (shown on page 127) or **Lesson Master 3-2B** (shown on pages 128–129).

Assessment

Written Communication Have students measure each others' heights in feet and inches. Then have each student convert his or her height into both inches and centimeters. Have students show in writing what they did to make each conversion. [Height is measured accurately. Explanation of conversion is clear and concise.]

Extension

Give **pairs of students** a road map, and have them determine the approximate number of miles represented by one inch. Then have them find straight-line distances between various points on the map.

Technology Connection You may wish to have students use the *Spreadsheet Workshop* to make a table for converting feet to miles. Students should enter the label "Feet" in cell A1, "Miles" in cell B1, any number of feet in A2, and the formula A2 / 5280 in cell B2. The program will display the number of miles.

▸ **LESSON MASTER 3-2 B** *page 2*

In 10-13, tell whether you would probably measure each item to the nearest inch, foot, or mile.

10. dimensions of a postage stamp ____ inch
11. length of a building ____ feet
12. thickness of the earth's crust ____ mile
13. height of a stereo speaker ____ inch

Uses Objective G: Convert within the U.S. system of measurement.

In 14-17, fill in the blank.

14. 36 inches = 1 yard **15.** 12 inches = 1 foot
16. 5,280 feet = 1 mile **17.** 3 feet = 1 yard

In 18 and 19, show the steps you use for each conversion. Student work is not shown.

18. $7\frac{1}{2}$ yards to feet: $7\frac{1}{2}$ yd = $22\frac{1}{2}$ ft
19. 5 miles to feet: 5 mi = 26,400 ft

Uses Objective I: Convert from inches to centimeters.

20. How many centimeters are in 1 inch? 2.54 cm

In 21 and 22, show the steps you use for each conversion. Student work is not shown.

21. 5 inches to centimeters: 5 in. = 12.7 cm
22. 2 feet to centimeters: 24 in. = 60.96 cm

23. Jorge is 75" tall. Is he taller than 6 feet? yes

24. Cristina is 5 feet 7 inches tall. How tall is she in centimeters? 170.18 cm

Adapting to Individual Needs

Challenge

Have students solve the problem given below. Either give them the distance around the earth (about 24,900 miles at the equator) and the length of a dollar bill ($6\frac{1}{8}$ in.), or have them research this information.

Suppose one billion dollar bills are laid end-to-end to form a continuous chain around the earth at the equator. Would the bills reach around the world? If so, how many times? [Yes, about 4 times]

Lesson 3-3

Objectives

F Give appropriate units for measuring weight and capacity in the U.S. system of measurement.

G Convert weight and capacity units within the U.S. system of measurement.

Resources

From the ***Teacher's Resource File***

- Lesson Master 3-3A or 3-3B
- Answer Master 3-3
- Assessment Sourcebook: Quiz for Lessons 3-1 through 3-3
- Teaching Aids
  - 25 Warm-up
  - 30 Customary Units of Weight and Capacity

Additional Resources

- Visuals for Teaching Aids 25, 30

Teaching Lesson 3-3

Warm-up

Diagnostic You have 30 seconds to fill in the blanks.

1. 1 ft = ____ in. **12**
2. 1 yd = ____ ft **3**
3. 1 mi = ____ ft **5280**
4. 1 in. = ____ cm **2.54**
5. 1 yd = ____ in. **36**

Notes on Reading

Students are expected to memorize conversion relationships given for units of weight and capacity.

History Connection Until 1960 our system of measurement was usually called the English System of

LESSON

3-3 *Weight and Capacity in the Customary System of Measurement*

It's worth its weight in gold. *Gold, like silver, is sold by the ounce. The price varies. In 1980, the price of gold was over $600 an ounce. In late 1993, the price was about $350 an ounce.*

In the customary or U.S. system of measurement, there are many units. So people refer to tables to check relationships between unfamiliar units. Still, you should know some relationships. Units of length were in the last lesson. Here are units of weight and capacity.

Conversion Equations for Customary Units of Weight and Capacity

For weight:	1 pound (lb) = 16 ounces (oz)
	1 short ton = 2000 pounds
For capacity (liquid or dry volume):	1 cup (c) = 8 fluid ounces (fl oz)
	1 pint (pt) = 2 cups
	1 quart (qt) = 2 pints
	1 gallon (gal) = 4 quarts

Notice that the word *ounce* appears in measures of both weight and capacity. To avoid confusion, the capacity measure is usually given in *fluid ounces.* The weight of one fluid ounce of water is one ounce, but this is not true for every liquid. You can tell whether weight or capacity is being measured by the context of the problem.

Example 1

A punch recipe calls for $3\frac{1}{2}$ pints of different juices. How many 1-cup servings will it make?

Solution

Start with the conversion equation relating pints and cups. 1 pint = 2 cups

Multiply both sides by 3.5. 3.5 × 1 pint = 3.5 × 2 cups

3.5 pints = 7 cups

3.5 pints = 7 cups, so there are 7 servings.

Lesson 3-3 Overview

Broad Goals The goal of this lesson is for students to become comfortable with the various units for weight and capacity used in the customary (U.S.) system.

Perspective Of all the customary units, perhaps the most confusing are those of capacity. They are not discussed as often as the geometric units of length, area, and volume, so students tend not to be as familiar with them. This lesson covers the relationships among fluid ounces, cups, pints, quarts, and gallons. These are quite important to know for cooking, and we believe everyone should know how to follow a recipe.

Every capacity is a volume. We usually use capacity when we want to measure how much something can hold and volume when we think of the space something occupies. If an object has a thin surface and is open at the top, its capacity, when filled, is about equal to its volume.

Sometimes many conversion equations are needed in the same problem.

Example 2

How many cups are in a gallon?

Solution

Start with the conversion equation for gallons and quarts.	1 gallon = 4 quarts
Now convert 4 quarts to pints.	1 quart = 2 pints
Multiply both sides by 4.	4 × 1 quart = 4 × 2 pints
	4 quarts = 8 pints
Lastly, convert 8 pints to cups.	1 pint = 2 cups
	8 × 1 pint = 8 × 2 cups
	8 pints = 16 cups

This shows that 1 gal = 4 qt = 8 pt = 16 cups. There are 16 cups in a gallon.

What's in mineral water? *Mineral water often contains such minerals as calcium, chlorine, iron, magnesium, potassium, sodium, and sulphur. Mineral water is consumed as a beverage and is used to help cure ailments.*

When there are many conversions in the same question, you may find it useful to organize your work as shown in Example 3.

Example 3

Mineral water comes in half-gallon jugs or a six-pack of 12-ounce bottles. Which contains more water? How much more?

Solution

To compare, we need both quantities in the same units. To avoid fractions, choose ounces. The six-pack of 12-ounce bottles contains a total of 6 × 12, or 72 ounces. For the half-gallon jugs, we need to convert gallons to quarts to pints to cups to (fluid) ounces.

1 gallon = 4 quarts, so
$\frac{1}{2}$ gallon = 2 quarts.

Since 1 quart = 2 pints,
2 quarts = 4 pints.

Now 1 pint = 2 cups,
so 4 pints = 8 cups.

Finally, 1 cup = 8 fluid ounces,
so 8 cups = 64 fluid ounces.

This shows that $\frac{1}{2}$ gal = 2 qt = 4 pt = 8c = 64 oz.

The six-pack contains 72 fluid ounces; the jug contains 64 fluid ounces. Thus the six-pack contains 8 fluid ounces more water.

Measurement because most units in both Great Britain and the United States were the same. Then Great Britain officially converted to the metric system, leaving the United States as the only major industrialized country not using the metric system.

In the 1970s, it was thought that the U.S. would convert to the metric system. Standards were set in some states and books were written "100% metric." At that time, many students learned only the metric system. This practice was shortsighted because students had to use the English system outside the classroom. We feel we must train students for the world of tomorrow which uses the metric system, but we cannot ignore their world of today which still uses the customary system, even if we do not like it. For this reason, both systems are used almost equally in this book.

Examples 2 and 3 *Activity 1* in *Optional Activities* below shows how the Substitution Principle can be used in place of the method shown in these examples.

You might ask students to name things that are measured in each unit. For example, what is measured in tons? [Sample responses: truck or road capacity; weight of a car] What is the size of the milk cartons served at school? [Usually a half pint] What unit is used for measuring the gasoline put into cars? [Gallon] What unit is used to measure the oil put into cars? [Quart]

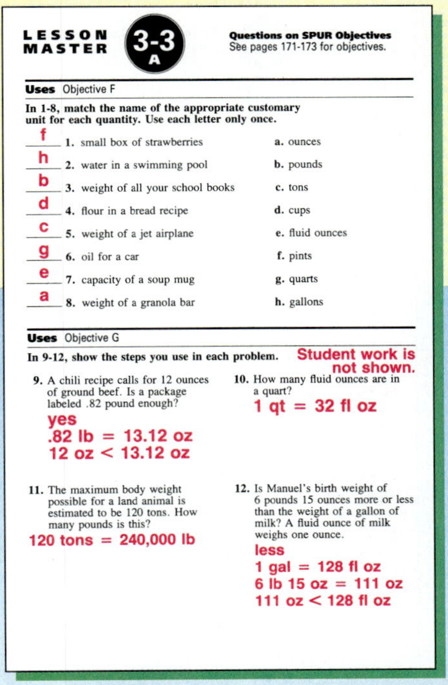

LESSON MASTER 3-3 A **Questions on SPUR Objectives**
See pages 171-173 for objectives.

Uses Objective F

In 1-8, match the name of the appropriate customary unit for each quantity. Use each letter only once.

f 1. small box of strawberries — a. ounces
h 2. water in a swimming pool — b. pounds
b 3. weight of all your school books — c. tons
d 4. flour in a bread recipe — d. cups
c 5. weight of a jet airplane — e. fluid ounces
g 6. oil for a car — f. pints
e 7. capacity of a soup mug — g. quarts
a 8. weight of a granola bar — h. gallons

Uses Objective G

In 9-12, show the steps you use in each problem. Student work is not shown.

9. A chili recipe calls for 12 ounces of ground beef. Is a package labeled .82 pound enough?
yes
.82 lb = 13.12 oz
12 oz < 13.12 oz

10. How many fluid ounces are in a quart?
1 qt = 32 fl oz

11. The maximum body weight possible for a land animal is estimated to be 120 tons. How many pounds is this?
120 tons = 240,000 lb

12. Is Manuel's birth weight of 6 pounds 15 ounces more or less than the weight of a gallon of milk? A fluid ounce of milk weighs one ounce.
less
1 gal = 128 fl oz
6 lb 15 oz = 111 oz
111 oz < 128 fl oz

Optional Activities

Activity 1 You might want to teach the conversions in **Examples 2 and 3** using the Substitution Principle. The work below shows how students can use the procedure to find the number of cups in one gallon (Example 2).

$$\begin{aligned} 1 \text{ gal} &= 4 \text{ qt} \\ &= 4 \cdot 2 \text{ pt} = 8 \text{ pt} \\ &= 8 \cdot 2 \text{ c} = 16 \text{ c} \end{aligned}$$

Activity 2 Using Physical Models
Materials: Balance; weights in ounces and pounds; cup, pint, quart, and gallon containers; other plastic containers; water

After discussing the conversion equations on page 130, you might want to give students an opportunity to weigh classroom objects in ounces and pounds and to find the capacities of various containers.

Additional Examples

1. A punch recipe calls for 3 quarts of orange juice and $1\frac{1}{2}$ quarts of soda water. How many cups of juice will this recipe make? **18 cups**
2. How many pints are in a gallon? **8 pints**
3. You can make 24 ounces of lemonade from a can of frozen concentrate. Is this more or less than a quart of lemonade? How much more or less? **Less, 8 ounces less**
4. A large truck weighs 12 tons. Should it be driven over a bridge with a posted weight limit of 20,000 pounds? **No**

Notes on Questions

Students might use **Teaching Aid 30** as a reference as they do their homework. It provides the conversion equations.

As the class discusses the questions, stress the importance of showing how the answers are derived. Explain that if this pattern is established early, it can make some of the more difficult questions easier to answer.

Question 3 To help students remember the conversion equation for gallons and quarts, explain that the name *quart* comes from the fact that it is a "quart-er" of a gallon.

LESSON MASTER 3-3 B Questions on SPUR Objectives

Uses Objective F: Give appropriate units for measuring weight and capacity in the U.S. system of measurement.

In 1-8, match the name of the appropriate customary unit for each quantity. Use each letter only once.

e	1. capacity of a laundry tub	a. fluid ounce
h	2. weight of a train car	b. cup
f	3. weight of a small bag of pretzels	c. pint
a	4. capacity of a soup can	d. quart
c	5. small box of raspberries	e. gallon
g	6. child's weight	f. ounce
d	7. oil for an automobile	g. pound
b	8. capacity of a chili bowl	h. ton

***Multiple choice.* In 9-12, choose the unit of measure that you would use to measure each item.**

9. capacity of a bucket (a) gallon (b) ounce — a
10. weight of a cat (a) ounce (b) pound — b
11. capacity of a cologne bottle (a) quart (b) fluid ounce — b
12. weight of a couch (a) pound (b) ton — a

QUESTIONS

Covering the Reading

In 1 and 2, consider the customary system of measurement.

1. Name five units in which an amount of milk could be measured. **cups, fluid ounces, pints, quarts, gallons**
2. Name three units of weight. **pounds, ounces, short tons**

In 3–6, copy and complete the conversion equation.

3. 1 gallon = __?__ quarts **4**
4. 1 quart = __?__ pints **2**
5. 1 lb = __?__ oz **16**
6. 1 short ton = __?__ pounds **2000**
7. How many cups are in 3 quarts? **12 cups**

In 8–11, do the conversions.

8. 7 tons to pounds **14,000 lb**
9. 8.3 gallons to quarts **33.2 qt**
10. $1\frac{1}{2}$ cups to fluid ounces **12 fluid oz**
11. $1\frac{1}{2}$ pounds to ounces **24 oz**
12. What sequence of conversions would change gallons to ounces? **gallons to quarts, quarts to pints, pints to cups, cups to ounces**

Applying the Mathematics

13. In Great Britain, one *gross ton* = one *long ton* = 2240 pounds. The heaviest ship ever built is the oil tanker *Jahre Viking* which weighs 622,420 long tons when fully loaded. How many pounds does the *Jahre Viking* weigh? **about 1,394,200,000 lb**
14. A quart contains how many fluid ounces? **32 fluid oz**

In 15–17, name the appropriate customary unit for each quantity.

15. the amount of flour in a recipe for cookies **cup**
16. the weight of an elephant **short ton or pound**
17. the amount of gas in a car gas tank **gallon**
18. You have a one-pint measuring vessel. How many times should you use it to fill a 10-gallon tank? **80 times**
19. A warning sign on a bridge is at the right. Can a truck weighing 8000 pounds safely cross the bridge? **No**
20. Which weighs more, a quarter-pound or a 6-ounce hamburger? **6-ounce hamburger**

Adapting to Individual Needs

Extra Help

Students who need extra help with this lesson will benefit from using the materials suggested in *Activity 2* in *Optional Activities* to verify the relationships shown on page 130 and then to measure weights and capacities.

English Language Development

Use pictures of common objects to reinforce students' recognition of customary units of weight and capacity. Students can participate by identifying the pictures appropriate for each unit. For example, students might associate pounds with a picture of a frozen turkey and quart with an orange-juice container.

21. Refer to the cartoon below. What should the chief cook tell Zero?
A gallon is not a unit of length; it is a unit of volume or capacity.

Question 12 Writing You may wish to ask several students to read the answers aloud.

Question 13 If students use a scientific calculator with an 8-digit display, their answers will appear in scientific notation: 1.3942×10^9.

The names of some units can be confusing. For example, there are various kinds of tons. One metric ton is 1000 kilograms or about 2200 pounds. This is not the same as one short ton (2000 pounds), but it is close to one gross ton (2240 pounds). The unit *long ton* is synonymous with *gross ton.*

Adapting to Individual Needs

Challenge

You might want to have students **use physical models or draw a picture** to show how to solve this problem: Suppose you have two containers. One holds exactly five cups and the other holds exactly three cups. How can you use these two containers to measure exactly four cups of water?

[Fill the 5-cup container. Use the water in it to fill the 3-cup container, and then empty the 3-cup container. Pour the 2 cups left in the 5-cup container into the 3-cup container. Refill the 5-cup container. Use this to fill the 3-cup container which already holds 2 cups. Then 4 cups will remain in the 5-cup container.]

▸ **LESSON MASTER 3-3 B** *page 2*

Uses Objective G: Convert weight and capacity units within the U.S. system of measurement.

In 13-18, show the steps in each problem.

13. How many 1-cup servings are there in $3\frac{1}{2}$ quarts of soup?
$3\frac{1}{2}$ qt = 14 c
14 1-cup servings

14. A truck hauls 6 tons of gravel. How many pounds is this?
6 tons = 12,000 lb
12,000 pounds

15. A recipe calls for 10 ounces of cheddar cheese. Is a $\frac{1}{2}$-pound chunk enough for the recipe?
$\frac{1}{2}$ lb = 8 oz
No, 8 ounces < 10 ounces.

16. Lanie filled her car with 10.7 gallons of gas. How many quarts is this?
10.7 gal = 42.8 qt
42.8 quarts

17. How many 1-ounce squares of fudge can be cut from $2\frac{1}{4}$ pounds?
$2\frac{1}{4}$ lb = 36 oz
36 squares

18. Which is more, 8 quarts of cream or 13 pints of cream?
8 qt = 16 pt
8 quarts is more.

Review Objectives A and E, Lessons 2-1, 2-2, and 2-4

In 19-24, write each product as a decimal.

19. $4 \times 1{,}000$ **4,000**

20. $.377 \times 100{,}000$ **37,700**

21. $.01 \times 648.3$ **6.483**

22. $0.52 \times .0001$ **.000052**

23. $10{,}000{,}000 \times 64.78$ **647,800,000**

24. $\frac{1}{1{,}000{,}000} \times 5{,}000$ **.005**

Follow-up for Lesson 3-3

Practice

For more questions on the SPUR objectives, use **Lesson Master 3-3A** (shown on page 131) or **Lesson Master 3-3B** (shown on pages 132–133).

Assessment

Quiz A quiz covering Lessons 3-1 through 3-3 is provided in the *Assessment Sourcebook.*

Group Assessment You might have each student write three conversion questions and find the answers. Then pairs of students can exchange questions (not the answers) with each student working his or her partner's problems. They should discuss any differences that arise in answers. [Questions show comprehension and variety. Answers are correct and clear. Discussion reveals understanding.]

Extension

You might have students investigate the relationship between *teaspoons* and *tablespoons* and name things measured with them. [1 fl oz = 2 tablespoons; 1 tablespoon = 3 teaspoons; sample responses: spices and extracts, butter, and medicines]

Project Update At this time students who selected Project 3, *Weighing a Collection*, on page 167, can decide on the item they are going to weigh and begin the project.

Review

22. Convert 6 yards $2\frac{1}{2}$ feet to inches. *(Lesson 3-2)* **246 in.**

23. How many feet are in a half mile? *(Lesson 3-2)* **2640 ft**

24. **a.** Find a door. Measure its height to the nearest inch.
b. Will 6-foot 6-inch Michael Jordan be able to walk through without ducking? *(Lessons 3-1, 3-2)* **a) Sample: 80 in.; b) Sample: 6′6″= 78 in., so Jordan could go through this doorway without ducking.**

25. To the nearest $\frac{1}{16}$ of an inch, how long is this pencil? *(Lesson 3-1)* **$4\frac{13}{16}$ in.**

Figures appear smaller than actual size in Teacher's Edition.

In 26 and 27, write the number in scientific notation. *(Lessons 2-3, 2-9)*

26. 117,490,000—the estimated population of Pakistan in 1991 **1.1749×10^8**

27. 0.013837 in.—the length of 1 point in typesetting **1.3837×10^{-2}**

28. 0% of the 500 students in a school are traveling to a game by bus. How many students is this? *(Lesson 2-5)* **0**

In 29–32, calculate in your head. *(Lessons 2-1, 2-4)*

29. 0.052 × 100 **5.2**

30. 3.446 × .0001 **0.0003446**

31. 15.36 × .1 **1.536**

32. 640 × 10,000 **6,400,000**

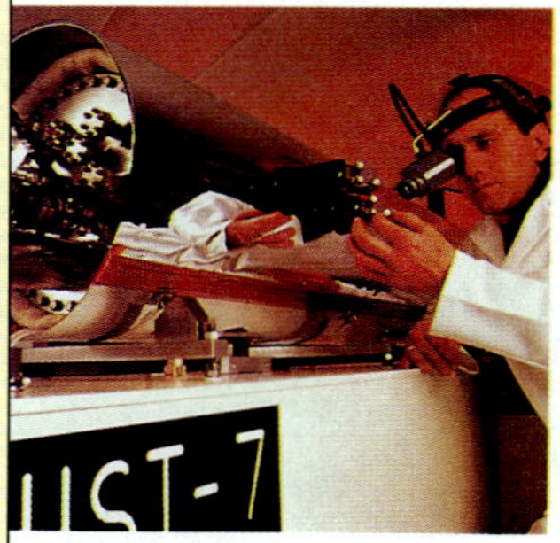

The time is right. *The National Institute of Standards of Technology has an atomic clock so accurate that it will neither gain nor lose one second in a million years. The clock is shown here with one of the developers, John P. Lowe. He is wearing an eyepiece that makes the clock's laser light visible.*

Exploration

33. All systems of measurement in common use today have the same units for time: 1 hour = 60 minutes, 1 minute = 60 seconds.

a. How many seconds are in an hour? **3600 seconds/hr**

b. How many seconds are in a day? **86,400 seconds/day**

c. How many seconds are in a 365-day year? **31,536,000 seconds/yr**

d. How many minutes are in a year? **525,600 minutes/yr**

e. If your heart beats 70 times a minute, how many times does it beat in a year? **36,792,000 times/yr**

f. If a heart beats 70 times a minute, how many times will it beat in 79 years, the average lifetime of a woman in the U.S.? **2.9066×10^9 or about 2,906,600,000 times**

34. An old song goes, "I love you, a bushel and a peck, a bushel and a peck and a hug around your neck, a hug around your neck and a barrel and a heap, a barrel and a heap and I'm talking in my sleep about you. . . ." Three units of capacity of fruits and grains are in the words to the song. What are they and how are they related? **A peck is 8 dry quarts; a bushel is 4 pecks or 32 dry quarts; a barrel is about 105 dry quarts. (A heap is an informal unit meaning "a lot.")**

Setting Up Lesson 3-4

Ask students to memorize the conversion equations presented on pages 135–136 of Lesson 3-4.

LESSON

3-4

The Metric System of Measurement

Countries Still Using Customary Units

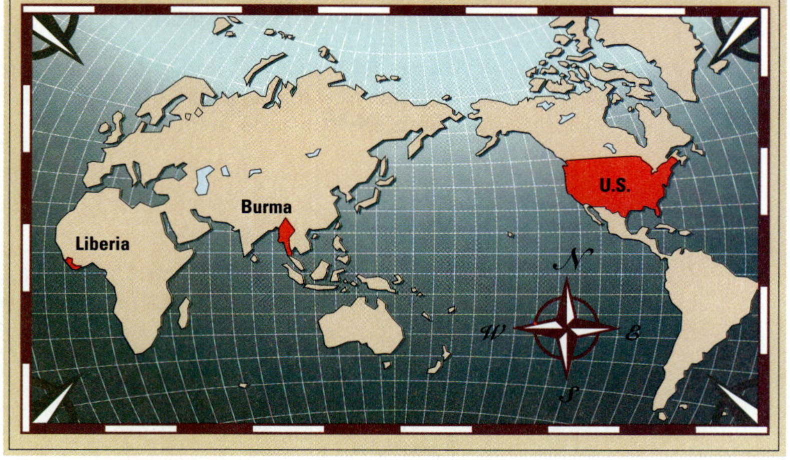

Not much company. *The only countries still using the customary system are Burma, Liberia, and the U.S. But even in the U.S., all new NASA projects and $1 billion in new construction for the General Services Administration use metrics.*

Why Was the Metric System Developed?

The U.S. system of measurement has three major weaknesses. First, the many units have names that do not help you know how the units are related. Second, the units are multiples of each other in no consistent manner. To see this, look again at the conversion equations in Lessons 3-2 and 3-3. You see the numbers 12, 3, 5280, 16, 2000, 8, 2, and 4. Third, in the decimal system these numbers are not as easy to work with as powers of 10 such as 100, 1000, 10,000, or .1, .01, and .001.

Other older measurement systems had the same weaknesses. So, in the late 1700s, a movement arose to design a better measurement system. The system devised is called the **international** or **metric system of measurement.** It is based on the decimal system and is by far the most widely used system of measurement in the world.

Some Important Units in the Metric System

Metric prefixes have fixed meanings related to place values in the decimal system. The table on page 137 identifies many of the prefixes. You have seen the three most common prefixes in units for measuring length: kilo- (1000), centi- $\left(\frac{1}{100} \text{ or } .01\right)$, and milli- $\left(\frac{1}{1000} \text{ or } .001\right)$.

The base unit of length is the **meter,** abbreviated **m.**

$$1 \text{ kilometer} = 1 \text{ km} = 1000 \text{ m}$$
$$1 \text{ centimeter} = 1 \text{ cm} = \frac{1}{100}, \text{ or } .01 \text{ m}$$
$$1 \text{ millimeter} = 1 \text{ mm} = \frac{1}{1000}, \text{ or } .001 \text{ m}$$

Lesson 3-4

Objectives

F Give appropriate units for measuring mass, length, and capacity in the metric system of measurement.
H Convert within the metric system.
N Give countries and approximate date of origin of the metric system.

Resources

From the ***Teacher's Resource File***

- Lesson Master 3-4A or 3-4B
- Answer Master 3-4
- Teaching Aids
  26 Warm-up
  31 Metric Units of Measure
- Technology Sourcebook
  Computer Master 3

Additional Resources

- Visuals for Teaching Aids 26, 31
- Spreadsheet Workshop

Teaching Lesson 3-4

Warm-up

Work with a partner. Choose the most sensible measure and explain your reasoning.

1. The length of a football field c
   a. 1100 cm **b.** 11 km **c.** 90 m
2. The capacity of a picnic cooler a
   a. 20 L **b.** 2400 cm **c.** 80 g
3. The area of the front of an envelope a
   a. 240 cm^2 **b.** 400 mm^2 **c.** 1 m^2
4. The mass of a shoe is about b
   a. 4 kg **b.** 0.4 kg **c.** 40 g

Lesson 3-4 Overview

Broad Goals The ability to deal with the language and common units of the metric system is the major goal of this lesson.

Perspective The gram is technically a measure of mass, not of weight; but throughout the world it is used as both in everyday affairs because, for practical purposes, mass and weight are proportional on the surface of the earth. The difference between mass and weight is easy to describe in this space age. An astronaut in a space lab is virtually weightless but he or she still has the same mass as on Earth. Mass measures the amount of "stuff" in an object; weight is a force. The weight of an object is the amount of gravity acting on that object times its mass. Astronauts have the same mass whether they are on Earth or in space. In space, because less gravity is acting on them, astronauts weigh much less than they do on Earth.

We abbreviate liter with a capital L. Students may see the abbreviation l (lower case el) elsewhere; we do not use it because it is very easily confused with the number 1 (one).

Notes on Reading

Even if students have read this lesson, it is so compact and so important that you might wish to have students read all but the table aloud in class. After each paragraph is read, ask if the ideas are clear.

You might use *Activity 2* in *Optional Activities* below to give students an opportunity to measure using metric units of mass and capacity.

Examples 1 and 2 These examples apply the technique used in previous lessons, the Multiplication Property of Equality. *Activity 1* in *Optional Activities* below shows how the Substitution Principle can be used instead.

The table on page 137 may strike students as being formidable, but emphasize that only the units in boldface are used consistently in the problems in this book. In reviewing the table, point out that the columns are in the order of place values. Note that the top half of the table includes all place values, but the bottom half only has a prefix for every three places.

Units of mass are multiples of the **gram,** abbreviated **g.** In everyday usage, the gram is also used to measure weight.

$$1 \text{ kilogram} = 1 \text{ kg} = 1000 \text{ g}$$
$$1 \text{ milligram} = 1 \text{ mg} = \tfrac{1}{1000}, \text{ or } .001, \text{ g}$$

The **liter,** abbreviated **L,** and milliliter (**mL**) are used to measure capacity or volume. Soft drinks today are often sold in 2-liter bottles. Smaller amounts are measured in milliliters.

$$1 \text{ milliliter} = 1\text{mL} = \tfrac{1}{1000}, \text{ or } .001, \text{ L}$$

Converting Within the Metric System

All conversions within the metric system can be done without a calculator because the multiples are powers of 10.

Example 1

How many meters are in 3.46 kilometers?

Solution

Start with the conversion equation for 1 km. It is easy to remember because kilo- means 1000. 1 km = 1000 m

Multiply both sides by 3.46. 3.46 x 1 km = 3.46 x 1000 m

Calculate. 3.46 km = 3460 m

Example 2

Change 89 milligrams to grams.

Solution

Start with the conversion equation for 1 mg.

Remember that milli- means $\frac{1}{1000}$ or .001. 1 mg = .001 g

Multiply both sides by 89. 89 x 1 mg = 89 x .001 g

89 mg = .089 g

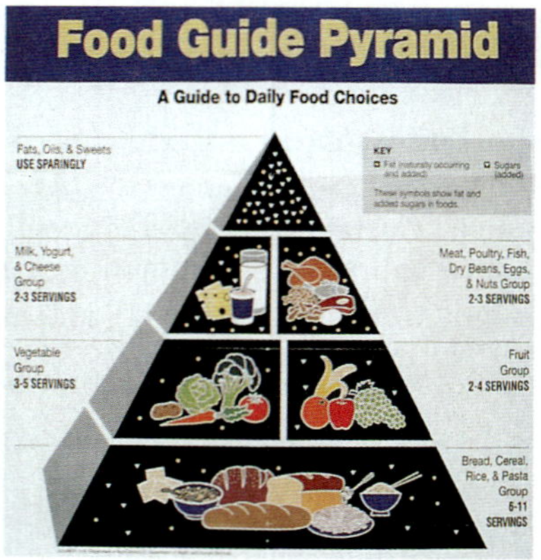

Every gram counts. *The Food Guide Pyramid suggests that everyone eat a variety of foods each day. Particularly good news for cereal lovers is that cereals are highly recommended in the grains category, as long as they contain no more than 2 grams of fat or 6 grams of sugar.*

Optional Activities

Activity 1 You might want to introduce **Examples 1 and 2** using the Substitution Principle.

Example 1 Substitute 1000 m for km.
3.46 km = 3.46 · 1000 m = 3460 m

Example 2 Substitute .001 g for mg.
89 mg = 89 · .001g = .089 g

Activity 2 Using Physical Models
Materials: Balance scale, metric weights, eyedropper, liter measure, plastic containers

After discussing the metric units of mass and capacity on page 137, you might have students **work in groups** to find the weights and capacities of different objects. This will give students who are not familiar with metric measures an opportunity to use them and become more familiar with them.

Activity 3 Technology Connection *Technology Sourcebook, Computer Master 3,* has students explore conversions among metric units. Students use the *Spreadsheet Workshop* to enter measurements and conversion formulas.

Many of the questions refer to this table. You should study it before reading the questions. The most commonly used units are in bold type.

The International or Metric System of Measurement

place value	thousands	hundreds	tens	ones	tenths	hundredths	thousandths
power of 10	10^3	10^2	10^1	10^0	10^{-1}	10^{-2}	10^{-3}
unit of length	**kilometer**	hectometer	dekameter	**meter**	decimeter	**centimeter**	**millimeter**
unit of mass	**kilogram**	hectogram	dekagram	**gram**	decigram	centigram	**milligram**
unit of capacity	kiloliter	hectoliter	dekaliter	**liter**	deciliter	centiliter	**milliliter**
Some Other Prefixes:							
place value	trillions	billions	millions		millionths	billionths	trillionths
power of 10	10^{12}	10^9	10^6		10^{-6}	10^{-9}	10^{-12}
prefix	tera-	giga-	mega-		micro-	nano-	pico-

Some Common Units:

Length: **kilometer (km)**—used for distances between towns and cities. 1 km ≈ 0.62 mi. The length of 10 football fields is about 1 kilometer.
meter (m)—used for rooms, heights, and fabrics. A doorknob is about 1 m high.
centimeter (cm)—used for small items. The diameter of an aspirin tablet is about 1 cm.
millimeter (mm)—used for very small items. The thickness of a dime is about 1 mm.

Mass: **kilogram (kg)**—used for heavier weights. A quart of milk weighs about 1 kg.
gram (g)—used for light items. An aspirin tablet weighs about 1 g.
milligram (mg)—used for very light items, such as vitamin content in food. A speck of sawdust weighs about 1 mg.

Capacity: **liter (L)**—used for soft drinks and other liquids. 1 liter ≈ 1.06 qt.
milliliter (mL)—used for small amounts such as perfume. 1 teaspoon ≈ 5 mL.

QUESTIONS

Covering the Reading

1. Name two weaknesses of the U.S. system of measurement. **The names of units do not tell how units are related; not easy to work with.**
2. Another name for the metric system is __?__. **international system of measurement**
3. Name three common units of length in the metric system. **meter, kilometer, centimeter**
4. Name three common units of mass in the metric system. **gram, kilogram, milligram**
5. Name two common units of capacity in the metric system. **liter, milliliter**

As students work in the metric system, they will soon appreciate the relationships among the units and the ease of converting from one unit to another using only multiples of 10. Stress that the common units accompanying the table give a useful frame of reference for relative size. Students should memorize the prefixes used in the metric system. To help them do this, you might want to have them complete the table on **Teaching Aid 31**.

Additional Examples

1. Convert 105 centimeters to meters. **1.05 m**
2. Convert 17.7 kilograms to grams. **17,700 g**
3. How many milliliters are in 1.5 liters? **1500 mL**
4. Give a sensible metric unit of measure for each item.
   a. weight of a dog **kg**
   b. capacity of a pool **kL**
   c. length of a pencil **cm**
   d. weight of a granola bar **g**
   e. capacity of a teaspoon **mL**

Notes on Questions

Questions 1–5 Use these questions to review the basic ideas of the lesson.

LESSON MASTER 3-4 A

Questions on SPUR Objectives
See pages 171-173 for objectives.

Uses Objectives F and H

In 1-4, fill in the chart. Do as much as possible from memory.

	Place Value	Thousands	Ones	Hundredths	Thousandths
1.	powers of ten	10^3	10^0	10^{-2}	10^{-3}
2.	unit of length	kilometer	meter	centimeter	millimeter
3.	unit of mass	kilogram	gram	centigram	milligram
4.	unit of capacity	kiloliter	liter	centiliter	milliliter

In 5-8, give a reasonable metric unit to measure each quantity.

5. amount of liquid in an eyedropper **milliliter**
6. the distance from Moscow to St. Petersburg **kilometer**
7. amount of salt in a serving of cereal **milligram**
8. capacity of a car's gas tank **liter**

In 9-12, show the steps used to answer each question. **Student work is not shown.**

9. How many grams are in $2\frac{1}{4}$ kg? **$2\frac{1}{4}$ kg = 2250 g**
10. Convert 650 mL to liters. **650 mL = .65 L**
11. How many meters are in 7.5 km? **7.5 km = 7500 m**
12. A bicycle wheel covers 2 m in one revolution. How many times will the wheel turn in a 10-km ride? **$10{,}000 \times \frac{1}{2}$ rev. = 5,000 rev.**

Culture Objective N

13. When and why was the metric system developed? **About 1760 the industrial revolution began, and accurate measurement was needed. The metric system, established in France in 1795, became legal in the U.S. in 1866.**

Notes on Questions

Question 24 Health Connection For people to reach and maintain healthy weight levels, the Dietary Guidelines for Americans recommend a diet that is high in carbohydrates and low in fat, sugar, and sodium. The Guidelines also recommend eating foods that provide adequate levels of vitamins, minerals, and fiber. You might suggest that students find more information about daily requirements for people their age.

Question 28 History Connection Hiroshima was founded in the 16th century, and it became a Japanese military center. It was also the first city in the world to be struck by an atomic bomb. Most of the city was destroyed, and more than 70,000 people died. Some students might want to research facts about Hiroshima today.

Question 29 The *second* is both the customary and metric unit of time. Parts of seconds, such as milliseconds and nanoseconds, use metric prefixes, but multiples of seconds (minutes and hours) do not.

Question 42 Some dictionaries and almanacs have tables that list monetary units from many countries. In *Webster's Ninth New Collegiate Dictionary*, the only unit that is not metric is the ouguiya, which in Mauritania equals 5 khoums.

LESSON MASTER 3-4 B — Questions on SPUR Objectives

Uses Objective F: Give appropriate units for measuring mass, length, and capacity in the metric system of measurement.

In 1-8, give a reasonable metric unit to measure each quantity.

1. the distance from Rome to Venice — kilometer
2. amount of liquid in a cologne sample — millimeter
3. amount of salt in a cup of soup — milligram
4. capacity of a punch bowl — liter
5. weight of a watermelon — kilogram
6. dimensions of a credit card — centimeter
7. length of a driveway — meter
8. weight of a small box of raisins — gram

In 9-12, fill in the chart. Do as much as possible from memory.

	Place Value	Thousands	Ones	Hundredths	Thousandths
9.	power of ten	10^3	10^0	10^{-2}	10^{-3}
10.	unit of length	kilometer	meter	centimeter	millimeter
11.	unit of mass	kilogram	gram	centigram	milligram
12.	unit of capacity	kiloliter	liter	centiliter	milliliter

In 13-16, match the prefix with the power of ten.

c 13. mega- a. 10^9
d 14. micro- b. 10^{-9}
b 15. nano- c. 10^6
a 16. giga- d. 10^{-6}

In 6–8, give the meaning of the prefix.

6. kilo- 1000 **7.** milli- $\frac{1}{1000}$ **8.** centi- $\frac{1}{100}$

In 9–11, write the abbreviation for the unit.

9. centimeter cm **10.** kilogram kg **11.** milliliter mL

In 12–17, convert.

12. 90 cm to meters .90 m **13.** 345 mL to liters .345 L **14.** 5 kg to grams 5000 g

15. 10 km to meters 10,000 m **16.** 48 mm to meters 0.048 m **17.** 60 mg to grams 0.06 g

18. Name something weighing approximately the given weight. Samples:
a. 1 kg quart of milk **b.** 1 g an aspirin tablet **c.** 1 mg a speck of sawdust

19. Name something about as long as the given length. Samples:
a. 1 m height of a doorknob **b.** 1 km about 10 football fields **c.** 1 mm thickness of a dime

20. Name something with about as much liquid in it as 1 liter. a quart of milk

In 21–23, give the power of 10 associated with the prefix.

21. centi- 10^{-2} **22.** milli- 10^{-3} **23.** kilo- 10^3

What country? *Signs like this one are posted in Australia, the native home of koala bears.*

Applying the Mathematics

In 24–26, choose the one best answer.

24. A high school freshman might weigh:
(a) 50 g (b) 50 mg (c) 50 kg (d) 500 g (c)

25. A high school freshman might be how tall?
(a) .7 m (b) 1.7 m (c) 2.2 m (d) 5.6 m (b)

26. A common dimension of camera film is:
(a) 35 km (b) 35 cm (c) 35 m (d) 35 mm (d)

27. Should most students be able to walk one kilometer in an hour? Explain your answer. Yes, 1 km is about .6 mile or 1056 yards. 1056 yd/hr or 53 ft/min is a leisurely pace.

28. The atomic bomb that the U.S. exploded on Hiroshima, Japan, in 1945 had a force equivalent to about 12.5 kilotons of TNT. How many tons is this? 12,500 tons

29. A millisecond is how many seconds? $\frac{1}{1000}$, or .001, second

30. The United States was the first country in the world (1792) to have a money system based on decimals. In this system:

$$1 \text{ dollar} = 100 \text{ cents}$$

$$\text{or equivalently, } 1 \text{ cent} = \frac{1}{100}, \text{ or } .01, \text{ dollar.}$$

a. Convert 56¢ to dollars. 0.56 dollar

b. Convert $13.49 to cents. 1349 cents

c. On September 17, 1983, UPI reported that a truck loaded with 7.6 million new pennies overturned on Interstate 80 in the mountains north of Sacramento, California. How many dollars is this? $76,000

Adapting to Individual Needs

Extra Help

Some students might find it easier to learn the metric units from this simplified chart. As they read each metric measure aloud, have them suggest things they might measure in the unit.

	thousands 1000	ones 1	hundredths .01	thousandths .001
length	**kilo**meter (km)	meter (m)	**centi**meter (cm)	**milli**meter (mm)
weight (mass)	**kilo**gram (kg)	gram (g)	**centi**gram (cg)	**milli**gram (mg)
capacity	**kilo**liter (kL)	liter (L)	**centi**liter (cL)	**milli**liter (mL)

Review

31. You have a 1-cup container. How many times would you have to use it to fill a half-gallon jug? *(Lesson 3-3)* **8 times**

In 32–35, complete each with the correct symbol <, =, or >. *(Lessons 3-2, 3-3)*

32. $2\frac{1}{2}$ pints __?__ 4 quarts **<** **33.** $3\frac{1}{2}$ feet __?__ 2 yards **<**

34. 2850 feet __?__ 1 mile **<** **35.** 1 lb __?__ 16 oz **=**

36. a. Find the length of the segment below to the nearest 0.1 cm. **1.7 cm**

Figures appear smaller than actual size in Teacher's Edition.

b. Write the length in millimeters. *(Lesson 3-1)* **17 mm**

37. Which measurement is more precise, one made to the nearest $\frac{1}{16}$ of an inch or one made to the nearest $\frac{1}{10}$ of an inch? Explain why. *(Lessons 1-4, 3-1)* **$\frac{1}{16}$ inch is more precise because $\frac{1}{16}$ inch is a smaller interval than $\frac{1}{10}$ inch.**

38. Order from smallest to largest: 10^{-4} 0 $\frac{1}{100}$. *(Lessons 1-2, 2-8)* **0, 10^{-4}, $\frac{1}{100}$**

39. The results of a survey of teenagers are shown at the right. Suppose there are 30 teenagers in your class, and they are representative of the students in the survey. How many of them would you expect to own each item?

Survey Results

	Percent of teenagers who own:
bicycle	85%
camera	80%
designer clothes	72%
TV set	52%

a. bicycle **25 or 26**

b. camera **24**

c. designer clothes *(Lesson 2-5)* **22**

40. Order from smallest to largest: 5^2 2^5 10^1. *(Lesson 2-2)* **10^1, 5^2, 2^5**

41. Write $\frac{2}{1000}$ cm, the approximate diameter of a cloud droplet, as a decimal. *(Lesson 1-8)* **0.002 cm**

42. a) Answers may vary. Sample: France, Belgium, Ivory Coast

b) Answers may vary. Sample: Mexico, Cuba, Bolivia

e) Answers may vary. Sample: Jordan, Kuwait, Iraq

Exploration

42. Almost every country in the world today has a decimal money system. Given are relationships between monetary units. Name a country in which these units are used.

a. 1 franc = 100 centimes **b.** 1 centavo = 100 pesos

c. 1 ruble = 100 kopecks **Russia** **d.** 1 yuan = 100 fen **China**

e. 1 dinar = 1000 fils **f.** 1 rupee = 100 paise **India**

g. 1 cedi = 100 pesewas **Zambia**

a, b, e) See above left.

Follow-up for Lesson 3-4

Practice

For more questions on SPUR objectives, use **Lesson Master 3-4A** (shown on page 137) or **Lesson Master 3-4B** (shown on pages 138–139).

Assessment

Oral Communication Show students objects and have them describe the metric units they would use for measuring them. For example, an envelope might suggest measuring the length in centimeters and the weight in grams. [Responses indicate level of understanding and facility with metric measures.]

Extension

Give students the following words which are related to metric prefixes: *centenarian, centennial, bicentennial, centigrade, century, decapod, decade, decagon, decathlon, millennium, kilowatt, kilowatt-hour, kilohertz.* Ask them to guess the meaning of each word based on their knowledge of the metric prefixes, and then have them check the meanings in a dictionary.

Project Update Project 1, *Metric Units,* on page 167, can be started at this time.

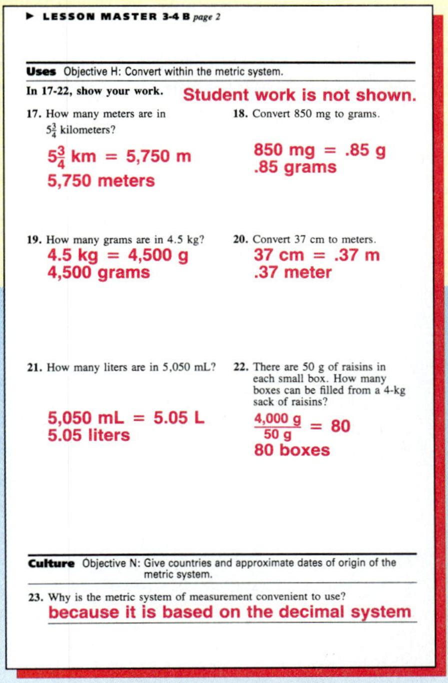

▸ LESSON MASTER 3-4 B *page 2*

Uses Objective H: Convert within the metric system.

In 17-22, show your work. **Student work is not shown.**

17. How many meters are in $5\frac{3}{4}$ kilometers? **$5\frac{3}{4}$ km = 5,750 m; 5,750 meters**

18. Convert 850 mg to grams. **850 mg = .85 g; .85 grams**

19. How many grams are in 4.5 kg? **4.5 kg = 4,500 g; 4,500 grams**

20. Convert 37 cm to meters. **37 cm = .37 m; .37 meter**

21. How many liters are in 5,050 mL? **5,050 mL = 5.05 L; 5.05 liters**

22. There are 50 g of raisins in each small box. How many boxes can be filled from a 4-kg sack of raisins? **$\frac{4,000 \text{ g}}{50 \text{ g}}$ = 80; 80 boxes**

Culture Objective N: Give countries and approximate dates of origin of the metric system.

23. Why is the metric system of measurement convenient to use? **because it is based on the decimal system**

Adapting to Individual Needs

English Language Development
Most students from other countries are more familiar with the metric system than the students who have grown up in this country. This is a good time to let these students help their classmates.

Setting Up Lesson 3-5

Materials If you assign Exploration Question 34 on page 144, have students bring empty cereal boxes to class. For Question 35 and the Extension activity, you may want to have a currency conversion table from a newspaper.

Lesson 3-5

Objectives

I Convert between different systems.

Resources

From the ***Teacher's Resource File***
- Lesson Master 3-5A or 3-5B
- Answer Master 3-5
- Teaching Aids
  26 Warm-up
  32 Conversions to Know
- Technology Sourcebook
  Calculator Master 6

Additional Resources
- Visuals for Teaching Aids 26, 32
- Cereal boxes

Teaching Lesson 3-5

Warm-up

Diagnostic You have one minute to fill in the blanks.

1. 1 gal = _____ qt **4**
2. 1 km = _____ m **1000**
3. 1 mi = _____ ft **5280**
4. 1 in. = _____ cm **2.54**
5. 1 mg = _____ g **.001**
6. 1 mL = _____ L **.001**

Notes on Reading

Using the three conversion relations given at the bottom of page 140, along with the fact that 1 in. = 2.54 cm exactly, any lengths, weights, or capacities can be converted between the systems.

LESSON

3-5 *Converting Between Systems*

A sporting chance. *Wrestlers in the Grand Sumo tournament at Kokugikan Hall, Tokyo, are known for their strong, immense bodies. Seven sumo wrestlers (rikishi) together, at 135 kg (about 300 lb) or more each, weigh more than a ton.*

Because using the metric system is so easy, almost every country in the world has adopted it. In the United States, science, medicine, and photography are almost all metric. Carpentry and other building trades usually use the U.S. system. The trend is to use metric units more often as time goes by. Some automobiles are manufactured with parts that conform to metric units. Others use customary units. Auto mechanics need tools for each system.

With two systems in use today, it is occasionally necessary to change from units in one system to units in the other. This change is called *converting between systems.* Converting between systems is like converting within one system. However, the numbers are usually not whole numbers.

Converting from Metric Units to Customary Units

You already know 1 inch = 2.54 centimeters exactly. Other conversions between the metric and U.S. systems are approximate. Remember that ≈ means "is approximately equal to."

Conversion Relations for Metric and U.S. Units

1 km	≈	.62 mi
1 kilogram	≈	2.2 pounds
1 liter	≈	1.06 quarts

Conversions may be done with these approximate relationships just as they are done with the exact relationships you saw in earlier lessons.

Lesson 3-5 Overview

Broad Goals One goal of this lesson is for students to be able to relate units in the metric and customary systems. Another is for them to be able to convert back and forth between the systems when necessary.

Perspective There are a number of reasons for conversion between systems, but four are fundamental. First, as long as the United States continues to use two systems, people need to know how to convert from one to the other. Second, conversion helps students conceptualize the metric system. Third, traditional measures exist even in countries that are metric (such as barrels of oil or picas to measure type size). Fourth, the monetary systems of countries differ even when their measurement systems are the same.

We recommend thinking metric when using metric units, thinking U.S. when using U.S. units, and occasionally thinking about the relationships between the two.

These Swedish girls might write to their pen pals and describe their enjoyment of St. Lucia Day, the Festival of Light.

Example 1

Your Swedish pen pal writes you that she weighs 50 kg. How much is this in pounds?

Solution

Start with the conversion relation relating pounds and kilograms. $1 \text{ kg} \approx 2.2 \text{ pounds}$

Multiply both sides by 50. $50 \times 1 \text{ kg} \approx 50 \times 2.2 \text{ pounds}$

$50 \text{ kg} \approx 110 \text{ pounds}$

Example 2

A 10K race is ten kilometers long. How long is this in miles?

Solution

Start with the conversion relation between kilometers and miles. $1 \text{ km} \approx 0.62 \text{ mi}$

Multiply both sides by 10. $10 \times 1 \text{ km} \approx 10 \times 0.62 \text{ mi}$

Compute. $10 \text{ km} \approx 6.2 \text{ mi}$

A 10K race is about 6.2 miles long.

You can use approximate and exact conversions in the same problem.

Example 3

Soft drinks often come in 2-liter bottles. About how many fluid ounces are in a 2-liter bottle?

Solution

The only conversion relation for capacity that you have seen is between liters and quarts.

$1 \text{ L} \approx 1.06 \text{ qt}$

Multiply both sides by 2.

$2 \text{ L} \approx 2.12 \text{ qt}$

Now change 2.12 quarts to fluid ounces. This is like what was done in Lesson 3-3.

Since $1 \text{ qt} = 2 \text{ pt}$,
$2.12 \text{ qt} = 4.24 \text{ pt}$.

Since $1 \text{ pt} = 2 \text{ c}$,
$4.24 \text{ pt} = 8.48 \text{ c}$.

Since $1 \text{ c} = 8 \text{ fl oz}$,
$8.48 \text{ c} = 67.84 \text{ fl oz}$.

So 2 liters ≈ 2.12 quarts = 4.24 pints = 8.48 cups = 67.48 ounces. There are about 67.48 fluid ounces in a 2-liter bottle.

A brief teacher-directed discussion is appropriate for pointing out the key difference between the conversions in this lesson and those in previous lessons, namely that some of the conversion relationships in this lesson are approximate. Even though they can be treated for most purposes as if they were exact, one must be careful when multiplying by large numbers, because any differences are magnified. For instance, 1 kg is not exactly 2.2 lb, but closer to 2.204623 lb. If the conversion 1 kg ≈ 2.2 lb is used, then 1 metric ton = 1000 kg ≈ 2200 lb; but if the conversion 1 kg ≈ 2.204623 lb is used, then 1 metric ton = 1000 kg ≈ 2204.623 lb, a difference of 4.623 lb. This could be significant in some applications.

Examples 1–3 Again, you may wish to show the conversions using the Substitution Principle.

The answers derived in **Examples 2–3** are useful for students to know.

You might want to use *Activity 1* in *Optional Activities* (below) to make students aware of everyday items that are measured with metric units.

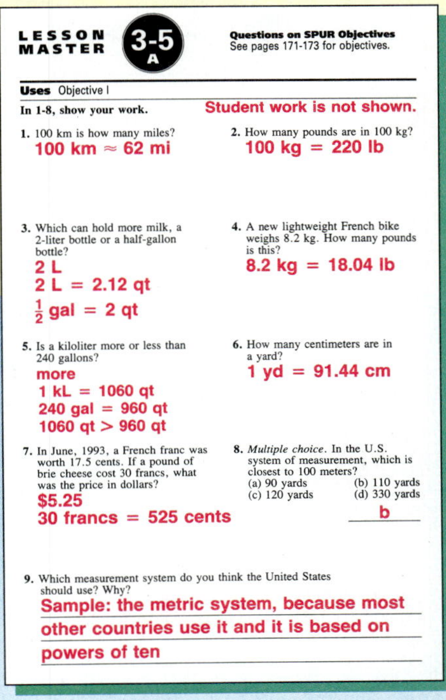

LESSON MASTER 3-5 A

Questions on SPUR Objectives
See pages 171-173 for objectives.

Uses Objective I

In 1-8, show your work. Student work is not shown.

1. 100 km is how many miles?
100 km ≈ 62 mi

2. How many pounds are in 100 kg?
100 kg = 220 lb

3. Which can hold more milk, a 2-liter bottle or a half-gallon bottle?
2 L
2 L = 2.12 qt
$\frac{1}{2}$ gal = 2 qt

4. A new lightweight French bike weighs 8.2 kg. How many pounds is this?
8.2 kg = 18.04 lb

5. Is a kiloliter more or less than 240 gallons?
more
1 kL = 1060 qt
240 gal = 960 qt
1060 qt > 960 qt

6. How many centimeters are in a yard?
1 yd = 91.44 cm

7. In June, 1993, a French franc was worth 17.5 cents. If a pound of brie cheese cost 30 francs, what was the price in dollars?
$5.25
30 francs = 525 cents

8. *Multiple choice.* In the U.S. system of measurement, which is closest to 100 meters?
(a) 90 yards (b) 110 yards
(c) 120 yards (d) 330 yards
b

9. Which measurement system do you think the United States should use? Why?
Sample: the metric system, because most other countries use it and it is based on powers of ten

Optional Activities

Activity 1 Finding Metric Measures
At the beginning of the lesson, you might suggest that students look for items at home that show measures in both metric and customary units, or only in metric units. Suggest that they bring some of the items to share with the class and that they write descriptions of the items they cannot bring to school.

Activity 2 Foreign Currency After discussing **Example 4,** you might have students **work in groups** with each group selecting a different country and investigating its currency. Each group might make a table describing the coins and bills used, and give equivalent values in U.S. dollars. Some students may also be able to bring in samples or pictures of the currency. Students might enjoy replacing advertisement prices with values in "their" currency.

Example 4 Point out that conversion equations for money change daily, and they may even vary from place to place in the same city. If you have a current currency conversion table available, have students find the conversion rate between dollars and pesos or between U.S. dollars and Canadian dollars.

Additional Examples

1. A recipe in a German cookbook calls for 1.5 kg of sausage. About how many pounds of meat is this? **≈3.3 lb**
2. A marathon race is about 42.2 km long. About how many miles is this? **≈ 26.2 mi**
3. A one-liter carton of milk contains about how many cups of milk? **≈ 4.24 c**
4. When Louise was in England, the pound was equal in value to about $1.59. Convert the 42 pounds she spent for a sweater into dollars. **≈ $66.78**

Notes on Questions

When students work on the questions, you might have them use **Teaching Aid 32** which shows the conversion relations between systems.

Questions 7–9 Make sure that students have written the symbol ≈ and have read each answer correctly.

Questions 10–11 Answers should have either the word *about* or the symbol ≈ to indicate approximation.

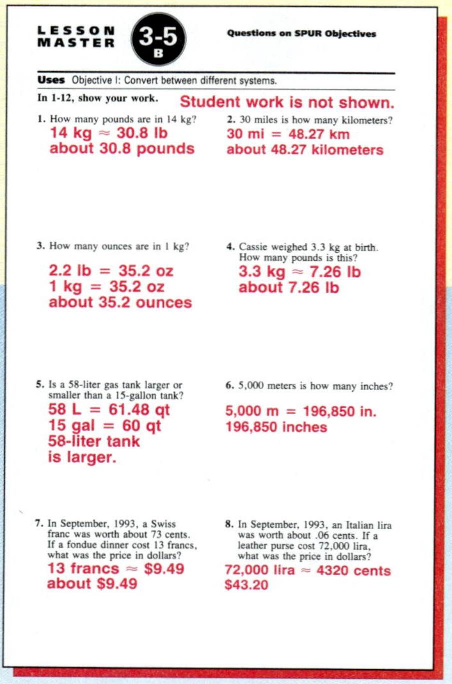

LESSON MASTER 3-5 B Questions on SPUR Objectives

Uses Objective I: Convert between different systems.

In 1-12, show your work. **Student work is not shown.**

1. How many pounds are in 14 kg?
   14 kg ≈ 30.8 lb
   about 30.8 pounds
2. 30 miles is how many kilometers?
   30 mi = 48.27 km
   about 48.27 kilometers
3. How many ounces are in 1 kg?
   2.2 lb = 35.2 oz
   1 kg = 35.2 oz
   about 35.2 ounces
4. Cassie weighed 3.3 kg at birth. How many pounds is this?
   3.3 kg ≈ 7.26 lb
   about 7.26 lb
5. Is a 58-liter gas tank larger or smaller than a 15-gallon tank?
   58 L = 61.48 qt
   15 gal = 60 qt
   58-liter tank is larger.
6. 5,000 meters is how many inches?
   5,000 m = 196,850 in.
   196,850 inches
7. In September, 1993, a Swiss franc was worth about 73 cents. If a fondue dinner cost 13 francs, what was the price in dollars?
   13 francs ≈ $9.49
   about $9.49
8. In September, 1993, an Italian lira was worth about .06 cents. If a leather purse cost 72,000 lira, what was the price in dollars?
   72,000 lira ≈ 4320 cents
   $43.20

Celebrate! *This Latino youth is participating in the Mexican* Cinco de Mayo *celebration. Serapes, like the brightly-colored one the youth is wearing, were once part of the* charro *or horseman's costume.*

Converting from One Currency to Another

Most countries have their own *monetary systems* with their own units for money. For instance, Mexico uses pesos. Canada uses the Canadian dollar, whose value is different from the U.S. dollar. If you travel to these or other countries, you will see prices in their units. Most American travelers want to know what these prices are in U.S. dollars, so they know what they are spending.

Example 4

In March of 1993, one Mexican peso was equal in value to about 32¢. If a serape cost 80 pesos at that time, what was its cost in dollars?

Solution

From the given information, the conversion relation is

$$1 \text{ peso} \approx \$.32.$$

Multiply both sides by 80.

$$80 \times 1 \text{ peso} \approx 80 \times \$.32$$

$$80 \text{ pesos} \approx \$25.60$$

The cost of the serape was about $25.60.

QUESTIONS

Covering the Reading

1. Name two professions in which a person in the U.S. would use the metric system more than the U.S. system. **Sample: photographer, doctor**
2. Name two professions in which a person in the U.S. currently would use U.S. units more than metric units. **Sample: carpenter, plumber**
3. What does the ≈ sign mean? **is approximately equal to**
4. What metric unit is a little larger than two pounds? **kilogram**
5. What U.S. unit is most like a liter? **quart**
6. One relationship between the U.S. and metric system is exact. What relationship is it? **1 inch = 2.54 centimeters**

In 7–9, give a relationship between:

7. kilograms and pounds. **1 kilogram ≈ 2.2 pounds**
8. liters and quarts. **1 liter ≈ 1.06 quarts**
9. kilometers and miles. **1 kilometer ≈ 0.62 mile**
10. 30K is the length of the longest cross-country skiing race for women in the Olympics. Convert this distance to miles. **≈ 18.6 miles**
11. The lightest class for weightlifting in the Olympics is for people who weigh under 52 kg. How many pounds is this? **≈ 114.4 lb**

Optional Activities

Activity 3 In *Technology Sourcebook, Calculator Master 6,* students explore conversions using constant keys and memory keys.

12. Is 900 milliliters more or less than a quart? less

13. In March of 1993, one Canadian dollar was equal in value to about .80 U.S. dollars. If an item cost $50 in a Canadian store at that time, estimate its cost in U.S. dollars. ≈ $40 U.S.

Applying the Mathematics

In 14–19, which is larger?

14. a pound or a kilogram
kilogram

15. a quart or a liter
liter

16. a meter or a yard
meter

17. a centimeter or an inch
inch

18. a kilometer or a mile
mile

19. a gram or an ounce
ounce

20. In March 1993, how many pesos equaled 1 dollar? Answer to the nearest whole number. ≈ 3

21. a. Write $\frac{5}{16}$ as a decimal. 0.3125
    b. A person needs a drill bit with a diameter of approximately $\frac{5}{16}$ in. If a bit with a metric measure must be used, what diameter is needed? 8 mm

22. An adult human brain weighs about 1.5 kg. Convert this to ounces.
≈ 52.8 oz

23. Convert 3 liters to cups. ≈ 12.72 cups

24. The monetary unit of Kenya is the shilling. In April of 1993, one shilling was worth about .020 U.S. dollar. At that rate, what was the cost in U.S. dollars of a hotel room for one night if the charge was 1500 shillings a night? ≈ $30 U.S.

Review

25. How many grams are in 4 kilograms? *(Lesson 3-4)*
4000 g

26. One centimeter is what percent of a meter? *(Lessons 2-6, 3-4)*
1%

27. A 5-lb bag of cat food has how many ounces of food in it? *(Lesson 3-3)* 80 ounces

28. A bucket holds 8 gallons. How many quarts will it hold? *(Lesson 3-3)*
32 quarts

29. How many inches are in a yard? *(Lesson 3-2)*
36 inches

30. Measure this segment to the nearest millimeter. *(Lesson 3-1)* 81 mm

Figures appear small than actual size in Teacher's Edition.

Multicultural Connection People who weigh under 52 kg compete in the flyweight division of the Olympic weightlifting competition. Suggest that interested students find information about the most recent Olympic weightlifting competition to learn what countries won medals in the various weight categories and what weights were lifted.

Questions 14–19 Error Alert These are very important questions, and not as easy as they look. For example, in Question 14, some students might assume that a kilogram is less than a pound because 1 kg ≈ 2.2 lb and 1 < 2.2. To help them see their error, point out that 1 kilogram is about 2.2 pounds.

Question 20 Students should refer to **Example 4** to find the value of a Mexican peso in March, 1993. Some students might find the answer to this question by dividing, others might use trial and error, and still others might reason that 1 peso ≈ 32¢, so 3 pesos ≈ 96¢.

Question 21b This is not an uncommon situation. Imported tools may have metric dimensions; items made in the United States may have customary dimensions. If a person wants to fix an item that is made using U.S. units with an imported tool, then they face this conversion problem.

Question 22 Some students may be surprised to learn that an adult brain weighs almost 4 pounds.

▸ LESSON MASTER 3-5 B *page 2*

9. Which is larger, an 8-ounce juice box or a 250-mL juice box?
250 mL = 8.48 oz
8.48 > 8
250 mL is larger.

10. How many grams are in 3 kg?
3 kg = 3000 g
3,000 grams

11. *Multiple choice.* In the U.S. system of measurement, which is closest to 800 m?
(a) 1 mile (b) $\frac{1}{2}$ mile
(c) 2 miles (d) $\frac{3}{4}$ mile
800 m ≈ .496 mi
b

12. *Multiple choice.* In the U.S. system of measurement, which is closest to 1,000 kg?
(a) 2.2 tons (b) $\frac{1}{2}$ ton
(c) 2 tons (d) 1 ton
1000 kg ≈ 2,200 lb
1 ton = 2000 lb
d

Review Objective J, Lesson 2-7

In 13-17, use the circle at the right.

13. Name the center. ______
14. Name a radius. $\overline{CY}, \overline{CW}, \overline{CZ}, \overline{CX}$
15. Name a diameter. $\overline{WX}$
16. Name the shaded sector. YCZ
17. Name an arc. $\overset{\frown}{WY}, \overset{\frown}{YZ}, \overset{\frown}{ZX}, \overset{\frown}{WX}$

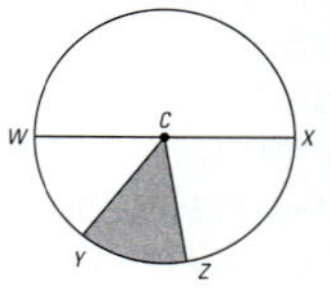

Adapting to Individual Needs

Challenge Multicultural Connection
Have students solve the following problem. Either give them the current exchange rate or have them research this information.

At a grocery store in Edmonton, 1 kilogram of chicken costs $6.49 in Canadian dollars. Find the equivalent cost of one pound of chicken in U.S. dollars. [About $2.30, based on an exchange rate of $1.00 (Canadian) ≈ $0.78 (U.S.)]

You might want students to write the steps they used to solve the problem. One approach involves this sequence of steps.

1. Find the cost of 1 kg in U. S. dollars:
   $1 Canadian ≈ $0.78 U.S.
   6.49 × $1 Canadian ≈ 6.49 × 0.78 U.S.
   $6.49 Canadian ≈ $5.06 U.S.
2. Since 1 kg costs $5.06 and 1 kg ≈ 2.2 lb, 2.2 lb costs about $5.06. Dividing $5.06 by 2.2 gives the cost of one pound, $2.30.

Notes on Questions

Question 31 Circle graphs will be studied again in Lesson 3-7.

Question 34 Students will need cereal boxes.

Follow-up for Lesson 3-5

Practice

For more questions on SPUR objectives, use **Lesson Master 3-5A** (shown on page 141) or **Lesson Master 3-5B** (shown on pages 142–143).

Assessment

Written Communication Have each student write a short letter to a real or imaginary person in another country, include at least three units of measure, one for weight, one for capacity, and one for distance. Have students give the measures in both customary and metric units. [Letters are coherent and contain the measures required.]

Extension

Multicultural Connection Two conversions that travelers often need to make involve money and distance. Have students **work in groups**, pretend they are visiting another country, and try to devise simple ways to mentally convert the money of the country to U.S. dollars and distances in kilometers to miles.

Project Update Project 2, *Other Traditional Units,* on page 167, involves other units of weight and capacity and is related to the content of this lesson.

31. From the circle graph below:

- **a.** Which age bracket has the fewest people? **60–64**
- **b.** Which age bracket has the most people? **30–39**
- **c.** How many people are between the ages of 5 and 19? **53.2 million**
- **d.** To the nearest 10%, what percent of people are 40 years of age or older? *(Lesson 2-7)* **40%**

32. Convert 0.136 to a fraction in lowest terms. *(Lesson 2-6)* $\frac{17}{125}$

33. What is 50% of 50? *(Lesson 2-5)* **25**

Exploration

34. On every cereal box, the amount of protein per serving is listed.

- **a.** Find a cereal box. How much protein per serving is listed?
- **b.** Is this amount given in U.S. units, metric units, or both?
- **c.** Is the weight of the box given in U.S. units, metric units, or both?

Answers will vary.

35. Find information about the current values of various units of currency from other countries. Has the value of a peso increased or decreased since March of 1993? **The answer may change with time.**

36. Examine the computer program in Question 29 of Lesson 3-2. Modify that program so that it converts a length in inches to a length in centimeters. Run your program a few times with values of your own choosing.

36) Sample:

```
10 PRINT "WHAT IS
   LENGTH IN
   INCHES?"
20 INPUT NINCHES
30 NCM =
2.54 * NINCHES
40 PRINT "THE
   NUMBER OF
   CM IS " NCM
50 END
```


Adapting to Individual Needs

English Language Development Prepare sets of index cards with each card containing a word or phrase associated with customary and metric units of length, weight, and capacity. Have students demonstrate their understanding of these terms by sorting the cards according to various criteria. For example, students might sort the cards into two piles—customary and metric; sort into three groups according to what the units measure (length, weight, capacity); or arrange the units from largest to smallest within each system.

Setting Up Lesson 3-6

Materials Students will need protractors for Lesson 3-6. The **Geometry Template** contains a protractor. Students will need straws if you use the Warm-up, and pictures from magazines if you use the Assessment.

LESSON

3-6 Measuring Angles

What Are Angles?

Think of rays of light coming from the sun. Each **ray** has the same starting point, called its **endpoint.** Each ray goes on forever in a particular direction. Only a part of any ray can be drawn.

Identified below are rays *SB* and *SA,* written $\overrightarrow{SB}$ and $\overrightarrow{SA}$. Notice that the first letter written when naming a ray is the endpoint of the ray. The second letter names another point on the ray. Two other rays are not identified.

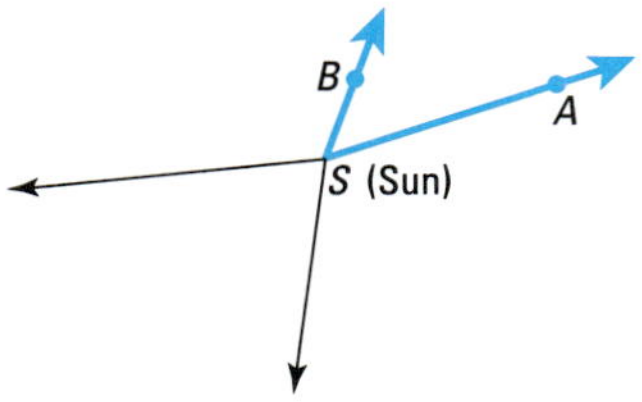

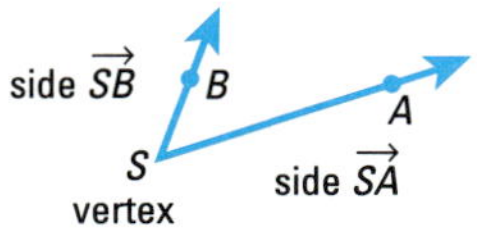

angle

The union of two rays with the same endpoint is an **angle.** The rays are the **sides** of the angle. The endpoint is the **vertex** of the angle. The sides of an angle go on forever; you can draw only part of them.

The symbol for angle is ∠. This symbol was first used by William Oughtred in 1657.

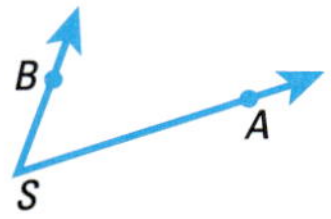

The angle above may be written as ***∠S, ∠ASB,*** or ***∠BSA.*** When three letters are used, the middle letter is the vertex. If an angle shares its vertex with any other angle, you must use three letters to name it. For instance, in the first drawing above, you should not name any angle ∠*S.* Which angle you meant would not be clear.

Lesson 3-6 Overview

Broad Goals The major goal of this lesson is measuring angles and drawing angles with given measures. This is a long lesson with many objectives, but the next lesson is quite brief.

Perspective Everyone knows that angles are important in the study of geometry. But they have many uses in the real world as well. For example, questions in this lesson demonstrate how angles can be used to indicate differences in direction, and in the next lesson, the In-class Activity on page 152 applies measures of angles to circle graphs. In Chapter 5, students find that angles and turns are closely related (an idea also used in Logo).

As with length, students should be given some leeway in measuring angles. Two degrees either way is usually acceptable.

Lesson 3-6

Objectives

B Measure an angle to the nearest degree using a protractor.

L Draw an angle with a given measure.

N Give countries and approximate dates of origin of current measuring devices.

Resources

From the ***Teacher's Resource File***

- Lesson Master 3-6A or 3-6B
- Answer Master 3-6
- Teaching Aids
  26 Warm-up
  33 Measuring Angles
- Technology Sourcebook, Computer Demonstration 3

Additional Resources

- Visuals for Teaching Aids 26, 33
- Geometry Workshop
- Protractor or Geometry Template
- Straws (Warm-up)
- Pictures from magazines (Assessment)

Teaching Lesson 3-6

Warm-up

Diagnostic You need straws and a protractor. Estimate each of the following angle measures with your straws. Then place the "straw angle" on a sheet of paper and draw the angle by tracing the inside of the straw angle. Finally, measure each angle to see how close it is to the given measure.

1. 30° **2.** 135° **3.** 45°
4. 110° **5.** 80° **6.** 170°

Check students' drawings.

Notes on Reading

You might want to use the activity in *Optional Activities* on page 146 to introduce this lesson.

There is a lot of reading in this lesson. Discuss one page of the lesson at a time, emphasizing the key points on each page. You might wish to discuss measuring an angle and then use **Teaching Aid 33** which asks students to measure angles. Use the first angle to demonstrate how to measure an angle; have students do each step as it is explained.

❶ After students have studied these angle measures, you might ask them to find angles in the classroom and approximate their degree measures. Some possible choices are the hands of the clock; tilt-style windows, if open; crossing support bars on chairs or desks; and the many 90° angles formed at the corners of doors, windows, chalkboards, or tiles.

❷ For students who do not understand the caution, use an overhead, and draw several angles with the same measure, but with sides of different lengths. Place the angles over one another to show that the measures of the angles are the same.

How Are Angles Measured?

Over 4000 years ago, the Babylonians wrote numbers in a system based on the number 60. So they measured with units based on 60. Even today, we use Babylonian ideas to measure time. That is why there are 60 minutes in an hour and 60 seconds in a minute.

We also use Babylonian ideas in measuring angles. The Babylonians divided a circle into 360 equally spaced units which we call **degrees.** (The number 360 equals 6 × 60 and is close to the number of days in a year.)

❶ The measures of angles range from 0° to 180°. Here are angles with measures from 10° to 180°, in multiples of 10°.

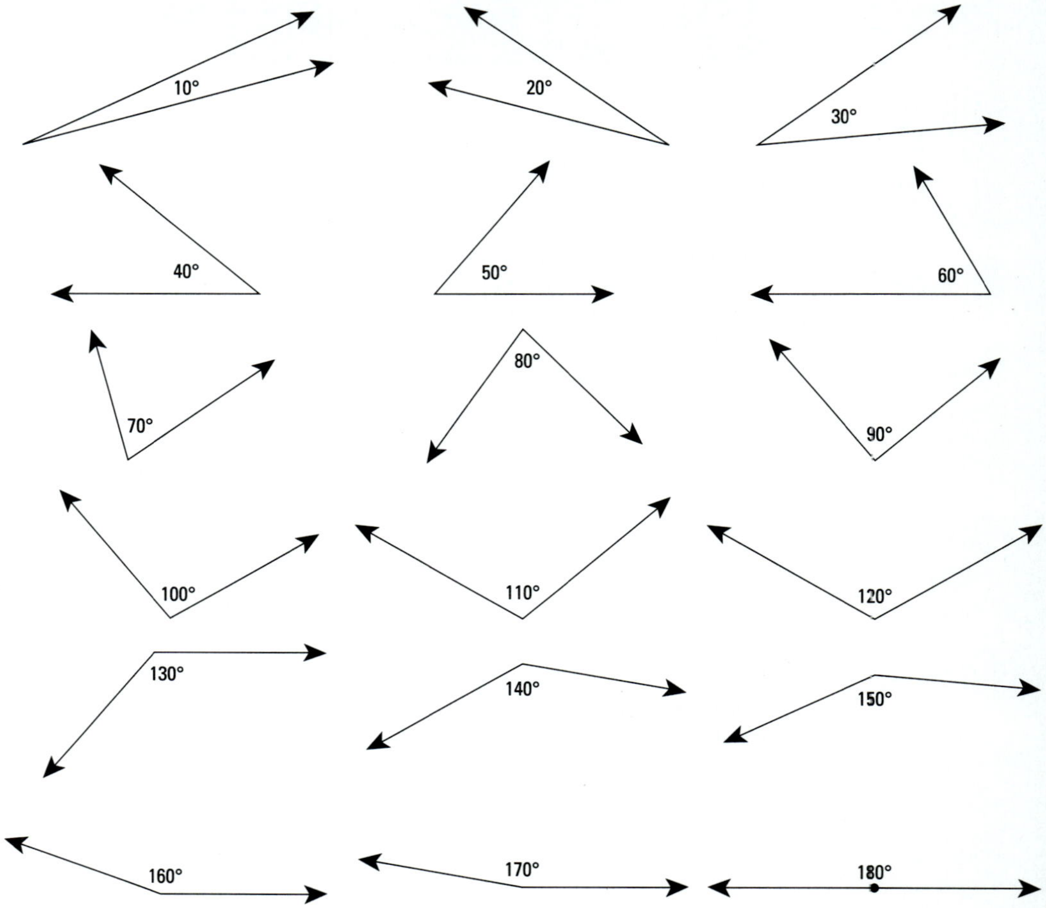

❷ *Caution:* The measure of an angle has nothing to do with the lengths of its sides. The measure is entirely determined by the difference in the directions of its rays.

Optional Activities

Activity 1 Use Physical Models

Materials: Square sheets of paper

You might introduce the lesson with this activity. Have each student fold a square sheet of paper in half so that the left edge folds on top of the right edge; then fold the paper in half again so that the bottom edge folds on the top edge; and finally, fold the paper diagonally so that the bottom and left edges meet. Tell them to open the paper and draw eight rays along the folds using the center as a common endpoint. Have them label the center *X* and one point on each of the rays using the letters *A* through *H*.

Use the diagram to illustrate the terms in this lesson. For example, *X* is the endpoint of $\overrightarrow{XH}$ and $\overrightarrow{XA}$, and the angle formed by them is called ∠*HXA* or ∠*AXH*. The endpoint is the *vertex* of the angle, and the rays are the *sides* of the angle. Have students name other angles. [Responses may vary. The union of any pair of rays with the same endpoint is an angle.]

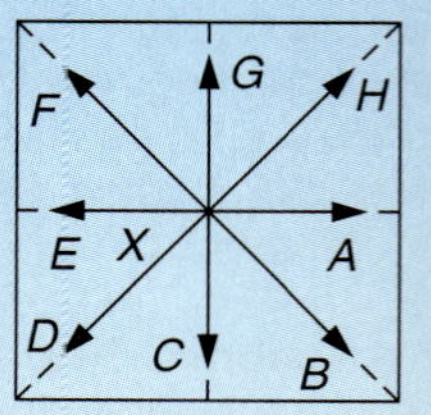

❸ Measuring Angles with a Protractor

A **protractor** is the most common instrument used for measuring angles. Many protractors look like the one pictured below, covering only half a circle. When protractors cover half of a circle, the degree measures on the outside go from 0° to 180°.

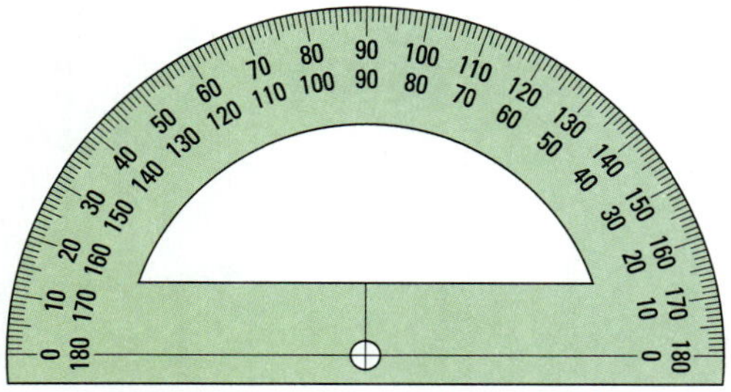

Every protractor has a segment connecting the 0° mark on one side to the 180° mark on the other. This segment is on the **base line** of the protractor. The middle point of this segment is called the **center** of the protractor. On the protractors in this lesson, the center is named V. On a protractor, V is usually marked by a hole, an arrow, or a + sign. There are almost always two curved scales on the outside of the protractor. One goes from 0° to 180°. The other goes from 180° to 0°.

The picture below shows how the protractor is placed on an angle.

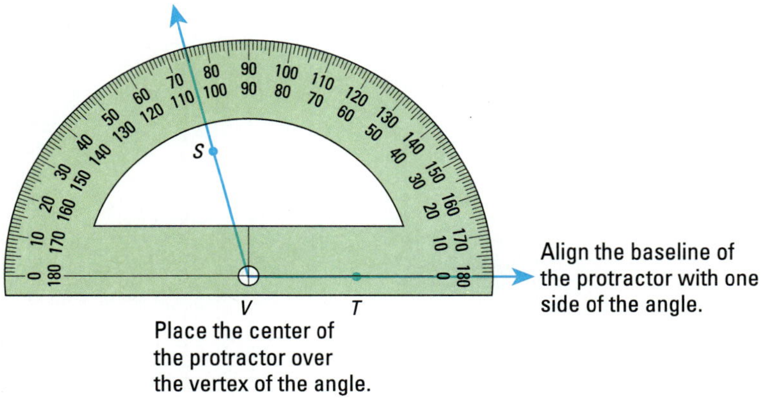

Example 1

What is the measure of $\angle SVT$ drawn above?

Solution

$\overrightarrow{VS}$ crosses the protractor at 105 and 75. It seems that the measure of $\angle SVT$ could be either 105° or 75°. Which measure is correct? The side $\overrightarrow{VT}$ crosses the *inner* scale at 0°. Therefore, the inner scale should be used to determine the measure of the angle. So, **The measure of $\angle SVT$ is 105°.**

❸ If students are having difficulty understanding the dual scales on their protractors, see *Extra Help* in *Adapting to Individual Needs* below.

Pacing You may be tempted to spend two days on this lesson. It is not necessary; Lesson 3-7 is purposely short and continues the discussion of angles and their measures.

Optional Activities

Activity 2 Technology Connection You may wish to demonstrate how to draw and measure angles on the computer, using *Technology Sourcebook, Computer Demonstration 3,* with the *Geometry Workshop.* Following the demonstration, have students draw various angles, estimate, and then check the measures using the Measure option.

Adapting to Individual Needs

Extra Help
Some students may need individual help if they are using a protractor for the first time. Go through the procedure of placing the protractor on the angle, choosing the correct scale to read, and then reading the measure. Then, as you observe, have students measure and draw angles.

English Language Development
Help students understand the vocabulary words associated with a protractor as you demonstrate how to use one. For example, "align" might be confused with "a line." You might also need to explain terms such as base line, center, inner scale, and outer scale.

The measure of $\angle A$ is written **m$\angle$*A*.** The measure of $\angle DEF$ is written **m$\angle$*DEF*.** So in Example 1, m$\angle SVT$ = 105°.

Example 2

What is m$\angle$*EVF?*

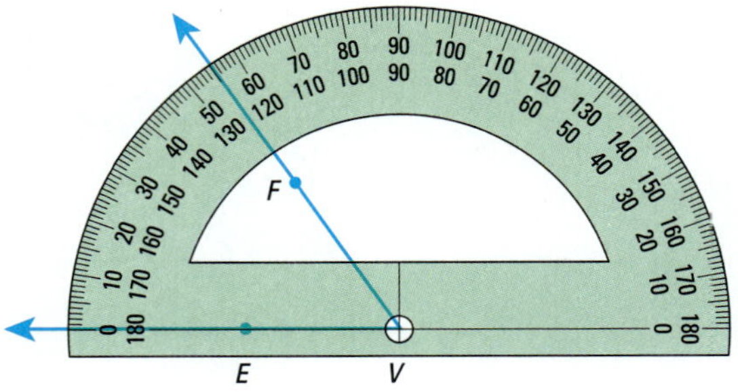

Solution

Examine where $\overrightarrow{VF}$ crosses the protractor. There are two numbers, 125° and 55°. Since side $\overrightarrow{VE}$ of the angle crosses the outer scale at 0°, pick the number in the outer scale. This is 55. Thus m$\angle$EVF = 55°.

Activity

Measure the angle drawn here to the nearest degree.

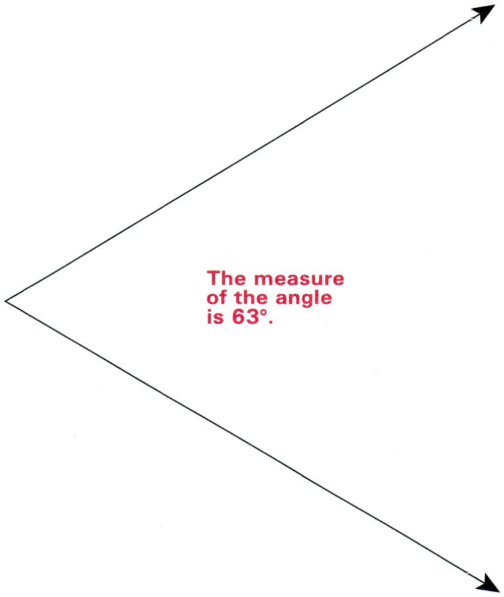

The measure of the angle is 63°.

If you get a measure between 60° and 70°, you probably know what you are doing.

Adapting to Individual Needs

Challenge

Explain that in navigation the angle of the line of direction of a plane or ship is given with respect to a north-south line. This angle is called the *heading.* For example, N30°W indicates a heading 30° west of north. Then pose this problem.

A plane flies with a heading of N30°E for 300 miles to point A. Then it changes course to a heading of N80°E for 300 more miles to point B. Make an accurate scale drawing and measure the angle of the line of direction from the starting point to point B. Then measure to find about how far the plane is from its starting point. [N55°E; about 550 miles]

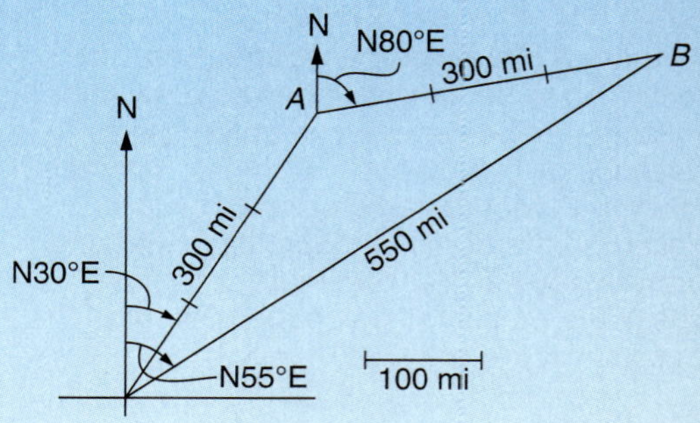

Example 3

Draw a 30° angle.

Solution

One solution is shown below.

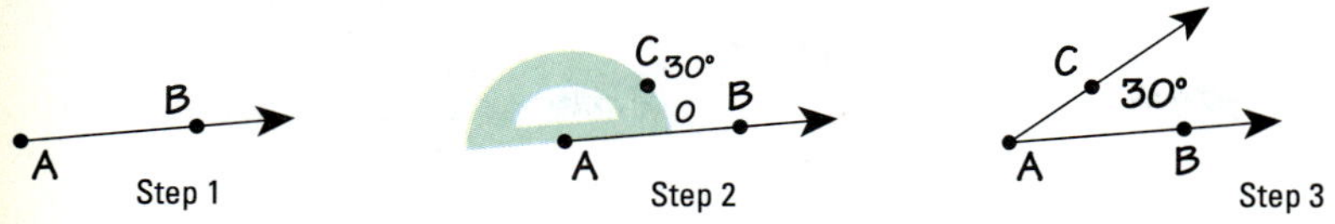

1. Draw a ray. We call our ray $\overrightarrow{AB}$. Then place the center of a protractor at *A,* with the base line of the protractor on $\overrightarrow{AB}$.
2. Using the scale that crosses $\overrightarrow{AB}$ at 0°, put a point at 30°. We call this point *C*.
3. Draw $\overrightarrow{AC}$. Then m∠*CAB* = 30°.

QUESTIONS

Covering the Reading

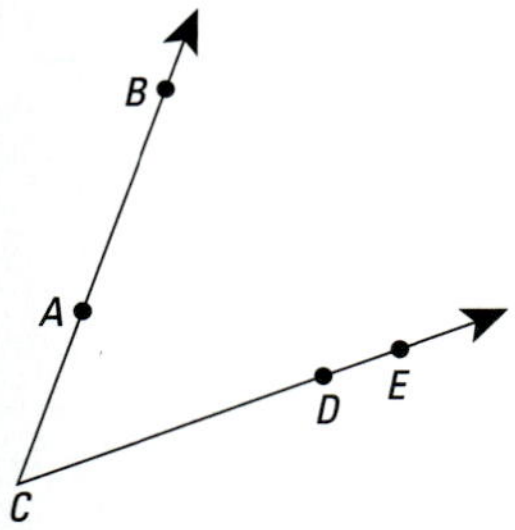

In 1–4, use the angle at the left.

1. Name the sides. $\overrightarrow{CB}$ **or** $\overrightarrow{CA}$ **and** $\overrightarrow{CD}$ **or** $\overrightarrow{CE}$
2. Name the vertex. ***C***
3. Which of the following are correct names for the angle?
   (a) ∠*ACE* (b) ∠*C* (c) ∠*ECA* (d) ∠*CBD*
   (e) ∠*ECB* (f) ∠*DBC* (g) ∠*ACD* (h) ∠*ACB*
   (a), (b), (c), (e) (g)
4. Which has the larger measure, ∠*BCE* or ∠*ACD*? **Neither, they are the same angle.**
5. Why did the Babylonians measure with units based on 60? **Their number system was based on 60.**

In 6–9, use the drawing.

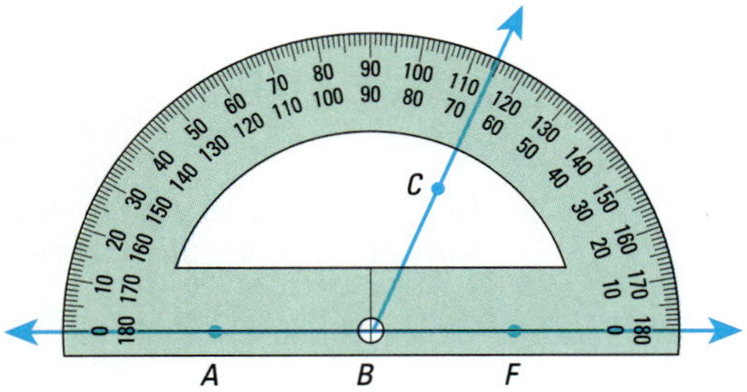

6. Name the base line of this protractor. $\overleftrightarrow{AF}$ **(or** $\overleftrightarrow{FA}$ **or** $\overleftrightarrow{AB}$ **or** $\overleftrightarrow{BA}$ **or** $\overleftrightarrow{BF}$ **or** $\overleftrightarrow{FB}$**)**
7. What point is at the center of this protractor? ***B***
8. What is the measure of ∠*ABC*? **114°**
9. What is the measure of ∠*CBF*? **66°**

Additional Examples

1. Draw two angles on a sheet of paper. Exchange papers with another student, and measure the angles on his or her paper. **Answers will vary.**
2. Draw an angle with a measure of 75°. **Check students' papers.**

Notes on Questions

Questions 1–3 The issue of naming rays and angles correctly is a detail overlooked by many students. Use these questions to emphasize the correct notation.

Question 6 Since there has been no formal discussion of lines or their proper symbols, accept any answer that indicates the student has the right idea.

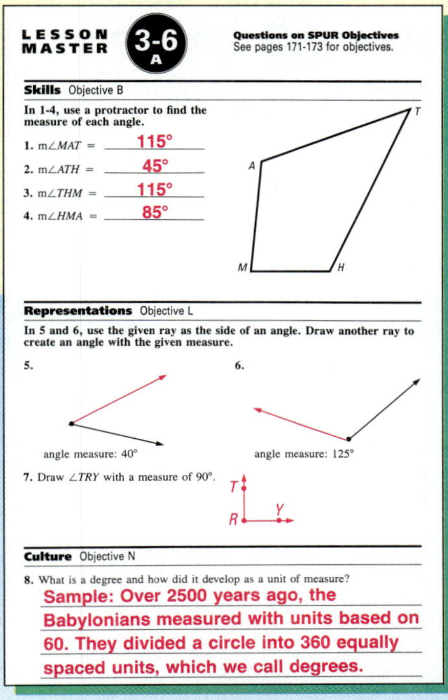

LESSON MASTER 3-6 A

Questions on SPUR Objectives
See pages 171-173 for objectives.

Skills Objective B

In 1-4, use a protractor to find the measure of each angle.

1. m∠*MAT* = **115°**
2. m∠*ATH* = **45°**
3. m∠*THM* = **115°**
4. m∠*HMA* = **85°**

Representations Objective L

In 5 and 6, use the given ray as the side of an angle. Draw another ray to create an angle with the given measure.

5. angle measure: 40°
6. angle measure: 125°
7. Draw ∠*TRY* with a measure of 90°.

Culture Objective N

8. What is a degree and how did it develop as a unit of measure? **Sample: Over 2500 years ago, the Babylonians measured with units based on 60. They divided a circle into 360 equally spaced units, which we call degrees.**

Notes on Questions

Questions 12–14 Error Alert Some students may read the wrong scale and incorrectly give the measure of the supplement of the angle. Stress that they should estimate whether the measure is greater than or less than 90° before measuring. Estimating in this way will also be used in Lesson 3-7.

Questions 21–23 Students may need help interpreting directions such as "South of West." Review the four principal directions, and make certain that everyone can draw them. Ask which is the principal direction in Question 21 [North], and show how to move 5° East of North [5° in a clockwise direction].

The *Challenge* in *Adapting to Individual Needs* on page 148 deals with headings in navigation.

Science Connection A tornado is a violent cyclonic (low-pressure) storm. The storm has an intense updraft near its center that enables it to lift heavy objects such as cars into the air. The paths of tornadoes average several hundred yards in width and 16 miles in length, but large deviations can occur. Tornadoes normally travel from 30 to 40 miles per hour. The winds around the center average nearly 300 miles per hour and have reached 500 miles per hour in the most violent storms. Some students might study newspaper weather reports to learn about current weather activity.

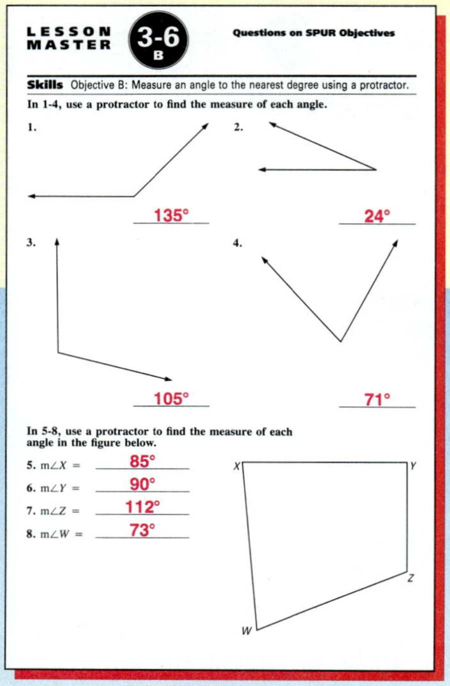

LESSON MASTER 3-6 B

Questions on SPUR Objectives

Skills Objective B: Measure an angle to the nearest degree using a protractor.

In 1-4, use a protractor to find the measure of each angle.

1. 135°

2. 24°

3. 105°

4. 71°

In 5-8, use a protractor to find the measure of each angle in the figure below.

5. m∠X = 85°

6. m∠Y = 90°

7. m∠Z = 112°

8. m∠W = 73°

10. m∠*AVB* stands for the __?__ of __?__ *AVB*. measure, angle

11. What measure did you get for the angle in the Activity of this lesson? 63°

In 12–14, use a protractor. Measure the angle to the nearest degree. (You may have to trace the angles and extend their sides.)

12.  165°

13. 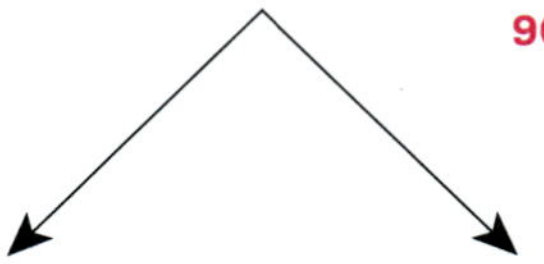 90°

14. 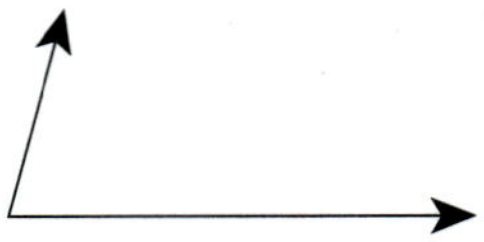 75°

16) 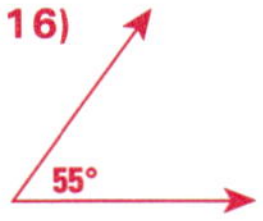

17) 

15. Who first used the symbol ∠ for an angle and when was this done? William Oughtred in 1657

In 16 and 17, draw an angle with the given measure. Use a protractor and ruler.

16. 55°

17. 162°

Applying the Mathematics

18. Point *X* is on $\overrightarrow{UV}$ drawn here. *True or false:* $\overrightarrow{UX}$ is the same ray as $\overrightarrow{UV}$. True

19. Which angle below has the largest angle measure, ∠*JGI*, ∠*IGH*, or ∠*JGH*? ∠JGH

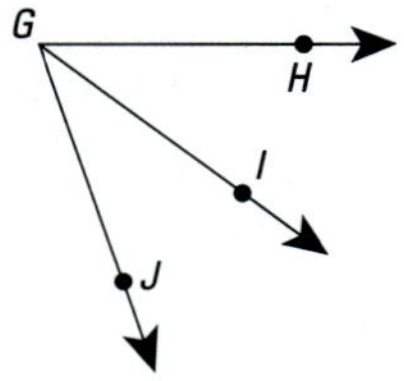

20. How many angles with vertex *E* are drawn below? (Be careful. Many students' answers are too low.) 6

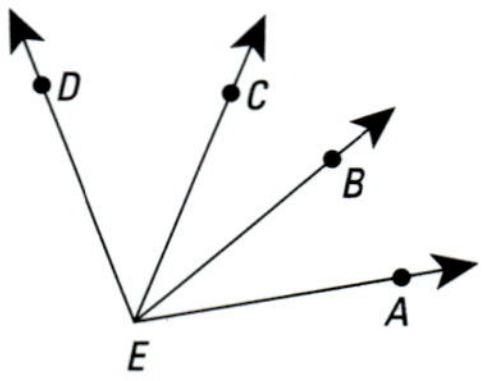

150

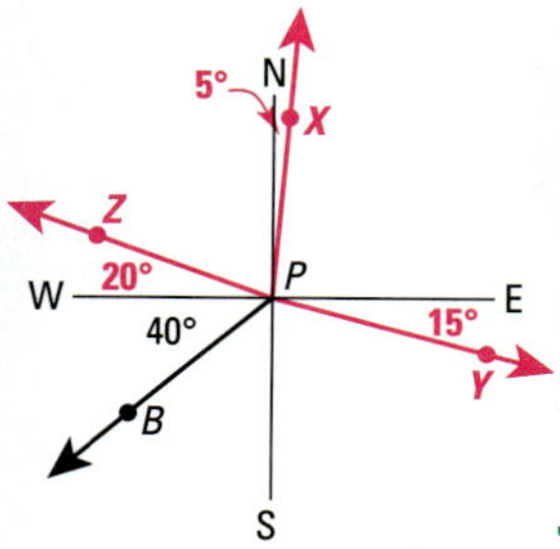

In 21–23, the ray $\overrightarrow{PB}$ represents the direction of a tornado seen 40° South of West. Copy the drawing at the left but make your drawing larger. Using a protractor, add the ray to your drawing.

21. $\overrightarrow{PX}$ to represent a UFO seen 5° East of North

22. $\overrightarrow{PY}$ to represent a whale sighted 15° South of East

23. $\overrightarrow{PZ}$ to represent a tanker observed 20° North of West

Review

24. While driving through Canada, Kirsten saw the sign below. About how many miles away was Toronto? *(Lesson 3-5)* **93 miles**

25. Convert 82 mm to meters. *(Lesson 3-4)* **0.082 m**

26. a. In the metric system, the amount of water in a bathtub could be measured in __?__. *(Lesson 3-4)* **liters**

b. In the U.S. system, the amount of water in a bathtub could be measured in __?__. *(Lesson 3-3)* **quarts or gallons**

27. Draw a line segment with a length of 7 cm. *(Lesson 3-1)*
Check students' drawings.

In 28–30, use the circle at the right. Name the following. *(Lesson 2-7)*

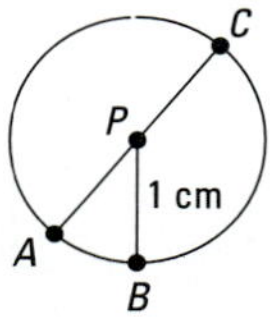

28. a radius **$\overline{PA}$ or $\overline{PB}$ or $\overline{PC}$**

29. a diameter **$\overline{AC}$**

30. The center **P**

31. Write 41.6 million in scientific notation. *(Lesson 2-3)* **4.16×10^7**

32. Roy found that 51 out of 68 people he polled liked the posters he made. Rewrite $\frac{51}{68}$ as a fraction in lowest terms. *(Lesson 1-10)* **$\frac{3}{4}$**

Exploration

33. Angles are not always measured in degrees. Two other units for measuring angles are the grad and the radian. Find out something about at least one of these units. **A grad is $\frac{1}{100}$ of a right angle or 0.9°. A radian is $\frac{180°}{\pi}$ or about 57.3°.**

Follow-up for Lesson 3-6

Practice

For more questions on SPUR objectives, use **Lesson Master 3-6A** (shown on page 149) or **Lesson Master 3-6B** (shown on pages 150–151).

Assessment

Written Communication
Materials: Pictures from magazines

Have each student select a picture and find three different examples of angles in the picture. Tell students to extend the sides of each angle on the picture and measure the angle. [Angles are clearly marked and the correct measure is given for each.]

Extension

Have students research instruments used to measure angles. They might choose the astrolabe which is pictured in the chapter opener, or a modern-day sextant. Most encyclopedias provide this information.

Project Update Project 6, *Computer Drawing Programs,* on page 168, relates to the content of this lesson.

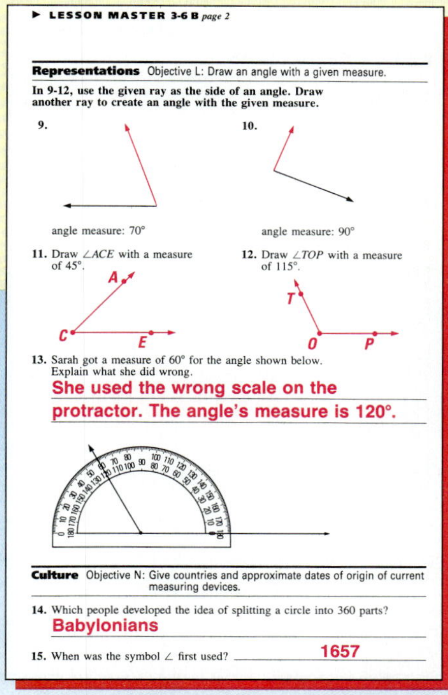

▸ **LESSON MASTER 3-6 B** *page 2*

Representations Objective L: Draw an angle with a given measure.

In 9-12, use the given ray as the side of an angle. Draw another ray to create an angle with the given measure.

9. angle measure: 70°

10. angle measure: 90°

11. Draw ∠*ACE* with a measure of 45°.

12. Draw ∠*TOP* with a measure of 115°.

13. Sarah got a measure of 60° for the angle shown below. Explain what she did wrong.
She used the wrong scale on the protractor. The angle's measure is 120°.

Culture Objective N: Give countries and approximate dates of origin of current measuring devices.

14. Which people developed the idea of splitting a circle into 360 parts?
Babylonians

15. When was the symbol ∠ first used? **1657**

Setting Up Lesson 3-7

Materials Students will continue to use protractors in Lesson 3-7. They will need compasses for the Extension.

In-class Activity

Resources

From the ***Teacher's Resource File***
- Teaching Aid 34: Make a Circle Graph

Additional Resources
- Visual for Teaching Aid 34

Remind students that a circle graph is a picture that shows the parts of a whole quantity. Making circle graphs usually requires a great deal of effort, and these days most people use computer software to draw all but the simplest of circle graphs. In this activity, students gather, record, and represent data obtained from the entire class. We recommend that students then **work in groups** to help each other make accurate graphs. Students can use the table on **Teaching Aid 34** to help them organize their data before graphing. You might need to help students complete one row of the table.

Display a variety of circle graphs in the classroom. Ask students to bring in circle graphs that they find, and add them to the display.

TEACHING AID 34
In-class Activity, Lesson 3-7

Make a Circle Graph

1. Record your data in the first two columns of the table. (The number of rows you will need depends on the data you gather.)
2. Record the percents for each entry in the third column
3. Record the number of degrees needed for each entry in the fourth column.
4. Make a circle graph to show the data.

Choices	Number of People with This Choice	Percent	Number of Degrees in Central Angle

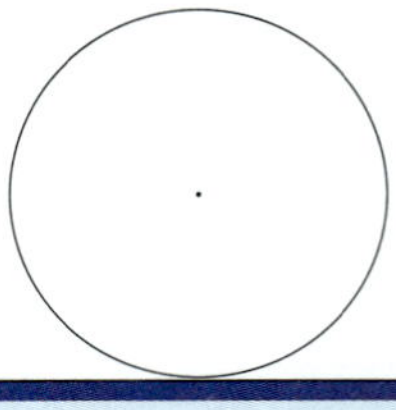

Introducing Lesson 3-7

Kinds of Angles

IN-CLASS ACTIVITY

A **central angle** of a circle is an angle with its vertex at the center of the circle. At the right, $\angle AOB$ is a central angle. It is the central angle of the shaded sector *AOB*. By drawing central angles, you can make circle graphs.

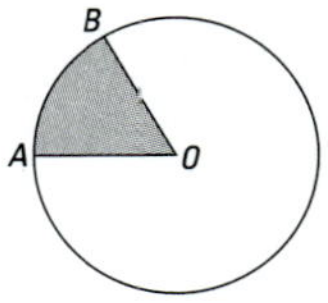

1 Take a survey of the favorite subjects of the students in your class. Then display the information in a circle graph.

2 For instance, suppose you survey 20 people. You might find the following preferences: 8, Math; 4, English; 5 Science; 3, Social Studies. So $\frac{8}{20}$, or 40%, prefer Math, and so on.

Put the numbers and percents into a table. Here is our example.

	Math	English	Science	Social Studies
Number	8	4	5	3
Percent	40%	20%	25%	15%

3 Display the information in a circle graph. Here is our display.

Since there are 360° in a circle, to find the number of degrees in 40% of a circle, find 40% of 360°. This is 144°. So we draw a 144° central angle for the Math sector. For the other central angles, the calculations are similar.

English:
20% of 360° = 0.20 × 360° = 72°

Science:
25% of 360° = 0.25 × 360° = 90°

Social Studies:
15% of 360° = 0.15 × 360° = 54°

4 Check. The sum of the measures of the central angles should be 360°.

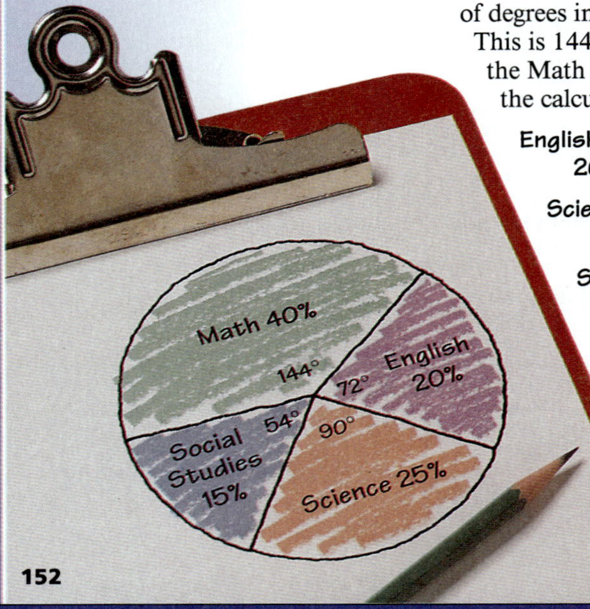

152

Optional Activities

Environmental Connection Have students use the data given at the right to draw a circle graph.

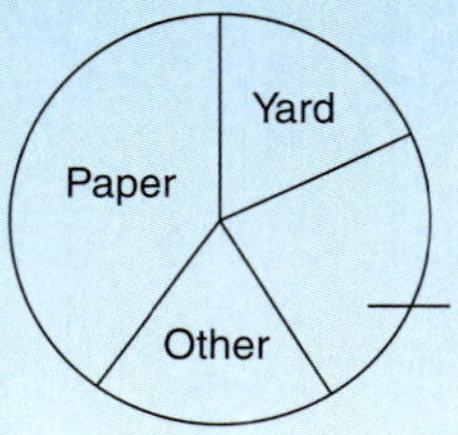

Municipal Solid Waste Generation
Source: EPA, 1990

Waste	Tons in Millions	
Paper	71.8	[40%; 144°]
Common Recyclables*	42.2	[23%; 83°]
Yard	31.6	[18%; 65°]
Other	34.0	[19%; 68°]

* Glass, metals, plastics

LESSON

3-7

Kinds of Angles

French connections. *The street called the Champs Elysée, as seen from the top of the Arc de Triomphe in Paris, France, intersects the circular road around the Arc at a right angle. Notice that the other streets in this photo also meet this road at right angles.*

Right Angles

Angles can be classified by their measures. If the measure of an angle is 90°, the angle is called a **right angle.** Some right angles are drawn below. The sides of this page form right angles at the corners. Many streets intersect at right angles.

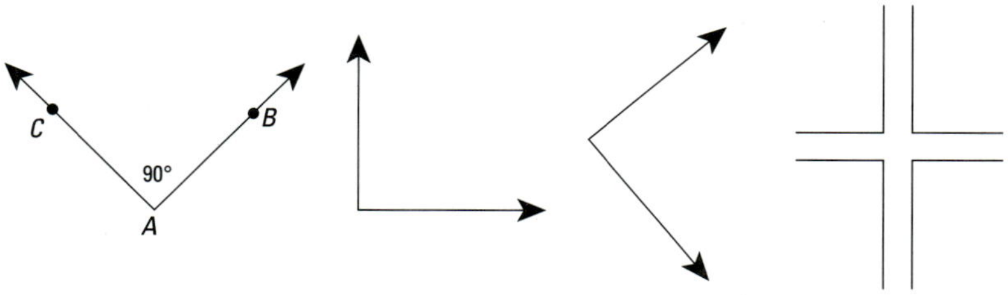

right angles

street intersection

Rays, segments, or lines that form right angles are called **perpendicular.** Above, $\overrightarrow{AC}$ is perpendicular to $\overrightarrow{AB}$. The streets drawn above are also perpendicular. Each long side of this page is perpendicular to each short side.

Lesson 3-7 Overview

Broad Goals This short, relatively easy lesson is designed to give students some extra time to practice with angle measures.

Perspective Being able to distinguish acute angles from obtuse angles gives students another way of choosing the correct measure from the two scales on most protractors. If an angle is seen to be obtuse and the choices on the protractor are 62° and 118°, the measure must be 118°.

Lesson 3-7

Objectives

C Distinguish between acute, right, and obtuse angles by sight or measure.

M Read, make, and interpret circle graphs.

Resources

From the ***Teacher's Resource File***

- Lesson Master 3-7A or 3-7B
- Answer Master 3-7
- Assessment Sourcebook: Quiz for Lessons 3-4 through 3-7
- Teaching Aids
  27 Warm-up
  35 United States Map (Challenge)
- Technology Sourcebook, Computer Master 4

Additional Resources

- Visuals for Teaching Aids 27, 35
- Geometry Workshop
- Protractor or Geometry Template
- Compass (Extension)

Teaching Lesson 3-7

Warm-up

Work in groups and find objects in the classroom that show acute angles and objects that show obtuse angles. List at least three examples of each kind of angle.

Notes on Reading

Since this lesson is devoted to vocabulary, you might wish to begin by discussing **Questions 38–39.** These questions give some outside context for the two words that are often confused, *acute* and *obtuse.*

The definition of *perpendicular* uses the words segments and lines, terms which require only an intuitive understanding at this time. As long as the notion of *perpendicular* is clear, you do not have to worry about distinctions between lines and segments until Lesson 5-9.

Additional Examples

You might want to use these examples when discussing the lesson. Have students refer to the questions in Lesson 3-6. Ask them to tell whether the angle seems to be acute, right, or obtuse.

1. $\angle ACD$ in Question 3 **Acute**
2. $\angle ABC$ in Questions 8 **Obtuse**
3. $\angle JGH$ in Question 19 **Acute**
4. $\angle CEA$ in Question 20 **Acute**
5. $\angle WPS$ in Questions 21-23 **Right**

Notes on Questions

You might review **Questions 1–15** in order to insure that the basic ideas of the lesson are clear to students.

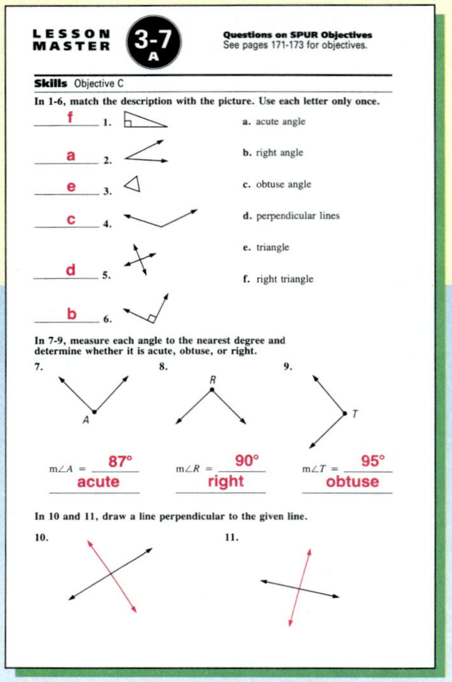
LESSON MASTER 3-7 A

Questions on SPUR Objectives
See pages 171-173 for objectives.

Skills Objective C

In 1-6, match the description with the picture. Use each letter only once.

f 1.
a 2.
e 3.
c 4.
d 5.
b 6.

a. acute angle
b. right angle
c. obtuse angle
d. perpendicular lines
e. triangle
f. right triangle

In 7-9, measure each angle to the nearest degree and determine whether it is acute, obtuse, or right.

7. $m\angle A =$ 87° acute
8. $m\angle R =$ 90° right
9. $m\angle T =$ 95° obtuse

In 10 and 11, draw a line perpendicular to the given line.

10.
11.

Acute and Obtuse Angles

If the measure of an angle is between 0° and 90°, the angle is called an **acute angle.** An **obtuse angle** is an angle whose measure is between 90° and 180°. Most of the time, you can tell whether an angle is acute or obtuse just by looking. If you are unsure, you can measure.

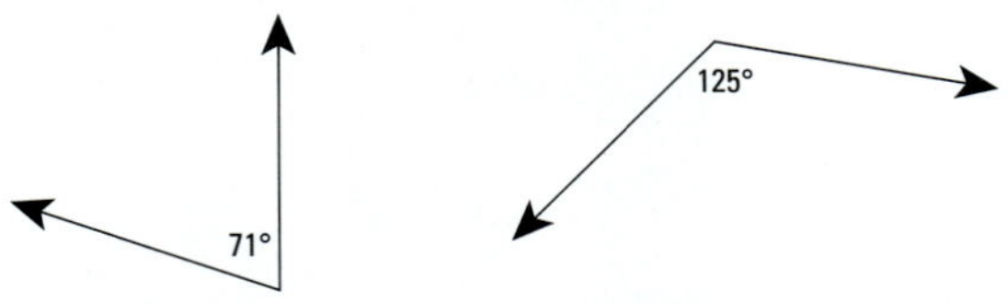

Triangles

A **triangle** gets its name because it is formed by parts of three angles. The triangle *TEN* drawn here has angles *T, E,* and *N.* Angle *T* is obtuse while angles *E* and *N* are acute. $\triangle AOK$ below ($\triangle$ is the symbol for triangle) is called a **right triangle** because one of its angles is a right angle.

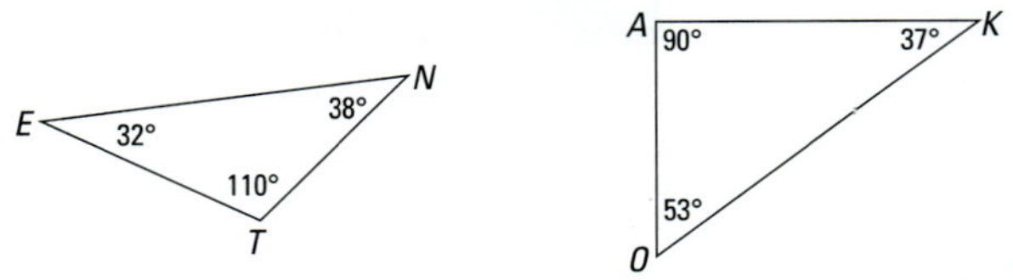

QUESTIONS

Covering the Reading

In 1–3, give a definition for the phrase. **See left.**

1. acute angle **2.** obtuse angle **3.** right triangle

1) an angle whose measure is between 0° and 90°

2) an angle whose measure is between 90° and 180°

3) a triangle with a right angle

4. Explain what is wrong with this sentence: Two angles are perpendicular if they form right angles. **Replace "Two angles" by "Two lines" because perpendicular is a relationship between two lines, not**

In 5–8, state whether an angle with the given measure is acute, right, or obtuse.

5. 40° **acute** **6.** 9° **acute** **7.** 140° **obtuse** **8.** 90° **right**

In 9–12, without measuring, tell whether the angle looks acute, right, or obtuse.

9. **right** **10.** **acute** **11.** **obtuse** **12.** **obtuse**

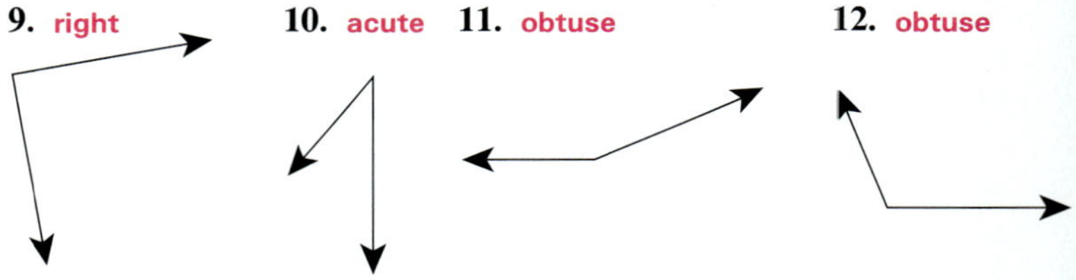

Optional Activities

Activity 1 Dangerous Intersections
Materials: Maps of a town or city

As an extension of **Question 40,** have students **work in pairs** and use a map of a town or city to find "dangerous" intersections. Suggest that they trace the angles formed by the streets and measure them.

Activity 2 History Connection
Materials: String, pegs or pins

After discussing right angles, you might explain that builders in ancient Egypt made right angles by stretching a rope around 3 pegs. The rope was separated into twelve equal parts by thirteen knots. Have students **work in groups,** mark a piece of heavy string in 12 equal parts, and stretch it around pegs or pins to show how this can be done. [Students should make a triangle with sides of 3, 4, and 5 units.]

13. *Multiple choice.* Which triangle looks like a right triangle? (c)

(a) (b) (c) (d)

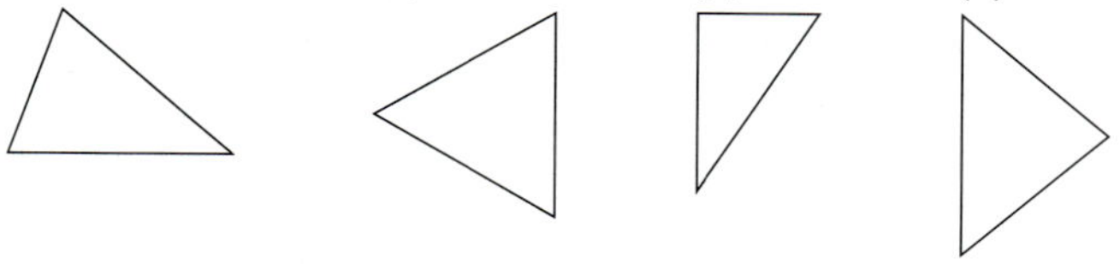

19)

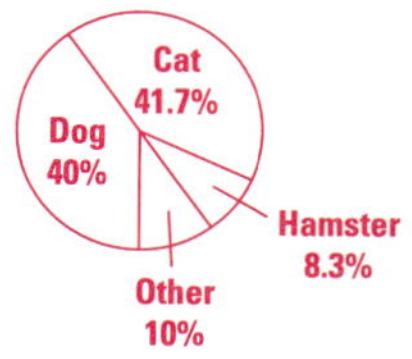

In 14 and 15, use the figure.

a. Tell whether the angle is acute or obtuse.

b. Give the measure of the angle.

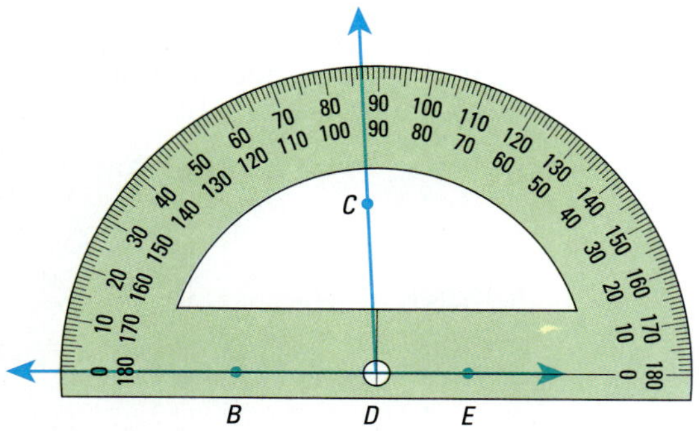

14. $\angle CDE$ a) obtuse; b) 93°

15. $\angle CDB$ a) acute; b) 87°

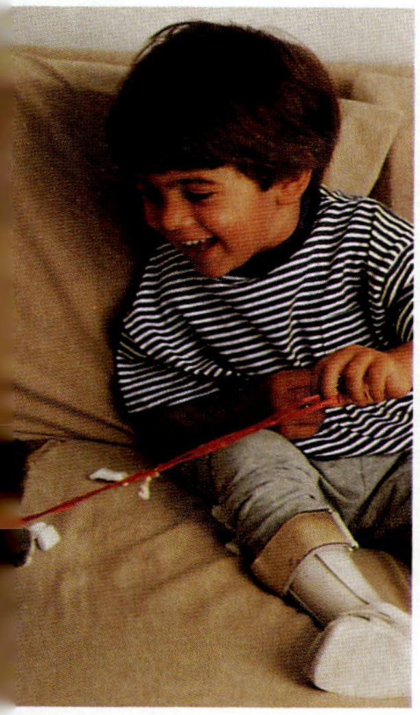

The purrfect pet. *Like many Americans, this boy prefers a cat for his pet. There are about 58 million pet cats in U.S. homes today. A bunch of cats is sometimes called a clowder of cats.*

Applying the Mathematics

In 16–18, refer to the In-class Activity on page 152 and the circle graph drawn there.

16. Define: central angle. an angle with its vertex at the center of the circle

17. What is the measure of the smallest central angle? 54°

18. Which central angles are acute, which right, which obtuse? acute: English, Social Studies; right: Science; obtuse: Math

19. Sixty students were asked to name their favorite pet. Their choices are given in the table below. Represent this information on a circle graph. See above left.

Pet	Number of students choosing that pet
Cat	25
Dog	24
Hamster	5
Other	6

Notes on Questions

Question 19 Multicultural Connection Today, cats have surpassed dogs as the most popular pets in the United States. The Siamese cat is the most popular shorthaired cat currently registered in the United States. Writings from Thailand indicate that the Siamese breed is well over two centuries old. Siamese cats were observed in Russia in the late 1700s, and the breed arrived in England by 1871. By the turn of the century, Siamese cats were in the United States, and the breed began to appear at American shows. Interested students may wish to research other breeds of cats or household pets and find out where they originated.

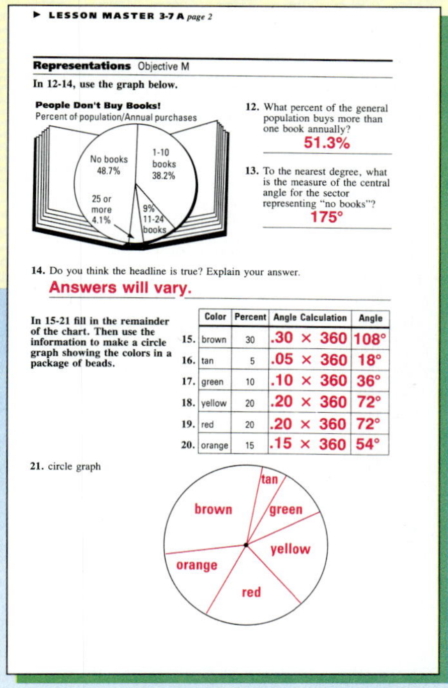

▸ **LESSON MASTER 3-7 A** *page 2*

Representations Objective M

In 12-14, use the graph below.

People Don't Buy Books!
Percent of population/Annual purchases

No books 48.7%
1-10 books 38.2%
25 or more 4.1%
9% 11-24 books

12. What percent of the general population buys more than one book annually? 51.3%

13. To the nearest degree, what is the measure of the central angle for the sector representing "no books"? 175°

14. Do you think the headline is true? Explain your answer. Answers will vary.

In 15-21 fill in the remainder of the chart. Then use the information to make a circle graph showing the colors in a package of beads.

	Color	Percent	Angle Calculation	Angle
15.	brown	30	.30 × 360	108°
16.	tan	5	.05 × 360	18°
17.	green	10	.10 × 360	36°
18.	yellow	20	.20 × 360	72°
19.	red	20	.20 × 360	72°
20.	orange	15	.15 × 360	54°

21. circle graph

brown, tan, green, yellow, red, orange

Adapting to Individual Needs

English Language Development

Write one vocabulary word per card on a set of index cards. Use words such as perpendicular, acute, obtuse, and right. Prepare enough sets so that students can **work in groups** of four. Distribute a set to each group and have students in the group list three real-life examples of each word on the other side of the card.

Extra Help

Materials: Index cards

Have students draw six angles with different measures. Ask students to compare each angle with a corner of an index card and tell if the angle they drew is acute, right, or obtuse.

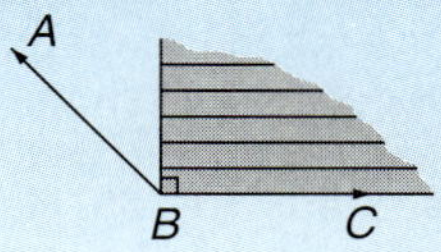

Notes on Questions

Question 25d Error Alert Many students forget that the hour hand moves halfway between 6 and 7 at the half hour. You might use a clock to illustrate this.

Question 26 The necessity of extending the sides presents problems for some students who still do not realize that the size of an angle does not change when the sides are extended.

Question 40 The measure of the smaller angle between two intersecting two-way streets is a measure of the safety of the intersection. The smaller the angle, the less safe the intersection is. For this reason, most city planners or engineers try to have streets intersect at right angles. This idea is also considered in *Activity 1* in *Optional Activities* on page 154, and is covered in more detail in Lesson 7-7.

Follow-up for Lesson 3-7

Practice

For more questions on SPUR objectives, use **Lesson Master 3-7A** (shown on pages 154–155) or **Lesson Master 3-7B** (shown on pages 156-157).

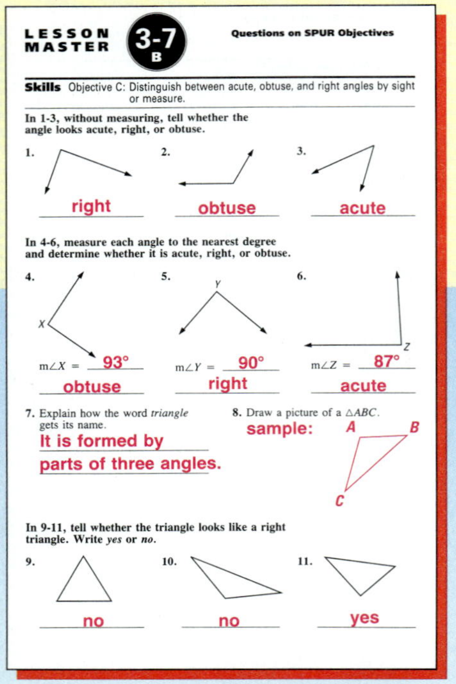

LESSON MASTER 3-7 B Questions on SPUR Objectives

Skills Objective C: Distinguish between acute, obtuse, and right angles by sight or measure.

In 1-3, without measuring, tell whether the angle looks acute, right, or obtuse.

1. right
2. obtuse
3. acute

In 4-6, measure each angle to the nearest degree and determine whether it is acute, right, or obtuse.

4. m∠X = 93° obtuse
5. m∠Y = 90° right
6. m∠Z = 87° acute

7. Explain how the word *triangle* gets its name. It is formed by parts of three angles.

8. Draw a picture of a △ABC. sample:

In 9-11, tell whether the triangle looks like a right triangle. Write *yes* or *no*.

9. no
10. no
11. yes

20. Find two examples of right angles different from those mentioned in this lesson. Samples: angle of ceiling with wall, corner of a window

21. Copy the line. Then using a ruler and protractor, draw a line perpendicular to the given line.

a.

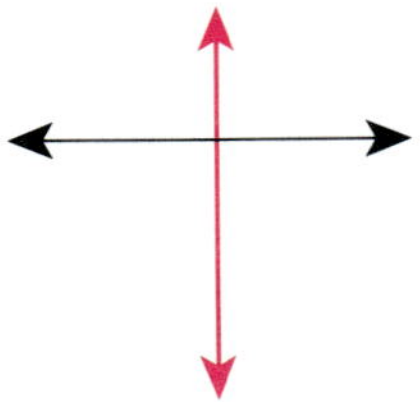

b.

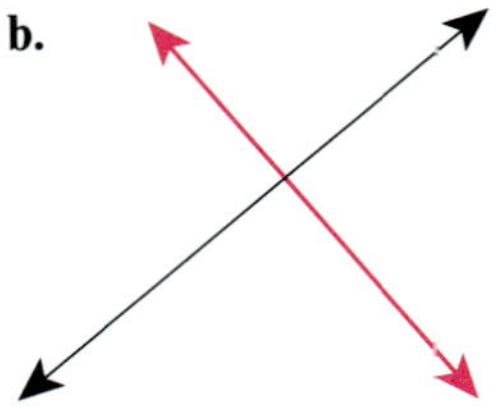

In 22–24, the picture is a closeup of the markings on a giraffe. See left.
a. Tell whether the angle is acute, right, or obtuse.
b. Measure the angle.

22 a) right
b) 90°

23 a) obtuse
b) 134°

24 a) acute
b) 60°

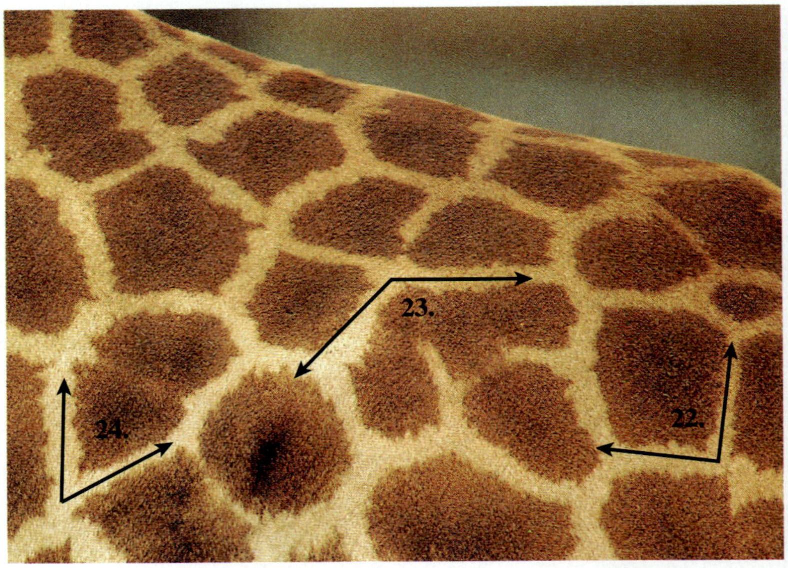

25. Name the type of angle and give the measure of the angle formed by the minute and hour hands of a watch at:
a. 1:00. acute, 30°
b. 4:00. obtuse, 120°
c. 9:00. right, 90°
d. 6:30. (Be careful!) acute, 15°

26. Find the measures of the three angles of $\triangle XYZ$. (You may want to copy the triangle and extend the lines of the sides before measuring.)

Figures appear smaller than actual size in Teacher's Edition.

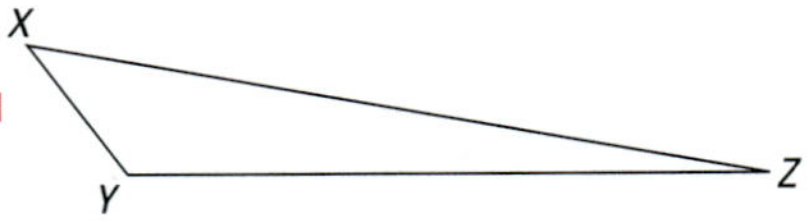

$m\angle X = 43°$, $m\angle Y = 127°$, $m\angle Z = 10°$

Adapting to Individual Needs

Challenge

Explain that a magnetic compass points to the magnetic North Pole, not the true North Pole. To correct for this, one must use the declination of his or her location. For example, if the declination is 15° east, the compass points 15° east of true north, and true north lies 15° to the left of the magnetic needle. Have students research the magnetic declinations in the United States and show them on **Teaching Aid 35**. Have them give the declination of their location.

Magnetic Declinations in the U. S.

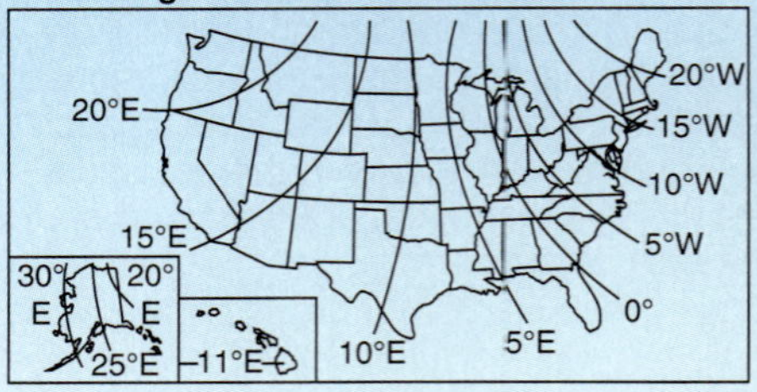

Review

27) 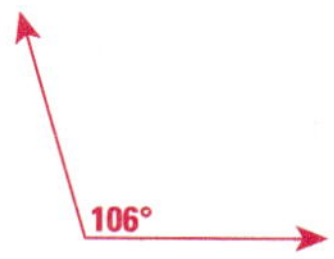

27. Accurately draw a 106° angle. *(Lesson 3-6)*

In 28–31, use <, =, or > to complete the relationship. *(Lessons 1-6, 3-4, 3-5)*

28. 2 meters __?__ 1 yard **>**

29. 1 kg __?__ 10,000 g **<**

30. 1 kg __?__ $4\frac{2}{3}$ lb **<**

31. 2 liters __?__ 1 gal **<**

In 32–34, complete the statement by using a reasonable metric unit. *(Lesson 3-4)*

32. In one day we rode 40 __?__ on our bikes. **km**

33. A cup can hold about 0.24 __?__ of water. **liter**

34. The meat she ate weighed 350 __?__. **grams**

35. Measure the longest side of triangle *XYZ* in Question 26 to the nearest $\frac{1}{4}$ inch. *(Lesson 3-1)* **$2\frac{1}{4}$ inches**

36. Tungsten wire four ten-thousandths of an inch in diameter is used to make filaments for light bulbs.
   a. Write this number as a decimal. **0.0004 in.**
   b. Write this number in scientific notation. *(Lessons 1-2, 2-9)* **4×10^{-4} in.**

37. According to one survey, teenage boys spend an average of 32% of their allowance on food. Teenage girls spend an average of 26% on food. If a boy and girl each receives $20, on average how much more does the boy spend on food? *(Lesson 2-5)* **$1.20**

Exploration

38. A person has acute appendicitis.
   a. What does this mean? **Sample: a sharp, severe case of appendicitis**
   b. Does this use of the word *acute* have any relation to the idea of acute angle? **Sample: An acute angle forms a sharp point.**

39. Look up the meaning of the word *obtuse* in the dictionary.
   a. What nonmathematical meaning does this word have?
   b. Is the nonmathematical meaning related to the idea of obtuse angle? **See below.**

40. a. Name a street intersection near your home or school in which the streets do not intersect at right angles.
   b. Approximately what are the measures of the angles formed by the streets?
   c. These kinds of intersections are usually not as safe as right angle intersections. Is anything done at the intersection you named to increase its safety? **Answers will vary.**

39a) Sample: slow in understanding, dull
b) Sample: An obtuse angle is dull in that it does not come to a sharp point.

Assessment

Quiz A quiz covering Lessons 3-4 through 3-7 is provided in the *Assessment Sourcebook.*

Written Communication Have students define and draw examples of the following terms from this lesson.
- right angle
- obtuse angle
- right triangle
- perpendicular
- acute angle

[Definitions are clear, and drawings are labelled correctly showing rays, lines, and angle measures.]

Extension

Technology Connection *Technology Sourcebook, Computer Master 4,* involves pairs of students creating triangles that have side *AB* as the diameter of a circle, and point *C* at a point on the circle. Students use *Geometry Workshop* to create various triangles and measure their angles. Students should discover that the triangles are always right triangles.

Project Update Students who have chosen Project 6, *Computer Drawing Programs,* on page 168, can continue to explore angles and triangles. Students who have chosen Project 5, *Circle Graph Summary,* can decide what they want to survey and when to take the survey.

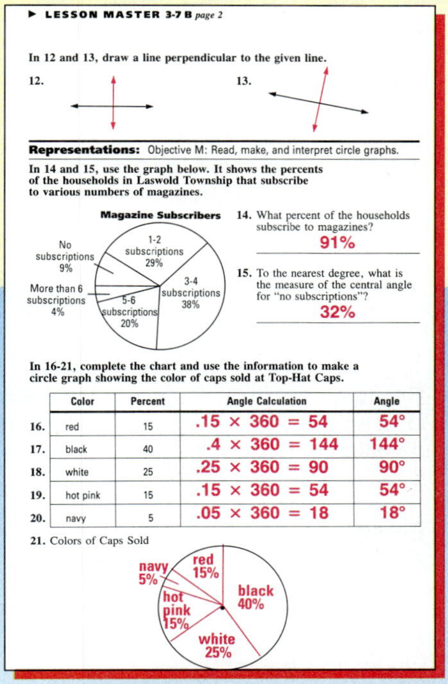

▶ **LESSON MASTER 3-7 B** *page 2*

In 12 and 13, draw a line perpendicular to the given line.

12. 13.

Representations: Objective M: Read, make, and interpret circle graphs.

In 14 and 15, use the graph below. It shows the percents of the households in Laswold Township that subscribe to various numbers of magazines.

14. What percent of the households subscribe to magazines? **91%**

15. To the nearest degree, what is the measure of the central angle for "no subscriptions"? **32%**

In 16-21, complete the chart and use the information to make a circle graph showing the color of caps sold at Top-Hat Caps.

	Color	Percent	Angle Calculation	Angle
16.	red	15	.15 × 360 = 54	54°
17.	black	40	.4 × 360 = 144	144°
18.	white	25	.25 × 360 = 90	90°
19.	hot pink	15	.15 × 360 = 54	54°
20.	navy	5	.05 × 360 = 18	18°

21. Colors of Caps Sold

Setting Up Lesson 3-8

Materials Students will need protractors for Lesson 3-8. There is a protractor on the **Geometry Template.**

Lesson 3-8

Objectives

D Find the area of a square given the length of one side.

J Find areas of squares in real contexts.

Resources

From the ***Teacher's Resource File***

- Lesson Master 3-8A or 3-8B
- Answer Master 3-8
- Teaching Aids
  27 Warm-up
  36 Centimeter grid
- Activity Kit, Activity 6

Additional Resources

- Visuals for Teaching Aids 27, 36

Teaching Lesson 3-8

Warm-up

Place the decimal point correctly in each product. Do not use a calculator.

1. $3.2 \times 3.2 = 1024$ **10.24**
2. $6.01 \times 6.01 = 361201$ **36.1201**
3. $7 \times 7 = 49$ **49.0**
4. $9.4 \times 9.4 = 8836$ **88.36**
5. $6.3^2 = 3969$ **39.69**
6. $7.25^2 = 525625$ **52.5625**

Notes on Reading

Notice that the figures showing a square centimeter and square inch are pictured in actual size in the Pupil's Edition so that they can compare them. It might also be helpful to students if you, or pairs of students, draw an actual sized square foot, square yard, and square meter on the chalkboard.

LESSON

3-8 *Measuring Area*

Shopping today? *Rental fees for retail stores, such as those shown here in the Mall of America in Bloomington, MN, are based upon location and area of the floorspace. In upscale malls, yearly rents may vary from $25 to $40 a square foot.*

The visual impact of a circle graph is based on *area.* The larger the percent being graphed, the larger the area of the sector.

What Is Area?

Area is a measure of the space inside a two-dimensional (flat) figure. You can think of area as a measure of how much is shaded within the figures drawn here.

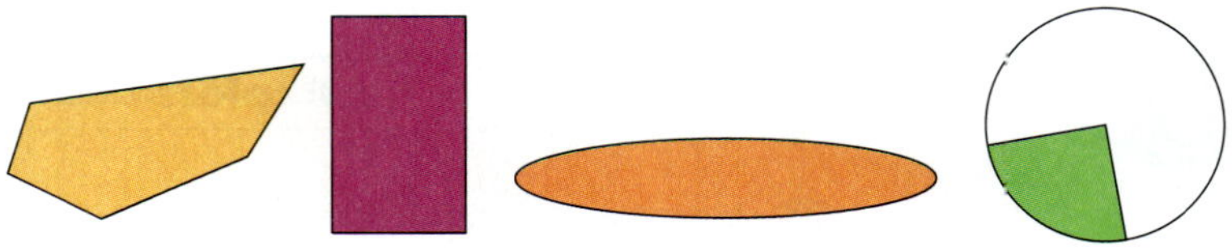

How Is Area Measured?

Regardless of how a figure is shaped, it is customary to measure its area in square units. Recall that a **square** is a four-sided figure with four right angles and four sides of equal length. The common units for measuring area are squares with sides of unit length.

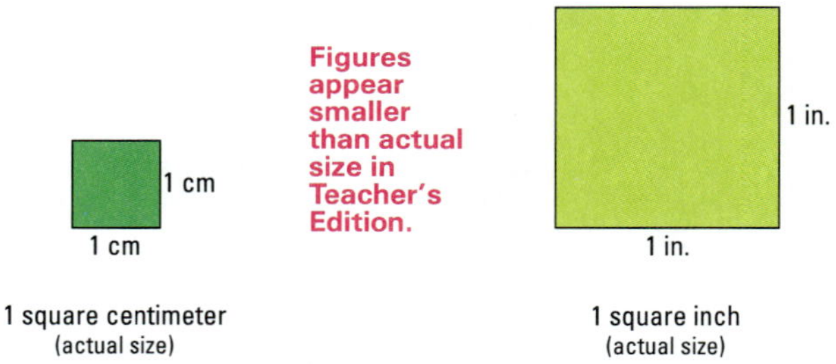

Figures appear smaller than actual size in Teacher's Edition.

Lesson 3-8 Overview

Broad Goals This lesson introduces the concept and units of area. Strictly speaking, despite the lesson title, area is usually not measured; it is calculated.

Perspective Some students may know that $A = s^2$, which is given on the top of page 160, is a *formula.* The word formula is not used until Lesson 4-7 when the formula $A = \ell w$ is introduced for the area of a rectangle. In Chapter 9, $A = \ell w$ is presented again as one of the basic uses of multiplication. Toward the end of the book, other area formulas are considered. Thus, the idea of area runs through many chapters.

Squares may be of any size. Large amounts of land in the U.S. are measured in square miles. Elsewhere in the world, area is measured in metric units. A **square kilometer** is the space taken up by a square whose sides are 1 km long. A **hectare** is the space taken up by a square whose sides are 100 meters long.

Figures with different shapes can have the same area. Each of these figures has shaded area equal to 2 square centimeters. But the lengths of their sides are quite different.

❶
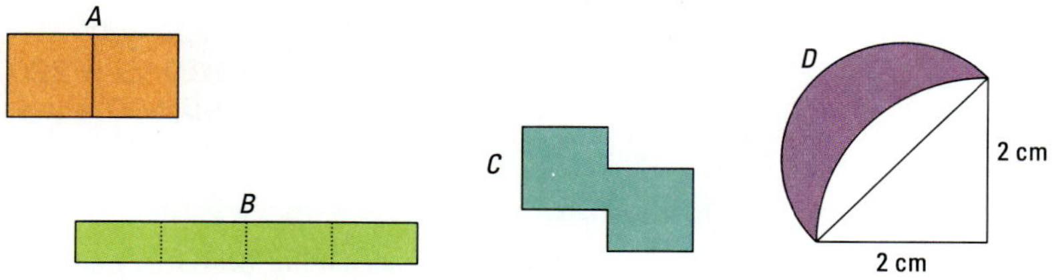

How Can Area Be Calculated?

There are three ways to find areas of figures. One way is to count square units. This will work in Figure *A* above. Another way is to cut and rearrange parts of figures. This will work in figures *B* and *C*. But if a figure is complicated, like the shaded part of *D*, formulas are needed. The simplest formula is that for the area of a square.

Each side of the square at the right has length 5 units. Counting shows that there are 25 square units.

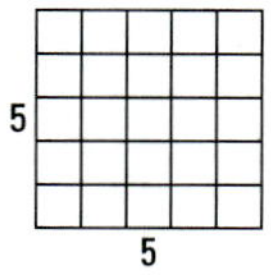

Each side of this square has length 5.5 units. Counting shows 25 whole square units, 10 half squares (which equal 5 whole squares), and an extra quarter square. This totals 30.25 square units.

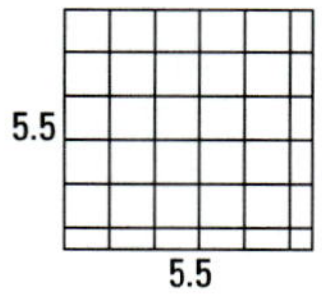

❷ Notice that $5^2 = 25$ and $5.5^2 = 30.25$.

> **The area of a square equals the second power of the length of one of its sides.**

For this reason, 5 to the second power, 5^2, is often read "5 squared." Also, for this reason, you can write square inches as in^2, square centimeters as cm^2, and square kilometers as km^2. You can write the equation:

$$\text{Area of a square} = (\text{length of side})^2$$

❶ Most students will understand why the area of each of figures A, B, and C is 2 square centimeters. However, they will probably have to accept the fact that the area of figure D has the same area. The following discussion shows why this is so; but it is too difficult for most students to understand at this level.

The non-shaded part of the figure, (the triangle and the segment of the circle) is a quarter circle with radius 2 cm. The area is:

$$\tfrac{1}{4}(\pi \cdot 2^2)\text{ cm}^2 = \pi\text{ cm}^2$$

Subtracting the area of the triangle gives the area of the segment of the circle:

$$\pi\text{ cm}^2 - 2\text{ cm}^2 = (\pi - 2)\text{ cm}^2$$

The circle segment and the shaded region form a half circle with the diameter equal to the hypotenuse of the triangle. Its area is:

$$\tfrac{1}{2} \cdot \pi \cdot \left(\tfrac{2\sqrt{2}}{2}\right)^2\text{ cm}^2 = \pi\text{ cm}^2$$

Now subtracting the area of the circle segment gives the area of the shaded part:

$$\pi - (\pi - 2)\text{ cm}^2 = 2\text{ cm}^2$$

❷ **Using a physical model**
Students can verify that the area is 30.25 square units by drawing the figure on the grid given on **Teaching Aid 36** and then demonstrating how the 10 half-squares form 5 whole squares.

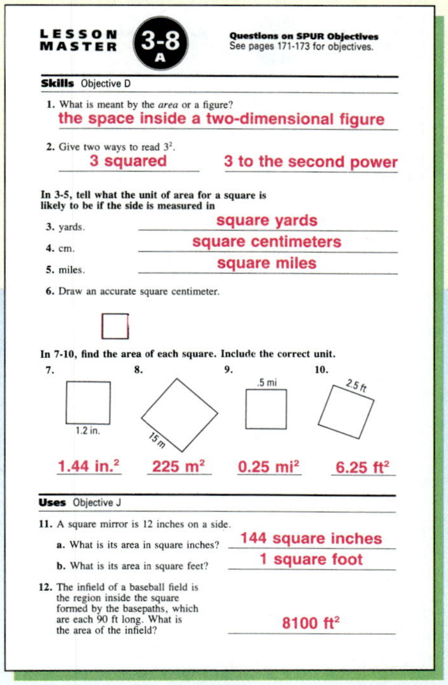
LESSON MASTER 3-8 A

Questions on SPUR Objectives
See pages 171-173 for objectives.

Skills Objective D

1. What is meant by the *area* of a figure? the space inside a two-dimensional figure

2. Give two ways to read 3^2. 3 squared; 3 to the second power

In 3-5, tell what the unit of area for a square is likely to be if the side is measured in

3. yards. square yards

4. cm. square centimeters

5. miles. square miles

6. Draw an accurate square centimeter.

In 7-10, find the area of each square. Include the correct unit.

7. 1.2 in. — 1.44 in.^2

8. 15 m — 225 m^2

9. .5 mi — 0.25 mi^2

10. 2.5 ft — 6.25 ft^2

Uses Objective J

11. A square mirror is 12 inches on a side.
   a. What is its area in square inches? 144 square inches
   b. What is its area in square feet? 1 square foot

12. The infield of a baseball field is the region inside the square formed by the basepaths, which are each 90 ft long. What is the area of the infield? 8100 ft^2

Video

Wide World of Mathematics The segment, *Huge Mall Opens*, examines the vastness of the largest shopping mall in the U.S.—the Mall of America in Bloomington, MN. Data related to the mall are presented to launch or extend a lesson on measuring area. Related questions and an investigation are provided in videodisc stills and in the Video Guide. A related CD-ROM activity is also available.

Videodisc bar codes

Search Chapter 14

Play

You can use *Activity 1* in *Optional Activities* (below) to extend the idea of cutting figures apart and rearranging the parts to find the area.

❸ You may wish to point out that a city block is often called "220 yards square." Explain that this is not the same as 220 square yards. Two hundred twenty yards square implies the region forms a square with sides of length 220 yards, but any shaped region might have an area of 220 square yards.

Additional Examples

1. Draw a square 2.5 units on a side. Show that its area is 6.25 square units.
   $4 + 1 + 1 + \frac{1}{4} = 6\frac{1}{4}$

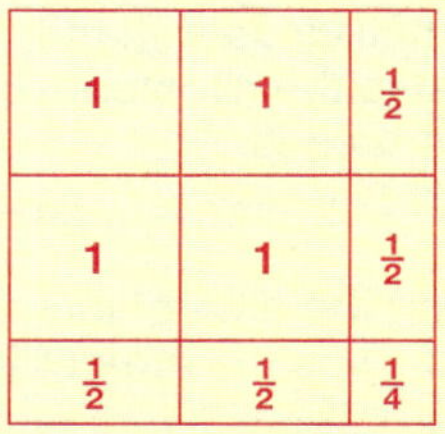

2. A standard floor tile is 9 inches on a side. Find its area. **81 in²**
3. A checkerboard is 8 units long and 8 units wide. How many unit squares are on it? **64**

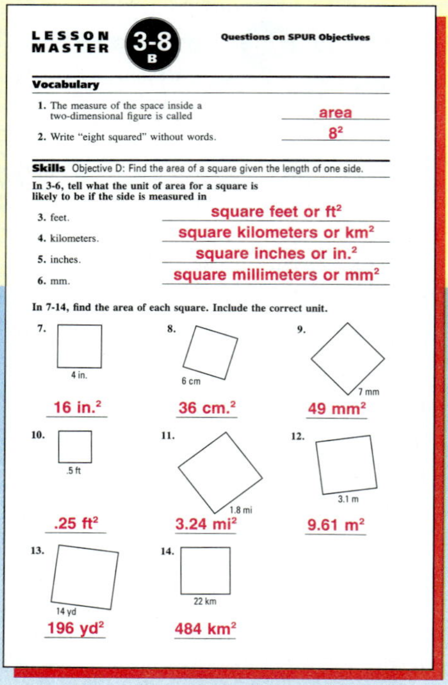

LESSON MASTER 3-8 B Questions on SPUR Objectives

Vocabulary

1. The measure of the space inside a two-dimensional figure is called ___ **area**
2. Write "eight squared" without words. ___ **8²**

Skills Objective D: Find the area of a square given the length of one side.

In 3-6, tell what the unit of area for a square is likely to be if the side is measured in

3. feet. **square feet or ft²**
4. kilometers. **square kilometers or km²**
5. inches. **square inches or in.²**
6. mm. **square millimeters or mm²**

In 7-14, find the area of each square. Include the correct unit.

7. 4 in. **16 in.²**
8. 6 cm **36 cm.²**
9. 7 mm **49 mm²**
10. .5 ft **.25 ft²**
11. 1.8 mi **3.24 mi²**
12. 3.1 m **9.61 m²**
13. 14 yd **196 yd²**
14. 22 km **484 km²**

The letter A is often used as an abbreviation for area. An abbreviation for the length of a side is s. Using these abbreviations, the area of a square can be described in a very short way.

$$A = s^2$$

Example

❸ Find the area of a city block 220 yards on a side.

Solution 1

$$\begin{aligned} \text{Area} &= (220 \text{ yd})^2 \\ &= 220 \text{ yd} \times 220 \text{ yd} \\ &= 48{,}400 \text{ square yards} \\ &= 48{,}400 \text{ yd}^2 \end{aligned}$$

Solution 2

Most scientific calculators have a [x²] key.
(On some calculators you must press [INV] or [F] before pressing this key.)

Key sequence: 220 [x²] [=]
Display: 48,400
Answer: The area is 48,400 yd².

QUESTIONS

Covering the Reading

1. What does area measure in a figure? **the space inside**
2. Suppose length is measured in centimeters. Area will most likely be measured in what units? **square centimeters**
3. What is a *square?* **a four-sided figure with four right angles and four sides of equal length**
4. Which of the following seem to be pictures of squares?

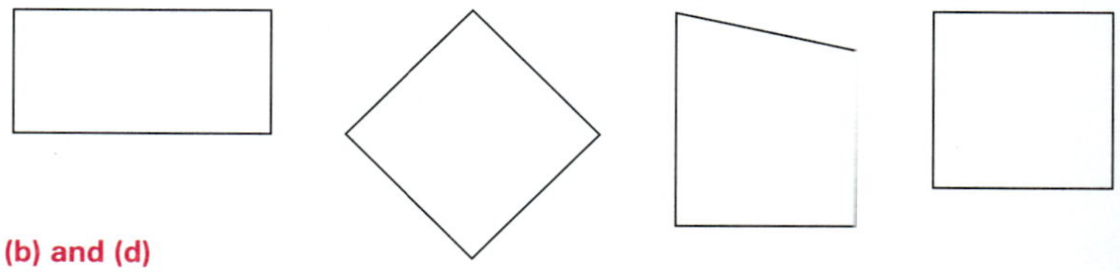

(b) and (d)

5. A square has a side of length 6.7 meters. Write a key sequence to find the area. **6.7 [yˣ] 2 [=] or 6.7 [x²]**
6. Give an example of a square you might find outside a mathematics class. **Sample: a city block**
7. A square is a __?__ -dimensional figure. **two**

Optional Activities

Activity 1 You might want to use *Activity 6* in the *Activity Kit* to introduce this lesson. In this activity, students cut figures apart, form squares, and find the areas.

Activity 2 Cutting Up Area
Materials: Grid paper, scissors, tape

After completing the lesson, you might have students draw and cut out two equal squares. Then cut one square into pieces and rearrange them to form another figure (pieces should not overlap). Ask students to give the area of the figure. They should realize that it has the same area as the square.

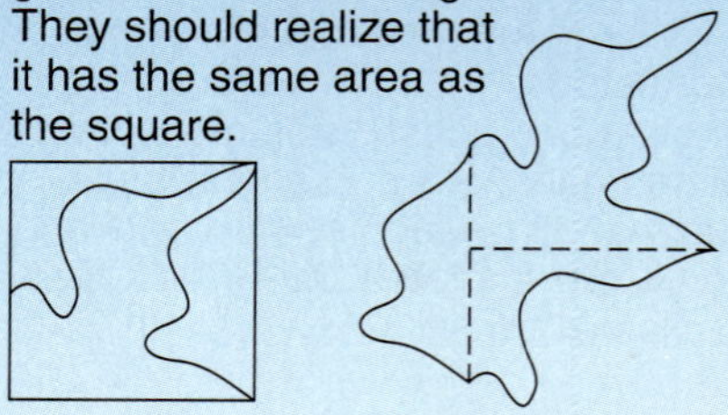

8. Give three ways to find the area of a figure. **count square units, cut and rearrange parts of figures, use formulas**

In 9–11, the length of a side of a square is given. Find the area of the square. Be sure to include the correct unit.

9. **10.** **11.**

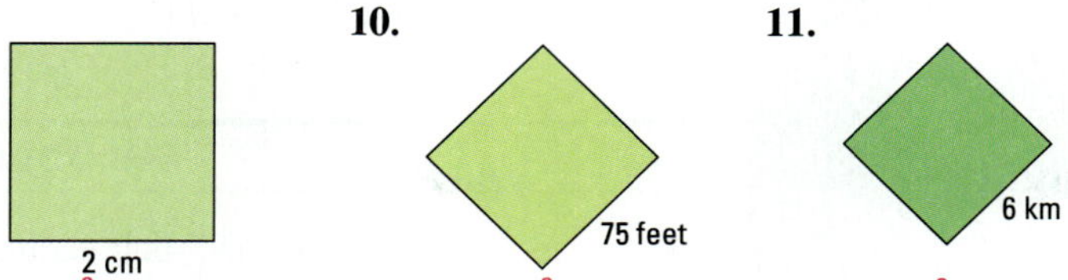

9. **4 cm^2** 10. **5625 ft^2** 11. **36 km^2**

12. 40^2 may be read "40 to the second power" or "40 __?__." **squared**

13. Consider the sentence $A = s^2$.
   a. What does A represent? **area of a square**
   b. What does s represent? **length of a side of a square**
   c. Write this sentence in words. **The area of a square equals the second power of the length of one of its sides.**

14. Find the area of a square that is 1.5 inches on a side. **2.25 in^2**

16 a, b)

Not actual size

c)

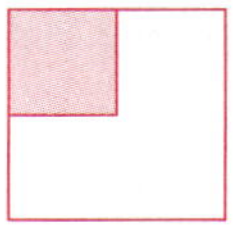

d)

Applying the Mathematics

15. The area of the figure drawn below at the left is how many square inches? **6 in^2**

16. a. Make an accurate drawing of 1 in^2.
   b. Shade 0.5 in^2.
   c. On another drawing, shade $\frac{1}{4}$ in^2.
   d. On still another drawing, shade 0.6 in^2.

17. Remember, there are 3 feet in a yard.
   a. Picture a square yard and split it up into square feet. **See below left.**
   b. How many square feet are in a square yard? **9 ft^2**

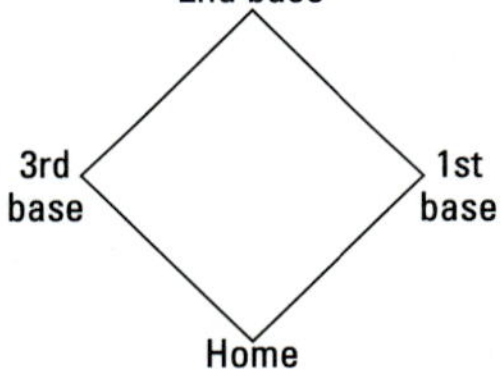

18. A baseball diamond is really a special diamond that is square in shape. The distance from home to 1st base is 90 ft. What is the area of the square? **8100 ft^2**

19. Name the unit of measure in which the floor area of a room would most likely be given.
   a. in the metric system **m^2**
   b. in the U.S. system **ft^2**

17 a)

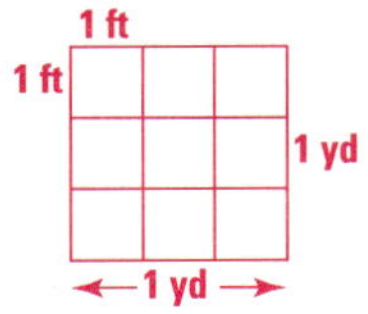

An acre is a unit of area equal to 43,560 square feet. Use this fact in Questions 20 and 21.

20. How many square feet are in 10 acres? **435,600 ft^2**

21. How many square feet are in a half-acre lot? **21,780 ft^2**

Notes on Questions

Question 4 Some students may think the figure in **part b** is not a square because it is tilted. Demonstrate how a square can be rotated, pointing out that the figure is still a square.

Question 17 Consumers usually measure room dimensions in feet, but carpeting is sold by the square yard. Converting square feet to square yards requires dividing by nine, not three, which significantly affects the estimated cost.

▶ LESSON MASTER 3-8 B *page 2*

15. In the space below, draw an accurate square inch.

16. In the space below, draw a square 2 cm on a side. Give the area of the square, including the correct unit. **4 cm^2**

Uses Objective J: Find areas of squares in real contexts.

17. A square garden is 24 yards on a side. Find its area. **576 yd^2**

18. A square tile is 1 foot on a side.
   a. What is its area in square feet? **1 ft^2**
   b. What is its area in square inches? **144 $in.^2$**

19. A square napkin is 17 inches on a side. Find its area. **289 $in.^2$**

20. A square tablecloth is 4.5 feet on a side. Find its area. **20.25 ft^2**

21. A square window is .8 m on a side. Find its area. **.64 m^2**

22. A quilt is made up of 96 squares, each 6 inches on a side. What is the total area of the quilt in square feet? **24 ft^2**

Review Objective C, Lesson 2-2

In 23-30, write each power as a decimal.

23. 2^8	**256**	24. 51^2	**2,601**
25. 3^4	**81**	26. 9^3	**729**
27. 1^{14}	**1**	28. 2.6^3	**17.576**
29. 0^{700}	**0**	30. $52{,}047.6^1$	**52,047.6**

Adapting to Individual Needs

Extra Help

Materials: Centimeter grid paper or **Teaching Aid 36**

To help students understand the meaning of area, have each student trace a closed palm of one of their hands on centimeter grid paper and then count the number of square centimeters *completely inside* the traced-hand figure. Then have students count all the squares needed to *completely cover* the figure. Explain that the actual area of the palm of their hand is between these two measurements.

Notes on Questions

Question 22b Science Connection A rain forest is generally composed of tall, broad-leaved evergreen trees, and it is usually found in the wet tropical uplands and lowlands around the equator. Rain forests have high annual rainfalls of more than 1800 mm (70 inches). The topography of rain forests varies, as do the soil conditions. Encourage interested students to research rain forests to learn about the various plant layers and the animals represented in the rain forest ecosystem.

Question 32 Encourage students to count all the squares with a particular area, then count all the squares with a different area, and so on, until they have counted them all. Students may not realize that squares of four different areas are represented.

Follow-up for Lesson 3-8

Practice

For more questions on SPUR objectives, use **Lesson Master 3-8A** (shown on page 159) or **Lesson Master 3-8B** (shown on pages 160–161).

Assessment

Oral / Written Communication
Area is a common topic in the middle elementary grades, so your students may be quite familiar with the ideas presented in this lesson. You might discuss with students what they considered new in this lesson and what they considered review. Or, you might ask them to write a paragraph describing what was new and what was review. [Discussion or paragraphs reveal any need for further development.]

Extension

Have students use the grid on **Teaching Aid 36** and draw different figures, each having the same area.

Project Update Project 4, *Large Edifices,* on page 168, relates to the content of this lesson and the next lesson. Students who selected this project can begin their research at this time.

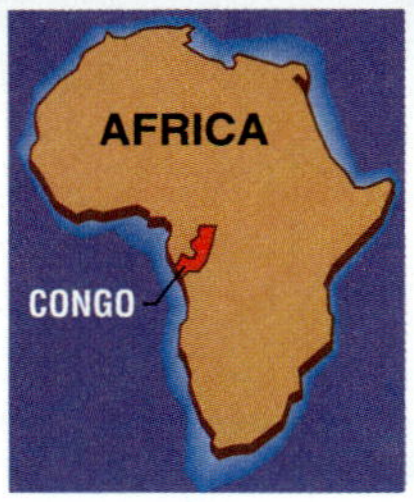

Where few have gone before. *The Ndoki rain forest in northern Congo is one of the last unexplored rain forests on Earth. Surrounded by swamps and the unnavigable Ndoki river, the rain forest is almost impossible to reach. So few humans have been to the Ndoki that the animals here, unlike in other parts of Africa, are not afraid of humans.*

22. a. How many hectares are in 1 square kilometer? **100 hectares = 1 km^2**

b. In the Republic of the Congo, commonly known as the Congo, is the 3 million hectare Ndoki (en-doe-key) rain forest. Is the Ndoki larger or smaller than Maryland? The state of Maryland has an area of about 27,100 km^2. **The Ndoki is larger than Maryland.**

Review

23. An angle has measure 19°. Is it acute, right, or obtuse? *(Lesson 3-7)* **acute**

24. Measure this angle to the nearest degree. *(Lesson 3-6)* **10°**

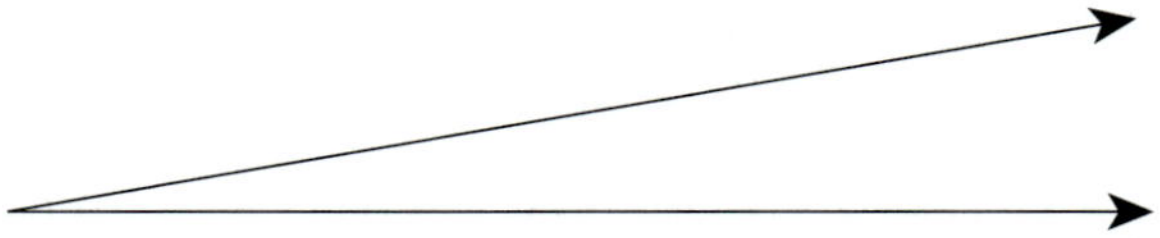

25. a. Sixty kilograms is about how many pounds? *(Lesson 3-5)* **≈ 132 lb**

b. Sixty kilograms is how many grams? *(Lesson 3-4)* **60,000 g**

26. Every spring, Indiana University holds a team bicycle race called the "Little 500." The women's course is 40.3 km long. About how many miles is this? *(Lesson 3-5)* **about 25 mi**

27. Measure the length of this printed line (from the *M* in "Measure" to the *o* in "to") to the nearest half centimeter. *(Lesson 3-1)* **11.5 cm**

28. Which is larger, 0 or 10^0? *(Lesson 2-8)* **10^0**

29. A school has 600 students. *(Lessons 2-4, 2-5, 2-6)*

a. Ten percent of the students is how many students? **60**

b. Use your answer in part **a** to find 20%, 40%, and 70% of the student body without doing another percent calculation. **120; 240; 420**

30. Round 2^{30} to the nearest million. *(Lessons 1-4, 2-2)* **1,074,000,000**

31. Complete the statement with $<$, $=$, or $>$. 13.26 _?_ $13\frac{4}{13}$. **$<$** *(Lessons 1-6, 1-9)*

Exploration

32. How many squares are in the pattern drawn below? **10**

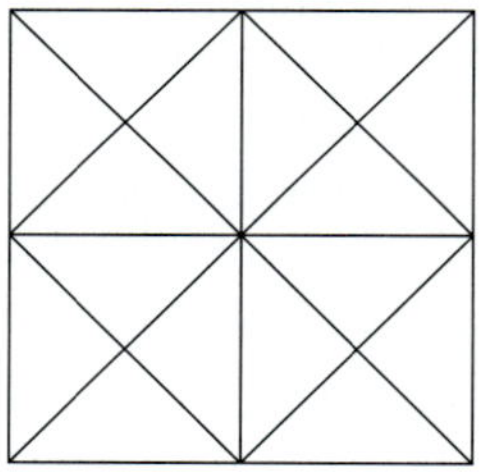

Adapting to Individual Needs

Challenge
Give the students the following problem.

A rectangular piece of carpeting is 135 inches long by 60 inches wide. How can the carpet be cut into two pieces of equal size and shape to cover a 90-inch square entry way? [One solution is given.]

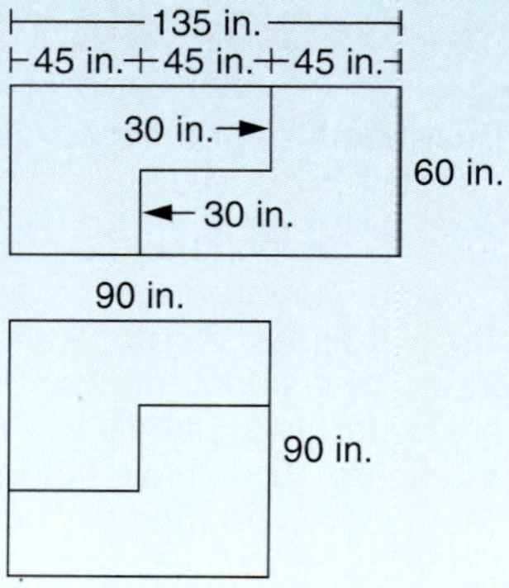

LESSON

3-9

Measuring Volume

Space is no problem here. *The Vehicle Assembly Building (VAB) at the Kennedy Space Center, Cape Canaveral, FL, is where space shuttles are prepared for launch. The VAB is 525 ft tall and has 4 bays with doors 460 ft high. Its capacity of 129.5 million cubic feet is greater than that of any other scientific building.*

What Is Volume?

Volume measures the space inside a three-dimensional or solid figure. Think of volume as measuring the amount a box, jar, or other container can hold. This is also called the container's **capacity.** Or think of volume as telling you how much material is in something that is solid. Whatever the shape of a figure, its volume is usually measured in **cubic units.** A **cube** is a figure with six faces, each face being a square. Sugar cubes, number cubes, and dice are examples of cubes. The most common units for measuring volume are cubes with edges of unit length.

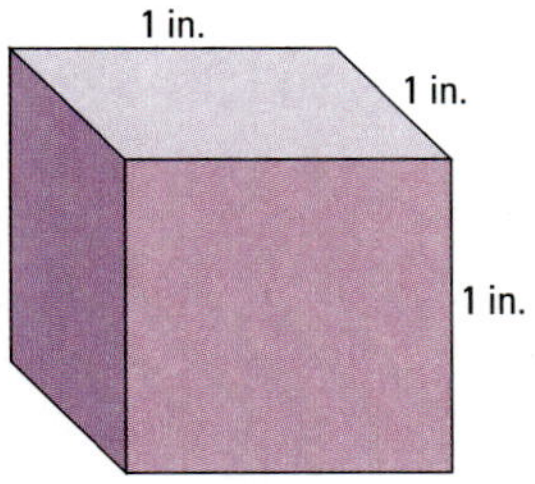

1 cubic inch

In a **cubic centimeter,** each edge has length 1 centimeter. Each face is a square with area 1 square centimeter.

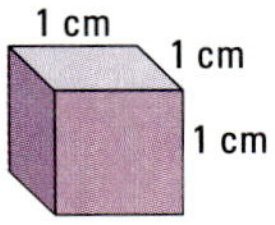

1 cubic centimeter

Notice that volume is quite different from area. Area is two-dimensional. The amount of paper it would take to cover the outside surface of the cube is an area, the *surface area* of the cube. Volume is three-dimensional. The *volume* of the cube indicates how much sand can be poured into the cube.

Lesson 3-9

Objectives

D Find the volume of a cube given the length of one edge.

J Find volumes of cubes in real contexts.

Resources

From the ***Teacher's Resource File***

- Lesson Master 3-9A or 3-9B
- Answer Master 3-9
- Teaching Aids
  - 27 Warm-up
  - 37 Square Foot, Cubic Foot (Question 20)
  - 38 Patterns for 1-inch Cube
- Activity Kit, Activity 7

Additional Resources

- Visuals for Teaching Aids 27, 37, 38
- 1000 centimeter cubes
- 1-liter containers

Lesson 3-9 Overview

Broad Goals This lesson is a companion to Lesson 3-8. Its purpose is to introduce the idea of volume and the units for measuring volume.

Perspective The volume of a rectangular solid is discussed in Chapter 9 as an example of a use of multiplication. At that time, volume is distinguished from surface area.

Until the Middle Ages, the only application known for powers was calculating areas and volumes. So when someone wrote the equivalent of 3^2 or 15^3, he or she was likely to be thinking of a square or a cube, which is how the words *squared* and *cubed* for these powers developed.

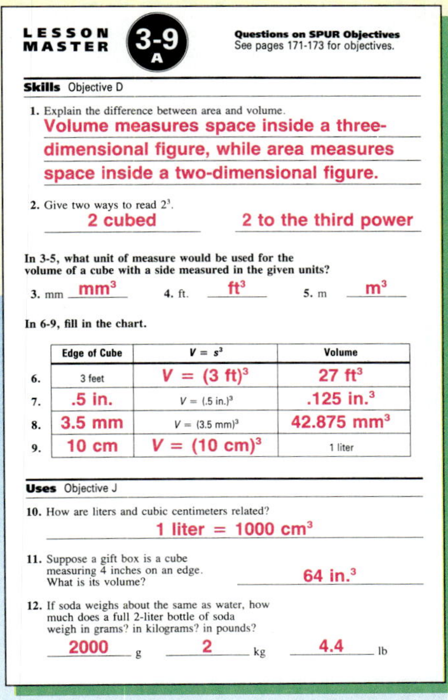

LESSON MASTER 3-9 A

Questions on SPUR Objectives
See pages 171-173 for objectives.

Skills Objective D

1. Explain the difference between area and volume.
Volume measures space inside a three-dimensional figure, while area measures space inside a two-dimensional figure.

2. Give two ways to read 2^3.
2 cubed   2 to the third power

In 3-5, what unit of measure would be used for the volume of a cube with a side measured in the given units?

3. mm mm^3 4. ft. ft^3 5. m m^3

In 6-9, fill in the chart.

	Edge of Cube	$V = s^3$	Volume
6.	3 feet	$V = (3\ ft)^3$	27 ft^3
7.	.5 in.	$V = (.5\ in.)^3$	.125 $in.^3$
8.	3.5 mm	$V = (3.5\ mm)^3$	42.875 mm^3
9.	10 cm	$V = (10\ cm)^3$	1 liter

Uses Objective J

10. How are liters and cubic centimeters related?
1 liter = 1000 cm^3

11. Suppose a gift box is a cube measuring 4 inches on an edge. What is its volume?
64 $in.^3$

12. If soda weighs about the same as water, how much does a full 2-liter bottle of soda weigh in grams? in kilograms? in pounds?
2000 g   2 kg   4.4 lb

Teaching Lesson 3-9

Warm-up

Work in groups. Solve the following problem.
Cheese wedges like the one at the left are packed in the wedge-shaped box at the right. How many wedges will fit in the box? Explain how you got your answer.

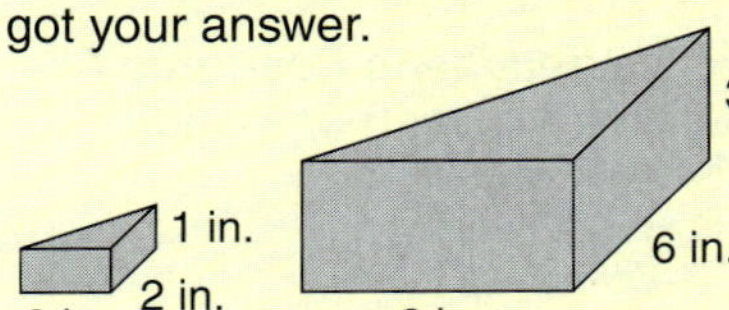

27 cheese wedges; the bottom layer contains 9 wedges and 3 layers fit in the box.

Notes on Reading

There is no substitute for stacking cubes in all sorts of ways to demonstrate volume. Thus, you might use *Activities 1 or 2* in *Optional Activities* (below) to introduce this lesson. **Teaching Aid 38** provides patterns for 1-inch cubes.

❶ You, or your students, might want to model the volume of a 1-liter cube using 1000 centimeter cubes. Even if only two or three layers can be modeled, the idea should be clear to students. Explain that a container the size of the model holds one liter, and show students other one-liter containers for comparison.

LESSON MASTER 3-9 B Questions on SPUR Objectives

Vocabulary

1. The measure of the space inside a three-dimensional figure is called **volume** or **capacity**.
2. Write "four cubed" without words. **4^3**

Skills Objective D: Find the volume of a cube given the length of one edge.

3. Explain the difference between 1 square inch and 1 cubic inch. You may draw sketches if you wish.
1 square inch is the measure of the area inside a square, 1 inch on a side; 1 cubic inch is the measure of the volume inside a cube, 1 inch on an edge. A square is 2-dimensional; a cube is 3-dimensional.
1 square inch
1 cubic inch

In 4-8, tell what the unit of volume for a cube is likely to be if the edge is measured in

4. cm. **cubic centimeters or cm^3**
5. kilometers. **cubic kilometers or km^3**
6. inches. **cubic inches or $in.^3$**
7. yd. **cubic yards or yd^3**
8. mi. **cubic miles or mi^3**
9. List three ways to find the volume of a cube.
Count cubes; cut and paste cubic units together; use a formula.

How Can Volume Be Calculated?

Volume can be calculated by counting cubes, by putting cubic units together, or with a formula. Below is a cube with edges of length 2 units. The picture is partially transparent and shows that there are two layers. The top layer has 2×2, or 4, cubes. So does the bottom layer. In all, there are $2 \times 2 \times 2$ or 2^3, or 8 cubes. So, the volume is 8 cubic units.

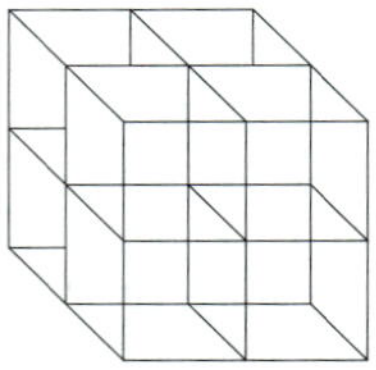

cube with edges of length 2 units

> **The volume of a cube equals the third power of the length of one of its edges.**

For this reason, 2^3, 2 to the third power, is often read "2 cubed." Also, for this reason, you can write cubic inches as in^3, cubic centimeters as cm^3, cubic meters as m^3, and so on. You can write the equation:

$$\text{Volume of a cube} = (\text{length of edge})^3$$

The letter V is an abbreviation for volume. An abbreviation for the length of an edge is e. Using these abbreviations, the above equation becomes

$$V = e^3.$$

❶ The Liter as a Unit of Volume

You have already learned that the liter is a metric unit of capacity. Since capacity is another word for volume, the liter is a unit of volume. It is defined as the volume of a cube that is 10 centimeters on each side.

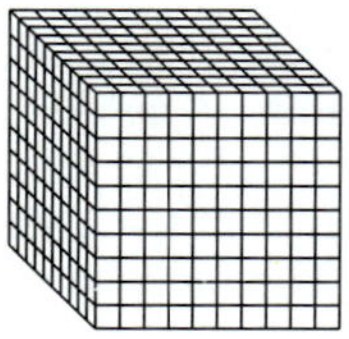

$$\begin{aligned}\text{Volume of cube} &= (10 \text{ cm})^3\\ &= 1000 \text{ cm}^3\\ &= 1 \text{ liter}\end{aligned}$$

Soft drinks are often sold in 2-liter bottles. Since 1 liter = 1000 cm^3, 2 liters = 2000 cm^3. Thus a 2-liter bottle has a volume of 2000 cm^3. Also, since 1 liter = 1000 cm^3, 1 milliliter = $\frac{1}{1000} \cdot 1000 \text{ cm}^3$. A milliliter is another name for cubic centimeter.

Optional Activities

Activity 1 You might use *Activity 7,* from the *Activity Kit* to introduce this lesson.

Activity 2
Materials: Rubik's Cube™

After a class discussion on volume, you might take a Rubik's Cube™ apart to show the equivalent of 27 cubic units: one in the middle of the spindle, 6 attached to the spindle, and 20 others.

Activity 3 One Cubic Mile As an extension of **Question 20**, you might ask students to find the number of cubic feet in one cubic mile. [147,197,952,000 cubic feet] Then have them suppose that a person needs a living space 8 ft by 8 ft by 8 ft, and find the number of people that could "live" in a cubic mile. [287,496,000 people, which is more people than live in the United States.]

QUESTIONS

Covering the Reading

1. What does volume measure in a 3-dimensional figure? the space inside
2. Suppose length is measured in meters. Volume will most likely be measured in what unit? cubic meters
3. What is a *cube?* a figure with 6 square faces
4. Draw a cube.

4) 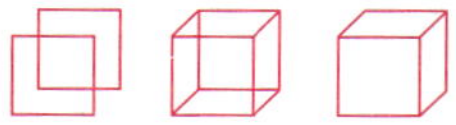

5. Give an example of a cube you might find outside a math class. Sample: sugar cube (or number cube or die)
6. A cube is a _?_-dimensional figure. 3
7. Name three ways to find the volume of a figure. counting cubes, putting cubic units together, using formulas
8. What does the volume of a cube equal? length of an edge cubed

In 9–11, find the volume of a cube with an edge of the given length. Use the correct unit in your answer.

9. 4 inches 64 in^3
10. 40 cm $64{,}000 \text{ cm}^3$
11. 7 yards 343 yd^3
12. A liter is defined as the volume of a cube with an edge of length _?_. 10 cm
13. How many cubic centimeters equal one liter? 1000 cm^3
14. A 2-liter bottle has a volume of _?_ cubic centimeters. 2000

Bon voyage! *The U.S.S. Abraham Lincoln is a nuclear-powered, U.S. Navy aircraft carrier. Besides having 4.5 acres of flight deck, the carrier is one of several warships with the largest full-load displacements in the world, namely 100,846 tons.*

Applying the Mathematics

15. **a.** Find the volume of a cube with edge 3.25 feet. 34.328125 ft^3
    b. The correct answer to part **a** is accurate to a millionth of a cubic foot. This is too precise for many uses. Round your answer to the nearest hundredth, the same precision as the original measure. 34.33 ft^3
16. Calculate six cubed plus five squared. 241
17. Arrange from smallest to largest: 1 liter, 89 cubic centimeters, and the volume of a cube with edge 9 cm. 89 cm^3, volume of cube with edge 9 cm, 1 liter

In 18 and 19, use the following information. You have learned that the liter (a unit of capacity) and the centimeter (a unit of length) are related. In the metric system, these two units are also related to the mass of water. Specifically, 1 cm^3 of water equals 1 mL of water and has a mass of 1 gram at 4°C. Its weight at sea level is 1 gram.

18. How much does a liter of water weigh? 1 kg
19. Suppose an aquarium is a cube 50 cm on a side.
    a. How much water will it hold? 125,000 mL
    b. How much will the water weigh in kilograms? 125 kg
    c. How much will the water weigh in pounds? ≈ 275 lb

The relationship between volume and the weight of water provides still another example of how much easier the metric system is than the U.S. system. In the U.S. system, a gallon of liquid is defined as having a capacity of exactly 231 cubic inches. So a pint contains exactly 28.875 cubic inches. The weight of a gallon of water is approximately 8.3 pounds. In the metric system, a liter is exactly 1000 cubic centimeters, a milliliter is exactly 1 cubic centimeter, and a liter of water weighs 1 kilogram at 4°C.

Additional Examples

You might want to use these examples when discussing the lesson. In 1–3, find the volume of a cube with an edge of the given length.

1. 3 in. 27 in^3
2. 9.5 ft 857.375 ft^3
3. 20 cm 8000 cm^3
4. Using trial and error, how long is the side of a cube if its volume is 64,000 cubic feet? 40 ft

Notes on Questions

The explanation given before **Questions 18 and 19** points out an important relationship within the metric system. If students know the capacity of a container of water in milliliters, they can determine the mass (weight) of the water by multiplying by 0.001. These questions point out the advantages of the metric system when dealing with water.

▶ **LESSON MASTER 3-9 B** *page 2*

In 10-20, fill in the chart.

	Edge of Cube	$V = s^3$	Volume
10.	7 feet	$V = (7 \text{ ft})^3$	343 ft^3
11.	4 cm	$V = (4 \text{ cm})^3$	64 cm^3
12.	5 mm	$V = (5 \text{ mm})^3$	125 mm^3
13.	2.7 m	$V = (2.7 \text{ m})^3$	19.683 m^3
14.	6.5 in.	$V = (6.5 \text{ in.})^3$	274.625 in.^3
15.	.5 yd	$V = (.5 \text{ yd})^3$	$.125 \text{ yd}^3$
16.	.2 mi	$V = (.2 \text{ mi})^3$	$.008 \text{ mi}^3$
17.	1 m	$V = (1 \text{ m})^3$	1 m^3
18.	24 cm	$V = (24 \text{ cm})^3$	$13{,}824 \text{ cm}^3$
19.	12 in.	$V = (12 \text{ in.})^3$	$1{,}728 \text{ in.}^3$
20.	2 ft	$V = (2 \text{ ft})^3$	8 ft^3

Uses Objective J: Find volumes of cubes in real contexts.

21. A box is a cube measuring 6 inches on an edge. What is its volume? 216 in.^3
22. A tool shed is a cube measuring 2.5 m on an edge. What is its volume? 15.625 m^3
23. The inside of an office-size refrigerator is a cube measuring 1.25 ft on an edge. To the nearest hundredth of a foot, what is the volume of the refrigerator? 1.95 ft^3
23. How many cubic centimeters are in 1 liter? $1{,}000 \text{ cm}^3$
24. A dose of cough syrup is 20 cm^3. How many milliliters is this? 20 mL

Adapting to Individual Needs

English Language Development

As an ongoing project, have students construct a class mobile showing formulas from this lesson. In Chapter 4, they can put on the area formula for a rectangle; in Chapter 5, the conversion formulas for temperature; and, in later chapters, other area and volume formulas. Hang the mobile in a corner of the room. Have students explain the formulas from time to time.

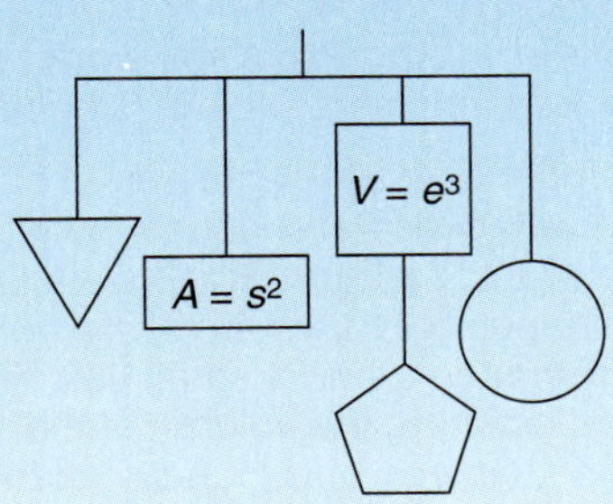

Notes on Questions

Question 20 The figures for this question are on **Teaching Aid 37.** As an extension, see *Activity 3* in *Optional Activities* on page 164.

Question 29 Multicultural Connection In 1958, when regular television broadcasting began in China, there were about 1000 television sets, and the Chinese government broadcast few programs other than those that it approved. By 1989, potential viewers of Chinese television numbered 600 million, and people had viewing choices from around the world. Suggest that students list programs about other countries that are available in their viewing area.

Follow-up for Lesson 3-9

Practice

For more questions on SPUR objectives, use **Lesson Master 3-9A** (shown on page 163) or **Lesson Master 3-9B** (shown on pages 164–165).

Assessment

Oral Communication Write the following units of measure on the board: square centimeter, square foot, square meter, square mile, cubic inch, and cubic yard. Ask students to name things they would measure using each unit and to explain their answers. [Responses indicate an understanding of the units of measure and the concepts of area and volume.]

Extension

Explain that the weight of a material can be found by multiplying its volume by its density. Then have students find the weight of the contents in a bathtub (5 ft by 2.5 ft by 1.5 ft) full of each of the following materials.

Material	Density (lb per in³)	Weight (to nearest lb)
Water	0.036	[1166]
Ice	0.033	[1069]
Aluminum	0.098	[3175]
Iron	0.280	[9072]

Project Update Project 4, *Large Edifices,* on page 168, relates to the content of this lesson.

20. You may want to draw a picture to help with these questions.
  a. How many square inches are there in a square foot? 144 in^2
  b. How many cubic inches are there in a cubic foot? 1728 in^3

Review

21. Give the area of the square drawn at the left. *(Lesson 3-8)* 100 cm^2

22. A band hired to play at a dance thinks that an area of at least 2000 m^2 is needed for the band and for dancing. Explain whether or not the school recreation room, a square 46.5 m on each side, will be large enough. *(Lesson 3-8)* The recreation room area is 2162 m^2 which is greater than 2000 m^2; so the room will be large enough.

23b)

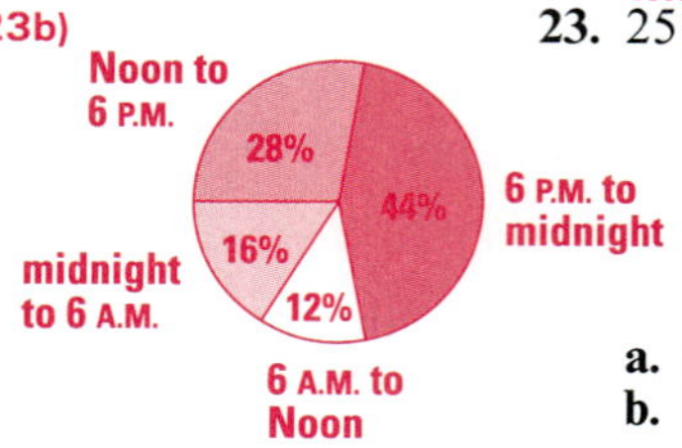

23. 25 people were asked, "What part of the day do you like best?"

4 answered midnight to 6 A.M.	a) 16%
3 answered 6 A.M. to noon	12%
7 answered noon to 6 P.M.	28%
11 answered 6 P.M. to midnight	44%

  a. Calculate the percent that gave each response.
  b. Put this information into a circle graph. *(Lessons 2-5, 3-7)*

24. Change 45 km to feet. *(Lesson 3-5)* ≈147,312 ft

25. *Multiple choice.* A 10-year-old boy who weighs 75 kg is likely to be:
  (a) underweight (b) about the right weight
  (c) overweight. *(Lesson 3-4)* (c)

26. 10^3 meters is how many kilometers? *(Lessons 2-2, 3-4)* 1 km

27. Change 6 yards to inches. *(Lesson 3-2)* 216 inches

28. Rewrite 3.4×10^{-4}
  a. as a decimal. **b.** as a fraction in lowest terms.
  (Lessons 2-6, 2-8) a) 0.00034; b) $\frac{17}{50,000}$

29. In the last 6 months of 1991, an average of 15,353,982 copies of *TV Guide* were sold weekly, the most of any weekly magazine in the U.S.
  a. Round this number to the nearest hundred thousand. 15,400,000
  b. Estimate how many copies were sold over the entire year 1991.
  c. Write your estimate in scientific notation. *(Lessons 1-4, 2-3)*
  Answers will vary. b) Sample: ≈ 800 million; c) 8×10^8

30. *Multiple choice.* Which is not an integer? *(Lessons 1-5, 1-8, 2-2)*
  (a) -4 (b) $\frac{8}{4}$ (c) 52 (d) 0 (e) $\frac{1}{2}$ (e)

Exploration

31. a. What happens to the volume of a cube if the length of an edge is doubled? Try some examples to see what happens. Caution: The volume is *not* doubled. The volume is multiplied by 8 or 2^3.
  b. Can you predict what will happen to the volume of a cube if the length of an edge is tripled? multiplied by 10? If the length of an edge is tripled, the volume is multiplied by 27 or 3^3. For an edge multiplied by 10, volume is multiplied by 10^3 or 1000.

Adapting to Individual Needs

Extra Help Using Physical Models
Materials: Centimeter cubes, small boxes

Have students **work in groups** to build shapes with centimeter cubes, noting the volume of each shape. Emphasize that different shapes can have the same volume. Then give each group a small box. Have students estimate the volume of the box in cubic centimeters, and then check their estimate using the cubes.

Challenge
Pose this problem to students: Suppose a cube like the one on the bottom of page 164 is made by gluing together 1000 centimeter cubes. If the outer surface is painted, how many centimeter cubes would have paint on

a. exactly 1 side? [384 cubes]
b. exactly 2 sides? [96 cubes]
c. exactly 3 sides? [8 cubes]
d. zero sides? [512 cubes]

A project presents an opportunity for you to extend your knowledge of a topic related to the material of this chapter. You should allow more time for a project than you do for typical homework questions.

1 Metric Units

There are metric units other than the ones we have used in this chapter. From an almanac, a science book, or some other source, find out what the seven base units for the metric system are. Identify all of the prefixes that are used (they range from 10^{18} to 10^{-18}). Name some other metric units that are defined from these units, and tell where they are used.

2 Other Traditional Units

The U.S., British, and metric systems are not the only systems of measurement that have ever been devised. For instance, until recently, in East Africa, the Swahili used a system with the following measures: shibiri, mkono, pima, kibaba, kisaga, pishi, wakia, ratli, frasili. Look in the book *Africa Counts,* by Claudia Zaslavsky, or in some other source to find out what these units represent. Write a report about this or some other measurement system different from the systems mentioned in this chapter.

3 Weighing a Collection

Often people collect things for charity drives, for recycling or for discard. Pick an item that is sometimes collected (for instance, clothes, newspapers, coins, bottle caps). If everyone in your school were to collect a certain number of these (you pick the number) what would the collection weigh? How much would it be worth? Repeat your analysis if every family in your community were to collect these. Discuss how you have determined your answers, and the problems (if any) that might occur if you tried to transport the collection.

Chapter 3 Projects

Chapter 3 projects relate to the content of the lessons as follows.

Project	Lesson(s)
1	3-4
2	3-1, 3-5
3	3-3
4	3-8, 3-9
5	3-6
6	3-6, 3-7
7	3-3

1 Metric Units Point out that identifying prefixes and identifying other metric units defined from the base units are not the same. Prefixes change the magnitude of the base unit, while metric units defined from base units measure an entirely different quantity. For instance, the dyne is a unit of force that would accelerate one gram one centimeter per one second per second.

2 Other Traditional Units *Africa Counts,* by Claudia Zaslavsky, published in 1973 by Lawrence Hill Books, Brooklyn, New York, is a fine reference.

3 Weighing a Collection Students should address all components of the project. They may find organizing their data in a table to be helpful.

Suggest that students contact recycling agencies to find the amount that is being paid for newspaper and aluminum. They might contact charitable organizations to find what types of items are being accepted, how the items should be packed, and whether or not the items will be picked up.

Possible responses

1. The seven base units (and what they measure) are: meter (length), kilogram (mass), second (time), ampere (electric current), kelvin (thermo dynamic temperature), mole (amount of substance), candela (luminous intensity). Some of the units derived from the base units are newton, a unit of force; watt, a unit of power; coulomb, a unit of electrical charge, and hertz, a unit of frequency.

Prefix	Power	Prefix	Power
exa	10^{18}	deci	10^{-1}
peta	10^{15}	centi	10^{-2}
tera	10^{12}	milli	10^{-3}
giga	10^{9}	micro	10^{-6}
mega	10^{6}	nano	10^{-9}
kilo	10^{3}	pico	10^{-12}
hecto	10^{2}	femto	10^{-15}
deka	10^{1}	atto	10^{-18}

2. The following information is a sample of what students might include in their projects. The Swahili measurement system included units of length, capacity, and weight. The basic unit of length is the shibiri, the distance from the tip of the thumb to the tip of the little finger when the hand is outstretched. A mkono is equal to two shibiri and a pima is equal to four

Responses continue on page 168

4 Large Edifices If students have difficulty drawing an accurate picture of the edifice they are reporting on, have them make a copy of it. Remind them that they may need to use more than one picture to describe the area and volume of the edifice. If available, a top view would be helpful. These types of drawings are often available in travel books or magazines.

5 Circle Graph Summary Students may refer to the In-class Activity of this chapter for an example of how to construct a circle graph. Advise students to make the circle large enough for some display.

6 Computer Drawing Programs Students may be surprised if other students have difficulty following the instructions they have written. Advise students to be as explicit as possible when writing directions for someone who has never used the software before. You might suggest indicating instructions step-by-step.

7 Units on Food You might suggest that students separate the foods into categories, such as canned goods, frozen items, liquid products, dry-packaged goods (ie. crackers, chips), and perishable food (ie. meat, cottage cheese). By listing foods under categories, students can see a commonality in the measures used.

PROJECTS 3 *(continued)*

4 Large Edifices

An edifice is a building or temple or monument or some other impressive structure. Over the ages, people have built many large edifices, including the pyramids of the Mayas, the Babylonians, or the Egyptians; the temples Angkor Wat in Cambodia or Machu Picchu in Peru; the Pentagon building in Washington; and the Kremlin in Russia. Pick one of these or some other famous large edifice. Look in encyclopedias for information regarding the edifice you picked. Draw an accurate picture of the edifice, labeling important points. Describe its area and volume, or areas and volumes related to it. Write a paragraph describing how and when the structure was built and what its use was or is.

5 Circle Graph Summary

Choose a topic of interest to you or to your class, such as lunch food, football, recycling, or homework. Write some questions about this topic that have a number of reasonable choices. (Think of the kind of question you would hear on the television program *Family Feud.*) Survey 25 or more people using these questions, and illustrate the distribution of answers to at least one of the questions in a circle graph. Then explain in words what you found.

6 Computer Drawing Programs

Locate drawing software for a computer that can draw angles and measure them, and that can draw angles of a specific measure. Explore this software with angles and triangles, and print out examples of your angles and measurements. After you have done some exploration, write instructions to a classmate on how to draw and measure angles with this software. If you can, test your instructions on a classmate who has never used the software to make sure that your instructions are clear.

7 Units on Food

Search the containers of all of the foods in your house for as many different units as you can find. Consider both U.S. customary and metric units. List all the quantities you find with different units and where they were found. Then write a summary that includes how you did your search and whether anything you found surprised you.

Additional responses, page 167.

mkono or eight shibiri. The basic unit of capacity is the kibaba, equivalent to a pint. A kisaga is equal to two kibaba and a pishi is equal to two kisaga or four kibaba. The basic unit of weight is the wakia. A ratti is equal to 16 wakia and a frasila is equal to 36 ratti.

3. Students should include at least the following in their responses: the item considered; the estimated weight of the collection and how the estimate was determined; the estimated value of the collection and how that value was determined; and some extrapolation of these values for the community as a whole.
4. The following information is a sample of the kind of material students might include in their projects. The temple Angkor Wat was completed in the 12th century. It is dedicated to the Hindu god Vishnu. It covers an area of 1500 meters × 1300 meters or 4920 feet × 4265 feet. French archeologists discovered the ruins of this temple in 1860. Machu Picchu is an ancient Inca city in the Andes of Peru. It is thought to have been built in the 1400s as a military post, agricultural area, or a religious sanctuary. The Pentagon is the building for the

Responses continued on page 169.

SUMMARY

The most common uses of numbers are as counts or measures. In this chapter, measures of length, area, volume (or capacity), mass (or weight), and angles are discussed.

There are two systems of measurement in use today in the United States. One is the metric system. The basic units in the metric system are the meter for length, the kilogram for mass, and the liter for capacity. The other system is called the U.S. or customary system. It uses inches, feet, miles, and so on, for length; ounces, pounds, and so on, for weight; ounces, cups, pints, quarts, gallons, and so on, for capacity. The metric system is generally easier to work with because its units are related to each other by powers of 10. So it is closely related to the decimal system. Conversion within one system or between systems can be done by beginning with known conversion equations and using the Multiplication Property of Equality.

Angles are measured the same way in both the metric and the U.S. systems. The degree, the common unit for angle measure, is based on splitting a circle into 360 equal parts. Thus, by using angle measures, circle graphs can be drawn. Angles can be classified by their measure. Units for area are usually squares based on units of length. Units for volume are usually cubes based on units of length.

VOCABULARY

You should be able to give a general description and a specific example of each of the following ideas.

Lesson 3-1
U.S. or customary system of measurement
inch
meter, centimeter, millimeter

Lesson 3-2
foot (ft), yard (yd), mile (mi),
inch (in.)
Multiplication Property of Equality

Lesson 3-3
ounce (oz), pound (lb), short ton,
cup (c), fluid ounce (fl oz)
pint (pt), quart (qt), gallon (gal)

Lesson 3-4
international or metric system of measurement
milli-, centi-, kilo-
meter (m)
gram (g)
liter (L)

Lesson 3-6
ray, $\overrightarrow{AB}$, endpoint of ray
angle, $\angle ABC$, sides of an angle,
vertex of an angle
degree (°)
protractor, base line of protractor,
center of protractor

Lesson 3-7
central angle
right angle, acute angle, obtuse angle
perpendicular
triangle, right triangle

Lesson 3-8
area
square, square units
hectare
in^2, cm^2, km^2, and so on

Lesson 3-9
volume, capacity
cube, cubic units
in^3, cm^3, m^3, and so on

Summary

The Summary gives an overview of the entire chapter and provides an opportunity for students to consider the material as a whole. Thus, the Summary can be used to help students relate and unify the concepts presented in the chapter.

Vocabulary

Terms, symbols, and properties are listed by lesson to provide a checklist of concepts a student must know. Emphasize to students that they should read the vocabulary list carefully before starting the Progress Self-Test. If students do not understand the meaning of a term, they should refer back to the indicated lesson.

Department of Defense of the United States government. It is in Arlington, Virginia. Construction began on the Pentagon in 1941 and was completed in 1943 at a cost of $83,000,000. building covers 29 acres or approximately 3,705,000 square feet.
The Kremlin in Moscow is the government center of Russia. Its name comes from the Russian word *kreml*, which means fortress. It was built in the late 1400s and early 1500s. It is a triangular enclosure with a perimeter of almost 1.5 miles. Accept any description of area or volume that a student can support from his or her findings.

5. Students' projects should include at least the question, the common answers, and a circle graph of reasonable size. If there are many different responses to the question, students may need to have a catch-all category in their circle graph entitled "Other." Still, since there are only 25 responses in all, they should include an explanation of the "other" responses.
6. Responses will vary depending on the software chosen and on the amount of detail. A good set of instructions will, at a minimum, describe steps in order.

Responses continued on page 170.

CHAPTER THREE

Progress Self-Test

For the development of mathematical competence, feedback and correction, along with the opportunity to practice, are necessary. The Progress Self-Test provides the opportunity for feedback and correction; the Chapter Review provides additional opportunities and practice. We cannot overemphasize the importance of these end-of-chapter materials. It is at this point that the material "gels" for many students, allowing them to solidify skills and understanding. In general, student performance should be markedly improved after these pages.

Assign the Progress Self-Test as a one-night assignment. Worked-out *solutions* for all questions are in the Selected Answers section of the student book. Encourage students to take the Progress Self-Test honestly, grade themselves, and then be prepared to discuss the test in class.

Additional Answers
6. Answers will vary. Sample: Since 1 foot = 12 inches, then 83 feet = 83 · 12 inches = 996 in.

Additional responses, page 168.
7. Responses will vary. In general, students will find that most dry perishable foods are measured in ounces, pounds, grams, and kilograms. Liquids are measured in ounces, pints, gallons, milliliters, or liters. Many products state measurements in both traditional and metric units.

PROGRESS SELF-TEST

See margin for answers not shown below.

After taking and correcting the Progress Self-Test, use your errors to help you decide what to study and review in this chapter.

1. Measure this segment to the nearest eighth of an inch. **$2\frac{5}{8}''$**

2. a. Draw a segment 6.4 centimeters long. **2a) Check students' drawings.**
   b. How long is your segment in millimeters? **64 mm**
3. Give the exact relationship between inches and centimeters. **1 in. = 2.54 cm**
4. Name the appropriate metric unit for measuring the weight or mass of a person. Explain why the unit you named is appropriate. **Kg is closest to pound.**
5. How many feet are there in $\frac{3}{4}$ of a mile? **3960 ft**
6. Give an example of the use of the Multiplication Property of Equality.
7. A kiloton is how many tons? **1000 tons**
8. 1103 mg = __?__ g **1.103**
9. 3 quarts = __?__ cups **12**
10. 3.2 pounds = __?__ ounces **51.2**
11. In the Olympics, there is a race called the 50K walk. To the nearest mile, how many miles is this? **31 mi**
12. To convert kilograms to pounds, what estimate can be used? **1 kg ≈ 2.2 lb**
13. Which is larger, 10 quarts or 9 liters? **10 qt**
14. The U.S. measuring system is derived from a system from what country? **England**
15. Measure angle *C* to the nearest degree. **135°**

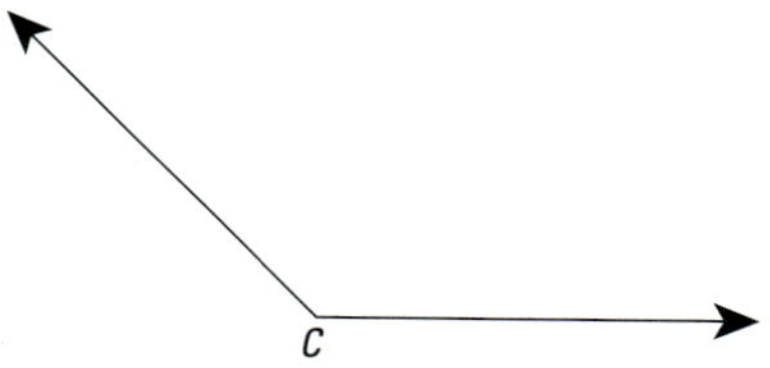

16. An acute angle has measure between __?__ and __?__ degrees. **0°, 90°**

17. Measure ∠*MNL* to the nearest degree. **70°**

Figures appear smaller than actual size in Teacher's Edition.

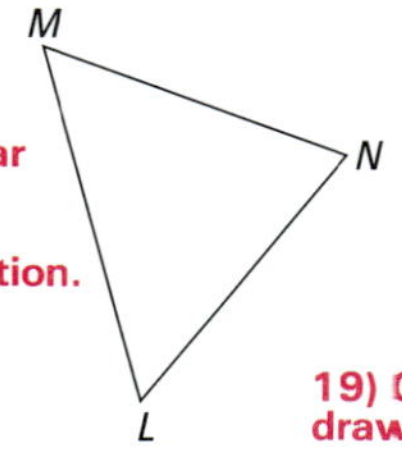

19) Check students' drawings.

18. An angle has measure 90°. Is this angle right, acute, or obtuse? **right**
19. Draw an angle with a measure of 80°.
20. Which angles of the triangle below seem to be acute, which right, which obtuse? **acute: ∠B, ∠C right: none obtuse: ∠A**

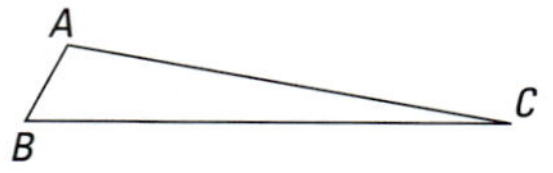

21. The circle graph shows the number of players in a string orchestra. If the graph is drawn correctly, what is the measure of the central angle for the violins sector? **150°**

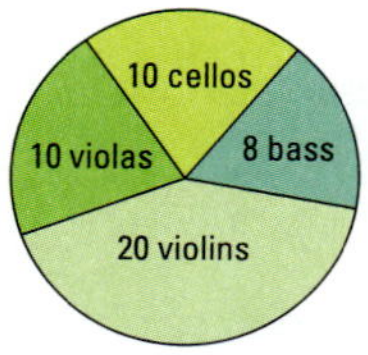

22) 20.25 in²

22. Find the area of a square with side 4.5 in.
23. If the side of a square is measured in cm, the area is usually measured in __?__. **cm²**
24. How are liters and cubic centimeters related? **1 L = 1000 cm³**
25. Give the volume of the cube drawn at the right. **125 cm³**

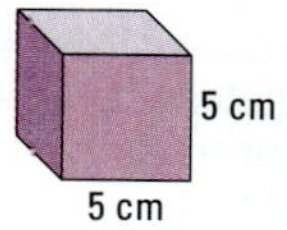

26. How many blocks, 2 cm on each edge, can be stored in a box 10 cm on each edge? **125**

CHAPTER REVIEW

Questions on SPUR Objectives

SPUR stands for **S**kills, **P**roperties, **U**ses, and **R**epresentations. The Chapter Review questions are grouped according to the SPUR Objectives for this chapter.

SKILLS DEAL WITH THE PROCEDURES USED TO GET ANSWERS.

Objective A. *Measure lengths to the nearest inch, half inch, quarter inch, or eighth of an inch, or to the nearest centimeter, or tenth of a centimeter.* (Lesson 3-1)

1. Measure the length of this segment to the nearest quarter inch. $1\frac{3}{4}$ in.

2. Measure the length of the above segment to the nearest tenth of a centimeter. 4.4 cm or 4.5 cm
3. Measure the segment below to the nearest centimeter. 7 cm

Figures appear smaller than actual size in Teacher's Edition

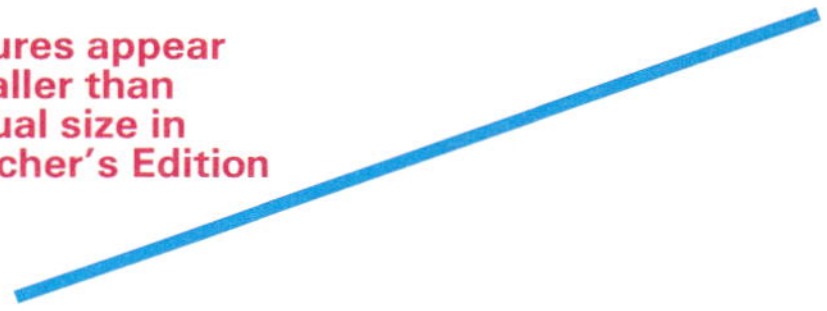

4. Measure the segment above to the nearest eighth of an inch. $2\frac{5}{8}$ in.

Objective B. *Measure angles to the nearest degree using a protractor.* (Lesson 3-6)

In 5–7, give the measure of the indicated angle in the drawing below.

5. ∠*Q* 65°
6. ∠*R* 153°
7. ∠*PSR* 39°

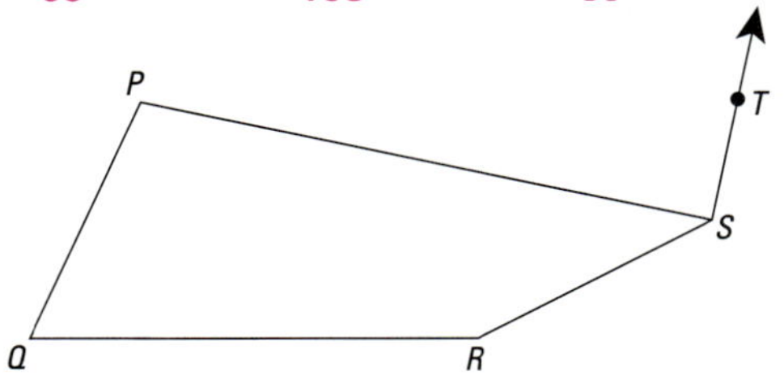

8. Jan van Eyck's *Portrait of a Man in a Red Turban* is contained very much within certain angles, as the diagram below shows. Give the measure of ∠*ADC*. 70°

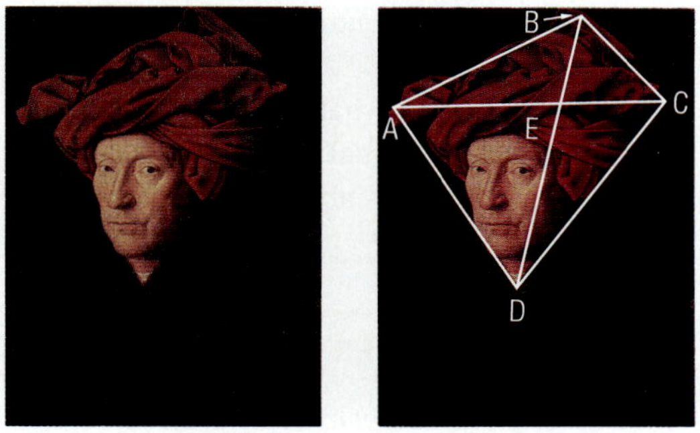

Jan van Eyck, *Portrait of a Man in a Red Turban*

Objective C. *Distinguish between acute, right, and obtuse angles by sight.* (Lesson 3-7)

9. Name an obtuse angle in the diagram over van Eyck's painting above.

In 10–12, use the figure of Questions 5–7.

10. Which angles seem to be acute? ∠*Q*, ∠*PSR*
11. Does ∠*RST* seem to be obtuse, acute, or right? obtuse
12. Name all angles that seem to be right angles. ∠*PST*

9) ∠*ABC*, ∠*BEA*, ∠*BCD*, or ∠*DEC*

Chapter 3 Review

Resources

From the ***Teacher's Resource File***

- Answer Master for Chapter 3 Review
- Assessment Sourcebook: Chapter 3 Test, Forms A–D Chapter 3 Test, Cumulative Form Comprehensive Test, Chapters 1–3

Additional Resources

- Quiz and Test Writer

The main objectives for the chapter are organized in the Chapter Review under the four types of understanding this book promotes—Skills, Properties, Uses, and Representations.

Whereas end-of-chapter material may be considered optional in some texts, in *Transition Mathematics,* we have selected these objectives and questions with the expectation that they will be covered. Students should be able to answer these questions with about 85% accuracy after studying the chapter.

You might assign these questions over a single night to help students prepare for a test the next day, or you might assign the questions over a two-day period. If you work the questions over two days, then we recommend assigning the *evens* for homework the first night so that students get feedback in class the next day and then assigning the *odds* the night before the test because answers are provided to the odd-numbered questions.

It is effective to ask students which questions they still do not understand, and use the day or days as a total class discussion of the material which the class finds most difficult.

CHAPTER THREE

Assessment

Evaluation The *Assessment Sourcebook* provides six forms of the Chapter 3 Test. Forms A and B present parallel versions in a short-answer format. Forms C and D offer performance assessment. The fifth test is Chapter 3 Test, Cumulative Form. About 50% of this test covers Chapter 3, 25% of it covers Chapter 2, and 25% of it covers Chapter 1. In addition to these tests, Comprehensive Test Chapter 1–3 gives roughly equal attention to all chapters covered thus far.

For information on grading, see *General Teaching Suggestions: Grading* in the *Professional Sourcebook* which begins on page T20 in Volume 1 of the Teacher's Edition.

Objective D. *Find areas of squares and volumes of cubes given the length of one side or edge.* *(Lessons 3-8, 3-9)*

13. Find the area of the square below. $4\ cm^2$

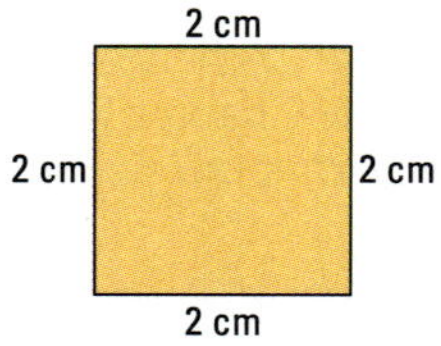

14. Find the area of a square with side 6.5 in.

15. If length is measured in meters, area is most easily measured in what unit? square meters

16. Find the volume of a cube with one edge of length 4 mm. $64\ mm^3$

17. To the nearest integer, find the volume of a cube with edge of length 3.75 in. $53\ in^3$

14) $42.25\ in^2$

PROPERTIES DEAL WITH THE PRINCIPLES BEHIND THE MATHEMATICS.

Objective E. *State and apply the Multiplication Property of Equality.* *(Lesson 3-2)*

18. State the Multiplication Property of Equality.

19. If 1 kg ≈ 2.2 lb, what does $\frac{1}{2}$ kg approximately equal? 1.1 lb

20. If 1 franc is worth about 19¢, how much are 30.5 francs worth? $5.80

21. *Multiple choice.* Below are three steps in converting 25 centimeters to meters. Which step uses the Multiplication Property of Equality?

(a) 1 cm = .01 m
(b) 25 · 1 cm = 25 · .01 m
(c) 25 cm = .25 m (b)

18) When equal quantities are multiplied by the same number, the resulting quantities are equal.

USES DEAL WITH APPLICATIONS OF MATHEMATICS IN REAL SITUATIONS.

Objective F. *Give appropriate units for measuring mass, length, and capacity in the U.S. or metric system of measurement.* *(Lessons 3-2, 3-3, 3-4)*

In 22–25, give an appropriate unit for measuring each quantity: **a.** in the metric system, **b.** in the U.S. system.

22. the distance from New York to London, England a) km; b) mi

23. the length of your foot a) cm; b) in.

24. the weight of a pencil a) g; b) oz

25. the capacity of a fish tank a) L; b) gal

Objective G. *Convert within the U.S. system of measurement.* *(Lessons 3-2, 3-3)* 1 qt = 2 pt

26. Give a relationship between pints and quarts.

27. How many ounces are in 1 pound? 16 oz

28. How are feet and miles related? 1 mi = 5280 ft

29. How many inches are in 2.5 yards? 90 in.

30. Convert 7.3 gallons into quarts. 29.2 qt

31. A road sign says: "Bridge ahead. Weight limit five tons." How many pounds is this? 10,000 lb

Objective H. *Convert within the metric system.* *(Lesson 3-4)*

32. What is the meaning of the prefix milli-?

33. How are centimeters and liters related?

34. 1 kilogram = __?__ grams 1000

35. Convert 200 cm to meters. 2 m

36. Convert 5.8 km to meters. 5800 m

37. Convert 265 mL to liters. 0.265 L

38. Convert 600 mg to grams. 0.6 g

32) one-thousandth
33) 1 liter = $1000\ cm^3$

56)

57)

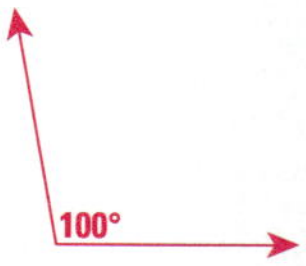

172

Objective I. *Convert between different systems.* *(Lessons 3-2, 3-5)*

39. Give an approximate relationship between pounds and kilograms. **1 kg ≈ 2.2 lb**

40. How are centimeters and inches related?

41. Which is longer, a mile or a kilometer? **mile**

42. Which is longer, a meter or a yard? **meter**

43. How many centimeters are in 2 feet? **60.96 cm**

44. In a guide book the distance between Paris and London is given as 343 km. How many miles is this? **about 212.66 mi**

45. How many quarts are in 6.8 liters? **≈ 7.2 qt**

40) 1 in. = 2.54 cm

46. In March of 1993, one Israeli shekel was worth about 37¢. So a blouse that cost 80 shekels was worth about how many dollars? **≈$29.60**

47. In March of 1993, one Irish punt was worth about $1.49. If a shillelagh sold for 2.98 punts, how much was that in U.S. dollars? **≈ $4.44**

Objective J. *Find areas of squares or volumes of cubes in real contexts.* *(Lessons 3-8, 3-9)*

48. A square table has a side of length 2.5 feet. Will a square tablecloth with an area of 6 square feet cover the table? **No**

49. How many cubes, 1 cm on an edge, will fit in a cubical container 12 cm on an edge? **1728 cubes**

REPRESENTATIONS DEAL WITH PICTURES, GRAPHS, OR OBJECTS THAT ILLUSTRATE CONCEPTS.

Objective K. *Draw a line segment of a given length.* *(Lesson 3-1)*

50. Draw a line segment with length 3.5 cm.

51. Draw a line segment with length $2\frac{1}{4}$ inches.

52. Draw a vertical line segment with length 4.375 inches.

53. Draw a horizontal line segment with length 7.8 cm. **50)-53) Check students' drawings.**

Objective L. *Draw an angle with a given measure.* *(Lesson 3-6)*

54. Draw an angle with a measure of 90°, in which neither side lies on a horizontal line.

55. Draw an angle with a measure of 37°.

56. Draw an angle with a measure of 145°.

57. Draw an angle with a measure of 100°.

54) Sample:

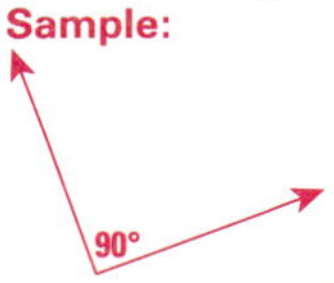

55)

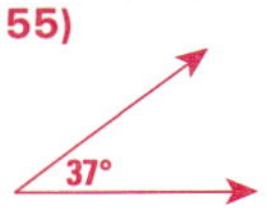

56-57) See page 172.

Objective M. *Read, make, and interpret circle graphs.* *(Lesson 3-7)*

In 58 and 59, the graph pictures the spending of $40.

Money Spent Last Week

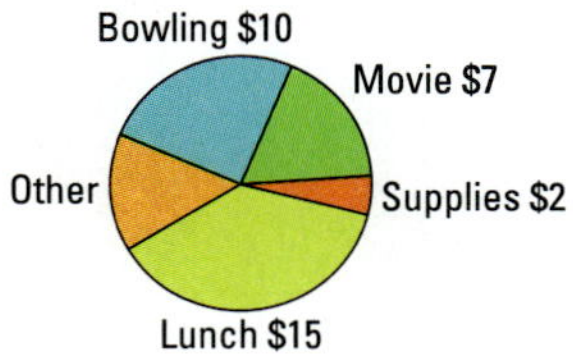

58. How much was spent on "other" things? **$6**

59. How can you tell that more than 25% of the money spent was for lunch?

60. Make a circle graph from the following information. The areas (in millions of square miles) of the continents of the world are: North America, 9.4; South America, 6.9; Europe, 3.8; Asia, 17.4; Africa 11.7; Australia, 3.3; Antarctica, 5.4. **See margin.**

59) More than $\frac{1}{4}$ of circle is for lunch.

CULTURE DEALS WITH THE PEOPLES AND THE HISTORY RELATED TO THE DEVELOPMENT OF MATHEMATICAL IDEAS.

Objective N. *Give countries and approximate dates of origin of current measuring ideas.* *(Lessons 3-1, 3-4, 3-6)*

61. When and where did the metric system originate? **France, 1790s**

62. How was the length of a yard first determined?

63. Our system for measuring angles is based on measuring done by what people? **Babylonians**

62) distance from tip of Henry I's nose to his fingertips

Additional Answers

60. Areas of Continents (in millions of square miles)

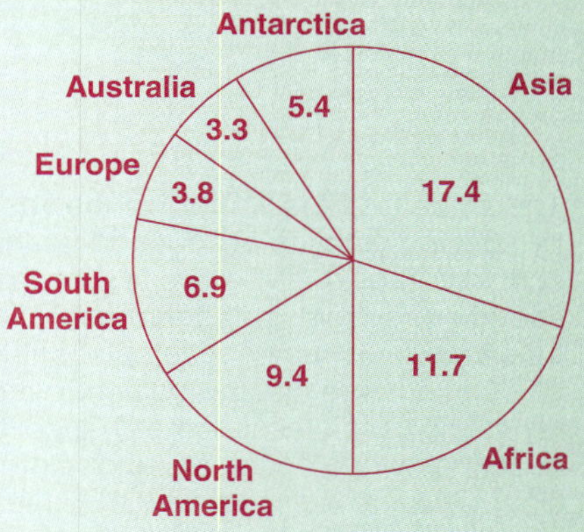

Setting Up Lesson 4-1

We strongly recommend that you assign Lesson 4-1, both reading and some questions, for homework the evening of the test. It gives students work to do after they have completed the test and keeps the class moving. If you do not do this consistently after tests, you may cover one less chapter over the course of the year.

Chapter 4 Planner

Adapting to Individual Needs

The student text is written for the vast majority of students. The chart at the right suggests two pacing plans to accommodate the needs of your students. Students in the Full Course should complete the entire text by the end of the year. Students in the Minimal Course will spend more time when there are quizzes and more time on the Chapter Review. Therefore, these students may not complete all of the chapters in the text.

Options are also presented to meet the needs of a variety of teaching and learning styles. For each lesson, the Teacher's Edition provides sections entitled: *Video* which describes video segments and related questions that can be used for motivation or extension; *Optional Activities* which suggests activities that employ materials, physical models, technology, and cooperative learning; and *Adapting to Individual Needs* which regularly includes **Challenge** problems, **English Language Development** suggestions, and suggestions for providing **Extra Help.** The Teacher's Edition also frequently includes an **Error Alert,** an **Extension,** and an **Assessment** alternative. The options available in Chapter 4 are summarized in the chart below.

Chapter 4 Pacing Chart

Day	Full Course	Minimal Course
1	4-1	4-1
2	4-2	4-2
3	4-3	4-3
4	4-4	4-4
5	Quiz*; 4-5	Quiz*; begin 4-5.
6	4-6	Finish 4-5.
7	4-7	4-6
8	4-8	4-7
9	Quiz*; 4-9	4-8
10	4-10	Quiz*; begin 4-9.
11	Self-Test	Finish 4-9.
12	Review	4-10
13	Test*	Self-Test
14		Review
15		Review
16		Test*

*in the Teacher's Resource File

In the Teacher's Edition...

Lesson	Optional Activities	Extra Help	Challenge	English Language Development	Error Alert	Extension	Cooperative Learning	Ongoing Assessment
4-1	●	●	●	●	●	●	●	Written/Oral
4-2	●	●	●	●	●	●	●	Oral
4-3	●	●	●	●	●	●	●	Oral/Written
4-4	●	●		●		●	●	Written
4-5	●	●	●	●		●	●	Written
4-6	●	●	●	●	●	●	●	Written/Oral
4-7	●	●	●	●		●	●	Written
4-8	●	●	●			●	●	Oral
4-9	●	●	●	●		●	●	Written
4-10	●	●	●	●	●	●	●	Group

In the Additional Resources...

	In the Teacher's Resource File								
Lesson	Lesson Masters, A and B	Teaching Aids*	Activity Kit*	Answer Masters	Technology Sourcebook	Assessment Sourcebook	Visual Aids**	Transition Mathematics Software	Video Segments
4-1	4-1	39		4-1	Demo 4		39, AM	Spreadsheet	
4-2	4-2	39, 42	8	4-2			39, 42, AM	Spreadsheet	
4-3	4-3	39		4-3			39, AM		
4-4	4-4	39		4-4		Quiz	39, AM		
4-5	4-5	40		4-5			40, AM		
4-6	4-6	40, 43		4-6	Calc 7		40, 43, AM		
4-7	4-7	40, 44		4-7	Comp 5		40, 44, AM	Spreadsheet	
In-class Activity		45		4-8			45, AM	Graphing/Probability	
4-8	4-8	41, 46	9	4-8		Quiz	41, 46, AM		4-8
4-9	4-9	41, 47		4-9	Comp 6		41, 47, AM	Graphing/Probability	
4-10	4-10	41, 48		4-10			41, 48, AM		
End of chapter				Review		Tests			

*Teaching Aids, except Warm-ups, are pictured on pages 174C and 174D. The activities in the Activity Kit are pictured on page 174C. Teaching Aid 45 which accompanies the In-class Activity is pictured with the lesson notes on page 213.

**Visual Aids provide transparencies for all Teaching Aids and all Answer Masters.

Also available is the Study Skills Handbook which includes study-skill tips related to reading, note-taking, and comprehension.

Integrating Strands and Applications

	4-1	4-2	4-3	4-4	4-5	4-6	4-7	4-8	4-9	4-10
Mathematical Connections										
Number Sense				●						
Algebra	●	●	●	●	●	●	●	●	●	●
Geometry				●			●	●	●	
Measurement				●	●		●			
Logic and Reasoning	●					●				●
Probability								●		
Statistics/Data Analysis			●					●		
Patterns and Functions		●	●	●	●					●
Interdisciplinary and Other Connections										
Science				●	●	●	●	●		●
Social Studies	●	●	●			●		●	●	●
Multicultural		●			●					
Technology	●	●		●	●	●	●		●	
Career							●			
Consumer	●		●			●	●			
Sports			●		●		●	●	●	

Teaching and Assessing the Chapter Objectives

				In the Assessment Sourcebook		
Chapter 4 Objectives (Organized into the SPUR categories—Skills, Properties, Uses, and Representations)	**Lessons**	**Progress Self-Test Questions**	**Chapter Review Questions**	**Chapter Test, Forms A and B**	**Chapter Test, Forms C**	**D**
Skills						
A: Use order of operations to evaluate numerical expressions.	4-1, 4-5, 4-6	1–5	1–14	12–14	1	
B: Evaluate algebraic expressions given the values of all variables.	4-4, 4-5, 4-6	6–8	15–24	15–17	4	✓
C: Find solutions to equations and inequalities involving simple arithmetic.	4-9, 4-10	9, 25, 26	25–30	18–23	4	✓
Properties						
D: Know the correct order of operations.	4-1, 4-5, 4-6	20	31–34	11	1	
E: Given instances of a pattern, write a description of the pattern using variables.	4-2	10, 11	35–37	4		
F: Give instances of a pattern described with variables.	4-2	31, 32	38–40	5	3	
Uses						
G: Given instances of a real-world pattern, write a description of the pattern using variables.	4-2	12	41, 42	3	3	✓
H: Write a numerical or algebraic expression for an English expression involving arithmetic operations.	4-3	16–19	43–50	6–10		
I: Calculate the value of a variable, given the values of other variables in a formula.	4-7	13–15, 19, 27, 28	51–54	26, 27	2	✓
J: Calculate probabilities and relative frequencies in a situation with known numbers of outcomes.	4-8	22, 23	55–60	28, 29	5	
Representations						
K: Graph the solutions to any inequality of the form $x < a$ and similar inequalities, and identify such graphs.	4-10	29, 30	61–68	24, 25	6	
Cultures						
L: Give rough dates and names of people for key ideas in arithmetic and algebra notation.	4-1, 4-2	21	69, 70	1		

Assessment Sourcebook
Quiz for Lessons 4-1 through 4-4
Quiz for Lessons 4-5 through 4-8
Chapter 4 Test, Forms A–D
Chapter 4 Test, Cumulative Form

Quiz and Test Writer
Multiple forms of chapter tests and quizzes; Challenges

Activity Kit

ACTIVITY 8 — PATTERNS AND VARIABLES. Use with **Lesson 4-2.**

Materials: 75 pennies
Group Size: Partners

Place a penny on your desk. Then make a ring of pennies around the first penny so that all of the pennies are touching. This arrangement is shown at the right.

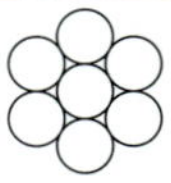

1. How many pennies are in the first ring around the original penny? ______
2. Make another ring around the first ring. Again, all of the pennies must be touching. How many pennies are in the second ring? ______
3. How many pennies do you think will be in the third ring? Make a third ring to check your prediction.

   Prediction: ______ Actual number: ______
4. Predict how many pennies will be in the fourth ring. Then test your prediction.

   Prediction: ______ Actual number: ______
5. Complete the statements below.

   The first ring has 6 pennies.
   The second ring has ☐ pennies.
   The third ring has ☐ pennies.
   The fourth ring has ☐ pennies.
6. Now complete these statements.

   The 1st ring has 1 • ☐ pennies.
   The 2nd ring has 2 • ☐ pennies.
   The 3rd ring has 3 • ☐ pennies.
   The 4th ring has 4 • ☐ pennies.
7. Study the pattern in Item 6 with other members of your group. Then, at the right, write statements like these for the 5th through 8th rings and for the 20th ring. Also give the number of pennies in each ring.
8. **Draw a Conclusion** Suppose *n* can stand for any of the counting numbers 1, 2, 3, ... Use the pattern you found to complete the statement at the right. The *n*th ring has *n* • ☐ pennies.

ACTIVITY 9 — PROBABILITY. Use with **Lesson 4-8.**

Materials: White pages of a phone book
Group Size: Small groups

You can do an experiment to estimate how likely it is that a person's last name has the same number of letters as your last name. Use the white pages of a phone book.

1. Each person in the group should look at any 20 nonconsecutive pages, such as 3, 6, 9, . . ., 60. Count the letters in the last name that is in the same location on each page. For example, you could check the 22nd name in the 3rd column on each page. Someone else in your group could look at the 4th name in the 1st column on pages 21, 23, 25, . . ., 59. Tally your findings in the chart at the right.

If your group read 80 last names and 6 of them had eight letters, the fraction $\frac{6}{80}$ is the *relative frequency* that a name in your group's sample has eight letters.

2. Give the relative frequency for last names in your sample that have the same number of letters as your last name. ______
3. Combine your tallies with those of the other members in your group, and record them in the chart. Then determine the relative frequency for each number.

Letters in Name	Your Tally	Group Tally	Relative Frequency
1			
2			
3			
4			
5			
6			
7			
8			
9			
10			
11			
12			
13			
14			
15 or more			

4. **Draw a Conclusion** Discuss and answer the following questions with the other groups in your class.

   a. Do any names have only 1 or 2 letters? more than 15 letters? ______

   b. Were all groups' relative frequencies about the same? ______

   c. What name length(s) have the greatest relative frequency? ______

Teaching Aids

TEACHING AID 39

Warm-up — Lesson 4-1

What number am I?

1. When you multiply me by two and subtract seventy-seven, I equal eleven.
2. When I am divided by nine and the quotient is multiplied by 13, I equal 286.
3. When I am added to 14, we make the largest prime number less than 53.

Warm-up — Lesson 4-2

Describe each pattern in words.

1. $-6 + 6 = 0$ $3.8 + -3.8 = 0$ $-\frac{1}{2} + \frac{1}{2} = 0$
2. $12 + 0 = 12$ $0.5 + 0 = 0.5$ $-7 + 0 = -7$
3. $-6.27 \times 1 = -6.27$ $\frac{1}{2} \times 1 = \frac{1}{2}$ $1 \times 2.2 = 2.2$

Warm-up — Lesson 4-3

Give words that suggest each operation.

1. Add 2. Subtract 3. Multiply 4. Divide

Warm-up — Lesson 4-4

Mental Mathematics Calculate.

1. $3^2 - 1$
2. $4 + 10 \times 10 - 4$
3. $4 \times 25 \div 2$
4. $7 + 3 + 5 \times 3$
5. $10^3 - 10^2$
6. $8 \times 3 \times 9 \times 0$

TEACHING AID 40

Warm-up — Lesson 4-5

Write a set of instructions telling how to make something. Explain why doing these steps in order is important.

Warm-up — Lesson 4-6

Calculator Write a decimal for each number.

1. $\frac{2 + 3}{125}$ 2. $\frac{40 + 50}{4 + 5}$ 3. $\frac{4632}{11 - 8}$ 4. $\frac{9.8}{0.63 + 0.07}$

Warm-up — Lesson 4-7

Find the area of each figure.

1.

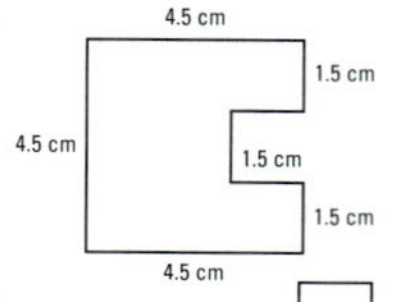

2.

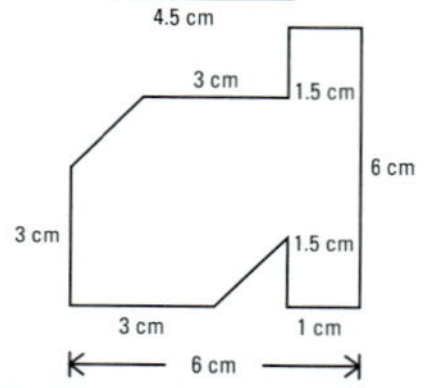

TEACHING AID 41

Warm-up — Lesson 4-8

Use a spinner with eight equal sections labeled 1 through 8. For each event listed below, (a) determine the probability assuming that the outcomes on the spinner are equally likely, and (b) spin the spinner 25 times to determine a relative frequency for the event.

1. An even number
2. A number divisible by 3
3. A number less than 9
4. A number greater than 8

Warm-up — Lesson 4-9

Solve.

1. $3x = 9$ 2. $17 + y = 20$ 3. $x + 6 = 12$
4. $m \div 2 = 5$ 5. $x - 1 = 7$ 6. $10 - r = 2$
7. $9n = 90$ 8. $45 \div x = 5$

Warm-up — Lesson 4-10

For 1–4, tell if the inequality is true or false.

1. $1 > 2$ 2. $1 < 2$
3. $1 \le 2$ 4. $1 \ge 2$

For each of 5–8, give three numbers that make the sentence true.

5. ______ < 2 6. ______ > 2
7. ______ ≤ 2 8. ______ $\ne 2$

TEACHING AID 42
Lesson 4-2

Patterns with Variables

Example 2

$1.43 + 2.9 = 2.9 + 1.43$
$12 + 37 = 37 + 12$
$\frac{8}{3} + \frac{7}{5} = \frac{7}{5} + \frac{8}{3}$
$a + b = b + a$

Using Example 2 Write 3 similar patterns for multiplication. Then write the pattern using the variables.

____ × ____ = ____ × ____
____ × ____ = ____ × ____
____ × ____ = ____ × ____
____ × ____ = ____ × ____

Example 3

1 person has 1 • 2 eyes.
1 people have 2 • 2 eyes in all.
3 people have 3 • 2 eyes in all.
4 people have 4 • 2 eyes in all.
p people have *p* • 2 eyes in all.

Using Example 3 Write a pattern that shows how many fingers *p* people have.

TEACHING AID 43
Lesson 4-6

Rules for Order of Operations

1. First, do operations within parentheses or other grouping symbols.
   - **A.** If there are nested grouping symbols, work in the innermost symbols first.
   - **B.** Remember that fraction bars are grouping symbols and can be different from / .
2. Within grouping symbols or if there are no grouping symbols:
   - **A.** First, take all powers.
   - **B.** Second, do all multiplications or divisions in order, from left to right.
   - **C.** Then do all additions or subtractions in order, from left to right.

TEACHING AID 44
Lesson 4-7

Additional Examples

1. Which rectangles have the same area?

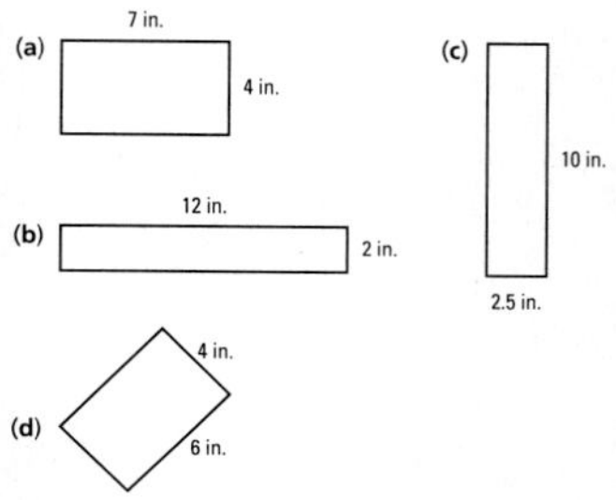

2. Find the area of a rectangle that is 1 meter long and 50 centimeters wide.
3. A photograph 20 inches square is framed. The framed photograph is 26 inches square. What is the area of the frame?

TEACHING AID 46
Lesson 4-8

Spinner

The diagram on the right shows how to make a spinner using a paper clip, a pencil, and the circle below.

Number	Frequency
1	
2	
3	
4	
5	
6	
7	
8	

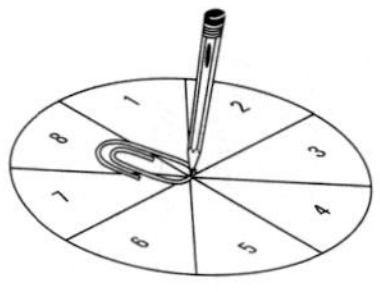

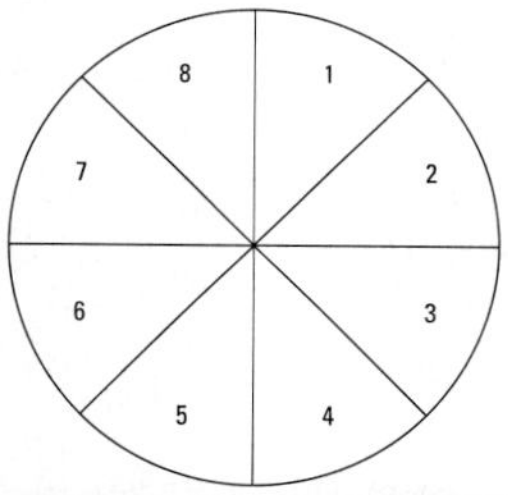

TEACHING AID 47
Lesson 4-9

Additional Examples

1. Mentally find the solution to each open sentence.
   - **a.** $12 + a = 12\frac{3}{4}$ **b.** $8 - 2.3 = b$ **c.** $100 - c = 53$
   - **d.** $\frac{d}{3} = 6$ **e.** $2e + 6 = 6$
2. *Multiple choice.* Choose the solution to each open sentence.
   - **a.** $\frac{15}{a} = 30$ (i) 2 (ii) $\frac{1}{2}$ (iii) 5 (iv) $\frac{1}{5}$
   - **b.** $100 = 2g - 6$ (i) 50 (ii) 5 (iii) 52 (iv) 53
   - **c.** $\frac{25}{h} = 6.25$ (i) 3 (ii) 4 (iii) 5 (iv) 6
3. A square-shaped room has an area of 100 square feet. Let *s* be the length of a side of the room. The value *s* is the solution to what open sentence? If you can, give the value.
4. Suppose the probability that a girl is picked at random out of a group of 50 students is .4.
   - **a.** What equation can you solve to find the number of girls in the group?
   - **b.** *Multiple choice.* How many girls are in the group?
     (i) 25 (ii) 30 (iii) 20 (iv) 50

TEACHING AID 48
Lesson 4-10

Questions 24, 26-32

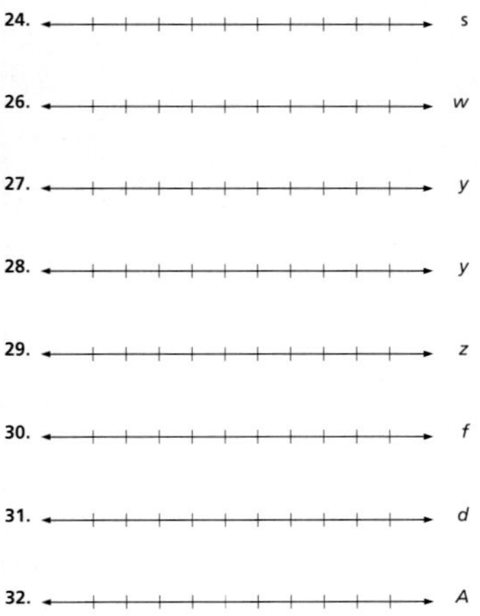

Chapter Opener 4

Pacing
Every lesson in this chapter is designed to be covered in one day. At the end of the chapter, you should plan to spend 1 day to review the Progress Self-Test, 1–2 days for the Chapter Review, and 1 day for a test. You may wish to spend a day on projects, and possibly a day is needed for quizzes. Therefore, this chapter should take 13–16 days. We strongly advise you not to spend more than 16 days on this chapter; there is ample opportunity to review ideas in later chapters.

Using Pages 174–175
The information in the chart on page 175 surprises many students. Explain that before the symbols shown here were established as part of the worldwide language of mathematics, the operations were stated with words and with other symbols. The invention of printing (in the 1450s by Gutenberg) increased the need for standard symbols and also made it possible for a particular symbol to be disseminated widely. The equal sign dates only from the 1550s. The up arrow, double asterisk, and carat symbols for powering have all been introduced since World War II because of the need to have unambiguous, easily typed symbols for operations.

Ask students when a particular symbol, such as ÷, was invented [1659], and who invented it [Johann Rahn]. Then ask them for the three different names for results of divisions. [fraction, quotient, ratio]

CHAPTER 4

Chapter 4 Overview
Algebra is generally thought of as using letters to represent numbers. In this sense, Chapter 4 begins our study of algebra. However, in earlier grades, students have been introduced to many ideas that lead naturally to algebra. For instance, they have had to fill in blanks in sentences like $4 + \_\_\_ = 7$; this is simply a different form of $4 + x = 7$. Students may have seen formulas for the area of a rectangle or square. They may have seen properties described with variables; one common example is the Commutative Property of Addition. We assume no previous exposure to these ideas; but if students have worked with them, you can build upon their experience.

This chapter could also be entitled "Notation," since the two major ideas introduced in the chapter relate to the ways in which things are written. The first idea, *order of operations*, is considered in Lessons 4-1, 4-5, and 4-6. For the second idea, *variable*, three uses are presented: in the description of patterns (Lesson 4-2); in formulas with a special application to relative frequency and probability (Lessons 4-7 and 4-8); and as unknowns (Lessons 4-9 and 4-10). The other lessons in the chapter introduce two important skills with variables: translating from English to variables (Lesson 4-3) and evaluating expressions (Lesson 4-4).

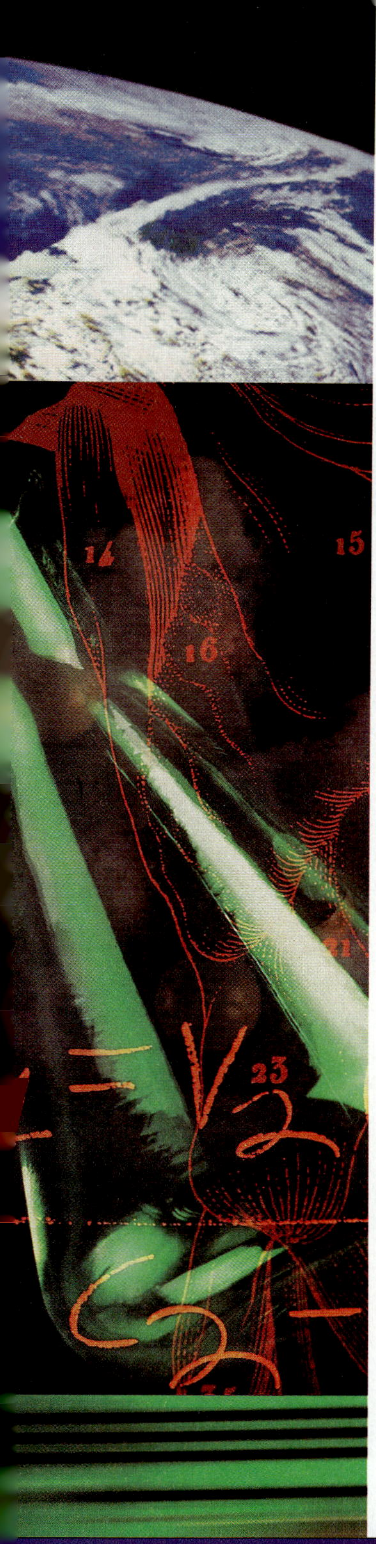

USES OF VARIABLES

Mathematics is, in many ways, a language. It is used to communicate information. It uses letters and symbols just as English, Spanish, Chinese, Hindi, Swahili, and other languages do. In the last 500 years, the symbols of mathematics have become an international language used in virtually all countries of the world. Just as our language changes over time, so does the language of mathematics. The table below shows some of the most important symbols of arithmetic, and who invented them. You can see that the language of mathematics has been developed by people from many different countries. The symbols invented since 1950 are used in computers and calculators worldwide.

Operation	Symbol	Name for Symbol	Inventor of Symbol (Year)	Name for Result
addition	+	plus	Johann Widman (German, 1498)	sum
subtraction	−	minus	Johann Widman (German, 1498)	difference
multiplication	×	times	William Oughtred (English, 1631)	product
	·	dot	Gottfried Leibniz (German, 1698)	product
	*	asterisk	(since 1950)	product
division	— as in $\frac{2}{3}$	bar or vinculum	al-Hassar (Arab, late 1100s)	fraction
	$\overline{)\ \ }$	into	Michael Stifel (German, 1544)	quotient
	÷	divided by	Johann Rahn (Swiss, 1659)	quotient
	: as in 2:3	colon	Gottfried Leibniz (German, 1684)	ratio
	/ as in 2/3	slash	Manuel A. Valdes (Mexican, 1784)	fraction
powering	3 as in 2^3	exponent	René Descartes (French, 1637)	power
	↑ as in 2 ↑ 3	up arrow	(since 1950)	power
	** as in 2**3	double*	(since 1950)	power
	^	carat	(since 1950)	power

In this chapter, you will learn about parentheses and variables. Parentheses ( ) are symbols for grouping. Variables are letters that stand for numbers or other objects, and have many uses.

You might also ask what else was going on in the world at the time these symbols were invented. [For instance, 1489 is three years before Columbus made his first voyage to the New World; 1784 is eight years after the United States adopted its Declaration of Independence.]

Photo Connections

The photo collage makes real-world connections to the content of the chapter: uses of variables.

Earth from Space: The language of mathematics spans the globe, bringing scientists and mathematicians together.

Multinational Flags: The letters and symbols of mathematics are utilized worldwide as an international language to communicate information.

Braille: Braille is a code of small raised dots on paper. It allows blind people to read by touch. Braille has won universal acceptance for all written languages and for mathematics, science, and computer notation.

Formula: Formulas are often used to communicate breakthroughs to the scientific community.

Electronic Circuit: An electronic circuit uses electricity as a method of carrying information. Properties of electricity are often expressed as equations.

Projects

At this time you might want to have students look over the projects on pages 229–230.

Although this chapter introduces many new concepts, these ideas will be considered again in later chapters. Students will have a great deal of practice with formulas; they will solve many sentences; and they will do extended work with finding patterns and translating from English to mathematical sentences and vice versa. Chapter 4 serves primarily as an introduction to these topics.

Lesson 4-1

Objectives

A Use order of operations to evaluate numerical expressions.

D Know the correct order of operations.

L Give rough dates and names of people for key ideas in arithmetic and algebra notation.

Resources

From the ***Teacher's Resource File***

- Lesson Master 4-1A or 4-1B
- Answer Master 4-1
- Teaching Aid 39: Warm-up
- Technology Sourcebook, Computer Demonstration 4

Additional Resources

- Visual for Teaching Aid 39
- Spreadsheet Workshop

Teaching Lesson 4-1

Warm-up

What number am I?

1. When you multiply me by two and subtract seventy-seven, I equal eleven. 44
2. When I am divided by nine and the quotient is multiplied by 13, I equal 286. 198
3. When I am added to 14, we make the largest prime number less than 53. 33

Notes on Reading

❶ There are several points to emphasize. First, it is possible to get different answers to the same question if there is no agreement about which operation to do first. You might have students

LESSON

4-1 *Order of Operations*

Order in the kitchen. *Cooks know the importance of mixing ingredients in the proper order. When baking a cake with egg whites, a cook must whip them and fold them into the batter just before baking. Changing the order may ruin the cake.*

Numerical Expressions

On the previous page is a table of symbols for the operations of arithmetic and algebra. There are many symbols, each with a precise meaning.

A **numerical expression** is a combination of symbols for numbers and operations that stands for a number. The **value** of a numerical expression is found by performing the operations. Performing the operations is called **evaluating the expression.** For example, the seven expressions here all have the same value, 2.

$$2 \qquad 5 - 3 \qquad 20/10 \qquad 5 \times 2 - 8 \qquad 2^1 \qquad 347.8 - 345.8 \qquad 10^0 + 10^0$$

❶ The Need for Rules for Order of Operations

The meaning of a numerical expression should be the same for everybody. But recall Lesson 1-5, where you were asked to evaluate $85 + 9 \times 2$ on your calculator. You keyed in

85 [+] 9 [×] 2 [=].

If you have a scientific calculator, the calculator multiplied first, making the problem $85 + 18 = 103$. A nonscientific calculator will probably add first; it will find $94 \times 2 = 188$.

Here is another confusing situation. Suppose you have \$25, spend \$10, and then spend \$4. You will wind up with

$$25 - 10 - 4 \text{ dollars.}$$

The situation tells you that the value of this expression is \$11. But someone else evaluating $25 - 10 - 4$ might first subtract the 4 from the 10. This would leave $25 - 6$, or \$19.

Lesson 4-1 Overview

Broad Goals The goal of this lesson is to cover the order of operations in algebraic expressions involving the operations of addition, subtraction, multiplication, division, and powering.

Perspective One of the reasons for requiring scientific calculators in this book is that the order of operations used in them is identical to that found in algebra. For example, to evaluate $2 + 3n$ when $n = 7$ on a scientific calculator, one can enter the numbers and operations in order from left to right and the value 23 will appear. In contrast, many four-function nonscientific calculators will give the value 35 to this key sequence. It is important to emphasize that scientific calculators use, and thereby reinforce, the order of operations found in algebra. You might also wish to note that many computer-programming languages use the order of operations given here.

The priority of parentheses in order of operations is introduced in Lesson 4-5, after students have learned the introductory rules. A summary of rules for order of operations is given in Lesson 4-6.

Calculating powers can also be confusing. Consider the expression 2×3^4. Some people might do the multiplication first, getting 6^4, which equals 1296. Others might first calculate the 4th power of 3, getting 2×81, which equals 162. These values are not even close to each other. To avoid confusion, rules are needed.

Rules for Order of Operations

The rules for order of operations tell the order in which operations should be done. These rules were not stated until this century, but they are now used throughout the world.

❷ **Rules for Order of Operations**

1. Calculate all powers in order, from left to right.
2. Next do multiplications or divisions in order, from left to right.
3. Then do additions or subtractions in order, from left to right.

To avoid mistakes, it is helpful to write each step clearly on a separate line. The examples below are done this way. After each example, you should check that your calculator evaluates expressions following these rules.

Example 1

Which value, 1296 or 162, is correct for the expression 2×3^4 discussed above?

Solution

Write the original expression. 2×3^4

Calculate the power before doing the multiplication. $= 2 \times 81$ $= 162$

162 is the correct value.

❸ **Activity 1**

Evaluate 2×3^4 on your calculator.

Scientific notation follows the rules for order of operations. An expression like 3.5×10^6 is evaluated by first taking the power, then multiplying.

$$3.5 \times 10^6$$
$$= 3.5 \times 1{,}000{,}000$$
$$= 3{,}500{,}000$$

evaluate $36 \div 3 + 1$. Then discuss the different answers: $(36 \div 3) + 1 = 13$ and $36 \div (3 + 1) = 9$.

Second, in expressions involving only addition and subtraction, neither operation has priority. Rather, you do the one which comes first as you work from left to right. The same holds true for expressions involving only multiplication and division. Stress that students must memorize the rules for order of operations.

❷ Some teachers use the mnemonic PMDAS (Please my dear Aunt Sally) to help students remember the rules for order of operations. This mnemonic is *misleading,* for it suggests that multiplications always precede divisions, and additions always precede subtractions. This is not the case in expressions such as $10 \div 2 \times 4$ and $15 - 6 + 3$.

❸ In Activities 1–5, students evaluate the same expressions given in **Examples 1–5** respectively, but now they use calculators. Before students do these activities, you might want to have them do the activity given below in *Optional Activities* to see how scientific and non-scientific calculators handle order of operations. Students should record the results of Activities 1–5 for use with **Question 19** on page 180.

If students have scientific calculators (which are recommended), they can enter the numbers and operations from left to right and the calculator will compute using the rules for order of operations. On non-scientific calculators, students must make adjustments and enter the numbers in the order in which the computation should be done. For example, to get the correct answer for $5 + 3 \times 4$ on a non-scientific calculator, they would enter $3 \times 4 + 5$.

Optional Activities

Activity 1

Materials: Scientific calculators and nonscientific calculators

Before students do the activities in the lesson, you might have them **work in pairs** with a scientific calculator and a non-scientific calculator. Have them compute the answers to the following problems with both calculators by entering each problem in order from left to right. [The first answer given appears on a scientific calculator; the second may appear on a non-scientific calculator.]

1.	$3 + 4 \times 5$	[23; 35]
2.	$6 - 2 \div 2$	[5; 2]
3.	$5 \times 3 - 1$	[14; 14]
4.	$18 + 12 \div 3$	[22; 10]
5.	$3 + 7 - 3$	[7; 7]
6.	$15 \times 9 \div 3$	[45; 45]
7.	$3 \times 3 + 5 \times 3$	[24; 42]

Discuss when different answers are obtained. [If an addition or subtraction is to the left of a multiplication or division, then it is likely that the answers will be different.] Ask students how they would have to enter Problems 1, 2, 4, and 7 on a non-scientific calculator to get the correct answers.

[1. 4 ⊗ 5 ⊕ 3 ⊜

2. 2 ⊘ 2 (M+) 6 ⊖ (MRC) ⊜

4. 12 ⊘ 3 ⊕ 18 ⊜

7. 3 ⊗ 3 (M+) 5 ⊗ 3 ⊕ (MRC) ⊜]

Social Studies Connection Rules that allow people to conduct meetings in an orderly manner are called *parliamentary procedure* because they come from the rules and customs of the British Parliament. The broad principles of parliamentary procedure, also known as parliamentary practice and rules of order, were established by the late 1600s. In 1876 a U.S. Army Engineer, Major Henry M. Robert, wrote what became the most popular book on parliamentary procedure, *Robert's Rules of Order.* The book presents rules of parliamentary procedure which help the presiding officer keep order during a meeting; they also help guide participants in transacting business and in accomplishing their purposes. Interested students might report on meetings held at school and in the community which use *Robert's Rules of Order.*

History Connection René Descartes (1596–1650) is regarded as the father of modern philosophy. His belief that all nature could be reduced to a system of mathematical principles was a sharp break with medieval thought. Descartes's well-known statement "I think, therefore I am" sought to establish knowledge on a foundation of absolute certainty.

Pacing Regardless of how many examples and exercises are given on order of operations, students can always use more. Keep in mind that there is practice in many lessons that follow this one, so although a few extra in-class examples are appropriate, resist the urge to spend an extra day on this lesson. If you only assigned *Covering the Reading* questions, you can go over the *Applying the Mathematics* questions with the class.

The next example applies the second of the rules for order of operations.

Example 2

Evaluate $100 \div 20 \times 2$.

Solution

Write the original expression. $100 \div 20 \times 2$

Multiplications and divisions have equal priority, so work from left to right, doing the division first.

$= 5 \times 2$

$= 10$

Activity 2

Do Example 2 on a calculator.

All multiplications or divisions are done before all additions or subtractions.

Example 3

Evaluate $85 + 9 \times 2$.

Solution

Write the original expression. $85 + 9 \times 2$

Multiply before adding. $= 85 + 18$

$= 103$

Activity 3

Verify Example 3 on your calculator.

Example 4

Evaluate $8 \times 12 - 3 \times 12$.

Solution

Write the original expression. $8 \times 12 - 3 \times 12$

Do *both* multiplications before the subtraction. $= 96 - 36$

$= 60$

Activity 4

Evaluate $8 \times 12 - 3 \times 12$ using a calculator.

The next example combines three operations and provides a good test of your calculator.

Optional Activities

Activity 2 Technology Connection You may wish to demonstrate how to use the *Spreadsheet Workshop* to explore order of operations, using *Technology Sourcebook, Computer Demonstration 4.* Following your demonstration, have students use the program to help them choose operation signs for equations such as the ones below.

1. 3 [×] 8 [−] 3 [−] 5 = 16

2. 6 [+] 5 [×] 3 [+] 7 = 28

Noted mathematician and philosopher. *René Descartes (1596-1650), a French mathematician and philosopher, was the first to use a raised number (exponent) to show powers, as in Example 5. His philosophy is known for the statement, "I think, therefore I am."*

Example 5

Evaluate $10 + 3 \times 4^2$.

Solution

Write the original expression.	$10 + 3 \times 4^2$
First evaluate the power.	$= 10 + 3 \times 16$
Now multiply.	$= 10 + 48$
Now add.	$= 58$

Activity 5

Evaluate $10 + 3 \times 4^2$ on your calculator using the key sequence indicated, and record the results. Do both key sequences produce the same results?

a. 10 [+] 3 [×] 4 [y^x] 2 [=]
b. 10 [+] 3 [×] 4 [x^2] [=]

QUESTIONS

Covering the Reading

1. a. $85 + 9 \times 2$ is an example of a __?__ expression. numerical
b. What is the value of this expression? 103

2. Finding the value of an expression is called __?__ the expression. evaluating

3. Why is there a need to have rules for order of operations? to avoid confusion when more than one operation is to be performed

4. Paulo had \$8.50 this morning. He spent \$3.75 for lunch and then spent \$2.09 for school supplies.
a. Use these numbers in a numerical expression telling how much money he had at the end of the day. 8.50 – 3.75 – 2.09
b. Evaluate the expression. \$2.66

In 5–8, an expression contains only the two given operations. Which one should you perform first?

5. division and addition division
6. a power and subtraction power
7. multiplication and division
8. addition and subtraction
7, 8) whichever is first from left to right

In 9–18, evaluate the expression. Show your work.

9. $55 - 4 \times 7$ $= 55 - 28 = 27$
10. $16 - 9 + 7$ $= 7 + 7 = 14$
11. $200 \div 10 \div 2$ $= 20 \div 2 = 10$
12. $6 + .03 \times 10$ $= 6 + .3 = 6.3$
13. $1000 - 3 \times 17^2$ $1000 - 3 \times 289 = 1000 - 867 = 133$
14. $1 \div 9 + 1 \div 7$ $= \frac{1}{9} + \frac{1}{7} = \frac{16}{63}$
15. $3 \times 9 - 2$ $= 27 - 2 = 25$
16. $4^2 + 8^3$ $= 16 + 512 = 528$
17. $2 \div 6 \times 9$ $= \frac{1}{3} \times 9 = 3$
18. 6×2^3 $= 6 \times 8 = 48$

14) about 0.254 on a calculator

Additional Examples

In 1-5, evaluate using the correct order of operations.

1. 5×2^5 160
2. $96 \div 5 \times 2$ 38.4
3. $300 \div 12 \times 5$ 125
4. $7 \times 14 - 5 \times 14$ 28
5. $100 - 5 \times 4^2$ 20
6. In computing 20 – 8 – 4, Christina got 8 and Maria got 16. How did each girl get her answer, and which girl was correct? Christina found 20 – 8, then 12 – 4; Maria found 8 – 4, then 20 – 4; Christina was correct.

Notes on Questions

Questions 5–8 Error Alert If students have difficulty remembering the correct order of operations, you might want to use the *Extra Help* suggestion given in *Adapting to Individual Needs* below.

LESSON MASTER 4-1 A

Questions on SPUR Objectives
See pages 233-235 for objectives.

Skills Objective A

In 1-9, evaluate each expression without a calculator.

1. $12 + 36 \div 9$ 16
2. $3.8 \times 10 \div 5$ 7.6
3. $8 + 6^2 \div 9 - 10$ 2
4. $6\frac{1}{2} + 9 \div 3$ $9\frac{1}{2}$
5. $2^3 + 4^2$ 24
6. $8 \times 6 - 7 \times 3$ 27
7. $\frac{51}{3} - 6 \cdot 2$ 5
8. $8 \cdot 2^3 - 5^2$ 39
9. $27 \div 3 + 6 \cdot 4.5 - 2$ 34

Properties Objective D

10. State three rules for order of operations.
(1) Calculate all powers in order, from left to right. (2) Multiply or divide in order, from left to right. (3) Add or subtract in order, from left to right.

11. Which operation should be done first in $24 \div 2 \times 4$? division; $24 \div 2$

12. Which operation should be done first in 4×3^2? powering; 3^2

Culture Objective L

13. *Multiple choice.* During what time period were computer symbols such as ↑ and ** developed? d
(a) before 1000 B.C. (b) 1 A.D. to 1000 A.D.
(c) 1200 A.D. to 1400 A.D. (d) since 1950

14. Why do mathematicians from different countries usually use the same symbols?
so they can communicate without speaking the same language

Adapting to Individual Needs

Extra Help
Some students will have trouble remembering the steps in the standard order of operations. These students might benefit from asking themselves a series of questions when evaluating expressions. Have them write these questions and instructions on an index card.

For each of the following questions, if the answer is *yes*, tell students to do the calculations in order from left to right. If the answer is *no*, they can go to the next question.

1. Are there any exponents?
2. Are there any multiplications or divisions?
3. Are there any additions or subtractions?

After using the card for a limited time, students should be able to work without it.

Notes on Questions

Questions 21–27 These questions apply to the table at the beginning of the chapter. This background is important to help students realize that mathematical symbols are all invented and to help them appreciate that mathematics is more than computational skills. These questions point out that symbols change and have changed, even in recent years. When students realize that questions will be asked on this material, they take it more seriously.

Question 38 After discussing this question, you may wish to ask students to think of two numbers whose difference equals their sum. [This will happen if the second number is 0.]

LESSON MASTER 4-1 B Questions on SPUR Objectives

Skills Objective A: Use order of operations to evaluate numerical expressions.

In 1-18, evaluate the expression without a calculator.

1. $8 \times 12 \div 4$ **24**
2. $14 + 10 \div 2$ **19**
3. $38 - 9 \times 3$ **11**
4. $100 \div 25 \div 2$ **2**
5. $45 \div 9 + 21 \div 7$ **8**
6. $30 + 4^3$ **94**
7. $10^2 - 3^4$ **19**
8. $35 + 8^2 \div 4 - 12$ **39**
9. $\frac{72}{9} - 2 \times 4$ **0**
10. $10 \times 2^5 - 7^2$ **271**
11. $6^2 \times 5 - 12^2 \div 16$ **171**
12. $375 \div 5^3$ **3**
13. $68 - 20 - 11$ **37**
14. $3 + 9 + 4 \cdot 8$ **44**
15. $12 + .08 \times 10^3$ **92**
16. $9^2 \div 3^4$ **1**
17. $90 - 2^3 \cdot 6$ **42**
18. $54 \div 3^2 + 7 \times 30 \div 5$ **48**

19. In which of Activities 1–4 in the lesson did your calculator give a value different from the example above it? **Answers will vary. With a scientific calculator, results should match examples.**

20. What results did you find for Activity 5? **With a scientific calculator, the result is 58.**

In 21–27, refer to the table on page 175.

21. Name three symbols that are used for multiplication. **×, ·, ***

22. Translate "three divided by nine" into symbols in 5 different ways. **$\frac{3}{9}$, 3 ÷ 9, 9)3, 3:9, 3/9**

23. How many years ago were the symbols we use for addition and multiplication invented and by whom? **See below.**

24. When you add, what is the result called? **sum**

25. When you subtract, what is the result called? **difference**

26. When you multiply, what is the result called? **product**

27. When you divide, what is the result called? **quotient**

Applying the Mathematics

In 28 and 29, write the numerical expression, then evaluate it.

28. the sum of 11 and 4.2 **11 + 4.2 = 15.2**

29. the product of 6 and 0.3 **6 × 0.3 = 1.8**

30. Which would you prefer: an allowance equal to the sum of the digits in the page number for this page or one equal to the product of those digits? **sum (1 · 8 · 0 = 0, while 1 + 8 + 0 = 9)**

31. Explain why the following sentence is confusing.

Calculate the sum of 2 and 4 divided by 8. **It is not clear whether 4 is added to 2 first or divided by 8 first.**

In 32–35, the expression is written in a computer language. Evaluate.

32. 2 * 3 + 8 **14**

33. 120 − 3 * 4/4 **117**

34. 200/2 * 10 − 4 **996**

35. 17 + 16 * 3 + 2 **67**

36. Why do you think mathematicians invent symbols? **Sample: to make things easier to understand**

37. *Multiple choice.* Which is largest?

(a) the sum of .1 and .2
(b) the product of .1 and .2
(c) .1 divided by .2
(d) the second power of .1

(c)

38. Find two numbers whose product is less than their sum. **Samples: 0 and 5, $\frac{1}{2}$ and 4, 1 and 3**

23) **+ invented about 500 years ago by Johann Widman;**
× invented about 350 years ago by William Oughtred;
· invented about 300 years ago by Gottfried Leibniz;
*** used in computer programs since 1950; inventor unknown**

Adapting to Individual Needs

English Language Development

Students who are just learning the English language might find the following chart helpful when learning order of operations.

in order, left to right →

a^n → × or ÷ → + or −

Review

39. Find the volume of a cube with an edge of length 5 inches. *(Lesson 3-9)* **125 in^3**

40. Use this angle.

a. Does the angle appear to be acute, right, or obtuse? *(Lesson 3-7)*
b. Measure the angle to the nearest degree. *(Lesson 3-6)* **120°**
a) obtuse

41. Draw a line segment with length 14.3 cm. *(Lesson 3-1)*
Check students' segments.

42. Write 0.00000 00000 06543 in scientific notation. *(Lesson 2-9)*
6.543×10^{-12}

43. Some insurance companies give a discount of 15% on homeowner's or renter's insurance if smoke detectors are installed. Suppose you need 3 smoke detectors and they cost $14.99 each. The insurance bill is $250 a year without smoke detectors. *(Lesson 2-5)*
a. How much will you save each year by installing smoke detectors?
b. What will be the total savings after five years?
See below.

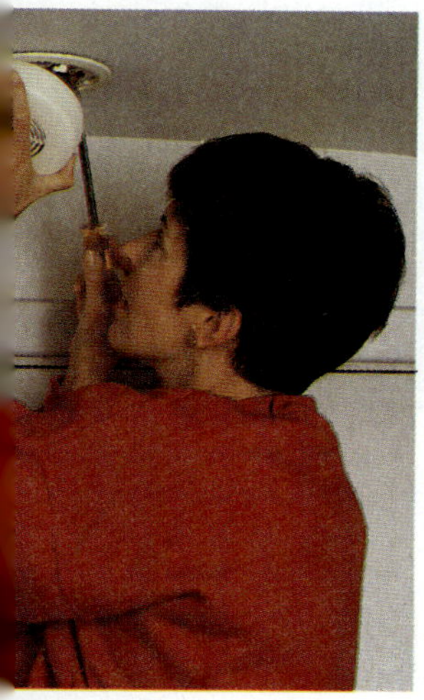

Life savers. *Smoke detectors are devices used to warn occupants of a building that a fire has started. The devices are inexpensive, easy to install, and save lives. But regardless of cost, every home should have at least one smoke detector installed.*

Exploration

44. Mathematics is a worldwide language, so mathematicians from different countries usually use the same symbols. Name some symbols outside mathematics that are used throughout the world.
Samples: music symbols, some traffic signs, airport signs

45. What is Esperanto? **a language invented about 100 years ago in an attempt to create a worldwide spoken and written language**

46. a. Ask a computer to evaluate the expressions of Questions 32–35. (Hint: For Question 32, you should type `?2*3 + 8` or `PRINT 2*3 + 8` and press RETURN.) **Outputs will be 14, 117, 996, 67.**
b. Does your computer follow the rules for order of operations stated in this lesson? If not, what rules does it seem to follow?
It should.

43a) The first year you will spend an additional $7.47 since the smoke detectors cost $44.97 and the insurance discount is only $37.50. The second through the fifth years, you will save $37.50 per year, or $150.00 over four years.
b) The total savings for five years will be $142.53.

Follow-up for Lesson 4-1

Practice

For more questions on SPUR Objectives, use **Lesson Master 4-1A** (shown on page 179) or **Lesson Master 4-1B** (shown on pages 180–181).

Assessment

Written/Oral Communication
Have pairs of students work together at the board to write an expression involving powers and at least two operations. Then have them evaluate the expressions. The class can decide whether or not each evaluation is correct. [Discussion will reveal any need for further development.]

Extension

You might give students problems such as the ones given below. Tell them to place an operation symbol in each box so that the expression equals the number.

1. 12 (÷) 3 (+) 8 (−) 2 = 10
2. 7 (×) 8 (÷) 4 (+) 4 = 18

Project Update Project 3, *Arithmetic Time Line,* on page 229, relates to the content of this lesson.

Adapting to Individual Needs

Challenge
Have students solve each problem:

1. A student wrote that $5^5 - 5^2 = 5^3$. Do you agree? Why or why not? [Sample answer: No; the student didn't follow the rules for order of operations. $5^5 = 3125$ and $5^2 = 25$. So the left side is $3125 - 25$, or 3100, which does not equal 5^3, or 125.]
2. Write a simpler expression for the following using only two digits: $5^4 + 5^4 + 5^4 + 5^4 + 5^4$ [5^5]

▶ **LESSON MASTER 4-1B** *page 2*

Properties Objective D: Know the correct order of operations.

19. In front of each rule below, write *1*, *2*, or *3*, to show the correct order of operations.
2 Do multiplications or divisions in order, from left to right.
3 Do additions or subtractions in order, from left to right.
1 Calculate all powers in order, from left to right.

20. Which operation should be done first in $56 - 2 + 4$? **subtraction; $56 - 2$**

21. Which operation should be done first in $56 - 2 \times 4$? **multiplication; 2×4**

22. Which operation should be done first in $56 - 2^4$? **powering; 2^4**

23. Which operation should be done first in $56 \div 2 \times 4$? **division; $56 \div 2$**

Culture Objective L: Give rough dates and names of people for key ideas in arithmetic and algebra notation.

24. *Multiple choice.* During what time period were the multiplication symbols × and · invented? **a**
(a) 1600s (b) before 1200 A.D.
(c) 1950s (d) 500 B.C.

25. Write any two mathematical symbols that were invented after 1950. ***, ↑, **, or ^**

Review Patterns (Previous course)

In 26-28, a sequence of numbers is given. Find a pattern and describe it in words. Then use the pattern to write the next three numbers in the sequence.

26. 6, 12, 18, 24 . . . **Add 6 to the previous number.** **30**, **36**, **42**

27. 1, 3, 7, 15, 31, . . . **Add 2^1, then 2^2, then 2^3, and so on.** **63**, **127**, **255**

28. 28, 14, 7, 3.5 . . . **Divide the previous number by 2.** **1.75**, **0.875**, **0.4375**

Lesson 4-2

Objectives

E Given instances of a pattern, write a description of the pattern using variables.

F Give instances of a pattern described with variables.

G Given instances of a real-world pattern, write a description of the pattern using variables.

L Give rough dates and names of people for key ideas in algebra notation.

Resources

From the ***Teacher's Resource File***

- Lesson Master 4-2A or 4-2B
- Answer Master 4-2
- Teaching Aids
  39 Warm-up
  42 Patterns with Variables
- Activity Kit, Activity 8

Additional Resources

- Visuals for Teaching Aids 39, 42
- Spreadsheet Workshop

Teaching Lesson 4-2

Warm-up

Describe each pattern in words.

1. $-6 + 6 = 0$ $\quad 3.8 + -3.8 = 0$
   $-\frac{1}{2} + \frac{1}{2} = 0$ **The sum of a number and its opposite is zero.**
2. $12 + 0 = 12$ $\quad -7 + 0 = -7$
   $0.5 + 0 = 0.5$ **The sum of a number and zero is that number.**
3. $-6.27 \times 1 = -6.27$ $\quad \frac{1}{2} \times 1 = \frac{1}{2}$
   $1 \times 2.2 = 2.2$ **The product of one and a number is that number.**

LESSON

4-2 Describing Patterns with Variables

Artistic and natural patterns. *The Navajo blanket shown was woven with various instances of the zig-zag pattern. The same kind of repeating pattern can be found in waves.*

What Are Patterns?

A **pattern** is a general idea for which there are many examples. An example of a pattern is called an **instance.** Here are three instances of a pattern with percent.

$$5\% = 5 \times .01$$
$$43.2\% = 43.2 \times .01$$
$$78\% = 78 \times .01$$

In Lesson 2-4, this pattern was described using English words:

The percent sign % means to multiply the number in front of it by .01.

But there is a simpler way to describe this pattern.

$$n\% = n \cdot .01$$

1 What Are Variables?

The letter n in the above equation is called a **variable.** *A variable is a symbol that can stand for any one of a set of numbers or other objects.* Here n can stand for any number. When n is 40, we write $n = 40$, and the instance becomes $40\% = 40 \cdot .01$.

Variables are usually letters. With variables, using × for multiplication could be confused with using the letter x. So the raised dot · is used instead.

Lesson 4-2 Overview

Broad Goals This lesson introduces variables through one of their major uses—the description of patterns.

Perspective This lesson contains the first transition from arithmetic to algebra. We have found that for about half the students, the descriptions of patterns using variables are easy. For the others, even the simplest examples are hard to understand. These students have difficulty with abstract thinking and need to build up this skill to be successful in algebra.

There are two weaknesses to first introducing variables to students as unknowns in equations such as $5n = 8$. First, this use does not convey the idea that a variable can stand for any one of many values. Second, it carries the connotation that the idea is mysterious—"seeking the unknown"—when variables are anything but mysterious to mathematicians.

There are often many different descriptions that apply to a pattern. Consider Question 16, for example. If a student writes $5 \cdot a = 3 \cdot b + 2 \cdot c$, the student has seen a pattern, but has missed the common element. The pattern $a \cdot b = c \cdot d + e \cdot f$ is even farther from what we would like, but it is not incorrect. For this reason, we usually tell students how many variables to use in their descriptions.

Describing Number Patterns with Variables

Descriptions with variables have two major advantages over descriptions using words. They look like the instances. Also, they are often shorter than the verbal descriptions. You can see this in Example 1.

❷ **Example 1**

Here are three instances of a pattern.

$$\frac{3}{3} = 1 \qquad \frac{657.2}{657.2} = 1 \qquad \frac{2/5}{2/5} = 1$$

a. Describe the pattern in words.
b. Describe the pattern with variables.

Solution

a. There is more than one way to write this in words. Here are two possible solutions.
   1. *If a number is divided by itself, the quotient is equal to one.*
   2. *If the numerator and denominator of a fraction are the same number, the value of the fraction is 1.*

b. First, write down everything that is the same in all three instances.

$$\frac{\;}{\;} = 1$$

Next, determine how many variables are needed. In this pattern, only one variable is needed because the numerator and denominator are the same in each instance.

$$\frac{r}{r} = 1$$

In Example 1, any other letter or symbol could be used in place of *r*.

Example 2

Describe the pattern with variables.

$$1.43 + 2.9 = 2.9 + 1.43$$
$$12 + 37 = 37 + 12$$
$$\frac{8}{3} + \frac{7}{5} = \frac{7}{5} + \frac{8}{3}$$

Solution

First, write everything that is the same in all the instances.

$$\_\_\_\_ + \_\_\_\_ = \_\_\_\_ + \_\_\_\_$$

Next, determine how many variables are needed. Because each instance has two different numbers, the pattern requires two variables. If *a* represents the first number and *b* represents the second, then

❸ $$a + b = b + a.$$

Because any letter may be used as a variable, there are many possible descriptions of a pattern. The sentence $a + b = b + a$ describes the same pattern as the sentence $y + z = z + y$.

Notes on Reading

Reading Mathematics You may wish to have students read this lesson aloud in class. As they do so, stop at each pattern, and ask them to describe the pattern in their own words before they read the explanation in the text or examine the description with variables. You may want to use **Teaching Aid 42** when discussing **Examples 2 and 3.**

❶ Students should become accustomed to seeing *any* letter used as a variable. However, mathematicians usually avoid the letters *l* (el) and *o* (oh) because they can be confused with 1 and 0.

❷ **Cooperative Learning** Work as a class to help students find patterns. First have them determine the elements that stay the same in each instance. Then have them note the changes from one instance to another. Finally, have students describe the pattern with variables and check the description against the instances given.

❸ Many patterns are properties that have names. For example, the Commutative Property of Addition is the pattern shown in **Example 2**. The names of the properties do not need to be discussed now. They will be studied in later chapters, at which time the names will be introduced.

LESSON MASTER 4-2 A

Questions on SPUR Objectives
See pages 233-235 for objectives.

Properties Objective E

In 1 and 2, three instances of a pattern are given. Describe the general pattern using one variable.

1. $3 + 3 = 2 \cdot 3 \qquad \frac{1}{4} + \frac{1}{4} = 2 \cdot \frac{1}{4} \qquad -4 + -4 = 2 \cdot -4$

$n + n = 2n$

2. $4 \cdot 1 = 4$
$9 \cdot 1 = 9$
$3.2 \cdot 1 = 3.2$

$n \cdot 1 = n$

Properties Objective F

In 3 and 4, give two instances of the pattern. Sample answers are given.

3. *w* weeks have $7 \cdot w$ days.
3 weeks have $7 \cdot 3$, or 21, days.
10 weeks have $7 \cdot 10$, or 70, days.

4. $\frac{x}{y} \cdot \frac{y}{x} = 1$
$\frac{5}{3} \cdot \frac{3}{5} = 1$
$\frac{10}{7} \cdot \frac{7}{10} = 1$

Uses Objective G

In 5 and 6, study the given instances of a pattern. Describe the general pattern using variables.

5. The value of three quarters is $3 \times .25$.
The value of six quarters is $6 \times .25$.
The value of nine quarters is $9 \times .25$.
value of *n* quarters is $n \times .25$

6. If Renato drives 300 miles at 60 mph, his trip takes $\frac{300}{60}$ hours.
If Renato drives 300 miles at 50 mph, his trip takes $\frac{300}{50}$ hours.
If Renato drives 300 miles at 55 mph, his trip takes $\frac{300}{55}$ hours.
If Renato drives 300 miles at *n* mph, his trip takes $\frac{300}{n}$ hours.

Culture Objective L

7. *Multiple choice.* Of what nationality was the mathematician who first used letters of the alphabet to describe patterns?
(a) American (b) Egyptian
(c) French (d) Greek
c

Optional Activities

Activity 1 You can use *Activity Kit, Activity 8,* as an introduction to Lesson 4-2. In this activity, students use physical models to show instances of a pattern. Then they write the pattern.

Activity 2 Technology Connection You may wish to have students use the *Spreadsheet Workshop* to explore how cell names can be used as variables. Have students enter numbers in cells A1, B1, and C1. In cell A2, have them use the Create Formula option to enter an expression such as A1 × B1 × C1. Point out that the cell names act as variables in the expression. If changes are made to the data in cells A1, B1, and C1, the value of the expression is updated.

Additional Examples

Describe the pattern of which these are instances. Use one variable.

1. $3 \cdot 1 = 3$
   $1.5 \cdot 1 = 1.5$
   $\frac{1}{2} \cdot 1 = \frac{1}{2}$
   $a \cdot 1 = a$
2. $2 \cdot 2 \cdot 2 = 2^3$
   $0.5 \cdot 0.5 \cdot 0.5 = (0.5)^3$
   $\frac{1}{3} \cdot \frac{1}{3} \cdot \frac{1}{3} = (\frac{1}{3})^3$
   $s \cdot s \cdot s = s^3$
3. One tripod has 3 legs.
   Two tripods have 6 legs in all.
   Three tripods have 9 legs in all.
   t tripods have $t \cdot 3$ legs in all.
4. $5 + 2 > 5$
   $8 + 2 > 8$
   $\frac{3}{4} + 2 > \frac{3}{4}$
   $a + 2 > a$

Notes on Questions

Question 15 Error Alert Some students may write a pattern for each instance, such as the following: $10 \cdot a = a$, $8.9 \cdot a = a$, and $15/5 \cdot a = a$. Remind these students to look for two things—what the instances have in common (the zeros) and what varies (10, 8.9, 15/5).

LESSON MASTER 4-2 B Questions on SPUR Objectives

Vocabulary

1. Explain what a *variable* is.
   A variable is a symbol that can stand for any one of a set of numbers or other objects.

Properties Objective E: Given instances of a pattern, write a description of the pattern using variables.

In 2-5, three instances of a pattern are given. Describe the general pattern using one variable.

2. $3 \cdot 6 = 6 + 6 + 6$
   $3 \cdot -10 = -10 + -10 + -10$
   $3 \cdot \frac{1}{2} = \frac{1}{2} + \frac{1}{2} + \frac{1}{2}$
   $3 \cdot n = n + n + n$
3. $38 \div 1 = 38$
   $-89.2 \div 1 = -89.2$
   $5\frac{3}{4} \div 1 = 5\frac{3}{4}$
   $n \div 1 = n$
4. 75% of 600 $= \frac{3}{4} \cdot 600$
   75% of $\frac{8}{15} = \frac{3}{4} \cdot \frac{8}{15}$
   75% of -54 $= \frac{3}{4} \cdot -54$
   75% of $n = \frac{3}{4} \cdot n$
5. $6 \cdot 10 = 10 \cdot 6$
   $.7 \cdot 24 = 24 \cdot .7$
   $\frac{1}{3} \cdot \frac{7}{8} = \frac{7}{8} \cdot \frac{1}{3}$
   $m \cdot n = n \cdot m$

Properties Objective F: Give instances of a pattern described with variables.

In 6-9, give two instances of the pattern. Sample answers are given.

6. d days have $24 \cdot d$ hours.
   6 days have $24 \cdot 6$ hours.
   10 days have $24 \cdot 10$ hours.
7. $a \cdot 0 = 0$
   $3 \cdot 0 = 0$
   $6.5 \cdot 0 = 0$
8. 50% of $n = \frac{n}{2}$
   50% of 9 $= \frac{9}{2}$
   50% of 20 $= \frac{20}{2}$
9. $b + b + b + b = 4 \cdot b$
   $2 + 2 + 2 + 2 = 4 \cdot 2$
   $10 + 10 + 10 + 10 = 4 \cdot 10$

A correct description of a pattern must work for all instances. The pattern in Example 2 works for all numbers. It works whether you use decimals or fractions. It is so important that it has a special name you may already know: the Commutative Property of Addition. You will study this property in the next chapter.

Describing Verbal Patterns with Variables

Patterns with words can also be described with variables.

Example 3

Describe the pattern using variables.

One person has 2 eyes.
Two people have 4 eyes in all.
Three people have 6 eyes in all.
Four people have 8 eyes in all.

Solution

First, rewrite the instances in a way that helps you see the pattern.

1 person has $1 \cdot 2$ eyes.
2 people have $2 \cdot 2$ eyes in all.
3 people have $3 \cdot 2$ eyes in all.
4 people have $4 \cdot 2$ eyes in all.

Second, write everything that is the same in all four instances.

___ people have ___ $\cdot$ 2 eyes in all.

Since the missing part in each instance is the same number, one variable is all that is needed.

p people have $p \cdot 2$ eyes in all.

He knew the laws of mathematics. *François Viète was a lawyer by profession, but he devoted himself to mathematics. He made major contributions in the areas of algebra, analytic geometry, and trigonometry.*

What Is Algebra?

Elementary algebra is the study of variables and the operations of arithmetic with variables. Mathematicians in many different ancient cultures, including Egyptian, Babylonian, Indian, and Chinese, solved problems that today would be solved using algebra. Greeks and Arabs first developed methods for solving problems we call algebra problems.

4 Algebra, the way it is done worldwide today, began in 1591. That was the year when François Viète (Fraw swah Vee yet), a French mathematician, first used letters of the alphabet to describe patterns. Viète's work quickly led to the invention of a great deal more mathematics. Within 100 years, the ideas behind almost all of elementary algebra and calculus had been discovered. (Notice how many symbols in the chart opening this chapter were invented in the 1600s.) For this reason, Viète is sometimes called the "father of algebra."

Adapting to Individual Needs

Extra Help

Be sure students understand that in the description of any pattern, different variables are used to represent different values. If the pattern involves the same number more than once, then the same variable should be used. For example, the pattern which represents the following equations can be described as $n - n = 0$.
$5 - 5 = 0$, $8 - 8 = 0$, $30 - 30 = 0$

Also, the pattern $3 \times 6 = 6 \times 3$, $4 \times 9 = 9 \times 4$, and $85 \times 2 = 2 \times 85$ can be described as $a \times b = b \times a$.

4) Samples: $\frac{2}{2} = 1$, $\frac{7.2}{7.2} = 1$. $(x \neq 0)$
5) Samples: $1.2\% = 1.2 \times .01$; $300\% = 300 \times .01$
6) Samples: 6 people have $6 \cdot 2$ eyes; 165 people have $165 \cdot 2$ eyes.
7) Samples: $\frac{1}{2} + \frac{3}{4} = \frac{3}{4} + \frac{1}{2}$; $0.8 + 6 = 6 + 0.8$

12) Samples: $12 + 4 = 5 + 4 + 7$; $12 + .01 = 5 + .01 + 7$; $12 + 1{,}080{,}299 = 5 + 1{,}080{,}299 + 7$; $12 + \frac{1}{2} = 5 + \frac{1}{2} + 7$
13) Samples: $6 \cdot 4 + 13 \cdot 4 = 19 \cdot 4$; $6 \cdot 9.7 + 13 \cdot 9.7 = 19 \cdot 9.7$; $6 \cdot 100 + 13 \cdot 100 = 19 \cdot 100$; $6 \cdot \frac{2}{3} + 13 \cdot \frac{2}{3} = 19 \cdot \frac{2}{3}$
14) Samples: For 2 days overdue, fine will be $20 + 2 \cdot 5$ cents. For 8 days overdue, fine will be $20 + 8 \cdot 5$ cents. For 15 days overdue, fine will be $20 + 15 \cdot 5$ cents. For 365 days overdue, fine will be $20 + 365 \cdot 5$ cents.

QUESTIONS

Covering the Reading

1. What is a variable? **a symbol that can stand for any one of a set of numbers or other objects**
2. What use of variables is explained in this lesson? **Variables can be used to describe patterns.**
3. Name two advantages of using variables to describe patterns. **They look like the instances; they are shorter.**

In 4–7, a pattern is described with variables. Give two instances of the pattern.

4. $\frac{x}{x} = 1$
5. $n\% = n \cdot .01$
6. p people have $p \cdot 2$ eyes.
7. $x + y = y + x$
8. Today's algebra problems were solved long ago by what peoples? **Greeks and Arabs**
9. What is elementary algebra? **the study of variables and arithmetic operations with them**
10. Who is sometimes called the "father of algebra," and why? **François Viète used letters of the alphabet to describe patterns.**
11. *Multiple choice.* Algebra was developed about how many years ago?
(a) 100 (b) 200 (c) 400 (d) 1700 **(c)**

Applying the Mathematics

In 12–14, give four instances of the pattern.

12. $12 + y = 5 + y + 7$
13. $6 \cdot a + 13 \cdot a = 19 \cdot a$
14. If your book is d days overdue, your fine will be $20 + d \cdot 5$ cents.

In 15–17, three instances of a general pattern are given. Describe the pattern using variables. Only one variable is needed for each description.

15. $10 \cdot 0 = 0$
$8.9 \cdot 0 = 0$
$\frac{15}{5} \cdot 0 = 0$ **$a \cdot 0 = 0$**
16. $5 \cdot 40 = 3 \cdot 40 + 2 \cdot 40$
$5 \cdot \frac{3}{8} = 3 \cdot \frac{3}{8} + 2 \cdot \frac{3}{8}$
$5 \cdot 0.2995 = 3 \cdot 0.2995 + 2 \cdot 0.2995$
$5 \cdot n = 3 \cdot n + 2 \cdot n$
17. In 3 years, we expect $3 \cdot 100$ more students and $3 \cdot 5$ more teachers.
In 4 years, we expect $4 \cdot 100$ more students and $4 \cdot 5$ more teachers.
In 1 year, we expect 100 more students and 5 more teachers.
In n years, we expect $n \cdot 100$ more students and $n \cdot 5$ more teachers.
18. Give three instances of the pattern $a \cdot b = b \cdot a$. **Samples: $7 \cdot \frac{1}{2} = \frac{1}{2} \cdot 7$; $6 \cdot 3 = 3 \cdot 6$; $5 \cdot 4.41 = 4.41 \cdot 5$**
19. Is $2 + 2 = 2 + 2$ an instance of the pattern $a + b = b + a$? Why or why not? **Yes, a and b can be the same number.**

Books on wheels. *In some areas, library books come to you. Traveling bookmobiles visit different neighborhoods, greatly enlarging the areas serviced by a library.*

Question 17 Notice that we do not do calculations such as $3 \cdot 100$ and $3 \cdot 5$ because that would disguise the pattern. In the real world, however, such operations would be performed, and the pattern would be more difficult to describe. Students need to be able to describe simple patterns from instances in the form given here before going on to more difficult situations.

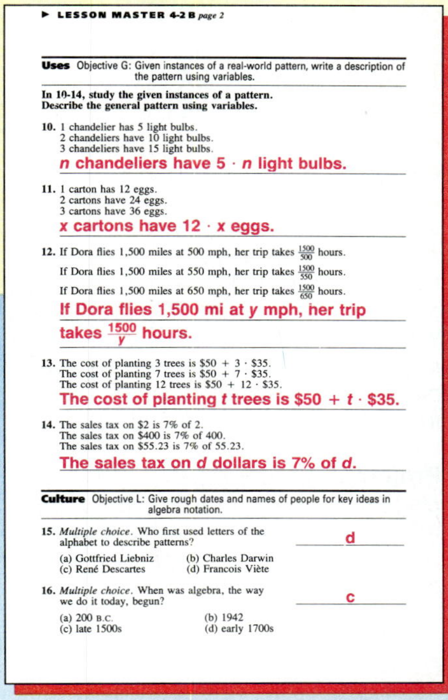

LESSON MASTER 4-2 B *page 2*

Uses Objective G: Given instances of a real-world pattern, write a description of the pattern using variables.

In 10-14, study the given instances of a pattern. Describe the general pattern using variables.

10. 1 chandelier has 5 light bulbs.
2 chandeliers have 10 light bulbs.
3 chandeliers have 15 light bulbs.
n chandeliers have $5 \cdot n$ light bulbs.
11. 1 carton has 12 eggs.
2 cartons have 24 eggs.
3 cartons have 36 eggs.
x cartons have $12 \cdot x$ eggs.
12. If Dora flies 1,500 miles at 500 mph, her trip takes $\frac{1500}{500}$ hours.
If Dora flies 1,500 miles at 550 mph, her trip takes $\frac{1500}{550}$ hours.
If Dora flies 1,500 miles at 650 mph, her trip takes $\frac{1500}{650}$ hours.
If Dora flies 1,500 mi at y mph, her trip takes $\frac{1500}{y}$ hours.
13. The cost of planting 3 trees is $\$50 + 3 \cdot \$35$.
The cost of planting 7 trees is $\$50 + 7 \cdot \$35$.
The cost of planting 12 trees is $\$50 + 12 \cdot \$35$.
The cost of planting t trees is $\$50 + t \cdot \$35$.
14. The sales tax on \$2 is 7% of 2.
The sales tax on \$400 is 7% of 400.
The sales tax on \$55.23 is 7% of 55.23.
The sales tax on d dollars is 7% of d.

Culture Objective L: Give rough dates and names of people for key ideas in algebra notation.

15. *Multiple choice.* Who first used letters of the alphabet to describe patterns? **d**
(a) Gottfried Liebniz (b) Charles Darwin
(c) René Descartes (d) Francois Viète
16. *Multiple choice.* When was algebra, the way we do it today, begun? **c**
(a) 200 B.C. (b) 1942
(c) late 1500s (d) early 1700s

Adapting to Individual Needs

English Language Development

Materials: Several markers, identical except for color

Write "The marker is ____." several times on the board. As you show students the markers, one at a time, ask them to name the color, and write it in one of the blanks. Explain that in each instance, only the color changes or varies; so the color can be called a *variable*. Ask what words in the sentences remain the same. [The marker is] Ask what varies. [The color] Have them tell the pattern. [The marker is *c*.] Next write $3 + 0 = 3$, $5 + 0 = 5$, and $21 + 0 = 21$ on the board. Have students point to the symbols that are the same in each instance [+, 0, =] and those that vary. [3, 5, 21] Then write the sentence again using a letter for the numbers that vary. Have students write sentences by replacing the variable with other numbers.

Notes on Questions

Question 22 You might point out that determining when a pattern is true often leads to the solving of an equation or an inequality. For this inequality, the pattern is *not* true when x is 0, 1, or between 0 and 1.

Questions 32–39 Students may show how each term follows from the previous one or they may describe all of the terms. For example, in Question 32, some students may say the pattern is "add 6" and others may say that the numbers are multiples of 6.

Follow-up for Lesson 4-2

Practice

For more questions on SPUR Objectives, use **Lesson Master 4-2A** (shown on page 183) or **Lesson Master 4-2B** (shown on pages 184–185).

Assessment

Oral Communication Have students **work in pairs** with one student describing a pattern using variables and the other giving three examples of the pattern. For example, one student might say, "t cars have $4 \times t$ wheels" and the other student might say, "One car has four wheels, two cars have eight wheels, and five cars have twenty wheels." [Each example will show a different type of pattern.]

Extension

✎ **Writing** Explain that the numbers in the sequences in **Questions 33 and 37** are called *square numbers and triangular numbers,* respectively. Have students try to discover why these names were given to the numbers and write a paragraph explaining their reasoning. [Sample: When using a pattern of dots, squares can be formed with square numbers and triangles can be formed with triangular numbers.]

Project Update Project 6, *The Beginning of Algebra,* on page 230, relates to the content of this lesson. Students choosing this project can begin their research.

20. Examine these four instances.

$$\frac{1}{3} + \frac{5}{3} = \frac{1+5}{3}$$
$$\frac{11}{3} + \frac{46}{3} = \frac{11+46}{3}$$
$$\frac{0}{3} + \frac{7}{3} = \frac{0+7}{3}$$
$$\frac{7}{4} + \frac{2}{4} = \frac{7+2}{4}$$

a) $\frac{x}{3} + \frac{y}{3} = \frac{x+y}{3}$
b) $\frac{x}{a} + \frac{y}{a} = \frac{x+y}{a}$

a. Describe the pattern of the first three instances using two variables.
b. Describe the pattern of all four instances using three variables.

21. Li noticed that 3 + .5 is not an integer, 4 + .5 is not an integer, and 7.8 + .5 is not an integer.
a. Describe a general pattern of these three instances.
b. Find an instance where the general pattern is not true.
c. Explain why the pattern is not always true. If b equals .5, 1.5, 2.5, and so on, the sum will be an integer.

21a) $b + .5$ is not an integer
b) 3.5 + .5 is an integer

22. Show that the pattern $x^2 > x$ is false by finding an instance that is not true. Sample: $0.1^2 < 0.1$

Review

In 23–28, evaluate. *(Lessons 2-2, 2-5, 4-1)*

23. $25\% \times 60 + 40$ 55
24. $7 \times 2 \times 8 - 7 \times 2$ 98
25. $60 + 40 \div 4 + 4$ 74
26. $12.5 - 11.5 \div 5$ 10.2
27. $72 - 4 \cdot 3^2$ 36
28. $170 - 5^3$ 45

In 29 and 30, translate into mathematical symbols. Then evaluate. *(Lessons 1-1, 1-2)*

29. fifty divided by one ten-thousandth 50/.0001 = 500,000

30. the product of five hundred and five hundredths $500 \cdot .05 = 25$

31. 300 centimeters is how many meters? *(Lesson 3-4)* 3 m

Exploration

In 32–39, examine the sequence of numbers.
a. Find a pattern. a, b) See margin.
b. Describe the pattern you have found in words or with variables.
c. Write the next term according to your pattern. See below.

32. 6, 12, 18, 24, 30, . . . 36
33. 1, 4, 9, 16, 25, . . . 36
34. 5, 6, 9, 10, 13, 14, . . . 17
35. $\frac{1}{3}, \frac{8}{3}, \frac{27}{3}, \frac{64}{3}, \frac{125}{3}, \ldots$ $\frac{216}{3}$
36. 2, 5, 8, 11, 14, . . . 17
37. 1, 3, 6, 10, 15, 21, . . . 28
38. 1, 1, 2, 3, 5, 8, 13, . . . 21
39. 4, 7, 13, 25, 49, . . . 97

32b) Sample: Add 6 to each number to get the next number.
33b) Sample: 1 squared, 2 squared, 3 squared, and so on.
34b) Sample: Begin with 5. Alternately add 1 and 3 to get the next number.
35b) Sample: Take the cube of each natural number, then divide by 3.
36b) Sample: Begin with 2; then add 3 to each number to get the next number.
37b) Sample: Begin with 1. Add 2, then 3, then 4, and so on.
38b) Sample: Begin with 1, 1. Add the two previous numbers to get the next.
39b) Sample: Begin with 4. Add 3, then 6, then 12, doubling what you add each time.

Adapting to Individual Needs

Challenge

Have students find the products given below. Then have then look for a pattern and test it with other numbers. Finally, suggest that they describe the pattern using a variable.
$[143 \times n \times 7 = 1000n + n]$
$143 \times 2 \times 7$ $[2002 = 1000 \cdot 2 + 2]$
$143 \times 3 \times 7$ $[3003 = 1000 \cdot 3 + 3]$
$143 \times 4 \times 7$ $[4004 = 1000 \cdot 4 + 4]$

LESSON

4-3

Translating Words to Algebraic Expressions

Silent translation. *Sign language is a visual language for the hearing impaired. The American Sign Language is the fourth most common language in the U.S.*

Algebraic Expressions

Recall from Lesson 4-1 that $4 + 52$, $9 - 6 \cdot 7$, and $\frac{1}{6}$ are numerical expressions. You know how to translate English into numerical expressions.

English expression	numerical expression
the sum of three and five	$3 + 5$
the product of two tenths and fifty	$.2 \times 50$

If an expression contains a variable alone or with number and operation symbols, it is called an **algebraic expression.** Here are some algebraic expressions.

$$t \qquad 3 \cdot a^2 \qquad z + \frac{400.3}{5} \qquad m - n + m$$

English expressions can be translated into algebraic expressions.

English expression	algebraic expression
the sum of a number and five	$n + 5$
the product of length and width	$\ell \cdot w$

The value of an algebraic expression depends on what is substituted for the variables. You will evaluate algebraic expressions in the next lesson.

Lesson 4-3

Objectives

H Write a numerical or algebraic expression for an English expression involving arithmetic operations.

Resources

From the ***Teacher's Resource File***
- Lesson Master 4-3A or 4-3B
- Answer Master 4-3
- Teaching Aid 39: Warm-up

Additional Resources
- Visual for Teaching Aid 39

Teaching Lesson 4-3

Warm-up

Give words that suggest each operation.

Sample answers are given.

1. Add **Plus, increased by, more than, sum**
2. Subtract **Minus, less, less than, decreased by**
3. Multiply **Times, product**
4. Divide **Divide by, divide into**

Notes on Reading

Reading Mathematics This is another good lesson to read aloud because it helps students hear the English expression as well as see it.

Lesson 4-3 Overview

Broad Goals In Lesson 4-2, students moved from arithmetic instances to writing general patterns using variables. In this lesson, they translate from instances and general patterns written in English to their arithmetic and algebraic counterparts.

Perspective In *Transition Mathematics,* students write algebraic expressions continually, so do not be concerned if students cannot do all of the translations immediately.

There are many phrases used for operations, and it takes time even for good students to become accustomed to all of them.

In this lesson, we continue to utilize the raised dot (·) for multiplication between a number and a variable. In the next lesson, we note that the raised dot can be (and almost always is) omitted.

Some phrases are ambiguous. For example, "the difference of a and b" could mean $a - b$, $b - a$, or $|a - b|$. Similarly, some people might interpret "the quotient of 5 and 40" to mean $\frac{40}{5}$, or 8. Others might divide the first number by the second, and give the answer $\frac{5}{40}$, or $\frac{1}{8}$, or 0.125. We try to avoid ambiguous statements. However, if they do appear, allow all reasonable answers.

❶ Most students know that they can add numbers in any order (because of the Commutative Property of Addition). Stress the importance of proper order in subtraction as illustrated here. Be sure students can differentiate between expressions such as *8 less than a number* and *8 less a number*. For students having difficulty, see *Extra Help* in *Adapting to Individual Needs* on page 189.

Error Alert Some students may want to include the phrase *difference of* as an expression for subtraction. Explain that this term is ambiguous, since *the difference of* -2 and 7 can mean -2 – 7 or 7 – -2.

Words Leading to Algebraic Expressions with Addition or Subtraction

Many English expressions can translate into the same algebraic expression. Below are some common English expressions and their translations. Notice that in subtraction you must be careful about the order of the numbers.

English expression	algebraic expression
a number *plus* five the *sum* of a number and 5 a number *increased* by five five *more than* a number *add* five to a number	$a + 5$ or $5 + a$
❶ a number *minus* eight *subtract* 8 from a number 8 *less than* a number a number *less* 8 a number *decreased by* 8	$h - 8$
eight *minus* a number *subtract* a number from 8 8 *less* a number 8 *decreased by* a number	$8 - n$

Often you have a choice of what letter to use for a number. We use the letter S in Example 1 because the word *salary* begins with that letter.

Example 1

A person's annual salary is S. It is increased by \$700. What is the new salary?

Solution

"Increase" means "add to." So add \$700 to S. The answer is S + \$700.

Example 2

Carmen is five years younger than her sister Anna. If Anna's age is A, what expression stands for Carmen's age?

Solution

Carmen's age is five less than Anna's.

Five less than A is $A - 5$. The answer is $A - 5$.

Optional Activities

Writing After discussing **Example 3**, you might have students **work in groups.** Each group should write ten English expressions which can be translated into algebraic expressions. Then have students trade expressions with another group, and write the algebraic expressions for that group's English expressions.

Words Leading to Algebraic Expressions with Multiplication or Division

Here are some English expressions for multiplication and division. In division, as in subtraction, you must be careful about the order of the numbers.

English expression	algebraic expression
two *times* a number the *product* of two and a number *twice* a number	$2 \cdot m$ or $m \cdot 2$
six *divided by* a number a number *divided into* six	$\frac{6}{u}$
a number *divided by* six six *divided into* a number	$\frac{u}{6}$

Some English expressions combine operations.

Example 3

Translate "five times a number, increased by 3."

Solution

Let n stand for the number.
Five times n is $5 \cdot n$.
$5 \cdot n$ increased by 3 is $5 \cdot n + 3$.

In Example 3, suppose there were no comma after the word *number.* The expression "five times a number increased by 3" would then be ambiguous. *Ambiguous* means the expression has more than one possible meaning. We would not know which to do first, to increase the number by 3, or to multiply the number by 5.

You can think of algebra as a language. As with any language, it is useful to be able to translate to and from other languages. Throughout this book, you will get a lot of practice in order to increase your ability to translate.

A country of many languages. *Nestled in the heart of Europe and bordering four other countries, Switzerland is a country with four national languages—German, French, Italian, and Romansh. The Swiss town shown is Spiez.*

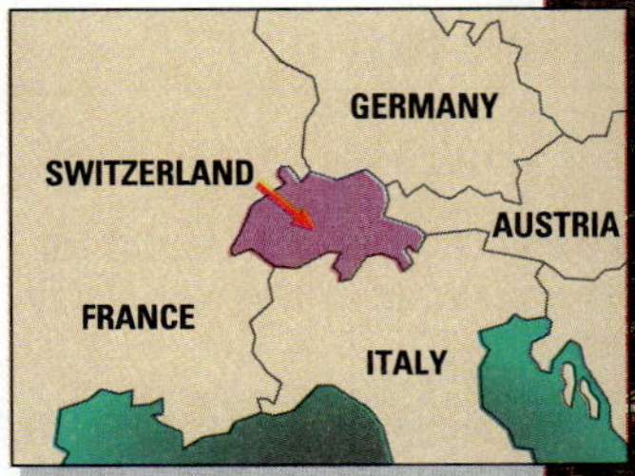

❷ Again emphasize the variety of English expressions for each algebraic expression. Use these examples to remind students that they can multiply in any order and to point out that this is not true for division.

Error Alert Some students may want to include the phrase *quotient of* as an expression for division. Explain that the quotient of 5 and 10 can mean $5 \div 10$ or $10 \div 5$.

Additional Examples

Translate each of the following situations into an algebraic expression.

1. A person weighing p kg gained 3.5 kg. What is his or her new weight? $p + 3.5$
2. The temperature dropped 10° during the past hour. If the temperature was d degrees an hour ago, what expression gives the temperature now? $d - 10$
3. A number n divided into one hundred $\frac{100}{n}$
4. Four times six, plus a number q $4 \times 6 + q$
5. The sum of eight and a number squared $8 + x^2$

Adapting to Individual Needs

Extra Help

Materials: Counters

Before or as you use the chart on page 188, you might want to use counters to model English expressions involving addition, subtraction, multiplication, and division. Emphasize the actions involved for each operation. You can show, for example, that *8 increased by 2* and *2 increased by 8* give the same result, but that *2 less 8 and 8 less 2* are quite different. After demonstrating some situations, have students **work in pairs,** and model other expressions for each operation.

LESSON MASTER 4-3 A

Questions on SPUR Objectives
See pages 233-235 for objectives.

Vocabulary

1. Describe in words the difference between a numerical expression and an algebraic expression.
A numerical expression contains only numbers and operation symbols, while an algebraic expression contains a variable alone or with numbers and operation symbols.

2. Write two possible word expressions for $\frac{24}{2}$.
samples: 24 divided by 2; 2 divided into 24

Uses Objective H

In 3-5, translate into mathematical symbols.

3. twelve less 8 $12 - 8$
4. twelve less than 8 $8 - 12$
5. Twelve is less than 8. $12 < 8$

In 6-12, translate into mathematical symbols. Use your favorite letter for algebraic expressions.

6. the product of 11 and 17 $11 \cdot 17$
7. 6 more than half a number $\frac{1}{2}n + 6$
8. six decreased by twice a number $6 - 2n$
9. 16 more than a number divided by 4 $\frac{n}{4} + 16$
10. the square of a number, decreased by 8 $n^2 - 8$
11. If Dawn can run n blocks per minute, how many blocks can she run in 5 minutes? $5 \times n$ blocks
12. Suppose your family phone bill for November was N dollars. Write an expression for the December bill if it is $25 higher. $N + 25$

Notes on Questions

Question 12 This question deals with the distinctions among *less, less than*, and *is less than*. Many students need practice differentiating these terms.

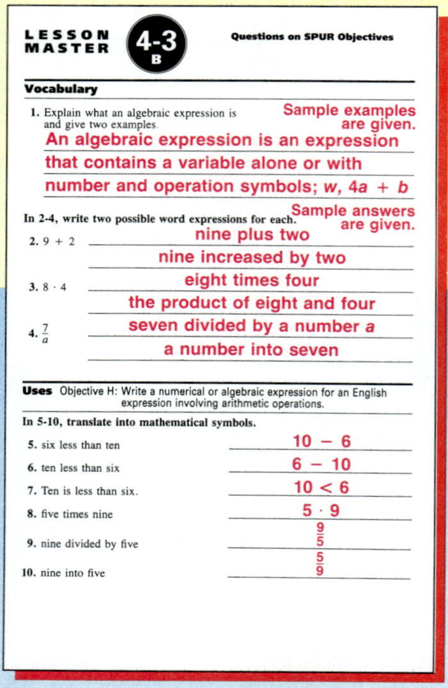

LESSON MASTER 4-3 B Questions on SPUR Objectives

Vocabulary

1. Explain what an algebraic expression is and give two examples. Sample examples are given.
An algebraic expression is an expression that contains a variable alone or with number and operation symbols; w, $4a + b$

In 2-4, write two possible word expressions for each. Sample answers are given.

2. $9 + 2$ nine plus two; nine increased by two
3. $8 \cdot 4$ eight times four; the product of eight and four
4. $\frac{7}{a}$ seven divided by a number a; a number into seven

Uses Objective H: Write a numerical or algebraic expression for an English expression involving arithmetic operations.

In 5-10, translate into mathematical symbols.

5. six less than ten $10 - 6$
6. ten less than six $6 - 10$
7. Ten is less than six. $10 < 6$
8. five times nine $5 \cdot 9$
9. nine divided by five $\frac{9}{5}$
10. nine into five $\frac{5}{9}$

QUESTIONS

Covering the Reading

1. What is the difference between a numerical expression and an algebraic expression? **1) A numerical expression contains only number and operation symbols; an algebraic expression contains a variable or variables as well.**

In 2–11, let n stand for the number. Then translate the English into an algebraic expression.

2. twice the number $2 \cdot n$
3. three more than the number $n + 3$ or $3 + n$
4. the number multiplied by four $n \cdot 4$ or $4 \cdot n$
5. the number less five $n - 5$
6. six less the number $6 - n$
7. seven less than the number $n - 7$
8. eight into the number $\frac{n}{8}$
9. the number divided by nine $\frac{n}{9}$
10. the number increased by ten $n + 10$
11. eleven decreased by the number $11 - n$

12. Translate into mathematics. Be careful. The answers are all different.
    a. six is less than a number $6 < n$
    b. six less than a number $n - 6$
    c. six less a number $6 - n$

13. A person's salary is currently S dollars a week. Write an expression for the new salary if:
    a. the person gets a raise of $50 a week. $S + 50$
    b. the salary is lowered by $12 a week. $S - 12$
    c. the salary is tripled. $3 \cdot S$

14. What is the meaning of the word *ambiguous?* **An ambiguous expression is one that has more than one possible meaning.**
15. Give an example of an English expression that is ambiguous. **Sample: five times a number increased by six**

In 16 and 17, give three possible English expressions for the algebraic expression.

16. $x + 10$ **10 more than a number; a number plus 10; a number increased by 10**
17. $2 - y$ **2 less a number; 2 decreased by a number; 2 minus a number**

18. Translate "a number times six, decreased by five" into an algebraic expression. $6 \cdot n - 5$

I love my new Cougar!

Applying the Mathematics

19. Tell why "fourteen less five plus three" is ambiguous. **It is not clear whether $14 - 5$ or $5 + 3$ is done first.**

In 20 and 21, translate into an algebraic expression. Use C to stand for the number. In working with a number between 0 and 1, the word *of* is often a signal to multiply.

20. half of the number $\frac{1}{2} \cdot C$
21. 6% of the number $.06 \cdot C$ or $6\% \cdot C$

Adapting to Individual Needs

English Language Development
Have students **work in pairs** and translate the following mathematical phrases and sentences into English:
$17 - n \quad n - 17 \quad 17 < n$.
Encourage them to use synonyms such as *minus* and *less*. Students may need help understanding, for example, the distinctions among "less," "less than," and "is less than."

22. Write two algebraic expressions for "a number times itself" using two different operations. $n \cdot n$; n^2

23. Much of what we know about mathematics in ancient Egypt comes from two documents written on papyrus, the *Ahmes Mathematical Papyrus* and the *Moscow Mathematical Papyrus*. Both documents were written around 1650 B.C. Problem 26 on the *Ahmes Papyrus* asks you to find a quantity such that when it is added to $\frac{1}{4}$ of itself, the result is 15. Translate the expression "a quantity added to $\frac{1}{4}$ of itself" into algebra. $x + \frac{1}{4} \cdot x$

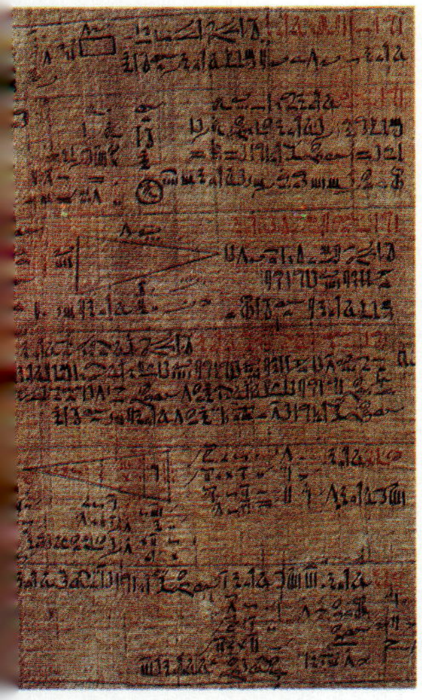

Key to the past. *Pictured here is part of the Ahmes Papyrus, named after the scribe who copied it. It is sometimes called the Rhind Papyrus, named after Alexander Rhind of Scotland who purchased it in 1851.*

24. "Trebled" means "multiplied by three."
 a. What does "quintupled" mean? multiplied by 5
 b. What is the word for "multiplying by four"? quadrupled

25. Why is the "quotient of 2 and 4" an ambiguous phrase?
It could mean $\frac{2}{4}$ or $\frac{4}{2}$.

Review

26. Give three instances of this pattern. *(Lesson 4-2)*

$$7 \cdot x - x = 6 \cdot x$$

$7 \cdot 1 - 1 = 6 \cdot 1$
$7 \cdot 200 - 200 = 6 \cdot 200$
$7 \cdot \frac{1}{2} - \frac{1}{2} = 6 \cdot \frac{1}{2}$

27. Three instances of a general pattern are given. Describe the pattern using one variable. *(Lesson 4-2)*

$$\frac{1 \text{ million}}{1} = 1 \text{ million}$$
$$\frac{10^2}{1} = 10^2$$
$$\frac{8.3}{1} = 8.3$$

$\frac{a}{1} = a$

28. Four instances of a general pattern are given. Describe the pattern using two variables. *(Lesson 4-2)*

$$4 + 5 + 12 - 5 = 4 + 12$$
$$\frac{1}{2} + 5 + \frac{1}{3} - 5 = \frac{1}{2} + \frac{1}{3}$$
$$1.7 + 5 + 6 - 5 = 1.7 + 6$$
$$0 + 5 + 0 - 5 = 0 + 0$$

$x + 5 + y - 5 = x + y$

In 29–31, evaluate each expression. Show your work. *(Lesson 4-1)*

29. $5^2 + 9^2$ 30. $2090 - 4 \times 16^2$ 31. $23 + .09 \times 11$

29) $5^2 + 9^2 = 25 + 81 = 106$
30) $2090 - 4 \times 256 = 2090 - 1024 = 1066$
31) $23 + .09 \times 11 = 23 + 0.99 = 23.99$

32. Find the volume of a cubical box with 10-foot edges. *(Lesson 3-9)* 1000 ft^3

33. a. Draw a triangle with three acute angles.
 b. Draw a triangle with a right angle.
 c. Draw a triangle with an obtuse angle. *(Lessons 3-6, 3-7)*

33) Samples:

a)

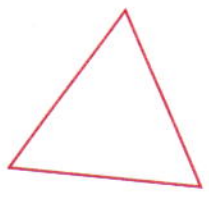

b)

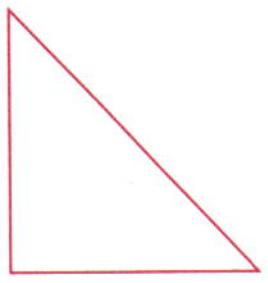

c)

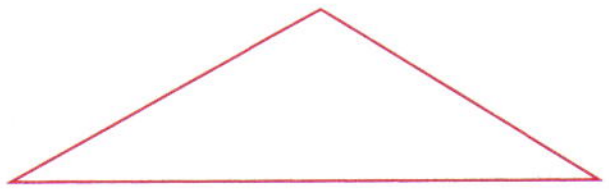

34. It is about 1110 km by air from Paris to Rome. In miles, about how far is it? *(Lesson 3-5)* about 688 miles

Question 23 History Connection Students might do some research on the two documents mentioned and report to the class. They may be interested in knowing that papyrus was a kind of writing paper first made by the Egyptians. The paper was made from the papyrus plant, a grasslike aquatic plant with blunt woody stems that can grow up to 15 feet high. Papyrus was used in the production of books, in both roll and scroll forms, and for correspondence and legal documents. By 300 A.D., less expensive plant fibers were introduced for the manufacture of paper.

Question 24 In an article on page 7 of the September 21, 1992, issue of *Sports Illustrated*, there were two appearances of the word "trebled". First: "... a total of $543,000 in damages ... was trebled as stipulated by federal antitrust law, to $1.63 million." Second, addressed to professional football players: "One other thing players should learn is the meaning of the word *trebled*. If the NFL owners don't make labor peace soon, these judgments could be the beginning of trouble^3 for them." Read these two excerpts to the class and ask which usage is correct. [The first is correct; the second is incorrect for trebled does not mean to take the 3rd power.]

Adapting to Individual Needs

Challenge
Have students solve each of the following problems.

1. A sidewalk vendor sells hot dogs for $1.50 apiece. On Saturday the vendor sells *x* hot dogs, and on Sunday the vendor sells *y* hot dogs. Write an expression to represent the total receipts for the weekend. [$1.50x + 1.50y$]
2. At a school play, adult tickets sold for $4 apiece and student tickets sold for $2 apiece. Write an expression to represent the total receipts for the play. [4A + 2S]

▸ **LESSON MASTER 4-3 B** *page 2*

In 11-24, translate into an algebraic expression.

11. the product of 7 and a number — $7b$
12. 16 more than a number — $n + 16$
13. 40 less a number — $40 - x$
14. a number divided by 13 — $\frac{n}{13}$
15. 27 less than a number — $w - 27$
16. the sum of a number and 1 — $a + 1$
17. 20 into a number — $\frac{c}{20}$
18. 16% of a number — $16\% \cdot t$ or $.16 \cdot t$
19. 11 increased by twice a number — $11 + 2x$
20. half a number less than 32 — $32 - \frac{1}{2}p$
21. the square of a number — d^2
22. Mario can read *x* pages per hour. How many can he read in 3 hours? — $3 \cdot x$ pages
23. Suppose a book cost *B* dollars. What is the cost of a radio if it costs $8 more than the book? — $B + 8$ dollars
24. If you divide *m* magazines equally into four piles, how many magazines are in each pile? — $\frac{m}{4}$ magazines

Review Objective A, Lesson 4-1

In 25-28, evaluate each expression mentally.

25. $8 + 5^2$ — 33
26. $4 \times 10 - 3 \times 9$ — 13
27. $58 - \frac{60}{15}$ — 54
28. $50 \div 5 \times 2$ — 20

Follow-up for Lesson 4-3

Practice

For more questions on SPUR Objectives, use **Lesson Master 4-3A** (shown on page 189) or **Lesson Master 4-3B** (shown on pages 190–191).

Assessment

Oral/Written Communication
Write these words and phrases (or similar ones) on the board: *divided into, more than, less, multiplied by, increased by, less than,* and *times*. Call on different students to use the words and phrases in expressions. The other students should write expressions using mathematical symbols. Call on students to write their algebraic expressions on the board, checking that they match the expressions given orally. [Oral expressions will be varied. Written expressions will show an ability to translate from words to symbols.]

Extension

✎ **Writing** Have students **work in pairs**. Students should write five algebraic expressions, each of which involves at least two operations and one or two variables. Then they should trade papers, and try to write a description of a situation that matches the expression. For example, a student might write the following description for 20 – 2*n*: If tickets to a school play cost $2 each and a person pays for tickets with a $20 bill, then 20 – 2*n* represents the change received.

37)
White: ≈ 200,000,000
Black: ≈ 30,000,000
American Indian, Eskimo, or Aleut: ≈ 2,000,000
Asian or Pacific Islander ≈ 7,000,000
Other races: ≈ 10,000,000
Hispanic: ≈ 22,000,000

35. Measure this segment to the nearest eighth of an inch. *(Lesson 3-1)*

Segment appears slightly reduced in Teacher's edition.

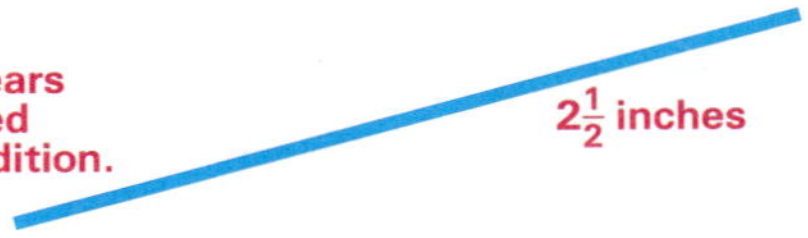

$2\frac{1}{2}$ inches

36. **a.** Give a word name for 10^{-5}. one hundred thousandth
b. Give a decimal for 10^{-5}. .00001
c. Give a fraction for 10^{-5}. *(Lesson 2-8)* $\frac{1}{100,000}$

37. According to the U.S. Bureau of the Census, the 1990 resident population of 248,709,873 was distributed approximately as follows:

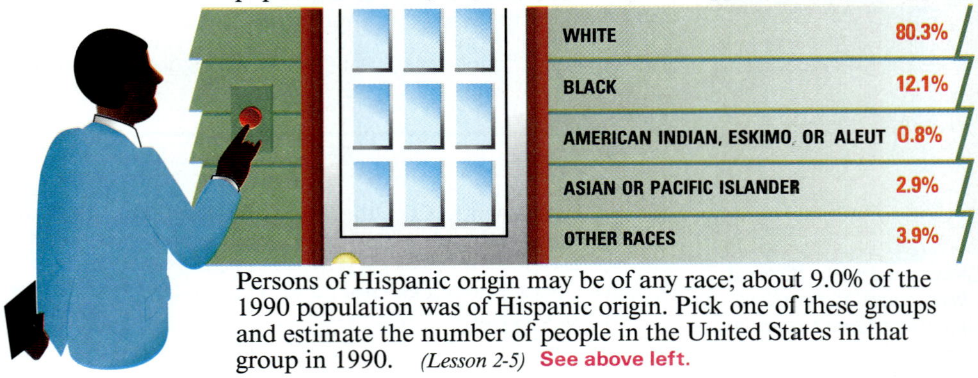

Persons of Hispanic origin may be of any race; about 9.0% of the 1990 population was of Hispanic origin. Pick one of these groups and estimate the number of people in the United States in that group in 1990. *(Lesson 2-5)* See above left.

38. Compare the two sides of each line listed below. Without calculating, decide if <, =, or > makes each sentence true. Be ready to justify your choice. *(Previous course, Lesson 1-9)*

a. = 13 × 17 × 9 __?__ 17 × 9 × 13
b. = 218 + 617 + 314 + 8 __?__ 617 + 314 + 8 + 218
c. > 373 + 936 + 475 __?__ 327 + 934 + 306
d. = 208 + 208 + 208 __?__ 3 × 208
e. = 42 + 43 + 44 __?__ 43 × 3
f. = 52 × 25 __?__ 25 × 52
g. > 530 ÷ 8 __?__ 530 ÷ 10
h. > 1840 ÷ 65 __?__ 1820 ÷ 65
i. < 67 × 73 __?__ 76 × 73

Exploration

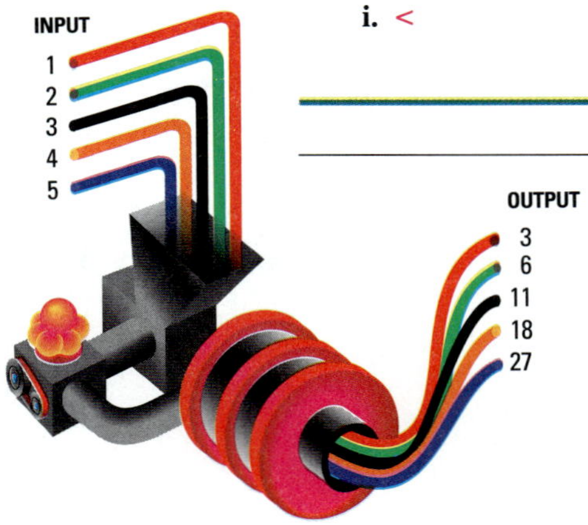

39. This machine performs the same operations with each input number, resulting in the output numbers in the order given. If a number *n* is input into the machine, what is the output? $n^2 + 2$

192

LESSON

4-4

Evaluating Algebraic Expressions

Libraries use mathematics. *Library fines, book inventories, and budgets may be determined using algebraic expressions. Shown here is the main floor of Harper Memorial Library, one of several libraries at the University of Chicago.*

A library charges 20¢ if a book is not returned on time. Added to the fine is 5¢ for each day overdue. Now let n be the number of days overdue. Then the fine is

$$20 + 5 \cdot n \text{ cents.}$$

The fine can now be calculated for any number of days overdue. For a book 13 days overdue, just replace n by 13. The fine is

$$20 + 5 \cdot 13 \text{ cents.}$$

This computes to 85¢.

We say that 13 days is the **value of the variable** n. We can write $n = 13$. The quantity 85¢ is the **value of the expression.** We have evaluated the expression by letting $n = 13$ and finding the value of the resulting expression.

Example 1

Find the value of the expression $25 - 3 \cdot n$ when:

a. $n = 2$. **b.** $n = 8$.

Solution

a. Substitute 2 for n. Then evaluate the resulting arithmetic expression.

When $n = 2$, $25 - 3 \cdot n = 25 - 3 \cdot 2 = 19$.

b. Substitute 8 for n.

When $n = 8$, $25 - 3 \cdot n = 25 - 3 \cdot 8 = 1$.

Lesson 4-4

Objectives

B Evaluate algebraic expressions given the values of all variables.

Resources

From the ***Teacher's Resource File***

- Lesson Master 4-4A or 4-4B
- Answer Master 4-4
- Assessment Sourcebook: Quiz for Lessons 4-1 through 4-4
- Teaching Aid 39: Warm-up

Additional Resource

- Visual for Teaching Aid 39

Teaching Lesson 4-4

Warm-up

Mental Mathematics Calculate.

1. $3^2 - 1$ **8**
2. $4 + 10 \times 10 - 4$ **100**
3. $4 \times 25 \div 2$ **50**
4. $7 + 3 + 5 \times 3$ **25**
5. $10^3 - 10^2$ **900**
6. $8 \times 3 \times 9 \times 0$ **0**

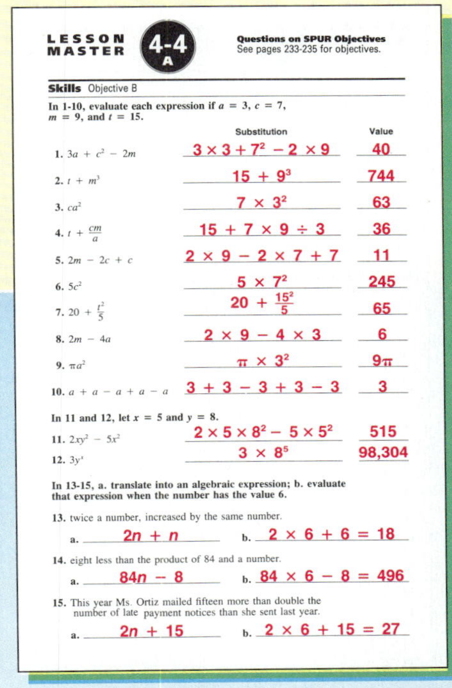

LESSON MASTER 4-4 A

Questions on SPUR Objectives
See pages 233-235 for objectives.

Skills Objective B

In 1-10, evaluate each expression if $a = 3$, $c = 7$, $m = 9$, and $t = 15$.

	Substitution	Value
1. $3a + c^2 - 2m$	$3 \times 3 + 7^2 - 2 \times 9$	40
2. $t + m^3$	$15 + 9^3$	744
3. ca^2	7×3^2	63
4. $t + \frac{cm}{a}$	$15 + 7 \times 9 \div 3$	36
5. $2m - 2c + c$	$2 \times 9 - 2 \times 7 + 7$	11
6. $5c^2$	5×7^2	245
7. $20 + \frac{t^2}{5}$	$20 + \frac{15^2}{5}$	65
8. $2m - 4a$	$2 \times 9 - 4 \times 3$	6
9. πa^2	$\pi \times 3^2$	9π
10. $a + a - a + a - a$	$3 + 3 - 3 + 3 - 3$	3

In 11 and 12, let $x = 5$ and $y = 8$.

11. $2xy^2 - 5x^2$	$2 \times 5 \times 8^2 - 5 \times 5^2$	515
12. $3y^x$	3×8^5	98,304

In 13-15, a. translate into an algebraic expression; b. evaluate that expression when the number has the value 6.

13. twice a number, increased by the same number.
 a. $2n + n$ b. $2 \times 6 + 6 = 18$

14. eight less than the product of 84 and a number.
 a. $84n - 8$ b. $84 \times 6 - 8 = 496$

15. This year Ms. Ortiz mailed fifteen more than double the number of late payment notices than she sent last year.
 a. $2n + 15$ b. $2 \times 6 + 15 = 27$

Lesson 4-4 Overview

Broad Goals This lesson deals with the converse of the idea of the preceding lessons; instead of being given instances and coming up with a general pattern, here the general pattern is given and instances are found for various values of the variable.

Perspective Evaluating algebraic expressions is a relatively easy skill. In Russian texts translated by UCSMP, it is the way algebra is introduced, and it occurs first at the beginning of grade 3.

An important idea in this lesson is the elimination of the symbol for multiplication in algebraic expressions. The symbol × resembles the variable x, and the · can be mistaken for a decimal point. Although a numerical expression such as 2×3 needs a symbol (so it can be differentiated from 23), this is not a problem with variables. Therefore, $6 \cdot t$ becomes $6t$.

Notes on Reading

Reading Mathematics Because the main idea of this lesson is conveyed almost exclusively through examples, you may want to review with your students how to read the examples. If you wish to discuss several replacements for the variable(s), see the suggestion in *Activity 2* in the *Optional Activities* below.

The deletion of symbols such as × and · affects our thinking. For example, the algebraic expression $4x + 3y$ can be thought of as an addition involving two products, $4x$ and $3y$. The omission of multiplication symbols creates an expression containing two terms, with multiplication occurring before addition.

Additional Examples

In 1–3, evaluate the expression for the given value(s) of the variable(s).

1. Find the value of the expression $12 - 2 \cdot m$ when
   a. $m = 1.5$. 9
   b. $m = 8$. −4
2. Find the value of each expression if $r = 5$.
   a. $9.4r$ 47
   b. $25 + 9r - r$ 65
   c. $2\pi r$ ≈31.4
3. Evaluate $3c - \frac{1}{2}d$ when
   a. $c = \frac{1}{2}$, $d = 3$. 0
   b. $c = 8$, $d = 16$. 16

LESSON MASTER 4-4 B Questions on SPUR Objectives

Vocabulary

1. Consider the algebraic expression $7a - 4$. Explain the difference between the value of the variable and the value of the expression.
The value of the variable is the number we substitute for *a*; the value of the expression is the value we get when we calculate $7a - 4$ with a value substituted for *a*.

Skills Objective B: Evaluate algebraic expressions given the values of all variables.

In 2-11, evaluate each expression if $a = 4$, $b = 8$, $n = 12$, and $p = 3.5$.

	Substitution	Value
2. $\frac{n}{2}$	$\frac{12}{2}$	6
3. $20 + a$	$20 + 4$	24
4. $6.2n$	$6.2 \cdot 12$	74.4
5. an	$4 \cdot 12$	48
6. p^2	3.5^2	12.25
7. $3b - 2n$	$3 \cdot 8 - 2 \cdot 12$	0
8. ab^2	$4 \cdot 8^2$	256
9. πn^2	$\pi \cdot 12^2 \approx 3.14 \cdot 12^2$	$144\pi \approx 452.39$
10. $b + np \div a$	$8 + 12 \cdot 3.5 \div 4$	18.5
11. $30 + n - n + n - n$	$30 + 12 - 12 + 12 - 12$	30

In 12-15, let $m = 3$ and $r = 6$.

	Substitution	Value
12. $8m + 2r$	$8 \cdot 3 + 2 \cdot 6$	36
13. r^4	6^4	1296
14. $mr^2 - 2m^2$	$3 \cdot 6^2 - 2 \cdot 3^2$	90
15. $5r^m$	$5 \cdot 6^3$	1,080

We have been using a dot to stand for multiplication. When one of the numbers being multiplied is a variable, the dot is usually not used.

With · for multiplication	Without ·
$6 \cdot t$	$6t$
$27 - 2 \cdot r + r$	$27 - 2r + r$
$4 \cdot x + 3 \cdot y$	$4x + 3y$

The rules for order of operations apply even when the multiplication symbol is absent.

Example 2

Find the value of each expression if $r = 5$.
a. $6r$ b. $27 - 2r + r$ c. πr^2

Solution

a. If $r = 5$, $6r = 6 \cdot 5 = 30$.

b. Do the multiplication before the subtraction or addition.

$$\text{If } r = 5,\ 27 - 2r + r = 27 - 2 \cdot 5 + 5 = 27 - 10 + 5 = 22$$

c. Do the power before the multiplication by π.

$$\text{If } r = 5,\ \pi r^2 = \pi \cdot 25 \approx 3.14 \cdot 25 \approx 78.5$$

When an expression contains more than one variable, you need a value for each variable to get a numerical value for the expression.

Example 3

Evaluate $4x + 3y$ when $x = 10$ and $y = 7$.

Solution

Substitute 10 for x and 7 for y.

$$4x + 3y = 4 \cdot 10 + 3 \cdot 7 = 40 + 21 = 61$$

QUESTIONS

Covering the Reading

1. *Multiple choice.* If $n = 3$, then $5 \cdot n =$
(a) 53 (b) 8 (c) 15 (d) none of these (c)

Optional Activities

Activity 1 What Makes Sense? As you discuss the expression $20 + 5 \cdot n$ for library fines, ask students to give other values for n. Ask what numbers *do not* make sense. [There is probably a maximum fine that is equal to the cost of replacing the book; 0 and negative values for n do not make sense.]

Activity 2 Making Tables As you discuss the examples, you might want to have students evaluate the expressions using other values for the variable, as shown in the table below for **Example 1**.

n	0	3	8	10
$25 - 3 \cdot n$	[25]	[16]	[1]	[-5]

2. Consider the expression $5 \cdot n$ from Question 1. Identify the:
   a. variable. n
   b. value of the variable. 3
   c. expression. $5 \cdot n$
   d. value of the expression. 15

3. What is the more common way of writing $5 \cdot n$? $5n$

4. Do the rules of order of operations apply to variables? Yes

5. Suppose that a book is n days overdue and the fine is $20 + 5n$ cents. Calculate the fine for a book that is:
   a. 1 day overdue. 25¢
   b. 6 days overdue. 50¢
   c. 20 days overdue. $1.20

6. The area of a circle with radius r is πr^2. Which example in this lesson calculates the area of a circle with radius 5? Example 2c

In 7–10, evaluate the expression when d is 5.

7. $d + d$ 10

8. $88 - 4d$ 68

9. $2 + 3d$ 17

10. $d\%$ 5%

In 11–14, give the value of the expression when $m = 5$ and $x = 9$.

11. $4m + 7x$ 83

12. $2mx$ 90

13. $1.6x + m^3$ 139.4

14. πx^2 81π or about 254.469

Applying the Mathematics

15. Let A be an age between 1 and 7 years. A boy of age A weighs, on the average, about $17 + 5A$ pounds.
    a. What is the average weight for 6-year-old boys? 47 lb
    b. What is the average weight for 2-year-old boys? 27 lb
    c. For each additional year of age, by how much does the average weight change? 5 lb

16. Suppose x is 4712 and y is 368.
    a. Evaluate $xy - yx$. 0
    b. Will the answer to part **a** change if the values of x and y are changed? Why or why not? No, because $xy = yx$ for any values of x and y.

17. a. Evaluate $2v + 1$ when v is 1, 2, 3, 4, and 5. 3, 5, 7, 9, and 11
    b. Your answers to part **a** should form a pattern. Describe the pattern in English. Sample: Begin with 3; add 2 to each number to get the next number.

In 18–20, an English expression is given.
a. Translate into an algebraic expression.
b. Evaluate that expression when the number has the value 10.

18. eight less than five times a number a) $5n - 8$; b) 42

19. the product of a number and 4, increased by nine a) $4n + 9$; b) 49

20. the third power of a number a) n^3; b) 1000

Notes on Questions

These questions can be reviewed rather quickly. You might wish to cover all of the questions in order to ensure that the basic ideas of the lesson are clear to students.

Question 10 In some circumstances, 5% would probably be changed to a decimal or a fraction. Yet in others, 5% could be an appropriate final answer.

Question 15c This question is adapted from the tests of the 1981–1982 National Assessment of Educational Progress given to 17-year-olds. Perhaps surprisingly, 53% of 17-year-olds who did *not* have algebra answered this item correctly. On the other hand, only 64% of students who had two years of algebra correctly answered the item! Thus it may require far less algebra to answer the question than one thinks.

▶ **LESSON MASTER 4-4 B** *page 2*

In 16-23, a. translate into an algebraic expression; b. evaluate that expression when the number has the value 9.

16. twice a number
    a. $2n$ b. 18

17. a number minus six
    a. $w - 6$ b. 3

18. the second power of a number
    a. a^2 b. 81

19. 22 more than 6 times a number
    a. $6x + 22$ b. 76

20. 13 less than the product of a number and 10
    a. $10c - 13$ b. 77

21. The number of trumpets in band has gone down by three.
    a. $t - 3$ b. 6 trumpets

22. Your hourly salary has been increased by $1.50 an hour.
    a. $w + 1.50$ b. $10.50 per hour

23. This year the total amount of snow was 4 inches more than twice the amount that fell last year.
    a. $2s + 4$ b. 22 inches

Review Objective E, Lessons 1-5, 1-6, 1-8, and Objective C, Lesson 2-2

In 24-27, write a key sequence for the given operations. Then write the value of the expression.

24. $22.4056 + 18.9$	22.4056 [+] 18.9 [=]	41.3056
25. 41×8	41 [×] 8 [=]	328
26. $972 \div 27 - 2.03$	972 [÷] 27 [−] 2.03 [=]	33.97
27. 4^6	4 [y^x] 6 [=]	4,096

Adapting to Individual Needs

Extra Help

Some students might benefit from using a table format to evaluate expressions. Use simple expressions as shown in the table at the right for $5n$. Ask students to write out the steps of their work, and have them read the results aloud. For example, "When n is 0, $5n$ is 0, when n is 3, $5n$ is 15," and so on.

n	0	3	6	8
$5n$	[0]	[15]	[30]	[40]

If students seem to understand when only one variable is involved, but struggle with expressions involving two variables, use tables like the one shown for $x + 3y$.

x	0	5	5	6
y	2	3	0	1
$x + 3y$	[6]	[14]	[5]	[9]

Question 28 In Chapter 6, this type of question would be done by applying the problem-solving strategy of *using simpler numbers.* In this lesson, the student is expected to try instances and to see the general pattern from the instances. The two approaches, although described differently, really are the same—trying to relate a seemingly complicated situation to something that is already understood.

Follow-up for Lesson 4-4

Practice

For more questions on SPUR Objectives, use **Lesson Master 4-4A** (shown on page 193) or **Lesson 4-4B** (shown on pages 194–195).

Assessment

Quiz A quiz covering Lesson 4-1 through Lesson 4-4 is provided in the *Assessment Sourcebook.*

Written Communication Have students **work in pairs,** and take turns giving each other an algebraic expression with the value of the variable(s) to be used when the partner evaluates the expression. The student giving the expression should check his or her partner's response. [The variety and complexity of the algebric expressions will show an understanding of the concept.]

Extension

Have students discuss the following questions.

1. When does $5a + 2b$ have the same value as $7a$? [When $a = b$]
2. When does $2x$ have the same value as $4y$? [When $x = 2y$]
3. When does mn have the same value as nm? [For all values of m and n]
4. When does $5x$ have the same value as $3x$? [When $x = 0$]
5. When does $x + 5$ have the same value as $x - 5$? [For no values of x]

Horse history. *Fossils found in Europe and North America indicate that horses date back at least 54 million years. Around 10,000 years ago, horses mysteriously disappeared from North America. Horses were then reintroduced by Spaniards in the early 16th century.*

Review

21. *Multiple choice.* Which is the largest? *(Lesson 4-3)*
(a) the sum of 10 and 1 (b) the product of 10 and 1
(b) 10 divided by 1 (d) 10 to the first power **(a)**

22. Four horses have $4 \cdot 4$ legs, $4 \cdot 2$ ears, and 4 tails. *(Lesson 4-2)*
a. Six horses have $6 \cdot 4$ legs, ? $\cdot$ 2 ears, and ? tails. **6, 6**
b. Eleven horses have ? legs, ? ears, and ? tails. **$11 \cdot 4$, $11 \cdot 2$, 11**
c. H horses have ? legs, ? ears, and ? tails. **$H \cdot 4$, $H \cdot 2$, H**

In 23 and 24, three instances of a pattern are given. Describe the pattern using one variable. *(Lesson 4-2)*

23. $5 + 0 = 5$
$43.0 + 0 = 43.0$
$\frac{1}{2} + 0 = \frac{1}{2}$ **$a + 0 = a$**

24. $1 \times 60\% = 60\%$
$1 \times 2 = 2$
$1 \times 1 = 1$ **$1 \times b = b$**

25. What is the metric prefix meaning $\frac{1}{1000}$? *(Lesson 3-4)* **milli-**

26. Convert $\frac{2.4}{10.24}$ into a simple fraction in lowest terms. *(Lesson 2-6)* **$\frac{15}{64}$**

27. *Multiple choice.* Which two of these refer to the same numbers? *(Lessons 1-1, 1-8)*
(a) the whole numbers (b) the natural numbers
(c) the integers (d) the positive integers **(b) and (d)**

Exploration

28. A library decides to charge m cents for an overdue book and A more cents for every day the book is overdue. What will be the fine for a book that is d days overdue? **$m + A \cdot d$**

29. Computers can evaluate algebraic expressions. Here is a program that evaluates a particular expression.

```
10 PRINT "GIVE VALUE OF YOUR VARIABLE"
20 INPUT X
30 V = 30 * X - 12
40 PRINT "VALUE OF THE EXPRESSION IS " V
50 END
```

a. What expression does the above program evaluate? **$30x - 12$**
b. What value does the computer give if you input 3.5 for X? **93**
c. Modify the program so that it evaluates the expression $25X + X^4$ and test your program when $X = 1$, $X = 2$, and $X = 17$. What values do you get? **Change line 30 to: 30 V = 25 * X + X ^ 4**
When X = 1, V = 26; when X = 2, V = 66; when X = 17, V = 83,946.

Adapting to Individual Needs

English Language Development
Materials: Envelopes and coins

You might use this activity to help students understand the meaning of *value of the variable* and *value of the expression.* Have 3 students come to the front of the room. Give each an envelope, and tell the class that each envelope contains the same amount of money. Write $3 \cdot e$ on the board. Ask students what they think 3 represents [3 envelopes or 3 students], what e represents [the amount of money in each envelope], and what $3 \cdot e$ represents [the total amount of money]. Explain that the *value of the variable* is the amount of money in each envelope. Have students open the envelopes to determine this value. Then the *value of the expression* is 3 times this amount. Repeat the activity by putting other amounts of money in the envelopes.

LESSON

4-5

Parentheses

Winter wonderland. *The queen of the Quebec Winter Carnival is crowned in front of a genuine ice castle in Quebec, Canada. The annual carnival, attracting 500,000 tourists, is held in early February when the average temperature of 12°F, or -11°C, ensures the ice will remain firm.*

A Formula That Uses Parentheses

Here are the directions given in an almanac for converting Fahrenheit temperatures (the U.S. everyday temperature scale) to Celsius (the temperature scale used by all scientists and people almost everywhere outside the U.S.).

To convert Fahrenheit to Celsius,
subtract 32 degrees and multiply by 5, divide by 9.

With algebra, this description can be shortened. Let F be the Fahrenheit temperature. First subtract 32 from F, resulting in

$$F - 32.$$

Now this entire expression is to be multiplied by 5 and divided by 9. This is equivalent to multiplying by $\frac{5}{9}$. Parentheses are used to show this multiplication.

$$\frac{5}{9} \cdot (F - 32)$$

The parentheses signify that the subtraction of 32 is done first. If there were no parentheses, the multiplication would be done first.

> **Order of Operations Parentheses Rule**
> Work inside parentheses before doing anything else.

Lesson 4-5

Objectives

A Use order of operations to evaluate numerical expressions.
B Evaluate algebraic expressions given the values of all variables.
D Know the correct order of operations in expressions.

Resources

From the ***Teacher's Resource File***
- Lesson Master 4-5A or 4-5B
- Answer Master 4-5
- Teaching Aid 40: Warm-up

Additional Resources
- Visual for Teaching Aid 40

Teaching Lesson 4-5

Warm Up

Writing Write a set of instructions telling how to make something. Explain why doing these steps in order is important.
Answers will vary.

Notes on Reading

❶ **Reading Connection** You might bring several current almanacs to class and discuss some of the information they contain.

Lesson 4-5 Overview

Broad Goals This lesson extends the ideas of the preceding lessons to arithmetic and algebraic expressions with parentheses.

Perspective There are three fundamental reasons for using parentheses. One reason is to change the order of operations. If an addition is to be done before a multiplication, then the numbers being added must be in parentheses. A second reason is to separate or group an expression for the purpose of identification. This is somewhat like using commas to separate a phrase from the rest of a sentence. A third reason is to write expressions on *one* line in order to enter them into the computer or calculator. Thus, instead of using a fraction bar for division, which itself is a grouping symbol, parentheses are needed. (This idea is discussed in the next lesson.) The use of grouping symbols is a traditional skill that has increased in importance with technology.

In Lesson 4-6, brackets [ ] are introduced as grouping symbols having the same meaning as parentheses. Using brackets is fine for paper and pencil work, but calculators and many computer languages do not accept brackets.

Multicultural Connection
The word *thermometer* means "heat measure." The earliest known thermometer was made by Italian scientist Galileo Galilei about 1593. It was not until 1724 that German-born Gabriel Daniel Fahrenheit developed a thermometer in which the freezing point of water was calibrated at 32°F. In 1741, Swedish astronomer Andres Celsius established a scale in which the freezing point of water was 100°C and the boiling point of water was 0°C. In 1745, this scale was reversed by Swedish botanist Carl Linnaeus, producing the centigrade scale.

Cooperative Learning Because this lesson contains mostly examples, as a class discuss the key point of each example. **Example 1** uses parentheses in a formula. In **Example 2**, parentheses are used to indicate the need to perform the addition before the multiplication; in **Example 3,** they are used to indicate that the multiplication is performed before the powering. **Example 4** teaches that no symbol between parentheses means multiplication. (Note that the symbol must be put in when using a calculator, as in Solution 2.) **Example 5** illustrates the use of nested parentheses.

Example 1

What is the Celsius equivalent of a Fahrenheit temperature of 68°?

Solution

Using the information on page 197, the Celsius equivalent is

$$\frac{5}{9} \cdot (F - 32),$$

where $F = 68$. So substitute 68 for F.

$$\begin{aligned}\frac{5}{9} \cdot (F - 32) &= \frac{5}{9} \cdot (68 - 32)\\ &= \frac{5}{9} \cdot (36)\\ &= \frac{5}{9} \cdot 36\\ &= 20\end{aligned}$$

68° Fahrenheit is equal to 20° Celsius.

In the Solution to Example 1 we removed the parentheses around 36. You can drop parentheses in an expression whenever doing so does not change the value of the expression.

As with other order-of-operation problems, it is useful to write the steps of calculations vertically as shown in the examples below.

Example 2

Simplify $7 + 9 \cdot (2 + 3)$.

Solution

Write the original expression.	$7 + 9 \cdot (2 + 3)$
Work inside () first.	$= 7 + 9 \cdot (5)$
Drop the parentheses.	$= 7 + 9 \cdot 5$
Now evaluate as before.	$= 7 + 45$
	$= 52$

Work inside parentheses even before taking powers.

Example 3

Evaluate $6 + 5 \cdot (4x)^3$ when $x = 2$.

Solution

Write the original expression.	$6 + 5 \cdot (4x)^3$
Substitute 2 for x.	$= 6 + 5 \cdot (4 \cdot 2)^3$
Work inside ().	$= 6 + 5 \cdot (8)^3$
Powering comes next.	$= 6 + 5 \cdot 512$
Multiplication comes next.	$= 6 + 2560$
Addition comes last.	$= 2566$

Optional Activities

When does $F = C$? As an extension of **Example 1**, you might have students use trial and error to find the temperature at which the Fahrenheit value is the same as the Celsius value. If you want to give students a hint, tell them it is a negative number. [–40°]

The dot for multiplication is generally not used with parentheses. For the expression in Example 3, it is more common to see $6 + 5(4x)^3$. The 5 next to the parentheses signals multiplication.

Example 4

Evaluate $(y + 15)(11 - 2y)$ when $y = 3$.

Solution 1

Write the original expression.	$(y + 15)(11 - 2y)$
Substitute 3 for y everywhere y occurs.	$= (3 + 15)(11 - 2 \cdot 3)$
Work inside (). Follow order of operations.	$= (18)(11 - 6)$
	$= 18 \cdot 5$
	$= 90$

Using Parenthesis Keys on Calculators

Most scientific calculators have parenthesis keys [( ] and [ )]. To use these keys, enter the parentheses where they appear in the problem.

Remember you may need to key in [×] even though the times sign is not written in the problem. Here is how Example 4 would be done with a calculator.

Solution 2

Key in: [( ] 3 [+] 15 [ )] [×] [( ] 11 [−] 2 [×] 3 [ )] [=].

The problem is not very difficult, but the calculator solution requires many key strokes. So unless the numbers are quite complicated, most people prefer not to use a calculator for this kind of problem.

Nested Parentheses

It is possible to have parentheses inside parentheses. These are called **nested parentheses.** With nested parentheses, work inside the innermost parentheses first.

Example 5

Simplify $300 - (40 + .6(30 - 8))$.

Solution

Write the original expression.	$300 - (40 + .6(30 - 8))$
Work in the innermost () first.	$= 300 - (40 + .6(22))$
Multiply before adding.	$= 300 - (40 + 13.2)$
Work inside the remaining ().	$= 300 - (53.2)$
	$= 246.8$

Some calculators enable you to nest parentheses; some do not. You should explore your calculator to see what it allows. (See Question 39.)

As you discuss the examples, some students might wonder why it is necessary to know rules for order of operations if parentheses can be used to indicate order. Use the following example to show that the rules make it possible to write an expression in simpler form:

$8((9 \times 7) - (6 \times 3) + 5) =$

$8(9 \times 7 - 6 \times 3 + 5)$

Explain that without the standard order of operations, three sets of parentheses are needed. However, since the standard order dictates that multiplication is to be done before addition or subtraction, two of those sets can be eliminated.

Students should record the results of the Activity following **Example 5. Question 23** on page 200 asks for a key sequence to evaluate the expression.

Additional Examples

1. Find the Celsius equivalent of a Fahrenheit temperature of 100°. **About 37.8°**

Evaluate each expression.

2. $8 \cdot (7 - 2) + 4$ **44**
3. $(13 + n)^3$ when $n = 2$ **3375**
4. $(3 + c)(s^2 - 3)$ when $c = 2$ and $s = 5$ **110**
5. $500 - 3(4 + .25(2 \cdot 4))$ **482**

LESSON MASTER 4-5 A

Questions on SPUR Objectives
See pages 233-235 for objectives.

Skills Objectives A and B

In 1-7, evaluate each expression.

1. $15 + 5(21 - 9)$ **75**
2. $4(16 - 2) + 36 + 2(10 - 8)$ **96**
3. $(4^3 + 4(11 - 2)) - (21 \cdot 2^2)$ **16**
4. $4(3x + 19) - 7$, when $x = 7$ **153**
5. $250 - (30 + 5 \cdot 12)$ **160**
6. $(2m + n)(4n)$, when $m = 3.5$ and $n = .25$ **7.25**
7. $5 + y[2 + y(1 + y)]$, when $y = 10$ **1125**
8. *Multiple choice.* Begin with a number t. Subtract 3. Multiply the difference by the square of t. What number results?
   (a) $2t(3 - t)$ (b) $2t(t - 3)$
   (c) $t^2(t - 3)$ (d) $t^2(3 - t)$ **c**
9. Rewrite the following sentence, inserting parentheses to make it true.
   $45 - 7 \times 6 - 2 - 6 = 11$ **$45 - 7 \times (6 - 2) - 6 = 11$**

Properties Objective D

10. When you evaluate the following expression, what operation should you do first, subtraction or squaring? $(7 - 2)^2$ **subtraction; $7 - 2$**
11. When you evaluate $5(15(8^2 - 24) \div 12) - 6^3$, what arithmetic should you do
    a. first? **8^2** b. second? **$64 - 24$**
    c. third? **$15 \times 40 \div 12$** d. fourth? **6^3**
    e. fifth? **5×50** f. sixth? **$250 - 216$**
12. Write a key sequence for evaluating $10 + 3(7 + 8)$.
    10 [+] 3 [×] [( ] 7 [+] 8 [ )] [=]

Adapting to Individual Needs

Extra Help

Students who are using the index-card questions suggested in *Extra Help* for Lesson 4-1, on page 178, should revise their lists, inserting "Are there any parentheses?" as question 1.

Then use the three expressions at the right to help students see that parentheses are sometimes necessary to indicate a variance from the standard order. Point out that the same numbers are used in each expression, but the use of parentheses changes the value.

$9 + 4 \times 3 - 1$	$(9 + 4)3 - 1$	$9 + 4(3 - 1)$
$9 + 12 - 1$	$13 \times 3 - 1$	$9 + 4 \times 2$
$21 - 1$	$39 - 1$	$9 + 8$
20	38	17

Note that it is not necessary to write $9 + 4 \times 3 - 1$ as $9 + (4 \times 3) - 1$ because of the standard order of operations.

Notes on Questions

When students evaluate expressions in this lesson, they should write all steps, as shown in the examples. Writing out steps forces students to think about the proper order, and it eliminates many careless mistakes.

LESSON MASTER 4-5 B Questions on SPUR Objectives

Skills Objective A: Use order of operations to evaluate numerical expressions.

In 1-14, evaluate each expression.

1.	$8(12 - 7)$	40
2.	$(17 + 6) \times (11 - 9)$	46
3.	$37 - (5 + 18)$	14
4.	$90 + 3(14 - 4)$	120
5.	$6(2 + 7) + 4(15 + 1)$	118
6.	$100 - (45 + 3 \cdot 8)$	31
7.	$9^2 + (48 + 22)$	151
8.	$65 - (2 \cdot 3^3)$	11
9.	$[15 + 2(25 - 7)] - (13 + 4)$	34
10.	$(7 \cdot 8)^2$	3,136
11.	$12 + 2(8 - 3)^3$	262
12.	$216 - (2^6 - 8(7 + 1))$	216
13.	$(9 + 1)^5 + (11 - 7)^2$	100,016
14.	$((3 + 1)^3 + 6)^2$	4,900

In 15-18, rewrite each sentence, inserting parentheses to make it true.

15.	$9 \times 4 + 6 = 90$	$9 \times (4 + 6) = 90$
16.	$28 - 20 - 3 - 4 = 7$	$28 - (20 - 3) - 4 = 7$
17.	$80 - 6 \times 7 - 3 = 41$	$80 - (6 \times 7 - 3) = 41$
18.	$7^2 + 5 \times 3 + 4 = 84$	$7^2 + 5 \times (3 + 4) = 84$

The given expression in Example 5 is too long for some calculators. With these calculators, you may have to evaluate the expression a little at a time.

Activity

Describe how to evaluate $300 - (40 + .6(30 - 8))$ on your calculator.

QUESTIONS

Covering the Reading

1. What is one reason for using parentheses? **to indicate operations that should be done before all others**

In 2–5, *true or false.*

2. $5 + 4 \cdot 3 = (5 + 4) \cdot 3$ **False**
3. $5 + 4 \cdot 3 = 5 + (4 \cdot 3)$ **True**
4. $5(3) = 15$ **True**
5. $2 + (4) = 8$ **False**
6. *Multiple choice.* When evaluating an expression with parentheses, how should you begin?
   (a) First do additions or subtractions, from left to right.
   (b) First do multiplications or divisions, from left to right.
   (c) First work inside parentheses.
   (d) First take powers.
   (e) Work from left to right regardless of the operation. **(c)**

In 7–12, evaluate.

7. $4 + 3(7 + 9)$ **52**
8. $(12)(3 + 4)$ **84**
9. $10 + 20 \div (2 + 3 \cdot 6)$ **11**
10. $40 - (30 - 5)$ **15**
11. $(6 + 6)(6 - 6)$ **0**
12. $3(2 + 4)^5$ **23,328**
13. a. Multiplication occurs twice in the expression $2(5 + 4n)$. What are these places? **between 2 and (5 + 4*n*); between 4 and *n***
    b. Suppose $n = 8$. Write the key sequence that will evaluate $2(5 + 4n)$ on your calculator. **2 [×] [(] 5 [+] 4 [×] 8 [)] [=]**
14. Find the Celsius equivalent of 122° Fahrenheit. **50°C**

In 15–20, $a = 2$, $b = 3$, and $c = 5$. Evaluate each expression.

15. $0.30(c - b)$ **0.6**
16. $(a + b)(7a + 2b)$ **100**
17. $(a + 100b) - (7a - 2b)$ **294**
18. $20a + 5(c - 3)$ **50**
19. $a^{(b + c)}$ **256**
20. $2(a + 2b)^3$ **1024**
21. What are *nested* parentheses? **parentheses inside parentheses**
22. a. To simplify $1000 - (100 - (10 - 1))$, what should you do first?
    b. Simplify $1000 - (100 - (10 - 1))$. **a) Evaluate (10 − 1). b) 909**
23. Give a key sequence for evaluating $300 - (40 + .6(30 - 8))$ on your calculator. **Answers may vary. Sample: 300 [−] [(] 40 [+] .6 [×] [(] 30 [−] 8 [)] [)] [=]**

Adapting to Individual Needs

English Language Development

Materials: A set of nested objects, such as nested boxes or nested dolls

Students just learning English might have trouble understanding the word *nested.* Show them a set of nested boxes or dolls. Explain that a set of things that fit within one another is said to be nested. Therefore, a set of parentheses within another set is nested. Then write the expression in **Example 5** on the board, and highlight the innermost or nested set of parentheses:

$300 - (40 + .6\mathbf{(30 - 8)})$

Multicultural Connection A traditional Russian doll, the *matreshka*, is a set of hollow wooden dolls that fit inside one another. If some of your students have sets of these dolls, you might ask them to give the class some background information about them.

Applying the Mathematics

In 24 and 25, let $a = 10$ and $b = 31$. Which expression has the larger value?

24. $b - (a - 2)$ or $b - a - 2$ $b - (a - 2)$

25. $a + 4(b + 3)$ or $(a + 4)b + 3$ $(a + 4)b + 3$

In 26 and 27, when $n = 3$, do the two expressions have the same value?

26. $4(n + 2)$ and $4n + 8$ Yes

27. $33 - 7n$ and $(33 - 7)n$ No

28. *Multiple choice.* Begin with a number n. Add 5 to it. Multiply the sum by 4. What number results?
(a) $n + 5 \cdot 4$
(b) $4(n + 5)$
(c) $n + 5 + n \cdot 4$
(d) $n + 5 + (n + 5)4$ (b)

29. To convert a Celsius temperature C to its Fahrenheit equivalent, you can multiply the temperature by 9, divide the product by 5, and then add 32.

a. *Multiple choice.* Which algebraic expression describes this rule?
(i) $\frac{9(C + 32)}{5}$
(ii) $9C + \frac{32}{5}$
(iii) $\frac{9C}{5} + 32$
(iv) $\frac{9C + 32}{5}$ (iii)

b. What is the Fahrenheit equivalent of 23° Celsius? 73.4°

30. Three instances of a pattern are given. Describe the general pattern using three variables.

$$11(3 + 2) = 11 \cdot 3 + 11 \cdot 2$$
$$5(12 + 19.3) = 5 \cdot 12 + 5 \cdot 19.3$$
$$2(0 + 6) = 2 \cdot 0 + 2 \cdot 6$$
$a(b + c) = ab + ac$

31. Evaluate $2(3 + n(n + 1) + 5)$ when $n = 14$. 436

In 32 and 33, insert parentheses to make the sentence true.

32. $16 - 15 - 9 = 10$ $16 - (15 - 9) = 10$

33. $16 - 8 - 4 - 2 = 14$ $16 - (8 - 4 - 2) = 14$

35a) T = number of touchdowns; E = number of extra points; F = number of field goals; S = number of safeties

Review

In 34 and 35, consider the expression $6T + E + 3F + 2S$. *(Lessons 4-3, 4-4)*

34. Evaluate this expression when $T = 3$, $E = 2$, $F = 1$, and $S = 0$. 23

35. This expression has something to do with scoring in football. The letters T, E, F, and S have been chosen carefully. With these hints,

a. what precisely do T, E, F, and S stand for? See above left.

b. what does the value of the expression tell you? the total score

36. Three instances of a pattern are given. Describe the general pattern using one variable. *(Lesson 4-2)*

$3^4 = 3 \cdot 3 \cdot 3 \cdot 3$ $6^4 = 6 \cdot 6 \cdot 6 \cdot 6$ $1^4 = 1 \cdot 1 \cdot 1 \cdot 1$

$n^4 = n \cdot n \cdot n \cdot n$

37. In many places in the Midwest, a township is a square, 6 miles on a side. What is the area of a township? *(Lesson 3-8)* 36 mi^2

Safety! *The official is signalling a "safety," giving 2 points to the team on defense. Typically, a safety is scored when the ball carrier is tackled in his own end zone or when a blocked punt goes out of the end zone. The scoring team then gains possession of the ball.*

Questions 32–33 Encourage students to use trial and error to devise some sort of method for inserting trial parentheses. (The problem-solving strategy of trial and error is described in detail in Chapter 6.) For example, in **Question 33,** suggest that students first try parentheses around the first two terms, then around the next two terms, and finally around the last two terms. If none of these arrangements work, they could try parentheses around three terms at a time.

Adapting to Individual Needs

Challenge

Have students use the rules given below to write an expression for each of the numbers 1 through 10.

a. Use only the digits 1 through 4, the four operations (+, –, ×, ÷), standard order of operations, and parentheses.

b. Use each number once, and only once, in each expression.

c. An operation can only be used once in an expression, but all four operations need not be used.

d. The numbers and operations can be used in any order.

[Sample answers:
$1 = (4 + 1 - 3) \div 2$ $2 = (3 \times 2 - 4) \div 1$
$3 = (3 + 4 - 1) \div 2$ $4 = 3 - 1 + 4 \div 2$
$5 = (4 + 3 - 2) \div 1$ $6 = 1 + 4 \times 2 - 3$
$7 = 4 \times 3 \div 2 + 1$ $8 = 4 + (3 - 1) \times 2$
$9 = 3 \times 2 + 4 - 1$ $10 = 2 \times 4 - 1 + 3$]

▶ **LESSON MASTER 4-5 B** *page 2*

Skills Objective B: Evaluate algebraic expressions given the values of all variables.

In 19-26, evaluate each expression if $a = 10$, $b = 4.2$, and $c = 8$.

19. $7(a + b)$ 99.4

20. $(2c)^2$ 256

21. $(a + b)(a - c)$ 28.4

22. $(100b - 16) + (100 - ac)$ 424

23. $4 + 7 \cdot (ab)^2$ 12,352

24. $3(a - c)^7$ 384

25. $b^{(a - c)}$ 17.64

26. $(3(a + 2))^2$ 1,296

Properties Objective D: Know the correct order of operations in expressions.

27. When you evaluate $(8 - 4)^2$, what operation should you do first, subtraction or squaring? subtraction; $8 - 4$

28. When you evaluate $9 \cdot (6 + 11)$, what operation should you do first, multiplication or addition? addition; $6 + 11$

29. When you evaluate $7(13(10^2 - 36) \div 8) - 22$, what arithmetic should you do

a. first? 10^2; 100
b. second? $100 - 36$; 64
c. third? 13×64; 832
d. fourth? $832 \div 8$; 104
e. fifth? 7×104; 728
f. sixth? $728 - 22$; 706

30. *Multiple choice.* Begin with the number y. Subtract 8. Multiply the difference by the square of y. What number results?
(a) $y^2(8 - y)$
(b) $y^2(y - 8)$
(c) $2y(8 - y)$
(d) $2y(y - 8)$
b

Follow-up for Lesson 4-5

Practice

For more questions on SPUR Objectives, use **Lesson Master 4-5A** (shown on page 199) or **Lesson Master 4-5B** (shown on pages 200–201).

Assessment

Written Communication Write 18 – 9 ÷ 3 × 6 on the board. Then ask each student to write the expression three times and to place parentheses and/or nested parentheses in the expression so that the expression has three different values. Then have them give the value for each arrangement.

Sample answers: 18, $17\frac{1}{2}$, 90

Extension

Questions such as 32 and 33 are fun for some students. You might have students **work in groups,** and ask each group to find as many different values of the expression 36 ÷ 2 × 3 + 24 ÷ 4 as they can by inserting parentheses in different places.

Sample answers:
36 ÷ (2 × 3) + 24 ÷ 4 = 12
(36 ÷ (2 × 3) + 24) ÷ 4 = 7.5
36 ÷ (2 × 3 + 24 ÷ 4) = 3

Project Update Project 2, *A Parentheses Problem*, on page 229, relates to the content of this lesson. Students choosing this project can begin constructing their solutions. Some students may want to **work in groups** to discuss possible strategies to use.

38. A person types a line in 5.7 seconds. Another person types it in one tenth of a second less time. What is the second person's time? *(Lesson 1-2)* **5.6 seconds**

Exploration

39. Use the following exercise to find out how many nested parentheses with operations inside your calculator will allow. Key in

100 – (1 – (2 – (3 – (4 . . . and so on.

When your calculator shows an error message, the last number keyed in is the calculator's limit. What is your calculator's limit? **See below.**

40. This program finds values of the expression in Example 4 of this lesson.

```
10 PRINT "GIVE VALUE OF YOUR VARIABLE"
20 INPUT Y
30 V = (Y + 15) * (11 - 2 * Y)
40 PRINT "VALUE OF EXPRESSION IS " V
50 END
```

a. Run the program when $Y = 3$ to check that it gives the value of Example 4. **Answer should be 90.**

b. Run the program for at least five other values of Y. **Answers will vary due to choice for INPUT in line 20.**

41. Modify the program in Question 40 so that it gives the Celsius equivalent of any Fahrenheit temperature.

```
20 INPUT F
30 C = (5/9) * (F - 32)
40 PRINT "CELSIUS EQUIVALENT IS " C
```

39) An error message for 4 or 5 nested parentheses is typical.

LESSON

4-6

Grouping Symbols

Inside out. *Just as we must simplify complicated expressions by working within innermost parentheses first, the animal must find a way out of the innermost section first.*

Brackets

Parentheses are the most common **grouping symbols. Brackets [ ]** are grouping symbols sometimes used when there are nested parentheses. As grouping symbols, brackets and parentheses mean the same thing.

$5[x + 2y(3 + z)]$ and $5(x + 2y(3 + z))$ are identical.

Many people find brackets clearer than a second pair of parentheses. But some calculators and computer languages do not allow brackets.

Example 1

Simplify $2[4 + 6(3 \cdot 5 - 4)] - 3(30 - 3)$.

Solution

Write the original expression.	$2[4 + 6(3 \cdot 5 - 4)] - 3(30 - 3)$
Evaluate the innermost () first.	$= 2[4 + 6(15 - 4)] - 3(30 - 3)$
Now there are no nested groupings.	$= 2[4 + 6 \cdot 11] - 3(30 - 3)$
	$= 2[4 + 66] - 3(30 - 3)$
	$= 2 \cdot 70 - 3 \cdot 27$
Do multiplication before subtraction.	$= 140 - 81$
	$= 59$

The Fraction Bar

Another important grouping symbol is the *fraction bar.* You may not have realized that the fraction bar acts like parentheses. Here is how it works.

Lesson 4-6

Objectives

A Use order of operations to evaluate numerical expressions.
B Evaluate algebraic expressions with grouping symbols given the values of all variables.
D Know the correct order of operations.

Resources

From the ***Teacher's Resource File***

- Lesson Master 4-6A or 4-6B
- Answer Master 4-6
- Teaching Aids
  40 Warm-up
  43 Rules for Order of Operations
- Technology Sourcebook, Calculator Master 7

Additional Resources

- Visuals for Teaching Aids 40, 43

Teaching Lesson 4-6

Warm-up

Calculator Write a decimal for each number.

1. $\frac{2+3}{125}$ **0.04**
2. $\frac{40+50}{4+5}$ **10**
3. $\frac{4632}{11-8}$ **1544**
4. $\frac{9.8}{0.63+0.07}$ **14**

Notes on Reading

Once again the reading is not much more than a sequence of examples. Each example illustrates an important aspect of the study of order of operations, so again you might ask students what the examples illustrate. **Example 1** shows nested grouping symbols.

Lesson 4-6 Overview

Broad Goals This second lesson on grouping symbols covers brackets, fraction bars, and parentheses within fractions.

Perspective Students may wonder why they need brackets if they can use nested parentheses. The reason is clarity. With brackets, it is easier to find the middle set of parentheses. However, brackets are not used as often as in the past for grouping. The fundamental reason for this is that there are only so many keys on any computer keyboard and only so many symbols that are easy to write and available for use. Brackets are also used on occasion to denote the greatest integer function; that is, [x] denotes the greatest integer less than or equal to x.

In this book, we sometimes use an underline for grouping. For example, we might write that $\underline{a - b}$ is the result when b is taken away from a. Similarly, any underline written to designate a blank to be filled in can also be thought of as acting like a vinculum.

At one time, it was common to use braces { } as grouping symbols. However, since braces are used to denote sets, it is confusing to also use them as grouping symbols. Also, many computer languages do not accept braces.

Example 2 is a simple fraction-bar problem. **Example 3** complicates the fraction bar with a variable, and an order-of-operation issue must be considered. **Solution 2** for **Example 3** demonstrates how complicated the problem becomes when one uses a calculator. **Example 4** shows how all the rules for order of operation are used in one problem.

❶ **History Connection** The fraction bar is called a *vinculum* (see the chart on page 175) and is a grouping symbol that is still in common use. In Europe, the square root of *xy* may be written $\sqrt{}(xy)$. However, in the United States it is written $\sqrt{xy}$; the vinculum is instead of the parentheses. Most people think of the vinculum as part of the square root symbol and do not realize that it is a grouping symbol.

❷ When discussing **Examples 2 through 4,** emphasize that the computations in the numerator and denominator must be done before dividing to evaluate the fractions. In particular, caution students against cancelling the variables or the 1s in **Example 3**.

❶ Suppose you want to calculate the average of 10, 20, and 36. The average is given by the expression

$$\frac{10 + 20 + 36}{3}.$$

If you write this fraction using the slash, /, like this,

$$10 + 20 + 36/3,$$

then, by order of operations, the division will be done first and only the 36 will be divided by 3. So you need to use parentheses.

$$\frac{10 + 20 + 36}{3} = (10 + 20 + 36)/3$$

In this way the slash, /, and the fraction bar, –, are different. (Of course, with something as simple as $\frac{1}{2}$ or 1/2, there is no difference.) A fraction bar always operates as if it has unwritten parentheses. Because the fraction bar is a grouping symbol, you *must* evaluate the numerator and denominator of a fraction separately before dividing.

❷ **Example 2**

Simplify $\frac{4 + 9}{2 + 3}$.

Solution

Think $\frac{(4 + 9)}{(2 + 3)}$ and get $\frac{13}{5}$.

Example 3

Evaluate $\frac{4n + 1}{3n - 1}$ when $n = 11$.

Solution 1

Write the original expression.	$\frac{4n + 1}{3n - 1}$
Substitute.	$= \frac{4 \cdot 11 + 1}{3 \cdot 11 - 1}$
Work separately in the numerator and denominator.	$= \frac{44 + 1}{33 - 1}$
	$= \frac{45}{32}$

Solution 2

If you use a calculator to evaluate $\frac{4 \cdot 11 + 1}{3 \cdot 11 - 1}$, you must insert parentheses to ensure that the entire numerator is divided by the entire denominator. One possible key sequence is shown here.

[( ] 4 [×] 11 [+] 1 [ )] [÷] [( ] 3 [×] 11 [−] 1 [ )] [=]

A calculator displays 1.40625, the decimal equivalent to $\frac{45}{32}$.

At times, as in Example 3, using a calculator may be more complicated and time-consuming than evaluating with paper and pencil. Also, it loses the fraction. So in evaluating a fraction, it is not always efficient to use a calculator.

Optional Activities

Activity 1
Materials: One-inch squares of paper

You might want to review the terms *mean* or *average* before students answer **Questions 16–19.** The following simple activity might help students understand that the average or the mean of a set of data is the sum of the items divided by the number of items.

Have students **work in groups** of 4, 5, or 6, to find the average number of letters in the first names of the people in their group. Each student is to write each of the letters of his or her first name on a different square and arrange his or her squares in a row. Ask one student in each group to record the number of letters in each first name. To find the average, have students move the letters until they all have the same number of letters in their rows. Extra letters should be set aside. The number of letters in each row is the average. Next, have the recorder calculate the average to verify the number. You might repeat the activity by asking students to find the average number of letters in their last names.

Activity 2 Technology Connection In *Technology Sourcebook, Calculator Master 7,* students explore and evaluate continued fractions.

Parentheses in Fractions

Parentheses in the numerator or denominator of a fraction are like the innermost of nested parentheses. So work with them first.

Example 4

Evaluate $x + \frac{100(4 + 2x) - 25}{200 - x}$ when $x = 50$.

Solution

First substitute 50 for x wherever x appears.

$$50 + \frac{100(4 + 2 \cdot 50) - 25}{200 - 50}$$

Work inside the parentheses first.

$$= 50 + \frac{100(104) - 25}{200 - 50}$$
$$= 50 + \frac{10{,}400 - 25}{150}$$
$$= 50 + \frac{10{,}375}{150}$$
$$= 50 + 69.1\overline{6}$$
$$= 119.1\overline{6}$$

❸ **Summary of Rules of Order of Operations**

1. First, do operations within parentheses or other grouping symbols. If there are nested grouping symbols, work within the innermost symbols first. Remember that fraction bars are grouping symbols and can be different from /.
2. Within grouping symbols or if there are no grouping symbols:
   - **A.** First, take all powers.
   - **B.** Second, do all multiplications or divisions in order, from left to right.
   - **C.** Then do all additions or subtractions in order, from left to right.

QUESTIONS

Covering the Reading

1. What are the symbols [ ] called? **brackets**
2. *True or false.* $2[x + 4]$ and $2(x + 4)$ mean the same thing. **True**
3. When are the symbols [ ] usually used? **when there are nested grouping symbols**
4. Name three different grouping symbols. **parentheses, brackets, and fraction bars**
5. When there are grouping symbols within grouping symbols, what should you do first? **work within the innermost symbols**

❸ The Summary of Rules for Order of Operations is found on **Teaching Aid 43.**

Additional Examples

Evaluate each expression.

1. $5[12 - 8(3 \cdot 2 - 5)] - 1.5(10 - 4)$ **11**
2. $\frac{7 \cdot 8}{3+1}$ **14**
3. $\frac{1+4a}{2a-3}$ when $a = 6$ **$\frac{25}{9}$ or $2.\overline{7}$**
4. $\frac{5(3m+4)+30}{15-m}$ when $m = 10$ **40**
5. Write the key sequence needed to evaluate $\frac{5+3 \cdot 7}{4+9}$

The following sequence works on many scientific calculators.

[(] 5 [+] 3 [×] 7 [)] [÷]

[(] 4 [+] 9 [)] [=]

Adapting to Individual Needs

Extra Help

If some students are having difficulty, you or another student might watch as they do their work. Suggest that they highlight the computation they plan to do first. If their choice is not correct, review the Rules of Order of Operations. If their choice is correct, have them rewrite the problem with the computed number. Then have them highlight the next computation, and so on, until the work is completed. Emphasize the necessity of writing each step.

LESSON MASTER 4-6 A — **Questions on SPUR Objectives** See pages 233-235 for objectives.

Skills Objectives A and B

In 1-5, evaluate each expression.

1. $35 - \frac{12}{3} + 8$ **39**
2. $25 - [16 \div (4 \cdot 2)]$ **23**
3. $\frac{2[(7 \cdot 3) + 6]}{26 \div 13}$ **27**
4. $\frac{8^x}{4^y}$ if $x = 2$ and $y = 3$ **1**
5. $50 \div [4x - (6^y \div y)]$ if $x = 5$ and $y = 2$ **25**
6. Rewrite the number sentence below, inserting parentheses to make it a true sentence.
   $45 - 3 \cdot 2 \div 3 = 13$ **$(45 - (3 \cdot 2)) \div 3 = 13$**
7. a. Write an expression for the sentence below.
   b. Evaluate your expression when the number is 8.
   The sum of 20 and a number, divided by the sum of 6 and the number
   a. **$\frac{20 + n}{6 + n}$** b. **2**

Properties Objective D

8. When evaluating $\frac{13 - 3}{2 + 3}$, what operation should you do
   a. first? **13 − 3**
   b. second? **2 + 3**
   c. third? **10 ÷ 5**
9. Write $\frac{20 + 4 \cdot 15}{6 + 4}$ on one line. **$(20 + 4 \cdot 15) \div (6 + 4)$**
10. Write a key sequence for evaluating $3[4(9 - 5) - 2 + 3^3]$.
    3 [×] [(] 4 [×] [(] 9 [−] 5 [)] [−] 2 [+] 3 [y^x] 3 [)] [=]

Notes on Questions

Question 12 Error Alert Students might write $\frac{560}{136.5}$, $\frac{1120}{273}$, 4.102564, or $4.\overline{102564}$. Accept all but the first answer as correct. Remind students that a decimal in a numerator or denominator of a fraction should be removed as discussed in Lesson 2-7.

Questions 16–19 This is an appropriate time to review the mean. At this time, you may want to have students do the activity in *Optional Activities* on page 204. Ask students to give a formula for the mean of two numbers *a* and *b* and a formula for the mean of four numbers, *a*, *b*, *c*, *d*. [$\frac{a+b}{2}$; $\frac{a+b+c+d}{4}$] It is important that students see these formulas, for they illustrate how common it is to find fractions in formulas.

Question 28 Ask how 4% of 150 million can be calculated mentally. [Sample: 1% of 150 is 1.5. Then 4% is 4 · 1.5, or 6, million.]

Health Connection You might explain that airbags only provide protection in frontal collisions because the impact is distributed over a wider area of the body.

Question 31 The famous "four 4s" problem presented here is extended in the *Challenge* in *Adapting for Individual Needs* on page 207.

LESSON MASTER 4-6 B **Questions on SPUR Objectives**

Skills Objective A: Use order of operations to evaluate numerical expressions.

In 1-8, evaluate each expression.

1. $\frac{20 + 30}{10 - 5}$ 10
2. $84 - [36 \div (2 \cdot 6)]$ 81
3. $15 + \frac{28}{7} - 9$ 10
4. $58 - \frac{66 + 22}{11}$ 50
5. $7[(5 - 2)^2 + 1)]$ 70
6. $[4(8 - 3)]^3$ 8,000
7. $\frac{72}{6^2} + 3^4$ 83
8. $4(6 + 10) - [48 \div (2 + 6)]$ 58

In 9 and 10, rewrite each number sentence, inserting parentheses and brackets, to make it a true sentence.

9. $48 \div 4 \cdot 10 - 8 = 6$ $48 \div [4 \cdot (10 - 8)] = 6$
10. $80 - 8 + 2 \cdot 6 = 20$ $80 - [(8 + 2) \cdot 6] = 20$

Skills Objective B: Evaluate algebraic expressions with grouping symbols given the values of all variables.

In 11-16, evaluate each expression if $d = 2$, $e = 5$, and $f = 6$.

11. $\frac{8d}{e - 1}$ 4
12. $ef - \frac{e + f}{11}$ 29
13. $3[(f - d)^2 + 3]$ 57
14. $100 \div [e^2 \div (f - e)]$ 4
15. $\frac{2^e}{2^d}$ 8
16. $[4^d(3e - 8)]$ 112

In 6–8, simplify. Show your work.

6. $3[2 + 4(5 - 2)]$ $= 3[2 + 4 \cdot 3] = 3[14] = 42$

7. $39 - [20 \div 4 + 2(3 + 6)]$ $= 39 - [5 + 2 \cdot 9] = 39 - [23] = 16$

8. $[(3 - 1)^3 + (5 - 1)^4]^2$ $= [2^3 + 4^4]^2 = [8 + 256]^2 = [264]^2 = 69{,}696$

9. a. Write a key sequence for evaluating the expression of Question 6 on your calculator.
a) 3 [×] [(] 2 [+] 4 [×] [(] 5 [−] 2 [)] [)] [=]

b. Which do you think is the better method for Question 6: paper and pencil, or calculator? Explain your choice.
b) Answers will vary.

10. *Multiple choice.* Written on one line, $\frac{20 + 2 \cdot 30}{6 + 4} =$
(a) $20 + 2 \cdot 30/6 + 4$.
(b) $20 + 2 \cdot 30/(6 - 4)$.
(c) $(20 + 2 \cdot 30)/6 + 4$.
(d) $(20 + 2 \cdot 30)/(6 + 4)$. (d)

In 11 and 12, simplify. Show each step.

11. $\frac{50 + 40}{50 - 40} = \frac{90}{10} = 9$

12. $\frac{560}{7(6 + 3 \cdot 4.5)} = \frac{560}{7(19.5)} = \frac{560}{136.5} = 4.\overline{102564}$

13. a. Write a key sequence for evaluating Question 12 on your calculator.
13a) 560 [÷] [(] 7 [×] [(] 6 [+] 3 [×] 4.5 [)] [)] [=]

b. Which do you think is the better method for doing Question 12: paper and pencil, or calculator?
b) Answers will vary.

In 14 and 15, evaluate when $a = 5$ and $x = 4$. Show each step.

14. $\frac{a + 3x}{a + x} = \frac{5 + 3 \cdot 4}{5 + 4} = \frac{5 + 12}{9} = \frac{17}{9}$ or $1\frac{8}{9}$ or $1.\overline{8}$

15. $\frac{5x - 2}{(x - 1)(x - 2)} = \frac{5 \cdot 4 - 2}{(4 - 1)(4 - 2)} = \frac{20 - 2}{3 \cdot 2} = \frac{18}{6} = 3$

Applying the Mathematics

In 16–19, recall that the **mean** or **average** of a collection of numbers is their sum divided by the number of numbers in the collection.

16. Write an expression for the mean of *a, b, c, d,* and *e.* $\frac{a + b + c + d + e}{5}$

17. A bookcase has three shelves with 42, 37, and 28 books on them. What is the average number of books on a shelf of this bookcase?
$35.\overline{6} \approx 36$ books

18. A student scores 83, 91, 86, and 89 on 4 tests. What is the average?
87.25

19. Grades can range from 0 to 100 on tests. A student scores 85 and 90 on the first two tests.
a. What is the lowest the student can average for all 3 tests? $58.\overline{3} \approx 58$
b. What is the highest the student can average for the 3 tests?
$91.\overline{6} \approx 92$

In 20 and 21, show each step in evaluating the expression.

20. $5[x + 2y(3 + 2z)]$ when $x = 1$, $y = 2$, and $z = 3$
20) $5[1 + 2 \cdot 2 \cdot (3 + 2 \cdot 3)] = 5[1 + 4(3 + 6)] = 5[1 + 4 \cdot 9] = 5[1 + 36] = 5 \cdot 37 = 185$

21. $\frac{x + 3y}{z} + \frac{4y + z}{3x}$ when $x = 3$, $y = 2$, and $z = 1$ $\frac{3 + 3 \cdot 2}{1} + \frac{4 \cdot 2 + 1}{3 \cdot 3} = \frac{9}{1} + \frac{9}{9} = 10$

In 22 and 23, insert grouping symbols to make the equation true.

22. $3 + 5 \cdot 6 - 8 \cdot 2 = 80$
$[(3 + 5) \cdot 6 - 8] \cdot 2 = 80$

23. $3 \cdot 8 - 6/2 + 3 = 12$
$(3 \cdot 8 - 6)/2 + 3 = 12$

24. Write the algebraic expression of Example 4 on one line.
$x + (100(4 + 2x) - 25)/(200 - x)$

Adapting to Individual Needs

English Language Development
If students are using the chart suggested in *English Language Development* on page 180, you might have them add a square before [a^n] with a parentheses symbol or note indicating that they must start with the innermost grouping symbols and work outward.

Review

25. Translate into mathematical symbols. *(Lesson 4-3)*

a. the sum of thirty and twenty **30 + 20**

b. three more than a number **$n + 3$**

c. a number decreased by one tenth **$n - .1$**

26. Here are four instances of a pattern. Describe the pattern using 1 variable. *(Lesson 4-2)*

$$2 \cdot 3 + 2 \cdot 3 = 4 \cdot 3$$
$$2(7.2) + 2(7.2) = 4(7.2)$$
$$2 \cdot \frac{3}{8} + 2 \cdot \frac{3}{8} = 4 \cdot \frac{3}{8}$$
$$2(6\%) + 2(6\%) = 4(6\%)$$

$2a + 2a = 4a$

27. Suppose a formal garden is made up of squares as in the array below.

Each of the squares is 8 feet on a side. A bag of organic fertilizer covers 25 square yards and costs \$6.95. How much will it cost to fertilize the entire garden? *(Lesson 3-8)*
\$20.85 (Purchase 3 bags.)

28. According to the *New York Times,* June 26, 1992, about 4% of the 150 million cars on the road in the U.S. in 1992 had airbags. Estimate the number of U.S. cars with airbags in 1992. *(Lesson 2-5)*
6 million

29. The U.S. budget deficit in 1991 was about \$268,729 million. (Source: *The World Almanac and Book of Facts* 1993.)

a. Write this number as a decimal. **268,729,000,000**

b. Round this number to the nearest billion. **269 billion**

c. Write the original number in scientific notation. **2.68729×10^{11}**
(Lessons 1-4, 2-1, 2-3)

30. Arrange the numbers $7\frac{2}{3}$, $7\frac{3}{5}$, and 7.65 in correct order with the symbol > between them. *(Lessons 1-6, 1-9)* **$7\frac{2}{3} > 7.65 > 7\frac{3}{5}$**

Exploration

31. The numerical expression $4 + \frac{4}{4} - 4$ uses four 4s and has a value of 1. Find numerical expressions using only four 4s that have the values of each integer from 2 to 10. You may use any operations and grouping symbols.

31) Sample:
2 = (4 ÷ 4) + (4 ÷ 4)
3 = (4 + 4 + 4) ÷ 4
4 = 4 + 4(4 − 4)
5 = (4 · 4 + 4) ÷ 4
6 = (4 + 4) ÷ 4 + 4
7 = 4 + 4 − (4 ÷ 4)
8 = 4 · 4 − (4 + 4)
9 = 4 + 4 + 4 ÷ 4
10 = (44 − 4) ÷ 4

Follow-up for Lesson 4-6

Practice

For more questions on SPUR Objectives, use **Lesson Master 4-6A** (shown on page 205) or **Lesson Master 4-6B** (shown on pages 206–207).

Assessment

Written/Oral Communication Have students **work in groups** and prepare three example problems, showing the steps they would follow to evaluate them. Students' problems should have grouping symbols, including the fraction bar. Provide time for groups to compare and discuss some of their examples. [Example problems and the discussion will reveal if there is a need for further development.]

Extension

Have students **work in groups** to obtain goal numbers given "resources." Each resource must be used once. Putting digits such as 3 and 5 together to make 35 is not allowed. Then have each group make up similar problems for another group to solve.

Resources: 1, 3, 5, 5, 6, +, +, ×, ( ).

1. Make 100. [5 (3 × 6 + 1) + 5 = 100]
2. Make the greatest possible number. [6 × 5 (5 + 3 + 1) = 270]

▶ **LESSON MASTER 4-6 B** *page 2*

In 17-19, a. translate into an algebraic expression; b. evaluate that expression when the number has the value 10.

17. a number divided by the difference of 7 minus 5
a. $\frac{x}{7-5}$ b. 5

18. 6 into the sum of the number and 2
a. $\frac{n+2}{6}$ b. 2

19. the second power of the quotient of 80 divided by twice a number
a. $\left(\frac{80}{2a}\right)^2$ b. 16

Properties Objective D: Know the correct order of operations.

20. To evalute $[42 - (3 + 7)]^2$, what operation should you do
a. first? addition; 3 + 7
b. second? subtraction; 42 − 10
c. third? squaring; 32^2

21. To evaluate $\frac{15 - 6}{1 + 2}$, what operation should you do
a. first? subtraction; 15 − 6
b. second? addition; 1 + 2
c. third? division; 9 ÷ 3

In 22 and 23, write each expression on one line.

22. $\frac{5 + 16}{10 - 7}$ (5 + 16) ÷ (10 − 7)

23. $\frac{44 - 4}{2 + 3 \cdot 6}$ (44 − 4) ÷ (2 + 3 · 6)

In 24 and 25, write a key sequence for evaluating each expression.
Sample answers are given.

24. $\frac{20 + 6}{11 + 2}$
(20 + 6) ÷ (11 + 2) =; 2

25. $2[6(7 + 1) - 3 + 4^2]$
7 + 1 = × 6 − 3 + 4 y^x 2 = × 2 =; 122

Adapting to Individual Needs

Challenge

The "four 4s" problem can be extended by having students write as many integers as they can from 11 to 100 using the directions in **Question 31.**

This activity should not be given a specific time limit or be terminated in a single class. Students should be allowed to work on it over a series of days, both at home and in school. As students work, you might have them make and update a class list of the numbers found. [If decimal points, juxtaposition (as in 44), parentheses, repetends, square-root symbols, and factorials are allowed, as well as +, –, ×, ÷, and powering, then all the numbers from 1 to 100 can be written.]

Lesson 4-7

Objectives

I Calculate the value of a variable, given the values of the other variables in a formula.

Resources

From the ***Teacher's Resource File***
- Lesson Master 4-7A and 4-7B
- Answer Master 4-7
- Teaching Aids
  40 Warm-up
  44 Additional Examples
- Technology Sourcebook, Computer Master 5

Additional Resources
- Visuals for Teaching Aids 40, 44
- Spreadsheet Workshop
- Nutrition information from food products (Assessment)
- Pizza menus (Extension)

Teaching Lesson 4-7

Warm-up

Find the area of each figure.

1. 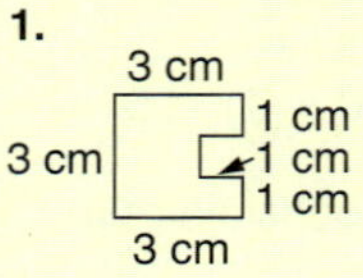

2. 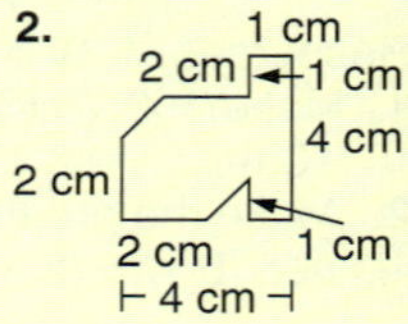

8 cm² **12 cm²**

Notes on Reading

The initial discussion of a formula described with variables uses the area of a rectangle because most students already know this formula.

LESSON

4-7 Formulas

Formulas in a can. *Due to the wide range of colors of paint that people desire, paint sellers often stock several base paints. Then they mix these colors according to exact formulas to create the desired colors.*

A Formula for the Area of a Rectangle

The rectangle drawn here has an actual length of about 6.3 cm, a width of about 2.5 cm, and area about 15.75 cm^2.

Figures in Teacher's Edition are slightly reduced.

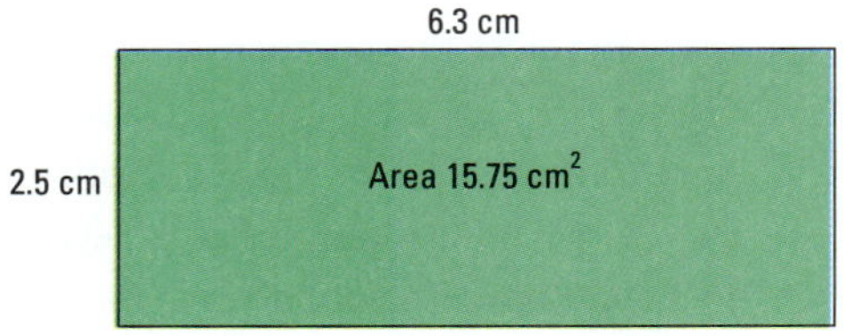

The length, width, and area are related by a simple pattern.

Area = length times width

Using the variables A for area, ℓ for length, and w for width,

$$A = \ell w.$$

❶ (Remember that multiplication signs are usually not written between variables.) The sentence $A = \ell w$ is a **formula** for the area of a rectangle **in terms of** its length and width.

Formulas are very useful. For instance, the formula $A = \ell w$ works for *any* rectangle. So suppose a rectangular field has length of 110 ft and a width of 30 ft. Then its area can be calculated using the formula.

$$\begin{aligned} A &= 110 \text{ ft} \cdot 30 \text{ ft} \\ &= 3300 \text{ ft}^2 \end{aligned}$$

Lesson 4-7 Overview

Broad Goals Here students are introduced to a third use of variables—they stand for numbers or quantities in formulas.

Perspective Formulas illustrate a particularly important use of variables, and the work with order of operations in the previous two lessons is applied here. Formulas exist to provide an automatic way of calculating some number or quantity. Consequently, it is not easy to strike the proper balance between a student's appreciating the usefulness of formulas and having the attitude that mathematics is just finding the right formula and plugging in values.

Three aspects of the approach used here help develop a constructive attitude toward formulas. First, we begin with formulas that have a geometric representation to illustrate their immediate utility. Second, the need for consistency in units is stressed. Third, by using the area of a square, the lesson provides a formula for the difference of the areas of the squares that many students could derive for themselves.

Although much is done in this lesson with the area of a rectangle, ready knowledge of the formula is not expected until Chapter 9.

Units in Formulas

Remember, area is typically measured in *square* units. It is therefore important when using the formula $A = \ell w$ that the length and width are given in the *same* units. For instance, suppose a rectangle has width 3 inches and length 4 feet. You should first either change inches to feet or feet to inches to calculate the area. Then you will get a sensible unit for measuring area, square inches or square feet.

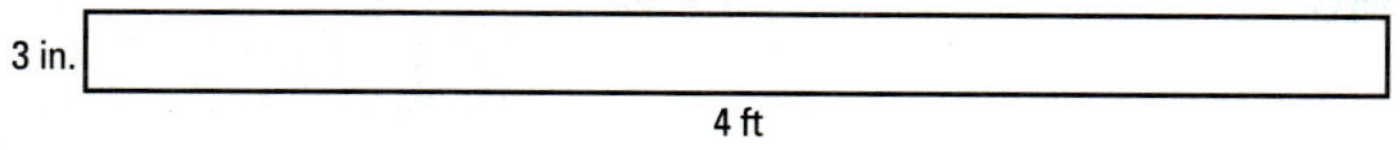

$$\begin{aligned} \text{Area} &= 3 \text{ in.} \times 4 \text{ ft} \\ &= 3 \text{ in.} \times 48 \text{ in.} \\ &= 144 \text{ in}^2 \end{aligned}$$

❷ **Activity**

Find the area of the front cover of your textbook.

Step 1: First, measure the length and width of the front cover to the nearest tenth of a centimeter.

Step 2: Use the area formula to find the area.

Repeat Steps 1 and 2 with measurements made to the nearest quarter inch.

Choosing Letters in Formulas

Letters in formulas are chosen carefully. Usually they are the first letters of the quantities they represent. That is why we use A for area, ℓ for length, and w for width. But be careful. In formulas, capital and small letters often stand for *different* things.

❸ **Example**

The area A of the shaded region can be found by the formula $A = S^2 - s^2$. Find the area if $S = 1.75$ in. and $s = 1.25$ in.

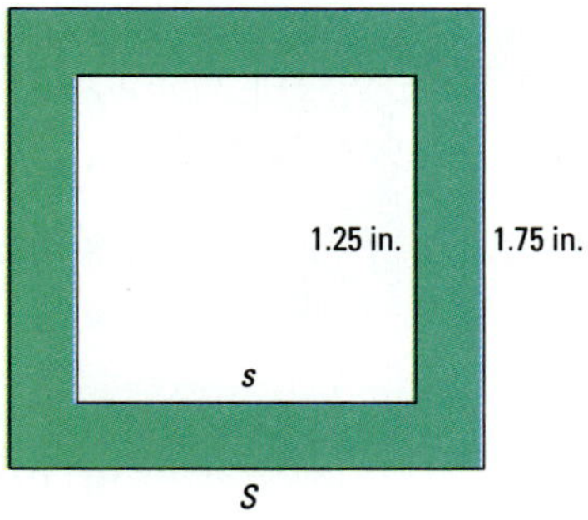

Solution

Substitute 1.75 in. for S and 1.25 in. for s in the formula. The unit of the answer is square inches.

$$\begin{aligned} A &= S^2 - s^2 \\ &= (1.75 \text{ in.})^2 - (1.25 \text{ in.})^2 \\ &= 3.0625 \text{ in}^2 - 1.5625 \text{ in}^2 \\ &= 1.5 \text{ in}^2 \end{aligned}$$

Notice that the description involves a careful indication of why certain letters are used.

❶ The phrase "in terms of" is one that is used often in mathematics and throughout this book. For example, in solving $ax = b$ for x, we say that we have found x "in terms of a and b." Be sure that students know the meaning of this phrase.

❷ When discussing the activity, ask students why they might get different answers for the area even if they do the activity correctly. [Samples: no measurements of length can be exact; people might round differently; rulers might not be calibrated exactly the same.] Compare students' answers; you might even want to list them all and find the mean (average).

❸ We have found that substitution into formulas is not an easy task for some students. It is a good idea to have students follow the steps shown in the example: first write the formula on one line, then show the substitution on the next line, and finally show the evaluation based on order of operations on subsequent lines. Students will use this procedure throughout the text.

It is important for students to develop a curiosity about the derivation of formulas they use and to consider the background as important as the formula itself. The formula $A = S^2 - s^2$ has the added pedagogical purpose of using upper and lower case letters to mean different things.

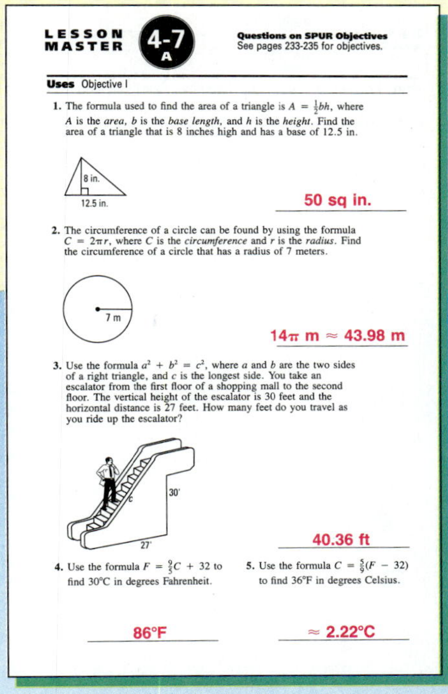
LESSON MASTER 4-7 A

Questions on SPUR Objectives
See pages 233-235 for objectives.

Uses Objective I

1. The formula used to find the area of a triangle is $A = \frac{1}{2}bh$, where A is the *area*, b is the *base length*, and h is the *height*. Find the area of a triangle that is 8 inches high and has a base of 12.5 in.

8 in. / 12.5 in.

50 sq in.

2. The circumference of a circle can be found by using the formula $C = 2\pi r$, where C is the *circumference* and r is the *radius*. Find the circumference of a circle that has a radius of 7 meters.

7 m

14π m $\approx$ 43.98 m

3. Use the formula $a^2 + b^2 = c^2$, where a and b are the two sides of a right triangle, and c is the longest side. You take an escalator from the first floor of a shopping mall to the second floor. The vertical height of the escalator is 30 feet and the horizontal distance is 27 feet. How many feet do you travel as you ride up the escalator?

c / 30' / 27'

40.36 ft

4. Use the formula $F = \frac{9}{5}C + 32$ to find 30°C in degrees Fahrenheit.

86°F

5. Use the formula $C = \frac{5}{9}(F - 32)$ to find 36°F in degrees Celsius.

$\approx$ 2.22°C

Optional Activities

After introducing the formula $A = lw$, you may want to ask students these questions. Have students substitute numbers until they can give a general answer to each question.

1. What happens to the area of a rectangle
   - a. when the length is doubled and the width remains the same? [The area is doubled.]
   - b. when both the length and the width are doubled? [The area is multiplied by 4.]
2. What happens to the area of a rectangle
   - a. when the length is tripled and the width remains the same? [The area is tripled.]
   - b. when both the length and the width are tripled? [The area is multiplied by 9.]

4 Many students do not appreciate the need to represent capital and small letters differently. Here is where the mathematics teacher must become a teacher of penmanship! Ask students to write capital and small letters noting which letters might appear the same, such as a capital *C* and a small *c*. Do not expect students to use the particular style of small letters we use; clarity of communication is more important and more realistic than conformity.

Additional Examples

You may want to use **Teaching Aid 44,** which contains all of the following additional examples.

1. Which rectangles have the same area? **b and d**

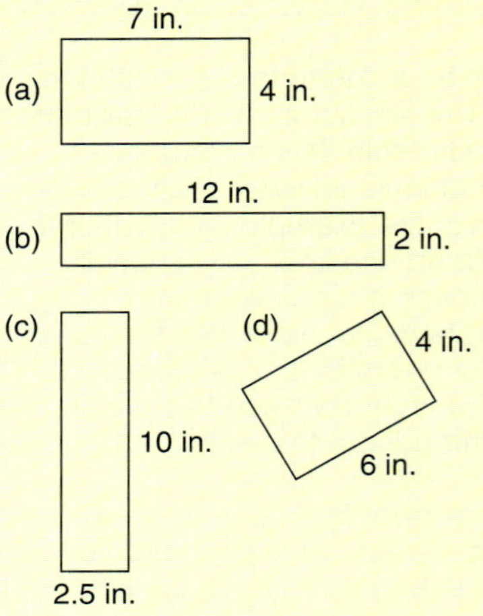

LESSON MASTER 4-7 B Questions on SPUR Objectives

Uses Objective I: Calculate the value of a variable, given the values of the other variables in a formula.

1. The perimeter of a rectangle can be found by using the formula $P = 2(\ell + w)$, where *P* is the *perimeter*, ℓ *is the length*, and *w* is the *width*. Find the perimeter of a rectangle that is 9 feet long and 6.5 feet wide.

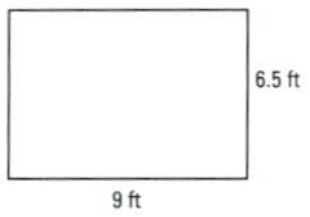

31 ft

2. The area of a circle can be found by using the formula $A = \pi r^2$, where *A* is the *area* and *r* is the *radius*. Find the area of a circle that has a radius of 8 inches.

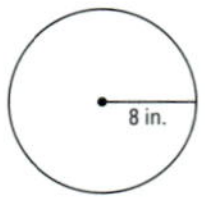

64π in.^{2} ≈ 201.06 in.^{2}

3. Use the formula $a^2 + b^2 = c^2$, where *a* and *b* are the lengths of two sides of a right triangle and *c* is the length of the longest side of the right triangle. A rectangular park is 3 blocks by 4 blocks. If you walk through the park from one corner straight to the opposite corner, how far do you walk?

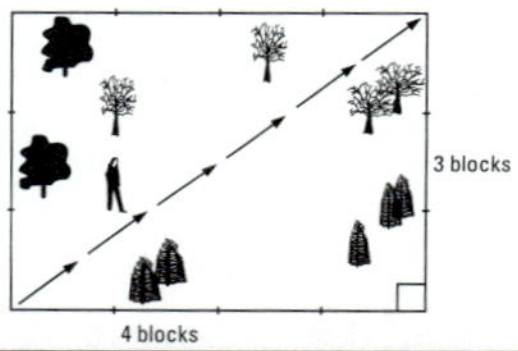

5 blocks

4 Writing Letters in Formulas

Because capital and small letters can mean different things, in algebra you should not change capital letters to small letters, or vice versa. And you need to learn to write small letters differently from capitals, not just smaller. Do this by writing the small letters with curves and hooks. Here are the most confusing letters, and one way to write them.

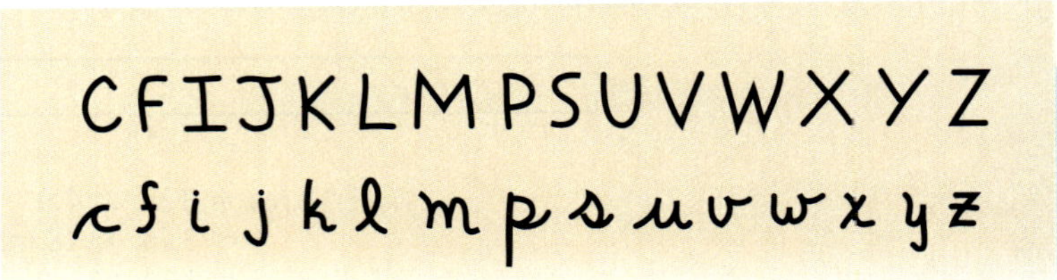

QUESTIONS

Covering the Reading

1. The formula $A = \ell w$ gives the _?_ of a rectangle in terms of its _?_ and _?_. **area, length, width**
2. How do the letters in the formula of Question 1 make that question easier to answer? **The variables are the first letters of the appropriate words.**
3. What is the area of a rectangle that is 43 cm long and 0.1 cm wide? **4.3 cm^2**
4. **a.** What is the area of a rectangle that is 3 in. long and 4 ft wide?
   b. What does part **a** tell you about units in formulas?

   a) 1 ft^2 or 144 in^2; b) Units in formulas must be the same.

In 5–7, use the formula $A = S^2 - s^2$ in the Example.

5. Do *S* and *s* stand for the same thing? **No**
6. What do *S* and *s* stand for? ***S* is the length of a side of the larger square; *s* is the length of a side of the smaller square.**
7. Give the area between the two squares drawn at the left. **3.77 cm^2**

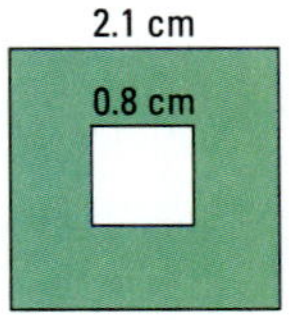

8. In a formula, why should you not change a capital letter to a small letter? **The capital letter and small letter may mean different things.**
9. **a.** Write the alphabet from A to Z in capital letters.
   b. Write the alphabet in small letters. Make sure your small letters look different from (not just smaller than) the capital letters.
   a,b) Check students' lists.
10. Refer to the Activity in this lesson. What values do you get for the area of the front cover of this book? **538.2 cm^2; ≈ 83.3 in^2**
    Sample: $\ell \approx 26$ cm, $w \approx 20.7$ cm, $A \approx 538.2$ cm^2; $\ell \approx 10\frac{1}{4}$ in., $w \approx 8\frac{1}{8}$ in., $A \approx 83.3$ in^2

Adapting to Individual Needs

Extra Help

If students are consistently getting incorrect results when using formulas, it is often because of incorrect substitutions or carelessness when evaluating. First have students copy the formula, and then substitute the given information. After checking to make sure they have substituted and evaluated correctly, students should look back at the problem situation to see if their answer makes sense.

English Language Development

People in different cultures write the alphabet in different ways. You might have an English-speaking student(s) with good penmanship write the alphabet in capital and small letters on the board. Then have any student(s) who know another language in which letters are written differently, show the class how to write them in this language.

Applying the Mathematics

11. A gardener wishes to surround a square garden by a walkway one meter wide. The garden is 5 meters on a side. How much ground will the gardener have to clear for the walkway? **24 m^2**

12. One cube is inside another as shown below.

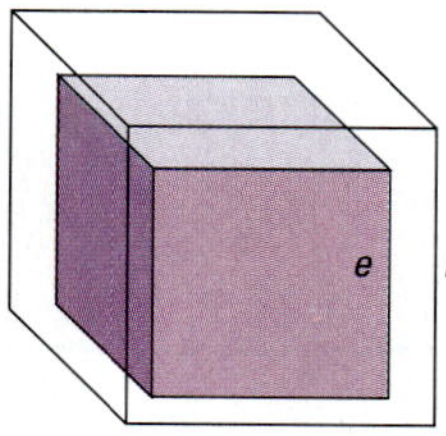

a. If the edges of the cubes have lengths E and e, what is the volume of the space between them? **$E^3 - e^3$**

b. If a cube with edge of 4″ is put inside a cube with edge of 5″, what is the volume between them? **61 in^3**

In 13–16, use this information. When a team wins W games and loses L games, then its winning percentage P is given by the formula

$$P = \frac{W}{W + L}.$$

This number is always converted to a decimal. Then it is rounded to the nearest thousandth. Calculate the winning percentage for each team.

13. the 1993 NCAA women's basketball champion Texas Tech, who had a season record of 31 wins and 3 losses **0.912**

14. the 1992 U.S. Olympic Men's basketball team, who won all 8 games they played **1.000**

15. a volleyball team that wins 7 games and loses 7 games **0.500**

16. a team that wins 3 games and loses 12 **0.200**

Pictured here are the Lady Raiders of Texas Tech University, the 1993 NCAA women's basketball champs.

In 17 and 18, use the formula $T = t - \frac{2f}{1000}$. This formula gives the estimated air temperature T (in degrees Fahrenheit) at an altitude of f feet when the ground temperature is t. Suppose it is 75°F at ground level.

17. Find the temperature at an altitude of 1000 ft. **73°**

18. Find the temperature at an altitude of 3000 ft. **69°**

2. Find the area of a rectangle that is 1 meter long and 50 centimeters wide.
5000 cm^2 or 0.5 m^2

3. A photograph 20 inches square is framed. The framed photograph is 26 inches square. What is the area of the frame? **276 in^2**

Notes on Questions

Question 4 You might want to have students do this problem in two ways. Then you can take the opportunity to talk about the number of square inches in a square foot.

3 in. × 48 in. = 144 sq in.
$\frac{1}{4}$ ft × 4 ft = 1 sq ft

Question 12 Most students are surprised to learn that a 4-inch cube fills only about half the space inside a 5-inch cube. If students do not believe this, you might **use physical models.** First, model a 4-inch cube with 64 cubes. Then add cubes to model a 5-inch cube, noting how many more cubes this takes. [61 more for a total of 125 cubes]

Questions 13–16 You might have students answer similar questions about local teams.

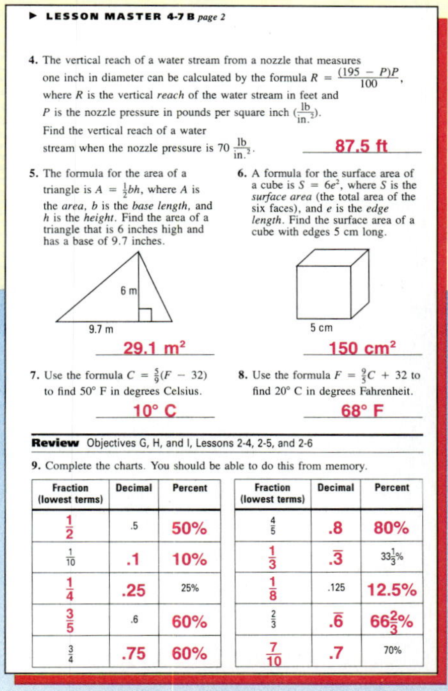

▶ **LESSON MASTER 4-7 B** *page 2*

4. The vertical reach of a water stream from a nozzle that measures one inch in diameter can be calculated by the formula $R = \frac{(195 - P)P}{100}$, where R is the vertical *reach* of the water stream in feet and P is the nozzle pressure in pounds per square inch $(\frac{lb}{in.^2})$. Find the vertical reach of a water stream when the nozzle pressure is 70 $\frac{lb}{in.^2}$. **87.5 ft**

5. The formula for the area of a triangle is $A = \frac{1}{2}bh$, where A is the *area*, b is the *base length*, and h is the *height*. Find the area of a triangle that is 6 inches high and has a base of 9.7 inches.

6 m
9.7 m

29.1 m^2

6. A formula for the surface area of a cube is $S = 6e^2$, where S is the *surface area* (the total area of the six faces), and e is the *edge length*. Find the surface area of a cube with edges 5 cm long.

5 cm

150 cm^2

7. Use the formula $C = \frac{5}{9}(F - 32)$ to find 50° F in degrees Celsius. **10° C**

8. Use the formula $F = \frac{9}{5}C + 32$ to find 20° C in degrees Fahrenheit. **68° F**

Review Objectives G, H, and I, Lessons 2-4, 2-5, and 2-6

9. Complete the charts. You should be able to do this from memory.

Fraction (lowest terms)	Decimal	Percent
$\frac{1}{2}$	.5	50%
$\frac{1}{10}$	.1	10%
$\frac{1}{4}$	.25	25%
$\frac{3}{5}$	.6	60%
$\frac{3}{4}$	.75	60%

Fraction (lowest terms)	Decimal	Percent
$\frac{4}{5}$	.8	80%
$\frac{1}{3}$	$.\overline{3}$	$33\frac{1}{3}\%$
$\frac{1}{8}$	.125	12.5%
$\frac{2}{3}$	$.\overline{6}$	$66\frac{2}{3}\%$
$\frac{7}{10}$	.7	70%

Adapting to Individual Needs

Challenge

Various rules can be used to determine the correct medicine dosage for children when the adult dosage has been specified. In each formula at the right, A is the age of the child in years, d is the adult dosage, and c is the child's dosage. (Source: *A Sourcebook of Applications of School Mathematics*, NCTM, 1980, p. 103)

Young's rule: $c = \frac{A}{A+12}d$

Cowling's rule: $c = \frac{A+1}{24}d$

Suppose the adult dosage for a certain medicine is 10 milligrams. Have students determine the dosage for a 5-year-old child and a 12-year-old child using both rules. [Young's rule: 2.94 grams; 5 grams Cowling's rule: 2.5 grams; 5.42 grams]

Notes on Questions

Question 20 Poll your students regarding the answers they give. In many classes, every choice is picked by at least one student.

Follow-up for Lesson 4-7

Practice

For more questions on SPUR Objectives, use **Lesson Master 4-7A** (shown on page 209) or **Lesson Masters 4-7B** (shown on pages 210–211).

Assessment

Written Communication

Materials: Nutrition information labels from a variety of food products

Have each student select two different food labels and use the formula $P = \frac{9F}{C}$ to find the percentage P of Calories from fat in one serving of food when F is the number of grams of fat listed and C is the number of Calories in a serving. [Correct solutions for both problems indicate an understanding of subsitution and order of operations.]

Extension

Technology Connection You might give students a pizza menu. *Technology Sourcebook, Computer Master 5*, has students use the *Spreadsheet Workshop* to enter formulas and make comparisons of the area of various pizzas. The formula $A = \pi r^2$ gives the area A of a circle in terms of the radius, r.

Project Update Project 1, *The Bricklayer's Formula*, on page 229, relates to the content of this lesson. Students choosing this project might decide what buildings they are going to measure. You may want students to **work in groups.**

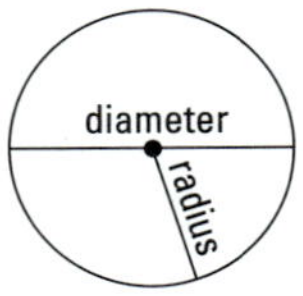

19. Write a formula that expresses the relationship between a radius and a diameter of a circle. Sample: $d = 2r$ or $r = \frac{1}{2}d$

20. *Multiple choice.* In a *Bill James Baseball Abstract,* the expression $\frac{2(HR \times SB)}{HR + SB}$ is called the Power/Speed number. A newspaper writer once incorrectly wrote the expression as $2[HR \times SB]/HR + SB$. What was wrong with the newspaper expression?

(a) It used brackets instead of parentheses.
(b) It should have used parentheses around $HR + SB$.
(c) It used a × sign for multiplication.
(d) It was written on one line.
(e) It used HR and SB instead of single letters for variables. (b)

Review

In 21–24, evaluate each expression. *(Lessons 4-5, 4-6)*

21. $9 + 5(3 + 2 \cdot 7)$ 94

22. $3 + 4 \cdot 5^2$ 103

23. $12 - 4x$ when $x = .5$ 10

24. $8/(8/(2 + 6))$ 8

25. Put into the correct order of operations. *(Lessons 4-1, 4-5)*
(a) multiplications or divisions from left to right
(b) powers
(c) inside parentheses
(d) additions or subtractions from left to right (c), (b), (a), (d)

In 26–29, put one of the symbols >, =, or < in the blank. *(Lessons 1-7, 1-9, 2-2, 4-4)*

26. -5 __?__ -5.1 >

27. 4.09 __?__ $4\frac{1}{11}$ <

28. $x + 14$ __?__ $x - 14$ when $x = 20$. >

29. a^3 __?__ a^2 when $a = 0.7$. <

30. One liter is how many cubic centimeters? *(Lesson 3-9)* 1000 cm^3

31. Convert 6 kilograms to grams. *(Lesson 3-5)* 6000 g

32. Change $\frac{8}{4}$, $\frac{9}{4}$, $\frac{10}{4}$, $\frac{11}{4}$, and $\frac{12}{4}$ to decimals. *(Lesson 1-6)*
2, 2.25, 2.5, 2.75, 3.0

Exploration

33. Look in a newspaper to find the wins, losses, and winning percentage for a particular team in your area. Use the formula from Questions 13–16 to see if you get the same percentage as the one you find in the newspaper. Answers may vary.

212

Setting Up Lesson 4-8

Materials: **Teaching Aid 46,** paper clips, pencils

The *Warm-up* for Lesson 4-8 requires students to use a spinner with 8 equal sections. If you do not have such spinners available in your classroom, students can make them using **Teaching Aid 46** and paper clips.

Introducing Lesson 4-8

Relative Frequency

IN-CLASS ACTIVITY

When you toss a coin there are two possible *outcomes,* "heads" and "tails." You expect heads to occur about 50% of the time and tails the other 50% of the time. However, this does not always happen. See what happens in your class.

The **frequency** of an outcome is the number of times the outcome occurs. If you toss the coin N times and an outcome occurs with frequency F, the **relative frequency** of the outcome is $\frac{F}{N}$.

First, work alone.

1
- **a.** Toss a coin 10 times, writing down an H or T each time the coin is tossed.
- **b.** Record the frequency of heads.
- **c.** Determine the relative frequency of heads.
- **d.** Write the relative frequency as a percent.
- **e.** If you continue, do you think you will get about the same relative frequency of heads and tails in the long run? Why or why not?

2
- **a.** Repeat step 1 four more times, for a total of 50 tosses.
- **b.** Calculate the total frequency of heads for the 50 tosses.
- **c.** Determine the relative frequency of heads for the 50 tosses.
- **d.** Write the relative frequency as a percent.
- **e.** Now do you think you will get about the same number of heads and tails in the long run? Why or why not?

Now work in a group of 3 or 4 students.

3
- **a.** Combine your results with those of the others in your group.
- **b.** How many tosses were made altogether?
- **c.** How many of these were heads?
- **d.** Determine the relative frequency of heads for all the tosses made by those in your group.
- **e.** In the long run, what percent of tosses do you think will be heads?

Finally, work together as a class.

4 Combine the results of your group with all other groups in your class. Repeat step 3.

5 A coin is considered to be fair if in the long run the relative frequency of heads is $\frac{1}{2}$. Do you think the coins tossed in your class were fair? Explain why you think the way you do.

In-class Activity

Resources

From the ***Teacher's Resource File***
- Teaching Aid 45: Relative Frequency

Additional Resources
- Visual for Teaching Aid 45
- Coins
- Graphing and Probability Workshop (for probability experiments)

Some books use the terms *experimental probability* and *theoretical probability.* We call these concepts *relative frequency* and *probability* respectively, so that the distinction will be clear.

A relative frequency is a statistic derived from an experiment and will vary with further experiments. It receives its name because it is the quotient of two frequencies. A probability is a number derived from assumptions (such as equal likelihood) or relative frequencies.

For example, consider the tossing of a coin. From the assumption that the two sides are equally likely, we obtain the probability of heads being one half and the probability of tails being one half. When the coin is tossed, we obtain relative frequencies of these events which may or may not be close to one half. If they are not close, we might change the assumptions that lead to the probability.

TEACHING AID 45
In-class Activity, Lesson 4-8

Relative Frequency

a. Tosses (Record H and T)	b. Frequency of H	c. Relative Frequency of H	d. Relative Frequency of H as a Percent

Answers to Questions 1-5 will vary . Answers here are based on the sample given.

1. a. Sample: HTHHHTTHTH
   b. 6 c) $\frac{6}{10}$ d) 60%
   e. Maybe. This relative frequency is based on only 10 tosses. Combining these tosses with 10 more tosses might give a relative frequency of 50%.
2. a. Sample:
   HTHTTTTHTH HTHTTTHHHT
   THTHTTHHTH TTTTHHTTHT
   b. 23 c. $\frac{23}{50}$ d. 46%
   e. Maybe. The percent is close to 50%.
3. b. Sample: 200 c. Sample 103
   d. $\frac{103}{200} = 51.5\%$ e. 50%
4. b. Sample: 1225 c. Sample: 601
   d. $\frac{601}{1225} \approx 49.1\%$
5. Sample: Since the relative frequency is close to 50%, the coins might be fair.

Lesson 4-8

Objectives

J Calculate probabilities and relative frequencies in a situation with known numbers of outcomes.

Resources

From the ***Teacher's Resource File***
- Lesson Master 4-8A or 4-8B
- Answer Master 4-8
- Assessment Sourcebook: Quiz for Lessons 4-5 through 4-8
- Teaching Aids
  41 Warm-up
  46 Spinner
- Activity Kit, Activity 9

Additional Resources
- Visuals for Teaching Aids 41, 46

Teaching Lesson 4-8

Warm-up

Activity Students can make a spinner using **Teaching Aid 46**, paper clips, and a pencil.

Use a spinner with eight equal sections labeled 1 through 8. For each event listed below, (a) determine the probability assuming that the outcomes on the spinner are equally likely, and (b) spin the spinner 25 times to determine a relative frequency for the event. **Answers to part a are given; answers to part b will vary.**

1. An even number $\frac{1}{2}$
2. A number divisible by 3 $\frac{1}{4}$
3. A number less than 9 1
4. A number greater than 8 0

LESSON

4-8 *Probability*

Rain expected today? *The probability of rain in this girl's neighborhood was 70% on the day this picture was taken. Weather forecasts are predictions of what might happen—and thus should be taken seriously.*

What Is Probability?

A **probability** is a number from 0 to 1 which tells you how likely something is to happen. A probability of 0 means that the event is impossible. A probability of $\frac{1}{5}$ means that in the long run it is expected the event will happen about 1 in 5 times. A probability of 70% means that the event is expected to happen about 70% of the time. A probability of 1, the highest probability possible, means that the event *must* happen.

The closer a probability is to 1, the more likely the event. Since 70% is greater than $\frac{1}{5}$, an event with a probability of 70% is more likely than one with a probability of $\frac{1}{5}$. This can be pictured on a number line.

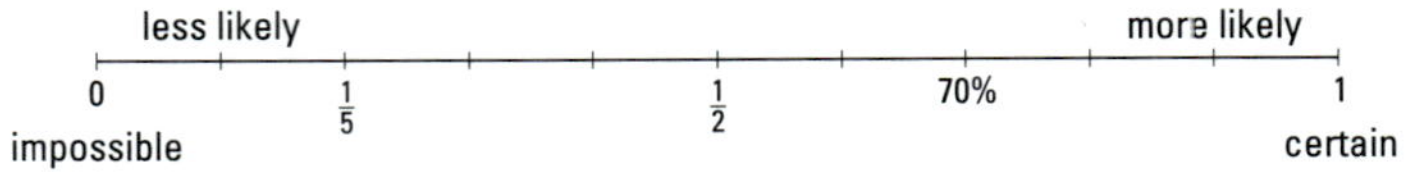

Probabilities can be written as fractions, decimals, or percents, or any other way that numbers are written.

Example 1

Suppose the weather bureau says there is a 1 in 3 chance of rain tomorrow. It reports a 40% precipitation probability the day after tomorrow. On which day does the weather bureau think rain is more likely?

Solution

The "1 in 3 chance of rain tomorrow" means the probability is $\frac{1}{3}$. To compare $\frac{1}{3}$ with 40%, change both numbers to decimals.

$\frac{1}{3} = 0.\overline{3}$ and 40% = 0.4, so 40% is larger, and rain is more likely the day after tomorrow.

Lesson 4-8 Overview

Broad Goals This lesson, and the in-class activity that precedes it, introduce students to the related ideas of probability and relative frequency.

Perspective These are the main properties of probability to be garnered from this lesson:
1. A probability is a number from 0 to 1 that indicates what we think the likelihood of an event is.
2. The closer a probability is to 1, the more likely an event is expected to occur.
3. A probability of 0 means an event is impossible. A probability of 1 means the event must occur.
4. If there are N equally likely outcomes, and E of these are an event, then the probability of the event is $\frac{E}{N}$.

The main properties of relative frequency are similar to those for probability.
1. A relative frequency is a number from 0 to 1 that indicates how often an event occurred.
2. The closer a relative frequency is to 1, the more relatively often the event occurs.
3. A relative frequency of 0 means an event did not occur. A relative frequency of 1 means it occurred every time it could.
4. If an event occurred F times out of N possible repetitions of an experiment, then the relative frequency of the event was $\frac{F}{N}$.

Determining a Probability

There are three common ways that people determine probabilities.

(1) Guess. This is not a great method, but sometimes it is the only thing you can do. For instance, suppose you would like a ten-speed bicycle for your birthday. You tell your friend you think the probability of getting the bike is only about 25%. This means that you think there is a 1 in 4 chance (since $\frac{1}{4}$ = 25%) you will get the bike. You are guessing at the probability because you have no other way to determine it.

(2) Perform an experiment and choose a probability close to the relative frequency you found. Suppose you thought some of the coins tossed in the In-class Activity on page 213 might be unbalanced. If the coin tossing led to 1224 heads in 2500 tosses, the relative frequency is then $\frac{F}{N} = \frac{1224}{2500} = 48.96\%$. You could choose the probability of heads for these coins to be 49%. Others might choose 50%. A probability estimated from a relative frequency may be different for different people. But it is more likely to be close to what would happen in the long run than a guess would be. Also, the more times an experiment is repeated, the closer the relative frequency should be to the probability.

❶ *(3) Assume outcomes are equally likely.* In many situations, people assume outcomes are equally likely. For instance, when you toss a coin, there are 2 possible outcomes. One of these is heads. If the outcomes are equally likely, the probability the event will occur is $\frac{1}{2}$.

Probabilities when Outcomes Are Assumed to Be Equally Likely

Consider tossing a dime and a quarter. Pictured here are the four possible outcomes.

Assume the outcomes are equally likely. Only one outcome has zero heads, so the probability of getting zero heads is $\frac{1}{4}$. There is also only one way to get two heads. So, the probability of getting 2 heads is $\frac{1}{4}$. Exactly one head can appear in two different ways: the dime can show heads and the quarter tails, or the quarter can show heads and the dime tails. So the probability of getting exactly one head is $\frac{2}{4} = \frac{1}{2}$.

When all outcomes of a situation like "tossing two coins" have the same probability, the outcomes are called **random.** The coins are said to be **fair,** or **unbiased.** In this lesson, dice and coins are assumed to be fair.

Notes on Reading

In addition to the experiments in the lesson, you might also want to use those in *Optional Activities* on page 216.

Either before or after students do the experiments, summarize the properties of probability and relative frequency as given in the *Overview* on page 214.

❶ When discussing *equally likely,* explain that probabilities are theoretical. A coin (or die, or spinner, or other object) in an experiment is called *fair* or *unbiased* when the outcomes are equally likely. There is no way to tell that an actual coin is fair. Testing a coin in experiments, such as the one performed in the *In-class Activity* on page 213, suggests that a coin is fair because the experiments show nearly equal relative frequencies of heads and tails. However, the coin could still be slightly biased. In theory, we would like probabilities to be very close to numbers derived from relative frequencies that we have experienced.

Pacing Although there is much to cover in this lesson, the next lesson is short. Discussion of this lesson can spill over into the next day.

Video

Wide World of Mathematics The segment, *Hurricane Prediction,* shows how forecasters estimate the probability that a hurricane will hit a particular area. Included are footage and interviews related to Hurricane Andrew. Motivation is provided to launch a lesson on probability. Related questions and investigation are provided in videodisc stills and in the Video Guide. A related CD-ROM activity is also available.

Videodisc Bar Codes

Search Chapter 19

Play

LESSON MASTER 4-8 A

Questions on SPUR Objectives
See pages 233-235 for objectives.

Uses Objective J

In 1-5, complete the table, describing the probability.

	In Words	As a Decimal	As a Percent	As a Fraction
1.	cannot happen	0	0%	$\frac{0}{n}$
2.	must happen	1	100%	$\frac{n}{n}$
3.	has a "50-50" chance	.5	50%	$\frac{1}{2}$
4.	will happen 3 times out of 4	.75	75%	$\frac{3}{4}$
5.	has 2 chances in 3 of happening	$.\overline{6}$	$66.\overline{6}\%$	$\frac{2}{3}$

6. a. How can you determine which event is more likely: event A with a probability of $\frac{11}{16}$ or event B with a probability of $\frac{2}{3}$?
determine which fraction is closer to 1
b. Which event is more likely? event A

7. A stack of index cards is numbered 1 to 50, and then shuffled and put into a box. What is the probability that 4 will be a factor of a card drawn from the box? $\frac{12}{50} = \frac{6}{25} = 24\%$

8. You have bought 10 tickets to a prize drawing. If n tickets were sold, what is the probability that you will win the raffle? $\frac{10}{n}$

9. Describe in your own words the differences between the probability of an event and the relative frequency of an event.
sample: Probability is the number of times an event is expected to happen divided by the number of things that can happen. Relative frequency of an event is the ratio of the number of times the event actually occurs to the number of times it could occur.

Additional Examples

1. Meg thinks the probability that gym class will be outside tomorrow is 90%. Bill thinks the probability is $\frac{4}{5}$. Who thinks that outdoor gym class is more likely? **Meg**
2. Suppose a fair die is tossed once. What is the probability of tossing an even number? $\frac{1}{2}$
3. The names of the students in your class are written on slips of paper and put into a hat. To decide who will give the first oral report, your teacher takes one name from the hat.
   a. What is the probability that a boy will give the report?
   b. What is the probability that a girl will give the report?
   c. What is the probability that you will give the report?
   d. Put the three calculated probabilities in order.
   Answers will vary. If there are b boys and g girls in your class, the probabilities for a–c are: $\frac{b}{b+g}$, $\frac{g}{b+g}$, $\frac{1}{b+g}$. The answer to d depends on which is greater, the number of boys or the number of girls.

Any collection of outcomes from the same situation is called an **event.** For instance, when tossing a single die the event "an even number is tossed" is the collection of outcomes 2, 4, and 6. When outcomes are equally likely, there is a simple formula for finding the probability of an event.

Probability Formula for Equally Likely Outcomes
Suppose a situation has N equally likely possible outcomes and an event includes E of these. Let P be the probability that the event will occur. Then
$$P = \frac{E}{N}.$$

Example 2

Suppose a fair die is tossed once. What is the probability of tossing a 5 or a 6?

Solution

Determine the number of possible outcomes. In this situation there are 6, as shown at the left.

The event in this situation is "tossing a 5 or a 6." The event includes two of the six outcomes. So The probability is $\frac{2}{6}$, or $\frac{1}{3}$.

Outcomes are not always equally likely. Consider the probability that you will find $1,000,000 on your way home today. There are two outcomes: finding the money and not finding it. If the outcomes were equally likely, the probability of each would be $\frac{1}{2}$. But "finding $1,000,000 today" and "not finding $1,000,000 today" are not equally-likely outcomes. The probability of finding the money is clearly much less than the probability of not finding it. In this case, you cannot use $P = \frac{E}{N}$.

QUESTIONS

Covering the Reading

1. A six-sided die was tossed 100 times. The numbers that showed up are given here, along with the number of times each occurred.

1	16 times	3	18 times	5	17 times
2	19 times	4	12 times	6	18 times

   a. What is the frequency of the outcome "5 showed up"? **17**
   b. What is the relative frequency of the outcome "5 showed up"? **$\frac{17}{100}$ or 17%**
   c. If the outcomes were equally likely, what would be the probability of each outcome? **$\frac{1}{6}$ or $0.1\overline{6}$ or ≈17%**
   d. Do you think this die is fair? Explain your answer. **Sample: It seems fair. The relative frequency of each outcome is close to 17%.**
2. A probability can be no larger than __?__ and no smaller than __?__. **1; 0**
3. If an event is impossible, its probability is __?__. **0**
4. What is the probability of a sure thing? **1**

LESSON MASTER 4-8 B Questions on SPUR Objectives

Uses Objective J: Calculate probabilities and relative frequencies in a situation with known numbers of outcomes.

In 1-6, complete the table, describing the probability.

	In Words	As a Fraction	As a Decimal	As a Percent
1.	1 in 5 chance	$\frac{1}{5}$	**.2**	**20%**
2.	certain to happen	**1**	1	**100%**
3.	3 chances out of 4	**$\frac{3}{4}$**	.75	**75%**
4.	impossible	$\frac{0}{n}$	**0**	**0%**
5.	"50-50" chance	**$\frac{1}{2}$**	**.5**	50%
6.	1 in 3 chance	**$\frac{1}{3}$**	$.\overline{3}$	$.\overline{3}$%

7. Write the Probability Formula. Then explain what each variable represents.
$P = \frac{E}{N}$
P is the probability that the event will occur. N is the number of equally likely possible outcomes. E is a particular one or more of the N outcomes.

In 8-10, the probabilities of two events are given. Tell which event is more likely to happen.

8. The probability of event A is $\frac{1}{2}$.
The probability of event B is $\frac{2}{3}$. **B**
9. The probability of event C is $\frac{1}{2}$.
The probability of event D is $\frac{1}{4}$. **C**
10. The probability of event E is $\frac{3}{4}$.
The probability of event F is is 70%. **E**

Optional Activities

Activity 1 You might want to use *Activity Kit, Activity 9*, as an additional probability experiment.

Activity 2 Fair Games
Materials: A die for every student

After completing the lesson, students might play this game. Pairs of students, A and B, take turns tossing two dice and recording whether the product of the two numbers is even (A gets a point) or odd (B gets a point). The first player to reach 10 points wins. Ask students if they think the game is fair and to explain why. [No. The probability of an even product is $\frac{3}{4}$, and the probability of an odd product is $\frac{1}{4}$.]

Next, vary the game so that even or odd *sums* determine who gets a point. Ask if the game is fair. [Yes, because both probabilities are $\frac{1}{2}$.]

5. Suppose event A has a probability of $\frac{1}{2}$ and event B has a probability of $\frac{1}{3}$. Which event is more likely? **A**

6. The weather bureau reports a 70% precipitation probability for tomorrow and a $\frac{3}{5}$ chance of thunderstorms the day after tomorrow. Which is thought to be more likely, precipitation tomorrow or thunderstorms the day after? **precipitation tomorrow**

7. Identify three ways in which people determine probabilities.

8. Write the formula for finding the probability of an event in a situation with equally likely outcomes. $P = \frac{E}{N}$

9. A fair die is tossed. What is the probability of getting a 1, 2, 5, or 6? $\frac{4}{6}$ or $\frac{2}{3}$

7) (1) Guess; (2) perform an experiment and choose a probability close to the relative frequency found; (3) assume outcomes are equally likely.

Applying the Mathematics

10. Toss a die 30 times. Record the number of times each number appears.
    a. What was your relative frequency of the event "tossing a 5 or a 6"?
    b. How does your relative frequency compare to the probability found in Example 2?

11. Explain the difference between relative frequency and probability.

10a) Answers will vary. The relative frequency is found by dividing the frequency of 5 or 6 landing face up by the number of tosses, 30, or $\frac{F}{30}$.
b) Compare the value of $\frac{F}{30}$ to the probability $\frac{1}{3}$.

11) Relative frequency is a number $\frac{F}{N}$ from 0 to 1 that indicates how many times (F) an event occurred out of N repetitions of an experiment that has taken place. Probability is a number from 0 to 1 that indicates what we think is the likelihood of an event.

In 12 and 13, imagine a situation where fifty raffle tickets are put into a hat. Each ticket has the same probability of being selected to win the raffle prize.

12. If one of these tickets is yours, what is the probability you will win the raffle? $\frac{1}{50}$

13. If you and two friends have one ticket apiece, what is the probability that one of you will win the raffle? $\frac{3}{50}$

14. A person says, "There is a negative probability that my uncle will leave me a million dollars." What is wrong with that statement?
A probability must be a number from 0 to 1, so it can't be negative.

15. A spinner in a game is pictured below. Assume all directions of the spinner are equally likely. Also assume radii that look perpendicular are.

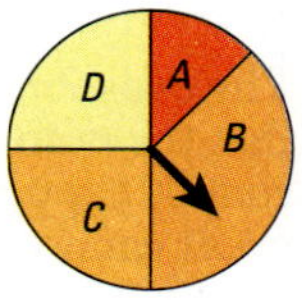

    a. If the angle which forms region A has measure 45°, what is the probability that the spinner will land in region A? $\frac{1}{8}$
    b. Determine the probabilities of landing in the other regions. **B: $\frac{3}{8}$; C: $\frac{1}{4}$; D: $\frac{1}{4}$**

16. What way of determining probability is being used in Question 15?
Assume outcomes (all directions of the spinner) are equally likely.

Notes on Questions

Questions 12–13 Social Studies Connection If you have a lottery in your area, you might want to discuss the chances of winning and what the government's share of the lottery revenue finances.

The first lotteries appeared in Europe in the 15th century and were attempts to raise money to fortify defenses or aid the poor. Today, Australia is called the home of the state lottery. Its lotteries are used to finance public programs and projects. New South Wales has lottery sales of more than 1,000,000 tickets a week, and the proceeds have financed projects including the spectacular Sydney Opera House.

Question 15 This question shows a situation in which the probability is not the ratio of counts, but of measures (or, equivalently, the ratio of the areas of the sectors). Point out that only regions C and D are the same size. In order to determine the probabilities, one can compare the sizes of the angles that form the regions. Here the greatest probability is that the spinner will land in the region B. [$\frac{135}{360}$, or $\frac{3}{8}$]

▸ **LESSON MASTER 4-8 B** *page 2*

11. Ten cards numbered 1 to 10 are shuffled and put in a box. What is the probability that a card drawn from the box will show a number less than 4? $\frac{3}{10}$

12. A spinner in a game is pictured below. Assume the spinner is a fair spinner. The angles which form the regions have the measures given at the right. Determine the probability of landing on each region.

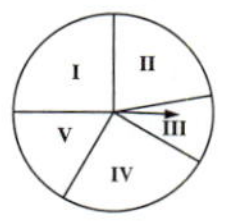

Region I: 90° $\frac{1}{4}$
Region II: 80° $\frac{2}{9}$
Region III: 40° $\frac{1}{9}$
Region IV: 90° $\frac{1}{4}$
Region V: 60° $\frac{1}{6}$

13. You have bought 12 tickets to a raffle. If n tickets were sold, what is the probability that you will win? $\frac{12}{n}$

14. If the probability of your being on the honor roll is 75%, what is the probability that you will *not* be on the honor roll? **25%**

15. Suppose there is a 1 in 5 chance that the cafeteria will not serve soup today. What is the probability that soup *will* be served in the cafeteria today? $\frac{4}{5}$

16. List three common ways for determining probabilities. Give an example of each. **Samples are given.**
Guess that you have a 75% chance of making the team. Perform an experiment and choose a probability close to the relative frequency; you might plant 200 seeds and if 181 germinate, the probability that a seed will germinate is about 90%. Assume outcomes are equally likely; if you roll a die, each face probably has the same probability of landing up.

Adapting to Individual Needs

Extra Help

Materials: A bag and two sets of different-colored marbles

Use a bag and two different colored marbles (such as green and blue) to model each situation. Put the suggested number of marbles in the bag, and discuss the probability of drawing a green marble and the probability of drawing a blue marble for each situation.

1. 0 green, 0 blue [green = 0, blue = 0]
2. 1 green, 0 blue [green = 1, blue = 0]
3. 1 green, 1 blue [green = $\frac{1}{2}$, blue = $\frac{1}{2}$]
4. 2 green, 1 blue [green = $\frac{2}{3}$, blue = $\frac{1}{3}$]
5. 2 green, 2 blue [green = $\frac{1}{2}$, blue = $\frac{1}{2}$]

Notes on Questions

Questions 17–18 These questions deal with the probability of the *complement* of an event—the probability that an event will not occur.

Follow-up for Lesson 4-8

Practice

For more questions on SPUR Objectives, use **Lesson Master 4-8A** (shown on page 215) or **Lesson Master 4-8B** (shown on pages 216–217).

Assessment

Quiz A quiz covering Lesson 4-5 through Lesson 4-8 is provided in the *Assessment Sourcebook.*

Oral Communication Write the numbers 0, $\frac{1}{4}$, 50%, and 1 on the board. For each number, have students give two examples of events that might have this probability. Discuss students' answers. [Examples are suitable and discussion yields insight into the understanding of the concept.]

Extension

Explain that *odds* are related to probabilities. When the probability of something happening is $\frac{E}{N}$, the odds of its happening are E to $N - E$, and the odds against its happening are $N - E$ to E. For instance, if you are expected to wear particular shoes 2 days out of 3, then the odds *for* that happening are 2 to 1, and the odds *against* it are 1 to 2. Ask students to find examples of the odds of something happening or against something happening. Some almanacs give odds for card games.

Project Update Project 4, *An Experiment with Dice,* on page 230, relates to the content of this lesson.

In 17 and 18, use this property: if the probability that an event will occur is p, then the probability that the event will not occur is $1 - p$.

17. Suppose the probability that your teacher will give a test next Friday is 80%. What is the probability that your teacher will not give a test next Friday? **20%**

18. You listen to a radio station for an hour. You estimate that $\frac{1}{10}$ is the probability that your favorite song will be played. What is the probability that your favorite song will not be played? $\frac{9}{10}$

Review

19. Which rectangle has greater area? *(Lesson 4-7)* **the 8.6 by 6.8 rectangle**

20. The area of a circle with radius r is $A = \pi r^2$. Find the area of a circle with radius 3 meters, to the nearest hundredth of a square meter. *(Lessons 1-3, 4-7)* **28.27 m²**

21. Suppose $y = 3.2$ and $x = 1.5$. Evaluate each expression. *(Lesson 4-6)*
a. $4x$ **6** **b.** $4y - 10$ **2.8** **c.** $[40 - (4y - 10)]/(4x)$ **6.2**

22. a. 6 miles + 1000 feet = __?__ feet **32,680**
b. 6 meters + 1000 centimeters = __?__ meters *(Lessons 3-1, 3-4)* **16**

23. The St. Gotthard Tunnel in Switzerland is the longest car tunnel in the world. Its length is about 16.4 km. About how many miles is this? *(Lesson 3-4)* **about 10.2 miles**

Turn on the lights. *The St. Gotthard road tunnel, pictured above, was opened in 1980 as a companion to the St. Gotthard rail tunnel opened in 1882. Switzerland relies on tunnels to aid passage through its mountainous regions.*

24. According to one source, 60% of Americans don't exercise regularly. Using 250,000,000 for the U.S. population, estimate the number of people in the United States who do exercise regularly. *(Lesson 2-5)* **100,000,000**

Exploration

25. The **odds for** an event happening is expressed as the number of ways that the event can happen to the number of ways that the event cannot happen. The **odds against** an event is the number of ways the event cannot happen to the number of ways the event can happen. For instance, suppose a fair die is tossed once. The odds for tossing a six are 1 to 5. The odds against tossing a six are 5 to 1.

a. Suppose Carol estimates that the odds for her passing the next math test are 10 to 1. What is Carol's estimate of the probability that she will pass? $\frac{10}{11}$ **or** $.\overline{90}$ **or** $\approx$ **91%**

b. Find an example of odds in a newspaper or magazine article. Write a probability question based on the odds you found. **Answers will vary.**

Adapting to Individual Needs

Challenge

Give students these problems.

1. The letters A, C, and T are written on three identical slips of paper and put into a hat. Then three slips are drawn at random, one at a time. What is the probability that they will be drawn in the order C, A, T? [$\frac{1}{6}$]
2. Repeat the activity in Question 1 using the letters A, H, M, T. What is the probability that they will be drawn in the order M, A, T, H? [$\frac{1}{24}$]

Most students will find the answers by listing all the possibilities. You might want to ask if they can see another way. [The letters A, C, T can be arranged in 3 × 2 × 1, or 6, different ways, one of which is CAT. The letters A, H, M, T can be arranged in 4 × 3 × 2 × 1, or 24, different ways, one of which is MATH.]

LESSON

4-9

Open Sentences

Problem solving. *An entertainment committee may solve an equation to determine the number of tickets that must be sold to cover the costs of an event. The event might include the Jesse White Tumblers shown above.*

What Is an Open Sentence?

A sentence with an equal sign = is called an **equation.** Here are some equations.

$27 = 9(4 - 1)$ $\quad 1 + 1 = 3$ $\quad x + 7 = 50$

The left equation is true. The middle equation is false. The right equation may be true or false, depending on what you substitute for x. If you substitute 57, the equation is false, because

57 + 7 does not equal 50.

If you substitute 43 for x, the equation is true.

$$43 + 7 = 50$$

The equation $x + 7 = 50$ is an example of an *open sentence.* An **open sentence** is a sentence containing one or more variables. An open sentence can be true or false, depending on what you substitute for the variables. The *solution* to this open sentence is 43. A **solution** to an open sentence is a value of a variable that makes the sentence true.

Finding Solutions to Open Sentences

Sometimes you can find some solutions to open sentences in your head.

Example 1

Find the solution to the open sentence $40 - A = 38$.

Solution

Since $40 - 2 = 38$, the number 2 is the solution. You can also write $A = 2$.

Lesson 4-9

Objectives

C Find solutions to equations involving simple arithmetic.

Resources

From the ***Teacher's Resource File***
- Lesson Master 4-9A or 4-9B
- Answer Master 4-9
- Teaching Aids
  41 Warm-up
  47 Number Line (Additional Examples)
- Technology Sourcebook, Computer Master 6

Additional Resources
- Visuals for Teaching Aids 41, 47
- Graphing and Probability Workshop

Teaching Lesson 4-9

Warm-up

Diagnostic Solve.

1. $3x = 9$ $\quad x = 3$
2. $17 + y = 20$ $\quad y = 3$
3. $x + 6 = 12$ $\quad x = 6$
4. $m \div 2 = 5$ $\quad m = 10$
5. $x - 1 = 7$ $\quad x = 8$
6. $10 - r = 2$ $\quad r = 8$
7. $9n = 90$ $\quad n = 10$
8. $45 \div x = 5$ $\quad x = 9$

Notes on Reading

Reading Mathematics Although this is not a difficult lesson for students to read on their own, you might want to have them read this lesson aloud in class. Then you can assess their ability to read equations. Since solutions in this lesson are found

Lesson 4-9 Overview

Broad Goals This lesson introduces (or reviews) the use of variables as unknowns in the context of solving an equation. At this time, students are expected to solve the equations mentally or to choose from possible solutions. No algorithms for solving equations are given.

Perspective Variables have the feeling of *knowns* when they appear in patterns or formulas, and for this reason they are not threatening. Though students have had experience with variables in patterns and formulas, the use of variables as *unknowns* is usually the first thing that comes to mind when algebra is discussed. We have purposely waited until the end of the chapter to introduce this use because we feel that the idea of *unknown* conveys a mysteriousness about variables that we wish to avoid.

The purpose of this lesson is only to introduce the *idea* of unknowns. The questions are designed to give a nonthreatening view of finding unknowns. Do *not* work on ways to solve sentences at this time. Many later lessons are devoted to solving equations.

This lesson also anticipates the discussion of the trial-and-error strategy in Chapter 6.

either by inspection or through multiple choice, the examples are not threatening and can be viewed as puzzles. With this approach, students think about unknowns in a positive way, and look at the equation as a whole, thinking about a sensible solution instead of following a series of mechanical steps for isolating the answer.

Example 2 After testing 0.5 and finding that $30 \cdot 0.5 > 6$, some students may realize that the solution is less than 0.5, and therefore it is not necessary to test 5.

Activity 1 in *Optional Activities* below suggests another way students might record their work for multiple-choice questions like **Example 2.** *Activity 2* poses a problem related to **Example 3**.

If you are given a set of choices, you can find solutions by trying each choice to see if it works.

Example 2

Multiple choice. Which number is a solution to $30m = 6$?
(a) 24 (b) 0.5 (c) 5 (d) 0.2

Solution

The solution is the value that makes the sentence true. Substitute to find the solution.
(a) $30 \cdot 24 = 720$, so 24 is not a solution.
(b) $30 \cdot 0.5 = 15$, so 0.5 is not a solution.
(c) $30 \cdot 5 = 150$, so 5 is not a solution.
(d) $30 \cdot 0.2 = 6$, so 0.2 is a solution.
Choice (d) is the correct choice.

How Formulas Lead to Open Sentences

One of the most important skills in algebra is finding solutions to open sentences. This skill is important because open sentences occur often in situations where decisions have to be made.

Example 3

A store is to have an area of 10,000 square feet. But it can be only 80 feet wide. Let ℓ be the length of the store. The value of ℓ is the solution to what open sentence?

Solution

Drawing a picture can help. We know $A = \ell w$. The given information tells us that $A = 10{,}000$ and $w = 80$. Substitute 10,000 for A and 80 for w in the formula. ℓ is the solution to the open sentence $10{,}000 = \ell \cdot 80$.

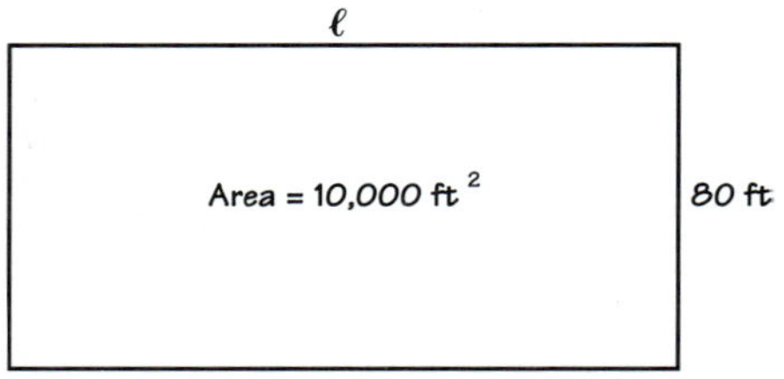

The solution to $10{,}000 = \ell \cdot 80$ is not obvious. The variable ℓ is called the **unknown.** Finding values of the unknown (or unknowns) that make the sentence true is called **solving the sentence.** At this point, you are expected to be able to solve only very simple sentences. The sentences will be the kind you can solve in your head, or ones with a set of choices for solutions.

Optional Activities

Activity 1 As students try choices in solving equations, they might make a table to record their work. The table below relates to **Example 2.**

m	$30m$	Is the value of m a solution?
24	$30 \cdot 24 = 720$	No
0.5	$30 \cdot 0.5 = 15$	No
5	$30 \cdot 5 = 150$	No
0.2	$30 \cdot 0.2 = 6$	Yes

Activity 2 As a follow-up for **Example 3**, you might give students similar problems involving sentences they can solve mentally. For example, have students imagine that a rectangular table top has an area of 24 ft^2.

1. List all possible integer solutions to $24 = \ell w$. [24,1; 12, 2; 6, 4; and 8, 3]
2. List some non-integer solutions. [Samples: 15, 1.6; 10, 2.4; 9.6, 2.5]
3. If ℓ has a value of 6, what are possible values of w? [4]

Activity 3 Technology Connection *Technology Sourcebook, Computer Master 6,* involves simulations with spinners. Students use the *Graphing and Probability Workshop* to find relative frequency for an experiment that is repeated many times. Students should discover that repeating a simulation hundreds of times usually gives a result that is fairly close to the actual probability.

Example 4

Multiple choice. If a basketball team loses 10 games, how many games must it win to have a winning percentage of .600?
(a) 6 (b) 15 (c) 16 (d) 25

Solution

From Questions 13–16 of Lesson 4-7, if a team wins W games and loses L games, then its winning percentage P is given by the formula $P = \frac{W}{W + L}$.
Here $P = .600$ and $L = 10$. So the sentence to solve is $.600 = \frac{W}{W + 10}$.
Now test each choice until you find the solution.

Activity

Finish Example 4.

QUESTIONS

Covering the Reading

1. What is an *equation?* **a sentence with an equal sign**
2. Give an example of an equation that is false. **Sample: 1 + 1 = 3**
3. What is an *open sentence?* **a sentence containing one or more variables**
4. Give an example of an open sentence. **Sample: $x + 7 = 50$**
5. Define: solution to an open sentence. **a value of the variable that makes the sentence true**
6. What is meant by *solving* an open sentence? **finding values of the unknown (or unknowns) that make the sentence true**
7. *Multiple choice.* The solution to $4x + 3 = 12$ is
   (a) 2.25. (b) 0.
   (c) 2.5. (d) 1. **(a)**
8. *Multiple choice.* A solution to $4n^2 = 64$ is
   (a) 1. (b) 2.
   (c) 4. (d) 8. **(c)**

In 9–12, solve the sentence in your head.

9. $18 + A = 19$ **1**
10. $2B = 10$ **5**
11. $C = 5 - .1$ **4.9**
12. $4 = 3.5 + t$ **.5**
13. Rhee Taylor wants a store with an area of 1000 square meters. The store can be only 40 meters wide. Rhee wants to know how many meters long the store should be.
    a. What equation can Rhee solve to find the length ℓ of the store?
    b. Which of these is the solution: 25 m, 960 m, 1040 m, or 4000 m?
    a) $40\ell = 1000$; b) 25 m
14. What is the answer to the question of Example 4? **(b) 15**

Additional Examples

You may want to use **Teaching Aid 47,** which contains all of the following additional examples.

1. Mentally find the solution to each open sentence.
   a. $12 + a = 12\frac{3}{4}$ **$\frac{3}{4}$**
   b. $8 - 2.3 = b$ **5.7**
   c. $100 - c = 53$ **47**
   d. $\frac{d}{3} = 6$ **18**
   e. $2e + 6 = 6$ **0**
2. *Multiple choice.* Choose the solution to each open sentence.
   a. $\frac{15}{a} = 30$ **ii**
      (i) 2 (ii) $\frac{1}{2}$ (iii) 5 (iv) $\frac{1}{5}$
   b. $100 = 2g - 6$ **iv**
      (i) 50 (ii) 5 (iii) 52 (iv) 53
   c. $\frac{25}{h} = 6.25$ **ii**
      (i) 3 (ii) 4 (iii) 5 (iv) 6
3. A square-shaped room has an area of 100 square feet. Let s be the length of a side of the room. The value s is the solution to what open sentence? If you can, give the value.
   $100 = s^2$; 10 feet
4. Suppose the probability that a girl is picked at random out of a group of 50 students is .4.
   a. What equation can you solve to find the number of girls in the group?
      $\frac{n}{50} = .4$
   b. *Multiple choice.* How many girls are in the group? **iii**
      (i) 25 (ii) 30 (iii) 20 (iv) 50

LESSON MASTER 4-9 A
Questions on SPUR Objectives
See pages 233-235 for objectives.

Skills Objective C

Multiple choice. **In 1-6, choose the correct solution to the equation.**

1. $2x^2 + 7 = 57$
   (a) 25 (b) 15
   (c) 10 (d) 5 **d**
2. $16 - y = 8.8$
   (a) 8.2 (b) 8
   (c) 7.8 (d) 7.2 **d**
3. $\frac{1}{4}x = 21$
   (a) 5.25 (b) 40
   (c) 84 (d) 100 **c**
4. $t - 2.05 = 12$
   (a) 9.95 (b) 12.05
   (c) 14.5 (d) 14.05 **d**
5. $15 = .3y + 3$
   (a) .4 (b) 4
   (c) 40 (d) 60 **c**
6. $70 + 4y - 8 = 90$
   (a) 12 (b) 7
   (c) 5 (d) 3 **b**

In 7-17, give a solution for each equation.

7. $\frac{x}{4} = 0$ **$x = 0$**
8. $m + 16 = 40$ **$m = 24$**
9. $y(9 - 2) = 14$ **$y = 2$**
10. $l - 25 = 35$ **$l = 60$**
11. $8a = 48$ **$a = 6$**
12. $y^2 = 49$ **$y = \pm 7$**
13. There are p planets in our solar system. **$p = 9$**
14. One yard equals f feet. **$f = 3$**
15. There are h hours in one day. **$h = 24$**
16. There are c centimeters in a meter. **$c = 100$**
17. Your household has t telephones. **Answers will vary.**

Adapting to Individual Needs

Extra Help

If students have trouble understanding that an open sentence can be made true or false depending on the substitution, give them an open sentence that uses a blank box instead of a variable. For example, $19 + n = 28$ could be written $19 + \square = 28$. Then students can write the sentence several times and fill the box with different numbers until they find the solution.

Notes on Questions

Questions 17 and 21 Open sentences in English raise the question of whether multiple solutions are possible with algebraic sentences—anticipating inequalities in the next lesson. Each of these questions has more than one correct answer.

Question 24 Students should substitute to see which value of n is the solution.

Questions 26–27 Emphasize that when a variable appears more than once in an equation, the variable must stand for the same number in each place.

Question 39 A chart and a calculator will be useful in answering this question. First ask students which whole numbers can be multiplied to give 100. [1 and 100, 2 and 50, 4 and 25, 5 and 20, 10 and 10] Since the numbers being multiplied in this problem, $(x + 1)$ and $(x + 2)$, are close in value, x must have a value less than 10. Help the students set up a chart like the one below to try out their proposed values. To determine the consecutive integers, tenths, and hundredths, students must compare their products of $(x + 1)(x + 2)$ with the required product of 100.

x	$x + 1$	$x + 2$	$(x + 1)(x + 2)$

LESSON MASTER 4-9 B Questions on SPUR Objectives

Vocabulary

1. A sentence with an equal sign is called a(n) equation.
2. A sentence with variables that can be true or false, depending on what is substituted for the variables, is called a(n) open sentence.

Skills Objective C: Find solutions to equations involving simple arithmetic.

Multiple choice. **In 3-10, choose the correct solution to the equation.**

3. $3.8 + x = 8.6$
   (a) 5.8 (b) 4.8 (c) 5.2 (d) 4.6 — b
4. $4b^2 = 100$
   (a) 5 (b) 2.5 (c) 12.5 (d) 10 — a
5. $7 + 2x = 15$
   (a) 6 (b) $1.\overline{6}$ (c) 4 (d) 8 — c
6. $y - 11.02 = 7$
   (a) 18.02 (b) 17.98 (c) 4 (d) 18.2 — a
7. $21 = .7m + 7$
   (a) 3 (b) .2 (c) 2 (d) 20 — d
8. $48 - 3c^2 = 0$
   (a) 16 (b) 4 (c) 48 (d) 8 — b
9. $\frac{1}{5}w = 32$
   (a) 160 (b) 16 (c) 6.4 (d) 31.8 — a
10. $45 + 5x - 10 = 85$
    (a) 50 (b) 5 (c) 1.9 (d) 10 — d

15. *Multiple choice.* If a volleyball team wins 12 games, how many games can it lose and still have a winning percentage of .750?
    (a) 3 (b) 4 (c) 8 (d) 9 **(b)**

Applying the Mathematics

Architectural splendor. *The Renaissance Center in downtown Detroit, Michigan, houses a circular 73-story hotel and four 39-story office buildings.*

In 16–19, give one solution to each of these nonmathematical open sentences.

16. ___?___ is currently President of the United States. **Bill Clinton**
17. In population, ___?___ is a bigger city than Detroit. **Sample: Los Angeles**
18. A trio has ___?___ members. **three**
19. An octet has ___?___ members. **eight**

In 20–23, give at least one solution.

20. There are y millimeters in a meter. **1000**
21. x is a negative integer. **Sample: -9**
22. You move the decimal point two places to the right when multiplying by m. **100**
23. The number one million, written as a decimal, is a 1 followed by z zeros. **6**
24. *Multiple choice.* Let n be the number of days a book is overdue. Let F be the fine. Suppose $F = .20 + .05n$ dollars, the situation described in Lesson 4-4. When the fine F is \$1.00, what number of days is the book overdue?
    (a) 20 (b) 15 (c) 16 (d) 25 **(c)**
25. Suppose $y = 2x + 3$. When $x = 4$, what value of y is a solution? **11**

In 26–31, find a solution to the sentence in your head.

26. $n + n = 16$ **8**
27. $m \cdot m = 16$ **4**
28. $z - 4 = 99$ **103**
29. $y \cdot 25 = 25$ **1**
30. $\frac{1}{2}w = \frac{5}{2}$ **5**
31. $p + 2\frac{1}{3} = 5\frac{1}{3}$ **3**

Adapting to Individual Needs

English Language Development

For this lesson you might want to focus on the terms: *equation, open sentence,* and *solution.* On the board, write the sentences for **a**, **b**, and **c**, shown at the right. Then, under each, write the corresponding mathematical sentence or *equation.* Talk about whether each equation is true [a] or false [b], and when a person can't tell [c]. Finally explain that equation **c** is an *open sentence* because it is *open* to being true or false depending on the replacement for n. Have students make replacements, establishing that the replacement that makes the sentence true is the *solution.*

a. Two plus four equals six.
Equation: $2 + 4 = 6$ [true]

b. Five plus eight equals twelve.
Equation: $5 + 8 = 12$ [false]

c. A number plus six equals ten.
Equation: $n + 6 = 10$ [can't tell]

Review

32. An organization has a raffle and sells n tickets. You have bought 5 of the tickets. What is the probability that you will win the raffle? *(Lesson 4-8)* **$5/n$**

33. Slips of paper numbered 1 to 100 are put into a hat. A slip is taken from the hat. What is the probability that the number is a multiple of 3? *(Lesson 4-8)* **$\frac{33}{100}$ or .33**

34. The sum of the integers from 1 to n is given by the expression $\frac{n(n+1)}{2}$.
- **a.** Evaluate the expression when $n = 5$. **15**
- **b.** Verify your answer to part **a** by adding the integers from 1 to 5.
- **c.** Find the sum of the integers from 1 to 100. *(Lessons 4-6, 4-7)*

b) 1 + 2 + 3 + 4 + 5 = 15; c) 5050

35. Evaluate this rather complicated expression. *(Lesson 4-6)*

$$\frac{6(2 + 4^3)^2 - 3^2}{40 - 13 \cdot 3}$$ **26,127**

36. Lynette used her calculator to find the average of the three numbers 83, 91, and 89. The answer came out higher than any of the numbers. Explain why Lynette must have made a mistake. *(Lesson 4-6)* **See below.**

37. Put the three quantities into one sentence with two inequality signs: 5 km, 500 m, 50,000 mm. *(Lessons 1-9, 3-4)*

$5 \text{ km} > 500 \text{ m} > 50{,}000 \text{ mm}$ or $50{,}000 \text{ mm} < 500 \text{ m} < 5 \text{ km}$

38. In 1991, the world population was estimated by the Bureau of the Census as 5.423 billion. *(Lessons 1-4, 2-1, 2-3)*
- **a.** Round this number to the nearest ten million. **5,420,000,000**
- **b.** Write your answer to part **a** in scientific notation. **5.42×10^9**

Exploration

39. Estimate a solution to $(x + 1)(x + 2) = 100$
- **a.** between consecutive integers. **between 8 and 9**
- **b.** between consecutive tenths. **between 8.5 and 8.6**
- **c.** between consecutive hundredths. **between 8.51 and 8.52**

36) Sample: The average of three numbers cannot be smaller than the least number in the group or larger than the greatest number in the group.

Follow-up for Lesson 4-9

Practice

For more questions on SPUR Objectives, use **Lesson Master 4-9A** (shown on page 221) or **Lesson Master 4-9B** (shown on pages 222–223).

Assessment

Written Communication Have students **work in pairs.** Ask each student to write three open sentences with four choices for answers (including the solution) for each sentence. Then have students solve their partners' sentences and discuss their answers. [Open sentences contain variables and vary in the operations used. Discussion clarifies understanding.]

Extension

Have students find how much each person will receive.

A woman will divide $5000 among her brother, a niece, and a nephew. First each person will receive $500. Then the remainder of the money will be divided as follows: the brother will receive three times as much as the nephew, who will receive the same amount as the niece. [5000 = 1500 + 3*x* + *x* + *x*; the brother receives $2600, both the niece and the nephew receive $1200]

▶ LESSON MASTER 4-9 B *page 2*

In 11-30, give a solution for each equation.

11. $x + 20 = 35$ **$x = 15$**
12. $\frac{a}{8} = 0$ **$a = 0$**
13. $y - 11 = 30$ **$y = 41$**
14. $4f = 28$ **$f = 7$**
15. $d(2 + 6) = 24$ **$d = 3$**
16. $0 + r = 13$ **$r = 13$**
17. $n^2 = 36$ **$n = 6$**
18. $u \cdot 72 = 72$ **$u = 1$**
19. $a + a = 18$ **$a = 9$**
20. $\frac{50}{x} = 25$ **$x = 2$**
21. There are y years in a decade. **$y = 10$**
22. January has d days. **$d = 31$**
23. There are c cups in a pint. **$c = 2$**
24. There are s students in class today. **Answers will vary.**
25. Every insect has l legs. **$l = 6$**
26. Each state in the United States has s senators. **$s = 2$**
27. A triangle has a angles. **$a = 3$**
28. I am i inches tall. **Answers will vary.**
29. Intelligent life has been discovered on p planets. **$p = 1$**
30. A right angle measures d degrees. **$d = 90$**

Review Objective H, Lesson 1-9

In 31-42, use the $<$, $>$, or $=$ symbol correctly in each blank.

31. $-4 \; > \; -7$
32. $3.62 \; < \; 3.\overline{6}$
33. $0 \; < \; 0.00012$
34. $0.0413 \; < \; 0.413$
35. $-7.18 \; < \; 0$
36. $9.5 \; = \; 9.50$
37. $-8.9 \; < \; 2.1$
38. $-4.02 \; < \; -3.8$
39. $-0.51 \; > \; -0.511$
40. $-174 \; > \; -192$
41. $\frac{3}{10} \; > \; \frac{1}{8}$
42. $-\frac{1}{5} \; > \; -\frac{1}{4}$

Adapting to Individual Needs

Challenge

Find the values of the unknowns so that the sum of the numbers in each row, column, and diagonal are the same. [The sum is 34. $a = 14$; $b = 12$; $c = 7$; $d = 9$; $e = 3$; $f = 16$]

1	15	*a*	4
b	6	*c*	*d*
8	10	11	5
13	*e*	2	*f*

Lesson 4-10

Objectives

C Find solutions to simple inequalities.

K Graph the solutions to any inequality of the form $x < a$ and similar inequalities, and identify such graphs.

Resources

From the ***Teacher's Resource File***

- Lesson Master 4-10A or 4-10B
- Answer Master 4-10
- Teaching Aids
  41 Warm-up
  48 Questions 24, 26–32

Additional Resources

- Visuals for Teaching Aids 41, 48

Teaching Lesson 4-10

Warm-up

Diagnostic For 1–4, tell if the inequality is true or false.

1. $1 > 2$ **False** **2.** $1 < 2$ **True**
3. $1 \le 2$ **True** **4.** $1 \ge 2$ **False**

For each of 5–8, give three numbers that make the sentence true.
Answers will vary

5. ___ < 2 **6.** ___ > 2
7. ___ ≤ 2 **8.** ___ $\ne 2$

5. Any number less than 2
6. Any number greater than 2
7. 2 or any number less than 2
8. Any number but 2

LESSON

4-10 *Inequalities*

Slow down! *It is unsafe to drive at a speed that* is greater than *the speed limit. The fine in many states for speeding* is greater than or equal to *$75.*

❶ What Is an Inequality?

An **inequality** is a sentence with one of the following symbols.

$\ne$	is not equal to
$<$	is less than
$\le$	is less than or equal to
$>$	is greater than
$\ge$	is greater than or equal to

$5 > -7$ is an inequality that is true. So is $5 \ge -7$. An example of an inequality that is false is $3 < 2$. The inequality $50\% \ne 0.5$ is also false.

The inequality $x < 30$ is an open sentence, neither true nor false. The number 20 is a solution, because $20 < 30$. The number -14 is also a solution, since $-14 < 30$. However, 30 is not a solution, because $30 < 30$ is not true. Also, 554 is not a solution, because 554 is not less than 30.

Inequalities that are open sentences usually have many solutions. The solutions are often easier to graph than to list.

Graphing Simple Inequalities

Example 1

Graph all solutions to $y < 2$.

Solution

Any number less than 2 is a solution. So there are infinitely many of them. Among the solutions are 0, 1, 1.5, -5, -4.3, and -2,000,000.

Lesson 4-10 Overview

Broad Goals The goals in this lesson are to introduce the idea of solving an inequality and the idea of graphing all the solutions of an inequality.

Perspective Solving inequalities presents difficulties for many students. One problem is that students have to deal with sentences that have many solutions; some students are so accustomed to having one answer to mathematical questions that they cannot fathom how something such as $y < 2$ can have infinitely many solutions. This is why we introduce inequalities so quickly after equations. We do not ask students to graph the solutions to equations in one variable; it is too much work for too little payoff. But we do ask students to graph solutions to inequalities because such graphs convey a lot of information.

Some books have used the word *inequation* rather than inequality. This is a nice idea, for it reinforces the commonalties in sentence-solving, but the word *inequality* is imbedded in the language of mathematics.

Recall that to graph a single number means to darken a dot on the number line. To graph all of the numbers on a part of the number line, thicken that part of the line. So here we thicken the part of the line with numbers that are less than 2. The open circle around the tick mark for 2 indicates that 2 is not a solution. It is not true that $2 < 2$. The thickened arrowhead below indicates that the solutions go on forever in that direction. Put a y at the right of the number line to indicate the variable.

$y < 2$

❷ Remember that $2 > y$ means the same as $y < 2$. So the graph of all solutions to $2 > y$ is identical to the graph of $y < 2$.

Example 2

Graph all solutions to $x \geq -1$.

Solution

Any number greater than or equal to -1 is a solution. Therefore, that part of the line is thickened. Since -1 is a solution, the circle at -1 is filled in. Here is the graph.

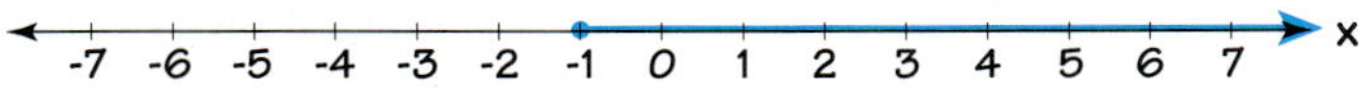

$x \geq -1$

❸ Graphing Double Inequalities

On some interstate highways, a car's speed must be from 45 mph to 55 mph. The graph of all possible legal speeds s is the graph of solutions to the double inequality $45 \leq s \leq 55$. This can be read as: "s is greater than or equal to 45 and s is less than or equal to 55" or "s ranges from 45 to 55." Another way to write this is with $\geq$ signs. $55 \geq s \geq 45$. Some solutions are 48, 50.3, 51, 55, 45, and 49. Because both 45 and 55 are solutions, the circles at 45 and 55 are filled in.

$45 \leq s \leq 55$

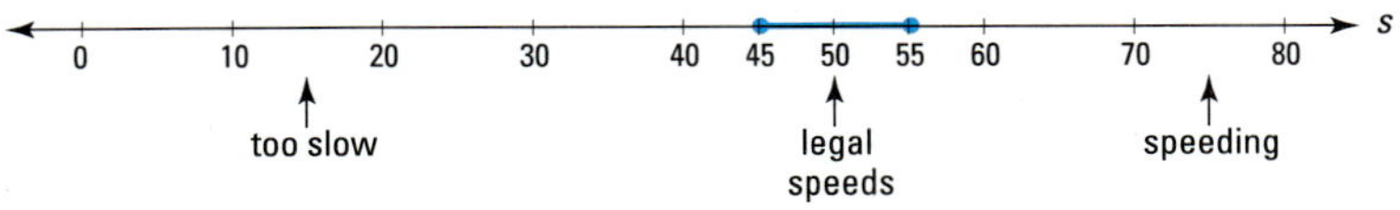

If 55 were not included, the sentence would be $45 \leq s < 55$. The graph would have an open circle at 55.

$45 \leq s < 55$

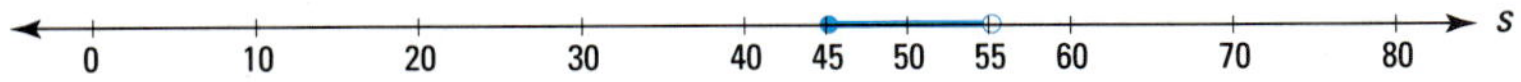

Notes on Reading

When you discuss the examples and answers to the questions for this lesson, you might want to use **Teaching Aid 48** which contains number lines for graphing.

❶ If students have difficulty understanding these symbols, see the *Extra Help* suggestions in *Adapting to Individual Needs* on page 226.

❷ Emphasize that $2 < y$ and $y > 2$ are two ways of stating the same thing. You may wish to call them *equivalent,* because they have the same solutions. We formally introduce that term in Chapter 7.

❸ You might ask what inequality describes speeding. [$s > 55$] What inequality describes going too slow? [$s < 45$]

Ecology Connection Ask students if they know about the "Adopt-a-Highway" program and, if so, to tell the class about it. Interested students can contact local highway authorities to learn if there is such a program in their area, and, if so, to find out how they can participate. The idea of local volunteers cleaning roadways is credited to James Evans, a Texas highway official. In 1984, Texas was spending almost $25 million a year collecting trash generated by motorists. Evans challenged civic clubs to "adopt" stretches of highways and to clean them on a regular basis. Today most states have or are planning similar programs.

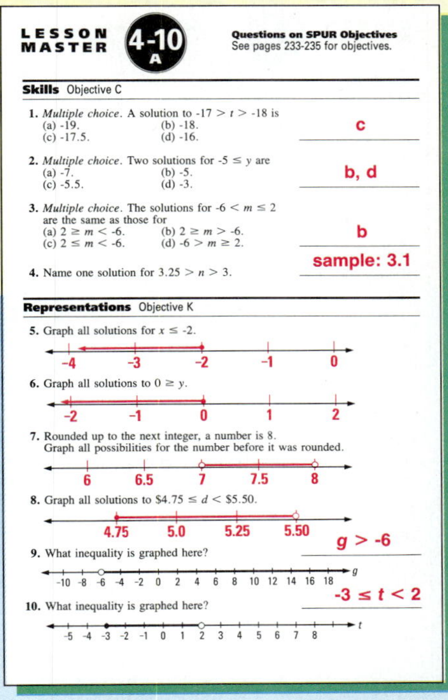

LESSON MASTER 4-10 A **Questions on SPUR Objectives** See pages 233-235 for objectives.

Skills Objective C

1. *Multiple choice.* A solution to $-17 > t > -18$ is
(a) -19. (b) -18.
(c) -17.5. (d) -16.
c

2. *Multiple choice.* Two solutions for $-5 \leq y$ are
(a) -7. (b) -5.
(c) -5.5. (d) -3.
b, d

3. *Multiple choice.* The solutions for $-6 < m \leq 2$ are the same as those for
(a) $2 \geq m < -6$. (b) $2 \geq m > -6$.
(c) $2 \leq m < -6$. (d) $-6 > m \geq 2$.
b

4. Name one solution for $3.25 > n > 3$. **sample: 3.1**

Representations Objective K

5. Graph all solutions for $x \leq -2$.
-4 -3 -2 -1 0

6. Graph all solutions to $0 \geq y$.
-2 -1 0 1 2

7. Rounded up to the next integer, a number is 8. Graph all possibilities for the number before it was rounded.
6 6.5 7 7.5 8

8. Graph all solutions to $\$4.75 \leq d < \$5.50$.
4.75 5.0 5.25 5.50

9. What inequality is graphed here? **$g > -6$**
-10 -8 -6 -4 -2 0 2 4 6 8 10 12 14 16 18 g

10. What inequality is graphed here? **$-3 \leq t < 2$**
-5 -4 -3 -2 -1 0 1 2 3 4 5 6 7 8 t

Optional Activities

Students might benefit from seeing the inequality in **Example 3** graphed in steps. You can ask them to break the inequality into two parts: $-4 < m$ and $m \leq 5$. Draw three identical number lines in a column, as shown at the right. Graph $-4 < m$ on the first line, $m \leq 5$ on the next line, and finally $-4 < m \leq 5$. Use vertical dotted lines through -4 and 5 to show how all three are related.

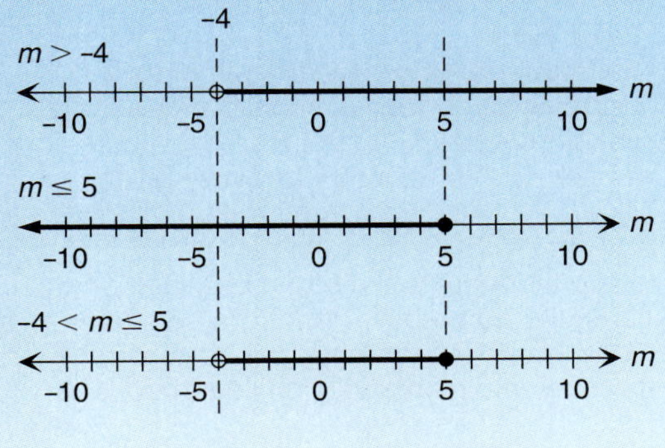

❹ The English language is not as precise as the mathematical notation for inequalities. In English, the word *between* sometimes means to include the endpoints and sometimes means to exclude them. If you wish precise language, you might use "from *a* to *b*" when you wish to include the endpoints, and "between *a* and *b*" when you wish to exclude them. There is no simple language for the inequality in **Example 3** where exactly one endpoint is included. Students can read $-4 < m \le 5$ as "*m* is greater than −4 and is less than or equal to 5" or "*m* ranges from −4 to 5, not including −4."

You might use the activities in *Optional Activities*, on page 225, to show students how a double inequality is the graph of the intersection of two inequalities.

Additional Examples

In 1–2, graph all the solutions to each inequality.

1. $m < 5$

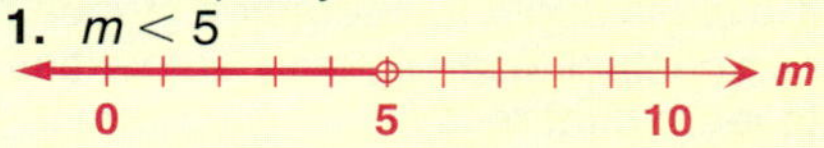

2. $s \ge 0$

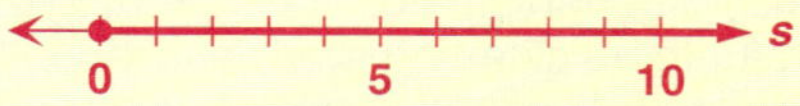

3. Write an inequality for the following graph. $6 < r \le 9$

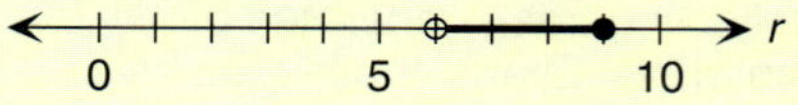

4. Graph $4\frac{1}{2} \le w \le 6\frac{1}{2}$

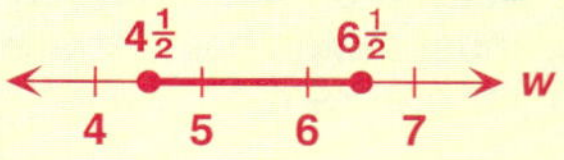

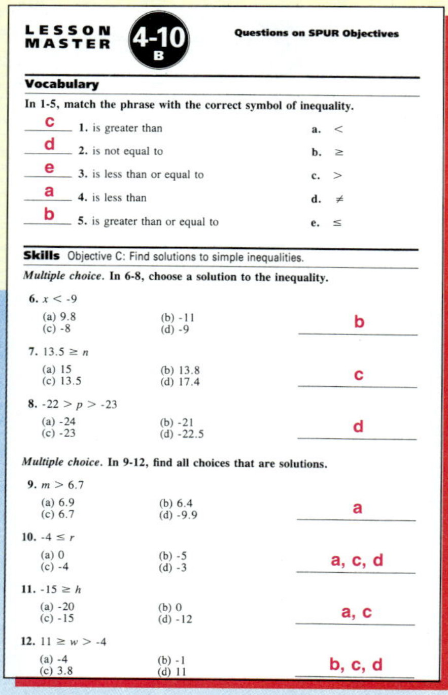

LESSON MASTER 4-10 B — Questions on SPUR Objectives

Vocabulary

In 1-5, match the phrase with the correct symbol of inequality.

c 1. is greater than — a. <
d 2. is not equal to — b. ≥
e 3. is less than or equal to — c. >
a 4. is less than — d. ≠
b 5. is greater than or equal to — e. ≤

Skills Objective C: Find solutions to simple inequalities.

Multiple choice. In 6-8, choose a solution to the inequality.

6. $x < -9$ (a) 9.8 (b) -11 (c) -8 (d) -9 — b

7. $13.5 \ge n$ (a) 15 (b) 13.8 (c) 13.5 (d) 17.4 — c

8. $-22 > p > -23$ (a) -24 (b) -21 (c) -23 (d) -22.5 — d

Multiple choice. In 9-12, find all choices that are solutions.

9. $m > 6.7$ (a) 6.9 (b) 6.4 (c) 6.7 (d) -9.9 — a

10. $-4 \le r$ (a) 0 (b) -5 (c) -4 (d) -3 — a, c, d

11. $-15 \ge h$ (a) -20 (b) 0 (c) -15 (d) -12 — a, c

12. $11 \ge w > -4$ (a) -4 (b) -1 (c) 3.8 (d) 11 — b, c, d

If neither 45 nor 55 were included, the sentence would be $45 < s < 55$. There would be open circles at both 45 and 55.

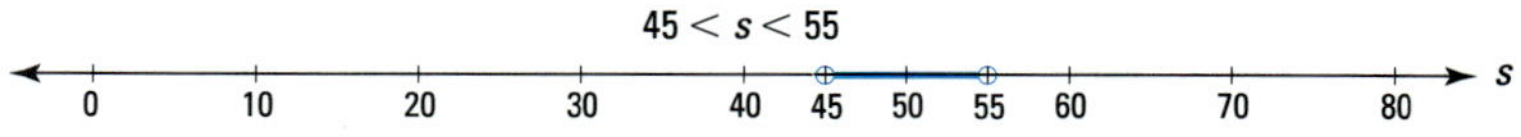

❹ **Example 3**

Write an inequality for the following graph. Use *m* as the variable.

Solution

The solutions are the numbers from -4 to 5, including 5 but not including -4.
One double inequality is $-4 < m \le 5$.
Another correct answer is $5 \ge m > -4$.

QUESTIONS

Covering the Reading

1. What is an inequality? a sentence with one of the symbols, <, >, ≤, ≥, or ≠

In 2–5, give the meaning of the symbol.

2. > is greater than

3. ≥ is greater than or equal to

4. < is less than

5. ≤ is less than or equal to

6. Write an inequality that means the same thing as $y > 5$. $5 < y$

In 7 and 8, is the sentence an open sentence?

7. $3y \ge 90$ Yes

8. $2 \le 9$ No

In 9–12, *true or false.*

9. $-2 < 1$ True

10. $3 < \frac{6}{2}$ False

11. $-5 \ge 5$ False

12. $6 \ne 5 + 1$ False

In 13–16, name one solution to the sentence. Samples are given.

13. $A > 5000$ 5001

14. $n \le -5$ -13

15. $6\frac{1}{2} < d < 7\frac{1}{4}$ $6\frac{3}{4}$

16. $55 \ge s \ge 45$ 47

17. *Multiple choice.* The solutions to which sentences are graphed here?

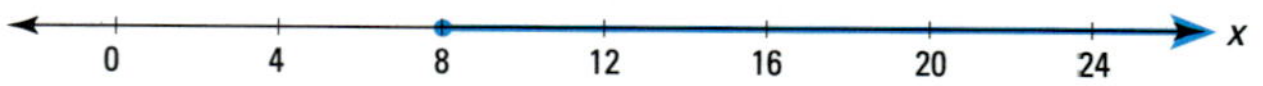

(a) $x > 8$ (b) $x < 8$ (c) $x \ge 8$ (d) $x \le 8$ (c)

Adapting to Individual Needs

Extra Help

For students who have trouble graphing inequalities correctly, the following activity might be helpful. Write these open sentences on the board in the order given.

$x = 3, \quad x < 3, \quad x \le 3, \quad x > 3, \quad x \ge 3$

Have students make 5 number lines and label the numbers −7 through 7 on each line. Have them graph $x = 3$ on the first number line by drawing a filled-in dot at 3. Then ask them what will be different about the graph for $x < 3$. [The dot at 3 will be open and the number line will be darkened to the left of 3.] Have them graph this inequality on the second number line. Continue this pattern of questioning and graphing. When the graphs are complete, ask students to describe the solutions. For $x = 3$, they should see that 3 is the only solution. For $x < 3$ the answer "any number less than 3" would indicate understanding.

18. Write a sentence whose solutions are graphed below. $n < 100$

19. Fill in the inequality symbols that describe the graph below.

-2.5 _?_ x _?_ 2 $\leq, <$

In 20–23, match the sentence with the graph of its solutions.

20. $1 \leq m \leq 4$ (c)

21. $1 < m < 4$ (b)

22. $1 < m \leq 4$ (d)

23. $1 \leq m < 4$ (a)

(a)

(b)

(c)

(d)

24. The legal speeds s on some interstate highways range from 45 mph to 65 mph. Graph all legal speeds.

24)

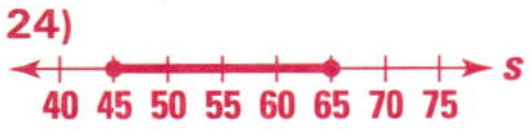

Applying the Mathematics

25. *Multiple choice.* Which sentence has the same solutions as $6 < a \leq 9\frac{2}{3}$?

(a) $9\frac{2}{3} < a \leq 6$

(b) $9\frac{2}{3} > a \geq 6$

(c) $9\frac{2}{3} \leq a < 6$

(d) $9\frac{2}{3} \geq a > 6$ (d)

In 26–29, graph all the solutions to the sentence.

26. $w < \frac{40}{3}$

27. $-6 \leq y$

28. $-2 < y < 3$

29. $-1 \geq z \geq -5$

26)

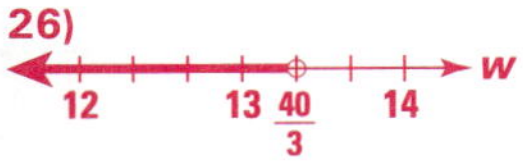

27)

28)

29)

In 30–32, a situation is given.

a. What inequality describes the situation?

b. Give three solutions to the inequality.

c. Graph all possible solutions.

30. The speed limit is 55 mph. A person is driving f miles per hour and is speeding. a) $f > 55$; b) Samples: 57, 60, 65

30c)

31. A person earns d dollars a year. The amount d is less than \$25,000 a year. a) $0 \leq d < 25{,}000$; b) Samples: 4.32, 5132, 24,999.99

31c)

32. The area is A. Rounded up to the next hundred, A is 500. a) $400 < A \leq 500$; b) Samples: 490, 439.36, 460

32c)

Notes on Questions

You might want to have students use **Teaching Aid 48** which provides blank number lines for Questions 24, 26 through 32.

Questions 20–23 Error Alert The choice of an open or closed circle on inequality graphs is hard for some students. It is easy to forget about this detail after thinking hard about the other parts of the graph. Remind students to check their work by rereading the inequality and comparing it to the graph.

Question 32 Error Alert Since this question is quite different from anything else in the lesson, be sure students understand the question. Some students may quickly write the answer as $A < 500$. These students need to review the meaning of *rounding up*. Then, they must decide that any number over 400, but not including 400, up to and including 500 will work. Finally, this information must be written as an inequality and graphed. If students still have trouble, isolate the steps causing the difficulty.

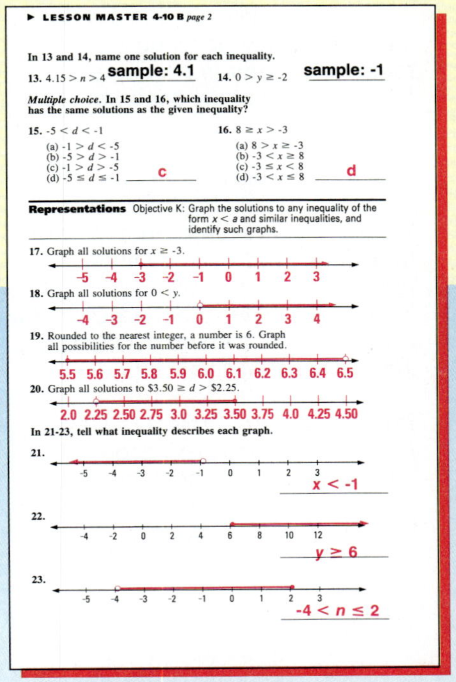

▶ LESSON MASTER 4-10 B *page 2*

In 13 and 14, name one solution for each inequality.

13. $4.15 > n > 4$ sample: 4.1

14. $0 > y \geq -2$ sample: -1

***Multiple choice.* In 15 and 16, which inequality has the same solutions as the given inequality?**

15. $-5 < d < -1$
(a) $-1 > d < -5$
(b) $-5 > d > -1$
(c) $-1 > d > -5$
(d) $-5 \leq d \leq -1$ c

16. $8 \geq x > -3$
(a) $8 > x \geq -3$
(b) $-3 < x \geq 8$
(c) $-3 \leq x < 8$
(d) $-3 < x \leq 8$ d

Representations Objective K: Graph the solutions to any inequality of the form $x < a$ and similar inequalities, and identify such graphs.

17. Graph all solutions for $x \geq -3$.
-5 -4 -3 -2 -1 0 1 2 3

18. Graph all solutions for $0 < y$.
-4 -3 -2 -1 0 1 2 3 4

19. Rounded to the nearest integer, a number is 6. Graph all possibilities for the number before it was rounded.
5.5 5.6 5.7 5.8 5.9 6.0 6.1 6.2 6.3 6.4 6.5

20. Graph all solutions to $\$3.50 \geq d > \$2.25$.
2.0 2.25 2.50 2.75 3.0 3.25 3.50 3.75 4.0 4.25 4.50

In 21-23, tell what inequality describes each graph.

21. -5 -4 -3 -2 -1 0 1 2 3
$x < -1$

22. -4 -2 0 2 4 6 8 10 12
$y \geq 6$

23. -5 -4 -3 -2 -1 0 1 2 3
$-4 < n \leq 2$

Adapting to Individual Needs

English Language Development

Materials: Index cards

Students with limited English proficiency may understand the concepts of this lesson but have trouble translating the symbols. You might suggest that they write a symbol on one side of an index card and the English translation on the other side. They might also draw a picture to help them distinguish *greater than*, *less than*, and *equal to*.

Bigger than More than Greater than	Smaller than Less than	Same as Equal to

Follow-up for Lesson 4-10

Practice

For more questions on SPUR Objectives, use **Lesson Master 4-10A** (shown on page 225) or **Lesson Master 4-10B** (shown on pages 226–227).

Assessment

Group Assessment For this assessment, **students work in groups of 4.** Each student needs a recording sheet to show his or her graph and a slip of paper that is passed around the group. Each student writes his or her name and an inequality on a slip of paper. Then the slips are exchanged until each student in the group has graphed each inequality. Finally, the students compare their graphs. You might suggest that students each make a recording sheet by folding a piece of paper in fourths, writing a group member's name in each section, and drawing the corresponding graph in that section. [Students graph the solutions to any simple inequality accurately.] Reverse the procedure by having students draw graphs of inequalities on slips of paper and then write the corresponding inequalities on the recording sheets. [Students correctly write inequalities represented by graphs.]

Extension

Writing Have students write inequalities that describe all classroom temperatures t in degrees Fahrenheit that they think would be

a. too hot. [Sample: $t > 75°$]
b. too cold. [Sample: $t < 65°$]
c. comfortable. [$65 \le t \le 75°$]

Then you might have students **work in groups,** and try to think of other real-world situations that involve inequalities. Have them describe the situations in writing, and include the inequalities they think apply.

Project Update Project 5, *Using Inequality Symbols,* on page 230, relates to the content of this lesson. Students choosing this project can begin writing their stories.

33. Let P be a probability.
a. Write an inequality showing all possible values of P. $0 \le P \le 1$
b. Graph the inequality.

Review

In 34–36, suppose it costs 30¢ for the first minute and 18¢ for each additional minute on a long-distance phone call. Then $c = .30 + .18(m - 1)$, where c is the total cost and m is the number of minutes talked. *(Lessons 4-5, 4-9)*

34. Calculate c when $m = 6$. **$1.20**

35. What will it cost to talk for 10 minutes? **$1.92**

36. *Multiple choice.* For $2.10, how long can you talk?
(a) 7 minutes (b) 9 minutes
(c) 10 minutes (d) 11 minutes **(d)**

37. If the probability that an event will occur is x, what is the probability it will not occur? *(Lesson 4-8)* **1 – x**

In 38 and 39, evaluate the expression when $a = 3$, $b = 5$, and $c = 7$. *(Lessons 4-4, 4-5, 4-6)*

38. $3(c + 10b - a^2)$ **144**

39. $a[a + b(b + c)]$ **189**

40. Give three instances of this pattern: There are $6n$ legs on n insects. *(Lesson 4-2)* **Sample: There are 6 · 3 legs on 3 insects. There are 6 · 108 legs on 108 insects. There are 6 · 1 million legs on 1 million insects.**

41. Three instances of a general pattern are given. Describe the pattern using two variables. *(Lesson 4-2)*

$\frac{31.4}{2} \cdot \frac{2}{31.4} = 1$ $\frac{7}{8} \cdot \frac{8}{7} = 1$ $\frac{100}{11} \cdot \frac{11}{100} = 1$

$\frac{a}{b} \cdot \frac{b}{a} = 1$

ET, phone home.
Imagine ET's phone bill if he were charged by the kilometer for his very long-distance phone call!

Exploration

42. Describe a real-life situation that can lead to each inequality. The letter used is a hint to one possible description.
a. $13 \le a \le 19$ **b.** $w > 250$ **c.** $d > 1.5$
Samples: a) a is the age of a teenager. b) The weight of that football player is greater than 250 pounds. c) If you live more than 1.5 miles from school, you can take the school bus for no cost.

Adapting to Individual Needs

Challenge
Have students study the following open sentences. Then have them determine if the sentences are *always true, sometimes true,* or *never true.* Remind students to try negative as well as positive replacements for the variables.

1. If $x < y$, then $x + a < y + a$.
[always true]

2. If $x > y$, then $x + y > x - y$.
[sometimes true]

3. If $x < y$ and $y < z$, then $x < z$.
[always true]

4. If $x < 0$ and $y < 0$, then $x + y > x - y$.
[never true]

Now have students make up three open sentences: one that is always true; one that is sometimes true; and one that is never true.

PROJECTS 4 CHAPTER FOUR

A project presents an opportunity for you to extend your knowledge of a topic related to the material of this chapter. You should allow more time for a project than you do for typical homework questions.

1 The Bricklayer's Formula

The formula $N = 7LH$ gives the number of bricks needed in a wall of length L feet and height H feet. Go with a tape measure to a brick building in your neighborhood. Consider a part of the wall with length and height that you should call L and H. How many bricks are in that part of the wall? Does the formula $N = 7LH$ work for that part of the wall? Try other parts of the wall. If the formula does not work, suggest a formula that will work for this wall.

2 A Parentheses Problem

Consider the subtraction problem $4 - 2 - 1$. Parentheses can be placed in two different places and the answer you get is different. $(4 - 2) - 1 = 1$ but $4 - (2 - 1) = 3$. How many different answers can you get by placing parentheses in $8 - 4 - 2 - 1$? Be careful—you can use more than one set of parentheses and you can put parentheses inside other parentheses. How many different answers can you get by placing parentheses in $16 - 8 - 4 - 2 - 1$? Write down any patterns you see in the answers you get, and use them to predict how many answers you might get for $32 - 16 - 8 - 4 - 2 - 1$.

3 Arithmetic Time Line

On page 175 dates are given for the invention of many of the symbols of arithmetic. Organize this information on a number line of dates (known as a time line). On this time line, put dates of at least ten other important events that happened around these times. Make your time line big enough so that it is easy for someone else to see and read. (You may need to use poster board.)

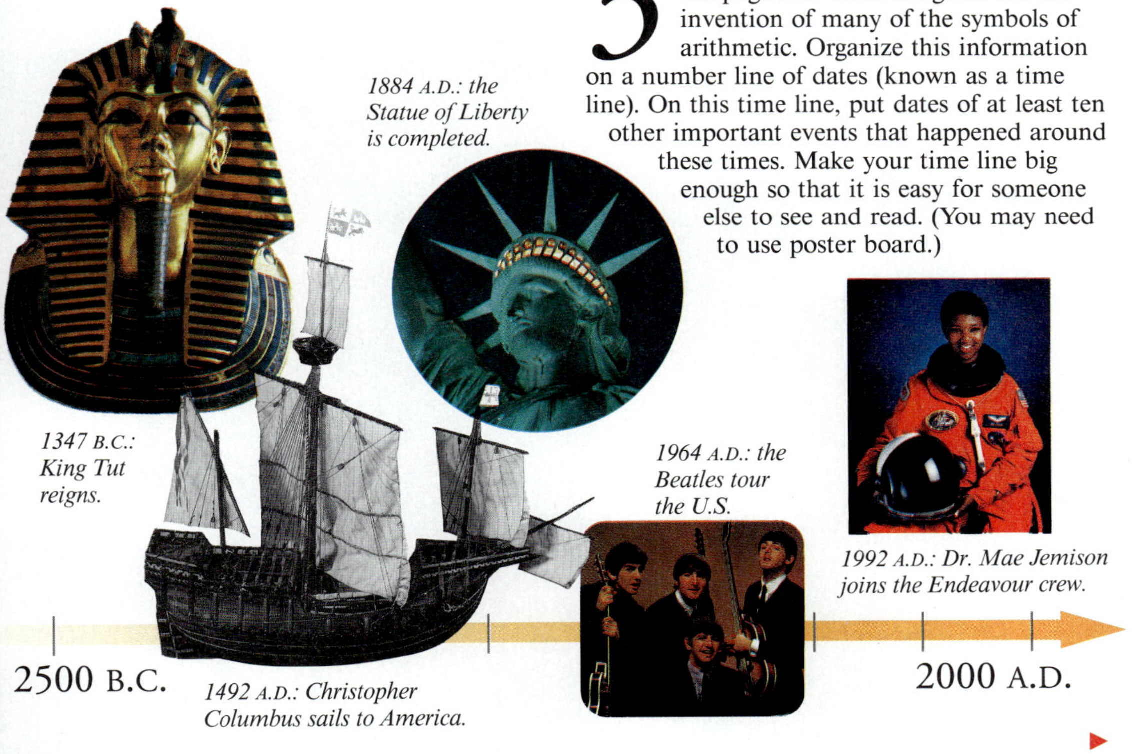

Chapter 4 Projects

Chapter 4 projects relate to the content of the lessons as follows.

Project	Lesson(s)
1	4-7
2	4-5, 4-6
3	4-1
4	4-8
5	4-10
6	4-2, 4-9

1 The Bricklayer's Formula You might tell students that a standard brick is 8 inches ($\frac{2}{3}$ feet) long and 2.5 inches ($\frac{5}{24}$ feet) wide. The bricklayer's formula will provide a good estimate of the number of standard bricks needed.

2 A Parentheses Problem Suggest that students systematically vary the placement of parentheses and the number of subtractions that the parentheses enclose, as well as the number of pairs of parentheses. If students need help getting started with $8 - 4 - 2 - 1$, you might want to discuss the use of more than one set of parentheses, $(8 - 4) - (2 - 1)$, and the use of nested parentheses, $8 - ((4 - 2) - 1) = 7$. Once students see a pattern, they will need to examine every possible combination of parentheses only to check. Encourage students to express the patterns they see by using variables.

3 Arithmetic Time Line You may want students to put the dates of invention of arithmetic symbols on one side of the time line and the ten other important events on the other side. Students may use the chronological tables found in history books, encyclopedias, or almanacs, as sources for the events they add to the line.

Possible responses

1. **The work might include a picture or drawing of the wall measured, perhaps including the number of rows of bricks. Students should indicate how they counted the number of bricks in the wall. How did they count partial bricks? Formulas suggested by students working with other units and nonstandard brick sizes may vary considerably.**

Responses continue on page 230.

4 An Experiment with Dice To determine whether or not the dice are fair, students determine the relative frequency of each of the numbers 1 through 6, and compare that with the probability of $\frac{1}{6}$. The dice should be considered fair if the relative frequencies are close to $\frac{1}{6}$. Let students discuss and judge how far off relative frequencies may be before considering them unfair, and then support their arguments for fairness or unfairness.

5 Using Inequality Symbols To motivate students, have them brainstorm ideas that focus on quantities, on degrees of personal values, or on degrees of skills. You could initiate the brainstorming by suggesting topics such as money, physical objects, love, food consumption, musical talent, or special movie effects.

6 The Beginning of Algebra Recommend the use of mathematics history books as sources. Encyclopedias provide succinct, limited information, so do not be surprised if several students turn in similar reports. Have students name their sources.

PROJECTS 4 *(continued)*

4 An Experiment with Dice

Test whether some dice you have are fair. Pick one die and toss it at least 100 times, recording the number that comes up each time. Count the number of times that 1, 2, 3, 4, 5, and 6 each come up. Compare the relative frequencies with the probability $\frac{1}{6}$ that these numbers would come up if your die was fair. Repeat this experiment with another die. Do you think your dice are fair? Explain why you think the way you do.

5 Using Inequality Symbols

Write a short true or fantasy story in which you use all of the inequality symbols ($\neq$, $<$, $\leq$, $>$, $\geq$). You might write about a place to visit, a sports event, or a type of vacation.

6 The Beginning of Algebra

Among the people who contributed to the beginnings of algebra were a Greek, Diophantus, and an Arab, al-Khowarizmi. Look in an encyclopedia or other reference book and write a short essay about each of these great mathematicians.

Additional responses, page 229.

2. Responses may vary. Many students will find that the expression $8 - 4 - 2 - 1$ yields four different values when the position of the parentheses is varied: 1, 3, 5, and 7. For $16 - 8 - 4 - 2 - 1$ there are 8 different values: 1, 3, 5, 7, 9, 11, 13, and 15. Some students will describe their findings as the odd integers 1 through 7 and 1 through 15, respectively. Students with a greater level of understanding might describe one or both of the following patterns: each solution is the set of odd integers 1, 3, 5, . . ., $2^n - 1$ where 2^n is the first number in the given expression. The number of different values possible for the given expression is 2^{n-1}, half the value of the first number in the expression. For instance, the expression $32 - 16 - 8 - 4 - 2 - 1$ has 16 different possible values: 1, 3, 5, . . . , 31.

SUMMARY

A variable is a symbol that can stand for any one set of numbers or other objects. Usually a variable is a single letter. Algebra is the study of variables and operations on them. An algebraic expression is an expression with one or more variables in it. Algebraic expressions are often found in equations and inequalities.

Numerical and algebraic expressions may contain a number of operations. To avoid confusion, mathematicians have agreed upon rules for order of operations. To operate in an order different from that given by these rules, parentheses and other grouping symbols are used.

Introduced in this chapter are four uses of variables:

(1) Variables enable *patterns* to be described. For example, n people have $2n$ eyes. Descriptions with variables tend to be shorter and look like the instances of the pattern.

(2) Variables describe *properties* of numbers. For example, $a + b = b + a$.

(3) Variables are shorthand for quantities in *formulas.* For example, $A = \ell w$ is shorthand for area = length × width. $P = \frac{E}{N}$ gives the probability P that an event will occur if a situation has N equally likely possible outcomes, of which E are included in the event.

(4) Variables may be *unknowns.* For instance, suppose the area of a rectangle is 4 square meters and its length is 3 meters. Then the width w is the solution to the equation $4 = 3w$. The value of w can be found by solving this sentence.

VOCABULARY

You should be able to give a general description and a specific example of each of the following ideas.

Lesson 4-1
symbols +, −, ×, /, and so on, for operations
numerical expression
value
evaluating an expression
order of operations

Lesson 4-2
pattern
instance
variable
symbol · for multiplication
algebra

Lesson 4-3
algebraic expression

Lesson 4-4
value of a variable
value of an expression

Lesson 4-5
parentheses, ( )
nested parentheses

Lesson 4-6
grouping symbols
brackets, [ ]
mean, average

Lesson 4-7
formula
one variable in terms of others

Lesson 4-8
frequency, relative frequency
probability
outcome
event
random
fair, unbiased

Lesson 4-9
equation
open sentence
solution
unknown
solving an open sentence

Lesson 4-10
inequality symbols ≤, ≥, ≠

Summary

The Summary gives an overview of the entire chapter and provides an opportunity for students to consider the material as a whole. Thus, the Summary can be used to help students relate and unify the concepts presented in the chapter.

Vocabulary

Terms, symbols, and properties are listed by lesson to provide a checklist of concepts a student must know. Emphasize to students that they should carefully read the vocabulary list before starting the Progress Self-Test. If students do not understand the meaning of a term, they should refer back to the indicated lesson.

3. In addition to the dates of the invention of the symbols given on page 176, the time line might include dates of discoveries or inventions, world disasters, or significant social, political, or economic events. Some sample dates follow.

1215 - Magna Carta
1286 - Invention of eyeglasses
1348 - Black plague
1453 - Fall of Constantinople
1492 - Columbus sails to America
1620 - Plymouth Rock
1679 - Writ of Habeas Corpus
1789 - French Revolution
1863 - Emancipation Proclamation
1917 - Russian Revolution

4. Results of tests nearly always show that the dice are fair. Students might tend to limit the range of results they would find acceptable; generally, any frequencies between 11 and 22 out of 100 tosses are considered as within an acceptable range.

Responses continue on page 232.

CHAPTER FOUR

Progress Self-Test

For the development of mathematical competence, feedback and correction, along with the opportunity to practice, are necessary. The Progress Self-Test provides the opportunity for feedback and correction; the Chapter Review provides additional opportunities and practice. We cannot overemphasize the importance of these end-of-chapter materials. It is at this point that the material "gels" for many students, allowing them to solidify skills and understanding. In general, student performance should be markedly improved after these pages.

Assign the Progress Self-Test as a one-night assignment. Worked-out *solutions* for all questions are in the Selected Answers section of the student book. Encourage students to honestly take the Progress Self-Test grade themselves, and then be prepared to discuss the test in class.

Advise students to pay special attention to those Chapter Review questions (pages 233–235) which correspond to questions missed on the Progress Self-Test.

Answers

26. Any number between -5 and -4 is a solution. Some are $-4.2, -4.9, -4\frac{1}{2}$.

27. Units in formulas must be consistent for the answer to make sense. For example, to find the area of a rectangle given the dimensions of the length and the width, if $w = 3$ inches and $l = 4$ feet, the area A cannot be 12 of either unit, even though $A = lw$.

29.

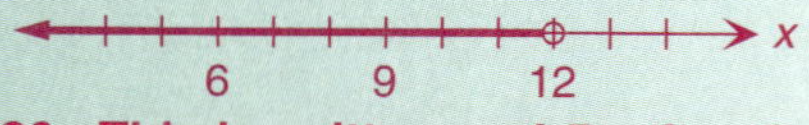

30. This is written as $4.5 \le k < 6$

31. Samples: If your age is 10 years, your sister is 10 – 5 or 5 years. If you age is 14, your sister's age is 14 – 5 or 9 years.

32. Samples: $30 + 2 - 30 = 2$; $7.3 + 6.2 - 7.3 = 6.2$.

PROGRESS SELF-TEST

Take this test as you would take a test in class. You will need a ruler. Then check your work with the solutions in the Selected Answers section in the back of the book.

See margin for answers not shown below.

In 1–4, evaluate the expression.

1. $6 + 8 \cdot 7 + 9$ **71** **2.** $(40-5)+(60-10)$ **85**

3. $75 - 50 - 3 - 1$ **21** **4.** $5 + 3 \cdot 4^2$ **53**

5. Round to the nearest integer: $\frac{100 + 2 \cdot 5}{10 + 5}$. **7**

In 6–8, evaluate when $a = 3$, $b = 4$, $x = 10$, and $y = 100$.

6. $x + 3y$ **310** **7.** $(a + b)(b - a)$ **7**

8. $y + 5[y + 4(y + 3)]$ **2660**

9. *Multiple choice.* Which is a solution to $(4x)^2 = 64$? **(a)**
(a) 2 (b) 4 (c) 8 (d) 16

In 10–12, three instances of a pattern are given. Describe the pattern using variables.

10. Use one variable. **$10 \cdot a = 6 \cdot a + 4 \cdot a$**
$10 \cdot 5 = 6 \cdot 5 + 4 \cdot 5$
$10 \cdot 8.2 = 6 \cdot 8.2 + 4 \cdot 8.2$
$10 \cdot 0.04 = 6 \cdot 0.04 + 4 \cdot 0.04$

11. Use two variables. **$a + b = b + a$**
$2 + 8 = 8 + 2$
$3.7 + 7.3 = 7.3 + 3.7$
$0 + 4 = 4 + 0$

12. Use one variable.
In one year, we expect the town to grow by 200 people.
In two years, we expect the town to grow by $2 \cdot 200$ people.
In three years, we expect the town to grow by $3 \cdot 200$ people. **In y years, we expect the town to grow by $y \cdot 200$ people.**

In 13 and 14, the formula $c = 23n + 6$ gives the cost of first-class postage in 1993; c is the cost in cents; n is the weight in ounces of the mail, rounded up to the nearest ounce.

13. If $n = 5$, find c. **121¢ or $1.21**

14. Find the cost in dollars and cents of mailing a 9-oz letter first-class. **$2.13**

15. In the formula $p = s - c$, calculate p if $s = \$45$ and $c = \$22.37$. **$22.63**

In 16–19, translate into a numerical or algebraic expression or sentence.

16. the product of twelve and sixteen **12×16**

17. forty is less than forty-seven **$40 < 47$**

18. a number is greater than or equal to zero **$n \ge 0$**

19. a number is divided into nine **$\frac{9}{a}$**

20. *Multiple choice.* Written on one line, $\frac{W}{W + L}$ is equal to:
(a) $W/W + L$ (b) $W/(W + L)$
(c) $(W/W) + L$ (d) $(W + L)/W$ **(b)**

21. *Multiple choice.* Most of the symbols we use for arithmetic operations were invented
(a) before 1 A.D.
(b) between 1 and 1000 A.D.
(c) between 1000 and 1800 A.D.
(d) since 1800 A.D. **(c)**

22. Suppose a box landed face up 8 of the first 50 times it was dropped. What is the relative frequency that the box landed face up? **$\frac{8}{50}$ or .16**

23. In the band, 5 boys and 7 girls play clarinet. If the director chooses 1 of these students at random to play a solo, what is the probability that the student will be a boy? **$\frac{5}{12}$ or $.41\overline{6}$**

24. *Multiple choice.* A sentence that means the same as $2 < y$ is
(a) $2 \le y$. (b) $y > 2$.
(c) $y \ge 2$. (d) $y < 2$. **(b)**

In 25 and 26, find a solution to the sentence.

25. $6x = 42$ **7** **26.** $-5 < y < -4$

27. Why must units in formulas be consistent? Give an example to support your answer.

28. If $x = 7y$ and $y = 3$, what is the value of x? **21**

29. Graph all solutions to $x < 12$.

30. Below are the solutions to what sentence? **$4.5 \le k < 6$**

In 31 and 32, give two instances of the pattern.

31. If your age is A years, your sister's age is $A - 5$ years.

32. $x + y - x = y$

Additional responses, page 229.

5. Students' stories will differ greatly in length, plot, quality of the writing, and any other dimension you might wish to examine. Look for each of the inequality symbols. You might wish to allow some latitude in how these symbols are interpreted in the story. Remember that this is the first time many students will have used such symbols.

6. The following information is a sample of what students might include in their projects. Students might present part or all of the information; some may include additional information. Diophantus of Alexandria (c. 200 A.D.) wrote *Arithmetica,* a collection of 150 application-type algebra problems and their solutions. He introduced abbreviated notation and algebraic symbols. Al-Khowarizmi published

232

 CHAPTER FOUR

CHAPTER REVIEW

Questions on SPUR Objectives

SPUR stands for **S**kills, **P**roperties, **U**ses, and **R**epresentations. The Chapter Review questions are grouped according to the SPUR Objectives for this chapter.

SKILLS DEAL WITH THE PROCEDURES USED TO GET ANSWERS.

Objective A. *Use order of operations to evaluate numerical expressions.* *(Lessons 4-1, 4-5, 4-6)*

In 1–14, evaluate the given expression.

1. $235-5\times4$ **215**

2. $32\div16\div8\times12$ **3**

3. $2+3^4$ **83**

4. $4\times2^3+\frac{28}{56}$ **32.5**

5. $5+8\times3+2$ **31**

6. $100-\frac{80}{5}-1$ **83**

7. $1984-(1947-1929)$

8. $40-30/(20-10/2)$ **38**

9. $6+8(12+7)$ **158**

10. $(6+3)(6-4)$ **18**

11. $3+[2+4(6-3\cdot2)]$ **5**

12. $4[7-2(2+1)]$ **4**

13. $\frac{4+5\cdot2}{13\cdot5}$ $\frac{14}{65}=0.215\ldots$

14. $\frac{3^3}{3^2}$ **3**

7) 1966

Objective B. *Evaluate algebraic expressions given the values of all variables.* *(Lessons 4-4, 4-5, 4-6)*

15. If $x = 4$, then $6x = \underline{\ ?\ }$. **24**

16. If $m = 7$, evaluate $3m + (m + 2)$. **30**

17. Find the value of $2 + a + 11$ when $a = 5$. **18**

18. Find the value of $3x^2$ when $x = 10$. **300**

19. Evaluate $2(a + b - c)$ when $a = 11$, $b = 10$, and $c = 9$. **24**

20. Find the value of $x^3 + 2^y$ when $x = 5$ and $y = 5$. **157**

21. Evaluate $(3m + 5)(2m - 4)$ when $m = 6$. **184**

22. Evaluate $(3m + 5) - (2m - 4)$ when $m = 6$. **15**

23. Evaluate $\frac{3a + 2b}{2a + 4b}$ when $a = 1$ and $b = 2.5$.

24. Find the value of $x + [1 + x(2 + x)]$ when $x = 7$. **71**

23) $\frac{8}{12}$ **or** $.\overline{6}$

Objective C. *Find solutions to equations and inequalities involving simple arithmetic.* *(Lessons 4-9, 4-10)*

25. *Multiple choice.* Which of these is a solution to $3x + 11 = 26$?
(a) 15 (b) 5 (c) 45 (d) 37 **(b)**

26. *Multiple choice.* Which of these is a solution to $y > -5$?
(a) -4 (b) -5 (c) -6 (d) -7 **(a)**

27. Find a solution to $3x = 12$. **4**

28. Find a solution to $100 - t = 99$. **1**

29. What is a solution to $y + 8 = 10$? **2**

30. What value of m works in $20 = m \cdot 4$? **5**

PROPERTIES DEAL WITH THE PRINCIPLES BEHIND THE MATHEMATICS.

Objective D. *Know the correct order of operations.* *(Lessons 4-1, 4-5, 4-6)*

31. An expression contains only two operations, a powering and a multiplication. Which should you do first? **powering**

32. *True or false.* If an expression contains nested parentheses, you should work the outside parentheses first. **False**

33) (d)

33. *Multiple choice.* Written on one line, $\frac{30+5}{30-5} =$
(a) $30 + 5/30 - 5$. (b) $(30 + 5)/30 - 5$.
(c) $30 + 5/(30 - 5)$. (d) $(30 + 5)/(30 - 5)$.

34. *Multiple choice.* In which expression can the grouping symbols be removed without changing its value?
(a) $10 - (7 - 2)$ (b) $(4 \cdot 87 \cdot 0) + 5$
(c) $10/(5 - 2^2)/2$ (d) $(9 \cdot 3)^2$ **(b)**

Chapter 4 Review

Resources

From the ***Teacher's Resource File***

- Answer Master for Chapter 4 Review
- Assessment Sourcebook: Chapter 4 Test, Forms A–D Chapter 4 Test, Cumulative Form

Additional Resources

- Quiz and Test Writer

The main objectives for the chapter are organized in the Chapter Review under the four types of understanding this book promotes—Skills, Properties, Uses, and Representations.

Whereas end-of-chapter material may be considered optional in some texts, in *Transition Mathematics* we have selected these objectives and questions with the expectation that they will be covered. Students should be able to answer these questions with about 85% accuracy after studying the chapter.

You may assign these questions over a single night to help students prepare for a test the next day, or you may assign the questions over a two-day period. If you work the questions over two days, then we recommend assigning the *evens* for homework the first night so that students get feedback in class the next day, and assigning the *odds* the night before the test, because answers are provided to the odd-numbered questions.

It is effective to ask students which questions they still do not understand, and use the day or days as a total class discussion of the material which the class finds most difficult.

the first extensive work in modern elementary algebra, *Hisab al-jabr w'al-muqabala,* about 830 A.D. Unlike Diophantus, Al-Khowarizmi proved general equations and denoted numbers and operations and variables in everyday language.

Assessment

Evaluation The *Assessment Sourcebook* provides five forms of the Chapter 4 Test. Forms A and B present parallel versions in a short-answer format. Forms C and D offer performance assessment. The fifth test is Chapter 4 Test, Cumulative Form. About 50% of this test covers Chapter 4, 25% of it covers Chapter 3, and 25% of it covers earlier chapters.

For information on grading, see *General Teaching Suggestions: Grading* in the *Professional Sourcebook* which begins on page T20 in Volume 1 of the Teacher's Edition.

Additional Answers

38. Sample: $5(3 + 4) = 5 \cdot 3 + 5 \cdot 4$;

39. Sample: $2 + 6 = 1 + 6 + 1$; $2 + .5 = 1 + .5 + 1$; $2 + \frac{1}{20} = 1 + \frac{1}{20} + 1$

40. Sample: $2 \cdot 4 - 3 = 4 \cdot 2 - 3$; $6 \cdot \frac{1}{3} - \frac{1}{2} = \frac{1}{3} \cdot 6 - \frac{1}{2}$

CHAPTER FOUR

Objective E. *Given instances of a pattern, write a description of the pattern using variables.* *(Lesson 4-2)*

35. Three instances of a pattern are given. Describe the general pattern using one variable. $5 \cdot x + 9 \cdot x = 14 \cdot x$

$$5 \cdot 12 + 9 \cdot 12 = 14 \cdot 12$$
$$5 \cdot 88 + 9 \cdot 88 = 14 \cdot 88$$
$$5 \cdot \pi + 9 \cdot \pi = 14 \cdot \pi$$

36. Three instances of a pattern are given. Describe the general pattern using three variables. $a + b - c = a - c + b$

$$6 + 7 - 8 = 6 - 8 + 7$$
$$10.2 + 0.5 - 0.22 = 10.2 - 0.22 + 0.5$$
$$30\% + 10\% - 20\% = 30\% - 20\% + 10\%$$

37. Four instances of a pattern are given. Describe the general pattern using two variables.

$$\frac{1}{9} + \frac{5}{9} = \frac{1 + 5}{9} \qquad \frac{0}{9} + \frac{25}{9} = \frac{0 + 25}{9}$$
$$\frac{11}{9} + \frac{44}{9} = \frac{11 + 44}{9} \qquad \frac{9}{9} + \frac{9}{9} = \frac{9 + 9}{9}$$

$\frac{a}{9} + \frac{b}{9} = \frac{a + b}{9}$

Objective F. *Give instances of a pattern described with variables.* *(Lesson 4-2)*

38. Give two instances of the pattern $5(x + y) = 5x + 5y$.

39. Give three instances of the pattern $2 + A = 1 + A + 1$.

40. Give two instances of the pattern $ab - c = ba - c$.

38–40) See page 235.

USES DEAL WITH APPLICATIONS OF MATHEMATICS IN REAL SITUATIONS.

Objective G. *Given instances of a real-world pattern, write a description of the pattern using variables.* *(Lesson 4-2)*

41. Three instances of a pattern are given. Describe the general pattern using variables.

If the weight is 5 ounces, the postage is 5¢ + 5 · 20¢.
If the weight is 3 ounces, the postage is 5¢ + 3 · 20¢.
If the weight is 1 ounce, the postage is 5¢ + 1 · 20¢. See below.

42. Four instances of a pattern are given. Describe the general pattern using variables.

One person has 10 fingers.
Two people have 2 · 10 fingers.
Seven people have 7 · 10 fingers.
One hundred people have 100 · 10 fingers.
p people have *p* · 10 fingers.

Objective H. *Write a numerical or algebraic expression for an English expression involving arithmetic operations.* *(Lesson 4-3)*

In 43–46, translate into mathematical symbols.

43. the sum of eighteen and twenty-seven $18 + 27$

44. fifteen less than one hundred thousand

45. the product of four and twenty, decreased by one $4 \cdot 20 - 1$ 44) $100{,}000 - 15$

46. seven less six $7 - 6$

41) If the weight is *w* ounces, the postage is 5¢ + *w* · 20¢.

In 47–50, translate into an algebraic expression.

47. seven more than twice a number $2x + 7$

48. a number divided by six, the quotient decreased by three $\frac{n}{6} - 3$

49. A number is less than five. $x < 5$

50. the product of thirty-nine and a number $39n$

Objective I. *Calculate the value of a variable, given the values of other variables in a formula.* *(Lesson 4-7)*

51. The formula $I = 100m/c$ is sometimes used to measure a person's IQ. The IQ is *I*, mental age is *m*, and chronological age is *c*. What is *I* if $m = 7$ and $c = 5.5$? ≈ 127

52. The formula $F = 1.8C + 32$ relates Fahrenheit (*F*) and Celsius (*C*) temperature. If *C* is 10, what is *F*? 50

53. The formula $A = bh$ gives the area *A* of a parallelogram in terms of its base *b* and height *h*. What is the area of a parallelogram with base 1 foot and height 6 inches?

54. The formula $C = 0.6n + 4$ estimates the temperature *C* in degrees Celsius when *n* is the number of cricket chirps in 15 seconds. If a cricket chirps 25 times in 15 seconds, what is an estimate for the temperature? 19°C

53) 72 in^2 or .5 ft^2

CHAPTER FOUR

Objective J. *Calculate probabilities and relative frequencies in a situation with known numbers of outcomes.* *(Lesson 4-8)*

55. What is the largest value that a probability can have? **1**

56. If an experiment has 3 equally likely outcomes, what is the probability of each outcome? $\frac{1}{3}$ **or** $.\overline{3}$

57. A grab bag has 10 prizes. Two are calculators. If you choose a prize without looking, what is the probability you will select a calculator? $\frac{2}{10}$ **or .2**

58. Fifty slips of paper numbered 1 to 50 are placed in a hat. A person picks a slip of paper out of the hat. What is the probability that the number on the slip ends in 4?

59. A coin was tossed 30 times and 16 times landed heads up. What was the relative frequency of *tails?* $\frac{14}{30}$ **or** $.4\overline{6}$ **58)** $\frac{5}{50}$ **or .1**

60. A survey of 200 voters after an election indicated that 105 of them voted for the Republican candidate, 60 for the Democrat, and 35 for others. What is the relative frequency that a voter in this survey voted Democrat? $\frac{60}{200}$ **or .3**

REPRESENTATIONS DEAL WITH PICTURES, GRAPHS, OR OBJECTS THAT ILLUSTRATE CONCEPTS.

Objective K. *Graph the solutions to any inequality of the form $x < a$ and similar inequalities, and identify such graphs.* *(Lesson 4-10)*

61. The solutions to what sentence are graphed here? $x \ge 2$ **or** $2 \le x$

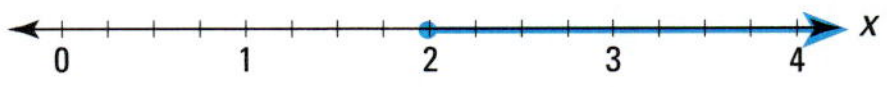

62. The solutions to what sentence are graphed here? $0 < y \le 3$ **or** $3 \ge y > 0$

38) Sample: $5(3 + 4) = 5 \cdot 3 + 5 \cdot 4$; $5(.6 + 1.3) = 5 \cdot .6 + 5 \cdot 1.3$

In 63–68, graph all solutions to the sentence on a number line.

63. $x < 24$

64. $y > 2$

65. $-4 \ge t$

66. $6 \le d$

67. $3 < x < 7$

68. $-1 > y \ge -2$

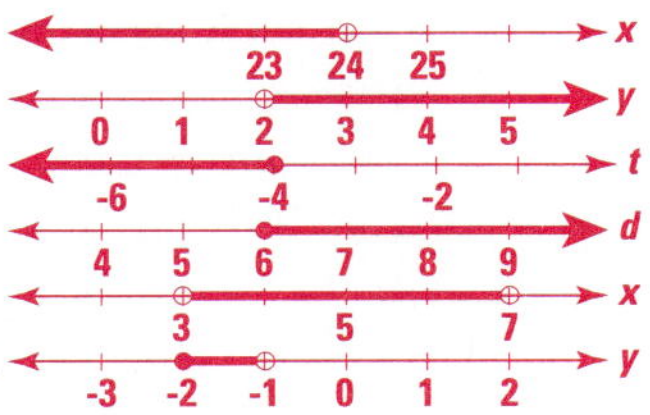

39) Sample: $2 + 6 = 1 + 6 + 1$; $2 + .5 = 1 + .5 + 1$; $2 + \frac{1}{20} = 1 + \frac{1}{20} + 1$

40) Sample: $2 \cdot 4 - 3 = 4 \cdot 2 - 3$; $6 \cdot \frac{1}{3} - \frac{1}{2} = \frac{1}{3} \cdot 6 - \frac{1}{2}$

CULTURE DEALS WITH THE PEOPLES AND THE HISTORY RELATED TO THE DEVELOPMENT OF MATHEMATICAL IDEAS.

Objective L. *Give rough dates and names of people for key ideas in arithmetic and algebra notation.* *(Lessons 4-1, 4-2)*

69. Write two arithmetic symbols used by computers but not much elsewhere. **Sample: *, ^**

70. *Multiple choice.* Who is sometimes called the "father of algebra"?
(a) Jacques Cousteau (b) Albert Einstein
(c) François Viète (d) Augustin-Louis Cauchy
(c)

Setting Up Lesson 5-1

We recommend that you assign Lesson 5-1, both reading and some questions, for homework the evening of the test. It gives students work to do after they have completed the test and keeps the class moving. If you do not do this consistently after tests, you may cover one less *chapter* over the course of the year.

Chapter 5 Planner

Adapting to Individual Needs

The student text is written for the vast majority of students. The chart at the right suggests two pacing plans to accommodate the needs of your students. Students in the Full Course should complete the entire text by the end of the year. Students in the Minimal Course will spend more time when there are quizzes and more time on the Chapter Review. Therefore, these students may not complete all of the chapters in the text.

Options are also presented to meet the needs of a variety of teaching and learning styles. For each lesson, the Teacher's Edition provides sections entitled: *Video* which describes video segments and related questions that can be used for motivation or extension; *Optional Activities* which suggests activities that employ materials, physical models, technology, and cooperative learning; and *Adapting to Individual Needs* which regularly includes **Challenge** problems, **English Language Development** suggestions, and suggestions for providing **Extra Help.** The Teacher's Edition also frequently includes an **Error Alert,** an **Extension,** and an **Assessment** alternative. The options available in Chapter 5 are summarized in the chart below.

Chapter 5 Pacing Chart

Day	Full Course	Minimal Course
1	5-1	5-1
2	5-2	5-2
3	5-3	5-3
4	5-4	5-4
5	Quiz*; 5-5	Quiz*; begin 5-5.
6	5-6	Finish 5-5.
7	5-7	5-6
8	5-8	5-7
9	Quiz*; 5-9	5-8
10	5-10	Quiz*; begin 5-9.
11	Self-Test	Finish 5-9.
12	Review	5-10
13	Test*	Self-Test
14		Review
15		Review
16		Test*

*in the Teacher's Resource File

In the Teacher's Edition...

Lesson	Optional Activities	Extra Help	Challenge	English Language Development	Error Alert	Extension	Cooperative Learning	Ongoing Assessment
5-1	●	●	●	●		●		Written
5-2	●	●	●	●		●	●	Group
5-3	●	●	●		●	●		Written/Oral
5-4	●	●		●		●	●	Oral
5-5	●	●	●	●	●	●	●	Oral/Written
5-6	●	●	●	●		●		Written
5-7	●	●	●	●		●	●	Group
5-8	●	●	●	●		●	●	Written
5-9	●	●	●	●		●		Written
5-10	●	●	●	●	●	●	●	Oral

In the Additional Resources...

	In the Teacher's Resource File								
Lesson	Lesson Masters, A and B	Teaching Aids*	Activity Kit*	Answer Masters	Technology Sourcebook	Assessment Sourcebook	Visual Aids**	Transition Mathematics Software	Video Segments
5-1	5-1	49, 52		5-1			49, 52, AM		
5-2	5-2	49		5-2			49, AM		
5-3	5-3	49	10	5-3			49, AM		5-3
In-class Activity				5-4			AM		
5-4	5-4	50, 53–55		5-4	Comp 7	Quiz	50, 53–55, AM	Geometry	
5-5	5-5	50		5-5			50, AM		
5-6	5-6	50, 56		5-6			50, 56, AM	Graphing/Probability	
5-7	5-7	51		5-7			51, AM		
5-8	5-8	51, 57	11	5-8		Quiz	51, 57, AM		
5-9	5-9	51, 58	12	5-9	Demo 5, Comp 8		51, 58, AM	Geometry	
5-10	5-10	51		5-10			51, AM		
End of chapter				Review		Tests			

*Teaching Aids, except Warm-ups, are pictured on pages 236C and 236D. The activities in the Activity Kit are pictured on page 236C.

**Visual Aids provide transparencies for all Teaching Aids and all Answer Masters.

Also available is the Study Skills Handbook which includes study-skill tips related to reading, note-taking, and comprehension.

Integrating Strands and Applications

	5-1	5-2	5-3	5-4	5-5	5-6	5-7	5-8	5-9	5-10
Mathematical Connections										
Number Sense								●		
Algebra	●	●	●		●		●	●	●	●
Geometry	●		●	●	●	●	●		●	●
Measurement	●		●			●		●		
Logic and Reasoning						●		●		
Probability						●		●		●
Patterns and Functions	●	●	●	●	●	●	●		●	●
Interdisciplinary and Other Connections										
Music					●					
Science	●	●	●	●	●	●	●	●		●
Social Studies	●		●	●			●		●	●
Multicultural	●	●	●	●				●		
Technology		●	●	●		●	●		●	
Consumer		●			●		●	●		
Sports					●	●	●			●

Teaching and Assessing the Chapter Objectives

				In the Assessment Sourcebook		
Chapter 5 Objectives (Organized into the SPUR categories—Skills, Properties, Uses, and Representations)	**Lessons**	**Progress Self-Test Questions**	**Chapter Review Questions**	**Chapter Test, Forms A and B**	**Chapter Test, Forms C**	**D**
Skills						
A: Add positive and negative numbers.	5-1, 5-3, 5-5	1, 2, 7, 12–15, 27	1–10	1, 4, 5, 7, 8, 14, 31	1, 3	✓
B: Calculate absolute value.	5-3	5, 6, 8	11–16	2, 5		✓
C: Apply properties of addition to simplify expressions.	5-2, 5-7	3, 4, 27	17–24	3, 6	3	
D: Solve equations of the form $x + a = b$.	5-8	9–11, 17	25–34	15–18	2	
E: Find the perimeter of a polygon.	5-10	22	35–39	27, 30	4	
Properties						
F: Identify the following properties of addition: Commutative Property of Addition, Associative Property of Addition, Additive Identity Property of Zero, Addition Property of Equality, Property of Opposites, Opposite of Opposites Property.	5-2, 5-7, 5-8	18, 19	40–43	9, 10	5	
G: Tell whether events are mutually exclusive or not.	5-6	21	44–48	11, 13	6	
H: Identify parts and give names of polygons	5-9	20	49–52	28, 29	4	
Uses						
I: Use the Putting-Together Model for Addition to form sentences involving addition.	5-1, 5-8, 5-10	24, 26, 28, 29	53–58	21, 22, 24, 25		✓
J: Use the Slide Model for Addition to form sentences involving addition.	5-1, 5-8	16	59–62	26	2	
K: Calculate the probability of mutually exclusive events or complements of events.	5-6	25, 31	63–68	12	6	
Representations						
L: Calculate magnitudes of turns given angle measures or revolutions.	5-4	32–34	69–72	19, 20	5	✓
M: Picture addition of positive and negative numbers using arrows on a number line.	5-1	30	73–75	23	1	

Assessment Sourcebook
Quiz for Lessons 5-1 through 5-4
Quiz for Lessons 5-5 through 5-8
Chapter 5 Test, Forms A–D
Chapter 5 Test, Cumulative Form

Quiz and Test Writer
Multiple forms of chapter tests and quizzes; Challenges

Activity Kit

ACTIVITY 10 — ADDING INTEGERS. Use with **Lesson 5-3.**

Materials: 15 integer tiles
Group Size: Small groups

Integer tiles can be used to help you add integers. One color of tile represents 1, and the other color of tile represents -1. Work on Items 1-5 independently and with your group on Item 6.

1. Show -6 + -2 by placing 6 negative tiles on your desk and then another 2 negative tiles. How would you express the sum? ______
2. Use tiles to model each sum. Then give the sum.
   a. -5 + -1 ______ **b.** -3 + -3 ______ **c.** -7 + -3 ______
3. **Draw a Conclusion** With your group, write a rule that tells how to add two negative integers.
4. Place one positive tile and one negative tile on your desk. What is the combined value of these tiles? ______

   This pair of tiles is called a *zero pair.* Zero pairs may be added to or taken away from other tiles without changing the total value of the tiles. Explain why this is so.

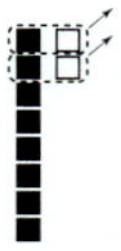

5. To show -8 + 2, place 8 negative tiles on your desk and then 2 positive tiles. Make as many zero pairs as you can and remove them. The remaining tiles show the sum, ______.
6. Use tiles to model each sum. Then give the sum.
   a. -7 + 5 ______ **b.** -3 + 6 ______ **c.** -5 + 5 ______
   d. 10 + -3 ______ **e.** 5 + -9 ______ **f.** -9 + 5 ______
7. **Draw a Conclusion** With your group, write a rule that tells how to add a positive integer and a negative integer.

ACTIVITY 11 — SOLVING $x + a = b$. Use with **Lesson 5-8.**

Materials: Envelope, paper clips
Group Size: Partners

1. Place two sheets of paper on the desk. Have your partner turn away as you place a secret number of paper clips into an envelope on the left sheet. Place 6 more clips next to the envelope. On the right sheet of paper, place the number of clips equal to the *total* number of clips on the left sheet. In our diagram, the total number of clips is 14. Your total number of clips should be different.

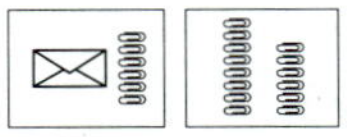

envelope + 6 clips = 14 clips

We let x represent the number of paper clips in the envelope. The equation that represents our situation above is $x + 6 = 14$.

2. Have your partner write the equation that represents the situation *you* created. ______

Our equation is solved below. Your partner should demonstrate how to solve *your* equation with *your* paper clips and envelope.

Remove 6 paper clips from each sheet of paper so that only the envelope is on the left.

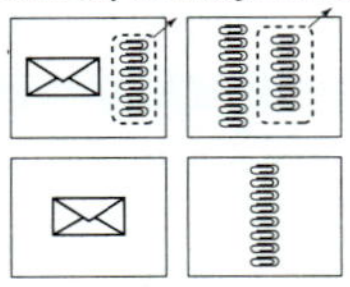

number of clips in envelope = 8

$x + 6 = 14$

Add -6 to both sides.

$x + 6 + -6 = 14 + -6$

$x + 0 = 8$

$x = 8$

3. Your partner should solve *your* equation. ______
4. Begin again. While you turn away, your partner should place some clips in the envelope on the left side and some more clips next to the envelope. The same total number of clips should be placed on the right side. Quantities should be different from those used in Item 1.
5. Now you should write the equation illustrated by the situation, demonstrate the solution with the envelope and clips, and solve the equation. Your partner should check your work.

ACTIVITY 12 — POLYGONS. Use with **Lesson 5-9.**

Materials: Scissors, paste, lightweight cardboard
Group Size: Small groups

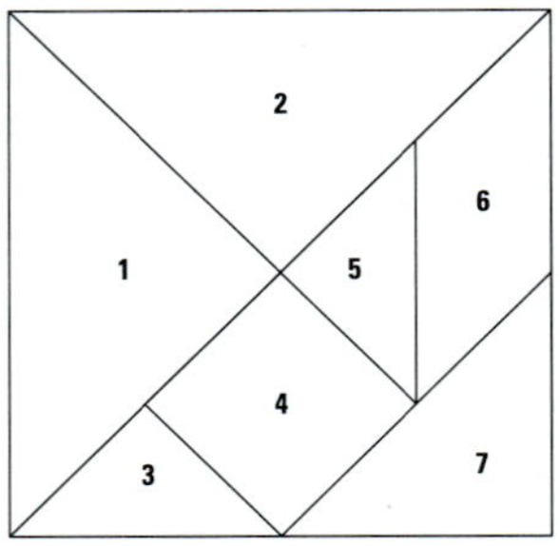

1. Cut out the large square above. Paste it onto cardboard and cut the square into the 7 polygons shown. These 7 pieces are known as *tangram* pieces.
2. Mix the pieces and try to make the square again, using all 7 pieces.

Combine the tangram pieces to make each polygon listed in the tables below. First, use the fewest pieces you can and record the number in the table. Then use the most pieces you can and record that number. Trace each polygon on a separate sheet of paper.

	Polygon	Fewest Pieces	Most Pieces
3.	triangle		
4.	quadrilateral		
5.	pentagon		
6.	hexagon		

	Polygon	Fewest Pieces	Most Pieces
7.	heptagon		
8.	octagon		
9.	nonagon		
10.	decagon		

Teaching Aids

TEACHING AID 49

Warm-up — Lesson 5-1

The following Swahili (Tanzanian) units of capacity were used in the early 1900s.

1 kisaga = 2 kibaba 1 pishi = 2 kisaga

Complete the following sentences.

1. 4 kibaba = ______ pishi
2. 2 pishi = ______ kibaba
3. 1 pishi + 1 kisaga = ______ kisaga
4. 1 pishi + 1 kisaga = ______ kibaba
5. 8 kibaba + 2 kisaga = ______ pishi

Warm-up — Lesson 5-2

Work in groups and write as many pairs of words as you can that have opposite meanings.

Warm-up — Lesson 5-3

For each situation, tell the net result.

1. The temperature goes up 16°C from -8°C.
2. An underwater diver who is at 10 feet below sea level descends 15 feet more.
3. A $30 deposit is made to a checking account that is $20 overdrawn.
4. An elevator in a building with many floor levels below ground is on the 5th level above ground and descends 8 levels.

TEACHING AID 50

Warm-up — Lesson 5-4

Solve.

1. Tell if each turn is a clockwise turn or a counterclockwise turn.
   a. A turn to the left b. A turn to the right
   c. A 30° turn d. A -30° turn
2. If you turn 90° counterclockwise and then turn 70° clockwise, what is the result?
3. If you turn 210° clockwise and then turn 180° counterclockwise, what is the result?

Warm-up — Lesson 5-5

Mental Mathematics For each fraction, give three equal fractions.

1. $\frac{1}{3}$ 2. $\frac{4}{5}$ 3. $\frac{5}{6}$ 4. $\frac{9}{10}$ 5. $\frac{1}{2}$ 6. $\frac{3}{4}$

Warm-up — Lesson 5-6

1. List all the possible outcomes for spinning these two spinners at the same time.
2. How many outcomes are there?

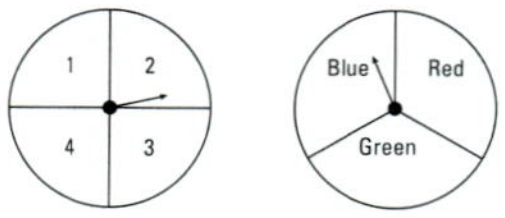

TEACHING AID 51

Warm-up — Lesson 5-7

Estimation Tell if each sum will be positive or negative.

1. -6 + 3 + 9 + -2 2. 12 + 0 + -6 + -12
3. 20 + -30 + -40 + 10 4. -5 + -5 + 2 + 3
5. -15 + 6 + 1 + 3 6. 9 + -3 + 6 + -4
7. -10 + 20 + -30 + 10 8. -7 + -4 + 5 + 8

Warm-up — Lesson 5-8

Find each missing number.

1. ______ + 3 = 8 2. ______ + -3 = 8
3. -7 + ______ = 8 4. -8 = 2 + ______
5. $\frac{2}{3}$ = ______ + $-\frac{1}{3}$ 6. 0 = -8 + ______

Warm-up — Lesson 5-9

Draw an angle for each of the following measures.

1. 90° 2. 30° 3. 45°
4. 120° 5. 180° 6. 75°

Warm-up — Lesson 5-10

For 1–2, use triangles *ABC* and *XYZ*.

1. Write an equation for the perimeter *p* of triangle *ABC*. Then find the perimeter.

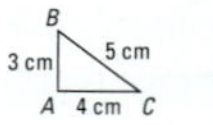

2. If the perimeter of triangle *WYZ* is 18 cm, write an equation to find the length of side *x*.

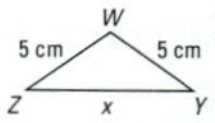

TEACHING AID 52
Lesson 5-1

Number Lines for Adding

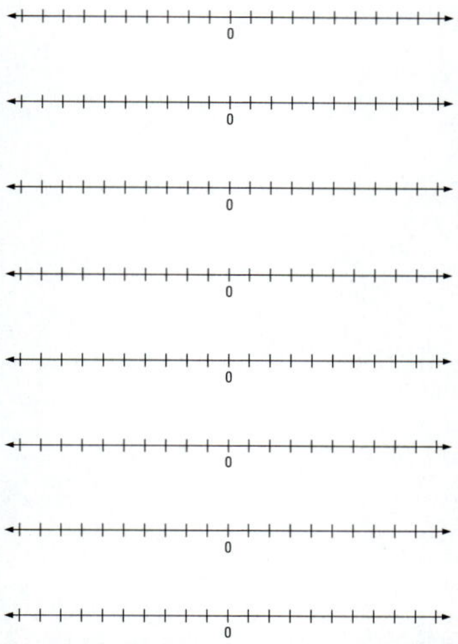

TEACHING AID 53
Lesson 5-4

Adding Angle Measures

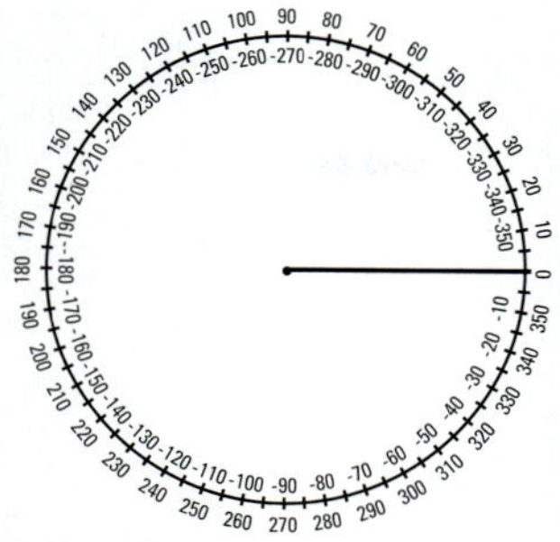

TEACHING AID 54
Lesson 5-4

Rotation

Fill in the boxes.

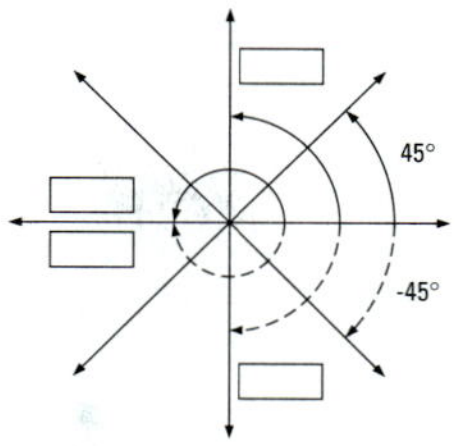

Show three different ways to combine turns so that the final result is a turn with a magnitude of 135°.

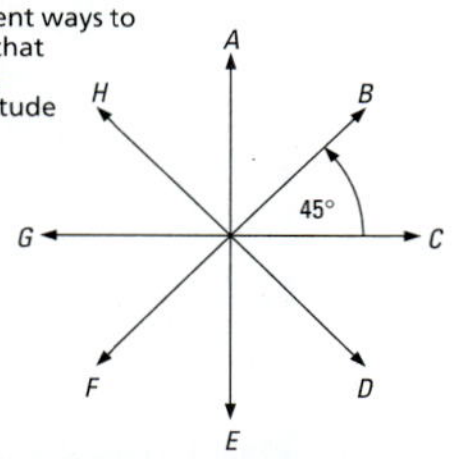

TEACHING AID 55
Lesson 5-4

Questions 8–11, 22–24

8–11.

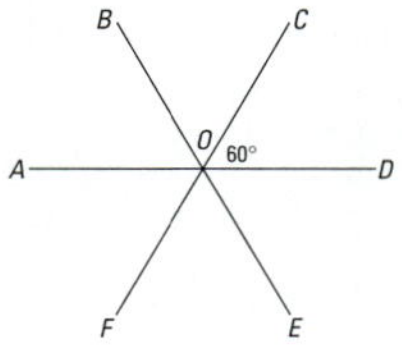

22–24.

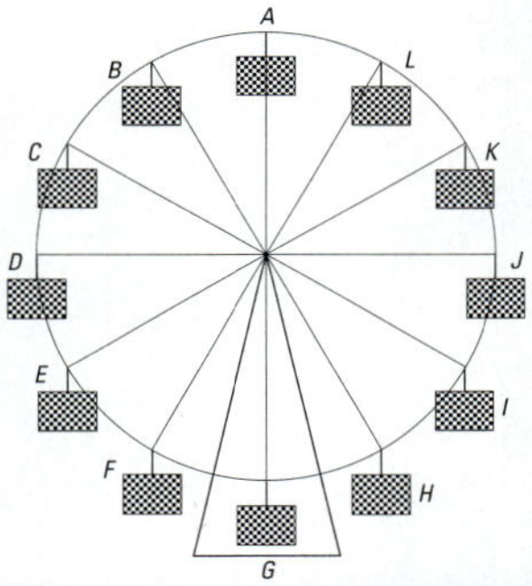

TEACHING AID 56
Lessons 5-6, 7-5, 9-3

Two-Dice Outcomes

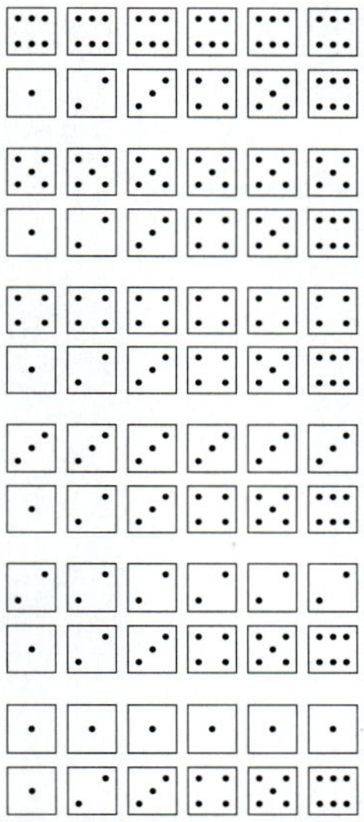

TEACHING AID 57
Lesson 5-8

Question 35

8			5
		3	0
		-1	
-4			-7

Challenge

How many ∆s are needed to balance 20 ▩s?

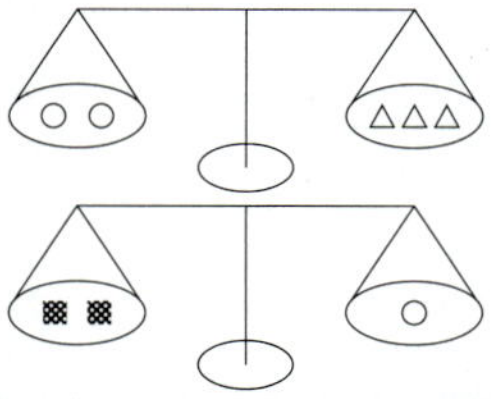

TEACHING AID 58
Lesson 5-9

Classification of Polygons

Number of Sides	Number of Vertices	Type of Polygon	Example
3	3	triangle	
4	4	quadrilateral	
5	5	pentagon	
6	6	hexagon	
7	7	heptagon	
8	8	octagon	
9	9	nonagon	
10	10	decagon	

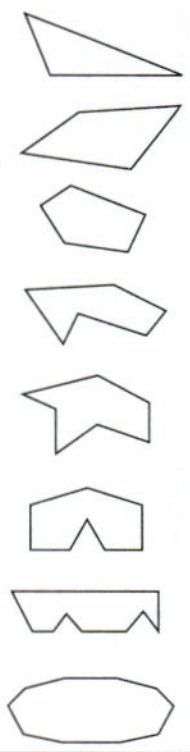

Chapter Opener 5

Pacing
All lessons in this chapter are designed to be covered in one day. Lesson 5-1 may seem long, but Lesson 5-2 is quite short. At the end of the chapter, you should plan to spend 1 day to review the Progress Self-Test, 1–2 days for the Chapter Review, and 1 day for a test. You may wish to spend a day on projects, and possibly a day is needed for quizzes. This chapter should therefore take 13–16 days.

Using Pages 236-237
Students may be surprised to see a chapter on addition; they may think it is babyish. You might point out that they are expected to know how to add whole numbers, fractions, and decimals before beginning this chapter. As you can see from the lesson titles, the new skills involve addition of positive and negative numbers (including fractions) and solving addition equations.

The article from which the table is taken is meant to be taken with a grain of salt. You might ask students what is strange about the table. Note that there are three oddities. First, the accuracy to which the times are taken is very uneven, ranging from times rounded to the nearest hour to times rounded to the nearest hundredth of a second. Second, there is not even a hint that two or more of these activities might be done at the same time. Third, parts of hours are inconsistently described —sometimes as decimals, sometimes as fractions, and sometimes in minutes.

CHAPTER 5

Chapter 5 Overview
Chapter 5 introduces an approach that recurs with the other basic operations in later chapters of this text. We have gathered many different ideas about addition and put them all together in this chapter. This chapter could be subtitled "Almost Everything You Need to Know About Addition in Order to Succeed in Algebra, Geometry, and Life." We do the same with subtraction in Chapter 7, with multiplication in Chapters 9 and 10, and with division in Chapter 11.

This chapter provides an excellent embodiment of the SPUR concept. The *Skills* cover adding positive and negative numbers (Lessons 5-1 to 5-3), adding positive and negative fractions (Lesson 5-5), and solving simple equations (Lesson 5-8). The *Properties* include properties of zero and opposites (Lesson 5-2), associativity and commutativity (Lesson 5-7), and those properties necessary for solving equations (Lesson 5-8). *Uses* are also important topics throughout the chapter. We introduce the putting-together and slide models for addition in Lesson 5-1. Addition of probabilities occurs in Lesson 5-6. Finding perimeter, a special case of the putting-together model, is in Lesson 5-10. The special application of the slide model to angle measure and turns is in Lesson 5-4. *Representations* of addition include the number line (Lessons 5-1 and 5-3), fraction circles (Lesson 5-5), and clockwise and counterclockwise turns (Lesson 5-4).

PATTERNS LEADING TO ADDITION

Karen S. Peterson wrote an article in *USA Today* in 1989 about the amount of time that experts say adults should spend on various activities. The table below is taken from that article.

Just how much can you fit into a day?	Experts suggest
Exercise	30 min.
Personal grooming	45 min.
Time with children	4 hrs.
Reading newspapers	45 min.
Pets	50 min.
Housekeeping/chores	1–2 hrs.
Work	7–10+ hrs.
Commuting	$1\frac{1}{2}$ hrs.
Errands	up to 2 hrs.
Grocery shopping	(men) 17.88 min. (women) 22.25 min.
Cooking, eating dinner	1 hr.
Entertaining	1 hr.
Dental care	18 min.
General time with spouse	6 hrs. 50 min.
Volunteering	30 min.
Time with plants	10 min.
Time for you	1 hr.
Reading a book	15 min.
Spiritual development	15 min.
Sleep	7.5 hrs.

Karen Peterson concluded that a person would need a day of about 42 hours to do everything the experts say you're supposed to do. To arrive at this conclusion, she had to add whole numbers, fractions, and decimals. She also had to worry about units. Of course, she was being funny. But she was also trying to be serious. Some people think they are not perfect unless they try to do everything the experts say. She used addition to point out that this was impossible.

In this chapter, you will study many other uses of addition.

Photo Connections

The photo collage makes real-world connections to the content of the chapter: patterns leading to addition.

Certificates: These stock certificates represent shares of stock traded in exchanges around the world. Increases and declines in stock prices are shown as positive and negative fractions.

Music: In music, there are half-notes, quarter-notes, and eighth-notes. Musicians base their compositions on these fractional notes.

Abacus: The abacus is an early form of adding machine which is still used today in some countries. Beads above the middle bar of an abacus count five each when lowered toward the bar and beads below the middle bar count one each when raised toward the bar. The patterns formed by the beads form a number.

The Louvre Pyramid: An Asian American architect I. M. Pei designed the giant pyramid which serves as an entrance to the Louvre. This combination of polygons stands in striking contrast to the rest of the museum which was constructed during the 1850s.

Watch: Setting this standard timepiece demonstrates a common form of combining turns.

Projects

At this time, you might want to have students look over the projects on pages 293–294.

Topics progress from simple to more complex. Uses of addition appear first as motivation for the continued study of addition. Familiar situations such as putting together are a good starting point. The uses lead to the necessary skills of adding fractions and integers. After the skills are covered, the properties are examined. All of these ideas are finally applied to solving of simple addition equations, which for many students is a new topic.

Lesson 5-1

Objectives

A Add positive and negative integers.
I Use the Putting-Together Model for Addition to form sentences involving addition.
J Use the Slide Model for Addition to form sentences involving addition.
M Picture addition of positive and negative numbers using arrows on a number line.

Resources

From the ***Teacher's Resource File***
- Lesson Master 5-1A or 5-1B
- Answer Master 5-1
- Teaching Aids
  49 Warm-up
  52 Number Lines for Adding

Additional Resources
- Visuals for Teaching Aids 49, 52

Teaching Lesson 5-1

Warm-up

Multicultural Connection The following Swahili (Tanzanian) units of capacity were used in the early 1900s.

1 kisaga = 2 kibaba
1 pishi = 2 kisaga

Complete the following sentences.

1. 4 kibaba = ___ pishi 1
2. 2 pishi = ___ kibaba 8
3. 1 pishi + 1 kisaga = ___ kisaga 3
4. 1 pishi + 1 kisaga = ___ kibaba 6
5. 8 kibaba + 2 kisaga = ___ pishi 3

LESSON

5-1 Models for Addition

Running water. *Niagara Falls, which lies on the U.S.-Canadian border, consists of two waterfalls—the American Falls in New York and the Horseshoe Falls in Ontario. The combined average water flow is about 212,200 cubic feet per second.*

Addition is important because adding gives answers in many actual situations. It is impossible to list all the uses of addition. So we give a general pattern that includes many of the uses. We call this general pattern a model for the operation. The two most important models for addition are called putting together and slide.

1 The Putting-Together Model for Addition

Here are three instances of the *Putting-Together Model for Addition.*

1. The two countries that share land borders with the United States are Canada and Mexico. In 1991, the population of Canada was estimated as 26,835,500 and the population of Mexico was estimated as 90,007,000. What was the total estimated population of these two countries in 1991?
2. Suppose a book is purchased for \$4.95 and the tax is \$0.30. What is the total cost?
3. Taken from a person's pay are 20% for taxes and 7.6% for social security. What percent is taken altogether?

The numbers put together may be large or small. They may be written as decimals, percents, or fractions. The general pattern is easy to describe using variables.

Putting-Together Model for Addition
Suppose count or measure x is put together with a count or measure y with the same units. If there is no overlap, then the result has count or measure $x + y$.

Lesson 5-1 Overview

Broad Goals This lesson introduces the idea of models for operations and uses the Putting-Together and Slide Models for Addition to explain addition of positive and negative numbers.

Perspective One of the unique features of this book is the use of *models for operations.* We generalize many uses of an operation in a model. You might think of a model as a property of applications that can be used in many situations.

We use models for a number of reasons. First, models help students to make sense out of applications. When they know all the models for an operation, they know all its basic uses. Second, models help students to choose an operation. Third, models can be used to verify properties. Fourth, models can be used to teach an operation. Recall that in the earliest grades, addition almost always starts with putting-together activities.

This is the first of several lessons on adding positive and negative numbers, so do not require mastery at this time. What is desired now is that students are able to think of situations involving addition of positive and negative numbers. Then the student can use the situations to add the numbers.

When the units are different and you want an answer in terms of a single unit, decide on an appropriate unit for your answer and then convert everything to that unit.

Example 1

2 meters + 46 centimeters

Solution

Either change everything to meters or change everything to centimeters.

Change to meters.	Change to centimeters.
2 meters + 46 centimeters	2 meters + 46 centimeters
= 2 meters + 0.46 meter	= 200 cm + 46 cm
= 2.46 meters	= 246 centimeters

The two answers, 2.46 meters and 246 centimeters, are equal.

Example 2

8 apples + 14 oranges

Solution

Apples cannot be changed to oranges, or vice versa. But they are both fruits.

8 apples + 14 oranges
= 8 pieces of fruit + 14 pieces of fruit
= 22 pieces of fruit

Numbers to be added are called **addends.** If one addend is unknown, the putting-together model can still be used. For instance:

You weigh y and a cat weighs c. If you step on a scale together, the total weight is $y + c$.

This idea can be applied to weigh a cat that is too small to be weighed on an adult scale.

First weigh yourself on the scale. Suppose you weigh 107.5 lb. Together you and the cat must weigh $(c + 107.5)$ lb. Now you pick up the cat and step on the scale again. Suppose the total weight is 113.25 lb. Then the cat's weight is the solution to the equation $c + 107.5 = 113.25$.

If you do not know how to solve an equation of this type, you will learn how to do so in Lesson 5-8.

When there is overlap in the addends, the total cannot be found by just adding. For example, imagine that 50 pages of a book have pictures and 110 pages have tables. You cannot conclude that 160 pages have either pictures or tables. Some pages might have both pictures and tables. You ❷ will deal with this situation in Chapter 7.

Notes on Reading

The major topic for discussion in this lesson is the purpose of models. Because students have little trouble deciding when to add in applications, and because most students have been taught to think of addition as putting-together, they may not appreciate the value of the Putting-Together Model for Addition.

❶ When discussing the Putting-Together Model for Addition, do not be concerned about whether the numbers are written as fractions or decimals or in any other form. The model works regardless of the form of the addends; $x + y$ seldom carries with it any knowledge of the way x and y are written.

Activity 1 in *Optional Activities* below gives students an additional opportunity to work with measures expressed in different units.

❷ After discussing the Putting-Together Model, you might describe other addition situations, such as those given below.

1. Write an addition expression that describes each situation.
   a. There were c students on the bus. After 5 more got on, how many students were on the bus? $c + 5$
   b. Dora planted t tulips and d daffodils. How many flowers did she plant? $t + d$
2. Write an equation that relates the three numbers.
   a. Louis had m marbles. After he bought 25 more, he had 108 marbles. $m + 25 = 108$
   b. Mrs. Ruiz bought 1.31 pounds of almonds and 1.42 pounds of pecans. Together the nuts weighed w pounds. $1.31 + 1.42 = w$

Optional Activities

Activity 1 How Do You Spend Your Day? This activity, which relates to the *Chapter Opener*, can be used anytime after discussing **Example 1.** Ask students to list how they allocate their time on a typical weekday or on a typical Saturday or Sunday. They can look at the categories in the table in the opener for possible activities to include. For example, they might change "General time with spouse" to "General time with family." You might want to have students list the information in three columns, listing the parts of hours in minutes, in fractions, and in decimals.

Discuss some of the activities on the students' lists. For example, what is the time range for sleeping? for reading? for housekeeping? What is the mean for each of these times?

Activity 2 To help reinforce the ideas presented in **Question 4,** write "5 feet 3 inches" on the board. Explain that this sum could be expressed 5'3", but this does not reflect adding 5 and 3. To add numbers and get a meaningful answer, the units must be the same. Have students express 5 feet 3 inches in feet and then in inches. [$5\frac{1}{4}$ ft; 63 in.] Then have each student express his or her height in these two ways.

❸ The Putting-Together Model would have to be distorted in order to apply to negative numbers. The Slide Model applies naturally. The introduction of addition with positive and negative numbers through both applications and slides on the number line provides two different ways of making the operation concrete for students.

The Slide Model may be new to students. Tell them that different models will be used in other lessons in this book. You might also discuss some of the advantages of models, as outlined in the *Overview* for this lesson.

Teaching Aid 52 can be used with the discussion of **Examples 3–5.**

❸ The Slide Model for Addition

Recall that negative numbers are used when a situation has two opposite directions. Examples are deposits and withdrawals in a savings account, ups and downs of temperatures or weight, profits and losses in business, and gains and losses in football or other games. In these situations, you may need to add negative numbers. Here is a situation that leads to the addition problem 10 + -12.

Unbelievably wet. *The boy and his grandfather are trying to cope with the Great Flood of 1993 along the banks of the Mississippi River. Due to spring and summer floods, the river was above flood stage for over $\frac{1}{3}$ of the year.*

Example 3

Flood waters rise 10 feet and then recede 12 feet. What is the end result?

Solution

Think of the waters sliding up and then sliding back down. Picture this with two vertical arrows, up for 10 and down for -12. Start the arrow for -12 where the arrow for 10 finished.

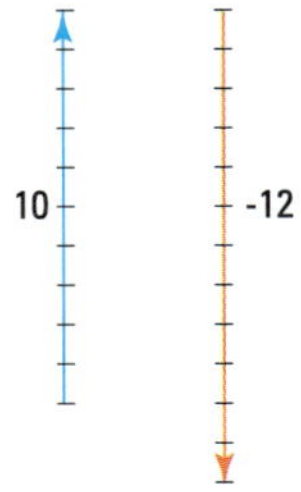

The arrow for -12 finishes 2 units below the starting position for the arrow for 10. In symbols, 10 + -12 = -2. **The end result is that the waters went down 2 feet.**

This example is an instance of the *Slide Model for Addition.* In the slide model, positive numbers are shifts or changes or slides in one direction. Negative numbers are slides in the opposite direction. The + sign means "followed by." The sum indicates the net result.

Slide Model for Addition
If a slide x is followed by a slide y, the result is a slide $x + y$.

Example 4

Tony spends $4 for dinner and then earns $7 for baby-sitting.
a. What is the net result of this?
b. What addition problem leads to this answer?

Solution

a. **Tony has $3 more than he had before dinner.**
b. **-4 + 7 gives the net result.** The -4 is for spending $4. The 7 is for earning $7.

Adapting to Individual Needs

Extra Help

To emphasize the relationship between real situations and the models for addition discussed in this lesson, ask students to tell whether each situation given to the right is an example of the Putting-Together Model or the Slide Model. Have them demonstrate the idea using objects on a number line. Allow for differences of opinion; the models are not mutually exclusive.

1. A diver descends to a depth of 20 feet and then rises 7 feet. [Slide]
2. Bill combined $10 he earned with $15 of his birthday money. [Putting together]
3. Sam spent $5 and then he earned $12. What is the net result? [Slide]
4. Amy's baby sister was 20 inches tall at birth. She has grown 1.5 inches since then. [Putting together]

Now ask students to make up and share examples of each model.

The solution to Example 4 can be pictured on a horizontal number line.

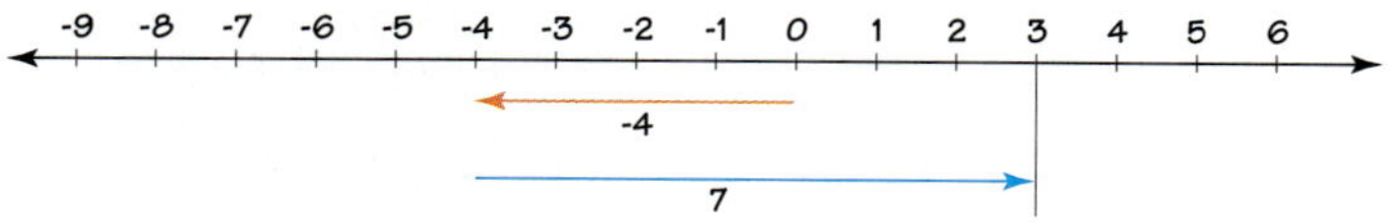

Start at 0. Think of -4 as a slide 4 units to the left. Draw the arrow pointing left. Think of 7 as an arrow going 7 units to the right but starting at -4. Where does the second arrow end? At 3, the sum.

Positive numbers are usually pictured as slides up or to the right. Negative numbers are usually pictured as slides down or to the left.

Example 5

a. Picture -3 + -2 on a horizontal number line.
b. What is the result?

Solution

a. Think of a slide 3 units to the left, followed by a slide 2 more units to the left.

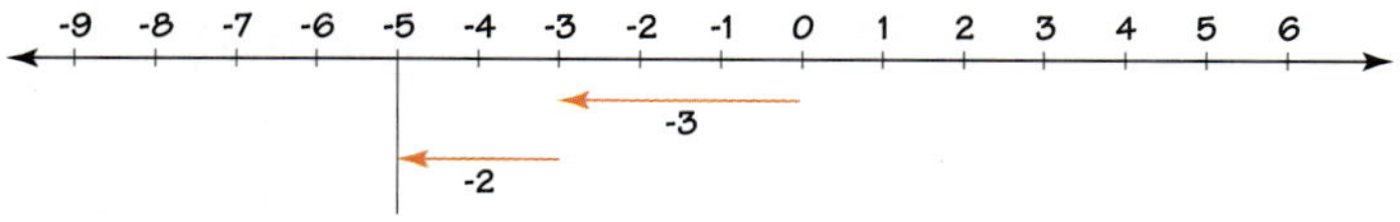

b. The result is a slide 5 units to the left. -3 + -2 = -5

The slide model can also be used with positive numbers. If the temperature goes up 9° and then goes up 7° more, the result is an increase of 16°. Of course you know this. You have known some instances of both the putting-together and slide models for many years.

QUESTIONS

Covering the Reading

1. What is an *addend?* a number to be added
2. State and give an example of the Putting-Together Model for Addition. See below.
3. Mary gets on a scale and weighs M kg. Craig gets on a scale and it registers 60 kg. Together they get on the scale and the scale shows 108 kg. Write an equation relating M, 60, and 108. $M + 60 = 108$

2) Suppose a count or measure x is put together with a count or measure y with the same units. If there is no overlap, then the result has count or measure $x + y$. Sample: If two letters weigh 15 g and 32 g, then their total weight is 47 g.

Additional Examples

1. Change 6 feet 9 inches to
   a. inches. 81
   b. feet. $6\frac{3}{4}$
2. Express 18 boys plus 17 girls as a sum using one number. Sample: 35 students
3. Maria earned $12 shoveling snow, but she used $8 to pay back a loan from her mother. What is the net result? She had $4 left.
4. A hot-air balloon rose 25 feet and then descended 45 feet.
   a. What was the effect of this? The balloon descended 20 ft.
   b. What addition problem leads to this answer? 25 + -45 gives the net result; 25 is for rising 25 feet and -45 is for descending 45 feet
5. Draw a picture using arrows to find each sum on a number line.
   a. 4 + -3 Sum: 1

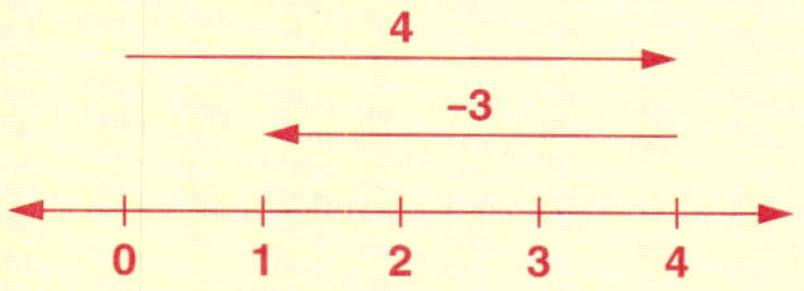

   b. -2.5 + -3.5 = ? Sum: -6

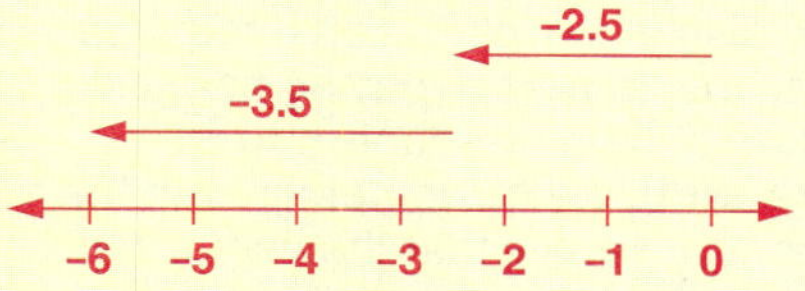

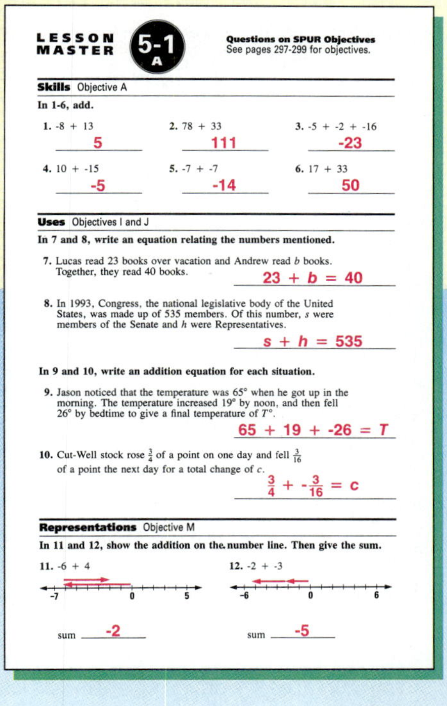

LESSON MASTER 5-1 A **Questions on SPUR Objectives** See pages 297-299 for objectives.

Skills Objective A

In 1-6, add.

1. -8 + 13 5	2. 78 + 33 111	3. -5 + -2 + -16 -23
4. 10 + -15 -5	5. -7 + -7 -14	6. 17 + 33 50

Uses Objectives I and J

In 7 and 8, write an equation relating the numbers mentioned.

7. Lucas read 23 books over vacation and Andrew read b books. Together, they read 40 books. $23 + b = 40$
8. In 1993, Congress, the national legislative body of the United States, was made up of 535 members. Of this number, s were members of the Senate and h were Representatives. $s + h = 535$

In 9 and 10, write an addition equation for each situation.

9. Jason noticed that the temperature was 65° when he got up in the morning. The temperature increased 19° by noon, and then fell 26° by bedtime to give a final temperature of T°. $65 + 19 + -26 = T$
10. Cut-Well stock rose $\frac{3}{4}$ of a point on one day and fell $\frac{3}{16}$ of a point the next day for a total change of c. $\frac{3}{4} + -\frac{3}{16} = c$

Representations Objective M

In 11 and 12, show the addition on the number line. Then give the sum.

11. -6 + 4   -7 0 5   sum -2
12. -2 + -3   -6 0 6   sum -5

Adapting to Individual Needs

English Language Development
Materials: Egg carton, thermometer, coins, envelopes, beaker, water

Many of the situations described in this lesson can be modeled with objects rather than words. As you model a situation, point out the words and directions associated with both positive and negative actions.

1. To show the addition of different units, you might use egg cartons to show 1 dozen plus 4 objects. Ask how many dozen there are and how many objects there are. [$1\frac{1}{3}$ dozen; 16 objects]
2. You could use coins and an envelope to model, for example, (m + 15) cents, ($m + n$) cents, and $m + 15 = 32$.
3. To illustrate the slide model for addition, you might use a beaker, water, and a thermometer.

Notes on Questions

Question 4 The unit issue as illustrated again in this question is subtle. It is also considered in *Activity 2* in *Optional Activities* on page 239.

Questions 11–16 Students can use the number lines on **Teaching Aid 52** to draw their pictures.

Questions 19 and 23 There is *insufficient information* to answer these questions. Some students may spend a great deal of time trying to figure out one numerical answer, for they often assume there is always enough information given to answer all questions. That is not the case in life in general and in this book in particular.

Question 20 Even though this question contains overlapping information—the brothers are brothers of both sisters—students can find out how many children are in the family.

Questions 27–29 Students must learn these generalizations. You might illustrate them with actual situations.

Question 31 This question should be discussed for its consumer applications. In **part a,** paying half price on a \$2 item discounts it to \$1. In **part b,** if a customer ignores the cents, it seems that the item is half price. But the discount is only about a third, not a half.

LESSON MASTER 5-1 B Questions on SPUR Objectives

Skills Objective A: Add positive and negative numbers.

In 1-12, add.

1.	-4 + 12	8
2.	21 + 88	109
3.	15 + -20	-5
4.	-3 + -2 + -11	-16
5.	44 + 18	62
6.	-9 + -9	-18
7.	-7 + -6	-13
8.	-6 + -3 + -6	-15
9.	-9 + 6	-3
10.	16 + -8	8
11.	47 + 50 + 139	236
12.	-7 + -2 + 5	-4

Uses Objective I: Use the Putting-Together Model for Addition to form sentences involving addition.

In 13-16, write an addition equation for each situation.

13. Maria had 17 CDs. She received c more for her birthday. Now she has 21 CDs. $17 + c = 21$

14. Geraldo spent 66 dollars on a new outfit. Jeans cost j dollars and a sweatshirt cost s dollars. $j + s = 66$

15. This year there are 515 students at Covington Junior High School. There are 269 girls and b boys. $269 + b = 515$

16. Judi spent 40 minutes washing her dad's car and 1 hour waxing it. Altogether, the job took m minutes. $40 + 60 = m$

6) Sample: If the temperature rises 12° and then falls 4°, the net result is an increase of 8°.

11a)

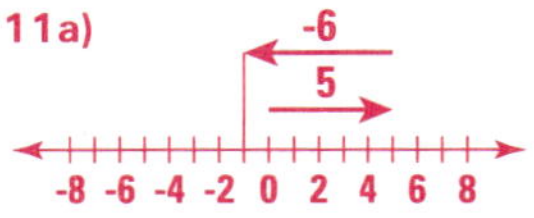

12a)

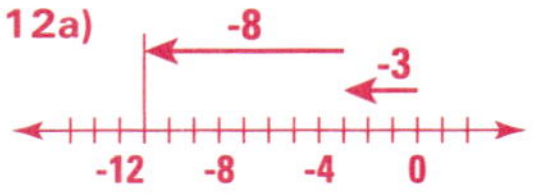

4. Carla says you can add apples and oranges. Peter says you cannot. Who is right? Justify your answer. Both are. If units are "pieces of fruit," Carla is right. If units are unchanged, Peter is right.
5. Write 3 meters + 4 centimeters as one quantity. 3.04 m or 304 cm
6. State and give an example of the Slide Model for Addition. If a slide x is followed by a slide y, the result is a slide $x + y$.

In 7–10, what does the phrase mean in the slide model?

7. a positive number slide to the right or up
8. a negative number slide to the left or down
9. the + sign followed by
10. the sum the net result
11. a. Draw a picture of 5 + -6 using arrows and a number line.
    b. 5 + -6 = ? -1
12. a. Draw a picture of -3 + -8 using arrows and a number line.
    b. -3 + -8 = ? -11

In 13–16, a situation is given. **a.** What question related to the situation can be answered by addition? **b.** What is the answer to that addition? (Draw a picture if you need to.)

13. The temperature fell 5°, then fell 3° more. a) What was the end result? b) -8°
14. A person gets a paycheck for \$250, then buys a coat for \$150. a) How much money is left? b) \$100
15. Flood waters rise 15 feet, recede 19 feet, then rise 5 feet 4 inches. a) Where are the flood waters now? b) $1\frac{1}{3}$ ft or 16 in. higher than they were.
16. In making a cake, a person puts in $\frac{1}{2}$ teaspoon of salt. Then the person forgets and puts in another $\frac{1}{2}$ teaspoon of salt. a) How much salt was put in? b) 1 teaspoon
17. Examine the table on page 237.
    a. Add up all the times experts suggest. Sample: about 40 hours
    b. Refer to your answer to part **a,** and explain why an adult cannot spend the suggested time on each activity. There are only 24 hours in a day.

Applying the Mathematics

18. Joe needs to buy a new pair of basketball shoes. He estimates that it will take $\frac{1}{2}$ hour to bike to the mall and 20 minutes to purchase the shoes. How long should he allow for shopping? 1 hr 20 min or $1\frac{1}{3}$ hr or 80 minutes
19. Together Dan and Diane have \$20. Together Diane and Donna have \$15. How much do the three of them have in total? There may be overlap. The total is at least \$20 and at most \$35.
20. Rosa has 2 brothers and 1 sister. Her sister Maria has 2 brothers and 1 sister. How many children are in the family? 4
21. Michelle has b brothers and s sisters. How many children are in the family? $b + s + 1$
22. Of the 25 students in Ms. Jones's class, 36% are on a school team, 40% are in the band or chorus, and 28% are in some other school activity.
    a. Is this possible? Yes
    b. Why or why not? Some students may be in more than one activity.

Adapting to Individual Needs

Challenge

Give students the following problems. In 1952, the U.S.S. United States crossed the Atlantic Ocean in 3 days, 10 hours, and 40 minutes, setting a speed record for a ship.

1. How many hours did the crossing take? [$82\frac{2}{3}$ hours]
2. How many minutes did the crossing take? [4960 minutes]

23. Last year in Springfield it rained or snowed on 140 days. The sun shone on s days. Can s be determined from this information? Why or why not? **No, rain or snow and sun could appear on the same day.**

24. Suppose the temperature was 58°F when you woke up at 7:00 A.M., then rose 23° from 7:00 A.M. to 2:00 P.M. and fell 8° from 2:00 P.M. to 6:00 P.M. What was the temperature at 6:00 P.M.? **73°**

25. What is the result of walking north 300 feet, then south 120 feet, and then north 40 feet? **a point 220 ft north of the starting point**

26. Give an inequality relating the three numbers mentioned. The bench will support at most 250 pounds. Mike weighs M pounds. Nina weighs 112 pounds. The bench will hold both of them. **$M + 112 \leq 250$**

In 27–29, tell whether the sum is always, sometimes, or never positive.

27. Two negative numbers are added. **never positive**

28. Two positive numbers are added. **always positive**

29. A positive number and a negative number are added. **sometimes positive**

Review

30. Tell whether the number is a solution to $0 \leq x < 50$. Write *yes* or *no*. *(Lesson 4-10)*
a. 35.2 **yes** **b.** -4 **no** **c.** 50 **no**
d. 0 **yes** **e.** 1/100 **yes** **f.** 60% **yes**

31. The percent p of discount on an item can be calculated by using the formula $p = 100(1 - n/g)$. In this formula, g is the original price, and n is the new price. Find the percent of discount on an item reduced from:
a. \$2 to \$1. **50%** **b.** \$2.95 to \$1.95. *(Lesson 4-7)* **≈ 33.9%**

32. How many degrees are there in the given figure? *(Lesson 3-7)*
a. a right angle **90°** **b.** half a circle **180°** **c.** an acute angle **between 0° and 90°**

33. Round 99.3% to the nearest whole number. (Hint: Watch out!) *(Lesson 2-4)* **1**

34. *True or false.* $-10 \leq -8$ *(Lesson 1-9)* **True**

35. If climbing up 2 meters is represented by the number 2, what number will represent each event? *(Lesson 1-8)*
a. climbing down 6 meters **-6** **b.** staying at the same height **0**

Exploration

36. Ask two adults how much time they spent yesterday on the activities listed in the table on page 237. How do their times compare with the times suggested by experts? **Answers will vary.**

37. When 1 cup of sugar is added to 1 cup of water, the result is not 2 cups of the mixture. Why not? **The sugar is dissolved in the water and the total volume is less than 2 cups.**

But I have only two hands! *Doing several things at once is one way to get everything done.*

Follow-up for Lesson 5-1

Practice

For more questions on SPUR Objectives, use **Lesson Master 5-1A** (shown on page 241) or **Lesson Master 5-1B** (shown on pages 242–243).

Assessment

Written Communication Have students write a paragraph explaining the Putting-Together Model and the Slide Model for Addition. Ask them to include a sample problem that illustrates each model. If students are keeping a journal, have them include this assessment in it. [Paragraphs give clear, concise explanations of each model. Samples clearly illustrate each model.]

Extension

Give students these problems.

1. A camera and case cost \$100. The camera is worth \$90 more than the case. How much is the case worth? **\$5**
2. Maria spent \$30 for two CDs. One cost \$3 more than the other. How much did each CD cost? **\$13.50 and \$16.50**

Project Update Project 6, *Financial Log,* on page 294, relates to the content of this lesson.

▶ LESSON MASTER 5-1B *page 2*

Uses Objective J: Use the Slide Model for Addition to form sentences involving addition.

In 17-20, write an addition equation for each situation.

17. Last week the river rose 7 feet. This week it went down 10 feet. Over the two-week period, the level of the river changed c feet. **$7t - 10 = c$**

18. At midnight the temperature was 45°. By 8 a.m. it fell 8° to a temperature of T degrees. **$45 + -8 = T$**

19. The Hawks gained 8 yards in the first down, and lost 5 yards in the second down, for a total change of y yards. **$8 + -5 = y$**

20. Chia weighed 112 pounds at the beginning of last month. She gained 2 pounds that month and then lost 4 pounds this month. Now she weighs p pounds. **$112 + 2 + -4 = p$**

Representations Objective M: Picture addition of positive and negative numbers using arrows on a number line.

In 21-23, picture the addition on the number line. Then give the sum.

21. -5 + 8

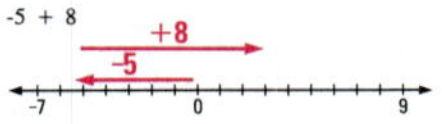

sum **3**

22. 4 + -7

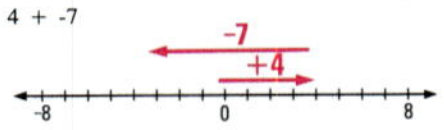

sum **-3**

23. -2 + -6

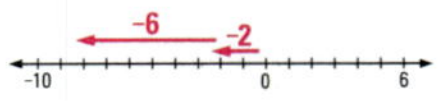

sum **-8**

Lesson 5-2

Objectives

C Apply properties of addition to simplify expressions.

F Identify the Additive Identity Property of Zero, the Property of Opposites, and the Opposite of Opposites Property.

Resources

From the ***Teacher's Resource File***
- Lesson Master 5-2A or 5-2B
- Answer Master 5-2
- Teaching Aid 49: Warm-up

Additional Resources
- Visual for Teaching Aid 49

Teaching Lesson 5-2

Warm-up

Work in groups and write as many pairs of words as you can that have opposite meanings.

After students have worked for a few minutes, put a master list on the board. Circle any pairs that can be associated with mathematics, such as positive–negative, add–subtract, multiply–divide, and plus–minus.

Notes on Reading

Writing This is a good lesson for students to read on their own. One way to guarantee that students give the properties careful attention is to have them write a description of each property in words. For example, they might write that the Additive Identity Property of Zero says that

LESSON

5-2 Zero and Opposites

Profits add up. *At some garage sales, children earn money selling homemade refreshments.*

Adding Zero

Suppose you have \$25. If you earn \$4, then you will have 25 + 4, or 29, dollars. If you spend \$4, you will have 25 + -4, or 21 dollars. If you do nothing, you will have 25 + 0, or 25, dollars. When you add 0 to a number, the result is the original number. We say that adding 0 to a number keeps the identity of that number. So 0 is called the **additive identity.**

Additive Identity Property of Zero
For any number n, $n + 0 = n$.

For example, $-\frac{1}{2} + 0 = -\frac{1}{2}$, 77% + 0 = 77%, and 0 + 3.469 = 3.469.

Adding Opposites

Remember that 5 and -5 are called opposites. They are called opposites because if 5 stands for gaining 5 pounds, then -5 stands for its opposite, losing 5 pounds. Now suppose you gain 5 pounds and then lose 5 pounds. This is a slide model situation. So the result is found by adding 5 + -5.

You know the result! If you gain 5 pounds and then lose 5 pounds, the result is no change in weight. This verifies that 5 + -5 = 0.

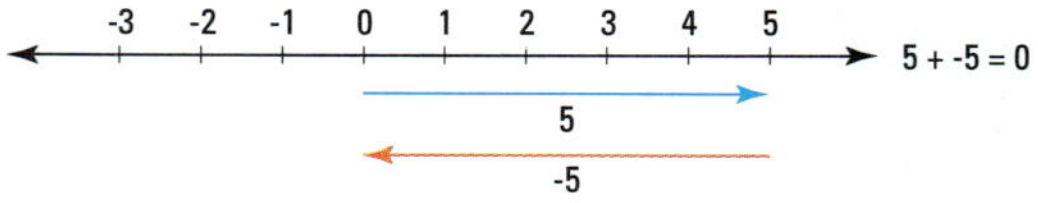

The same result occurs regardless of what number you use. The sum of a number and its opposite is 0. In symbols, $-n$ is the opposite of n. Some people call the general pattern the Property of Opposites.

Lesson 5-2 Overview

Broad Goals This lesson provides more practice on addition of positive and negative numbers and covers three important properties of zero and opposites.

Perspective The three properties highlighted on pages 244 and 245 do not have names that are universally used. You may wish to use your own favorite names, but be flexible enough to allow a student to use the names given in the text as well.

There are no new skills, and the properties, with the possible exception of the Opposite of Opposites Property, are general statements of patterns the students already know.

Property of Opposites
For any number n, $n + -n = 0$.

The word "inverse" means opposite. Because of the property of opposites, the numbers n and $-n$ are called additive inverses of each other. For example, the additive inverse of 40 is -40. The additive inverse of -40 is 40. The additive inverse of -6.3 is 6.3. This can be written as -(-6.3) = 6.3. The parentheses are used so that it is clear that there are two dashes. Because 0 + 0 = 0, the opposite of 0 is zero. That is, -0 = 0. Some people call $n + -n = 0$ the Additive Inverse Property.

The Opposite of an Opposite

The opposite of the opposite of any number is the number itself. We call this the Opposite of Opposites Property, or the Op-op Property for short. Your class may wish to make up a different name.

Opposite of Opposites (Op-op) Property
For any number n, $-(-n) = n$.

Honoring the harvest. *The Mayas created an advanced civilization based on agriculture. Today, Mayas of Oaxaca, Mexico, enjoy the* Guelaguetza, *honoring the corn harvest.*

To verify the Opposite of Opposites Property on a calculator, display any number. Now press the [+/–] key twice. After the first pressing, you will get the opposite of the number. After the second pressing, the original number will appear.

Caution: When x is negative, $-x$ is positive. For instance, if $x = -3$, then $-x = -(-3) = 3$. For this reason, we read $-x$ as "the opposite of x," not as "negative x."

See	Read
-3	negative 3 or opposite of 3
$-t$	opposite of t

As important as zero and negative numbers are, it took a long time to discover them. The Mayas of Central America are the first known culture to have a symbol for zero, dating from about the year 300. Negative numbers were first seen as solutions to equations by some Western European mathematicians in the late 1400s.

QUESTIONS

Covering the Reading

1. Why is zero called the additive identity? Adding zero to a number keeps the identity of that number.
2. Add: 0 + 3 + 0 + 4. 7
3. Another name for additive inverse is _?_. opposite

adding zero to a number doesn't change the value of that number.

Science Connection If a galvanometer is available from the science department, allow students to experiment by moving the magnet through the coil. Ask students to describe the reading on the galvanometer as the magnet moves. Ideally the reading should be zero when the center of the magnet is in the center of the coil.

If you plan to use integer tiles to teach computation with integers, you might want to use the activity in *Optional Activities* on this page to illustrate the Property of Opposites.

Additional Examples

You might want to use the following examples as you discuss the lesson.

1. What property is illustrated?
   a. 0 + -9 = -9 Additive Identity Property of Zero
   b. 10 + -10 = 0 Property of Opposites
   c. –(–12) = 12 Opposite of Opposites Property
2. Find the sum.
   a. -6 + 6 0
   b. 0 + -1 -1
   c. 0 + -4 + 0 + -5 -9
   d. $y + 0 + -y$ 0

Optional Activities

Summing Up Opposites

Materials: Integer counters

You might introduce this lesson with the following activity. Have students **work in groups.** Give each group equal numbers of positive and negative integer counters. Relate the use of the counters to football yardage. Suggest that one color represents a gain of one yard and the other color represents a loss of one yard. Ask what the net change in position would be if a team gained one yard and then lost one yard. [0] Have students model other situations that result in a net change of zero. Students should conclude that a pair of tiles—one of each color—represents opposites and so their sum is 0.

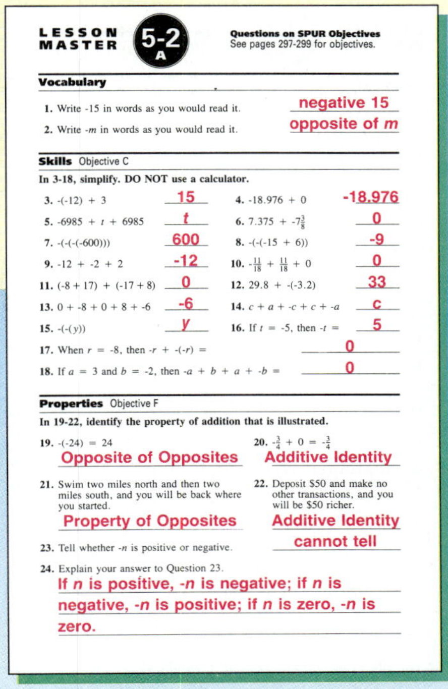

LESSON MASTER 5-2 A
Questions on SPUR Objectives
See pages 297-299 for objectives.

Vocabulary

1. Write -15 in words as you would read it. negative 15
2. Write $-m$ in words as you would read it. opposite of m

Skills Objective C

In 3-18, simplify. DO NOT use a calculator.

3. -(-12) + 3 15
4. -18.976 + 0 -18.976
5. -6985 + t + 6985 t
6. 7.375 + $-7\frac{3}{8}$ 0
7. -(-(-(-600))) 600
8. -(-(-15 + 6)) -9
9. -12 + -2 + 2 -12
10. $-\frac{11}{18} + \frac{11}{18} + 0$ 0
11. (-8 + 17) + (-17 + 8) 0
12. 29.8 + -(-3.2) 33
13. 0 + -8 + 0 + 8 + -6 -6
14. $c + a + -c + c + -a$ c
15. $-(-(y))$ y
16. If $t = -5$, then $-t$ = 5
17. When $r = -8$, then $-r + -(-r)$ = 0
18. If $a = 3$ and $b = -2$, then $-a + b + a + -b$ = 0

Properties Objective F

In 19-22, identify the property of addition that is illustrated.

19. -(-24) = 24 Opposite of Opposites
20. $-\frac{3}{4} + 0 = -\frac{3}{4}$ Additive Identity
21. Swim two miles north and then two miles south, and you will be back where you started. Property of Opposites
22. Deposit $50 and make no other transactions, and you will be $50 richer. Additive Identity
23. Tell whether $-n$ is positive or negative. cannot tell
24. Explain your answer to Question 23. If n is positive, $-n$ is negative; if n is negative, $-n$ is positive; if n is zero, $-n$ is zero.

Notes on Questions

Questions 11–14 Students may answer these questions by giving the general pattern with variables (for example, in **Question 11,** they might say $a + -a = 0$), or they might give the name of the property. Either answer is correct.

Questions 27–28 These questions lead to an important generalization.

Question 35 This question relates to solving equations, a topic which is introduced in Lesson 5-8.

LESSON MASTER 5-2 B Questions on SPUR Objectives

Vocabulary

1. Write -y in words as you would read it. opposite of y
2. Write -9 in words as you would read it. Give two different answers. negative nine opposite of nine

Skills Objective C: Apply properties of addition to simplify expressions.

In 3-20, simplify. DO NOT use a calculator.

3. 0 + 19.0057	19.0057	4. -67 + 67	0
5. -(-15)	15	6. -581 + x + 581	x
7. -(-(33))	33	8. -(-7 + 10)	-3
9. -(-(12 + -6))	6	10. -(-(-(-(-55))))	-55
11. -(-(-(u)))	-u	12. (-9 + 4) + (9 + -4)	0
13. $-\frac{13}{15} + \frac{13}{15}$	0	14. 0 + 88.76 + -88.76	0
15. $-\frac{7}{12} + 0 + \frac{7}{12} + -18$	-18	16. $-b + e + -e + e + b$	e
17. $-m + 0 + m$	0	18. $-\frac{3}{4} + .75$	0
19. -(-18) + 22	40	20. $-\frac{18}{25} + \frac{17}{3} + 0 + -\frac{17}{3}$	$-\frac{18}{25}$

In 21-28, evaluate the expression given that $s = 3$ and $t = -7$.

21. $-s$	-3	22. $-t$	7
23. $-14 + -s$	-17	24. $-t + -7$	0
25. $-t + -(-t)$	0	26. $s + -t$	10
27. $-s + t$	-10	28. $s + -t + -s + t$	0

In 4–7, give the additive inverse of each number.

4. 70 -70 **5.** -13 13 **6.** $-\frac{1}{2}$ $\frac{1}{2}$ **7.** $-x$ x

8. State the Property of Opposites. For any number n, $n + -n = 0$.

9. Describe a real situation that illustrates 7 + -7 = 0.

9) Seven people came to a party; then seven left. There is no change in the number at the party.

10. State the Opposite of Opposites Property. For any number n, $-(-n) = n$.

In 11–14, an instance of what property is given?

11. 2 + -2 = 0 Property of Opposites

12. -9.4 = 0 + -9.4 Additive Identity Property of Zero

13. 7 = -(-7) Opposite of Opposites Property

14. 0 = 1 + -1 Property of Opposites

In 15 and 16, a situation is given.

a. Translate the words into an equation involving addition.

b. An instance of what property is given?

15. Withdraw $25, then make no other withdrawal or other deposit, and you have decreased the amount in your account by $25.
a) -25 + 0 = -25; b) Additive Identity Property of Zero

16. Walk 40 meters east, then 40 meters west, and you are back where you started. a) 40 + -40 = 0; b) Property of Opposites

17. When does $-n$ stand for a positive number? when n is negative

18. If $x = -10$, give the value of $-x$. 10

Applying the Mathematics

In 19–22, perform the additions.

19. -51 + -9 + 51 + 2 -7

20. $x + 0 + -x$ 0

21. $a + b + -b + b + -a$ b

22. $-\frac{8}{3} + -\frac{2}{7} + 0 + \frac{2}{7} + \frac{8}{3} + \frac{14}{11}$ $\frac{14}{11}$

In 23–26, simplify.

23. -(-(-5)) -5

24. -(-(-(-6))) 6

25. $-(-(-x))$ $-x$

26. -(-(-7 + 1)) -6

27. Suppose you have entered the number 5 on your calculator. After you press the [+/−] key 50 times, what number will be displayed? 5

28. Suppose you have entered the number -6 on your calculator. Then you press the [+/−] key n times.

a. For what values of n will 6 be displayed? odd

b. For what values of n will -6 be displayed? even

In 29–32, evaluate the expression given that $a = 4$ and $b = -5$.

29. $-a + -b$ 1

30. $-b + 18$ 23

31. $a + -b$ 9

32. $a + b + -b + -a$ 0

Adapting to Individual Needs

Extra Help

Some students might find it helpful to think of adding opposites as *doing and undoing.* For example, write 5 + −5 = 0 on the board. Tell students to think of 5 as 5 steps forward and −5 as 5 steps backward. Then have a volunteer walk 5 steps forward and *undo* this action by walking 5 steps backward. Have another volunteer similarly demonstrate −5 + 5.

English Language Development

To help students understand the term *opposite*, show them several things that are the same and then contrast this with an opposite. For example, use black and white crayons, big and small boxes, empty and full containers, or long and short pencils.

Review

Like a bird. *Hang gliders are generally launched from the tops of hills. Changes in altitude are affected by wind currents.*

In 33 and 34 a situation is given.
a. What is the result for each situation?
b. What addition problem gets that result? *(Lesson 5-1)*

33. The temperature is $-11°$ and then goes up $2°$. **a) The temperature is $-9°$. b) $-11 + 2$**

34. A person is \$150 in debt and takes out another loan of \$100. **a) The person is \$250 in debt. b) $-150 + -100$**

In 35 and 36, give an equation or inequality with addition to relate the three numbers. *(Lesson 5-1)*

35. We were at an altitude of t meters. We went down 35 meters in altitude. Our altitude is now 60 meters below sea level. **$t + -35 = -60$**

36. We need \$50 to buy an anniversary gift for our parents. You have Y dollars. I have \$14.50. Together we have more than enough. **$Y + 14.50 > 50$**

37. A rope d inches in diameter can lift a maximum of about w pounds, where $w = 5000d(d + 1)$. *(Lesson 4-6)*

a. About how many pounds can a rope of diameter 1″ lift? **10,000 lb**

b. About how many pounds can a rope with a diameter of one-half inch lift? **3750 lb**

c. A rope has diameter $\frac{9}{16}$ inch. Can it lift 5,000 pounds? **No**

38. Put in order from smallest to largest. *(Lessons 2-2, 2-8)*
3.2×10^4 9.7×10^{-5} 5.1×10^7
9.7×10^{-5}; 3.2×10^4; 5.1×10^7

Exploration

39. Opposites are common outside of mathematics. You know that fast and slow are opposites, and so are big and little. Each of the eight animal names given here has a meaning other than as an animal. Identify the four pairs of opposites.

donkey dove hawk mouse
tiger elephant bear bull

dove and hawk (war politics)
bear and bull (stock market)
donkey and elephant (political parties)
mouse and tiger (aggression)

Follow-up for Lesson 5-2

Practice

For more questions on SPUR Objectives, use **Lesson Master 5-2A** (shown on page 245) or **Lesson Master 5-2B** (shown on pages 246–247).

Assessment

Group Assessment Have students **work in groups** and write five addition problems that use the properties discussed in this lesson. Then have the groups exchange papers, identify the property or properties used in each problem, and solve the problem. [Each of the three properties are exhibited in the problems. Problems are identified and solved correctly.]

Extension

Writing Science Connection You might have students investigate *absolute zero* and write a paragraph describing it. [Absolute zero is the theoretical temperature at which substances would have no heat whatever, and all molecules would stop moving. It is −273.16 degrees Celsius, −459.69 degrees Fahrenheit, and 0 degrees Kelvin.]

Project Update Project 3, *The Mayas*, on page 293, relates to the content of this lesson.

▶ **LESSON MASTER 5-2 B** *page 2*

Properties Objective F: Identify the Additive Identity Property of Zero, the Property of Opposites, and the Opposite of Opposites Property.

In 29-34, identify the property of addition that is illustrated.

29. $-\frac{7}{8} + \frac{7}{8} = 0$ **Property of Opposites**

30. $0 + -44.093 = -44.093$ **Additive Identity Property of Zero**

31. $0 = 22\frac{1}{2} + -22\frac{1}{2}$ **Property of Opposites**

32. $-(-19) = 19$ **Opposite of Opposites Property**

33. Walk eight miles east and then walk eight miles west, and you will be back where you started. **Property of Opposites**

34. Withdraw \$25 and make no other transactions, and your bank balance will be \$25 less than it was. **Additive Identity**

35. How can you tell whether $-m$ is positive, negative, or equal to zero?
If m is positive, $-m$ is negative. If m is negative, $-m$ is positive. If $m = 0$, $-m = 0$.

Review Addition and subtraction of decimals (Previous course)

In 36 and 37, solve each problem.

36. Kartik bought 2.8 pounds of cheddar and 1.35 pounds of brick cheese. How much heavier was the cheddar than the brick cheese? **1.45 pounds**

37. Use estimation to decide if \$35 is enough money to buy a watch for \$9.79, a scarf for \$12.19, and a back pack for \$17.98? **no**

38. Write a problem that involves addition of decimals.
sample: Pam hiked 3.2 km the first day, 4.8 km the second, and 2.5 km the third. In all, how far did Pam hike?

39. Write a problem that involves subtraction of decimals.
sample: Sue needs \$18. She already has \$14.72 How much more does she need?

Adapting to Individual Needs

Challenge
Use a 12-hour clock to show that 2 hours after 11 o'clock is 1 o'clock. Explain that in *clock addition*, 11 + 2 = 1. Then have students make an addition table for clock numbers. Ask them which number on the clock is the additive identity [12], and have them determine pairs of additive inverses. [Any pair with a sum of 12]

+	1	2	3	4	5	6	7	8	9	10	11	12
1	2	3	4	5	6	7	8	9	10	11	12	1
2	3	4	5	6	7	8	9	10	11	12	1	2
3	4	5	6	7	8	9	10	11	12	1	2	3
4	5	6	7	8	9	10	11	12	1	2	3	4
5	6	7	8	9	10	11	12	1	2	3	4	5
6	7	8	9	10	11	12	1	2	3	4	5	6
7	8	9	10	11	12	1	2	3	4	5	6	7
8	9	10	11	12	1	2	3	4	5	6	7	8
9	10	11	12	1	2	3	4	5	6	7	8	9
10	11	12	1	2	3	4	5	6	7	8	9	10
11	12	1	2	3	4	5	6	7	8	9	10	11
12	1	2	3	4	5	6	7	8	9	10	11	12

Lesson 5-3

Objectives

A Add positive and negative decimals.

B Calculate absolute value.

Resources

From the ***Teacher's Resource File***

- Lesson Master 5-3A or 5-3B
- Answer Master 5-3
- Teaching Aid 49: Warm-up
- Activity Kit, Activity 10

Additional Resources

- Visual for Teaching Aid 49

Teaching Lesson 5-3

Warm-up

For each situation, tell the net result.

1. The temperature goes up 16°C from –8°C. **The temperature is 8°C.**
2. An underwater diver who is at 10 feet below sea level descends 15 feet more. **The diver is 25 feet below sea level.**
3. A $30 deposit is made to a checking account that is $20 overdrawn. **The balance in the checking account is $10.**
4. An elevator in a building with many floor levels below ground is on the 5th level above ground and descends 8 levels. **The elevator is 3 levels below ground.**

LESSON

5-3 *Rules for Adding Positive and Negative Numbers*

Take stock in this. *A stock exchange enables investors to buy and sell bonds or shares of stocks. The prices of stocks and bonds can go up or down, resulting in positive or negative changes.*

Adding Without Using Rules

Suppose you want to add -50 and 30. In Lesson 5-1, you learned two ways of doing this. One way is to think of a situation using the numbers -50 and 30.

I spend $50 and I earn $30.
What is the net result?

The net result is that you have $20 less than when you started.

A second way is to represent -50 and 30 with arrows on a number line.

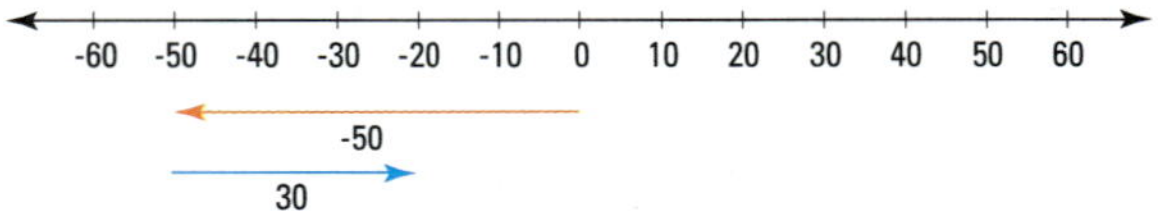

The bottom arrow ends under the -20 on the number line. Like the spending and earning idea, it shows that -50 + 30 = -20.

The Absolute Value of a Number

It isn't always easy to think of a situation for an addition problem, and it can be time consuming to draw a number line and arrows. So it helps to have a rule for adding positive and negative numbers. This rule is described using an idea called the *absolute value of a number.*

The **absolute value** of a number *n*, written $|n|$, is the distance of *n* from 0 on the number line. The absolute value of *n* is also the length of the arrow that describes *n*.

Lesson 5-3 Overview

Broad Goals This lesson has two objectives. The first is to introduce absolute value. The second is to use absolute value to give a definite rule for adding positive and negative numbers.

Perspective In this lesson we give the usual arithmetic description of absolute value and the geometric description which states that the absolute value of a number is its distance from zero. The arithmetic description has the advantage of being easily described algebraically, but the geometric description prepares students for more of the applications of absolute value and holds for complex numbers as well as real numbers. There are three rules in this lesson for adding positive and negative numbers. The algebraic descriptions of these rules are shown at the right. However, due to the complexity of these descriptions, we describe the rules in words rather than with algebra.

If $a > 0$ and $b > 0$,
then $a + b = |a| + |b|$.
If $a < 0$ and $b < 0$,
then $a + b = -(|a| + |b|)$.
If $a < 0$ and $b > 0$,
then $a + b = |b| - |a|$ if $|b| \geq |a|$,
and $a + b = -(|a| - |b|)$ if $|a| > |b|$.

Consider the numbers -2, $-\frac{1}{3}$, 0, 3.8, and 5.

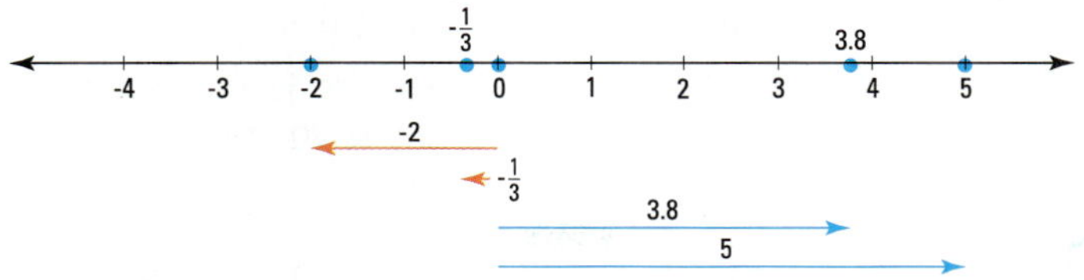

Number	Distance from 0	Length of Arrow	Absolute Value
-2	2	2	2
$-\frac{1}{3}$	$\frac{1}{3}$	$\frac{1}{3}$	$\frac{1}{3}$
0	0	0	0
3.8	3.8	3.8	3.8
5	5	5	5

❶ Notice how simple it is to calculate absolute value.

The absolute value of a positive number is that number. The absolute value of 5 is 5. In mathematical symbols, this is written $|5| = 5$. The absolute value of 3.8 is 3.8, so $|3.8| = 3.8$. The absolute value of 4 million is 4 million.

The absolute value of a negative number is the opposite of that number. The absolute value of -2 is 2. In symbols, $|-2| = 2$. The absolute value of $-\frac{1}{3}$ is $\frac{1}{3}$, so $\left|-\frac{1}{3}\right| = \frac{1}{3}$. The absolute value of -4000 is 4000. The absolute value of zero is 0. $|0| = 0$.

❷ A Rule for Adding Two Negative Numbers

Using the idea of absolute value, it is possible to state rules for adding positive and negative numbers. If the numbers are both positive, no rule is needed. You have been adding positive numbers since first grade. For instance, 7 + 4 = 11.

Suppose the numbers are both negative, as in -7 + -4. How are they added? First, you can add 7 and 4. (You have added the absolute values of the numbers.) Now put the negative sign on. (You have taken the opposite.)

> To add two negative numbers, add their absolute values and then take the opposite.

Notes on Reading

You may wish to have students read this lesson aloud in class. However, if they have read it before class, review these important ideas: the definition of absolute value, the rule for adding two negative numbers, and the rule for adding a positive and negative number.

❶ Absolute value is so easy to calculate that many students do not realize what they are doing. As a result, absolute values involving variables can be very confusing. It is very helpful to split the idea of absolute value into two parts: when the number is not negative; and when the number is negative.

Error Alert Ask students to explain absolute value in their own words after they read the explanation in the text. Do *not* let students say, "The absolute value is the number without its sign." Repeatedly stress that the absolute value of a negative number is the *opposite* of that number. Do not use the phrase "the negative of the number" for $-x$, because that reinforces the notion that when $|x| = -x$, $-x$ is negative.

❷ Three rules are given in this lesson. The two on this page include the trivial case in which the numbers are both positive and the case in which both numbers are negative.

LESSON MASTER 5-3 A

Questions on SPUR Objectives
See pages 297-299 for objectives.

Skills Objectives A and B

In 1-16, simplify.

1. $\|-16\|$	16	2. $\|42.5\|$	42.5
3. $\|-16\| + \|14\|$	30	4. $\|-16 + 14\|$	2
5. -16.5 + 20 + -4.5	-1	6. -30 + 45 + -10	5
7. $-\|-105\|$	-105	8. -11 + -7 + -10	-28
9. -28.02 + -.8	-28.82	10. $\|-1\| + \|0\| + \|14\|$	15
11. 57 + -2.3 + 5	59.7	12. $\|9 + -5 + -8\|$	4
13. 93 + -7	86	14. -62.3 + -8.2 + 10	-60.5
15. $\|17\| + -\|9\|$	8	16. -18.9 + -16.4	-35.3

17. *True or false.* When adding a group of numbers that are all negative, the sum will always be negative. true

18. *True or false.* $|a|$ always equals $-a$. false

19. *True or false.* $|0|$ is positive. false

20. Are the values of (a) and (b) equal? Explain why or why not.
(a) $|28| + |-12|$ (b) $|28 + -12|$
No. (a) requires that the absolute value of each number be taken first, then added. (b) requires addition first, then take the absolute value of the sum. $|28| + |-12| = 28 + 12 = 40$. $|28 + -12| = |16| = 16$.

Video

Wide World of Mathematics The segment, *Integer Football,* shows how the yardage results of successive plays on a football field can be used to model the addition of integers. The segment may be used to launch a lesson or to provide additional practice on the addition of integers. Related questions and an investigation are provided in videodisc stills and in the Video Guide. A related CD-ROM activity is also available.

Videodisc Bar Codes

Search Chapter 24

Play

❸ The third rule, and most complicated, is the case when one number is positive and the other is negative. Students should not be forced to learn the rules; for most students they are far more complicated than real-world models or number-line representations. From a skill standpoint, the rules exist for those students who, even after seeing slide-model situations and number-line representations, need an algorithm.

If you wish to show addition of positive and negative numbers using integer tiles, see *Optional Activities* below.

Additional Examples

1. Add 8.5 and –10 **–1.5**
2. –62 + 14 = ? **–48**
3. Use your calculator to find 597.5 + –386.2. **211.3**
4. Simplify.
   a. $\left|\frac{3}{4}\right|$ $\frac{3}{4}$
   b. | –.5 | **.5**
   c. | 2 | **2**
   d. – | 2 | **–2**

LESSON MASTER 5-3 B — Questions on SPUR Objectives

Skills Objective A: Add positive and negative decimals.

In 1-18, add.

1. 4 + -11 — **-7**
2. -6 + -22 — **-28**
3. -7 + 20 — **13**
4. -33 + 18 — **-15**
5. 85 + -40 — **45**
6. -77 + -100 — **-177**
7. -9 + 53 — **44**
8. 7.3 + .81 — **8.11**
9. -5.5 + -9 — **-14.5**
10. -.07 + 15 — **14.93**
11. -44.08 + -.6 — **-44.68**
12. 29.8 + -14.4 — **15.4**
13. -8 + -17 + -12 — **-37**
14. -20 + 65 + -30 — **15**
15. 31 + -4.7 + 60 — **86.3**
16. -5.9 + -22.8 + 100 — **71.3**
17. -8.6 + 2.2 + -9.1 — **-15.5**
18. .7 + -.88 + .1 — **-.08**

Skills Objective B: Calculate absolute values.

In 19-38, simplify.

19. |-23| — **23**
20. |54| — **54**
21. |100| — **100**
22. |-100| — **100**
23. |-.0072| — **.0072**
24. |50.1| — **50.1**
25. |0| — **0**
26. -|-904| — **-904**
27. |-13| + |17| — **30**
28. |-13 + 17| — **4**
29. -|-18| + -|-10| — **-28**
30. |16| + -|20| — **-4**
31. |3.8 + -4.4| — **.6**
32. |-.84| + |.33| — **1.17**
33. |9 + -7 + -4| — **2**
34. -|-9| + |9| + |-5| — **5**
35. |10| + |-21| + |20| — **51**
36. |-9.1 + -12| — **21.1**
37. -|3.6 + -.2| — **-3.4**
38. |-30| + -|6.1| + 127 — **150.9**

❸ A Rule for Adding a Positive and a Negative Number

The big advantage of the idea of absolute value comes when one addend is positive and one is negative.

Consider 13 + -40. You are 13 points ahead but you lose 40 points. How do you stand? If you don't know the answer, arrows can help.

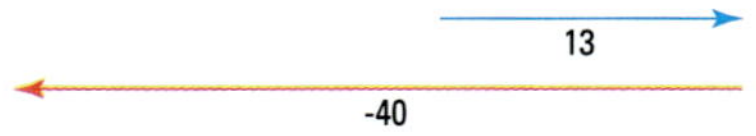

Let's analyze this. The sum is certainly going to be negative. This is because -40 has a larger absolute value than 13.

How far negative? Just subtract 13 from 40. So the sum is -27. Here is the process described in words.

> To add a positive number and a negative number, take their absolute values. The sum is in the direction of the number with the larger absolute value. Subtract the smaller absolute value from the larger to find out how far the sum is in that direction.

Example 1

Add 5 and -8.9 using the above rule.

Solution

First take the absolute values. |5| = 5 and |-8.9| = 8.9. Since -8.9 has the larger absolute value, the sum is negative. Now subtract the smaller absolute value from the larger. 8.9 – 5 = 3.9. So the sum is -3.9.

Example 2

76 + -5 = ?

Solution

The absolute values of the addends are 76 and 5. Since 76 has the larger absolute value, the sum is positive. Now subtract the absolute values.
76 – 5 = 71. So the sum is 71.

You may be able to find sums of positive and negative numbers without using the above rule. As long as you do not make errors, this is fine.

Activity

The ± or +/– key on a calculator changes a number to its opposite. The following key sequence can be used to add -3 and -2. Should the answer be positive or negative? Answer in your mind before going on. Key in 3 ± + 2 ± = on your calculator.

Enter the addition problem -263 + 159 on your calculator. Is the result positive or negative?

Optional Activities

Activity You can use *Activity Kit, Activity 10,* to introduce Lesson 5-3. In this activity, students use integer tiles to add integers and work together to develop a rule for adding integers. The activity also presents a physical interpretation to the concept of absolute values.

QUESTIONS

Covering the Reading

1. *Multiple choice.* Which are ways of finding the sum of positive and negative numbers?
   (a) Think of a situation fitting the slide model for addition.
   (b) Use arrows and a number line.
   (c) Take absolute values and use a rule.
   (d) All of the above are valid ways. **(d)**

In 2–5, give the absolute value of the number.

2. -58 **58** **3.** 4.01 **4.01** **4.** 0 **0** **5.** -11 **11**

In 6–9, simplify.

6. $|12|$ **12** **7.** $|-20|$ **20** **8.** $|0.0032|$ **0.0032** **9.** $|0|$ **0**

10c) 40 [+/−] [+] 41 [=]
11c) 7.3 [+/−] [+] 0.8 [+/−] [=]
12c) 6 [+] 7 [=]

In 10–12, an addition problem is given.
a. Without adding, tell whether the sum is positive or negative.
b. Add.
c. Check using a calculator. Show the key sequence you used.

10. -40 + 41 **a) positive b) 1** **11.** -7.3 + -0.8 **a) negative b) -8.1** **12.** 6 + 7 **a) positive b) 13**

In 13–18, *true or false.*

13. The sum of two positive numbers is always positive. **True**

14. The sum of two negative numbers is always negative. **True**

15. The sum of a negative number and a positive number is always negative. **False**

16. The absolute value of a number is always positive. **False; zero is neither positive or negative.**

17. The numbers 50 and -50 have the same absolute value. **True**

18. The absolute value of a negative number is the opposite of that number. **True**

In 19–22, find the sum.

19. 3 + -6 **-3** **20.** -10 + -4 **-14** **21.** -1.7 + -.85 **-2.55** **22.** -473 + 2920 **2447**

Applying the Mathematics

In 23–32, simplify.

23. $-2\frac{1}{3} + 1\frac{2}{3}$ $\mathbf{-\frac{2}{3}}$

24. $5 + -\frac{3}{4}$ $\mathbf{4\frac{1}{4}}$

25. -3 + 8 + -7 + -9 + 7 **-4**

26. 11 + -86 + -11 + -7 + 105 **12**

27. $-|-2|$ **-2**

28. $-\left|\frac{15}{2}\right|$ $\mathbf{-\frac{15}{2}}$

29. $|-0.74| + -|-0.74|$ **0**

30. $|3| + |-3|$ **6**

31. $|3| - |-3|$ **0**

32. $-|2.5| + |-6.8|$ **4.3**

Notes on Questions

Questions 10–12 Students should learn how to add positive and negative numbers both with and without a calculator. They should understand that using a calculator for simple additions is a waste of time.

Since it is so easy to make a mistake when entering negative numbers on a calculator, students should always check their calculator answers by thinking about a realistic situation involving the numbers.

Question 16 This question provides an opportunity to discuss the burden of stating something as always true. Zero is the only counterexample to the statement, but that one counterexample is enough to make the entire sentence false.

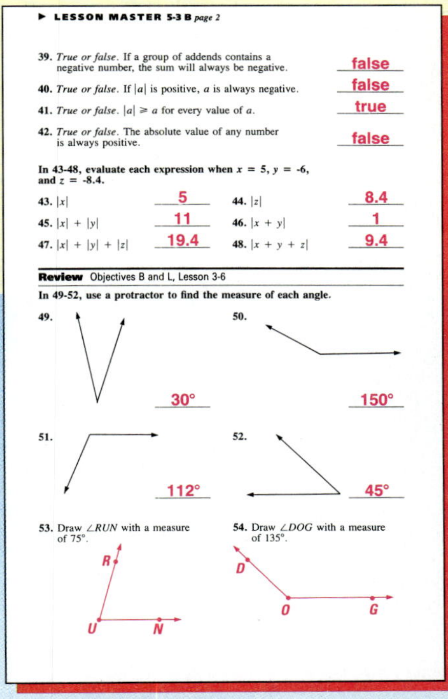
► LESSON MASTER 5-3 B *page 2*

39. *True or false.* If a group of addends contains a negative number, the sum will always be negative. **false**

40. *True or false.* If $|a|$ is positive, a is always negative. **false**

41. *True or false.* $|a| \geq a$ for every value of a. **true**

42. *True or false.* The absolute value of any number is always positive. **false**

In 43-48, evaluate each expression when $x = 5$, $y = -6$, and $z = -8.4$.

43. $|x|$ **5** 44. $|z|$ **8.4**
45. $|x| + |y|$ **11** 46. $|x + y|$ **1**
47. $|x| + |y| + |z|$ **19.4** 48. $|x + y + z|$ **9.4**

Review Objectives B and L, Lesson 3-6

In 49-52, use a protractor to find the measure of each angle.

49. **30°** 50. **150°**
51. **112°** 52. **45°**

53. Draw $\angle RUN$ with a measure of 75°.
54. Draw $\angle DOG$ with a measure of 135°.

Adapting to Individual Needs

Extra Help

Some students may benefit from seeing several real-world examples relating to absolute value. Emphasize that absolute value refers to the distance the number is from zero, *regardless of direction.* For example, the opposite of 5 feet above sea level is 5 feet below sea level, just as the opposite of 5 is –5. However, both positions are a distance of 5 feet from sea level, just as both 5 and –5 have an absolute value of 5.

Be sure students understand that the greater of two integers does not necessarily have the greater absolute value. For example, 8 is greater than –12, but 12 feet below sea level is a greater distance from sea level (zero) than 8 feet above sea level, so | -12 | > | 8 |.

Follow-up for Lesson 5-3

Practice

For more questions on SPUR Objectives, use **Lesson Master 5-3A** (shown on page 249) or **Lesson Master 5-3B** (shown on pages 250–251).

Assessment

Written/Oral Communication Tell students to imagine that they have to explain how to add a positive number and a negative number to a friend who knows about positive and negative numbers but does not know how to add them. Ask students to use real-life situations in their explanations. Then have each student write a brief description of his or her explanation and the corresponding problem. [Each explanation gives a real-life situation with diagrams and/or equations to describe it.]

Extension

Multicultural Connection Shuffleboard is a game that originated in England around the 13th century. Have students research the game rules and make up a play-by-play description of a set of four shots that result in a negative score.

Project Update Project 6, *Financial Log,* on page 294, relates to the content of this lesson.

33. *True or false.*
  a. When x is positive, $|x| = x$. True
  b. When x is negative, $|x| = -x$. True
  c. When $x = 0$, $|x| = x$. True

In 34 and 35, the absolute value sign occurs outside an expression. When this happens, $|\ \ |$ is acting as a grouping symbol as well as indicating absolute value. So work within the absolute value sign first.

34. What is the value of $|x + y|$ when $x = -5$ and $y = 4$? 1

35. *Multiple choice.* Which is *not* true?
  (a) $|10 + 32| = |10| + |32|$
  (b) $|10 + -32| = |10| + |-32|$
  (c) $|-10 + -32| = |-10| + |-32|$ (b)

36. Can the absolute value of a number ever be negative? Explain. See left below.

In 37 and 38, use this information. Values of exports are considered as positive quantities. Imports are considered as negative quantities. The total of exports and imports is called the *balance of trade.*

37. In 1991, the United States exported 421.730 billion dollars of goods and imported 487.129 billion dollars of goods. What was the balance of trade for the U.S. in 1991? -65.399 billion dollars or -$65,399,000,000

38. U.S. exports to Algeria in 1991 were 726.7 million dollars. The imports were 2,102.6 million dollars. What was the balance of trade with Algeria? -1375.9 million dollars or -$1,375,900,000

Shown above is Ghardaia Market in Algiers, Algeria. The U.S. is the biggest buyer of Algerian goods, purchasing nearly half the country's oil production. In return, Algeria imports machinery, raw materials, and most of its food.

Review

39. Evaluate $-h + 13$ for the given value of h. *(Lesson 5-2)*
  a. $h = 13$ 0 **b.** $h = -2$ 15 **c.** $h = 0$ 13

40. Translate into mathematical symbols. The sum of a number and its additive inverse is the additive identity. *(Lessons 4-3, 5-2)* $n + -n = 0$

41. Suppose a person is $150 in debt and pays off $50.
  a. What addition problem gives the result for this situation? -150 + 50
  b. What is that result? *(Lesson 5-1)* -100; the person is $100 in debt.

In 42 and 43, use the drawing at the left.

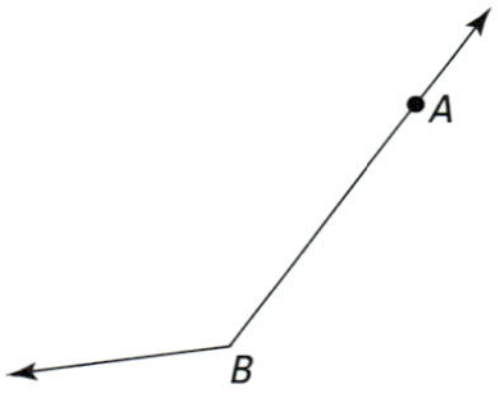

42. **a.** Without measuring, tell whether $\angle B$ is acute, obtuse, or right. obtuse
  b. Measure $\angle B$ to the nearest degree. *(Lessons 3-6, 3-7)* 134°

43. Measure the distance from A to B to the nearest $\frac{1}{8}$ inch. *(Lesson 3-1)* 1 inch

Exploration

44. Find three numbers that satisfy all of the following conditions.
  (1) The sum of the numbers is negative.
  (2) The sum of the numbers is greater than -1.
  (3) The sum of the absolute values of the numbers is larger than 1,000,000. Sample: -500,000; 500,000; and $-\frac{1}{2}$

36) No, when a number is positive, it equals its absolute value; the absolute value of 0 is defined to be zero; and the absolute value of a negative number is the opposite, which is positive.

Adapting to Individual Needs

Challenge

Show students these graphs.

$|x| = 3$

$|x| \geq 3$

$|x| \leq 3$

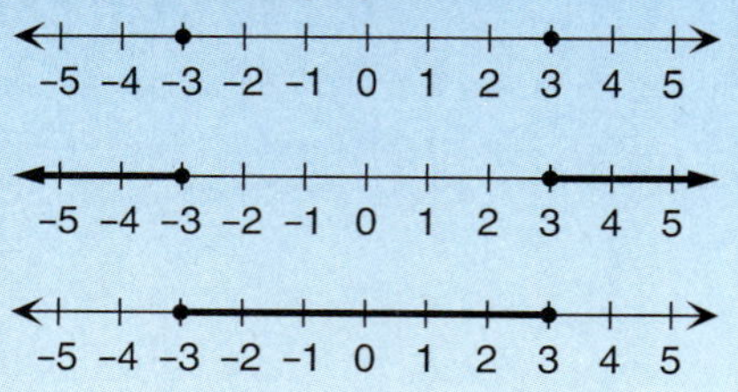

Now have students draw graphs for the following sentences.

1. $|x| = 2$
2. $|x| \geq 2$
3. $|x| \leq 2$
4. $|x| > 2$

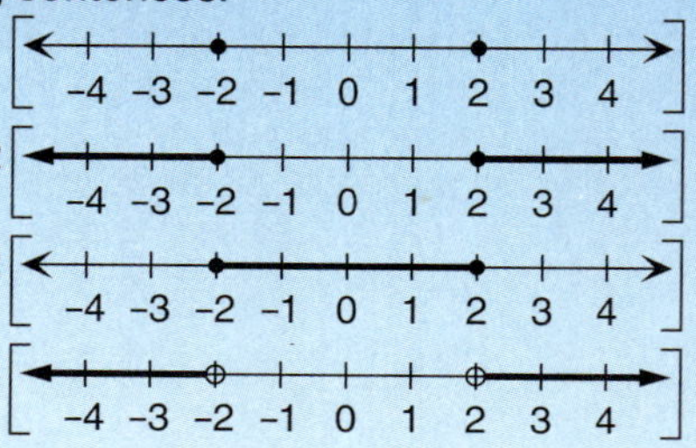

Introducing Lesson 5-4

Combining Turns

IN-CLASS ACTIVITY

Recall that a circle has 360°. If you turn all the way around, you have made one **full turn** or one **revolution.** A full turn has **magnitude** 360°.

Pictured below are two **quarter turns.** Each is $\frac{1}{4}$ of a revolution, or 90°.

Notice that the turns are in different directions. In the turn at left, think of standing at point *O* (the center of the turn) and looking at point *P*. Then turn so that you are looking at point *Q*. You have turned **counterclockwise,** the opposite of the way clock hands usually move. At right, imagine yourself at point *B*. Look first at point *A*, then turn to look at point *C*. You have turned 90° **clockwise.**

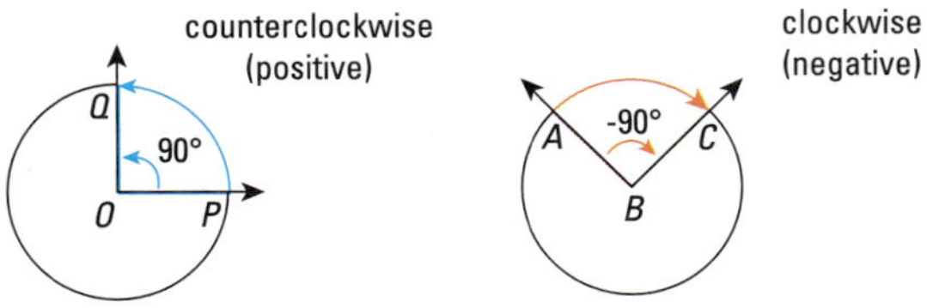

In most of mathematics, the counterclockwise direction is considered positive and the clockwise direction is negative. The turn with center *O* above is a turn with the positive magnitude 90°. The turn with center *B* is a turn of -90°.

1 Face the front of the room. Imagine that you are standing at the center of a circle on the floor. Turn 90° clockwise. If your entire class is doing this together, wait for signals from your teacher. What is in front of you?

2 Turn another 90° clockwise. What is in front of you?

3 Turn 45° counterclockwise. What is in front of you?

4 Begin again facing the front of the room. Your teacher will select an object in the room. Estimate how far (clockwise or counterclockwise) you have to turn to face the object directly.

5 Your teacher may select other objects. For each object, follow the directions of step 4.

6 Select 4 objects in the room. For each object, give the magnitude of a clockwise and a counterclockwise turn you would make to face each object. What is true about the magnitudes?

253

In-class Activity

Resources

From the ***Teacher's Resource File***

- Answer Master 5-4

Have students stand and face the front of the room. Tell them to make a full turn to the right. Then tell them to make a full turn to the left. Ask which is a clockwise turn as seen from the ceiling [to the right], and which is a counterclockwise turn [to the left].

Face the front of the room and show students a quarter turn clockwise by turning yourself 90° to the right and a quarter turn counterclockwise by turning 90° to the left. Then have students practice making quarter turns and half turns.

Answers

1–5. Answers will vary.

6. The sum of the absolute values of the two magnitudes for each object is 360°.

Optional Activities

Ask students if they have ever heard of or used "clock positions" to describe locations. Tell them to face the same direction, look straight ahead, and imagine they are looking at 12 o'clock. Explain that something that is about 30° to the right is at 1 o'clock, something that is about 60° to the left is at 10 o'clock, and so on. Name some things in the room and have students describe their positions. Students should realize that if they change their "straight ahead" position, the location descriptions will also change.

You might also ask students when they think using "clock positions" to locate an object might be useful. [Sample responses: when describing the location of a person in a crowd; when describing a location in the sky]

Lesson 5-4

Objectives

L Calculate magnitudes of turns given angle measures or revolutions.

Resources

From the ***Teacher's Resource File***

- Lesson Master 5-4A or 5-4B
- Answer Master 5-4
- Assessment Sourcebook: Quiz for Lessons 5-1 through 5-4
- Teaching Aids
  50 Warm-up
  53 Adding Angle Measures
  54 Rotations
  55 Questions
- Technology Sourcebook, Computer Master 7

Additional Resources

- Visuals for Teaching Aids 50, 53–55
- Geometry Workshop
- Toothpicks (Flat)

Teaching Lesson 5-4

Warm-up

Diagnostic Solve.

1. Tell if each turn is a clockwise turn or a counterclockwise turn.

a. A turn to the left
counterclockwise

b. A turn to the right
clockwise

c. A 30° turn
counterclockwise

d. A –30° turn
clockwise

LESSON

5-4 *Combining Turns*

Spirals, leaps, and spins. *In the 1992 Winter Olympics, Russians Natalia Mishkutienok and Artur Dmitriev of the Unified Team performed their turns and lifts with grace and precision. They won the gold medal in pair skating.*

Examples of Turns

In the picture below, the six small angles at M are drawn to have equal measures. Each angle has measure 60° because each is $\frac{1}{6}$ of 360°. Think of standing at M and facing point S. If you now turn clockwise to face point U, you have turned -120°. If you turn from facing S to face point X, you have turned 60°.

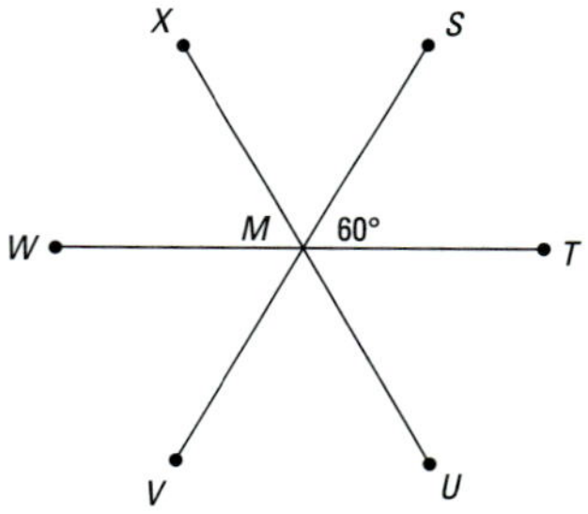

For any clockwise turn, there is a counterclockwise turn that ends in the same place. For instance, the -120° turn from S to U above can also be achieved by going 240° counterclockwise. So a turn of -120° is considered identical to a turn of 240°.

You can use protractors to help measure magnitudes of turns. But a protractor cannot tell you the direction of the turn.

254

Lesson 5-4 Overview

Broad Goals To obtain the results when turns are combined, one uses addition.

Perspective This lesson is very important for future work in geometry and trigonometry. In geometry, the idea is crucial to understanding relationships involving parallel lines and angle sums in polygons. In trigonometry, students are expected to understand clockwise and counterclockwise turns immediately. If they have never seen such turns before, they can get very confused.

Turn is a simpler name for *rotation*, one of the fundamental transformations that relate congruent figures. Although congruence is not mentioned in this lesson, there are hints of this concept.

It is important to be aware of the following subtle point. The physical turn is not the same as the mathematical turn. For example, physical turns of magnitudes –120° and 240° are obviously different. Customarily, mathematical turns are concerned only with where a point "winds up"; how it got there is not of concern. Thus, the mathematical turns of –120° and 240° are considered identical. In general, adding or subtracting 360° from the magnitude of a mathematical turn does not change that turn. Thus many questions in this lesson have numerous answers.

Following One Turn by Another

Turns are discussed in this chapter because addition is used in finding results of combining two turns. Pictured below is a 35° turn followed by a 90° turn. The result is a 125° turn. In general, if one turn is followed by another, the magnitude of the result is found by adding the magnitudes of the turns.

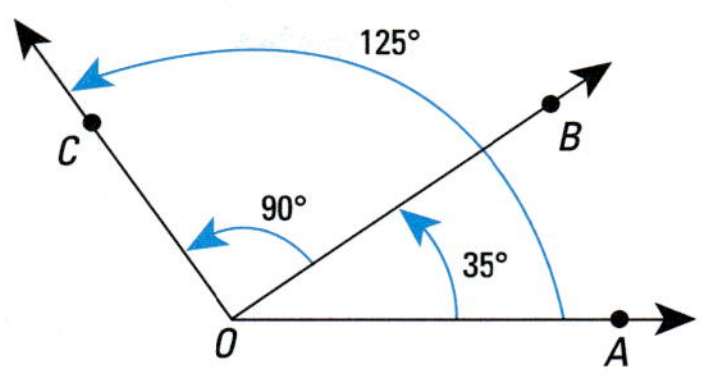

This addition property holds even if the turns are in opposite directions, but you then need to add positive and negative numbers. Shown below is a 60° turn followed by a -90° turn. The result is a -30° turn, or in other words, a turn of 30° clockwise.

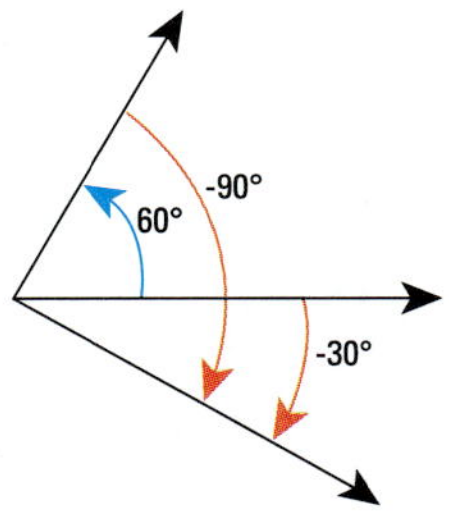

60° + -90° = -30°

> **Fundamental Property of Turns**
> If a turn of magnitude x is followed by a turn of magnitude y, the result is a turn of magnitude $x + y$.

Tops, figure skaters, gears, the earth, pinwheels, and phonograph records turn. All of these objects may turn many revolutions. So it is possible to have turns with magnitudes over 360°. For example, a dancer who spins $1\frac{1}{2}$ times around has spun 540°, since the dancer has made a full turn of 360° followed by a half turn of 180°.

2. If you turn 90° counterclockwise and then turn 70° clockwise, what is the result? **20° (a 20° counterclockwise turn)**

3. If you turn 210° clockwise and then turn 180° counterclockwise, what is the result? **-30° (a 30° clockwise turn.)**

Notes on Reading

You might want to use **Teaching Aid 53** to demonstrate the examples in the text.

Be sure students understand the difference between clockwise and counterclockwise turns of the same magnitude. Discuss the fact that if the magnitude of the turns have the same absolute value, then following one turn by the other gets a person back to his or her starting position. This is the Additive Inverse Property applied to turns.

To reinforce the ideas presented in the lesson, you might put the following diagram on the board, or use **Teaching Aid 54**. Have students fill in the boxes.

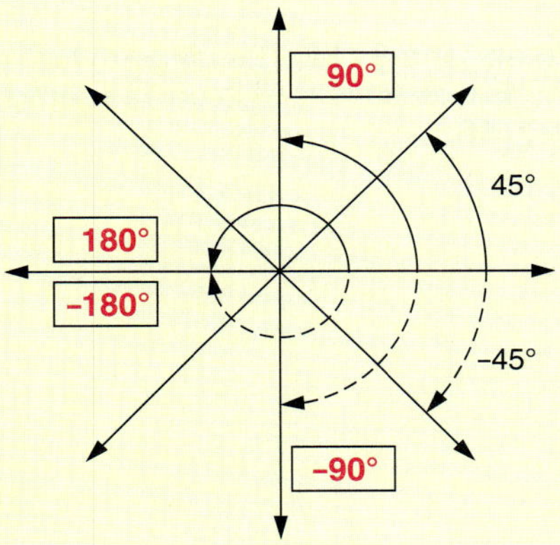

Optional Activities

Activity 1 After students answer **Question 3,** you might put the following drawing on the board. Note that when the propeller is rotated 180°, the blades and the numbers on the blades look the same. Have students find other numbers which read the same way when turned 180°. [Some numbers that contain 0, 1, 6, 8, and/or 9 as digits, such as, 101, 6009, 181]

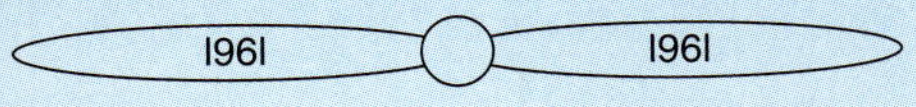

Activity 2 Spokes of a Wheel
Materials: Protractors

After students answer **Questions 22–24,** you might have them use protractors to draw a wheel with 10 equally-spaced spokes, labeling each spoke with a different capital letter. Then ask them to write and solve two problems about their drawings that are similar to Questions 22–24.

You may wish to have students **work in pairs**, exchange papers, and solve each other's problems.

Activity 3 Technology Connection You may wish to have students use the *Geometry Workshop* to explore angles and turns with *Technology Sourcebook, Computer Master 7.*

Additional Examples

You might use the following examples as you discuss this lesson.

1. If you turn 40° counterclockwise and then 70° clockwise, what turn is the result? **30° clockwise turn**
2. Consider a turn of 150°.
   a. Is this a clockwise or counterclockwise turn? **Counterclockwise**
   b. It is identical to a turn of what magnitude in the opposite direction? **-210°**
3. What is m∠*ABD*? **52°**

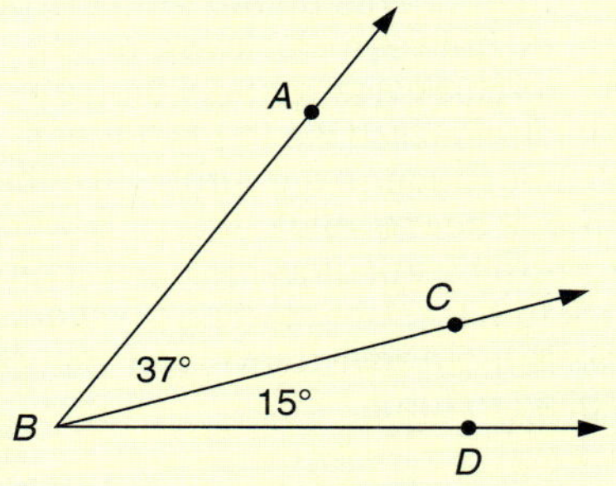

Notes on Questions

Question 3 Students might enjoy doing *Activity 1* in *Optional Activities,* on page 255, at this time.

Questions 8–11 The diagram for these questions is also on **Teaching Aid 55**.

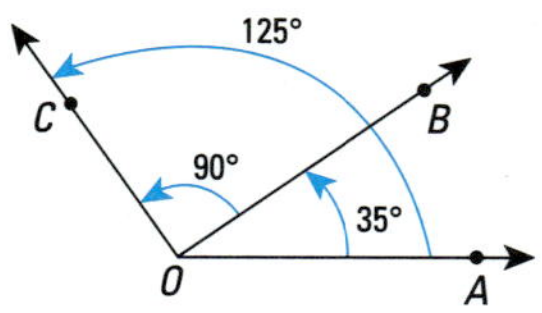

Adding Measures of Adjacent Angles

In the drawing at the left, ray $\overrightarrow{OB}$ is in the *interior* of ∠*AOC*. This ray is a side of two angles, *AOB* and *BOC*, that have no common interior points. The angles are called **adjacent angles.** The absolute values of the magnitudes of the turns are the measures of these angles. You can see that

$$m\angle AOB + m\angle BOC = m\angle AOC.$$
$$35° \quad + \quad 90° \quad = \quad 125°$$

This is called the *Angle Addition Property.*

Angle Addition Property
If $\overrightarrow{OB}$ is in the interior of ∠*AOC*, then m∠*AOB* + m∠*BOC* = m∠*AOC*.

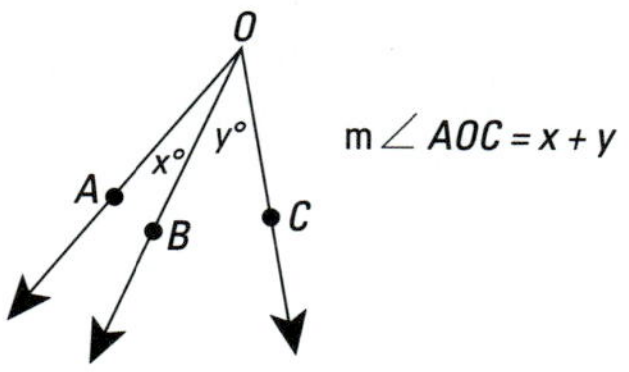

QUESTIONS

Covering the Reading

In 1–4, give the number of degrees in the turn.

1. a full turn **360°**
2. one revolution **360°**
3. a half turn **180°**
4. a quarter turn **90°**
5. In the drawing above, is the 35° turn clockwise or counterclockwise? **counterclockwise**
6. __?__ turns have positive magnitudes. **counterclockwise**
7. __?__ turns have negative magnitudes. **clockwise**

In 8–11, all small angles at *O* have the same measure. Give the magnitude of each turn around point *O*.

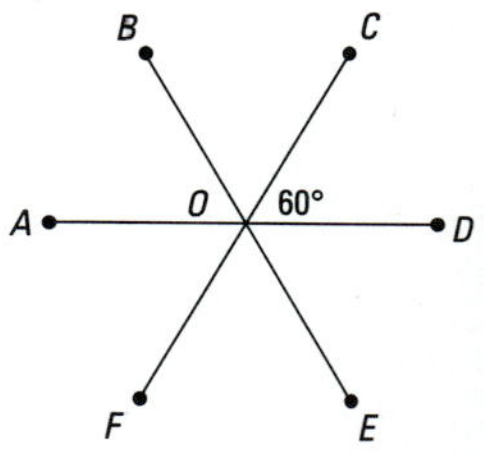

8. the counterclockwise turn from *D* to *B*. **120°**
9. the counterclockwise turn from *C* to *F*. **180°**
10. the clockwise turn from *D* to *E*. **-60°**
11. the clockwise turn from *A* to *F*. **-300°**
12. In the drawing of Questions 8–11, what is m∠*BOF*? **120° or 240°**
13. A turn of -80° ends in the same place as a turn of what positive magnitude? **280°**

Adapting to Individual Needs

Extra Help
Materials: **Teaching Aid 53**, toothpicks (flat)

To help students measure the magnitude of angles, have them **work in groups.** Give each group **Teaching Aid 53**. Tell students to use the toothpicks on the circle to represent the sides of the angles to duplicate the examples given in the lesson. Explain that the angle measures will be close, but not exactly the same as those in the text because of the nature of the materials being used. However, the process should help show the Angle-Addition Property.

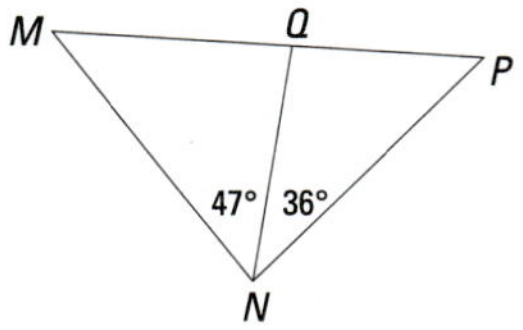

17) If a turn of magnitude *x* is followed by a turn of magnitude *y*, the result is a turn of magnitude *x* + *y*.

In 14–16, give the result of

14. a 90° turn followed by a 35° turn. 125° turn

15. a 90° turn followed by a -35° turn. 55° turn

16. a -5° turn followed by a -6° turn. -11° turn

17. State the Fundamental Property of Turns.

18. a. In the drawing at the left, how are $\angle MNQ$ and $\angle QNP$ related?
b. Find $m\angle MNP$. a) $m\angle MNP = m\angle MNQ + m\angle QNP$; b) 83°

Applying the Mathematics

19. An airplane pilot is flying along the line shown toward point *B*. When the plane reaches point *A*, the pilot changes course toward point *C*. Use a protractor to determine the magnitude of the turn that is needed. -29°

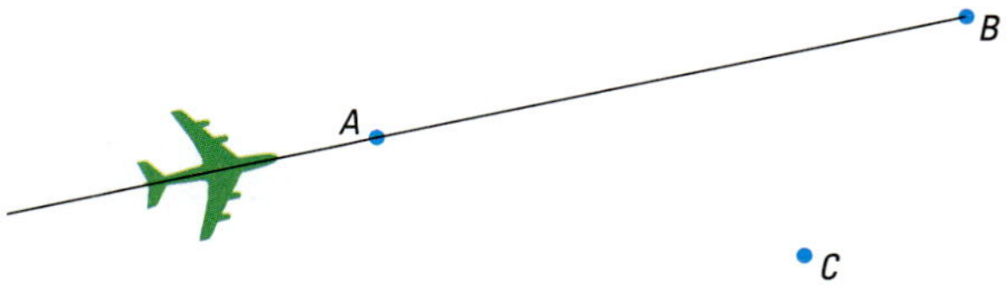

In 20 and 21, the highlighted spokes divide the wheel into equal sections. What is the measure of a central angle?

20. (rear wheel) 120°   **21.** (front wheel) 72°

Adapting to Individual Needs

English Language Development
Materials: Clock

You might use the hands of a clock to explain the meanings of *clockwise* and *counterclockwise*. Emphasize that the term *counter* means against or opposite, so counterclockwise is the opposite of clockwise. You can also use the clock hands to illustrate a *full turn* or *complete revolution*, a *half turn*, a *quarter turn*, and so on.

LESSON MASTER 5-4 A **Questions on SPUR Objectives**
See pages 297-299 for objectives.

Representations Objective L

1. How many degrees are in four revolutions? 1440°
2. What is the result of a 180° turn followed by a -45° turn? a 135° turn
3. A turn of magnitude -75° is a 75° clockwise turn.
4. $\overline{OA}$ is perpendicular to $\overline{TC}$. Write an equation that relates $\angle TOA$ and $\angle AOB$. $m\angle TOA = m\angle AOB + 30°$; $m\angle TOA + m\angle AOB + 30° = 180°$

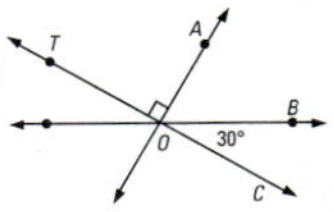

5. What is the approximate measure of the angle formed by the hands of a clock at 1:00? 30°

6. How far does the *minute* hand of a clock turn in
   a. one hour? 360°
   b. twenty minutes? 120°
7. How many degrees does the hour hand turn in
   a. forty minutes? 20° b. twenty minutes? 10°

In 8-10, all the small angles at *O* have the same measure. Consider turns around point *O*.

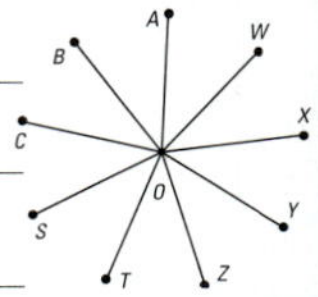

8. What is the magnitude of the clockwise turn from *B* to *Y*? 160°
9. What is the magnitude of the counterclockwise turn from *W* to *S*? 160°
10. If you are standing on *O* facing *T* and turn 160° clockwise, what letter will you be facing? A

Notes on Questions

Questions 22–24 These questions help develop spatial ability. They may be difficult for some students at first, but with practice such questions become easier. Students may benefit from moving their fingers from position to position on the Ferris wheel. The Ferris wheel diagram is also on **Teaching Aid 55.** *Activity 2* in *Optional Activities,* on page 255, also relates to **Questions 22–24.**

Question 26 Students might draw a clock face and think of how the hands move from 5 o'clock to 6 o'clock, for example. *Drawing a picture* is one of the problem-solving techniques discussed in Chapter 6.

Questions 29–34 Note that the answers to Questions 29–30 and 31–32 are different, but the answers to Questions 33–34 are the same. Students might explore if $-a + -b + -c$ is always equal to $-(a + b + c)$.

Question 41 *Quantum* is published by the National Science Teachers Association.

LESSON MASTER 5-4 B **Questions on SPUR Objectives**

Vocabulary

1. In the space below, draw and label a pair of *adjacent* angles.
sample:

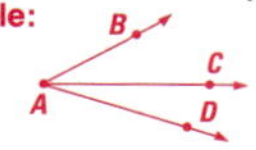

Give the names of the two adjacent angles you drew. ∠BAC ∠CAD

Representations Objective L: Calculate magnitudes of turns given angle measures or revolutions.

2. How many degrees are in two revolutions? 720°
3. *Multiple choice.* A turn of 90° is the same as
(a) a half turn (b) a quarter turn
(c) a full turn (d) one revolution
b
4. In which direction is a turn with a positive magnitude? counterclockwise
5. In which direction is a turn with a negative magnitude? clockwise
6. *True or false.* A clockwise turn of 55° is the same as a counterclockwise turn of 305°. true
7. *True or false.* A turn of 65° is the same as a counterclockwise turn of 295°. false
8. *True or false.* A counterclockwise turn of 110° is the same as a clockwise turn of 70°. false
9. *True or false.* A turn of 20° is the same as a turn of -340°. true

In 10-14, give each result.

10. A turn of 45° followed by a turn of 70°. a turn of 115°
11. A turn of -50° followed by a turn of 40°. a turn of -10°
12. A turn of 115° followed by a turn of -35°. a turn of 80°
13. A turn of -90° followed by a turn of -20°. a turn of -110°
14. A turn of 17° followed by a turn of -17°. a turn of 0°

In 22–24, a Ferris wheel is pictured. The spokes are equally spaced.

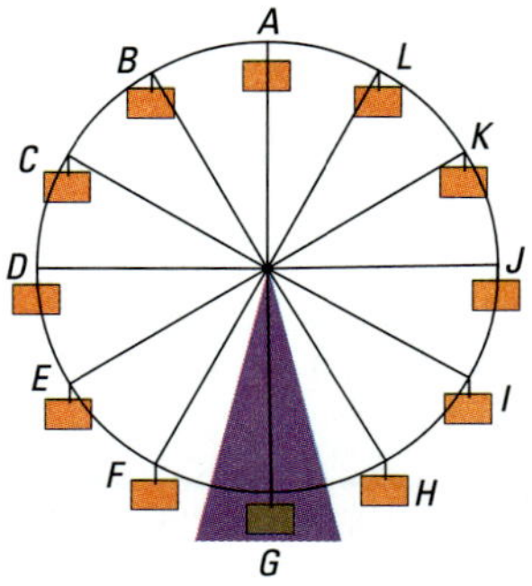

22. **a.** What magnitude turn will bring seat J to the position of seat L?
b. Where will seat B wind up on this turn? **a) 60° (or -300°); b) *D***

23. **a.** What magnitude turn will bring seat K to the position of seat G?
b. What magnitude turn will bring seat K back to its original position?
a) 240° (or -120°); b) 120° (or -240°)

24. If seat C is moved to the position of seat G, what seat will be moved to the top? ***I***

25. If $\overrightarrow{BC}$ and $\overrightarrow{BD}$ are perpendicular, how many degrees are in $\angle ABC$? **100°**

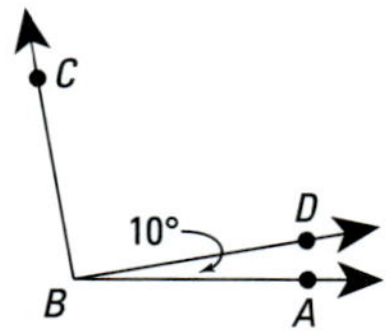

26. How many degrees does the hour hand of a clock turn in the given amount of time?
a. one hour **-30°** **b.** 10 minutes **-5°**

27. How many degrees are in 6 revolutions? **2160°**

28. Describe a situation involving turns that is not mentioned in this lesson. **Sample: automobile tires spinning on their axles**

Review

In 29–34, let a = -5, b = -6, and c = 20. Find the value of the expression. *(Lessons 4-1, 5-1, 5-2, 5-3)*

29. $a + b$ **-11** **30.** $a + -b$ **1** **31.** $|b + c|$ **14**

32. $|b| + |c|$ **26** **33.** $-a + -b + -c$ **-9** **34.** $-(a + b + c)$ **-9**

35. Consider this situation. It took Ralph 2 hours to do homework last night. He spent 45 minutes on math and m minutes on the rest. Give an equation that relates all the quantities in the situation. *(Lesson 5-1)* **45 + m = 120 (minutes), or $\frac{3}{4} + \frac{m}{60} = 2$ (hours)**

A big wheel. *George Washington Gale Ferris built his wheel after his design won a contest held by promoters of the Exposition. The wheel was 264 ft high and had 36 seats. But each "seat" held 60 people and was about the size of a bus!*

36. The first Ferris wheel was erected in 1893 by G.W.G. Ferris for the World's Columbian Exposition in Chicago. It was huge. The wheel and cars weighed 2100 tons; the levers and machinery weighed 2200 tons; and a full load of passengers weighed 150 tons. What was the total weight of the wheel and machinery with a full load of passengers? *(Lesson 5-1)* **2100 + 2200 + 150 = 4450 tons**

37. If Y stands for a year and time is measured in years, what stands for two years before Y? *(Lesson 4-3)* **$Y - 2$**

38. Four instances of a general pattern are given. Describe the general pattern using two variables. *(Lesson 4-2)*

$$3 + 4 + 3 = 4 + 2 \cdot 3$$
$$-2 + 9.1 + -2 = 9.1 + 2 \cdot -2$$
$$7 + 0 + 7 = 0 + 2 \cdot 7$$
$$\frac{2}{7} + \frac{3}{7} + \frac{2}{7} = \frac{3}{7} + 2 \cdot \frac{2}{7}$$

Sample: $x + y + x = y + 2 \cdot x$

39. How many meters are in 6 kilometers? *(Lesson 3-4)* **6000 m**

40. Write 63.2 million

a. as a decimal. **63,200,000**

b. in scientific notation. *(Lessons 2-1, 2-3)* **6.32×10^7**

Exploration

41. Here is a brainteaser from *Quantum,* a mathematics and science magazine for students.

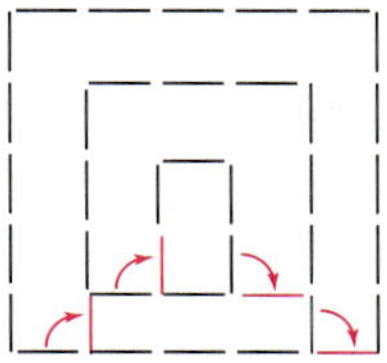

Starting from the inside, the above spiral of 35 toothpicks is wound clockwise. Move four toothpicks to rewind it counterclockwise.

Follow-up for Lesson 5-4

Practice

For more questions on SPUR Objectives, use **Lesson Master 5-4A** (shown on page 257) or **Lesson Master 5-4B** (shown on pages 258–259).

Assessment

Quiz A quiz covering Lesson 5-1 through Lesson 5-4 is provided in the *Assessment Sourcebook.*

Oral Communication Have students describe three different ways to combine turns so that the final result is a turn with a magnitude of 135°. The drawing is on **Teaching Aid 54.** [Descriptions contain both clockwise and counterclockwise turns.]

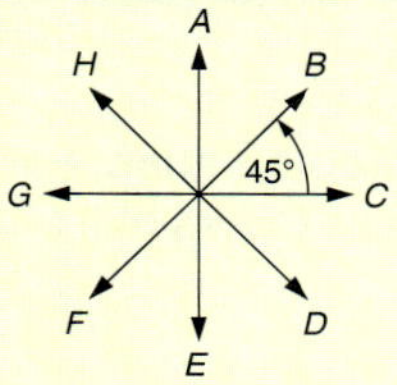

Extension

Multicultural Connection Patterns involving rotations can be found in Native American jewelry, Colonial American quilts, African carvings, and Chinese embroidery. Students might find examples of such patterns, display them, and describe the rotation(s) involved.

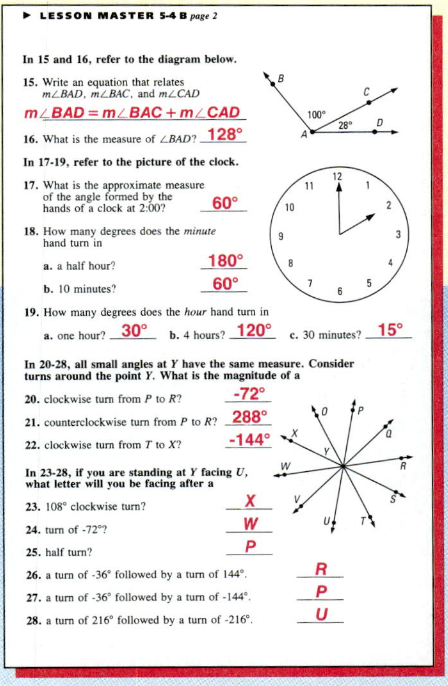

▶ **LESSON MASTER 5-4 B** *page 2*

In 15 and 16, refer to the diagram below.

15. Write an equation that relates $m\angle BAD$, $m\angle BAC$, and $m\angle CAD$
$m\angle BAD = m\angle BAC + m\angle CAD$

16. What is the measure of $\angle BAD$? **128°**

In 17-19, refer to the picture of the clock.

17. What is the approximate measure of the angle formed by the hands of a clock at 2:00? **60°**

18. How many degrees does the *minute* hand turn in

a. a half hour? **180°**

b. 10 minutes? **60°**

19. How many degrees does the *hour* hand turn in

a. one hour? **30°** b. 4 hours? **120°** c. 30 minutes? **15°**

In 20-28, all small angles at Y have the same measure. Consider turns around the point Y. What is the magnitude of a

20. clockwise turn from P to R? **-72°**

21. counterclockwise turn from P to R? **288°**

22. clockwise turn from T to X? **-144°**

In 23-28, if you are standing at Y facing U, what letter will you be facing after a

23. 108° clockwise turn? **X**

24. turn of -72°? **W**

25. half turn? **P**

26. a turn of -36° followed by a turn of 144°. **R**

27. a turn of -36° followed by a turn of -144°. **P**

28. a turn of 216° followed by a turn of -216°. **U**

Setting Up Lesson 5-5

Materials If you plan to use the *Assessment* suggested for Lesson 5-5, each group of students will need a newspaper.

Lesson 5-5

Objectives

A Add positive and negative numbers written as fractions.

Resources

From the ***Teacher's Resource File***
- Lesson Master 5-5A or 5-5B
- Answer Master 5-5
- Teaching Aid 50: Warm-up

Additional Resources
- Visual for Teaching Aid 50
- Newspapers (Assessment)

Teaching Lesson 5-5

Warm-up

Mental Mathematics For each fraction, give three equal fractions.
Sample fractions are given.

1. $\frac{1}{3}$ $\frac{2}{6}, \frac{5}{15}, \frac{6}{18}$
2. $\frac{4}{5}$ $\frac{8}{10}, \frac{20}{25}, \frac{40}{50}$
3. $\frac{5}{6}$ $\frac{10}{12}, \frac{15}{18}, \frac{20}{24}$
4. $\frac{9}{10}$ $\frac{18}{20}, \frac{45}{50}, \frac{90}{100}$
5. $\frac{1}{2}$ $\frac{2}{4}, \frac{5}{10}, \frac{10}{20}$
6. $\frac{3}{4}$ $\frac{6}{8}, \frac{15}{20}, \frac{30}{40}$

LESSON

5-5 Adding Positive and Negative Fractions

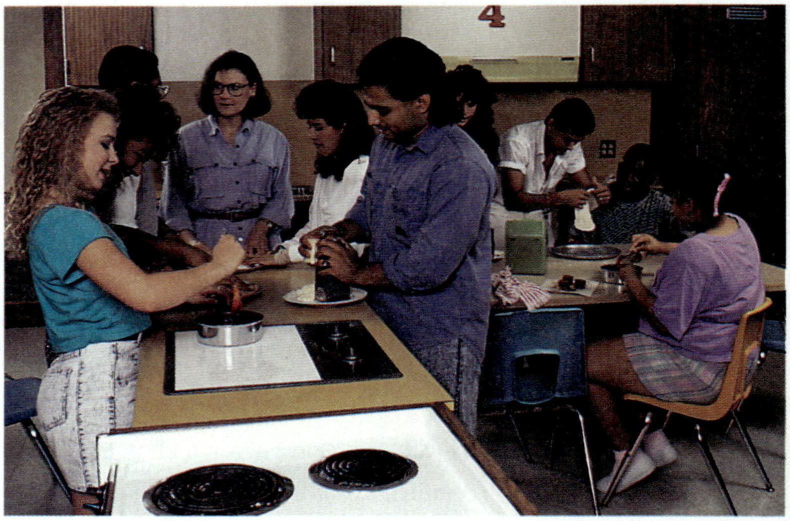

Using fractions. *Fractions are commonplace in food science or cooking classes.*

❶ Adding Fractions with the Same Denominator

Nanette put $\frac{1}{3}$ cup of milk in a casserole. She forgot and then put in another $\frac{1}{3}$ cup of milk. No, no, Nanette! To find the total amount of milk Nanette put in the casserole, think of thirds as units. By the Putting-Together Model for Addition:

$$1 \text{ third} + 1 \text{ third} = 2 \text{ thirds}$$
$$\frac{1}{3} + \frac{1}{3} = \frac{2}{3}$$

Nanette put $\frac{2}{3}$ cup milk in the casserole.

Milton jogs laps on a quarter-mile track. Two days ago he ran 3 laps or 3/4 mile. Yesterday he ran 9 laps. Today he ran 10 laps. My, my, Milton. The total amount he ran is:

$$3 \text{ laps} + 9 \text{ laps} + 10 \text{ laps} = 22 \text{ laps}$$
$$\frac{3}{4} + \frac{9}{4} + \frac{10}{4} = \frac{22}{4}$$

Milton ran $\frac{22}{4}$ miles altogether.

The general pattern is easy to see. To add fractions with the same denominator, add the numerators and keep the denominator the same. Here is a description of the pattern, using variables:

> **Adding Fractions Property**
> For all numbers a, b, and c, with $c \neq 0$, $\frac{a}{c} + \frac{b}{c} = \frac{a+b}{c}$.

Lesson 5-5 Overview

Broad Goals This lesson discusses the addition of positive and negative fractions, including the generalization to algebraic fractions with the same denominator.

Perspective The arithmetic in this lesson is review for most students. The algebra is new, but not difficult.

We introduce common denominators by making lists of equivalent fractions and then searching for a pair with the same denominator. Our goal is simply to get students to realize that they need to have like denominators in order to add fractions, rather than have them concentrate on finding the least common denominator. If students do not already know this skill, it will come with experience.

Some calculators do operations with both fractions and mixed numbers. Some of your students may own such calculators. You might let these students use them to check computations like those in Questions 10–14 and 20–23.

Example 1

Simplify $\frac{3}{x} + \frac{5}{x}$ and check your answer.

Solution

Using the Adding Fractions Property,

$$\frac{3}{x} + \frac{5}{x} = \frac{3+5}{x} = \frac{8}{x}.$$

Check

This should work for every value of x other than zero. So to check, we substitute some value for x. We pick 4, because fourths are terminating decimals and are easier to check than repeating decimals.

Does $\frac{3}{4} + \frac{5}{4} = \frac{8}{4}$? Check by rewriting the fractions as decimals.
Does $0.75 + 1.25 = 2$? Yes.

One good turn deserves another. *With just a few minutes between classes, students must make accurate clockwise and counterclockwise turns to quickly open their combination locks and grab their books.*

Example 2

A quarter turn counterclockwise is followed by a half turn clockwise. What is the result?

Solution 1

Draw a picture like the one below. Think of standing at O, facing P. After the quarter turn counterclockwise you will be facing Q. Then, after the half turn clockwise you will be facing R. **The result is a quarter turn clockwise.**

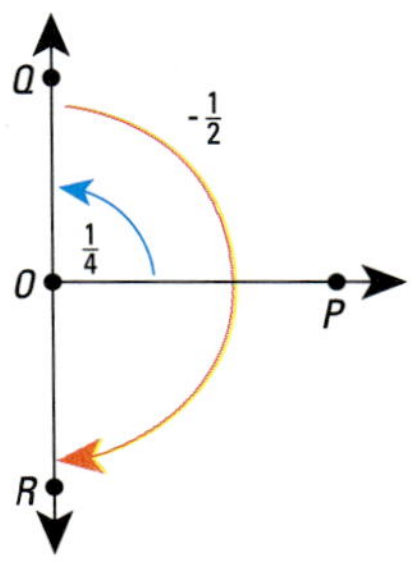

Solution 2

Use the Adding Fractions Property.

quarter turn counterclockwise + half turn clockwise	
$= \frac{1}{4} + -\frac{1}{2}$	Translate to fractions.
$= \frac{1}{4} + -\frac{2}{4}$	Change to common denominator.
❷ $= \frac{1 + -2}{4}$	Use the Adding Fractions Property. $(-\frac{2}{4} = \frac{-2}{4})$
$= -\frac{1}{4}$	Add 1 and -2.
= quarter turn clockwise	Translate back to words.

Notes on Reading

❶ **Error Alert** Some students may want to add fractions by adding not only the numerators but also the denominators. We tie addition to the Putting-Together Model to help students prevent this mistake, and a careful reading of the text is helpful in developing such understanding.

❷ In the solution, we use the equality $-\frac{2}{4} = \frac{-2}{4}$. At this point, students may not know enough about division to deduce the equality of $\frac{-a}{b}$ and $-\frac{a}{b}$. However, for special cases, you can have students verify the equality with a calculator.

Optional Activities

After discussing adding fractions with the same denominator, you might want to pose these problems to emphasize again that the units must be the same. Discuss whether the conclusions are valid, and have students explain why or why not.

1. Jerry and Liz bought a pizza. Each of them ate half of it. Conclusion: They ate the entire pizza. [Valid conclusion; they each ate one half of the same pizza. $\frac{1}{2} + \frac{1}{2} = 1$]
2. Mort and Todd each bought a pizza. Each person ate half his pizza. Conclusion: They each ate the same amount of pizza. [Not valid because there is no way of knowing whether the pizzas were the same size.]
3. Heidi bought a large pizza and Kim bought a small one. Each person ate half of her pizza. Conclusion: Heidi ate more pizza than Kim [Valid. Since Heidi's pizza is bigger, and they both ate half of their pizzas, Heidi ate more.]

❸ If your students are not proficient at adding fractions, you may wish to take some extra time to practice finding common denominators, finding least common denominators, and adding fractions. However, if your students are reasonably competent at this skill, do not spend extra time on it.

Some interesting results from the Second International Mathematics Study showed that a particular addition of fractions was correctly done by 85% of 8th graders at the beginning of the year; 100% of the teachers reported teaching the idea during the year, and at the end of the year 84% of students answered the same item correctly. This confirms the idea that, after a while, mastery is not increased by reviewing an idea in the same way it had previously been taught. We believe mastery is increased by using an idea in new contexts so as to develop new understandings.

❸ Adding Fractions with Different Denominators

$\frac{3}{8}$ $\frac{2}{6}$

In Example 2, the denominators are not the same. Here is another example of adding fractions with different denominators.

Bill ate 3 of 8 pieces of a personal spinach pizza and 2 of 6 pieces of a mushroom pizza the same size. How much pizza did he eat in all? Use the Equal Fractions Property to find equal fractions with the same denominator. One way to start is to write

$$\frac{3}{8} = \frac{6}{16} = \frac{9}{24} = \frac{12}{32} = \ldots$$
$$\frac{2}{6} = \frac{4}{12} = \frac{6}{18} = \frac{8}{24} = \ldots$$

Stop, as we have, when two fractions have the same denominator. The number 24 is a **common denominator.**

$$\frac{3}{8} + \frac{2}{6} = \frac{9}{24} + \frac{8}{24} = \frac{17}{24}$$

Bill ate the equivalent of $\frac{17}{24}$ of a whole pizza.

Notice that the common denominator 24 is a multiple of both 8 and 6. Other common multiples would be 48, 72, 96, and so on. Since 24 is the smallest common integer multiple of 8 and 6, it is called the **least common multiple (LCM)** of these numbers. You could use any common multiple as the common denominator. However, when the least common multiple is the common denominator, the numbers are smaller than with any other multiple.

Example 3

Add $\frac{5}{6} + \text{-}\frac{1}{2} + \frac{7}{3}$, and check.

Solution

You could find a common denominator by finding the product of the denominators: $6 \cdot 2 \cdot 3 = 36$. But that is much bigger than is needed. Since 6 is a multiple of the other denominators, 6 can be a common denominator.

$$\frac{5}{6} + \text{-}\frac{1}{2} + \frac{7}{3}$$
$$= \frac{5}{6} + \text{-}\frac{3}{6} + \frac{14}{6} \qquad \text{Since } \frac{1}{2} = \frac{1 \cdot 3}{2 \cdot 3} = \frac{3}{6} \text{ and } \frac{7}{3} = \frac{7 \cdot 2}{3 \cdot 2} = \frac{14}{6}.$$
$$= \frac{5 + \text{-}3 + 14}{6} \qquad \text{Adding Fractions Property}$$
$$= \frac{16}{6}$$
$$= \frac{8}{3}$$

▸

Adapting to Individual Needs

Extra Help

To emphasize the need for common denominators when adding fractions, review the apples-and-oranges example from Lesson 5-1. Remind students that they need to think of the denominators as units, as illustrated below.

3 apples + 2 apples = 5 apples

$\frac{3}{8} + \frac{4}{8}$ = 3 eighths + 4 eighths = 7 eighths

$\frac{1}{2} + \frac{3}{4}$ = 1 half + 3 fourths

= 2 fourths + 3 fourths = 5 fourths

$= \frac{2}{4} + \frac{3}{4} = \frac{5}{4}$

Thinking of the denominators as units will also help students remember that only the numerators are added. Be sure students understand that when adding positive and negative fractions with the same denominator, they also add the numerators and keep the common denominator.

Check

You can check using decimals even if the decimals repeat.

$$\frac{5}{6} \approx 0.833333$$
$$-\frac{1}{2} = -0.5$$
$$\frac{7}{3} \approx 2.333333$$

So the sum of the fractions is about
$0.833333 + -0.5 + 2.333333 = 2.666666$.
Since $\frac{8}{3} = 2.666666\ldots$, the answer checks.

Using a Fraction Calculator

There are calculators that can add fractions directly. On those calculators you do not have to find a common denominator. You just enter the fractions, add, and the answer is given as a fraction.

Changing Mixed Numbers to Simple Fractions

When adding an integer and a fraction, use the denominator of the fraction as the common denominator. With this process, you can change any mixed number to a simple fraction.

Example 4

Write $2\frac{3}{5}$ as a simple fraction.

Solution

4 Think of $2\frac{3}{5}$ as $2 + \frac{3}{5}$.

$$2 + \frac{3}{5} = \frac{2}{1} + \frac{3}{5}$$

Use 5 as common denominator.

$$= \frac{10}{5} + \frac{3}{5}$$
$$= \frac{13}{5}$$

To do Example 4, many people use a shortcut to find the numerator of the simple fraction: multiply 5 by 2, and then add 3.

QUESTIONS

Covering the Reading

1. On Monday, Mary ran 7 laps. On Tuesday, she ran 9 laps. If each lap is a quarter mile, how far in miles did Mary run? $\frac{16}{4}$ **miles or 4 miles**

2. Sam used $\frac{5}{2}$ cups of flour in one recipe and $\frac{3}{2}$ cups of flour in another. How much flour did he use altogether? $\frac{8}{2}$ **cups or 4 cups**

4 Some people prefer to refer to $2\frac{3}{5}$ as a "mixed number," while others prefer "mixed numeral." The former is far more common; the latter is technically more correct.

Additional Examples

1. Simplify $\frac{9}{a} + \frac{7}{a}$ $\frac{16}{a}$
2. A half turn clockwise is followed by a quarter turn counterclockwise.
   a. Draw a picture to show the result. **Drawings will vary. In the sample below, assume standing at O and facing N.**

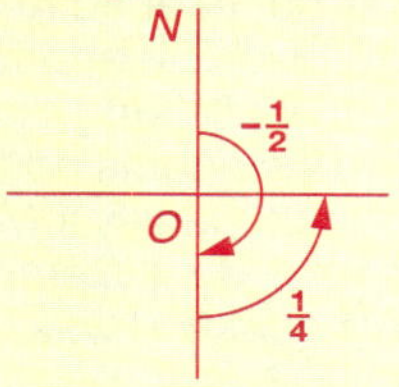

   b. Use the Adding Fractions Property to show the result. $-\frac{1}{2} + \frac{1}{4} = -\frac{1}{4}$, **or a quarter turn clockwise**
3. Find the sum. $\frac{1}{2} + -\frac{3}{4} + \frac{7}{8}$ $\frac{5}{8}$
4. Write $4\frac{5}{8}$ as a simple fraction. $\frac{37}{8}$
5. a. Find $-5\frac{3}{4} + 3\frac{1}{2}$ $-2\frac{1}{4}$
   b. Check your answer by using decimals. $-5.75 + 3.5 = -2.25$

Adapting to Individual Needs

English Language Development

You might want to give students additional help with terms such as *common multiple, least common multiple, common denominator,* and *least common denominator.* Make sure students understand that in these cases *common* means "shared," not "usual" or "ordinary."

A visual way to help students find the least common multiple, and thus the least common denominator, is shown below.

Denominators	Multiples
8	8, 16, (24), 32, 40, 48 . . .
12	12, (24), 36, 48, . . .

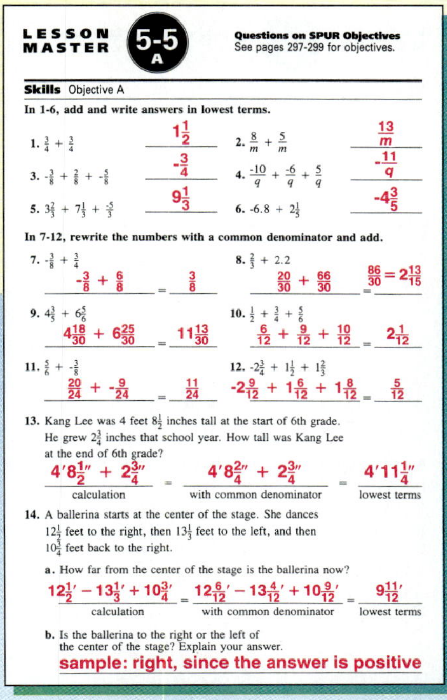

LESSON MASTER 5-5 A

Questions on SPUR Objectives
See pages 297-299 for objectives.

Skills Objective A

In 1-6, add and write answers in lowest terms.

1. $\frac{3}{4} + \frac{3}{4}$ $1\frac{1}{2}$
2. $\frac{8}{m} + \frac{5}{m}$ $\frac{13}{m}$
3. $-\frac{3}{8} + \frac{2}{8} + -\frac{5}{8}$ $-\frac{3}{4}$
4. $\frac{-10}{q} + \frac{-6}{q} + \frac{5}{q}$ $-\frac{11}{q}$
5. $3\frac{2}{3} + 7\frac{1}{3} + \frac{-5}{3}$ $9\frac{1}{3}$
6. $-6.8 + 2\frac{1}{5}$ $-4\frac{3}{5}$

In 7-12, rewrite the numbers with a common denominator and add.

7. $-\frac{3}{8} + \frac{3}{4}$ $-\frac{3}{8} + \frac{6}{8} = \frac{3}{8}$
8. $\frac{2}{3} + 2.2$ $\frac{20}{30} + \frac{66}{30} = \frac{86}{30} = 2\frac{13}{15}$
9. $4\frac{3}{5} + 6\frac{5}{6}$ $4\frac{18}{30} + 6\frac{25}{30} = 11\frac{13}{30}$
10. $\frac{1}{2} + \frac{3}{4} + \frac{5}{6}$ $\frac{6}{12} + \frac{9}{12} + \frac{10}{12} = 2\frac{1}{12}$
11. $\frac{5}{6} + -\frac{3}{8}$ $\frac{20}{24} + -\frac{9}{24} = \frac{11}{24}$
12. $-2\frac{3}{4} + 1\frac{1}{2} + 1\frac{2}{3}$ $-2\frac{9}{12} + 1\frac{6}{12} + 1\frac{8}{12} = \frac{5}{12}$

13. Kang Lee was 4 feet $8\frac{1}{2}$ inches tall at the start of 6th grade. He grew $2\frac{3}{4}$ inches that school year. How tall was Kang Lee at the end of 6th grade?
$4'8\frac{1}{2}'' + 2\frac{3}{4}''$ (calculation) = $4'8\frac{2}{4}'' + 2\frac{3}{4}''$ (with common denominator) = $4'11\frac{1}{4}''$ (lowest terms)

14. A ballerina starts at the center of the stage. She dances $12\frac{1}{2}$ feet to the right, then $13\frac{1}{3}$ feet to the left, and then $10\frac{3}{4}$ feet back to the right.
   a. How far from the center of the stage is the ballerina now?
   $12\frac{1}{2}' - 13\frac{1}{3}' + 10\frac{3}{4}'$ (calculation) = $12\frac{6}{12}' - 13\frac{4}{12}' + 10\frac{9}{12}'$ (with common denominator) = $9\frac{11}{12}'$ (lowest terms)
   b. Is the ballerina to the right or the left of the center of the stage? Explain your answer.
   sample: right, since the answer is positive

Notes on Questions

Question 6b The translation to decimals provides a nice check and also constitutes a nice way to do the addition in the first place.

Questions 20–23 Help students think about reasonable ways to approach these questions. Emphasize methods of checking the results: changing to decimals, adding the integers separately from the fractions, or thinking of a situation where the numbers stand for actual quantities.

Question 30 Ask if any of the given information is not needed to answer the question. [Yes. Either one of the descriptions is sufficient.] Then generalize and ask students how many children are in the family if Minnie has b brothers and s sisters. [$b + s + 1$] This last question was Question 21 of Lesson 5-1.

Question 33 Science Connection Students might enjoy researching other facts about the *Brachiosaurus*; they might also read about other dinosaurs and record some of their weights in scientific notation.

LESSON MASTER 5-5 B Questions on SPUR Objectives

Vocabulary

1. Explain what the least common multiple of two numbers is, and give an example. The least common multiple of two numbers is the smallest integer that is a multiple of each number. Sample example: 12 is the least common multiple of 4 and 6.

Skills Objective A: Add positive and negative numbers written as fractions.

In 2-13, add and write answers in lowest terms.

2. $\frac{2}{9} + \frac{5}{9}$ $\frac{7}{9}$
3. $\frac{3}{8} + \frac{3}{8}$ $\frac{3}{4}$
4. $\frac{7}{12} + \frac{11}{12}$ $\frac{3}{2}$, or $1\frac{1}{2}$
5. $-\frac{1}{4} + \frac{3}{4}$ $\frac{1}{2}$
6. $-\frac{4}{3} + -\frac{11}{3}$ -5
7. $\frac{3}{x} + \frac{4}{x}$ $\frac{7}{x}$
8. $\frac{2}{m} + -\frac{5}{m}$ $-\frac{3}{m}$
9. $-\frac{9}{10} + \frac{4}{10} + \frac{1}{10}$ $-\frac{2}{5}$
10. $\frac{-6}{y} + \frac{3}{y} + \frac{-5}{y}$ $-\frac{8}{y}$
11. $4\frac{7}{8} + -2\frac{3}{8}$ $\frac{5}{2}$, or $2\frac{1}{2}$
12. $3\frac{4}{5} + -1.2$ $2\frac{3}{5}$, or 2.6
13. $\frac{-7}{3} + \frac{-5}{3} + \frac{-2}{3}$ $-\frac{14}{3}$, or $-4\frac{2}{3}$

In 14-19, rewrite the numbers with a common denominator and add.

14. $\frac{1}{6} + \frac{1}{3}$ $\frac{1}{6} + \frac{2}{6} = \frac{3}{6} = \frac{1}{2}$
15. $\frac{3}{5} + \frac{1}{4}$ $\frac{12}{20} + \frac{5}{20} = \frac{17}{20}$
16. $8\frac{3}{5} + \frac{3}{8}$ $8\frac{24}{40} + \frac{15}{40} = \frac{359}{40}$, or $8\frac{39}{40}$
17. $\frac{3}{4} + \frac{1}{6} + \frac{7}{8}$ $\frac{18}{24} + \frac{4}{24} + \frac{21}{24} = \frac{43}{24}$, or $1\frac{19}{24}$
18. $-\frac{1}{3} + \frac{3}{4}$ $-\frac{4}{12} + \frac{9}{12} = \frac{5}{12}$
19. $6\frac{1}{2} + -4\frac{3}{4} + 2\frac{5}{6}$ $6\frac{6}{12} + -4\frac{9}{12} + 2\frac{10}{12} = \frac{55}{12}$, or $4\frac{7}{12}$

3a)

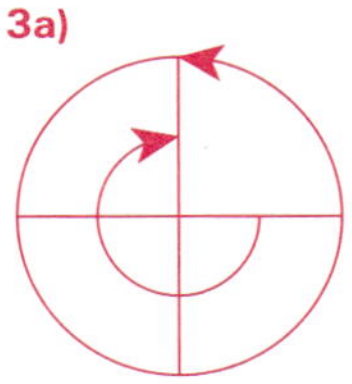

3. A $\frac{3}{4}$ clockwise turn is followed by a full turn counterclockwise.
   a. Draw a picture of this.
   b. What is the result? $\frac{1}{4}$ turn counterclockwise

4. Terri ate $\frac{1}{3}$ of one pizza and $\frac{1}{4}$ of another the same size. a) $\frac{1}{3} + \frac{1}{4}$
   a. What problem with fractions determines the total that Terri ate?
   b. Name five fractions equal to $\frac{1}{3}$. Samples: $\frac{2}{6}, \frac{3}{9}, \frac{4}{12}, \frac{5}{15}, \frac{6}{18}$
   c. Name five fractions equal to $\frac{1}{4}$. Samples: $\frac{2}{8}, \frac{3}{12}, \frac{4}{16}, \frac{5}{20}, \frac{6}{24}$
   d. What is the total amount of pizza that Terri ate? $\frac{7}{12}$

5. a. Find three common multiples of 5 and 7. Samples: 35, 70, 105
   b. What is the least common multiple of 5 and 7? 35
   c. Evaluate $\frac{2}{7} + \frac{3}{5}$. Show your work. $\frac{10}{35} + \frac{21}{35} = \frac{31}{35}$

6. a. Write $\frac{4}{5} + \frac{3}{10}$ as a single fraction. $\frac{11}{10}$
   b. Check by using decimals. $.8 + .3 = 1.1 = \frac{11}{10}$

In 7–14, write the sum as a simple fraction. Show each step in your work.

7. $\frac{50}{11} + \frac{5}{11}$ $\frac{55}{11}$ or 5
8. $\frac{13}{x} + \frac{4}{x}$ $\frac{17}{x}$
9. $\frac{3}{z} + -\frac{9}{z}$ $-\frac{6}{z}$
10. $\frac{-4}{9} + \frac{1}{3}$ $-\frac{1}{9}$
11. $\frac{8}{9} + \frac{1}{15}$ $\frac{43}{45}$
12. $\frac{5}{8} + \frac{2}{5}$ $\frac{41}{40}$
13. $\frac{11}{7} + \frac{6}{7} + -\frac{15}{7}$ $\frac{2}{7}$
14. $\frac{2}{3} + \frac{5}{3} + -\frac{5}{6}$ $\frac{3}{2}$
15. a. Write $4 + \frac{2}{5}$ as a simple fraction. $\frac{22}{5}$
    b. Write $4 + \frac{2}{5}$ as a mixed number. $4\frac{2}{5}$

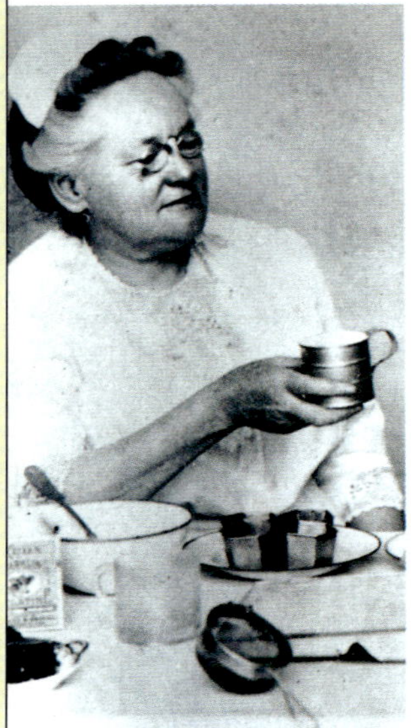

Bon appetit. *The* Fannie Farmer Cook Book *is the most famous American cookbook ever published. Over 3 million copies have been sold. Many of the recipes were tested and revised at Miss Farmer's Boston Cooking School.*

Applying the Mathematics

16. a. Divide to write $\frac{15}{4}$ as a mixed number. $3\frac{3}{4}$
    b. Draw a circle representation of $\frac{15}{4}$.

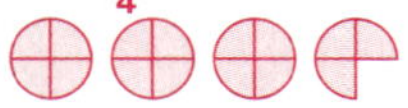

17. In 1896, Fannie Merritt Farmer (1857–1915) published the first cookbook that used standard measuring units such as teaspoons and cups. (Earlier cookbooks used such unclear terms as "a handful" or "a glass.") One of the relationships used in her cookbook is
    1 teaspoon = $\frac{1}{3}$ tablespoon.
    a. Add $\frac{1}{3}$ tablespoon to $\frac{2}{3}$ tablespoon. 1 tablespoon
    b. Convert the tablespoons to teaspoons in part **a** and add the corresponding quantities. 3 teaspoons
    c. Are your answers to parts **a** and **b** equal quantities? Why or why not? Yes. Since 1 tsp = $\frac{1}{3}$T, then 3 tsp = $3 \cdot \frac{1}{3}$T = 1T.

18. In music, two eighth notes take the same time as a quarter note. What addition of fractions explains this? $\frac{1}{8} + \frac{1}{8} = \frac{1}{4}$

19. In music, what amount of time is taken by a sixteenth note followed by an eighth note? $\frac{1}{16} + \frac{1}{8} = \frac{1}{16} + \frac{2}{16} = \frac{3}{16}$

Adapting to Individual Needs

Challenge

If your students are intrigued with the sum of the infinite series given in the *Extension* on page 265, have them find the sum of this infinite series: $\frac{1}{2} - \frac{1}{4} + \frac{1}{8} - \frac{1}{16} + \frac{1}{32} - \ldots$. [Now the pattern of partial sums is $\frac{1}{4}, \frac{3}{8}, \frac{5}{16}, \frac{11}{32}, \ldots$ The limit may not be so obvious; it is $\frac{1}{3}$.]

In 20–23, write the sum as a simple fraction. Show all your steps in writing out each solution.

20. $4\frac{3}{8} + 2\frac{1}{5}$ $\frac{263}{40}$

21. $4\frac{3}{8} + 2\frac{2}{3}$ $\frac{169}{24}$

22. $\frac{6}{7} + 3\frac{7}{12}$ $\frac{373}{84}$

23. $9.75 + \frac{1}{4} + 3$ $\frac{13}{1}$

24. Because of a rainstorm, the water level in a swimming pool rose by $1\frac{1}{2}''$. The following day, it was $2\frac{1}{4}''$ lower.

a. What was the total change in the water level? $-\frac{3}{4}''$

b. If the deep end of the pool was originally 9 ft deep, how deep was the water at the end of the second day? $107\frac{1}{4}''$ or $8'11\frac{1}{4}''$

34a) 28: 1, 2, 4, 7, 14, 28; 49: 1, 7, 49; 196: 1, 2, 4, 7, 14, 28, 49, 98, 196
b) 30: 1, 2, 3, 5, 6, 10, 15, 30; 40: 1, 2, 4, 5, 8, 10, 20, 40; 120: 1, 2, 3, 4, 5, 6, 8, 10, 12, 15, 20, 24, 30, 40, 60, 120
c) Divide the LCM by each factor of the two numbers. The factors of the LCM are all of these divisors and quotients.

31 b)

32 b)

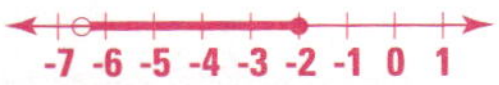

Review

25. A clockwise turn of 52° is followed by a counterclockwise turn of 120°. What is the result? *(Lesson 5-4)* a counterclockwise turn of 68°

In 26–29, simplify. *(Lessons 5-2, 5-3)*

26. $3 + -2 + -1$ 0

27. $-(-(-4.7))$ -4.7

28. $-6 + -8 + -10$ -24

29. $-6 + 8 + -10$ -8

30. Minnie has 5 brothers and 2 sisters. Her brother Dennis has 4 brothers and 3 sisters. How many children are in the family? *(Lesson 5-1)* 8

In 31 and 32, a sentence is given. **a.** Name one solution. **b.** Graph all solutions. *(Lesson 4-10)*

31. $x < 3$ a) Sample: 0

32. $-2 \geq y > -6.5$ a) Sample: -4

The biggest known dinosaur. *Shown here is a friendly Brachiosaurus as depicted in the movie* Jurassic Park.

33. The dinosaur known as *Brachiosaurus,* weighed over 30,000 kg.

a. Write this number in scientific notation. 3×10^4

b. About how much is this weight in pounds? *(Lessons 2-3, 3-5)* about 66,000 lb

Exploration

34. a. List all the factors of 28 and 49. Then list all the factors of the least common multiple of 28 and 49.

b. List all the factors of 30 and 40. Then list all the factors of the least common multiple of 30 and 40.

c. Suppose you know the factors of two numbers. Describe how to find the factors of the least common multiple of the numbers. See above left.

Follow-up for Lesson 5-5

Practice

For more questions on SPUR Objectives, use **Lesson Master 5-5A** (shown on page 263) or **Lesson Master 5-5B** (shown on pages 264–265).

Assessment

Oral/Written Communication Have students **work in groups.** Give each group a newspaper and ask them to find at least one instance in the newspaper in which adding positive and/or negative fractions could be used. Then have them write problems using this data. [The application of fractions for the selection is proper. The problems composed and solutions found are correct.]

Extension

Have students investigate the sum of the infinite series.

$\frac{1}{2} + \frac{1}{4} + \frac{1}{8} + \frac{1}{16} + \frac{1}{32} \ldots$

Tell them to begin by adding the first two terms, then the first three terms, and so on. [Many students will see that the pattern of partial sums, $\frac{3}{4}$, $\frac{7}{8}$, $\frac{15}{16}$, approaches 1.]

Project Update Project 2, *Fractions that Add to 1*, on page 293, relates to the content of this lesson.

▶ **LESSON MASTER 5-5 B** *page 2*

20. Gitesh's baby brother was $20\frac{1}{2}$ inches long when he was born. He grew $1\frac{3}{4}$ inches the first two months. How long was the baby at the age of 2 months?

$20\frac{1}{2} + 1\frac{3}{4}$ (calculation) = $20\frac{2}{4} + 1\frac{3}{4}$ (with common denominator) = $22\frac{1}{4}$ inches (lowest terms)

21. A cake recipe calls for $2\frac{2}{3}$ cups of flour. A brownie recipe calls for $1\frac{3}{4}$ cups of flour. How much flour is needed to make both the cake and brownies?

$2\frac{2}{3} + 1\frac{3}{4}$ (calculation) = $2\frac{8}{12} + 1\frac{9}{12}$ (with common denominator) = $4\frac{5}{12}$ cups (lowest terms)

22. At Pulaski Middle School, $\frac{1}{4}$ of the students will have their picture taken on Monday, $\frac{1}{8}$ on Tuesday, and $\frac{1}{4}$ on Wednesday. What fraction of the students will be photographed the first three days of the week?

$\frac{1}{4} + \frac{1}{8} + \frac{1}{4}$ (calculation) = $\frac{2}{8} + \frac{1}{8} + \frac{2}{8}$ (with common denominator) = $\frac{5}{8}$ of the students (lowest terms)

23. The first day after Mrs. Grabske bought some stock, the price rose $1\frac{1}{4}$ dollars per share. The second day it fell $2\frac{1}{2}$ dollars, and the third day it rose again $1\frac{3}{4}$ dollars.

a. What was the overall change in the price of a share of stock from the time Mrs. Grabske purchased it?

$1\frac{1}{4} + -2\frac{1}{2} + 1\frac{3}{4}$ (calculation) = $1\frac{1}{4} + -2\frac{2}{4} + 1\frac{3}{4}$ (with common denominator) = $\frac{1}{2}$ dollar (lowest terms)

b. Was the stock worth more or less than it was when Mrs. Grabske bought it? Explain your answer.
More; a positive sum means the value went up.

Review Objective J, Lesson 4-8

In 24-27, refer to the cards pictured. If a card is drawn at random, what is the probability that it will show

T R I
C E R A
T O P S

24. a P? $\frac{1}{11}$ **25.** an R? $\frac{2}{11}$

26. a T? $\frac{2}{11}$ **27.** a vowel? $\frac{4}{11}$

Setting Up Lesson 5-6

Materials: Students will need a pair of dice for **Question 29** on page 270 and *Graphing and Probability Workshop* for the *Extension.*

Lesson 5-6

Objectives

G Tell whether or not events are mutually exclusive.

K Calculate the probability of mutually exclusive events or complements of events.

Resources

From the ***Teacher's Resource File***

- Lesson Master 5-6A or 5-6B
- Answer Master 5-6
- Teaching Aids
  50 Warm-up
  56 Two-Dice Outcomes

Additional Resources

- Visuals for Teaching Aids 50, 56
- Graphing and Probability Workshop

LESSON MASTER 5-6 A **Questions on SPUR Objectives** See pages 297-299 for objectives.

Properties Objective G

1. What are *mutually exclusive* events?
   sample: Two events that can't occur together are said to be mutually exclusive.

2. Give an example of two events that are not mutually exclusive.
   sample: choosing a ball and choosing a blue ball

3. *Multiple choice.* Which of the following pairs of events are mutually exclusive?
   (a) The sun is shining. It is raining.
   (b) temperature above freezing; temperature below freezing
   (c) getting an A on your math test; getting a B on your math test
   (d) A number is divisible by 4. A number is divisible by 5.
   (e) Player A wins the chess match. Player B wins the chess match.
   (f) Manuel likes rap music. Manuel likes classical music.
   (g) Hanna has a pet dog. Hanna has a pet cat.
   (h) A turn is clockwise. A turn is counterclockwise.
   b, c, e, h

Uses Objective K

4. Ty Cobb has the highest career batting average in major-league baseball, .367. On a randomly selected time at bat, what was the probability Cobb did *not* get a hit?
   .633

LESSON 5-6 *Adding Probabilities*

Family fun. *You are on Pennsylvania Avenue on the game board. It is your turn to toss the dice. Do you know the probability of landing on Boardwalk (5 spaces away)?*

Certain situations lead to the adding of probabilities.

Example 1

Consider the spinner shown here. If all directions of the spinner are equally likely, what is the probability that the spinner will land either in region *A* or in region *B*?

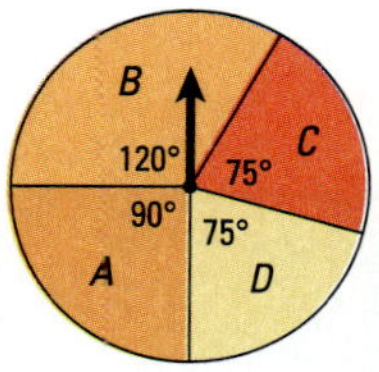

Solution

The circle has a total of 360°.

The probability of landing in A is $\frac{90}{360}$.

The probability of landing in B is $\frac{120}{360}$.

The probability of landing in region A or in region B is the sum of these two probabilities.

$$\frac{90}{360} + \frac{120}{360} = \frac{210}{360}$$
$$= \frac{7 \cdot 30}{12 \cdot 30} = \frac{7}{12}.$$

The probability that the spinner will land either in region A or in region B is $\frac{7}{12}$.

Check

$\frac{7}{12}$ is a little more than $\frac{6}{12}$, which is $\frac{1}{2}$. Do regions *A* and *B* cover a little more than half the circle? It seems so.

Lesson 5-6 Overview

Broad Goals The goal of this lesson is to be able to calculate the probability of *A* or *B* when *A* and *B* are mutually exclusive and to calculate the complement of *A*.

Perspective An offshoot of the Putting-Together Model for Addition is the calculation of the probability of mutually exclusive events. Mutual exclusion implies there is no overlap, so the connection between the two ideas is quite direct.

An event *E* and its complement, *not E,* are automatically mutually exclusive because *not E* contains exactly the outcomes that are not in E. Since the events *E* and *not E* include all possible outcomes, the probability of *E or not E* is 1. Since the probability of *E or not E* equals the sum of the probability of *E* and the probability of *not E,* the Probabilities of Complements property follows.

Probabilities of Mutually Exclusive Events

Addition works in Example 1 because the events "landing in region A" and "landing in region B" do not overlap. The spinner is not able to land in both regions at the same time. Two events which cannot occur at the same time are called **mutually exclusive.** This name comes from the fact that the occurrence of one event "excludes" the occurrence of the other event.

Example 2

Two normal dice are tossed at the same time. Assume the dice are fair.
Let C = one or more of the dice show a 1.
Let D = the sum of the numbers on the dice is 10.

a. Are C and D mutually exclusive events?
b. What is the probability of C or D occurring?

Solution

A display of all 36 possible outcomes from tossing two dice is helpful.

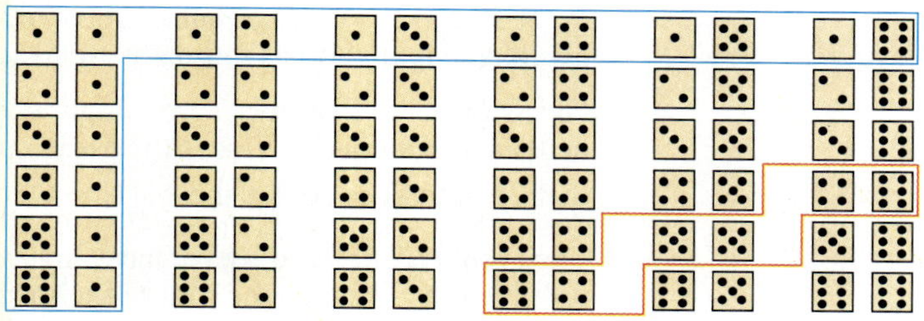

The outcomes in event C are outlined in blue. There are 11 outcomes in event C.

The outcomes in event D are outlined in orange. There are three possible ways of rolling a sum of 10, so event D has three outcomes.

a. *Since C and D have no outcomes in common, they are mutually exclusive.*

b. There are 14 outcomes in events C or D. Since the dice are fair, each outcome has probability $\frac{1}{36}$. *The probability that C or D will occur is* $\frac{14}{36}$.

The general pattern is quite simple.

Probability of *A or B*
If A and B are mutually exclusive events, the probability of the event *A or B* is the probability of A plus the probability of B.

Teaching Lesson 5-6

Warm-up

1. List all the possible outcomes for spinning these two spinners at the same time.

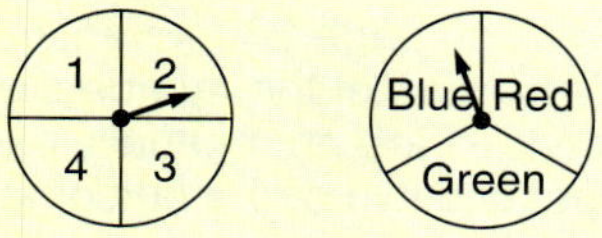

1, red	1, blue	1, green
2, red	2, blue	2, green
3, red	3, blue	3, green
4, red	4, blue	4, green

2. How many outcomes are there?
12 outcomes

Notes on Reading

Reading Mathematics There are three vocabulary ideas in this lesson. First, the word *or*, as used in *A or B*, has its usual mathematical meaning of "either one or the other or both." Next, the term *mutually exclusive* is from the word exclude. Finally, the word *complement* has a meaning analogous to the complement of an angle. With angles, a complement fills out a right angle. With events, a complement fills out a set of all outcomes.

Example 1 This is a straightforward example of adding probabilities.

Example 2 Teaching Aid 56 shows the 36 outcomes of tossing two dice,

▸ **LESSON MASTER 5-6 A** *page 2*

In 5-6, use the circle graph.

5. What is the probability that a randomly selected toy is given to a child under ten?
$\frac{15}{100} + \frac{22}{100} + \frac{27}{100}$ (calculation)
$\frac{16}{25}$, or 64% (answer)

6. Show two ways to find the probability that a randomly selected toy is given to someone ten or older.
$\frac{14}{100} + \frac{22}{100}$, $1 - \frac{16}{25}$ (calculation)
$\frac{9}{25}$, or 36% (answer)

Ages of Children Receiving Toys

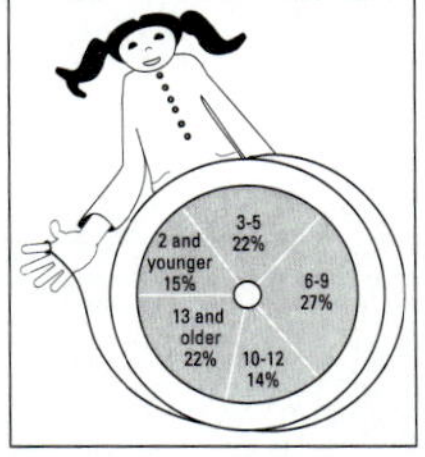

In 7 and 8, use the diagram, on page 267 of your book, of possible outcomes when tossing two dice.

7. What is the probability of rolling a sum less than 5 or greater than 10?
$\frac{6}{36} + \frac{3}{36}$ (calculation)
$\frac{1}{4}$, or 25% (answer)

8. What is the probability that the outcome will be doubles or a sum of seven?
$\frac{6}{36} + \frac{6}{36}$ (calculation)
$\frac{1}{3}$, or $33\frac{1}{3}$% (answer)

9. The probability that a newborn baby will be a boy is about 51.2%. What is the probability that a newborn will be a girl?
1 − .512 (calculation)
.488, or 48.8% (answer)

10. A bag contains 4 white, 6 green, and 8 yellow chips. What is the probability that a randomly selected chip will be white or yellow?
$\frac{4}{18} + \frac{8}{18}$ (calculation)
$\frac{2}{3}$, or $66\frac{2}{3}$% (answer)

Optional Activities

After discussing **Example 2,** you might want to give students more opportunities to work with the possible outcomes of tossing two dice. Have them use the picture in the text or **Teaching Aid 56** to find these answers.

1. What is the probability of tossing each sum? [Answer is below Question 3.]
2. What sum has the greatest probability of occurring? [7] the least probability? [2 or 12]
3. What is the probability the sum will be
a. even? [$\frac{18}{36}$, or $\frac{1}{2}$] **b.** odd? [$\frac{18}{36}$, or $\frac{1}{2}$]
c. even or odd? [$\frac{36}{36}$, or 1]

1.

Sum	2	3	4	5	6	7
Prob.	$\frac{1}{36}$	$\frac{2}{36}$	$\frac{3}{36}$	$\frac{4}{36}$	$\frac{5}{36}$	$\frac{6}{36}$

Sum	8	9	10	11	12
Prob.	$\frac{5}{36}$	$\frac{4}{36}$	$\frac{3}{36}$	$\frac{2}{36}$	$\frac{1}{36}$

without the outcomes for event *C* and event *D* identified. This teaching aid can be used with Example 2 and other similar examples you might want to present, such as those in *Optional Activities* below.

Although events *C* and *D* in Example 2 are mutually exclusive, other events could be described that are not. See Question 2 in the *Additional Examples* on page 268. Events *C* and *E* (the sum of the numbers on the dice is 7) are not mutually exclusive because two of the outcomes have both a one and a sum of 7. Events *D* and *E* are mutually exclusive since there is no overlap.

Example 3 Have students note the pitfalls of adding probabilities when there is some overlap.

Addition of probabilities does not work if the events are not mutually exclusive.

Example 3

Three of eight patients in the pediatrician's waiting room have sore throats and half have a fever. What is wrong with the following reasoning?
"$\frac{3}{8} + \frac{1}{2} = \frac{3}{8} + \frac{4}{8} = \frac{7}{8}$, so $\frac{7}{8}$ of the patients have either a sore throat or a fever."

Solution

Since it is possible that a patient has both a sore throat and a fever, the two events are not mutually exclusive. Because of the overlap, the putting-together model does not apply.

Probabilities of Complementary Events

For any event *E,* there is a corresponding event consisting of all the outcomes that are not in *E.* This event is called the **complement** of the event *E,* and is written as ***not E.*** You can see that an event and its complement are always mutually exclusive.

For instance, in Example 2, you might wish to know the probability that neither die shows a 1. This is the event *not C.* By counting, you can see that 25 outcomes do not show a 1, so the probability of *not C* is $\frac{25}{36}$.

The events *E* and *not E* never have any overlap and together include all possible outcomes. So the sum of their probabilities is 1. In the case of the events *C* and *not C* discussed above, $\frac{11}{36} + \frac{25}{36} = \frac{36}{36} = 1$.

Probabilities of Complements
The sum of the probabilities of any event *E* and its complement *not E* is 1.

For instance, if the probability of rain today is 30%, then the probability of no rain has to be 70%, since 30% + 70% = 1.

QUESTIONS

Covering the Reading

In 1–4, suppose the spinner in Example 1 is spun once.

1. a. What is the probability that the spinner will land in region *C*? $\frac{5}{24}$
   b. What is the probability that the spinner will land in region *D*? $\frac{5}{24}$
   c. What is the probability that the spinner will land in region *C* or region *D*? $\frac{5}{12}$
2. What is the probability that the spinner lands in region *A* or region *C*? $\frac{11}{24}$
3. What is the probability that the spinner will not land in region *B*? $\frac{2}{3}$

LESSON MASTER 5-6 B — Questions on SPUR Objectives

Properties Objective G: Tell whether or not events are mutually exclusive or not.

1. Give an example of two events that are mutually exclusive.
   sample: Luke weighs 140 pounds. Luke weighs less than 120 pounds.
2. *Multiple choice* Which of the following pairs of events are mutually exclusive?
   (a) We planted marigolds. We planted roses.
   (b) A number is divisible by 3. A number is divisible by 5.
   (c) Roger failed his math test. Roger passed his math test.
   (d) The first initial of your name is a vowel. The first initial of your name is G.
   (e) A number is divisible by 6. A number is between 26 and 29.
   (f) Your sister is a newborn. Your sister is a grandmother.
   (g) Your brother is a newborn. Your brother is an uncle.
   (h) Player A wins the tennis match. Player B wins the tennis match.
   (i) The plane flies toward the east. The plane flies toward the west.
   (j) Mr. Clearwater teaches math. Mr. Clearwater teaches art.
   (k) A number is less than 8. A number is greater than -5.
   (l) A number is greater than 8. A number is less than -5.
   c, d, e, f, h, i, l

Uses Objective K: Calculate the probability of mutually exclusive events or complements of events.

3. Ms. Rivera's boss says she has a 95% chance of receiving a promotion. What is the probability that she will *not* receive the promotion?
   100% − 95% (calculation) — 5% (answer)
4. Sue has .3 chance of winning a race, Jayminna has a .1 chance, and Lena has a .2 chance. What is the probability that either Jayminna or Sue will win?
   .1 + .3 (calculation) — .4 (answer)
5. In Crestville Commons, the probability that the first digit of a phone number is even is $\frac{7}{10}$. What is the probability that the first digit is odd?
   $1 - \frac{7}{10}$ (calculation) — $\frac{3}{10}$ (answer)

Adapting to Individual Needs

Extra Help

To help students understand that events are either mutually exclusive or overlapping, write the numbers 1 through 10 on slips of paper and put them into a bag. Have students imagine drawing a number, recording it, and returning the slip to the bag. Ask if the events "draw a multiple of 3" and "draw an even number" are mutually exclusive or overlapping. [Overlapping; 6 fits both descriptions.] Ask if the events "draw an even number" and "draw an odd number" are mutually exclusive or overlapping. [Mutually exclusive; no number fits both descriptions.] Then ask if the following events are mutually exclusive or overlapping.

1. Draw a one-digit number; draw a two-digit number. [Mutually exclusive]
2. Draw a multiple of 2; draw a multiple of 3. [Overlapping]
3. Draw a multiple of 5; draw a 2-digit number. [Overlapping]

4. Is it considered possible for the spinner to land in both regions A and D at the same time? **No**

5. Give an example of mutually exclusive events. **Sample: A tossed coin lands heads up. The coin lands tails up.**

6. Give an example of events that are not mutually exclusive. **Sample: Two dice show a sum of 10. One of the dice shows 6.**

In 7–9, consider the tossing of two fair dice. Tell whether or not events E and F are mutually exclusive.

7. E = one of the dice shows a 5.
F = the sum of the numbers on the dice is 6. **not mutually exclusive**

8. E = the sum of the numbers on the dice is 7.
F = the sum of the numbers on the dice is 8. **mutually exclusive**

9. E = the numbers on the two dice are equal.
F = the sum of the numbers on the dice is 7. **mutually exclusive**

In 10–12, an event is given.
a. Describe the complement of the event E.
b. Give the probability of the complement.

10. In the spinner situation of Example 1, E = the spinner will land in region B. **a) The spinner will not land in region B. b) $\frac{2}{3}$**

11. In the dice situation of Example 2, E = the sum of the numbers on the dice is 12. **a) The sum of the numbers on the dice is less than 12. b) $\frac{35}{36}$**

12. It is thought that the probability of rain tomorrow is 20%. **a) It will not rain tomorrow. b) 80%**

13. The probability of event A is $\frac{5}{8}$. The probability of event B is $\frac{2}{5}$. Explain why A and B cannot be mutually exclusive events.

13) If A and B were mutually exclusive, you could add their probabilities to obtain the probability of A or B. But the sum of the probabilities is $\frac{41}{40}$ which is greater than 1. This is impossible for a probability, so A and B cannot be mutually exclusive events.

Applying the Mathematics

14. If Joan's chance of winning the 100-m freestyle is .5 and Janie's is .3, explain how you know there is at least one other person in the race. **The sum of all the probabilities must equal 1, and .5 + .3 = .8.**

15. If the grades on the last quiz in history were 3 As, 6 Bs, 10 Cs, 1 D, and 3 Fs, what is the probability a randomly selected student passed the quiz? **$\frac{20}{23}$**

In 16–17, tell whether A and B are mutually exclusive events.

16. A: You have Nintendo®. B: You have a GameBoy™. **not mutually exclusive**

17. A: x is an integer evenly divisible by 3. B: x is an integer evenly divisible by 4. **not mutually exclusive**

Additional Examples

1. Use the spinner in **Example 1.** What is the probability that the spinner will land in
   a. Region C? **$\frac{5}{24}$**
   b. Region D? **$\frac{5}{24}$**
   c. Region C or Region D? **$\frac{5}{12}$**
2. Use the situation of **Example 2.** Let E = the sum of the numbers on the dice is 7.
   a. What is the probability of E? **$\frac{1}{6}$**
   b. How many outcomes are in event C or E? **15 outcomes**
   c. Are the events C and E mutually exclusive? **No**
   d. Are the events D and E mutually exclusive? **Yes**
3. The year 2000, a leap year, will be 52 weeks and 2 days long. It will begin on a Saturday and end on a Sunday. What is the probability that a random day in that year will fall on a weekend? **$\frac{106}{366}$**

Notes on Questions

Question 15 Using the ideas presented in this lesson, students would find the answer by adding the probabilities: $\frac{3}{23} + \frac{6}{23} + \frac{10}{23} + \frac{1}{23} = \frac{20}{23}$.

Another way to calculate the probability is to add the number of passing grades and divide by the number of students.

Question 17 The overlap is the set of integers evenly divisible by 12.

▶ **LESSON MASTER 5-6 B** *page 2*

In 6-8, use the circle graph at the right.

Ages of Houses in Lowvale

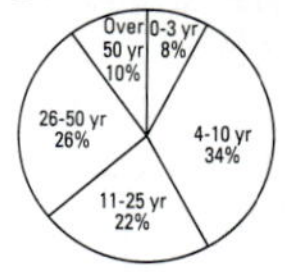

6. What is the probability that a house randomly selected is 0-10 years old?
   8% + 34% (calculation)
   42% (answer)
7. What is the probability that a house selected at random is over 25 years old?
   26% + 10% (calculation) **36%** (answer)
8. Show two ways to find the probability that a randomly selected house is 0-50 years old.
   8% + 34% + 22% + 26% (calculation) **100% − 10%** (calculation)
   90% (answer)

In 9 and 10, use the diagram, on page 267 of your book, of possible outcomes when tossing two dice.

9. What is the probability of tossing a sum less than 3 or greater than 8?
   $\frac{1}{36} + \frac{10}{36}$ (calculation) **$\frac{11}{36}$** (answer)
10. What is the probability that the sum will be 5 or an even number?
   $\frac{4}{36} + \frac{18}{36}$ (calculation) **$\frac{22}{36} = \frac{11}{18}$** (answer)
11. A bag contains 3 red, 6 green, 1 yellow, and 4 blue marbles.
   a. What is the probability that a randomly selected marble will be green or blue?
   $\frac{6}{14} + \frac{4}{14}$ (calculation) **$\frac{10}{14} = \frac{5}{7}$** (answer)
   b. What is the probability that a randomly selected marble will be not be yellow?
   $1 - \frac{1}{14}$ or $\frac{3}{14} + \frac{6}{14} + \frac{4}{14}$ (calculation) **$\frac{13}{14}$** (answer)

Adapting to Individual Needs

English Language Development
Discuss the difference between *and* and the inclusive *or.* Explain that: "We will go if it is sunny *and* warm." means we will go if it is *both* sunny *and* warm. "We will go if it is sunny *or* warm." means we'll go if it's sunny and warm, if it's just sunny (and not warm), or if it's just warm (and not sunny).

Give students examples of events that are mutually exclusive, and contrast them with things that overlap. For example, a number cannot be both 3 and even; these events are mutually exclusive. However a number can be both a multiple of 3 and even.

Notes on Questions

Question 20 The overlap is the double-fours. Therefore, the probability cannot be found by adding the probability of doubles to the probability of a sum of 8. Students can use the display in **Example 2** and count to find that the probability is $\frac{10}{36}$, or $\frac{5}{18}$.

Follow-up Lesson 5-6

Practice

For more questions on SPUR Objectives, use **Lesson Master 5-6A** (shown on pages 266–267) or **Lesson Master 5-6B** (shown on pages 268–269).

Assessment

Written Communication Have each student write a paragraph explaining how he or she would decide if two events are mutually exclusive and give an example of mutually exclusive events and another of two events that are not mutually exclusive. Then ask students to explain how to find the probability of either mutually exclusive event occurring. [Explanation of mutually exclusive events is clear and examples of exclusive and nonexclusive events are given. Procedure for finding probability is correct.]

Extension

Technology Connection You may wish to have students create various spinners using the *Graphing and Probability Workshop.* In a standard table, have students enter letter labels in Column 1 and degree measures with a sum of 360 in Column 2. Use the Circle Graph option to display the spinner. The data can be transformed to fractions to represent probabilities.

Project Update Project 4, *A Probability Experiment,* on page 294, relates to the content of this lesson. This project is an extension of **Question 29.**

18a) 2: $\frac{1}{36}$; 3: $\frac{2}{36}$; 4: $\frac{3}{36}$; 5: $\frac{4}{36}$; 6: $\frac{5}{36}$; 7: $\frac{6}{36}$; 8: $\frac{5}{36}$; 9: $\frac{4}{36}$; 10: $\frac{3}{36}$; 11: $\frac{2}{36}$; 12: $\frac{1}{36}$

b) $\frac{1}{36} + \frac{2}{36} + \frac{3}{36} + \frac{4}{36} + \frac{5}{36} + \frac{6}{36} + \frac{5}{36} + \frac{4}{36} + \frac{3}{36} + \frac{2}{36} + \frac{1}{36} = \frac{36}{36} = 1$

In 18–20, imagine that two fair dice are tossed.

18. a. List the probabilities of rolling each possible sum from 2 to 12.
b. Verify that the probabilities in part **a** add to 1.
c. What is the probability of a sum of 7 or a sum of 11? $\frac{2}{9}$

19. What is the probability of tossing a number that has three as a factor? $\frac{1}{3}$

20. What is the probability of tossing "doubles" (two of the same number) or a sum of 8? $\frac{5}{18}$

Review

21. Simplify $\frac{11}{6} + -\frac{2}{5}$. *(Lesson 5-5)* $\frac{43}{30}$ or $1\frac{13}{30}$

22. a. Evaluate $a + \frac{c}{3} - b$ when $a = \frac{20}{3}$, $b = \frac{17}{6}$, and $c = -10$. $\frac{3}{6}$
b. Write your answer to part **a** in lowest terms. *(Lessons 1-10, 5-5)* $\frac{1}{2}$

23. One package weighed $2\frac{1}{2}$ lb and the other weighed $2\frac{3}{4}$ lb. How much did they weigh altogether? *(Lessons 5-1, 5-5)* $\frac{21}{4}$ lb or $5\frac{1}{4}$ lb

24. On the spinner below $\overline{AO} \perp \overline{OB}$. Find the magnitude of the turn from A to B. *(Lesson 5-4)* -90° or 270°

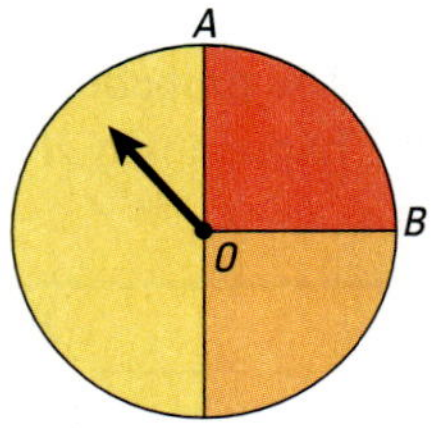

In 25–28, perform the addition.

25. 3 feet + 4 inches = __?__ inches **40**

26. 6 pounds + 13 ounces = __?__ ounces **109**

27. 4 meters + 351 millimeters = __?__ meters **4.351**

28. 100 grams + 2 kilograms = __?__ grams *(Lessons 3-2, 3-3, 3-4, 5-1)* **2100**

Exploration

29. Toss two dice 108 times, recording the sum each time.
a. Calculate your relative frequency for tossing a sum of 7 or a sum of 11. Answers will vary.
b. Compare this relative frequency with your answer to Question 18c. Explain why differences might have occurred. The relative frequency should be close to $\frac{2}{9}$ (24 occurrences of a 7 or 11 in 108 tosses). Differences might occur because probabilities tell only what is expected to occur in the long run, not what must occur.

Adapting to Individual Needs

Challenge

Have students answer each question.

1. How many outcomes are possible when three dice are tossed? [$6 \times 6 \times 6 = 216$]
2. Let A be the greatest possible sum when three dice are tossed. If the dice are fair, what is the probability of A? [$\frac{1}{216}$; the greatest sum, 18, occurs when all the dice show 6; this happens in 1 case out of 216.]
3. Let B be the least possible sum when three dice are tossed. If the dice are fair, what is the probability of B? [$\frac{1}{216}$; the least sum, 3, occurs when all the dice show 1, or in 1 case out of 216.]
4. Find the probability of A or B. [$\frac{1}{216} + \frac{1}{216} = \frac{1}{108}$]

LESSON

5-7

The Commutative and Associative Properties

Which way is up? *Switch them around and call them Curly, Moe, and Larry, or Moe, Curly, and Larry, or Moe, Larry, and Curly. But no matter how mixed up they become, they are still The Three Stooges.*

The Commutative Property of Addition

When two things have been put together, it does not make any difference which came first. Buying two items in different order results in the same total cost. Likewise, the order of slides or turns makes no difference. In football, gaining 3 yards and then losing 4 yards gives the same end result as first losing 4 yards and then gaining 3: $3 + -4 = -4 + 3$.

The general pattern was first given a name by François Servois in 1814. He used the French word *commutatif,* which means "switchable." The English name is the *commutative property.*

Commutative Property of Addition
For any numbers a and b, $a + b = b + a$.

The Associative Property of Addition

Think of spending \$5, earning \$14, and then spending \$20. The end result is given by the addition $-5 + 14 + -20$. From order of operations, you know you should work from left to right. But does it matter in which order the additions are done? Follow this experiment. By using parentheses, we can change which addition is to be done first.

Doing the left addition first is shown by:

$$(-5 + 14) + -20$$
$$= 9 + -20$$
$$= -11$$

Doing the right addition first is shown by:

$$-5 + (14 + -20)$$
$$= -5 + -6$$
$$= -11$$

The sums are equal.

$$(-5 + 14) + -20 = -5 + (14 + -20)$$

Lesson 5-7

Objectives

C Apply properties of addition to simplify expressions.
F Identify the Commutative and Associative Properties of Addition.

Resources

From the ***Teacher's Resource File***
- Lesson Master 5-7A or 5-7B
- Answer Master 5-7
- Teaching Aid 51: Warm-up

Additional Resources
- Visual for Teaching Aid 51

Teaching Lesson 5-7

Warm-up

Estimation Tell if each sum will be positive or negative.
1. $-6 + 3 + 9 + -2$ Positive
2. $12 + 0 + -6 + -12$ Negative
3. $20 + -30 + -40 + 10$ Negative
4. $-5 + -5 + 2 + 3$ Negative
5. $-15 + 6 + 1 + 3$ Negative
6. $9 + -3 + 6 + -4$ Positive
7. $-10 + 20 + -30 + 10$ Negative
8. $-7 + -4 + 5 + 8$ Positive

Lesson 5-7 Overview

Broad Goals Students practice adding two or more positive and negative numbers, utilizing the Commutative and Associative Properties of Addition.

Perspective Because the names for these properties are universal, students should memorize them. Students frequently misspell the word *commutative.* Tell them to think of the word *commuter.* Commuters also switch order: they go from home to work, then from work to home.

Because addition is commutative, we can say "add a and b" without reference to order. Because addition is both commutative and associative, we can also say, "add all the numbers" when more than two numbers are given. In Chapter 7, students learn that it is not appropriate to say, "subtract all of those numbers," and it is ambiguous to say "subtract a and b."

In the last example in this lesson, as with many previous examples in this chapter, we anticipate the discussion of subtraction of positive and negative numbers. Here students are being taught to use the addition $a + -b$. In Chapter 7, they will use $a - b$ for the same problem.

Notes on Reading

To create awareness of several critical details, you may want to read this lesson aloud with your students.

Examples 1–2 Direct attention to the subtle distinction between the Commutative and Associative Properties. Use the paragraph in *Applying the Properties* to stress the implications of both properties when taken together. Finally, emphasize that these properties make it possible to simplify additions containing several positive and negative numbers by first adding all the positives, then adding all the negatives, and finally combining the two sums.

Example 3 demonstrates the advantages of grouping the positive numbers, grouping the negative numbers, and then adding.

Students often confuse the Commutative and Associative Properties. Emphasize that commutativity refers to switching the order of the numbers to be added; associativity refers to switching the order in which the additions take place. You may also want to mention the word *association*, a group, and point out that the Associative Property concerns the way that numbers are *associated*, or grouped, in order to add them.

The genius of Sir William Rowan Hamilton was identified before he was 3. During his career, he made major contributions in mathematics and physics.

On the left-hand side, the 14 is associated with the -5 first. On the right-hand side, the 14 is associated with the -20. For this reason, in 1835, the Irish mathematician Sir William Rowan Hamilton called the general pattern the *associative property.*

Associative Property of Addition
For any numbers a, b, and c, $(a + b) + c = a + (b + c)$.

Distinguishing Between the Properties

Both the commutative property and the associative property have to do with changing order. The commutative property says you can change the order of the *numbers* being added. The associative property says you can change the order of the *operations.*

Example 1

Which property is demonstrated by 3 + (18 + -12) = 3 + (-12 + 18)?

Solution

All that has been changed is the order of numbers within parentheses. So this is an instance of the **Commutative Property of Addition.**

Example 2

Below is an instance of which property of addition?

150 + -73 + -22 + 8 = 150 + (-73 + -22) + 8

Solution

The order of the numbers has not been changed. On the left-hand side of the equation, we would add the 150 and the -73 first. On the right-hand side, we would add the -73 to the -22 first. So the order of additions has been changed. This can be done because of the **Associative Property of Addition.**

Applying the Properties

Because addition is both commutative and associative, when an expression involves *only* addition:

(1) addends can be put in any order before adding them;

(2) parentheses can be removed or put in whenever you wish;

(3) you can speak of adding three or more numbers.

Optional Activities

After discussing **Example 1,** you might have students do the following activity. Give students pairs of everyday activities and ask if they are commutative. That is, can their order be switched without changing the result? Then have students make up their own examples of activities that are commutative and activities that are not. Some examples are given at the right. Note that Activities A and B are not commutative; Activities B and C are.

A. Put toothpaste on your toothbrush.
B. Brush your teeth.
C. Wash your face.
D. Dry your face.
E. Go to school.
F. Go home from school.
G. Do homework.
H. Play baseball.
I. Watch television.
J. Eat dinner.

Example 3

Consider the following checking account, opened with \$150 on October 24. How much was in the account after the deposit of November 6?

DATE	DEPOSIT	WITHDRAWAL (check)
10-24	\$150.00	
10-27		\$70.00
10-31	100.00	
11-01		40.00
11-03		60.00
11-06	50.00	

Solution

In order, the deposits and withdrawals lead to the expression

$$150 + -70 + 100 + -40 + -60 + 50.$$

These numbers are all added, so they may be added in any order. It is easier to add positives to positives and negatives to negatives, so group all deposits together and all withdrawals together. Then find the positive total and the negative total.

$$= (150 + 100 + 50) + (-70 + -40 + -60)$$
$$= 300 + -170$$
$$= 130$$

There was \$130 in the account after the deposit of November 6.

QUESTIONS

Covering the Reading

1. Give an example of the Commutative Property of Addition. Sample: $3 + 2.4 = 2.4 + 3$
2. Give an example of the Associative Property of Addition. Sample: $(12 + 95) + 5 = 12 + (95 + 5)$
3. In an expression involving only additions, you can change the order of the additions. Which property implies this? Associative Property of Addition

In 4–7, *multiple choice.* Tell which property is illustrated.

(a) only the Commutative Property of Addition
(b) only the Associative Property of Addition
(c) both the commutative and associative properties
(d) neither the commutative nor the associative property

4. $\frac{2}{3} + \frac{3}{4} = \frac{3}{4} + \frac{2}{3}$ (a)
5. $8 + (36 + -24) + -16 = (8 + 36) + (-24 + -16)$ (b)
6. $3(4 + 9) = 3(9 + 4)$ (a)
7. $1 + 2 + 3 = 3 + 2 + 1$ (c)
8. In what century were the names commutative and associative first used? (Remember that the years 1901–2000 constitute the 20th century.) 19th century
9. Give a real-world situation that could lead someone to add many positive and negative numbers. Sample: gaining and losing weight

Additional Examples

In 1–2, tell what property of addition is illustrated.

1. a. $3 + 2 = 2 + 3$ Commutative
   b. $6 + (5 + 4) = (5 + 4) + 6$ Commutative
   c. $3 + (2 + 1) = (3 + 2) + 1$ Associative
2. a. $(6 + 53) + -53 = 6 + (53 + -53)$ Associative
   b. $19 + 8 + 7 + 6 = 19 + (8 + 7) + 6$ Associative
3. In golf, *par* is the standard score expected for a hole. Actual scores are recorded as strokes over or under par. On nine holes of golf, Pia scored one over par, two over par, par, a birdie (one under par), four over par, par, an eagle (two under par), two over par, and a birdie.
   a. Write the addition that gives the total result for Pia. $1 + 2 + 0 + -1 + 4 + 0 + -2 + 2 + -1 = 5$
   b. What is her score? Five strokes over par

Notes on Questions

Question 7 Students may wonder how the associative property can be illustrated if there are no parentheses. They need to consider the order in which addition takes place on each side of the equation to see how the associative property has been used. Because of order of operations, there is an implicit order $(1 + 2) + 3$ when $1 + 2 + 3$ is written and an implicit order $(3 + 2) + 1$ when $3 + 2 + 1$ is written.

LESSON MASTER 5-7 A

Questions on SPUR Objectives
See pages 297-299 for objectives.

Skills Objective C

In 1-9, simplify the sum.

1. $-3 + -5 + 7$ -1
2. $-\frac{1}{2} + \frac{2}{3} + -\frac{3}{4}$ $-\frac{7}{12}$
3. $3\frac{1}{2} + 2\frac{5}{6} + 1\frac{1}{2}$ $7\frac{5}{6}$
4. $\frac{4}{5} + a + -\frac{4}{5}$ a
5. $38 + 93 + -65 + 8$ 74
6. $1\frac{3}{4} + 3.8 + -2\frac{3}{4}$ 2.8
7. $-10 + -20 + -30 + 40$ -20
8. $2.5 + 8 + -2.5 + -3.2$ 4.8
9. $12 + 5 + -5 + -12$ 0

Properties Objective F

In 10-15, tell whether the equation illustrates the Commutative Property of Addition, the Associative Property of Addition, both properties, or neither property.

10. $(3 + 2) + 1 = 3 + (2 + 1)$ Associative Property
11. $-6 + (5 + -9) = -6 + (-9 + 5)$ Commutative Property
12. $5\frac{1}{3} + 2\frac{1}{2} = 2\frac{1}{2} + 5\frac{1}{3}$ Commutative Property
13. $\frac{2}{3} + \frac{5}{6} = \frac{4}{6} + \frac{5}{6}$ neither property
14. $3 \cdot 4 = 4 \cdot 3$ neither property
15. $3.5 + (-1.2 + 2.7) = (3.5 + 2.7) + -1.2$ both properties

Multiple choice. **In 16-20, choose the property used in each step of the solution to $5 + 2\frac{3}{4} + -5$.**

16. $5 + (2\frac{3}{4} + -5)$	e	(a) Additive Identity Property of Zero
17. $5 + (-5 + 2\frac{3}{4})$	d	(b) Property of Opposites
18. $(5 + -5) + 2\frac{3}{4}$	e	(c) Opposite of Opposites Property
19. $0 + 2\frac{3}{4}$	b	(d) Commutative Property of Addition
20. $2\frac{3}{4}$	a	(e) Associative Property of Addition

Adapting to Individual Needs

Extra Help

Tell students that, when asked to find the sum of many addends, they should look at the problem before starting to add. Explain that they can save themselves a lot of work by *reordering* and *associating* the addends. Point out that reordering refers to the Commutative Property of Addition and associating refers to the Associative Property of Addition. Then give students problems like those shown below and efficient ways to add the numbers. Samples are given.

1. $6 + -9 + 8 + -9 + -3 + 18 + 45 + -3 + -30 + -15$ [$6 + (-3 + -3) + (-9 + -9) + 18 + 45 + (-30 + -15) + 8 = 8$]
2. $-\frac{1}{8} + \frac{4}{5} + -\frac{3}{4} + \frac{5}{8} + \frac{3}{4} + -\frac{4}{5}$ [$(-\frac{1}{8}) + \frac{5}{8}) + (-\frac{3}{4} + \frac{3}{4}) + (\frac{4}{5} + -\frac{4}{5}) = \frac{1}{2}$]
3. $27 + \frac{3}{8} + -9 + \frac{5}{8} + -18 + 563$ [$27 + (-9 + -18) + (\frac{3}{8} + \frac{5}{8}) + 563 = 564$]

Notes on Questions

Question 12 This is an example of commutativity of addition of vectors. Ask students if the paths can be switched regardless of direction. [Yes]

Question 19 Students can apply the formula without knowing how to divide positive and negative numbers because the numerator happens to be positive. You might want to give an example with a negative numerator.

Question 35 Calculator Students will enjoy this exploration. **Part c** gives students practice in skills.

Follow-up for Lesson 5-7

Practice

For more questions on SPUR Objectives, use **Lesson Master 5-7A** (shown on page 273) or **Lesson Master 5-7B** (shown on pages 274–275).

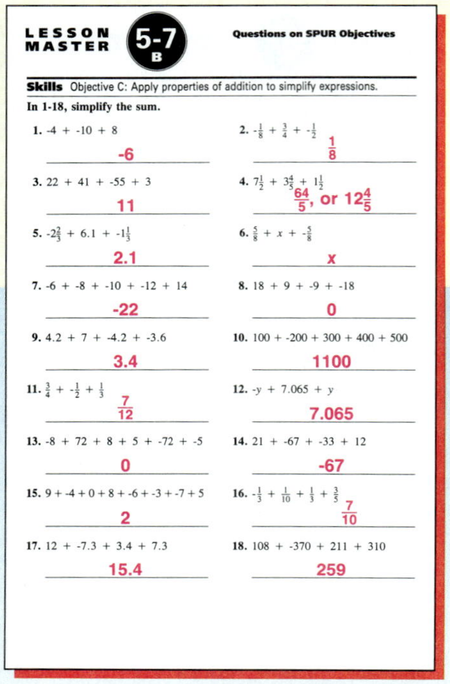

LESSON MASTER 5-7 B — Questions on SPUR Objectives

Skills Objective C: Apply properties of addition to simplify expressions.

In 1-18, simplify the sum.

1. $-4 + -10 + 8$ -6	**2.** $-\frac{1}{8} + \frac{3}{4} + -\frac{1}{2}$ $\frac{1}{8}$
3. $22 + 41 + -55 + 3$ 11	**4.** $7\frac{1}{2} + 3\frac{4}{5} + 1\frac{1}{2}$ $\frac{64}{5}$, or $12\frac{4}{5}$
5. $-2\frac{2}{3} + 6.1 + -1\frac{1}{3}$ 2.1	**6.** $\frac{5}{8} + x + -\frac{5}{8}$ x
7. $-6 + -8 + -10 + -12 + 14$ -22	**8.** $18 + 9 + -9 + -18$ 0
9. $4.2 + 7 + -4.2 + -3.6$ 3.4	**10.** $100 + -200 + 300 + 400 + 500$ 1100
11. $\frac{3}{4} + -\frac{1}{2} + \frac{1}{3}$ $\frac{7}{12}$	**12.** $-y + 7.065 + y$ 7.065
13. $-8 + 72 + 8 + 5 + -72 + -5$ 0	**14.** $21 + -67 + -33 + 12$ -67
15. $9 + -4 + 0 + 8 + -6 + -3 + -7 + 5$ 2	**16.** $-\frac{1}{3} + \frac{1}{10} + \frac{1}{3} + \frac{3}{5}$ $\frac{7}{10}$
17. $12 + -7.3 + 3.4 + 7.3$ 15.4	**18.** $108 + -370 + 211 + 310$ 259

10. On November 1, a person had $400 in a checking account. Here are the transactions for the next two weeks.

DATE	DEPOSIT	WITHDRAWAL (check)
11-03	$102.00	
11-05		$35.00
11-08		75.00
11-11	40.00	
11-12		200.00

a. What addition can you do to calculate the amount in the account at the end of the day on November 12?
b. How much was in the account at that time?
a) 400 + 102 + -35 + -75 + 40 + -200 b) $232

Applying the Mathematics

11. What does a negative answer to a problem like Question 10b mean? Your account is overdrawn.

12. Harry and Kerry start at the same place. Harry walks 300 meters east and then 500 meters west. Kerry walks 500 meters west and then 300 meters east. Do they end at the same place? Explain. Yes. Addition of distance is commutative; and east and west are opposites.

In 13 and 14, simplify.

13. $17 + -1 + -4$ 12

14. $0 + -3 + -2 + 4 + -6 + 1$ -6

In 15 and 16, add the given numbers.

15. 99, -46, 12, -99, 46, -12 0

16. $-\frac{3}{8}, -\frac{3}{8}, \frac{40}{3}, -\frac{3}{8}, -\frac{40}{3}, \frac{3}{8}$ $-\frac{3}{4}$

What do robots do? *Robots were first introduced as toys. Today, robots are indispensable in industry. The robot pictured above is applying adhesive to a new car window on a production line.*

17. A family keeps a weekly budget. During a five-week period, they are $12.50 over, $6.30 under, $21 over, $7.05 under, and $9.90 under. How are they doing? They are $10.25 over budget.

18. A robot turns 50°, -75°, 120°, -103°, and 17°. What is the total turn? 9°

19. The daily low temperatures last week were -1°, 5°, 6°, 4°, 3°, -4°, and -6°. Find the mean of these temperatures. 1°

In 20 and 21, tell whether the equation illustrates the Commutative Property of Addition, the Associative Property of Addition, or both.

20. $-3x + (4 + 3x) = -3x + (3x + 4)$ Commutative Prop. of Add.

21. $8x + -5y + 5y = 8x + (-5y + 5y)$ Associative Prop. of Add.

Review

22. Suppose an airplane flight has a 15% probability of being more than 10 minutes early, a 60% probability of being within 10 minutes of its scheduled arrival time, and a 25% probability of being over 10 minutes late. The plane is due at 8:10 P.M. a) 75%
a. What is the probability that the plane will land before 8:20 P.M.?
b. What is the probability that the plane will land after 8:00 P.M.? 85%
c. Are the events in parts **a** and **b** mutually exclusive? No
d. Are the events in parts **a** and **b** complements? *(Lesson 5-6)* No

Adapting to Individual Needs

English Language Development
To help students understand the difference between the terms commutative and associative, you might offer these definitions.

1. Commutative comes from the Latin *commutare*, which means to change. The Commutative Property says that the order of the numbers to be added can be changed. For example 42 + 73 can be changed to 73 + 42.

2. Associative comes from the Latin *associare,* which means to join in companionship. The Associative Property says that the way the numbers to be added are grouped (or associated) can be changed. For example, the numbers 97 + 43 + −43 can be grouped as (97 + 43) + −43 or as 97 + (43 + −43).

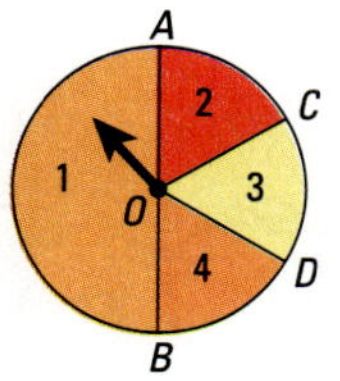

23. In the spinner at the left, $\overline{AB}$ is a diameter of the circle. $m\angle AOC = m\angle COD = m\angle BOD$.
  a. What is $m\angle AOC$? **60°**
  b. What is $m\angle AOD$? **120°**
  c. Name all acute angles.
  d. Name all right angles. **none**
  e. Name all obtuse angles in the picture. **∠AOD, ∠COB**
  f. If all positions of the pointer are equally likely, what is the probability the pointer will stop on an odd number? *(Lessons 3-7, 4-8, 5-4, 5-6)* **$\frac{2}{3}$** **c) ∠AOC, ∠COD, ∠DOB**

24. To open a lock, you turn it $2\frac{1}{2}$ turns clockwise and $1\frac{3}{4}$ turns counterclockwise. What is the result of these two turns? *(Lessons 5-4, 5-5)* **3/4 turn clockwise or -270°**

25. Refer to the picture of the Ferris wheel on page 258. If seat *B* is turned to the position of seat *G*, what seat will be moved to the top? *(Lesson 5-4)* ***H***

26. How many degrees does the second hand of a watch turn in 10 seconds? *(Lesson 5-4)* **-60°**

27. Give an instance of the Property of Opposites. *(Lesson 5-2)* **Sample: 5 + -5 = 0**

28. Another term for "additive inverse" is __?__. *(Lesson 5-2)* **opposite**

29. The temperature is $t°$ and goes down 3°. What is the end result? *(Lesson 5-1)* **(*t* – 3) degrees**

30. Morrie and Lori together have 7 tickets to a concert. Corey and Lori together have 5 tickets. How many tickets do Corey, Lori, and Morrie have altogether? *(Lesson 5-1)* **any number from 7 to 12**

31. Simplify: -5 + 6(3.7 + 1.3/2) – 4. *(Lesson 4-5)* **17.1**

32. At many professional athletic contests, fans are asked to guess the day's attendance from five choices displayed on the scoreboard. Assuming you guess randomly:
  a. What is the probability of picking the right number? **20%**
  b. Write the answer to part **a** as a percent, a decimal, and a fraction.
  c. If the correct attendance figure was 38,833, about how many people will guess the correct number? Round this answer for reasonable accuracy. *(Lessons 1-4, 2-6, 4-8)* **≈ 7800**
  b) 20%, .2, 1/5

33. How many feet are in 6.2 miles? *(Lesson 3-2)* **32,736**

34. State the Multiplication Property of Equality. *(Lesson 3-2)* **When equal quantities are multiplied by the same number, the resulting quantities are equal.**

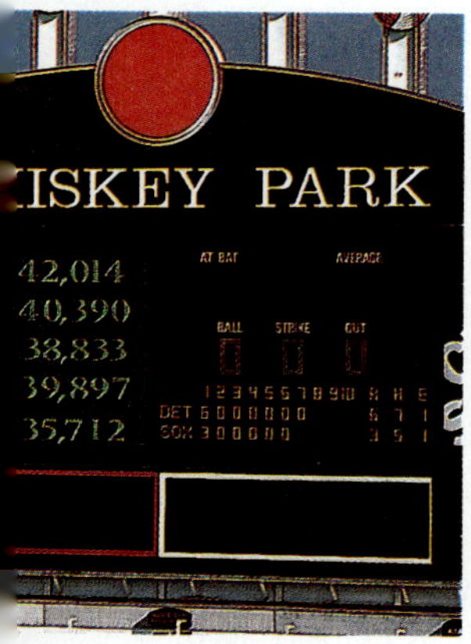

What's your best guess? *The fans at a baseball game are being asked to guess the attendance.*

Exploration

35. a. Add 203,275 + -89,635 + 265,164 on a simple or scientific calculator.
  b. Turn the calculator 180°. What word does the display spell?
  c. Find two negative numbers and a positive number whose sum on the calculator, when turned 180°, is ShOE.
  d. Make up a problem to spell a word on the calculator display.

35a) 378804;
b) hOBBLE;
c) Sum should be 3045. Sample: -999 + -2 + 4046.
d) Answers will vary.

Assessment

Group Assessment Have students **work in groups,** and take turns writing an example of either the Commutative or Associative Property of Addition. The other members of the group should decide which property is shown. [Examples reveal student understanding of the properties.]

Extension

Have students **work in groups** and discuss these questions about the sum of three numbers.

1. If all three numbers are positive, is the sum positive or negative? **Positive**
2. If two numbers are positive and one is negative, is their sum positive or negative? **Cannot be determined**
3. What are the other possibilities? Can the sign of their sum be determined? **If two are negative and one is positive, the sign of the sum cannot be determined. If all three are negative, the sum is negative.**

Students might also consider the sums of four or more numbers and discuss what can be said about the signs of the sums. **If all the addends have the same sign, then their sum will also have that sign. If the addends have different signs, the sign of the sum cannot be determined.**

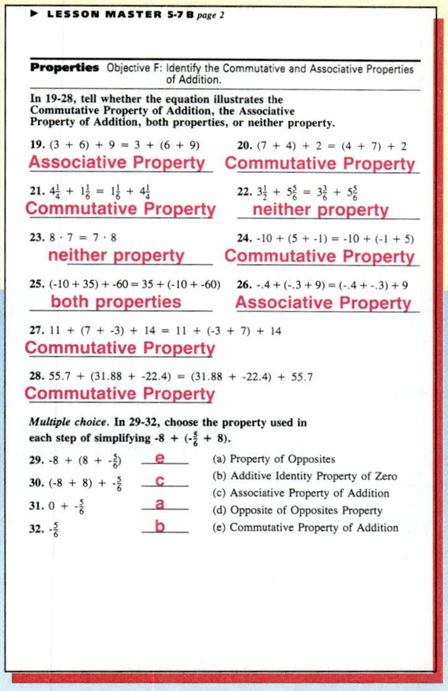
▸ **LESSON MASTER 5-7 B** *page 2*

Properties Objective F: Identify the Commutative and Associative Properties of Addition.

In 19-28, tell whether the equation illustrates the Commutative Property of Addition, the Associative Property of Addition, both properties, or neither property.

19. (3 + 6) + 9 = 3 + (6 + 9) **Associative Property**

20. (7 + 4) + 2 = (4 + 7) + 2 **Commutative Property**

21. $4\frac{1}{4} + 1\frac{1}{6} = 1\frac{1}{6} + 4\frac{1}{4}$ **Commutative Property**

22. $3\frac{1}{2} + 5\frac{5}{6} = 3\frac{3}{6} + 5\frac{5}{6}$ **neither property**

23. 8 · 7 = 7 · 8 **neither property**

24. -10 + (5 + -1) = -10 + (-1 + 5) **Commutative Property**

25. (-10 + 35) + -60 = 35 + (-10 + -60) **both properties**

26. -.4 + (-.3 + 9) = (-.4 + -.3) + 9 **Associative Property**

27. 11 + (7 + -3) + 14 = 11 + (-3 + 7) + 14 **Commutative Property**

28. 55.7 + (31.88 + -22.4) = (31.88 + -22.4) + 55.7 **Commutative Property**

***Multiple choice.* In 29-32, choose the property used in each step of simplifying $-8 + (-\frac{5}{6} + 8)$.**

29. $-8 + (8 + -\frac{5}{6})$ **e**

30. $(-8 + 8) + -\frac{5}{6}$ **c**

31. $0 + -\frac{5}{6}$ **a**

32. $-\frac{5}{6}$ **b**

(a) Property of Opposites
(b) Additive Identity Property of Zero
(c) Associative Property of Addition
(d) Opposite of Opposites Property
(e) Commutative Property of Addition

Adapting to Individual Needs

Challenge

If students made the clock-arithmetic addition table in the *Challenge* for Lesson 5-2, ask them if clock arithmetic is commutative, and if so, to give an example. [Yes. Sample: 7 + 6 = 1 and 6 + 7 = 1, so 7 + 6 = 6 + 7.] Then ask if it is associative, and if so, to give an example. [Yes. Sample: 8 + (9 + 11) = 8 + 8 = 4 and (8 + 9) + 11 = 5 + 11 = 4.]

Lesson 5-8

Objectives

D Solve equations of the form $x + a = b$.

F Identify the Addition Property of Equality.

I Use the Putting-Together Model for Addition to form sentences involving addition.

J Use the Slide Model for Addition to form sentences involving addition.

Resources

From the ***Teacher's Resource File***

- Lesson Master 5-8A or 5-8B
- Answer Master 5-8
- Assessment Sourcebook: Quiz for Lessons 5-5 through 5-8
- Teaching Aids
  51 Warm-up
  57 Question 35, Challenge
- Activity Kit, Activity 11

Additional Resources

- Visuals for Teaching Aids 51, 57

Teaching Lesson 5-8

Warm-up

Find each missing number.

1. ___ + 3 = 8 **5**
2. ___ + -3 = 8 **11**
3. -7 + ___ = 8 **15**
4. -8 = 2 + ___ **-10**
5. $\frac{2}{3}$ = ___ + $-\frac{1}{3}$ **1**
6. 0 = -8 + ___ **8**

LESSON 5-8 Solving $x + a = b$

❶ Examples of Equations of the Form $x + a = b$

Early in elementary school, you could see how to fill in the blank in

$$\_\_\_ + 3 = 4.$$

In algebra, usually the blank is replaced by a letter. If the sentence involves simple numbers, you should be able to find the solution mentally. For instance, in

$$x + 35 = 48$$

you should know that $x = 13$.

But some equations involve complicated numbers. Other equations involve only variables and no specific numbers at all. It helps to have a systematic way of solving these equations. On one side of both ___ + 3 = 4 and $x + 35 = 48$, a number is being added to an (unknown) variable. On the other side is a single number. These equations are *equations of the form* $x + a = b$. Think of x as the unknown. Think of a and b as known numbers.

A Useful Property for Solving Equations

One property of addition is particularly helpful in solving equations. Here is an example. Begin with equal numbers.

$$\frac{1}{4} = 0.25$$

If the same number is added to both sides, then the sums will be equal. For instance, if 3 is added to both sides:

$$3 + \frac{1}{4} = 3 + 0.25.$$

That is, $3\frac{1}{4} = 3.25$.

Lesson 5-8 Overview

Broad Goals This lesson offers an algorithm for solving a sentence of the form $x + a = b$. It involves adding the same number to both sides.

Perspective This lesson presents a method for solving a specific type of equation. We have postponed this presentation to promote mental calculation of solutions where appropriate and to develop the ability to translate words into an equation. By now, many students may have figured out all or part of this procedure on their own.

Throughout this book, we identify reasons for steps with names of properties. We do so to prepare students for algebra. Even though we give the steps, it is not crucial at this point that students know the reason for each step. However, students should know what it means to solve an equation, how to check solutions, and how to translate real situations into equations. The formal study of writing and solving equations should come in algebra courses.

Of course, you could add *any* number to both sides. The sums would still be equal. This property is a special form of the Substitution Principle first mentioned in Lesson 2-5.

> **Addition Property of Equality**
> If $a = b$, then $a + c = b + c$.

Using the Addition Property of Equality

The Addition Property of Equality says: If two numbers are equal, then you can add anything you want to both numbers and the sums will be equal. It is similar to the Multiplication Property of Equality. Here is how this property is used in solving equations.

❷ **Example 1**

Solve $x + -8 = 57$.

Solution

Add 8 to both sides. (You can do this because of the Addition Property of Equality.) Because addition is associative, you do not have to worry about grouping.

Original equation	$x + -8 = 57$
Use Addition Property of Equality	$x + -8 + 8 = 57 + 8$
Property of Opposites	$x + 0 = 57 + 8$
Additive Identity Property of Zero and simplification	$x = 65$

Check

Substitute 65 for x in the original equation. Does $65 + -8 = 57$? Yes. So 65 is the solution.

The key is to know what number to add to both sides. In Example 1, we added 8 to both sides. This caused the left side to simplify to just x.

You may be able to solve equations like these in your head. Still, you must learn the general strategy. More complicated problems require it.

In Example 1, after adding the same number to both sides, all you have to do is simplify the sides to find the solution. So there is only one step to remember.

> To solve an equation of the form $x + a = b$, add $-a$ to both sides and simplify.

Notes on Reading

If you want to introduce solving equations using manipulatives, see *Optional Activities* below.

❶ **Reading Mathematics** It is appropriate to have students read this lesson aloud in class so that they get practice in reading equations. To emphasize what "the form $x + a = b$" means, suggest that students think of a and b as *known* numbers and x as the *unknown* number. It may be helpful to have volunteers write a few equations of this type on the board.

A word of caution is in order. Once the steps used in solving equations are introduced, many students proceed mechanically through them. They do not take time to examine an equation to determine whether it can be solved mentally or whether it has an unusual feature that needs attention. Urge students to look closely at an equation *before* they begin solving it.

❷ Establishing the good habits given in this lesson can help the student in all sentence-solving. It is important that students write successive sentences with the equal signs underneath each other, and they should check answers whenever possible.

Optional Activities

Activity 1 Solving Equations with Integer Tiles. You might want to use *Activity Kit, Activity 11*, to introduce Lesson 5-8. In this activity students model equations of the form $x + a = b$ and demonstrate how to solve the equations using concrete materials.

Activity 2 Lima-Bean Equations
Materials: Plain and painted lima beans (or similar materials), 1 cup

You may prefer to use this activity instead of Activity 1. Tell students that the cup represents the unknown, each plain bean represents 1, and each painted bean represents −1. Note that a plain bean plus a painted bean represents $1 + -1$, or 0. Then show students how to solve equations such as $x + 2 = 5$ using these materials.

First put a cup and 2 plain beans on one side of the "=" sign and 5 plain beans on the other side. Then put 2 painted beans on each side and pair the 2 painted beans on each side with 2 plain beans and remove them. The result is x equals 3.

$x + 2 = 5$

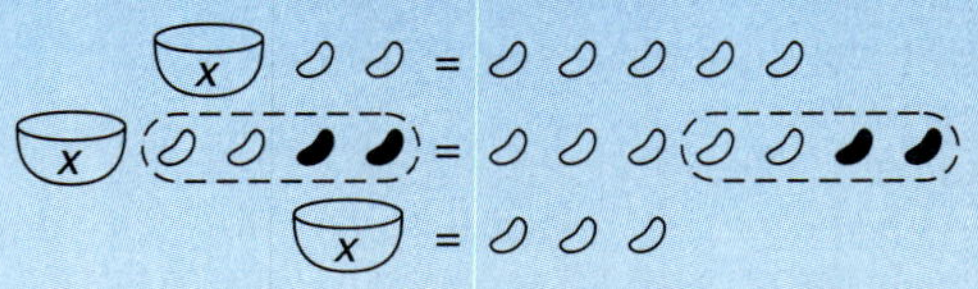

If a balance is available from the science department, you might want to demonstrate solving an equation like $x + 4 = 11$. Have 25 equal weights. Hide 7 of them in a bag and put the bag, along with 4 more weights, on one pan. Put 11 weights on the other pan (the scale should balance). Take 4 weights off each pan; it should still balance, and students should see that there are 7 weights in the bag.

Multicultural Connection You might tell students that the oldest type of scale known to us is the balance first used by the ancient Egyptians about 2500 B.C. The *steelyard* scale was developed by the Romans about 2000 years ago. It consists of a horizontal bar on a steelyard that has arms of unequal length. A pan or hook on the shorter arm holds the load. A small weight is moved along the longer arm until it balances the load. The load's weight is indicated on the markings along this arm. Interested students can read about advanced mechanical and electronic scales.

Picturing the Solving of $x + a = b$

Solving $x + a = b$ can be pictured with a balance scale. Think of x as the unknown weight of a sack. Various objects have been placed on the two pans of the scale. Because the scale is not tipped one way or the other, the total weights of the two sides are equal.

$$x + a = b$$

Clearly one way to find x is to remove a weight equal to a from both pans. This is like adding $-a$ to each side. The result is that $x = b + -a$.

In Example 2, no equation is given. An equation has to be found from the situation.

Example 2

The temperature was 4° this afternoon and now is -6°. By how much has it changed?

Solution

Let c be the change in temperature. (If c is positive, the temperature has gone up. If c is negative, the temperature has gone down.)

$$\text{Then} \quad 4 + c = -6.$$

Since 4 is added to c, we add -4 to both sides. This ensures that c will wind up alone on its side of the equation.

$$4 + c = -6$$
$$-4 + 4 + c = -4 + -6$$
$$0 + c = -10$$
$$c = -10$$

The change is -10°.

Check

To check, look at the original question. If the temperature was 4° and it changed -10°, is it now -6°? Since the answer is yes, -10° is the correct solution.

Adapting to Individual Needs

Extra Help

Some students may have trouble identifying the properties involved in solving equations. Before discussing Example 1 with these students, you might review these properties. Use several examples, and then ask students to state the property in their own words.

Addition Property of Equality
 Example: $4 = 4$, so $4 + 9 = 4 + 9$
 [If two numbers are equal, then you can add the same number to each and the sums are equal.]

Property of Opposites
 Example: $4 + -4 = 0$
 [The sum of a number and its opposite is zero.]

Additive Identity Property of Zero
 Example: $4 + 0 = 4$
 [The sum of zero and any number is the number.]

More Comments on Solving $x + a = b$

When solving an equation, it is important to organize your work carefully. Write each step *underneath* the previous step. Some teachers like students to name properties. Here the equation $x + 43 = -18$ is solved with the properties named where they are used.

❸

$x + 43 = -18$	(original equation)
$x + 43 + -43 = -18 + -43$	Addition Property of Equality
$x + 0 = -18 + -43$	Property of Opposites
$x = -18 + -43$	Additive Identity Property of Zero
$x = -61$	(arithmetic computation)

Check

Substitute -61 for x in the original equation.
Does $-61 + 43 = -18$? Yes. So -61 is the solution.

In solving an equation, the unknown can be on either side. (The sack can be on either side of the scale.) And since addition is commutative, the unknown may be the first or second addend on that side. So all four equations below have the same solution.

$x + 43 = -18 \qquad 43 + x = -18 \qquad -18 = x + 43 \qquad -18 = 43 + x$

QUESTIONS

Covering the Reading

1. Give the solution to $8 + \underline{\ ?\ } = 13$. 5
2. In algebra, the blank of Question 1 is usually replaced by what? a variable (a letter)
3. Begin with the true equation $\frac{4}{5} = 0.8$.
   a. Is it true that $6 + \frac{4}{5} = 6 + 0.8$? Yes
   b. Is it true that $-1 + \frac{4}{5} = -1 + 0.8$? Yes
   c. Is it true that $17.43 + \frac{4}{5} = 17.43 + 0.8$? Yes
   d. Parts **a** to **c** are instances of what property? Addition Property of Equality
4. Here are steps in the solution of the equation $3.28 = A + -5$. Give the reason for each step.
   $3.28 = A + -5$
   a. $3.28 + 5 = A + -5 + 5$ a) Addition Property of Equality
   b. $3.28 + 5 = A + 0$ b) Property of Opposites
   c. $3.28 + 5 = A$ c) Additive Identity Property of Zero
   d. $8.28 = A$ d) arithmetic computation
5. *Multiple choice.* Which equation does not have the same solution as the others? (b)
   (a) $13 + x = -6$ (b) $-6 + x = 13$ (c) $x + 13 = -6$ (d) $-6 = x + 13$

❸ A goal of sentence-solving is to skip unnecessary steps. Few adults would take four lines to solve the sentence $x + 43 = -18$. However, it is important that students at first see all steps. Ultimately students should be able to omit the third and fourth lines. But do not allow students to skip the second line too quickly; the number added to both sides is a critical part of finding the solution.

Additional Examples

1. Solve each equation.
   a. $p + 5 = 3$ **-2**
   b. $-8 + q = 10$ **18**
   c. $3 = r + \frac{1}{2}$ **$2\frac{1}{2}$**
   d. $10.6 = -5.2 + s$ **15.8**
2. William J. Cobb, who was a professional wrestler from Augusta, Georgia, went on a diet and lost 570 pounds over a period of $2\frac{1}{2}$ years. He weighed 232 pounds at the end of his diet.
   a. Write an equation of the form $x + a = b$ that you might use to find Cobb's original weight w. **$w + -570 = 232$**
   b. What was his original weight? **802 pounds**

Notes on Questions

Notice that there is great variety in **Questions 1–13.** This is done so that students have to think about what they are doing, and so that they do not solve the equations mechanically.

LESSON MASTER 5-8 A

Questions on SPUR Objectives
See pages 297-299 for objectives.

Skills, Properties Objectives D and F

In 1-10, show what you added to both sides as you solved the equation. Student work is not shown.

1. $p + 15 = 6$ $p = 9$
2. $-32 + q = -17$ $q = 15$
3. $5\frac{1}{2} = \frac{3}{4} + a$ $a = 4\frac{3}{4}$
4. $p + -5.23 = 6.4$ $p = 11.63$
5. $8 = -6 + m + 12$ $m = 2$
6. $-3.7 = 2.4 + v + -2.4$ $v = -3.7$
7. $d + 4.5 = 6 + -3.2 + 7.8$ $d = 6.1$
8. $\frac{1}{2} + h + -\frac{3}{8} = \frac{1}{4}$ $h = \frac{1}{8}$
9. Solve for x: $x + a = b$ $x = b - a$
10. Solve for p: $t = p + 2 + q$ $p = t - 2 - q$

Uses Objectives I and J

11. Stanley needs to do 50 hours of community service before graduation. He worked at the hospital for $10\frac{1}{2}$ hours, tutored a first grader for 15 hours, and cleaned the park for $12\frac{1}{4}$ hours. How many hours of work does he still need to complete?
    $10\frac{1}{2} + 15 + 12\frac{1}{4} + h = 50$ (equation) $12\frac{1}{4}$ hr (answer)
12. Annabelle's best time in the 100-meter dash is 14.4 seconds. The school record is 13.72 seconds. How much longer is her time than the school record?
    $13.72 + a = 14.4$ (equation) 0.68 sec (answer)

Adapting to Individual Needs

English Language Development
Explain the phrase "equations of the form $x + a = b$" by writing several equations of this form, such as $x + 5 = 7$, $r + -3 = 9$, $m + \frac{1}{2} = -3\frac{1}{2}$. Then contrast equations of this form with equations not of this form, such as $2n = 8$, $\frac{x}{3} = 7$, and $4y + 3 = 11$.

Be sure to stress that each of the equations $x + 5 = 7$, $5 + x = 7$, $7 = 5 + x$, and $7 = x + 5$, are equivalent and of the form $x + a = b$.

Notes on Questions

Questions 6–11 These equations are purposely difficult to solve in one's head so as to promote the use of the algorithm given in this lesson.

Question 19 Some students may answer this question without showing an equation. This is fine, but point out how the equation $103.52 + 35 + -12.50 + I = 130.05$ can help them to organize their work.

Question 35 This magic square is reproduced on **Teaching Aid 57.** Some students may try to find the answer without using the second condition which is needed to complete the first and last rows and the second and third columns.

LESSON MASTER 5-8 B — Questions on SPUR Objectives

Skills Objective D: Solve equations of the form $x + a = b$.

In 1-14, show what you added to both sides as you solved the equation. Student work is not shown.

1. $m + 13 = 10$ $m = -3$	**2.** $-40 + b = -17$ $b = 23$
3. $21 + h = -10$ $h = -31$	**4.** $-8 + d = 0$ $d = 8$
5. $18 = -5 + r$ $r = 23$	**6.** $g + 5.4 = 7.1$ $g = 1.7$
7. $\frac{7}{8} + a = \frac{15}{16}$ $a = \frac{1}{16}$	**8.** $-3.66 = w + 22$ $w = -25.66$
9. $e + 17 = 66 + 31$ $e = 80$	**10.** $8.2 + u + 1.4 = -7.3 + .6$ $u = -16.3$
11. $k + \frac{1}{4} = -\frac{1}{2} + \frac{5}{8}$ $k = -\frac{1}{8}$	**12.** $-122 + 77 = p + -40 + -5$ $p = 0$
13. Solve for x: $a + x = b$ $x = b - a$	**14.** Solve for v: $n = v + 4 + j$ $v = n - 4 - j$

6a) -86; b) 144; c) $144 + 86 = 230$

7a) 12; b) 19 c) $-12 + 19 = 7$

8a) 3.2; b) -2.7; c) $-5.9 = -2.7 + -3.2$

9a) $\frac{22}{3}$; b) $\frac{202}{3}$ c) $60 = \frac{202}{3} + -\frac{22}{3}$

10a) -431; b) -1243 c) $431 + -1243 = -812$

11a) $-\frac{1}{4}$; b) $\frac{3}{20}$; c) $\frac{3}{20} + \frac{1}{4} = \frac{8}{20} = \frac{2}{5}$

In 6–11, an equation is given. **a.** To solve the equation, what number should you add to each side of the equation? **b.** Find the solution. **c.** Check your answer.

6. $x + 86 = 230$ **7.** $-12 + y = 7$ **8.** $-5.9 = A + -3.2$

9. $60 = z + \frac{-22}{3}$ **10.** $431 + B = -812$ **11.** $C - \frac{1}{4} = \frac{2}{5}$

12. The temperature was $-15°$ yesterday and is $-20°$ today. Let c be the change in the temperature.
   a. What equation can be solved to find c? $-15 + c = -20$
   b. Solve that equation. $c = -5$
   c. Check your answer. $-15 + -5 = -20$

13. Suppose the temperature is two degrees below zero. By how much must it change to become three degrees above zero? 5°

Applying the Mathematics

14. If $a = b$, the Addition Property of Equality says that $a + c = b + c$. But it is also true that $c + a = c + b$. Why? because of the Commutative Property of Addition

In 15 and 16, first simplify one side of the equation. Then solve and check.

15. $A + 43 + -5 = 120$ **16.** $-35 = 16 + d + 5$

15) $A + 38 = 120$
$A = 82$
$82 + 43 + -5 = 120$

16) $-35 = 21 + d$
$d = -56$
$-35 = 16 + -56 + 5$

17. A family's income I satisfies the formula $I = F + M + C$, where F is the amount the father earns, M is the amount the mother earns, and C is the amount the children earn. If $I = 40{,}325$, $F = 18{,}800$, and $M = 20{,}500$, how much did the children earn? $1025

18. Roberto had $48.83. His mother gave him some money for his birthday. He then had $63.33.
   a. Write an equation to determine how much money Roberto got for his birthday. $48.83 + m = 63.33$
   b. Solve and check. $m = 14.50$; $48.83 + 14.50 = 63.33$

19. On Monday, Vito's savings account showed a balance of $103.52. He deposited $35 into the account Tuesday. Wednesday he withdrew $12.50. Thursday he asked the bank to tell him how much was in the account. They said that $130.05 was in the account. What happened is that the bank paid Vito some interest. How much interest? $4.03

20. George is G years old. Wilma is W years old.
   a. What will be George's age 10 years from now? $G + 10$
   b. What will be Wilma's age 10 years from now? $W + 10$
   c. If George and Wilma are the same age, how are G and W related?
   d. Translate into mathematics: If George and Wilma are the same age now, then they will be the same age 10 years from now.
   e. Part **d** of this question is an instance of what property?
   c) $G = W$; d) $G + 10 = W + 10$; e) Addition Property of Equality

21. Solve for b: $a + b = c$. $b = c + -a$

Adapting to Individual Needs

Challenge

Refer students to the balance scales on the top of page 278. Remind them that equal weights must be added to or removed from each side of the scale in order for the scale to be balanced. Then give them **Teaching Aid 57** which pictures the diagrams at the right, and ask how many △s are needed to balance 20 ■s? [15 △s]

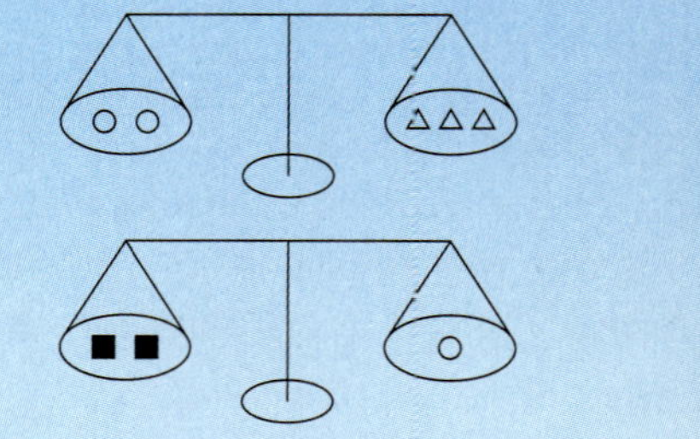

Review

22. Which property is used in getting to each step? *(Lessons 5-2, 5-7)*

$(5 + 7) + -5$

a. $= 5 + (7 + -5)$ a) Associative Property of Addition
b. $= 5 + (-5 + 7)$ b) Commutative Property of Addition
c. $= (5 + -5) + 7$ c) Associative Property of Addition
d. $= 0 + 7$ d) Property of Opposites
e. $= 7$ e) Additive Identity Property of Zero

23. You make a random choice from a hat filled with red, white, and blue chips. The probability of choosing a red chip is $\frac{2}{3}$. The probability of choosing a white chip is $\frac{1}{4}$.
a. What is the probability of choosing a red or white chip? $\frac{11}{12}$
b. Describe the complement of the event in part **a.** choosing a blue chip
c. Find the probability of the event you described in part **b.** *(Lesson 5-6)* $\frac{1}{12}$ or $.08\overline{3}$

24. If a $210\frac{1}{2}°$ counterclockwise turn is followed by a $150\frac{1}{8}°$ counterclockwise turn, what results? *(Lessons 5-4, 5-5)* a $360\frac{5}{8}°$ turn or a $\frac{5}{8}°$ turn

25. Consider the inequality $x < -3$.
a. Name a value of x that is a solution. Sample: -4
b. Name a value of x that is not a solution. *(Lesson 4-10)* Sample: 2

26. Simplify: $(4 \cdot 3 - 2 \cdot 1)(4 \cdot 3 + 2 \cdot 1)$. *(Lesson 4-5)* 140

In 27–29, translate into mathematics. *(Lesson 4-3)*

27. triple a number n $3n$

28. five less than a number t $t - 5$

29. a number B divided by twice a second number C $B/(2C)$ or $\frac{B}{2C}$

In 30 and 31, translate into English words. *(Lesson 3-6)*

30. $\overrightarrow{AB}$ the ray with endpoint A and containing B

31. $m\angle LNP = 35°$ The measure of angle LNP is thirty-five degrees.

32. Draw a line segment with length 73 mm. *(Lessons 3-1, 3-3)* Check students' drawings.

33. How many zeros follow the 1 in the decimal form of 10^{30}? *(Lesson 2-2)* 30

34. Approximate $\frac{7}{16}$ to the nearest hundredth. *(Lessons 1-4, 1-6)* ≈ 0.44

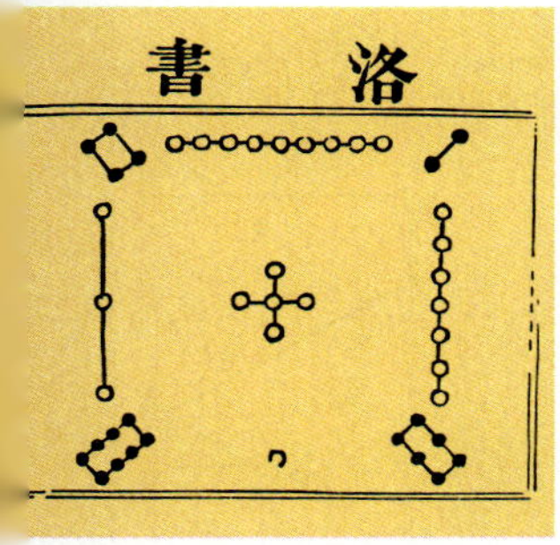

Where did it come from? *The earliest known magic squares came from China. According to tradition, the Emperor Yu received a magic square called the* Lo shu *from a divine tortoise in about 2900* B.C.

Exploration

35. A magic square is a square array of numbers in which the sum along every row, column or main diagonal is the same. Copy and complete the square at the right, such that
(1) Each row, column, and diagonal adds to 2.
(2) Each integer from -7 to 8 is used exactly once.

8	-5	-6	5
-3	2	3	0
1	-2	-1	4
-4	7	6	-7

Follow-up for Lesson 5-8

Practice

For more questions on SPUR Objectives, use **Lesson Master 5-8A** (shown on page 279) or **Lesson Master 5-8B** (shown on pages 280–281).

Assessment

Written Assessment Have students **work in pairs.** Have partners take turns writing an equation. Have the other student write three other equations that have the same solution. For example, if the first student writes $x + 3 = 6$, the other student could write $3 + x = 6$, $6 = 3 + x$, and $6 = x + 3$. Then have the students solve one of the equations together. [The equations are correct and discussion during the activity indicates students' understanding.]

Extension

You may want some students to investigate solutions to equations of the form $|x| + a = b$. Students can answer the following questions:

1. How many solutions can these equations have? at most two
2. If $a = b$, how many solutions are there? One
3. What happens if $b < a$? The equation has no solutions.

Setting up Lesson 5-9

The activity for Lesson 5-9 can be done in class, or you might want students to construct the hexagon as part of their homework. We suggest that you make the hexagon before students try to do it so that you are prepared for the possible trouble spots.

▸ **LESSON MASTER 5-8 B** *page 2*

Properties Objective F: Identify the Addition Property of Equality.

15. State the Addition Property of Equality.
If $a = b$, then $a + c = b + c$.

In 16-17, tell what was added to both sides to solve the equation.

16. $x + 11 = -20$, $x = -31$ — -11

17. $-27 + y = 14$, $y = 41$ — 27

Uses Objective I: Use the Putting-Together Model for Addition to form sentences involving addition.

18. Doug needs to get $50 in pledges for his school's walk-a-thon. Mrs. Dorsey pledged $8, Mr. Sanchez pledged $10, and his sister Doreen pledged $5. How much more money in pledges does Doug need?
equation: $50 = 8 + 10 + 5 + p$ answer: $27

19. Mrs. Chung's bank balance on March 1 was $560.64. On March 31 the balance was $788.04. During the month, she deposited $125, withdrew $60, and made one other transaction. Describe the other transaction.
equation: $560.64 + 125 - 60 + t = 788.04$ answer: deposit of $162.40

Uses Objective J: Use the Slide Model for Addition to form sentences involving addition.

20. This morning the temperature was eight degrees below zero. At noon it was four degrees above zero. By how much did it change?
equation: $-8 + c = 4$ answer: rose 12°

21. The level of the Great Horse River is three feet below flood stage. By how much must it rise to be three feet above flood stage?
equation: $-3 + c = 3$ answer: 6 feet

In-class Activity

You might want to have students **work in groups.** Each student should make the polygon, but if they are in groups, they can help each other.

Have students save their polygons for **Questions 20-24** in Lesson 5-9.

Introducing Lesson 5-9

Polygons

IN-CLASS ACTIVITY

With this activity, you will make a special hexagon. Start with an $8\frac{1}{2}''$ by $11''$ or $8''$ by $10\frac{1}{2}''$ piece of paper. Your teacher may guide you through the steps, so wait for instructions.

---

1 Hold your paper with the long side horizontal. Fold in half along the dotted line as shown.

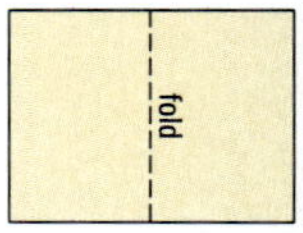

2 With the folded edge to the left, again fold the paper in half along the dotted line.

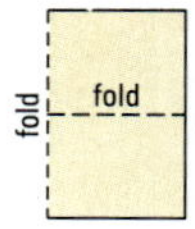

3 With the folds at the top and left, starting at the upper left, label the corners *J, K, L,* and *M*. (This rectangle has $\frac{1}{4}$ the area of the original sheet of paper.)

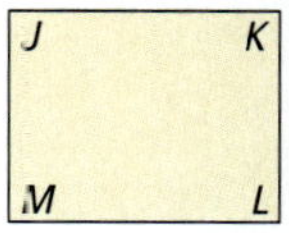

4 Pick up corner *K*. Move $\overline{JK}$ so that the measure of $\angle KJM$ is equal to the measure of $\angle KJN$. Be as careful as you can here.

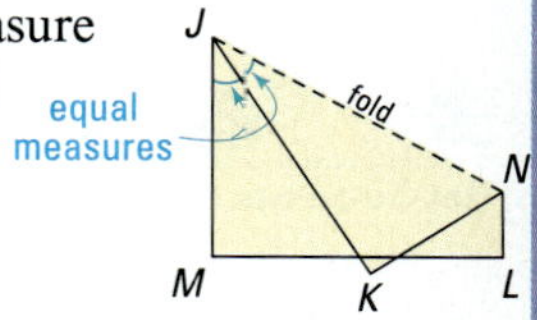

5 Pick up the corner *M* and fold it over $\overline{JK}$ to meet $\overline{JN}$. (If you have made $m\angle KJM = m\angle KJN$ in Step 4, this will work.)

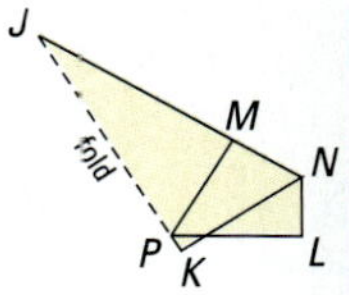

6 Cut through all the sheets of paper along $\overline{PM}$.

7 Unfold $\triangle JPM$. You now should have a hexagon to use for Questions 20–24 of Lesson 5-9. Label the vertices of your hexagon *H, E, X, A, G, N.*

282

Optional Activities

A Paper Pentagon

Materials: Strip of heavy paper 2 inches wide and 18 inches long

Students can tape 2-inch strips of paper together to make a strip 18 inches long. Have them use the strip to make a pentagon by carefully tying a knot in the center of the strip of paper, creasing the sides, and folding in the ends. Students can make larger or smaller pentagons by using wider or narrower strips of paper.

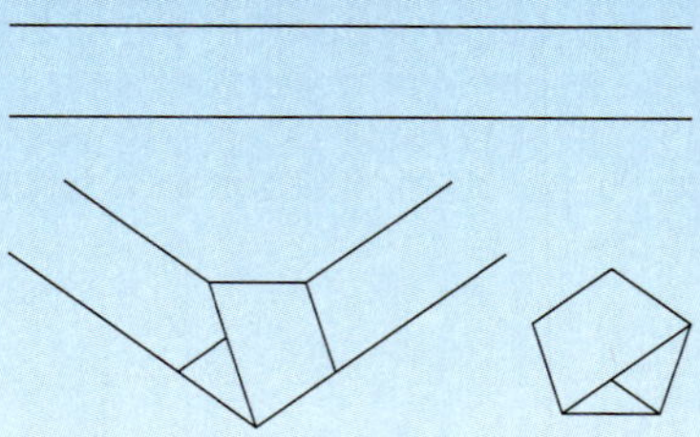

LESSON

5-9

Polygons

Hexagonal structures. *The hexagon is the polygonal shape of the Navajo hogan. Most hogans are log-and-mud structures built to face the rising sun.*

Naming Lines and Line Segments

Let A and B be any points. There is only one line containing both of them. The line goes on forever. To show this, when we draw a picture of a line, we put arrows at both ends. This line is written $\overleftrightarrow{AB}$ with the two-sided arrow above the letters.

❶ The points on $\overleftrightarrow{AB}$ that are between A and B, together with the points A and B themselves, make up a **line segment** or **segment,** written as $\overline{AB}$. A and B are the **endpoints** of $\overline{AB}$.

What Is a Polygon?

A **polygon** is a union of segments in which each segment intersects two others, one at each of its endpoints. The segments are called the **sides** of the polygon. Two sides meet at a **vertex** of the polygon. (The plural of vertex is **vertices.**) The number of sides of a polygon equals the number of its vertices. Polygons are classified by that number.

Lesson 5-9

Objectives

H Identify parts and give names of polygons.

Resources

From the ***Teacher's Resource File***

- Lesson Master 5-9A or 5-9B
- Answer Master 5-9
- Teaching Aids
  51 Warm-up
  58 Classification of Polygons
- Activity Kit, Activity 12
- Technology Sourcebook
  Computer Demonstration 5
  Computer Master 8

Additional Resources

- Visuals for Teaching Aids 51, 58
- Geometry Workshop
- Geometry Template
- Hexagon from the In-class Activity (Additional Examples and Questions 20–24)

Teaching Lesson 5-9

Warm-up

Draw an angle for each of the following measures. **Check students' drawings.**

1. 90° **2.** 30° **3.** 45°
4. 120° **5.** 180° **6.** 75°

Notes on Reading

❶ The distinction between $\overline{AB}$ and $\overleftrightarrow{AB}$ is customary in most textbooks. However, this distinction is not always made by mathematicians, who often use *AB* for both and rely

Lesson 5-9 Overview

Broad Goals This lesson reviews (or introduces, depending on student experience) the basic terminology of polygons.

Perspective A lesson on polygons is included at this time for four reasons. First, it is necessary for the discussion of perimeter that immediately follows. (Perimeter, or the sum of lengths, fits naturally in a chapter on addition.) Second, polygons provide a nice change of pace and a day for developing some terminology while at the same time continuing the practice of equation-solving. Third, we use polygons frequently in Chapter 6 as vehicles for studying problem solving. And fourth, polygons are obviously an important topic in geometry.

Just as most students like the names for big numbers, they like the names for polygons with various numbers of sides. There are special (though not important) names for 11-gons and 12-gons, but we delay introducing them until the next chapter.

on context to tell whether lines or segments are indicated.

❷ Make certain that students understand the need to learn the names of the polygons given in this chart. The chart is also reproduced on **Teaching Aid 58**.

Some people use the word *septagon* as the name for a 7-sided polygon. *Heptagon* is the more common name.

You might want to use one or more of the activities in *Optional Activities* at this time to give students more opportunities to work with polygons.

Additional Examples

You might use the following examples when you discuss the lesson.
Use the polygon below to answer Questions 1-4.

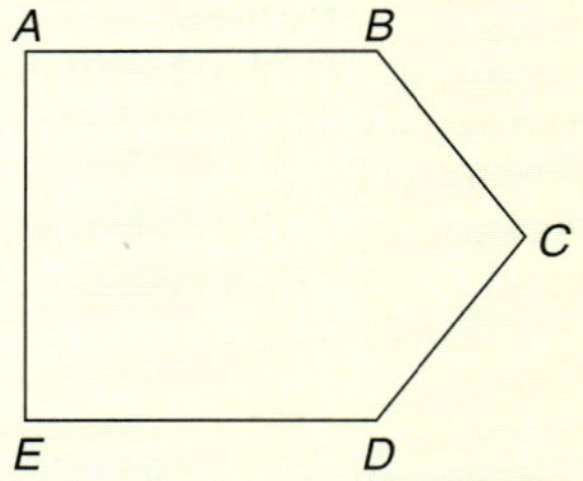

1. How many sides does the polygon have? How many vertices? **5, 5**
2. What type of polygon is it? **Pentagon**
3. Use the vertices to name the polygon. **Sample: *BCDEA***
4. How many angles does the polygon have? **5**
5. Now answer questions 1-4 using the polygon you made in the *In-class Activity.*
   1. 6 sides, 6 vertices;
   2. hexagon
   3. Sample: *HEXAGN*
   4. 6 angles

Number of sides	Number of vertices	Type of polygon	Example
3	3	triangle	
4	4	quadrilateral	
5	5	pentagon	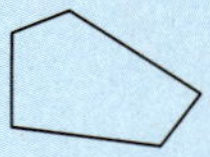
6	6	hexagon	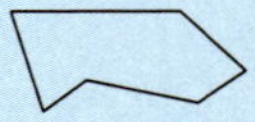
❷ 7	7	heptagon	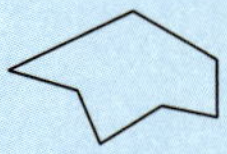
8	8	octagon	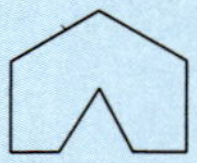
9	9	nonagon	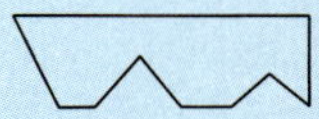
10	10	decagon	

Polygons with more than 10 sides do not always have special names. A polygon with 11 sides is called an 11-gon. A polygon with 42 sides is called a 42-gon. In general, a polygon with n sides is called an ***n*-gon.**

Naming Polygons

Polygons are named by giving their vertices in order around the figure. The polygon below is *WTUV.* You could also call it *TUVW, WVUT,* or five other names. *WTVU* is not a correct name for this polygon because the vertices *W, T, V,* and *U* are not in order.

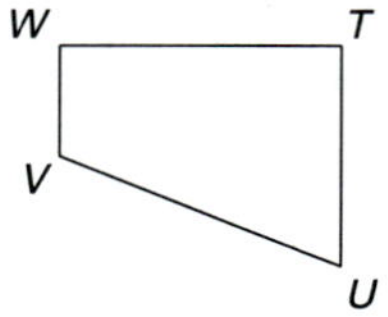

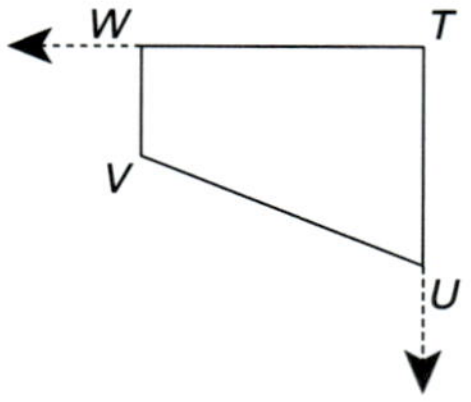

Extend two sides of a polygon drawn from a particular vertex to be rays with the vertex as the endpoint. These rays form an **angle of the polygon.** Every polygon has as many angles as it has sides or vertices. In polygon *WTUV,* angles *W* and *T* look like right angles. Angle *U* is acute. Angle *V* is obtuse.

Optional Activities

Activity 1 Tangrams In *Activity 12* in *Activity Kit,* students combine tangram pieces to form polygons. You can use this activity after students have learned the names for the polygons.

Activity 2 Drawing Polygons
Materials: Geometry Template

After students learn the names of polygons, you might have them use their **Geometry Templates** to draw polygons. For each polygon, have them measure its smallest angle, its largest angle, its shortest side, and its longest side. Then have them try to draw each of the following polygons. [It is impossible to draw the one described in 2; those in 1 and 3–5 are possible to draw.]

1. A quadrilateral that is not a rectangle with two 90° angles
2. A pentagon with four right angles
3. A hexagon with four right angles
4. A hexagon with all obtuse angles
5. A hexagon with three acute angles

Activity 3 Technology Connection You may wish to use *Computer Demonstration 5* to show students how to create polygons using the *Geometry Workshop.* Following the demonstration, you could assign *Technology Sourcebook, Computer Master 8.*

QUESTIONS

Covering the Reading

1. The line through points *A* and *B* is written _?_. $\overleftrightarrow{AB}$

2. The line segment with endpoints *C* and *D* consists of what points? all the points on $\overleftrightarrow{CD}$ between and including *C* and *D*

3. The line segment with endpoints *F* and *E* is written _?_. $\overline{FE}$ or $\overline{EF}$

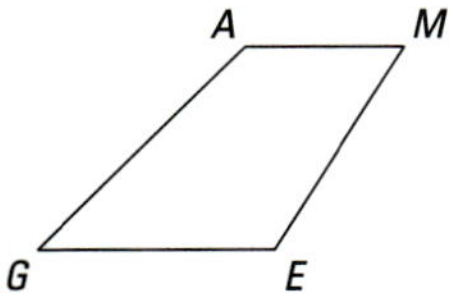

4. Refer to the polygon pictured at the left.
   a. Name this polygon. a) Sample: *GAME*
   b. Name its sides. $\overline{GA}$, $\overline{AM}$, $\overline{ME}$, $\overline{EG}$
   c. Name its vertices. *G, A, M, E*
   d. Name its angles. ∠*G*, ∠*A*, ∠*M*, ∠*E*
   e. What type of polygon is this? quadrilateral

In 5–12, what name is given to a polygon with the given number of sides?

5. 5 pentagon
6. 6 hexagon
7. 7 heptagon
8. 8 octagon
9. 9 nonagon
10. *n* *n*-gon
11. 11 11-gon
12. 1994 1994-gon

13. How many angles does a 12-gon have? 12

14. A decagon has _?_ sides, _?_ angles, and _?_ vertices. 10, 10, 10

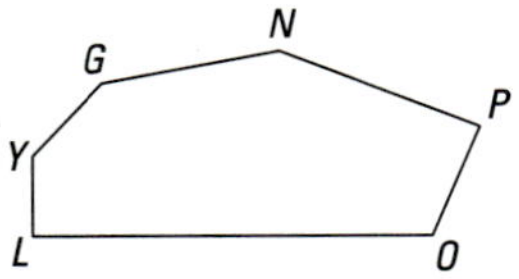

15. Refer to the figure at the left.
   a. Give three possible names for this polygon. Samples: *POLYGN, LOPNGY, GNPOLY*
   b. What type of polygon is this? hexagon

Applying the Mathematics

16. A square is what type of polygon mentioned in this lesson? quadrilateral

17. Temples in the Bahá'í religion have 9 sides. Suppose you view a Bahá'í temple from directly overhead. The outline of the temple will have what shape? nonagon

18. A famous building just outside of Washington, DC, is pictured below. A clue to its name is given by its shape. What is its name? The Pentagon

Notes on Questions

Question 4 Check that students have used the correct notation for each part of the question.

Question 18 History Connection You might ask students if they know what government agency is headquartered in the Pentagon. [The headquarters for the United States Department of Defense] You might also want to give students some information about the building. It was designed by George Edwin Bergstrom, and the entire structure cost 83 million dollars. When it was completed in 1943, it was the largest office building in the world. The Pentagon covers 34 acres and has 3.7 million square feet of usable floor space. Students might enjoy reading about the Pentagon and sharing interesting data that they find.

Adapting to Individual Needs

Extra Help

If students are having difficulty identifying the polygons in the table, you might direct them to sketch each figure, and then give the number of sides and the number of angles. Then give the name of the polygon, emphasizing the prefix and how it relates to the number of sides and angles. For some prefixes, students should be able to suggest other words with the same prefix.

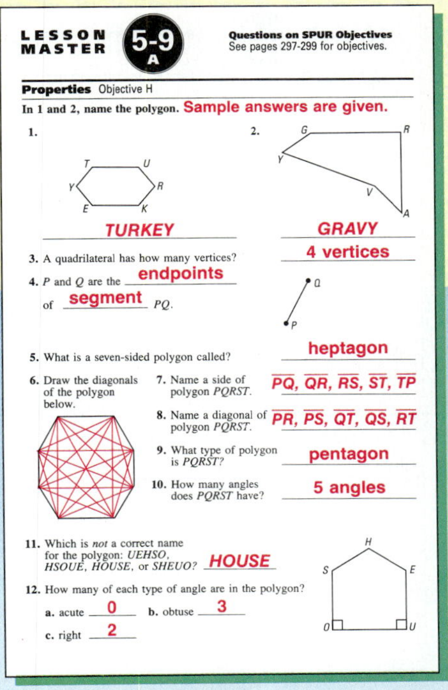

LESSON MASTER 5-9 A

Questions on SPUR Objectives
See pages 297-299 for objectives.

Properties Objective H

In 1 and 2, name the polygon. Sample answers are given.

1. TURKEY
2. GRAVY

3. A quadrilateral has how many vertices? 4 vertices

4. *P* and *Q* are the endpoints of segment *PQ*.

5. What is a seven-sided polygon called? heptagon

6. Draw the diagonals of the polygon below.

7. Name a side of polygon *PQRST*. $\overline{PQ}$, $\overline{QR}$, $\overline{RS}$, $\overline{ST}$, $\overline{TP}$

8. Name a diagonal of polygon *PQRST*. $\overline{PR}$, $\overline{PS}$, $\overline{QT}$, $\overline{QS}$, $\overline{RT}$

9. What type of polygon is *PQRST*? pentagon

10. How many angles does *PQRST* have? 5 angles

11. Which is *not* a correct name for the polygon: *UEHSO, HSOUE, HOUSE,* or *SHEUO*? *HOUSE*

12. How many of each type of angle are in the polygon?
   a. acute 0
   b. obtuse 3
   c. right 2

Notes on Questions

Question 19 Even though the word *diagonal* is introduced in the questions, we expect students to remember its meaning.

Questions 20–24 Students will need the hexagon they made in the *In-class Activity* for these questions.

✎ **Writing** You might ask students to read the descriptions they wrote for **Question 24.**

19. A **diagonal** of a polygon is a segment that connects two vertices of the polygon but is not a side of the polygon. For example, $\overline{AC}$ and $\overline{BD}$ are the diagonals of quadrilateral *ABCD* drawn below.

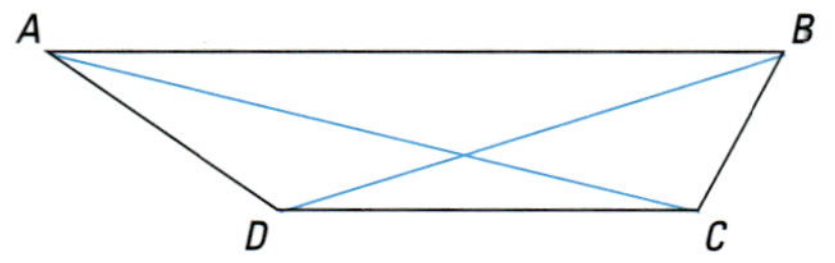

a. Draw a pentagon *PQRST* and name its diagonals.
b. How many diagonals does it have? 5
a) Check students' drawings. $\overline{PR}$, $\overline{PS}$, $\overline{QT}$, $\overline{QS}$, $\overline{TR}$

In 20–24, use the hexagon you made in the In-class Activity preceding this lesson.

20. Measure ∠*H*, ∠*E*, and ∠*X*. Compare your measures with those of a neighbor. Make a conjecture about the measures of ∠*A*, ∠*G*, and ∠*N*. Measure the angles. How do they compare to the measures of angles *H*, *E*, *X*? Can you make a conjecture about the angles of *HEXAGN*? What is the approximate sum of the measures of angles *H*, *E*, *X*, *A*, *G*, and *N*? Sample: Each angle is approximately 120°. The sum of the angles is approximately 720°.

21. Measure $\overline{HE}$, $\overline{EX}$, and $\overline{XA}$ to the nearest centimeter. Compare your measures with those of a neighbor. Make a conjecture about the lengths of $\overline{AG}$, $\overline{GN}$, and $\overline{NH}$. Do you see a pattern? If so, what is it? Sample: All sides are approximately the same length.

22. $\overline{HX}$ is a diagonal. List the other diagonals of *HEXAGN*. Measure their lengths to the nearest centimeter. $\overline{HX}$, $\overline{HA}$, $\overline{HG}$, $\overline{EA}$, $\overline{EG}$, $\overline{EN}$, $\overline{XG}$, $\overline{XN}$, $\overline{AN}$

22) Hexagon from $8\frac{1}{2}'' \times 11''$ paper: diagonals $HX = XG = GH = EA = AN = NE \approx 22$ cm; $EG = XN = AH \approx 25$ cm. From $8'' \times 10\frac{1}{2}''$ paper, $HX = \ldots = NE \approx 20$ cm; $EG = XN = AH \approx 23$ cm.

23. Explain why $\overline{XA}$ is not a diagonal. $\overline{XA}$ joins two consecutive vertices and is a side of the polygon. A diagonal is not a side, so $\overline{XA}$ is not a diagonal.

24. Write a paragraph describing some characteristics of *HEXAGN*. Answers will vary.

Review

25. *Multiple choice.* Which equation does not have the same solution as the others? *(Lesson 5-8)*
(a) $23 = 60 + y$ (b) $y + 60 = 23$
(c) $23 = y + 60$ (d) $y + 23 = 60$ (d)

In 26–29, solve and check. *(Lesson 5-8)*

26. $x + 12 = -10$ $x = -22$; $-22 + 12 = -10$

27. $300 = 172 + (45 + w)$ $w = 83$; $300 = 172 + (45 + 83)$

28. $-1 + -2 + m + -3 + -4 = -100$ $m = -90$; $-1 + -2 + -90 + -3 + -4 = -100$

29. $d + -1.3 = 6.8$ $d = 8.1$; $8.1 + -1.3 = 6.8$

30. Given are steps in solving the general equation $a + x = b$ for *x*. Give the reason why each step is correct. *(Lessons 5-2, 5-8)*

$a + x = b$
a. $-a + a + x = -a + b$ a) Addition Property of Equality
b. $0 + x = -a + b$ b) Property of Opposites
c. $x = -a + b$ c) Additive Identity Property of Zero

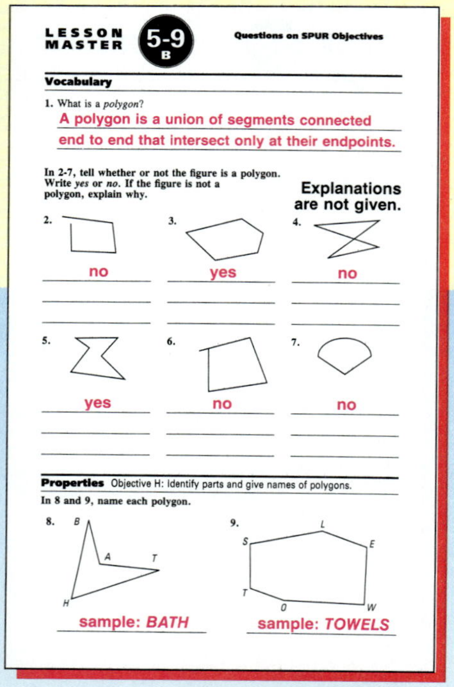

Adapting to Individual Needs

English Language Development
You might have students give the names of familiar polygons (triangle, quadrilateral, pentagon, hexagon, and octagon) in their native languages. Ask if any parts of the names relate to the number of sides and angles in the polygon.

31. A sofa has length s inches. If the sofa were 3 inches longer, it would be 8 feet long. *(Lessons 4-3, 5-8)*
  a. Give an equation of the form $a + x = b$ that involves the three quantities mentioned in the previous two sentences.
  b. Solve that equation for s.
  a) 8 ft = 96 in., so $s + 3 = 96$; b) $s = 93$ inches

Exploration

32) $\approx$ 9.1 cm or $3\frac{9}{16}$ in.

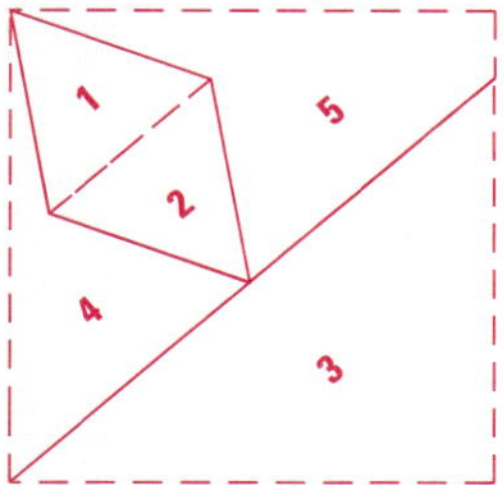

32. Find the area of the six-pointed star below using the following steps.
  a. Trace the figure below onto a piece of paper.
  b. Cut the figure into the 5 pieces shown.
  c. Rearrange the pieces and measure to find the area. The new figure is a square. $A \approx 83\text{ cm}^2$, or $\approx 13\text{ in}^2$.

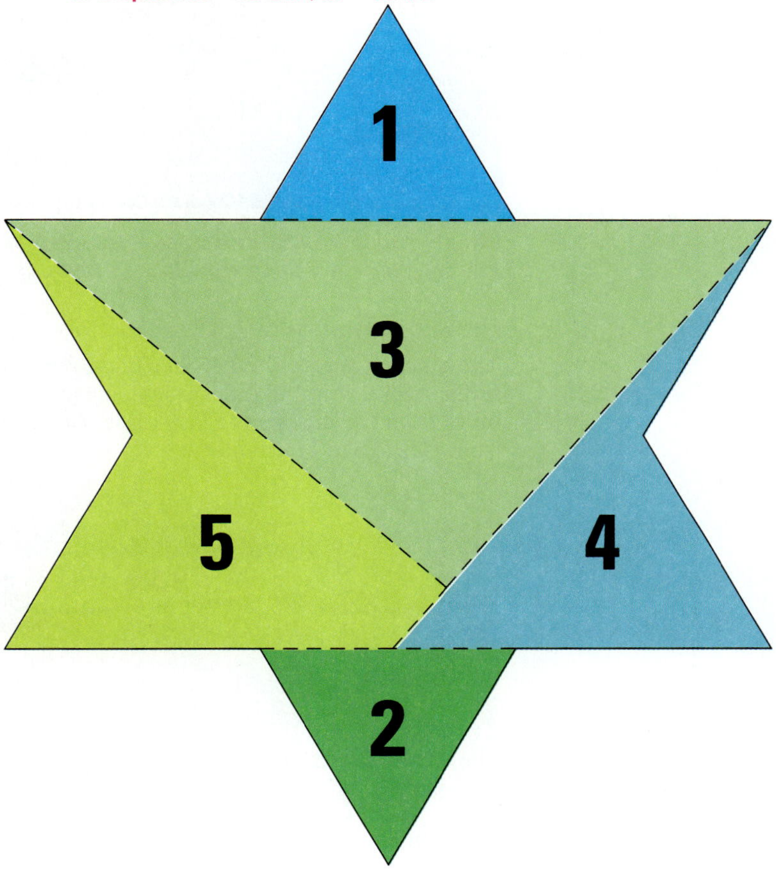

Follow-up for Lesson 5-9

Practice

For more questions on SPUR Objectives, use **Lesson Master 5-9A** (shown on page 285) or **Lesson Master 5-9B** (shown on pages 286–287).

Assessment

Written Assessment Have each student write a paragraph explaining how word associations could help them remember the names of polygons. [For example, students could write that they remember that a quadrilateral has four sides because the prefix *quadri-* reminds them of a quarter, and there are four quarters in a dollar.]

Extension

Ask students how many different ways there are to name a triangle. [6 names; for example, *ABC*, *BCA*, *CAB*, *CBA*, *ACB*, and *BAC*] Then ask how many ways there are to name an *n*-gon. [2*n*]. Students might have fun choosing letters for the vertices of a quadrilateral so that some of the different names for the quadrilateral form words. (A good name is *ITEM*, which also gives *MITE*, *TIME*, and *EMIT*.)

Project Update Project 1, *Polygons in Architecture*, on page 293, relates to the content of this lesson.

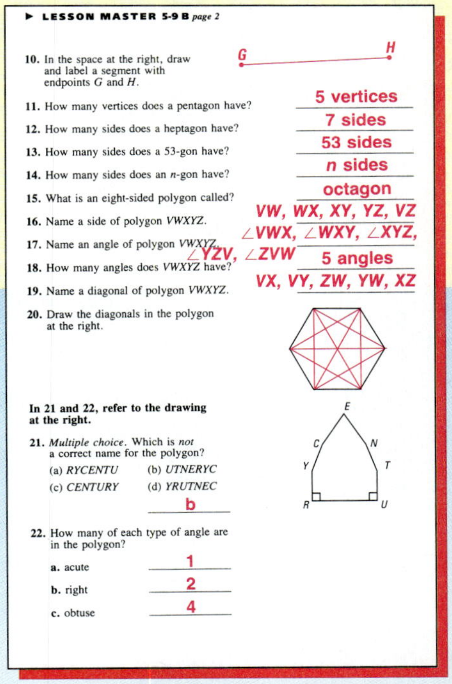
▶ LESSON MASTER 5-9 B *page 2*

10. In the space at the right, draw and label a segment with endpoints G and H.
11. How many vertices does a pentagon have? 5 vertices
12. How many sides does a heptagon have? 7 sides
13. How many sides does a 53-gon have? 53 sides
14. How many sides does an n-gon have? n sides
15. What is an eight-sided polygon called? octagon
16. Name a side of polygon $VWXYZ$. VW, WX, XY, YZ, VZ
17. Name an angle of polygon $VWXYZ$. ∠VWX, ∠WXY, ∠XYZ, ∠YZV, ∠ZVW
18. How many angles does $VWXYZ$ have? 5 angles
19. Name a diagonal of polygon $VWXYZ$. VX, VY, ZW, YW, XZ
20. Draw the diagonals in the polygon at the right.

In 21 and 22, refer to the drawing at the right.

21. *Multiple choice.* Which is *not* a correct name for the polygon?
  (a) *RYCENTU* (b) *UTNERYC*
  (c) *CENTURY* (d) *YRUTNEC*
  b
22. How many of each type of angle are in the polygon?
  a. acute 1
  b. right 2
  c. obtuse 4

Adapting to Individual Needs

Challenge

Materials: Grid paper

Have students copy the two figures shown on a grid at the far right onto their grid paper, cut out the five pieces, and rearrange them to form a square.

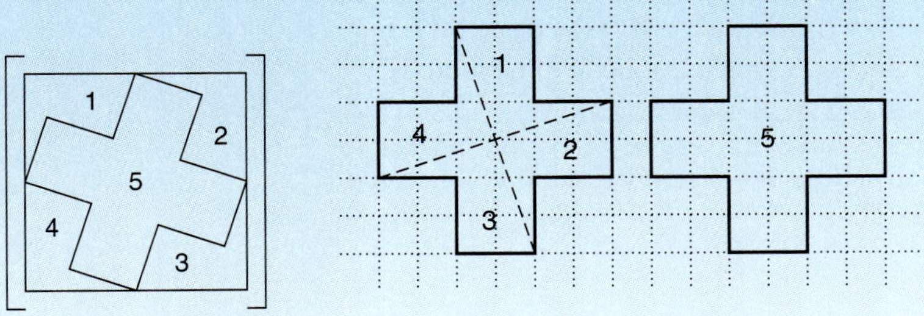

Lesson 5-10

Objectives

E Find the perimeter of a polygon.
I Use the Putting-Together Model to relate lengths.

Resources

From the ***Teacher's Resource File***

- Lesson Master 5-10A or 5-10B
- Answer Master 5-10
- Teaching Aid 51: Warm-up

Additional Resources

- Visual for Teaching Aid 51
- Geometry Templates

Teaching Lesson 5-10

Warm-up

Diagnostic For 1–2, use triangles ABC and WYZ.

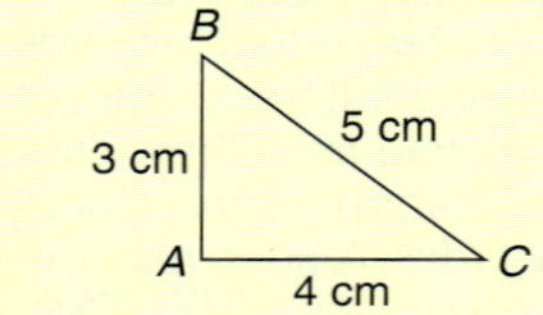

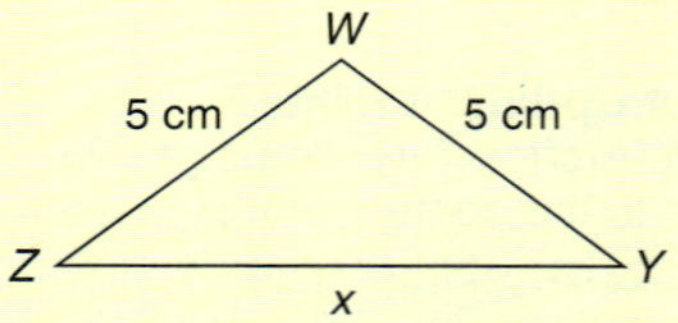

1. Write an equation for the perimeter p of triangle ABC. Then find the perimeter.
   $p = 3 + 4 + 5$, 12 cm
2. If the perimeter of triangle WYZ is 18cm, write an equation to find the length of side x.
   $18 = x + 5 + 5$, 8 cm

LESSON

5-10 *Adding Lengths*

Winning by a length or a nose? *Hundreds of thousands of people travel to Louisville each year to see the Kentucky Derby at Churchill Downs.*

An Example of Adding Lengths

The quickest way to drive from Chicago to Louisville is to go through Indianapolis. It is 185 miles from Chicago to Indianapolis. It is 114 miles from Indianapolis to Louisville. Along this route, how far is it from Chicago to Louisville?

The answer is easy to find. Just add.

$$185 + 114 = 299$$

It is 299 driving miles from Chicago to Louisville.

The general pattern is an instance of the Putting-Together Model for Addition. If you have two lengths x and y, the total length is $x + y$.

Lesson 5-10 Overview

Broad Goals The goal is to give students practice with formulas for perimeters of polygons and to relate these ideas to equations involving addition.

Perspective Many students know perimeter from earlier courses. For those to whom it is new, this content is easy to learn.

In this lesson, students learn the fourth, and last, symbol using AB when A and B are points. $\overrightarrow{AB}$ was introduced in Lesson 3-5; $\overline{AB}$ and $\overleftrightarrow{AB}$ were introduced in Lesson 5-9. The symbol for length, AB, is the hardest to learn because it stands for a number, not a geometric figure. Furthermore, AB does not mean A times B.

What Is Meant by Perimeter?

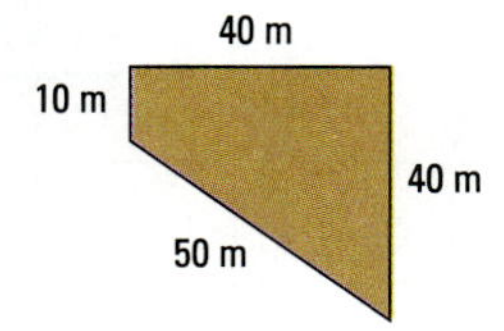

There are many situations in which more than two lengths are put together. Imagine walking around the building outlined at the left. You will have walked 40 + 40 + 50 + 10 meters. This is the idea behind *perimeter.*

> The **perimeter** of a polygon is the sum of the lengths of the sides of the polygon.

Let the sides of a pentagon have lengths v, w, x, y, and z. If the perimeter is p, then $p = v + w + x + y + z$.

Now suppose $v = 12$, $w = 19$, $x = 15$, $z = 22$, and the perimeter $p = 82$. The situation is pictured below. What is the value of y? You can solve an equation to find out.

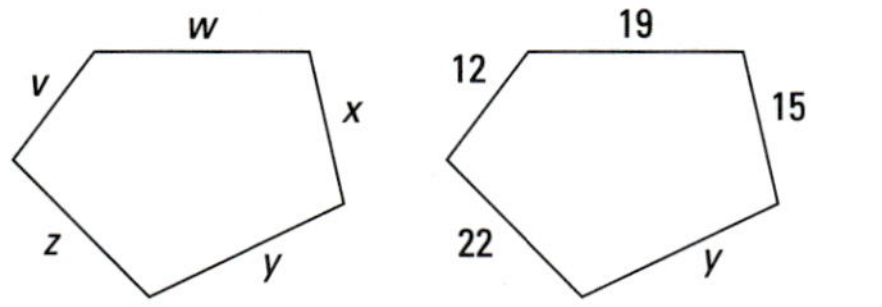

Begin with the general formula.	$p = v + w + x + y + z$
Substitute.	$82 = 12 + 19 + 15 + y + 22$
Simplify.	$82 = 68 + y$
Add -68 to both sides.	$-68 + 82 = -68 + 68 + y$
Simplify.	$14 = y$

Naming the Distance Between Two Points

Recall that if A and B are points, we use the following symbols.

$\overleftrightarrow{AB}$ line through A and B

$\overline{AB}$ segment with endpoints A and B

$\overrightarrow{AB}$ ray with endpoint A and containing B

There is one other related symbol. The symbol ***AB*** (with nothing over it) stands for the *length* of the segment AB. (It makes no sense to multiply points. So when A and B are points, putting the letters next to each other does not mean multiplication.) Here are some examples of this notation. The perimeter of triangle PQR is $PQ + QR + RP$.

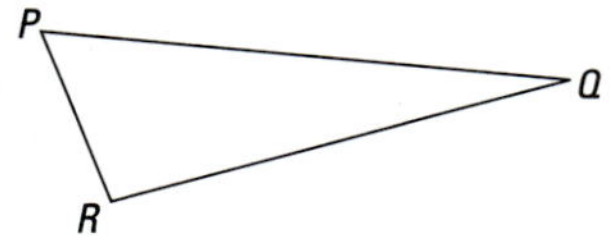

At the right, B is on $\overline{AC}$.

$AB + BC = AC$

$12 + 24 = AC$

$36 = AC$

Notes on Reading

Emphasize the definition of perimeter. The word is derived from the Greek words *peri,* meaning "around" and *meter,* meaning "measure."

Showing students examples of perimeter and area that are significantly different numerically should emphasize that these are different ideas. For example, consider a square whose sides have a large numerical length, perhaps 125 feet. Its area is 125^2, or 15,625, square feet. Its perimeter is 500 feet. You might want to remind students that the area of a region is given in square units.

Make sure students understand the differences among $\overrightarrow{AB}$, $\overline{AB}$, $\overleftrightarrow{AB}$, and AB.

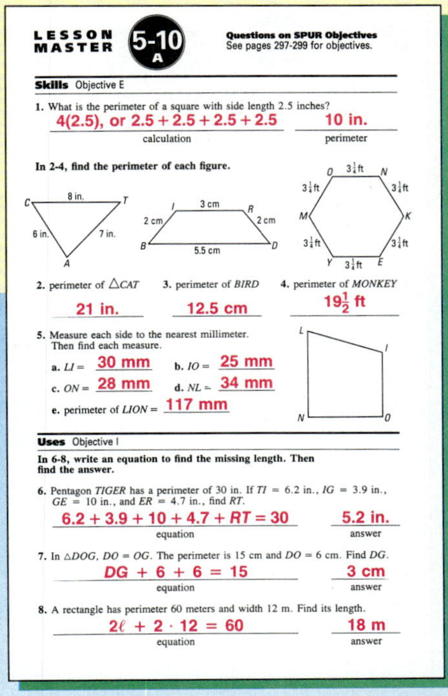

LESSON MASTER 5-10 A

Questions on SPUR Objectives
See pages 297-299 for objectives.

Skills Objective E

1. What is the perimeter of a square with side length 2.5 inches?
4(2.5), or 2.5 + 2.5 + 2.5 + 2.5 (calculation) 10 in. (perimeter)

In 2-4, find the perimeter of each figure.

2. perimeter of $\triangle CAT$ 21 in.
3. perimeter of *BIRD* 12.5 cm
4. perimeter of *MONKEY* $19\frac{1}{2}$ ft

5. Measure each side to the nearest millimeter. Then find each measure.
a. LI = 30 mm b. IO = 25 mm
c. ON = 28 mm d. NL = 34 mm
e. perimeter of *LION* = 117 mm

Uses Objective I

In 6-8, write an equation to find the missing length. Then find the answer.

6. Pentagon *TIGER* has a perimeter of 30 in. If TI = 6.2 in., IG = 3.9 in., GE = 10 in., and ER = 4.7 in., find RT.
$6.2 + 3.9 + 10 + 4.7 + RT = 30$ (equation) 5.2 in. (answer)

7. In $\triangle DOG$, $DO = OG$. The perimeter is 15 cm and DO = 6 cm. Find DG.
$DG + 6 + 6 = 15$ (equation) 3 cm (answer)

8. A rectangle has perimeter 60 meters and width 12 m. Find its length.
$2\ell + 2 \cdot 12 = 60$ (equation) 18 m (answer)

Optional Activities

Activity 1 Map Distances
Materials: Road maps

After completing the lesson, have students **work in groups,** using a road map. Tell them to imagine they are going to take a trip, passing through at least three cities. Have them draw straight lines between pairs of cities and estimate the distance using information given on the map. Then have them find the total distance for the trip.

Activity 2 History Connection As a variation of *Activity 1,* have students identify well-known United States highways or expressways, such as the Lincoln Highway which goes from New York City to San Francisco, or the Pennsylvania Turnpike. Have them identify points along the highway, and estimate the distance between them. Also have them estimate the total length of the highway. Some students might draw a picture to show their information.

Additional Examples

You might want to use the following examples as you discuss the lesson.

In 1–3, find the perimeter of each polygon.

1. **a.** A triangle with sides 5 ft, 12 ft, and 13 ft **30 ft**
   b. A triangle with sides x, y, and z. $x + y + z$
2. A rectangle with length ℓ and width w
   $\ell + w + \ell + w$ or $2\ell + 2w$
3. A pentagon with sides $1\frac{1}{4}$ ft, 8 in., $1\frac{1}{2}$ ft, 1 ft, and 10 in.
   63 in. or $5\frac{1}{4}$ ft
4. Write the correct symbol for each set of points:

   a. All points on the ray with endpoint A and containing B $\overrightarrow{AB}$
   b. All points on the line through A and B $\overleftrightarrow{AB}$
   c. All points on the ray with endpoint B and containing A $\overrightarrow{BA}$
   d. All points on both $\overrightarrow{AB}$ and $\overrightarrow{BA}$ $\overline{AB}$
   e. The distance between A and B AB
5. Which of the answers in Question 4 stands for a number? Which stand for sets of points? **e; a, b, c, d**

LESSON MASTER 5-10 B Questions on SPUR Objectives

Vocabulary

1. What is the *perimeter* of a polygon?
   The perimeter of a polygon is the sum of the lengths of the sides of the polygon.

Skills Objective E: Find the perimeter of a polygon.

2. What is the perimeter of a square with side length 1.5 inches?
   $4 \cdot 1.5$ or $1.5 + 1.5 + 1.5 + 1.5$ (calculation) 6 inches (perimeter)

In 3-6, find the perimeter of each figure.

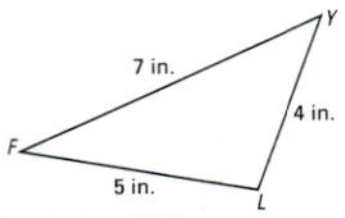

3. perimeter $\triangle FLY$
   16 in.

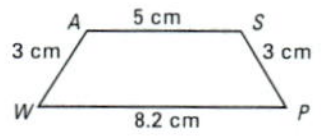

4. perimeter of $WASP$
   19.2 cm

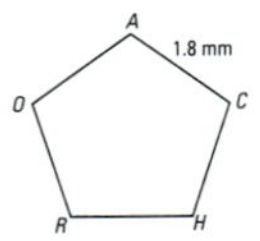

5. perimeter of regular pentagon $ROACH$ (all sides equal in length)
   9 mm

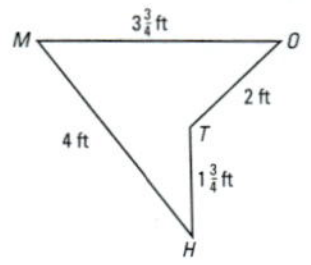

6. perimeter of $MOTH$
   $11\frac{1}{2}$ ft

QUESTIONS

Covering the Reading

1. On Route 1 along the California coast, San Luis Obispo is located between San Francisco and Los Angeles. A map shows that San Francisco is 227 miles from San Luis Obispo. Los Angeles is 195 miles from San Luis Obispo. By this route, how far is it from San Francisco to Los Angeles? **422 miles**

2. The situation in Question 1 is an instance of what model for addition? **the Putting-Together Model**

In 3–6, P and Q are points.
a. Give the meaning of the symbol.
b. Draw a picture (if possible) of the figure the symbol stands for.

3. $\overleftrightarrow{PQ}$ **a) the line through P and Q**
4. $\overrightarrow{PQ}$ **a) the ray from P through Q**
5. $\overline{PQ}$ **a) the segment with endpoints P and Q**
6. PQ **a) the length of segment PQ**

3b)

4b)

5b)

6b) not possible

In 7–10, use the drawing. B is on $\overline{AC}$.

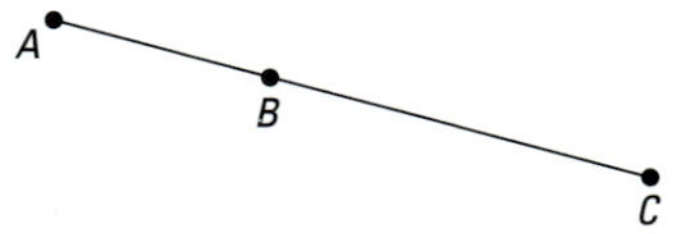

7. If $AB = 5$ and $BC = 3$, what is AC? **8**
8. If $AB = x$ and $BC = y$, what is AC? **$x + y$**
9. If $AB = x$ and $BC = 3$, what is AC? **$x + 3$**
10. If $AB = 14.3$ cm, $BC = t$ cm, and $AC = v$ cm, how are 14.3, t, and v related? **$14.3 + t = v$**
11. What is the perimeter of a polygon? **the sum of the lengths of its sides**

In 12 and 13, give the perimeter of the polygon.

12.

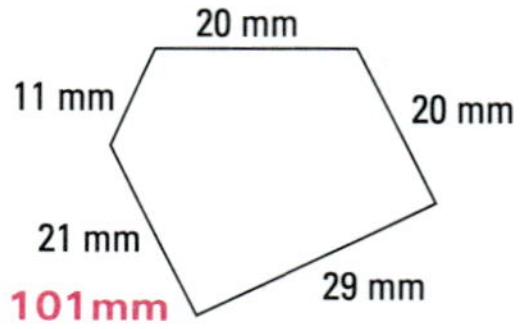

101mm

13.

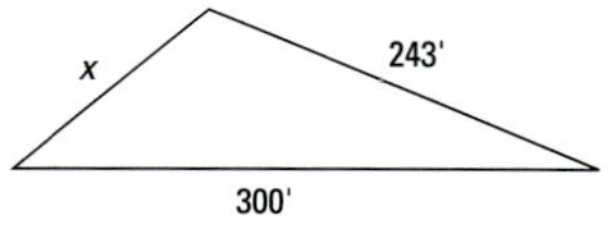

(x + 543) ft

14. Suppose the perimeter of the triangle in Question 13 is 689 feet.
    a. What equation can you solve to find x? **$x + 543 = 689$**
    b. Solve the equation. **146 ft**

Adapting to Individual Needs

Extra Help

Materials: Grid paper

Some students have trouble distinguishing between area and perimeter. To help them understand the difference, have each student use the grid lines to draw a rectangle on grid paper. Then have them trace around the rectangle again, and count the units to find the distance around it. Ask if this number represents the perimeter or area. [Perimeter] Then have students shade the rectangle, counting the number of square units shaded. Ask if this number represents perimeter or area. [Area] Finally have students describe, in their own words, the differences between perimeter and area. If they have difficulty, you might provide additional examples.

Applying the Mathematics

In 15 and 16,
a. Write an equation that will help answer the question.
b. Solve the equation.

15. Two sides of a pentagon have length 9 and two sides have length 5. The perimeter of the pentagon is 30. What is the length of the fifth side? a) $9 + 9 + 5 + 5 + x = 30$; b) 2

16. A race is to be 10 km long. The organizers want the runners to run along a bicycle path that is 2800 meters long and a final leg that is 650 meters long. How long must the rest of the course be? a) $2800 + 650 + x = 10{,}000$; b) 6550 meters

17. Two sides of a triangle ABC have the same length, and $AB = 40$. The perimeter of triangle ABC is 100. What are the possible lengths for $\overline{BC}$ and $\overline{AC}$? 40 and 20; 30 and 30; 20 and 40

How much is enough? *In Leo Tolstoy's short story,* How Much Land Does a Man Need?, *a farmer pays 1,000 rubles for as much land as he wants. The catch is that he must walk the perimeter of the land in one day.*

18. *Multiple choice.* Only one of these equations is not true. Which one is it?

(a) $\overleftrightarrow{AB} = \overleftrightarrow{BA}$ (b) $\overrightarrow{AB} = \overrightarrow{BA}$
(c) $\overline{AB} = \overline{BA}$ (d) $AB = BA$ (b)

19. A square has one side of length 5 m.
a. Is this enough information to find its perimeter? Yes
b. If so, find it. If not, tell why there is not enough information. 20 m

20. Use the drawing at the left. B is on $\overline{AC}$. If $AC = 1$ ft and $BC = 1$ in., what is AB? 11 inches

Review

21) Sample:

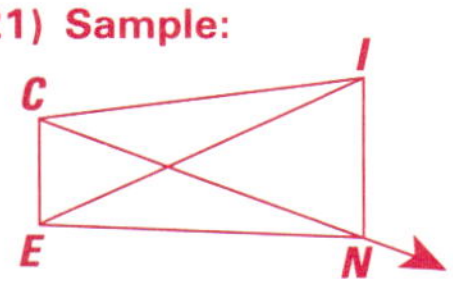

21. Draw a polygon called $NICE$ and put $\overrightarrow{CN}$ and $\overline{IE}$ on your drawing. *(Lesson 5-9)*

22. The temperature was -22° yesterday and 10° today. Let t be the change in the temperature.
a. What equation can be used to find t? $-22 + t = 10$
b. Solve the equation. $t = 32$
c. Check your answer. *(Lesson 5-8)* $-22 + 32 = 10$

6. Give the symbol involving F and G for each.
a. The distance from base of flagpole F to a corner of the garage G FG
b. A light beam from flashlight F through gate keyhole G $\overrightarrow{FG}$
c. A section of rope held taut between Frances, F, and George, G $\overline{FG}$
d. All points on $\overrightarrow{FG}$ or $\overrightarrow{GF}$ $\overleftrightarrow{FG}$

Notes on Questions

Question 17 Many students are so used to thinking a math problem has a unique solution that they will not consider the additional possibilities. One way to approach this problem is to emphasize the assumption made to get the first answer, and then ask if it is possible to start with a different assumption. For example, students may assume that AB is one of the two equal lengths. If that is so, then $AC = 20$ and $BC = 40$, or $AC = 40$ and $BC = 20$. A different assumption is that the other two sides have the same length. If that is the case, then $AC = BC = 30$.

Question 18 Error Alert Some students may have difficulty understanding the differences in notation for lines, rays, segments, and length. Suggest that these students draw a picture of each situation.

▶ **LESSON MASTER 5-10 B** *page 2*

In 7-18, give the measure of each side to the nearest millimeter. Then find the perimeter.

7. FL 49 mm 8. LE 33 mm
9. EA 49 mm 10. AF 33 mm
11. perimeter of $FLEA$ 164 mm
12. SP 31 mm 13. PI 32 mm
14. ID 35 mm 15. DE 30 mm
16. ER 27 mm 17. RS 20 mm
18. perimeter of $SPIDER$ 175 mm

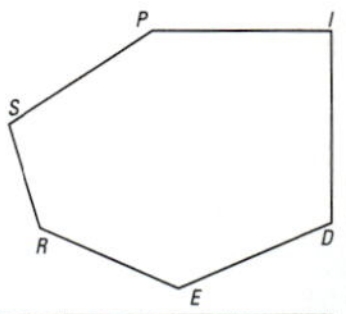

Uses Objective I: Use the Putting-Together Model to relate lengths.

In 19-22, write an equation. Then answer the question.

19. At the right, U and G are on $\overline{SB}$. If $SB = 11$ in., $SG = 6.1$ in., and $GU = 1.8$ in., how long is $\overline{UB}$?

$11 = 6.1 + 1.8 + x$ (equation) 3.1 in. (answer)

20. In $\triangle ANT$, $AN = NT$. The perimeter is 18 m and $AN = 8$ m. Find AT.

$18 = 8 + 8 + x$ (equation) 2 m (answer)

21. Quadrilateral $TICK$ has a perimeter of 34 cm. If $IC = 9.3$ cm, $CK = 4.8$ cm, and $KT = 11.7$ cm, what is TI?

$34 = 9.3 + 4.8 + 11.7 + x$ (equation) 8.2 cm (answer)

22. A hexagon has 3 sides of length 75 mm, 2 sides of length 100 mm, and a perimeter of 600 mm. What is the length of the remaining side?

$600 = 75 + 75 + 75 + 100 + 100 + x$ (equation) 175 mm (answer)

Adapting to Individual Needs

English Language Development
You might want to use pictures rather than words to help students distinguish among the terms *line, ray,* and *segment.* Make sure they understand that the arrow means that the line (or ray) extends indefinitely (on and on) in the direction of the arrow, and that a dot represents a point.

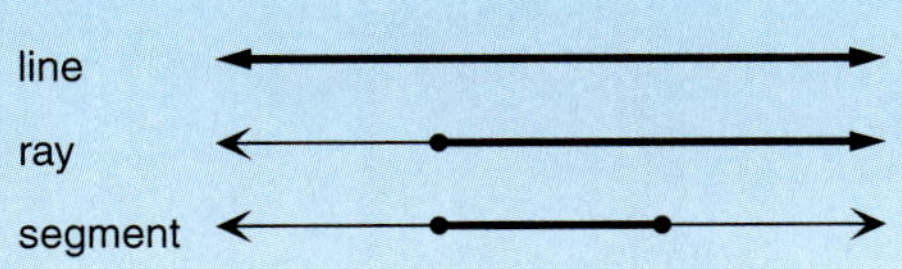

Notes On Questions

Question 34 Students might **work in groups.** As a hint, you can tell them that there are only eight triangles.

Literature Connection Students might enjoy reading the short story referred to in the photo caption entitled *How Much Land Does a Man Need?* by Count Leo Tolstoy. Tolstoy was a Russian author, probably best known for his novel *War and Peace.*

Follow-up for Lesson 5-10

Practice

For more questions on SPUR Objectives, use **Lesson Master 5-10A** (shown on page 289) or **Lesson Master 5-10B** (shown on pages 290–291).

Assessment

Oral Assessment Ask students to explain how to find the length of a side of a polygon if they know the perimeter and the lengths of all of the other sides. [Find the sum of the known lengths and subtract this from the perimeter.] Ask them to give an example of when knowing the length of only one side of a polygon would allow them to find the perimeter of the polygon. [The sides of the polygon have the same length.]

Extension

Have students try to draw a triangle with sides of 3 cm, 4 cm, and 8 cm. Then have them **work in groups** to try other sets of three lengths, and to decide when it is possible to draw a triangle. **When the sum of the lengths of the two shorter sides is greater than the length of the longest side.**

23. Suppose the probability of rain is $\frac{1}{50}$, and the probability of no rain is x.

a. What equation can be solved to find x? $\frac{1}{50} + x = 1$

b. Solve this equation. *(Lessons 5-6, 5-8)* $x = \frac{49}{50}$

24. Solve $-0.3 + A = 6.3$. *(Lesson 5-8)* $A = 6.6$

25. The sum of 23.6 and some number is 40.05. Find the number. *(Lesson 5-8)* **16.45**

26. Perform the intended operations. *(Lesson 5-2)*

a. $-6 + -(-6)$ **0**

b. $-(-x) + -(-y)$ $x + y$

In 27 and 28, graph the solutions to the inequality. *(Lesson 4-10)*

27. $1 \le x < 5$

27)

28. $y \ge -\frac{3}{2}$

28)

29. Ernestine is E years old. Alfredo is A years old. *(Lesson 4-3)*

a. How old was Ernestine 4 years ago? $E + -4$

b. How old was Alfredo 4 years ago? $A + -4$

c. Translate into mathematics: If Ernestine and Alfredo are the same age now, then they were the same age four years ago.

d. Part **c** of this question is an instance of what property?

c) If $E = A$, then $E + -4 = A + -4$. d) Addition Property of Equality.

In 30–33, use the drawing.

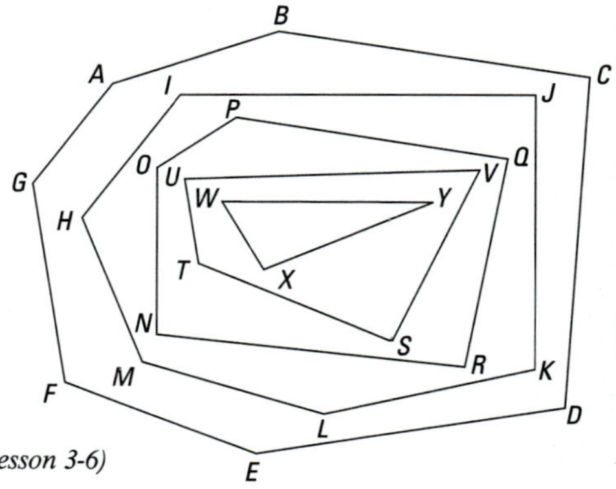

30. Measure the lengths of all sides of the quadrilateral to the nearest millimeter. *(Lesson 3-1)*

30) TS = 25 mm; SV = 23 mm; VU = 35 mm; UT = 10 mm

31. Which angles of the heptagon seem to be obtuse? *(Lessons 3-7, 5-9)* **all**

32. Which angles of the pentagon seem to be acute? *(Lessons 3-7, 5-9)* $\angle Q$

33. Measure angle TSV. *(Lesson 3-6)* **94°**

Exploration

34. Find the length of sides in all triangles satisfying *all* these conditions.

(1) The perimeter is 40.
(2) No side has length under 10.
(3) All sides have different lengths.
(4) The lengths of all sides are integers.
(Hint: Organize your work.)

10,11,19 — 10,12,18 — 10,13,17 — 10,14,16 — 11,12,17 — 11,13,16 — 11,14,15 — 12,13,15

Adapting to Individual Needs

Challenge

Have students find the perimeter of the following diagram.

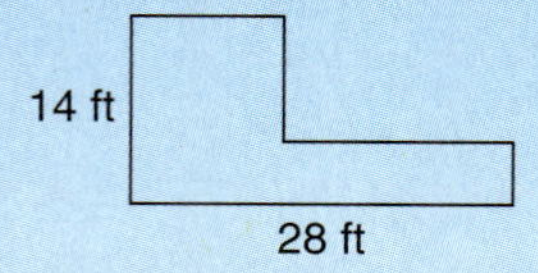

[Draw the dashed lines to form a rectangle. The dashed lines have the same lengths as the two unknown sides of the original figure. The perimeter is 84 ft.]

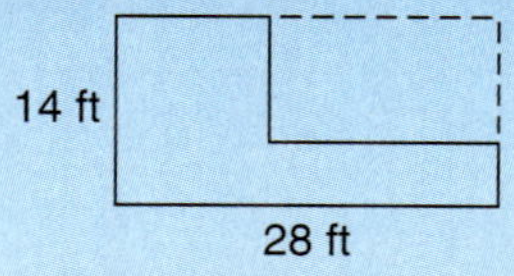

You might have students draw other figures with the left side 14 feet long, the bottom 28 feet long, and the perimeter 84 feet. Then have them generalize about these figures. [If you start at A, and draw horizontal and vertical lines to the right and down to B, the figure will fit the conditions.]

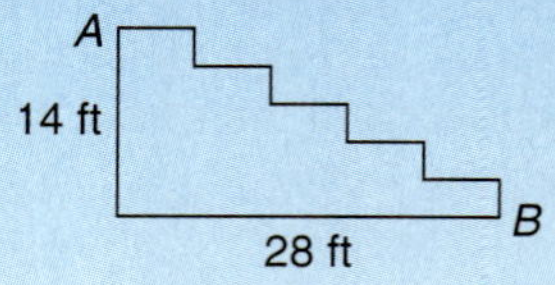

A project presents an opportunity for you to extend your knowledge of a topic related to the material of this chapter. You should allow more time for a project than you do for typical homework questions.

1 Polygons in Architecture

In Lesson 5-9 there is a picture of the Pentagon building outside of Washington DC, a building that received its name from its shape. But a building does not have to have the shape or name of a polygon in order to have polygons in it. Take photographs or draw pictures of buildings near where you live and identify various kinds of polygons on them.

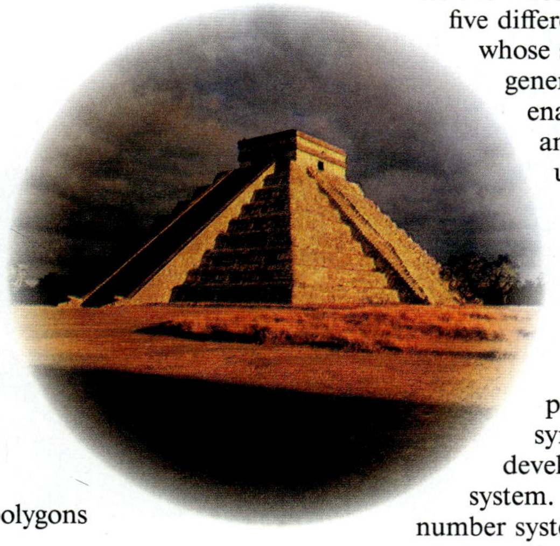

2 Fractions that Add to 1

The fractions $\frac{1}{2}$, $\frac{1}{3}$, and $\frac{1}{6}$ are *unit fractions* (their numerators are 1) and their sum is 1. Find four different unit fractions whose sum is 1. Then find five different unit fractions whose sum is 1. Try to find a general procedure that could enable a person to find any number of different unit fractions whose sum is 1.

3 The Mayas

The Mayas, who are the first known people to have a symbol for zero, developed their own number system. Find out about this number system and write an essay on what you find.

Chapter 5 Projects

Chapter 5 projects relate to the content of the lessons as follows.

Project	Lesson(s)
1	5-9
2	5-5
3	5-2
4	5-6
5	5-4
6	5-1, 5-3

1 Polygons in Architecture Students should look for polygons that encompass the entire structure, overlapping polygons, and polygons that make up parts of the buildings. This may include shapes that form or are parts of windows, doors, roofs, patios, decks, and chimneys. Students might also distingush those from shapes that are not polygons, such as circles, ovals, and shapes that are a combination of curved and straight sides.

2 Fractions That Add To 1 If students need help getting started, suggest that they look at the denominators of the fractions in the example to find a pattern. This observation should help students write the required sets of fractions. Further patterns will emerge from the three sets of fractions, allowing students to formulate a general procedure for writing these fractions.

3 The Maya Students might use encyclopedias, mathematics-history books, or books on Mayan culture as resources. Suggest that students include in their essays instructions on how to write various numerals using Mayan symbols.

Responses

1. **Responses will vary.**
2. **There are many such sets of fractions. One set is $\frac{1}{2}+\frac{1}{4}+\frac{1}{6}+\frac{1}{12}=1$ and $\frac{1}{2}+\frac{1}{4}+\frac{1}{8}+\frac{1}{12}+\frac{1}{24}=1$. In this set and the example, the biggest fraction is $\frac{1}{2}$; the denominator of the smallest fraction is the least common denominator of all fractions in the set; the denominator of the smallest fraction in any set is double the denominator of the next smallest fraction; the smallest fraction in any set is the second last fraction in the next set. For the given set of fractions, students might observe that the first term always appears to be $\frac{1}{2}$; some students might recognize that the remaining terms can be found by doubling the denominators of the previous set. Some students may discover other examples; for instance, $\frac{1}{2}+\frac{1}{3}+\frac{1}{7}+\frac{1}{42}=1$ and $\frac{1}{2}+\frac{1}{3}+\frac{1}{7}+\frac{1}{42}+\frac{1}{1806}=1$. Accept any explanations that students can justify.**

Responses continue on page 294.

4 A Probability Experiment Point out to students that they will first need to find the eight possible outcomes of tossing three coins and from that the probabilities. Then they need to find a way to assign the random numbers in equal probabilities to the eight possible outcomes.

5 Turns in Sport Remind students that clockwise turns are considered negative and counterclockwise turns are considered positive. Usually, with humans, we think of these turns as seen from above, so a left turn is counterclockwise. Students may need to talk to physical education teachers to obtain references for this project. Some students may choose to describe turns as clockwise or counterclockwise instead of using a positive or negative sign.

6 Financial Log Some students may want to use a spreadsheet to record the money they receive and spend. Instruction on how to create spreadsheets is given in Lesson 6-6. (Any student wishing to use a spreadsheet for this project may act as a peer tutor when you teach Lesson 6-6.)

PROJECTS 5 *(continued)*

4 A Probability Experiment

Extend the Lesson 5-6 Exploration by using a computer or calculator to generate at least 500 random numbers. Assign those numbers in equal probabilities to the eight outcomes possible when tossing three coins. Compare the relative frequencies you found for obtaining 0, 1, 2, and 3 heads with the probabilities of these events.

5 Turns in Sport

In gymnastics, diving, throwing the discus, and some other sports, a competitor may do a number of turns while competing. Select a sport and analyze some of these turns mathematically, giving the magnitude and direction of each turn.

6 Financial Log

Keep track of the money you receive and the money you spend—to the penny—over a week-long period in an organized table. Consider all receipts as positive and expenses as negative, and explain how addition of positive and negative numbers can indicate how you are doing.

294

Additional responses, page 293.

3. **The following information is a sample of what students might include in their projects. The Maya developed a place-value number system that allowed them to write very large numbers. They used a seashell symbol to represent zero and used it as a place-value holder. A dot represented the number 1 and a horizontal line represented the number 5. The system was based on powers of 20. Numbers were written in a column and were read from top to bottom. The bottom line represented the numbers 1 through 19. The second line represented multiples of 20, 20 to 399. The third line, however, did not represent the multiples of 20 × 20, but the multiples of 18 × 20, the fourth line the multiples of 18 × 20 × 20, and so on. There were 20 days in a Mayan month and 18 months in a year. It is thought that this is why the Mayan number system is not strictly a base 20 number system.**

SUMMARY

A large variety of situations lead to addition. These situations are of two types: putting together or slide. Some situations can be interpreted as either of these types.

In a putting-together situation, a count or measure x is put together with a count or measure y. If x and y have the same units and there is no overlap, the result has count or measure $x + y$. Probabilities of mutually exclusive events can be added to find the probability that either one or the other event will occur. When the lengths of the sides of a polygon are put together, the result is the perimeter of the polygon. In a putting-together situation, x and y must be positive or zero.

In slide situations, a slide x is followed by a slide y. The result is a slide $x + y$. There may be changes forward or back, up or down, in or out, clockwise or counterclockwise. One direction is positive, the other negative. So in a slide situation, x and y can be positive, zero, or negative.

From these situations, you can see many properties of addition. Zero is the additive identity. Every number has an opposite or additive inverse. Addition is both commutative and associative.

Suppose you know one addend a and the sum b and would like to find the other addend. Then you are trying to find x in the equation $x + a = b$. This sentence can be solved using the Addition Property of Equality and the other properties of addition.

VOCABULARY

You should be able to give a general description and a specific example of each of the following ideas.

Lesson 5-1
Putting-Together Model for Addition
addend
Slide Model for Addition

Lesson 5-2
additive identity
Additive Identity Property of Zero
additive inverse
Property of Opposites
Opposite of Opposites (Op-Op) Property
± or +/–

Lesson 5-3
absolute value, | |

Lesson 5-4
revolution, full turn, quarter turn
clockwise, counterclockwise
magnitude of turn
Fundamental Property of Turns
adjacent angles
Angle Addition Property

Lesson 5-5
Adding Fractions Property
common denominator
least common multiple (LCM)

Lesson 5-6
mutually exclusive
complement of an event
probability of *A or B*
probabilities of complements

Lesson 5-7
Commutative Property of Addition
Associative Property of Addition

Lesson 5-8
Addition Property of Equality
equation of the form $x + a = b$

Lesson 5-9
line segment, segment, $\overline{AB}$,
endpoints, $\overleftrightarrow{AB}$
polygon, side, vertex (vertices), angle of polygon
triangle, quadrilateral, pentagon, hexagon, . . . , *n*-gon
diagonal of a polygon

Lesson 5-10
perimeter
AB for length $\overline{AB}$

Summary

The Summary gives an overview of the entire chapter and provides an opportunity for students to consider the material as a whole. Thus, the Summary can be used to help students relate and unify the concepts presented in the chapter.

Vocabulary

Terms, symbols, and properties are listed by lesson to provide a checklist of concepts a student must know. Emphasize to students that they should read the vocabulary list carefully before starting the Progress Self-Test. If students do not understand the meaning of a term, they should refer back to the indicated lesson.

4. The eight possible outcomes of tossing three coins are : TTT, HTT, THT, TTH, THH, HTH, HHT, and HHH. The probabilities of obtaining 0, 1, 2, and 3 heads with a fair coin are $\frac{1}{8}$, $\frac{3}{8}$, $\frac{3}{8}$, and $\frac{1}{8}$, respectively. Most students will find relative frequencies close to the probabilities.
5. The following information is a sample of what students might include in their projects. Throwing a discus results in one 540° counterclockwise turn for right-handed throwers. In gymnastics, completing a cartwheel requires a 360° turn. Spins in figure skating may involve anywhere from a few to 15 or 20 revolutions clockwise or counterclockwise. A diver attempting a triple somersault dive will make a 1080° clockwise turn.
6. Responses will vary.

Progress Self-Test

For the development of mathematical competence, feedback and correction, along with the opportunity to practice, are necessary. The Progress Self-Test provides the opportunity for feedback and correction; the Chapter Review provides additional opportunities and practice. We cannot overemphasize the importance of these end-of-chapter materials. It is at this point that the material "gels" for many students, allowing them to solidify skills and understanding. In general, student performance should be markedly improved after these pages.

Assign the Progress Self-Test as a one-night assignment. Worked-out *solutions* for all questions are in the Selected Answers section of the student book. Encourage students to take the Progress Self-Test honestly, grade themselves, and then be prepared to discuss the test in class.

Advise students to pay special attention to those Chapter Review questions (pages 297–299) which correspond to questions missed on the Progress Self-Test.

CHAPTER FIVE

PROGRESS SELF-TEST

Take this test as you would take a test in class. Then check your work with the solutions in the Selected Answers section in the back of the book.

In 1–7, simplify.

1. $3 + -10$ -7

2. $-460 + -250$ -710

3. $-9.8 + -(-1)$ -8.8

4. $x + y + -x + 4$ $y + 4$

5. $|-8|$ 8

6. $|-2 + 1| + |0|$ 1

7. $-6 + 42 + -11 + 16 + -12$ 29

8. Evaluate $|-A + 8|$ when $A = -3$. 11

In 9–11, solve.

9. $x + 43 = 31$ $x = -12$

10. $-2.5 + y = -1.2$ $y = 1.3$

11. $8 = -2 + z + -5$ $z = 15$

In 12–15, write as a single fraction in lowest terms.

12. $\frac{53}{12} + \frac{11}{12}$ $\frac{16}{3}$

13. $\frac{5}{x} + \frac{10}{x}$ $\frac{15}{x}$

14. $\frac{17}{9} + -\frac{8}{3}$ $\frac{-7}{9}$

15. $\frac{1}{4} + \frac{3}{8} + \frac{2}{16}$ $\frac{3}{4}$

In 16 and 17, Sally was 20 points behind. Now she is 150 points ahead. Let c be the change in Sally's status. 16) $-20 + c = 150$

16. What equation can be solved to find c?

17. Solve that equation. $c = 170$

18. $(2 + 3) + 4 = 2 + (3 + 4)$ is an instance of what property? Assoc. Prop. of Addition

19. Give an instance of the Addition Property of Zero. Sample: $19 + 0 = 19$

20. A polygon with 6 sides is called a __?__. hexagon

21. Give an example of two mutually exclusive events and tell why they are mutually exclusive. See below.

22. A pentagon has two sides of length 3 cm and three sides of length 4 cm. What is its perimeter? 18 cm

23. *Multiple choice.* If L and K are points, which symbol stands for a number?

(a) LK (b) $\overline{LK}$ (c) $\overrightarrow{LK}$ (d) $\overleftrightarrow{LK}$ (a)

21) Sample: A toss of a die shows a 6. A toss of the same die shows a 2. Since these two events cannot occur at the same time, they are mutually exclusive events.

24. Ms. A's class has m students. Mr. B's class has n students. Together there are 50 students in the classes. How are m, n, and 50 related? $m + n = 50$

25. Anita and Ajay will play a game of chess. The probability that Anita will win is 50%. The probability that Ajay will win is 45%. What is the probability of a draw? 5%

26. An iron bar is 3 cm longer than 5 meters. In meters, how long is the bar? 5.03 m

27. Is $-5.498765432101 + 5.498765432102$ positive, negative, or zero? positive

In 28 and 29, use the figure below. A is on $\overline{MP}$.

28. If $MA = 16$ and $AP = 8$, what is MP? 24

29. If $MA = 2.3$ and $MP = 3$, what is PA? 0.7

30. Picture the addition problem $-3 + 2$ on a number line and give the sum. -1

31. What is the probability of getting a number less than 3 on one toss of a fair die? 1/3

32. What is the result when a 50° clockwise turn is followed by a 250° counterclockwise turn? a 200° counterclockwise turn

In 33 and 34, use the figure below. Assume all small angles with vertex O have the same measure.

33. What is $m\angle VOW$? 72°

34. If you are standing at O facing U and turn to X, what is the magnitude of your turn? (clockwise) -144° or (counterclockwise) 216°

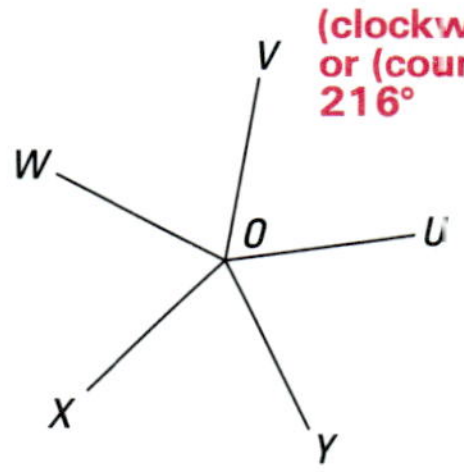

30)

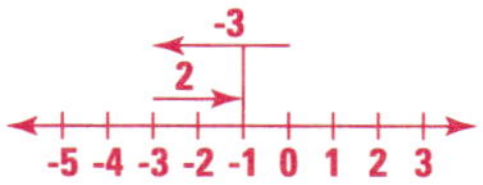

296

CHAPTER FIVE

CHAPTER REVIEW

Questions on SPUR Objectives

SPUR stands for **S**kills, **P**roperties, **U**ses, and **R**epresentations. The Chapter Review questions are grouped according to the **SPUR** Objectives for this chapter.

SKILLS DEAL WITH THE PROCEDURES USED TO GET ANSWERS.

Objective A. *Add positive and negative numbers.* *(Lessons 5-1, 5-3, 5-5)*

In 1–10, perform the addition.

1. $-16 + 4$ **-12**
2. $-7 + -8 + -9$ **-24**
3. $7 + -2.4 + 5$ **9.6**
4. $-31 + 32$ **1**
5. $\frac{6}{11} + 2\frac{5}{11}$ **3**
6. $\frac{12}{17} + -\frac{12}{17}$ **0**
7. $6 + -\frac{8}{9}$ $\frac{46}{9}$
8. $\frac{2}{3} + \frac{6}{7}$ $\frac{32}{21}$
9. $\frac{1}{2} + \frac{1}{3} + -\frac{1}{4}$ $\frac{7}{12}$
10. $\frac{40}{c} + \frac{-10}{c}$ $\frac{30}{c}$

Objective B. *Calculate absolute value.* *(Lesson 5-3)*

In 11–16, simplify.

11. $|-12|$ **12**
12. $|4 + -9 + -2|$ **7**
13. $|0| + |3| + |-5|$ **8**
14. $-|7| + |4|$ **-3**
15. $-|-8 + 7|$ **-1**
16. $|x + y|$, when $x = 40$ and $y = -40$ **0**

Objective C. *Apply properties of addition to simplify expressions.* *(Lessons 5-2, 5-7)*

In 17–22, simplify.

17. $-(-(-17))$ **-17**
18. $-(-4) + 3$ **7**
19. $-40 + 0$ **-40**
20. $(86 + -14) + (-86 + 14)$ **0**
21. $-(-(0 + \frac{2}{7}))$ $\frac{2}{7}$
22. $\frac{11}{4} + y + -\frac{11}{4}$ ***y***

23. When $a = -42$, find $-a + 6$. **48**

24. If $b = \frac{3}{5}$, find the value of $b + -b$. **0**

Objective D. *Solve equations of the form $x + a = b$.* *(Lesson 5-8)*

In 25–34, solve.

25. $x + -32 = -12$ $x = 20$
26. $6.3 = t + 2.9$ $t = 3.4$
27. $\frac{10}{3} + y = \frac{1}{3}$ $y = -3$
28. $0 + a = 4 + 1$ $a = 5$
29. $3 + c + -5 = 36$
30. $-8 = 14 + (d + -6)$
31. $7034 = v + 1112$
32. $312.9 = 163.4 + b$
33. $-1 + e = \frac{1}{6}$ $e = \frac{7}{6}$
34. $-\frac{11}{5} + w = -\frac{4}{5}$ $w = \frac{7}{5}$

29) $c = 38$
30) $d = -16$
31) $v = 5922$
32) $b = 149.5$

Objective E. *Find the perimeter of a polygon.* *(Lesson 5-10)*

35. What is the perimeter of a square in which one side has length 3? **12**

36. If $x = 23$, what is the perimeter of the polygon *ABCDE*? **80**

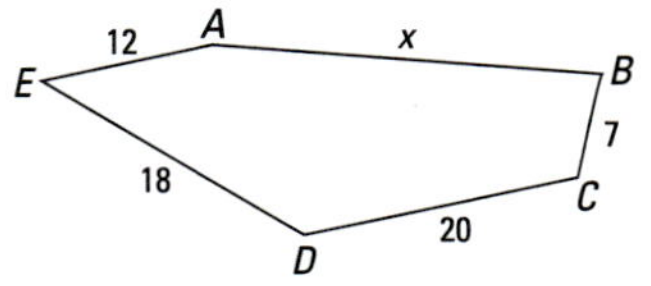

37. Measure the sides of polygon *GHIJ* to find its perimeter to the nearest centimeter. **16 cm**

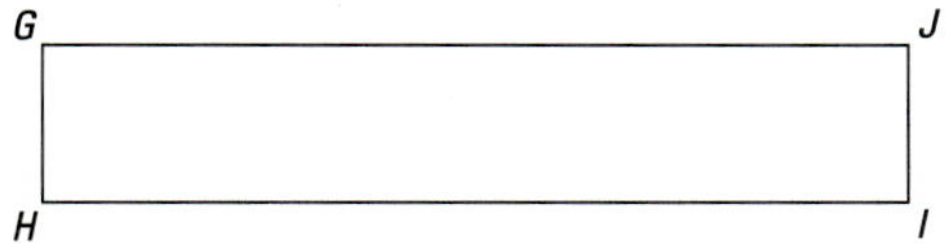

38. An octagon has 3 sides of length 7 and 5 sides of length 6. What is its perimeter? **51**

39. For polygon *ABCDE* of Question 36, if the perimeter is 82, what equation can be solved to find x? $12 + 18 + 20 + 7 + x = 82$

Chapter 5 Review

Resources

From the ***Teacher's Resource File***

- Answer Master for Chapter 5 Review
- Assessment Sourcebook: Chapter 5 Test, Forms A–D Chapter 5 Test, Cumulative Form

Additional Resources

- Quiz and Test Writer

The main objectives for the chapter are organized in the Chapter Review under the four types of understanding this book promotes— Skills, Properties, Uses, and Representations.

Whereas end-of chapter material may be considered optional in some texts, in *UCSMP Transition Mathematics,* we have selected these objectives and questions with the expectation that they will be covered. Students should be able to answer these questions with about 85% accuracy after studying the chapter.

You may assign these questions over a single night to help students prepare for a test the next day, or you may assign the questions over a two-day period. If you work the questions over two days, then we recommend assigning the *evens* for homework the first night so that students get feedback in class the next day, then assigning the *odds* the night before the test, because answers are provided to the odd-numbered questions.

It is effective to ask students which questions they still do not understand, and use the day or days as a total class discussion of the material which the class finds most difficult.

Assessment

Evaluation The *Assessment Sourcebook* provides five forms of the Chapter 5 Test. Forms A and B present parallel versions in a short-answer format. Forms C and D offer performance assessment. The fifth test is Chapter 5 Test, Cumulative Form. About 50% of this test covers Chapter 5, 25% covers Chapter 4, and 25% covers earlier chapters.

For information on grading, see *General Teaching Suggestions: Grading* in the *Professional Sourcebook* which begins on page T20 in Volume 1 of the Teacher's Edition.

PROPERTIES DEAL WITH THE PRINCIPLES BEHIND THE MATHEMATICS.

Objective F. *Identify the following properties of addition: Commutative Property of Addition, Associative Property of Addition, Additive Identity Property of Zero, Addition Property of Equality, Property of Opposites, Opposite of Opposites Property.* *(Lessons 5-2, 5-7, 5-8)*

In 40–43, an instance of what property of addition is given?

40. 3.53 meters + 6.74 meters = 6.74 meters + 3.53 meters **Commutative Property of Addition**

41. Since 30% = $\frac{3}{10}$, it is also true that $\frac{1}{2} + 30\% = \frac{1}{2} + \frac{3}{10}$. **Addition Prop. of Equality**

42. -941 + 941 = 0 **Property of Opposites**

43. (1 + 2) + 3 = (2 + 1) + 3 **Commutative Property of Addition**

Objective G. *Tell whether events are mutually exclusive or not.* *(Lesson 5-6)*

In 44–48, what events are mutually exclusive?

44. It is raining outside. It is not raining outside.

45. I am a student. I have a job. **not mutually exclusive**

46. Mathematics is Beth's favorite subject. English is Gilbert's favorite subject. **not mutually exclusive**

44) mutually exclusive

47. Mathematics is Greg's favorite subject. English is Greg's favorite subject. **mutually exclusive**

48. If the probability of one event is $\frac{1}{2}$ and of another is $\frac{3}{4}$, explain why they cannot be mutually exclusive. **Their probabilities add to more than 1.**

Objective H. *Identify parts and give names of polygons.* *(Lesson 5-9)*

49. Which is not a correct name for the polygon below? *LAKE, LEAK, KALE, ELAK* ***LEAK***

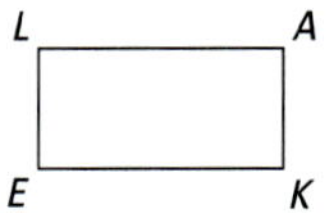

50. Name the two diagonals of the polygon in Question 49. $\overline{LK}$, $\overline{EA}$

51. The polygon in Question 49 has __?__ vertices and __?__ sides. **4, 4**

52. Name a side of the polygon *ABCDE*. $\overline{AB}$, $\overline{BC}$, $\overline{CD}$, $\overline{DE}$, **or** $\overline{EA}$

USES DEAL WITH APPLICATIONS OF MATHEMATICS IN REAL SITUATIONS.

Objective I. *Use the Putting-Together Model for Addition to form sentences involving addition.* *(Lessons 5-1, 5-8, 5-10)*

53. Bob rode his bicycle a mile and a half to school. Then he rode $\frac{3}{5}$ of a mile to his friend's house. Altogether he rode *M* miles. What equation connects these distances?

54. You have read *x* books this year. A friend has read *y* books. Together you have read 16 books. What equation connects *x*, *y*, and 16?

55. In the Johannson family, Dad earned *D* dollars last year. Mom earned *M* dollars. The children earned *C* dollars. The total family income was *T* dollars. What equation relates *D*, *M*, *C*, and *T*? $T = D + M + C$

53) $1\frac{1}{2} + \frac{3}{5} = M$ **54)** $x + y = 16$

In 56–58, use the figure shown. *B* is on $\overline{AC}$.

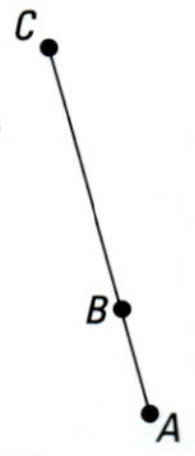

56. What equation connects *AB*, *BC*, and *AC*? $AB + BC = AC$

57. If *AB* = *x* and *BC* = 3, what is *AC*?

58. Let *AC* = 10.4 and *BC* = 7.8.

a. What equation can be used to find *AB*? $AB + 7.8 = 10.4$

b. What is *AB*? **2.6**

57) $AC = x + 3$

Objective J. *Use the Slide Model for Addition to form sentences involving addition.* *(Lessons 5-1, 5-8)*

59. Charyl's stock rose $\frac{3}{8}$ of a point on one day and fell $\frac{1}{4}$ point the next day.

a. What addition gives the total change in Charyl's stock? **3/8 + -1/4**

b. What is the total change? **1/8 point**

60. Bernie gained 5 pounds one week, lost 7 the next, and lost 3 the next.
  a. What addition gives the total change in Bernie's weight? 5 + -7 + -3
  b. What is the total change? -5 pounds

61. A scuba diving team was 60 feet below sea level then came up 25 feet.
  a. What addition tells where the team wound up? -60 + 25
  b. Where did they wind up? 35 ft below sea level

62. The temperature was -3° and changed c° to reach -10°. What is c? -7

Objective K. *Calculate the probability of mutually exclusive events or complements of events.* *(Lesson 5-6)*

63. From prior experience, we estimate that when Frank comes up to bat in a baseball game, he has a 12% probability of hitting a single, a 6% probability of hitting a double, a 2% probability of hitting a triple, and a 4% probability of hitting a home run. These are the only possible hits. What is the probability Frank will get a hit when he bats? 24%

64. If Lee works hard, he has a $\frac{1}{3}$ probability of getting an A, a $\frac{1}{2}$ probability of getting a B, and a $\frac{1}{6}$ probability of getting a C. If Lee works hard, will he pass? Yes, the probabilities add to 1.

In 65 and 66, assume the spinner below is spun once. All angles at the center have equal measure. Assume all positions of the arrow are equally likely.

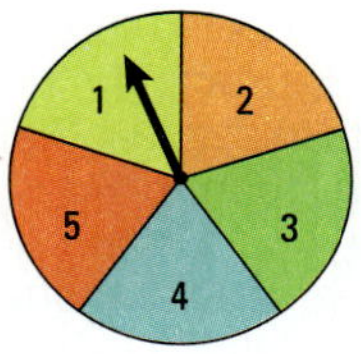

65. What is the probability that the spinner will land in an even-numbered region? $\frac{2}{5}$

66. What is the probability that the spinner will land in an odd-numbered region? $\frac{3}{5}$

67. Explain why the events in Questions 65 and 66 are complements. See below.

68. A weighted quarter is tossed. Let E = heads will occur. Suppose the probability of E is $\frac{3}{5}$.
  a. Describe the event that is the complement of E. Tails occurs.
  b. Give the probability of that event. $\frac{2}{5}$

67) They are mutually exclusive and together include all outcomes.

REPRESENTATIONS DEAL WITH PICTURES, GRAPHS, OR OBJECTS THAT ILLUSTRATE CONCEPTS.

Objective L. *Calculate magnitudes of turns given angle measures or revolutions.* *(Lesson 5-4)*

In 69–71, all small angles at O have the same measure. Think of turns around the point O.

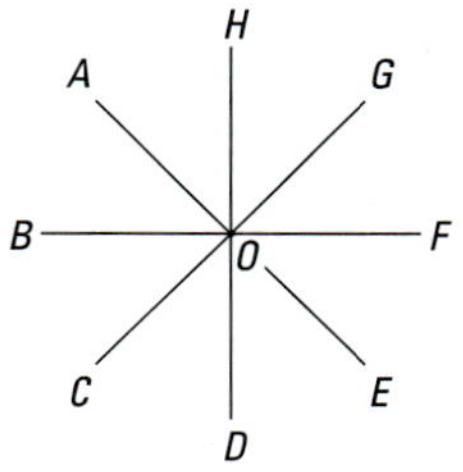

69. What is the magnitude of the turn from F to A? 135° or -225°

70. What is the magnitude of the turn from E to C? -90° or 270°

71. Suppose you are facing H and turn 315° clockwise and then 45° counterclockwise.
  a. What point will you then be facing? B
  b. How much will you have turned? -270° or 90°

72. If you turn 90° counterclockwise, and then turn 40° clockwise, what is the result? a 50° counterclockwise turn

Objective M. *Picture addition of positive and negative numbers using arrows on a number line.* *(Lesson 5-1)*

73. Picture the addition -5 + 8 on a number line and give the sum. See margin.

74. Picture the addition 17 + -4 on a number line and give the sum. See margin.

75. Picture the addition -3.5 + -6.5 on a number line and give the sum. See margin.

Additional Answers

73.

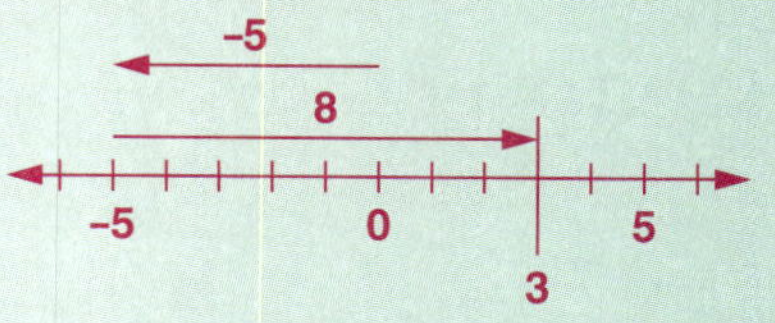

74.

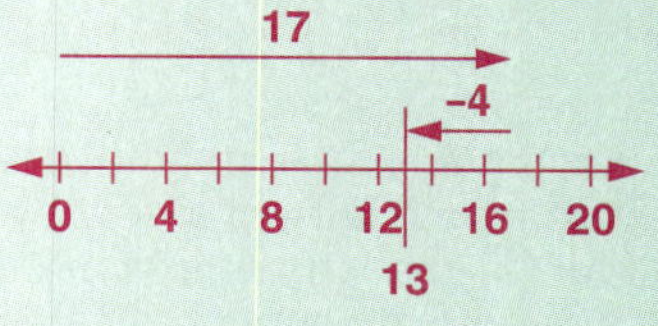

75.

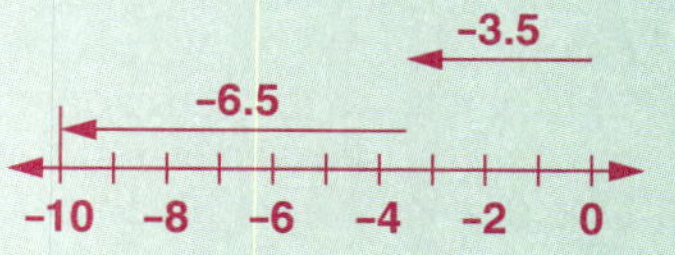

Setting Up Lesson 6-1

We recommend that you assign Lesson 6-1, both reading and some questions, for homework the evening of the test. It gives students work to do after they have completed the test and keeps the class moving. If you do not do this consistently after tests, you may cover one less chapter over the course of the year.

Chapter 6 Planner

Adapting to Individual Needs

The student text is written for the vast majority of students. The chart at the right suggests two pacing plans to accommodate the needs of your students. Students in the Full Course should complete the entire text by the end of the year. Students in the Minimal Course will spend more time when there are quizzes and more time on the Chapter Review. Therefore, these students may not complete all of the chapters in the text.

Options are also presented to meet the needs of a variety of teaching and learning styles. For each lesson, the Teacher's Edition provides sections entitled: *Video* which describes video segments and related questions that can be used for motivation or extension; *Optional Activities* which suggests activities that employ materials, physical models, technology, and cooperative learning; and *Adapting to Individual Needs* which regularly includes **Challenge** problems, **English Language Development** suggestions, and suggestions for providing **Extra Help.** The Teacher's Edition also frequently includes an **Error Alert,** an **Extension,** and an **Assessment** alternative. The options available in Chapter 6 are summarized in the chart below.

Chapter 6 Pacing Chart

Day	Full Course	Minimal Course
1	6-1	6-1
2	6-2	6-2
3	6-3	6-3
4	Quiz*; 6-4	Quiz*; begin 6-4.
5	6-5	Finish 6-4.
6	6-6	6-5
7	Quiz*; 6-7	6-6
8	Self-Test	Quiz*; begin 6-7.
9	Review	Finish 6-7.
10	Test*	Self-Test
11	Comprehensive Test*	Review
12		Review
13		Test*
14		Comprehensive Test*

*in the Teacher's Resource File

In the Teacher's Edition...

Lesson	Optional Activities	Extra Help	Challenge	English Language Development	Error Alert	Extension	Cooperative Learning	Ongoing Assessment
6-1	●	●	●	●		●	●	Written
6-2	●	●	●	●		●	●	Group
6-3	●	●	●	●	●	●	●	Oral/Written
6-4	●	●	●	●		●	●	Written
6-5	●	●	●	●		●	●	Group
6-6	●	●	●	●	●	●	●	Written
6-7	●	●	●	●		●	●	Group

In the Additional Resources...

	In the Teacher's Resource File								
Lesson	Lesson Masters, A and B	Teaching Aids*	Activity Kit*	Answer Masters	Technology Sourcebook	Assessment Sourcebook	Visual Aids**	Transition Mathematics Software	Video Segments
6-1	6-1	59, 61, 62		6-1			59, 61, 62, AM		
6-2	6-2	59		6-2			59, AM	Spreadsheet	
6-3	6-3	59		6-3		Quiz	59, AM		
6-4	6-4	59	13	6-4	Demo 6, Comp 9, Calc 8		59, AM	Spreadsheet	
6-5	6-5	60, 63, 64	14	6-5	Calc 9		60, 63, 64, AM		
6-6	6-6	60, 65, 66		6-6	Comp 10	Quiz	60, 65, 66, AM	Spreadsheet	
6-7	6-7	60	15	6-7			60, AM		6-7
End of chapter				Review		Tests			

*Teaching Aids, except Warm-ups, are pictured on pages 300C and 300D. The activities in the Activity Kit are pictured on page 300C.

**Visual Aids provide transparencies for all Teaching Aids and all Answer Masters.

Also available is the Study Skills Handbook which includes study-skill tips related to reading, note-taking, and comprehension.

Integrating Strands and Applications

	6-1	6-2	6-3	6-4	6-5	6-6	6-7
Mathematical Connections							
Number Sense				●	●		
Algebra				●	●	●	●
Geometry	●	●	●	●	●		●
Measurement	●		●	●			
Logic and Reasoning	●	●		●	●	●	●
Patterns and Functions					●	●	●
Interdisciplinary and Other Connections							
Science						●	
Social Studies	●	●		●		●	
Multicultural					●		●
Technology		●	●	●	●	●	
Career						●	
Consumer	●	●			●	●	●
Sports			●				●

Teaching and Assessing the Chapter Objectives

				In the Assessment Sourcebook		
Chapter 6 Objectives (Organized into the SPUR categories—Skills, Properties, Uses, and Representations)	**Lessons**	**Progress Self-Test Questions**	**Chapter Review Questions**	**Chapter Test, Forms A and B**	**Chapter Test, Forms C**	**Chapter Test, Forms D**
Skills						
A: Know the general strategies used by good problem solvers.	6-1	5, 17	1–3	4		✓
B: Determine solutions to sentences by trial and error.	6-4	11	4–7	7–9		✓
Properties						
C: Determine whether a number is prime or composite.	6-2	6	8–11	2	3	
D: Find the meaning of unknown words.	6-2	1	12, 13	1	3	✓
E: Make a table to find patterns and make generalizations.	6-5	4, 13, 15, 16	14, 15	17	4	✓
F: Work with a special case to determine whether a pattern is true.	6-7	14	16, 17	16		
G: Use special cases to determine that a property is false or to give evidence that it is true.	6-7	7, 10	18, 19	10	1	
Uses						
H: Use simpler numbers to answer a question requiring only one operation.	6-7	9	20, 21	11		
I: Use drawings to solve real problems.	6-3	3, 12	22–25	5	2	
Representations						
J: Use a spreadsheet to answer questions in real situations.	6-6	8, 18	26, 27	12–14	4	✓
K: Draw a diagram to aid in solving geometric problems.	6-3	2	28–31	3, 6, 15	2	

Assessment Sourcebook
Quiz for Lessons 6-1 through 6-3
Quiz for Lessons 6-4 through 6-6
Chapter 6 Test, Forms A–D
Chapter 6 Test, Cumulative Form
Comprehensive Test, Chapters 1-6

Quiz and Test Writer
Multiple forms of chapter tests and quizzes; Challenges

Activity Kit

ACTIVITY 13

TRIAL AND ERROR
Use with **Lesson 6-4.**

Materials: 27 centimeter cubes (9 each of 3 different colors), colored pencils
Group Size: Partners

1. You and your partner are to try to arrange the 27 centimeter cubes to form one large cube in which no color is repeated within any row or any column. Use your colored pencils to show your answer below.

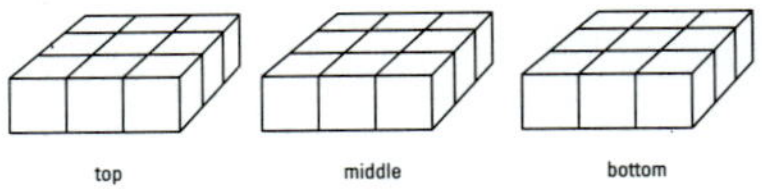

2. Now try to arrange the cubes so that every row and every column has exactly two cubes of the same color. Show your answer below.

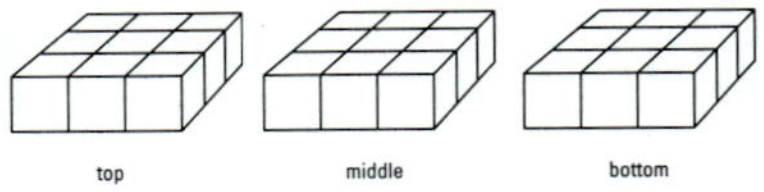

3. Describe how you and your partner tried to solve Items 1 and 2.

ACTIVITY 14

MAKE A TABLE
Use with **Lesson 6-5.**

Materials: 75 centimeter cubes in two colors, shoe box
Group Size: Small groups

1. In your group, stack the centimeter cubes in a corner of the shoe box, following Steps a–d.
   - **a.** Start with 1 cube and place it in a corner of the box. Call this cube **Set 1**. You *added* 1 cube and there is a *total* of 1 cube in the box. Fill in the table for **Set 1**.
   - **b.** Now use cubes of a different color. Place a cube on or next to each of the 3 exposed faces of the first cube—just enough cubes so that you can not see the first cube. In the table, enter the number of cubes you added and the total number of cubes now in the box for **Set 2**.
   - **c.** Use cubes that are a different color from the cubes in **Set 2**. Place just enough cubes so that you cannot see **Set 2**. In the table, enter the number of cubes you added and the total number of cubes now in the box for **Set 3**.
   - **d.** Repeat Steps a–d for **Sets 4–6** and complete the table.

Set	1	2	3	4	5	6
Number of Cubes Added						
Total Number of Cubes in Box						

2. Did you add the same number of cubes each time? ____________
3. Study the table you made. Describe a pattern for determining how many cubes will be added to the box for any particular set.
4. Use this pattern to help you determine the total number of cubes in the box after each of these sets is made.

Set 7 ________ **Set 8** ________ **Set 9** ________

ACTIVITY 15

SIMPLER PROBLEMS
Use with **Lesson 6-7.**

Materials: 7 centimeter cubes
Group Size: Small groups

Your group is to consider the following problem: In how many different ways can 25 centimeter cubes be arranged in 3 stacks?

1. One way to approach this problem is to try a simpler problem. Count all arrangements possible with 3 cubes, 4 cubes, and 5 cubes. Record the data in the appropriate boxes in the table below.

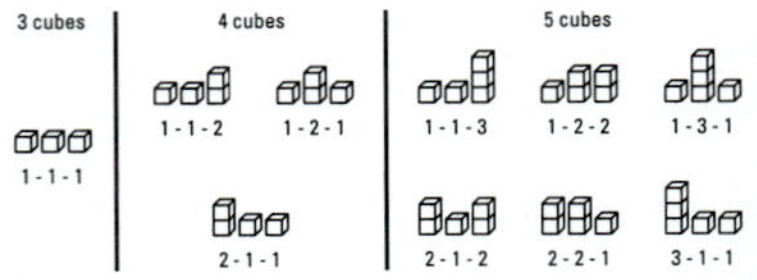

Number of Cubes	3	4	5	6	7	8	9	10
Number of Possible Arrangements								

2. Use cubes to find all the different ways you can arrange 6 cubes in 3 stacks. Then find all the ways to arrange 7 cubes in 3 stacks. Record the data in the table.
3. Look for a pattern in the table. Describe the pattern.
4. Use your pattern to predict the number of different ways 8 cubes, 9 cubes, and 10 cubes can be arranged in 3 stacks. Record the numbers in the table.
5. Now answer the original question: In how many different ways can 25 cubes be arranged in 3 stacks? ____________

Teaching Aids

TEACHING AID 59

Warm-up
Lesson 6-1

Work in groups to solve the following problem. In a tournament, the first person to win 3 games out of 5 is the winner. In how many ways is it possible for a player to be a winner? For example, if *W* means win and *L* means lose, one possibility is *WLWW* (that is, a player wins games 1, 3, and 4).

Warm-up
Lesson 6-2

Use each word or phrase in a sentence.

1. Prime number
2. Factor
3. Negative number
4. Hexagon

Warm-up
Lesson 6-3

Draw the shapes described.

1. A rectangle with a width that is twice the length
2. Three concentric circles
3. A nine-sided polygon that has at least three sides of equal length

Warm-up
Lesson 6-4

Solve each problem.

1. A rectangle has an area of 12 square inches and a perimeter of 16 inches. Find its dimensions.
2. A triangle has a perimeter of 17 inches. The longest side is 3 inches longer than one side and twice as long as the other. Find the length of each side.

TEACHING AID 60

Warm-up
Lesson 6-5

Find the number of dimes and quarters in Sam's pocket. All the dimes can be exchanged for dollar bills. There are twice as many dimes as quarters. The value of the coins is less than $5.00 but more than $2.00.

Warm-up
Lesson 6-6

Make a table showing how much you would earn for 1 through 5 hours of baby-sitting. Include hourly rates of $2 an hour, $3 an hour, and $4 an hour. Shade the place in the table that shows how much you would earn if you were paid $3 an hour for 4 hours. Explain how to find this location in your table.

Warm-up
Lesson 6-7

For each question, tell if the result is (a) always even, (b) always odd, or (c) sometimes even, sometimes odd.

1. The sum of two even integers
2. The sum of two odd integers
3. The sum of an even and an odd integer
4. The product of an even and an odd integer
5. Twice an integer
6. Three times an integer
7. The square of an integer
8. The sum of an integer and its square

TEACHING AID 61

Lesson 6-1

Problem-Solving Advice

General Advice for Solving Problems

In this chapter you will learn many strategies for solving problems. But you must do three things.

1. Take your time. Few people solve problems fast.
2. Don't give up. You will never solve a problem if you do not try. Do something!
3. Be flexible. If at first you don't succeed, try another way. And if the second way does not work, try a third way.

How Do Good Problem Solvers Solve Problems?

In a famous book called *How to Solve It,* Polya described what good problems solvers do.

- They *read the problem carefully.* They try to understand every word. They make sure they know what is asked for. They reread. They make certain that they are using the correct information. They look up words they do not know.
- They *devise a plan.* They even plan their guesses. They arrange information in tables. They draw pictures. They compare the problem to other problems they know. They decide to try something.
- They *carry out the plan.* They attempt to solve. They work with care. They write things down so they can read them later. If the attempt does not work, they go back to read the problem again.
- They *check work.* In fact, they check their work at every step. The do not check by repeating what they did. They check estimating or by trying to find another way of doing the problem.

Additional Examples

1. How many different whole numbers can you make with the digits 1, 2, 3, and 4? Any number you make can have one to four digits in it. You cannot repeat a digit in any number you make.
2. How many triangles are in this drawing?

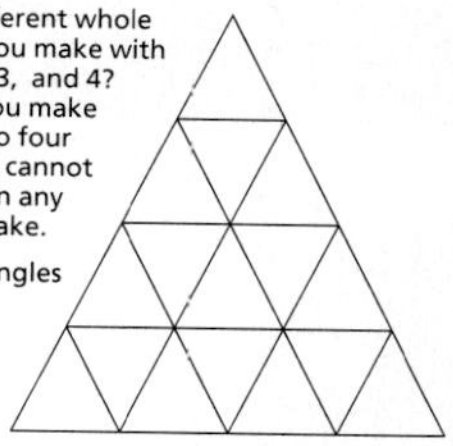

Extension

Continue the pattern. How many squares are in the *n*th diagram? ______________

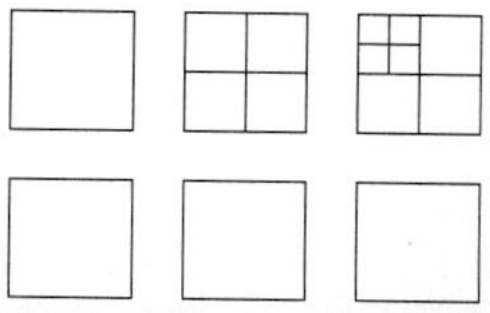

Cost of Phone Calls

Cost per first minute(s) ______________

Cost for each additional minute ______________

Number of Minutes	Cost of Phone Calls

Checkerboard

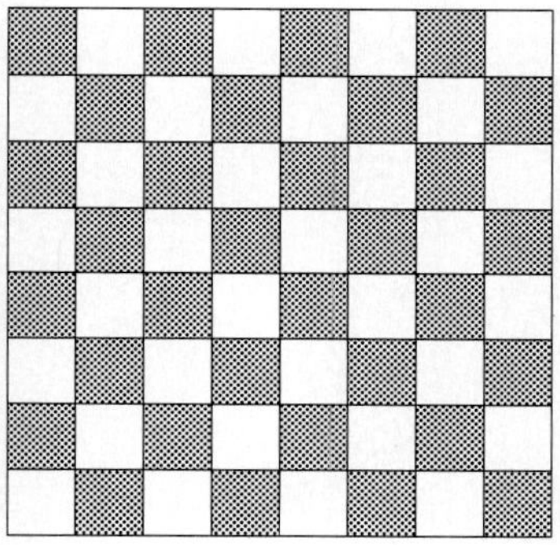

Spreadsheet

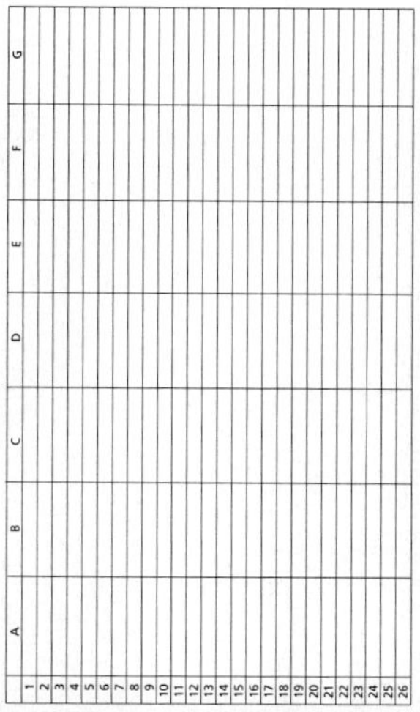

Additional Examples

1. Create a spreadsheet that resembles the table of sides and diagonals from Lesson 6-5.
2. a. Use the spreadsheet form and enter the formula =A9 + 1 in cell A10. What do you see?
   b. Copy the formula from cell A10 onto cells A11 through A15. What do you see?
   c. Enter the formula =B9 + A9−1 in cell B10. What do you see?
   d. Copy the formula from cell B10 into cells B11 through B15. What do you see?
   e. According to this pattern, what is the number of diagonals in a 15-gon?
3. Use the spreadsheet to determine the number of diagonals in a 25-sided polygon.
4. Suppose a rental car agency charges $31.95 per day plus $.30 a mile beyond 200 miles to rent a car.
   a. Create the following skeleton for the spreadsheet.

	A	B
1	miles	cost
2	200	31.95
3		

   b. Type =A2 + 1 in cell A3, and =B2 + .30 in cell B3. What do you see in A? in B?
   c. Create enough additional rows on the spreadsheet so that you can determine the cost of driving this car 234 miles in a single day.

Chapter Opener 6

Pacing

We recommend spending 10-13 days on this chapter. A test covering Chapters 1–6 is provided in the *Assessment Sourcebook*. This comprehensive test can be used as a midyear exam.

Using Pages 300 – 301

There are many quotes about problem solving. We have chosen two from the most famous writer about mathematical problem solving, George Polya. Polya also wrote that one learns to solve problems by solving problems. This is akin to the phrase on the opening page of this book: mathematics is not a spectator sport.

Ask students to tell why they think each quote is included. Here are our answers. The first quote is to point out that a problem is not supposed to be something that is automatic. The second quote, however, indicates that it is natural for people to want to confront tasks that are not automatic; at times all people would rather be creative than be robots. The third quote indicates that errors can be expected in the process of solving problems, and that one learns from errors.

You may wish to ask students to explain what is funny—or not so funny, depending on the point of view—about the comic strip. Point out that asking for help or for a rule to follow is often an appropriate way to confront a problem. Tell students that, in this chapter, they will examine ways to approach problem solving without help from others.

CHAPTER 6

Chapter 6 Overview

All of *Transition Mathematics* works to develop problem-solving competence. This is because we agree with the long-standing positions of the National Council of Supervisors of Mathematics and the National Council of Teachers of Mathematics that problem solving should be a major component of every mathematics program. In the NCTM Curriculum Standards, problem solving is one of the three aspects of the study of mathematics.

What is a problem? Today's generally accepted definition, which is described in Lesson 6-1, is that a problem is an unresolved question for which the potential solver does not have an algorithm. Under this definition, a standard word problem may or may not be a problem for a given student. Thus, in order to teach problem solving, one must use situations or questions that students have not seen before.

We devote an entire chapter to teaching the many processes involved in problem solving because it is important at times to focus on the strategies and not on bits of mathematics. By bringing these lessons together, we heighten the importance of problem solving. The rest of the book, both before and after this chapter, applies the ideas found here.

This chapter discusses both general and specific problem-solving strategies.

PROBLEM-SOLVING STRATEGIES

McGURK'S MOB

To solve a problem is to find a way where no way is known off-hand, to find a way out of a difficulty, to find a way around an obstacle, to attain a desired end that is not immediately attainable, by appropriate means.

—George Polya (1887–1985)

Solving problems is human nature itself.

—Polya

The person who makes no mistakes usually makes nothing.

—Anonymous

When *Transition Mathematics* was first written, few students had encountered problem-solving strategies in their prior mathematics experiences. You might wish to read the list of section titles and ask students if they have studied these ideas. This will give your students some feel for the content they will encounter and inform you as to the variety of earlier experiences they have had.

Photo Connections

The photo collage makes real-world connections to the content of the chapter: problem solving techniques.

Computer Keyboard and Circuit Boards: Computers are tools used within a variety of problem-solving strategies. The speed of computers allows problem solvers to test more solutions than they previously might have tested in a lifetime.

Drawing Tools: A picture can be worth a thousand words. Drawing tools help students and many professionals present a visual representation of a problem. Preparing the drawing leads to a careful consideration of all aspects of the problem.

Wastebasket: A wastebasket suggests that finding the answers to problems can include a lot of trial and error.

Puzzle: People have different strategies for working jigsaw puzzles A common thread running through this and all problem solving is: begin! Select one point and start. You'll never solve it if you don't try.

Maze: A maze represents a network of paths through which one traverses while searching for the solution to a problem. If one strategy does not work, try another.

Projects

At this time you might want to have students look over the projects on pages 338–339.

Lesson 6-1 contains the most general advice. Lessons 6-2 through 6-7 are each devoted to a particular problem-solving strategy. Each strategy is applied to at least one typical kind of question a student should be able to answer. Each section also has examples of atypical problems utilizing that strategy.

Because this chapter concentrates on process, *reward* process. Encourage your students to use *chatter* to communicate their thought processes while solving problems. Some examples of chatter are: "I'm going to try the simplest numbers I know." "There seem to be three possibilities." Chatter can alert you to misconceptions and incomplete understandings, and it also may demonstrate wonderful insights.

Problem solving takes time and is not necessarily easy. Some students will not master the content in this chapter, but you should give credit for attempts, partial answers, and ingenuity. Students are so accustomed to rules and single answers that they may not know how to proceed when there are no rules. The goal is for them to experience the delight of solving a problem unlike any they've seen before.

Many teachers have told us that this is their favorite chapter in the book.

Lesson 6-1

Objectives

A Know the general strategies followed by good problem solvers.

Resources

From the ***Teacher's Resource File***

- Lesson Master 6-1A or 6-1B
- Answer Master 6-1
- Teaching Aids
  59 Warm-up
  61 Problem-Solving Advice
  62 Additional Example 2, Extension

Additional Resources

- Visuals for Teaching Aids 59, 61, 62

Teaching Lesson 6-1

Warm-up

Work in groups to solve the following problem.

In a tournament, the first person to win 3 games out of 5 is the winner. In how many ways is it possible for a player to be a winner? For example, if *W* means win and *L* means lose, one possibility is *WLWW* (that is, a player wins games 1, 3, and 4).
10 ways

LESSON

6-1 *Being a Good Problem Solver*

Amazing Maize Maze. *When solving problems, you need not feel as if you are lost in a maze. Strategies can help you find solutions. Shown here is the* Amazing Maize Maze, *carved from a cornfield in Annville, Pennsylvania.*

What Is an Algorithm?

In Chapter 5, you learned how to solve any equation of the form $x + a = b$ for x. The method was to add $-a$ to each side and then simplify. This method is an example of an *algorithm.* An **algorithm** is a sequence of steps that leads to a desired result.

Not all algorithms are short. The algorithm called *long division* can involve many steps.

```
       .75
  34)25.50
     23 8
      1 70
      1 70
```

You know another algorithm for dividing decimals. It is the calculator algorithm. It is much easier to describe the algorithm for division on a calculator than the long division algorithm. This key sequence describes the algorithm.

Key sequence:	25.50	÷	34	=
Display:	25.50	25.50	34.	0.75

There is another way to think about algorithms. An algorithm is something that a computer can be programmed to do.

How Do Problems Differ from Exercises?

An **exercise** is a question that you know how to answer. For you, adding whole numbers is an exercise because you know an algorithm for addition. A **problem** for you is a question you do not know how to answer. It is a question for which you have no algorithm. Many people think that if they do not have an algorithm, then they cannot solve a problem. But that isn't true. By following some advice, almost anyone can become a better problem solver.

Lesson 6-1 Overview

Broad Goals This lesson defines *problem* and gives advice about how to approach a problem. It is meant to provide background and to ease students into problem solving.

Perspective A full chapter is devoted to problem-solving strategies because knowledge of algorithms alone is not enough to solve problems. If there is an algorithm for a question, then the question can be (and today usually is) answered by computer or calculator. The important skill is to decide what to do when there is no algorithm. The goal of this chapter is to teach students how to proceed when, in the past, they might have given up.

To some students, this lesson may seem to have no content because there are no algorithms to learn and no examples to study, but its messages on page 303 are just as important as examples.

❶ General Advice for Solving Problems

In this chapter you will learn many strategies for solving problems. But you must do three things.

1. Take your time. Few people solve problems fast. (If a person solves a problem fast, then it may not have been a problem for that person!)
2. Don't give up. You will never solve a problem if you do not try. Do something! (In the cartoon on page 301, Rick and the man give up too soon.)
3. Be flexible. If at first you don't succeed, try another way. And if the second way does not work, try a third way.

George Polya was a mathematician at Stanford University who was famous for his writing about solving problems. He once wrote:

> Solving problems is a practical skill like, let us say, swimming. We acquire any practical skill by imitation and practice. Trying to swim, you imitate what other people do with their hands and feet to keep their heads above water, and, finally, you learn to swim by practicing swimming. Trying to solve problems, you have to observe and to imitate what other people do when solving problems and, finally, you learn to do problems by doing them.

How Do Good Problem Solvers Solve Problems?

In a famous book called *How to Solve It,* Polya described what good problem solvers do.

- They *read the problem carefully.* They try to understand every word. They make sure they know what is asked for. They reread. They make certain that they are using the correct information. They look up words they do not know.
- They *devise a plan.* They even plan their guesses. They arrange information in tables. They draw pictures. They compare the problem to other problems they know. They decide to try something.
- They *carry out the plan.* They attempt to solve. They work with care. They write things down so they can read them later. If the attempt does not work, they go back to read the problem again.
- They *check work.* In fact, they check their work at every step. They do not check by repeating what they did. They check by estimating or by trying to find another way of doing the problem.

These are the kinds of strategies you will study in this chapter. You will also learn about some important problems and some fun problems.

Notes on Reading

❶ In class, emphasize the strategies and steps to reinforce the messages given and help students take this advice seriously. The procedures listed on this page are reproduced on **Teaching Aid 61**.

Tell students that what constitutes a problem for some people may not be a problem for them, and vice versa. They may find some of the questions in this chapter very easy and some quite hard. Encourage and reward sincere attempts by students to tackle hard problems.

At times students have probably been encouraged to work quickly. All standardized tests reward that type of behavior. Remind them it is often necessary to "slow down" when trying to solve a problem. Also, give them adequate time so that they don't feel pressured.

Problem solving requires flexibility; yet we often teach students a particular algorithm for solving a problem and sometimes discourage the use of alternate algorithms. So, though the advice in this lesson may seem obvious, it's not always easy to practice what is preached.

After discussing the reading, you might want to use *Activity 1* in *Optional Activities* below.

LESSON MASTER 6-1 A

Questions on SPUR Objectives
See pages 342-343 for objectives.

Skills Objective A

1. Write a paragraph describing four steps good problem solvers use.
They read the problem carefully. They devise a plan. They carry out the plan. They check their work.

In 2-4, what advice would you give to your friend who approached a problem this way? Sample answers are given.

2. After reading the problem once, Lily sat and stared at it for 15 minutes.
She should reread the problem.

3. Juan hurried through Lesson 6-1 so he could go swimming.
Few people solve problems quickly.

4. Rachel needed to multiply to solve a problem. Her answer wasn't sensible. When she multiplied again she got the same answer.
Check by estimating; use another method.

In 5-7, try these problems. Be ready to explain how you got your answer. Sample strategies are given.

5. One number is 8 more than another number. If their sum is 50, what is the smaller number?
Use trial and error; solve $n + (n + 8) = 50$.
21

6. Suppose 32 players enter a chess tournament. If a player is eliminated when he or she loses a match, how many matches are needed to produce a winner?
Make a table to show matches in each round. 31 matches

7. In how many ways can $79 be paid exactly using only $5 bills and $2 bills?
Make a table showing combinations of $5s and $2s. 8 ways

Optional Activities

Activity 1 Writing After students complete the reading, you might ask them to write an essay describing the hardest problem they have ever tackled. (It does not have to be a problem that they have solved.) You may wish to collect the essays and read some to the class.

Activity 2 History Connection After discussing the algorithms, you might have students research other multiplication algorithms besides the commonly used one shown for **Questions 15 and 16.** Two possible algorithms are Russian peasant multiplication and lattice multiplication. Most encyclopedias and mathematics history books will have information on these subjects. Have students give presentations on how to use the methods.

Additional Examples

You might want to use these examples when discussing the lesson. **Teaching Aid 62** contains the triangle diagram.

1. How many different whole numbers can you make with the digits 1, 2, 3, and 4? Any number you make can have one to four digits in it. You cannot repeat a digit in any number you make. **A total of 64 numbers: 24 with four digits, 24 with three digits, 12 with two digits, and 4 with one digit.**
2. How many triangles are in this drawing?

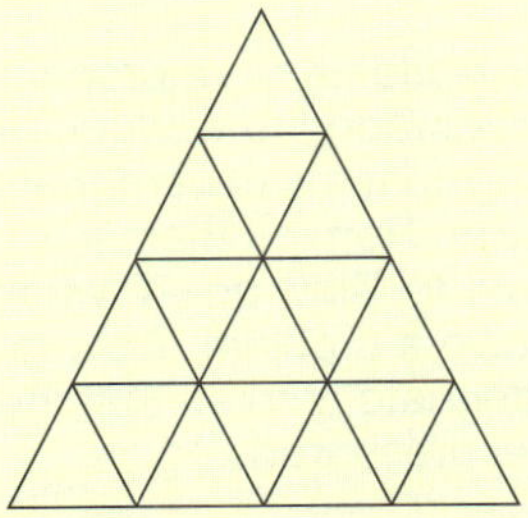

16 little triangles, 7 four times as big, 3 nine times as big, 1 sixteen times as big, for a total of 27 triangles

Notes on Questions

Questions 15–16 This algorithm is usually called *partial product multiplication.* In some countries, it is called *long multiplication. Activity 2* in *Optional Activities* on page 303 asks students to investigate other algorithms for multiplication.

LESSON MASTER 6-1 B Questions on SPUR Objectives

Skills Objective A: Understand the general strategies followed by good problem solvers.

1. Describe the difference between an exercise and a problem. You may use examples if you wish.
   sample: An exercise is a question you know how to answer, such as 6 + 4. A problem is a question you do not know how to answer, such as finding the number of diagonals in a decagon.

In 2-4 what advice would you give to your friend who approached a problem in this way. Sample answers are given

2. Matsue hurried through a set of problems so she could watch a favorite television show.
   Take your time.
3. Nathan tried addition to solve a problem. His answer wasn't reasonable. So he tried addition again and got the same answer.
   Be flexible; try another way.
4. Lynn read a problem once and then just sat and stared at it. After 20 minutes she gave up.
   Don't give up; do something.
5. How is learning to swim similar to learning how to solve problems?
   You imitate the skills of other people who know how to swim or how to solve problems. Then you practice swimming or practice solving problems.

QUESTIONS

Covering the Reading

1. What is an algorithm? **a sequence of steps that leads to a desired result**
2. Give an example of an algorithm. **Sample: long division**
3. What is a *problem?* Give an example of a question that for you is a problem. **a question you do not know how to answer; examples of questions will vary.**
4. What is an *exercise?* Give an example of a question that for you is an exercise. **a question you know how to answer; examples of questions will vary.**

In 5–7, what problem-solving advice is suggested by the traffic sign?

5. 

Take your time.

6. 

Don't give up.

7. 

Be flexible.

8. Who was George Polya? **a mathematician famous for writing about solving problems**

George Polya (1887–1985)

9. What famous book did Polya write? ***How to Solve It***

In 10–12, tell what the person should have done.

10. Monty tried one way to do the problem. When that did not work, he tried the same way again. **He should have tried another way (be flexible).**
11. Priscilla said to herself, "I've never seen any problem like that before. I won't be able to do it." **She should try something (don't give up).**
12. Adam wrote down an answer very quickly and went on to the next problem. **He should take more time (take your time).**

304

Adapting to Individual Needs

Extra Help

If students need extra help, you might want to guide them through selected problems by considering simpler cases first. For example, before students consider the number of whole numbers they can make with the digits 1, 2, 3, and 4 in *Additional Example 1*, have them first consider the number they can make with the digit 1 [1], with the digits 1 and 2 [4], and with the digits 1, 2, and 3. [15]

For *Additional Example 2*, have students first consider the top row, then the top two rows, and so on, before tackling the problem given.

Similar adjustments can be made to help students understand how to approach **Questions 17–21.**

13. What four things do successful problem solvers do when solving a problem? They read the problem carefully, devise a plan, carry it out, and check their work.

14. Suppose you want to devise a plan to solve a problem. What are some of the things you can do? Guess, arrange information in tables, draw pictures, compare to similar problems, try something.

Applying the Mathematics

In 15 and 16, refer to the algorithm pictured below.

```
     34.2
     5.67
    -----
    2394
   2052
  1710
  -------
  193.914
```

15. What question does this algorithm answer? What is 34.2 × 5.67?

16. Write the calculator algorithm that answers the same question. 34.2 [×] 5.67 [=]

17. Consider the letters *L, U, N, C, H*. Make two-letter monograms with these letters, such as *LU, UL, LL*. How many two-letter monograms are there? (Hint: Make an organized list.) 25

18. You can buy stickers for the digits from 0 through 9 at most hardware stores. They can be used for house addresses and room numbers. Suppose you buy stickers for all the digits in all the integers from 1 through 100.
   a. What digit will be used most? 1
   b. What digit will be used least? 0

19. Trains leave Union Station every hour from 7 A.M. through 7 P.M. bound for Kroy. How many trains is that in a day? 13

20. Suppose in Question 19, trains left every *half* hour, from 7 A.M. through 7 P.M. How many trains is that in a day? 25

21. Theo wants to buy a newspaper from a newspaper vending machine. The newspaper costs \$0.55. The machine takes nickels, dimes, and quarters. He has 4 dimes, 6 nickels, and 3 quarters. List all the different ways Theo can buy the newspaper.

21)

quarters	dimes	nickels
2	0	1
1	3	0
1	2	2
1	1	4
1	0	6
0	4	3
0	3	5

Review

22. Simplify $\frac{2}{3} + \frac{5}{7} - \frac{1}{14}$. *(Lessons 5-3, 5-5)* $\frac{55}{42}$

23. Find the value of $3 + 4a$ when $a = 2.5$. *(Lesson 4-4)* 13

24. A cube has how many edges? *(Lesson 3-8)* 12

25. What is the volume of a cube with an edge of length 5 centimeters? *(Lesson 3-8)* 125 cubic centimeters

Questions 17–18 It is more important for students to try these problems than it is for them to arrive at the exact answer. You may want students to **work in groups** and compare their solution methods.

You might ask students to write a generalization for the number of two-letter monograms that can be made from *n* letters. If students try the problem for 2, 3, and 4 letters, they should see that the number of monograms is n^2.

Generalization is an important problem-solving strategy. When a problem is solved, it is important to ask if the answer can be generalized. In some cases the generalization is easy, such as n^2 for **Question 17.** Other generalizations, such as $n + n(n-1) + n(n-1)(n-2) + \ldots + n!$ for *Additional Example 1,* are more difficult. For *Additional Example 2,* we have found no simple formula.

Questions 19–20 Each of these questions is a common type of counting question in which one must count everything from *a* to *b*, including the endpoints.

Question 21 *Make an organized list* is a useful strategy for this problem. The key word in the strategy is "organized." If a list is not organized, then it is more difficult to tell when the solution has been found.

Adapting to Individual Needs

English Language Development
In the problem-solving lessons in this chapter, you might have students **work in groups,** pairing students who have limited English proficiency with students whose reading skills are stronger. As students solve problems, be sure they can answer questions such as, "What facts do I know?" and "What am I trying to find out?"

► **LESSON MASTER 6-1 B** *page 2*

In 6-9, try these problems. Give a brief explanation of how you got your answer. Sample explanations are given.

6. How many 2-digit numbers are there that have no digits greater than 5?
30 numbers; make a list.
10–15 20–25
30–35 40–45
50–55

7. One number is 9 less than another. If their product is 36, what are the two numbers?
3 and 12; use trial and error.

8. How many different ways can 40¢ be made with fewer than 8 coins?
7 ways; make a list.
25 + 10 + 5
25 + 10 + 1 + 1 + 1 + 1 + 1
25 + 5 + 5 + 5
10 + 10 + 10 + 10
10 + 10 + 10 + 5 + 5
10 + 10 + 5 + 5 + 5 + 5
10 + 5 + 5 + 5 + 5 + 5 + 5

9. Arrange the digits 1-6 in the circles so that each side of the triangle adds up to 10.
Use trial and error.

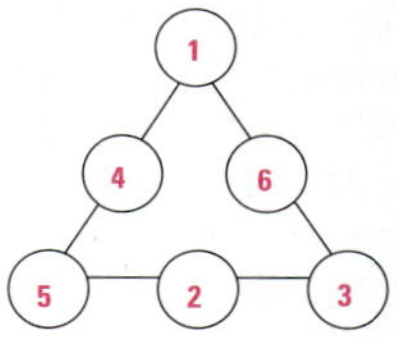

Follow-up for Lesson 6-1

Practice

For more questions on SPUR Objectives, use **Lesson Master 6-1A** (shown on page 303) or **Lesson Master 6-1B** (shown on pages 304–305).

Assessment

Written Assessment Ask students to write a letter to their parents explaining how good problem solvers solve problems. Ask them to include a comment on why access to calculators and/or computers will not necessarily make them good problem solvers. [Letter includes one or more strategies, the need for persistence, examples, and an explanation that calculators and computers are the tools used to compute answers.]

Extension

Give students the following series of diagrams, or have them use **Teaching Aid 62.** Ask them to find the total number of squares in each diagram. [1, 5, 9] Then have them continue drawing diagrams until they see a pattern. Have them try to describe the number of squares in the *n*th diagram. [1 + 4(*n* – 1)]

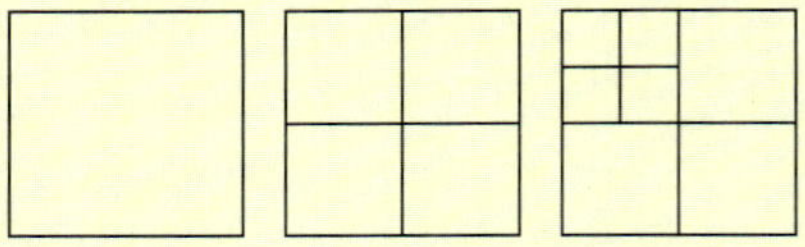

Project Update Project 3, *Problem Solving,* on page 338, and Project 4, *Cryptarithms,* on page 339, relate to the content of this lesson.

26. Here are changes in populations for the ten largest cities in the United States from 1980 to 1990.

New York	250,925
Los Angeles	518,548
Chicago	-221,346
Houston	35,415
Philadelphia	-102,633
San Diego	235,011
Detroit	-175,365
Dallas	102,799
Phoenix	193,699
San Antonio	150,053

a. Which cities lost in population from 1980 to 1990?

b. What was the total change in population for these ten cities combined? *(Lessons 1-8, 5-7)*
a) Chicago, Philadelphia, Detroit; b) 987,106

27. How many feet are in 5 miles? *(Lesson 3-2)* **26,400 feet**

28. One-sixth is equal to _?_ percent. *(Lesson 2-6)* **$16.\overline{6}$ or $16\frac{2}{3}$**

29. Of the 5.4 billion people on Earth in 1991, about 1% lived in Egypt. How many people is this? *(Lessons 2-1, 2-5)* **about 54 million**

30. Give the fraction in lowest terms equal to the given percent.

a. 10% $\frac{1}{10}$ **b.** 75% $\frac{3}{4}$
c. 25% $\frac{1}{4}$ **d.** $66\frac{2}{3}$% *(Lesson 2-4)* $\frac{2}{3}$

Exploration

31. In this addition problem each letter stands for a different digit. The sum is 10440. Find the digits. **There are many possible answers.**

	Sample:
U	3
CAN	782
DO	45
THIS	9610
10440	10440

Adapting to Individual Needs

Challenge
Materials: Dot paper

Have students draw the first triangle shown at the right on dot paper. Then have them "fill" the triangle with smaller triangles by connecting dots. Finally, have them count the total number of triangles in their figures. [Drawings and the total number of triangles will vary. A sample with 18 triangles is shown.]

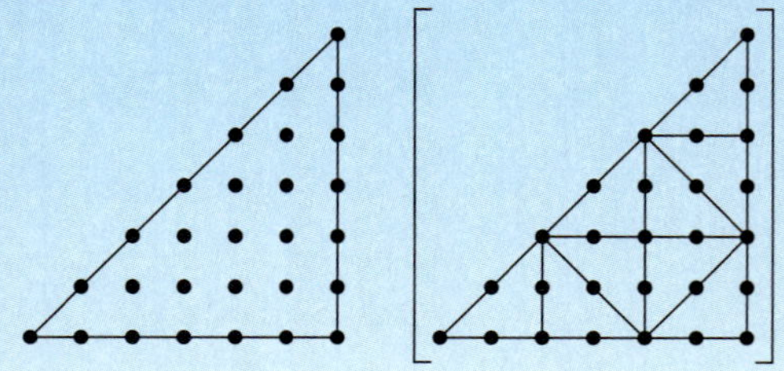

Setting Up Lesson 6-2

Materials: For Lesson 6-2, students will need dictionaries or other resource books in which mathematics terminology is defined.

LESSON

6-2

Read Carefully

A sign of the times? *Drivers at the intersection shown above need to read carefully and obey only those signs that apply to them. The photo above was taken at an intersection in Muncie, Indiana.*

General Advice About Reading

To solve a problem, you must understand it. So, if the problem is written down, you must *read it carefully.* Here are three things to do to get the necessary information from reading.

1. Know the meaning of all words and symbols in the problem.
2. Sort the information into what is needed and what is not needed.
3. Determine if there is enough information to solve the problem.

Example 1

List the ten smallest positive composite integers.

Strategy

To answer this question, you must know the meaning of "positive composite integer." In this book, we have already discussed the positive integers. So the new word here is "composite." Our dictionary has many definitions of "composite," but only one of "composite number." Here is that definition: "Any number exactly divisible by one or more numbers other than itself and 1; opposed to *prime number.*" So a composite number is a positive integer that is not prime nor equal to 1. Now the problem can be solved.

Solution

The positive integers are 1, 2, 3, 4, ... Those that are prime are 2, 3, 5, 7, 11, 13, 17, and so on. The ten smallest composites are the others: 4, 6, 8, 9, 10, 12, 14, 15, 16, 18.

Lesson 6-2

Objectives

C Determine whether a number is prime or composite.

D Find the meaning of unknown words.

Resources

From the ***Teacher's Resource File***

- Lesson Master 6-2A or 6-2B
- Answer Master 6-2
- Teaching Aid 59: Warm-up

Additional Resources

- Visual for Teaching Aid 59
- Spreadsheet Workshop
- Dictionaries or books in which mathematical terms are defined

Teaching Lesson 6-2

Warm-up

Use each word or phrase in a sentence. **Samples are given.**

1. Prime number **A prime number has exactly two factors, 1 and itself.**
2. Factor **Seven is a factor of twenty-one.**
3. Negative number **A negative number is less than zero.**
4. Hexagon **A hexagon has six sides and six angles.**

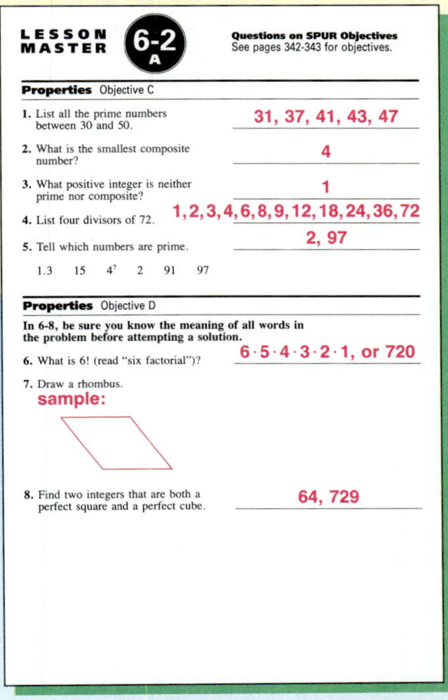
LESSON MASTER 6-2 A

Questions on SPUR Objectives
See pages 342-343 for objectives.

Properties Objective C

1. List all the prime numbers between 30 and 50. **31, 37, 41, 43, 47**
2. What is the smallest composite number? **4**
3. What positive integer is neither prime nor composite? **1**
4. List four divisors of 72. **1, 2, 3, 4, 6, 8, 9, 12, 18, 24, 36, 72**
5. Tell which numbers are prime. **2, 97**

   1.3 15 4^7 2 91 97

Properties Objective D

In 6-8, be sure you know the meaning of all words in the problem before attempting a solution.

6. What is 6! (read "six factorial")? **6 · 5 · 4 · 3 · 2 · 1, or 720**
7. Draw a rhombus. **sample:**
8. Find two integers that are both a perfect square and a perfect cube. **64, 729**

Lesson 6-2 Overview

Broad Goals Like Lesson 6-1, this lesson provides general advice about problem solving. It emphasizes reading for comprehension and reminds students to look up words they do not know.

Perspective This lesson focuses on students finding the meaning of words they do not know. Some students may never have done this before. Likewise, students may never have confronted a problem in math class in which there is more information than is needed to solve it, or a problem that cannot be solved because there is too little information. Yet, in real life, these two situations occur more often than those in which only the necessary information is given.

After this lesson, students should know the meanings of *prime*, *composite*, *divisor*, *factor*, and *natural number*.

Notes on Reading

There are many sources for finding definitions of terms, as in **Example 1.** Many books, including this one, have both an index and a glossary. Have students look carefully in both sections. If students cannot find a word in the glossary, suggest that they look in a regular dictionary, a mathematical dictionary, an encyclopedia, or other mathematics books.

Examples 2 and 3 These examples deal with common situations that arise in real-world problem solving—those in which there is information not needed to solve the problem and those in which there is not enough information to solve the problem.

Reading Connection A report in the April 12, 1993, issue of *Publisher's Weekly* shows that 65% of United States households bought at least one book in the period from April 1991 to March 1992. You might ask students to name a book or books they have read for pleasure in the past month.

Finding the Meanings of Words and Symbols

If you do not know the meaning of a word, look it up in a dictionary. Your school may have a mathematics dictionary, one that specializes in mathematical terms. Some mathematics books have glossaries or indexes in the back that can help you locate words.

Some terms have more than one meaning even in mathematics. The word *divisor* can mean *the number divided by* in a division problem. (In 12 ÷ 5 = 2.4, 5 is the divisor.) But *divisor* also means *a number that divides another number with a zero remainder.* For example, 7 is a divisor of 21. In this situation *divisor* has the same meaning as *factor.*

Some symbols have more than one meaning. The dash (-) can mean subtraction. It can also mean "the opposite of." However, in phone numbers, like 555-1212, it has no meaning other than to separate the number to make it easier to remember. You must look at the situation to determine which meaning is correct in a given problem.

Sorting Information into What Is Needed

Here is an example of a problem with too much information. Can you tell what information is not needed?

Example 2

Last year the Williams family decided that they should try to read more. So they kept track of the books they read. Mrs. Williams read 20 books. Mr. Williams read 16 books. Their son Jed read 12 books. Their daughter Josie read 14 books, and their daughter Julie read 7 books. How many books did these children of Mr. and Mrs. Williams read altogether?

Solution

Did you see that the problem asks only about the *children?* The information about the books read by Mr. and Mrs. Williams is not needed. *The children read 12 + 14 + 7 books, for a total of 33 books.*

Sometimes too little information is given to answer a question.

Example 3

Read Example 2 again. How many children do the Williamses have?

Solution

Do you think 3? Reread the problem. Nowhere does it say that these are the only children. *The Williamses have at least 3 children.*

LESSON MASTER 6-2 B Questions on SPUR Objectives

Properties Objective C: Determine whether a number is prime or composite.

1. List all prime numbers between 20 and 45. 23, 29, 31, 37, 41, 43
2. How many even prime numbers are there? 1
3. Is 1 prime or composite? Explain your answer. neither; 1 has only one factor. A prime number has exactly 2 factors; a composite number has more than 2 factors.
4. List the composite numbers between 5 and 25. 6, 8, 9, 10, 12, 14, 15, 16, 18, 20, 21, 22, 24
5. What number is a divisor of every positive integer? 1
6. Tell which of these number are prime. 18 6^3 5.1 51 59 19 — 59, 19
7. Which of these number is a divisor of 102? 4 8 17 21 22 14 — 17

In 8-17, list all of the positive integers that are factors of the number. Then tell if the number is prime or composite.

8. 54 — 1, 2, 3, 6, 9, 18, 27, 54; composite
9. 60 — 1, 2, 3, 4, 5, 6, 10, 12, 15, 20, 30, 60; composite
10. 67 — 1, 67; prime
11. 91 — 1, 7, 13, 91; composite
12. 71 — 1, 71; prime
13. 49 — 1, 7, 49; composite
14. 55 — 1, 5, 11, 55; composite
15. 79 — 1, 79; prime
16. 100 — 1, 2, 4, 5, 10, 20, 25, 50, 100; composite
17. 112 — 1, 2, 4, 7, 8, 14, 16, 28, 56, 112; composite

Optional Activities

Activity 1 History Connection After students complete **Question 20,** you might tell them that over 2200 years ago, Euclid wrote this definition of a perfect number:

> A perfect number is a whole number that is equal to the sum of all its divisors (factors) except itself.

Euclid himself found four examples of perfect numbers. You might have students do some research and find the first four perfect numbers. [6, 28, 496, and 8128] In their research, they might also find the fifth perfect number, 33,550,336. Ask students why they think the fifth number was found only recently. [Sample response: Before computers, calculations in the search for perfect numbers were done by hand. Computers have made the search easier.]

QUESTIONS

Covering the Reading

1. What three things should you do when you read a problem?

1) Know the meaning of all words and symbols in the problem, sort out unneeded information, and see if there is enough information to solve the problem.

2. Can a word have more than one mathematical meaning? Yes

3. Give an example of a mathematical symbol that has more than one meaning. Example: the dash -

4. Which of the following numbers is not a composite integer?
   6 7 8 9 10 7

5. Which of the following numbers is not a prime number?
   11 13 15 17 19 15

6. List the ten smallest positive prime numbers. 2, 3, 5, 7, 11, 13, 17, 19, 23, 29

7. Which of the following numbers is a divisor of 91?
   3 5 7 9 11 7

8. Which of the following numbers is a factor of 91?
   13 15 17 19 21 13

In 9–11, refer to Example 2.

9. How many books did Mr. and Mrs. Williams read altogether? 36

10. What word seems to hint that the Williamses have more than three children? "these" (children)

11. Of the three Williams children named, who is the youngest? Not enough information is given.

12. Name two places to look to find a definition of a mathematical term. Samples: dictionary, mathematical dictionary, glossary

Applying the Mathematics

In 13–15, use this definition. A *natural number* is one of the numbers 1, 2, 3, 4, ...

13. *Multiple choice.* Which of (a) to (c) is the same as natural number?
   (a) whole number
   (b) integer
   (c) positive integer
   (d) none of these (c)

14. Name all natural numbers that are solutions to $10 > x \geq 7$. 7, 8, 9

15. How many natural numbers are solutions of $v < 40$? 39

16. List all the divisors of 36. 1, 2, 3, 4, 6, 9, 12, 18, 36

17. In the fraction $\frac{24}{35}$, which number is the divisor: 24 or 35? 35

18. Explain why 7^5 is not a prime number. It is divisible by 7.

Additional Examples

1. Look up any words you do not know. Then solve the problem.
   a. Draw a tangent to a circle.

   Sample: 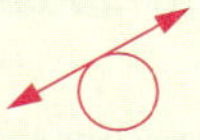

   b. Find two different meanings of the word *cone*. One meaning should describe a geometric figure. Sample: fruit of pine trees; a solid that tapers to a point from a flat, circular base

2. Leah has 5 nickels, 2 quarters, 6 dimes, and two one-dollar bills in her purse. How much money does she have in coins? $1.35

3. At Hallowed Hall High, the sophomore class has 100 fewer students than the freshman class, the junior class has three fourths the number in the freshman class, and the senior class is 60% of the freshman class. How many students attend Hallowed Hall High?
   Not enough information; you need to know the size of the freshman class.

Notes on Questions

Questions 13–15 Students may need to review the meanings of *whole number* and *integer*. In some books, zero is considered to be a natural number. If a student finds such a book, you may wish to point out that even in mathematics, words can be defined differently.

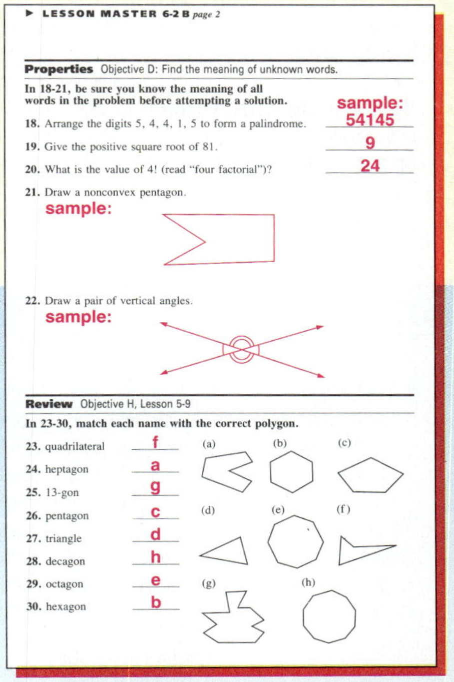

▶ LESSON MASTER 6-2 B *page 2*

Properties Objective D: Find the meaning of unknown words.

In 18-21, be sure you know the meaning of all words in the problem before attempting a solution.

18. Arrange the digits 5, 4, 4, 1, 5 to form a palindrome. sample: 54145

19. Give the positive square root of 81. 9

20. What is the value of 4! (read "four factorial")? 24

21. Draw a nonconvex pentagon.
    sample:

22. Draw a pair of vertical angles.
    sample:

Review Objective H, Lesson 5-9

In 23-30, match each name with the correct polygon.

23. quadrilateral f
24. heptagon a
25. 13-gon g
26. pentagon c
27. triangle d
28. decagon h
29. octagon e
30. hexagon b

(a) (b) (c) (d) (e) (f) (g) (h)

Optional Activities

Activity 2 Technology Connection You may wish to have students use the *Spreadsheet Workshop* to find prime numbers less than 100. When students select the Prime Finder option, a chart of whole numbers from 2 to 99 is displayed. Multiples of numbers can be erased easily, thus allowing students to identify primes.

Adapting to Individual Needs

English Language Development
A lesson in which students must look up the meanings of words gives students for whom English is their native language a taste of what students just learning English experience on a daily basis. Have students **work in pairs** to discuss how to find and interpret the meanings of words they do not know.

Notes on Questions

Questions 22–25 Be sure students recognize that **Questions 22–23** contain instances of the patterns described in **Questions 24–25.**

Follow-up for Lesson 6-2

Practice

For more questions on SPUR Objectives, use **Lesson Master 6-2A** (shown on page 307) or **Lesson Master 6-2B** (shown on pages 308–309).

Assessment

Group Assessment Have students **work in pairs.** Have each student write a problem that has too much or too little information and give it to his or her partner. If there is not enough information, the partner must supply what is missing and solve the problem. If the problem has too much information, the partner should solve it and tell which information was not needed. [Writes an appropriate problem. Interprets correctly and writes a proper solution for a problem.]

Extension

Have students find the value of $n^2 + n + 11$ when n is 1, 2, 3, and 4. [13, 17, 23, and 31] Ask them if they think the result is always prime. [Maybe] Then have them **work in groups** to find a value for n that will cause the result to be composite. [For $n = 10$, the result is 121, which is not prime.]

Project Update Project 6, *Special Numbers,* on page 339, relates to the content of this lesson.

19) 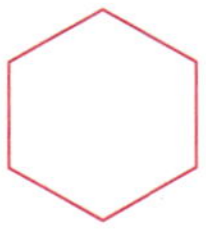

20) (A perfect number is an integer that is the sum of all of its factors excluding the integer itself.)

21) (Twin primes are two consecutive odd numbers that are both primes.)

In 19–21, you may need to look in a dictionary or other source.

19. Draw a regular hexagon. (A regular hexagon is a 6-sided polygon whose angles all have same measure and sides all have same length.)

20. Give an example of a perfect number. Sample: 6 (6 = 1 + 2 + 3)

21. Give an example of a pair of twin primes. Sample: 29 and 31

In 22 and 23, use the following information. The class in room 25 had 23 students last year and has 27 students this year. The class in room 24 had 25 students last year and has 26 students this year. There are 22 students this year and there were 28 students last year in room 23.

22. What was the total number of students in these classrooms last year? 76

23. In which year were there more students in these classrooms? last year

In 24 and 25, use the following information. The class in room a had b students last year and has c students this year. The class in room d had e students last year and has f students this year. There are g students this year and there were h students last year in room i.

24. What was the total number of students in these classrooms last year? $b + e + h$

25. In which year were there more students in these classrooms? Not enough information. If $b + e + h > c + f + g$, then last year; if $b + e + h < c + f + g$, then this year.

Review

26. What are Polya's four steps in problem solving? *(Lesson 6-1)* Read the problem carefully, devise a plan, carry out the plan, check work.

27. How many diagonals does a hexagon have? *(Lesson 5-9)* 9

28. Solve for x: $x + 3 + y = y + 8$. *(Lesson 5-8)* $x = 5$

29. In a Scrabble® tournament, a person played six different people with the following results: won by 12, lost by 30, won by 65, won by 47, lost by 3, and lost by 91. What was the total point difference between this person and the other six people combined? *(Lesson 5-3)* 0

30. Simplify $-(-(-(-y)))$. *(Lesson 5-3)* y

31. Simplify $5 + -(-(-3 + 4 \cdot 2))$. *(Lessons 4-5, 5-2)* 10

32. Name two segments in the drawing at the left that look perpendicular. *(Lesson 3-7)* $\overline{ED}$ and $\overline{DC}$ or $\overline{CD}$ and $\overline{CB}$

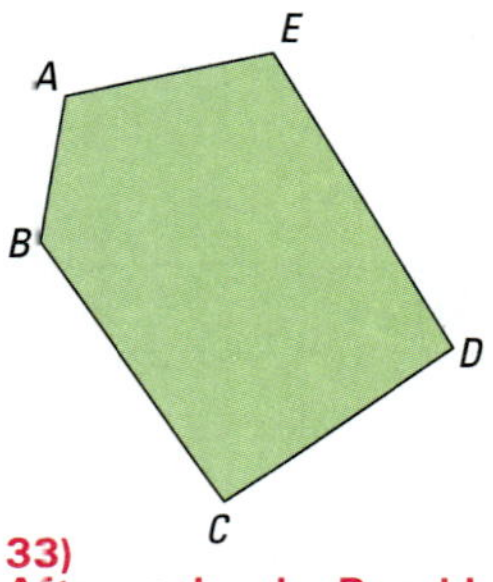

Exploration

33. Ronald has a truckload of fewer than 5000 apples. He sold exactly 20% of them to Mary. Next he sold exactly 20% of the remaining apples to Gregory. Next he sold exactly 20% of those remaining to Carolyn. He sold exactly 20% of those remaining to Joy. Then he sold exactly 20% of those remaining to Anne. If Ronald cannot sell a fraction of an apple, how many apples did he begin with? How many does he have now? Explain your answers.

33) After each sale, Ronald had $\frac{4}{5}$ of what he had before the sale. He made five sales, so he ended up with $\frac{4}{5} \cdot \frac{4}{5} \cdot \frac{4}{5} \cdot \frac{4}{5} \cdot \frac{4}{5}$, or $\frac{1024}{3125}$, of a truckload. Since he began with a whole number of apples less than 5000 and ended with a whole number of apples, the original number of apples is a number less than 5000 that is divisible by 3125. So Ronald started with 3125 apples and ended up with $\frac{1024}{3125} \times 3125$, or 1024 apples.

Adapting to Individual Needs

Challenge

Solving a common type of puzzle, the logic puzzle, requires careful reading, as well as organization. Give students the puzzle at the right. After they solve it, they might make up similar puzzles for classmates to solve. Or, they might try to solve a harder logic puzzle found in a commercial puzzle book.

Each of five people brought one of the following items to Stacy's party: chips, soda, pretzels, ice cream, and cookies. Who brought which item? [Julio, chips; Amy, soda; Neil, ice cream; Betsy, cookies; Latasha, pretzels]

(1) Julio's item was not served cold.
(2) Amy brought either soda, chips, or pretzels.
(3) Either Neil or Betsy brought cookies.
(4) Latasha brought pretzels.
(5) Betsy did not bring ice cream.

Setting Up Lesson 6-3

Materials: If you use the *Assessment* in Lesson 6-3, students will need installation or assembly instructions for a variety of things such as model cars, bicycles, telephones, and window shades.

LESSON

6-3

Draw a Picture

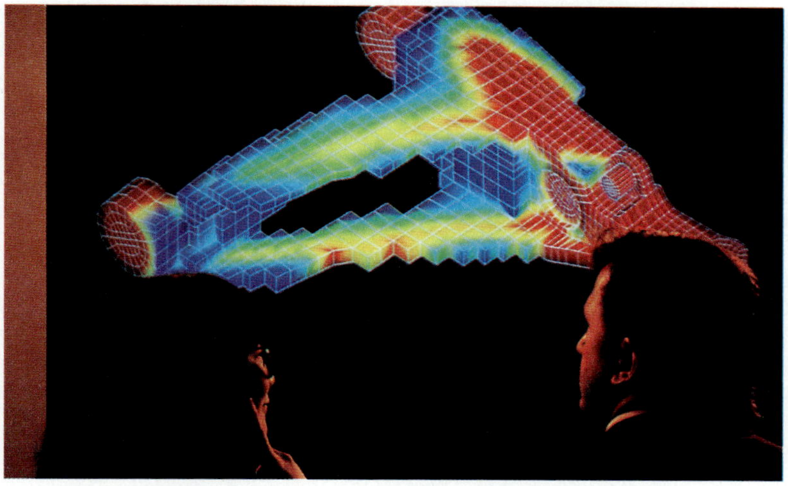

Picture perfect. *Designers of automobiles can create, test, and modify plans using computer-aided design programs. This picture from Ford Motor Company shows a computerized image of the lower control arm of an automobile.*

Pictures for Geometry Problems

You can understand every word in a problem yet still not be able to solve it immediately. One useful strategy is to *draw a picture.* This is particularly helpful when the problem involves a geometric figure.

Activity 1

How many diagonals does a heptagon have?

Strategy

One strategy is obvious. Draw a heptagon and draw its diagonals. Count the diagonals as you draw them.

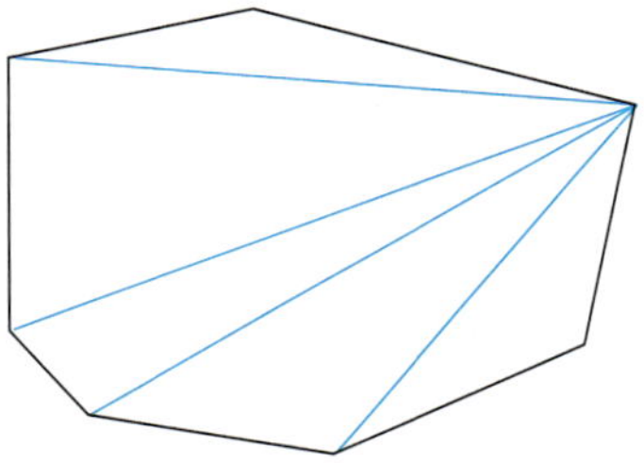

Trace the heptagon above and draw the remaining diagonals, counting as you draw. How many diagonals does a heptagon have?

Suppose you did not remember that a heptagon has 7 sides, or suppose you forget what a diagonal is. Then you could look in the glossary of this book. Or you could look in a dictionary.

Lesson 6-3

Objectives

I Use drawings to solve real-world problems.

K Draw a diagram to aid in solving geometric problems.

Resources

From the ***Teacher's Resource File***
- Lesson Master 6-3A or 6-3B
- Answer Master 6-3
- Assessment Sourcebook: Quiz for Lessons 6-1 through 6-3
- Teaching Aid 59: Warm-up

Additional Resources
- Visual for Teaching Aid 59
- Installation or assembly instructions (Assessment)

Teaching Lesson 6-3

Warm-up

Draw the shapes described.
Answers will vary. Check students' drawings.

1. A rectangle with a width that is twice the length
2. Three concentric circles
3. A nine-sided polygon that has at least three sides of equal length

Lesson 6-3 Overview

Broad Goals The main goal of this lesson is to convince students that drawing a picture is a valid and quite useful strategy in solving many problems, both geometric and otherwise.

Perspective In spite of the adage "a picture is worth a thousand words" (the oldest source is Chinese and states that a picture is worth *more* than a thousand words), it is often difficult to get many students to draw even the most obvious diagrams. Yet pictures or diagrams are helpful in devising a course of action and in avoiding careless mistakes in many types of problems. You will do your students, yourself, and their future math teachers a great service if you can convince your students to make liberal use of this tool. Devoting an entire lesson to this strategy emphasizes its usefulness. Also, awarding credit for the diagram in a solution will help.

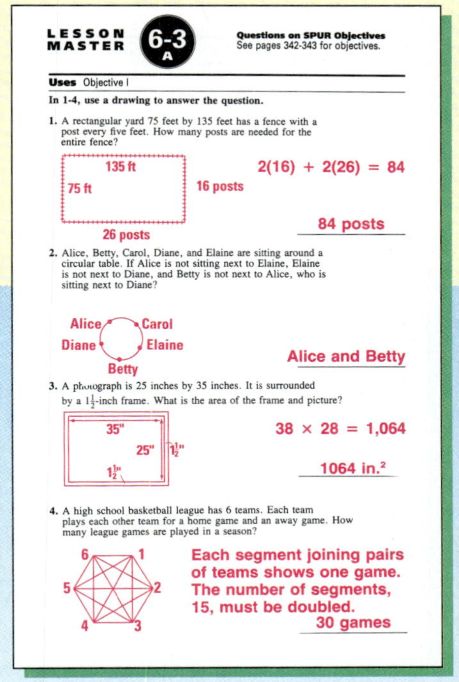

LESSON MASTER 6-3 A **Questions on SPUR Objectives** See pages 342-343 for objectives.

Uses Objective I

In 1-4, use a drawing to answer the question.

1. A rectangular yard 75 feet by 135 feet has a fence with a post every five feet. How many posts are needed for the entire fence?

135 ft, 75 ft, 16 posts, 26 posts

$2(16) + 2(26) = 84$

84 posts

2. Alice, Betty, Carol, Diane, and Elaine are sitting around a circular table. If Alice is not sitting next to Elaine, Elaine is not next to Diane, and Betty is not next to Alice, who is sitting next to Diane?

Alice, Carol, Diane, Elaine, Betty

Alice and Betty

3. A phuıograph is 25 inches by 35 inches. It is surrounded by a $1\frac{1}{2}$-inch frame. What is the area of the frame and picture?

35", 25", $1\frac{1}{2}$", $1\frac{1}{2}$"

$38 \times 28 = 1{,}064$

1064 in.^{2}

4. A high school basketball league has 6 teams. Each team plays each other team for a home game and an away game. How many league games are played in a season?

6, 1, 5, 2, 4, 3

Each segment joining pairs of teams shows one game. The number of segments, 15, must be doubled.

30 games

Notes on Reading

Point out that there are three general kinds of situations for which drawing a picture is appropriate. First, there are geometric situations, as in **Activity 1 and Questions 6, 7, and 10.** Second, there are situations with known representations, such as **Example 1**, where the picture might not be obvious at first, but once students see the connection, they should start thinking of situations in terms of diagrams. The third situation, as exemplified by the ordering idea in **Question 8**, does not seem at first glance to involve a picture. Nonetheless, a diagram helps solve the problem.

Students should record the results of **Activities 1 and 2** for use with **Questions 1 and 10** on pages 312 and 313.

Additional Examples

1. How many diagonals does a pentagon have? **5 diagonals; check to see that students have drawn pentagons.**
2. There are 5 players in a chess tournament. Each player must play every other contestant once. How many games will be played? **10 games; students can use the picture from Question 1.**
3. To go directly from Yellville to Harrison is 26 miles. To make the same trip through Diamond City is 41 miles. If it is 23 miles from Yellville to Diamond City, how far is it from Diamond City to Harrison? **18 miles; students' drawings will vary.**

▸ **LESSON MASTER 6-3 A** *page 2*

Representations Objective K

In 5-8, draw a diagram to solve the problem.

5. P, O, I, N, T, and S appear in that order on $\overline{PS}$. If $PS = 23$, $PO = 3$, $IS = 12$, $TS = 6$ and $IN = 2$, find OI and OT.

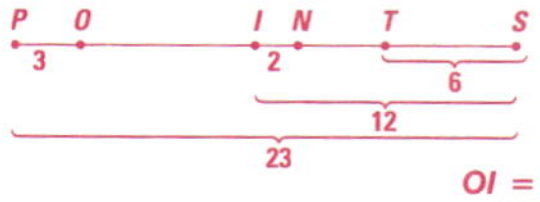

$OI = 8$, $OT = 14$

6. How many rectangles are formed by three horizontal and four vertical lines?

6 small rectangles: 1
4 small rectangles: 2
3 small rectangles: 2
2 small rectangles: 7
1 small rectangle: 6

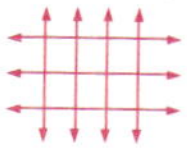

18 rectangles

7. Five points are located on a circle. How many different line segments can you draw joining pairs of these points?

10 line segments

8. The midpoints of each side of $\triangle NOT$ are connected to make a smaller triangle inside $\triangle NOT$. If the area of $\triangle NOT$ is 16 in.^{2}, what is the area of the smaller triangle?

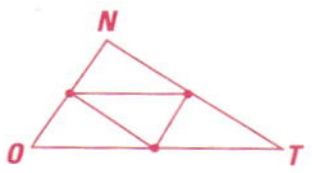

Area of smaller triangle is one fourth area of $\triangle NOT$.

4 in.^{2}

Pictures for Problems That Are Not Geometric

Even when a problem is not geometric, a drawing can still help. Example 1 uses the heptagon drawing in a way that may surprise you.

Example 1

Seven teams are to play each other in a tournament. How many games are needed?

Solution

Name the teams A, B, C, D, E, F, and G. Use these letters to name points in a drawing. When A plays D, draw the segment $\overline{AD}$. So each segment between two points represents a different game.

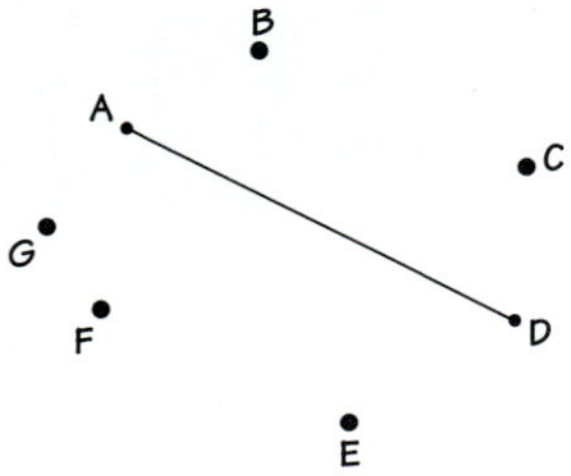

The number of games played is the number of segments that can be drawn. But the segments are the sides and diagonals of a heptagon. A heptagon has 7 sides. Your work in Activity 1 should have shown that there are 14 diagonals in a heptagon. So there are 21 segments altogether. *Twenty-one games are needed for the tournament.*

Activity 2

List each of the 21 games needed for the tournament. (Identify each game by a segment.)

Drawing a picture is a very important problem-solving idea. You may never have thought of picturing teams as we did, but there are many types of problems for which drawing a picture is a helpful, but not obvious, way to find a solution.

QUESTIONS

Covering the Reading

1. How many diagonals does a heptagon have? **14**
2. Seven teams A, B, C, D, E, F, and G are to play each other in a tournament.
   a. How many games are needed? **21**
   b. List the games that are needed. ***AB, AC, AD, AE, AF, AG, BC, BD, BE, BF, BG, CD, CE, CF, CG, DE, DF, DG, EF, EG, FG***

Optional Activities

Materials: Centimeter cubes or sugar cubes, marker or tape

Many geometric models are three-dimensional pictures. Consequently, when discussing **Question 24,** you might ask students to make a model using actual cubes. **Divide students into groups** and give each group 27 centimeter cubes or sugar cubes. Have them make a 3 × 3 × 3 cube and use a marker or tape to show the faces that would be painted. Then ask the following questions. Are there any small cubes which will be painted on four sides? [No] How many small cubes will be painted on exactly three sides? [8] on exactly two sides? [12] on only one side? [6] How many small cubes have no painted sides? [1] How might you check your answers? [Altogether there are 54 painted sides; 3 × 8 + 2 × 12 + 1 × 6 = 24 + 24 + 6 = 54.]

3. How many diagonals does a quadrilateral have? 2

4. Four teams are to play each other in a volleyball tournament. How many games are needed? 6

Net result—volleyball. *Volleyball was invented in 1895 by a physical-education teacher, William G. Morgan, in Holyoke, Massachusetts. Volleyball is now an international sport, with more than 170 nations belonging to the Federation Internationale de Volleyball.*

Applying the Mathematics

5. Eight teams are to play each other two times in a season. How many games are needed? 56

6. Have you heard this problem? If you haven't, watch out. A snail wants to climb out of a hole that is 10 feet deep. The snail climbs up 2 feet each day and falls back 1 foot each night. How many days will it take the snail to climb out of the hole? 9

In 7–10, drawing a picture will help.

7. A square dog pen is 10 feet on a side. There is a post in each corner. There are posts every 2 feet on each side. How many posts are there in all? 20

8. Bill is older than Wanda and younger than Jill. Jill is older than Chris and younger than Pete. Chris is older than Wanda. Bill is younger than Pete. Chris is older than Bill. Who is youngest? Wanda

9. Amy is driving along Interstate 55 in Illinois from Collinsville to Joliet. She will pass through Litchfield and then through Atlanta. The distance from Collinsville to Litchfield is half the distance from Litchfield to Atlanta. The distance from Atlanta to Joliet is three times the distance from Collinsville to Litchfield. The distance from Atlanta to Joliet is 114 miles. How far is it from Collinsville to Joliet? 228 miles

10. The Sherman family has a pool 30 feet long and 25 feet wide. There is a walkway 4.5 feet wide around the pool.
   a. What is the perimeter of the pool? 110 feet
   b. What is the perimeter of the outside edge of the walkway? 146 feet

Notes on Questions

Question 2b It is important that students' lists be organized, otherwise they may not see how similar problems can be solved. We named the seven teams A, B, C, D, E, F, and G to suggest that an alphabetical organization might be suitable. Naming the games by the two-letter words AB, AC, and so on, in alphabetical order, shows that one can begin the list with the six games played by team A, then add the five games played by B that do not involve A, then add the four games played by C that do not involve A or B, and so on. The sum, $6 + 5 + 4 + 3 + 2 + 1$, shows a pattern that is easy to generalize to larger or smaller numbers of given teams. The number of games needed by n teams is the sum of the integers from 1 to $n - 1$.

Question 7 Students need to realize that the corner posts are on two sides.

Questions 8–9 Error Alert Students who have difficulty drawing diagrams for these problems need to reread the facts, evaluating each bit of information in terms of the other pieces of information.

Question 10b Ask students to write a generalization for the perimeter. [If the pool's dimensions are ℓ and w and the width of the walkway is y, the perimeter is $2\ell + 2w + 8y$.]

Adapting to Individual Needs

Extra Help
Be sure students understand that the pictures they draw can be simple sketches. For instance, in **Example 1,** a point represents a team and a segment connecting two points represents a game. Emphasize that the purpose of drawing a picture is to make problem solving easier. Suggest that students use different-colored pencils within a drawing if they help to clarify the problem.

English Language Development
You might pair each student with limited English proficiency with a strong reader. The strong reader can read the problems and explain the meaning of any words or ideas his or her partner does not understand. Drawing a picture helps convey the meaning of many words and ideas. Then both students can solve the problems together.

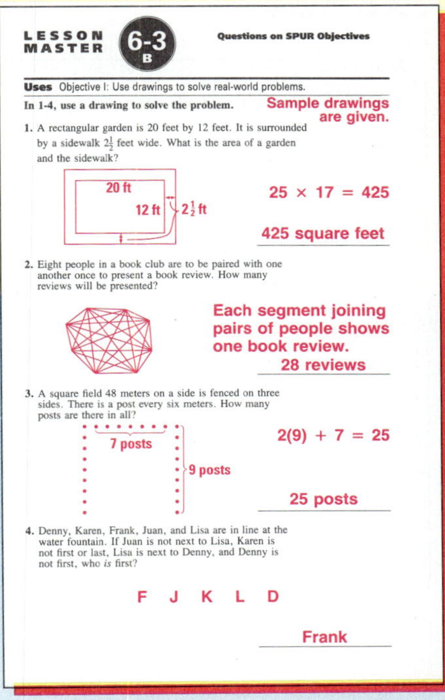
LESSON MASTER 6-3 B Questions on SPUR Objectives

Uses Objective I: Use drawings to solve real-world problems.

In 1-4, use a drawing to solve the problem. Sample drawings are given.

1. A rectangular garden is 20 feet by 12 feet. It is surrounded by a sidewalk $2\frac{1}{2}$ feet wide. What is the area of a garden and the sidewalk?

20 ft, 12 ft, $2\frac{1}{2}$ ft

$25 \times 17 = 425$

425 square feet

2. Eight people in a book club are to be paired with one another once to present a book review. How many reviews will be presented?

Each segment joining pairs of people shows one book review.

28 reviews

3. A square field 48 meters on a side is fenced on three sides. There is a post every six meters. How many posts are there in all?

7 posts, 9 posts

$2(9) + 7 = 25$

25 posts

4. Denny, Karen, Frank, Juan, and Lisa are in line at the water fountain. If Juan is not next to Lisa, Karen is not first or last, Lisa is next to Denny, and Denny is not first, who *is* first?

F J K L D

Frank

Notes on Questions

Question 24 Students can model this situation as suggested in *Optional Activities* on page 312.

Follow-up for Lesson 6-3

Practice

For more questions on SPUR Objectives, use **Lesson Master 6-3A** (shown on pages 311–312) or **Lesson Master 6-3B** (shown on pages 313–314).

Assessment

Quiz A quiz covering Lessons 6-1 through 6-3 is provided in the *Assessment Sourcebook.*

Oral/Written Communication Have students **work in groups**. Give each group the installation or assembly instructions for an item. Tell students to read the instructions without looking at the pictures or drawings that accompany them. Then have students explain how pictures help them understand the directions. [Explanation includes examples of how the pictures help with the instructions.]

Extension

Project Update Project 1, *Diagonals of Regular Polygons,* on page 338, relates to the content of this lesson.

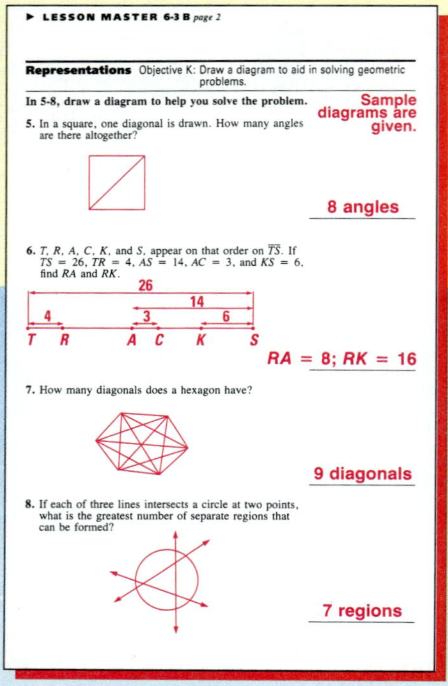
▸ LESSON MASTER 6-3 B *page 2*

Representations Objective K: Draw a diagram to aid in solving geometric problems.

In 5-8, draw a diagram to help you solve the problem. Sample diagrams are given.

5. In a square, one diagonal is drawn. How many angles are there altogether? **8 angles**

6. *T, R, A, C, K,* and *S*, appear on that order on $\overline{TS}$. If $TS = 26$, $TR = 4$, $AS = 14$, $AC = 3$, and $KS = 6$, find *RA* and *RK*.

RA = 8; RK = 16

7. How many diagonals does a hexagon have? **9 diagonals**

8. If each of three lines intersects a circle at two points, what is the greatest number of separate regions that can be formed? **7 regions**

Review

11. Name two places to look if you do not know the meaning of a mathematical term. *(Lesson 6-2)* **Samples: glossary, dictionary**

12. List all the natural number factors of 40. *(Lesson 6-2)* **1, 2, 4, 5, 8, 10, 20, 40**

13. List the natural numbers between 8.4 and 4.2. *(Lesson 6-2)* **5, 6, 7, 8**

14. List all even prime numbers. Explain your answer. *(Lesson 6-2)* **2; all other even numbers are divisible by 2.**

In 15 and 16, suppose that Sarah has S dollars and Dana has D dollars. Translate into English. *(Lesson 5-8)*

15. $S = D$ **Sarah and Dana have the same number of dollars.**

16. If $S = D$, then $S + 2 = D + 2$. **See below.**

17. When $a = -3$ and $b = 6$, what is the value of $-(a + b)$? *(Lessons 4-5, 5-3)* **-3**

18. What is the absolute value of -30? *(Lesson 5-3)* **30**

19. Find the value of $6x^4$ when $x = 3$. *(Lesson 4-4)* **486**

20. 10 pounds is about how many kilograms? *(Lesson 3-5)* **≈ 4.5 kg**

21. Which is larger, 45 centimeters or 800 millimeters? *(Lesson 3-4)* **800 mm**

22. What number will you get if you enter this key sequence?
20 [y^x] 3 [×] 2 [÷] [(] 5 [÷] 4 [)] [=] *(Lessons 1-5, 2-2)* **12,800**

23. Round 56.831 to the nearest hundredth. *(Lesson 1-4)* **56.83**

Exploration

24. 27 small cubes are arranged to form one big 3 × 3 × 3 cube. Then the entire big cube is dipped in paint. How many small cubes will now be painted on exactly two sides? **12 cubes**

25. One local soccer league has 5 teams and another has 6 teams. Each team in the first league is to play each team in the second league once. How many games are needed? **30 games**

16) If Sarah and Dana have the same number of dollars, they will still have the same number of dollars after each receives $2 more.

Adapting to Individual Needs

Challenge

Give students this problem to solve.

Six people are seated at a round table. Each person reaches out and shakes the hand of one other person. No pair of joined hands may cross any other pair. In how many different ways is this possible? [5 ways; see the sample diagrams at the right.] Which pairs cannot shake hands? [1 and 5, 1 and 3, 2 and 4, 2 and 6, 3 and 5, and 4 and 6]

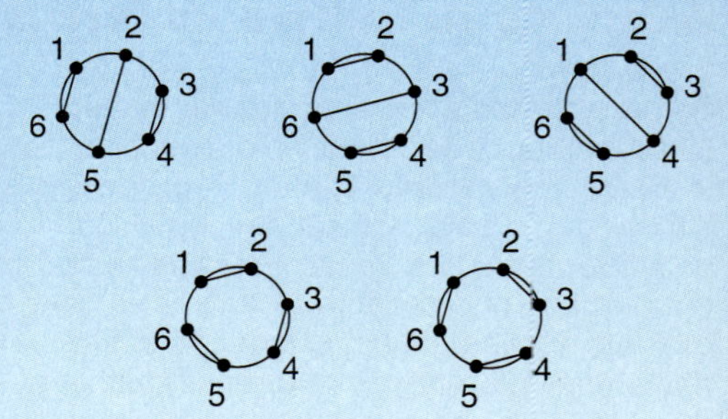

LESSON

6-4

Trial and Error

Try, try again. *The strategy of trial and error is necessary in order to solve a jigsaw puzzle. If a piece does not fit, don't give up—try another piece.*

Trial and error is a problem-solving strategy everyone uses at one time or another. In trial and error, you try an answer. (The word *trial* comes from *try.*) If the answer is in error, you try something else. You keep trying until you get a correct answer.

Trial and error is a particularly good strategy if a question has only a few possible answers.

Example 1

Which of the numbers 4, 5, and 6 is a solution to $(n + 3)(n - 2) = 36$?

Strategy

This type of equation is not discussed in this book. You probably do not know how to solve it. You have no algorithm. So it is a problem for you. However, since there are only three choices for a value of n, trial and error is a suitable strategy.

Solution

Try the numbers one at a time.
Try 4. Does $(4 + 3)(4 - 2) = 36$? Does $7 \cdot 2 = 36$? No, $14 \neq 36$.
Try 5. Does $(5 + 3)(5 - 2) = 36$? Does $8 \cdot 3 = 36$? No, $24 \neq 36$, but 24 is closer than 14.
Try 6. Does $(6 + 3)(6 - 2) = 36$? Does $9 \cdot 4 = 36$? Yes.
So 6 is a solution.

Lesson 6-4

Objectives

B Determine solutions to sentences by trial and error.

Resources

From the ***Teacher's Resource File***
- Lesson Master 6-4A or 6-4B
- Answer Master 6-4
- Teaching Aid 59: Warm-up
- Activity Kit, Activity 13
- Technology Sourcebook, Computer Demonstration 6, Computer Master 9, Calculator Master 8

Additional Resources
- Visual for Teaching Aid 59
- Spreadsheet Workshop

Teaching Lesson 6-4

Warm-up

Solve each problem.

1. A rectangle has an area of 12 square inches and a perimeter of 16 inches. Find its dimensions. **2 in. by 6 in.**
2. A triangle has a perimeter of 17 inches. The longest side is 3 inches longer than one side and twice as long as the other. Find the length of each side. **4 in., 5 in., and 8 in.**

Notes on Reading

See *Activity 1* in *Optional Activities* on page 316 for an alternate way to introduce this lesson. In class discussion, emphasize the following three points in case students over-

Lesson 6-4 Overview

Broad Goals This lesson provides the opportunity to discuss the general problem-solving strategy of trial and error.

Perspective *Trial and error* is called "guess and check" or "test and check" in some books. It has a long history of use outside the classroom as well as in it. Justice Louis Brandeis of the United States Supreme Court wrote in a 1932 decision: ". . . this court has often overruled its earlier decisions. The Court bows to the lessons of experience and the force of better reasoning, recognizing that the process of trial and error, so fruitful in the physical sciences, is appropriate also in the judicial function."

Although the discussion emphasizes testing an answer, in reality one often uses trial and error to select a strategy. That is, a person will try strategy 1, and if it does not work, he or she will use strategy 2, and so on. This approach works well if there are only a few possible options.

Trial and error may be a particularly appropriate strategy to use on a multiple-choice test because it is no more than the simple logic of ruling out possibilities. The good multiple-choice test taker often rules out choices rather than doing the problem in a straightforward way. That person is making use of *all* the information given.

looked them in the reading. First, trial and error works best when there are a limited number of possible solutions. This is illustrated in **Examples 1 and 2. Example 1** is similar to a multiple-choice question, and in **Example 2** it is clear that the polygon with 9 diagonals cannot have very many sides.

Second, sometimes a thoughtful look at a trial that did not work can give clues about a trial that might work. For example, after a trial, students might ask themselves if the answer is greater than or less than their guess and if it is close to or very different from their guess. The answers to these questions can help them to make a better next guess.

Third, organized guessing and a written record of the results improves the efficiency and value of this strategy. **Example 3** illustrates the last two points.

Example 3 serves still another purpose. Many students are intrigued that computers may solve problems by trial and error. For some skeptics, this lends legitimacy to the strategy.

Organizing the Trials

Trial and error works best if the trials are organized. So try possible answers in some logical order and write down your results, noting even the errors. A wrong answer or patterns in wrong answers may lead you to a right answer.

Example 2

A polygon has exactly 9 diagonals. How many sides does the polygon have?

Strategy

Combine two strategies. Draw pictures of various polygons with their diagonals, starting with a triangle. Keep adding a side until a polygon with 9 diagonals is found. Count the diagonals as you draw them.

Solution

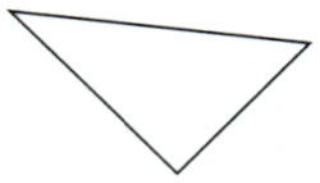

A triangle has 0 diagonals.

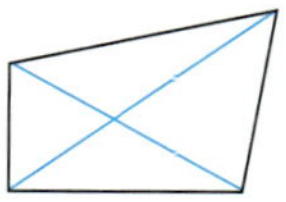

A quadrilateral has 2 diagonals.

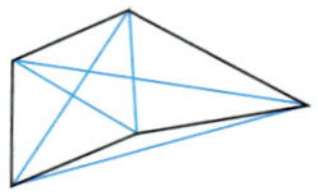

A pentagon has 5 diagonals.

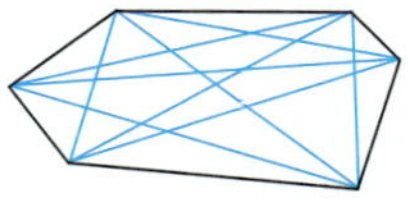

A hexagon has 9 diagonals.

A polygon with 9 diagonals has 6 sides.

Using Technology

Computers and calculators are able to do a lot of calculations very quickly. When there are many possible solutions or complicated calculations, it may be worth the effort to program a computer to do a trial-and-error search. The FOR-NEXT-STEP command sets up a loop to test several values for a variable. FOR assigns a beginning value and an ending value to a variable. NEXT increases the value of the variable by the amount indicated in STEP. If the increase is 1, the STEP part of the command is not needed.

Example 3

Estimate, to the nearest tenth, the positive value of x that satisfies $x^2 + x = 10$.

Solution

First try to estimate x.

Let $x = 1$: $1^2 + 1 = 2$, so 1 is too small.
Let $x = 2$: $2^2 + 2 = 6$, so 2 is too small.
Let $x = 3$: $3^2 + 3 = 12$, so 3 is too big.
Thus $2 < x < 3$.

Optional Activities

Activity 1 You might want to use *Activity Kit, Activity 13,* to introduce this lesson or as a follow-up to the lesson. In this activity, students use trial and error to build a large cube out of smaller ones. Each row and column must show different colors. Then students build a cube in which each row and column have two cubes of the same color.

Activity 2 Technology Connection You may wish to use *Technology Sourcebook, Computer Demonstration 6,* to show students how to use trial and error with the *Spreadsheet Workshop.* Then you could assign *Technology Sourcebook, Computer Master 9.*

Activity 3 Technology Connection *Technology Sourcebook, Calculator Master 8,* involves students in a trial-and-error strategy as they organize and record guesses for solutions to equations and problems involving area and number theory.

Finding x to the nearest tenth requires a more difficult calculation, so a computer program is appropriate.

The following program evaluates and prints $x^2 + x$ for 2.0, 2.1, 2.2, 2.3, . . . , 3.0.

```
10 FOR X = 2 TO 3 STEP .1
20 LET Y = X ^ 2 + X
30 PRINT X, Y
40 NEXT X
50 END
```

When this program is run, the computer will print a table with two columns of numbers. The left column is x. The right column is $x^2 + x$.

2	6
2.1	6.51
2.2	7.04
2.3	7.59
2.4	8.16
2.5	8.75
2.6	9.36
2.7	9.99
2.8	10.64
2.9	11.31
3	12

Read the columns to see that $x^2 + x$ is closest to 10 when $x \approx 2.7$. In fact, since $2.71^2 + 2.71 > 10$, $2.7 < x < 2.71$.

To the nearest tenth, the value of x that satisfies $x^2 + x = 10$ is 2.7.

Some graphing calculators have the capability to make tables like the one in Example 3.

QUESTIONS

Covering the Reading

1. Describe the problem-solving strategy called "trial and error." **Try an answer. If it doesn't work, try another one.**
2. When is trial and error a useful strategy? **when there are only a few possible answers**
3. When using trial and error, what can you do to make the strategy work well? **Organize the trials. Try possible answers in a logical order and write down all results.**

In 4–7, which of the numbers 1, 2, 3, 4, or 5 is a solution?

4. $(x + 7)(x + 2)(x + 3) = 300$ **3**
5. $3y - 2 + 5y = 30$ **4**
6. $1 + \frac{4}{3} = 2$ **3**
7. $11 - x = 7 + x$ **2**
8. What polygons have 5 diagonals? **pentagons**
9. A polygon has 14 diagonals. How many sides does it have? **7**
10. Can a polygon have exactly 10 diagonals? Explain your answer.

10) No, a hexagon has 9 diagonals and a heptagon has 14. The number of diagonals increases as the number of sides increases.

Additional Examples

You might want to use these examples when discussing the lesson.

1. Find the smallest positive integer solution to $x^2 - 7x + 12 = 0$. **3**
2. Is it possible to plant 7 trees so that they lie on 5 lines, 3 of them on each line? **Yes; see sample diagram below.**

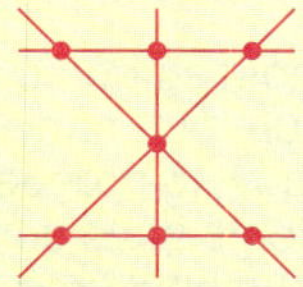

3. Find the number to one decimal place whose cube is closest to 13. **2.4**
4. Find the largest prime number less than 120. **113**

Adapting to Individual Needs

Extra Help

Before using the examples in the book, some students may benefit from answering some easy trial-and-error questions, such as those at the right. For each question, help students determine the approximate size of the trial number by asking questions such as: Will the answer(s) be close to 1, 10, or 100? Why? What is a good number to try first? How does the result of trying this number help in picking the second trial number? Should the second trial be greater than or less than the first? Why? About how much greater or less? Also make sure students understand the need for recording all of their trials in an organized way.

1. The sum of two number is 25 and their product is 100. What are the numbers? [5 and 20]
2. Find 5 coins with a value of 57¢. [2 quarters, 1 nickel, 2 pennies]
3. Find x, if $x^2 = 529$. [23]

LESSON MASTER 6-4 A

Questions on SPUR Objectives
See pages 342-343 for objectives.

Skills Objective B

1. Why is it useful to write down even your errors when using trial and error? **sample: so that you don't repeat the mistakes**

In 2-7, use a trial-and-error strategy.

2. Find a prime number between 110 and 120. **113**
3. Find the solution to the equation $3x - 4 = 8$. **x = 4**
4. The sum of four consecutive integers is 334. What is the greatest of these integers? **85**
5. If n and d are positive integers and $\frac{n}{d} = 3$, what is the least possible value of $n + d$? **4**
6. Use each of 6, 7, 8, and 9 exactly once, and find the two two-digit numbers with the greatest possible product. **96 · 87 = 8,352**
7. Find the number C, to the nearest tenth, so that $C \cdot C \cdot C = 15$. **2.5**

Notes on Questions

Question 13 If students recognize that the sum of the ones digits must end in zero, they can eliminate several trials.

Question 20 Students will probably have to look up the word *dodecagon* in a dictionary.

Question 28 For most students this question is a lot of fun, but many of them have no idea how to proceed. However, once students have solved a problem like this, the next time they encounter a similar problem, it will be easier. Students will solve a similar problem involving multiplication in Lesson 6-7.

One of the quiz shows on the Children's Television Workshop, *Square One TV*™, employs a problem like **Question 28** with a probability twist. The numbers are found by spinning a wheel, and teams must put each number in a place as it comes up. The team with the largest sum wins.

LESSON MASTER 6-4 B Questions on SPUR Objectives

Skills Objective B: Determine solutions to sentences by trial and error.

1. For what kinds of problems is the trial-and-error strategy helpful? It is a good strategy if a question has only a few possible answers.

In 2-10, use trial and error.

2. Find a number between 80 and 90 that has both 3 and 7 as factors. 84

3. Find the number N to the nearest tenth, so that $N \cdot N \cdot N = 18$. $N = 2.6$

4. Find the solution to the equation $7m - 4 = 31$. $m = 5$

5. The product of three consecutive integers is 210. What is the least of these integers? $5;\ 5 \cdot 6 \cdot 7 = 210$

11. In Example 3, how do you know the computer should check numbers between 2 and 3? 2 is too small an estimate; 3 is too big.

12. Use the information in Example 3 to estimate to the nearest tenth the value of x that satisfies $x^2 + x = 7$. $x \approx 2.2$

Applying the Mathematics

In 13–17, trial and error is a useful strategy.

13. Choose one number from each row so that the sum of the numbers is 300.

Row 1:	147	152	128
Row 2:	132	103	118
Row 3:	63	35	41

147, 118, 35

14. Joel was 13 years old in a year in the 1980s when he noticed that his age was a factor of the year. In what year was Joel born? 1976

15. What two positive integers whose sum is 14 have the smallest product? 13 and 1

16.
```
10 FOR N = 1 TO 100
20 IF (N+3) * (N-2) = 696 THEN PRINT N
30 NEXT N
40 END
```

a. What does this program find?

b. Modify the program so that it finds all integer solutions between 1 and 50 to the equation $x(x + 40) = 329$.

c. Modify the program so that it finds all integer solutions between -100 and 100 to $n(n + 18) = \frac{25(3n + 28)}{n}$.

16a) Integer solutions to $(n + 3)(n - 2) = 696$ between 1 and 100

b)
```
10 FOR X = 1 TO 50
20 IF X * (X + 40) = 329
   THEN PRINT X
30 NEXT X
40 END
```

c)
```
10 FOR N = -100 TO 100
20 IF N * (N + 18) =
   (25 * (3 * N + 28))/N
   THEN PRINT N
30 NEXT N
40 END
```

17. Write a computer program to find a positive integer solution to $x^3 + x^2 + x = 2954$. Be sure the program will print the answer. If you have access to a computer, run your program.

17) Sample:
```
10 FOR X = 1 TO 20
20 IF X ^ 3 + X ^ 2 + X =
   2954 THEN PRINT X
30 NEXT X
40 END
```

18. Describe a situation where you have used trial and error to solve a problem outside of math class. Answers will vary.

Review

19. Kenneth is older than Ali and Bill. Carla is younger than Ali and older than Bill. Don is older than Carla but younger than Kenneth. Don is Ali's older brother. If the ages of these people are 11, 12, 13, 14, and 15, who is the 13-year-old? *(Lesson 6-3)* Ali

Adapting to Individual Needs

English Language Development

Students learning a language often use trial and error in communication. They might say something one way and, realizing they are not being understood, try another way. You might have students who are just learning English talk about experiences they have had trying to communicate with classmates.

20. How many sides are in a dodecagon? *(Lesson 6-2)* **12**

21. List all composite numbers between 11 and 23. *(Lesson 6-2)*
12, 14, 15, 16, 18, 20, 21, 22

22. Give an example of the Associative Property of Addition. *(Lesson 5-7)*
Sample: (2 + 3) + 7 = 2 + (3 + 7)

23. Add: $\frac{1}{10} + -\frac{2}{5} + \frac{7}{18}$. Write your answer as a simple fraction.
(Lessons 5-1, 5-3, 5-5) $\frac{4}{45}$

24. Evaluate $2xy + \frac{x}{z}$ when $x = 3$, $y = 4$, and $z = 1.5$. *(Lesson 4-4)* **26**

25. To the nearest tenth of a foot, how many feet are in 50 inches?
(Lesson 3-2) **4.2 feet**

26. Consider the number 5.843%. *(Lessons 1-2, 1-4, 2-4)*
   a. Convert this number to a decimal. **0.05843**
   b. Round the number in part **a** to the nearest thousandth. **0.058**
   c. Between what two integers is this number? **0 and 1**

27. Repeat Question 26 for the number $\frac{99}{70}$. *(Lessons 1-4, 1-6)*
a) $1.4\overline{142857}$; b) 1.414; c) 1 and 2

Exploration

28. Put one of the digits 0, 1, 2, 3, 4, 5, 6, 7, 8, 9, in each circle, using each digit only once. This will form two five-digit numbers.
   a. Make the sum as large as possible. (For example, 53,812 and 64,097 use all the digits, but their sum of 117,909 is easy to beat.)
   b. Make the difference the smallest possible positive number.

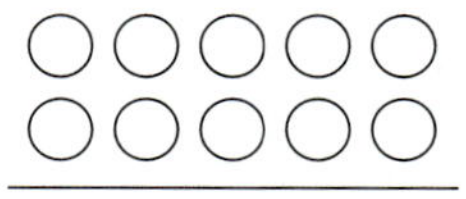

a. Sample: 97531 + 86420 = 183951 **(Each digit of the top number may be switched with the digit below it.)**

b. 50123 − 49876 = 247

Follow-up for Lesson 6-4

Practice

For more questions on SPUR Objectives, use **Lesson Master 6-4A** (show on page 317) or **Lesson Master 6-4B** (shown on pages 318–319).

Assessment

Written Assessment Have students write a paragraph explaining how they would use trial and error to solve a problem. [Explanation includes the idea of organizing trials and using errors to find the correct answer, an example, methods of organizing, and the need for persistence.]

Extension

Writing Have students **work in pairs.** Have each student write a problem which can be solved by using trial and error and then exchange problems with their partners who are to solve them.

Project Update Project 4, *Cryptarithms*, on page 339, relates to the content of this lesson.

Adapting to Individual Needs

Challenge

History Connection Srinivasa Ramanujan, the great Indian mathematician, noticed that 1729 is the smallest prime number that can be written as the sum of two cubes in two ways. One way is $1^3 + 12^3$. Have students find the other way. [$10^3 + 9^3$]

Setting Up Lesson 6-5

Materials: If you plan to use the *Assessment* suggested for Lesson 6-5, students will need lists of long-distance phone costs from your area to other locations. These costs are given in the front of some phone books or they can be obtained from telephone companies.

▸ LESSON MASTER 6-4 B *page 2*

6. Which of the numbers 3, 6, 8, or 11, is the solution to the equation $5m + 2(m - 1) = 54$. **8**

7. What are the smallest composite positive integers x and y such that $\frac{x}{y} = 5$? **$x = 20, y = 4$**

8. Which two of the numbers 12, 27, 31, and 33 have a product between 375 and 400? **12, 33; 12 · 33 = 396**

9. Which number between 20 and 40 has the greatest number of factors? **36; 1, 2, 3, 4, 6, 9, 12, 18, 36**

10. The product of three consecutive odd integers is 1287. What is the greatest of these integers? **13; 9 · 11 · 13 = 1287**

Lesson 6-5

Objectives

E Make a table to find patterns and make generalizations.

Resources

From the ***Teacher's Resource File***
- Lesson Master 6-5A or 6-5B
- Answer Master 6-5
- Teaching Aids
  60 Warm-up
  63 Cost of Phone Calls
  64 Checkerboard (Question 19)
- Activity Kit, Activity 14
- Technology Sourcebook, Calculator Master 9

Additional Resources
- Visuals for Teaching Aids 60, 63, 64
- Long-distance phone rates

Teaching Lesson 6-5

Warm-up

Find the number of dimes and quarters in Sam's pocket. All the dimes can be exchanged for dollar bills. There are twice as many dimes as quarters. The value of the coins is less than \$5.00 but more than \$2.00.
20 dimes, 10 quarters

LESSON

6-5 *Make a Table*

Using a Table to Solve a Problem

Vadim thought he knew everything about diagonals and polygons. But this question had him stumped:

How many diagonals does a 13-gon have?

He read the question carefully. It was easy to understand. He drew a picture of a 13-gon.

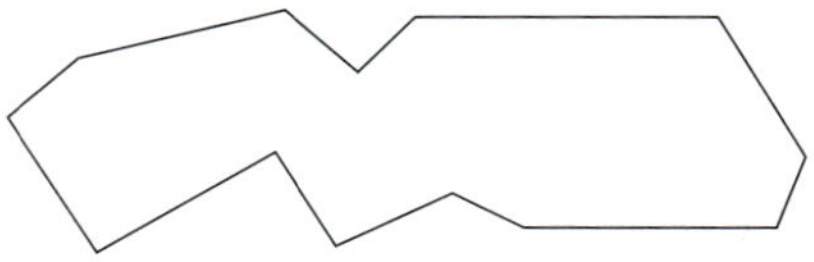

He started drawing diagonals and quickly gave up this approach. He thought about trial and error. He even thought about guessing. He had used all of the strategies of the last three lessons. What could he do?

Sometimes it helps to *make a table.* You saw one table in Example 3 of Lesson 6-4. A **table** is an arrangement with rows and columns. Making a table is just one way of organizing what you know. Vadim's friend Rose recalled the following information from Example 2 of Lesson 6-4. She wrote down a table with two columns.

Number of sides	Number of diagonals
3	0
4	2
5	5
6	9
7	14

Lesson 6-5 Overview

Broad Goals This lesson instructs students in creating tables and making generalizations from them.

Perspective This and the following two lessons discuss problem-solving strategies that are exceedingly useful in algebra. The message here is that it is much easier to make generalizations from a table than from unorganized data. So a table can reduce a complicated problem to one of describing patterns with variables, the focus of Lesson 4-2. Once described, the generalization can be used to answer a specific question or sometimes other similar questions.

This lesson explains one of the fundamental ways in which arithmetic leads to algebra—through patterns. We cannot overemphasize its importance. The time spent on this lesson should require the careful attention of students.

Optional Activities

Activity 1 You might want to use *Activity 14* in the *Activity Kit* to introduce this lesson. In this activity, students stack centimeter cubes in the corner of a shoe box and find a pattern as more cubes are added.

She noticed that the number of diagonals increases by 2, then 3, then 4, then 5. She figured that if the pattern continued, then these would be the next three rows of the table.

8	20
9	27
10	35

She checked her work by drawing an octagon. It did have 20 diagonals. So she continued the pattern and answered Vadim's question. (You are asked to do this yourself in the questions following this lesson.)

Reasons for Making a Table

In solving problems, there are three reasons for making a table.

1. A table organizes your thoughts.
2. It helps you find patterns.
3. It can help you to make a *generalization.*

Using a Table to Make a Generalization

A **generalization** is a statement that is true about many instances. The following story is about making a generalization.

Francie lives in Phoenix. She has a telephone in her room. She pays for all long-distance calls she makes. One Sunday she called her cousin Meg in San Diego. As they talked, Francie forgot about the time. They talked for at least an hour! She called her long-distance operator for rates and found that it cost \$.25 for the first minute and \$.18 for each additional minute. She had a problem.

> What is the cost of a one-hour phone call, if the first minute costs \$.25 and each additional minute costs \$.18?

Francie began by making a table.

Number of minutes talked	Cost of phone call
1	\$.25
2	.43
3	.61
4	.79
5	.97

It wasn't working at all. Yet the pattern was simple. You add .18 to get the next cost. But she wanted to know the cost for 60 minutes. She did not want to add .18 all those times. She might make a mistake, even with a calculator.

Notes on Reading

You might want to use *Activity 1* in *Optional Activities* below to introduce this lesson.

You also might wish to have students read this lesson aloud in class. As they read, display the tables and go over them carefully searching for patterns. Stress that making a table and looking for a pattern takes time.

1 Don't volunteer answers for the next two lines in Rose's table unless the students have done *Covering the Reading.* **Questions 1 and 2** in that section ask for the number of diagonals in a 10-gon and an 11-gon.

An expression for the number of diagonals is $\frac{n(n-3)}{2}$, but students are not expected to find this generalization at this time.

Optional Activities

Activity 2

Materials: Newspapers and magazines

After students have read the lesson, you might have them **work in groups** and look through newspapers and magazines to find examples of organized lists, such as tables, charts, and graphs. Then have them select one list and discuss whether the way the data are organized makes them easier to understand. They might also suggest other ways in which the data could have been organized.

Activity 3 Technology Connection In *Technology Sourcebook, Calculator Master 9,* students make a table recording patterns that lead to finding the sum of the exterior angles of an *n*-gon.

LESSON MASTER 6-5 A

Questions on SPUR Objectives
See pages 342-343 for objectives.

Properties Objective E

In 1-4, make a table to help you answer each question.

1. The Cruzes have an account to save for the family vacation. They started with \$175 in the account and added \$25 each week. How much was in the account after 6 weeks? after 15 weeks? after *n* weeks? after a year?

Week	Added	Total
1	25	200
2	25	225
3	25	250
⋮	⋮	⋮

\$325; \$550; \$175 + \$25*n*; \$1,475

2. What is the first odd natural number? the second? the fifth? the *n*th? the 156th?

1st	2nd	3rd	. . .
1	3	5	. . .

1; 3; 9; $2n - 1$; 311

3. Maria's parents wanted to encourage her to save for college. They agreed to match the amount of money in her account at the end of every school year. If she saved \$600 each of the four years she was in high school and withdrew only the interest, how much did Maria have when she graduated?

Yr.	Begin.	Maria	Parents	Ending
1	0	600	600	1200
2	1200	600	1800	3600
3	3600	600	4200	8400
4	8400	600	9000	18,000

\$18,000

4. Complete this chart.

1	2^0	1
2	$2^0 + 2^1$	$1 + 2 = 3$
3	$2^0 + 2^1 + 2^2$	$1 + 2 + 4 = 7$
4	$2^0 + 2^1 + 2^2 + 2^3$	$1 + 2 + 4 + 8 = 15$
5	$2^0 + 2^1 + 2^2 + 2^3 + 2^4$	$1 + 2 + 4 + 8 + 16 = 31$
6	$2^0 + 2^1 + 2^2 + \ldots + 2^5$	$1 + 2 + 4 + \ldots + 32 = 63$
n	$2^0 + 2^1 + 2^2 + \ldots + 2^n$	$1 + 2 + \ldots + 2^{n-1} = 2^n - 1$

❷ The second table, involving the cost of a phone call, displays a subtle strategy for coming up with an algebraic formula. Notice that Francie works out all the arithmetic. George does not, and, because he doesn't, the original information is present in his table. George does less work and also generates a more effective table.

Students can fill in the table on **Teaching Aid 63** using either Francie's method or George's method for finding the costs. Then they can continue using the table as they answer **Questions 4–7.**

Making a Table is an exceedingly useful strategy. Carefully review the examples in class to make sure everyone understands. Students should also be aware that making tables and looking for patterns are time-consuming activities.

Additional Examples

You might want to use these examples when discussing the lesson.

1. In a concert hall, there are 25 seats in the first row. In each succeeding row, there is an additional seat on each end of the row. Therefore, the second row has 27 seats, the third row 29 seats, and so on. How many seats are in the 6th row? the 25th row? the *n*th row? **35 seats; 73 seats; 25 + 2(*n* – 1)**

❷ George helped Francie by rewriting the costs to show a different pattern.

Number of minutes talked	Cost of phone call
1	\$.25
2	.25 + .18
3	.25 + 2 · .18
4	.25 + 3 · .18
5	.25 + 4 · .18

"Look across the rows," he said. "See what stays the same and what changes." George noted that in the right column, the only number that changes is the number multiplied by .18. It is always one less than the number in the left column. So,

60	.25 + 59 · .18

"Now you can calculate the cost." Francie did the calculations.

.25 + 59 · .18 = 10.87

The cost of her phone call was over \$10.87!

George and Francie then realized that the table makes it possible to write a formula—a general pattern—for the cost.

m	$.25 + (m - 1) \cdot .18$

If Francie spoke for m minutes, it would cost $.25 + (m - 1) \cdot .18$ dollars, not including tax.

The formula enables you to find the cost for any number of minutes easily. It is a generalization made from the pattern the instances formed in the table.

QUESTIONS

Covering the Reading

In 1–3, use information given in this lesson.

1. How many diagonals does a 10-gon have? **35**
2. How many diagonals does an 11-gon have? **44**
3. Answer the question Vadim could not answer. **65 diagonals**

In 4–7, refer to the story with Francie in this lesson.

4. If Francie had talked to her cousin Meg for only 5 minutes, what would have been the cost of the phone call? **\$0.97**
5. If Francie had talked to her cousin Meg for 30 minutes, what would have been the cost of the call? **\$5.47**
6. In the story about Francie, what generalization did George and Francie make? **The cost of an *m*-minute call for Francie is .25 + (*m* – 1) · .18 dollars.**

LESSON MASTER 6-5 B **Questions on SPUR Objectives**

Vocabulary

1. What is a generalization?
A generalization is a statement that is true for many instances.

2. List three reasons for making a table.
sample: A table organizes your thoughts; it helps you to find patterns; and it can help you make generalizations.

Properties Objective E: Make a table to find patterns and make generalizations.

In 3-6, make a table to help you answer each question.

3. The Fong family has started a college fund for their new baby. They started with \$700 the first month and plan to add \$75 each month. How much will be in the account after 6 months? after 12 months? after *n* months? after 10 years?

Months	In Account
1	\$700
2	\$700 + \$75
3	\$700 + 2 · \$75
4	\$700 + 3 · \$75
5	\$700 + 4 · \$75
6	\$700 + 5 · \$75
12	\$700 + 11 · \$75
n	\$700 + (*n* – 1)\$75
120	\$700 + 119 · \$75

6 mo: \$1075; 12 mo: \$1525; *n* mo: \$700 + (*n* – 1)\$75; 10 yr: \$9625

4. What is the first positive multiple of 5? the second? the fifth? the *n*th? the 127th?

No. of Multiple	1	2	3	4	5	*n*	127
Multiple	5	10	15	20	25	5*n*	635

1st: 5; 2nd: 10; 5th: 25; *n*th: 5*n*; 127th: 635

Adapting to Individual Needs

Extra Help

As suggested earlier, some students have trouble because they have not learned to approach a situation in an organized way. Use tables like the one on **Teaching Aid 63** and work with students to ensure they fill it in properly.

Encourage students who are unable to express generalizations using variables, to explain them in their own words.

English Language Development

The problems involving phone rates and postal rates might prompt a discussion of such rates in other countries. Encourage students who have come from other countries to share with the class the telephone and postal rates in these countries, as well as the rates between the United States and these countries.

7. For a two-hour phone call to Meg, what would it cost Francie? **\$21.67**

8. a. What is a *generalization?*
   b. Give an example. **a) a statement that is true about many instances; b) Sample: Every polygon has an equal number of sides and angles.**

9. Erich wants to call his cousin Inge in Germany. The cost for a late-night call is \$1.45 for the first minute and 81¢ for each additional minute.
   a. Make a table indicating the cost for calls lasting 1, 2, 3, 4, and 5 minutes.
   b. What is the cost of a 25-minute call? **\$20.89**
   c. What is the cost of a call lasting *m* minutes? **1.45 + (m – 1) · .81 dollars**

9a)

Number of minutes	Cost
1	\$1.45
2	\$1.45 + .81
3	\$1.45 + 2 · .81
4	\$1.45 + 3 · .81
5	\$1.45 + 4 · .81

Applying the Mathematics

10. Make a table to help answer this question: In a 50-gon, all the diagonals from *one* particular vertex are drawn. How many triangles are formed? **48 triangles**

10)

Number of sides	Number of triangles
3	1
4	2
5	3
6	4
.	.
.	.
.	.
n	$n - 2$

11. In 1993, it cost 29¢ to mail a one-ounce first-class letter. It cost 23¢ for each additional ounce or part of an ounce up to 11 ounces.
    a. What was the cost to mail a letter weighing 4 ounces? **98¢**
    b. What was the cost to mail a letter weighing 9.5 ounces? **\$2.36**
    c. What was the cost to mail a letter weighing *w* ounces, if *w* is a whole number? **.29 + (w – 1) · .23 dollars**

12. Calculate enough of the sums

$$1 + 2$$
$$1 + 2 + 4$$
$$1 + 2 + 4 + 8$$
$$\vdots$$

so that you see a pattern in the sums and can give the answer to

$$2^0 + 2^1 + 2^2 + 2^3 + \ldots + 2^{20}$$

without adding. (You are allowed to use a calculator, but not the [+] key on it.) **$2^{21} - 1 = 2{,}097{,}151$**

The Pacific Northwest is known for its flowers. Shown here is Farmers' Market in Seattle, Washington.

Review

13. To drive from Seattle to Chehalis, you must first drive from Seattle to Tacoma, then from Tacoma to Olympia, and finally from Olympia to Chehalis. It is 4 miles farther from Seattle to Tacoma than from Tacoma to Olympia. And it is 4 miles farther from Tacoma to Olympia than from Olympia to Chehalis. If it is 84 miles from Seattle to Chehalis, how far is it from Tacoma to Olympia? *(Lessons 6-3, 6-4)* **28 miles**

2. Consider the pattern of sums of odd integers:
   1 = 1
   1 + 3 = 4
   1 + 3 + 5 = 9
   a. Make three more rows of the pattern.
   1 + 3 + 5 + 7 = 16
   1 + 3 + 5 + 7 + 9 = 25
   1 + 3 + 5 + 7 + 9 + 11 = 36
   b. Explain the pattern using words or variables.
   The sum of the first *n* positive odd integers is n^2.
   c. Find the sum of
   1 + 3 + 5 + 7 + . . . + 91 + 93 + 95 + 97 + 99.
   (This is the sum of the positive odd integers less than 100.)
   50^2 or 2500

Notes on Questions

Questions 4–7 Students can use the table on **Teaching Aid 63** with these questions.

Question 10 Point out that making a table with entries to 50 is inefficient and misses the point of the lesson. Stress that the table should be used to find patterns and make generalizations. After students see the generalization, it is no longer necessary to test 50 instances.

▶ **LESSON MASTER 6-5 B** *page 2*

5. Mrs. Herrera is saving for her retirement through a special company fund. At the end of each year, the company adds to the fund half the amount Mrs. Herrera has in the fund. If Mrs. Herrera pays \$2,000 into the fund each year, how much will be in the fund after 5 years?

No. of Years	Balance
1	\$2,000 + \$1,000 = \$3,000
2	\$5,000 + \$2,500 = \$7,500
3	\$9,500 + \$4,750 = \$14,250
4	\$16,250 + \$8,125 = \$24,375
5	\$26,375 + \$13,187.50 = \$39,562.50

\$39,562.50

6. Complete this chart.

	Odd Numbers	Sum
1	1	$1 = 1^2$
2	1, 3	$1 + 3 = 4 = 2^2$
3	1, 3, 5	$1 + 3 + 5 = 9 = 3^2$
4	1, 3, 5, 7	$1 + 3 + 5 + 7 = 16 = 4^2$
5	1, 3, 5, 7, 9	$1 + 3 + 5 + 7 + 9 = 25 = 5^2$
6	1, 3, 5, 7, 9, 11	$1 + 3 + 5 + \ldots + 11 = 36 = 6^2$
7	1, 3, 5, 7, 9, 11, 13	$1 + 3 + 5 + \ldots + 13 = 49 = 7^2$
n	1, 3, 5, . . ., $2n - 1$	$1 + 3 + 5 + \ldots + 2n - 1 = n^2$

Adapting to Individual Needs

Challenge

Have students use *Additional Example 2* to write the generalization for the sum of the first *n* odd numbers and the first *n* nonzero even numbers. [n^2; $n(n + 1)$] Then have them find these sums.

1. The first 500 odd numbers (the odd numbers 1 through 1000) [250,000]
2. The first 500 even numbers (the even numbers 1 through 1000) [250,500]
3. The whole numbers 1 through 1000 [500,500]
4. The whole numbers 1 through 1,000,000? [500,000,500,000]

To find the answer to Question 3, students can add their answers to Questions 1 and 2. They can find the answer to Question 4 in a similar way. Some students might also try to find a generalization for the sum of the first *n* nonzero whole numbers. It is $\frac{n(n+1)}{2}$.

Notes on Questions

Question 14 Finding an intelligent process for narrowing the possible solutions is more interesting than finding the answer. The power, 343, is odd and ends in 3, so *x* and *y* must be odd and cannot be 5. For 1, the power would be too small and for 9 it would probably be too big. Thus, the possibilities to test are powers of 3 and 7.

Question 19 Students can use **Teaching Aid 64** with this question.

Follow-up for Lesson 6-5

Practice

For more questions on SPUR Objectives, use **Lesson Master 6-5A** (shown on page 321) or **Lesson Master 6-5B** (shown on pages 322–323).

Assessment

Group Assessment

Materials: List of long-distance telephone rates

Have students **work in groups**. Give each group a list of long-distance phone rates. Have them decide where they want to call, determine the rate(s) that apply, and then find the cost of both a 10-minute call and an *m*-minute call. [Creates an organized table and cites an appropriate generalization for *m*.]

Extension

Multicultural Connection

After students answer **Question 19,** you might want to tell the class more about the game of Checkers. Checkers, also called draughts, is one of the world's oldest games. Early forms of Checkers were played by the Egyptian pharaohs around 1600 B.C. The Greek writers Homer and Plato mentioned the games in their writings. Around the 12th century, the game was adapted to the 64-square board. By the 16th century, it evolved to be similar to the game of checkers we know today. Then you might have students choose a game they like to play and prepare a report describing winning strategies for the game.

Project Update Project 1, *Diagonals of a Regular Polygon,* on page 338, relates to the content of this lesson.

14. $x^y = 343$ and x and y are integers between 1 and 10. Find x and y. *(Lessons 2-2, 6-4)* **x = 7 and y = 3**

15.
```
10 FOR X = 10 TO 30 STEP .5
20 IF X ^ 4 + X ^ 2 = 360900.3125 THEN PRINT "X =";X
30 NEXT X
40 END
```
a. What problem does this program solve?
b. How many values for x will it test? **41**
c. If you have a computer, run the program and record the output. *(Lesson 6-4)* **X = 24.5**

15a) It tests the numbers from 10 to 30 at .5 intervals as possible solutions to the equation $x^4 + x^2 = 360900.3125$.

16. One type of polygon is the *undecagon.* How many sides does an undecagon have? *(Lesson 6-2)* **11**

17. Mabel was 5 pounds overweight. Now she is 3 pounds underweight. Let c be the change in her weight.
a. Write an equation relating 5, 3, and c. **$5 + c = {}^-3$**
b. Find c. *(Lesson 5-8)* **$c = {}^-8$ pounds**

18. List all the factors of 54. *(Lesson 1-10)* **1, 2, 3, 6, 9, 18, 27, 54**

Exploration

19. Find the number of squares on a regular 8 × 8 checkerboard. (Include squares of all possible sizes.) **204**

Setting Up Lesson 6-6

Lesson 6-6 is an activity-based lesson; it is meant to be read while having access to a computer. Should computers not be available on the day you reach the lesson, you may delay the lesson until after Lesson 6-7. However, the questions can be answered without a computer.

We strongly recommend that you do these activities yourself before having your students do them.

LESSON

6-6

Use a Spreadsheet

Spreading the workload. *Many companies use computer spreadsheets to help them keep track of their inventory. This woman is checking to see if the store's inventory matches the computer records.*

What Is a Spreadsheet?

A **spreadsheet** is a table, usually with many rows and columns. In 1978, the first electronic spreadsheet, VisiCalc, was created by Dan Bricklin and Bob Frankston. Before this time, spreadsheets were used primarily by accountants and other people to keep track of income and expenses for companies. Now there are spreadsheet programs available for every computer and some calculators can deal with them. They are used by many people to organize, explore, and analyze information. Spreadsheets have become all-purpose tools for storing information and solving problems.

	A	B	C	D
1				
2				
3				
4				
5	Gym Shorts			
6			24	
7				

Spreadsheets are made up of **columns** and **rows.** Columns are vertical and labeled by capital letters. Rows are horizontal and are labeled by numbers. The intersection of each column and row is a **cell.** The label Gym Shorts is located in cell A5 which is in column A and row 5. In cell C6 is the number 24.

Lesson 6-6

Objectives

J Use a spreadsheet to answer questions in real situations.

Resources

From the ***Teacher's Resource File***

- Lesson Master 6-6A or 6-6B
- Answer Master 6-6
- Assessment Sourcebook: Quiz for Lessons 6-4 through 6-6
- Teaching Aids
  60 Warm-up
  65 Spreadsheet
  66 Additional Examples
- Technology Sourcebook, Computer Master 10

Additional Resources

- Visuals for Teaching Aids 60, 65, 66
- Spreadsheet Workshop

Teaching Lesson 6-6

Warm-up

Make a table showing how much you would earn for 1 through 5 hours of baby-sitting. Include hourly rates of $2 an hour, $3 an hour, and $4 an hour. Shade the place in the table that shows how much you would earn if you were paid $3 an hour for 4 hours. Explain how to find this location in your table. **Sample table shown below. To find $3 for 4 hr in this table, go across the $3 row to the 4 hr column.**

	1 hr	2 hr	3 hr	4 hr	5 hr
$2	$2	$4	$6	$8	$10
$3	$3	$6	$9	$12	$15
$4	$4	$8	$12	$16	$20

Lesson 6-6 Overview

Broad Goals Students should learn how a spreadsheet works and how it can be used to make tables that solve problems.

Perspective For hundreds of years, financial records have been kept in spreadsheets. What is different about computer spreadsheets is that they can be easily programmed so that filling certain cells automatically fills others. Thus, sums, products, square roots, and virtually any of the common operations normally done with numbers can be automatically put into cells. It is like programming, but it is the easiest programming imaginable.

The language used in this lesson is that found with Microsoft Excel™. There may be slight differences with other software. In Excel, the equal sign is the signal that the entry into a cell will be a formula rather than the symbols typed. For example, typing "= B6 * C6" in cell D6 tells the computer to multiply the number in cell B6 by the number in cell C6 and to put the product into cell D6. Typing "B6 * C6" simply places the symbols into cell D6.

As in computer programs, everything is written on one line, so the slash / is used for division, ^ is used for powers, and parentheses are used if the denominator consists of more than one term.

Notes on Reading

It is intended that this reading be done with access to a computer. You can save time by loading the spreadsheet software onto each machine before class begins. All students should have an opportunity to enter data and formulas. It is possible that some of your students may have worked with spreadsheet packages in another class or at home. If so, they can help others learn how to use spreadsheets.

You should be aware that **Activity 1** gives students practice in typing and in using the proper language to describe the cells in a spreadsheet. Step 1 in **Activity 2** shows the first formula. Step 2 introduces the idea of copying a formula from one cell to another. **Activity 3** completes the work from **Activity 2.** Copying a formula from one cell to another saves enormous amounts of time and is used in **Activity 4** to create a table that answers a question from Lesson 6-5.

If computers are not available, you might use the suggestions given in *Activity 1* in *Optional Activities* below.

Students should record the results of **Activities 1–4** for use with questions on pages 329–331.

Entering Information into a Spreadsheet

To use a spreadsheet, you must know how to enter information into its cells. Here is a sample spreadsheet for a school supply store.

	A	B	C	D	E	F	G
1		January	Sales				
2							
3	Item	Unit Price	Number Sold	Total Sales			
4							
5	Gym Shorts	6.00	15				
6	Shirts	8.00	24				
7	Sweatshirts	12.00	32				
8	Tablets	.60	38				
9	Pencils	.10	123				
10	Folders	.50	21				
11							
12	Monthly Sales						

Activity 1

Create the spreadsheet shown above.

Step 1

Turn on your computer and load in your spreadsheet package. The cell which is highlighted or in a different color is called the **active cell.** It is the cell that takes the information you type. You can change the active cell by pressing the arrow keys: → for right, ← for left, ↑ for up, and ↓ for down. With some machines, you can change cells by using a mouse.

Step 2

Use the arrow keys or mouse to make cell B1 the active cell.
Type: January
Make C1 the active cell.
Type: Sales
Make A3 the active cell.
Continue typing until you have entered all of columns A, B, and C. If you make a mistake, use the arrow keys to go back, and then type over your mistakes.

Cells can hold formulas as well as numbers and words. Each formula indicates how a number in a particular place in the spreadsheet is computed from other numbers in the spreadsheet. When a number is changed, the computer uses the formula to change the other numbers in the spreadsheet automatically.

Optional Activities

Activity 1 If you do not have access to computers for this lesson, you still might want to discuss the lesson as a class activity. Have students **work in groups.** Give all students copies of the spreadsheet on **Teaching Aid 65.** On one copy have them reproduce the spreadsheet shown on page 326. Then have them manually compute and insert the information given in Activities 1, 2, and 3 on pages 326 and 327 in the Pupil's Edition.

Students can use other copies of the spreadsheet for Activity 4 and the questions. You will want to alter some of the spreadsheet activities if students are working manually. For example, Activity 4 asks students to find the cost of a 60-minute phone call. You might limit it to a 10-minute call.

Activity 2 Technology Connection *Technology Sourcebook, Computer Master 10,* has students use the *Spreadsheet Workshop* to compare membership plans for a health club. One plan has a $50 monthly fee and a $1 fee per visit. The second plan has no monthly fee and a $4 fee per visit. Students use the spreadsheet to decide which plan is less expensive for certain numbers of visits.

Activity 2

Use the spreadsheet you created in Activity 1 to calculate total sales.

	A	B	C	D
1		January	Sales	
2				
3	Item	Unit Price	Number Sold	Total Sales
4				
5	Gym Shorts	6.00	15	=B5*C5

Step 1

Each number in column D, Total Sales, is the product of a value in column B and a value in column C. For instance, the Total Sales for Gym Shorts is the product of the number in cell B5 and the number in cell C5. So in cell D5, enter the formula = B5 * C5. Now press the enter key.

	A	B	C	D
1		January	Sales	
2				
3	Item	Unit Price	Number Sold	Total Sales
4				
5	Gym Shorts	6.00	15	90.00

You should see 90, or 90.00, displayed in cell D5.

Note: Different spreadsheets have different methods for entering formulas. Some choices are: an equal sign (=) in front of the formula, parentheses, or an arithmetic operator. You will need to know what your spreadsheet requires.

Step 2

Fill in cells D6 through D10. One way to do this is to type = B6 * C6 in cell D6, = B7 * C7 in cell D7, and so on. However, most spreadsheets have a way of copying formulas from one cell to another. The command may be called COPY, FILL, or REPLICATE. Use this command to copy cell D5. Now paste it onto cells D6, D7, D8, D9, and D10. You should see the correct values for Total Sales appear in the appropriate cells.

Row 12 of the spreadsheet can now be completed.

Activity 3

Find the Monthly Sales Total for the data you entered in Activity 1.

Activate cell D12 and enter the formula needed. What were the total sales?

Adapting to Individual Needs

Extra Help

As you discuss the reading, be sure students understand what the formulas tell the computer to do and why. For example, before students can understand the formula for computing the total sales in **Activity 2** (Step 1), they must understand the mathematics behind computing this number, i.e. multiplying the price per item (unit price) by the number of items sold. You might also emphasize that the formula = B5 * C5, rather than 6 × 15, is written in cell D5 because 6 or 15 might change. For example, suppose 8 more sales need to be included for January. Changing cell C5 to 23 will automatically change cell D5 to 138.00 if the formula is used. Without the formula, 23 × 6.00 has to be calculated and the product entered in D5.

Notes on Reading

In **Activity 4,** if you are using the *Spreadsheet Workshop* with this lesson, give students these instructions to do in place of Steps 2 and 3. In cell A3, enter 60. In cell B3, enter the formula .25 + (A3 – 1)*.18. To find the price for a different number of minutes, simply change the number in cell A3.

Additional Examples

These additional examples require a computer. **Teaching Aid 66** contains all of these examples.

1. Create a spreadsheet that resembles the table of sides and diagonals from Lesson 6-5.

	A	B
1	No. of sides	No. of diagonals
2	3	0
3	4	2
4	5	5
5	6	9
6	7	14
7	8	20
8	9	27
9	10	35

2. **a.** Use the spreadsheet form and enter the formula = A9 + 1 in cell A10. What do you see? **11**
   b. Copy the formula from cell A10 onto cells A11 through A15. What do you see? **12, 13, 14, 15, 16**
   c. Enter the formula = B9 + A9 – 1 in cell B10. What do you see? **44**
   d. Copy the formula from cell B10 onto cells B11 through B15. What do you see? **54, 65, 77, 90, 104**
   e. According to this pattern, what is the number of diagonals in a 15-gon? **90 diagonals**

(Additional Examples continue on page 329.)

Saving and Updating a Spreadsheet

You should save your work on a **data disk.** Sometimes, you will also want a printed copy of the table you have produced. The commands used for saving and printing vary with the computer and with the spreadsheet package being used. Make sure you know how to save and print with the package you use.

Once formulas are in a spreadsheet, any change in the cells used in the formula will result in automatic recalculation. For example, suppose 27 shirts rather than 24 shirts had been sold. If 27 is typed in cell C6, cell D6 will automatically change to 216. To update the spreadsheet for February, you could change cell B1 to February and put the February sales figures in column C. If any unit prices change, then update column B. The totals in column D for February will be calculated automatically.

Problem Solving with a Spreadsheet

The next activity shows the power of a spreadsheet to solve mathematical problems. Here is a question from Lesson 6-5.

Activity 4

Use a spreadsheet to determine the cost of a one-hour phone call, if the first minute costs $.25 and each additional minute costs $.18.

Step 1

Create the following skeleton for the spreadsheet.

	A	B
1	Minutes	Cost
2	1	.25
3		
4		
5		
6		

Step 2

To enter the consecutive integers 2, 3, 4, 5, . . . in the cells of column A, first type = A2 + 1 in cell A3. Then copy that cell onto cells A4 to A61.

Step 3

To increase each consecutive value in column B by .18, type = B2 + .18 in cell B3. Then copy that cell onto cells B4 through B61. The answer to the question of the activity should be found in row 61.

Adapting to Individual Needs

English Language Development

Students just learning English may have used spreadsheets and understand how they work, but may have difficulty with the terminology. For these students, give special attention to terms like *cells, active cells, columns*, and *rows* as they relate to the spreadsheet.

QUESTIONS

Covering the Reading

1. What is a spreadsheet? a table made up of columns and rows

2. Explain two uses of a spreadsheet. Sample: to organize information and to solve problems

In 3–5, what is displayed in the given cell of the spreadsheet in Activity 1?

3. C5 15 4. A10 Folders 5. B8 .60

In 6 and 7, refer to the spreadsheet in Activity 1.

6. Give the heading for row 7. Sweatshirts

7. Give the heading for column B. January

8. What is meant by the active cell? the highlighted cell; it takes the information you type

9. How do you change the active cell? by pressing the arrow keys or using a mouse

In 10 and 11, refer to the spreadsheet in Activity 2.

10. a. What is the formula for cell D8? =B8*C8
 b. What values appear in the other cells of column D? D5 = 90, D6 = 192, D7 = 384, D8 = 22.8, D9 = 12.3, D10 = 10.5

11. What happens within the spreadsheet if the value in cell B7 is changed to 15? cell D7 changes to 480

12. Formulas are entered with a symbol typed in front of them. What symbol do you need to use on your computer? = (Answers may vary.)

13. a. What formula did you type for Activity 3?
 b. What is the result?
 a) = D5 + D6 + D7 + D8 + D9 + D10; b) 711.60

14. When were electronic spreadsheets first introduced? 1978

In 15 and 16, refer to Activity 4.

15. What formulas are entered in cells A6 and B6? in A6: = A5 + 1; in B6: = B5 +.18

16. What formula is in row 51? in A51: = A50 + 1; in B51: = B50 + .18

3. Use the spreadsheet to determine the number of diagonals in a 25-sided polygon. 275

4. Suppose a rental car agency charges \$31.95 per day plus \$.30 a mile beyond 200 miles to rent a car.
 a. Create the following skeleton for the spreadsheet.

	A	B
1	miles	cost
2	200	31.95
3		

 b. Type = A2 + 1 in cell A3, and = B2 + .30 in cell B3. What do you see in A? In B? 201; 32.25
 c. Create enough additional rows on the spreadsheet so that you can determine the cost of driving this car 234 miles in a single day. \$42.15

Adapting to Individual Needs

Challenge
Health Connection

Materials: Nutritional information for common foods

Have students explain how using a spreadsheet might help them keep track of calories or show them if they are getting all the nutrients their bodies need. [Answers will vary. Students might include example formulas for calculating nutritional information such as calories, fat, and cholesterol.] If computers are available, students might make the spreadsheet. Then they can keep track of nutritional information about the foods they eat over a period of time, such as a week.

LESSON MASTER 6-6 A

Questions on SPUR Objectives
See pages 342-343 for objectives.

Representations Objective J

1. Give two reasons why use of spreadsheets is so common. They are useful for organizing data; information is clear; more computers are in use.

2. Complete this spreadsheet using 4% as the sales-tax rate.

	A	B	C	D
1	Item	Price	Sales Tax	Total Cost
2	CD	14.75	.59	15.34
3	Baseball	3.25	.13	3.38
4	Jeans	29.50	1.18	30.68
5	Mom's birthday	20.00	.80	20.80
6	Total	67.50	2.70	70.20

3. What is in cell A4? "Jeans" 4. "Price" is in what cell? B1

5. What formula could you use in cell C2? =B2*.04

6. What formula could you use in cell D2? =B2+C2

7. What formula could you use in cell B6? =B2+B3+B4+B5

8. Describe how you would finish filling in the cells of the spreadsheet after completing Questions 5, 6, and 7.
C3 =B3*.04; C4 =B4*.04; C5 =B5*.04; C6 = C2+C3+C4+C5; D3 =B3+C3; D4 =B4+C4; D5 =B5+C5; D6 =D2+D3+D4+D5

9. What appears in cell D6? (Use a spreadsheet, if possible.) \$70.20

10. Design a spreadsheet to determine the test average of five students on 3 exams and use formulas wherever possible. If you have access to a computer, enter and print your spreadsheet. Three rows are shown.

	A	B	C	D	E
1	St.	T1	T2	T3	Average
2	a				(B2 + C2 + D2)/3
3	b				(B3 + C3 + D3)/3
4	c				(B4 + C4 + D4)/3

Notes on Questions

Question 21 This is the only question of the set that asks students to create a spreadsheet. If computers are not available, students should still show what a spreadsheet would look like, and they should attempt to answer **part b**. They could use the spreadsheet on **Teaching Aid 65.**

Questions 22–23 If you are using the *Spreadsheet Workshop*, have students substitute *x***x* for *x*^2 and so on. In **Question 23,** answers will take the form: **part a** is A2*A2, **part b** is A3*B3, **part c** is A4*C4, and **part d** is B2*C2.

Question 24 The power of the spreadsheet is that only the cells in column B need to be changed manually. The cells in column D will automatically change with them.

Question 25 Students could create a spreadsheet to answer specific cases, but the spreadsheet does not display the formulas in a way that makes it easy to answer **part c.**

Question 27 Trial and error is a reasonable strategy to use because there are few such numbers.

Question 28 Error Alert Some students might write $\frac{1}{1}$, thinking that "lowest terms" means writing a fraction. We believe that when a fraction equals an integer, the answer should not be written in fraction form unless the situation requires the fraction.

LESSON MASTER 6-6 B **Questions on SPUR Objectives**

Representations Objective J: Use a spreadsheet to answer questions in real situations.

1. Describe a situation where it would be helpful to use a spreadsheet.
sample: keeping track of orders and sales

2. Use this spreadsheet to determine 12% shipping and handling costs.

	A	B	C	D
1	Item	Price	Shipping and Handling	Total Cost
2	Toaster	29.75	3.57	33.32
3	Shoes	54.99	6.60	61.59
4	Cookbook	12.40	1.49	13.89
5	Tape deck	169.50	20.34	189.84
6	Total	266.64	32.00	298.64

a. What is in cell A3? "Shoes"

b. "Price" is in what cell? B1

c. What formula could you use in cell C2? =B2*.12

d. What formula could you use in cell D2? =B2+C2

e. What formula could you use in cell B6? =B2+B3+B4+B5

f. Describe how you would complete filling in the cells of the spreadsheet after completing parts c, d, and e.
Multiply each B cell by .12 to get C cells. Then add each B cell and C cell to its right to get D cell to their right. To find C6, add C2, C3, C4, and C5. To find D6, add B6 and C6.

g. What appears in cell D6? (Use a spreadsheet, if possible.) 298.64

Applying the Mathematics

In 17–20, use the spreadsheet for Nautilus Subs shown below.

	A	B	C	D	E	F	G
1	Sandwich	Quantity	Small	Quantity	Large	Item Total	
2							
3	Tuna Salad		3.00		4.35		
4	Ham & Cheese		3.25		4.65		
5	Turkey		3.75		5.65		
6	Roast Beef		4.00		5.95		
7	Italian		4.75		6.75		
8							
9	Beverages						
10							
11	Soda		.60		.75		
12	Milk		.40		.55		
13	Coffee		.50		.65		
14							
15					Subtotal:		
16					Tax:		
17							
18					Total:		

17. Fill in the blanks to give a formula for cell F3.
= B3 * C3 + D3 * E3

18. What is a formula for cell F15?
= F3 + F4 + F5 + F6 + F7 + F11 + F12 + F13

19. If the tax is 5%, what is a formula for cell F16? = .05*F15

20. Nancy and Chuck plan to stop at Nautilus Subs for dinner.

a. If they order a large turkey sandwich, a small tuna salad sandwich, two large sodas, and one small milk, what entries will the cashier make in the spreadsheet? In D5: 1; in B3: 1; in D11: 2; in B12: 1

b. What is the formula in cell F18? = F15 + F16

c. What will be shown in that cell? 11.0775

21. a. Create a spreadsheet that lists times and costs for a phone call to Nigeria if the cost is $1.19 for the first minute and 79¢ for each additional minute.

b. What will it cost for a 27-minute phone call? $21.73

21a)

	A	B
1	Minutes	Cost
2	1	1.19
3		
4		

Cell A3 is =A2+1 and so on; cell B3 is =B2+.79 and so on.

In 22 and 23, use the spreadsheet shown below.

	A	B	C	D	E
1	X				
2	2	4	8	16	32
3	3	9	27	81	243
4	5	25	125	625	3125

22. Give a heading for each column.
a. B x^2 **b.** C x^3 **c.** D x^4 **d.** E x^5

23. Give the formula that is in each indicated cell.
a. B2 =A2^2 **b.** C3 =A3^3 **c.** D4 =A4^4 **d.** E2 =A2^5

24. Consider the school supply store spreadsheet in this lesson. Suppose that there is an 8% increase in the price of all clothing sold at the store. What spreadsheet cells need to change value and what are the new prices?
cells B5 through B7; B5 = 6.48, B6 = 8.64, B7 = 12.96

Review

25. Admission to Video-Rama, which includes one game token, costs \$4.75. Additional game tokens cost \$.35 each.
a. How much is one admission with three tokens? **\$5.45**
b. How much is one admission with 4 tokens? **\$5.80**
c. What is the cost of one admission with t tokens? *(Lesson 6-5)*
$4.75 + (t - 1) \cdot .35$

26. Find all sets of three integers which satisfy all of the following:
Condition 1: The numbers are different.
Condition 2: The sum of the numbers is 0.
Condition 3: No number is greater than 4.
Condition 4: No number is less than -4. *(Lesson 6-4)*
-4, 4, 0; -4, 1, 3; -3, 3, 0; -3, 2, 1; -2, 2, 0; -1, 1, 0; 3, -2, -1; 4, -3, -1

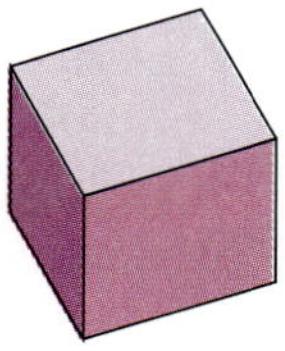

27. Hidden inside the box at the left are two numbers between 10 and 99. The difference between the numbers is 54. The sum of the digits in each number is 10. What are the two numbers? *(Lesson 6-4)*
91 and 37, or 82 and 28, or 73 and 19

In 28–31, write answers in lowest terms. *(Lesson 5-5)*

28. $\frac{5}{6} + \frac{1}{6}$ **1**

29. $2\frac{3}{4} + 1\frac{2}{3}$ **$\frac{53}{12}$ or $4\frac{5}{12}$**

30. $-\frac{1}{3} + \frac{1}{4} + \frac{1}{5}$ **$\frac{7}{60}$**

31. $5 + 2\frac{1}{4}$ **$7\frac{1}{4}$ or $\frac{29}{4}$**

Exploration

32. Spreadsheets contain many built-in commands and functions. Explore the commands that enable you to obtain quickly the sum and the mean of numbers in a row or column. Write a short summary of what you find.

32) Samples:
SUM(F1: F4) for F1+F2+F3+F4
MEAN(F1: F4) for $\frac{F1+F2+F3+F4}{4}$
Answers may vary.

Follow-up for Lesson 6-6

Practice

For more questions on SPUR Objectives, use **Lesson Master 6-6A** (shown on page 329) or **Lesson Master 6-6B** (shown on pages 330–331).

Assessment

Quiz A quiz covering Lessons 6-4 through 6-6 is provided in the *Assessment Sourcebook.*

Written Communication Have students write a paragraph describing several situations where they feel a spreadsheet would be useful; and, if computers are available, create a spreadsheet for one of their suggestions. [Possible uses are keeping track of money they have earned, saved, and spent; personal sports statistics; and grades for their classes.]

Extension

Many students have family members, friends, or acquaintances who use spreadsheet programs in their work. You might have students interview these people to find as many types of applications as they can for spreadsheet programs.

Project Update Project 2, *Spreadsheets*, on page 338, relates to the content of this Lesson.

▸ **LESSON MASTER 6-6 B** *page 2*

3. Complete the spreadsheet. What formula could be used for
a. column B? **=2*A**
b. column C? **=2*A−1 or B−1**
c. column D? **=B*C**

	A	B	C	D
1	1	2	1	2
2	2	4	3	12
3	3	6	5	30
4	4	8	7	56
5	5	10	9	90
6	6	12	11	132
7	7	14	13	182
8	8	16	15	240

4. Design a spreadsheet to determine the average attendance in six classrooms during three days. Use formulas wherever possible. If you have access to a computer, enter and print your spreadsheet with made-up numbers for the entries. **samples:**

	A	B	C	D	E
1	Classroom	Day 1	Day 2	Day 3	Average
2	Room 1				
3	Room 2				
4	Room 3				
5	Room 4				
6	Room 5				
7	Room 6				
8	Average				

B8=(B2+B3+B4+B5+B6+B7)/6
C8=(C2+C3+C4+C5+C6+C7)/6
D8=(D2+D3+D4+D5+D6+D7)/6
E2=(B2+C2+D2)/3
E3=(B3+C3+D3)/3
E4=(B4+C4+D4)/3
E5=(B5+C5+D5)/3
E6=(B6+C6+D6)/3
E7=(B7+C7+D7)/3
E8+(B8+C8+D8)/3

Lesson 6-7

Objectives

F Work with a special case to determine whether a pattern is true.

G Use special cases to determine that a property is false or to give evidence that it is true.

H Use simpler numbers to answer a question requiring only one operation.

Resources

From the ***Teacher's Resource File***

- Lesson Master 6-7A or 6-7B
- Answer Master 6-7
- Teaching Aid 60: Warm-up
- Activity Kit, Activity 15

Additional Resources

- Visual for Teaching Aid 60

Teaching Lesson 6-7

Warm-up

Diagnostic For each question, tell if the result is (a) always even, (b) always odd, or (c) sometimes even, sometimes odd.

1. The sum of two even integers a
2. The sum of two odd integers a
3. The sum of an even and an odd integer b
4. The product of an even and an odd integer a
5. Twice an integer a
6. Three times an integer c
7. The square of an integer c
8. The sum of an integer and its square a

LESSON

6-7 *Special Cases and Simpler Numbers*

An Example of Testing a Special Case

Elaine was not sure whether the pattern

$$x(y + z) = xy + xz$$

is true for all numbers x, y, and z. So she tried some numbers. She substituted 10 for x, 3 for y, and 2 for z. She wrote:

Does $10(3 + 2) = 10 \cdot 3 + 10 \cdot 2$?

Following the rules for order of operations, she simplified. She wrote:

Does $10(5) = 30 + 20$?
Yes.

Elaine found that the equation is true for this *special case.* A **special case** is an instance of a pattern used for some definite purpose. Elaine was using a strategy called *testing a special case.*

Special cases help to test whether a property or generalization is true.

Example 1

Is it true that $-(a + b) = -a + -b$ for any numbers a and b?

Strategy

Work with a special case. Let $a = 3$ and $b = 2$.

Does $-(3 + 2) = -3 + -2$?
Does $-(5) = -5$? Yes.

This case may be too special. Both numbers are positive. So try another special case, this time substituting a negative number. Let $a = -4$ and $b = 7$. Now substitute.

Lesson 6-7 Overview

Broad Goals In this lesson, students learn how to use special cases and simpler numbers to test generalizations.

Perspective The strategy *use a special case* is exactly the same as an instance of a generalization used for a definite purpose. A generalization usually has many instances, and if one is replaced by another with simpler numbers for the purpose of solving a problem, we call the strategy *try simpler numbers*. Since instances of generalizations were discussed in Chapter 4, the new content here is the selection of these instances.

Almost all students who have difficulty with problems involving complicated numbers can do the same problem when the numbers are simple. Needless to say, mastering this strategy may increase scores on standardized tests far more than many days spent on individual skills! In solving real problems, trying simpler numbers is an alternate strategy to using models for operations. By trying simpler numbers, students can answer these questions by induction from the simpler cases rather than by deduction from a generalization. However, therein lies a potential difficulty: induction is not guaranteed to be valid. That is why better students learn both inductive and deductive strategies.

Does -(-4 + 7) = -(-4) + -7?
Does -(3) = 4 + -7? Again, yes. But it wasn't as obvious this time.

You might want to try other special cases.

Solution

We have evidence that the property is true.
We still do not know for certain that it is true.

Caution:
Even if several special cases of a pattern are true, the pattern may not always be true.

Trying a special case can show you that a pattern is not always true.

Example 2

Is x^2 always greater than or equal to x?

Strategy

Try several special cases.

Solution

Try x = 6. $6^2 = 36$, which is greater than 6.
Try x = 13. $13^2 = 169$, which is greater than 13.

So you might think $x^2 \geq x$ is always true.

But now try x = 0.5.
$0.5^2 = 0.25$, which is less than 0.5.
x^2 is not always greater than or equal to x.

Using Special Cases to Make Choices

Suppose you know that only one of a small number of possibilities is true. Then working with a special case can help you pick the right one.

Example 3

Multiple choice. In an n-gon, how many diagonals can be drawn from one vertex?

(a) n (b) $n - 2$ (c) $n - 3$ (d) $\frac{n}{2}$

Strategy

Pick a special case where n is a small number that is easy to work with. We want a polygon with diagonals, so we need $n \geq 4$. Reword the question for the special case when n is 4.

Notes on Reading

You might want to use *Activity 1* in *Optional Activities* on page 334 to introduce this lesson.

Reading Mathematics There is quite a bit of detail in this lesson and the ideas presented may be new to some students. Therefore, you may wish to read this lesson in class with your students, and do the questions in *Covering the Reading* as the corresponding content in the lesson is mentioned.

The variety in the five examples illustrates the power of these strategies. **Example 1** uses special cases to see if a generalization is probably true. In **Example 2,** special cases are used to show a generalization to be false. **Example 3** uses special cases to select the correct generalization from a few possibilities (a strategy for multiple-choice tests). **Examples 4 and 5** show how the use of simpler numbers can help solve a problem and also arrive at a generalization.

Stress the difficulty of proving a generalization true and the ease of proving one false. The few cases in **Example 1** do *not* prove the generalization true, but one case in **Example 2** shows that $x^2 \geq x$ is false. Summarize this idea for students: even if there are many true instances of a pattern, the generalization may not always be true. However, *just one* false instance is enough to make the generalization false. You may wish to introduce the term *counterexample.* A counterexample is an instance which shows that a generalization is false. A key difficulty in learning the strategy of **Example 3** is in determining what are reasonable "simpler numbers" for a given situation. Explain that this skill comes with practice; a number that is simple in one situation may not be simple in another.

Video

Wide World of Mathematics The segment, *Student Engineers,* highlights a group of engineering students who volunteer their time to solve problems faced by individuals with disabilities. The segment provides motivation to launch a lesson on the use of problem-solving strategies. Related questions and an investigation are provided in videodisc stills and in the Video Guide. A related CD-ROM activity is also available.

Videodisc Bar Codes

Search Chapter 29

Play

Additional Examples

1. Is it true that, regardless of the value of m, $m^3 \cdot m^2 = m^5$? **Special cases show that it appears true.**
2. Is $\frac{10}{x}$ $(x \neq 0)$ always less than or equal to 10? **No; it is greater than 10 when x is less than 1.**
3. *Multiple choice.* If n teams are to play each other in a tournament, how many games are needed? **b**

   (a) $n(n-1)$

   (b) $\frac{n(n-1)}{2}$

   (c) $n(n-3)$

   (d) $\frac{n(n-3)}{2}$

In 4–5, try simpler numbers.

4. The area of a rectangle is 10.32 square inches. If its length is 4.3 inches, what is its width? **If the area were 12 and the length 4, then the width would have to be $\frac{12}{4} = 3$. Thus, divide to show $\frac{10.32}{4.3} = 2.4$ in.**
5. If the area of a rectangle is A and the length is ℓ, what is the width w? $\frac{A}{\ell} = w$

Solution

Special case

Multiple choice. In a 4-gon, how many diagonals can be drawn from one vertex?

(a) 4 (b) $4 - 2$ (c) $4 - 3$ (d) $\frac{4}{2}$

Draw a picture to answer the question for the special case.

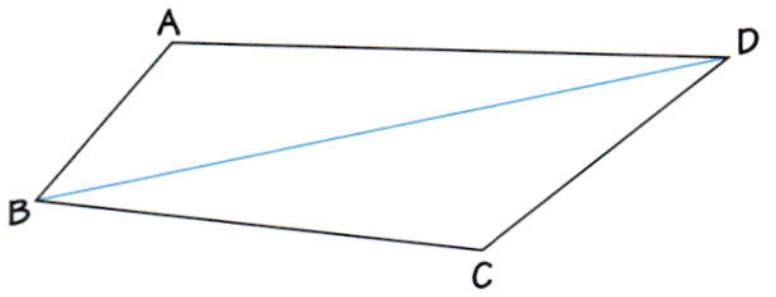

There is only one diagonal from 1 vertex in a quadrilateral (a 4-gon). *Choice (c) is correct for the quadrilateral. So choice (c) n – 3 is correct for an n-gon.*

Check

Try another special case, perhaps a pentagon. Are there $5 - 3$ diagonals from each vertex in a 5-gon? Yes.

Solving Problems by Trying Simpler Numbers

A strategy similar to trying a special case is called *try simpler numbers.* The idea is that complicated numbers or variables may make it hard to devise a plan, so substitute simpler numbers. Simpler numbers often make it easier to see the steps required to solve the problem. Then you can use these same steps with the complicated numbers or variables.

A long tour. *The Tour de France is a famous bicycle race that lasts about 24 days. The participants travel about 4000 km, or about 2500 miles, throughout Europe.*

Example 4

Steve can bike one mile in 8 minutes. If he can keep up this rate, how far will he ride in one hour?

Strategy

The numbers are complicated. There are minutes and hours—that makes things more difficult. Modify the problem so that the numbers are simpler and you can answer the question. Then look for a pattern.

Modified problem

Steve can bike one mile in 10 minutes. If he can keep up this rate, how far will he bike in 60 minutes (1 hour)?

Solution to Modified Problem

The answer to this new problem is 6 miles. (Do you see why?)

Solution

The answer 6 to the modified problem is 60 divided by 10. This suggests that the original problem can be solved by division. Dividing the corresponding numbers of the original problem, the number of miles is 60/8.

Steve can bike 60 ÷ 8, or 7.5 miles in an hour.

Optional Activities

Activity 1 You might want to use *Activity Kit, Activity 15,* to introduce this lesson. Students use the problem-solving strategy of trying simpler numbers to determine the number of different arrangements of 25 cubes in 3 stacks.

Activity 2 Multicultural Connection After discussing **Example 4,** you might want to tell students that bicycles were first made in the early 19th century, and they developed as an important means of transportation. Even today, in some countries such as China, bicycles are more numerous than cars. Traveling and sightseeing by bicycle is very popular in England, Germany, and France. Bicycles are also used for racing in many countries. You might suggest this activity: Devise a bicycle course that is one mile long and have another person time you as you ride the course at a comfortable pace. Using the data, calculate how far you could ride in one hour.

Example 5

Therese can bike one mile in t minutes. At this rate, how far can she bike in u minutes?

Strategy

This is similar to Example 4 except that variables are used instead of numbers. Replace the numbers with variables to find the answer.

Solution

When u was 60 and t was 10, the answer was $\frac{60}{10}$.

Therese can bike u/t miles.

QUESTIONS

Covering the Reading

1. What is a special case of a pattern? an instance of a pattern used for some definite purpose

In 2–4, consider the pattern $-(a + b) = -a + -b$.

2. Give an instance of this pattern. Sample: $-(4 + 3) = -4 + -3$
3. Let $a = -5$ and $b = -11$. Is this special case true? Yes
4. Let $a = 4.8$ and $b = 3.25$. Is this special case true? Yes
5. *True or false.* If more than two special cases of a pattern are true, then the pattern is true. False
6. Consider the pattern $x^2 \geq x$.
   a. Give two instances that are true. Samples: $5^2 \geq 5$, $1^2 \geq 1$
   b. Give an instance that is false.
   c. What do parts **a** and **b** tell you about special cases? Although many special cases may be true, the general pattern may be false.

6b) Let x be any number between 0 and 1.

7. *True or false.* When a special case of a pattern is not true, then the general pattern is not true. True

In 8–12, consider the following pattern: In an n-gon, $n - 3$ diagonals can be drawn from one vertex.

8. a. When $n = 4$, to what kind of polygon does the pattern refer?
   b. Is the pattern true for that kind of polygon?
   a) quadrilateral; b) Yes
9. a. When $n = 7$, to what kind of polygon does the pattern refer?
   b. Is the pattern true for that kind of polygon?
   a) heptagon; b) Yes
10. a. What value of n refers to a hexagon? 6
    b. Is the pattern true for hexagons? Yes
11. a. What value of n refers to a triangle? 3
    b. Is the pattern true for triangles? Yes
12. Show, by drawing, that this pattern is true for an octagon.

12)

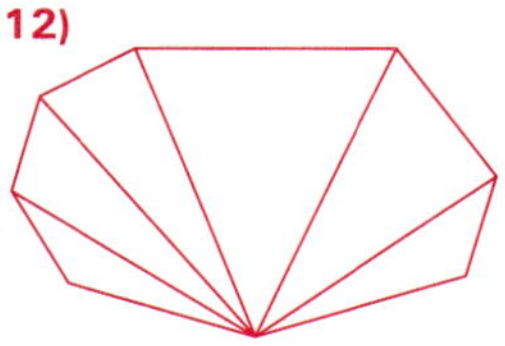

Notes on Questions

If these questions are truly problems (and not exercises) for your students, they may be difficult and time-consuming.

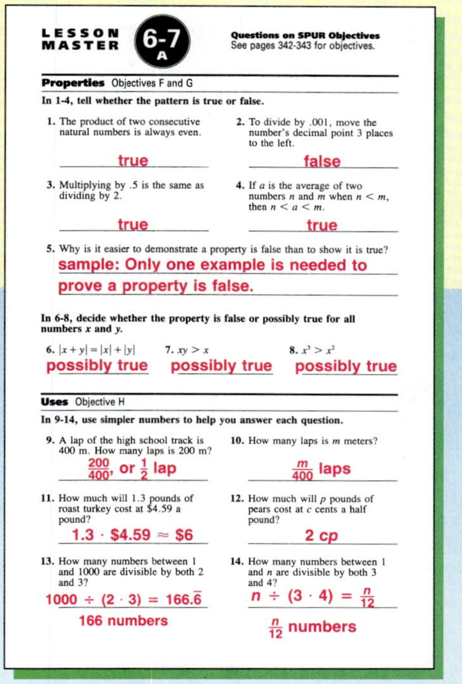

LESSON MASTER 6-7 A

Questions on SPUR Objectives
See pages 342-343 for objectives.

Properties Objectives F and G

In 1-4, tell whether the pattern is true or false.

1. The product of two consecutive natural numbers is always even. true
2. To divide by .001, move the number's decimal point 3 places to the left. false
3. Multiplying by .5 is the same as dividing by 2. true
4. If a is the average of two numbers n and m when $n < m$, then $n < a < m$. true
5. Why is it easier to demonstrate a property is false than to show it is true? sample: Only one example is needed to prove a property is false.

In 6-8, decide whether the property is false or possibly true for all numbers x and y.

6. $|x + y| = |x| + |y|$ possibly true
7. $xy > x$ possibly true
8. $x^3 > x^2$ possibly true

Uses Objective H

In 9-14, use simpler numbers to help you answer each question.

9. A lap of the high school track is 400 m. How many laps is 200 m? $\frac{200}{400}$, or $\frac{1}{2}$ lap
10. How many laps is m meters? $\frac{m}{400}$ laps
11. How much will 1.3 pounds of roast turkey cost at \$4.59 a pound? $1.3 \cdot \$4.59 \approx \$6$
12. How much will p pounds of pears cost at c cents a half pound? 2 cp
13. How many numbers between 1 and 1000 are divisible by both 2 and 3? $1000 \div (2 \cdot 3) = 166.\overline{6}$ 166 numbers
14. How many numbers between 1 and n are divisible by both 3 and 4? $n \div (3 \cdot 4) = \frac{n}{12}$ $\frac{n}{12}$ numbers

Adapting to Individual Needs

Extra Help

Work with students who are having difficulty, or pair them with students who have grasped the ideas in the lesson. Spend extra time on each example. For **Examples 1 and 2,** have students try instances until they are convinced of the results. For **Example 3,** draw a triangle, a quadrilateral, and a pentagon on the board and have students check each of the multiple-choice responses. After they see that choice c works for each of these cases, draw an octagon on the board and see if it works for that figure. In **Example 4,** help students understand that "simpler numbers" are not always smaller numbers. In some cases, they could be rounded numbers, such as the multiples of 10 used in this example.

Notes on Questions

Question 19 Students may need help interpreting "sum of all whole numbers from 1 to *n*." Give an example, such as the sum of all whole numbers from 1 to 4 is 1 + 2 + 3 + 4, or 10, and then students can pick their own special case. To check, students can use another special case.

Some students might recognize this generalization as one they found in the *Challenge* in Lesson 6-5.

Question 22 Students may need to consider smaller combinations to find a pattern.

Question 25 Some students might measure angles to demonstrate that 360° is the correct choice.

Question 34 Trying simpler numbers does not give the solution but gives guidelines to follow. What if a 2-digit number is multiplied by a 1-digit number, and the digits are 1, 2, and 3? Then the largest product is 21 × 3, not 31 × 2. What if the digits are 7, 8, and 9? Then the largest product is 87 × 9, not 97 × 8. This suggests two properties of the answer—the digits should decrease from left to right, and the largest digit should be in the smaller number. This suggests that the answer is of the form 87__ × 9___. Then students can try a 3-digit number multiplied by a 2-digit number, where the digits are 5, 6, 7, 8, and 9.

LESSON MASTER 6-7 B Questions on SPUR Objectives

Properties Objective F: Work with a special case to determine whether a pattern is true.

In 1-6, tell whether the pattern is true or false.

1. The product of any two odd numbers is odd. true
2. The sum of any two prime numbers is even. false
3. To divide a number by .01, move the number's decimal point 2 places to the left. false
4. Multiplying by .25 is the same as dividing by 4. true
5. When a natural number is multiplied by another number, the product is greater than the natural number. false
6. The number of centimeters in a given distance is greater than the number of inches. true

Properties Objective G: Use special cases to determine that a property is false or to give evidence that it is true.

7. What should you do to demonstrate that a property is false? Find a special case that is not true.

In 8-12, the variables can stand for any numbers. Decide whether the property is false or possibly true.

8. $|x| > 0$ false
9. $2a > a$ false
10. $2m + 3m = 5m$ possibly true
11. $a^2 + b^2 = (a + b)^2$ false
12. $-|k| \leq 0$ possibly true

In 13 and 14, use the formula from Example 5.

13. Buzz can bike one mile in 7 minutes. At this rate, how far can he bike in an hour? $\frac{60}{7}$ or $8\frac{4}{7}$ miles

14. Kristin can bike one mile in M minutes. At this rate, how far can she bike in 30 minutes? $\frac{30}{M}$ miles

15. *True or false.* A simpler number is always a smaller number. False

Applying the Mathematics

16. Tell how many miles per gallon the car is getting.

a. Isaac drove 250 miles on 10 gallons of gas. 25 miles per gallon

b. Judy drove 250 miles on 11.2 gallons of gas. ≈ 22.3 mi per gal

c. Ken drove m miles on 11.2 gallons of gas. $\frac{m}{11.2}$ mi per gal

d. Louise drove m miles on g gallons of gas. $\frac{m}{g}$ mi per gal

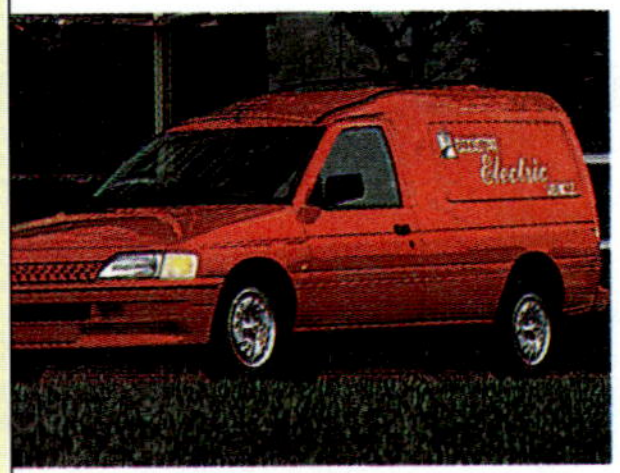

Electrical vehicle technology holds great promise for the future. This electric van, being tested by utility and delivery companies, is expected to be technically and commercially viable by the year 2000.

17a) Sample: if m = 2, -(-2 + 9) = 2 + -9; true; b) Sample: if m = -4, -(-(-4) + 9) = -4 + -9; true

17. Consider the pattern $-(-m + 9) = m + -9$.

a. Test a special case with a positive number. See below left.

b. Test a special case with a negative number. See below left.

c. Decide whether the pattern is possibly true or definitely not always true. possibly true

18. Which is easier, showing a pattern is true or showing a pattern is false? Explain your answer. Showing a pattern is false is easier. You need only one special case to show a pattern is false.

19. *Multiple choice.* Use special cases to help you select. The sum of all the whole numbers from 1 to n is

(a) $n + 1$. (b) $n + 2$.
(c) $\frac{n(n+1)}{2}$. (d) n^2. (c)

20. *Multiple choice.* Use special cases to help you select.
For all whole numbers w, n, and d, where $d \neq 0$, $w + \frac{n}{d} =$

(a) $\frac{dw + n}{d}$. (b) wn/d.
(c) $\frac{w + n}{w + d}$. (d) $\frac{w + n}{d}$. (a)

In 21–25, if you cannot answer the question, try a special case or use simpler numbers.

21. A roll of paper towels originally had R sheets. If Z sheets are used, how many sheets remain? $R - Z$

22. There are 8 boys and 7 girls at a party. A photographer wants to take a picture of each boy with each girl. How many pictures are required? 56

23. A coat costs $49.95. You give the clerk G dollars. How much change should you receive? $G - 49.95$ dollars

24. How should you move the decimal point in order to divide a decimal by .001? three places to the right

Adapting to Individual Needs

English Language Development
Make sure students understand the difference between a special case and a general case. In **Example 1,** $-(a + b) = -a + -b$ is a general case. Instances where a and b are replaced with numbers give special cases. Emphasize that all of the instances that students can find show that the general case is true. Similarly, in **Example 2,** $x^2 \geq x$ is the general case. Note that showing that a special case is true does not prove the general case is true, as shown in **Example 1.** However, showing that a special case is false proves that the general case is false, as shown in **Example 2.**

25. *Multiple choice.* The sum of the measures of the four angles of any quadrilateral is
(a) 180°. (b) 360°. (c) 540°. (d) 720°. (b)

Review

In 26–28, use the following spreadsheet. *(Lessons 4-6, 6-6)*

	A	B	C	D
1		Student	Grades	
2	Name	Test 1	Test 2	Average
3	John	86	78	
4	Paul	55	80	
5	George	97	94	
6	James	23	18	
7	Average			=(B11+C11)/2

26. Write the formula that calculates John's test average, and name the cell in which the formula is entered. =(B3+C3)/2; in cell D3

27. What formula should be entered in cell B7 to calculate the group's average on Test 1? =(B3+B4+B5+B6)/4

28. **a.** In which cell will the formula used to calculate the group's average on Test 2 be entered? C7
b. What formula should be entered there? =(C3+C4+C5+C6)/4

29. A downtown parking lot charges \$1.00 for the first hour and \$.50 for each additional hour or part of an hour. *(Lesson 6-5)*
a. What will it cost to park from 9 A.M. to 4:45 P.M.? \$4.50
b. At this rate, what does it cost for h hours of parking, when h is a whole number? $1.00 + (h - 1) \cdot .50$ dollars

30. The number 17 is a divisor of x, and $925 < x < 950$. Find x. *(Lesson 6-4)* $x = 935$

31. Virginia's garden is in the shape of a triangle. Each side of the triangle is 12 feet long. There is a stake at each corner. There are stakes every 3 feet on each side. How many stakes are there in all? *(Lesson 6-3)* 12

32. Evaluate a^{b+c} when $a = 5$, $b = 2$, and $c = 4$. *(Lessons 2-2, 4-4)* 15,625

33. Would an adult be more likely to weigh 10 kg, 70 kg, or 170 kg? *(Lesson 3-3)* 70 kg

Exploration

(9) (6) (4) (2) (1)
× (8) (7) (5) (3)
8 4 3 9 7 3 0 1 3

34. Put the digits 1, 2, 3, 4, 5, 6, 7, 8, and 9 in the circles at the left to make the largest product possible.

Follow-up for Lesson 6-7

Practice

For more questions on SPUR Objectives, use **Lesson Master 6-7A** (shown on page 335) or **Lesson Master 6-7B** (shown on pages 336–337).

Assessment

Group Assessment You might have students **work in groups**, summarize the strategies they learned in the chapter, and give examples that use each strategy. [Summary will be similar to the *Summary* on page 340. Examples will vary.]

Extension

As an extension of **Question 25,** have students find the sum of the measures of the angles of a triangle, a quadrilateral, a pentagon, a hexagon, and so on, until they can find a pattern. [180°, 360°, 540°, 720°, and so on] Then have them give the generalization [$180(a - 2)$, where a is the number of angles (or sides) in the polygon] and use it to find the sum of the measures of all the angles in a 25-sided polygon. [4140°]

Project Update Project 5, *Special Cases that Work, But Generalizations that Do Not*, on page 339, relates to the content of this lesson.

► **LESSON MASTER 6-7 B** *page 2*

Uses Objective H: Use simpler numbers to answer a question requiring only one operation.

In 13-18, use simpler numbers to help you answer each question.

13. If a serving of cereal weighs 40 grams, how many servings is 120 grams? 3 servings

14. If a serving a cereal weighs 40 grams, how many servings is 20 grams? $\frac{1}{2}$ serving

15. If a serving of cereal weighs 40 grams, how many servings is g grams? $\frac{g}{40}$ servings

16. If a serving of cereal weighs s grams, how many servings is g grams? $\frac{g}{s}$ servings

17. If Jake reads a page in a novel in 1.5 minutes, how many pages can he read in a half hour? 20 pages

18. If Jake reads a page in a novel in m minutes, how many pages can he read in h hours? $\frac{60h}{m}$ pages

Adapting to Individual Needs

Challenge
Have students solve these problems and explain their thinking. [Sample explanations are given.]

1. What is the ones digit in 4^{48}?
[$4^1 = 4$, $4^2 = 16$, $4^3 = 64$, $4^4 = 256$, $4^5 = 1024$, $4^6 = 4096$, and so on. It appears that the ones digits alternate between 4 for odd powers and 6 for even powers. So the ones digit in 4^{48} is 6.]
2. What is the 120th odd positive integer?
[The even integers 2, 4, 6, 8, . . ., can be generated, replacing n in $2n$, by 1, 2, 3, ... The odd integers, 1, 3, 5, 7, . . ., can be generated by replacing n in $2n - 1$ by 1, 2, 3, ... Therefore, the 120th odd integer is 2(120) −1 or 239.]
3. Find 3333^2 and 33333^2 without computing. [Use a calculator to find $3^2 = 9$, $33^2 = 1089$, and $333^2 = 110889$. Then use the pattern: $3333^2 = 11108889$ and $33333^3 = 1111088889$.]

Chapter 6 Projects

Chapter 6 projects relate to the content of the lessons as follows.

Project	Lesson(s)
1	6-3, 6-5
2	6-6
3	6-1
4	6-1, 6-4
5	6-7
6	6-2

1 Diagonals of Regular Polygons If the polygons are not regular, the lengths of the diagonals will not reflect any pattern. Students can use **Geometry Templates** to draw regular polygons. If students need help, suggest that they make a chart and list information, such as the name of the polygon, the number of sides, the total number of diagonals, and the number of different lengths of diagonals. If students list polygons in the order of increasing number of sides, they should notice a pattern.

2 Spreadsheets Suggest that students make a spreadsheet organizing data from a hobby or sport they may participate in. Applying the spreadsheet function to their own data will give students a better understanding of what the spreadsheet program can and cannot do.

3 Problem Solving Some appropriate books are: *Problem Solving: Concepts and Methods for Community Organizations* by Ralph Brody, Human Sciences Publishers, 1982; *Problem Solving for Teens: An Interactive Approach to Real-Life Problem Solving* by Barbara J. Gray, LinguiSystems, 1990; *Problem-Solving Techniques Helpful in Math and Science* by Charles A. Reeves, National Council of Teachers of Mathematics, 1987.

Discourage students from simply reproducing the summary of the steps to solve problems as given in the book they choose.

PROJECTS 6 CHAPTER SIX

A project presents an opportunity for you to extend your knowledge of a topic related to the material of this chapter. You should allow more time for a project than you do for typical homework questions.

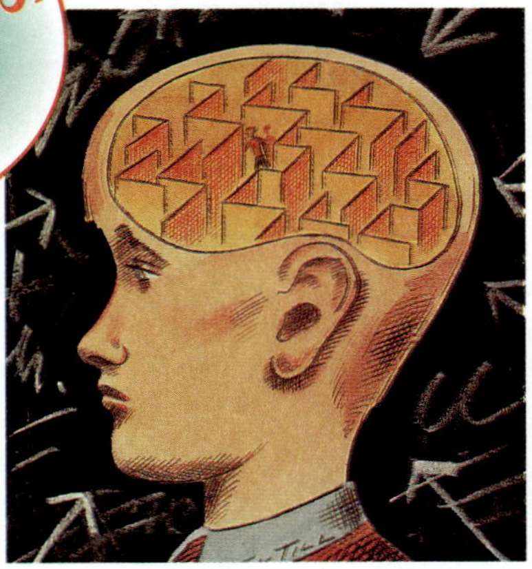

1 Diagonals of Regular Polygons

A *regular polygon* is one in which all sides have the same length and all angles have the same measure. Many of the diagonals of regular polygons are of the same length. For instance, the nine diagonals of a regular hexagon have only two different lengths: 3 are longer and 6 are shorter. Explore the diagonals of regular polygons. How many different lengths are there in the diagonals of a regular n-gon?

2 Spreadsheets

Explore one of the best-selling spreadsheets, such as Microsoft Excel® or Lotus 1-2-3®. Write an essay describing what these spreadsheets can do.

3 Problem Solving

Being able to solve problems is important in almost every walk of life. Books have been written for people who want to solve problems in their work, in their personal lives, or in various subjects. Find a book that talks about solving problems. Summarize the main advice given in that book.

338

Responses

1. There are $\frac{n}{2} - 1$ different lengths of diagonals in a regular n-gon when n is even. When n is odd, there are $\frac{n-1}{2}$ different lengths of diagonals.

2. The following information is a sample of what students might include in their projects. Most spreadsheets come with tools for creating worksheets, charts, databases, and macros. Worksheets allow the user to organize and explore information. Charting tools help visualize and analyze worksheet data. Standard database operations allow you to manage a database on a worksheet. Macros

4 Cryptarithms

Question 31 in Lesson 6-1 is a type of problem known as a *cryptarithm.* Cryptarithms are normally solved with a good amount of trial and error combined with a knowledge of arithmetic. Sometimes there is more than one solution. One of the

most famous of these problems was (according to a story) sent by a boy in college to his father:

```
  S E N D
+ M O R E
---------
M O N E Y
```

His father responded:

```
    U S E
+ L E S S
---------
S O N N Y
```

Solve these cryptarithms. That is, find out what digit each letter stands for in these addition problems. In each problem, each different letter stands for a different digit. The same letter may stand for different digits in the two problems.

5 Special Cases that Work, but Generalizations that Do Not

3 is an odd number and 3 is prime. 5 is an odd number and 5 is prime. 7 is an odd number and 7 is prime. A person might be tempted to make the generalization that all odd numbers are prime. But of course they are not. Make up *ten* examples of situations in which some special cases have a certain property, but the generalization is not true. Not all of your examples have to be mathematical.

6 Special Numbers

Find the meaning of each of the following terms. Give at least two examples of each. Explain why the term is appropriate for these numbers.

abundant number
deficient number
amicable numbers
relatively prime numbers

4 Cryptarithms Remind students that a letter represents the same number whenever it appears in a particular cryptarithm, but it might represent another number in another cryptarithm.

To help students get started solving the first cryptarithm, suggest that they work from left to right. The only sensible value for M is 1. If M = 1, it follows that S = 9 and O = 0. If O = 0, and no two letters have the same value, the fact that E + O = N tells that the sum of N and R must be greater than 10, and that N = E + 1. If students try various combinations to find E and N, then finding D and Y is easy.

The second cryptarithm can be solved in a similar way. The leftmost digit, S, must be 1. Then it follows that N = 2 because S + S = N. Now, working from left to right, find that L = 9, O = 0, and U + E = 12. Several different values for U, E, and Y will solve the cryptarithm.

5 Special Cases that Work, but Generalizations that Do Not Encourage students to find as many mathematical examples as they can. Students may be tempted to provide generalizations that are considered stereotypes. That is not the intention of the project.

6 Special Numbers If students do not know the meaning of these words, have them use a dictionary to find the common usage definition of each term. Students will probably need a mathematics dictionary to determine the mathematical meanings.

are sets of instructions like computer programs that you can create and store. Creating macros is the key to customizing standard functions. Once macros are created, they can automate frequently performed tasks.

3. Responses will vary.
4.

SEND	9567		
MORE	1085		
MONEY	10652		
USE	715	517	814
LESS	9511	9711	9411
SONNY	10226	10228	10225

5. One sample of each type is given.

It was sunny on Monday, it was sunny on Tuesday, and it is sunny today, so it will be sunny tomorrow.

The sum of two prime numbers is even. This is not true when 2 is added to any other prime number.

Responses continue on page 340.

Summary

The Summary gives an overview of the entire chapter and provides an opportunity for students to consider the material as a whole. Thus, the Summary can be used to help students relate and unify the concepts presented in the chapter.

Vocabulary

Terms, symbols, and properties are listed by lesson to provide a checklist of concepts a student must know. Emphasize to students that they should read the vocabulary list carefully before starting the Progress Self-Test. If students do not understand the meaning of a term, they should refer back to the indicated lesson.

SUMMARY

If you have an algorithm for answering a question, it is an exercise for you. If not, then the question is a problem for you. Problems are frustrating unless you know strategies that can help you approach them. This chapter discusses six general strategies. They are:

1. Read the problem carefully. Look up definitions for any unfamiliar words. Determine if enough information is given. Sort information into what is needed and what is not needed.
2. Draw an accurate picture.
3. Use trial and error. Use earlier trials to help in choosing better later trials.
4. Make a table to organize your thoughts. Use the table to find patterns. Use the table to make generalizations. A spreadsheet may be a good way to make your table.
5. Use special cases to help decide whether a pattern is true.
6. Try simpler numbers. Generalize to more complicated numbers or variables.

These strategies can help in understanding a problem, in devising a plan, in solving, and in checking. Good problem solvers take their time. They do not give up. They are flexible. And they continually check their work.

VOCABULARY

You should be able to give a general description and a specific example of each of the following ideas.

Lesson 6-1
algorithm, exercise, problem

Lesson 6-2
prime number, composite number
divisor, factor
natural number

Lesson 6-4
trial and error

Lesson 6-5
table
generalization

Lesson 6-6
spreadsheet
row, cell, column
active cell
replicate
data disk

Lesson 6-7
special case
testing a special case
try simpler numbers

Response, page 339

6. **The following information is a sample of what students might include in their projects. Abundant means plentiful. An abundant number is an integer which is greater than the sum of its divisors (not including the number itself as a divisor); 72 and 100 are two abundant numbers. Deficient means not sufficient in quantity. A deficient number is an integer which is less than the sum of its divisors (not including the number itself); 32 and 50 are deficient. Amicable means having a friendly attitude. Amicable numbers are two integers, each of which is the sum of the divisors (excluding the number itself) of the other; 220 and 284 are amicable numbers. Relatively means in relation to something else. Two integers are relatively prime if they have no factors in common besides one. Any two consecutive integers are relatively prime.**

PROGRESS SELF-TEST

Take this test as you would take a test in class. Then check your work with the solutions in the Selected Answers section in the back of the book.

1. Name two places to find the meaning of the term "trapezoid."
2. How many diagonals does an octagon have?
3. There are six players in a singles tennis tournament. Each player will compete with each of the others. How many matches will be played? 15
4. What two positive integers whose product is 24 will have the smallest sum? 4 and 6
5. *True or false.* If you know an algorithm for multiplying fractions, then multiplying fractions is a problem for you. False
6. List the prime numbers between 50 and 60.
7. Consider the sentence $|x| + |y| = |x + y|$. Find values of x and y that make this sentence false.
8. What is an advantage of using an electronic spreadsheet over a handwritten table?
9. How much will 1.62 pounds of hamburger cost if the price is \$1.49 per pound? \$2.42
10. *True or false.* If a special case of a pattern is true, then the general pattern may still be true. True

1) Samples: dictionary, glossary in a math book
2) 20

6) 53, 59
7) If one value is positive and one is negative, the pattern will be false. For instance, $|-5| + |3| = 5 + 3 = 8$, but $|-5 + 3| = |-2| = 2$.
8) Sample: The calculations are done automatically by a computer.

11. What integer between 5 and 10 is a solution to $(x - 3) + (x - 4) = 9$? 8
12. Donna has some disks numbered 1, 2, 3, 4, and so on. She arranges them in order in a circle, equally spaced. If disk 3 is directly across from disk 10, how many disks are in the circle? 14
13. When all the possible diagonals are drawn, an n-gon has $n + 3$ diagonals. What is n? 6
14. How many decimal places and in which direction should you move a decimal point in order to divide by .01? 2 places to the right
15. Brianna was given \$1000 by her parents to spend during her first year of college. She decided to spend \$25 a week. Make a table to show how much she will have left after 1, 2, 3, and 4 weeks.
16. In the situation of Question 15, how much will Brianna have after 31 weeks? \$225
17. Auni carefully read a problem, prepared a table to help solve the problem, and worked until she reached a conclusion. She wrote her answer and went on to the next problem. What step in good problem solving did Auni omit? Check your work.
18. Name two situations in which an electronic spreadsheet would be helpful. Samples: organizing and storing 16 test scores for a class; keeping track of monthly sales for a store

15)

weeks	amount left
1	1000–25
2	$1000-2 \cdot 25$
3	$1000-3 \cdot 25$
4	$1000-4 \cdot 25$

Progress Self-Test

For the development of mathematical competence, feedback and correction, along with the opportunity to practice, are necessary. The Progress Self-Test provides the opportunity for feedback and correction; the Chapter Review provides additional opportunities for practice. We cannot overemphasize the importance of these end-of-chapter materials. It is at this point that the material "gels" for many students, allowing them to solidify skills and understanding. In general, student performance should be markedly improved after these pages.

Assign the Progress Self-Test as a one-night assignment. Worked-out *solutions* for all questions are in the Selected Answers section of the student book. Encourage students to take the Progress Self-Test honestly, grade themselves, and then be prepared to discuss the test in class.

Advise students to pay special attention to those Chapter Review questions (pages 342–343) which correspond to questions missed on the Progress Self-Test.

Chapter 6 Review

Resources

From the ***Teacher's Resource File***

- Answer Master for Chapter 6 Review
- Assessment Sourcebook: Chapter 6 Test, Forms A–D Chapter 6 Test, Cumulative Form Comprehensive Test, Chapters 1–6

Additional Resources

- Quiz and Test Writer

The main objectives for the chapter are organized in the Chapter Review under the four types of understanding this book promotes—Skills, Properties, Uses, and Representations.

Whereas end-of chapter material may be considered optional in some texts, in *UCSMP Transition Mathematics* we have selected these objectives and questions with the expectation that they will be covered. Because this is a chapter on problems, you should not expect the kind of performance that you have received with exercises in preceding chapters. Students should be able to answer these questions with about 85% accuracy after studying the chapter if you give partial credit.

You may assign these questions over a single night to help students prepare for a test the next day, or you may assign the questions over a two-day period. If you work the questions over two days, then we recommend assigning the *evens* for homework the first night so that students get feedback in class the next day, then assigning the *odds* the night before the test, because answers are provided to the odd-numbered questions.

It is effective to ask students which questions they still do not understand and use the day or days as a total class discussion of the material which the class finds most difficult.

CHAPTER REVIEW

Questions on SPUR Objectives

SPUR stands for **S**kills, **P**roperties, **U**ses, and **R**epresentations. The Chapter Review questions are grouped according to the SPUR Objectives for this chapter.

SKILLS DEAL WITH THE PROCEDURES USED TO GET ANSWERS.

Objective A. *Know the general strategies used by good problem solvers.* *(Lesson 6-1)*

1. *Multiple choice.* Which advice should you follow to become a better problem solver?
   (a) Check work by answering the question the same way you did it.
   (b) Be flexible.
   (c) Skip over words you don't understand as long as you can write an equation.
   (d) none of (a) through (c) **(b)**
2. If you can apply an algorithm to a problem, then the problem becomes an __?__. **exercise**
3. Nancy multiplied 1487 × 309 on her calculator. What would be a good way for her to check her answer? **Sample: Divide the answer by 1487 or 309.**

Objective B. *Determine solutions to sentences by trial and error.* *(Lesson 6-4)*

4. Which integer between 10 and 20 is a solution to $3x + 15 = 66$? **17**
5. *Multiple choice.* Which number is not a solution to $n^2 \geq n$?
   (a) 0 (b) 0.5
   (c) 1 (d) 2 **(b)**
6. Choose one number from each row so that the sum of the numbers is 255.

88	84	9	**84**
69	79	76	**69**
108	104	102	**102**

7. What number between 1000 and 1050 has 37 as a factor? **1036**

PROPERTIES DEAL WITH THE PRINCIPLES BEHIND THE MATHEMATICS.

Objective C. *Determine whether a number is prime or composite.* *(Lesson 6-2)*

8. Explain why 2.3×10^4 is composite.
9. Is 49 prime or composite? Explain your answer. **Composite; 7 is a factor.**
10. Is 47 prime or composite? Explain your answer. **Prime; only 1 and 47 are factors.**
11. List all composite numbers n with $20 < n < 30$. **21, 22, 24, 25, 26, 27, 28**

8) 2.3×10^4 **must have a factor of 10.**

Objective D. *Find the meaning of unknown words.* *(Lesson 6-2)*

12. What is a tetrahedron?
13. What is a perfect number?

12) a three-dimensional figure with four triangular faces
13) a number that equals the sum of its divisors except itself

Objective E. *Make a table to find patterns and make generalizations.* *(Lesson 6-5)*

14. Mandy is saving to buy a present for her parents' anniversary. She has $10 now and will add $5 a week. **a) $70; b) 10 + 5*w* dollars**
    a. How much will she save in 12 weeks?
    b. How much will she save in w weeks?
15. Consider 2, 4, 8, 16, 32, . . . (the positive integer powers of 2). Make a table listing all the factors of these numbers. How many factors does 256 have?

15)

2	**1, 2**
4	**1, 2, 4**
8	**1, 2, 4, 8**
16	**1, 2, 4, 8, 16**
32	**1, 2, 4, 8, 16, 32**

256 has 9 factors.

CHAPTER SIX

Objective F. *Work with a special case to determine whether a pattern is true.* *(Lesson 6-7)*

16. Is there any *n*-gon with $n + 2$ diagonals?

17. To divide a decimal by 1 million, you can move the decimal point __?__ places to the __?__. **6, left**

16) No, a 5-gon has 5 diagonals, a 6-gon has 9; thereafter the number of diagonals increases.
18) There is more evidence that the property is true.
19) Sample: If x = 2 and y = 3, then $5x + 5y \neq 10xy$.

Objective G. *Use special cases to determine that a property is false or to give evidence that it is true.* *(Lesson 6-7)*

18. Let $a = 5$ and $b = -4$ to test whether $2a + b = a + (b + a)$. Is the property false or do you have more evidence that it is true?

19. Show that $5x + 5y$ is not always equal to $10xy$ by choosing a special case.

USES DEAL WITH APPLICATIONS OF MATHEMATICS IN REAL SITUATIONS.

Objective H. *Use simpler numbers to answer a question requiring only one operation.* *(Lesson 6-7)*

20. If you fly 430 miles in 2.5 hours, how fast have you gone? **172 mph**

21. If you buy 7.3 gallons of gas at a cost of $1.19 per gallon, what is your total cost (to the penny)? **$8.69**

Objective I. *Use drawings to solve real problems.* *(Lesson 6-3)*

22. Nine teams are to play each other in a tournament. How many games are needed? **36**

23. Five hockey teams are to play each other two times in a season. How many games are needed? **20**

24. Bill is older than Becky. Becky is younger than Bob. Bob is older than Barbara. Barbara is older than Bill. Who is second oldest? **Barbara**

25. Interstate 25 runs north and south through Wyoming and Colorado. Denver is 70 miles from Colorado Springs and 112 miles from Pueblo. Cheyenne is 171 miles from Colorado Springs and 101 miles from Denver. Pueblo is 42 miles from Colorado Springs. Cheyenne is north of Denver. Which of these four cities, all on Interstate 25, is farthest south? **Pueblo**

REPRESENTATIONS DEAL WITH PICTURES, GRAPHS, OR OBJECTS THAT ILLUSTRATE CONCEPTS.

Objective J. *Use a spreadsheet to answer questions in real situations.* *(Lesson 6-6)*

26. Jenny scored 82 on test 1, 84 on test 2, and 60 on test 3. Tom scored 93 on test 1, 85 on test 2, and 90 on test 3. David scored 75 on test 1, 100 on test 2, and 86 on test 3. Sara scored 99 on test 1, 100 on test 2, and 87 on test 3. Their teacher needs to know the average grade for each student and the average grade for each test. Design a spreadsheet to show this information.

27. A plumber charges $18.75 for a service call and $11 for every 15 minutes of labor. Design a spreadsheet that will show the costs for the plumber's time from 0 minutes to 6 hours, in 15-minute increments.

26–27) See margin below.

Objective K. *Draw a diagram to aid in solving geometric problems.* *(Lesson 6-3)*

28. How many diagonals does a hexagon have?

29. How many diagonals does a decagon have?

30. All the diagonals of a pentagon are drawn. Into how many sections is the interior divided? **11 regions is the maximum.**

31. In polygon *ABCDEFGHI* all diagonals from *A* are drawn. How many triangles are formed? **7**

28) 9
29) 35

Assessment

Evaluation The *Assessment Sourcebook* provides six forms of the Chapter 6 Test. Forms A and B present parallel versions in a short-answer format. Forms C and D offer performance assessment. The fifth test is Chapter 6 Test, Cumulative Form. About 50% of this test covers Chapter 6, 25% of it covers Chapter 5, and 25% of it covers earlier chapters. In addition to these tests, Comprehensive Test Chapter 1-6 gives roughly equal attention to all chapters covered thus far.

For information on grading, see *General Teaching Suggestions: Grading* in the *Professional Sourcebook* which begins on page T20 in Volume 1 of the Teacher's Edition.

Additional Answers, page 343

26.

	A	B	C	D	E
1	Student	Test 1	Test 2	Test 3	Average
2	Jenny	82	84	60	75.33
3	Tom	93	85	90	89.33
4	David	75	100	86	87
5	Sara	99	100	87	95.33
6	Average	87.25	92.25	80.75	

Cell	Equation
B6	= (B2 + B3 + B4 + B5)/4
C6	= (C2 + C3 + C4 + C5)/4
D6	= (D2 + D3 + D4 + D5)/4
E2	= (B2 + C2 + D2)/3
E3	= (B3 + C3 + D3)/3
E4	= (B4 + C4 + D4)/3
E5	= (B5 + C5 + D5)/3

27.

	A	B
1	Minutes	Cost
2	0	18.75
3	15	29.75
4	30	40.75
5	45	51.75
6	60	62.75

Cell	Equation
A3	= A2 + 15
B3	= B2 + 11
•	•
•	•
•	•
A26	= A25 + 15
B26	= B25 + 11

Table of Contents

Professional Sourcebook: SECTION 1 OVERVIEW OF UCSMP

The Reasons for UCSMP

Recommendations for Change

The mathematics curriculum has undergone changes in every country of the world throughout this century, as a result of an increasing number of students staying in school longer, the need for a greater number of technically competent workers and citizens, and major advances in mathematics itself. In the last twenty years, these developments have accelerated due to the widespread appearance of computers with their unprecedented abilities to handle and display information.

In the last 100 years, national groups have examined the curriculum periodically in light of these changes in society. A study of reports before 1970 can be found in *A History of Mathematics Education in the United States and Canada,* the 30th Yearbook of the National Council of Teachers of Mathematics, 1970. A summary of reports from 1970 to 1984 can be found in Z. Usiskin, "We Need Another Revolution in Secondary School Mathematics," in *The Secondary School Mathematics Curriculum,* the 1985 Yearbook of NCTM.

The most recent era of reports can be said to have begun in the years 1975-1980, with the publication of reports by various national mathematics organizations calling attention to serious problems in the education of our youth. These reports from inside mathematics education were joined by governmental and private reports through the 1980s decrying the state of American education and providing broad recommendations for school practice. Two of the most notable of these reports for their specific remarks about mathematics education appeared in the year that UCSMP began.

1983: National Commission on Excellence in Education. *A Nation At Risk.*

> The teaching of mathematics in high school should equip graduates to: (a) understand geometric and algebraic concepts; (b) understand elementary probability and statistics; (c) apply mathematics in everyday situations; and (d) estimate, approximate, measure, and test the accuracy of their calculations. In addition to the traditional sequence of studies available for college-bound students, new, equally demanding mathematics curricula need to be developed for those who do not plan to continue their formal education immediately. (p. 25)

1983: College Board (Project EQuality). *Academic Preparation for College: What Students Need to Know and Be Able to Do.*

> All students (college-bound or not) should have:
>
> The ability to apply mathematical techniques in the solution of real-life problems and to recognize when to apply those techniques.
>
> Familiarity with the language, notation, and deductive nature of mathematics and the ability to express quantitative ideas with precision.
>
> The ability to use computers and calculators.
>
> Familiarity with the basic concepts of statistics and statistical reasoning.
>
> Knowledge in considerable depth and detail of algebra, geometry, and functions. (p. 20)

The specific remarks about school mathematics in these documents for the most part mirror what appeared in the earlier reports. Thus, given what seemed to be a broad consensus on the problems and desirable changes in pre-college mathematics instruction, it was decided, at the outset of UCSMP, that UCSMP would not attempt to form its own set of recommendations, but undertake the task of translating the existing recommendations into the reality of classrooms and schools. It was also decided that UCSMP would look at the best that other countries had to offer, and so in 1983 UCSMP began to translate materials from Japan and some countries of Eastern Europe known for excellence in mathematics education.

Universities for many years have recognized that mathematics encompasses far more than algebra, geometry, and analysis. The term mathematical sciences is an umbrella designation which includes traditional mathematics as well as a number of other disciplines. The largest of these other disciplines today are statistics, computer science, and applied mathematics, not coincidentally the areas in which recent reports have recommended greater emphasis. In 1983, the Conference Board of the Mathematical Sciences produced a report, *The Mathematical Sciences Curriculum: What Is Still Fundamental and What Is Not.* The UCSMP Grades 7–12 curriculum is the first mathematical sciences curriculum for average students in the United States.

In the middle 1980s, as the first edition of UCSMP secondary textbooks were being developed and tested, studies comparing the achievement of secondary school students in the U.S. with the achievement of students in other countries verified our conception that we were quite a bit behind those countries in performance.

The Second International Mathematics Study (SIMS) was conducted in 1981–1982 and involved 23 populations in 21 countries. At the eighth-grade level, virtually all students attend school in all those countries, and our students scored at or below the international average on all five subtests: arithmetic, measurement, algebra, geometry, and statistics. We are far below the top: Japan looked at the test and decided it was too easy for their 8th-graders, and so they gave it at 7th grade. Still, the median Japanese 7th-grader performed at the 95th percentile of the Unites States 8th-graders. SIMS recommended steps to renew school mathematics in the United States.

At the 12th-grade level in 1981–82, about 13% of our population was enrolled in precalculus or calculus; the mean among developed countries is about 16%. Thus, the U.S. no longer kept more students in mathematics than other developed countries, yet our advanced placement students did not perform well when compared to their peers in other countries. SIMS found:

1987: Second International Mathematics Study (SIMS). *The Underachieving Curriculum.*

> In the U.S., the achievement of the Calculus classes, the nation's best mathematics students, was at or near the average achievement of the advanced secondary school mathematics students in other countries. (In most countries, all advanced mathematics students take calculus. In the U.S., only about one-fifth do.) The achievement of the U.S. Precalculus students (the majority of twelfth grade college-preparatory students) was substantially below the international average. In some cases the U.S. ranked with the lower one-fourth of all countries in the Study, and was the lowest of the advanced industrialized countries. (*The Underachieving Curriculum,* p. *vii*)

The situation has been even worse for those who do not take precalculus mathematics in high school. Such students either have performed poorly in their last mathematics course, a situation which has caused them not to go on in mathematics, or they were performing poorly in junior high school and had to take remedial mathematics as 9th-graders. If these students go to college, they invariably take remedial mathematics, which is taught at a faster pace than in high school, and the failure rates in such courses often exceed 40%. If they do not go to college but join the job market, they lack the mathematics needed to understand today's technology. It is no understatement to say that **UCSMP has received its funding from business and industry because those who leave schooling to join the work force are woefully weak in the mathematics they will need.**

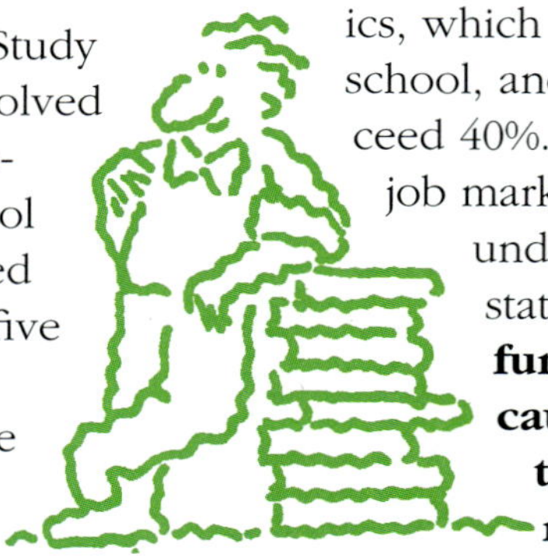

SIMS recommended:

> A fundamental revision of the U.S. school mathematics curriculum, in both form and substance, is needed. This activity should begin at the early grades of the elementary school.
>
> With respect to form, the excessive repetition of topics from year to year should be eliminated. A more focused organization of the subject matter, with a more intense treatment of topics, should be considered.
>
> Concerning substance, the continued dominating role of arithmetic in the junior high school curriculum results in students entering high school with very limited mathematical backgrounds. The curriculum for all students should be broadened and enriched by the inclusion of appropriate topics in geometry, probability and statistics, as well as algebra. (*The Underachieving Curriculum,* p. *xii*)

These SIMS results have been confirmed in other studies comparing students at the eighth grade levels. In a study conducted by the Educational Testing Service in 1988–89, U.S. eighth-grade students were last in average mathematics proficiency compared with students in Ireland, South Korea, Spain, the United Kingdom, and Canada (Center for the Assessment of Educational Progress, *A World of Differences,* 1989).

Why do we perform so poorly? National Assessment results have shown that emphasizing algebra and geometry leads to higher test scores for eighth graders (U.S. Department of Education, National Center for Education Statistics, *The State of Mathematics Achievement: NAEP's 1990 Assessment of the Nation and the Trial Assessment of the States,* 1992). Historically, schools in the United States have delayed concentrated study of algebra and geometry longer than schools in other countries of the world.

The UCSMP secondary curriculum implements the curriculum recommendations of the Second International Mathematics Study.

In 1986, the National Council of Teachers of Mathematics began an ambitious effort to detail the curriculum it would like to see in schools. The "NCTM Standards," as they have come to be called, involve both content and methodology. The long Curriculum and Evaluation Standards document is divided into four sections, K–4, 5–8, 9–12, and Evaluation. Space limits our discussion here to just a few quotes from the 9–12 standards.

1989: National Council of Teachers of Mathematics. *Curriculum and Evaluation of Standards for School Mathematics.*

> The standards for grades 9–12 are based on the following assumptions:
>
> Students entering grade 9 will have experienced mathematics in the context of the broad, rich curriculum outlined in the K–8 standards.
>
> The level of computational proficiency suggested in the K–8 standards will be expected of all students; however, no student will be denied access to the study of mathematics in grades 9–12 because of a lack of computational facility.
>
> Although arithmetic computation will not be a direct object of study in grades 9–12, conceptual and procedural understandings of number, numeration, and operations, and the ability to make estimations and approximations and to judge the reasonableness of results will be strengthened in the context of applications and problem solving, including those situations dealing with issues of scientific computation.
>
> Scientific calculators with graphing capabilities will be available to all students at all times.
>
> A computer will be available at all times in every classroom for demonstration purposes, and all students will have access to computers for individual and group work.
>
> At least three years of mathematical study will be required of all secondary school students.
>
> These three years of mathematical study will revolve around a core curriculum differentiated by the depth and breadth of the treatment of topics and by the nature of applications.
>
> Four years of mathematical study will be required of all college-intending students.
>
> These four years of mathematical study will revolve around a broadened curriculum that includes extensions of the core topics and for which calculus is no longer viewed as the capstone experience.
>
> All students will study appropriate mathematics during their senior year. (pp. 124–125)

In 1991, NCTM came out with a second Standards document, concerned with the development of teachers and classroom teaching processes. Space limits our discussion to just a few quotes from the Standards for Teaching Mathematics section of this document.

1991: National Council of Teachers of Mathematics. *Professional Standards for Teaching Mathematics.*

> The standards for teaching are based on four assumptions about the practice of mathematics teaching:
>
> 1. The goal of teaching mathematics is to help all students develop mathematical power . . .
> 2. What students learn is fundamentally connected with *How* they learn.
> 3. All students can learn to think mathematically.

4. Teaching is a complex practice and hence not reducible to recipes or prescriptions. (pp. 21–22)

The teacher of mathematics should pose tasks that are based on —

sound and significant mathematics;

knowledge of students' understandings, interests, and experiences;

knowledge of the range of ways that diverse students learn mathematics;

and that

engage students' intellect;

develop students' mathematical understandings and skills;

stimulate students to make connections and develop a coherent framework for mathematical ideas;

call for problem formulation, problem solving, and mathematical reasoning;

promote communication about mathematics;

represent mathematics as an ongoing human activity;

display sensitivity to, and draw on, students' diverse background experiences and dispositions;

promote the development of all students' dispositions to do mathematics. (p. 25)

The UCSMP secondary curriculum is the first full mathematics curriculum that is consistent with the recommendations of the NCTM standards.

In 1989, the Mathematical Sciences Education Board (MSEB), a committee of the National Research Council that coordinates efforts for improvement of mathematics education in the United States, came out with the report *Everybody Counts,* emphasizing the need for the mathematics curriculum to be appropriate for as many students as possible. This thrust reflects the UCSMP position that as many students as possible be accommodated with the curriculum taken by those who go to college. It represents a change in thinking from the two-tiered system recommended in A Nation at Risk.

Following up and elaborating on the NCTM Evaluation Standards, many national reports have dealt with issues related to assessment. Among these are three MSEB reports: *For Good Measure* (1991), *Measuring Up* (1993), and *Measuring What Counts* (1993). The themes of these reports are that we need to change assessment instruments to be aligned with new curricula, to incorporate a variety of ways in which students can demonstrate their knowledge of mathematics, and to ensure that assessments are used in positive ways to enhance learning and teaching rather than in negative ways to keep students from having future opportunities to learn. (For further discussion of assessment, see pages T49–T52 of this Professional Sourcebook.)

Some changes have already occurred in assessment. The SAT, mathematics achievement, and Advanced Placement calculus exams of the Educational Testing Service now allow any calculator without a QWERTY keyboard. Some states have altered their testing to focus on applying mathematics and higher order thinking rather than on skills out of context.

Many of the ideas of recent reports are summarized in a 1991 MSEB report, *Reshaping School Mathematics: A Philosophy and Framework for Curriculum.* Six changes are identified there as affecting the context of mathematics education:

- Changes in the need for mathematics.
- Changes in mathematics and how it is used.
- Changes in the role of technology.
- Changes in American society.
- Changes in understanding of how students learn.
- Changes in international competitiveness.

In the UCSMP secondary curriculum we have attempted to respond to each of these changes.

Accomplishing the Goals

The three general problems in mathematics education in the United States lead to three major goals of the UCSMP secondary mathematics curriculum.

General Problem 1: Students do not learn enough mathematics by the time they leave school.

Specifically:

(A) Many students lack the mathematics background necessary to succeed in college, on the job, or in daily affairs.

(B) Even those students who possess mathematical skills are not introduced to enough applications of the mathematics they know.

(C) Students do not get enough experience with problems and questions that require some thought before answering.

(D) Many students terminate their study of mathematics too soon, not realizing the importance mathematics has in later schooling and in the marketplace.

(E) Students do not read mathematics books and, as a result, do not learn to become independent learners capable of acquiring mathematics outside of school when the need arises.

Goal 1: Upgrade students' achievement.

General Problem 2: The school mathematics curriculum has not kept up with changes in mathematics and the ways in which mathematics is used.

Specifically:

(A) Many mathematics curricula have not taken into account today's calculator and computer technology.

(B) Students who do succeed in secondary school mathematics are prepared for calculus, but are not equipped for the other mathematics they will encounter in college.

(C) Statistical ideas are found everywhere, from newspapers to research studies, but are not found in most secondary school mathematics curricula.

(D) The emergence of computer science has increased the importance of a background in discrete mathematics.

(E) Mathematics is not applied to areas outside the realm of the physical sciences, as much as within the field itself, but these applications are rarely taught and even more rarely tested.

(F) Estimation and approximation techniques are important in all of mathematics, from arithmetic on.

Goal 2: Update the mathematics curriculum.

General Problem 3: Too many students have been sorted out of the mathematics needed for employment and further schooling.

Specifically:

(A) Tracks make it easy to go down levels but almost impossible to go up.

(B) Remedial programs tend to put students further behind instead of catching them up.

(C) Enrichment classes often cover many topics, such as probability, statistics, discrete mathematics, and applications, and with activities of broader scope that are appropriate and important for all students.

(D) Courses for better students are often taught following the belief that the difficulty of a course is more important than its content, and with the view that if all survive, then the course was not a good one.

(E) Relative standards and preset numbers of students who go into special classes are incorrectly used as absolute indicators of ability to perform.

Goal 3: Increase the number of students who take mathematics beyond algebra and geometry.

We at UCSMP believe that these goals can be accomplished, because they already have been realized in some school districts. But substantial reworking of the curriculum has to be involved.

It is not enough simply to insert applications, a bit of statistics, and take students a few times a year to a computer. Currently the greatest amount of time in arithmetic is spent on calculation, in algebra on manipulating polynomials and rational expressions, in geometry on proof, in advanced algebra and later courses on functions. These topics are the most affected by technology.

It is also not enough to raise graduation requirements, although that is the simplest action to take. Increases in requirements characteristically lead to one of two situations. If the courses are kept the same, the result is typically a greater number of failures and an even greater number of dropouts. If the courses are eased, the result is lower performance for many students as they are brought through a weakened curriculum.

The fundamental problem, as SIMS noted, is the curriculum, and the fundamental problem in the curriculum is *time*. There is not enough time in the current 4-year algebra-geometry-algebra-precalculus curriculum to prepare students for calculus. The data reported by Bert Waits and Frank Demana in the *Mathematics Teacher* (January, 1988) are typical. Of students entering Ohio State University with exactly four years of college preparatory high-school mathematics, only 8% placed into calculus on the Ohio State mathematics placement test. The majority placed into pre-calculus, with 31% requiring one semester and 42% requiring two semesters of work. The remaining 19% placed into remedial courses below precalculus. Thus, even with the current curriculum, four years are not enough to take a typical student from algebra to calculus.

Today even most students who take four years of college preparatory mathematics successfully in high schools do not begin college with calculus. Given that the latest recommendations ask for students to learn more mathematics, *we believe five years of college preparatory mathematics beginning with algebra are necessary to provide the time for students to learn the mathematics they need for college in the 1990s.* Thus we do not believe the current NCTM Curriculum Standards for grades 9–12 can be accomplished in four years.

The time can be found by starting reform in grades 6-8. Examining textbooks of the early 1980s, Jim Flanders found that over half the pages in grades 6-8 are totally review ("How Much of the Content in Mathematics Textbook is New?" *Arithmetic Teacher*, September, 1987). This amount of review, coupled with the magnitude of review in previous years, effectively decelerates students at least 1–2 years compared to students in other countries. It explains why almost all industrialized countries of the world, except U.S. and Canada (and some French-speaking countries who do geometry before algebra), can begin concentrated study of algebra and geometry in the 7th or 8th grade.

In stark contrast to the review in grades 6-8, Flanders found that almost 90% of the pages of first-year algebra texts have content new to the student. This finding indicates why so many students in the U.S. have difficulty in first-year algebra. The student, having sat for years in mathematics classes where little was new, is overwhelmed. Some people interpret the overwhelming as the student "not being ready" for algebra, but we interpret it as the student being swamped by the pace. When you have been in a classroom in which at most only 1 of 3 days is devoted to anything new, you are not ready for a new idea every day. Thus we believe that algebra should be taught one year earlier to most students than is currently the case (Z. Usiskin, "Why Elementary Algebra Can, Should, and Must Be an Eighth-Grade Course for Average Students", *Mathematics Teacher*, September 1987).

Some school districts are attempting to do away with tracking by placing all students in the same classes, and with very similar expectations. We believe this is too simplistic a solution. Almost all of the very many schools that have implemented the UCSMP secondary curriculum with all their students *at the same time* have found that student differences in interests, cultural background, and learning style can be handled by their teachers who take advantage of the richness of the UCSMP textbooks and the wealth of teaching suggestions and ancillary materials that accompany them. Even so, they have almost all had to create slower-paced sections for students who enter with the least knowledge or who are unwilling to do homework. And they almost all realize that many students could have begun the curriculum a year earlier than the other students.

The most successful school districts realize that complex problems seldom have simple solutions. We believe strongly that the UCSMP curriculum is appropriate for virtually all students, but not at the same time. No student should be deprived of the opportunity to be successful in any of the courses, but no child who is ready should have to wait a year or two to begin the curriculum. Our evidence is strong that the national percentiles that we show on page T29 are good predictors of readiness for UCSMP courses. We recommend that school districts follow these percentiles by strongly recommending that students who fit them take our courses, and having a gray area in which students who miss these percentiles by small amounts or who very much wish to take our courses are allowed to take them. We strongly urge school districts to emphasize the importance of entering knowledge by strengthening their curricula in the preceding years, and stress that students must do homework *every day* when studying from UCSMP materials.

Finally, because UCSMP materials are not like traditional materials, we urge that school districts provide sufficient in-service training on the newer ideas incorporated in them. Teachers differ in ability, entering knowledge, preferred teaching style, and cultural background almost as much as students differ. Some love cooperative learning; others have never used it. Some are computer experts; others are neophytes. Some enjoy using manipulative materials; others avoid them. Some have had courses in statistics and discrete mathematics; others have not. Some are already trying writing and alternate assessment in their classrooms; others have not heard of these things. No single in-service can handle such variety. We encourage school districts to send teachers to professional conferences where teachers have choices on what to attend, to take advantage of in-service opportunities offered by UCSMP and ScottForesman, in addition to holding periodic meetings on site to discuss local issues. Like their students, teachers need time to learn.

The UCSMP Secondary Curriculum

The Six UCSMP Courses

Each UCSMP course is designed for the equivalent of a school year of at least 170 days in which mathematics is taught for at least 45 minutes (preferably 50 minutes or more) each day. All of the courses have the following general features: wider scope of content; continual emphasis on applications to the real world and to problem solving; up-to-date use of calculators and computers; a multi-dimensional (SPUR) approach to understanding; and review and mastery strategies for enhancing performance. These are described below and on pages *iv-v* of the Student Edition.

***Transition Mathematics* (TM)** weaves three themes—applied arithmetic, pre-algebra and pre-geometry—by focusing on arithmetic operations in mathematics and the real world. Variables are used as pattern generalizers, abbreviations in formulas, and unknowns in problems, and are represented on the number line and graphed in the coordinate plane. Basic arithmetic and algebraic skills are connected to corresponding geometry topics.

Algebra has a scope far wider than most other algebra texts. Applications motivate all topics. Exponential growth and compound interest are covered. Statistics and geometry are settings for work with linear expressions and sentences. Probability provides a context for algebraic fractions, functions, and set ideas. Technology for graphing is assumed to be available.

Geometry integrates coordinates and transformations throughout, and gives strong attention to measurement formulas and three-dimensional figures in the first two-thirds of the book. Work with proof-writing follows a carefully sequenced development of the logical and conceptual precursors to proof. Geometry drawing technology is highly recommended.

Advanced Algebra emphasizes facility with algebraic expressions and forms, especially linear and quadratic forms, powers and roots, and functions based on these concepts. Students study logarithmic, trigonometric, polynomial, and other special functions both for their abstract properties and as tools for modeling real-world situations. A geometry course or its equivalent is a prerequisite, for geometric ideas are utilized throughout. Technology for graphing functions is assumed to be available to students

***Functions, Statistics, and Trigonometry* (FST)** integrates statistical and algebraic concepts, and previews calculus in work with functions and intuitive notions of limits. Technology is assumed available for student use in plotting functions, analyzing data, and simulating experiments. Enough trigonometry is available to constitute a standard precalculus course in trigonometry and circular functions.

***Precalculus and Discrete Mathematics* (PDM)** integrates the background students must have to be successful in calculus (advanced work with functions and trigonometry, an introduction to limits and other calculus ideas), with the discrete mathematics (number systems, combinatorics, recursion, graphs) helpful in computer science. Mathematical thinking, including specific attention to formal logic and proof, is a theme throughout. Automatic graphing technology is assumed available for students.

Target Populations

We believe that all high-school graduates should take courses through *Advanced Algebra*, that all students planning to go to college should take courses through *Functions, Statistics, and Trigonometry*, and that students planning majors in technical areas should take all six UCSMP courses.

The critical juncture is when first-year algebra is completed. All qualified students should be afforded the possibility of taking *Transition Mathematics* in 6th grade so as to maximize the potential for them to complete *Algebra* in 7th grade and thus take calculus in high school without any acceleration.

The fundamental principle in placing students into courses is that entry should not be based on age, but on mathematical knowledge. Our studies indicate that with a standard curriculum, about 10% of students nationally are ready for *Transition Mathematics* at 6th grade, about another 40% at 7th grade, another 20% at 8th grade, and another 10–15% at 9th grade. We caution that these percentages are national, not local percentages, and the variability in our nation is enormous. We have tested the materials in school districts where few students are at grade level, where *Transition Mathematics* is appropriate for no more than the upper half of 8th-graders. We have tested also in school districts where as many as 90% of the students have successfully used *Transition Mathematics* in 7th grade. School districts have increased the percentages at the 6th and 7th grade by strengthening the mathematics curriculum in grades K–5 or K–6.

We also caution that the percentages are not automatic. Students who do not reach 7th-grade competence until the 9th-grade level often do not possess the study habits necessary for successful completion of these courses. At the 9th-grade level, *Transition Mathematics* has been substituted successfully either for a traditional pre-algebra course or for the first year of an algebra course spread out over two years. It does not work as a substitute for a general mathematics course in which there is no expectation that students will take algebra the following year.

On page T29 is a chart identifying the courses and the populations for which they are intended. The percentiles are national percentiles on a 7th-grade standardized mathematics test using 7th-grade norms, and apply to potential *Transition Mathematics* students. Page T29 also provides advice for starting in the middle of the series.

Left column: These students are often more interested in school, and they should be offered the Challenges suggested in the Teacher's Edition. Teachers may also wish to enrich courses for these students further with problems from mathematics contests.

2nd column: These students should be expected to take mathematics at least through the 11th grade, by which time they will have the mathematics needed for all college majors except those in the hard sciences and engineering. For that they will have the opportunity to take 12th-grade mathematics.

3rd column: Students in the 30th–70th percentile can complete *Advanced Algebra* by taking three years of high school mathematics. Currently over half of these students go to college. By completing *FST,* they will have studied the kind of mathematics needed for any major.

Grade	**The top 10% of students** are ready for *Transition Mathematics* in 6th grade. These students can proceed through the entire curriculum by the 11th grade and take calculus in the 12th grade.	**Students in the 50th–90th percentile** on a 7th-grade standardized mathematics test should be ready to take *Transition Mathematics* in 7th grade.	Students who do not reach the 7th-grade level in mathematics until the 8th grade **(in the 30th–70th percentile)** begin *Transition Mathematics* in 8th grade.	Students who do not reach the 7th-grade level in mathematics until the 9th grade **(in the 15th–50th percentile)** begin *Transition Mathematics* in 9th grade.
6	Transition Mathematics			
7	Algebra	Transition Mathematics		
8	Geometry	Algebra	Transition Mathematics	
9	Advanced Algebra	Geometry	Algebra	Transition Mathematics
10	Functions, Statistics, and Trigonometry	Advanced Algebra	Geometry	Algebra
11	Precalculus and Discrete Mathematics	Functions, Statistics, and Trigonometry	Advanced Algebra	Geometry
12	Calculus (not available through UCSMP)	Precalculus and Discrete Mathematics	Functions, Statistics, and Trigonometry	Advanced Algebra

Right column: Students in the 15th–50th percentile should not be tracked into courses that put them further behind. Rather they should be put into this curriculum and counseled on study skills. The logic is simple: Students who are behind in mathematical knowledge need to work harder at it, not less, in order to catch up.

Starting in the Middle of the Series

Every UCSMP course has been designed so that it could be used independently of other UCSMP courses. Accordingly, about half of the testing of UCSMP courses after *Transition Mathematics* has been with students who have not had any previous UCSMP courses. We have verified that any of the UCSMP courses can be taken successfully following the typical prerequisite courses in the standard curriculum.

Starting with UCSMP *Algebra* No additional prerequisites other than those needed for success in any algebra course are needed for success in UCSMP *Algebra.*

Students who have studied *Transition Mathematics* tend to cover more of UCSMP *Algebra* than other students because they have been introduced to more of the applications of algebra.

UCSMP *Algebra* prepares students for any standard geometry course.

Starting with UCSMP *Geometry* No additional prerequisites other than those needed for success in any geometry course are needed for success in UCSMP *Geometry.*

UCSMP *Geometry* can be used with faster, average, and slower students who have these prerequisites. Prior study of *Transition Mathematics* and UCSMP *Algebra* ensures this background, but this content is also found in virtually all existing middle school or junior high school texts. Classes of students who have studied UCSMP *Algebra* tend to cover more UCSMP *Geometry* than other classes because they know more geometry and are better at the algebra used in geometry. Students who have studied UCSMP *Geometry* are ready for any second-year algebra text.

Starting with UCSMP *Advanced Algebra* UCSMP *Advanced Algebra* can be used following any standard geometry text.

Students who have had UCSMP *Geometry* before UCSMP *Advanced Algebra* tend to be better prepared in the transformations and coordinate geometry they will need in this course, and geometry courses using other books should be careful to cover this content.

Students who have studied UCSMP *Advanced Algebra* are prepared for courses commonly found at the senior level, including trigonometry or precalculus courses.

Starting with *Functions, Statistics, and Trigonometry* *FST* assumes that students have completed a second-year algebra course. Students who have studied some trigonometry, like that found in UCSMP *Advanced Algebra*, will be at an advantage. No additional prerequisites other than those found in any second-year algebra text are needed for success in *FST*.

FST provides the background for success in a non-proof-oriented calculus, such as is often taken by business or social studies majors in college, but not for a proof-oriented calculus.

Starting with *Precalculus and Discrete Mathematics* *PDM* can be taken successfully by students who have had *FST*, by students who have had typical senior level courses that include study of trigonometry and functions, and by top students who have successfully completed *full* advanced algebra and trigonometry courses.

PDM provides the background necessary for any typical calculus course, either at the high school or college level, including advanced placement calculus courses at either the AB or BC level.

Professional Sourcebook: SECTION 2 ABOUT *TRANSITION MATHEMATICS*

Goals of *Transition Mathematics*

Transition Mathematics attacks three content areas—arithmetic, algebra, and geometry—simultaneously. In each area we want to upgrade student performance in mathematics as we update the curriculum. We want more students to be better able to apply arithmetic, and to be successful in future years in both algebra and geometry study. If there were a subtitle for this book, it would be:

Applied Arithmetic, Pre-Algebra, and Pre-Geometry.

We have other, more lofty goals. We want students to view their study of mathematics as worthwhile, as full of interesting and entertaining information, as related to almost every endeavor. We want them to realize that mathematics is still growing and is changing fast. We want them to look for and recognize mathematics in places they haven't before, to use the library, to search through newspapers or almanacs, to get excited by knowledge. We want students to develop personal self-confidence, positive attitudes, and effective study skills in mathematics.

Who Should Take *Transition Mathematics?*

This book works with students who, *regardless of age*, enter the course knowing at least as much arithmetic as the typical entering 7th grader nationally. We call this "entering 7th-grade competence." Without a calculator, this student has the following arithmetic competence at a minimum:

(1) is proficient at whole number arithmetic;

(2) can multiply fractions and can add or subtract fractions with the same denominator, but may not be so good at adding or subtracting with different denominators or with division of fractions;

(3) can add or subtract decimals when in columns, but may not be so good when they are on a horizontal line; can multiply decimals but cannot divide them with accuracy;

(4) has seen percentages but only knows the simplest things about them.

The student at entering 7th-grade competence will have measured lengths and will be familiar with both customary and metric measures of length and weight, and will know the names of common geometric figures. This student will also be familiar with the idea of number lines.

If a student does not fit at least these minimums, this book assumes too much and the teacher will be frustrated by having to review so much from previous years. Older students – those in 9th grade or above – who are in a course where this book is used have usually experienced years of frustration in courses where they have performed poorly and years of boredom from encountering so little new material. They particularly need a teacher who has the patience and the determination to guide them through. Like all *Transition Mathematics* students, these students should also be in a program where algebra is the next course, and they must be willing to work in this one. The pace of *Transition Mathematics* has been set with the expectation that students will do homework every night to prepare them for the work load in their later mathematics courses.

Problems *Transition Mathematics* Addresses

The general problems addressed by the UCSMP secondary curriculum are discussed in Section 1, on pages T21–T30. More specifically, *Transition Mathematics* responds to six serious problems which cannot be treated by small changes in content or approach.

Problem 1: *Large numbers of students are not able to apply the arithmetic they know.*

Historically, many courses at this level have concentrated on paper and pencil arithmetic skills, in the mistaken belief that with arithmetic skill automatically comes competence in the ability to apply that skill. By such review, students are decelerated in their mathematical education at a time when their minds are especially curious and desirous of tackling new ideas.

The *Transition Mathematics* response: Since the evidence is that students do have whole number arithmetic in hand, this is not reviewed again. Instead, from Chapter 1 on, the uses of numbers and operations are given very strong emphasis. These uses are the foundation upon which we build to provide motivation for studying algebra and geometry. There is a careful sequence. Numbers represent things. The models for the operations deal with these numbers. So at first there are simple uses, and then more complex ones. Our evidence is that this *structured approach to applications* provides the basics which students can use in all future endeavors when applying arithmetic. By reviewing arithmetic in this way, with algebraic and geometric contexts emphasized, students gain considerable knowledge of algebra and geometry without loss of arithmetic skills and concepts.

Problem 2: *The mathematics curriculum has been lagging behind today's widely available and inexpensive technology.*

When *Transition Mathematics* was first developed, its requirement that students have a scientific calculator was considered quite bold. Now there is unanimous sentiment in recent national reports on mathematics education in favor of the use of calculators in all mathematics courses. There is also unanimous sentiment for the incorporation of computers, but thus far no agreement on how that should be done.

The *Transition Mathematics* response: We continue to use scientific calculators starting in the first chapter. There are important reasons for using scientific calculators rather than simpler 4-function calculators (see pages T39–T40). If a student is to buy a calculator, it should be one that will be useful for more than a single year of study.

The evidence from our evaluations of *Transition Mathematics* is that students gain considerably in arithmetic skills during the year. They are particularly able to do better than other students when allowed to use calculators, a circumstance which more and more the outside world requires. Teachers report that they are able to cover much more content because they do not have to waste time waiting for students to do complicated arithmetic that does not contribute to the ideas behind the solving of problems.

In the second edition, we include significant work with spreadsheets because of their importance in the real world, but also because they involve many of the important concepts students should learn at this level: the organization of data; the use of various types of graphs and charts; the significance of algebraic language and formulas. We introduce graphics calculators in the last chapter to show students the power of technology they should encounter in their next year of study.

Problem 3: *Too many students fail algebra.*

It is too much to expect students to learn all of traditional first-year algebra in a single year. Students who have not had prior experience with algebra rarely master all the concepts of first-year algebra in a single year, and they often fail because both the pace and the number of new concepts overwhelm them.

The *Transition Mathematics* response: With regard to content, we work not only on the transition into algebra, but also on the important concepts of algebra. The evidence from our studies is that students using *Transition Mathematics* knew much more algebra at the end of their year than students in comparison classes. Thus, though we expect students to do well in algebra even if they have not had *Transition Mathematics*, we expect much better performance from those who have had that kind of rich experience.

With regard to the introduction of new ideas, we suggest in *Transition Mathematics* the same kind of pace that students will encounter the next year in any algebra course. This prepares students for the nightly homework and the daily introduction of new ideas. The lessons are shorter in *Transition Mathematics* than in UCSMP *Algebra*, but the evidence is that students, though often requiring a period of adjustment, are able to make the adjustment well in *Transition Mathematics* and those habits carry over into their next mathematics courses.

Problem 4: *Even students who succeed in algebra often do poorly in geometry.*

The evidence is that the knowledge of geometry among American 8th-graders and among entering geometry students is atrocious. As with algebra, it is too much to expect students to learn all of geometry in a single year in high school. The best predictor of success with proof is a student's geometry knowledge at the beginning of a course.

The *Transition Mathematics* response: *Transition Mathematics* devotes considerable attention to geometry, with particular attention paid to the numerical relationships involving lines, angles, and polygons. The evidence from our studies of *Transition Mathematics* validates the UCSMP integration of geometry into these courses. In the first edition *Transition Mathematics* summative evaluation, students in comparison classes showed no increase in geometry knowledge from September to June. However, students using *Transition Mathematics* knew almost as much at the end of the year as typical students entering a 10th grade geometry class.

Problem 5: *Students don't read.*

Students using traditional texts tell us they don't read because (1) the text is uninteresting, and (2) they don't have to read because the teacher explains it for them. But students *must* learn to read for future success in mathematics.

The *Transition Mathematics* response to (1) above: We have paid careful attention to the explanations, examples, and questions in each lesson. So every lesson of this book contains reading and questions covering the reading. *Transition Mathematics* is more than a resource for questions; it is a resource for information, for examples of how to do problems, for the history of major ideas, for applications of the ideas, for connections between ideas in one place in the book and in another, and for motivation.

Our response to (2) above is to encourage teachers not to explain everything *in advance* to students. Because students can read and understand the *Transition Mathematics* text, the teacher has the freedom to teach in a variety of ways, and it is not necessary to explain every day what the textbook says. The teacher can concentrate on helping students with difficult new symbols and vocabulary, or on developing further examples, explanations, and investigations tailored to his or her class. More detailed information about reading can be found on pages T45–T47.

First-time teachers of *Transition Mathematics* are often skeptical at first about the amount of reading. As the year progresses, they tend to join those who have taught *Transition Mathematics* in viewing the reading as one of the strongest features of this series. Some teachers feel that *Transition Mathematics* teaches reading comprehension; almost all who use the book feel that the requirement to read helps develop thinkers who are more critical and aware.

Problem 6: *Students are not skillful enough, regardless of what they are taught.*

The evidence is that students are rather skillful at routine problems but not with problems involving complicated numbers, different wordings, or new contexts. It is obvious that in order to obtain such skill, students must see problems with all sorts of numbers, a variety of wordings, and many different contexts. We also ask that students do certain problems mentally, which expands the level of competence expected of students.

Encountering such problems is not enough. *Transition Mathematics* employs a **four-stage approach to develop skill**.

Stage 1 involves a concentrated introduction to the ideas surrounding the skill: why it is needed, how it is done, and the kinds of problems that can be solved with it. Most books are organized to have this stage, because teachers recognize that explanations of an idea require time. At the end of this stage, typically only the best students have the skill. But in *Transition Mathematics* this is only the beginning.

Stage 2 occupies the following lessons in the chapter and consists of questions designed to establish some competence in the skill. These are found in the review exercises. By the end of the lessons of the chapter, most students should have some competence in the skills, but some may not have enough.

Stage 3 involves mastery learning. At the end of each chapter is a Progress Self-Test for students to take and judge how they are doing. Worked-out solutions are included to provide feedback and help to the student. This is followed by a Chapter Review, organized by objectives, to enable students to acquire those skills they didn't have when taking the Progress Self-Test. Teachers are expected to spend 1–3 days on these sections to give students time to reach mastery. By the end of this stage, students should have gained mastery at least at the level of typical students covering the content.

Stage 4 continues the review. Vital skills, such as measuring or working with percent, receive consistent emphasis throughout the book. The evidence is striking. *Transition Mathematics* students attain arithmetic skills virtually equivalent to those students who are learning only arithmetic all year. They attain algebra and geometry skills and concepts far above comparable students. (See pages T52–T56 on research)

What's New in the Second Edition

The publication of the complete six-year UCSMP series has given another perspective on each text and its role in the long-term development of mathematical concepts and competence. National reports that have been issued since the publication of the first test version of *Transition Mathematics* in 1985 have stressed the importance of many of the innovations present in UCSMP texts. Widespread availability of computer spreadsheets indicates that this course could incorporate technology beyond the scientific calculator. At the same time, the elementary curriculum has changed in many schools, and we can expect slightly better student competence with certain ideas.

The second edition of *Transition Mathematics* has also benefited from user reports, focus group discussions, and ScottForesman surveys of users from all regions throughout the United States. This information has verified the immense popularity of the book and the overwhelming good feelings it has generated among its users. Thus, though many changes have been made, the second edition maintains the overall structure and features of the first edition.

The person familiar with the first edition of *Transition Mathematics* will note the following changes:

- Colored headers appear in the lessons to help outline the reading and to present it in more manageable chunks.
- Each chapter includes a set of Projects to provide students opportunities to explore concepts in a more in-depth way. Students may find it beneficial to work on the Projects in small groups. (See pages T41–T42.)
- Activities are included to provide students with more hands-on experiences. Many of the activities are suitable for small-group work.
- The use of spreadsheets has been introduced.
- There is a greater emphasis on probability.
- Solutions to Examples are printed in a special font to help model what students should write when they do the Questions.
- A larger number of questions require student writing. (See pages T48–T49.)
- A global, multicultural view of mathematics is enhanced with new photos from around the world. Informative captions are now included.
- Graphic displays are drawn with a contemporary look to emphasize that the data in the text are like that found in newspapers, magazines, and other sources outside the classroom.
- An enhanced Teacher's Edition now provides daily suggestions for adapting to individual needs, optional activities, and assessment alternatives.
- An augmented ancillary package offers two sets of Lesson Masters, performance tests and forms for authentic assessment, and an expanded Technology Sourcebook.
- Interactive multimedia components, emphasizing real-world applications, are designed to further enhance instruction and provide motivation.

Professional Sourcebook: SECTION 3 GENERAL TEACHING SUGGESTIONS FOR *TRANSITION MATHEMATICS*

Transition Mathematics is the core of a mathematics course. It is not meant to stand alone without a teacher or without other materials. Nor does it attempt to prescribe a single way of teaching mathematics. We have seen the first edition of this text used effectively with a variety of models of teaching—from direct instruction through cooperative learning, and we expect the second edition to be at least as flexible.

We feel a need to restate one of the assumptions of the *Professional Standards for Teaching Mathematics* (NCTM, 1991), that "teaching is a complex practice and hence not reducible to recipes or prescriptions." The suggestions which follow should not be construed as rigid: students, teachers, classes, and schools vary greatly. But the suggestions should not be ignored. They come from extensive discussions with teachers of earlier versions of these materials, written comments from experienced users of the first edition, and from test results. We encourage you to read them, and to try as many of them as you can in your classroom.

Planning

It hardly needs to be said that good teaching begins with careful planning. In this section we concentrate on features that may be different from other books from which you have taught.

First Steps

1. Find out more about these materials. If you have not already done so, skim Section 1 and read Section 2 of this Professional Sourcebook. These sections will inform you if your students are among the typical *Transition Mathematics* students, and they give the motivation for many of the features you will find. Also read pages *iv-v* of the Student Edition for additional information on UCSMP and *Transition Mathematics*.

2. Make certain that you have all the materials you need. A list of components that are available with the Second Edition of *Transition Mathematics* is on page T19 of this book. If you do not have all the materials, contact your local ScottForesman representative or call ScottForesman at 1-800-554-4411.

Before the school year starts you should assemble some resources for your teaching. Some materials you will want to have in your classroom throughout the year are: a dictionary, an atlas, an almanac, and either a globe or a large world map for the wall.

3. Check that your students will have all the materials they need. In addition to pencils and paper, all students are expected to have a scientific calculator, a ruler calibrated in centimeters and inches, and a protractor. A list of specifications is given in the "To the Student" section on pages 1–3. Be certain to cover this section with your students.

4. Familiarize yourself with the general layout of the two-part Teacher's Edition (this part and one other). Part 1 of the Teacher's Edition contains Chapters 1–6. Part 2 contains Chapters 7–13. At the beginning of each chapter are four extra pages (tinted) that display pacing schedules, objectives, available materials, and overall notes for the chapter. Following Chapter 6 in Part 1 are the Selected Answers (for Chapters 1–6) and the Glossary and Index to the entire Student Edition. In Part 2, Chapter 13 is is followed by the Selected Answers (for Chapters 7–13), and again the Glossary and Index.

5. Familiarize yourself with the features of the Student Edition. There are 13 chapters, with from 6–10 lessons each. Each chapter begins with a 2-page chapter opener that serves as an introduction and is meant to be read. Then come the lessons, each with reading followed by four types of questions: Covering the Reading, Applying the Mathematics, Review, and

Exploration. At the end of the chapter are Projects. (See pages T41–T42.) Each chapter ends with a Summary and list of new Vocabulary for the chapter, a Progress Self-Test, and a Chapter Review. The Progress Self-Test and Chapter Review are not optional; they are designed to focus students' attentions to the important material and objectives of the chapter. (See pages T38–T39.) The Selected Answers section (pages 732–754) in the student edition provides answers to odd-numbered Applying the Mathematics and Review Questions.

6. Consider sending information about *Transition Mathematics* home with your students. A letter or flyer to parents conveys your and your school district's concern for their child and at the same time can let them know your expectations regarding materials and homework. Suggestions concerning what form a letter or flyer can take, and what to put in it are provided below. These suggestions come from mailings sent to us by UCSMP users.

Sample Letter to Parents

Because the adoption of books is generally done by a school or school district, it may be best if the letter comes from the mathematics department, the mathematics department chair or supervisor, or the principal. The letter should be on school or school district stationery. Here are the kinds of information schools have conveyed:

UCSMP beliefs/philosophy Mathematics is valuable to the average citizen. All students can learn a significant amount of mathematics. We can learn from other countries. A major cause of our problems lies in the curriculum. The mathematics curriculum can make better use of time by spending less time on review (from previous years) and outmoded content and skills. Calculators and computers render some content obsolete, make other content more important, and change the ways we should view still other content. The scope of mathematics should expand at all levels. The classroom should draw examples from the real world. To make significant changes in any school, teachers, administrators, and parents must work together.

Features of UCSMP texts that parents will notice Students are expected to read. They are expected to use calculators. There are a variety of problems in each question set rather than a single type of problem repeated a large number of times. *It is best if each feature is followed by a sentence or two with a rationale for that feature. Such information may be found throughout this Sourcebook.*

Materials students need This can be similar to the list found in the "To The Student" section of the student book (pages 1–3). This should include a list of the features of the calculators students should have, and information on how students can obtain such calculators (whether from the school or from a local store). If possible, include prices.

How parents can help It is wise to include statements that describe the roles of parents in their child's education, particularly because at this level, parents are sometimes given the feeling that they no longer are integral. Here are some suggestions: Encourage your child to read the textbook. Check with your children to see that they have the supplies they need. See that your children are doing homework every night. Encourage determination and perseverance; if your child is having a problem, ask your child to tell you what he or she knows about the idea. Monitor your child's absences (perhaps include the school's absence policy). Contact the teacher as soon as a problem arises; do not wait. Encourage your child to seek help whenever necessary (give places to get help).

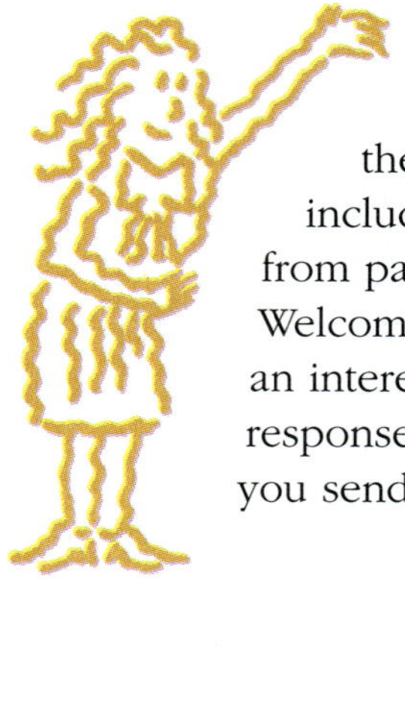

With this letter, some school districts include their mathematics course sequence. Some indicate their grading policies. Whatever you include, you should expect responses from parents who seek clarification. Welcome each response as a sign of an interested parent and because the responses will help you in drafting what you send next year.

Planning for Teaching

Planning for teaching with *Transition Mathematics* is similar to the planning you might do for any mathematics class.

Global planning can be done by looking over the Table of Contents and setting goals for each grading period. The chapters in this book are meant to be covered in order, at a pace of about one lesson per day, and we suggest that first-time users adhere to this pattern. This means that most teachers should be able to cover about 12 chapters. This amounts to approximately two chapters each marking period if you give grades every six weeks, or three chapters per marking period if you give grades every nine or ten weeks. Teachers of very well-prepared students in schools which do not lose much instructional time to other matters are likely to be able to cover more, and those who are teaching underprepared students in classes with numerous interruptions may cover less.

To get an overview of the content in each chapter, read the Chapter Overview on the tinted pages in this Teacher's Edition; read the lesson titles; and scan the Summary and Vocabulary, Progress Self-Test, and Chapter Review at the end of the chapter. Collectively these will give you a good idea of what the chapter is about, and how much of the content will be new to you or your students. Make a tentative schedule for working through the chapter. Be sure to leave 2 or 3 days for review before the chapter test (see *Strategies for Mastery* on pages T38–T39).

Read each lesson in the Student Edition. Then read the Overview, the Notes on Reading, the Notes on the Questions, and other side and bottom notes in the Teacher's Edition. They indicate the Resources you may need for the lesson. They also provide ideas for various ways of approaching the lesson. They will help you decide what instructional modes (whole-class discussion, small-group work, demonstration, lecture, etc.) you might use, how you might go over the assignment from the previous day, how you could sequence the class activities from opening to closing, and what assignment you can make for the next class.

Do all of the Questions before assigning them. Note any questions with directions which might need clarification to your students, or any questions which you think are particularly important or exceptionally difficult.

Pace

There is a natural tendency, when using a new book, to go more slowly, to play it safe should you forget something. Teachers using these materials for the first time have almost invariably said that they would move more quickly the next year. Do not be afraid to move quickly. As in all UCSMP texts, virtually all lessons in *Transition Mathematics* are intended to be read and discussed in one day.

Students adjust to the pace set by the teacher. It is especially important that Chapter 1 be taught at a one-day-per-lesson pace. At the end of the chapter, spend a few days on the Progress Self-Test and Chapter Review to cinch the major skills. We know from our studies that this pace produces the highest performance levels. Students need to be exposed to content in order to learn it.

Some classes in our studies of this book went very slowly; their teachers seemed reluctant to move to any new content. Where this happens, the students get into a rut. Better students are bored because they know the material. Slower students are frustrated because they are being asked to spend more time on the stuff they don't know. They all get discouraged and perform far lower than any other comparable students at the end of the year. We can state this rather strongly: If you want to guarantee poor performance, go slowly through a book.

There are times when it will be difficult to maintain this pace. But be advised: a slow pace can make it too easy to lose perspective and difficult to relate ideas. You need to get to later content to realize why you were asked to learn earlier content! If you spend too much time in the lessons, you may find that your slowest students may have learned more by having gone through content slowly, but all the other students will have learned less. The wise teacher strikes a balance, goes quickly enough to keep things interesting but slowly enough to have time for explanations.

David R. Johnson's booklets *Every Minute Counts* and *Making Minutes Count Even More* give excellent practical suggestions on making use of class time.

Average students should be able to complete 12 chapters of *Transition Mathematics*. Classes with better than average students have usually been able to complete the entire text. If you find in spring that you have been going through the chapters more slowly than recommended, rather than omitting entire chapters, we suggest omitting certain lessons. However, please be aware that these lessons are reviewed later. You will need to adjust your homework assignments accordingly.

Assignments

We recommend that a typical homework assignment be one of the following:

1. read Lesson n; write answers to all Questions in Lesson n; or
2. read Lesson n; write answers to Questions Covering the Reading in Lesson n, and Applying the Mathematics, Review, and Exploration in Lesson $n - 1$.

Thus virtually every day students should be expected to do the equivalent of a complete set of questions from a lesson. At times you will want to preview the reading, but for typical classes this should not be a regular part of the plan. (See *Using the Reading*, pages T46–T47.)

The Questions in each lesson have been designed to cover the key skills, properties, uses and representations in the lesson. Questions were not written with an odd-even assignment plan in mind. Skipping questions may lead to gaps in student understanding. The Exploration questions may be assigned for all to do, or left as optional work for extra credit.

We also recommend that assignments be given on the days following chapter tests. If this is not done, then there will be up to 13 days without homework, the equivalent of a complete chapter's work.

Taking Review Into Account

Every lesson includes a set of Review questions. These questions serve a variety of purposes. First, they develop competence in a topic. Because we do not expect students to master a topic on the day they are introduced to it, these questions, coming on the days after introduction, help to solidify the ideas. Second, they maintain competence from preceding chapters. This review is particularly effective with topics that have not been studied for some time.

At times, we are able to give harder questions in reviews than we could expect students to be able to do on the day they were introduced to the topic. Thus the reviews sometimes serve as questions which integrate ideas from previous lessons.

Finally, we occasionally review an idea that has not been discussed for some time, just before it is to surface again in a lesson. The notes on the Questions usually alert you to this circumstance.

Teachers of classes that perform the best assign all the Review questions, give students the answers each day, and discuss them when needed. Those who do not assign all reviews tend to get poorer performance; their students never get enough practice to solidify and master the ideas and, even when mastered, the ideas are forgotten. *The Review questions must be assigned to ensure optimum performance.*

Strategies for Mastery

Some students master the content of one lesson in one day; but many do not. Why then do we suggest that you spend only one day per lesson? We do so because the combination of Review questions in each lesson and the end-of-chapter material has proved to be a powerful vehicle for achieving mastery, while allowing teachers and students to cover a substantial amount of material.

The mastery strategy used at the end of each chapter of *Transition Mathematics* is one that has been validated by a great deal of research. Its components are a Progress Self-Test (the "formative test" in the parlance of some mastery learning literature), solutions to that test in the student's textbook (the "feedback"), review questions tied to the same objectives used to make up the self-test (the "correctives"), and finally a chapter test covering the same objectives.

Following the strategy means assigning the Progress Self-Test as a homework assignment to be done *under simulated test conditions.* The next day should be devoted to answering student questions about the problems and doing some problems from the Chapter Review if there is time.

For most classes, as a second night's assignment, we suggest the even-numbered questions from the Chapter Review. Neither solutions nor answers to the even-numbered questions are in the student text, so students will have to work on their own without these aids. The next day, discuss these questions in class.

Give the test on the third day. The odd-numbered Chapter Review questions, for which answers are given in the student text, can be useful for studying for that test. In some classes, a third day before the test may be needed. If so, either the odd-numbered Chapter Review questions, selected Lesson Masters, or questions generated by the *Quiz and Test Writer* software can be used as sources of problems.

We strongly recommend that, except for classes of exceptionally talented students (where less review may be needed), teachers follow this strategy. The evidence is substantial that it promotes higher levels of performance.

Using Technology

We use calculators and computers in UCSMP fundamentally because they are tools important to most users of mathematics today, whether on the job or in one's personal life. The popularity of their use is because they make important mathematical ideas accessible to students at an early age and to people who might otherwise find mathematics difficult; they relieve the drudgery of calculation, particularly with numbers and equations encountered in realistic contexts; and they facilitate exploration and open-ended problem solving by making multiple instances easy to examine. Furthermore, as indicated in Section 4 (Research and Development), our use of technology has resulted in no loss of paper-and-pencil skill in arithmetic, and has freed up time in the curriculum to spend on other topics that lead to overall better performance by UCSMP students.

Calculators Hand-held calculators first appeared in 1971. Not until 1976 did the price for a four-function calculator come below $50 (equivalent to well over $100 today). Still, in 1975, a national commission recommended that hand calculators be used on all tests starting in eighth grade, and in 1980 the National Council of Teachers of Mathematics recommended that calculators be used in all grades of school from kindergarten on. The SATs, Achievement, and Advanced Placement tests of the College Board already allow all standard scientific and graphing calculators. Several standardized test batteries are being developed with calculators. And slowly but surely calculators are being expected on more and more licensing exams outside of school.

The business and mathematics education communities generally believe that paper-and-pencil algorithms are becoming obsolete. Do not be surprised. The long division algorithm we use was born only in the late 1400s; it can have a death as well.

It is wonderful to live in the age when calculators have been developed that quickly and efficiently do arithmetic. This frees us to use arithmetic more and, as teachers, to spend more time on mental arithmetic, estimation, and problem solving. It is inevitable that calculators will be considered as natural as pencils for doing mathematics. A century from now people will be amazed when they learn that some students as recently as the 1990s went to schools where calculators were not used. Students of the future would no doubt consider it cruel and unusual punishment.

Transition Mathematics assumes the student has a *scientific* calculator, one that can display numbers in scientific notation. This is required for the large and small numbers found throughout the book. There is also need for the π, square root, power, and parentheses keys found on such calculators. The order of operations on a scientific calculator is the same as in algebra, so this kind of calculator motivates and reinforces algebra skills. CAUTION: Some calculators that do fractions are *not* scientific calculators.

Students will overuse calculators. Part of learning to use any machine is to make mistakes: using it when you shouldn't, not using it when you should. Anyone who has a word processor has used it for short memos that could much more easily have been handwritten. Anyone who has a microwave has used it for food that could have been cooked either in a conventional oven or on top of the stove.

The overuse dies down, but it takes some months. In the meantime, stress this important idea. There are three ways to get answers to arithmetic problems: by paper and pencil, mentally, or by using some automatic means (a table, a calculator, a trusty friend, etc.). Some problems require more than one of these means, but the wise applier of arithmetic knows when to use each of these ways.

Generally this means that good arithmeticians do a lot of calculations mentally, either because they are basic facts (e.g., 3×5) or because they follow simple rules (e.g., $2/3 \times 4/5$ or 100×4.72). They may not use a calculator on these because the likelihood of making an error entering or reading is greater than the likelihood of making a mental error. As a rule, we seldom say, "Do not use calculators here." We want students to learn for themselves when calculator use is appropriate and when it is not. However, you may feel the need to prod some students to avoid the calculator. An answer of 2.9999999 to $\sqrt{9}$ should be strongly discouraged.

Many lessons include questions to be done "in your head." These are designed to develop skill in mental arithmetic and show students situations in which mental calculation is an appropriate approach to calculation. You may wish to give quizzes on these kinds of problems and have a "no calculator" rule for these problems.

Further information about the UCSMP approach to calculators is found in an article by Dan Hirschhorn and Sharon Senk in the 1992 NCTM Yearbook.

Graphics calculators Even at this level, you may have a student or a few students who own graphics calculators. We recommend graphics calculators for use in later UCSMP courses, and they are discussed in Chapter 13 of *Transition Mathematics*. They have all the calculator operations we expect in a scientific calculator. They also have the advantage of displaying numbers in computations. However, their order of operations is often different from that found in scientific calculators, and key sequences for scientific calculators will often not work with them.

Computers The computer is a powerful tool for you to use in your classroom to demonstrate the relationships, patterns, properties, and algorithms of arithmetic. From the very first chapter of this book, computer exercises appear. Do not ignore the computer questions even if you do not have computers available. The goal is not to teach computer programming, but to use the computer as a tool. Students are not surprised that the computer can do difficult tasks, but many students are surprised that a computer can do easy things, for instance, act as a calculator.

Some questions ask students to use a computer. If students do not have access to a computer, exercise caution in your assigning of such questions. As mathematical tools, a desirable computer has the ability to deal with a good amount of data and to display graphs with accuracy and precision. ScottForesman has published *Transition Mathematics Software Tools* for IBM, Macintosh, and Apple II computers. The package includes the following three programs: Geometry Workshop, Graphing and Probability Workshop, and Spreadsheet Workshop.

The BASIC computer language was selected for use in this book because it is packaged for the computers which are most popular in American schools. The programs have been kept short so that students can type them relatively quickly. It is not necessary for every student to type and run the program. Most programs can be used as classroom demonstrations.

Computer educators have recommended that students be required to provide a block structure to programs; document their programs with abundant remarks; and declare variables. Since this is a mathematics course, not a programming course, you should emphasize the *computational* steps of a program. Can the students follow the steps of a program and tell what the output will be? Can the student modify a given program to solve an exercise with different values?

Whether you are a novice or expert in BASIC, we encourage you to try the programs we provide on your own system. Each version of BASIC and each computer has slightly different characteristics, and our generic programs may need to be modified slightly for your system.

Projects

Based on very positive responses from teachers and students of both *Functions, Statistics, and Trigonometry* and *Precalculus and Discrete Mathematics* to the projects in those books, and numerous requests from teachers for some similar activities for this course, we have developed projects for each chapter of the second edition of *Transition Mathematics*. Each project is an extended activity, often open-ended, meant to take the student several hours to complete. Some provide an opportunity to engage in library research; others require that students draw or build something; some require the student to collect data through surveys or measurements; others involve independent work with computers. The projects are designed for the wide range of interests and abilities one might find in a class of average students.

The projects serve many purposes.

(a) Students experience using real data in a mode comparable to that actually used by people in business, science, and many other careers.

(b) Students understand that a higher level of persistence than normal is expected. Too often in mathematics the greatest demand we make of students is to apply 5–10 minutes of effort on a single task. Longer-term projects demand more persistence and stretch a student's personal level of expectation.

(c) Projects, with some allowances for student choice, provide a sense of ownership of a task.

(d) Projects provide a chance for students to share their learning publicly in a visual or oral presentation.

(e) Projects provide an opportunity for students to apply graphic, writing, and oral talents in mathematical situations.

(f) Projects provide an alternative way to assess students' achievement.

The Projects appear immediately after the last lesson in the chapter, but we do not recommend that they be done immediately after the last lesson has been completed. Typically this would interrupt the flow of the chapter. You can schedule work on them in a number of ways. Here are two suggestions: (1) Assign one project when you reach the middle of a chapter, due in the middle of the next chapter. (2) Assign one project per grading period from any of the chapters covered in that period. Some teachers are more comfortable limiting the students choice of projects at the beginning (e.g., do any one of projects 2 or 5); other teachers want to give students free choice at all times. Do whatever makes sense for you and your class.

Transition Mathematics students will need more guidance in the development of their first few projects than will older, more mature students. Be very specific and clear on what you expect (e.g., length of paper, format of poster, number of minutes of oral presentation, etc.). If possible, show sample student work. Tell students how you will grade their work. You may want to use the first project as a trial run, with somewhat relaxed grading standards. Then you can show work you consider exemplary, and work which is good but not exemplary in preparation for the second project. English, social studies, or art teachers, the school librarian, or the computer teacher who teaches word processing can often assist with advice on how to structure assigning or grading projects.

Here are two suggested ways to grade projects: (1) Give a certain number of points for various parts of the project, e.g. 20 points for completing all required work, 20 points for the mathematical content, 5 points for neatness and organization, and 5 points for mechanics of the paper (spelling, grammar, etc.); then convert the total number of points (in the previous case as a percent of 50) to the grading scale you use on other assignments. Teachers using this type of grading scheme often give a small number of bonus points for creativity. (2) Use a holistic approach. Develop a set of general criteria (often called a rubric), and sort the papers into categories based on your criteria. This is the way many English and social studies teachers grade papers. See Stenmark (1989, 1991) for descriptions of rubrics with four and seven categories developed in California for use in a new state mathematics assessment program.

We recommend that however you use the projects, please do not avoid them. They often have impact far beyond the mathematics classroom. Teachers from one school remarked that by the end of the year graphs like those that had been made for projects were appearing in the school yearbook! In fact, you may find students to be encouraged if they are given time to put together a first-rate presentation to be displayed on a bulletin board or a school display case.

Teaching

Teaching Models and Strategies

Traditionally teachers have relied heavily on lecture, supervised practice, and recitation of answers as their dominant modes of instruction. When these dominate instruction, the mathematics studied is often limited to simple algorithms which can be easily mimicked, and students learn to depend almost exclusively on the teacher as the sole source of their information.

In recent years the importance of communication skills in all school subjects has been noted. To achieve these skills students must read, write, and speak *to each other* in class. These skills are in line with the broader curricular and process goals of *Transition Mathematics* and are more easily developed in classrooms which are dominated less by the teacher, that is, in classrooms in which students are actively engaged throughout the period.

Thus, in effective UCSMP classrooms, one sees smaller amounts of lecture, recitation, and individual seatwork than in comparison classes, and more discussions in small groups or with the whole class, individual or group work with calculators, computers, or other physical materials, and opportunities for students to do extended projects outside of class. Also, students read more of the book outside of class because they realize that this reading enables more to go on inside class.

The notes with each lesson in this Teacher's Edition provide a variety of teaching ideas, grouped under the following categories: Warm-up, Notes on Reading, Additional Examples, Optional Activities, Notes on Questions, Adapting to Individual Needs, Assessment, and Extension. All lessons contain more ideas than can be used in one period. None of the lists is exhaustive; there are, no doubt, many other ways to teach the lesson.

You should use your professional judgment to select and sequence the activities you think are appropriate for the length of your class period and your students' needs. This selection needs to be made before you enter class. We note that teachers who have never used group work, manipulatives, or technology often assume that they are very time-consuming. Our experience is that when well-planned ahead of time, many such activities can be done in relatively short periods of time, and we encourage you to try them. Also, you should understand that when a particular type of activity is done for the first time, it always takes longer because students need more guidance. The second time to the computer lab, or using group work, or presenting projects, or bringing out some manipulatives should go more easily than the first.

A variety of teaching models and strategies have been effectively used in the classroom by UCSMP teachers. Some teachers have students read each lesson and do all the questions before class. Then the teacher and students (sometimes in small groups, sometimes as the entire class) discuss the lesson and engage in various activities related to it during the next period. Some teachers preview the next day's lesson with some guidance as to the key points they think their students will need in reading or doing the questions. Some teachers begin the reading of the next lesson in class.

With less-prepared students, teachers need to adjust strategies. Most teachers do more reading out loud in class, and engage in more manipulative activities and use more Lesson Masters. Group work is often more important in these classes.

To give you a better picture of the variety of instructional techniques employed in classes using UCSMP materials, we have included reprints of the articles, "A 'Typical Day' in a *Transition Mathematics* Classroom," and "Using Cooperative Reading Strategies," both written by experienced *Transition Mathematics* teachers.

A "TYPICAL DAY" IN A *TRANSITION MATHEMATICS* CLASSROOM

by Sharon Mallo, Lake Park High School, Roselle, IL

No matter how much our textbooks may or may not change over the years, one fact remains: students have different learning styles, and teachers need to address each of them. Therefore, there's really no "typical day" in the classroom. In my classroom, means of presentation vary from lesson to lesson, with common threads woven in for continuity and class management. The threads that tie my teaching strategies together are those that reinforce good mathematics study skills and those that help students "learn how to learn."

The UCSMP program gives me an easy-to-use, flexible tool through which to accomplish these goals. I'd like to show you some of the ways I use the supplementary materials and options in the program for presenting lessons—particularly the UCSMP Lesson Masters, Computer Masters, Teaching Aids, and Activities Sourcebook. Each class begins with a warm-up activity, followed by coverage of the previous day's homework. These two activities take up no more than half of the class period. Next, there is a introduction to the new lesson, followed by a related activity.

Warm-up Activity

The warm-up activity usually consists of the Lesson Master from the previous day's lesson being handed out as students arrive. I ask students to work out some or all of the questions, depending on the length of the master. This allows me to identify students who are having difficulty with the Lesson Master. I give individual help, reteach, and/or ask students to help each other as I circulate. For example, on the day I will be teaching Lesson 4-2, I will use Lesson Master 4-1 as the warm-up. This lesson on order of operations allows me to say "No calculators" and check for understanding.

The warm-up can also be cooperative, such as with Lesson 5-4 on turns. I'll have each student use a protractor to draw with ten equally spaced spokes, and label each spoke with a different letter like on the Ferris wheel in questions 22–24 from the homework. Each student writes three problems about his/her diagram. Then students exchange papers and solve the problems.

The warm-up can also be a lead-in for today's lesson or a problem-solving activity that will later tie into today's lesson.

Going Over Homework

One of my most import requirements is that students correct each answer on their homework and write out the steps for answers they've gotten wrong. Using the answers found at the back of the book to correct their work is part of the assignment. Students have already marked problems they need help with before coming to class. After we've done the warm-up activity, I'll put answers on the overhead projector. Then we discuss problems I've chosen as the most important or students have identified as stumbling blocks. Three or four times during chapter, I have students discuss their questions within their cooperative groups, (Groups have one high, two middle, and one low student, and they change after every two chapter tests.)

Students need a reason to be concerned about whether or not their homework answers are correct and, more importantly, how to get the correct answer. I give an unannounced Homework Quiz once or twice a week. Students use their own notebooks of homework assignments and a clean sheet of paper—no textbook. They divide their papers into four or six sections:

Lesson 4-2	
#8	#12
#18	#22

Lesson 5-6	**Lesson 5-7**
#14	#18
Lesson 5-8	**Lesson 5-8**
#14	#30
Lesson 5-9	**Lesson 5-9**
#18	#24

I do the same on a transparency to show them which questions I want. Students are to copy the correct answer for each question from their notebooks. If they've made the corrections in their notebooks, each student should have a perfect paper.

It takes five to ten minutes to correct a set of these quizzes. Scores are low at the beginning but they steadily get better.

Presenting a Lesson

The method I choose to present a lesson depends on the difficulty of the content and the applications. For instance, Lesson 4-2 is one that the class usually reads together. I stop students at each example. Using Teaching Aid 42 and different-colored overhead pens, we choose a variable and fill in the blanks of the patterns. Then we reverse the problem where I write the pattern on the overhead and we identify the variable. Students take turns making up instances.

If the students are able to read a lesson on their own, either in school or at home, I focus their reading. Vocabulary words (not their definitions) are pointed out. Sometimes I write an additional example from the margin of the Teacher's Edition and tell student that they should have an idea of how to solve it once they've read the lesson. Now they have a purpose for reading.

When students have read a difficult lesson in class, I put one of the additional examples on the overhead. (Some are already on transparencies in the Teaching Aids.) Then I ask students to find the parallel example in the reading. This is one of the hardest things for them to do when they get stuck on a problem at home, so we practice it in class.

I do lectures and give notes on a lesson about 10-15 percent of the time. This is usually after students have read the lesson and done the "Covering the Reading" questions. The most common assignment I give is to complete the Applying the Mathematics, Review, and Exploration Questions of a given lesson and then to read or re-read the following lesson and do Covering the Reading. Occasionally, they read a lesson and do all the questions, and once in a while I develop an assignment from outside the book.

As you can see, there is no "typical day" in my classroom. With *Transition Mathematics,* my students have much stronger number sense by the end of the year. They are working with all types of numbers: fractions, decimals, integers, and percents—*every day* in practice problems, literal examples, and applications. They're not afraid to tackle problems, and they're learning how to learn.

Sharon Mallo has been teaching Transition Mathematics *in the Chicago area since 1984. She is an author on the Second Edition of* Transition Mathematics.

USING COOPERATIVE READING STRATEGIES:

Students helping each other understand their textbook

by Tom Stone, Sheldon High School, Eugene, OR

There are many ways in which cooperative learning strategies can be used effectively in the mathematics classroom. Because of the important role reading plays in determining students' success in the UCSMP program, I would like to focus on this application of these strategies and to share some ways that the use of cooperative learning groups can help students learn good reading habits.

First, let me briefly explain my classroom organization. My students are familiar with two seating arrangements: 1) individual seating in six rows of desks, and 2) group seating with each set of four desks formed into a tight square. Each student in the group is assigned a number, 1 through 4. I do this for management purposes which should become clear later. The following scenarios illustrate how I use small-group instruction to help my students with their reading. (All section references are to UCSMP *Geometry*.)

Scenario 1 (Key Ideas)

Students are seated individually. After identifying a few vocabulary words they will encounter, I assign the reading of Section 1-3 in the textbook. Students read the material individually and take notes as they go along. When they have had time to finish, they move into their groups. Using his/her notes, Student 1 in each group selects a major idea from the reading and shares it with the group. After several minutes, Student 2 in each group discusses another idea found in the reading. This is continued until all four students in each group have had an opportunity to share. In this way, students receive important practice identifying the key ideas from a given section of their book.

Scenario 2 (Share the Pain)

Say the reading of Section 7-5 is to be done outside of class as part of the homework assignment. It includes two examples that I expect will be difficult for my students to read. Therefore, I have them encounter the challenging part of the reading in class in teams before they try to handle it on their own outside of class. I assign the reading of the first example to Students 1 and 2 in each group and the second example to Students 3 and 4. After students have completed the reading, they move into their groups. Students 1 and 2 discuss their understanding of the first example while Students 3 and 4 do the same with the second example. Now all students should be able to comprehend the reading of the section on their own.

Scenario 3 (Experts)

Section 9-7 breaks down into four main ideas. Student 1 is assigned to read the first ideas, Student 2 the second, and so on. Upon finishing the reading, students move into their groups and each student takes a turn presenting to the rests of the group. Then students begin working on the problem set for the section. Each student acts as the "expert" for questions related to the idea for which he/she was responsible.

Scenario 4 (The Set-up)

Let's suppose my geometry class is going to learn about traversability of networks (as in the Konigsberg Bridge problem) tomorrow, Today, I have students move into their groups and I give each team a worksheet with five figures. After determining which figures are traversable and which are not, teams list the number of even and odd vertices for each figure. Finally, each group writes out and tests a conjecture for the connection between traversability and the number of even and/or odd vertices in a figure. Tomorrow, the students will be well prepared to read about the applications of traversability in networks.

The above scenarios are only a few examples of how small-group instruction and cooperative-learning strategies can be used to help students develop the skill needed for reading mathematics. Equally important, they provide variety in lesson structure. I hope that the ideas presented here are helpful and can serve as catalysts for generating more ideas that can be put to effective use in the classroom.

Tom Stone taught UCSMP courses in the Oregon area for many years. He was chosen as the 1991 Oregon Secondary Mathematics Teacher of the Year by the American Electronic Association.

Using the Reading

In order to become an independent learner of mathematics, a student must learn to learn mathematics from reading. You should expect students to read all lessons. At the beginning of the course, this may require time in class. Do not expect overnight changes in behavior from students who have never read their math book before. Some will read immediately, others in a few days, others in a few weeks, and still others after a couple of months. Teachers of *Transition Mathematics* report that by the end of the year almost all of their students are reading. Teachers of later UCSMP courses report that this behavior continues without the amount of prodding needed in this course. It is an effort well-spent.

Because students may never have been asked to read mathematics, they may ask why they have to read. We tell them: You must read because you must learn to learn for success in all future courses that use mathematics, not just in mathematics; because you must learn to learn for success in life outside of school and on any job; because the reading will help you understand the uses of mathematics; because the reading contains interesting information; because the reading tells you how the material from one lesson is related to other material in the book; because there is not enough time in class to spend doing something that you can do in a study period or at home.

Students often do not know how to read a mathematics text. They read too quickly and they gloss over little words ("if," "but,","not," and so on) that may be very important to the meaning of a statement. They may not realize that text and graphics are often related and they should move back and forth from one to the other. Students may not be able to read 2^5 (2 to the 5th power) or $x + 5 = 9$ (x plus 5 is equal to 9), for they may have no vocabulary for symbols such as +, –, ×, ÷, =, or <. (Many of us have trouble reading Greek letters such as ψ or μ, because we have never had to give their names out loud.) For many students the same is true for common mathematical symbols. Thus it is important to have students read out loud as well as to give them assignments that involve reading.

To teach students how to read mathematics, we suggest that at the beginning of the school year some class time be spent each day reading the lesson in class. Some days you can have students read out loud, and provide feedback on their ability to read technical words and symbols correctly. (In general, it is not a good idea to call on students in any particular obvious order. That just gets some students nervous that their turn is coming up, and encourages others not to pay attention, because they are likely not to be called on.) Be sure to point out how the colored headers in the lessons help outline the important concepts and provide an overview (advance organizer) of what they are about to read.

You might have students answer the Questions Covering the Reading orally, and point out how these questions are meant to test comprehension of the material in the text. The answers for these questions can be found literally in the reading or by mimicking worked examples. The questions can be used as oral exercises during or after oral reading of the text, or as part of a written assignment. Once students are comfortable with the format of the lessons, we suggest you begin to expect that reading be done outside of class on a regular basis.

Some days you may want to ask some questions that set up the reading of the lesson. Other days you might give a brief summary of the key ideas in the reading, have students read silently in class, and then ask them to identify where in the exposition those main ideas are covered. Once students have become somewhat comfortable with reading on their own, you can rely more and more on them to summarize or probe keys ideas without your assistance.

To help stress the importance of reading as a tool for learning mathematics, some teachers give brief (2–5 minute) "reading quizzes" at the beginning of class. These may consist of a request for a summary of the key ideas in the text, or the answers to several even-numbered questions from the homework. Doing so for 3 or 4 consecutive days early in the year lets students know you are serious about their attempts to do the reading and to answer the questions. Allowing students to use their notes, but not their book, encourages students to take good notes, and to organize their solutions to homework problems.

Although we believe that reading their text is an important strategy by which students learn mathematics, we know that it is not the only way they learn. In particular, if you want to give a brief overview of the new lesson before students read it, please do. We do, however, wish to discourage the practice of *always* explaining how to do questions before the students have had the opportunity to learn on their own. Particularly counterproductive is to tell students that certain problems do not have to be tried "because we have not yet done them in class." This only teaches students that they cannot learn on their own and to be dependent on you.

Students learn enormous amounts from discussing alternate strategies to problems with you and their classmates, from engaging in well-constructed activities, and from doing open-ended explorations and projects. By teaching students to read outside of class, you are free to use class time more creatively and effectively than if you were compelled to develop all major ideas yourself in class.

Going Over Homework Questions

Feedback to student work is very important, and to positively reinforce the doing of homework it is important to go over questions. We are frequently asked how we want the teacher to go over the questions. Our response is that there are multiple ways to do so. We recommend that each teacher use a couple of methods regularly so students can get used to a routine, and a couple of others occasionally for variety.

Below are some of the more commonly used techniques which we support:

1. Show answers (using the Answer Masters provided) on an overhead projector at beginning of period; have students correct their own papers (you can use time to take roll); have whole class discussion on questions that were particularly troublesome.
2. Same as (1) above; but after students have checked their own papers, have them form groups of 2 to 4 to discuss what they missed; after a few minutes have a whole class discussion only on questions the groups could not resolve.
3. Have students form small groups; provide one copy of answers on paper to each group; have groups discuss what they missed; after a few minutes have a whole class discussion only on questions the groups could not resolve.
4. Read all answers out loud; have students correct their own papers; when done reading answers, have whole class discussion to explain questions that were particularly troublesome.
5. Have students write the numbers of the questions they could not answer on the board as they come into class; have them put tick marks after numbers to indicate how many students want to discuss that one; have student volunteers do those problems on the board, and explain their work; explain how to do the ones no student could solve.
6. Preselect questions which you feel are particularly important or may be particularly troublesome; have a whole class discussion about those.

It is important to remember that "going over the homework" should be more than providing correct answers. It is a wonderful opportunity to consider alternate solution strategies, to address any misconceptions that are uncovered, to relate ideas in one question to ideas in another, and to extend ideas in the questions via "what if" questions. In short, it is an opportunity to have the kind of rich classroom discourse described in the NCTM's Professional Teaching Standards. Many ideas are given in the Notes on Questions for each lesson.

Writing in Mathematics

The NCTM *Curriculum and Evaluation Standards* stress the importance of students' ability to communicate mathematics. Through writing, communication opens up in the classroom on a variety of levels. As they write, students apply concepts to their own experience; construct meaning for mathematical symbols, procedures, and concepts; and internalize meaning as they explore and examine mathematical ideas in words.

At times, writing may consist simply of the steps in answering a question, but to be most effective it should be more than that. It can include comments about what was being done, why a particular strategy was chosen, and how the student felt about the question. The careful examination of thought that writing requires may lead students to see the process of thinking as more important than the ability to quote rules; consequently, mathematics becomes a richer pastime. Furthermore, students will be developing a skill that many of them will need throughout their lives, the ability to explain what they are thinking to others.

In *Transition Mathematics* we begin the multi-year process of asking students on occasion to write explanations of what they are doing. Do not be surprised if at first students' explanations are vague, imprecise, or too brief. Writing good explanations takes time, experience, and guidance, and students may have never been asked to write in their previous mathematics classes. You can encourage greater thoroughness and effectiveness by discussing good explanations in the text with your students. The solutions of the examples in each lesson are excellent models. The portions of the solutions that you may expect students to write are printed in a special font.

To be considered important by students, writing must be discussed in class. Reading good student efforts aloud in class can encourage good writing. Having students read their own efforts can inform them about whether others understood what they wrote.

There are different forms which writing may take. *Chatter* refers to writing explanations of procedures a student used to solve a problem. It can communicate a student's thought process, and can therefore alert you (and the student!) to hidden misconceptions and incomplete understandings as well as to wonderful insights. Arthur Powell of Rutgers University suggests that chatter be written in a separate column of the page from the actual solution of the problem.

Journal writing is believed by some people to be one of the most effective methods of writing to learn mathematics; however, *informal explorative writing* in class and on homework (not necessarily in a bound or spiral notebook) achieves similar results. Journals and informal explorative writing allow students to put concepts in their own words, to speculate on extensions to problems, and to relate material they are learning to what they already know. This kind of writing allows students to write freely without worrying excessively over mechanics. It also can focus students' minds. Writing at the beginning of a period can interest and involve students in a topic; writing at the end of a period can help them to summarize and organize what happened that day.

Here is some general advice: If you use journals with 7th or 8th graders, you may wish to keep the journals in the classroom; asking young students to remember yet another item to bring to class may prove difficult for them and frustrating to you. For this reason, informal explorative writing on ideas and on homework may prove to be a better option.

In general, undirected journal writing does not provoke as much focus or response from students as carefully and thoughtfully worded questions, sometimes called *prompts*. The more concise the prompt, the better. Longer, more complex prompts that are intended to yield more writing often do not.

Collect journals regularly to communicate to students that they are important. You do not have to collect all journals at the same time. (Reading students' writing is often not as time-consuming as you might think, and it can be very interesting.) Give credit for journals, but don't grade them. When giving credit, look for frequency and length of entries and for self-initiated topics. Give feedback on the writing to students; comments indicate that you care. Do not emphasize mechanics or grammar. Above all, be patient and flexible.

Do not penalize students when they don't write. When students have difficulty writing, claiming they do not know what to say, you might try *freewriting*, an activity where the goal is simply to empty thoughts on the page without censoring. Write yourself and share what you wrote with your students.

It is appropriate to keep examples of student writing of mathematics in a portfolio along with other examples of student work.

Dealing with Individual Differences

Every student differs from all others in many ways. Differences in ability, entering knowledge, willingness to work, interest, learning style, and cultural background are the most commonly referred by teachers and researchers.

In Section 1 of this Professional Sourcebook, we pointed out that not enough is known about individual differences in ability to make judgments based on them. Individual differences in entering knowledge are far better predictors. These differences are great enough to warrant differences in what is offered to students at a particular grade level, and based on them we suggest that students take *Transition Mathematics* at different ages. However, a wide range of entering knowledge exists within every class and needs to be considered when teaching.

For all students, we have included an enormous variety of activities, questions, and contexts to bring out the brilliance, surprise, applicability, and structure of mathematics, and to appeal to students with the panoply of cultural backgrounds found in the United States. Note the many cultural activities in this Teacher's Edition as well. You should take these into account, because familiar contexts are critical to the understanding of mathematics, the contributions of various cultures are important in conveying the universality of mathematical ideas, and because it helps students to develop a sense of ownership of these ideas. Differences in interest can be handled by giving students choice of the end-of-chapter Projects, by asking students to elaborate on questions and or ideas they particularly liked, and by other optional activities.

For better-prepared students, or students with more willingness to work, you may wish to offer, assign, and discuss:

- Challenge and Extension problems and activities contained in the Teacher's Notes;
- Technology activities from the *Technology Sourcebook*;
- Contest problems from such sources as MathCounts or the American Junior High School Mathematics Examination (AJHSME)

For students needing more preparation or with limited language development, consider using:

- Suggestions for additional practice contained in these Teacher's Notes;
- Manipulative activities from the *Activities Sourcebook*;
- English Language Development and Extra Help activities provided in these Teacher's Notes.

We must stress that *many of these ideas should be used with all your students.* In particular, manipulative, technology, and other activities are appropriate for all students, and all students need some practice in order to develop high levels of competence.

Assessment

The Evaluation Standards provide some sensible guidelines for student assessment. The first is Alignment. Simply put, this standard suggests that you assess what you teach. In particular, because the *Transition Mathematics* course has much broader goals than most other courses at this level, many tests, quizzes, final exams, and other forms of assessment you have used in the past will not be appropriate for this course.

The second Evaluation Standard is Multiple Forms of Assessment. This standard reminds us that no single instrument is perfect. Each test or assignment provides only a small picture of what each student knows. A teacher who wants to develop mathematical power must use instruments which reflect the broad range of goals of the curriculum.

The third Evaluation Standard is Purposes of Assessment. This standard reminds the reader that instruments developed for one purpose usually are not appropriate for another purpose. Specifically, traditional standardized tests are usually not appropriate for evaluating students at the end of any single mathematics course because they are usually not well-aligned with the objectives of the course. The best measure of success of a student is the extent to which the student has accomplished the goals and objectives of the individual course.

Assessment Options

To help you accomplish the above goals, the *Assessment Sourcebook* (in the Teacher's Resource File) provides a wide variety of assessment instruments. These include Quizzes, Chapter Tests, Cumulative Tests (by chapter), Comprehensive Tests, and several types of alternative assessment. The Chapter Tests include parallel traditional Forms A and B, in which most questions are short-answer, and Forms C and D, which provide more open-ended performance assessment. The *Quiz and Test Writer* software enables you to produce a virtually unlimited number of versions for a quiz or chapter test. The Teacher's Edition provides additional assessment suggestions and activities.

Tests, quizzes, or homework assignments provide only a small picture of what each student knows. In order to help you develop your students' abilities to do open-ended questions or longer more elaborate tasks, you should consider the Exploration questions at the end of each lesson and the Projects at the end of each chapter as part of your assessment toolkit. (The grading of Projects is discussed on page T42.)

Understanding— The SPUR Approach

"Understanding" is an easy goal to have, for who can be against it? Yet understanding means different things to different people. In UCSMP texts an approach to the development of mathematical power is taken that we call the SPUR approach. The SPUR approach involves four different aspects, or dimensions, of understanding.

Skills: For many people, understanding mathematics means simply knowing *how* to get an answer to a problem with no help from any outside source. But in classrooms, when we speak of understanding how to use a calculator or a computer, we mean using a computer to do something for us. In UCSMP texts, these are both aspects of the same kind of understanding, the understanding of algorithms (procedures) for getting answers. This is the S of SPUR, the Skills dimension, and it ranges from the rote memorization of basic facts to the development of new algorithms for solving problems.

Properties: During the 1960s, understanding *why* became at least as important as understanding *how*. Mathematicians often view this kind of understanding as the ultimate goal. For instance, mathematics courses for prospective elementary school teachers assume these college students can do arithmetic and instead teach the properties and principles behind that arithmetic. This is the P of SPUR, the Properties dimension, and it ranges from the rote identification of properties to the discovery of new proofs.

Uses: To the person who applies mathematics, neither knowing how to get an answer nor knowing the mathematical reasons behind the process is as important as being able to *use* the answer. For example, a person does not possess full understanding of linear equations until that person can apply them appropriately in real situations. This dimension ranges from the rote application of ideas (for instance, when you encounter a take-away situation, subtract) to the discovery of new applications or models for mathematical ideas. *Transition Mathematics* is notable for its attention to this dimension of understanding.

Representations: To some people, even having all three dimensions of understanding given above does not comprise full understanding. They require that students represent a concept and deal with the concept in that representation in some way. Ability to use concrete materials and models, or graphs and other pictorial representations demonstrates this dimension of understanding. This is the R of SPUR, the Representations dimension, and it ranges from the rote manipulation of objects to the invention of new representations of concepts.

There are continual arguments among educators as to which dimension should come first and which should be emphasized. For each there are people for whom that type of understanding is preeminent, and who believe that the other types do not convey the *real* understanding of mathematics.

Each dimension has aspects that can be memorized and the potential for the highest level of creative thinking. Also, each dimension has its easy aspects and its difficult ones. Some skills (for example, long division) take at least as long to learn as geometry proofs; some uses are as easy as putting together beads. Furthermore, some students prefer applications, some would rather do manipulative skills, some most want to know the theory, and still others like the models and representations best. Thus we believe that the most effective teaching allows students opportunities in all these dimensions.

For a specific example of what understanding means in these four dimensions, consider what would constitute evidence of the understanding of $\frac{2}{3} \bullet \frac{4}{5}$.

Skills understanding means knowing a way to obtain a solution. (Obtain $\frac{8}{15}$ by some means.)

Properties understanding means knowing properties which you can apply. (Identify or justify the steps in obtaining $\frac{8}{15}$, such as $\frac{2}{3} \bullet \frac{4}{5} = (2 \bullet \frac{1}{3}) \bullet (4 \bullet \frac{1}{5})$, using the relationship of $\frac{a}{b}$ for division.)

Uses understanding means knowing situations in which you could apply this multiplication. (If $\frac{2}{3}$ of students would know how to set up this question, and $\frac{4}{5}$ of those could get the problem right, what portion of students would get the correct answer?)

Representations understanding means having a representation of the solving process or a graphical way of interpreting the solution. (Consider an array of dots with 3 rows and 5 columns. Color 2 of the 3 rows red and 4 of the 5 columns blue. What portion of the points is colored both red and blue?)

The SPUR approach is not a perfect sorter of knowledge; many ideas and many problems involve more than one dimension. Some understandings do not fit any of these dimensions. At times we add a fifth dimension C—the Culture dimension—for it provides still another way of looking at knowledge.

In this book, you see the SPUR categorization at the end of each chapter with the Chapter Review questions. The Progress Self-Test for each chapter and the Lesson Masters (in the Teacher's Resource File) are also keyed to these objectives. We never ask students (or teachers) to categorize tasks into the various kinds of understanding; that is not a suitable goal. The categorization is meant only to be a convenient and efficient way to ensure that the book provides the opportunity for teachers to teach and for students to gain a broader and deeper understanding of mathematics than is normally the case.

Grading

No problem seems more difficult than the question of grading. If a teacher has students who perform so well that they all deserve *A*s and the teacher gives them *A*s as a result, the teacher will probably not be given plaudits for being successful but will be accused of being too easy. This suggests that the grading scale ought to be based on a fixed level of performance, which is what we recommend. We recommend this because the performance that gives an *A* in one school or with one teacher may only rate a *C* in another, and we think it unfair.

Seldom in this book are there ten similar questions in a row. To teach students to be flexible, questions have all sorts of wordings. The problems are varied because that's the way problems come in later courses and in life outside of school. We believe a student should be able to do each set of objectives at about the 85% mastery level. An 85% score on a test deserves no less than a high *B*, and probably an *A*. In the past, our tests have often led us to the following curve: 85–100 = *A*, 72–84 = *B*, 60–71 = *C*, 50–59 = *D*, 0–49 = *F*. Such a low curve alarms some teachers, but students in UCSMP courses generally learn more mathematics overall than students in comparison classes. We believe that the above grading policy rewards students fairly for work well done.

Some teachers have said our suggested grading scale is too easy. Maybe they have better students. They simply raise our scale. Why? Must every class have *D* students? Wouldn't it be nice if all students got *A*s?

One January a teacher of *Transition Mathematics* presented us with a problem. She had to make out grades for the fall semester. Her quandary was as follows: "I've never had a class that learned so much, but my grades are lower." Later she said, "I have students who are failing. But I can't switch them to another class [using another book at the same level] because they know too much." Her problem is not unusual: scores on tests of higher order thinking are generally lower than scores on tests of routine skills. To encourage students, we often make a basketball analogy. In a traditional course, all the shots students ever have are lay-ups (exercises) and an occasional free throw (easy problems). They shoot these over and over again, from the same spot ("Do the odds from 1–49."). In *Transition Mathematics*, almost every question is a different shot (a problem), some close in, some from middle distance, a few from half-court. To expect percentages of correct shots to be the same is unrealistic.

We have found that a word to your students about why your grading scale is "different" is helpful. They may be so accustomed to another grading scale that they feel they are doing poorly, while you think they are doing well.

Some teachers have found that because of the way that the Review questions maintain and improve performance, cumulative tests at the end of each marking period give students an opportunity to do well. *The Assessment Sourcebook* has cumulative tests for each chapter beginning with Chapter 2. When you want to practice one specific shot to make it automatic, we suggest focusing in on a few topics for quizzes.

Two final points: First, let students know what they need to know in order to get good grades. All research on the subject indicates that telling students what they are supposed to learn increases the amount of material covered and tends to increase performance. Second, have confidence in your students. Do not arbitrarily consign some of them to low grades. Let them know that it is possible for all of them to get *A*s if they learn the material. If students perform well on tests, it has a real effect on interest and motivation. As the newer evaluation documents stress, you should endeavor to use grading as a vehicle for breeding success as well as for evaluating students.

Professional Sourcebook: SECTION 4 RESEARCH AND DEVELOPMENT OF *TRANSITION MATHEMATICS*

Development of the First Edition

The development of the first edition of each UCSMP text was in four stages. First, the overall goals for each course were created by UCSMP in consultation with a national advisory board of distinguished professors, and through discussion with classroom teachers, school administrators, and district and state mathematics supervisors. At the second stage, UCSMP selected authors who wrote first drafts of the courses. Half of all UCSMP authors currently teach mathematics in secondary schools, and all authors and editors for the first five courses have secondary school teaching experience. After teaching by the authors, selected teachers, and revision by the authors and UCSMP editors, materials entered the third stage in the text development. Classes of teachers not connected with the project used the books, and independent evaluators closely studied student achievement, attitudes, and issues related to implementation. The fourth stage consisted of a wider comparative evaluation.

The specific ideas for *Transition Mathematics* originated as a result of two previous projects directed by Zalman Usiskin at the University of Chicago. The first was a NSF-sponsored project which developed a first-year algebra text entitled *Algebra Through Applications with Probability and Statistics.* The text was distributed by the National Council of Teachers of Mathematics in a two-volume paperback version from 1979-85. Many of its ideas are found in this book and in UCSMP *Algebra.* In developing that text, we found that one of the major reasons students had so much trouble applying algebra was that they did not know how to apply arithmetic beyond the arithmetic of adding and subtracting whole numbers.

In the years 1979–82, the Cognitive Development and Achievement in Secondary School Geometry project did much testing of senior high school geometry students. It was found in these studies that the geometry knowledge of students entering a high school geometry course was very low. Yet the best predictor of success in that course, be it with proof or with performance on a standardized test at the end of the year, was incoming geometry knowledge.

As a result, Dr. Usiskin planned a course to precede an algebra course that would incorporate the ideas of applying arithmetic and the geometry students needed for success later. The course began with a traditional look. In the middle of the year, dissatisfied with the performance of the students, the continual review strategy used in the elementary school curricula of many foreign countries was used. The SPUR mastery sequence also entered the course at that time.

In 1984–85, a formative evaluation of a revised version of *Transition Mathematics* was conducted with 20 classes from 10 schools in the city of Chicago and suburbs. Classes at each of grades 7, 8, and 9 were represented. The results were so positive that the features of *Transition Mathematics* became incorporated into the UCSMP *Algebra* and *Advanced Algebra* texts, whose first drafts were written in the summer of 1985. That summer, *Transition Mathematics* was revised for a second time, though most of the revisions were minor, befitting the success of the year.

First Edition Summative Evaluation and Test Results

In 1985–86, a carefully controlled study involving 1048 students in 41 *Transition Mathematics* classes and 976 students in 38 matched comparison classes. Included were 7th grade, 8th grade, and senior high school classes. The 35 schools included 7 Chicago Public schools, 10 from the metropolitan Chicago area, and 18 were from 9 states coast to coast. Small town and rural areas were represented.

A detailed report of this study is available from UCSMP. Herein is a summary: Matching criteria eliminated 18 of the 40 pairs. Of the 20 pairs that remained, 7 were 7th grade, 10 were 8th grade, and only 3 were 9th grade. Three tests were given. First was a standardized test, the American Testronics *High School Subjects Test: General Mathematics* (HSST) 40-question multiple-choice test, chosen because it seems rather representative of such tests, and was new and thus less likely to be familiar to any teacher. Students in all classes were tested for two other complete periods, during which they were given three additional tests: The 60-item Orleans-Hanna algebra readiness test, a 19-item geometry readiness test used in an earlier study at the University of Chicago, and a test of selected items designed specifically to cover the unique features of *Transition Mathematics.* The HSST test was given without calculators to most students and with calculators to others.

Because it was felt that each class is a unique situation, the analysis of all tests was done at the class level using the well-matched pairs. For all grades, the results showed that when calculators were not allowed, the *Transition Mathematics* classes performed at the same level as the comparison classes. However, when all students were allowed to use calculators, students in the *Transition Mathematics* classes scored about 11.3% higher than students in

comparison classes. UCSMP students also scored significantly higher on the algebra and geometry readiness tests.

Here are selected other results found, as given in the summary of the report available from UCSMP: Student attitudes were not significantly different in the two groups. Students felt the real-life explanations were good, the text was challenging and interesting, and the problems difficult but fun. Some students did find the problems too difficult and sometimes confusing. Reading was a problem early in the school year for teachers and students: students were unaccustomed to reading mathematics and considerable persuasion was required. Over time, reading became less problematic and teachers felt that the benefits outweighed the difficulties encountered at the beginning of the year.

Teachers also responded positively to the curriculum and even when implementation difficulties were encountered, teachers still endorsed the ideas and intents of the curriculum. *Transition Mathematics* teachers liked the substantive aspects of the text, and many commented particularly on the value of the chapter on problem solving.

The summative evaluation convinced us that the approach is not only sound but quite effective and that no major changes should be made in the materials. However, many minor changes were made before publication of the first edition, based either on careful readings given to the materials by UCSMP and ScottForesman editors, on the test results above, or on remarks on detailed forms returned by the teachers in the summative evaluation.

Second Edition Studies

To help in preparation for the second edition, during the school year 1991–92, ScottForesman asked a small number of *Transition Mathematics* users to evaluate each chapter of the text as they completed it. ScottForesman also mailed a series of questionnaires during the year to a larger number of users. The results from these surveys were used to help in the planning and writing of the second edition materials.

Over the years 1989–92, UCSMP had also kept notes on comments made by many users of *Transition Mathematics*. All second edition authors are experienced teachers of *Transition Mathematics* who had made presentations about the book to school districts. Thus they had both first-hand experience and many discussions about the materials with other teachers. Writing of the first draft of the second edition began in the summer and continued through the fall of 1992.

In the 1992–93 school year, 26 classes in 12 schools participated in a formal study of the second edition materials. The schools were chosen to reflect the wide range of students who are currently using *Transition Mathematics*. Teachers completed detailed forms evaluating the materials. Their students were tested along with students from 25 comparable classes at the same grade level in the same school. Because we felt that the first edition studies had compared *Transition Mathematics* with traditional textbooks, most of the comparable classes in the second edition studies used first edition *Transition Mathematics* materials. To our knowledge, this is the first time that a book has been compared with an earlier edition of itself.

From these classes, we were able to obtain 16 pairs of classes between which there were no significant differences on pretest scores of those students who took all tests. In four of these pairs, the comparison class used texts other than UCSMP materials. In the other twelve pairs, the comparison class used the first edition of *Transition Mathematics*. The small total number of students is due to the requirement that for a student to be included in this analysis, that student had to be present for all pretests and posttests. This ensures that the student was present for the entire year.

The pretest and one posttest used the same *High School Subjects Test: General Mathematics* (HSST) that was used in the first edition summative evaluation. The Algebra posttest is a test designed by UCSMP over basic algebra. The Geometry posttest is a test of readiness for geometry written at the University of Chicago for a nationwide study in 1980–81. All students were allowed to use calculators on the Algebra and Geometry tests, but only on the Algebra test was a calculator deemed to have any potential use.

Mean Scores of Students in Matched Pairs The table shown below contains the mean scores (standard deviations in parentheses) from the groups of students in the 16 matched pairs of classes. Posttest means are adjusted for the slight differences in the pretest means.

Mean scores in boldface are significantly higher than the corresponding scores. The algebra posttest mean is significantly higher at the .05 level; the geometry posttest mean is significantly higher at the .002 level. No other differences are statistically significant.

Range of Mean Scores Mean scores do not convey the vast range in means among the classes in this study. Results repeated what we have found in every large study we have ever conducted, that mean *posttest* scores in some classes were lower than mean *pretest* scores in other classes using the same book. There was also a vast range in the mean amount of growth that took place over the year, and that variable showed remarkable school effects. That is, comparison and second edition classes in the same school tended either both to show large increases or both to show small increases. This indicates how important school climate is if one wishes to improve achievement, regardless of the materials used.

Comparison of Individual Matched Pairs of Classes Because of the small numbers of students in classes, the difference between the means of two classes has to be reasonably large for that difference to be statistically significant. Still, there were some significant differences between individual matched pairs of classes on the posttests, after adjustment for differences on the HSST pretest.

Here are all the significant differences (at the .05 level) found when comparing the 12 UCSMP 2nd edition classes with their matched UCSMP 1st edition classes in the same schools:

- On the HSST posttest, two UCSMP 2nd edition classes outperformed their 1st edition counterparts at the .05 level.
- On the Algebra posttest, a different two UCSMP 2nd edition classes outperformed their counterparts, while in one pair the UCSMP 1st edition classes outperformed the UCSMP 2nd edition classes.
- On the Geometry posttest, one significant difference went each way.

This suggests a slight trend favoring UCSMP 2nd edition classes to UCSMP 1st edition classes on general mathematics and algebra, and no difference in geometry.

Here are all the significant differences (at the .05 level) found when comparing the four UCSMP 2nd edition classes with their matched classes using other texts in the same schools:

- On the HSST posttest, there were no significant differences either way in any pair.
- On the Algebra posttest, two of the four UCSMP 2nd edition classes significantly outperformed their counterparts.
- On the Geometry posttest, three of the four UCSMP 2nd edition classes significantly outperformed their counterparts.

Thus, on none of the posttest measures did a non-UCSMP class significantly perform its matched UCSMP counterpart. This confirms the results found

Mean Scores of Students in Matched Pairs

Group	N	Pretest HSST	Posttest HSST	Posttest Algebra	Posttest Geometry
UCSMP 2nd Edition	237	19.32 (6.23)	24.95 (7.42)	11.51 (4.00)	11.14 (3.68)
UCSMP 1st Edition	229	18.89 (6.60)	23.31 (8.36)	11.28 (4.23)	10.74 (3.92)
UCSMP 2nd Edition	56	17.55 (6.74)	22.89 (8.64)	**9.91** (4.76)	**9.62** (3.94)
Other Texts	53	17.60 (7.00)	22.83 (8.46)	8.00 (4.63)	7.40 (3.56)

for the students as a whole, namely that students in UCSMP classes hold their own on arithmetic performance and greatly improve their algebra and geometry performance when compared to students in non-UCSMP classes.

Breakdown by Grade Level The scores were also broken down by grade level: 7th, 8th, or 9th and above. Four significant differences were found: At the 7th-grade level, on the HSST test, students in the six UCSMP 2nd Edition classes (adjusted mean 24.78) significantly outperformed (at the .02 level) their counterpart 1st Edition classes (adjusted mean 22.42).

No significant differences were found in any of the tests among the four matched pairs at the 8th-grade level. At the 9th-grade level, there were only two matched pairs. On the Algebra posttest, both UCSMP 2nd edition classes outperformed their counterparts, one a UCSMP 1st edition class, the other using another text. On the Geometry posttest, the UCSMP 2nd edition class outperformed the class using another text. These results, though based on a small sample, confirm our belief that, particularly at the 9th-grade level, prealgebra classes in non-UCSMP materials focus too much attention on reviewing arithmetic, and do not give students the algebra and geometry that would help them in later courses.

Taken as a whole, these results confirm conclusions from the first edition studies, namely that ***Transition Mathematics*** **students maintain paper-and-pencil arithmetic skills (the main thrust of the HSST tests), while significantly enriching their algebra and geometry backgrounds over students in non-UCSMP materials.**

Continuing Research and Development

Since November of 1985, UCSMP has sponsored an annual "User's Conference" at the University of Chicago at which users and prospective users of its materials can meet with each other and with authors. This conference now includes all components of the project. It provides a valuable opportunity for reports on UCSMP materials from those not involved in formal studies. Since August of 1989, UCSMP has sponsored an inservice on its texts open to all those who will be using the materials the next school year. We encourage users to attend these conferences.

Both ScottForesman and UCSMP welcome comments on our books. Please address comments either to Mathematics Product Manager, ScottForesman, 1900 East Lake Avenue, Glenview, IL 60025, or to Zalman Usiskin, Director, UCSMP, 5835 S. Kimbark Avenue, Chicago, IL 60637.

Professional Sourcebook: SECTION 5 BIBLIOGRAPHY

References for Sections 1–4 of Professional Sourcebook

Center for the Assessment of Educational Progress. *A World of Differences.* Princeton, NJ: Educational Testing Service, 1989.

College Board. *Academic Preparation for College: What Students Need To Know and Be Able To Do.* New York: College Board, 1983.

Flanders, James. "How Much of the Content in Mathematics Textbooks Is New?" *Arithmetic Teacher,* September 1987, pp. 18–23.

Hirschhorn, Daniel B. and Senk, Sharon L. "Calculators in the UCSMP Curriculum for Grades 7 and 8." In *Calculators in Mathematics Education,* edited by James T. Fey and Christian R. Hirsch, pp. 79–90. Reston, VA: National Council of Teachers of Mathematics, 1992.

Johnson, David R. *Every Minute Counts.* Palo Alto, CA: Dale Seymour Publications, 1982.

Johnson, David R. *Making Minutes Count Even More.* Palo Alto, CA: Dale Seymour Publications, 1986.

Jones, Philip and Coxford, Arthur F. A *History of Mathematics Education in the United States and Canada*. 30th Yearbook of the National Council of Teachers of Mathematics. Reston, VA: NCTM, 1970.

McNight, Curtis, et al. *The Underachieving Curriculum: Assessing U.S. School Mathematics from an International Perspective.* Champaign, IL: Stipes Publishing Company, 1987.

National Commission on Excellence in Education. *A Nation at Risk: The Imperative for Educational Reform.* Washington, DC: U.S. Department of Education, 1983.

National Council of Teachers of Mathematics. *Curriculum and Evaluation Standards for School Mathematics.* Reston, VA: National Council of Teachers of Mathematics, 1989.

National Council of Teachers of Mathematics. *Professional Standards for Teaching Mathematics.* Reston, VA: National Council of Teachers of Mathematics, 1991

National Research Council. *Everybody Counts.* Washington, DC: National Academy Press, 1989.

National Research Council. *For Good Measure.* Washington, DC: National Academy Press, 1991.

National Research Council. *Measuring Up: Prototypes for Mathematics Assessment.* Washington, DC: National Academy Press, 1993.

National Research Council. *Measuring What Counts.* Washington, DC: National Academy Press, 1993.

National Research Council. *Reshaping School Mathematics: A Philosophy and Framework for Curriculum.* Washington, DC: National Academy Press, 1991.

Polya, George. *How To Solve It.* Princeton, NJ: Princeton University Press, 1952.

Stenmark, Jean Kerr. *Assessment Alternatives in Mathematics.* Berkeley, CA: EQUALS, 1989.

Stenmark, Jean Kerr, editor. *Mathematics Assessment: Myths, Models, Good Questions, and Practical Suggestions.* Reston, VA: National Council of Teachers of Mathematics, 1991.

Waits, Bert, and Demana, Franklin. "Is Three Years Enough?" *Mathematics Teacher,* January 1988, pp. 11–15.

Sources for Additional Problems

The Diagram Group. *Comparisons.* New York. St. Martin's Press, 1980. This is an excellent source of visual and numerical data on such quantities as distance, area and volume, and time and speed.

Eves, Howard. *An Introduction to the History of Mathematics.* 5th ed. Philadelphia. Saunders College Publishing, 1983. This comprehensive history includes references to recent 20th century mathematics, such as the proof ofthe four color theorem. There is an outstanding collection of problems.

Hoffman, Mark, editor. *The World Almanac and Book of Facts,* 1994. New York: World Almanac, 1994.

Johnson, Otto, executive ed. *The 1994 Information Please Almanac.* Boston: Houghton Mifflin Company, 1994.Almanacs are excellent sources of data for problems.

Joint Committee of the Mathematical Association of America and the National Council of Teachers of Mathematics. *A Sourcebook of Applications of School Mathematics.* Reston, VA: National Council of Teachers of Mathematics, 1980. This comprehensive source of applied problems is organized in sections by mathematical content (advanced arithmetic through combinatorics and probability). It is a must for every high school mathematics teacher.

Kastner, Bernice. Applications of Secondary School Mathematics. Reston, Va.: National Council of Teachers of Mathematics, 1978. This short paperback book provides interesting applications in physics, chemistry, biology, economics, and other fields. There is a chapter on mathematical modeling.

The Mathematics Teacher. National Council of Teachers of Mathematics. 1906 Association Drive, Reston, VA, 22091. This journal is an excellent source of applications and other teaching suggestions. We believe that every secondary school mathematics teacher should join the NCTM and read this journal regularly.

Phillips, Elizabeth, et al. *Patterns and Functions.* Reston, VA: National Council of Teachers of Mathematics, 1991. As part of the NCTM's Addenda Series for Grades 5–8, this booklet gives teachers ideas and materials to support the Patterns and Functions strand of the Curriculum and Evaluation Standards. Many examples involve "hands on" activities.

Sharron, Sidney, and Reys, Robert E., editors. *Applications in School Mathematics.* Reston, Va.: NCTM, 1979. This NCTM yearbook is a collection of essays on applications, ways of including applications in the classroom, mathematical modeling, and other issues related to applications. There is an extensive bibliography on sources of applications.

The UMAP Journal, Consortium for Mathematics and Its Applications Project, Inc. 271 Lincoln Street, Suite Number 4, Lexington, Ma. 02173. This journal is a wonderful source of applications, although many of them are at the college level. COMAP also publishes a quarterly newsletter called Consortium that includes "The HiMAP Pull-Out Section." Consortium provides information on COMAP modules which are appropriate for high schools.

U.S. Bureau of the Census. Statistical Abstract of the United States: 1994. 112th ed. Washington, D.C., 1993. This outstanding data source, published annually since 1878, summarizes statistics on the United States, and provides reference to other statistical publications.

LESSON 1-1 (pp. 4–9)
15. a. 50 **b.** stars **17. a.** Salinas-Seaside-Monterey, California **b.** Pensacola, Florida **19.** 600,000,000 **21.** 506 **23.** 9,999 **25. a.** 10 **b.** 100

LESSON 1-2 (pp. 10–15)
21. three hundred twenty-four and sixty-six hundredths **23.** Sample: 44.61 **25. a.** and **c. See below. b.** 10.39 seconds **27.** sixty-five thousandths, sixty-five, sixty-five thousand **29.** 6 **31.** 31,068 **33.** count: 76; counting unit: trombones

25. a. and **c.**

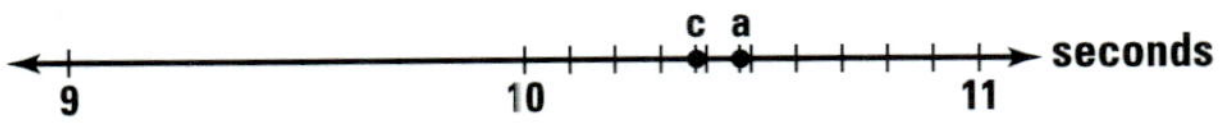

LESSON 1-3 (pp. 16–20)
11. 0.97531246 **13. a.** 6000 **b.** 5000 **c. See below. 15. a.** 1.610 **b.** 1.609 **17.** High. You want everyone to have some cake. **19.** Low. You don't want the cable to break. **21.** 5.001, 5.01, 5.1 **23.** (c) **25.** Sample: 5.99 **27. a.** *Q* **b.** *R* **c.** *Y* **29.** 4,030,000

13.

LESSON 1-4 (pp. 21–25)
11. 2.5 **13. a.** 3.7 **b.** 3.67 **c.** 3.667 **d.** 3.6667 **15. a.** $20.97 **b.** $21, 3¢ off **17.** $24 **19.** 921 **21. a.** 9550 **b.** 9650 **23.** $1.54 **25.** 3.7 **27.** Sample: 3.3 **29.** These numbers are equal so there is no number between them. **31.** count: 12; counting unit: eggs

LESSON 1-5 (pp. 26–30)
9. [C] or [AC] or [clear] **11.** [0.1234568]; 7 decimal places. Answers may vary. **13.** 0.909 **15.** 56 **17.** 99999999. Answers may vary. **19.** Answers will vary. **21. a.** .440 **b.** .441 **c.** .405 **23.** 53.5 seconds **25.** 21 **27.** three million, four hundred twelve thousand, six hundred seventy **29.** 299,997

LESSON 1-6 (pp. 31–36)
23. a. 0.1875″ **b.** shorter **25. a.** and **b. See below. 27.** $\frac{2}{11}, \frac{2}{9}, \frac{2}{7}$ **29. a.** Sample: 59.131824 **b.** 59.132 **31.** 9.8979 **33.** 34.0079 **35.** 2916 gallons

25.

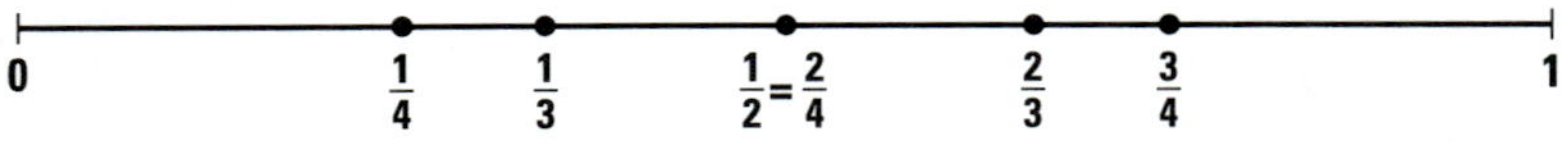

LESSON 1-7 (pp. 37–40)
13. $2\frac{3}{5}, 3\frac{2}{5}, 5\frac{2}{3}$ **15.** 12.533 **17.** longer **19. See below. 21. a.** Sample: $\frac{11}{12}$ **b.** Sample: $\frac{1.4}{7}$ **23.** 100 **25.** True **27. a.** counts: 27 and 206 **b.** counting units: small bones and bones

19.

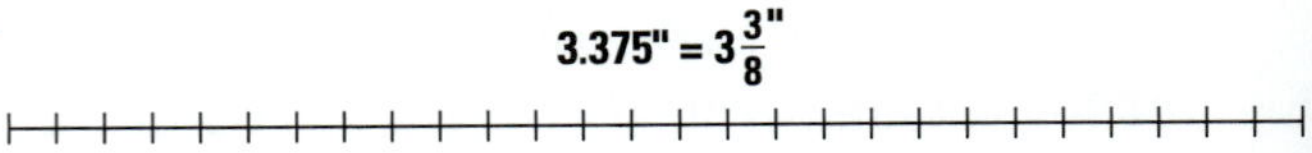

LESSON 1-8 (pp. 41–45)
15. a. −1 **b.** 1 **c.** −2 **d.** 2 **17.** *Q* **19.** none **21.** $-1, 0, \frac{1}{2}, \frac{3}{2}$ **23.** −1 **25.** −60.5 **27.** −9.3 **29.** 6 [+] 3 [×] 4 [÷] 2 [=] [6.] [6.] [3.] [3.] [4.] [12.] [2.] [12.] **31.** 1.2 or $1\frac{1}{5}$ **33.** 462,000.01

LESSON 1-9 (pp. 46–49)
21. a. See below. b. 1 > −2000 **23.** > **25.** = **27.** < **29.** < **31.** 62.1 > 6.21 > 0.621 or 0.621 < 6.21 < 62.1 **33.** 99.2 < 99.8 < 100.4 or 100.4 > 99.8 > 99.2 **35.** 1, 2, 3, 4 **37.** 6.283 **39.** $26

21. a.

LESSON 1-10 (pp. 50–54)
15. a. $\frac{3}{11} = \frac{21}{77}, \frac{2}{7} = \frac{22}{77}, \frac{22}{77} > \frac{21}{77}$, so $\frac{2}{7} > \frac{3}{11}$. **b.** $\frac{3}{11} = .\overline{27}$ and $\frac{2}{7} = .\overline{285714}$; $.\overline{285714} > .\overline{27}$; so $\frac{2}{7} > \frac{3}{11}$. **17.** $\frac{2}{8} = \frac{1}{4}$ **19.** Samples: $\frac{2}{2}, \frac{3}{3}, \frac{5}{5}$ **21.** $\frac{7}{4}$ **23. a.** 1 row of 60 chairs, 2 rows of 30 chairs, 3 rows of 20 chairs, 4 rows of 15 chairs, 5 rows of 12 chairs, 6 rows of 10 chairs, 10 rows of 6 chairs, 12 rows of 5 chairs, 15 rows of 4 chairs, 20 rows of 3 chairs, 30 rows of 2 chairs, 60 rows of 1 chair **b.** These numbers are all the factors of 60. **25.** Samples: $-\frac{1}{2}$, −0.2, −0.05 **27.** 1782.4 **29.** 4.12 **31. a.** 0.4; **b.** 0.625; **c.** 0.75; **d.** $0.\overline{3}$; **e.** $0.8\overline{3}$

CHAPTER 1 PROGRESS SELF-TEST (p. 58)
1. 700,000 **2.** 45.6 **3.** 0.25 **4.** $15\frac{13}{16} = 15 + \frac{13}{16} = 15 + 0.8125 = 15.8125$ **5.** 6 **6.** three-thousandths **7.** Write each number to three decimal places and compare: $.\overline{6}$ = .600, .66 = .660, $.\overline{6}$ = .666 . . . , .606 = .606. This indicates that $.\overline{6}$ is the largest. **8.** Change each fraction to a decimal and compare. $\frac{1}{2}$ = .5, $\frac{2}{5}$ = .4, $\frac{3}{10}$ = .3, and $\frac{1}{3}$ = .333 . . . . So $\frac{3}{10}$ is smallest. **9.** 98.7 **10.** 99 **11.** −80 ft > −100 ft; the negative numbers are below sea level and the > sign means "is higher than." **12.** Each interval on the number line represents $\frac{1}{4}$. Therefore *M* is $\frac{2}{4}$ or $\frac{1}{2}$. **13.** Each interval is $\frac{1}{4}$ or 0.25. *F* corresponds to −1.25. **14.** Rewrite the numbers as 16.50 and 16.60. Any decimal beginning with 16.5 . . . is between. **15.** Rewrite the numbers as −2.3900 and −2.3910. Any decimal beginning with −2.390 . . . is between. **16.** < **17.** =; 24 hundredths is the same as 240 thousandths. **18.** <; $4\frac{4}{15}$ = 4.2666 . . . , and $4.2\overline{6}$ < 4.93 **19.** > ; on a number line, since −4 is to the right of −5, −4 is greater than −5. **20.** 0.6 = $\frac{6}{10}$. Any fraction equal to $\frac{6}{10}$ is equal to 0.6. Sample: $\frac{3}{5}$ **21.** Any number other than . . . , −3, −2, −1, 0, 1, 2, 3, ... For example, $\frac{1}{2}$, 0.43, or $-5.\overline{3}$. **22.** The store will round up. You will pay 18¢. **23.** 3 + 9 = 12 **24.** 3.456 [×] 2.345 [=] **25.** 6 [×] [π] [=] is a calculator sequence that yields 18.849556 . . . . Rounded to the nearest integer, the answer is 19. **26.** 47 **27.** On a number line, divide the interval between 7 and 8 into 10 equal intervals; then each interval

represents 0.1. Place a dot at 7, 7.7, and 8 and label each point. **See below for graph.** **28.** Divide a vertical number line into 10 equal intervals from $^{-}5$ to 5. One interval represents 1°. Place dots at $^{-}4$, 0, and 5, and label each in degrees. **See right for graph.**
29. Sample: the number of people watching a parade **30.** Sample: There are <u>4300</u> <u>people</u> watching the parade. **31.** The numbers are 0.1, 0.000001, 0.000000001, and 0.001. Of these, 0.1 is largest.
32. 18 is divisible by 1, 2, 3, 6, 9, and 18; so these are the factors of 18. **33.** Multiply the numerator and denominator of $\frac{6}{1}$ by 5. This gives $\frac{30}{5}$. **34.** 3 is a factor of both 12 and 21. So $\frac{12}{21} = \frac{12/3}{21/3} = \frac{4}{7}$. **35.** (c)

27.

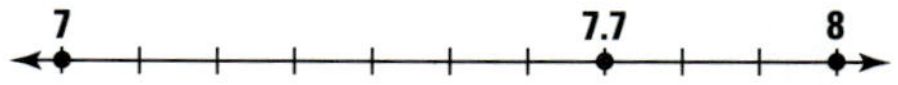

28.

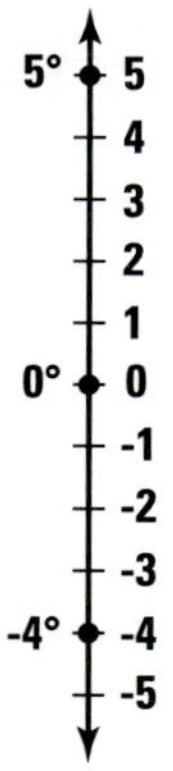

The chart below keys the **Progress Self-Test** questions to the objectives in the **Chapter Review** on pages 59–61 or to the **Vocabulary** (Voc.) on page 57. This will enable you to locate those **Chapter Review** questions that correspond to questions you missed on the **Progress Self-Test.** The lesson where the material is covered is also indicated on the chart.

Question	**1**	**2**	**3**	**4**	**5**	**6**	**7**	**8**	**9**	**10**
Objective	A	A	G	F	A	A	B	B	D	D
Lesson	1-1	1-2	1-6	1-7	1-2	1-2	1-2, 1-6	1-6	1-3	1-4
Question	**11**	**12**	**13**	**14**	**15**	**16**	**17**	**18**	**19**	**20**
Objective	L	M	M	C	C	H	H	H	H	G
Lesson	1-8	1-2	1-8	1-2	1-8	1-9	1-9	1-9	1-9	1-6
Question	**21**	**22**	**23**	**24**	**25**	**26**	**27**	**28**	**29**	**30**
Objective	Voc.	K	D	E	E	I	M	M	K	Voc.
Lesson	1-8	1-4	1-4	1-5	1-5	1-6	1-2	1-8	1-3	1-1
Question	**31**	**32**	**33**	**34**	**35**					
Objective	B	J	J	J	N					
Lesson	1-2	1-10	1-10	1-10	1-1					

CHAPTER 1 REVIEW (pp. 59–61)

1. 4003 **3.** 120,000,000 **5.** 75.6 **7.** five hundred thousand, four hundred **9.** three and forty-one thousandths **11.** largest: 400,001; smallest: $^{-}$.40000000001 **13.** 0.2, 0.19, 0, $^{-}$0.2 **15.** $\frac{1}{7}, \frac{1}{9}, \frac{1}{11}$ **17.** $4\frac{1}{6}$, $3\frac{1}{3}$, $2\frac{2}{3}$ **19.** Sample: 73.05 **21.** Sample: 6.995 **23.** Sample: 0 **25.** 5.84 **27.** 0.595959 **29.** 6.8 **31.** $^{-}$2.5 **33.** $^{-}$20 **35.** 48 **37.** 561.605 **39.** Sample: 5 (+/−) **41.** 2.2 **43.** $6.\overline{571428}$ **45.** .75 **47.** .2 **49.** Sample: $\frac{4}{5}$ **51.** Sample: $\frac{1}{4}$ **53.** > **55.** .667 > $\frac{2}{3}$ > .6

57. 1 **59.** $6.8\overline{9}$ **61.** Sample: $\frac{4}{14}$ and $\frac{6}{21}$ **63.** $\frac{4}{3}$ **65.** 29,000 **67.** 50¢ or $.50 **69.** Sample: An estimate might be easier to work with. **71.** $^{-}$75,000 < 10,000 **73.** **See below.** **75.** **See below.** **77. a.** .1 or $\frac{1}{10}$ **b.** 4.7 **79.** (c)

73.

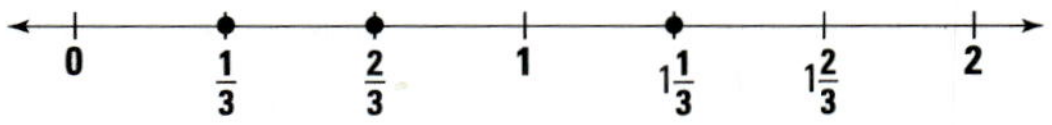

75.

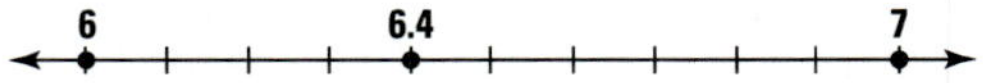

LESSON 2-1 (pp. 62–67)

27. Sample: You can round 1.43 up to 2 or down to 1. Multiply the 1 and 2 by 10,000. The answer should be between 10,000 and 20,000. **29. a.** 9,300,000,000 **b.** 9,320,000,000 **31.** 3.4 billion; 3,400,000,000 **33.** 5.2 billion or 5.3 billion; 5,200,000,000 or 5,300,000,000 **35.** 27.8 billion **37.** the word name "quadrillion," or next whole number 1,000,000,000,001, or $1,000,000,000,000.01 **39. a.** .125 **b.** .1 **c.** .02 **d.** .01 **41.** 2.649

LESSON 2-2 (pp. 68–72)

19. 999 **21.** 10^4, ten thousand, 10,000; 10^5, hundred thousand, 100,000 **23. a.** 4; **b.** 4 **25.** Samples: $6^2 + 8^2 = 100$; $26^2 - 24^2 = 100$ **27.** True **29.** 2,500,000,000 **31.** 1,800,000 **33.** 13 **35.** $^{-}$459.67 **37.** 2 **39.** 3 × 9 = 27

LESSON 2-3 (pp. 73–77)

15. 4.18×10^5 or 418,000 lb **17. a.** Sample: (9.9999 99) for 9.9999×10^{99} **b.** Sample: (−9.9999 99) for -9.9999×10^{99} **19. a.** Find 3×10^5. Enter 3 (EE) 5 or 3 (×) 10 (y^x) 5. **b.** Enter 1000 in scientific notation. Enter 1 (EE) 3. **c.** Find 2^5. Enter 2 (y^x) 5. **21.** 6 **23. a.** *Q* **b.** *E* **c.** *S* **d.** *C* **25.** Samples: $\frac{9}{10}, \frac{27}{30}$

LESSON 2-4 (pp. 78–83)
39. $\frac{1}{100}$ or .01 **41.** 0.04387 **43.** $\frac{150}{100}$ or $1\frac{1}{2}$ or 1.50; $\frac{1795}{100}$ or $\frac{359}{20}$ or 17.95 **45.** (b) **47.** 0.001, $\frac{1}{1000}$ **49.** Volkswagen/Audi **51.** 0% **53. a.** 14,570,000; 12,472,000; 15,200,000 **b.** 1.457×10^7; 1.2472×10^7; 1.52×10^7 **55.** 8^3

LESSON 2-5 (pp. 84–88)
13. Sample: "We are with you totally." **15. a.** 50 million **b.** 75 million **c.** 100 million **d.** 125 million **17.** 36 or 37 **19.** lose; 48.8% is less than 50% which is half **21.** 1.8 million **23. a.** 990 **b.** 99 **c.** 9.9 **d.** 0.99 **25. a.** 10^{15} **b.** 10^4 **27.** 8,300,000 **29.** 4.8 **31.** $\frac{12}{25}$ **33.** 0.7853

LESSON 2-6 (pp. 89–92)
11. a. 350% **b.** $1.58 **13.** **See below.** **15.** $\frac{16}{5}$; 320% **17.** $\frac{27}{100}$; 27% **19.** $\frac{11}{25}$; 0.44 **21.** $\frac{3}{80}$ **23.** $\frac{1}{3}$ off **25.** 32.34 **27.** 240,000 **29.** 8.8×10^6 **31.** 5.256×10^5 **33.** one quadrillion

13.

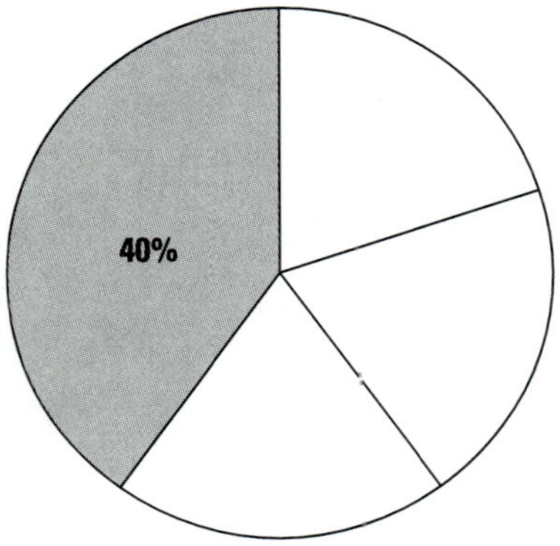

LESSON 2-7 (pp. 93–98)
15. the percent of people who wake up a certain way **17.** by alarm or clock radio **19. a.** $\frac{40}{60}$ or $\frac{2}{3}$ **b.** $66\frac{2}{3}$% **c.** **See below.** **21. a.** 30% **b.** $\frac{25}{50}$ or $\frac{1}{2}$ **c.** **See below.** **23. a.** .35 **b.** 35% **25.** .125, $\frac{125}{1000}$ or $\frac{1}{8}$ **27.** If the numerator and denominator of a fraction are multiplied by the same nonzero number, the resulting fraction is equal to the original one. **29.** five and thirty-four hundredths

19. c.

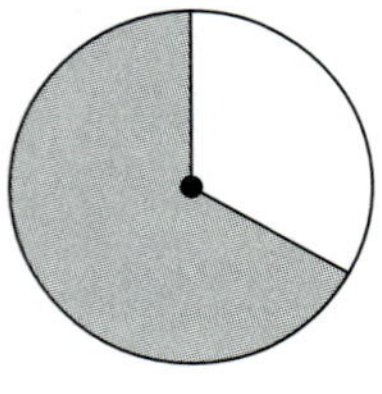

21. c.

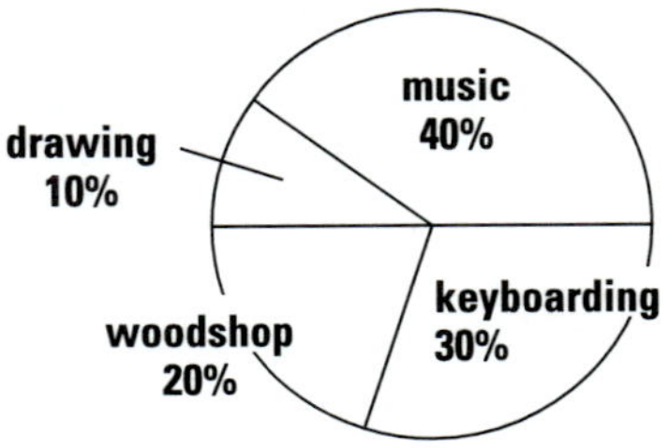

LESSON 2-8 (pp. 99–103)
19. (f) **21.** The zero power of any number other than 0 equals 1. **23. a.** 1 **b.** 1 **c.** When 10 to a power is multiplied by 10 to the opposite of the power, the product is 1. **25. a.** 1000 meters **b.** .01 meter or one hundredth of a meter **c.** .001 meter or one thousandth of a meter **27.** 9^2 or 3^4 **29.** 2^5 **31.** 58.0% of 13.50 million = 7.83 million or 7,830,000 **33.** West, Northeast **35. a.** $\frac{3}{16}$ **b.** 18.75% **37.** Multiply the number by .1. **39.** ninth

LESSON 2-9 (pp. 104–108)
11. a. 0.00000 001 centimeter **b.** 0.00000 000529 centimeter **13. a.** 5×10^{-2} **b.** .05 **15.** = **17. a.** 10^6 **b.** 10^{-6} **19.** millimeter, centimeter, kilometer **21.** The team lost more often. **23.** −19.7 **25. a.** $0.001 or 0.1¢ **b.** $0.0001 **c.** $0.0111 **d.** $0.01 **27.** 4.5005005×10^9 **29. a.** **See below.** **b.** Yes **31.** Low; too much baggage would endanger the safety of the passengers.

29. a.

CHAPTER 2 PROGRESS SELF-TEST (pp. 112)

1. Move the decimal point 8 places to the right. 2,351,864,000 **2.** $\frac{34}{100} \times 600 = 204$ **3.** 32×10^{-9} = 0.00000 0032 **4.** Move the decimal point 5 places to the left. 0.0082459 **5.** 0.001 × 77 = 0.077 **6.** Move the decimal point 5 places to the right. 345,689,100 **7.** Move the decimal point 3 places to the left. 0.002816 **8.** 0.00000 01 **9.** 8% = 8 × .01 = 0.08 **10.** 216 **11.** base; exponent **12. a.** 125 [y^x] 6 [=] **b.** [3.8147 12] Answers may vary. **13.** 3,814,700,000,000 **14.** radius **15.** 100% **16.** Place a decimal point between the 2 and 1. You must move the decimal point 10 places to the right to get the given number. So the scientific notation is 2.107×10^{10}. **17.** Place a decimal point to the right of the 8. Move the decimal point 8 places to the left to get the given number. So 0.00000 008 equals 8×10^{-8}. **18.** 4.5 [EE] 13 or 4.5 [×] 10 [y^x] 13 [=] **19.** First write in scientific notation: 1.23456×10^{-7}. Then enter either 1.23456 [EE] 7 [+/−] or 1.23456 [×] 10 [y^x] 7 [+/−] [=]. **20.** In the order given, the numbers equal 256, 125, and 243. So from smallest to largest, they are: 5^3, 3^5, 4^4. **21.** First change to a decimal. 40% = 0.40. This number is between 0 and 1. **22. a.** $4.73 = \frac{4.73}{1} = \frac{473}{100}$ **b.** $\frac{473}{100}$ = 473% **23.** $\frac{1}{3}$ **24. a.** cassette tapes (53.6%) **b.** 100% − 42.3% = 57.7% **c.** 3.3% of 801 million = .033 × 801 million = 26.433 million ≈ 26.4 million **25.** 30% × 150 = .3 × 150 = 45 **26.** You save 0.25 × $1699 = $424.75. Subtract from $1699 to get the sale price, $1274.25 ≈ $1274. **27.** 0.8 × 20 = 16. This is the number correct. So 20 − 16 = 4 is the number missed. **28.** 22.4 is not between 1 and 10. **29.** 6, since 10^6 = 1,000,000 **30.** $\frac{3}{5}$ = 60%, $\frac{1}{10}$ = 10%, so $\frac{3}{5} - \frac{1}{10}$ = 60% − 10%. **31.** 250 billion = 250,000,000,000 = 2.5×10^{11}

The chart below keys the **Progress Self-Test** questions to the objectives in the **Chapter Review** on pages 113–115 or to the **Vocabulary** (Voc.) on page 111. This will enable you to locate those **Chapter Review** questions that correspond to questions you missed on the **Progress Self-Test.** The lesson where the material is covered is also indicated on the chart.

Question	**1**	**2**	**3**	**4**	**5**	**6**	**7**	**8**	**9**	**10**
Objective	A	G, K	B	E	E	A	E	D	G	C
Lesson	2-1	2-5	2-8	2-4	2-4	2-2	2-4	2-8	2-4	2-2
Question	**11**	**12**	**13**	**14**	**15**	**16**	**17**	**18**	**19**	**20**
Objective	Voc.	N	C	J	O	F	F	N	N	C
Lesson	2-2	2-3	2-2	2-7	2-7	2-3	2-9	2-3	2-9	2-2
Question	**21**	**22**	**23**	**24**	**25**	**26**	**27**	**28**	**29**	**30**
Objective	G, H	I	H	O	M	M	M	L	D	K
Lesson	2-4	2-6	2-4	2-7	2-5	2-5	2-5	2-3	2-2	2-5
Question	**31**									
Objective	F									
Lesson	2-3									

CHAPTER 2 REVIEW (pp. 113–115)

1. 320,000 **3.** 25,000 **5.** 30,000,000 **7.** 29,314,000,000 **9.** 0.00000 46 **11.** 64 **13.** ≈ 429,980,000 **15.** 100,000 **17.** 0.0001 **19.** one billion **21.** twelfth **23.** 0.00000 00273 **25.** 0.075 **27.** 8 **29.** 4.8×10^5 **31.** 1.3×10^{-4} **33.** 3,000,000,000,000,000,000,000,000,000,000,000 **35.** 0.15 **37.** 0.09 **39.** 75 **41.** 6.2 **43.** 50% **45.** $\frac{3}{10}$ **47.** Sample: $\frac{57}{10}$ **49.** 86% **51.** about 42.9% **53.** $\overline{AC}$, $\overline{BC}$ or $\overline{DC}$ **55.** C **57.** $\overrightarrow{AB}$ or $\overrightarrow{AD}$ or $\overrightarrow{BD}$ **59.** If two numbers are equal, one can be substituted for the other in any computation without changing the results of the computation. **61.** $\frac{1}{2}$ and .5 **63.** 23 is not between 1 and 10 **65.** \$15.90 **67.** \$24,960 (about \$25,000) **69.** Sample: 3.2 (EE) 10 **71. a.** Sample: 2 (y^x) 45 (=) **b.** ≈ 3.5184×10^{13} **73.** ≈ 3.3516×10^{13} **75.** Sample: 1.93 (EE) 15 (+/−) **77.** 6% **79.** percent of adults who sleep more than 7.5 hours up to 8.5 hours

LESSON 3-1 (pp. 116–124)

21. (d) **23.** (c) **25.** **See below.** **27.** **See below.** **29.** 45% **31.** 5^6

25. **6 cm ≈ $2\frac{3}{8}$ in.**

27. **12.4 cm**

LESSON 3-2 (pp. 125–129)

15. a. 1 rod = 16.5 ft **b.** 1 furlong = 660 ft **c.** 6600 ft **17.** 120 strides **19.** 282 in. **21. a.** $3\frac{3}{8}$ in. **b.** 9 cm **23. a.** 10,000 **b.** \$600 per student **c.** $\$1.5 \times 10^8$; \$150,000,000 **25. a.** −2, −1.5, −1 **b.** $-2 < -1.5 < -1$ or $-1 > -1.5 > -2$ **27.** 900

LESSON 3-3 (pp. 130–134)

13. about 1,394,200,000 lb **15.** cup **17.** gallon **19.** No **21.** A gallon is not a unit of length; it is a unit of volume or capacity. **23.** 2640 ft **25.** $4\frac{13}{16}$ inches **27.** 1.3837×10^{-2} **29.** 5.2 **31.** 1.536

LESSON 3-4 (pp. 135–139)

25. (b) **27.** Yes **29.** $\frac{1}{1000}$ or .001 second **31.** 8 times **33.** $<$ **35.** $=$ **37.** Since $\frac{1}{16}$ inch is a smaller interval than $\frac{1}{10}$ inch, a measurement to the nearest $\frac{1}{16}$ inch is more precise. **39. a.** 25 or 26 **b.** 24 **c.** 22 **41.** 0.002 cm

LESSON 3-5 (pp. 140–144)

15. liter **17.** inch **19.** ounce **21. a.** 0.3125 **b.** 8 mm **23.** ≈ 12.72 cups **25.** 4000 g **27.** 80 ounces **29.** 36 in. **31. a.** 60 – 64 **b.** 30 – 39 **c.** 53.2 million **d.** 40% **33.** 25

LESSON 3-6 (pp. 145–151)

19. $\angle JGH$ **21 and 23.** **See below.** **25.** 0.082 m **27.** **See below.** **29.** $\overrightarrow{AC}$ **31.** 4.16×10^7

21 and 23. Sample:

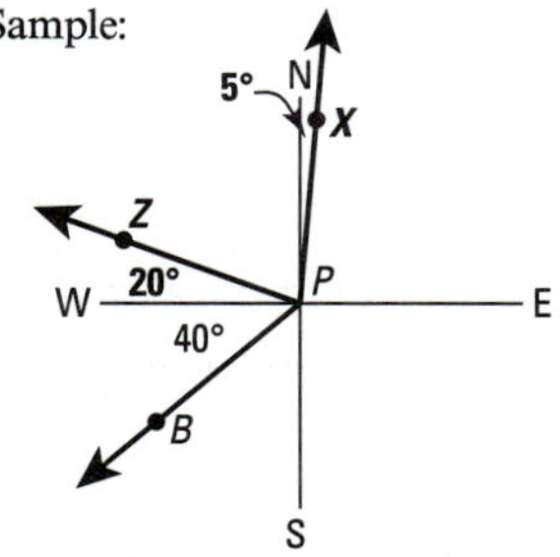

27. **7 cm**

LESSON 3-7 (pp. 152–157)

17. 54°
19. **See right.** **21.** **See below.**
23. **a.** obtuse; **b.** 134°
25. **a.** acute, 30°; **b.** obtuse, 120°; **c.** right, 90°; **d.** acute, 15°
27. **See below.** **29.** < **31.** < **33.** liter
35. $2\frac{1}{4}$ inches **37.** $1.20

19.

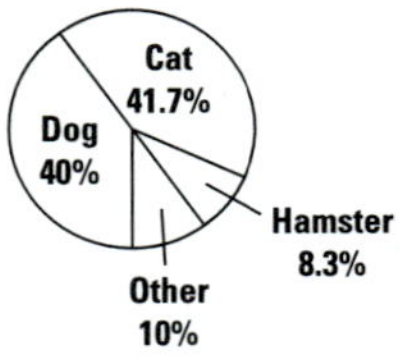

21. **a, b.** Sample:

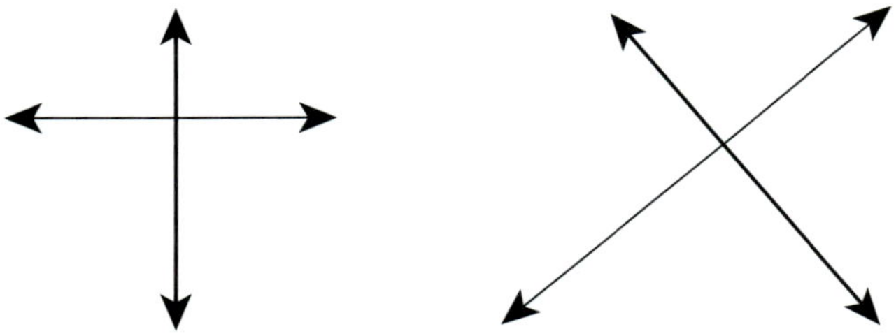

27.

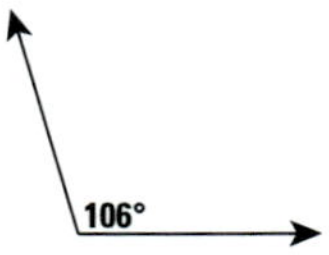

LESSON 3-8 (pp. 158–162)

15. 6 in^2 **17.** **a.** **See right.** **b.** 9 ft^2
19. **a.** m^2 **b.** ft^2
21. 21,780 ft^2 **23.** acute
25. **a.** ≈ 132 lb **b.** 60,000 g
27. 11.5 cm **29.** **a.** 60 **b.** 120; 240; 420 **31.** <

17. **a.**

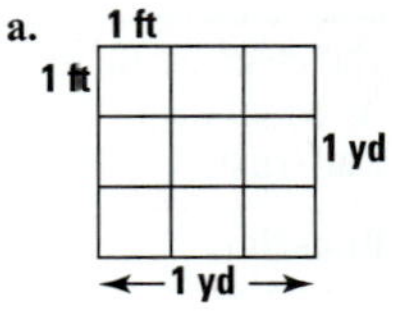

LESSON 3-9 (pp. 163–166)

15. **a.** 34.328125 ft^3 **b.** 34.33 ft^3 **17.** 89 cubic centimeters, volume of a cube with edge 9 cm, 1 liter **19.** **a.** 125,000 mL **b.** 125 kg **c.** ≈ 275 lb **21.** 100 cm^2 **23.** **a.** 16%, 12%, 28%, and 44% **b.** **See below.** **25.** (c) **27.** 216 inches **29.** **a.** 15,400,000 **b.** Answers will vary. Sample: ≈ 800,000,000 copies **c.** Answers will vary. Sample: 8×10^8

23. **b.**

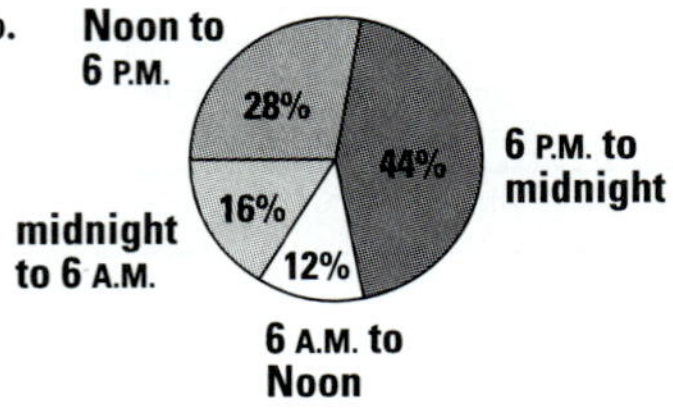

CHAPTER 3 PROGRESS SELF-TEST (p. 170)

1. $2\frac{5}{8}''$ **2.** **a.** **See right.** **b.** 64 mm **3.** 1 in. = 2.54 cm
4. kilogram **5.** $\frac{3}{4}$ mile = $\frac{3}{4} \times$ 5280 ft = 0.75 × 5280 ft = 3960 ft
6. Answers will vary: Sample: Since 1 foot = 12 inches, then 83 feet = 83 · 12 inches = 996 inches. **7.** 1000 tons **8.** 1103 mg = 1103 × .001 g = 1.103 g **9.** 1 quart = 2 pints, so 3 quarts = 6 pints. 1 pint = 2 cups, so 6 pints = 12 cups. Thus 3 quarts = 12 cups. **10.** 1 pound = 16 ounces, so 3.2 pounds = 3.2 × 16 ounces = 51.2 ounces **11.** 1 km ≈ .62 mi so 50 km ≈ 50 × .62 mi = 31 mi **12.** 1 kg ≈ 2.2 lb **13.** 9 liters = 9 × 1 liter ≈ 9 × 1.06 quarts = 9.54 quarts. So 10 quarts is larger. **14.** England **15.** 135° **16.** 0°; 90° **17.** 70° **18.** right **19.** **See right.** **20.** Angles *B* and *C* are acute. There are no right angles. Angle *A* is obtuse. **21.** 20 violins out of 48 players is $\frac{20}{48}$ or $\frac{5}{12}$. $\frac{5}{12}$ of 360° = 150°. **22.** Area = $(4.5 \text{ in.})^2 = 20.25 \text{ in}^2$ **23.** square centimeters **24.** 1 liter = 1000 cubic centimeters **25.** V = $(5 \text{ cm})^3 = 125 \text{ cm}^3$ **26.** Volume of the box is $(10 \text{ cm})^3 = 1000 \text{ cm}^3$. Volume of each block is $(2 \text{ cm})^3 = 8 \text{ cm}^3$. Divide the volume of the big box by the volume of one block, $\frac{1000 \text{ cm}^3}{8 \text{ cm}^3} = 125$. So 125 blocks will fit in the box.

2. **a.**

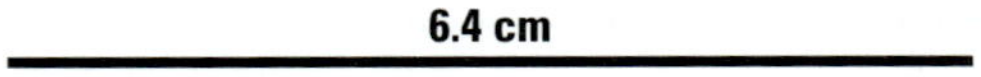

19.

The chart below keys the **Progress Self-Test** questions to the objectives in the **Chapter Review** on pages 171–173 or to the **Vocabulary** (Voc.) on page 169. This will enable you to locate those **Chapter Review** questions that correspond to questions you missed on the **Progress Self-Test.** The lesson where the material is covered is also indicated on the chart.

Question	**1**	**2**	**3**	**4**	**5**	**6**	**7**	**8**	**9**	**10**
Objective	A	K, H	I	F	G	E	H	H	G	G
Lesson	3-1	3-1, 3-4	3-2	3-3	3-2	3-2	3-4	3-4	3-3	3-3
Question	**11**	**12**	**13**	**14**	**15**	**16**	**17**	**18**	**19**	**20**
Objective	I	I	I	N	B	B	Voc.	Voc.	L	C
Lesson	3-5	3-5	3-5	3-1	3-6	3-6	3-7	3-7	3-6	3-7
Question	**21**	**22**	**23**	**24**	**25**	**26**				
Objective	M	D	Voc.	H	D	J				
Lesson	3-7	3-8	3-8	3-4	3-9	3-9				

CHAPTER 3 REVIEW (pp. 171–173)

1. $1\frac{3}{4}$ in. **3.** 7 cm **5.** 65° **7.** 39° **9.** ∠*ABC*, ∠*BEA*, ∠*BCD*, ∠*DEC* **11.** obtuse **13.** 4 cm^2 **15.** square meters **17.** 53 in^3 **19.** 1.1 lb **21.** (b) **23. a.** cm **b.** in. **25. a.** liters **b.** gallons **27.** 16 ounces **29.** 90 inches **31.** 10,000 lb **33.** 1 liter = 1000 cm^3 **35.** 2 m **37.** 0.265 L **39.** 1 kg ≈ 2.2 lb **41.** mile **43.** 60.96 cm **45.** 7.208 ≈ 7.21 qt **47.** ≈$4.44 **49.** 1728 cubes **51. See right. 53. See right. 55. See right. 57. See right. 59.** More than $\frac{1}{4}$ of the circle is shaded for lunch. **61.** France, 1790s **63.** Babylonians

51. 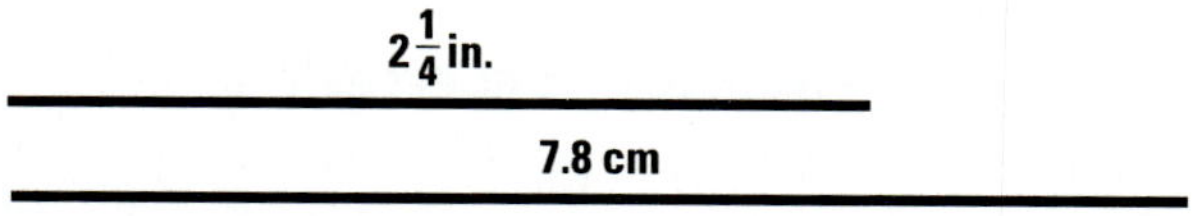

53.

55. **57.** 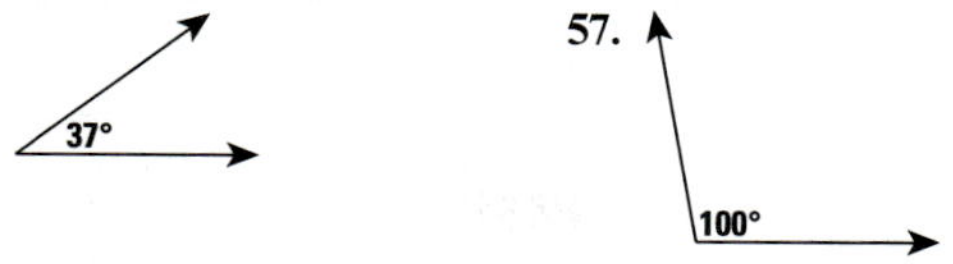

LESSON 4-1 (pp. 174–181)

29. 6 × 0.3 = 1.8 **31.** It is not clear whether 4 is added to 2 first or divided by 8 first. **33.** 117 **35.** 67 **37.** (c) **39.** 125 in^3 **41. See below. 43. a.** The first year you will spend an additional $7.47 since the smoke detectors cost $44.97 and the insurance discount is only $37.50. The second through the fifth years, you will save $37.50 per year, or $150.00 over four years. **b.** The total savings for the five years will be $142.53.

41. 

LESSON 4-2 (pp. 182–186)

13. Samples: 6 · 4 + 13 · 4 = 19 · 4; 6 · 9.7 + 13 · 9.7 = 19 · 9.7; 6 · 100 + 13 · 100 = 19 · 100; $6 \cdot \frac{2}{3} + 13 \cdot \frac{2}{3} = 19 \cdot \frac{2}{3}$ **15.** $a \cdot 0 = 0$ **17.** In *n* years, we expect *n* · 100 more students and *n* · 5 more teachers. **19.** Yes. *a* and *b* can be the same number. **21. a.** *b* + .5 is not an integer **b.** 3.5 + .5 is an integer **c.** The pattern is not always true because if *b* = .5, 1.5, 2.5, and so on, the sum will be an integer. **23.** 55 **25.** 74 **27.** 36 **29.** 50/.0001 = 500,000 **31.** 3 m

LESSON 4-3 (pp. 187–192)

19. It is not clear whether 14 − 5 or 5 + 3 is done first. **21.** .06 · *C* or 6% · *C* **23.** $x + \frac{1}{4} \cdot x$ **25.** It could mean $\frac{2}{4}$ or $\frac{4}{2}$. **27.** $\frac{a}{1} = a$ **29.** $5^2 + 9^2 = 25 + 81 = 106$ **31.** 23 + .09 × 11 = 23 + 0.99 = 23.99 **33. See below. 35.** $2\frac{4}{8}$ in. or $2\frac{1}{2}$ in. **37.** about 200,000,000 White; about 30,000,000 Black; about 2,000,000 American Indian, Eskimo, or Aleut.; about 7,000,000 Asian or Pacific Islander; about 10,000,000 Other; about 22,000,000 Hispanic

33. Samples:

a. **b.** **c.**

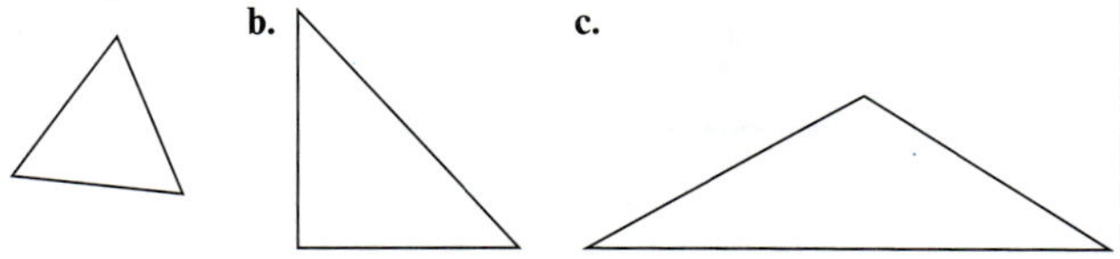

LESSON 4-4 (pp. 193–196)

15. a. 47 lb **b.** 27 lb **c.** 5 lb **17. a.** 3, 5, 7, 9, and 11 **b.** Sample: Begin with 3; add 2 to each number to get the next number. **19. a.** 4*n* + 9 **b.** 49 **21.** (a) **23.** *a* + 0 = *a* **25.** milli- **27.** (b) and (d)

LESSON 4-5 (pp. 197–202)

25. (*a* + 4)*b* + 3 **27.** No **29. a.** (iii) **b.** 73.4° **31.** 436 **33.** 16 − (8 − 4 − 2) = 14 **35. a.** *T* = number of touchdowns; *E* = number of extra points; *F* = number of field goals; *S* = number of safeties **b.** the total score **37.** 36 mi^2

LESSON 4-6 (pp. 203–207)

17. $35.\overline{6}$ ≈ 36 books **19. a.** $58.\overline{3}$ **b.** $91.\overline{6}$ **21.** $\frac{x + 3y}{z} + \frac{4y + z}{3x} = \frac{3 + 3 \cdot 2}{1} + \frac{4 \cdot 2 + 1}{3 \cdot 3} = \frac{3 + 6}{1} + \frac{8 + 1}{9} = \frac{9}{1} + \frac{9}{9} = 9 + 1 = 10$ **23.** (3 · 8 − 6)/2 + 3 = 12 **25. a.** 30 + 20 **b.** *n* + 3 **c.** *n* − .1 **27.** $20.85 (It will require 3 bags; some fertilizer will be left over.) **29. a.** 268,729,000,000 **b.** 269 billion **c.** 2.68729×10^{11}

LESSON 4-7 (pp. 208–212)

11. 24 m^2 **13.** 0.912 **15.** 0.500 **17.** 73° **19.** Sample: $d = 2r$ or $r = \frac{1}{2}d$ **21.** 94 **23.** 10 **25.** (c) inside parentheses, (b) powers, (a) multiplication or division from left to right, (d) addition or subtraction from left to right **27.** < **29.** < **31.** 6000 g

LESSON 4-8 (pp. 213–218)

11. Relative frequency is a number $\frac{F}{N}$ from 0 to 1 that indicates how many times (*F*) an event occurred out of *N* repetitions of an experiment that has taken place. Probability is a number from 0 to 1 that indicates what we think is the likelihood of an event. **13.** $\frac{3}{50}$ **15. a.** $\frac{1}{8}$; **b.** *B*: $\frac{3}{8}$; *C*: $\frac{1}{4}$; *D*: $\frac{1}{4}$ **17.** 20% **19.** the 8.6 by 6.8 rectangle **21. a.** 6 **b.** 2.8 **c.** 6.2 **23.** about 10.2 miles

LESSON 4-9 (pp. 219–223)

17. Sample: Los Angeles **19.** eight **21.** Sample: −9 **23.** 6 **25.** 11 **27.** 4 **29.** 1 **31.** 3 **33.** $\frac{33}{100}$ or .33 **35.** 26,127 **37.** 5 km > 500 m > 50,000 mm or 50,000 mm < 500 m < 5 km

LESSON 4-10 (pp. 224–228)

25. (d) **27. See below. 29. See below. 31. a.** $0 \le d < 25{,}000$ **b.** Samples: 4.32, 5132, 24,999.99 **c. See below. 33. a.** $0 \le P \le 1$ **b. See below. 35.** $1.92 **37.** 1 − *x* **39.** 189 **41.** $\frac{a}{b} \cdot \frac{b}{a} = 1$

27. 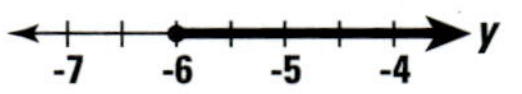

29. 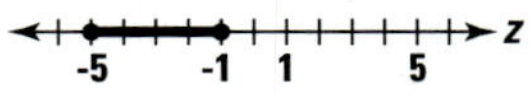

31. c. 

33. b. 

CHAPTER 4 PROGRESS SELF-TEST (p. 232)

1. $6 + 56 + 9 = 71$ **2.** $35 + 50 = 85$ **3.** $25 - 3 - 1 = 22 - 1 = 21$ **4.** $5 + 3 \cdot 16 = 5 + 48 = 53$ **5.** $\frac{100 + 10}{10 + 5} = \frac{110}{15} = 7.\overline{3} \approx 7$ **6.** $10 + 3 \cdot 100 = 10 + 300 = 310$ **7.** $(3 + 4)(4 - 3) = 7 \cdot 1 = 7$ **8.** $100 + 5[100 + 4(100 + 3)] = 100 + 5[100 + 4 \cdot 103] = 100 + 5[100 + 412] = 100 + 5 \cdot 512 = 100 + 2560 = 2660$ **9.** $(4x)^2 = 64$; (a) $(4 \cdot 2)^2 = 8^2 = 64$; so 2 is a solution. (b) $(4 \cdot 4)^2 = 16^2 = 256 \neq 64$; so 4 is not a solution. (c) $(4 \cdot 8)^2 = 32^2 = 1024 \neq 64$, so 16 is not a solution. (d) $(4 \cdot 16)^2 = 64^2 \neq 64$, so 16 is not a solution. The correct answer is (a). **10.** $10 \cdot a = 6 \cdot a + 4 \cdot a$ **11.** $a + b = b + a$ **12.** In y years we expect the town to grow by $y \cdot 200$ people. **13.** $c = 23 \cdot 5 + 6 = 115 + 6 = 121$¢, or \$1.21 **14.** $c = 23 \cdot 9 + 6 = 207 + 6 = 213$¢, or \$2.13 **15.** $p = \$45 - \$22.37 = \$22.63$ **16.** 12×16 **17.** $40 < 47$ **18.** $n \geq 0$ or $0 \leq n$ **19.** $\frac{9}{a}$ **20.** $\frac{W}{W + L} = W/(W + L)$; The correct answer is (b).

21. (c) **22.** 8 is the number of times the event occurred; 50 is the number of total outcomes. So the relative frequency is $\frac{8}{50}$, or .16. **23.** The total number of students is $5 + 7 = 12$. Since 5 students are boys, the probability a boy is chosen is $\frac{5}{12}$ or $.41\overline{6}$. **24.** (b) **25.** $6 \cdot 7 = 42$, so $x = 7$. **26.** Any number between −5 and −4 is a solution. Some sample solutions are −4.2, −4.9, $-4\frac{1}{2}$. **27.** Units in formulas must be consistent for the answer to make sense. For example, to find the area of a rectangle given the dimensions of the length and the width, if $w = 3$ inches and $\ell = 4$ feet, the area A cannot be 12 of either unit, even though $A = \ell w$. **28.** $x = 7 \cdot 3 = 21$ **29. See below.** **30.** This is written as $4.5 \leq k < 6$ **31.** Samples: If your age is 10 years, your sister's age is $10 - 5$ or 5 years. If your age is 14, your sister's age is $14 - 5$ or 9 years. **32.** Samples: $30 + 2 - 30 = 2$; $7.3 + 6.2 - 7.3 = 6.2$.

29.
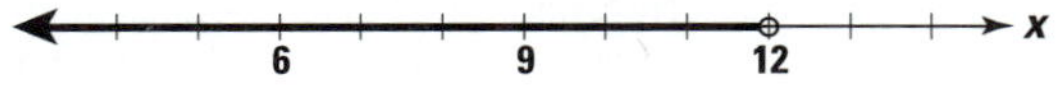

The chart below keys the **Progress Self-Test** questions to the objectives in the **Chapter Review** on pages 233–235 or to the **Vocabulary** (Voc.) on page 231. This will enable you to locate those **Chapter Review** questions that correspond to questions you missed on the **Progress Self-Test.** The lesson where the material is covered is also indicated on the chart.

Question	**1**	**2**	**3**	**4**	**5**	**6**	**7**	**8**	**9**	**10**
Objective	A	A	A	A	A	B	B	B	C	E
Lesson	4-1	4-5	4-1	4-1	4-6	4-4	4-5	4-6	4-9	4-2
Question	**11**	**12**	**13**	**14**	**15**	**16**	**17**	**18**	**19**	**20**
Objective	E	G	I	I	H	H	H	H	I	D
Lesson	4-2	4-2	4-7	4-7	4-3	4-3	4-3	4-3	4-7	4-6
Question	**21**	**22**	**23**	**24**	**25**	**26**	**27**	**28**	**29**	**30**
Objective	L	J	J	Voc.	C	C	I	I	K	K
Lesson	4-1	4-8	4-8	4-10	4-9	4-10	4-7	4-7	4-10	4-10
Question	**31**	**32**								
Objective	F	F								
Lesson	4-2	4-2								

CHAPTER 4 REVIEW (pp. 233–235)

1. 215 **3.** 83 **5.** 31 **7.** 1966 **9.** 158 **11.** 5 **13.** $\frac{14}{65} = 0.215\ldots$ **15.** 24 **17.** 18 **19.** 24 **21.** 184 **23.** $\frac{8}{12}$ or $\frac{2}{3}$ or $.\overline{6}$ **25.** (b) **27.** 4 **29.** 2 **31.** powering **33.** (d) **35.** $5 \cdot x + 9 \cdot x = 14 \cdot x$ **37.** $\frac{a}{9} + \frac{b}{9} = \frac{a + b}{9}$ **39.** Sample: $2 + 6 = 1 + 6 + 1$; $2 + .5 = 1 + .5 + 1$; $2 + \frac{1}{20} = 1 + \frac{1}{20} + 1$ **41.** If the weight is w ounces, the postage is 5¢ + w · 20¢. **43.** $18 + 27$ **45.** $4 \cdot 20 - 1$ **47.** $2x + 7$ **49.** $x < 5$ **51.** ≈ 127 **53.** 72 in^2 or .5 ft^2 **55.** 1 **57.** $\frac{2}{10}$ or $\frac{1}{5}$ or .2 **59.** $\frac{14}{30}$ or $\frac{7}{15}$ or $.4\overline{6}$ **61.** $x \geq 2$ or $2 \leq x$ **63. See right.** **65. See right.** **67. See right.** **69.** Sample: *, ^

63.

65.
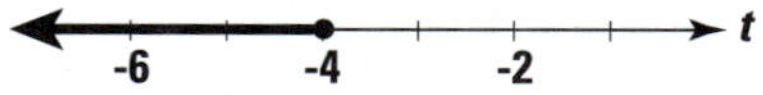

67.

LESSON 5-1 (pp. 236–243)

19. Not enough information to tell. There may be overlap, so we cannot add the amounts to give an answer. The total is at least \$20 and at most \$35. **21.** $b + s + 1$ **23.** No, rain and sun could appear on the same day, as could snow and sun. **25.** a point 220 ft north of the starting point **27.** never positive **29.** sometimes positive **31. a.** 50% **b.** ≈ 33.9% **33.** 1 **35. a.** -6 **b.** 0

LESSON 5-2 (pp. 244–247)

19. -7 **21.** b **23.** -5 **25.** $-x$ **27.** 5 **29.** 1 **31.** 9 **33. a.** The temperature is $-9°$. **b.** $-11 + 2$ **35.** $t + -35 = -60$ **37. a.** 10,000 lb **b.** 3750 lb **c.** No

LESSON 5-3 (pp. 248–252)

23. $-\frac{2}{3}$ **25.** -4 **27.** -2 **29.** 0 **31.** 0 **33. a.** True **b.** True **c.** True **35.** (b) **37.** -65.399 billion dollars or $-\$65{,}399{,}000{,}000$ **39. a.** 0 **b.** 15 **c.** 13 **41. a.** $-150 + 50$ **b.** -100; the person is \$100 in debt. **43.** 1 in.

LESSON 5-4 (pp. 253–259)

19. $-29°$ **21.** 72° **23. a.** 240° (or $-120°$) **b.** 120° (or $-240°$) **25.** 100° **27.** 2160° **29.** -11 **31.** 14 **33.** -9 **35.** $45 + m = 120$ (minutes), or $\frac{3}{4} + m = 2$ (hours) **37.** $Y - 2$ **39.** 6000 m

LESSON 5-5 (pp. 260–265)

17. a. 1 tablespoon **b.** 3 teaspoons **c.** Yes. Since 1 tsp = $\frac{1}{3}$ tbsp, 3 tsp = $3 \cdot \frac{1}{3}$ tbsp = 1 tbsp. **19.** $\frac{1}{16} + \frac{1}{8} = \frac{1}{16} + \frac{2}{16} = \frac{3}{16}$ **21.** $\frac{35}{8} + \frac{8}{3} = \frac{105}{24} + \frac{64}{24} = \frac{169}{24}$ **23.** $9\frac{3}{4} + \frac{1}{4} + 3 = 10 + 3 = 13$ or $\frac{13}{1}$ **25.** a counterclockwise turn of 68° **27.** -4.7 **29.** -8 **31. a.** Sample: 0 **b.** See below. **33. a.** 3×10^4 **b.** about 66,000 lb

31. b.

LESSON 5-6 (pp. 266–270)

15. $\frac{20}{23}$ **17.** not mutually exclusive **19.** $\frac{1}{3}$ **21.** $\frac{43}{30}$ or $1\frac{13}{30}$ **23.** $\frac{21}{4}$ lb or $5\frac{1}{4}$ lb **25.** 40 **27.** 4.351

LESSON 5-7 (pp. 271–275)

11. Your account is overdrawn. **13.** 12 **15.** 0 **17.** They are \$10.25 over budget. **19.** 1° **21.** Associative Property of Addition **23. a.** 60° **b.** 120° **c.** ∠AOC, ∠COD, ∠DOB **d.** There are none. **e.** ∠AOD, ∠COB **f.** $\frac{2}{3}$ **25.** H **27.** Sample: $5 + -5 = 0$ **29.** $(t - 3)$ degrees **31.** 17.1 **33.** 32,736

LESSON 5-8 (pp. 276–281)

15. $A + 38 = 120$, $A = 82$, $82 + 43 + -5 = 120$ **17.** \$1025 **19.** \$4.03 **21.** $b = c + -a$ **23. a.** $\frac{11}{12}$ **b.** choosing a blue chip **c.** $b = \frac{1}{12}$ or $.08\overline{3}$ **25. a.** Sample: -4 **b.** Sample: 2 **27.** $3n$ **29.** $B/(2C)$ or $\frac{B}{2C}$ **31.** The measure of angle LNP is thirty-five degrees. **33.** 30

LESSON 5-9 (pp. 282–287)

17. nonagon **19. a.** See below for drawing. $\overline{PR}$, $\overline{PS}$, $\overline{QT}$, $\overline{QS}$, $\overline{TR}$ **b.** 5 **21.** Sample: All sides are approximately the same length. **23.** $\overline{XA}$ joins two consecutive vertices and is a side of the polygon. A diagonal is not a side of the polygon, so $\overline{XA}$ is not a diagonal. **25.** (d) **27.** $w = 83$; $300 = 172 + (45 + 83)$ **29.** $d = 8.1$; $8.1 + -1.3 = 6.8$ **31. a.** 8 ft = 96 in., so an equation is $s + 3 = 96$ **b.** $s = 93$ inches

19. a. Sample:

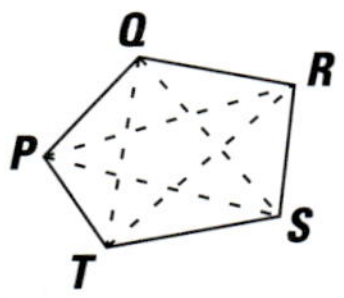

LESSON 5-10 (pp. 288–292)

15. a. $9 + 9 + 5 + 5 + x = 30$ **b.** 2 **17.** 40 and 20; 30 and 30; 20 and 40 **19. a.** Yes **b.** 20 m **21.** See below. **23. a.** $\frac{1}{50} + x = 1$ **b.** $x = \frac{49}{50}$ **25.** 16.45 **27.** See below. **29. a.** $E + -4$ **b.** $A + -4$ **c.** If $E = A$, then $E + -4 = A + -4$. **d.** Addition Property of Equality **31.** all **33.** 94°

21. Sample:

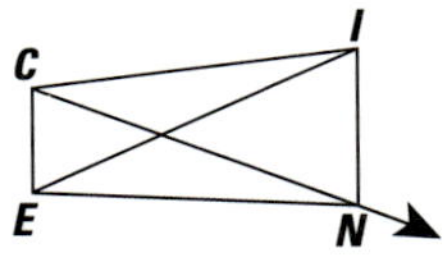

27.

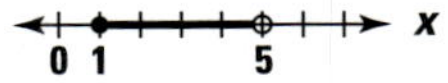

CHAPTER 5 PROGRESS SELF-TEST (p. 296)

1. -7 **2.** -710 **3.** $-9.8 + -(-1) = -9.8 + 1 = -8.8$ **4.** $x + y + -x + 4 = x + -x + y + 4 = 0 + y + 4 = y + 4$ **5.** 8 **6.** $|-2 + 1| + |0| = |-1| + 0 = |-1| = 1$ **7.** $-6 + 42 + -11 + 16 + -12 = -6 + -11 + -12 + 42 + 16 = -29 + 58 = 29$ **8.** $|-(-3) + 8| = |3 + 8| = |11| = 11$ **9.** Add -43 to both sides; $x = -12$ **10.** Add 2.5 to both sides; $y = 1.3$ **11.** $8 = z + -7$; add 7 to both sides; $z = 15$ **12.** $\frac{53}{12} + \frac{11}{12} = \frac{(53 + 11)}{12} = \frac{64}{12} = \frac{16}{3}$ **13.** $\frac{5}{x} + \frac{10}{x} = \frac{(5 + 10)}{x} = \frac{15}{x}$ **14.** 9 is the common denominator. So $\frac{-8}{3} = \frac{-24}{9}$ and $\frac{17}{9} + \frac{-24}{9} = \frac{(17 + -24)}{9} = \frac{-7}{9}$. **15.** Notice that $\frac{2}{16} = \frac{1}{8}$. So 8 is the common denominator and $\frac{2}{8} + \frac{3}{8} + \frac{1}{8} = \frac{6}{8} = \frac{3}{4}$. **16.** $-20 + c = 150$ **17.** Add 20 to both sides; $c = 170$ **18.** Associative Property of Addition **19.** One instance is $19 + 0 = 19$. There are many others. **20.** hexagon **21.** Sample: A toss of a die shows a 6 and a toss of the same die shows a 2. Since these two events cannot occur at the same time, they are mutually exclusive. **22.** 3 cm + 3 cm + 4 cm + 4 cm + 4 cm = 18 cm **23.** (a) is the answer. (b) is a segment, (c) is a ray, (d) is a line. **24.** $m + n = 50$ **25.** The probabilities must add to 100%. $50\% + 45\% + d = 100\%$; $95\% + d = 100\%$; $d = 5\%$ **26.** 5 m + .03 m = 5.03 m **27.** positive, since the absolute value of the second addend is larger than the absolute value of the first addend **28.** $MP = MA + AP = 16 + 8 = 24$ **29.** $MA + PA = MP$, so $2.3 + PA = 3$. Add -2.3 to both sides to get $PA = 0.7$. **30.** See below. The sum is -1. **31.** The probability of getting a 1 is $\frac{1}{6}$ and the probability of getting a 2 is $\frac{1}{6}$. Since these are mutually exclusive events, you can add the probabilities. $\frac{1}{6} + \frac{1}{6} = \frac{2}{6} = \frac{1}{3}$. **32.** $-50° + 250° = 200°$; a 200° counterclockwise turn **33.** $\frac{360}{5} = 72°$ **34.** either a clockwise turn of $-72 + -72 = -144$ or a counterclockwise turn of $72 + 72 + 72 = 216°$

30.

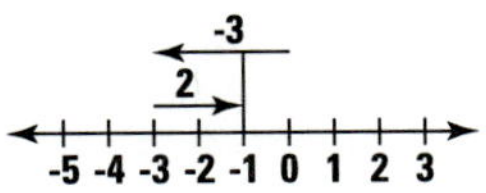

The chart below keys the **Progress Self-Test** questions to the objectives in the **Chapter Review** on pages 297–299 or to the **Vocabulary** (Voc.) on page 295. This will enable you to locate those **Chapter Review** questions that correspond to questions you missed on the **Progress Self-Test.** The lesson where the material is covered is also indicated on the chart.

Question	**1**	**2**	**3**	**4**	**5**	**6**	**7**	**8**	**9**	**10**
Objective	A	A	C	C	B	B	A	B	D	D
Lesson	5-3	5-3	5-2	5-2	5-3	5-3	5-3	5-3	5-8	5-8
Question	**11**	**12**	**13**	**14**	**15**	**16**	**17**	**18**	**19**	**20**
Objective	D	A	A	A	A	J	D	F	F	H
Lesson	5-8	5-5	5-5	5-5	5-5	5-1	5-8	5-7	5-2	5-9
Question	**21**	**22**	**23**	**24**	**25**	**26**	**27**	**28**	**29**	**30**
Objective	G	E	Voc.	I	K	I	A, C	I	I	M
Lesson	5-6	5-10	5-10	5-1	5-6	5-10	5-2, 5-3	5-10	5-10	5-1
Question	**31**	**32**	**33**	**34**						
Objective	K	L	L	L						
Lesson	5-6	5-4	5-4	5-4						

CHAPTER 5 REVIEW (pp. 297–299)

1. −12 **3.** 9.6 **5.** 3 **7.** $\frac{46}{9}$ **9.** $\frac{7}{12}$ **11.** 12 **13.** 8 **15.** −1 **17.** −17 **19.** −40 **21.** $\frac{2}{7}$ **23.** 48 **25.** $x = 20$ **27.** $y = -3$ **29.** $c = 38$ **31.** $v = 5922$ **33.** $e = \frac{7}{6}$ **35.** 12 **37.** 16 cm **39.** $12 + 18 + 20 + 7 + x = 82$ **41.** Addition Property of Equality **43.** Commutative Property of Addition **45.** not mutually exclusive **47.** mutually exclusive **49.** *LEAK* **51.** 4, 4 **53.** $1\frac{1}{2} + \frac{3}{5} = M$ **55.** $T = D + M + C$ **57.** $AC = x + 3$ **59. a.** $\frac{3}{8} + -\frac{1}{4}$ **b.** $\frac{1}{8}$ point **61. a.** $-60 + 25$ **b.** 35 feet below sea level **63.** 24% **65.** $\frac{144}{360} = \frac{2}{5}$ **67.** They are mutually exclusive and together include all outcomes. **69.** 135° or −225° **71. a.** *B* **b.** 90° or −270°

73.

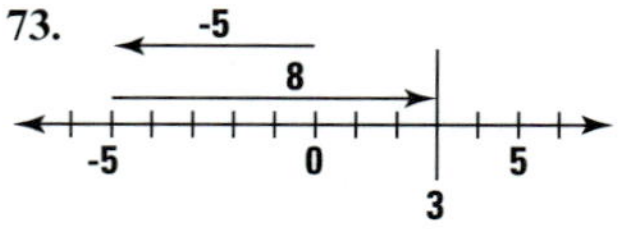

75.

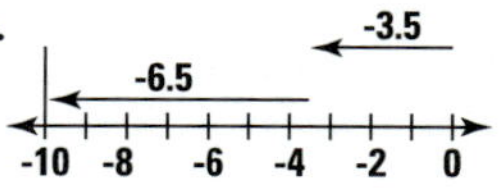

LESSON 6-1 (pp. 300–306)

15. What is 34.2 × 5.67? **17.** 25 **19.** 13 trains

21.

quarters	dimes	nickels
2	0	1
1	3	0
1	2	2
1	1	4
1	0	6
0	4	3
0	3	5

23. 13 **25.** 125 cm^3 **27.** 26,400 feet **29.** about 54 million

LESSON 6-2 (pp. 307–310)

13. (c) **15.** 39 **17.** 35 **19.** (A regular hexagon is a 6-sided polygon whose angles all have same measure, and sides all have same length.) **See below for drawing.** **21.** Sample: 29 and 31. (Twin primes are two consecutive odd numbers that are both primes.) **23.** last year **25.** Not enough information. If $b + e + h > c + f + g$, then last year; if $b + e + h < c + f + g$, then this year. **27.** 9 **29.** 0 **31.** 10

19.

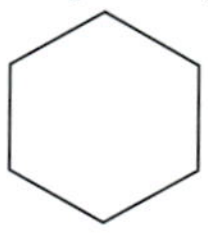

LESSON 6-3 (pp. 311–314)

5. 56 games **7.** 20 posts **9.** 228 miles **11.** Samples: glossary, dictionary **13.** 5, 6, 7, 8 **15.** Sarah and Dana have the same number of dollars. **17.** −3 **19.** 486 **21.** 800 mm **23.** 56.83

LESSON 6-4 (pp. 315–319)

13. 147, 118, 35 **15.** 13 and 1

17. Sample:

```
10  FOR X = 1 TO 20
20  IF X ^ 3 + X ^ 2 + X = 2954 THEN PRINT X
30  NEXT X
40  END
```

19. Ali **21.** 12, 14, 15, 16, 18, 20, 21, 22 **23.** $\frac{4}{45}$ or $0.0\overline{8}$ **25.** 4.2 feet **27. a.** $1.4\overline{142857}$ **b.** 1.414 **c.** 1 and 2

LESSON 6-5 (pp. 320–324)

11. a. 98¢ **b.** $2.36 **c.** $.29 + (w - 1) \cdot .23$ dollars **13.** 28 miles **15. a.** It tests the numbers between and including 10 and 30 at .5 intervals as possible solutions to the equation $x^4 + x^2 = 360900.3125$. **b.** 41 **c.** output: $x = 24.5$ **17. a.** $5 + c = -3$ **b.** $c = -8$ pounds

LESSON 6-6 (pp. 325–331)

17. B3, D3, E3 **19.** =.05*F15

21. a.

	A	B
1	Minutes	Cost
2	1	1.19
3		
4		

Cell A3 is =A2+1 and so on; cell B3 is =B2+.79 and so on.

b. \$21.73 **23. a.** =A2^2 **b.** =A3^3 **c.** =A4^4 **d.** =A2^5 **25. a.** \$5.45 **b.** \$5.80 **c.** 4.75 + $(t - 1) \cdot .35$ dollars **27.** 91 and 37, or 82 and 28, or 73 and 19. **29.** $\frac{53}{12}$ or $4\frac{5}{12}$ **31.** $7\frac{1}{4}$ or $\frac{29}{4}$

LESSON 6-7 (pp. 332–337)

17. a. Sample: if $m = 2$, $-(-2 + 9) = 2 + -9$, true **b.** Sample: if $m = -4$, $-(-(-4) + 9) = -4 + -9$, true **c.** possibly true **19.** (c) **21.** $R - Z$ **23.** $G - 49.95$ dollars **25.** (b) **27.** =(B3+B4+B5+B6)/4 **29. a.** \$4.50 **b.** $1.00 + (h - 1) \cdot .50$ dollars **31.** 12 stakes **33.** 70 kg

CHAPTER 6 PROGRESS SELF-TEST (p. 341)

1. any two of dictionary, glossary in a math book, encyclopedia **2.** An octagon has 20 diagonals. **See right for drawing.** **3.** Name the teams *A, B, C, D, E,* and *F.* Draw all the segments connecting these points. The figure created is a hexagon. The number of games is equal to the number of diagonals plus the number of sides in the hexagon. That is 9 + 6 = 15 games. **See right for drawing.** **4.** Use trial and error. The sums of each pair of factors of 24 are: 1 + 24 = 25; 2 + 12 = 14; 3 + 8 = 11 and 4 + 6 = 10. So 4 and 6 give the smallest sums. **5.** False. If you know an algorithm for an operation, you know how to answer the question. So multiplying fractions is only an exercise, not a problem. **6.** 53, 59 **7.** If one value is positive and one is negative, the pattern will be false. For instance, $|-5| + |3| = 5 + 3 = 8$, but $|-5 + 3| = |-2| = 2$. **8.** Sample: The calculations are done automatically by a computer. **9.** 2 pounds at \$3 per pound cost \$6, so multiplication gives the answer. \$1.49 per pound · 1.62 pounds = \$2.4138, which rounds up to \$2.42. **10.** True **11.** By trial and error, $(8 - 3) + (8 - 4) = 5 + 4 = 9$, so 8 is the solution. **12.** Read carefully and draw a picture. There must be 6 more dots on the right side between 3 and 10, for a total of 14 dots. **See right for drawing.** **13.** Use trial and error. A 3-gon has 0 diagonals, a 4-gon has 2 diagonals, a 5-gon has 5 diagonals, a 6-gon has 9 diagonals. So $n = 6$. **14.** Use a special case. $\frac{.05}{.01} = 5$, which means that the decimal point is moved two places to the right.

15.

weeks	amount left
1	1000 − 25
2	1000 − 2 · 25
3	1000 − 3 · 25
4	1000 − 4 · 25

16. After 31 weeks, Brianna will have 1000 − 31 · 25 dollars left. That computes to \$225. **17.** After you find an answer, you should check your work. **18.** Samples: organizing and storing 16 test scores for a class; keeping track of monthly sales for a store.

2.

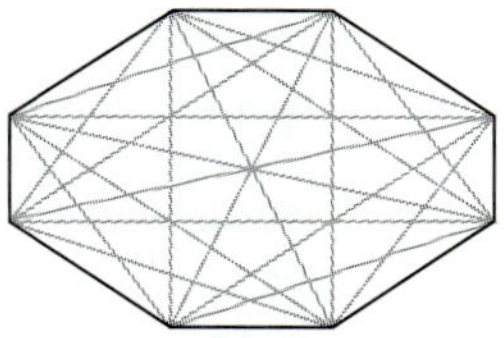

3.

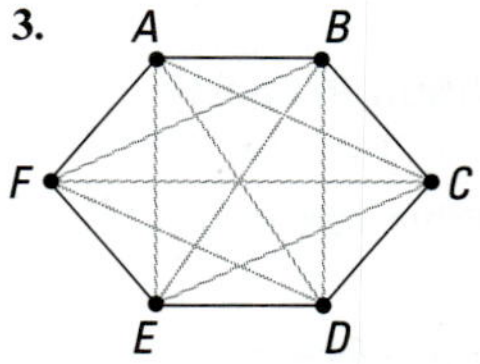

12.

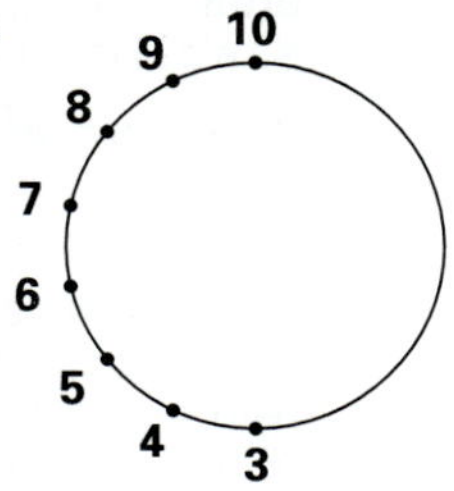

The chart below keys the **Progress Self-Test** questions to the objectives in the **Chapter Review** on pages 342–343 or to the **Vocabulary** (Voc.) on page 340. This will enable you to locate those **Chapter Review** questions that correspond to questions you missed on the **Progress Self-Test.** The lesson where the material is covered is also indicated on the chart.

Question	**1**	**2**	**3**	**4**	**5**	**6**	**7**	**8**	**9**	**10**
Objective	D	K	I	E	A, Voc.	C	G	J	H	G
Lesson	6-2	6-3	6-3	6-5	6-1	6-2	6-7	6-6	6-7	6-7
Question	**11**	**12**	**13**	**14**	**15**	**16**	**17**	**18**		
Objective	B	I	E	F	E	E	A	J		
Lesson	6-4	6-3	6-5	6-7	6-5	6-5	6-1	6-6		

CHAPTER 6 REVIEW (pp. 342–343)

1. (b) **3.** Sample: Divide answer by 1487 or 309. **5.** (b) **7.** 1036 **9.** composite; 7 is a factor **11.** 21, 22, 24, 25, 26, 27, 28 **13.** a number that equals the sum of its divisors except itself **15.** 2 1,2
4 1, 2, 4
8 1, 2, 4, 8
16 1, 2, 4, 8, 16
32 1, 2, 4, 8, 16, 32
256 has 9 factors.
17. 6, left **19.** Sample: If $x = 2$ and $y = 3$, then $5x + 5y \neq 10xy$. **21.** \$8.69 **23.** 20 games **25.** Pueblo

27.

	A	B
1	Minutes	Cost
2	0	18.75
3	15	29.75
4	30	40.75
5	45	51.75
6	60	62.75

Cell	Equation
A3	= A2 + 15
B3	= B2 + 11
.	.
.	.
.	.
A26	= A25 + 15
B26	= B25 + 11

29. 35 **31.** 7 triangles

absolute value The distance that a number is from 0 on the number line. (248)

acre (a) A unit of area equal to 43,560 square feet. (162)

acute angle An angle with a measure less than 90°. (154)

addend A number to be added. In *a* + *b*, *a* and *b* are addends. (239)

Adding Fractions Property For all numbers *a*, *b*, and *c*, with $c \neq 0$, $\frac{a}{c} + \frac{b}{c} = \frac{a+b}{c}$. (260)

Addition Property of Equality If $a = b$, then $a + c = b + c$. (277)

additive identity The number zero. (244)

Additive Identity Property of Zero For any number *n*, $n + 0 = n$. (244)

additive inverse A number whose sum with a given number is 0. Also called *opposite.* (245)

adjacent angles Angles that share a common side and have no common interior points. (256)

algebra See *elementary algebra.*

Algebraic Definition of Division For all numbers *a* and nonzero numbers *b*, $a \cdot \frac{1}{b} = \frac{a}{b} = a \div b$. (483)

Algebraic Definition of Subtraction For any numbers *x* and *y*, $x - y = x + {}^-y$. Also called the *Adding Opposites Property* or the *Add-Opp Property.* (353)

algebraic expression An expression that contains either a variable alone or with number and operation symbols. (187)

algorithm A finite sequence of steps that leads to a desired result. (302)

alternate exterior angles Angles formed by two lines and a transversal that are on opposite sides of the transversal but not between the two given lines. (382)

alternate interior angles Angles formed by two lines and a transversal that are between the two given lines and on opposite sides of the transversal. (382)

altitude The perpendicular segment from a vertex of a triangle to the opposite side of the triangle. Also see *height.* (572)

ambiguous Having more than one possible meaning. (189)

angle The union of two rays with the same endpoint. (145)

Angle Addition Property If $\overrightarrow{OB}$ is in the interior of $\angle AOC$, then $m\angle AOB + m\angle BOC = m\angle AOC$. (256)

Arabic numerals See *Hindu-Arabic numerals.*

arc of a circle A part of a circle connecting two points (called the **endpoints** of the arc) on the circle. (94)

area A measure of the space inside a two-dimensional figure. (158)

Area Formula for a Circle Let *A* be the area of a circle with radius *r*. Then $A = \pi r^2$. (666)

Area Formula for a Sector Let *A* be the area of a sector of a circle with radius *r*. Let *m* be the measure of the central angle of the sector in degrees. Then $A = \frac{m}{360} \cdot \pi r^2$. (667)

Area Formula for a Trapezoid Let *A* be the area of a trapezoid with bases b_1 and b_2 and height *h*. Then $A = \frac{1}{2} \cdot h(b_1 + b_2)$. (579)

Area Formula for Any Triangle Let *b* be the length of a side of a triangle with area *A*. Let *h* be the length of the altitude drawn to that side. Then $A = \frac{1}{2}bh$. (572)

Area Formula for a Right Triangle Let *A* be the area of a right triangle with legs of lengths *a* and *b*. Then $A = \frac{1}{2}ab$. (470)

Area Model for Multiplication The area of a rectangle with length ℓ units and width *w* units is $\ell \cdot w$ (or ℓw) square units. (469)

array See *rectangular array.*

Associative Property of Addition For any numbers *a*, *b*, and *c*, $(a + b) + c = a + (b + c)$. (272)

Associative Property of Multiplication For any numbers *a*, *b*, and *c*, $(ab)c = a(bc)$. (479)

automatic drawer Technology that can be used to draw geometric figures. (400)

automatic grapher A computer program or calculator that is used to make coordinate graphs. (458)

average See *mean.*

ball A sphere together with all the points inside it. (680)

bar graph A display in which numbers are represented by bars whose lengths correspond to the magnitude of the numbers being represented. (415)

base **1** In a power x^y, *x*. (68) **2** The side of a triangle perpendicular to an altitude. (572) **3** The bottom of a box, or rectangular solid. (476) **4** In a trapezoid, one of the parallel sides. (578) **5** In a cylindric solid, one of the plane regions translated to form the solid. (675)

base line of a protractor A segment on a protractor connecting a 0° mark with a 180° mark opposite which is placed over one side of the angle being measured. (147)

billion In the United States, a word name for the number 1,000,000,000 or 10^9. (65)

billionth A word name for the number 0.00000 0001 or 10^{-9}. (101)

box See *rectangular solid.*

brackets [ ] **1** Grouping symbols that indicate that all arithmetic operations inside are to be done first. As grouping symbols, brackets mean exactly the same thing as parentheses. (203) **2** A notation sometimes used for the greatest integer function. (720)

capacity See *volume.*

ceiling function symbol See *rounding up symbol.*

cell In a spreadsheet, the intersection of a column and a row. (325)

center of a circle See *circle.*

center of a protractor The midpoint of the base line on a protractor. The center is placed over the vertex of the angle being measured. (147)

center of a sphere See *sphere.*

center of gravity The center of gravity of a set of points is the point whose first coordinate is the mean of the first coordinates of the given points, and whose second coordinate is the mean of the second coordinates of the given points. (609)

centi- A prefix meaning $\frac{1}{100}$. (137)

central angle of a circle An angle whose vertex is the center of the circle. (152)

certain event An event with probability one. (214)

circle The set of all points in a plane a given distance (its **radius**) from a fixed point in the plane (its **center**). (94)

circle graph A display in which parts of a whole are represented by sectors whose areas are proportional to the fraction of the whole taken up by each part. Also called *pie chart.* (93)

circular cylinder A cylindric solid whose bases are circles. Also called *cylinder.* (670)

circumference A circle's perimeter. (659)

clockwise The same direction as that in which the hands of a clock normally move. (253)

coincide To occupy the same position as. (442)

column One of the vertical arrangements of items in a table, rectangular array, or spreadsheet. (325)

common denominator A number that is a multiple of the denominator of every fraction in a collection of fractions. (262)

Commutative Property of Addition For any numbers *a* and *b*, $a + b = b + a$. (271)

Commutative Property of Multiplication For any numbers *a* and *b*, $ab = ba$. (470)

Comparison Model for Subtraction $x - y$ is how much more *x* is than *y*. (348)

complement of an event The event consisting of all outcomes not in the given event. (268)

complementary angles Two angles whose measures add to 90°. (376)

composite number Any positive integer exactly divisible by one or more positive integers other than itself or 1; opposed to *prime number.* (307)

congruent figures Figures having the same size and shape. Figures that are the image of each other under a reflection, rotation, or translation, or any combination of these. (436)

contraction A size change with a magnitude whose absolute value is between 0 and 1. (511)

conversion factor A rate factor that equals the number 1, used for converting quantities given in one unit to a quantity given in another unit. (495)

convex polygon A polygon in which every diagonal lies inside the polygon. (451)

coordinate graph A display in which an ordered pair of numbers is displayed as a dot located relative to a fixed point called the **origin.** (420)

corresponding angles Any pair of angles in similar locations in relation to a transversal intersecting two lines. (382)

corresponding sides Any pair of sides in the same relative positions in two figures. (626)

count A whole number tally of particular things. (7)

counterclockwise The direction opposite to that in which the hands of a clock normally move. (253)

counting unit The name of the particular things being tallied in a count. (7)

cube A three-dimensional figure with six square faces. (163)

cup (c) A unit of capacity in the U.S. system of measurement equal to 8 fluid ounces. (130)

customary system See *U.S. system of measurement.*

cylinder See *circular cylinder.*

cylindric solid The set of points between a plane region (its **base**) and its translation image in space, including the region and its image. (675)

cylindric surface The surface of a cylindric solid. (675)

data disk A disk used to store computer information. (328)

decagon A ten-sided polygon. (284)

deci- A prefix meaning $\frac{1}{10}$. (137)

decimal notation A notation in which numbers are written using ten digits and each place stands for a power of 10. (6)

decimal system A system in which numbers are written in decimal notation. (6)

degree A unit of angle measure equal to $\frac{1}{360}$ of a full revolution. (146)

deka- A prefix meaning 10. (137)

denominator In a fraction, the divisor. The number *b* in the fraction $\frac{a}{b}$. (31)

diagonal of a polygon A segment that connects two vertices of the polygon but is not a side of the polygon. (286)

diameter **1** Twice the radius of a circle or sphere. **2** A segment connecting two points on a circle that contains the center of the circle. (94) **3** A segment connecting two points on a sphere that contains the center of the sphere. (680)

diamond See *rhombus.*

difference The result of a subtraction. (347)

digit One of the ten symbols 0, 1, 2, 3, 4, 5, 6, 7, 8, 9 used in the decimal system to stand for the first ten whole numbers. (3)

dimension **1** The length or width of a rectangle. (469) **2** The number of rows or the number of columns in an array. (469) **3** The length, width, or height of a box. (476)

display **1** Numbers or other symbols that appear on the screen of a calculator or computer. (26) **2** A diagram, graph, table, or other visual arrangement used to organize, present, or represent information. (407)

Distributive Property of Multiplication over Addition For any numbers *a*, *b*, and *x*, $ax + bx = (a + b)x$ and $x(a + b) = xa + xb$. (556)

Distributive Property of Multiplication over Subtraction For any numbers *a*, *b*, and *x*, $ax - bx = (a - b)x$ and $x(a - b) = xa - xb$. (557)

dividend The number in a quotient that is being divided. In the division $a \div b$, *a* is the dividend. (31)

divisible An integer *a* is divisible by an integer *b* when $\frac{a}{b}$ is an integer. Also called *evenly divisible*. (34)

divisor **1** The number by which you divide in a quotient. In the division $a \div b$, *b* is the divisor. (31) **2** A number that divides into another number with zero remainder. Also called *factor*. (308)

dodecagon A 12-sided polygon (319)

double bar graph A display in which two bar graphs are combined into a single display. (416)

edges The sides of the faces of a rectangular solid. (476)

elementary algebra The study of variables and the operations of arithmetic with variables. (184)

ending decimal See *terminating decimal*.

endpoint of a ray See *ray*.

entering Pressing a key on a calculator to enter numbers, operations, or other symbols. (27)

Equal Fractions Property If the numerator and denominator of a fraction are both multiplied (or divided) by the same nonzero number, then the resulting fraction is equal to the original one. (51)

equally likely outcomes Outcomes in a situation where the likelihood of each outcome is assumed to be equal. (215)

equation A sentence with an equal sign. (219)

equilateral triangle A triangle whose sides all have the same length and whose angles all have the same measure. (452)

equivalent equations Equations that have the same solutions. (363)

equivalent formulas Formulas that have the same solutions. (364)

estimate **1** A number which is near another number. Also called *approximation*. **2** To obtain an estimate. (16)

evaluating an algebraic expression Replacing each variable with a particular number (the **value of the variable**) and then evaluating the resulting numerical expression. (193)

evaluating a numerical expression Carrying out the operations in a numerical expression to find the value of the expression. (176)

evenly divisible See *divisible*.

event Any collection of outcomes from the same experiment. (216)

exercise A question that you know how to answer. (302)

expansion A size change with a magnitude whose absolute value is greater than 1. (505)

exponent In a power x^y, *y*. (68)

exponential form A number written as a power. The form x^y. (99)

exterior angles Angles formed by two lines and a transversal that have no points between the two given lines. (382)

extremes In the proportion $\frac{a}{b} = \frac{c}{d}$, the numbers *a* and *d*. (620)

faces See *rectangular solid*.

factor **1** A number that divides evenly into another number. Also called *divisor*. (308) **2** To find the factors of a particular number. (51)

fair An object or experiment in which all outcomes are equally likely. Also called *unbiased*. (215)

finite decimal See *terminating decimal*.

first coordinate See *ordered pair*.

floor function symbol See *rounding down symbol*.

fluid ounce (fl oz) A unit of capacity in the U.S. system of measurement equal to $\frac{1}{128}$ of a gallon. Often called simply *ounce*. (130)

foot (ft) A unit of length in the U.S. system of measurement equal to twelve inches. (125)

formula A sentence in which one variable is written in terms of other variables. (208)

Formula for Circumference of a Circle In a circle with diameter *d* and circumference *C*, $C = \pi d$. (659)

fraction A symbol of the form $\frac{a}{b}$ which represents the quotient when *a* is divided by *b*. (31)

fraction bar The horizontal line in a fraction that indicates the operation of division. (31)

frequency of an outcome The number of times an outcome occurs. (213)

full turn A turn of 360°. Also called *revolution*. (253)

Fundamental Property of Turns If a turn of magnitude *x* is followed by a turn of magnitude *y*, the result is a turn of magnitude $x + y$. (255)

fundamental region A figure whose congruent copies make up a tessellation. Also called *fundamental shape*. (452)

fundamental shape See *fundamental region*.

furlong (fur) A unit of length in the U.S. system of measurement equal to 40 rods. (128)

gallon (gal) A unit of capacity in the U.S. system of measurement equal to 4 quarts. One gallon is equal to 231 cubic inches. (130)

generalization A statement that is true about many instances. (321)

giga- A prefix meaning one billion. (137)

gram (g) A unit of mass in the metric system equal to $\frac{1}{1000}$ of a kilogram. (136)

greatest common factor (GCF) The largest number that is a factor of every number in a given collection of numbers. (52)

greatest integer function symbol See *rounding down symbol*.

gross ton A unit of weight in the U.S. system of measurement equal to 2240 pounds. Also called *long ton*. (132)

grouping symbols Symbols such as parentheses, brackets, or fraction bars that indicate that certain arithmetic operations are to be done before others in an expression. (203)

half turn A turn of magnitude 180°. (253)

hectare (ha) A metric unit of area equal to 10,000 m^2. (159)

hecto- A prefix meaning 100. (137)

height **1** The perpendicular distance from any vertex of a triangle to the side opposite that vertex. (572) **2** The distance between the bases of the trapezoid. (578) **3** The distance between the bases of a cylinder or prism. (676) Also called *altitude.*

heptagon A seven-sided polygon. (284)

hexagon A six-sided polygon. (284)

Hindu-Arabic numerals The numerals 0, 1, 2, 3, 4, 5, 6, 7, 8, 9 used throughout the world today to represent numbers in the decimal system. (3)

hour (h) A unit of time equal to 60 minutes. (130)

hundred A word name for the number 100 or 10^2. (65)

hundred-thousandth A word name for 0.00001 or 10^{-5}. (12)

hundredth A word name for 0.01 or 10^{-2}. (11)

hypotenuse The longest side of a right triangle. (470)

image The result of applying a transformation to a figure. (435)

impossible event An event with probability zero. (214)

inch (in.) The basic unit of length in the U.S. system of measurement. One inch equals 2.54 centimeters exactly. (119)

independent events Two events *A* and *B* are independent events when and only when *Prob(A and B)* = *Prob(A)* · *Prob(B).* (489)

inequality A sentence with one or more of the symbols $\neq$, $<$, $\leq$, $>$, $\geq$. (224)

inequality symbols Any one of the symbols $\neq$ (not equal to), $<$ (is less than), $\leq$ (is less than or equal to), $>$ (is greater than), or $\geq$ (is greater than or equal to). (224)

infinite repeating decimal A decimal in which a digit or group of digits to the right of the decimal point repeat forever. (33)

instance A particular example of a pattern. (182)

integer A number which is a whole number or the opposite of a whole number. Any of the numbers 0, 1, -1, 2, -2, 3, -3, ... (43)

integer division Dividing an integer *a* by a positive integer *b* to yield an integer quotient and an integer remainder less than *b.* (592)

interior angles Angles formed by two lines and a transversal that have some points between the two given lines. (382)

international system of measurement See *metric system.*

irrational number A real number that cannot be written as a simple fraction. (660)

key in To press a key on a calculator to enter numbers or perform operations. (27)

key sequence A description of the calculator keys and the order in which they must be pressed to perform a particular computation. (27)

kilo- A prefix meaning 1000. (137)

kilogram (kg) The base unit of mass in the metric system. (136)

lateral area The area of the surface of a cylindric solid excluding the bases. (670)

least common denominator (LCD) The least common multiple of the denominators of every fraction in a given collection of fractions. (262)

least common multiple (LCM) The smallest number that is a multiple of every number in a given collection of integers. (262)

legs of a right triangle The sides of a right triangle that are on the sides of the right angle, or the lengths of these sides. (470)

light-year The distance that light travels in a year. (74)

like terms Terms that involve the same variables to the same powers. (532)

linear equation An equation of the form $y = ax + b$. An equation equivalent to $ax + b = cx + d$. (694)

linear pair Two angles that share a common side and whose non-common sides are opposite rays. (374)

line of symmetry A line over which the reflection image of a figure coincides with its preimage. Also called *symmetry line.* (446)

line segment A pair of given points *A* and *B* (the **endpoints** of the line segment) along with all the points on $\overleftrightarrow{AB}$ between *A* and *B*. Also called *segment.* (283)

liter (L) A unit of volume in the metric system equal to 1000 cm^3. (136)

long ton See *gross ton.*

lowest terms A fraction is in lowest terms when the numerator and denominator have no factors in common except 1. (51)

magic square A square array of numbers in which the sum along every row, column, or main diagonal is the same. (281)

magnitude **1** An amount measuring the size of a turn. (253) **2** The distance between a point and its translation image. (435) **3** A size change factor. (507)

make a table A problem-solving strategy in which information is organized in a table to make it easier to find patterns and generalizations. (320)

mean The sum of the numbers in a collection divided by the number of numbers in the collection. Also called *average.* (206)

means In the proportion $\frac{a}{b} = \frac{c}{d}$, the numbers *b* and *c*. (620)

Means-Extremes Property In any true proportion, the product of the means equals the product of the extremes. If $\frac{a}{b} = \frac{c}{d}$, then $b \cdot c = a \cdot d$. (621)

GLOSSARY

measure A real number indicating an amount of some quantity. (10)

median In a collection consisting of an odd number of numbers arranged in numerical order, the middle number. In a collection of an even number of numbers arranged in numerical order, the average of the middle two numbers. (411)

mega- A prefix meaning one million. (137)

meter (m) The basic unit of length in the metric system, defined as the length that light in vacuum travels in $\frac{1}{299,792,458}$ of a second. (119)

metric system A decimal system of measurement with the meter as its base unit of length and the kilogram as its base unit of mass. Also called *international system of measurement.* (118)

micro- A prefix meaning one millionth. (137)

mile (mi) A unit of length in the U.S. system of measurement equal to 5280 feet. (125)

milli- A prefix meaning $\frac{1}{1000}$. (137)

million A word name for the number 1,000,000 or 10^6. (65)

millionth A word name for 0.000001 or 10^{-6}. (12)

minuend In a subtraction problem, the number from which another number is subtracted. In $a - b$, the minuend is a. (347)

minute A unit of time equal to 60 seconds. (130)

mirror See *reflection image.*

mixed number The sum of a whole number and a fraction. (37)

mode The mode of a collection of objects is the object that appears most often. (411)

Multiplication of Fractions Property For all numbers a and c, and nonzero numbers b and d, $\frac{a}{b} \cdot \frac{c}{d} = \frac{ac}{bd}$. (484)

Multiplication of Unit Fractions Property For all nonzero numbers a and b, $\frac{1}{a} \cdot \frac{1}{b}$. (483)

Multiplication Property of Equality When equal quantities are multiplied by the same number, the resulting quantities are equal. (125)

Multiplication Property of -1 For any number x, $-1 \cdot x = -x$. (501)

Multiplication Property of Zero For any number x, $0 \cdot x = 0$. (502)

Multiplicative Identity Property of One For any number x, $1 \cdot x = x$. (507)

multiplicative inverse A number whose product with a given number is 1. Also called *reciprocal.* (483)

mutually exclusive events Events that cannot occur at the same time. (267)

nano- A prefix meaning one billionth. (137)

natural number Any of the numbers 1, 2, 3, ... Also called *positive integer.* (43) (Some people like to include 0 as a natural number.)

negative integer Any of the numbers -1, -2, -3, ... (43)

negative numbers The opposites of the positive numbers. Numbers that are graphed to the left of zero on a horizontal number line. (41)

nested parentheses Parentheses inside parentheses. (199)

net A plane pattern for a three-dimensional figure. (561)

***n*-gon** A polygon with n sides. (284)

nonagon A nine-sided polygon. (284)

numerator In a fraction, the dividend. The number a in the fraction $\frac{a}{b}$. (31)

numerical expression A combination of symbols for numbers and operations that stands for a number. (176)

obtuse angle An angle with a measure greater than 90°. (154)

octagon An eight-sided polygon. (284)

odds against an event The ratio of the number of ways an event cannot occur to the number of ways that event can occur. (218)

odds for an event The ratio of the number of ways an event can occur to the number of ways that event cannot occur. (218)

open sentence A sentence containing one or more variables that can be true or false, depending on what is substituted for the variables. (219)

Opposite of Opposites Property (Op-op Property) For any number n, $-(-n) = n$. (245)

opposite A number whose sum with a given number is 0. Also called *additive inverse.* (245)

opposite angles In a quadrilateral, two angles that do not share a side. (388)

opposite rays Two rays that have the same endpoint and whose union is a line. (374)

opposite sides In a quadrilateral, two sides that do not share a vertex. (388)

ordered pair A pair of numbers or objects (x, y) in which the first number x is designated the **first coordinate** and the second number y is designated the **second coordinate.** (422)

Order of Operations The rules for carrying out arithmetic operations: **1.** Work first inside parentheses or other grouping symbols. **2.** Inside grouping symbols or if there are no grouping symbols: **a.** First take all powers; **b.** Second, do all multiplications or divisions in order, from left to right; **c.** Finally, do all additions or subtractions in order, from left to right. (177)

origin The point (0, 0) in a coordinate graph. (424)

ounce (oz) A unit of weight in the U.S. system of measurement, equal to $\frac{1}{16}$ of a pound. (130)

outcome A possible result of an experiment. (213)

palindrome An integer which reads the same forward or backward. (433)

parabola The shape of all graphs of equations of the form $y = ax^2$. (691)

parallel Two lines in a plane are parallel if they have no points in common or are identical. (331)

parallelogram A quadrilateral with two pairs of parallel sides. (388)

parentheses ( ) Grouping symbols that indicate that all arithmetic operations inside are to be done first. (197)

pattern A general idea for which there are many examples. (182)

pentagon A five-sided polygon. (284)

percent A number written using the percent sign %. The percent sign indicates that the number preceding it should be multiplied by 0.01 or $\frac{1}{100}$. (79)

perfect number A positive integer *n* for which the sum of all its factors, except *n*, is equal to *n*. (310)

perimeter The sum of the lengths of the sides of a polygon. (289)

perpendicular Two rays, segments, or lines that form right angles. (153)

pi (π) The ratio of the circumference to the diameter of any circle. (12)

pico- A prefix meaning one trillionth. (137)

pie chart See *circle graph.*

pint (pt) A unit of capacity in the U.S. system of measurement equal to 2 cups. (130)

place value The number that each digit in a decimal stands for. For instance, in the decimal 123.45 the place value of the digit 2 is twenty. (7)

polygon A union of segments (its **sides**) in which each segment intersects two others, one at each of its endpoints. (283)

positive integer Any of the numbers 1, 2, 3, ... Also called *natural number.* (43)

positive numbers Numbers that are graphed to the right of zero on a horizontal number line. (43)

pound (lb) A unit of weight in the U.S. system of measurement equal to 16 ounces. One pound is approximately 455 grams. (130)

power The result of x^y. (68)

preimage A figure to which a transformation has been applied. (435)

prime number A positive integer other than 1 that is divisible only by itself and 1. (307)

prism A cylindric solid whose bases are polygons. (671)

Probabilities of Complements The sum of the probabilities of any event *E* and its complement *not E* is 1. (268)

probability A number from 0 to 1 that tells how likely an event is to happen. (214)

Probability Formula for Equally Likely Outcomes Suppose a situation has *N* equally likely possible outcomes and an event includes *E* of these. Let *P* be the probability that the event will occur. Then $P = \frac{E}{N}$. (216)

Probability of *A or B* If *A* and *B* are mutually exclusive events, the probability of *A* plus the probability of *B*. (267)

problem A question for which you do not have an algorithm to arrive at an answer. (302)

problem-solving strategies Strategies such as *read carefully, make a table, trial and error, draw a picture, try special cases,* and *check work* that good problem solvers use when solving problems. (303)

product The result of multiplication. (175)

Properties of Parallelograms In a parallelogram, opposite sides have the same length; opposite angles have the same measure. (388)

Property of Opposites For any number *n*, $n + -n = 0$. Sometimes called the *additive inverse property.* (245)

Property of Reciprocals For any nonzero number *a*, *a* and $\frac{1}{a}$ are reciprocals. That is, $a \cdot \frac{1}{a} = 1$. (484)

proportion A statement that two fractions are equal. (615)

proportional thinking The ability to get or estimate an answer to a proportion without solving an equation. (630)

protractor An instrument for measuring angles. (147)

Putting-Together Model for Addition Suppose a count or measure *x* is put together with a count or measure *y* with the same units. If there is no overlap, then the result has count or measure $x + y$. (238)

Putting-Together with Overlap Model If a quantity *x* is put together with a quantity *y,* and there is overlap *z*, the result is the quantity $x + y - z$. (368)

Pythagorean Theorem Let the legs of a right triangle have lengths *a* and *b*. Let the hypotenuse have length *c*. Then $a^2 + b^2 = c^2$. (652)

quadrant One of the four regions of the coordinate plane determined by the *x*- and *y*- axes. (424)

quadrilateral A four-sided polygon. (284)

quadrillion A word name for the number 1,000,000,000,000,000 or 10^{15}. (65)

quadrillionth A word name for the number 0.00000 00000 00001 or 10^{-15}. (101)

quart (qt) A unit of capacity in the U.S. system of measurement equal to 2 pints. (130)

quarter turn A turn of 90°. (253)

quintillion A word name for the number 1,000,000,000,000,000,000 or 10^{18}. (65)

quintillionth A word name for the number 0.00000 00000 00000 001 or 10^{-18}. (101)

quotient The result of dividing one number by another. (31)

Quotient-Remainder Formula Let *n* be an integer and *d* be a positive integer. Let *q* be the integer quotient and let *r* be the remainder after dividing *n* by *d*. Then $n = d \cdot q + r$. (593)

quotient-remainder form The result of an integer division expressed as an integer quotient and an integer remainder. (593)

radical sign The symbol $\sqrt{\ }$ used to denote a positive square root. (647)

radius **1** The distance that all points in a circle are from the center of the circle. **2** A segment connecting the center of a circle to any point on the circle. (94) **3** The distance that all points on a sphere are from the center of the sphere. **4** A segment connecting the center of a sphere to any point on the sphere. (680)

random experiment An experiment in which all outcomes are equally likely. (215)

range In a collection of numbers, the difference between the largest number and the smallest number. (411)

rate The quotient of two quantities with different units. A quantity whose unit contains the word "per" or "for each" or some synonym. (493)

GLOSSARY

rate factor A rate used in a multiplication. (494)

Rate Factor Model for Multiplication The product of (a $unit_1$) and $\left(b \frac{unit_2}{unit_1}\right)$ is (ab $unit_2$), signifying the total amount of $unit_2$ in the situation. (494)

Rate Model for Division If a and b are quantities with different units, then $\frac{a}{b}$ is the amount of quantity a per quantity b. (598)

rate unit The unit in a rate. (493)

ratio The quotient of two quantities with the same units. (611)

Ratio Comparison Model for Division If a and b are quantities with the same units, then $\frac{a}{b}$ compares a to b. (611)

rational number A number that can be written as a simple fraction. (660)

ray A part of a line starting at one point (the **endpoint** of the ray) and continuing forever in a particular direction. (145)

real-number division Dividing one real number a by a nonzero real number b to yield the single real number $\frac{a}{b}$. (592)

real number A number that can be written as a decimal. (641)

reciprocal A number whose product with a given number is 1. Also called *multiplicative inverse.* (483)

rectangle A parallelogram with a right angle. (388)

rectangular array An arrangement of objects into rows and columns. Also called *array.* (469)

rectangular solid A three-dimensional figure with six **faces** that are all rectangles. Also called *box.* (476)

reflection A transformation in which the image of each point lies on a line perpendicular to a fixed line called the **reflection line,** or **mirror,** and is the same distance from the reflection line as the preimage point. (440)

reflection line See *reflection.*

reflection symmetry The property that a figure coincides with its image under a reflection over a line called a **line of symmetry.** Also called *symmetry with respect to a line.* (446)

regular polygon A convex polygon in which all sides have the same length and all angles have the same measure. (338)

relative frequency The frequency of a particular outcome divided by the total number of times an experiment is performed. (213)

Repeated Addition Property of Multiplication If n is a positive integer, then
$nx = x + x + \ldots + x$. (531)
(n addends)

repeating decimal A decimal in which a digit or group of digits to the right of the decimal point repeat forever. (33)

repetend The digits in a repeating decimal that repeat forever. (33)

revolution A turn of 360°. Also called *full turn.* (253)

rhombus A quadrilateral with all sides the same length. Also called *diamond.* (388)

right angle An angle with a measure of 90°. (153)

right triangle A triangle with a right angle. (154)

rod (rd) A unit of length in the U.S. system of measurement equal to $5\frac{1}{2}$ yards. (128)

rotation symmetry The property that a figure coincides with its own image under a rotation of less than 360°. (451)

rounding down Making an estimate that is smaller than the actual value. (16)

rounding down symbol The symbol $\lfloor\ \rfloor$ used to indicate that the number inside is to be rounded down to the preceding integer. Also called the *floor function symbol* or the *greatest integer function symbol.* (720)

rounding to the nearest Making an estimate to a particular decimal place by either rounding up or rounding down, depending on which estimate is closer to the actual value. (21)

rounding up Making an estimate that is larger than the actual value. (16)

rounding up symbol The symbol $\lceil\ \rceil$ used to indicate that the number inside is to be rounded up to the next integer. Also called the *ceiling function symbol.* (720)

row One of the horizontal arrangements of items in a table, rectangular array, or spreadsheet. (325)

scale of a map The conversion factor used to convert real-world distances to distances on the map. (515)

scientific calculator A calculator which displays very large or very small numbers in scientific notation and which has powering, factorial, square root, negative, reciprocal, and other keys. (26)

scientific notation A notation in which a number is expressed as a number greater than or equal to 1 and less than 10 multiplied by an integer power of 10. A notation in which a number is written in the form $decimal \times 10^{exponent}$ with $1 \leq decimal < 10$. (74)

second coordinate See *ordered pair.*

second The fundamental unit of time in the metric and customary systems of measurement. (134)

sector A region bounded by an arc of a circle and the two radii to the endpoints of the arc. (94)

segment See *line segment.*

short ton A unit of weight in the U.S. system of measurement equal to 2000 pounds. Sometimes simply called *ton.* (130)

side **1** In an angle, one of the two rays that make up an angle. (145) **2** In a polygon, one of the line segments that make up the polygon, or the length of a side. (145) **3** In a rectangular solid, a face of the solid. (476)

similar figures Two figures that have the same shape, but not necessarily the same size. (507)

simple fraction A fraction with a whole number as its numerator and a nonzero whole number as its denominator. (31)

size change factor The number k by which the coordinates of the preimage are multiplied in a size change. (507)

Size Change Model for Multiplication (two-dimensional version) Under a size change of magnitude k, the image of (x, y) is (kx, ky). (507)

Size Change Model for Multiplication Let k be a nonzero number without a unit. Then ka is the result of applying a **size change of magnitude** $\boldsymbol{k}$ to the quantity a. (506)

slash The symbol / used to indicate division. (31)

slide image See *translation image.*

Slide Model for Addition If a slide x is followed by a slide y, the result is a slide $x + y$. (240)

Slide Model for Subtraction If a quantity x is decreased by an amount y, the resulting quantity is $x - y$. (352)

slope The amount of change in the height of a line as you move one unit to the right. For a line with equation $y = ax + b$, the slope is a. (711)

solution to an open sentence A value of the variable or variables in an open sentence that makes the sentence true. (219)

solve a proportion To find the values of all variables in a proportion that make the proportion true. (616)

solving a sentence Finding the values of the unknown or unknowns that make the sentence true. (220)

special case An instance of a pattern used for some definite purpose. (332)

sphere The set of points in space at a given distance (its **radius**) from a given point (its **center**). (680)

spreadsheet **1** A table. **2** A computer program in which data is presented in a table, and calculations upon entries in the table can be made. (325)

square A four-sided figure with four right angles and four sides of equal length. (158)

square root If $A = s^2$, then s is called a square root of A. (646)

statistic A number used to describe a set of numbers. (411)

stem-and-leaf display A display of a collection of numbers in which the digits in certain place values are designated as the **stems** and digits in lower place values are designated as the **leaves** and placed side-by-side next to the stems. (409)

step function symbols The symbols $\lfloor\ \rfloor$ and $\lceil\ \rceil$. (722)

Substitution Principle If two numbers are equal, then one can be substituted for the other in any computation without changing the results of the computation. (84)

subtrahend The number being subtracted in a subtraction. In $a - b$, the subtrahend is b. (347)

sum The result of an addition. (175)

supplementary angles Two angles whose measures add to 180°. (376)

Surface Area and Volume Formulas for a Sphere In a sphere with radius r, surface area S, and volume V, $S = 4\pi r^2$ and $V = \frac{4}{3}\pi r^3$. (680)

surface area The sum of the areas of the faces of a solid. (562)

symmetric figure A figure that coincides with its image under a reflection or rotation. (446)

symmetry line A reflection line over which the image of a reflection symmetric figure coincides with the preimage. Also called *line of symmetry.* (446)

symmetry with respect to a line See *reflection symmetry.*

table An arrangement of numbers or symbols into rows and columns. (320)

tablespoon (T) A unit of capacity in the U.S. system of measurement equal to $\frac{1}{2}$ of a fluid ounce. (264)

Take-Away Model for Subtraction If a quantity y is taken away from an original quantity x with the same units, the quantity left is $x - y$. (346)

teaspoon (tsp) A unit of capacity in the U.S. system of measurement equal to $\frac{1}{3}$ of a tablespoon. (264)

ten A word name for the number 10. (65)

ten-millionth A word name for 0.0000001 or 10^{-7}. (12)

ten-thousandth A word name for 0.0001 or 10^{-4}. (12)

tenth A word name for 0.1 or 10^{-1}. (11)

tenths place In a decimal, the first position to the right of the decimal point. (11)

tera- A prefix meaning one trillion. (137)

terminating decimal A decimal with only a finite number of nonzero decimal places. Also called *ending decimal* or *finite decimal.* (89)

tessellation A filling up of a two-dimensional space by congruent copies of a figure that do not overlap. (452)

test a special case A problem-solving strategy in which one or more special cases are examined to formulate a generalization or determine whether a property or generalization is true. (332)

theorem A statement that follows logically from other statements. (652)

thousand A word name for the number 1,000 or 10^3. (65)

thousandth A word name for 0.001 or 10^{-3}. (12)

ton (t) A unit of weight in the U.S. system equal to 2000 pounds. Also called *short ton.* (130)

transformation A one-to-one correspondence between a first set (the **preimage**) and a second set (the **image**). (440)

translation image The result of adding a number h to each first coordinate and a number k to each second coordinate of all the points of a figure. Also called *slide image.* (435)

transversal A line intersecting both of a pair of lines. (382)

trapezoid A quadrilateral with at least one pair of parallel sides. (577)

trial and error A problem-solving strategy in which potential solutions are tried and discarded repeatedly until a correct solution is found. (315)

triangle A three-sided polygon. (154)

Triangle-Sum Property In any triangle, the sum of the measures of the angles is 180°. (394)

trillion A word name for the number 1,000,000,000,000 or 10^{12}. (65)

trillionth A word name for the number 0.00000 00000 01 or 10^{-12}. (101)

truncate To discard all digits to the right of a particular place. To round down to a particular decimal place. (17)

try simpler numbers A problem-solving strategy in which numbers in a problem are replaced with numbers that are easier to work with so that a general method of solution can be found. (334)

twin primes Two consecutive odd numbers that are both prime numbers. (310)

unbiased See *fair.*

undecagon An eleven-sided polygon. (324)

uniform scale A scale in which the numbers are equally spaced so that each interval represents the same value. (416)

unit cube A cube whose edges are 1 unit long. (477)

unit fraction A fraction with a 1 in its denominator and a nonzero integer in its denominator. (483)

unit of measure A standardized amount with which measures can be compared. (10)

unit square A square whose sides are 1 unit long. (468)

U.S. system of measurement A system of measurement evolved from the British Imperial system in which length is measured in inches, feet, yards, miles and other units, weight is measured in ounces, pounds, tons, and other units, and capacity is measured in ounces, cups, pints, quarts, gallons, and other units. Also called *customary system.* (119)

unknown A variable in an open sentence for which the sentence is to be solved. (220)

unlike terms Terms that involve different variables or the same variable with different exponents. (532)

value of a numerical expression The result of carrying out the operations in a numerical expression. (176)

variable A symbol that can stand for any one of a set of numbers or other objects. (182)

Venn diagram A diagram using circles to represent sets and the relationships between them. (367)

vertex **1** The common endpoint of the two rays that make up the angle. (145) **2** A point common to two sides of a polygon. (283) **3** One of the points at which two or more edges meet. (476)

vertical angles Angles formed by two intersecting lines, but that are not a linear pair. (375)

Volume Formula for a Cylindric Solid The volume of a cylindric solid with height h and base with area B is given by $V = Bh$. (676)

volume The measure of the space inside a three-dimensional figure. Also called *capacity.* (163)

whole number Any of the numbers 0, 1, 2, 3, ... (6)

window The part of the coordinate plane that appears on the screen of an automatic grapher. (698)

***x*-axis** The first (usually horizontal) number line in a coordinate graph. (424)

***x*-coordinate** The first coordinate of an ordered pair. (424)

***y*-axis** The second (usually vertical) number line in a coordinate graph. (424)

***y*-coordinate** The second coordinate of an ordered pair. (424)

yard (yd) A unit of length in the U.S. system of measurement equal to 3 feet. (125)

NOTES